The Sporting News

HOCKEY REGISTER

1998-99 EDITION

Editors/Hockey Register
MARK BONAVITA
BRENDAN ROBERTS

Contributing Editor/Hockey Register
LARRY WIGGE

The Sporting News

Efrem Zimbalist III, President and Chief Executive Officer, Times Mirror Magazines; **James H. Nuckols**, President, The Sporting News; **Francis X. Farrell**, Senior Vice President, Publisher; **John D. Rawlings**, Senior Vice President, Editorial Director; **John Kastberg**, Vice President, General Manager; **Kathy Kinkeade**, Vice President, Operations; **Steve Meyerhoff**, Executive Editor; **Mike Huguenin**, Assistant Managing Editor; **Craig Carter**, Statistical Editor; **Marilyn Kasal**, Production Director; **Mike Bruner**, Prepress Director; **Terry Shea**, Database Analyst; **Michael Behrens**, Art Director, Special Projects; **Christen Webster**, Macintosh Production Artist; **Amanda Kuehner, Steve Siegel** and **David Walton**, Editorial Interns.

A Times Mirror
Company

ON THE COVER: Steve Yzerman. (Cover designed by Michael Behrens. Photos by Albert Dickson/THE SPORTING NEWS.)

Spine photo: Eric Lindros.

Editorial assistance provided by Igor Kuperman of the Phoenix Coyotes.

ISBN: 0-89204-598-1

10 9 8 7 6 5 4 3 2 1

CONTENTS

Veteran players and top prospects 6
    This section includes all veteran NHL players who appeared in at least one NHL game during the 1997-98 season, top prospects and other players signed with a NHL team as of August 4, 1998.

1998 top draft picks 415
    This section includes all players selected in the first six rounds of the 1998 NHL draft.

Head coaches 442

National Hockey League statistical leaders 460

EXPLANATION OF AWARDS

NHL AWARDS: Alka-Seltzer Plus Award: plus/minus leader. **Art Ross Trophy:** leading scorer. **Bill Masterton Memorial Trophy:** perseverance, sportsmanship and dedication to hockey. **Bud Light/NHL Man of the Year:** service to community; called Budweiser/NHL Man of the Year prior to 1990-91. **Budweiser/NHL Man of the Year:** service to community; renamed Bud Light/NHL Man of the Year in 1990-91. **Calder Memorial Trophy:** rookie of the year. **Conn Smythe Trophy:** most valuable player in playoffs. **Dodge Performance of the Year Award:** most outstanding achievement or single-game performance. **Dodge Performer of the Year Award:** most outstanding performer in regular season. **Dodge Ram Tough Award:** highest combined total of power-play, shorthanded, game-winning and game-tying goals. **Emery Edge Award:** plus/minus leader; awarded from 1982-83 through 1987-88. **Frank J. Selke Trophy:** best defensive forward. **Hart Memorial Trophy:** most valuable player. **Jack Adams Award:** coach of the year. **James Norris Memorial Trophy:** outstanding defenseman. **King Clancy Memorial Trophy:** humanitarian contributions. **Lady Byng Memorial Trophy:** most gentlemanly player. **Lester B. Pearson Award:** outstanding player as selected by NHL Players' Association. **Lester Patrick Trophy:** outstanding service to hockey in U.S. **Trico Goaltender Award:** best save percentage. **Vezina Trophy:** best goaltender; awarded to goalkeeper(s) having played minimum of 25 games for team with fewest goals scored against prior to 1981-82. **William M. Jennings Trophy:** goalkeeper(s) having played minimum of 25 games for team with fewest goals scored against.

MINOR LEAGUE AWARDS: Baz Bastien Trophy: top goaltender (AHL). **Bobby Orr Trophy:** best defenseman (CHL); awarded prior to 1984-85. **Bob Gassoff Award:** most improved defenseman (CHL); awarded prior to 1984-85. **Commissioner's Trophy:** coach of the year (IHL). **Dudley (Red) Garrett Memorial Trophy:** rookie of the year (AHL). **Eddie Shore Plaque:** outstanding defenseman (AHL). **Fred Hunt Memorial Award:** sportsmanship, determination and dedication (AHL). **Garry F. Longman Memorial Trophy:** outstanding rookie (IHL). **Governors Trophy:** outstanding defenseman (IHL). **Harry (Hap) Holmes Memorial Trophy:** goaltender(s) having played minimum of 25 games for team with fewest goals scored against (AHL); awarded to outstanding goaltender prior to 1983-84. **Jack Butterfield Trophy:** Calder Cup playoffs MVP (AHL). **Jake Milford Trophy:** coach of the year (CHL); awarded prior to 1984-85. **James Gatschene Memorial Trophy:** most valuable player (IHL). **James Norris Memorial Trophy:** outstanding goaltender (IHL). **John B. Sollenberger Trophy:** leading scorer (AHL); originally called Wally Kilrea Trophy, later changed to Carl Liscombe Trophy until summer of 1955. **Ken McKenzie Trophy:** outstanding U.S.-born rookie (IHL). **Ken McKenzie Trophy:** top rookie (CHL); awarded to scoring leader from 1992-93. **Leo P. Lamoureux Memorial Trophy:** leading scorer (IHL); originally called George H. Wilkinson Trophy from 1946-47 through 1959-60. **Les Cunningham Plaque:** most valuable player (AHL). **Louis A.R. Pieri Memorial Award:** top coach (AHL). **Max McNab Trophy:** playoff MVP (CHL); awarded prior to 1984-85. **N.R. (Bud) Poile Trophy:** playoff MVP (IHL); originally called Turner Cup Playoff MVP from 1984-85 through 1988-89. **Phil Esposito Trophy:** leading scorer (CHL); awarded prior to 1984-85. **Terry Sawchuk Trophy:** top goaltenders (CHL); awarded prior to 1984-85. **Tommy Ivan Trophy:** most valuable player (CHL); awarded prior to 1984-85. **Turner Cup Playoff MVP:** playoff MVP (IHL); renamed N.R. (Bud) Poile Trophy in 1989-90.

MAJOR JUNIOR LEAGUE AWARDS: Association of Journalists for Major Junior League Hockey Trophy: top pro prospect (QMJHL); renamed Michael Bossy Trophy in 1983-84. **Bill Hunter Trophy:** top defenseman (WHL); called Top Defenseman Trophy prior to 1987-88 season. **Bob Brownridge Memorial Trophy:** top scorer (WHL); later renamed Bob Clarke Trophy. **Bobby Smith Trophy:** scholastic player of the year (OHL). **Bob Clarke Trophy:** top scorer (WHL); originally called Bob Brownridge Memorial Trophy. **Brad Hornung Trophy:** most sportsmanlike player (WHL); called Frank Boucher Memorial Trophy for most gentlemanly player prior to 1987-88 season. **Dave Pinkney Trophy:** top team goaltending (OHL). **Del Wilson Trophy:** top goaltender (WHL); called Top Goaltender Trophy prior to 1987-88 season. **Des Instructeurs Trophy:** rookie of the year (QMJHL); awarded to top rookie forward since 1981-82 season; renamed Michel Bergeron Trophy in 1985-86. **Dunc McCallum Memorial Trophy:** coach of the year (WHL). **Eddie Powers Memorial Trophy:** scoring champion (OHL). **Emile (Butch) Bouchard Trophy:** best defenseman (QMJHL). **Emms Family Award:** rookie of the year (OHL). **Four Broncos Memorial Trophy:** most valuable player as selected by coaches (WHL); called Most Valuable Player Trophy prior to 1987-88 season. **Frank Boucher Memorial Trophy:** most gentlemanly player (WHL); renamed Brad Hornung Trophy during 1987-88 season. **Frank J. Selke Trophy:** most gentlemanly player (QMJHL). **F.W. (Dinty) Moore Trophy:** rookie goalie with best goals-against average (OHL). **George Parsons Trophy:** sportsmanship in Memorial Cup (Can.HL). **Guy Lafleur Trophy:** most valuable player during playoffs (QMJHL). **Hap Emms Memorial Trophy:** outstanding goaltender in Memorial Cup (Can.HL). **Jacques Plante Trophy:** best goaltender (QMJHL). **Jean Beliveau Trophy:** leading point scorer (QMJHL). **Jim Mahon Memorial Trophy:** top-scoring right winger (OHL). **Jim Piggott Memorial Trophy:** rookie of the year (WHL); originally called Stewart (Butch) Paul Memorial Trophy. **Leo Lalonde Memorial Trophy:** overage player of the year (OHL). **Marcel Robert Trophy:** top scholastic/athletic performer (QMJHL). **Matt Leyden Trophy:** coach of the year (OHL). **Max Kaminsky Trophy:** outstanding defenseman (OHL); awarded to most gentlemanly player prior to 1969-70. **Michael Bossy Trophy:** top pro prospect (QMJHL); originally called Association of Journalists for Major Junior League Hockey Trophy from 1980-81 through 1982-83. **Michel Bergeron Trophy:** top rookie forward (QMJHL); awarded to rookie of the year prior to 1980-81 season. **Michel Briere Trophy:** most valuable player (QMJHL). **Most Valuable Player Trophy:** most valuable player (WHL); renamed Four Broncos Memorial Trophy during 1987-88 season. **Raymond Lagace Trophy:** top rookie defenseman or goaltender (QMJHL). **Red Tilson Trophy:** outstanding player (OHL). **Shell Cup:** awarded to offensive player of the year and defensive player of the year (QMJHL). **Stafford Smythe Memorial Trophy:** most valuable player of Memorial Cup (Can.HL). **Stewart (Butch) Paul Memorial Trophy:** rookie of the year (WHL); renamed Jim Piggott Memorial Trophy during 1987-88 season. **Top Defenseman Trophy:** top defenseman (WHL); renamed Bill Hunter Trophy during 1987-88 season. **Top Goaltender Trophy:** top goaltender (WHL); renamed Del Wilson Trophy during 1987-88 season. **William Hanley Trophy:** most gentlemanly player (OHL).

COLLEGE AWARDS: Hobey Baker Memorial Award: top college hockey player in U.S. **Senator Joseph A. Sullivan Trophy:** outstanding player in Canadian Interuniversity Athletic Union.

OTHER AWARDS: Golden Puck Award: Sweden's Player of the Year. **Golden Stick Award:** Europe's top player. **Izvestia Trophy:** leading scorer (Soviet Union).

EXPLANATION OF FOOTNOTES AND ABBREVIATIONS

*   League leader.
†   Tied for league lead.
‡   Overtime loss.
§   Led or tied for league lead, but total figure is divided between two different teams. Actual league-leading or league-tying figure is mentioned in "Statistical Notes" section.
... Statistic unavailable, unofficial or mathematically impossible to calculate.
—   Statistic inapplicable.

POSITIONS: C: center. **D:** defenseman. **G:** goaltender. **LW:** left winger. **RW:** right winger.

STATISTICS: A: assists. **Avg.:** goals-against average. **G:** goals. **GA:** goals against. **Gms.:** games. **L:** losses. **Min.:** minutes. **PIM.:** penalties in minutes. **+/-:** plus-minus. **PP:** power-play goals. **Pts:** points. **SH:** shorthanded goals. **SO:** shutouts. **T:** ties. **W:** wins.

TEAMS: Bloom. Jefferson: Bloomington Jefferson. **Chem. Litvinov:** Chemopetrol Litvinov. **Chem. Litvinov Jrs.:** Chemopetrol Litvinov Juniors. **Culver Mil. Acad.:** Culver Military Academy. **Czech. Olympic team:** Czechoslovakian Olympic team. **Det. Little Caesars:** Detroit Little Caesars. **Djur. Stockholm:** Djurgarden Stockholm. **Dynamo-Energ. Yek.:** Dynamo-Energiya Yekaterinburg. **Dynamo Ust-Kameno.:** Dynamo Ust-Kamenogorsk. **Fin. Olympic team:** Finnish Olympic team. **German Oly. team:** German Olympic team. **HC Ceske Bude.:** HC Ceske Budejovice. **HK 32 Lip. Mikulas:** HK 32 Liptovsky Mikulas. **IS Banska Byst.:** IS Banska Bystrica. **Krylja Sov. Moscow:** Krylja Sovetov Moscow. **Mass.-Lowell:** Massachusetts-Lowell. **Metal. Cherepovets:** Metallurg Cherepovets. **Metal. Magnitogorsk:** Metallurg Magnitogorsk. **Metallurg-2 Novok.:** Metallurg-2 Novokuznetsk. **MoDo Ornsk. Jrs.:** Modo Ornskoldsvik Jrs. **Motor Ceske Bude.:** Motor Ceske Budejovice. **N. Yarmouth Acad.:** North Yarmouth Academy. **N. Michigan Univ.:** Northern Michigan University. **NW Americans Jr. B:** Northwest Americans Junior B. **Poji. Pardubice Jrs.:** Pojistovna Pardubice Juniors. **Prin. Edward Island:** Prince Edward Island. **Rus. Olympic team:** Russian Olympic team. **Sault Ste. Marie:** Sault Sainte Marie. **Sever. Cherepovets:** Seversta Cherepovets. **Slovakian Oly. team:** Slovakian Olympic team. **Sov. Olympic team:** Soviet Olympic team. **Spisska N.V.:** Spisska Nova Ves. **Stad. Hradec Kralove:** Stadion Hradec Kralove. **Swed. Olympic team:** Swedish Olympic team. **Tor. Nizhny Nov.:** Torpedo Nizhny Novgorod. **Torpedo Ust-Kam.:** Torpedo Ust-Kamenogorsk. **Unif. Olympic team:** Unified Olympic team. **Univ. of West. Ontario:** University of Western Ontario. **V. Frolunda Goteborg:** Vastra Frolunda Goteborg.

LEAGUES: AAHL: All American Hockey League. **ACHL:** Atlantic Coast Hockey League. **AHL:** American Hockey League. **AJHL:** Alberta Junior Hockey League. **AMHL:** Alberta Minor Hockey League. **AUAA:** Atlantic Universities Athletic Association. **BCJHL:** British Columbia Junior Hockey League. **CAHL:** Central Alberta Hockey League. **CAJHL:** Central Alberta Junior Hockey League. **Can. College:** Canadian College. **Can.HL:** Canadian Hockey League. **CCHA:** Central Collegiate Hockey Association. **CHL:** Central Hockey League. **CIS:** Commonwealth of Independent States. **CJHL:** Central Junior A Hockey League. **COJHL:** Central Ontario Junior Hockey League. **CPHL:** Central Professional Hockey League. **CWUAA:** Canada West University Athletic Association. **Conn. H.S.:** Connecticut High School. **Czech.:** Czechoslovakia. **Czech Rep.:** Czechoslovakia Republic. **ECAC:** Eastern College Athletic Conference. **ECAC-II:** Eastern College Athletic Conference, Division II. **ECHL:** East Coast Hockey League. **EEHL:** Eastern European Hockey League. **EHL:** Eastern Hockey League. **EURO:** Euroliga. **Fin.:** Finland. **Ger.:** Germany. **GWHC:** Great Western Hockey Conference. **Hoc. East:** Hockey East. **IHL:** International Hockey League. **III. H.S.:** Illinois High School. **Indiana H.S.:** Indiana High School. **Int'l:** International. **KIJHL:** Kootenay International Junior Hockey League. **Mass. H.S.:** Massachusetts High School. **Md. H.S.:** Maryland High School. **Met. Bos.:** Metro Boston. **Mich. H.S.:** Michigan High School. **Minn. H.S.:** Minnesota High School. **MJHL:** Manitoba Junior Hockey League. **MTHL:** Metro Toronto Hockey League. **NAHL:** North American Hockey League. **NAJHL:** North American Junior Hockey League. **N.B. H.S.:** New Brunswick High School. **NCAA-II:** National Collegiate Athletic Association, Division II. **N.D. H.S.:** North Dakota High School. **NEJHL:** New England Junior Hockey League. **NHL:** National Hockey League. **N.H. H.S.:** New Hampshire High School. **N.J. H.S.:** New Jersey High School. **Nia. D. Jr. C:** Niagara District Junior C. **NSJHL:** Nova Scotia Junior Hockey League. **N.S. Jr. A:** Nova Scotia Junior A. **N.Y. H.S.:** New York High School. **NYMJHL:** New York Major Junior Hockey League. **NYOHL:** North York Ontario Hockey League. **ODHA:** Ottawa & District Hockey Association. **OHA:** Ontario Hockey Association. **OHA Jr. A:** Ontario Hockey Association Junior A. **OHA Mjr. Jr. A:** Ontario Hockey Association Major Junior A. **OHA Senior:** Ontario Hockey Association Senior. **OHL:** Ontario Hockey League. **O.H.S.:** Ohio High School. **OJHA:** Ontario Junior Hockey Association. **OJHL:** Ontario Junior Hockey League. **OMJHL:** Ontario Major Junior Hockey League. **OPJHL:** Ontario Provincial Junior Hockey League. **OUAA:** Ontario Universities Athletic Association. **PCJHL:** Peace Caribou Junior Hockey League. **PEIHA:** Prince Edward Island Hockey Association. **PEIJHL:** Prince Edward Island Junior Hockey League. **Penn. H.S.:** Pennsylvania High School. **QMJHL:** Quebec Major Junior Hockey League. **R.I. H.S.:** Rhode Island High School. **Rus. Div II, III:** Russian Division II, III. **SAJHL:** Southern Alberta Junior Hockey League. **SJHL:** Saskatchewan Junior Hockey League. **Sask. H.S.:** Saskatchewan High School. **SOJHL:** Southern Ontario Junior Hockey League. **Swed. Jr.:** Sweden Junior. **Switz.:** Switzerland. **TBAHA:** Thunder Bay Amateur Hockey Association. **TBJHL:** Thunder Bay Junior Hockey League. **UHL:** United Hockey League. **USHL:** United States Hockey League. **USHS:** United States High School. **USSR:** Union of Soviet Socialist Republics. **V. Frolunda Goteborg:** Vastra Frolunda Goteborg. **Vt. H.S.:** Vermont High School. **W. Germany, W. Ger.:** West Germany. **WCHA:** Western Collegiate Hockey Association. **WCHL:** Western Canada Hockey League. **WHA:** World Hockey Association. **WHL:** Western Hockey League. **Wisc. H.S.:** Wisconsin High School. **Yukon Sr.:** Yukon Senior.

VETERANS AND TOP PROSPECTS

A

AALTO, ANTTI   C   MIGHTY DUCKS

PERSONAL: Born March 4, 1975, in Lappeenrana, Finland. ... 6-2/190. ... Shoots left. ... Name pronounced AN-tee AL-toh.
TRANSACTIONS/CAREER NOTES: Selected by Mighty Ducks of Anaheim in sixth round (sixth Mighty Ducks pick, 134th overall) of NHL entry draft (June 26, 1993).

Season Team	League	Gms.	G	A	Pts.	PIM	+/-	PP	SH	Gms.	G	A	Pts.	PIM
					REGULAR SEASON							PLAYOFFS		
91-92—SaiPa Jr.	Finland	19	10	10	20	38	...	...	...	—	—	—	—	—
—SaiPa	Finland	20	6	6	12	20	...	...	...	—	—	—	—	—
92-93—SaiPa	Finland	23	6	8	14	14	...	...	...	—	—	—	—	—
—TPS Jr.	Finland	14	6	8	14	18	...	...	...	—	—	—	—	—
—TPS Turku	Finland	1	0	0	0	0	...	...	...	—	—	—	—	—
93-94—TPS Turku	Finland	33	5	9	14	16	...	...	...	10	1	1	2	4
94-95—TPS Turku	Finland	44	11	7	18	18	...	...	...	5	0	1	1	2
95-96—TPS Turku	Finland	40	15	16	31	22	...	...	...	11	3	5	8	14
—Kiekko-67	Finland Dv.II	2	0	2	2	2	...	...	...	—	—	—	—	—
96-97—TPS Turku	Finland	44	15	19	34	60	...	...	...	11	5	6	11	31
97-98—Cincinnati	AHL	29	4	9	13	30	...	...	...	—	—	—	—	—
—Anaheim	NHL	3	0	0	0	0	-1	0	0	—	—	—	—	—
NHL Totals (1 year)		3	0	0	0	0	-1	0	0	—	—	—	—	—

ABRAHAMSSON, ELIAS   D   BRUINS

PERSONAL: Born June 15, 1977, in Uppsala, Sweden. ... 6-3/227. ... Shoots left. ... Name pronounced uh-LEE-uhz ay-bruh-HAM-suhn.
TRANSACTIONS/CAREER NOTES: Selected by Boston Bruins in fifth round (sixth Bruins pick, 132nd overall) of NHL entry draft (June 22, 1996).

Season Team	League	Gms.	G	A	Pts.	PIM	+/-	PP	SH	Gms.	G	A	Pts.	PIM
					REGULAR SEASON							PLAYOFFS		
93-94—Uppsala	Swed. Dv.II	1	0	0	0	0	...	...	...	—	—	—	—	—
94-95—Halifax	QMJHL	25	0	3	3	41	...	...	...	—	—	—	—	—
95-96—Halifax	QMJHL	64	3	11	14	268	...	...	...	6	2	2	4	8
96-97—Halifax	QMJHL	30	4	11	15	221	...	...	...	18	4	8	12	74
97-98—Providence	AHL	29	0	1	1	47	...	...	...	—	—	—	—	—

ADAMS, GREG   LW

PERSONAL: Born August 1, 1963, in Nelson, B.C. ... 6-3/198. ... Shoots left. ... Full name: Greg G. Adams. ... Son-in-law of George Swarbrick, right winger with three NHL teams (1967-68 through 1970-71).
COLLEGE: Northern Arizona.
TRANSACTIONS/CAREER NOTES: Signed as free agent by New Jersey Devils (June 25, 1984). ... Tore tendon in right wrist (April 1986). ... Traded by Devils with G Kirk McLean to Vancouver Canucks for C Patrik Sundstrom, fourth-round pick in 1988 draft (LW Matt Ruchty) and the option to flip second-round picks in 1988 draft; Devils exercised option and selected LW Jeff Christian and Canucks selected D Leif Rohlin (September 10, 1987). ... Fractured ankle (February 1989). ... Fractured cheekbone (January 4, 1990); missed 12 games. ... Sprained left knee (October 17, 1990); missed 12 games. ... Sprained forearm, wrist and abdomen (February 27, 1991). ... Suffered concussion (October 8, 1991); missed one game. ... Suffered charley horse (January 16, 1993); missed nine games. ... Suffered charley horse (February 15, 1993); missed 22 games. ... Suffered stress fracture in hand requiring minor surgery (December 14, 1993); missed 14 games. ... Bruised foot (February 22, 1994); missed one game. ... Traded by Canucks with RW Dan Kesa and fifth-round pick (traded to Los Angeles) in 1995 draft to Dallas Stars for RW Russ Courtnall (April 7, 1995). ... Fractured hand (March 2, 1996); missed 11 games. ... Broke toe (April 7, 1996); missed final four games of season. ... Suffered herniated disc in neck (December 21, 1996); missed 30 games. ... Strained groin (April 4, 1997); missed one game. ... Bruised ribs (November 16, 1997); missed 11 games. ... Injured knee (December 23, 1997); missed 20 games. ... Injured neck (April 6, 1998); missed two games.
HONORS: Played in NHL All-Star Game (1988).
MISCELLANEOUS: Failed to score on a penalty shot (vs. Alain Chevrier, January 7, 1988; vs. Alan Bester, January 9, 1989; vs. Jacques Cloutier, December 10, 1989; vs. Bill Ranford, December 1, 1991; vs. Curtis Joseph, January 25, 1992).
STATISTICAL PLATEAUS: Three-goal games: 1991-92 (1). ... Four-goal games: 1987-88 (1). ... Total hat tricks: 2.

Season Team	League	Gms.	G	A	Pts.	PIM	+/-	PP	SH	Gms.	G	A	Pts.	PIM
					REGULAR SEASON							PLAYOFFS		
80-81—Kelowna	BCJHL	47	40	50	90	16	...	...	...	—	—	—	—	—
81-82—Kelowna	BCJHL	45	31	42	73	24	...	...	...	—	—	—	—	—
82-83—N. Arizona Univ.	Indep.	29	14	21	35	46	...	...	...	—	—	—	—	—
83-84—N. Arizona Univ.	Indep.	47	40	50	90	16	...	...	...	—	—	—	—	—
84-85—Maine	AHL	41	15	20	35	12	...	...	...	11	3	4	7	0
—New Jersey	NHL	36	12	9	21	14	-14	5	0	—	—	—	—	—
85-86—New Jersey	NHL	78	35	42	77	30	-6	10	0	—	—	—	—	—
86-87—New Jersey	NHL	72	20	27	47	19	-16	6	0	—	—	—	—	—
87-88—Vancouver	NHL	80	36	40	76	30	-24	12	0	—	—	—	—	—
88-89—Vancouver	NHL	61	19	14	33	24	-21	9	0	7	2	3	5	2
89-90—Vancouver	NHL	65	30	20	50	18	-8	13	0	—	—	—	—	—
90-91—Vancouver	NHL	55	21	24	45	10	-5	5	1	5	0	0	0	2
91-92—Vancouver	NHL	76	30	27	57	26	8	13	1	6	0	2	2	4
92-93—Vancouver	NHL	53	25	31	56	14	31	6	1	12	7	6	13	6
93-94—Vancouver	NHL	68	13	24	37	20	-1	5	1	23	6	8	14	2
94-95—Vancouver	NHL	31	5	10	15	12	1	2	2	—	—	—	—	—
—Dallas	NHL	12	3	3	6	4	-4	1	0	5	2	0	2	0

Season Team	League	Gms.	G	A	Pts.	PIM	+/-	PP	SH	Gms.	G	A	Pts.	PIM
					REGULAR SEASON							PLAYOFFS		
95-96—Dallas	NHL	66	22	21	43	33	-21	11	1	—	—	—	—	—
96-97—Dallas	NHL	50	21	15	36	2	27	5	0	3	0	1	1	0
97-98—Dallas	NHL	49	14	18	32	20	11	7	0	12	2	2	4	0
NHL Totals (14 years)		852	306	325	631	276	-42	110	7	73	19	22	41	16

A

ADAMS, KEVYN — C — MAPLE LEAFS

PERSONAL: Born October 8, 1974, in Washington, D.C. ... 6-1/195. ... Shoots right.
HIGH SCHOOL: Clarence (N.Y.).
COLLEGE: Miami of Ohio.
TRANSACTIONS/CAREER NOTES: Selected by Boston Bruins in first round (first Bruins pick, 25th overall) of NHL entry draft (June 26, 1993). ... Signed as free agent by Toronto Maple Leafs (August 1, 1997).
HONORS: Named to CCHA All-Star second team (1994-95).

Season Team	League	Gms.	G	A	Pts.	PIM	+/-	PP	SH	Gms.	G	A	Pts.	PIM
					REGULAR SEASON							PLAYOFFS		
90-91—Niagara	NAJHL	55	17	20	37	24	...	...	...	—	—	—	—	—
91-92—Niagara	NAJHL	40	25	33	58	51	...	...	...	—	—	—	—	—
92-93—Miami of Ohio	CCHA	41	17	16	33	18	...	...	...	—	—	—	—	—
93-94—Miami of Ohio	CCHA	36	15	28	43	24	...	...	...	—	—	—	—	—
94-95—Miami of Ohio	CCHA	38	20	29	49	30	...	...	...	—	—	—	—	—
95-96—Miami of Ohio	CCHA	36	17	30	47	30	...	...	...	—	—	—	—	—
96-97—Grand Rapids	IHL	82	22	25	47	47	...	...	...	5	1	1	2	4
97-98—Toronto	NHL	5	0	0	0	7	0	0	0	—	—	—	—	—
—St. John's	AHL	58	17	21	38	99	...	...	...	4	0	0	0	4
NHL Totals (1 year)		5	0	0	0	7	0	0	0					

AFINOGENOV, MAXIM — RW — SABRES

PERSONAL: Born September 4, 1979, in Moscow, U.S.S.R. ... 5-11/176. ... Shoots left.
TRANSACTIONS/CAREER NOTES: Selected by Buffalo Sabres in third round (third Sabres pick, 69th overall) of NHL entry draft (June 21, 1997).

Season Team	League	Gms.	G	A	Pts.	PIM	+/-	PP	SH	Gms.	G	A	Pts.	PIM
					REGULAR SEASON							PLAYOFFS		
95-96—Dynamo Moscow	CIS	1	0	0	0	0	...	...	...	—	—	—	—	—
96-97—Dynamo Moscow	Russian	29	6	5	11	10	...	...	...	4	0	2	2	0
—Dynamo-2 Moscow	Rus. Div. III	14	9	2	11	10	...	...	...	—	—	—	—	—
97-98—Dynamo Moscow	Russian	35	10	5	15	53	...	...	...	—	—	—	—	—

AITKEN, JOHNATHAN — D — BRUINS

PERSONAL: Born May 24, 1978, in Sherwood Park, Alta. ... 6-4/205. ... Shoots left. ... Name pronounced AYT-kihn.
TRANSACTIONS/CAREER NOTES: Selected by Boston Bruins in first round (first Bruins pick, eighth overall) of NHL entry draft (June 22, 1996).
HONORS: Named to WHL (East) All-Star second team (1997-98).

Season Team	League	Gms.	G	A	Pts.	PIM	+/-	PP	SH	Gms.	G	A	Pts.	PIM
					REGULAR SEASON							PLAYOFFS		
94-95—Medicine Hat	WHL	53	0	5	5	71	...	...	...	—	—	—	—	—
95-96—Medicine Hat	WHL	71	6	14	20	131	...	...	...	5	1	0	1	6
96-97—Brandon	WHL	65	4	18	22	211	...	...	...	6	0	0	0	4
97-98—Brandon	WHL	69	9	25	34	183	...	...	...	18	0	8	8	67

ALBELIN, TOMMY — D — FLAMES

PERSONAL: Born May 21, 1964, in Stockholm, Sweden. ... 6-1/200. ... Shoots left. ... Name pronounced AL-buh-leen.
TRANSACTIONS/CAREER NOTES: Selected by Quebec Nordiques in eighth round (seventh Nordiques pick, 152nd overall) of NHL entry draft (June 8, 1983). ... Traded by Nordiques to New Jersey Devils for fourth-round pick (LW Niclas Andersson) in 1989 draft (December 12, 1988). ... Injured right knee (March 2, 1990); missed four games. ... Injured groin (November 21, 1992); missed two games. ... Suffered from urinary infection (1993-94 season); missed nine games. ... Bruised thigh (December 16, 1995); missed six games. ... Traded by Devils with D Cale Hulse and RW Jocelyn Lemieux to Calgary Flames for D Phil Housley and D Dan Keczmer (February 26, 1996). ... Strained groin (November 9, 1996); missed four games. ... Reinjured groin (November 25, 1996); missed two games. ... Strained abdominal muscle (December 7, 1996); missed five games. ... Suffered concussion (November 11, 1997); missed three games. ... Pulled groin (November 27, 1997); missed three games. ... Reinjured groin (December 9, 1997); missed four games. ... Injured ribs (February 2, 1998); missed three games.
HONORS: Named to Swedish League All-Star team (1986-87).
MISCELLANEOUS: Member of Stanley Cup championship team (1995).

Season Team	League	Gms.	G	A	Pts.	PIM	+/-	PP	SH	Gms.	G	A	Pts.	PIM
					REGULAR SEASON							PLAYOFFS		
82-83—Djur. Stockholm	Sweden	17	2	5	7	4	...	...	...	6	1	0	1	2
83-84—Djur. Stockholm	Sweden	37	9	8	17	36	...	...	...	4	0	1	1	2
84-85—Djur. Stockholm	Sweden	32	9	8	17	22	...	...	...	8	2	1	3	4
85-86—Djur. Stockholm	Sweden	35	4	8	12	26	...	...	...	—	—	—	—	—
86-87—Djur. Stockholm	Sweden	33	7	5	12	49	...	...	...	2	0	0	0	0
87-88—Quebec	NHL	60	3	23	26	47	-7	0	0	—	—	—	—	—
88-89—Halifax	AHL	8	2	5	7	4	...	...	...	—	—	—	—	—
—Quebec	NHL	14	2	4	6	27	-6	1	0	—	—	—	—	—
—New Jersey	NHL	46	7	24	31	40	18	1	1	—	—	—	—	—

Season Team	League	REGULAR SEASON								PLAYOFFS				
		Gms.	G	A	Pts.	PIM	+/-	PP	SH	Gms.	G	A	Pts.	PIM
89-90—New Jersey	NHL	68	6	23	29	63	-1	4	0	—	—	—	—	—
90-91—Utica	AHL	14	4	2	6	10	...	...	...	—	—	—	—	—
—New Jersey	NHL	47	2	12	14	44	1	1	0	3	0	1	1	2
91-92—New Jersey	NHL	19	0	4	4	4	7	0	0	1	1	1	2	0
—Utica	AHL	11	4	6	10	4	...	...	...	—	—	—	—	—
92-93—New Jersey	NHL	36	1	5	6	14	0	1	0	5	2	0	2	0
93-94—Albany	AHL	4	0	2	2	17	...	...	...	—	—	—	—	—
—New Jersey	NHL	62	2	17	19	36	20	1	0	20	2	5	7	14
94-95—New Jersey	NHL	48	5	10	15	20	9	2	0	20	1	7	8	2
95-96—New Jersey	NHL	53	1	12	13	14	0	0	0	—	—	—	—	—
—Calgary	NHL	20	0	1	1	4	1	0	0	4	0	0	0	0
96-97—Calgary	NHL	72	4	11	15	14	-8	2	0	—	—	—	—	—
97-98—Calgary	NHL	69	2	17	19	32	9	1	0	—	—	—	—	—
—Swedish Oly. team	Int'l	3	0	0	0	4	...	...	...	—	—	—	—	—
NHL Totals (11 years)		614	35	163	198	359	43	14	1	53	6	14	20	18

ALFREDSSON, DANIEL   RW   SENATORS

PERSONAL: Born December 11, 1972, in Grums, Sweden. ... 5-11/194. ... Shoots right.
TRANSACTIONS/CAREER NOTES: Selected by Ottawa Senators in sixth round (fifth Senators pick, 133rd overall) of NHL entry draft (June 29, 1994). ... Strained abdominal muscle (January 29, 1997); missed six games. ... Injured right ankle (November 3, 1997); missed eight games. ... Fractured right fibula (December 11, 1997); missed 13 games.
HONORS: Played in NHL All-Star Game (1996-1998). ... Won Calder Memorial Trophy (1995-96). ... Named to NHL All-Rookie team (1995-96).
STATISTICAL PLATEAUS: Three-goal games: 1995-96 (1).

Season Team	League	REGULAR SEASON								PLAYOFFS				
		Gms.	G	A	Pts.	PIM	+/-	PP	SH	Gms.	G	A	Pts.	PIM
91-92—Molndal Hockey	Swed. Dv.II	32	12	8	20	43	...	...	...	—	—	—	—	—
92-93—Vastra Frolunda	Sweden	20	1	5	6	8	...	...	...	—	—	—	—	—
93-94—Vastra Frolunda	Sweden	39	20	10	30	18	...	...	...	4	1	1	2	—
94-95—Vastra Frolunda	Sweden	22	7	11	18	22	...	...	...	—	—	—	—	...
95-96—Ottawa	NHL	82	26	35	61	28	-18	8	2	—	—	—	—	—
96-97—Ottawa	NHL	76	24	47	71	30	5	11	1	7	5	2	7	6
97-98—Ottawa	NHL	55	17	28	45	18	7	7	0	11	7	2	9	20
—Swedish Oly. team	Int'l	4	2	3	5	2	...	...	...	—	—	—	—	—
NHL Totals (3 years)		213	67	110	177	76	-6	26	3	18	12	4	16	26

ALLAN, CHAD   D   CANUCKS

PERSONAL: Born July 12, 1976, in Davidson, Sask. ... 6-1/195. ... Shoots left.
HIGH SCHOOL: Marion Graham (Regina, Sask.).
TRANSACTIONS/CAREER NOTES: Selected by Vancouver Canucks in third round (fourth Canucks pick, 65th overall) of NHL entry draft (June 29, 1994).
HONORS: Named to WHL (East) All-Star first team (1994-95). ... Named to WHL (Central/East) All-Star second team (1995-96).

Season Team	League	REGULAR SEASON								PLAYOFFS				
		Gms.	G	A	Pts.	PIM	+/-	PP	SH	Gms.	G	A	Pts.	PIM
91-92—Saskatoon	WHL	1	0	0	0	2	...	...	...	—	—	—	—	—
92-93—Saskatoon	WHL	69	2	10	12	67	...	...	...	9	0	0	0	25
93-94—Saskatoon	WHL	70	6	16	22	123	...	...	...	16	1	1	2	21
94-95—Saskatoon	WHL	63	14	29	43	95	...	...	...	9	0	3	3	2
95-96—Saskatoon	WHL	57	8	30	38	106	...	...	...	4	0	0	0	5
96-97—Syracuse	AHL	73	3	10	13	83	...	...	...	3	0	1	1	0
97-98—Syracuse	AHL	73	2	10	12	121	...	...	...	5	0	0	0	4

ALLEN, CHRIS   D   PANTHERS

PERSONAL: Born May 8, 1978, in Blenheim, Ont. ... 6-2/192. ... Shoots right.
TRANSACTIONS/CAREER NOTES: Selected by Florida Panthers in third round (second Panthers pick, 60th overall) of NHL entry draft (June 22, 1996).
HONORS: Named to Can.HL All-Star first team (1997-98). ... Won Max Kaminsky Trophy (1997-98). ... Named to OHL All-Star first team (1997-98).

Season Team	League	REGULAR SEASON								PLAYOFFS				
		Gms.	G	A	Pts.	PIM	+/-	PP	SH	Gms.	G	A	Pts.	PIM
92-93—Blenheim Jr. C	OHA	3	0	0	0	0	...	...	...	—	—	—	—	—
93-94—Leamington	Jr. B	52	6	20	26	38	...	...	...	—	—	—	—	—
94-95—Kingston	OHL	43	3	5	8	15	...	...	...	2	0	0	0	0
95-96—Kingston	OHL	55	21	18	39	58	...	...	...	6	0	2	2	8
96-97—Kingston	OHL	61	14	29	43	81	...	...	...	5	1	2	3	4
—Carolina	AHL	9	0	0	0	2	...	...	...	—	—	—	—	—
97-98—Kingston	OHL	66	38	57	95	91	...	...	...	10	4	2	6	6
—Florida	NHL	1	0	0	0	2	0	0	0	—	—	—	—	—
NHL Totals (1 year)		1	0	0	0	2	0	0	0					

ALLISON, JAMIE · D · FLAMES

PERSONAL: Born May 13, 1975, in Lindsay, Ont. ... 6-1/195. ... Shoots left.
TRANSACTIONS/CAREER NOTES: Selected by Calgary Flames in second round (second Flames pick, 44th overall) of NHL entry draft (June 26, 1993). ... Suffered concussion (December 20, 1996); missed three games. ... Fractured thumb (January 9, 1998); missed 11 games. ... Suffered concussion (March 28, 1998); missed 10 games.

		REGULAR SEASON								PLAYOFFS				
Season Team	League	Gms.	G	A	Pts.	PIM	+/-	PP	SH	Gms.	G	A	Pts.	PIM
90-91—Waterloo Jr. B	OHA	45	3	8	11	91	...	...	...	—	—	—	—	—
91-92—Windsor	OHL	59	4	8	12	52	...	...	...	4	1	1	2	2
92-93—Detroit	OHL	61	0	13	13	64	...	...	...	15	2	5	7	23
93-94—Detroit	OHL	40	2	22	24	69	...	...	...	17	2	9	11	35
94-95—Detroit	OHL	50	1	14	15	119	...	...	...	18	2	7	9	35
—Calgary	NHL	1	0	0	0	0	0	0	0	—	—	—	—	—
95-96—Saint John	AHL	71	3	16	19	223	...	...	...	14	0	2	2	16
96-97—Saint John	AHL	46	3	6	9	139	...	...	...	5	0	1	1	4
—Calgary	NHL	20	0	0	0	35	-4	0	0	—	—	—	—	—
97-98—Saint John	AHL	16	0	5	5	49	...	...	...	—	—	—	—	—
—Calgary	NHL	43	3	8	11	104	3	0	0	—	—	—	—	—
NHL Totals (3 years)		64	3	8	11	139	-1	0	0					

ALLISON, JASON · C · BRUINS

PERSONAL: Born May 29, 1975, in North York, Ont. ... 6-3/205. ... Shoots right.
TRANSACTIONS/CAREER NOTES: Selected by Washington Capitals in first round (second Capitals pick, 17th overall) of NHL entry draft (June 26, 1993). ... Injured ankle (February 15, 1997); missed one game. ... Traded by Capitals with G Jim Carey, C Anson Carter and third-round pick (RW Lee Goren) in 1997 draft to Boston Bruins for C Adam Oates, RW Rick Tocchet and G Bill Ranford (March 1, 1997). ... Injured hip (March 1, 1998); missed one game.
HONORS: Won Can.HL Player of the Year Award (1993-94). ... Won Can.HL Top Scorer Award (1993-94). ... Won Red Tilson Trophy (1993-94). ... Won William Hanley Trophy (1993-94). ... Won Eddie Powers Memorial Trophy (1993-94). ... Named to Can.HL All-Star first team (1993-94). ... Named to OHL All-Star first team (1993-94).
MISCELLANEOUS: Failed to score on a penalty shot (vs. Dominik Hasek, April 10, 1997).
STATISTICAL PLATEAUS: Three-goal games: 1997-98 (2).

		REGULAR SEASON								PLAYOFFS				
Season Team	League	Gms.	G	A	Pts.	PIM	+/-	PP	SH	Gms.	G	A	Pts.	PIM
91-92—London	OHL	65	11	18	29	15	...	...	...	7	0	0	0	0
92-93—London	OHL	66	42	76	118	50	...	...	...	12	7	13	20	8
93-94—London	OHL	56	55	87	*142	68	...	...	...	5	2	13	15	13
—Washington	NHL	2	0	1	1	0	1	0	0	—	—	—	—	—
—Portland	AHL	6	2	1	3	0	...	...	...	—	—	—	—	—
94-95—London	OHL	15	15	21	36	43	...	...	...	—	—	—	—	—
—Washington	NHL	12	2	1	3	6	-3	2	0	—	—	—	—	—
—Portland	AHL	8	5	4	9	2	...	...	...	7	3	8	11	2
95-96—Washington	NHL	19	0	3	3	2	-3	0	0	—	—	—	—	—
—Portland	AHL	57	28	41	69	42	...	...	...	6	1	6	7	9
96-97—Washington	NHL	53	5	17	22	25	-3	1	0	—	—	—	—	—
—Boston	NHL	19	3	9	12	9	-3	1	0	—	—	—	—	—
97-98—Boston	NHL	81	33	50	83	60	33	5	0	6	2	6	8	4
NHL Totals (5 years)		186	43	81	124	102	22	9	0	6	2	6	8	4

ALVEY, MATT · RW · BRUINS

PERSONAL: Born May 15, 1975, in Troy, N.Y. ... 6-5/200. ... Shoots right.
COLLEGE: Lake Superior State (Mich.).
TRANSACTIONS/CAREER NOTES: Selected by Boston Bruins in second round (second Bruins pick, 51st overall) of NHL entry draft (June 26, 1993).

		REGULAR SEASON								PLAYOFFS				
Season Team	League	Gms.	G	A	Pts.	PIM	+/-	PP	SH	Gms.	G	A	Pts.	PIM
90-91—Springfield Jr. B	NEJHL	—	12	20	32	—	...	...	—	—	—	—	—	—
91-92—Springfield Jr. B	NEJHL	32	22	35	57	34	...	...	...	—	—	—	—	—
92-93—Springfield Jr. B	NEJHL	38	22	37	59	85	...	...	...	—	—	—	—	—
93-94—Lake Superior	CCHA	41	6	8	14	16	...	...	...	—	—	—	—	—
94-95—Lake Superior	CCHA	25	4	7	11	32	...	...	...	—	—	—	—	—
95-96—Lake Superior	CCHA	38	14	8	22	40	...	...	...	—	—	—	—	—
96-97—Lake Superior	CCHA	18	10	8	18	49	...	...	...	—	—	—	—	—
—Pensacola	ECHL	7	1	2	3	0	...	...	...	3	0	0	0	4
97-98—Charlotte	ECHL	38	17	15	32	37	...	...	...	7	3	1	4	6

AMONTE, TONY · LW/RW · BLACKHAWKS

PERSONAL: Born August 2, 1970, in Weymouth, Mass. ... 6-0/195. ... Shoots left. ... Full name: Anthony Lewis Amonte. ... Name pronounced ah-MAHN-tee.
HIGH SCHOOL: Thayer Academy (Braintree, Mass.).
COLLEGE: Boston University.
TRANSACTIONS/CAREER NOTES: Selected by New York Rangers in fourth round (third Rangers pick, 68th overall) of NHL entry draft (June 11, 1988). ... Separated shoulder (December 29, 1990). ... Traded by Rangers with rights to LW Matt Oates to Chicago Blackhawks for LW Stephane Matteau and RW Brian Noonan (March 21, 1994). ... Pulled groin (1993-94 season); missed three games. ... Played in Europe during 1994-95 NHL lockout.

HONORS: Named to Hockey East All-Rookie team (1989-90). ... Named to NCAA All-Tournament team (1990-91). ... Named to Hockey East All-Star second team (1990-91). ... Named NHL Rookie of the Year by THE SPORTING NEWS (1991-92). ... Named to NHL All-Rookie team (1991-92). ... Played in NHL All-Star Game (1997 and 1998).
MISCELLANEOUS: Failed to score on a penalty shot (vs. Kelly Hrudey, January 27, 1994; vs. Guy Hebert, February 1, 1998).
STATISTICAL PLATEAUS: Three-goal games: 1991-92 (1), 1995-96 (1), 1996-97 (2). Total: 4.

Season Team	League	REGULAR SEASON								PLAYOFFS				
		Gms.	G	A	Pts.	PIM	+/-	PP	SH	Gms.	G	A	Pts.	PIM
86-87—Thayer Academy	Mass. H.S.	25	25	32	57	...	...	...	...	—	—	—	—	—
87-88—Thayer Academy	Mass. H.S.	28	30	38	68	...	...	...	...	—	—	—	—	—
88-89—Team USA Juniors	Int'l	7	1	3	4	...	...	...	...	—	—	—	—	—
89-90—Boston University	Hockey East	41	25	33	58	52	...	...	...	—	—	—	—	—
90-91—Boston University	Hockey East	38	31	37	68	82	...	...	...	—	—	—	—	—
—New York Rangers	NHL	—	—	—	—	—	—	—	—	2	0	2	2	2
91-92—New York Rangers	NHL	79	35	34	69	55	12	9	0	13	3	6	9	2
92-93—New York Rangers	NHL	83	33	43	76	49	0	13	0	—	—	—	—	—
93-94—New York Rangers	NHL	72	16	22	38	31	5	3	0	—	—	—	—	—
—Chicago	NHL	7	1	3	4	6	-5	1	0	6	4	2	6	4
94-95—Fassa	Italy	14	22	16	38	10	...	...	...	—	—	—	—	—
—Chicago	NHL	48	15	20	35	41	7	6	1	16	3	3	6	10
95-96—Chicago	NHL	81	31	32	63	62	10	5	4	7	2	4	6	6
96-97—Chicago	NHL	81	41	36	77	64	35	9	2	6	4	2	6	8
97-98—Chicago	NHL	82	31	42	73	66	21	7	3	—	—	—	—	—
—U.S. Olympic Team	Int'l	4	0	1	1	4	...	...	...	—	—	—	—	—
NHL Totals (8 years)............		533	203	232	435	374	85	53	10	50	16	19	35	32

ANDERSON, CRAIG   D   RANGERS

PERSONAL: Born January 6, 1976, in Minneapolis. ... 6-2/180. ... Shoots left.
HIGH SCHOOL: Park Center (Minn.).
COLLEGE: Wisconsin.
TRANSACTIONS/CAREER NOTES: Selected by New York Rangers in eighth round (10th Rangers pick, 208th overall) of NHL entry draft (June 29, 1994).
HONORS: Named to WCHA All-Star first team (1997-98).

Season Team	League	REGULAR SEASON								PLAYOFFS				
		Gms.	G	A	Pts.	PIM	+/-	PP	SH	Gms.	G	A	Pts.	PIM
93-94—Park Center H.S.	Minn. H.S.	24	24	18	42	...	...	...	...	—	—	—	—	—
94-95—Univ. of Wisconsin	WCHA					Did not play.				—	—	—	—	—
95-96—Univ. of Wisconsin	WCHA	15	1	3	4	2	...	...	...	—	—	—	—	—
96-97—Univ. of Wisconsin	WCHA	34	3	8	11	22	...	...	...	—	—	—	—	—
97-98—Univ. of Wisconsin......	WCHA	40	12	30	42	24	...	...	...	—	—	—	—	—

ANDERSON, MIKE   RW   CAPITALS

PERSONAL: Born December 24, 1976, in Edina, Minn. ... 6-1/186. ... Shoots right. ... Full name: Michael Anderson.
COLLEGE: Minnesota.
TRANSACTIONS/CAREER NOTES: Selected by Washington Capitals in seventh round (10th Capitals pick, 180th overall) of NHL entry draft (June 22, 1996).

Season Team	League	REGULAR SEASON								PLAYOFFS				
		Gms.	G	A	Pts.	PIM	+/-	PP	SH	Gms.	G	A	Pts.	PIM
95-96—Univ. of Minnesota......	WCHA	28	3	6	9	51	...	...	...	—	—	—	—	—
96-97—Univ. of Minnesota......	WCHA	42	9	11	20	46	...	...	...	—	—	—	—	—
97-98—Univ. of Minnesota......	WCHA	31	12	13	25	62	...	...	...	—	—	—	—	—

ANDERSSON, ERIK   RW   FLAMES

PERSONAL: Born August 19, 1971, in Stockholm, Sweden. ... 6-3/210. ... Shoots left. ... Full name: Erik Folke Andersson.
COLLEGE: Denver.
TRANSACTIONS/CAREER NOTES: Selected by Los Angeles Kings in sixth round (fifth Kings pick, 112th overall) of NHL entry draft (June 16, 1990). ... Returned to draft pool by Kings and selected by Calgary Flames in third round (sixth Flames pick, 70th overall) of NHL entry draft (June 21, 1997). ... Suffered concussion (October 17, 1997); missed 12 games. ... Injured back (February 7, 1998); missed remainder of the season.

Season Team	League	REGULAR SEASON								PLAYOFFS				
		Gms.	G	A	Pts.	PIM	+/-	PP	SH	Gms.	G	A	Pts.	PIM
89-90—Danderyd	Swed. Dv.II	30	14	5	19	16	...	...	...	—	—	—	—	—
90-91—AIK Solna..................	Sweden	32	1	1	2	10	...	...	...	—	—	—	—	—
91-92—AIK Solna..................	Sweden	3	0	0	0	0	...	...	...	—	—	—	—	—
92-93—						Did not play.				—	—	—	—	—
93-94—Univ. of Denver..........	WCHA	38	10	20	30	42	...	...	...	—	—	—	—	—
94-95—Univ. of Denver..........	WCHA	42	12	19	31	42	...	...	...	—	—	—	—	—
95-96—Univ. of Denver..........	WCHA	39	12	35	47	40	...	...	...	—	—	—	—	—
96-97—Univ. of Denver..........	WCHA	39	17	17	34	42	...	...	...	—	—	—	—	—
97-98—Calgary	NHL	12	2	1	3	8	-4	0	0	—	—	—	—	—
NHL Totals (2 years)............		12	2	1	3	8	-4	0	0					

ANDERSSON, MIKAEL   RW   LIGHTNING

PERSONAL: Born May 10, 1966, in Malmo, Sweden. ... 5-11/184. ... Shoots left. ... Full name: Bo Mikael Andersson. ... Brother of Niklas Andersson, left winger, San Jose Sharks system. ... Name pronounced mih-KEHL AN-duhr-suhn.
TRANSACTIONS/CAREER NOTES: Selected by Buffalo Sabres in first round (first Sabres pick, 18th overall) of NHL entry draft (June 9, 1984). ... Sprained ankle (March 3, 1987); missed three weeks. ... Twisted ankle (March 1988). ... Sprained neck and shoulder (December 1988). ... Selected by Hartford Whalers in 1989 NHL waiver draft (October 2, 1989). ... Bruised left knee (December 13, 1989). ... Reinjured knee (February 9, 1990). ... Pulled right hamstring (March 8, 1990). ... Reinjured hamstring (March 17, 1990). ... Reinjured hamstring (April 1990). ... Underwent surgery to left knee (May 14, 1990). ... Suffered from the flu (October 4, 1990); missed two games. ... Pulled groin (January 1991). ... Injured toe (October 26, 1991); missed one game. ... Injured groin (December 17, 1991); missed three games. ... Suffered chip fracture to foot (April 12, 1992). ... Signed as free agent by Tampa Bay Lightning (July 8, 1992). ... Suffered back spasms (November 21, 1992); missed four games. ... Injured left rotator cuff (October 27, 1993); missed three games. ... Played in Europe during 1994-95 NHL lock-out. ... Injured groin (March 4, 1995); missed four games. ... Sprained ankle (April 8, 1995); missed six games. ... Injured left knee (November 25, 1995); missed two games. ... Injured left knee (December 3, 1995); missed one game. ... Suffered tendinitis in left knee (December 19, 1995); missed two games. ... Pulled hamstring (November 19, 1996); missed two games. ... Bruised shoulder (December 16, 1996); missed six games. ... Injured back (April 5, 1997); missed remainder of season. ... Suffered from the flu (October 29, 1997); missed one game. ... Strained groin (December 21, 1997); missed three games. ... Suffered from the flu (January 31, 1998); missed five games.
MISCELLANEOUS: Scored on a penalty shot (vs. Robb Stauber, December 15, 1992).
STATISTICAL PLATEAUS: Three-goal games: 1992-93 (1).

		REGULAR SEASON								PLAYOFFS				
Season Team	League	Gms.	G	A	Pts.	PIM	+/-	PP	SH	Gms.	G	A	Pts.	PIM
82-83—Vastra Frolunda	Sweden	1	1	0	1	...	...	...	...	—	—	—	—	—
83-84—Vastra Frolunda	Sweden	12	0	2	2	6	...	...	...	—	—	—	—	—
84-85—Vastra Frolunda	Sweden	32	16	11	27	18	...	...	...	6	3	2	5	2
85-86—Rochester	AHL	20	10	4	14	6	...	...	...	—	—	—	—	—
—Buffalo	NHL	32	1	9	10	4	0	0	0	—	—	—	—	—
86-87—Rochester	AHL	42	6	20	26	14	...	...	...	9	1	2	3	2
—Buffalo	NHL	16	0	3	3	0	-2	0	0	—	—	—	—	—
87-88—Rochester	AHL	35	12	24	36	16	...	...	...	—	—	—	—	—
—Buffalo	NHL	37	3	20	23	10	7	0	1	1	1	0	1	0
88-89—Buffalo	NHL	14	0	1	1	4	-1	0	0	—	—	—	—	—
—Rochester	AHL	56	18	33	51	12	...	...	...	—	—	—	—	—
89-90—Hartford	NHL	50	13	24	37	6	0	1	2	5	0	3	3	2
90-91—Hartford	NHL	41	4	7	11	8	0	0	0	—	—	—	—	—
—Springfield	AHL	26	7	22	29	10	...	...	...	18	†10	8	18	12
91-92—Hartford	NHL	74	18	29	47	14	18	1	3	7	0	2	2	6
92-93—Tampa Bay	NHL	77	16	11	27	14	-14	3	2	—	—	—	—	—
93-94—Tampa Bay	NHL	76	13	12	25	23	8	1	1	—	—	—	—	—
94-95—Vastra Frolunda	Sweden	7	1	0	1	31	...	...	...	—	—	—	—	—
—Tampa Bay	NHL	36	4	7	11	4	-3	0	0	—	—	—	—	—
95-96—Tampa Bay	NHL	64	8	11	19	2	0	0	0	6	1	1	2	0
96-97—Tampa Bay	NHL	70	5	14	19	8	1	0	3	—	—	—	—	—
97-98—Tampa Bay	NHL	72	6	11	17	29	-4	0	1	—	—	—	—	—
—Swed. Olympic team...	Int'l	4	1	1	2	0	...	...	...	—	—	—	—	—
NHL Totals (13 years).........		659	91	159	250	126	10	6	13	19	2	6	8	8

ANDERSSON, NIKLAS   LW

PERSONAL: Born May 20, 1971, in Kunglav, Sweden. ... 5-9/180. ... Shoots left. ... Brother of Mikael Andersson, right winger, Tampa Bay Lightning.
TRANSACTIONS/CAREER NOTES: Selected by Quebec Nordiques in third round (fifth Nordiques pick, 68th overall) of NHL entry draft (June 17, 1989). ... Signed as free agent by New York Islanders (July 15, 1994). ... Sprained shoulder (February 5, 1997); missed two games. ... Suffered sore foot (March 29, 1997); missed two games. ... Signed as free agent by San Jose Sharks (September 10, 1997).
STATISTICAL PLATEAUS: Three-goal games: 1995-96 (1).

		REGULAR SEASON								PLAYOFFS				
Season Team	League	Gms.	G	A	Pts.	PIM	+/-	PP	SH	Gms.	G	A	Pts.	PIM
87-88—Frolunda	Sweden	15	5	5	10	...	...	...	...	—	—	—	—	—
88-89—Frolunda	Sweden	30	13	24	37	...	...	...	...	—	—	—	—	—
89-90—Frolunda	Sweden	38	10	21	31	14	...	...	...	—	—	—	—	—
90-91—Frolunda	Sweden	22	6	10	16	16	...	...	...	—	—	—	—	—
91-92—Halifax.......................	AHL	57	8	26	34	41	...	...	...	—	—	—	—	—
92-93—Halifax.......................	AHL	76	32	50	82	42	...	...	...	—	—	—	—	—
—Quebec	NHL	3	0	1	1	2	0	0	0	—	—	—	—	—
93-94—Cornwall	AHL	42	18	34	52	8	...	...	...	15	8	13	21	10
94-95—Denver	IHL	66	22	39	61	28	...	...	...	—	—	—	—	—
95-96—Utah	IHL	30	13	22	35	25	...	...	...	—	—	—	—	—
—New York Islanders....	NHL	47	14	12	26	12	-3	3	2	—	—	—	—	—
96-97—New York Islanders.....	NHL	74	12	31	43	57	4	1	1	—	—	—	—	—
97-98—Kentucky	AHL	37	10	28	38	54	...	...	...	—	—	—	—	—
—San Jose....................	NHL	5	0	0	0	2	-1	0	0	—	—	—	—	—
—Utah..........................	IHL	21	6	20	26	24	...	...	...	4	3	1	4	4
NHL Totals (4 years)...........		129	26	44	70	73	0	4	3					

ANDREYCHUK, DAVE   LW   DEVILS

PERSONAL: Born September 29, 1963, in Hamilton, Ont. ... 6-4/220. ... Shoots right. ... Full name: David Andreychuk. ... Name pronounced AN-druh-chuhk.

A

TRANSACTIONS/CAREER NOTES: Selected by Buffalo Sabres as underage junior in first round (third Sabres pick, 16th overall) of NHL entry draft (June 9, 1982). ... Sprained knee (March 1983). ... Fractured collarbone (March 1985). ... Twisted knee (September 1985). ... Injured right knee (September 1986). ... Strained left knee ligaments (November 27, 1988). ... Broke left thumb (February 18, 1990). ... Suspended two off-days and fined $500 by NHL for cross-checking (November 16, 1992). ... Traded by Sabres with G Daren Puppa and first-round pick in 1993 draft (D Kenny Jonsson) to Toronto Maple Leafs for G Grant Fuhr and fifth-round pick (D Kevin Popp) in 1995 draft (February 2, 1993). ... Injured knee (December 27, 1993); missed one game. ... Separated shoulder (December 2, 1995); missed five games. ... Suffered from the flu (December 27, 1995); missed one game. ... Underwent thumb surgery (January 15, 1996); missed two games. ... Traded by Maple Leafs to New Jersey Devils for second-round pick (D Marek Posmyk) in 1996 draft and undisclosed pick in 1999 draft (March 13, 1996). ... Bruised left foot (October 23, 1997); missed six games.
HONORS: Played in NHL All-Star Game (1990 and 1994). ... Named to THE SPORTING NEWS All-Star second team (1993-94).
MISCELLANEOUS: Failed to score on a penalty shot (vs. Clint Malarchuk, November 22, 1986; vs. Darcy Wakaluk, February 7, 1992; vs. Tim Cheveldae, April 8, 1995). ... Played with Team Canada in World Junior Championships (1982-83).
STATISTICAL PLATEAUS: Three-goal games: 1987-88 (3), 1988-89 (1), 1989-90 (1), 1991-92 (1), 1992-93 (1). Total: 7. ... Four-goal games: 1991-92 (1), 1992-93 (1). Total: 2. ... Five-goal games: 1985-86 (1). ... Total hat tricks: 10.

Season Team	League	REGULAR SEASON								PLAYOFFS				
		Gms.	G	A	Pts.	PIM	+/-	PP	SH	Gms.	G	A	Pts.	PIM
80-81—Oshawa	OMJHL	67	22	22	44	80	...	...	...	10	3	2	5	20
81-82—Oshawa	OHL	67	58	43	101	71	...	...	...	3	1	4	5	16
82-83—Oshawa	OHL	14	8	24	32	6	...	...	...	—	—	—	—	—
—Buffalo	NHL	43	14	23	37	16	6	3	0	4	1	0	1	4
83-84—Buffalo	NHL	78	38	42	80	42	20	10	0	2	0	1	1	2
84-85—Buffalo	NHL	64	31	30	61	54	-4	14	0	5	4	2	6	4
85-86—Buffalo	NHL	80	36	51	87	61	3	12	0	—	—	—	—	—
86-87—Buffalo	NHL	77	25	48	73	46	2	13	0	—	—	—	—	—
87-88—Buffalo	NHL	80	30	48	78	112	1	15	0	6	2	4	6	0
88-89—Buffalo	NHL	56	28	24	52	40	0	7	0	5	0	3	3	0
89-90—Buffalo	NHL	73	40	42	82	42	6	18	0	6	2	5	7	2
90-91—Buffalo	NHL	80	36	33	69	32	11	13	0	6	2	2	4	8
91-92—Buffalo	NHL	80	41	50	91	71	-9	*28	0	7	1	3	4	12
92-93—Buffalo	NHL	52	29	32	61	48	-8	*20	0	—	—	—	—	—
—Toronto	NHL	31	25	13	38	8	12	*12	0	21	12	7	19	35
93-94—Toronto	NHL	83	53	46	99	98	22	21	5	18	5	5	10	16
94-95—Toronto	NHL	48	22	16	38	34	-7	8	0	7	3	2	5	25
95-96—Toronto	NHL	61	20	24	44	54	-11	12	2	—	—	—	—	—
—New Jersey	NHL	15	8	5	13	10	2	2	0	—	—	—	—	—
96-97—New Jersey	NHL	82	27	34	61	48	38	4	1	1	0	0	0	0
97-98—New Jersey	NHL	75	14	34	48	26	19	4	0	6	1	0	1	4
NHL Totals (16 years)		1158	517	595	1112	842	103	216	8	94	33	34	67	112

ANTIPOV, VLADIMIR RW MAPLE LEAFS

PERSONAL: Born January 17, 1978, in Appatity, U.S.S.R. ... 5-11/180. ... Shoots left.
TRANSACTIONS/CAREER NOTES: Selected by Toronto Maple Leafs in fourth round (sixth Maple Leafs pick, 103rd overall) of NHL entry draft (June 22, 1996).

Season Team	League	REGULAR SEASON								PLAYOFFS				
		Gms.	G	A	Pts.	PIM	+/-	PP	SH	Gms.	G	A	Pts.	PIM
95-96—Torpedo-2 Yaroslavl	CIS Div. II	...	14	11	25	...	...	...	...	—	—	—	—	—
96-97—Torpedo Yaroslavl	Russian	27	6	4	10	22	...	...	...	2	0	0	0	0
97-98—Torpedo Yaroslavl	Russian	41	9	3	12	57	...	...	...	—	—	—	—	—

ANTOSKI, SHAWN LW

PERSONAL: Born May 25, 1970, in Brantford, Ont. ... 6-4/235. ... Shoots left. ... Name pronounced an-TAH-skee.
TRANSACTIONS/CAREER NOTES: Injured knee ligament (December 1988). ... Separated shoulder (March 1989). ... Selected by Vancouver Canucks in first round (second Canucks pick, 18th overall) of NHL entry draft (June 17, 1989). ... Suffered sore back (December 1991). ... Fractured knuckle (December 15, 1993); missed eight games. ... Sprained thumb (January 19, 1994); missed three games. ... Suffered sore hand (April 1, 1994); missed three games. ... Traded by Canucks to Philadelphia Flyers for LW Josef Beranek (February 15, 1995). ... Suffered from the flu (March 2, 1995); missed four games. ... Injured shoulder (October 22, 1995); missed one game. ... Strained hamstring (December 18, 1995); missed two games. ... Sprained right ankle (January 9, 1996); missed two games. ... Suffered from the flu (January 22, 1996); missed one game. ... Signed as free agent by Pittsburgh Penguins (July 31, 1996). ... Traded by Penguins with D Dmitri Mironov to Mighty Ducks of Anaheim for C Alex Hicks and D Fredrik Olausson (November 19, 1996). ... Strained left hip (November 20, 1996); missed 19 games. ... Strained hip (January 8, 1997); missed 10 games. ... Underwent hernia surgery (February 4, 1997); missed remainder of season. ... Suffered depressed skull fracture in car accident (November 24, 1997); missed remainder of season.

Season Team	League	REGULAR SEASON								PLAYOFFS				
		Gms.	G	A	Pts.	PIM	+/-	PP	SH	Gms.	G	A	Pts.	PIM
87-88—North Bay	OHL	52	3	4	7	163	...	...	...	—	—	—	—	—
88-89—North Bay	OHL	57	6	21	27	201	...	...	...	9	5	3	8	24
89-90—North Bay	OHL	59	25	31	56	201	...	...	...	5	1	2	3	17
90-91—Milwaukee	IHL	62	17	7	24	330	...	...	...	5	1	2	3	10
—Vancouver	NHL	2	0	0	0	0	-2	0	0	—	—	—	—	—
91-92—Milwaukee	IHL	52	17	16	33	346	...	...	...	5	2	0	2	20
—Vancouver	NHL	4	0	0	0	29	-1	0	0	—	—	—	—	—
92-93—Hamilton	AHL	41	3	4	7	172	...	...	...	—	—	—	—	—
—Vancouver	NHL	2	0	0	0	0	0	0	0	—	—	—	—	—
93-94—Vancouver	NHL	55	1	2	3	190	-11	0	0	16	0	1	1	36
94-95—Vancouver	NHL	7	0	0	0	46	-4	0	0	—	—	—	—	—
—Philadelphia	NHL	25	0	0	0	61	0	0	0	13	0	1	1	10
95-96—Philadelphia	NHL	64	1	3	4	204	-4	0	0	7	1	1	2	28
96-97—Pittsburgh	NHL	13	0	0	0	49	0	0	0	—	—	—	—	—
—Anaheim	NHL	2	0	0	0	2	1	0	0	—	—	—	—	—
97-98—Anaheim	NHL	9	1	0	1	18	1	0	0	—	—	—	—	—
NHL Totals (8 years)		183	3	5	8	599	-20	0	0	36	1	3	4	74

ARMSTRONG, CHRIS   D   PREDATORS

PERSONAL: Born June 26, 1975, in Regina, Sask. ... 6-0/184. ... Shoots left.
HIGH SCHOOL: Vanier Collegiate (Moose Jaw, Sask.).
TRANSACTIONS/CAREER NOTES: Selected by Florida Panthers in third round (third Panthers pick, 57th overall) of NHL entry draft (June 26, 1993). ... Selected by Nashville Predators in NHL expansion draft (June 26, 1998).
HONORS: Named to Can.HL All-Star second team (1993-94). ... Named to WHL (East) All-Star first team (1993-94). ... Named to WHL (East) All-Star second team (1994-95).

Season Team	League	REGULAR SEASON Gms.	G	A	Pts.	PIM	+/-	PP	SH	PLAYOFFS Gms.	G	A	Pts.	PIM
91-92—Moose Jaw	WHL	43	2	7	9	19	...	...	...	4	0	0	0	0
92-93—Moose Jaw	WHL	67	9	35	44	104	...	...	...	—	—	—	—	—
93-94—Moose Jaw	WHL	64	13	55	68	54	...	...	...	10	1	3	4	2
—Cincinnati	IHL	1	0	0	0	0	...	...	...	10	2	12	14	22
94-95—Moose Jaw	WHL	66	17	54	71	61	...	...	...	9	1	3	4	10
—Cincinnati	IHL	—	—	—	—	—	...	...	...					
95-96—Carolina	AHL	78	9	33	42	65	...	...	...	—	—	—	—	—
96-97—Carolina	AHL	66	9	23	32	38	...	...	...	—	—	—	—	—
97-98—Fort Wayne	IHL	79	8	36	44	66	...	...	...	4	0	2	2	4

ARMSTRONG, DEREK   C   RANGERS

PERSONAL: Born April 23, 1973, in Ottawa. ... 5-11/188. ... Shoots right.
HIGH SCHOOL: Lo-Ellen Park Secondary School (Sudbury, Ont.).
TRANSACTIONS/CAREER NOTES: Selected by New York Islanders in sixth round (fifth Islanders pick, 128th overall) of NHL entry draft (June 20, 1992). ... Suffered food poisoning (January 28, 1997); missed one game. ... Signed as free agent by Ottawa Senators (July 10, 1997). ... Signed as free agent by New York Rangers (July 20, 1998).

Season Team	League	REGULAR SEASON Gms.	G	A	Pts.	PIM	+/-	PP	SH	PLAYOFFS Gms.	G	A	Pts.	PIM
89-90—Hawkesbury	COJHL	48	8	10	18	30	...	...	...	—	—	—	—	—
90-91—Hawkesbury	COJHL	54	27	45	72	49	...	...	...	—	—	—	—	—
91-92—Sudbury	OHL	66	31	54	85	22	...	...	...	9	2	2	4	2
92-93—Sudbury	OHL	66	44	62	106	56	...	...	...	14	9	10	19	26
93-94—Salt Lake City	IHL	76	23	35	58	61	...	...	...	—	—	—	—	—
94-95—Denver	IHL	59	13	18	31	65	...	...	...	6	0	2	2	0
95-96—Worcester	AHL	51	11	15	26	33	...	...	...	4	2	1	3	0
—New York Islanders	NHL	19	1	3	4	14	-6	0	0	—	—	—	—	—
96-97—New York Islanders	NHL	50	6	7	13	33	-8	0	0	—	—	—	—	—
—Utah	IHL	17	4	8	12	10	...	...	...	6	0	4	4	4
97-98—Detroit	IHL	10	0	1	1	2	...	...	...	—	—	—	—	—
—Hartford	AHL	54	16	30	46	40	...	...	...	15	2	6	8	22
—Ottawa	NHL	9	2	0	2	9	1	0	0	—	—	—	—	—
NHL Totals (3 years)		78	9	10	19	56	-13	0	0					

ARNOTT, JASON   C/RW   DEVILS

PERSONAL: Born October 11, 1974, in Collingworth, Ont. ... 6-3/220. ... Shoots right. ... Name pronounced AHR-niht.
HIGH SCHOOL: Henry Street (Whitby, Ont.).
TRANSACTIONS/CAREER NOTES: Selected by Edmonton Oilers in first round (first Oilers pick, seventh overall) of NHL entry draft (June 26, 1993). ... Suffered from tonsillitis (November 3, 1993); missed one game. ... Bruised sternum (November 27, 1993); missed one game. ... Sprained back (December 7, 1993); missed one game. ... Underwent appendectomy (December 28, 1993); missed three games. ... Suffered from the flu (February 22, 1995); missed one game. ... Suffered concussion (March 23, 1995); missed two games. ... Strained knee (April 19, 1995); missed two games. ... Suspended one game by NHL for game misconduct penalties (April 22, 1995). ... Suffered concussion and lacerated face (October 8, 1995); missed seven games. ... Sprained knee (February 11, 1996); missed nine games. ... Strained knee (March 19, 1996); missed one game. ... Suffered inner ear infection (April 8, 1996); missed one game. ... Fractured ankle (December 27, 1996); missed seven games. ... Injured ankle (January 22, 1997); missed two games. ... Suffered from the flu (February 12, 1997); missed two games. ... Strained lower back (March 23, 1997); missed four games. ... Injured shoulder (December 10, 1997); missed five games. ... Reinjured shoulder (January 2, 1998); missed two games. ... Traded by Oilers with D Bryan Muir to New Jersey Devils for RW Bill Guerin and RW Valeri Zelepukin (January 4, 1998). ... Suffered back spasms (March 21, 1998); missed one game. ... Injured hip (April 8, 1998); missed three games. ... Reinjured hip (April 16, 1998); missed two games.
HONORS: Named NHL Rookie of the Year by THE SPORTING NEWS (1993-94). ... Named to NHL All-Rookie team (1993-94). ... Played in NHL All-Star Game (1997).
STATISTICAL PLATEAUS: Three-goal games: 1994-95 (1), 1995-96 (1). Total: 2.

Season Team	League	REGULAR SEASON Gms.	G	A	Pts.	PIM	+/-	PP	SH	PLAYOFFS Gms.	G	A	Pts.	PIM
89-90—Stayner	Jr. C	34	21	31	52	12	...	...	...	—	—	—	—	—
90-91—Lindsay Jr. B	OHA	42	17	44	61	10	...	...	...	—	—	—	—	—
91-92—Oshawa	OHL	57	9	15	24	12	...	...	...	—	—	—	—	—
92-93—Oshawa	OHL	56	41	57	98	74	...	...	...	13	9	9	18	20
93-94—Edmonton	NHL	78	33	35	68	104	1	10	0	—	—	—	—	—
94-95—Edmonton	NHL	42	15	22	37	128	-14	7	0	—	—	—	—	—
95-96—Edmonton	NHL	64	28	31	59	87	-6	8	0	—	—	—	—	—
96-97—Edmonton	NHL	67	19	38	57	92	-21	10	1	12	3	6	9	18
97-98—Edmonton	NHL	35	5	13	18	78	-16	1	0	—	—	—	—	—
—New Jersey	NHL	35	5	10	15	21	-8	3	0	5	0	2	2	0
NHL Totals (5 years)		321	105	149	254	510	-64	39	1	17	3	8	11	18

ARSENAULT, DAVID   G   RED WINGS

PERSONAL: Born March 21, 1977, in West Germany. ... 6-1/165. ... Catches left. ... Name pronounced AHR-sih-noh.
TRANSACTIONS/CAREER NOTES: Selected by Detroit Red Wings in fifth round (sixth Red Wings pick, 126th overall) of NHL entry draft (July 8, 1995).

					REGULAR SEASON							PLAYOFFS					
Season Team	League	Gms.	Min	W	L	T	GA	SO	Avg.	Gms.	Min.	W	L	GA	SO	Avg.
94-95—St. Hyacinthe	QMJHL	19	862	3	10	0	75	0	5.22	—	—	—	—	—	—	—
—Drummondville	QMJHL	12	478	2	5	0	40	0	5.02	2	122	0	2	8	0	3.93
95-96—Drummondville	QMJHL	21	1177	8	10	1	89	0	4.54	—	—	—	—	—	—	—
—Chicoutimi	QMJHL	6	207	1	1	1	14	0	4.06	5	108	0	1	10	0	5.56
96-97—Oshawa	OHL	41	2316	24	9	5	106	2	2.75	17	1027	11	6	46	*1	*2.69
97-98—Adirondack	AHL	10	563	3	5	0	41	0	4.37	—	—	—	—	—	—	—
—Toledo	ECHL	22	1261	13	4	‡3	60	0	2.85	—	—	—	—	—	—	—

ARVEDSON, MAGNUS   LW   SENATORS

PERSONAL: Born November 25, 1971, in Karlstad, Sweden. ... 6-2/198. ... Shoots left. ... Name pronounced AHR-vihd-suhn.
TRANSACTIONS/CAREER NOTES: Selected by Ottawa Senators in fifth round (fourth Senators pick, 119th overall) of NHL entry draft (June 21, 1997). ... Strained groin (October 17, 1997); missed seven games. ... Strained groin (November 29, 1997); missed three games. ... Suffered concussion (December 16, 1997); missed five games. ... Strained left shoulder (January 11, 1998); missed one game. ... Injured groin (March 20, 1998); missed three games.

				REGULAR SEASON							PLAYOFFS			
Season Team	League	Gms.	G	A	Pts.	PIM	+/-	PP	SH	Gms.	G	A	Pts.	PIM
91-92—Orebro	Swed. Dv.II	32	12	21	33	30	...	...	...	7	4	4	8	4
92-93—Orebro	Swed. Dv.II	36	11	18	29	34	...	...	...	6	2	1	3	0
93-94—Farjestad Karlstad	Sweden	16	1	7	8	10	...	...	...	—	—	—	—	—
94-95—Farjestad Karlstad	Sweden	36	1	7	8	45	...	...	...	4	0	0	0	6
95-96—Farjestad Karlstad	Sweden	39	10	14	24	42	...	...	...	8	0	3	3	10
96-97—Farjestad Karlstad	Sweden	48	13	11	24	36	...	...	...	14	4	7	11	8
97-98—Ottawa	NHL	61	11	15	26	36	2	0	1	11	0	1	1	6
NHL Totals (1 year)		61	11	15	26	36	2	0	1	11	0	1	1	6

ASHAM, ARRON   C   CANADIENS

PERSONAL: Born April 13, 1978, in Portage, Man. ... 5-11/176. ... Shoots right.
TRANSACTIONS/CAREER NOTES: Selected by Montreal Canadiens in third round (third Canadiens pick, 71st overall) of NHL entry draft (June 22, 1996).

				REGULAR SEASON							PLAYOFFS			
Season Team	League	Gms.	G	A	Pts.	PIM	+/-	PP	SH	Gms.	G	A	Pts.	PIM
94-95—Red Deer	WHL	62	11	16	27	126	...	...	...	—	—	—	—	—
95-96—Red Deer	WHL	70	32	45	77	174	...	...	...	10	6	3	9	20
96-97—Red Deer	WHL	67	45	51	96	149	...	...	...	16	12	14	26	36
97-98—Red Deer	WHL	67	43	49	92	153	...	...	...	5	0	2	2	8
—Fredericton	AHL	2	1	1	2	0	...	...	...	2	0	1	1	0

ASKEY, TOM   G   MIGHTY DUCKS

PERSONAL: Born October 4, 1974, in Kenmore, N.Y. ... 6-2/185. ... Catches left.
COLLEGE: Ohio State.
TRANSACTIONS/CAREER NOTES: Selected by Mighty Ducks of Anaheim in eighth round (eighth Ducks pick, 186th overall) of NHL entry draft (June 26, 1993).
HONORS: Named to CCHA All-Star second team (1995-96).

					REGULAR SEASON							PLAYOFFS					
Season Team	League	Gms.	Min	W	L	T	GA	SO	Avg.	Gms.	Min.	W	L	GA	SO	Avg.
92-93—Ohio State	CCHA	25	1235	2	19	0	125	0	6.07	—	—	—	—	—	—	—
93-94—Ohio State	CCHA	27	1488	3	19	4	103	0	4.15	—	—	—	—	—	—	—
94-95—Ohio State	CCHA	26	1387	4	19	2	121	0	5.23	—	—	—	—	—	—	—
95-96—Ohio State	CCHA	26	1340	8	11	4	68	0	3.04	—	—	—	—	—	—	—
96-97—Baltimore	AHL	40	2239	17	18	2	140	1	3.75	3	138	0	3	11	0	4.78
97-98—Cincinnati	AHL	32	1753	10	16	4	104	3	3.56	—	—	—	—	—	—	—
—Anaheim	NHL	7	273	0	1	2	12	0	2.64	—	—	—	—	—	—	—
NHL Totals (1 year)		7	273	0	1	2	12	0	2.64							

ATCHEYNUM, BLAIR   RW   PREDATORS

PERSONAL: Born April 20, 1969, in Estevan, Sask. ... 6-1/196. ... Shoots right. ... Name pronounced ATCH-ih-nuhm.
TRANSACTIONS/CAREER NOTES: Selected by Swift Current Broncos in special compensation draft to replace players injured and killed in a December 30, 1986 bus crash (February 1987). ... Traded by Broncos to Moose Jaw Warriors for D Tim Logan (February 1987). ... Selected by Hartford Whalers in third round (second Whalers pick, 52nd overall) of NHL entry draft (June 17, 1989). ... Suffered concussion (January 12, 1991). ... Selected by Ottawa Senators in NHL expansion draft (June 18, 1992). ... Signed as free agent by Worcester Icecats (December 2, 1994). ... Signed as free agent by Cape Breton of AHL (September 8, 1995). ... Signed as free agent by St. Louis Blues (August 12, 1997). ... Fractured finger (March 1, 1998); missed 17 games. ... Selected by Nashville Predators in NHL expansion draft (June 26, 1998).
HONORS: Won Brad Hornung Trophy (1988-89). ... Named to WHL (East) All-Star first team (1988-89). ... Named to AHL All-Star first team (1996-97).

Season Team	League	Gms.	G	A	Pts.	PIM	+/-	PP	SH	Gms.	G	A	Pts.	PIM
85-86—North Battleford.........	SJHL	35	25	20	45	50	...	...	...	—	—	—	—	—
86-87—Saskatoon..................	WHL	21	0	4	4	4	...	...	...	—	—	—	—	—
—Swift Current	WHL	5	2	1	3	0	...	...	...	—	—	—	—	—
—Moose Jaw	WHL	12	3	0	3	2	...	...	...	—	—	—	—	—
87-88—Moose Jaw	WHL	60	32	16	48	52	...	...	...	—	—	—	—	—
88-89—Moose Jaw	WHL	71	70	68	138	70	...	...	...	7	2	5	7	13
89-90—Binghamton	AHL	78	20	21	41	45	...	...	...	—	—	—	—	—
90-91—Springfield	AHL	72	25	27	52	42	...	...	...	13	0	6	6	6
91-92—Springfield	AHL	62	16	21	37	64	...	...	...	6	1	1	2	2
92-93—New Haven	AHL	51	16	18	34	47	...	...	...	—	—	—	—	—
—Ottawa	NHL	4	0	1	1	0	-3	0	0	—	—	—	—	—
93-94—Portland...................	AHL	2	0	0	0	0	...	...	...	—	—	—	—	—
—Springfield	AHL	40	18	22	40	13	...	...	...	6	0	2	2	0
—Columbus	ECHL	16	15	12	27	10	...	...	...	—	—	—	—	—
94-95—Minnesota.................	IHL	17	4	6	10	7	...	...	...	—	—	—	—	—
—Worcester	AHL	55	17	29	46	26	...	...	...	—	—	—	—	—
95-96—Cape Breton	AHL	79	30	42	72	65	...	...	...	—	—	—	—	—
96-97—Hershey	AHL	77	42	45	87	57	...	...	...	13	6	11	17	6
97-98—St. Louis	NHL	61	11	15	26	10	5	0	1	10	0	0	0	2
NHL Totals (2 years)..........		65	11	16	27	10	2	0	1	10	0	0	0	2

AUBIN, JEAN-SEBASTIEN   G   PENGUINS

PERSONAL: Born July 19, 1977, in Montreal. ... 5-11/174. ... Catches right. ... Name pronounced AH-ban.
TRANSACTIONS/CAREER NOTES: Selected by Pittsburgh Penguins in third round (second Penguins pick, 76th overall) of NHL entry draft (July 8, 1995).

Season Team	League	REGULAR SEASON							PLAYOFFS					
		Gms.	Min	W	L	T	GA	SO	Avg.	Gms.	Min.	W	L	GA	SO	Avg.
94-95—Sherbrooke	QMJHL	27	1287	13	10	1	73	1	3.40	3	185	1	2	11	0	3.57
95-96—Sherbrooke	QMJHL	40	2084	18	14	2	127	0	3.66	4	174	1	3	16	0	5.52
96-97—Sherbrooke	QMJHL	4	249	3	1	0	8	0	1.93	—	—	—	—	—	—	—
—Moncton.....................	QMJHL	23	1311	9	13	0	72	1	3.30	—	—	—	—	—	—	—
—Laval	QMJHL	11	532	2	6	1	41	0	4.62	2	128	0	2	10	0	4.69
97-98—Syracuse	AHL	8	380	2	4	1	26	0	4.11	—	—	—	—	—	—	—
—Dayton	ECHL	21	1177	15	2	‡2	59	1	3.01	3	142	1	1	4	0	1.69

AUBIN, SERGE   C

PERSONAL: Born February 15, 1975, in Val d'Or, Que. ... 6-0/180. ... Shoots left. ... Name pronounced AH-ban.
TRANSACTIONS/CAREER NOTES: Selected by Pittsburgh Penguins in seventh round (ninth Penguins pick, 161st overall) of NHL entry draft (June 29, 1994).

Season Team	League	REGULAR SEASON								PLAYOFFS				
		Gms.	G	A	Pts.	PIM	+/-	PP	SH	Gms.	G	A	Pts.	PIM
92-93—Drummondville	QMJHL	65	16	34	50	30	...	...	...	8	0	1	1	16
93-94—Granby......................	QMJHL	63	42	32	74	80	...	...	...	7	2	3	5	8
94-95—Granby......................	QMJHL	60	37	73	110	55	...	...	...	11	8	15	23	4
95-96—Cleveland	IHL	2	0	0	0	0	...	...	...	2	0	0	0	0
—Hampton Roads...........	ECHL	62	24	62	86	74	...	...	...	3	1	4	5	10
96-97—Cleveland	IHL	57	9	16	25	38	...	...	...	2	0	0	0	0
97-98—Syracuse....................	AHL	55	6	14	20	57	...	...	...	—	—	—	—	—
—Hershey	AHL	5	2	1	3	0	...	...	...	7	1	3	4	6

AUCOIN, ADRIAN   D   CANUCKS

PERSONAL: Born July 3, 1973, in London, Ont. ... 6-1/194. ... Shoots right. ... Name pronounced oh-COYN.
COLLEGE: Boston University.
TRANSACTIONS/CAREER NOTES: Selected by Vancouver Canucks in fifth round (seventh Canucks pick, 117th overall) of NHL entry draft (June 20, 1992). ... Sprained shoulder (January 10, 1997); missed six games. ... Strained groin (October 30, 1997); missed five games. ... Reinjured groin (November 12, 1997); missed 10 games. ... Sprained ankle (December 13, 1997); missed seven games.
MISCELLANEOUS: Member of silver-medal-winning Canadian Olympic team (1994).

Season Team	League	REGULAR SEASON								PLAYOFFS				
		Gms.	G	A	Pts.	PIM	+/-	PP	SH	Gms.	G	A	Pts.	PIM
91-92—Boston University	Hockey East	33	2	10	12	62	...	...	...	—	—	—	—	—
92-93—Canadian nat'l team ...	Int'l	42	8	10	18	71	...	...	...	—	—	—	—	—
93-94—Canadian nat'l team ...	Int'l	59	5	12	17	80	...	...	...	—	—	—	—	—
—Can. Olympic Team.....	Int'l	4	0	0	0	2	...	...	...	—	—	—	—	—
—Hamilton	AHL	13	1	2	3	19	...	...	...	4	0	2	2	6
94-95—Syracuse....................	AHL	71	13	18	31	52	...	...	...	—	—	—	—	—
—Vancouver..................	NHL	1	1	0	1	0	1	0	0	4	1	0	1	0
95-96—Syracuse....................	AHL	29	5	13	18	47	...	...	...	—	—	—	—	—
—Vancouver..................	NHL	49	4	14	18	34	8	2	0	6	0	0	0	2
96-97—Vancouver..................	NHL	70	5	16	21	63	0	1	0	—	—	—	—	—
97-98—Vancouver..................	NHL	35	3	3	6	21	-4	1	0	—	—	—	—	—
NHL Totals (4 years)..........		155	13	33	46	118	5	4	0	10	1	0	1	2

AUDET, PHILIPPE — LW — RED WINGS

PERSONAL: Born June 4, 1977, in Ottawa. ... 6-2/175. ... Shoots left. ... Name pronounced oh-DEHT.
TRANSACTIONS/CAREER NOTES: Selected by Detroit Red Wings in second round (second Red Wings pick, 52nd overall) of NHL entry draft (July 8, 1995).
HONORS: Won Ed Chynoweth Trophy (1995-96). ... Named to Memorial Cup All-Star team (1995-96). ... Named to QMJHL All-Star first team (1996-97).

Season Team	League	REGULAR SEASON								PLAYOFFS				
		Gms.	G	A	Pts.	PIM	+/-	PP	SH	Gms.	G	A	Pts.	PIM
94-95—Granby	QMJHL	62	19	17	36	93	...	...	...	7	1	3	4	4
95-96—Granby	QMJHL	67	40	43	83	162	...	...	...	21	12	18	30	32
96-97—Granby	QMJHL	67	52	56	108	150	...	...	...	4	4	1	5	25
—Adirondack	AHL	3	1	1	2	0	...	...	...	1	1	0	1	0
97-98—Adirondack	AHL	50	7	8	15	43	...	...	...	1	0	0	0	0

AUDETTE, DONALD — RW — SABRES

PERSONAL: Born September 23, 1969, in Laval, Que. ... 5-8/184. ... Shoots right. ... Name pronounced aw-DEHT.
TRANSACTIONS/CAREER NOTES: Selected by Buffalo Sabres in ninth round (eighth Sabres pick, 183rd overall) of NHL entry draft (June 17, 1989). ... Broke left hand (February 11, 1990); missed seven games. ... Bruised thigh (September 1990). ... Bruised thigh (October 1990); missed five games. ... Tore left knee ligaments (November 16, 1990). ... Underwent surgery to left knee (December 10, 1990). ... Sprained ankle (December 14, 1991); missed eight games. ... Injured knee (March 31, 1992). ... Underwent knee surgery prior to 1992-93 season; missed first 22 games of season. ... Tore knee cartilage (September 23, 1995); missed 11 games. ... Broke tip of right thumb (November 8, 1995); missed two games. ... Injured right knee (December 1, 1995); missed seven games. ... Underwent right knee surgery (January 26, 1996); missed remainder of season. ... Strained groin (October 26, 1996); missed five games. ... Suffered concussion (October 22, 1997); missed seven games.
HONORS: Won Guy Lafleur Trophy (1988-89). ... Named to QMJHL All-Star first team (1988-89). ... Won Dudley (Red) Garrett Memorial Trophy (1989-90). ... Named to AHL All-Star first team (1989-90).
MISCELLANEOUS: Failed to score on a penalty shot (vs. Felix Potvin, November 21, 1996).
STATISTICAL PLATEAUS: Three-goal games: 1994-95 (1), 1995-96 (1). Total: 2.

Season Team	League	REGULAR SEASON								PLAYOFFS				
		Gms.	G	A	Pts.	PIM	+/-	PP	SH	Gms.	G	A	Pts.	PIM
86-87—Laval	QMJHL	66	17	22	39	36	...	...	...	14	2	6	8	10
87-88—Laval	QMJHL	63	48	61	109	56	...	...	...	14	7	12	19	20
88-89—Laval	QMJHL	70	76	85	161	123	...	...	...	17	*17	12	29	43
89-90—Rochester	AHL	70	42	46	88	78	...	...	...	15	9	8	17	29
—Buffalo	NHL	0	0	0	0	0	0	0	0	2	0	0	0	0
90-91—Rochester	AHL	5	4	0	4	2	...	...	...	—	—	—	—	—
—Buffalo	NHL	8	4	3	7	4	-1	2	0	—	—	—	—	—
91-92—Buffalo	NHL	63	31	17	48	75	-1	5	0	—	—	—	—	—
92-93—Buffalo	NHL	44	12	7	19	51	-8	2	0	8	2	2	4	6
—Rochester	AHL	6	8	4	12	10	...	...	...	—	—	—	—	—
93-94—Buffalo	NHL	77	29	30	59	41	2	16	1	7	0	1	1	6
94-95—Buffalo	NHL	46	24	13	37	27	-3	13	0	5	1	1	2	4
95-96—Buffalo	NHL	23	12	13	25	18	0	8	0	—	—	—	—	—
96-97—Buffalo	NHL	73	28	22	50	48	-6	8	0	11	4	5	9	6
97-98—Buffalo	NHL	75	24	20	44	59	10	10	0	15	5	8	13	10
NHL Totals (9 years)		409	164	125	289	323	-7	64	1	48	12	17	29	32

AUGER, VINCENT — C — AVALANCHE

PERSONAL: Born March 7, 1975, in Quebec City. ... 5-10/175. ... Shoots left.
COLLEGE: Cornell.
TRANSACTIONS/CAREER NOTES: Selected by Quebec Nordiques in ninth round (11th Nordiques pick, 231st overall) of NHL entry draft (June 26, 1993). ... Nordiques franchise moved to Colorado and renamed Avalanche for 1995-96 season (June 21, 1995).

Season Team	League	REGULAR SEASON								PLAYOFFS				
		Gms.	G	A	Pts.	PIM	+/-	PP	SH	Gms.	G	A	Pts.	PIM
92-93—Hawkesbury	COJHL	52	41	36	77	104	...	...	...	—	—	—	—	—
93-94—Cornell University	ECAC	29	11	13	24	33	...	...	...	—	—	—	—	—
94-95—Cornell University	ECAC							Did not play.						
95-96—Cornell University	ECAC	23	5	15	20	22	...	...	...	—	—	—	—	—
96-97—Cornell University	ECAC	26	11	7	18	36	...	...	...	—	—	—	—	—
97-98—Cornell University	ECAC	4	2	5	7	4	...	...	...	—	—	—	—	—

AXELSSON, P.J. — RW — BRUINS

PERSONAL: Born February 26, 1975, in Kungalv, Sweden. ... 6-1/174. ... Shoots left. ... Full name: Per-Johan Axelsson. ... Name pronounced AK-sihl-suhn.
TRANSACTIONS/CAREER NOTES: Selected by Boston Bruins in seventh round (seventh Bruins pick, 177th overall) of NHL entry draft (June 8, 1995).

Season Team	League	REGULAR SEASON								PLAYOFFS				
		Gms.	G	A	Pts.	PIM	+/-	PP	SH	Gms.	G	A	Pts.	PIM
93-94—Frolunda	Sweden	11	0	0	0	4	...	...	...	4	0	0	0	0
94-95—Frolunda	Sweden	8	2	1	3	6	...	...	...	—	—	—	—	—
95-96—Frolunda	Sweden	36	15	5	20	10	...	...	...	13	3	0	3	10
96-97—Vastra Frolunda	Sweden	50	19	15	34	34	...	...	...	3	0	2	2	0
97-98—Boston	NHL	82	8	19	27	38	-14	2	0	6	1	0	1	0
NHL Totals (1 year)		82	8	19	27	38	-14	2	0	6	1	0	1	0

BABENKO, YURI   C   AVALANCHE

PERSONAL: Born January 2, 1978, in Penza, U.S.S.R. ... 6-0/185. ... Shoots left.
TRANSACTIONS/CAREER NOTES: Selected by Colorado Avalanche in second round (second Avalanche pick, 51st overall) of NHL entry draft (June 22, 1996).

		REGULAR SEASON								PLAYOFFS				
Season Team	League	Gms.	G	A	Pts.	PIM	+/-	PP	SH	Gms.	G	A	Pts.	PIM
95-96—Soviet Wings	CIS	21	0	0	0	16	...	...	...	—	—	—	—	—
96-97—Soviet Wings	USSR	4	1	0	1	4	...	...	...	—	—	—	—	—
—Soviet Wings 2	Rus. Div. 3	26	8	10	18	24	...	...	...	—	—	—	—	—
—CSKA	Rus. Div. 2	24	3	3	6	12	...	...	...	—	—	—	—	—
97-98—Plymouth	OHL	59	22	34	56	22	...	...	...	15	3	7	10	24

BABYCH, DAVE   D   FLYERS   B

PERSONAL: Born May 23, 1961, in Edmonton. ... 6-2/215. ... Shoots left. ... Full Name: David Michael Babych. ... Brother of Wayne Babych, right winger for four NHL teams (1978-79 through 1986-87). ... Name pronounced BAB-ihch.
TRANSACTIONS/CAREER NOTES: Selected by Winnipeg Jets as underage junior in first round (first Jets pick, second overall) of NHL entry draft (June 11, 1980). ... Separated shoulder (March 1984). ... Suffered back spasms (December 1984). ... Traded by Jets to Hartford Whalers for RW Ray Neufeld (November 21, 1985). ... Injured hip (January 1987); missed 12 games. ... Cut right hand (March 16, 1989); missed six games. ... Bruised neck (March 1990). ... Underwent surgery to right wrist (October 29, 1990); missed 44 games. ... Broke right thumb (February 8, 1991); missed remainder of season. ... Selected by Minnesota North Stars in NHL expansion draft (May 30, 1991). ... Traded by North Stars to Vancouver Canucks for D Craig Ludwig as part of a three-club deal in which Canucks sent D Tom Kurvers to Islanders for Ludwig (June 22, 1991). ... Suffered sore back (November 3, 1991); missed one game. ... Suffered hernia (September 22, 1992); missed 22 games. ... Sprained knee (December 7, 1992); missed 12 games. ... Suffered from the flu (March 20, 1993); missed one game. ... Suffered facial lacerations (April 4, 1993); missed three games. ... Suffered facial lacerations (December 15, 1993); missed two games. ... Bruised foot (February 13, 1994); missed one game. ... Suffered injury (February 5, 1995); missed three games. ... Injured foot (December 8, 1995); missed 23 games. ... Suffered illness (February 23, 1996); missed one game. ... Injured hand (February 29, 1996); missed one game. ... Injured ankle (April 1, 1996); missed three games. ... Strained groin (December 3, 1996); missed three games. ... Strained back and hip (October 9, 1997); missed nine games. ... Strained back (November 4, 1997); missed 15 games. ... Traded by Canucks with sixth-round pick (G Antero Nittymaki) in 1998 draft to Philadelphia Flyers for third-round pick (RW Justin Morrison) in 1998 draft (March 24, 1998). ... Fractured left foot (April 9, 1998); missed final six games of regular season.
HONORS: Won AJHL Top Defenseman Trophy (1977-78). ... Won AJHL Rookie of the Year Trophy (1977-78). ... Named to AJHL All-Star first team (1977-78). ... Won WHL Top Defenseman Trophy (1979-80). ... Named to WHL All-Star first team (1979-80). ... Played in NHL All-Star Game (1983 and 1984).
STATISTICAL PLATEAUS: Three-goal games: 1991-92 (1).

		REGULAR SEASON								PLAYOFFS				
Season Team	League	Gms.	G	A	Pts.	PIM	+/-	PP	SH	Gms.	G	A	Pts.	PIM
77-78—Portland	WCHL	6	1	3	4	4	...	...	...	—	—	—	—	—
—Fort Saskatchewan	AJHL	56	31	69	100	37	...	...	...	—	—	—	—	—
78-79—Portland	WHL	67	20	59	79	63	...	...	...	25	7	22	29	22
79-80—Portland	WHL	50	22	60	82	71	...	...	...	8	1	10	11	2
80-81—Winnipeg	NHL	69	6	38	44	90	-61	3	0	—	—	—	—	—
81-82—Winnipeg	NHL	79	19	49	68	92	-11	11	0	4	1	2	3	29
82-83—Winnipeg	NHL	79	13	61	74	56	-10	7	0	3	0	0	0	0
83-84—Winnipeg	NHL	66	18	39	57	62	-31	10	0	3	1	1	2	0
84-85—Winnipeg	NHL	78	13	49	62	78	-16	6	0	8	2	7	9	6
85-86—Winnipeg	NHL	19	4	12	16	14	-1	2	0	—	—	—	—	—
—Hartford	NHL	62	10	43	53	36	1	7	1	8	1	3	4	14
86-87—Hartford	NHL	66	8	33	41	44	-16	7	0	6	1	1	2	14
87-88—Hartford	NHL	71	14	36	50	54	-25	10	0	6	3	2	5	2
88-89—Hartford	NHL	70	6	41	47	54	-5	4	0	4	1	5	6	2
89-90—Hartford	NHL	72	6	37	43	62	-16	4	0	7	1	2	3	0
90-91—Hartford	NHL	8	0	6	6	4	-4	0	0	—	—	—	—	—
91-92—Vancouver	NHL	75	5	24	29	63	-2	4	0	13	2	6	8	10
92-93—Vancouver	NHL	43	3	16	19	44	6	3	0	12	2	5	7	6
93-94—Vancouver	NHL	73	4	28	32	52	0	0	0	24	3	5	8	12
94-95—Vancouver	NHL	40	3	11	14	18	-13	1	0	11	2	2	4	14
95-96—Vancouver	NHL	53	3	21	24	38	-5	3	0	—	—	—	—	—
96-97—Vancouver	NHL	78	5	22	27	38	-2	2	0	—	—	—	—	—
97-98—Vancouver	NHL	47	0	9	9	37	-11	0	0	—	—	—	—	—
—Philadelphia	NHL	6	0	0	0	12	2	0	0	5	1	0	1	4
NHL Totals (18 years)		1154	140	575	715	948	-220	84	1	114	21	41	62	113

BACH, RYAN   G   RED WINGS

PERSONAL: Born October 21, 1973, in Sherwood Park, Alta. ... 6-1/195. ... Catches left. ... Full Name: Ryan David Bach. ... Name pronounced BAHK.
HIGH SCHOOL: Notre Dame College (Welland, Ont.).
COLLEGE: Colorado College.
TRANSACTIONS/CAREER NOTES: Selected by Detroit Red Wings in 11th round (11th Red Wings pick, 262nd overall) of NHL entry draft (June 20, 1992).
HONORS: Named to NCAA All-America West second team (1994-95). ... Named to WCHA All-Star first team (1994-95). ... Named to NCAA All-America West first team (1995-96). ... Named to WCHA All-Star first team (1995-96).

		REGULAR SEASON							PLAYOFFS					
Season Team	League	Gms.	Min	W	L	T	GA	SO	Avg.	Gms.	Min.	W	L	GA	SO	Avg.
91-92—Notre Dame	SJHL	33	1862	16	11	6	124	0	4.00	—	—	—	—	—	—	—
92-93—Colorado College	WCHA	4	239	1	3	0	11	0	2.76	—	—	—	—	—	—	—

Season Team	League	REGULAR SEASON								PLAYOFFS						
		Gms.	Min	W	L	T	GA	SO	Avg.	Gms.	Min.	W	L	GA	SO	Avg.
93-94—Colorado College..........	WCHA	30	1733	17	7	5	105	0	3.64	—	—	—	—	—	—	—
94-95—Colorado College..........	WCHA	27	1522	18	5	1	83	0	3.27	—	—	—	—	—	—	—
95-96—Colorado College..........	WCHA	23	1390	17	4	2	62	2	2.68	—	—	—	—	—	—	—
96-97—Adirondack..................	AHL	13	451	2	3	1	29	0	3.86	1	46	0	0	3	0	3.91
—Toledo	ECHL	20	1168	5	11	‡3	74	0	3.80	—	—	—	—	—	—	—
—Utica.............................	Col.HL	2	119	0	1	1	8	0	4.03	—	—	—	—	—	—	—
97-98—Houston	IHL	43	2453	26	9	‡6	95	5	2.32	—	—	—	—	—	—	—

BACUL, ROBIN — RW — SENATORS

PERSONAL: Born August 6, 1979, in Ostrava, Czechoslavakia. ... 6-1/174. ... Shoots right.
TRANSACTIONS/CAREER NOTES: Selected by Ottawa Senators in seventh round (sixth Senators pick, 173rd overall) of 1997 NHL entry draft.

Season Team	League	REGULAR SEASON								PLAYOFFS				
		Gms.	G	A	Pts.	PIM	+/-	PP	SH	Gms.	G	A	Pts.	PIM
96-97—Slavia Praha................	Czech Rep.	6	0	0	0	0	...	...	...	—	—	—	—	—
—Slavia Praha Jrs.	Czech Rep.	33	28	15	43	0	...	...	...	—	—	—	—	—
97-98—Chicoutimi	QMJHL	49	10	14	24	34	...	...	...	6	0	0	0	20

BAKER, JAMIE — C — MAPLE LEAFS

PERSONAL: Born August 31, 1966, in Nepean, Ont. ... 5-11/195. ... Shoots left. ... Full Name: James Paul Baker.
HIGH SCHOOL: J.S. Woodsworth (Nepean, Ont.).
COLLEGE: St. Lawrence (N.Y.).
TRANSACTIONS/CAREER NOTES: Selected by Quebec Nordiques in NHL supplemental draft (June 10, 1988). ... Broke left ankle (December 30, 1988). ... Sprained ankle (January 9, 1992); missed two games. ... Signed as free agent by Ottawa Senators (September 2, 1992). ... Sprained ankle (December 15, 1992); missed six games. ... Bruised foot (February 22, 1993); missed one game. ... Signed as free agent by San Jose Sharks (August 18, 1993). ... Suffered slight groin pull (October 16, 1993); missed 10 games. ... Suffered from the flu (February 26, 1995); missed two games. ... Injured shoulder (March 15, 1995); missed three games. ... Suffered from concussion (December 16, 1995); missed two games. ... Suffered from body aches (March 3, 1996); missed one game. ... Suffered from the flu (April 4, 1996); missed two games. ... Traded by Sharks with fifth-round pick (C Peter Cava) in 1996 draft to Toronto Maple Leafs for D Todd Gill (June 14, 1996). ... Separated shoulder (December 6, 1996); missed five games. ... Cut head (March 1, 1997); missed 12 games.
MISCELLANEOUS: Failed to score on a penalty shot (vs. Patrick Roy, March 28, 1996).

Season Team	League	REGULAR SEASON								PLAYOFFS				
		Gms.	G	A	Pts.	PIM	+/-	PP	SH	Gms.	G	A	Pts.	PIM
85-86—St. Lawrence Univ.......	ECAC	31	9	16	25	52	...	...	...	—	—	—	—	—
86-87—St. Lawrence Univ.......	ECAC	32	8	24	32	59	...	...	...	—	—	—	—	—
87-88—St. Lawrence Univ.......	ECAC	38	26	28	54	44	...	...	...	—	—	—	—	—
88-89—St. Lawrence Univ.......	ECAC	13	11	16	27	16	...	...	...	—	—	—	—	—
89-90—Quebec	NHL	1	0	0	0	0	-1	0	0	—	—	—	—	—
—Halifax	AHL	74	17	43	60	47	...	...	...	6	0	0	0	7
90-91—Quebec	NHL	18	2	0	2	8	-4	0	1	—	—	—	—	—
—Halifax	AHL	50	14	22	36	85	...	...	...	—	—	—	—	—
91-92—Halifax	AHL	9	5	0	5	12	...	...	...	—	—	—	—	—
—Quebec	NHL	52	7	10	17	32	-5	3	0	—	—	—	—	—
92-93—Ottawa	NHL	76	19	29	48	54	-20	10	0	—	—	—	—	—
93-94—San Jose	NHL	65	12	5	17	38	2	0	0	14	3	2	5	30
94-95—San Jose	NHL	43	7	4	11	22	-7	0	1	11	2	2	4	12
95-96—San Jose	NHL	77	16	17	33	79	-19	2	6	—	—	—	—	—
96-97—Toronto	NHL	58	8	8	16	28	2	1	0	—	—	—	—	—
97-98—Chicago	IHL	53	11	34	45	80	...	...	...	22	4	5	9	42
—Toronto	NHL	13	0	5	5	10	1	0	0	—	—	—	—	—
NHL Totals (9 years)............		403	71	78	149	271	-51	16	8	25	5	4	9	42

BALES, MIKE — G — STARS

PERSONAL: Born August 6, 1971, in Saskatoon, Sask. ... 6-1/180. ... Catches left. ... Full Name: Michael Raymond Bales.
COLLEGE: Ohio State.
TRANSACTIONS/CAREER NOTES: Selected by Boston Bruins in fifth round (fourth Bruins pick, 105th overall) of NHL entry draft (June 16, 1990). ... Signed as free agent by Ottawa Senators (July 4, 1994). ... Signed as free agent by Buffalo Sabres (August 14, 1997). ... Signed as free agent by Dallas Stars (July 8, 1998).

Season Team	League	REGULAR SEASON								PLAYOFFS						
		Gms.	Min	W	L	T	GA	SO	Avg.	Gms.	Min.	W	L	GA	SO	Avg.
88-89—Estevan	SJHL	44	2412	...	...	...	197	1	4.90	—	—	—	—	—	—	—
89-90—Ohio State	CCHA	21	1117	6	13	2	95	0	5.10	—	—	—	—	—	—	—
90-91—Ohio State	CCHA	*39	*2180	11	24	3	*184	0	5.06	—	—	—	—	—	—	—
91-92—Ohio State	CCHA	36	2061	11	20	5	*180	0	5.24	—	—	—	—	—	—	—
92-93—Providence	AHL	44	2363	22	17	0	166	1	4.21	2	118	0	2	8	0	4.07
—Boston	NHL	1	25	0	0	0	1	0	2.40	—	—	—	—	—	—	—
93-94—Providence	AHL	33	1757	9	15	4	130	0	4.44	—	—	—	—	—	—	—
94-95—Prin. Edward Island	AHL	45	2649	25	16	3	160	2	3.62	9	530	6	3	24	2	2.72
—Ottawa...........................	NHL	1	3	0	0	0	0	0	0.00	—	—	—	—	—	—	—
95-96—Prin. Edward Island	AHL	2	118	0	2	0	11	0	5.59	—	—	—	—	—	—	—
—Ottawa...........................	NHL	20	1040	2	14	1	72	0	4.15	—	—	—	—	—	—	—
96-97—Baltimore	AHL	46	2544	13	21	8	130	3	3.07	—	—	—	—	—	—	—
—Ottawa...........................	NHL	1	52	0	1	0	4	0	4.62	—	—	—	—	—	—	—
97-98—Rochester	AHL	39	2230	13	19	5	127	0	3.42	—	—	—	—	—	—	—
NHL Totals (4 years)............		23	1120	2	15	1	77	0	4.13							

B

BANCROFT, STEVE — D — FLAMES

PERSONAL: Born October 6, 1970, in Toronto. ... 6-1/214. ... Shoots left.
TRANSACTIONS/CAREER NOTES: Underwent surgery to left shoulder (April 1989). ... Selected by Toronto Maple Leafs in first round (third Maple Leafs pick, 21st overall) of NHL entry draft (June 17, 1989). ... Traded by Maple Leafs to Boston Bruins for LW Rob Cimetta (November 9, 1990). ... Traded by Bruins with 11th-round pick in 1993 draft (traded to Winnipeg Jets who selected LW Russell Hewson) to Chicago Blackhawks for 11th-round pick in 1992 draft (LW Yevgeny Pavlov) and 12th-round pick in 1993 draft (January 8, 1992). ... Traded by Blackhawks with undisclosed pick in 1993 draft to Jets for C Troy Murray (February 21, 1993); Jets received 11th-round pick in 1993 draft (LW Russell Hewson) to complete deal. ... Selected by Florida Panthers in NHL expansion draft (June 24, 1993). ... Signed as free agent by Pittsburgh Penguins (August 2, 1993). ... Loaned by Penguins to St. John's of AHL (March 29, 1995). ... Signed as free agent by Los Angeles Ice Dogs (August 30, 1995). ... Traded by Las Vegas of IHL to St. John's of AHL, Calgary Flames organization, for D Keith McCambridge, D Sami Helenias and LW Paxton Schulte (March 23, 1998).

		REGULAR SEASON								PLAYOFFS				
Season Team	League	Gms.	G	A	Pts.	PIM	+/-	PP	SH	Gms.	G	A	Pts.	PIM
86-87—St. Catharines Jr. B.....	OHA	11	5	8	13	20	...	...	...	—	—	—	—	—
87-88—Belleville	OHL	56	1	8	9	42	...	...	...	—	—	—	—	—
88-89—Belleville	OHL	66	7	30	37	99	...	...	...	5	0	2	2	10
89-90—Belleville	OHL	53	10	33	43	135	...	...	...	11	3	9	12	38
90-91—Newmarket	AHL	9	0	3	3	22	...	...	...	—	—	—	—	—
—Maine........................	AHL	53	2	12	14	46	...	...	...	2	0	0	0	2
91-92—Maine.....................	AHL	26	1	3	4	45	...	...	...	—	—	—	—	—
—Indianapolis	IHL	36	8	23	31	49	...	...	...	—	—	—	—	—
92-93—Indianapolis	IHL	53	10	35	45	138	...	...	...	—	—	—	—	—
—Chicago.....................	NHL	1	0	0	0	0	0	0	0	—	—	—	—	—
—Moncton	AHL	21	3	13	16	16	...	...	...	5	0	0	0	16
93-94—Cleveland	IHL	33	2	12	14	58	...	...	...	—	—	—	—	—
94-95—Fort Wayne	IHL	50	7	17	24	100	...	...	...	—	—	—	—	—
—Detroit.......................	IHL	6	1	3	4	0	...	...	...	—	—	—	—	—
—St. John's..................	AHL	4	2	0	2	2	...	...	...	5	0	3	3	8
95-96—Los Angeles.............	IHL	15	3	10	13	22	...	...	...	—	—	—	—	—
—Chicago.....................	IHL	64	9	41	50	91	...	...	...	9	1	7	8	22
96-97—Chicago.................	IHL	39	6	10	16	66	...	...	...	—	—	—	—	—
—Las Vegas	IHL	36	9	28	37	64	...	...	...	3	0	0	0	2
97-98—Las Vegas	IHL	70	15	44	59	148	...	...	...	—	—	—	—	—
—Saint John	AHL	9	0	4	4	12	...	...	...	19	2	11	13	30
NHL Totals (1 year)............		1	0	0	0	0	0	0	0					

BANHAM, FRANK — RW — MIGHTY DUCKS

PERSONAL: Born April 14, 1975, in Calahoo, Alta. ... 6-0/190. ... Shoots right.
TRANSACTIONS/CAREER NOTES: Selected by Washington Capitals in sixth round (fourth Capitals pick, 147th overall) of NHL entry draft (June 26, 1993). ... Signed as free agent by Mighty Ducks of Anaheim (January 22, 1996).
HONORS: Named to WHL (Central/East) All-Star first team (1995-96).

		REGULAR SEASON								PLAYOFFS				
Season Team	League	Gms.	G	A	Pts.	PIM	+/-	PP	SH	Gms.	G	A	Pts.	PIM
91-92—Saskatoon.................	WHL	71	29	33	62	55	...	...	...	9	2	7	9	8
92-93—Saskatoon.................	WHL	71	29	33	62	55	...	...	...	9	2	7	9	8
93-94—Saskatoon.................	WHL	65	28	39	67	99	...	...	...	16	8	11	19	36
94-95—Saskatoon.................	WHL	70	50	39	89	63	...	...	...	8	2	6	8	12
95-96—Saskatoon.................	WHL	72	*83	69	152	116	...	...	...	4	6	0	6	2
—Baltimore...................	AHL	9	1	4	5	0	...	...	...	7	1	1	2	2
96-97—Baltimore.................	AHL	21	11	13	24	4	...	...	...	—	—	—	—	—
—Anaheim...................	NHL	3	0	0	0	0	-2	0	0	—	—	—	—	—
97-98—Cincinnati.................	AHL	35	7	8	15	39	...	...	...	—	—	—	—	—
—Anaheim...................	NHL	21	9	2	11	12	-6	1	0	—	—	—	—	—
NHL Totals (2 years)...........		24	9	2	11	12	-8	1	0					

BANNISTER, DREW — D — MIGHTY DUCKS

PERSONAL: Born September 4, 1974, in Belleville, Ont. ... 6-2/200. ... Shoots right.
HIGH SCHOOL: Bawating Collegiate School (Sault Ste. Marie, Ont.).
TRANSACTIONS/CAREER NOTES: Selected by Tampa Bay Lightning in second round (second Lightning pick, 26th overall) of NHL entry draft (June 20, 1992). ... Injured ribs (November 27, 1996); missed one game. ... Bruised shoulder (March 15, 1997); missed one game. ... Traded by Lightning with sixth-round pick (C Peter Sarne) in 1997 draft to Edmonton Oilers for D Jeff Norton (March 18, 1997). ... Traded by Oilers to Mighty Ducks of Anaheim for D Bobby Dollas (January 9, 1998).
HONORS: Named to Memorial Cup All-Star team (1991-92). ... Named to OHL All-Star second team (1993-94).

		REGULAR SEASON								PLAYOFFS				
Season Team	League	Gms.	G	A	Pts.	PIM	+/-	PP	SH	Gms.	G	A	Pts.	PIM
90-91—Sault Ste. Marie	OHL	41	2	8	10	51	...	...	...	4	0	0	0	0
91-92—Sault Ste. Marie	OHL	64	4	21	25	122	...	...	...	16	3	10	13	36
92-93—Sault Ste. Marie	OHL	59	5	28	33	114	...	...	...	18	2	7	9	12
93-94—Sault Ste. Marie	OHL	58	7	43	50	108	...	...	...	14	6	9	15	20
94-95—Atlanta	IHL	72	5	7	12	74	...	...	...	5	0	2	2	22
95-96—Atlanta	IHL	61	3	13	16	105	...	...	...	3	0	0	0	4
—Tampa Bay	NHL	13	0	1	1	4	-1	0	0	—	—	—	—	—
96-97—Tampa Bay	NHL	64	4	13	17	44	-21	1	0	—	—	—	—	—
—Edmonton	NHL	1	0	1	1	0	-2	0	0	12	0	0	0	30
97-98—Edmonton	NHL	34	0	2	2	42	-7	0	0	—	—	—	—	—
—Anaheim...................	NHL	27	0	6	6	47	-2	0	0	—	—	—	—	—
NHL Totals (3 years)............		139	4	23	27	137	-33	1	0	12	0	0	0	30

B

BARNABY, MATTHEW RW SABRES

PERSONAL: Born May 4, 1973, in Ottawa. ... 6-0/188. ... Shoots left.
TRANSACTIONS/CAREER NOTES: Selected by Buffalo Sabres in fourth round (fifth Sabres pick, 83rd overall) of NHL entry draft (June 20, 1992). ... Suffered lower back spasms (March 28, 1995); missed one game. ... Suspended one game by NHL for accumulating three game misconduct penalties (March 31, 1996). ... Injured groin (April 3, 1996); missed five games. ... Sprained knee ligament (April 2, 1997); missed final six games of regular season and four playoff games. ... Injured sternum (October 10, 1997); missed five games. ... Strained shoulder (February 2, 1998); missed one game.

			REGULAR SEASON							PLAYOFFS				
Season Team	League	Gms.	G	A	Pts.	PIM	+/-	PP	SH	Gms.	G	A	Pts.	PIM
90-91—Beauport	QMJHL	52	9	5	14	262	...	...	...	—	—	—	—	—
91-92—Beauport	QMJHL	63	29	37	66	*476	...	...	...	—	—	—	—	—
92-93—Victoriaville	QMJHL	65	44	67	111	*448	...	...	...	6	2	4	6	44
—Buffalo	NHL	2	1	0	1	10	0	1	0	1	0	1	1	4
93-94—Buffalo	NHL	35	2	4	6	106	-7	1	0	3	0	0	0	17
—Rochester	AHL	42	10	32	42	153	...	...	...	—	—	—	—	—
94-95—Rochester	AHL	56	21	29	50	274	...	...	...	—	—	—	—	—
—Buffalo	NHL	23	1	1	2	116	-2	0	0	—	—	—	—	—
95-96—Buffalo	NHL	73	15	16	31	*335	-2	0	0	—	—	—	—	—
96-97—Buffalo	NHL	68	19	24	43	249	16	2	0	8	0	4	4	36
97-98—Buffalo	NHL	72	5	20	25	289	8	0	0	15	7	6	13	22
NHL Totals (6 years)		273	43	65	108	1105	13	4	0	27	7	11	18	79

BARNES, STU C PENGUINS

PERSONAL: Born December 25, 1970, in Edmonton. ... 5-11/174. ... Shoots right. ... Full Name: Stu D. Barnes.
TRANSACTIONS/CAREER NOTES: Selected by Winnipeg Jets in first round (first Jets pick, fourth overall) of NHL entry draft (June 17, 1989). ... Traded by Jets to Florida Panthers for C Randy Gilhen (November 26, 1993). ... Strained left calf (January 1, 1994); missed one game. ... Suffered lacerations and bruises in and around left eye (February 15, 1995); missed seven games. ... Sprained left knee (March 10, 1996); missed 10 games. ... Traded by Panthers with D Jason Woolley to Pittsburgh Penguins for C Chris Wells (November 19, 1996). ... Injured hip (April 11, 1997); missed one game. ... Suffered back spasms (October 9, 1997); missed one game. ... Strained hip flexor (April 16, 1998); missed one game.
HONORS: Won Jim Piggott Memorial Trophy (1987-88). ... Named to WHL All-Star second team (1987-88). ... Won Four Broncos Memorial Trophy (1988-89). ... Named to WHL All-Star first team (1988-89).
MISCELLANEOUS: Failed to score on a penalty shot (vs. Peter Sidorkiewicz, February 23, 1993; vs. Ron Hextall, March 8, 1998).
STATISTICAL PLATEAUS: Three-goal games: 1991-92 (1), 1997-98 (1). Total: 2.

			REGULAR SEASON							PLAYOFFS				
Season Team	League	Gms.	G	A	Pts.	PIM	+/-	PP	SH	Gms.	G	A	Pts.	PIM
86-87—St. Albert	AJHL	57	43	32	75	80	...	...	...	—	—	—	—	—
87-88—New Westminster	WHL	71	37	64	101	88	...	...	...	5	2	3	5	6
88-89—Tri-City	WHL	70	59	82	141	117	...	...	...	7	6	5	11	10
89-90—Tri-City	WHL	63	52	92	144	165	...	...	...	7	1	5	6	26
90-91—Canadian nat'l team	Int'l	53	22	27	49	68	...	...	...	—	—	—	—	—
91-92—Winnipeg	NHL	46	8	9	17	26	-2	4	0	—	—	—	—	—
—Moncton	AHL	30	13	19	32	10	...	...	...	11	3	9	12	6
92-93—Moncton	AHL	42	23	31	54	58	...	...	...	—	—	—	—	—
—Winnipeg	NHL	38	12	10	22	10	-3	3	0	6	1	3	4	2
93-94—Winnipeg	NHL	18	5	4	9	8	-1	2	0	—	—	—	—	—
—Florida	NHL	59	18	20	38	30	5	6	1	—	—	—	—	—
94-95—Florida	NHL	41	10	19	29	8	7	1	0	—	—	—	—	—
95-96—Florida	NHL	72	19	25	44	46	-12	8	0	22	6	10	16	4
96-97—Florida	NHL	19	2	8	10	10	-3	1	0	—	—	—	—	—
—Pittsburgh	NHL	62	17	22	39	16	-20	4	0	5	0	1	1	0
97-98—Pittsburgh	NHL	78	30	35	65	30	15	15	1	6	3	3	6	2
NHL Totals (7 years)		433	121	152	273	184	-14	44	2	39	10	17	27	8

BARNEY, SCOTT C KINGS

PERSONAL: Born March 27, 1979, in Oshawa, Ont. ... 6-4/198. ... Shoots right.
TRANSACTIONS/CAREER NOTES: Selected by Los Angeles Kings in second round (third Kings pick, 29th overall) of NHL entry draft (June 21, 1997).

			REGULAR SEASON							PLAYOFFS				
Season Team	League	Gms.	G	A	Pts.	PIM	+/-	PP	SH	Gms.	G	A	Pts.	PIM
94-95—North York	MTHL	41	16	19	35	88	...	...	...	—	—	—	—	—
95-96—Peterborough	OHL	60	22	24	46	52	...	...	...	24	6	8	14	38
96-97—Peterborough	OHL	64	21	33	54	110	...	...	...	9	0	3	3	16
97-98—Peterborough	OHL	62	44	32	76	60	...	...	...	4	1	0	1	6

BARON, MURRAY D CANUCKS

PERSONAL: Born June 1, 1967, in Prince George, B.C. ... 6-3/222. ... Shoots left. ... Full Name: Murray D. Baron.
HIGH SCHOOL: Kamloops (B.C.).
COLLEGE: North Dakota.
TRANSACTIONS/CAREER NOTES: Selected by Philadelphia Flyers as underage player in eighth round (seventh Flyers pick, 167th overall) of NHL entry draft (June 21, 1986). ... Separated left shoulder (October 5, 1989). ... Underwent surgery to have bone spur removed from foot (April 1990). ... Traded by Flyers with C Ron Sutter to St. Louis Blues for C Rod Brind'Amour and C Dan Quinn (September 22, 1991). ...

B

Injured shoulder (December 3, 1991); missed seven games. ... Broke foot (March 22, 1993); missed remainder of regular season. ... Injured groin (December 1, 1993); missed three games. ... Injured groin (December 11, 1993); missed three games. ... Injured knee (March 7, 1994); missed one game. ... Injured knee (April 18, 1995); missed last nine games of regular season. ... Traded by Blues with LW Shayne Corson and fifth-round pick (D Gennady Razin) in 1997 draft to Montreal Canadiens for C Pierre Turgeon, C Craig Conroy and D Rory Fitzpatrick (October 29, 1996). ... Bruised eye (November 21, 1996); missed one game. ... Traded by Canadiens with RW Chris Murray to Phoenix Coyotes for D Dave Manson (March 18, 1997). ... Fractured foot (April 6, 1997); missed remainder of regular season. ... Tore tricep (November 17, 1997); missed 37 games. ... Signed as free agent by Vancouver Canucks (July 14, 1998).

		REGULAR SEASON									PLAYOFFS				
Season Team	League	Gms.	G	A	Pts.	PIM	+/-	PP	SH		Gms.	G	A	Pts.	PIM
84-85—Vernon	BCJHL	37	5	9	14	93	...	...	...		—	—	—	—	—
85-86—Vernon	BCJHL	49	15	32	47	176	...	...	...		7	1	2	3	13
86-87—U. of North Dakota	WCHA	41	4	10	14	62	...	...	...		—	—	—	—	—
87-88—U. of North Dakota	WCHA	41	1	10	11	95	...	...	...		—	—	—	—	—
88-89—U. of North Dakota	WCHA	40	2	6	8	92	...	...	...		—	—	—	—	—
—Hershey	AHL	9	0	3	3	8	...	...	...		—	—	—	—	—
89-90—Hershey	AHL	50	0	10	10	101	...	...	...		—	—	—	—	—
—Philadelphia	NHL	16	2	2	4	12	-1	0	0		—	—	—	—	—
90-91—Hershey	AHL	6	2	3	5	0	...	...	...		—	—	—	—	—
—Philadelphia	NHL	67	8	8	16	74	-3	3	0		—	—	—	—	—
91-92—St. Louis	NHL	67	3	8	11	94	-3	0	0		2	0	0	0	2
92-93—St. Louis	NHL	53	2	2	4	59	-5	0	0		11	0	0	0	12
93-94—St. Louis	NHL	77	5	9	14	123	-14	0	0		4	0	0	0	10
94-95—St. Louis	NHL	39	0	5	5	93	9	0	0		7	1	1	2	2
95-96—St. Louis	NHL	82	2	9	11	190	3	0	0		13	1	0	1	20
96-97—St. Louis	NHL	11	0	2	2	11	-4	0	0		—	—	—	—	—
—Montreal	NHL	60	1	5	6	107	-16	0	0		1	0	0	0	0
—Phoenix	NHL	8	0	0	0	4	0	0	0		—	—	—	—	—
97-98—Phoenix	NHL	45	1	5	6	106	-10	0	0		6	0	2	2	6
NHL Totals (9 years)		525	24	55	79	873	-44	3	0		44	2	3	5	52

BARRASSO, TOM   G   PENGUINS

PERSONAL: Born March 31, 1965, in Boston. ... 6-3/210. ... Catches right. ... Full Name: Thomas Barrasso. ... Name pronounced buh-RAH-soh.
HIGH SCHOOL: Acton (Mass.)-Boxborough.
TRANSACTIONS/CAREER NOTES: Selected by Buffalo Sabres in first round (first Sabres pick, fifth overall) of NHL entry draft (June 8, 1983). ... Suffered chip fracture of ankle (November 1987). ... Pulled groin (April 9, 1988). ... Traded by Sabres with third-round pick in 1990 draft (RW Joe Dziedzic) to Pittsburgh Penguins for D Doug Bodger and LW Darrin Shannon (November 12, 1988). ... Pulled groin muscle (January 17, 1989). ... Injured shoulder (March 1989). ... Underwent surgery to right wrist (October 30, 1989); missed 21 games. ... Pulled groin (February 1990). ... Granted leave of absence to be with daughter as she underwent cancer treatment in Los Angeles (February 9, 1990). ... Rejoined the Penguins (March 19, 1990). ... Bruised right hand (October 29, 1991); missed two games. ... Bruised right ankle (December 26, 1991); missed three games. ... Suffered back spasms (March 1992); missed three games. ... Suffered from chicken pox (January 14, 1993); missed nine games. ... Strained groin (October 7, 1993); missed four games. ... Injured hip (November 18, 1993); missed 12 games. ... Underwent surgery on right wrist (January 20, 1995); missed first 43 games of season. ... Suffered sore wrist (May 3, 1995); missed one game. ... Pulled groin (December 7, 1995); missed eight games. ... Pulled groin and injured shoulder (February 6, 1996); missed four games. ... Suffered recurring shoulder problem (October 25, 1996); missed remainder of season. ... Strained leg muscle (November 5, 1997); missed one game. ... Strained quadriceps (December 29, 1997); missed five games. ... Hyperextended elbow (March 5, 1998); missed three games. ... Suffered from the flu (March 26, 1998); missed three games. ... Bruised knee (April 7, 1998); missed one game. ... Bruised finger (April 16, 1998); missed one game.
HONORS: Won Vezina Trophy (1983-84). ... Won Calder Memorial Trophy (1983-84). ... Named to THE SPORTING NEWS All-Star second team (1983-84, 1984-85 and 1987-88). ... Named to NHL All-Star first team (1983-84). ... Named to NHL All-Rookie team (1983-84). ... Shared William M. Jennings Trophy with Bob Sauve (1984-85). ... Named to NHL All-Star second team (1984-85 and 1992-93). ... Played in NHL All-Star Game (1985). ... Named to THE SPORTING NEWS All-Star first team (1992-93).
RECORDS: Shares NHL single-season playoff records for most wins by a goaltender—16 (1992); and most consecutive wins by a goaltender—11 (1992).
MISCELLANEOUS: Member of Stanley Cup championship team (1991 and 1992). ... Holds Pittsburgh Penguins all-time records for most games played by goalie (399), most wins (202) and most shutouts (17). ... Stopped penalty shot attempt (vs. Bryan Trottier, January 5, 1985; vs. Doug Smail, October 10, 1989). ... Allowed penalty shot goal (vs. Marcel Dionne, March 9, 1984; vs. Scott Pearson, March 16, 1991; vs. Robert Reichel, October 24, 1996). ... Member of U.S. National Junior Team (1983).

		REGULAR SEASON									PLAYOFFS						
Season Team	League	Gms.	Min	W	L	T	GA	SO	Avg.		Gms.	Min.	W	L	GA	SO	Avg.
81-82—Acton-Boxborough HS..	Mass. H.S.	23	1035	...	...	...	32	7	1.86		—	—	—	—	—	—	—
82-83—Acton-Boxborough HS..	Mass. H.S.	23	1035	...	...	...	17	10	0.99		—	—	—	—	—	—	—
83-84—Buffalo	NHL	42	2475	26	12	3	117	2	2.84		3	139	0	2	8	0	3.45
84-85—Rochester	AHL	5	267	3	1	1	6	1	1.35		—	—	—	—	—	—	—
—Buffalo	NHL	54	3248	25	18	10	144	*5	*2.66		5	300	2	3	22	0	4.40
85-86—Buffalo	NHL	60	*3561	29	24	5	214	2	3.61		—	—	—	—	—	—	—
86-87—Buffalo	NHL	46	2501	17	23	2	152	2	3.65		—	—	—	—	—	—	—
87-88—Buffalo	NHL	54	3133	25	18	8	173	2	3.31		4	224	1	3	16	0	4.29
88-89—Buffalo	NHL	10	545	2	7	0	45	0	4.95		—	—	—	—	—	—	—
—Pittsburgh	NHL	44	2406	18	15	7	162	0	4.04		11	631	7	4	40	0	3.80
89-90—Pittsburgh	NHL	24	1294	7	12	3	101	0	4.68		—	—	—	—	—	—	—
90-91—Pittsburgh	NHL	48	2754	27	16	3	165	1	3.59		20	1175	12	7	51	†1	*2.60
91-92—Pittsburgh	NHL	57	3329	25	22	9	196	1	3.53		*21	*1233	*16	5	*58	1	2.82
92-93—Pittsburgh	NHL	63	3702	*43	14	5	186	4	3.01		12	722	7	5	35	2	2.91
93-94—Pittsburgh	NHL	44	2482	22	15	5	139	2	3.36		6	356	2	4	17	0	2.87
94-95—Pittsburgh	NHL	2	125	0	1	1	8	0	3.84		2	80	0	1	8	0	6.00
95-96—Pittsburgh	NHL	49	2799	29	16	2	160	2	3.43		10	558	4	5	26	1	2.80
96-97—Pittsburgh	NHL	5	270	0	5	0	26	0	5.78		—	—	—	—	—	—	—
97-98—Pittsburgh	NHL	63	3542	31	14	13	122	7	2.07		6	376	2	4	17	0	2.71
NHL Totals (15 years)		665	38166	326	232	76	2110	30	3.32		100	5794	53	43	298	5	3.09

BASSEN, BOB   C   FLAMES

PERSONAL: Born May 6, 1965, in Calgary. ... 5-10/180. ... Shoots left. ... Son of Hank Bassen, goaltender with Chicago Blackhawks (1954-55 through 1955-56), Detroit Red Wings (1960-61 through 1966-67) and Pittsburgh Penguins (1967-68); and brother of Mark Bassen, center with Philadelphia Flyers (1989-90 and 1990-91) and St. Louis Blues (1991-92 through 1994-95) organizations. ... Name pronounced BAZ-ihn.
HIGH SCHOOL: Sir Winston Churchill (Calgary).
TRANSACTIONS/CAREER NOTES: Signed as free agent by New York Islanders (October 19, 1984). ... Injured knee (October 12, 1985). ... Traded by Islanders with D Steve Konroyd to Chicago Blackhawks for D Gary Nylund and D Marc Bergevin (November 25, 1988). ... Selected by St. Louis Blues in 1990 waiver draft for $25,000 (October 2, 1990). ... Broke right foot (December 4, 1992); missed 22 games. ... Broke finger (January 28, 1993); missed nine games. ... Traded by Blues with C Ron Sutter and D Garth Butcher to Quebec Nordiques for D Steve Duchesne and RW Denis Chasse (January 23, 1994). ... Lacerated left eye (March 30, 1994); missed one game. ... Injured back (February 18, 1995); missed one game. ... Signed as free agent by Dallas Stars (July 18, 1995). ... Injured knee (September 30, 1995); missed first 69 games of season. ... Underwent surgery to repair herniated disc in neck (September 28, 1996); missed 36 games. ... Bruised thigh (November 10, 1997); missed one game. ... Injured hand (January 12, 1998); missed four games. ... Injured knee (February 7, 1998); missed 18 games. ... Traded by Stars to Calgary Flames for C Aaron Gavey (July 14, 1998).
HONORS: Named to WHL (East) All-Star first team (1984-85). ... Named to IHL All-Star first team (1989-90).

Season Team	League	Gms.	G	A	Pts.	PIM	+/-	PP	SH	Gms.	G	A	Pts.	PIM
				REGULAR SEASON								PLAYOFFS		
82-83—Medicine Hat	WHL	4	3	2	5	0	...	...	...	3	0	0	0	4
83-84—Medicine Hat	WHL	72	29	29	58	93	...	...	...	14	5	11	16	12
84-85—Medicine Hat	WHL	65	32	50	82	143	...	...	...	10	2	8	10	39
85-86—New York Islanders	NHL	11	2	1	3	6	...	...	...	3	0	1	1	0
—Springfield	AHL	54	13	21	34	111	...	...	...	—				
86-87—New York Islanders	NHL	77	7	10	17	89	-17	0	0	14	1	2	3	21
87-88—New York Islanders	NHL	77	6	16	22	99	8	1	0	6	0	1	1	23
88-89—New York Islanders	NHL	19	1	4	5	21	0	0	0	—				
—Chicago	NHL	49	4	12	16	62	5	0	0	10	1	1	2	34
89-90—Indianapolis	IHL	73	22	32	54	179	...	...	...	12	3	8	11	33
—Chicago	NHL	6	1	1	2	8	1	0	0	—				
90-91—St. Louis	NHL	79	16	18	34	183	17	0	2	13	1	3	4	24
91-92—St. Louis	NHL	79	7	25	32	167	12	0	0	6	0	2	2	4
92-93—St. Louis	NHL	53	9	10	19	63	0	0	1	11	0	0	0	10
93-94—St. Louis	NHL	46	2	7	9	44	-14	0	1	—				
—Quebec	NHL	37	11	8	19	55	-3	1	0	—				
94-95—Quebec	NHL	47	12	15	27	33	14	0	1	5	2	4	6	0
95-96—Michigan	IHL	1	0	0	0	4	...	...	...	—				
—Dallas	NHL	13	0	1	1	15	-6	0	0	—				
96-97—Dallas	NHL	46	5	7	12	41	5	0	0	7	3	1	4	4
97-98—Dallas	NHL	58	3	4	7	57	-4	0	0	17	1	0	1	12
NHL Totals (13 years)		697	86	139	225	943	18	2	5	92	9	15	24	132

BAST, RYAN   D   FLYERS

PERSONAL: Born August 27, 1975, in Spruce Grove, Alta. ... 6-2/190. ... Shoots left.
TRANSACTIONS/CAREER NOTES: Signed as free agent by Philadelphia Flyers (May 18, 1998).
HONORS: Named to AHL All-Star first team (1997-98).

Season Team	League	Gms.	G	A	Pts.	PIM	+/-	PP	SH	Gms.	G	A	Pts.	PIM
				REGULAR SEASON								PLAYOFFS		
93-94—Portland	WHL	6	0	0	0	4	...	...	...	—				
—Prince Albert	WHL	47	2	8	10	139	...	...	...	—				
94-95—Prince Albert	WHL	42	1	10	11	149	...	...	...	14	0	3	3	13
95-96—Swift Current	WHL	72	9	18	27	203	...	...	...	6	1	0	1	21
96-97—Toledo	ECHL	12	2	2	4	75	...	...	...	—				
—Las Vegas	IHL	49	2	3	5	266	...	...	...	—				
—Saint John	AHL	12	0	0	0	21	...	...	...	5	0	0	0	4
97-98—Saint John	AHL	77	3	8	11	187	...	...	...	21	0	1	1	55

BATES, SHAWN   C   BRUINS

PERSONAL: Born April 3, 1975, in Melrose, Mass. ... 5-11/205. ... Shoots right.
HIGH SCHOOL: Medford (Mass.).
COLLEGE: Boston University.
TRANSACTIONS/CAREER NOTES: Selected by Boston Bruins in fourth round (fourth Bruins pick, 103rd overall) of NHL entry draft (June 26, 1993). ... Involved in car accident (November 8, 1997); missed one game.
HONORS: Named to Hockey East All-Rookie team (1993-94).

Season Team	League	Gms.	G	A	Pts.	PIM	+/-	PP	SH	Gms.	G	A	Pts.	PIM
				REGULAR SEASON								PLAYOFFS		
90-91—Medford H.S.	Mass. H.S.	22	18	43	61	6	...	...	...	—				
91-92—Medford H.S.	Mass. H.S.	22	38	41	79	10	...	...	...	—				
92-93—Medford H.S.	Mass. H.S.	25	49	46	95	20	...	...	...	—				
93-94—Boston University	Hockey East	41	10	19	29	24	...	...	...	—				
94-95—Boston University	Hockey East	38	18	12	30	48	...	...	...	—				
95-96—Boston University	Hockey East	40	28	22	50	54	...	...	...	—				
96-97—Boston University	Hockey East	41	17	18	35	64	...	...	...	—				
97-98—Boston	NHL	13	2	0	2	2	-3	0	0	—				
—Providence	AHL	50	15	19	34	22	...	...	...	—				
NHL Totals (1 year)		13	2	0	2	2	-3	0	0					

BATTAGLIA, BATES　　　　LW　　　　HURRICANES

PERSONAL: Born December 13, 1975, in Chicago. ... 6-2/185. ... Shoots left. ... Full Name: Jonathon Battaglia. ... Name pronounced buh-TAG-lee-uh.
HIGH SCHOOL: Lake Superior State (Mich.).
TRANSACTIONS/CAREER NOTES: Selected by Mighty Ducks of Anaheim in sixth round (sixth Mighty Ducks pick, 132nd overall) of NHL entry draft (June 29, 1994). ... Traded by Mighty Ducks with fourth-round pick (C Josef Vasicek) in 1998 draft to Hartford Whalers for C Mark Janssens (March 18, 1997).

		REGULAR SEASON								PLAYOFFS				
Season Team	League	Gms.	G	A	Pts.	PIM	+/-	PP	SH	Gms.	G	A	Pts.	PIM
93-94—Caledon	Jr. A	44	15	33	48	104	...	...	...	—	—	—	—	—
94-95—Lake Superior	CCHA	38	6	15	21	34	...	...	...	—	—	—	—	—
95-96—Lake Superior	CCHA	40	13	22	35	48	...	...	...	—	—	—	—	—
96-97—Lake Superior	CCHA	38	12	27	39	80	...	...	...	—	—	—	—	—
97-98—New Haven	AHL	48	15	21	36	48	...	...	...	1	0	0	0	0
—Carolina	NHL	33	2	4	6	10	-1	0	0	—	—	—	—	—
NHL Totals (1 year)		33	2	4	6	10	-1	0	0					

BAUMGARTNER, GREGOR　　　　C　　　　CANADIENS

PERSONAL: Born July 13, 1979, in Leoben, Austria. ... 6-1/179. ... Shoots left.
COLLEGE: Clarkson (N.Y.).
TRANSACTIONS/CAREER NOTES: Selected by Montreal Canadiens in second round (second Canadiens pick, 37th overall) of NHL entry draft (June 21, 1997).
HONORS: Named to QMJHL All-Rookie team (1996-97).

		REGULAR SEASON								PLAYOFFS				
Season Team	League	Gms.	G	A	Pts.	PIM	+/-	PP	SH	Gms.	G	A	Pts.	PIM
95-96—Clarkson	ECAC	7	0	1	1	0	...	...	...	—	—	—	—	—
96-97—Laval	QMJHL	68	19	45	64	15	...	...	...	3	0	0	0	0
97-98—Laval	QMJHL	68	31	51	82	10	...	...	...	16	5	12	17	6

BAUMGARTNER, KEN　　　　LW　　　　BRUINS

PERSONAL: Born March 11, 1966, in Flin Flon, Man. ... 6-1/205. ... Shoots left. ... Full Name: Ken James Baumgartner.
TRANSACTIONS/CAREER NOTES: Selected by Buffalo Sabres as underage junior in 12th round (12th Sabres pick, 245th overall) of NHL entry draft (June 15, 1985). ... Traded by Sabres with D Larry Playfair and RW Sean McKenna to Los Angeles Kings for D Brian Engblom and C Doug Smith (January 29, 1986). ... Traded by Kings with C Hubie McDonough to New York Islanders for RW Mikko Makela (November 29, 1989). ... Suspended one game by NHL for fighting (April 5, 1990). ... Fractured right orbital bone (December 19, 1991); missed 14 games. ... Traded by Islanders with C Dave McLlwain to Toronto Maple Leafs for C Claude Loiselle and RW Daniel Marois (March 10, 1992). ... Broke bone in wrist (February 28, 1994); missed remainder of season. ... Underwent shoulder surgery (January 31, 1995); missed remainder of season. ... Traded by Maple Leafs to Mighty Ducks of Anaheim for fourth-round pick (traded to Montreal) in 1996 draft (March 20, 1996). ... Bruised shoulder (October 12, 1996); missed one game. ... Injured ankle (December 1, 1996); missed three games. ... Fractured right hand (February 9, 1997); missed 11 games. ... Signed as free agent by Boston Bruins (July 1, 1997).

		REGULAR SEASON								PLAYOFFS				
Season Team	League	Gms.	G	A	Pts.	PIM	+/-	PP	SH	Gms.	G	A	Pts.	PIM
83-84—Prince Albert	WHL	57	1	6	7	203	...	...	...	—	—	—	—	—
84-85—Prince Albert	WHL	60	3	9	12	252	...	...	...	13	1	3	4	*89
85-86—Prince Albert	WHL	70	4	23	27	277	...	...	...	20	3	9	12	112
86-87—Chur	Switzerland					Statistics unavailable.				6	0	0	0	60
—New Haven	AHL	13	0	3	3	99	...	...	...	6	0	0	0	60
87-88—Los Angeles	NHL	30	2	3	5	189	5	0	0	5	0	1	1	28
—New Haven	AHL	48	1	5	6	181	...	...	...	—	—	—	—	—
88-89—Los Angeles	NHL	49	1	3	4	288	-9	0	0	5	0	0	0	8
—New Haven	AHL	10	1	3	4	26	...	...	...	—	—	—	—	—
89-90—Los Angeles	NHL	12	1	0	1	28	-10	0	0	—	—	—	—	—
—New York Islanders	NHL	53	0	5	5	194	6	0	0	4	0	0	0	27
90-91—New York Islanders	NHL	78	1	6	7	282	-14	0	0	—	—	—	—	—
91-92—New York Islanders	NHL	44	0	1	1	202	-10	0	0	—	—	—	—	—
—Toronto	NHL	11	0	0	0	23	1	0	0	—	—	—	—	—
92-93—Toronto	NHL	63	1	0	1	155	-11	0	0	7	1	0	1	0
93-94—Toronto	NHL	64	4	4	8	185	-6	0	0	10	0	0	0	18
94-95—Toronto	NHL	2	0	0	0	5	0	0	0	—	—	—	—	—
95-96—Toronto	NHL	60	2	3	5	152	-5	0	0	—	—	—	—	—
—Anaheim	NHL	12	0	1	1	41	0	0	0	—	—	—	—	—
96-97—Anaheim	NHL	67	0	11	11	182	0	0	0	11	0	1	1	11
97-98—Boston	NHL	82	0	1	1	199	-14	0	0	6	0	0	0	14
NHL Totals (11 years)		627	12	38	50	2125	-67	0	0	48	1	2	3	106

BAUMGARTNER, NOLAN　　　　D　　　　CAPITALS

PERSONAL: Born March 23, 1976, in Calgary. ... 6-1/200. ... Shoots right.
HIGH SCHOOL: Norkam Secondary (Kamloops, B.C.).
TRANSACTIONS/CAREER NOTES: Selected by Washington Capitals in first round (first Capitals pick, 10th overall) of NHL entry draft (June 28, 1994).
HONORS: Named to Memorial Cup All-Star team (1993-94 and 1994-95). ... Won Can.HL Defenseman of the Year Award (1994-95). ... Won Bill Hunter Trophy (1994-95 and 1995-96). ... Named to Can.HL All-Star first team (1994-95). ... Named to WHL (West) All-Star first team (1994-95 and 1995-96).

Season Team	League	REGULAR SEASON								PLAYOFFS				
		Gms.	G	A	Pts.	PIM	+/-	PP	SH	Gms.	G	A	Pts.	PIM
92-93—Kamloops	WHL	43	0	5	5	30	...	...	...	11	1	1	2	0
93-94—Kamloops	WHL	69	13	42	55	109	...	...	...	19	3	14	17	33
94-95—Kamloops	WHL	62	8	36	44	71	...	...	...	21	4	13	17	16
95-96—Washington	NHL	1	0	0	0	0	-1	0	0	1	0	0	0	10
—Kamloops	WHL	28	13	15	28	45	...	...	...	16	1	9	10	26
96-97—Portland	AHL	8	2	2	4	4	...	...	...	—	—	—	—	—
97-98—Portland	AHL	70	2	24	26	70	...	...	...	10	1	4	5	10
—Washington	NHL	4	0	1	1	0	0	0	0	—	—	—	—	—
NHL Totals (2 years)		5	0	1	1	0	-1	0	0	1	0	0	0	10

B

BEAUDOIN, NIC — LW — AVALANCHE

PERSONAL: Born December 25, 1976, in Ottawa. ... 6-3/205. ... Shoots left. ... Name pronounced boh-DWAI.
TRANSACTIONS/CAREER NOTES: Missed much of 1994-95 season due to knee injury. ... Selected by Colorado Avalanche in second round (second Avalanche pick, 51st overall) of NHL entry draft (July 8, 1995).

Season Team	League	REGULAR SEASON								PLAYOFFS				
		Gms.	G	A	Pts.	PIM	+/-	PP	SH	Gms.	G	A	Pts.	PIM
92-93—Ottawa	Tier II Jr. A	51	13	22	35	62	...	...	...	—	—	—	—	—
93-94—Detroit	OHL	63	9	18	27	32	...	...	...	17	1	2	3	13
94-95—Detroit	OHL	11	1	3	4	16	...	...	...	21	5	7	12	16
95-96—Detroit	OHL	60	26	33	59	78	...	...	...	16	8	10	18	35
96-97—Hershey	AHL	34	4	3	7	51	...	...	...	—	—	—	—	—
97-98—Canadian nat'l team	Int'l	49	10	16	26	107	...	...	...	—	—	—	—	—

BEAUREGARD, STEPHANE — G

PERSONAL: Born January 10, 1968, in Cowansville, Que. ... 5-11/190. ... Catches right. ... Name pronounced steh-FAN BOH-rih-GAHRD.
TRANSACTIONS/CAREER NOTES: Selected by Winnipeg Jets in third round (third Jets pick, 52nd overall) of NHL entry draft (June 11, 1988). ... Suffered hip flexor (October 29, 1991); missed four games. ... Traded by Jets to Buffalo Sabres for C Christian Ruuttu and future considerations (June 15, 1992). ... Traded by Sabres with future considerations to Chicago Blackhawks for G Dominik Hasek (August 7, 1992). ... Traded by Blackhawks to Jets for C Christian Ruuttu and future considerations (August 10, 1992). ... Traded by Jets to Philadelphia Flyers for third-round pick in 1993 draft and fifth-round pick in 1994 draft (October 1, 1992). ... Traded by Flyers to Jets for third-round pick in 1993 draft and future considerations (February 8, 1993); trade nullified by NHL, citing league bylaw that prohibits trading player within month of waiver draft and reacquiring him later in season (February 9, 1993). ... Traded by Flyers to Jets for fourth-round pick in 1993 draft and fifth-round pick in 1994 draft (June 11, 1993). ... Suffered from the flu (October 26, 1993); missed two games. ... Signed as free agent by San Francisco Spiders of IHL (August 14, 1995). ... Signed as free agent by Washington Capitals (August 31, 1997).
HONORS: Won Jacques Plante Trophy (1987-88). ... Won Raymond Lagace Trophy (1987-88). ... Won Marcel Robert Trophy (1987-88). ... Named to QMJHL All-Star first team (1987-88). ... Named to IHL All-Star first team (1995-96). ... Won James Gatschene Memorial Trophy (1995-96).

Season Team	League	REGULAR SEASON								PLAYOFFS						
		Gms.	Min	W	L	T	GA	SO	Avg.	Gms.	Min.	W	L	GA	SO	Avg.
86-87—St. Jean	QMJHL	13	785	6	7	0	58	0	4.43	5	260	1	3	26	0	6.00
87-88—St. Jean	QMJHL	*66	*3766	38	20	3	229	2	*3.65	7	423	3	4	34	0	4.82
88-89—Moncton	AHL	15	824	4	8	2	62	0	4.51	—	—	—	—	—	—	—
—Fort Wayne	IHL	16	830	9	5	‡0	43	0	3.11	9	484	4	4	21	*1	*2.60
89-90—Fort Wayne	IHL	33	1949	20	8	‡3	115	1	3.54	—	—	—	—	—	—	—
—Winnipeg	NHL	19	1079	7	8	3	59	0	3.28	4	238	1	3	12	0	3.03
90-91—Winnipeg	NHL	16	836	3	10	1	55	0	3.95	—	—	—	—	—	—	—
—Moncton	AHL	9	504	3	4	1	20	1	2.38	1	60	1	0	1	0	1.00
—Fort Wayne	IHL	32	1761	14	13	‡2	109	0	3.71	*19	*1158	10	9	57	2	2.95
91-92—Winnipeg	NHL	26	1267	6	8	6	61	2	2.89	—	—	—	—	—	—	—
92-93—Philadelphia	NHL	16	802	3	9	0	59	0	4.41	—	—	—	—	—	—	—
—Hershey	AHL	13	794	5	5	3	48	0	3.63	—	—	—	—	—	—	—
93-94—Winnipeg	NHL	13	418	0	4	1	34	0	4.88	—	—	—	—	—	—	—
—Moncton	AHL	37	2083	18	11	6	121	1	3.49	21	*1304	†12	*9	58	*2	2.67
94-95—Springfield	AHL	24	1381	10	11	3	73	2	3.17	—	—	—	—	—	—	—
95-96—San Francisco	IHL	69	4022	36	24	‡8	207	1	3.09	4	241	1	3	10	0	2.49
96-97—Quebec	IHL	67	3945	35	20	‡11	174	4	2.65	9	498	5	3	19	0	2.29
97-98—Chicago	IHL	18	918	10	6	‡0	49	1	3.20	14	820	10	4	36	1	2.63
NHL Totals (5 years)		90	4402	19	39	11	268	2	3.65	4	238	1	3	12	0	3.03

BEDDOES, CLAYTON — C — SENATORS

PERSONAL: Born November 10, 1970, in Bentley, Alta. ... 5-11/190. ... Shoots left. ... Name pronounced BEH-dohs.
HIGH SCHOOL: Bentley (Alta.).
COLLEGE: Lake Superior State (Mich.).
TRANSACTIONS/CAREER NOTES: Signed as free agent by Boston Bruins (May 24, 1994). ... Suffered bruised ribs (December 14, 1996); missed 10 games. ... Signed as free agent by Ottawa Senators (July 17, 1997).
HONORS: Named to NCAA All-America West second team (1993-94). ... Named to CCHA All-Star second team (1993-94).

Season Team	League	REGULAR SEASON								PLAYOFFS				
		Gms.	G	A	Pts.	PIM	+/-	PP	SH	Gms.	G	A	Pts.	PIM
90-91—Lake Superior	CCHA	45	14	28	42	26	...	...	...	—	—	—	—	—
91-92—Lake Superior	CCHA	42	16	28	44	26	...	...	...	—	—	—	—	—
92-93—Lake Superior	CCHA	45	18	40	58	32	...	...	...	—	—	—	—	—
93-94—Lake Superior	CCHA	44	23	31	54	56	...	...	...	—	—	—	—	—

Season Team	League	REGULAR SEASON								PLAYOFFS				
		Gms.	G	A	Pts.	PIM	+/-	PP	SH	Gms.	G	A	Pts.	PIM
94-95—Providence	AHL	65	16	20	36	39	...	...	...	13	3	1	4	18
95-96—Boston	NHL	39	1	6	7	44	-5	0	0	—	—	—	—	—
—Providence	AHL	32	10	15	25	24	...	...	...	4	2	3	5	0
96-97—Boston	NHL	21	1	2	3	13	-1	0	0	—	—	—	—	—
—Providence	AHL	36	11	23	34	60	...	...	...	7	2	0	2	4
97-98—Detroit	IHL	65	22	24	46	63	...	...	...	22	5	10	15	16
NHL Totals (2 years)		60	2	8	10	57	-6	0	0					

BEGIN, STEVE — C — FLAMES

PERSONAL: Born June 17, 1978, in Trois-Rivieres, Que. ... 5-11/185. ... Shoots left.
TRANSACTIONS/CAREER NOTES: Selected by Calgary Flames in second round (third Flames pick, 40th overall) of NHL entry draft (June 22, 1996). ... Injured shoulder (October 10, 1997); missed six games.

Season Team	League	REGULAR SEASON								PLAYOFFS				
		Gms.	G	A	Pts.	PIM	+/-	PP	SH	Gms.	G	A	Pts.	PIM
95-96—Val-d'Or	QMJHL	64	13	23	36	218	...	...	...	13	1	3	4	33
96-97—Val-d'Or	QMJHL	58	13	33	46	207	...	...	...	10	0	3	3	8
—Saint John	AHL	—	—	—	—	—	...	...	...	4	0	2	2	6
97-98—Calgary	NHL	5	0	0	0	23	0	0	0	—	—	—	—	—
—Val-d'Or	QMJHL	35	18	17	35	73	...	...	...	15	2	12	14	34
NHL Totals (1 year)		5	0	0	0	23	0	0	0					

BELAK, GRAHAM — D — AVALANCHE

PERSONAL: Born August 1, 1979, in Battleford, Sask. ... 6-4/206. ... Shoots left. ... Brother of Wade Belak, defenseman, Colorado Avalanche. ... Name pronounced BEE-lak.
TRANSACTIONS/CAREER NOTES: Selected by Colorado Avalanche in second round (second Avalanche pick, 53rd overall) of NHL entry draft (June 21, 1997).

Season Team	League	REGULAR SEASON								PLAYOFFS				
		Gms.	G	A	Pts.	PIM	+/-	PP	SH	Gms.	G	A	Pts.	PIM
96-97—Edmonton	WHL	61	3	5	8	46	...	...	...	—	—	—	—	—
97-98—Edmonton	WHL	47	5	5	10	168	...	...	...	—	—	—	—	—

BELAK, WADE — D — AVALANCHE

PERSONAL: Born July 3, 1976, in North Battleford, Sask. ... 6-5/223. ... Shoots right. ... Brother of Graham Belak, defenseman, Colorado Avalanche. ... Name pronounced BEE-lak.
HIGH SCHOOL: North Battleford (Sask.) Comprehensive.
TRANSACTIONS/CAREER NOTES: Selected by Quebec Nordiques in first round (first Nordiques pick, 12th overall) of NHL entry draft (June 28, 1994). ... Nordiques franchise moved to Colorado and renamed Avalanche for 1995-96 season (June 21, 1995). ... Pulled abdominal muscle (March 5, 1998); missed six games.

Season Team	League	REGULAR SEASON								PLAYOFFS				
		Gms.	G	A	Pts.	PIM	+/-	PP	SH	Gms.	G	A	Pts.	PIM
91-92—North Battleford	SJHL	57	6	20	26	186	...	...	...	—	—	—	—	—
92-93—North Battleford	SJHL	32	3	13	16	142	...	...	...	—	—	—	—	—
93-94—Saskatoon	WHL	69	4	13	17	226	...	...	...	16	2	2	4	43
94-95—Saskatoon	WHL	72	4	14	18	290	...	...	...	9	0	0	0	36
—Cornwall	AHL	—	—	—	—	—	...	...	...	11	1	2	3	40
95-96—Saskatoon	WHL	63	3	15	18	207	...	...	...	4	0	0	0	9
—Cornwall	AHL	5	0	0	0	18	...	...	...	2	0	0	0	2
96-97—Colorado	NHL	5	0	0	0	11	-1	0	0	—	—	—	—	—
—Hershey	AHL	65	1	7	8	320	...	...	...	16	0	1	1	61
97-98—Colorado	NHL	8	1	1	2	27	-3	0	0	—	—	—	—	—
—Hershey	AHL	11	0	0	0	30	...	...	...	—	—	—	—	—
NHL Totals (2 years)		13	1	1	2	38	-4	0	0					

BELANGER, ERIC — C — KINGS

PERSONAL: Born December 16, 1977, in Sherbrooke, Que. ... 5-11/166. ... Shoots left. ... Name pronounced buh-LAH-zhay.
TRANSACTIONS/CAREER NOTES: Selected by Los Angeles Kings in fourth round (fifth Kings pick, 96th overall) of NHL entry draft (June 22, 1996).

Season Team	League	REGULAR SEASON								PLAYOFFS				
		Gms.	G	A	Pts.	PIM	+/-	PP	SH	Gms.	G	A	Pts.	PIM
94-95—Beauport	QMJHL	71	12	28	40	24	...	...	...	—	—	—	—	—
95-96—Beauport	QMJHL	59	35	48	83	18	...	...	...	20	13	14	27	6
96-97—Beauport	QMJHL	31	13	37	50	30	...	...	...	—	—	—	—	—
—Rimouski	QMJHL	31	26	41	67	36	...	...	...	4	2	3	5	10
97-98—Fredericton	AHL	56	17	34	51	28	...	...	...	4	2	1	3	2

BELANGER, KEN — LW — ISLANDERS

PERSONAL: Born May 14, 1974, in Sault Ste. Marie, Ont. ... 6-4/225. ... Shoots left. ... Name pronounced buh-LAH-zhay.
TRANSACTIONS/CAREER NOTES: Selected by Hartford Whalers in seventh round (seventh Whalers pick, 153rd overall) of NHL entry draft (June 20, 1992). ... Traded by Whalers to Toronto Maple Leafs for ninth-round pick (RW Matt Ball) in 1994 draft (March 18, 1994). ... Traded

B

by Maple Leafs with G Damian Rhodes to New York Islanders for C Kirk Muller (January 23, 1996). ... Suffered concussion (February 6, 1996); missed two games. ... Suffered concussion (February 12, 1996); missed remainder of season. ... Suffered concussion (October 13, 1997); missed four games. ... Injured hand (November 15, 1997); missed three games. ... Suffered from the flu (November 26, 1997); missed three games. ... Reinjured hand (January 8, 1998); missed two games. ... Underwent thumb surgery (January 14, 1998); missed 22 games.

Season Team	League	REGULAR SEASON								PLAYOFFS				
		Gms.	G	A	Pts.	PIM	+/-	PP	SH	Gms.	G	A	Pts.	PIM
91-92—Ottawa	OHL	51	4	4	8	174	...	...	...	11	0	0	0	24
92-93—Ottawa	OHL	34	6	12	18	139	...	...	...	—	—	—	—	—
—Guelph	OHL	29	10	14	24	86	...	...	...	5	2	1	3	14
93-94—Guelph	OHL	55	11	22	33	185	...	...	...	9	2	3	5	30
94-95—St. John's	AHL	47	5	5	10	246	...	...	...	4	0	0	0	30
—Toronto	NHL	3	0	0	0	9	0	0	0	—	—	—	—	—
95-96—St. John's	AHL	40	16	14	30	222	...	...	...	—	—	—	—	—
—New York Islanders	NHL	7	0	0	0	27	-2	0	0	—	—	—	—	—
96-97—Kentucky	AHL	38	10	12	22	164	...	...	...	4	0	1	1	27
—New York Islanders	NHL	18	0	2	2	102	-1	0	0	—	—	—	—	—
97-98—New York Islanders	NHL	37	3	1	4	101	1	0	0	—	—	—	—	—
NHL Totals (4 years)		65	3	3	6	239	-2	0	0					

BELFOUR, ED   G   STARS

PERSONAL: Born April 21, 1965, in Carman, Man. ... 5-11/182. ... Catches left. ... Full Name: Edward Belfour.
COLLEGE: North Dakota.
TRANSACTIONS/CAREER NOTES: Signed as free agent by Chicago Blackhawks (June 18, 1987). ... Strained hip muscle (1993-94 season); missed four games. ... Sprained knee (January 31, 1996); missed one game. ... Injured back (February 19, 1996); missed three games. ... Traded by Blackhawks to San Jose Sharks for G Chris Terreri, D Michal Sykora and RW Ulf Dahlen (January 25, 1997). ... Injured knee ligament (February 1, 1997); missed 13 games. ... Suffered bulging disc in back (March 1, 1997); missed seven games. ... Signed as free agent by Dallas Stars (July 2, 1997). ... Strained lower back (February 2, 1998); missed three games.
HONORS: Named top goaltender in MJHL (1985-86). ... Named to NCAA All-America West second team (1986-87). ... Named to NCAA All-Tournament team (1986-87). ... Named to WCHA All-Star first team (1986-87). ... Shared Garry F. Longman Memorial Trophy with John Cullen (1987-88). ... Named to IHL All-Star first team (1987-88). ... Named Rookie of the Year by THE SPORTING NEWS (1990-91). ... Won Vezina Trophy (1990-91 and 1992-93). ... Won Calder Memorial Trophy (1990-91). ... Won William M. Jennings Trophy (1990-91, 1992-93 and 1994-95). ... Won Trico Goaltender Award (1990-91). ... Named to THE SPORTING NEWS All-Star first team (1990-91). ... Named to NHL All-Star first team (1990-91 and 1992-93). ... Named to NHL All-Rookie team (1990-91). ... Played in NHL All-Star Game (1992, 1993, 1996 and 1998). ... Named to THE SPORTING NEWS All-Star second team (1992-93 and 1994-95).
RECORDS: Shares NHL single-season playoff record for most consecutive wins by goaltender—11 (1992).
MISCELLANEOUS: Stopped penalty shot attempt (vs. Steve Maltais, February 25, 1993; vs. Roman Oksiuta, February 4, 1994; vs. Mark Howe, March 22, 1994). ... Allowed penalty shot goal (vs. Philippe Bozon, April 3, 1993; vs. Steve Larmer, January 16, 1994).
STATISTICAL NOTES: Led NHL with .910 save percentage (1990-91).

Season Team	League	REGULAR SEASON								PLAYOFFS						
		Gms.	Min	W	L	T	GA	SO	Avg.	Gms.	Min.	W	L	GA	SO	Avg.
85-86—Winkler	MJHL	48	2880	...	...	...	124	1	2.58	—	—	—	—	—	—	—
86-87—U. of North Dakota	WCHA	34	2049	29	4	0	81	3	2.37	—	—	—	—	—	—	—
87-88—Saginaw	IHL	61	*3446	32	25	‡0	183	3	3.19	9	561	4	5	33	0	3.53
88-89—Chicago	NHL	23	1148	4	12	3	74	0	3.87	—	—	—	—	—	—	—
—Saginaw	IHL	29	1760	12	10	‡0	92	0	3.14	5	298	2	3	14	0	2.82
89-90—Canadian nat'l team	Int'l	33	1808	...	...	...	93	...	3.09	—	—	—	—	—	—	—
—Chicago	NHL	—	—	—	—	—	—	—	—	9	409	4	2	17	0	2.49
90-91—Chicago	NHL	*74	*4127	43	19	7	170	4	*2.47	6	295	2	4	20	0	4.07
91-92—Chicago	NHL	52	2928	21	18	10	132	†5	2.70	18	949	12	4	39	1	*2.47
92-93—Chicago	NHL	*71	*4106	41	18	11	177	*7	2.59	4	249	0	4	13	0	3.13
93-94—Chicago	NHL	70	3998	37	24	6	178	†7	2.67	6	360	2	4	15	0	2.50
94-95—Chicago	NHL	42	2450	22	15	3	93	†5	2.28	16	1014	9	†7	37	1	2.19
95-96—Chicago	NHL	50	2956	22	17	10	135	1	2.74	9	666	6	3	23	1	*2.07
96-97—Chicago	NHL	33	1966	11	15	6	88	1	2.69	—	—	—	—	—	—	—
—San Jose	NHL	13	757	3	9	0	43	1	3.41	—	—	—	—	—	—	—
97-98—Dallas	NHL	61	3581	37	12	10	112	9	*1.88	17	1039	10	7	31	1	*1.79
NHL Totals (10 years)		489	28017	241	159	66	1202	40	2.57	85	4981	45	35	195	4	2.35

BELLOWS, BRIAN   LW   CAPITALS

PERSONAL: Born September 1, 1964, in St. Catharines, Ont. ... 5-11/210. ... Shoots right.
TRANSACTIONS/CAREER NOTES: Separated shoulder (November 1981); coached Kitchener Rangers for two games while recovering (became the youngest coach in OHL history at 17 years old). ... Selected by Minnesota North Stars as underage junior in first round (first North Stars pick, second overall) of NHL entry draft (June 9, 1982). ... Suffered tendinitis in elbow (October 1984). ... Injured wrist (October 1986); missed 13 games. ... Strained abdominal muscles (February 1989); missed 20 games. ... Bruised left knee (September 1990). ... Strained hip and groin (December 18, 1990). ... Traded by North Stars to Montreal Canadiens for RW Russ Courtnall (August 31, 1992). ... Injured neck (December 3, 1992); missed two games. ... Injured rib cage (November 20, 1993); missed seven games. ... Separated shoulder (February 18, 1995); missed two games. ... Separated shoulder (February 25, 1995); missed five games. ... Traded by Canadiens to Tampa Bay Lightning for C Marc Bureau (June 29, 1995). ... Injured groin (January 3, 1996); missed one game. ... Suffered hip pointer (March 21, 1996); missed two games. ... Strained back (October 31, 1996); missed two games. ... Reinjured back (November 6, 1996); missed two games. ... Traded by Lightning to Mighty Ducks of Anaheim for sixth-round pick (D Andrei Skopintsev) in 1997 draft (November 19, 1996). ... Played in Germany during 1997-98 season. ... Signed as free agent by Washington Capitals (March 26, 1998).
HONORS: Named to Memorial Cup All-Star team (1980-81). ... Won George Parsons Trophy (1981-82). ... Named to OHL All-Star first team (1981-82). ... Played in NHL All-Star Game (1984, 1988 and 1992). ... Named to THE SPORTING NEWS All-Star second team (1989-90). ... Named to NHL All-Star second team (1989-90).
MISCELLANEOUS: Member of Stanley Cup championship team (1993). ... Co-captain of Minnesota North Stars (1983-84). ... Holds Dallas Stars franchise all-time record for most goals (342).

STATISTICAL PLATEAUS: Three-goal games: 1987-88 (1), 1988-89 (1), 1989-90 (1), 1990-91 (1), 1991-92 (1), 1995-96 (1). Total: 6. ... Four-goal games: 1985-86 (1), 1991-92 (1), 1992-93 (1). Total: 3. ... Total hat tricks: 9.

		REGULAR SEASON								PLAYOFFS				
Season Team	League	Gms.	G	A	Pts.	PIM	+/-	PP	SH	Gms.	G	A	Pts.	PIM
80-81—Kitchener	OMJHL	66	49	67	116	23	...	...	...	16	14	13	27	13
81-82—Kitchener	OHL	47	45	52	97	23	...	...	...	15	16	13	29	11
82-83—Minnesota	NHL	78	35	30	65	27	-12	15	1	9	5	4	9	18
83-84—Minnesota	NHL	78	41	42	83	66	-2	14	5	16	2	12	14	6
84-85—Minnesota	NHL	78	26	36	62	72	-18	8	1	9	2	4	6	9
85-86—Minnesota	NHL	77	31	48	79	46	16	11	0	5	5	0	5	16
86-87—Minnesota	NHL	65	26	27	53	34	-13	8	1	—	—	—	—	—
87-88—Minnesota	NHL	77	40	41	81	81	-8	21	1	—	—	—	—	—
88-89—Minnesota	NHL	60	23	27	50	55	-14	7	0	5	2	3	5	8
89-90—Minnesota	NHL	80	55	44	99	72	-3	21	1	7	4	3	7	10
90-91—Minnesota	NHL	80	35	40	75	43	-13	17	0	23	10	19	29	30
91-92—Minnesota	NHL	80	30	45	75	41	-20	12	1	7	4	4	8	14
92-93—Montreal	NHL	82	40	48	88	44	4	16	0	18	6	9	15	18
93-94—Montreal	NHL	77	33	38	71	36	9	13	0	6	1	2	3	2
94-95—Montreal	NHL	41	8	8	16	8	-7	1	0	—	—	—	—	—
95-96—Tampa Bay	NHL	79	23	26	49	39	-14	13	0	6	2	0	2	4
96-97—Tampa Bay	NHL	7	1	2	3	0	-4	0	0	—	—	—	—	—
—Anaheim	NHL	62	15	13	28	22	-11	8	0	11	2	4	6	2
97-98—Berlin	Germany	31	15	17	32	...	...	...	...	—	—	—	—	—
—Washington	NHL	11	6	3	9	6	-3	5	0	21	6	7	13	6
NHL Totals (16 years)		1112	468	518	986	692	-113	190	11	143	51	71	122	143

BENDA, JAN — LW

PERSONAL: Born March 28, 1972, in Reef, Belgium ... 6-2/208. ... Name pronounced YAHN BEHN-duh.
TRANSACTIONS/CAREER NOTES: Signed as free agent by Washington Capitals (October 1, 1997).

		REGULAR SEASON								PLAYOFFS				
Season Team	League	Gms.	G	A	Pts.	PIM	+/-	PP	SH	Gms.	G	A	Pts.	PIM
94-95—Richmond	ECHL	62	21	39	60	187	...	...	...	17	8	2	10	50
96-97—Sparta Praha	Czech Rep.	49	7	21	28	61	...	...	...	10	1	1	2	12
97-98—Washington	NHL	9	0	3	3	6	1	0	0	—	—	—	—	—
—Portland	AHL	62	25	29	54	90	4	...	...	8	0	7	7	6
—German Oly. team	Int'l	4	3	0	3	8	...	...	...	—	—	—	—	—
NHL Totals (1 year)		9	0	3	3	6	1	0	0					

BENOIT, MATHIEU — RW — DEVILS

PERSONAL: Born July 12, 1979, in St. Clet, Que. ... 5-11/200. ... Shoots right.
TRANSACTIONS/CAREER NOTES: Selected by New Jersey Devils in seventh round (sixth Devils pick, 188th overall) of NHL entry draft (June 21, 1997).

		REGULAR SEASON								PLAYOFFS				
Season Team	League	Gms.	G	A	Pts.	PIM	+/-	PP	SH	Gms.	G	A	Pts.	PIM
95-96—Chicoutimi	QMJHL	61	6	14	20	17	...	...	...	17	0	0	0	0
96-97—Chicoutimi	QMJHL	64	35	36	71	22	...	...	...	—	—	—	—	—
97-98—Chicoutimi	QMJHL	59	56	61	117	32	...	...	...	6	2	3	5	2

BENYSEK, LADISLAV — D — OILERS

PERSONAL: Born March 24, 1975, in Olomouc, Czechoslavakia ... 6-2/200. ... Shoots left. ... Name pronounced BEHN-ih-shehk.
TRANSACTIONS/CAREER NOTES: Selected by Edmonton Oilers in 11th round (16th Oilers pick, 266th overall) of NHL entry draft (June 29, 1994).

		REGULAR SEASON								PLAYOFFS				
Season Team	League	Gms.	G	A	Pts.	PIM	+/-	PP	SH	Gms.	G	A	Pts.	PIM
93-94—HC Olomouc	Czech Rep.				Statistics unavailable.									
94-95—Cape Breton	AHL	58	2	7	9	54	...	...	...	—	—	—	—	—
95-96—HC Olomouc	Czech Rep.	33	1	4	5	...	...	...	...	—	—	—	—	—
96-97—HC Olomouc	Czech Rep.	14	0	1	1	8	...	...	...	—	—	—	—	—
—Sparta Praha	Czech Rep.	36	5	5	10	28	...	...	...	—	—	—	—	—
97-98—Edmonton	NHL	2	0	0	0	0	-2	0	0	—	—	—	—	—
—Hamilton	AHL	53	2	14	16	29	...	...	...	9	1	1	2	2
NHL Totals (1 year)		2	0	0	0	0	-2	0	0					

BERANEK, JOSEF — LW — OILERS

PERSONAL: Born October 25, 1969, in Litvinov, Czechoslovakia. ... 6-2/190. ... Shoots left. ... Name pronounced JOH-sehf buh-RAH-nehk.
TRANSACTIONS/CAREER NOTES: Selected by Edmonton Oilers in fourth round (third Oilers pick, 78th overall) of NHL entry draft (June 17, 1989). ... Traded by Oilers with D Greg Hawgood to Philadelphia Flyers for D Brian Benning (January 16, 1993). ... Bruised left shoulder (January 30, 1994); missed three games. ... Played in Europe during 1994-95 NHL lockout. ... Traded by Flyers to Vancouver Canucks for LW Shawn Antoski (February 15, 1995). ... Sprained thumb (February 2, 1996); missed two games. ... Injured thumb (February 17, 1996); missed one game. ... Signed as free agent by Vancouver Canucks (September 8, 1996). ... Traded by Canucks to Pittsburgh Penguins for future considerations (March 18, 1997). ... Bruised shoulder (March 24, 1997); missed one game. ... Strained groin (April 8, 1997); missed two games. ... Traded by Penguins to Oilers for D Bobby Dollas and C Tony Hrkac (June 16, 1998).
STATISTICAL PLATEAUS: Three-goal games: 1994-95 (1).

B

Season Team	League	REGULAR SEASON Gms.	G	A	Pts.	PIM	+/-	PP	SH	PLAYOFFS Gms.	G	A	Pts.	PIM
87-88—CHZ Litvinov	Czech.	14	7	4	11	12	...	...	...	—	—	—	—	—
88-89—CHZ Litvinov	Czech.	32	18	10	28	47	...	...	...	—	—	—	—	—
—Czechoslovakia Jr.	Czech.	5	2	7	9	2	...	...	...	—	—	—	—	—
89-90—Dukla Trencin	Czech.	49	16	21	37	...	...	...	...	—	—	—	—	—
90-91—CHZ Litvinov	Czech.	50	27	27	54	98	...	...	...	—	—	—	—	—
91-92—Edmonton	NHL	58	12	16	28	18	-2	0	0	12	2	1	3	0
92-93—Edmonton	NHL	26	2	6	8	28	-7	0	0	—	—	—	—	—
—Cape Breton	AHL	6	1	2	3	8	...	...	...	—	—	—	—	—
—Philadelphia	NHL	40	13	12	25	50	-1	1	0	—	—	—	—	—
93-94—Philadelphia	NHL	80	28	21	49	85	-2	6	0	—	—	—	—	—
94-95—Vsetin	Czech Rep.	16	7	7	14	26	...	...	...	—	—	—	—	—
—Philadelphia	NHL	14	5	5	10	2	3	1	0	—	—	—	—	—
—Vancouver	NHL	37	8	13	21	28	-10	2	0	11	1	1	2	12
95-96—Vancouver	NHL	61	6	14	20	60	-11	0	0	3	2	1	3	0
96-97—Vsetin	Czech Rep.	39	19	24	43	115	...	...	...	3	3	2	5	4
—Pittsburgh	NHL	8	3	1	4	4	-1	1	0	5	0	0	0	2
97-98—Vsetin	Czech Rep.	45	24	27	51	92	...	...	...	10	2	8	10	14
—Czech Rep. Olympic	Int'l	6	1	0	1	4	...	...	...	—	—	—	—	—
NHL Totals (6 years)		324	77	88	165	275	-31	11	0	31	5	3	8	14

BERARD, BRYAN   D   ISLANDERS

PERSONAL: Born March 5, 1977, in Woonsocket, R.I. ... 6-1/190. ... Shoots left. ... Name pronounced buh-RAHRD.
HIGH SCHOOL: Mount St. Charles (Woonsocket, R.I.).
COLLEGE: University of Michigan-Dearborn.
TRANSACTIONS/CAREER NOTES: Selected by Ottawa Senators in first round (first Senators pick, first overall) of NHL entry draft (July 8, 1995). ... Traded by Senators with C Martin Straka to New York Islanders for D Wade Redden and G Damian Rhodes (January 23, 1996). ... Strained groin (October 16, 1997); missed one game. ... Reinjured groin (November 10, 1997); missed two games. ... Reinjured groin (November 15, 1997); missed three games. ... Bruised elbow (March 24, 1998); missed one game.
HONORS: Won Can.HL Rookie of the Year Award (1994-95). ... Won Can.HL Top Draft Prospect Award (1994-95). ... Won Emms Family Trophy (1994-95). ... Won Max Kaminsky Trophy (1994-95 and 1995-96). ... Won OHL Top Draft Prospect Award (1994-95). ... Named to Can.HL All-Star first team (1994-95 and 1995-96). ... Named to Can.HL All-Rookie team (1994-95). ... Named to OHL All-Star first team (1994-95 and 1995-96). ... Won Can.HL Defenseman of the Year Award (1995-96). ... Named NHL Rookie of the Year by THE SPORTING NEWS (1996-97). ... Won Calder Memorial Trophy (1996-97). ... Named to NHL All-Rookie team (1996-97).

Season Team	League	REGULAR SEASON Gms.	G	A	Pts.	PIM	+/-	PP	SH	PLAYOFFS Gms.	G	A	Pts.	PIM
91-92—Mt. St. Charles H.S.	R.I.H.S.	32	3	15	18	10	...	...	...	—	—	—	—	—
92-93—Mt. St. Charles H.S.	R.I.H.S.	32	8	12	20	18	...	...	...	—	—	—	—	—
93-94—Mt. St. Charles H.S.	R.I.H.S.	32	11	36	47	5	...	...	...	—	—	—	—	—
94-95—Detroit	OHL	58	20	55	75	97	...	...	...	21	4	20	24	38
95-96—Detroit	OHL	56	31	58	89	116	...	...	...	17	7	18	25	41
96-97—New York Islanders	NHL	82	8	40	48	86	1	3	0	—	—	—	—	—
97-98—New York Islanders	NHL	75	14	32	46	59	-32	8	1	—	—	—	—	—
—U.S. Olympic Team	Int'l	2	0	0	0	0	...	...	...	—	—	—	—	—
NHL Totals (2 years)		157	22	72	94	145	-31	11	1					

BEREHOWSKY, DRAKE   D   OILERS

PERSONAL: Born January 3, 1972, in Toronto. ... 6-2/211. ... Shoots right. ... Name pronounced BAIR-ih-HOW-skee.
TRANSACTIONS/CAREER NOTES: Injured knees and underwent reconstructive surgery (October 13, 1989); missed remainder of season. ... Selected by Toronto Maple Leafs in first round (first Maple Leafs pick, 10th overall) of NHL entry draft (June 16, 1990). ... Sprained knee (April 15, 1993); missed remainder of season. ... Underwent knee surgery prior to 1994-95 season; missed first four games of season. ... Traded by Maple Leafs to Pittsburgh Penguins for D Grant Jennings (April 7, 1995). ... Signed as free agent by Edmonton Oilers (September 29, 1997).
HONORS: Won Can.HL Defenseman of the Year Award (1991-92). ... Won Max Kaminsky Trophy (1991-92). ... Named to Can.HL All-Star first team (1991-92). ... Named to OHL All-Star first team (1991-92).

Season Team	League	REGULAR SEASON Gms.	G	A	Pts.	PIM	+/-	PP	SH	PLAYOFFS Gms.	G	A	Pts.	PIM
87-88—Barrie Jr. B	OHA	40	10	36	46	81	...	...	...	—	—	—	—	—
88-89—Kingston	OHL	63	7	39	46	85	...	...	...	—	—	—	—	—
89-90—Kingston	OHL	9	3	11	14	28	...	...	...	—	—	—	—	—
90-91—Toronto	NHL	8	0	1	1	25	-6	0	0	—	—	—	—	—
—Kingston	OHL	13	5	13	18	28	...	...	...	—	—	—	—	—
—North Bay	OHL	26	7	23	30	51	...	...	...	10	2	7	9	21
91-92—North Bay	OHL	62	19	63	82	147	...	...	...	21	7	24	31	22
—Toronto	NHL	1	0	0	0	0	0	0	0	—	—	—	—	—
—St. John's	AHL	—	—	—	—	—	...	...	...	6	0	5	5	21
92-93—Toronto	NHL	41	4	15	19	61	1	1	0	—	—	—	—	—
—St. John's	AHL	28	10	17	27	38	...	...	...	—	—	—	—	—
93-94—Toronto	NHL	49	2	8	10	63	-3	2	0	—	—	—	—	—
—St. John's	AHL	18	3	12	15	40	...	...	...	—	—	—	—	—
94-95—Toronto	NHL	25	0	2	2	15	-10	0	0	—	—	—	—	—
—Pittsburgh	NHL	4	0	0	0	13	1	0	0	1	0	0	0	0
95-96—Cleveland	IHL	74	6	28	34	141	...	...	...	3	0	3	3	6
—Pittsburgh	NHL	1	0	0	0	0	1	0	0	—	—	—	—	—
96-97—San Antonio	IHL	16	3	4	7	36	...	...	...	—	—	—	—	—
—Carolina	AHL	49	2	15	17	55	...	...	...	—	—	—	—	—
97-98—Edmonton	NHL	67	1	6	7	169	1	1	0	12	1	2	3	14
—Hamilton	AHL	8	2	0	2	21	...	...	...	—	—	—	—	—
NHL Totals (7 years)		196	7	32	39	346	-15	4	0	13	1	2	3	14

BERENZWEIG, BUBBA   D   ISLANDERS

PERSONAL: Born August 8, 1977, in Arlington Heights, Ill. ... 6-2/195. ... Shoots left. ... Full Name: Andrew Berenzweig.
HIGH SCHOOL: Buffalo Grove (Ill.), then Loomis-Chaffee Prep School (Windsor, Conn.).
COLLEGE: Michigan.
TRANSACTIONS/CAREER NOTES: Selected by New York Islanders in fifth round (fifth Islanders pick, 109th overall) of NHL entry draft (June 22, 1996).
HONORS: Named to NCAA All-Tournament team (1997-98). ... Named to CCHA All-Star second team (1997-98).

		REGULAR SEASON							PLAYOFFS				
Season Team	League	Gms.	G	A	Pts.	PIM	+/-	PP	SH	Gms.	G	A	Pts.	PIM
94-95—Loomis-Chaffee	Conn. H.S.	23	19	23	42	24	...	...	...	—	—	—	—	—
95-96—Univ. of Michigan	CCHA	42	4	8	12	4	...	...	...	—	—	—	—	—
96-97—Univ. of Michigan	CCHA	38	7	12	19	49	...	...	...	—	—	—	—	—
97-98—Univ. of Michigan	CCHA	43	6	10	16	28	...	...	...	—	—	—	—	—

BEREZIN, SERGEI   RW   MAPLE LEAFS

PERSONAL: Born November 5, 1971, in Voskresensk, U.S.S.R. ... 5-10/197. ... Shoots right. ... Name pronounced BAIR-ih-zihn.
TRANSACTIONS/CAREER NOTES: Selected by Toronto Maple Leafs in 10th round (eighth Maple Leafs pick, 256th overall) of NHL entry draft (June 29, 1994). ... Injured hand (November 19, 1996); missed one game. ... Underwent hand surgery (December 3, 1996); missed six games. ... Strained knee (December 23, 1996); missed two games.
HONORS: Named to NHL All-Rookie team (1996-97).

		REGULAR SEASON							PLAYOFFS				
Season Team	League	Gms.	G	A	Pts.	PIM	+/-	PP	SH	Gms.	G	A	Pts.	PIM
90-91—Khimik Voskresensk	USSR	30	6	2	8	4	...	...	...	—	—	—	—	—
91-92—Khimik Voskresensk	CIS	36	7	5	12	10	...	...	...	—	—	—	—	—
92-93—Khimik Voskresensk	CIS	38	9	3	12	12	...	...	...	2	1	0	1	0
93-94—Khimik Voskresensk	CIS	40	31	10	41	16	...	...	...	—	—	—	—	—
—Russian nat'l team	Int'l	6	2	1	3	2	...	...	...	—	—	—	—	—
—Russian Oly. team	Int'l	8	3	2	5	2	...	...	...	—	—	—	—	—
94-95—Koln	Germany	43	38	19	57	8	...	...	...	18	17	8	25	18
—Russian nat'l team	Int'l	6	7	1	8	4	...	...	...	—	—	—	—	—
95-96—Koln	Germany	45	49	31	80	8	...	...	...	14	13	9	22	4
—Russian nat'l team	Int'l	8	4	5	9	2	...	...	...	—	—	—	—	—
96-97—Toronto	NHL	73	25	16	41	2	-3	7	0	—	—	—	—	—
—Russian nat'l team	Int'l	2	1	0	1	0	...	...	...	—	—	—	—	—
97-98—Toronto	NHL	68	16	15	31	10	-3	3	0	—	—	—	—	—
NHL Totals (2 years)		141	41	31	72	12	-6	10	0					

BERG, AKI   D   KINGS

PERSONAL: Born July 28, 1977, in Turku, Finland. ... 6-3/202. ... Shoots left. ... Full Name: Aki-Petteri Berg. ... Name pronounced AH-kee BUHRG.
TRANSACTIONS/CAREER NOTES: Selected by Los Angeles Kings in first round (first Kings pick, third overall) of NHL entry draft (July 8, 1995). ... Suffered charley horse (January 25, 1997); missed one game. ... Suffered concussion (February 3, 1997); missed two games. ... Sprained left ankle (April 9, 1997); missed final two games of regular season. ... Bruised right foot (December 4, 1997); missed one game. ... Sprained right wrist (March 10, 1998); missed two games.
MISCELLANEOUS: Member of bronze-medal-winning Finnish Olympic team (1998).

		REGULAR SEASON							PLAYOFFS				
Season Team	League	Gms.	G	A	Pts.	PIM	+/-	PP	SH	Gms.	G	A	Pts.	PIM
92-93—TPS Jr.	Finland	39	18	24	42	59	...	...	...	—	—	—	—	—
93-94—TPS Jr.	Finland	21	3	11	14	24	...	...	...	7	0	0	0	10
—TPS Turku	Finland	6	0	3	3	4	...	...	...	—	—	—	—	—
94-95—Kiekko-67	Finland Dv.II	20	3	9	12	34	...	...	...	—	—	—	—	—
—TPS Jr.	Finland	8	1	0	1	30	...	...	...	—	—	—	—	—
—TPS Turku	Finland	5	0	0	0	4	...	...	...	—	—	—	—	—
95-96—Los Angeles	NHL	51	0	7	7	29	-13	0	0	—	—	—	—	—
—Phoenix	IHL	20	0	3	3	18	...	...	...	2	0	0	0	4
96-97—Los Angeles	NHL	41	2	6	8	24	-9	2	0	—	—	—	—	—
—Phoenix	IHL	23	1	3	4	21	...	...	...	—	—	—	—	—
97-98—Los Angeles	NHL	72	0	8	8	61	3	0	0	4	0	3	3	0
—Fin. Olympic Team	Int'l	6	0	0	0	6	...	...	...	—	—	—	—	—
NHL Totals (3 years)		164	2	21	23	114	-19	2	0	4	0	3	3	0

BERG, BILL   LW   RANGERS

PERSONAL: Born October 21, 1967, in St. Catharines, Ont. ... 6-1/205. ... Shoots left. ... Full Name: William Berg. ... Brother of Bob Berg, left winger with Los Angeles Kings and New York Rangers organizations (1990-91 through 1995-96).
TRANSACTIONS/CAREER NOTES: Broke ankle (March 1985). ... Selected by New York Islanders as underage junior in third round (third Islanders pick, 59th overall) of NHL entry draft (June 21, 1986). ... Injured knee (October 1986). ... Separated shoulder (May 1990). ... Fractured left foot (November 9, 1991); missed 12 games. ... Claimed on waivers by Toronto Maple Leafs (December 3, 1992). ... Injured hip flexor (November 18, 1993); missed one game. ... Sprained knee (February 6, 1995); missed 16 games. ... Broke leg (October 26, 1995); missed 33 games. ... Traded by Maple Leafs with LW Sergio Momesso to New York Rangers for LW Nick Kypreos and RW Wayne Presley (February 29, 1996). ... Strained groin (November 12, 1996); missed nine games. ... Bruised foot (February 15, 1997); missed two games. ... Broke fibula (April 22, 1997); missed remainder of playoffs. ... Sprained right knee (November 28, 1997); missed 12 games. ... Sprained elbow (January 8, 1998); missed one game.
MISCELLANEOUS: Moved from defense to left wing (1990).

Season Team	League	REGULAR SEASON								PLAYOFFS				
		Gms.	G	A	Pts.	PIM	+/-	PP	SH	Gms.	G	A	Pts.	PIM
84-85—Grimsby Jr. B	OHA	42	10	22	32	153	...	...	...	—	—	—	—	—
85-86—Toronto	OHL	64	3	35	38	143	...	...	...	4	0	0	0	19
—Springfield	AHL	4	1	1	2	4	...	...	...	—	—	—	—	—
86-87—Toronto	OHL	57	3	15	18	138	...	...	...	—	—	—	—	—
87-88—Springfield	AHL	76	6	26	32	148	...	...	...	—	—	—	—	—
—Peoria	IHL	5	0	1	1	8	...	...	...	7	0	3	3	31
88-89—New York Islanders	NHL	7	1	2	3	10	-2	1	0	—	—	—	—	—
—Springfield	AHL	69	17	32	49	122	...	...	...	—	—	—	—	—
89-90—Springfield	AHL	74	12	42	54	74	...	...	...	15	5	12	17	35
90-91—New York Islanders	NHL	78	9	14	23	67	-3	0	0	—	—	—	—	—
91-92—New York Islanders	NHL	47	5	9	14	28	-18	1	0	—	—	—	—	—
—Capital District	AHL	3	0	2	2	16	...	...	...	—	—	—	—	—
92-93—New York Islanders	NHL	22	6	3	9	49	4	0	2	—	—	—	—	—
—Toronto	NHL	58	7	8	15	54	-1	0	1	21	1	1	2	18
93-94—Toronto	NHL	83	8	11	19	93	-3	0	0	18	1	2	3	10
94-95—Toronto	NHL	32	5	1	6	26	-11	0	0	7	0	1	1	4
95-96—Toronto	NHL	23	1	1	2	33	-6	0	0	—	—	—	—	—
—New York Rangers	NHL	18	2	1	3	8	0	0	1	10	1	0	1	0
96-97—New York Rangers	NHL	67	8	6	14	37	2	0	2	3	0	0	0	2
97-98—New York Rangers	NHL	67	1	9	10	55	-15	0	0	—	—	—	—	—
NHL Totals (9 years)		502	53	65	118	460	-53	2	6	59	3	4	7	34

BERGEVIN, MARC   D   BLUES

PERSONAL: Born August 11, 1965, in Montreal. ... 6-1/213. ... Shoots left. ... Name pronounced BUHR-jih-vihn.
TRANSACTIONS/CAREER NOTES: Selected by Chicago Blackhawks as underage junior in third round (third Blackhawks pick, 59th overall) of NHL entry draft (June 8, 1983). ... Sprained neck (March 18, 1987). ... Traded by Blackhawks with D Gary Nylund to New York Islanders for D Steve Konroyd and C Bob Bassen (November 25, 1988). ... Bruised ribs (November 25, 1989). ... Broke hand (May 1990). ... Traded by Islanders to Hartford Whalers for future considerations; Islanders later received fifth-round pick in 1992 draft (C Ryan Duthie) to complete deal (October 31, 1990). ... Signed as free agent by Tampa Bay Lightning (July 9, 1992). ... Injured foot (March 18, 1993); missed one game. ... Bruised back (November 19, 1993); missed one game. ... Injured elbow (March 10, 1995); missed one game. ... Suffered from sore neck (April 22, 1995); missed three games. ... Traded by Lightning with RW Ben Hankinson to Detroit Red Wings for LW Shawn Burr and third-round pick (traded to Boston) in 1996 draft (August 17, 1995). ... Suffered from the flu (November 1, 1995); missed one game. ... Injured groin (April 7, 1996); missed three games. ... Signed as free agent by St. Louis Blues (July 9, 1996). ... Injured ankle (December 13, 1997); missed one game.

Season Team	League	REGULAR SEASON								PLAYOFFS				
		Gms.	G	A	Pts.	PIM	+/-	PP	SH	Gms.	G	A	Pts.	PIM
82-83—Chicoutimi	QMJHL	64	3	27	30	113	...	...	...	—	—	—	—	—
83-84—Chicoutimi	QMJHL	70	10	35	45	125	...	...	...	—	—	—	—	—
—Springfield	AHL	7	0	1	1	2	...	...	...	—	—	—	—	—
84-85—Chicago	NHL	60	0	6	6	54	-9	0	0	6	0	3	3	2
—Springfield	AHL	—	—	—	—	—	...	...	...	4	0	0	0	0
85-86—Chicago	NHL	71	7	7	14	60	0	0	0	3	0	0	0	0
86-87—Chicago	NHL	66	4	10	14	66	4	0	0	3	1	0	1	2
87-88—Chicago	NHL	58	1	6	7	85	-19	0	0	—	—	—	—	—
—Saginaw	IHL	10	2	7	9	20	...	...	...	—	—	—	—	—
88-89—Chicago	NHL	11	0	0	0	18	-3	0	0	—	—	—	—	—
—New York Islanders	NHL	58	2	13	15	62	2	1	0	—	—	—	—	—
89-90—New York Islanders	NHL	18	0	4	4	30	-8	0	0	—	—	—	—	—
—Springfield	AHL	47	7	16	23	66	...	...	...	17	2	11	13	16
90-91—Hartford	NHL	4	0	0	0	4	-3	0	0	—	—	—	—	—
—Capital District	AHL	7	0	5	5	6	...	...	...	—	—	—	—	—
—Springfield	AHL	58	4	23	27	85	...	...	...	18	0	7	7	26
91-92—Hartford	NHL	75	7	17	24	64	-13	4	1	5	0	0	0	2
92-93—Tampa Bay	NHL	78	2	12	14	66	-16	0	0	—	—	—	—	—
93-94—Tampa Bay	NHL	83	1	15	16	87	-5	0	0	—	—	—	—	—
94-95—Tampa Bay	NHL	44	2	4	6	51	-6	0	1	—	—	—	—	—
95-96—Detroit	NHL	70	1	9	10	33	7	0	0	17	1	0	1	14
96-97—St. Louis	NHL	82	0	4	4	53	-9	0	0	6	1	0	1	8
97-98—St. Louis	NHL	81	3	7	10	90	-2	0	0	10	0	1	1	8
NHL Totals (14 years)		859	30	114	144	823	-80	5	2	50	3	4	7	36

BERRY, RICK   D   AVALANCHE

PERSONAL: Born November 4, 1978, in Brandon, Man. ... 6-1/192. ... Shoots left.
TRANSACTIONS/CAREER NOTES: Selected by Colorado Avalanche in third round (third Avalanche pick, 55th overall) of NHL entry draft (June 21, 1997).

Season Team	League	REGULAR SEASON								PLAYOFFS				
		Gms.	G	A	Pts.	PIM	+/-	PP	SH	Gms.	G	A	Pts.	PIM
95-96—Seattle	WHL	59	4	9	13	103	...	...	...	1	0	0	0	0
96-97—Seattle	WHL	72	12	21	33	125	...	...	...	15	3	7	10	23
97-98—Spokane	WHL	59	9	21	30	131	...	...	...	17	1	4	5	26

BERTUZZI, TODD   LW   CANUCKS

PERSONAL: Born February 2, 1975, in Sudbury, Ont. ... 6-3/224. ... Shoots left. ... Name pronounced buhr-TOO-zee.
HIGH SCHOOL: Bishop MacDonnell (Guelph, Ont.).

TRANSACTIONS/CAREER NOTES: Selected by New York Islanders in first round (first Islanders pick, 23rd overall) of NHL entry draft (June 26, 1993). ... Injured eye (February 22, 1996); missed two games. ... Suspended three games by NHL for attempting to break free of a linesman (April 2, 1996). ... Bone chips in elbow (November 23, 1996); missed one game. ... Traded by Islanders with D Bryan McCabe and third-round pick (LW Jarkko Ruutu) in 1998 draft to Vancouver Canucks for C Trevor Linden (February 6, 1998). ... Bruised thigh (March 17, 1998); missed four games.

HONORS: Named to OHL All-Star second team (1994-95).

Season Team	League	REGULAR SEASON								PLAYOFFS				
		Gms.	G	A	Pts.	PIM	+/-	PP	SH	Gms.	G	A	Pts.	PIM
91-92—Guelph	OHL	47	7	14	21	145	...	...	...	—	—	—	—	—
92-93—Guelph	OHL	59	27	32	59	164	...	...	...	5	2	2	4	6
93-94—Guelph	OHL	61	28	54	82	165	...	...	...	9	2	6	8	30
94-95—Guelph	OHL	62	54	65	119	58	...	...	...	14	*15	18	33	41
95-96—New York Islanders	NHL	76	18	21	39	83	-14	4	0	—	—	—	—	—
96-97—New York Islanders	NHL	64	10	13	23	68	-3	3	0	—	—	—	—	—
—Utah	IHL	13	5	5	10	16	...	...	...	—	—	—	—	—
97-98—New York Islanders	NHL	52	7	11	18	58	-19	1	0	—	—	—	—	—
—Vancouver	NHL	22	6	9	15	63	2	1	1	—	—	—	—	—
NHL Totals (3 years)		214	41	54	95	272	-34	9	1					

BERUBE, CRAIG   LW   CAPITALS

PERSONAL: Born December 17, 1965, in Calahoo, Alta. ... 6-1/215. ... Shoots left. ... Name pronounced buh-ROO-bee.

TRANSACTIONS/CAREER NOTES: Signed as free agent by Philadelphia Flyers (March 19, 1986). ... Sprained left knee (March 1988). ... Traded by Flyers with RW Scott Mellanby and C Craig Fisher to Edmonton Oilers for RW Dave Brown, D Corey Foster and the NHL rights to RW Jari Kurri (May 30, 1991). ... Traded by Oilers with G Grant Fuhr and RW/LW Glenn Anderson to Toronto Maple Leafs for LW Vincent Damphousse, D Luke Richardson, G Peter Ing, C Scott Thornton and future considerations (September 19, 1991). ... Traded by Maple Leafs with D Alexander Godynyuk, RW Gary Leeman, D Michel Petit and G Jeff Reese to Calgary Flames for C Doug Gilmour, D Jamie Macoun, LW Kent Manderville, D Ric Nattress and G Rick Wamsley (January 2, 1992). ... Traded by Flames to Washington Capitals for fifth-round pick (C Darryl LaFrance) in 1993 draft (June 26, 1993). ... Suffered from the flu (March 31, 1995); missed three games. ... Broke jaw (September 14, 1995); missed seven games. ... Suffered mild concussion (November 10, 1995); missed four games. ... Suspended 10 games by NHL for coming off bench to fight (December 22, 1995). ... Injured right knee (March 22, 1996); missed 11 games. ... Suspended two games and fined $1,000 by NHL for slashing incident (January 19, 1997). ... Injured hip (October 15, 1997); missed seven games. ... Suspended one game by NHL for directing a racial slur at LW Peter Worrell (November 25, 1997).

Season Team	League	REGULAR SEASON								PLAYOFFS				
		Gms.	G	A	Pts.	PIM	+/-	PP	SH	Gms.	G	A	Pts.	PIM
82-83—Williams Lake	PCJHL	33	9	24	33	99	...	...	...	—	—	—	—	—
—Kamloops	WHL	4	0	0	0	0	...	...	...	—	—	—	—	—
83-84—New Westminster	WHL	70	11	20	31	104	...	...	...	8	1	2	3	5
84-85—New Westminster	WHL	70	25	44	69	191	...	...	...	10	3	2	5	4
85-86—Kamloops	WHL	32	17	14	31	119	...	...	...	—	—	—	—	—
—Medicine Hat	WHL	34	14	16	30	95	...	...	...	25	7	8	15	102
86-87—Hershey	AHL	63	7	17	24	325	...	...	...	—	—	—	—	—
—Philadelphia	NHL	7	0	0	0	57	2	0	0	5	0	0	0	17
87-88—Hershey	AHL	31	5	9	14	119	...	...	...	—	—	—	—	—
—Philadelphia	NHL	27	3	2	5	108	1	0	0	—	—	—	—	—
88-89—Hershey	AHL	7	0	2	2	19	...	...	...	—	—	—	—	—
—Philadelphia	NHL	53	1	1	2	199	-15	0	0	16	0	0	0	56
89-90—Philadelphia	NHL	74	4	14	18	291	-7	0	0	—	—	—	—	—
90-91—Philadelphia	NHL	74	8	9	17	293	-6	0	0	—	—	—	—	—
91-92—Toronto	NHL	40	5	7	12	109	-2	1	0	—	—	—	—	—
—Calgary	NHL	36	1	4	5	155	-3	0	0	—	—	—	—	—
92-93—Calgary	NHL	77	4	8	12	209	-6	0	0	6	0	1	1	21
93-94—Washington	NHL	84	7	7	14	305	-4	0	0	8	0	0	0	21
94-95—Washington	NHL	43	2	4	6	173	-5	0	0	7	0	0	0	29
95-96—Washington	NHL	50	2	10	12	151	1	1	0	2	0	0	0	19
96-97—Washington	NHL	80	4	3	7	218	-11	0	0	—	—	—	—	—
97-98—Washington	NHL	74	6	9	15	189	-3	0	0	21	1	0	1	21
NHL Totals (12 years)		719	47	78	125	2457	-58	2	0	65	1	1	2	184

BEUKEBOOM, JEFF   D   RANGERS

PERSONAL: Born March 28, 1965, in Ajax, Ont. ... 6-5/230. ... Shoots right. ... Nephew of Ed Kea, defenseman with Atlanta Flames (1973-74 through 1978-79) and St. Louis Blues (1979-80 through 1982-83); and cousin of Joe Nieuwendyk, center, Dallas Stars. ... Name pronounced BOO-kuh-BOOM.

TRANSACTIONS/CAREER NOTES: Selected by Edmonton Oilers as underage junior in first round (first Oilers pick, 19th overall) of NHL entry draft (June 8,1983). ... Injured knee (December 1984). ... Lacerated knuckle (October 24, 1987). ... Suspended 10 games by NHL for leaving the bench (October 2, 1988). ... Sprained right knee (January 1989). ... Suffered hairline fracture of ankle (February 22, 1991); missed two games. ... Traded by Oilers to New York Rangers for D David Shaw (November 12, 1991), completing deal in which Oilers traded C Mark Messier with future considerations to Rangers for C Bernie Nicholls, LW Louie DeBrusk, RW Steven Rice and future considerations (October 4, 1991). ... Strained back (March 16, 1992); missed one game. ... Injured knee (December 21, 1992); missed one game. ... Bruised ankle (February 1, 1993); missed one game. ... Suspended one game by NHL for hitting from behind (May 25, 1994). ... Suffered neck spasms (March 5, 1995); missed one game. ... Bruised chest (March 18, 1995); missed three games. ... Suffered from the flu (February 15, 1997); missed two games. ... Fractured left ankle (December 16, 1997); missed 12 games. ... Suffered stress fracture of left leg (March 16, 1998); missed three games. ... Reinjured left leg (April 1, 1998); missed one game.

HONORS: Named to OHL All-Star first team (1984-85).

MISCELLANEOUS: Member of Stanley Cup championship team (1987, 1988, 1990 and 1994). ... Failed to score on a penalty shot (vs. Richard Tabaracci, October 6, 1990).

Season Team	League	REGULAR SEASON								PLAYOFFS				
		Gms.	G	A	Pts.	PIM	+/-	PP	SH	Gms.	G	A	Pts.	PIM
81-82—Newmarket	OPJHL	49	5	30	35	218	...	...	...	—	—	—	—	—
82-83—Sault Ste. Marie	OHL	70	0	25	25	143	...	...	...	16	1	14	15	46
83-84—Sault Ste. Marie	OHL	61	6	30	36	178	...	...	...	16	1	7	8	43
84-85—Sault Ste. Marie	OHL	37	4	20	24	85	...	...	...	16	4	6	10	47
85-86—Nova Scotia	AHL	77	9	20	29	175	...	...	...	—	—	—	—	—
—Edmonton	NHL	—	—	—	—	—	—	—	—	1	0	0	0	4
86-87—Nova Scotia	AHL	14	1	7	8	35	...	...	...	—	—	—	—	—
—Edmonton	NHL	44	3	8	11	124	7	1	0	—	—	—	—	—
87-88—Edmonton	NHL	73	5	20	25	201	27	1	0	7	0	0	0	16
88-89—Cape Breton	AHL	8	0	4	4	36	...	...	...	—	—	—	—	—
—Edmonton	NHL	36	0	5	5	94	2	0	0	1	0	0	0	2
89-90—Edmonton	NHL	46	1	12	13	86	5	0	0	2	0	0	0	0
90-91—Edmonton	NHL	67	3	7	10	150	6	0	0	18	1	3	4	28
91-92—Edmonton	NHL	18	0	5	5	78	4	0	0	—	—	—	—	—
—New York Rangers	NHL	56	1	10	11	122	19	0	0	13	2	3	5	*47
92-93—New York Rangers	NHL	82	2	17	19	153	9	0	0	—	—	—	—	—
93-94—New York Rangers	NHL	68	8	8	16	170	18	1	0	22	0	6	6	50
94-95—New York Rangers	NHL	44	1	3	4	70	3	0	0	9	0	0	0	10
95-96—New York Rangers	NHL	82	3	11	14	220	19	0	0	11	0	3	3	6
96-97—New York Rangers	NHL	80	3	9	12	167	22	0	0	15	0	1	1	34
97-98—New York Rangers	NHL	63	0	5	5	195	-25	0	0	—	—	—	—	—
NHL Totals (13 years).........		759	30	120	150	1830	116	3	0	99	3	16	19	197

BICANEK, RADIM — D — SENATORS

PERSONAL: Born January 18, 1975, in Uherske Hradiste, Czechoslovakia. ... 6-1/210. ... Shoots left. ... Name pronounced RA-deem bih-CHAN-ihk.
TRANSACTIONS/CAREER NOTES: Selected by Ottawa Senators in second round (second Senators pick, 27th overall) of NHL entry draft (June 26, 1993).

Season Team	League	REGULAR SEASON								PLAYOFFS				
		Gms.	G	A	Pts.	PIM	+/-	PP	SH	Gms.	G	A	Pts.	PIM
92-93—Jihlava	Czech.	43	2	3	5	...	...	...	...	—	—	—	—	—
93-94—Belleville	OHL	63	16	27	43	49	...	...	...	12	2	8	10	21
94-95—Belleville	OHL	49	13	26	39	61	...	...	...	16	6	5	11	30
—Ottawa	NHL	6	0	0	0	0	3	0	0	—	—	—	—	—
—Prin. Edward Island	AHL	—	—	—	—	—	...	...	...	3	0	1	1	0
95-96—Prin. Edward Island	AHL	74	7	19	26	87	...	...	...	5	0	2	2	6
96-97—Worcester	AHL	44	1	15	16	22	...	...	...	—	—	—	—	—
—Ottawa	NHL	21	0	1	1	8	-4	0	0	7	0	0	0	8
97-98—Ottawa	NHL	1	0	0	0	0	0	0	0	—	—	—	—	—
—Detroit........................	IHL	9	1	3	4	16	...	...	...	—	—	—	—	—
—Manitoba....................	IHL	42	1	7	8	52	...	...	...	—	—	—	—	—
NHL Totals (3 years)...........		28	0	1	1	8	-1	0	0	7	0	0	0	8

BIENVENUE, DANIEL — LW — SABRES

PERSONAL: Born June 10, 1977, in Val d'Or, Que. ... 6-0/196. ... Shoots left. ... Name pronounced bee-EHN-vih-NOO.
TRANSACTIONS/CAREER NOTES: Selected by Buffalo Sabres in fifth round (eighth Sabres pick, 123rd overall) of NHL entry draft (July 8, 1995).

Season Team	League	REGULAR SEASON								PLAYOFFS				
		Gms.	G	A	Pts.	PIM	+/-	PP	SH	Gms.	G	A	Pts.	PIM
93-94—Chicoutimi	QMJHL	42	2	7	9	4	...	...	...	0	0	0	0	0
94-95—Val-d'Or	QMJHL	67	27	14	41	40	...	...	...	—	—	—	—	—
95-96—Val-d'Or	QMJHL	67	30	42	72	65	...	...	...	13	6	1	7	0
96-97—Val-d'Or	QMJHL	20	4	4	8	22	...	...	...	13	6	5	11	29
97-98—Rochester	AHL	10	0	0	0	17	...	...	...	—	—	—	—	—
—South Carolina............	ECHL	50	10	11	21	4	...	...	...	—	—	—	—	—

BIERK, ZAC — G — LIGHTNING

PERSONAL: Born September 17, 1976, in Peterborough, Ont. ... 6-4/205. ... Catches left. ... Name pronounced BUHRK.
HIGH SCHOOL: Thomas A. Stewart S.S. (Peterborough, Ont.).
TRANSACTIONS/CAREER NOTES: Selected by Tampa Bay Lightning in ninth round (eighth Lightning pick, 212th overall) of NHL entry draft (July 8, 1995).
HONORS: Won Leo Lalonde Memorial Trophy (1996-97). ... Named to Can.HL All-Star second team (1996-97). ... Named to OHL All-Star first team (1996-97).
MISCELLANEOUS: Allowed a penalty shot goal (vs. Robert Reichel, January 14, 1998).

Season Team	League	REGULAR SEASON							PLAYOFFS					
		Gms.	Min	W	L	T	GA	SO	Avg.	Gms.	Min.	W	L	GA	SO	Avg.
93-94—Peterborough...............	Tier II Jr. A	4	205				17	0	4.98	—	—	—	—	—	—	—
—Peterborough...............	OHL	9	423	0	4	2	37	0	5.25	1	33	0	0	7	0	12.73
94-95—Peterborough...............	OHL	35	1798	12	15	5	118	0	3.94	6	301	2	3	24	0	4.78
95-96—Peterborough...............	OHL	58	3292	31	16	6	174	2	3.17	*22	*1383	*14	†7	*83	0	3.60
96-97—Peterborough...............	OHL	49	2744	*28	16	0	151	2	3.30	11	666	6	5	35	0	3.15
97-98—Adirondack..................	AHL	12	558	1	6	1	36	0	3.87	—	—	—	—	—	—	—
—Tampa Bay	NHL	13	433	1	4	1	30	0	4.16	—	—	—	—	—	—	—
NHL Totals (1 year)..............		13	433	1	4	1	30	0	4.16							

BILLINGTON, CRAIG   G

PERSONAL: Born September 11, 1966, in London, Ont. ... 5-10/170. ... Catches left.
TRANSACTIONS/CAREER NOTES: Selected by New Jersey Devils as underage junior in second round (second Devils pick, 23rd overall) of NHL entry draft (June 9, 1984). ... Suffered from mononucleosis (July 1984). ... Injured hamstring (February 15, 1992); missed two games. ... Strained knee (March 11, 1992); missed six games. ... Underwent arthroscopic knee surgery (April 13, 1992). ... Suffered from sore throat (March 27, 1993); missed one game. ... Traded by Devils with C/LW Troy Mallette and fourth-round pick in 1993 draft (C Cosmo Dupaul) to Ottawa Senators for G Peter Sidorkiewicz and future considerations (June 20, 1993); Senators sent LW Mike Peluso to Devils to complete deal (June 26, 1993). ... Injured knee (January 27, 1995); missed 17 games. ... Traded by Senators to Boston Bruins for eighth-round pick (D Ray Schultz) in 1995 draft (April 7, 1995). ... Signed as free agent by Florida Panthers (September 4, 1996). ... Selected by Colorado Avalanche in NHL waiver draft for cash (September 30, 1996). ... Sprained knee ligament (November 19, 1996); missed seven games.
HONORS: Won Bobby Smith Trophy (1984-85). ... Named to OHL All-Star first team (1984-85). ... Played in NHL All-Star Game (1993).
MISCELLANEOUS: Holds Ottawa Senators all-time record for most games played by goaltender (72). ... Stopped penalty shot attempt (vs. Rick Tocchet, January 6, 1987).

		REGULAR SEASON							PLAYOFFS						
Season Team	League	Gms.	Min	W	L	T	GA	SO	Avg.	Gms.	Min.	W	L	GA	SO	Avg.
82-83—London Diamonds	OPJHL	23	1338	...	...	...	76	0	3.41	—	—	—	—	—	—	—
83-84—Belleville	OHL	44	2335	20	19	0	162	1	4.16	1	30	0	0	3	0	6.00
84-85—Belleville	OHL	47	2544	26	19	0	180	1	4.25	14	761	7	5	47	†1	3.71
85-86—Belleville	OHL	3	180	2	1	0	11	0	3.67	†20	1133	9	6	*68	0	3.60
—New Jersey	NHL	18	701	4	9	1	77	0	6.59	—	—	—	—	—	—	—
86-87—Maine	AHL	20	1151	9	8	2	70	0	3.65	—	—	—	—	—	—	—
—New Jersey	NHL	22	1114	4	13	2	89	0	4.79	—	—	—	—	—	—	—
87-88—Utica	AHL	*59	*3404	22	27	8	*208	1	3.67	—	—	—	—	—	—	—
88-89—New Jersey	NHL	3	140	1	1	0	11	0	4.71	—	—	—	—	—	—	—
—Utica	AHL	41	2432	17	18	6	150	2	3.70	4	219	1	3	18	0	4.93
89-90—Utica	AHL	38	2087	20	13	1	138	0	3.97	—	—	—	—	—	—	—
90-91—Canadian nat'l team	Int'l	34	1879	17	14	2	110	2	3.51	—	—	—	—	—	—	—
91-92—New Jersey	NHL	26	1363	13	7	1	69	2	3.04	—	—	—	—	—	—	—
92-93—New Jersey	NHL	42	2389	21	16	4	146	2	3.67	2	78	0	1	5	0	3.85
93-94—Ottawa	NHL	63	3319	11	*41	4	*254	0	4.59	—	—	—	—	—	—	—
94-95—Boston	NHL	8	373	5	1	0	19	0	3.06	1	25	0	0	1	0	2.40
—Ottawa	NHL	9	472	0	6	2	32	0	4.07	—	—	—	—	—	—	—
95-96—Boston	NHL	27	1380	10	13	3	79	1	3.43	1	60	0	1	6	0	6.00
96-97—Colorado	NHL	23	1200	11	8	2	53	1	2.65	1	20	0	0	1	0	3.00
97-98—Colorado	NHL	23	1162	8	7	4	45	1	2.32	1	1	0	0	0	0	...
NHL Totals (10 years)		264	13613	88	122	23	874	7	3.85	6	184	0	2	13	0	4.24

BIRON, MARTIN   G   SABRES

PERSONAL: Born August 15, 1977, in Lac St. Charles, Que. ... 6-1/154. ... Catches left. ... Name pronounced bih-RAH.
TRANSACTIONS/CAREER NOTES: Selected by Buffalo Sabres in first round (second Sabres pick, 16th overall) of NHL entry draft (July 8, 1995).
HONORS: Won Can.HL Goaltender of the Year Award (1994-95). ... Won Raymond Lagace Trophy (1994-95). ... Won Mike Bossy Trophy (1994-95). ... Won Jacques Plante Trophy (1994-95). ... Named to Can.HL All-Star first team (1994-95). ... Named to Can.HL All-Rookie team (1994-95).

		REGULAR SEASON							PLAYOFFS						
Season Team	League	Gms.	Min	W	L	T	GA	SO	Avg.	Gms.	Min.	W	L	GA	SO	Avg.
94-95—Beauport	QMJHL	56	3193	29	16	9	132	3	2.48	16	902	8	7	37	4	2.46
95-96—Beauport	QMJHL	55	3207	29	17	7	152	1	2.84	*19	1132	*12	†8	64	0	3.39
—Buffalo	NHL	3	119	0	2	0	10	0	5.04	—	—	—	—	—	—	—
96-97—Beauport	QMJHL	18	935	6	10	1	62	1	3.98	—	—	—	—	—	—	—
—Hull	QMJHL	16	972	11	4	1	43	2	2.65	6	326	3	1	19	0	3.50
97-98—Rochester	AHL	41	2312	14	18	6	113	*5	2.93	4	239	1	3	16	0	4.02
—South Carolina	ECHL	2	86	0	1	‡1	3	0	2.09	—	—	—	—	—	—	—
NHL Totals (1 year)		3	119	0	2	0	10	0	5.04							

BLACK, JAMES   C/LW   BLACKHAWKS

PERSONAL: Born August 15, 1969, in Regina, Sask. ... 5-11/190. ... Shoots left.
TRANSACTIONS/CAREER NOTES: Selected by Hartford Whalers in fifth round (fourth Whalers pick, 94th overall) of NHL entry draft (June 17, 1989). ... Traded by Whalers to Minnesota North Stars for C Mark Janssens (September 3, 1992). ... North Stars franchise moved from Minnesota to Dallas and renamed Stars for 1993-94 season. ... Traded by Stars with seventh-round pick in 1994 draft (RW Steve Webb) to Buffalo Sabres for RW Gord Donnelly (December 15, 1993). ... Cut forehead (October 27, 1993); missed five games. ... Signed as free agent by Chicago Blackhawks (August 10, 1995). ... Injured hand (October 22, 1997); missed six games. ... Sprained knee (November 8, 1997); missed three games.

		REGULAR SEASON							PLAYOFFS				
Season Team	League	Gms.	G	A	Pts.	PIM	+/-	PP	SH	Gms.	G	A	Pts.	PIM
87-88—Portland	WHL	72	30	50	80	50	...	...	...	—	—	—	—	—
88-89—Portland	WHL	71	45	51	96	57	...	...	...	19	13	6	19	28
89-90—Hartford	NHL	1	0	0	0	0	0	0	0	—	—	—	—	—
—Binghamton	AHL	80	37	35	72	34	...	...	...	—	—	—	—	—
90-91—Hartford	NHL	1	0	0	0	0	0	0	0	—	—	—	—	—
—Springfield	AHL	79	35	61	96	34	...	...	...	18	9	9	18	6
91-92—Springfield	AHL	47	15	25	40	33	...	...	...	10	3	2	5	18
—Hartford	NHL	30	4	6	10	10	-4	1	0	—	—	—	—	—
92-93—Minnesota	NHL	10	2	1	3	4	0	0	0	—	—	—	—	—
—Kalamazoo	IHL	63	25	45	70	40	...	...	...	—	—	—	—	—

Season Team	League	REGULAR SEASON								PLAYOFFS				
		Gms.	G	A	Pts.	PIM	+/-	PP	SH	Gms.	G	A	Pts.	PIM
93-94—Dallas	NHL	13	2	3	5	2	-4	2	0	—	—	—	—	—
—Buffalo	NHL	2	0	0	0	0	0	0	0	—	—	—	—	—
—Rochester	AHL	45	19	32	51	28	...	...	...	4	2	3	5	0
94-95—Las Vegas	IHL	78	29	44	73	54	...	...	...	10	1	6	7	4
95-96—Indianapolis	IHL	67	32	50	82	56	...	...	...					
—Chicago	NHL	13	3	3	6	16	1	0	0	8	1	0	1	2
96-97—Chicago	NHL	64	12	11	23	20	6	0	0	5	1	1	2	2
97-98—Chicago	NHL	52	10	5	15	8	-8	2	1	—	—	—	—	—
NHL Totals (8 years)		186	33	29	62	60	-9	5	1	13	2	1	3	4

BLAKE, ROB   D   KINGS

B

PERSONAL: Born December 10, 1969, in Simcoe, Ont. ... 6-3/222. ... Shoots right. ... Full Name: Robert Bowlby Blake.
COLLEGE: Bowling Green State.
TRANSACTIONS/CAREER NOTES: Dislocated shoulder (April 1987). ... Selected by Los Angeles Kings in fourth round (fourth Kings pick, 70th overall) of NHL entry draft (June 11, 1988). ... Sprained knee (April 1990). ... Injured knee (February 12, 1991); missed two games. ... Injured shoulder (October 8, 1991); missed 11 games. ... Sprained knee ligaments (November 28, 1991); missed six games. ... Suffered from the flu (January 23, 1992); missed one game. ... Suffered from the flu (February 13, 1992); missed one game. ... Strained shoulder (March 14, 1992); missed four games. ... Broke rib (December 19, 1992); missed three games. ... Bruised lower back (April 3, 1993); missed final five games of regular season and one playoff game. ... Strained groin (January 23, 1995); missed 11 games. ... Strained groin (March 11, 1995); missed 12 games. ... Strained groin (April 7, 1995); missed one game. ... Suffered partial tear of left knee ligaments (October 20, 1995); missed 76 games. ... Fractured hand (December 26, 1996); missed 11 games. ... Suspended two games and fined $1,000 by NHL for high-sticking incident (February 5, 1997). ... Suffered tendinitis in left knee (February 22, 1997); missed seven games.
HONORS: Named to CCHA All-Star second team (1988-89). ... Named to NCAA All-America West first team (1989-90). ... Named to CCHA All-Star first team (1989-90). ... Named to NHL All-Rookie team (1990-91). ... Played in NHL All-Star Game (1994). ... Named to play in NHL All-Star Game (1997); replaced by LW Dimitri Khristich due to injury. ... Named to THE SPORTING NEWS All-Star team (1997-98). ... Won James Norris Memorial Trophy (1997-98). ... Named to NHL All-Star first team (1997-98).
MISCELLANEOUS: Captain of Los Angeles Kings (1996-97 and 1997-98). ... Failed to score on a penalty shot (vs. Dwayne Roloson, April 13, 1998).

Season Team	League	REGULAR SEASON								PLAYOFFS				
		Gms.	G	A	Pts.	PIM	+/-	PP	SH	Gms.	G	A	Pts.	PIM
86-87—Stratford Jr. B	OHA	31	11	20	31	115	...	...	...	—	—	—	—	—
87-88—Bowling Green	CCHA	36	5	8	13	72	...	...	...	—	—	—	—	—
88-89—Bowling Green	CCHA	46	11	21	32	140	...	...	...	—	—	—	—	—
89-90—Bowling Green	CCHA	42	23	36	59	140	...	...	...	—	—	—	—	—
—Los Angeles	NHL	4	0	0	0	4	0	0	0	8	1	3	4	4
90-91—Los Angeles	NHL	75	12	34	46	125	3	9	0	12	1	4	5	26
91-92—Los Angeles	NHL	57	7	13	20	102	-5	5	0	6	2	1	3	12
92-93—Los Angeles	NHL	76	16	43	59	152	18	10	0	23	4	6	10	46
93-94—Los Angeles	NHL	84	20	48	68	137	-7	7	0	—	—	—	—	—
94-95—Los Angeles	NHL	24	4	7	11	38	-16	4	0	—	—	—	—	—
95-96—Los Angeles	NHL	6	1	2	3	8	0	0	0	—	—	—	—	—
96-97—Los Angeles	NHL	62	8	23	31	82	-28	4	0	—	—	—	—	—
97-98—Los Angeles	NHL	81	23	27	50	94	-3	11	0	4	0	0	0	6
—Can. Olympic Team	Int'l	6	1	1	2	2	...	...	...	—	—	—	—	—
NHL Totals (9 years)		469	91	197	288	742	-38	50	0	53	8	14	22	94

BLANCHARD, SEAN   D   KINGS

PERSONAL: Born March 29, 1978, in Garson, Ont. ... 6-0/201. ... Shoots left.
TRANSACTIONS/CAREER NOTES: Selected by Los Angeles Kings in fourth round (fifth Kings pick, 99th overall) of NHL entry draft (June 21, 1997).
HONORS: Won Can.HL Defenseman of the Year Award (1996-97). ... Named to Can.HL All-Star first team (1996-97). ... Named to OHL All-Star first team (1996-97). ... Won Max Kaminsky Trophy (1996-97). ... Named to OHL All-Star first team (1997-98).

Season Team	League	REGULAR SEASON								PLAYOFFS				
		Gms.	G	A	Pts.	PIM	+/-	PP	SH	Gms.	G	A	Pts.	PIM
95-96—Ottawa	OHL	64	7	29	36	49	...	...	...	—	—	—	—	—
96-97—Ottawa	OHL	66	11	57	68	64	...	...	...	24	3	15	18	34
97-98—Ottawa	OHL	57	13	51	64	43	...	...	...	13	0	5	5	27

BLOUIN, SYLVAIN   D   RANGERS

PERSONAL: Born May 21, 1974, in Montreal. ... 6-0/210. ... Shoots left. ... Name pronounced bloo-AN.
TRANSACTIONS/CAREER NOTES: Selected by New York Rangers in fourth round (fifth Rangers pick, 104th overall) of NHL entry draft (June 29, 1994). ... Loaned by Rangers to Chicago Wolves of IHL (October 6, 1994). ... Bruised hand (February 19, 1997); missed two games.

Season Team	League	REGULAR SEASON								PLAYOFFS				
		Gms.	G	A	Pts.	PIM	+/-	PP	SH	Gms.	G	A	Pts.	PIM
91-92—Laval	QMJHL	28	0	0	0	23	...	...	...	9	0	0	0	35
92-93—Laval	QMJHL	68	0	10	10	373	...	...	...	13	1	0	1	*66
93-94—Laval	QMJHL	62	18	22	40	*492	...	...	...	21	4	13	17	*177
94-95—Binghamton	AHL	10	1	0	1	46	...	...	...	2	0	0	0	24
—Chicago	IHL	1	0	0	0	2	...	...	...	—	—	—	—	—
—Charlotte	ECHL	50	5	7	12	280	...	...	...	3	0	0	0	6
95-96—Binghamton	AHL	71	5	8	13	*352	...	...	...	4	0	3	3	4
96-97—Binghamton	AHL	62	13	17	30	301	...	...	...	4	2	1	3	16
—New York Rangers	NHL	6	0	0	0	18	-1	0	0	—	—	—	—	—
97-98—Hartford	AHL	53	8	9	17	286	...	...	...	9	0	1	1	63
—New York Rangers	NHL	1	0	0	0	5	0	0	0	—	—	—	—	—
NHL Totals (2 years)		7	0	0	0	23	-1	0	0					

BODGER, DOUG D KINGS

PERSONAL: Born June 18, 1966, in Chemainus, B.C. ... 6-2/215. ... Shoots left. ... Name pronounced BAH-juhr.
TRANSACTIONS/CAREER NOTES: Selected by Pittsburgh Penguins as underage junior in first round (second Penguins pick, ninth overall) of NHL entry draft (June 9, 1984). ... Underwent surgery to remove bone chip on left foot (April 1985). ... Sprained knee (December 1987). ... Strained left knee (October 1988). ... Traded by Penguins with LW Darrin Shannon to Buffalo Sabres for G Tom Barrasso and third-round pick (RW Joe Dziedzic) in 1990 draft (November 12, 1988). ... Sprained left knee (October 1989); missed eight games. ... Injured shoulder (December 28, 1990); missed four games. ... Separated left shoulder (February 17, 1991); missed 18 games. ... Reinjured left shoulder (March 30, 1991). ... Injured eye (February 11, 1992); missed seven games. ... Suffered sore back (December 2, 1993); missed four games. ... Suffered from the flu (March 19, 1995); missed one game. ... Bruised shoulder (April 28, 1995); missed last three games of season. ... Traded by Sabres to San Jose Sharks for RW Martin Spanhel and first- (traded to Winnipeg) and fourth-round (traded to Buffalo) picks in 1996 draft (November 16, 1995). ... Injured knee (January 17, 1996); missed three games. ... Injured groin (February 23, 1996); missed four games. ... Injured shoulder (November 8, 1997); missed two games. ... Traded by Sharks with LW Dody Wood to New Jersey Devils for RW John MacLean and D Ken Sutton (December 7, 1997). ... Fractured right index finger (February 26, 1998); missed two games. ... Traded by Devils to Los Angeles Kings for fourth-round pick (LW Pierre Dagenais) in 1998 draft (June 18, 1998).
HONORS: Named to WHL All-Star second team (1982-83). ... Named to WHL (West) All-Star first team (1983-84).

		REGULAR SEASON								PLAYOFFS				
Season Team	League	Gms.	G	A	Pts.	PIM	+/-	PP	SH	Gms.	G	A	Pts.	PIM
82-83—Kamloops	WHL	72	26	66	92	98	...	...	...	7	0	5	5	2
83-84—Kamloops	WHL	70	21	77	98	90	...	...	...	17	2	15	17	12
84-85—Pittsburgh	NHL	65	5	26	31	67	-24	3	0	—	—	—	—	—
85-86—Pittsburgh	NHL	79	4	33	37	63	3	1	0	—	—	—	—	—
86-87—Pittsburgh	NHL	76	11	38	49	52	6	5	0	—	—	—	—	—
87-88—Pittsburgh	NHL	69	14	31	45	103	-4	13	0	—	—	—	—	—
88-89—Pittsburgh	NHL	10	1	4	5	7	6	0	0	—	—	—	—	—
—Buffalo	NHL	61	7	40	47	52	9	6	0	5	1	1	2	11
89-90—Buffalo	NHL	71	12	36	48	64	0	8	0	6	1	5	6	6
90-91—Buffalo	NHL	58	5	23	28	54	-8	2	0	4	0	1	1	0
91-92—Buffalo	NHL	73	11	35	46	108	1	4	0	7	2	1	3	2
92-93—Buffalo	NHL	81	9	45	54	87	14	6	0	8	2	3	5	0
93-94—Buffalo	NHL	75	7	32	39	76	8	5	1	7	0	3	3	6
94-95—Buffalo	NHL	44	3	17	20	47	-3	2	0	5	0	4	4	0
95-96—Buffalo	NHL	16	0	5	5	18	-6	0	0	—	—	—	—	—
—San Jose	NHL	57	4	19	23	50	-18	3	0	—	—	—	—	—
96-97—San Jose	NHL	81	1	15	16	64	-14	0	0	—	—	—	—	—
97-98—San Jose	NHL	28	4	6	10	32	0	0	0	—	—	—	—	—
—New Jersey	NHL	49	5	5	10	25	-1	3	0	5	0	0	0	0
NHL Totals (14 years)		993	103	410	513	969	-31	61	1	47	6	18	24	25

BODTKER, STEWART C CANUCKS

PERSONAL: Born September 15, 1976, in Vancouver. ... 6-1/175. ... Shoots right. ... Full Name: Stewart Warwick Bodtker.
COLLEGE: Colorado College.
TRANSACTIONS/CAREER NOTES: Selected by Vancouver Canucks in seventh round (seventh Canucks pick, 170th overall) of NHL entry draft (July 8, 1995).

		REGULAR SEASON								PLAYOFFS				
Season Team	League	Gms.	G	A	Pts.	PIM	+/-	PP	SH	Gms.	G	A	Pts.	PIM
93-94—Penticton	BCJHL	44	11	20	31	60	...	...	...	—	—	—	—	—
94-95—Colorado College	WCHA	32	6	4	10	24	...	...	...	—	—	—	—	—
95-96—Colorado College	WCHA	42	6	7	13	40	...	...	...	—	—	—	—	—
96-97—Colorado College	WCHA	43	19	17	36	71	...	...	...	—	—	—	—	—
97-98—Colorado College	WCHA	30	11	15	26	50	...	...	...	—	—	—	—	—

BOGAS, CHRIS D MAPLE LEAFS

PERSONAL: Born November 12, 1976, in Cleveland. ... 6-0/202. ... Shoots right.
COLLEGE: Michigan State.
TRANSACTIONS/CAREER NOTES: Selected by Toronto Maple Leafs in sixth round (10th Maple Leafs pick, 148th overall) of NHL entry draft (June 22, 1996).
HONORS: Named to CCHA All-Rookie team (1995-96).

		REGULAR SEASON								PLAYOFFS				
Season Team	League	Gms.	G	A	Pts.	PIM	+/-	PP	SH	Gms.	G	A	Pts.	PIM
94-95—Omaha	USHL	42	5	11	16	78	...	...	...	—	—	—	—	—
95-96—Michigan State	CCHA	38	1	20	21	55	...	...	...	—	—	—	—	—
96-97—Michigan State	CCHA	40	7	4	11	58	...	...	...	—	—	—	—	—
97-98—Michigan State	CCHA	44	4	10	14	75	...	...	...	—	—	—	—	—

BOHONOS, LONNY RW MAPLE LEAFS

PERSONAL: Born May 20, 1973, in Winnipeg. ... 5-11/190. ... Shoots right. ... Name pronounced boh-HAH-nohz.
TRANSACTIONS/CAREER NOTES: Signed as free agent by Vancouver Canucks (May 31, 1994). ... Traded by Canucks to Toronto Maple Leafs for C Brandon Convery (March 7, 1998).
HONORS: Won Bob Clarke Trophy (1993-94). ... Won Brad Hornung Trophy (1993-94). ... Named to Can.HL All-Star first team (1993-94). ... Named to WHL (West) All-Star first team (1993-94).

B

Season Team	League	REGULAR SEASON								PLAYOFFS				
		Gms.	G	A	Pts.	PIM	+/-	PP	SH	Gms.	G	A	Pts.	PIM
91-92—Moose Jaw	WHL	8	1	1	2	0	...	...	...	—	—	—	—	—
92-93—Seattle	WHL	46	13	13	26	27	...	...	...	—	—	—	—	—
—Portland	WHL	27	20	17	37	16	...	...	...	15	8	13	21	19
93-94—Portland	WHL	70	*62	*90	*152	80	...	...	...	10	8	11	19	13
94-95—Syracuse	AHL	67	30	45	75	71	...	...	...	—	—	—	—	—
95-96—Syracuse	AHL	74	40	39	79	82	...	...	...	16	14	8	22	16
—Vancouver	NHL	3	0	1	1	0	1	0	0	—	—	—	—	—
96-97—Syracuse	AHL	41	22	30	52	28	...	...	...	3	2	2	4	4
—Vancouver	NHL	36	11	11	22	10	-3	2	0	—	—	—	—	—
97-98—Vancouver	NHL	31	2	1	3	4	-9	0	0	—	—	—	—	—
—Syracuse	AHL	17	12	12	24	8	...	...	...	—	—	—	—	—
—Toronto	NHL	6	3	3	6	4	1	0	0	—	—	—	—	—
—St. John's	AHL	11	7	9	16	10	...	...	...	2	1	1	2	2
NHL Totals (3 years)		76	16	16	32	18	-10	2	0					

BOIKOV, ALEXANDRE   D   SHARKS

PERSONAL: Born February 7, 1975, in Chelyabinsk, U.S.S.R. ... 6-0/190. ... Shoots left. ... Name pronounced BOY-kahf.
TRANSACTIONS/CAREER NOTES: Signed as free agent by San Jose Sharks (August 26, 1996).

Season Team	League	REGULAR SEASON								PLAYOFFS				
		Gms.	G	A	Pts.	PIM	+/-	PP	SH	Gms.	G	A	Pts.	PIM
93-94—Victoria	WHL	70	4	31	35	250	...	...	...	—	—	—	—	—
94-95—Prince George	WHL	46	5	23	28	115	...	...	...	—	—	—	—	—
—Tri-City	WHL	24	3	13	16	63	...	...	...	17	1	7	8	30
95-96—Tri-City	WHL	71	3	49	52	230	...	...	...	11	2	4	6	28
96-97—Kentucky	AHL	61	1	19	20	182	...	...	...	4	0	1	1	4
97-98—Kentucky	AHL	69	5	14	19	153	...	...	...	3	0	1	1	8

BOILEAU, PATRICK   D   CAPITALS

PERSONAL: Born February 22, 1975, in Montreal. ... 6-0/190. ... Shoots right. ... Name pronounced BOY-loh.
HIGH SCHOOL: CEGEP Lionel-Groulx (Que.).
TRANSACTIONS/CAREER NOTES: Selected by Washington Capitals in third round (third Capitals pick, 69th overall) of NHL entry draft (June 26, 1993).
HONORS: Named to Can.HL All-Rookie team (1992-93). ... Won Marcel Robert Trophy (1993-94). ... Won Can.HL Scholastic Player of the Year Award (1993-94).

Season Team	League	REGULAR SEASON								PLAYOFFS				
		Gms.	G	A	Pts.	PIM	+/-	PP	SH	Gms.	G	A	Pts.	PIM
92-93—Laval	QMJHL	69	4	19	23	73	...	...	...	13	1	2	3	10
93-94—Laval	QMJHL	64	13	57	70	56	...	...	...	21	1	7	8	24
94-95—Laval	QMJHL	38	8	25	33	46	...	...	...	20	4	16	20	24
95-96—Portland	AHL	78	10	28	38	41	...	...	...	19	1	3	4	12
96-97—Portland	AHL	67	16	28	44	63	...	...	...	5	1	1	2	4
—Washington	NHL	1	0	0	0	0	0	0	0	—	—	—	—	—
97-98—Portland	AHL	47	6	21	27	53	...	...	...	10	0	1	1	8
NHL Totals (1 year)		1	0	0	0	0	0	0	0					

BOMBARDIR, BRAD   D   DEVILS

PERSONAL: Born May 5, 1972, in Powell River, B.C. ... 6-1/205. ... Shoots left. ... Full Name: Luke Bradley Bombardir. ... Name pronounced BAHM-bahr-deer.
COLLEGE: North Dakota.
TRANSACTIONS/CAREER NOTES: Selected by New Jersey Devils in third round (fifth Devils pick, 56th overall) of NHL entry draft (June 16, 1990). ... Bruised left knee (November 29, 1997); missed six games.
HONORS: Named to AHL All-Star second team (1995-96).

Season Team	League	REGULAR SEASON								PLAYOFFS				
		Gms.	G	A	Pts.	PIM	+/-	PP	SH	Gms.	G	A	Pts.	PIM
88-89—Powell River	BCJHL	30	6	5	11	24	...	...	...	6	0	0	0	0
89-90—Powell River	BCJHL	60	10	35	45	93	...	...	...	8	2	3	5	4
90-91—U. of North Dakota	WCHA	33	3	6	9	18	...	...	...	—	—	—	—	—
91-92—U. of North Dakota	WCHA	35	3	14	17	54	...	...	...	—	—	—	—	—
92-93—U. of North Dakota	WCHA	38	8	15	23	34	...	...	...	—	—	—	—	—
93-94—U. of North Dakota	WCHA	38	5	17	22	38	...	...	...	—	—	—	—	—
94-95—Albany	AHL	77	5	22	27	22	...	...	...	14	0	3	3	6
95-96—Albany	AHL	80	6	25	31	63	...	...	...	3	0	1	1	4
96-97—Albany	AHL	32	0	8	8	6	...	...	...	16	1	3	4	8
97-98—New Jersey	NHL	43	1	5	6	8	11	0	0	—	—	—	—	—
—Albany	AHL	5	0	0	0	0	...	...	...	—	—	—	—	—
NHL Totals (1 year)		43	1	5	6	8	11	0	0					

BONDRA, PETER   RW   CAPITALS

PERSONAL: Born February 7, 1968, in Luck, U.S.S.R. ... 6-1/200. ... Shoots left. ... Name pronounced BAHN-druh.
TRANSACTIONS/CAREER NOTES: Selected by Washington Capitals in eighth round (ninth Capitals pick, 156th overall) of NHL entry draft (June 16, 1990). ... Dislocated left shoulder (January 17, 1991). ... Suffered recurring shoulder problems (February 13, 1991); missed 13

games. ... Injured throat (April 4, 1993); missed one game. ... Broke left hand (November 26, 1993); missed 12 games. ... Played in Europe during 1994-95 NHL lockout. ... Suffered from the flu (April 8, 1995); missed one game. ... Signed by Detroit Vipers of AHL during contract holdout (September 28, 1995); re-signed by Capitals (October 20, 1995). ... Separated shoulder (November 11, 1995); missed six games. ... Pulled groin (February 24, 1996); missed four games. ... Strained groin (December 4, 1996); missed three games. ... Suspended one game and fined $1,000 by NHL for kneeing incident (February 4, 1997). ... Suffered back spasms (April 1, 1997); missed one game. ... Injured foot (November 29, 1997); missed three games. ... Injured knee (April 8, 1998); missed two games.

HONORS: Played in NHL All-Star Game (1993 and 1996-1998).

MISCELLANEOUS: Failed to score on a penalty shot (vs. Mikhail Shtalenkov, December 13, 1996; vs. Stephane Fiset, April 4, 1998).

STATISTICAL PLATEAUS: Three-goal games: 1993-94 (1), 1994-95 (1), 1995-96 (2), 1996-97 (1), 1997-98 (1). Total: 6. ... Four-goal games: 1995-96 (2), 1996-97 (1). Total: 3. ... Total hat tricks: 9.

STATISTICAL NOTES: Led NHL with 13 game-winning goals (1997-98).

Season Team	League	REGULAR SEASON								PLAYOFFS				
		Gms.	G	A	Pts.	PIM	+/-	PP	SH	Gms.	G	A	Pts.	PIM
86-87—Kosice	Czech.	32	4	5	9	24	...	...	...	—	—	—	—	—
87-88—Kosice	Czech.	45	27	11	38	20	...	...	...	—	—	—	—	—
88-89—Kosice	Czech.	40	30	10	40	20	...	...	...	—	—	—	—	—
89-90—Kosice	Czech.	42	29	17	46	...	...	...	...	—	—	—	—	—
90-91—Washington	NHL	54	12	16	28	47	-10	4	0	4	0	1	1	2
91-92—Washington	NHL	71	28	28	56	42	16	4	0	7	6	2	8	4
92-93—Washington	NHL	83	37	48	85	70	8	10	0	6	0	6	6	0
93-94—Washington	NHL	69	24	19	43	40	22	4	0	9	2	4	6	4
94-95—HC Kosice	Slovakia	2	1	0	1	0	...	...	...	—	—	—	—	—
—Washington	NHL	47	*34	9	43	24	9	12	*6	7	5	3	8	10
95-96—Detroit	IHL	7	8	1	9	0	...	...	...	—	—	—	—	—
—Washington	NHL	67	52	28	80	40	18	11	4	6	3	2	5	8
96-97—Washington	NHL	77	46	31	77	72	7	10	4	—	—	—	—	—
97-98—Washington	NHL	76	†52	26	78	44	14	11	5	17	7	5	12	12
—Slovakian Oly. team	Int'l	2	1	0	1	25	...	...	...	—	—	—	—	—
NHL Totals (8 years)		544	285	205	490	379	84	66	19	56	23	23	46	40

BONIN, BRIAN   C   PENGUINS

PERSONAL: Born November 28, 1973, in St. Paul, Minn. ... 5-10/186. ... Shoots left. ... Name pronounced BAH-nihn.

HIGH SCHOOL: White Bear Lake (Minn.) Area.

COLLEGE: Minnesota.

TRANSACTIONS/CAREER NOTES: Selected by Pittsburgh Penguins in ninth round (ninth Penguins pick, 211th overall) of NHL entry draft (June 20, 1992).

HONORS: Named WCHA Player of the Year (1994-95 and 1995-96). ... Named to NCAA All-America West first team (1994-95 and 1995-96). ... Named to WCHA All-Star first team (1994-95 and 1995-96). ... Won Hobey Baker Memorial Award (1995-96).

Season Team	League	REGULAR SEASON								PLAYOFFS				
		Gms.	G	A	Pts.	PIM	+/-	PP	SH	Gms.	G	A	Pts.	PIM
91-92—White Bear Lake H.S.	Minn. H.S.	23	22	35	57	8	...	...	...	—	—	—	—	—
92-93—Univ. of Minnesota	WCHA	38	10	18	28	10	...	...	...	—	—	—	—	—
93-94—Univ. of Minnesota	WCHA	42	24	20	44	14	...	...	...	—	—	—	—	—
94-95—Univ. of Minnesota	WCHA	44	32	31	63	28	...	...	...	—	—	—	—	—
95-96—Univ. of Minnesota	WCHA	42	34	47	81	30	...	...	...	—	—	—	—	—
96-97—Cleveland	IHL	60	13	26	39	18	...	...	...	1	1	0	1	0
97-98—Syracuse	AHL	67	31	38	69	46	...	...	...	5	1	3	4	6

BONK, RADEK   C   SENATORS

PERSONAL: Born January 9, 1976, in Kronov, Czechoslovakia. ... 6-3/210. ... Shoots left. ... Name pronounced BAHNK.

TRANSACTIONS/CAREER NOTES: Selected by Ottawa Senators in first round (first Senators pick, third overall) of NHL entry draft (June 28, 1994). ... Injured ankle (April 26, 1995); missed last five games of season. ... Injured hand during 1995-96 season; missed one game. ... Suffered abdominal strain (November 8, 1996); missed six games. ... Broke left wrist (November 23, 1996); missed 23 games. ... Bruised knee (March 5, 1998); missed one game.

HONORS: Won Garry F. Longman Memorial Trophy (1993-94).

MISCELLANEOUS: Failed to score on a penalty shot (vs. Daren Puppa, January 13, 1996).

Season Team	League	REGULAR SEASON								PLAYOFFS				
		Gms.	G	A	Pts.	PIM	+/-	PP	SH	Gms.	G	A	Pts.	PIM
90-91—Opava	Czech.	35	47	42	89	25	...	...	...	—	—	—	—	—
91-92—ZPS Zlin	Czech Dv.II	45	47	36	83	30	...	...	...	—	—	—	—	—
92-93—ZPS Zlin	Czech.	30	5	5	10	10	...	...	...	—	—	—	—	—
93-94—Las Vegas	IHL	76	42	45	87	208	...	...	...	5	1	2	3	10
94-95—Las Vegas	IHL	33	7	13	20	62	...	...	...	—	—	—	—	—
—Ottawa	NHL	42	3	8	11	28	-5	1	0	—	—	—	—	—
—Prin. Edward Island	AHL	—	—	—	—	—	...	...	...	1	0	0	0	0
95-96—Ottawa	NHL	76	16	19	35	36	-5	5	0	—	—	—	—	—
96-97—Ottawa	NHL	53	5	13	18	14	-4	0	1	7	0	1	1	4
97-98—Ottawa	NHL	65	7	9	16	16	-13	1	0	5	0	0	0	2
NHL Totals (4 years)		236	31	49	80	94	-27	7	1	12	0	1	1	6

BONNI, RYAN   D   CANUCKS

PERSONAL: Born February 18, 1979, in Winnipeg. ... 6-4/190. ... Shoots left. ... Name pronounced BAH-nee.

TRANSACTIONS/CAREER NOTES: Selected by Vancouver Canucks in second round (second Canucks pick, 34th overal) of NHL entry draft (June 21, 1997).

Season Team	League	REGULAR SEASON								PLAYOFFS				
		Gms.	G	A	Pts.	PIM	+/-	PP	SH	Gms.	G	A	Pts.	PIM
95-96—Saskatoon	WHL	63	1	7	8	78	...	...	...	3	0	0	0	0
96-97—Saskatoon	WHL	69	11	19	30	219	...	...	...	—	—	—	—	—
97-98—Saskatoon	WHL	42	5	14	19	100	...	...	...	—	—	—	—	—

BONSIGNORE, JASON   C   LIGHTNING

PERSONAL: Born April 15, 1976, in Rochester, N.Y. ... 6-4/220. ... Shoots right. ... Name pronounced BAHN-seen-yohr.

TRANSACTIONS/CAREER NOTES: Selected by Edmonton Oilers in first round (first Oilers pick, fourth overall) of NHL entry draft (June 28, 1994). ... Suffered from the flu (October 30, 1995); missed three games. ... Traded by Oilers to Lightning with C Steve Kelly and D Bryan Marchment for D Roman Hamrlik and F Paul Comrie (December 30, 1997).

B

Season Team	League	REGULAR SEASON								PLAYOFFS				
		Gms.	G	A	Pts.	PIM	+/-	PP	SH	Gms.	G	A	Pts.	PIM
92-93—Newmarket	OHL	66	22	20	42	6	...	...	...	—	—	—	—	—
93-94—Newmarket	OHL	17	7	17	24	22	...	...	...	—	—	—	—	—
—Niagara Falls	OHL	41	15	47	62	41	...	...	...	—	—	—	—	—
—U.S. national team	Int'l	5	0	2	2	0	...	...	...	—	—	—	—	—
94-95—Niagara Falls	OHL	26	12	21	33	51	...	...	...	—	—	—	—	—
—Edmonton	NHL	1	1	0	1	0	-1	0	0	—	—	—	—	—
—Sudbury	OHL	23	15	14	29	45	...	...	...	17	13	10	23	12
95-96—Edmonton	NHL	20	0	2	2	4	-6	0	0	—	—	—	—	—
—Cape Breton	AHL	12	1	4	5	12	...	...	...	—	—	—	—	—
—Sudbury	OHL	18	10	16	26	37	...	...	...	—	—	—	—	—
96-97—Hamilton	AHL	78	21	33	54	78	...	...	...	7	0	0	0	4
97-98—Hamilton	AHL	8	0	2	2	14	...	...	...	—	—	—	—	—
—San Antonio	IHL	22	3	8	11	34	...	...	...	—	—	—	—	—
—Tampa Bay	NHL	35	2	8	10	22	-11	0	0	—	—	—	—	—
—Cleveland	IHL	6	4	0	4	32	...	...	...	8	1	1	2	20
NHL Totals (3 years)		56	3	10	13	26	-18	0	0					

BONVIE, DENNIS   D   OILERS

PERSONAL: Born July 23, 1973, in Antigonish, Nova Scotia ... 5-11/205. ... Shoots right. ... Name pronounced BAHN-vee.

TRANSACTIONS/CAREER NOTES: Signed as free agent by Edmonton Oilers (August 26, 1994).

Season Team	League	REGULAR SEASON								PLAYOFFS				
		Gms.	G	A	Pts.	PIM	+/-	PP	SH	Gms.	G	A	Pts.	PIM
90-91—Antigonish	N.S. Jr. A					Statistics unavailable.								
91-92—Kitchener	OHL	7	1	1	2	23	...	...	...	—	—	—	—	—
—North Bay	OHL	49	0	12	12	261	...	...	...	21	0	1	1	91
92-93—North Bay	OHL	64	3	21	24	316	...	...	...	5	0	0	0	34
93-94—Cape Breton	AHL	63	1	10	11	278	...	...	...	4	0	0	0	11
94-95—Cape Breton	AHL	74	5	15	20	422	...	...	...	—	—	—	—	—
—Edmonton	NHL	2	0	0	0	0	0	0	0	—	—	—	—	—
95-96—Edmonton	NHL	8	0	0	0	47	-3	0	0	—	—	—	—	—
—Cape Breton	AHL	38	13	14	27	269	...	...	...	—	—	—	—	—
96-97—Hamilton	AHL	73	9	20	29	*522	...	...	...	22	3	11	14	*91
97-98—Edmonton	NHL	4	0	0	0	27	0	0	0	—	—	—	—	—
—Hamilton	AHL	57	11	19	30	295	...	...	...	9	0	5	5	18
NHL Totals (3 years)		14	0	0	0	74	-3	0	0					

BORDELEAU, SEBASTIEN   C   PREDATORS

PERSONAL: Born February 15, 1975, in Vancouver. ... 5-11/188. ... Shoots right. ... Son of Paulin Bordeleau, head coach, Fredericton Canadiens of American Hockey League. ... Name pronounced BOHR-dih-loh.

TRANSACTIONS/CAREER NOTES: Selected by Montreal Canadiens in third round (third Canadiens pick, 73rd overall) of NHL entry draft (June 26, 1993). ... Pulled groin (January 13, 1997); missed one game. ... Strained hip flexor (November 17, 1997); missed two games. ... Bruised thigh (November 24, 1997); missed four games. ... Bruised testicles (January 24, 1998); missed two games. ... Strained hip flexor (Feburary 4, 1998); missed two games. ... Traded by Canadiens to Nashville Predators for future considerations (June 27, 1998).

HONORS: Named to QMJHL All-Star first team (1994-95).

Season Team	League	REGULAR SEASON								PLAYOFFS				
		Gms.	G	A	Pts.	PIM	+/-	PP	SH	Gms.	G	A	Pts.	PIM
91-92—Hull	QMJHL	62	26	32	58	91	...	...	...	5	0	3	3	23
92-93—Hull	QMJHL	60	18	39	57	95	...	...	...	10	3	8	11	20
93-94—Hull	QMJHL	60	26	57	83	147	...	...	...	17	6	14	20	26
94-95—Hull	QMJHL	68	52	76	128	142	...	...	...	18	13	19	32	25
95-96—Fredericton	AHL	43	17	29	46	68	...	...	...	7	0	2	2	8
—Montreal	NHL	4	0	0	0	0	-1	0	0	—	—	—	—	—
96-97—Fredericton	AHL	33	17	21	38	50	...	...	...	—	—	—	—	—
—Montreal	NHL	28	2	9	11	2	-3	0	0	—	—	—	—	—
97-98—Montreal	NHL	53	6	8	14	36	5	2	1	5	0	0	0	2
NHL Totals (3 years)		85	8	17	25	38	1	2	1	5	0	0	0	2

BOTTERILL, JASON   LW   STARS

PERSONAL: Born May 19, 1976, in Edmonton. ... 6-4/217. ... Shoots left. ... Name pronounced BAH-tuh-rihl.

HIGH SCHOOL: St. Paul's Prep (Concord, N.H.).

COLLEGE: Michigan.

TRANSACTIONS/CAREER NOTES: Selected by Dallas Stars in first round (first Stars pick, 20th overall) of NHL entry draft (June 28, 1994).
HONORS: Named to CCHA All-Rookie team (1993-94). ... Named to CCHA All-Star second team (1995-96). ... Named to NCAA All-America West second team (1996-97).

		REGULAR SEASON								PLAYOFFS				
Season Team	League	Gms.	G	A	Pts.	PIM	+/-	PP	SH	Gms.	G	A	Pts.	PIM
92-93—St. Paul's	USHL	22	22	26	48	...	...	...	...	—	—	—	—	—
93-94—Univ. of Michigan	CCHA	37	21	19	40	94	...	...	...	—	—	—	—	—
94-95—Univ. of Michigan	CCHA	34	14	14	28	117	...	...	...	—	—	—	—	—
95-96—Univ. of Michigan	CCHA	37	32	25	57	143	...	...	...	—	—	—	—	—
96-97—Univ. of Michigan	CCHA	42	37	24	61	129	...	...	...	—	—	—	—	—
97-98—Michigan	IHL	50	11	11	22	82	...	...	...	4	0	0	0	5
—Dallas	NHL	4	0	0	0	19	-1	0	0	—	—	—	—	—
NHL Totals (1 year)		4	0	0	0	19	-1	0	0	—	—	—	—	—

BOUCHARD, JOEL D PREDATORS

PERSONAL: Born January 23, 1974, in Montreal. ... 6-0/200. ... Shoots left.
TRANSACTIONS/CAREER NOTES: Selected by Calgary Flames in sixth round (sixth Flames pick, 129th overall) of NHL entry draft (June 20, 1992). ... Strained abdomen (September 30, 1997); missed one game. ... Suffered concussion (January 24, 1998); missed six games. ... Selected by Nashville Predators in NHL expansion draft (June 26, 1998).
HONORS: Named to QMJHL All-Star first team (1993-94).

		REGULAR SEASON								PLAYOFFS				
Season Team	League	Gms.	G	A	Pts.	PIM	+/-	PP	SH	Gms.	G	A	Pts.	PIM
90-91—Longueuil	QMJHL	53	3	19	22	34	...	...	...	8	0	1	1	11
91-92—Verdun	QMJHL	70	9	37	46	55	...	...	...	19	1	7	8	20
92-93—Verdun	QMJHL	60	10	49	59	126	...	...	...	4	0	2	2	4
93-94—Verdun	QMJHL	60	15	55	70	62	...	...	...	4	1	0	1	6
—Saint John	AHL	1	0	0	0	0	...	...	...	2	0	0	0	0
94-95—Saint John	AHL	77	6	25	31	63	...	...	...	5	1	0	1	4
—Calgary	NHL	2	0	0	0	0	0	0	0	—	—	—	—	—
95-96—Saint John	AHL	74	8	25	33	104	...	...	...	16	1	4	5	10
—Calgary	NHL	4	0	0	0	4	0	0	0	—	—	—	—	—
96-97—Calgary	NHL	76	4	5	9	49	-23	0	1	—	—	—	—	—
97-98—Calgary	NHL	44	5	7	12	57	0	0	1	—	—	—	—	—
—Saint John	AHL	3	2	1	3	6	...	...	...	—	—	—	—	—
NHL Totals (4 years)		126	9	12	21	110	-23	0	2	—	—	—	—	—

BOUCHER, BRIAN G FLYERS

PERSONAL: Born August 1, 1977, in Woonsocket, R.I. ... 6-1/180. ... Catches left. ... Name pronounced boo-SHAY.
HIGH SCHOOL: Mount St. Charles (Woonsocket, R.I.), then Kamiakin (Kennewick, Wash.).
TRANSACTIONS/CAREER NOTES: Selected by Philadelphia Flyers in first round (first Flyers pick, 22nd overall) of NHL entry draft (July 8, 1995).
HONORS: Named to WHL (West) All-Star second team (1995-96). ... Named to WHL (West) All-Star first team (1996-97). ... Won Del Wilson Trophy (1996-97).

		REGULAR SEASON								PLAYOFFS						
Season Team	League	Gms.	Min	W	L	T	GA	SO	Avg.	Gms.	Min.	W	L	GA	SO	Avg.
93-94—Mt. St. Charles H.S.	R.I.H.S.	23	1170	...	...	...	23	12	1.18	—	—	—	—	—	—	—
94-95—Wexford	Tier II Jr. A	8	425	...	...	...	23	0	3.25	—	—	—	—	—	—	—
—Tri-City	WHL	35	1969	17	11	2	108	1	3.29	13	795	6	5	50	0	3.77
95-96—Tri-City	WHL	55	3183	33	19	2	181	1	3.41	11	653	6	5	37	†2	3.40
96-97—Tri-City	WHL	41	2458	10	24	†6	149	1	3.64	—	—	—	—	—	—	—
97-98—Philadelphia	AHL	34	1901	16	16	3	101	0	3.19	2	31	0	0	1	0	1.94

BOUCHER, PHILIPPE D KINGS

PERSONAL: Born March 24, 1973, in St. Apollnaire, Que. ... 6-3/212. ... Shoots right. ... Name pronounced fih-LEEP boo-SHAY.
TRANSACTIONS/CAREER NOTES: Selected by Buffalo Sabres in first round (first Sabres pick, 13th overall) of NHL entry draft (June 22, 1991). ... Traded by Sabres with G Grant Fuhr and D Denis Tsygurov to Los Angeles Kings for D Alexei Zhitnik, D Charlie Huddy, G Robb Stauber and fifth-round pick (D Marian Menhart) in 1995 draft (February 14, 1995). ... Sprained wrist (February 25, 1995); missed final 31 games of season. ... Suffered tendinitis in right wrist (October 6, 1995); missed first 25 games of season. ... Injured left hand (February 19, 1996); missed four games. ... Sprained right shoulder (October 4, 1996); missed 10 games. ... Suffered from the flu (December 18, 1997); missed two games. ... Suffered illness (January 10, 1998); missed 12 games.
HONORS: Won Can.HL Rookie of the Year Award (1990-91). ... Won Raymond Lagace Trophy (1990-91). ... Won Michael Bossy Trophy (1990-91). ... Named to QMJHL All-Star second team (1990-91 and 1991-92).

		REGULAR SEASON								PLAYOFFS				
Season Team	League	Gms.	G	A	Pts.	PIM	+/-	PP	SH	Gms.	G	A	Pts.	PIM
90-91—Granby	QMJHL	69	21	46	67	92	...	...	...	—	—	—	—	—
91-92—Granby	QMJHL	49	22	37	59	47	...	...	...	—	—	—	—	—
—Laval	QMJHL	16	7	11	18	36	...	...	...	10	5	6	11	8
92-93—Laval	QMJHL	16	12	15	27	37	...	...	...	13	6	15	21	12
—Rochester	AHL	5	4	3	7	8	...	...	...	3	0	1	1	2
—Buffalo	NHL	18	0	4	4	14	1	0	0	—	—	—	—	—
93-94—Buffalo	NHL	38	6	8	14	29	-1	4	0	7	1	1	2	2
—Rochester	AHL	31	10	22	32	51	...	...	...	—	—	—	—	—
94-95—Rochester	AHL	43	14	27	41	26	...	...	...	—	—	—	—	—
—Buffalo	NHL	9	1	4	5	0	6	0	0	—	—	—	—	—
—Los Angeles	NHL	6	1	0	1	4	-3	0	0	—	—	—	—	—

Season Team	League	REGULAR SEASON								PLAYOFFS				
		Gms.	G	A	Pts.	PIM	+/-	PP	SH	Gms.	G	A	Pts.	PIM
95-96—Los Angeles	NHL	53	7	16	23	31	-26	5	0	—	—	—	—	—
—Phoenix	IHL	10	4	3	7	4	...	...	...	—	—	—	—	—
96-97—Los Angeles	NHL	60	7	18	25	25	0	2	0	—	—	—	—	—
97-98—Los Angeles	NHL	45	6	10	16	49	6	1	0	—	—	—	—	—
—Long Beach	IHL	2	0	1	1	4	...	...	...	—	—	—	—	—
NHL Totals (6 years)		229	28	60	88	152	-17	12	0	7	1	1	2	2

BOUGHNER, BOB D PREDATORS

PERSONAL: Born March 8, 1971, in Windsor, Ont. ... 6-0/206. ... Shoots right. ... Name pronounced BOOG-nuhr.

TRANSACTIONS/CAREER NOTES: Selected by Detroit Red Wings in second round (second Red Wings pick, 32nd overall) of NHL entry draft (June 17, 1989). ... Signed as free agent by Florida Panthers (August 10, 1994). ... Traded by Panthers to Buffalo Sabres for conditional pick in 1996 draft (February 1, 1996). ... Bruised left thigh (February 28, 1996); missed one game. ... Bruised shoulder (February 7, 1998); missed two games. ... Injured wrist (March 12, 1998); missed three games. ... Bruised foot (April 29, 1998); missed one game. ... Selected by Nashville Predators in NHL expansion draft (June 26, 1998).

Season Team	League	REGULAR SEASON								PLAYOFFS				
		Gms.	G	A	Pts.	PIM	+/-	PP	SH	Gms.	G	A	Pts.	PIM
87-88—St. Mary's Jr. B	OHA	36	4	18	22	177	...	...	...	—	—	—	—	—
88-89—Sault Ste. Marie	OHL	64	6	15	21	182	...	...	...	—	—	—	—	—
89-90—Sault Ste. Marie	OHL	49	7	23	30	122	...	...	...	—	—	—	—	—
90-91—Sault Ste. Marie	OHL	64	13	33	46	156	...	...	...	14	2	9	11	35
91-92—Adirondack	AHL	1	0	0	0	7	...	...	...	—	—	—	—	—
—Toledo	ECHL	28	3	10	13	79	...	...	...	5	2	0	2	15
92-93—Adirondack	AHL	69	1	16	17	190	...	...	...	—	—	—	—	—
93-94—Adirondack	AHL	72	8	14	22	292	...	...	...	10	1	1	2	18
94-95—Cincinnati	IHL	81	2	14	16	192	...	...	...	10	0	0	0	18
95-96—Carolina	AHL	46	2	15	17	127	...	...	...	—	—	—	—	—
—Buffalo	NHL	31	0	1	1	104	3	0	0	—	—	—	—	—
96-97—Buffalo	NHL	77	1	7	8	225	12	0	0	11	0	1	1	9
97-98—Buffalo	NHL	69	1	3	4	165	5	0	0	14	0	4	4	15
NHL Totals (3 years)		177	2	11	13	494	20	0	0	25	0	5	5	24

BOULERICE, JESSE D FLYERS

PERSONAL: Born August 10, 1978, in Plattsburgh, N.Y. ... 6-1/200. ... Shoots right.

TRANSACTIONS/CAREER NOTES: Selected by Philadelphia Flyers in fifth round (fourth Flyers pick, 133rd overall) of NHL entry draft (June 22, 1996).

Season Team	League	REGULAR SEASON								PLAYOFFS				
		Gms.	G	A	Pts.	PIM	+/-	PP	SH	Gms.	G	A	Pts.	PIM
95-96—Detroit	OHL	64	2	5	7	150	...	...	...	16	0	0	0	12
96-97—Detroit	OHL	33	10	14	24	209	...	...	...	—	—	—	—	—
97-98—Plymouth	OHL	53	20	23	43	170	...	...	...	13	2	4	6	35

BOURQUE, RAY D BRUINS

PERSONAL: Born December 28, 1960, in Montreal. ... 5-11/219. ... Shoots left. ... Full Name: Raymond Jean Bourque. ... Name pronounced BOHRK.

TRANSACTIONS/CAREER NOTES: Selected by Boston Bruins in first round (first Bruins pick, eighth overall) of NHL entry draft (August 9, 1979). ... Broke jaw (November 11, 1980). ... Injured left shoulder (October 1981). ... Fractured left wrist (April 21, 1982). ... Refractured left wrist and fractured left forearm (summer 1982). ... Broke bone over left eye (October 1982). ... Sprained left knee ligaments (December 10, 1988). ... Bruised right shoulder (October 17, 1990); missed four games. ... Fractured finger (May 5, 1992); missed remainder of playoffs. ... Injured back (December 19, 1992); missed two games. ... Injured ankle (January 21, 1993); missed three games. ... Injured knee (March 22, 1994); missed 11 games. ... Bruised shoulder (October 20, 1996); missed nine games. ... Strained abdominal muscle (December 14, 1996); missed five games. ... Bruised ankle (March 6, 1997); missed three games. ... Injured ankle (March 17, 1997); missed three games.

HONORS: Named to QMJHL All-Star first team (1977-78 and 1978-79). ... Won Frank J. Selke Trophy (1978-79). ... Won Emile (Butch) Bouchard Trophy (1978-79). ... Named NHL Rookie of the Year by THE SPORTING NEWS (1979-80). ... Won Calder Memorial Trophy (1979-80). ... Named to NHL All-Star first team (1979-80, 1981-82, 1983-84, 1984-85, 1986-87, 1987-88, and 1989-90 through 1993-94 and 1995-96). ... Named to THE SPORTING NEWS All-Star second team (1980-81, 1982-83, 1985-86 and 1988-89). ... Named to NHL All-Star second team (1980-81, 1982-83, 1985-86, 1988-89 and 1994-95). ... Played in NHL All-Star Game (1981-1986, 1988-1994 and 1996-1998). ... Named to THE SPORTING NEWS All-Star first team (1981-82, 1983-84, 1984-85, 1986-87, 1987-88 and 1989-90 through 1995-96). ... Won James Norris Memorial Trophy (1986-87, 1987-88, 1989-90, 1990-91 and 1993-94). ... Won King Clancy Memorial Trophy (1991-92). ... Named All-Star Game Most Valuable Player (1996).

MISCELLANEOUS: Co-captain of Boston Bruins (1985-86 through 1987-88). ... Captain of Bruins (1988-89 through 1997-98). ... Holds Boston Bruins all-time records for most points (1,410) and most assists (1,035). ... Scored on a penalty shot (vs. Chris Terreri, March 19, 1994). ... Failed to score on a penalty shot (vs. John Vanbiesbrouck, November 11, 1988).

STATISTICAL PLATEAUS: Three-goal games: 1982-83 (1).

Season Team	League	REGULAR SEASON								PLAYOFFS				
		Gms.	G	A	Pts.	PIM	+/-	PP	SH	Gms.	G	A	Pts.	PIM
76-77—Sorel	QMJHL	69	12	36	48	61	...	...	...	—	—	—	—	—
77-78—Verdun	QMJHL	72	22	57	79	90	...	...	...	4	2	1	3	0
78-79—Verdun	QMJHL	63	22	71	93	44	...	...	...	11	3	16	19	18
79-80—Boston	NHL	80	17	48	65	73	...	3	2	10	2	9	11	27
80-81—Boston	NHL	67	27	29	56	96	29	9	1	3	0	1	1	2
81-82—Boston	NHL	65	17	49	66	51	22	4	0	9	1	5	6	16

Season Team	League	REGULAR SEASON								PLAYOFFS				
		Gms.	G	A	Pts.	PIM	+/-	PP	SH	Gms.	G	A	Pts.	PIM
82-83—Boston	NHL	65	22	51	73	20	49	7	0	17	8	15	23	10
83-84—Boston	NHL	78	31	65	96	57	51	12	1	3	0	2	2	0
84-85—Boston	NHL	73	20	66	86	53	30	10	1	5	0	3	3	4
85-86—Boston	NHL	74	19	57	76	68	17	11	0	3	0	0	0	0
86-87—Boston	NHL	78	23	72	95	36	44	6	1	4	1	2	3	0
87-88—Boston	NHL	78	17	64	81	72	34	7	1	23	3	18	21	26
88-89—Boston	NHL	60	18	43	61	52	20	6	0	10	0	4	4	6
89-90—Boston	NHL	76	19	65	84	50	31	8	0	17	5	12	17	16
90-91—Boston	NHL	76	21	73	94	75	33	7	0	19	7	18	25	12
91-92—Boston	NHL	80	21	60	81	56	11	7	1	12	3	6	9	12
92-93—Boston	NHL	78	19	63	82	40	38	8	0	4	1	0	1	2
93-94—Boston	NHL	72	20	71	91	58	26	10	3	13	2	8	10	0
94-95—Boston	NHL	46	12	31	43	20	3	9	0	5	0	3	3	0
95-96—Boston	NHL	82	20	62	82	58	31	9	2	5	1	6	7	2
96-97—Boston	NHL	62	19	31	50	18	-11	8	1	—	—	—	—	—
97-98—Boston	NHL	82	13	35	48	80	2	9	0	6	1	4	5	2
—Can. Olympic Team	Int'l	6	1	2	3	4	...	...	...	—	—	—	—	—
NHL Totals (19 years)		1372	375	1035	1410	1033	...	150	14	168	35	116	151	137

BOWEN, JASON — D — OILERS

PERSONAL: Born November 11, 1973, in Courtenay, B.C. ... 6-4/208. ... Shoots left. ... Name pronounced BOH-ihn.
TRANSACTIONS/CAREER NOTES: Selected by Philadelphia Flyers in first round (second Flyers pick, 15th overall) of NHL entry draft (June 20, 1992). ... Suffered from hyphema in left eye (November 18, 1993); missed eight games. ... Separated left shoulder (January 30, 1994); missed 14 games. ... Traded by Flyers to Edmonton Oilers for F Brantt Myhres (October 15, 1997).

Season Team	League	REGULAR SEASON								PLAYOFFS				
		Gms.	G	A	Pts.	PIM	+/-	PP	SH	Gms.	G	A	Pts.	PIM
89-90—Tri-City	WHL	61	8	5	13	129	...	...	...	7	0	3	3	4
90-91—Tri-City	WHL	60	7	13	20	252	...	...	...	6	2	2	4	18
91-92—Tri-City	WHL	19	5	3	8	135	...	...	...	5	0	1	1	42
92-93—Tri-City	WHL	62	10	12	22	219	...	...	...	3	1	1	2	18
—Philadelphia	NHL	7	1	0	1	2	1	0	0	—	—	—	—	—
93-94—Philadelphia	NHL	56	1	5	6	87	12	0	0	—	—	—	—	—
94-95—Hershey	AHL	55	5	5	10	116	...	...	...	6	0	0	0	46
—Philadelphia	NHL	4	0	0	0	0	-2	0	0	—	—	—	—	—
95-96—Hershey	AHL	72	6	7	13	128	...	...	...	4	2	0	2	13
—Philadelphia	NHL	2	0	0	0	2	0	0	0	—	—	—	—	—
96-97—Philadelphia	AHL	61	10	12	22	160	...	...	...	—	—	—	—	—
—Philadelphia	NHL	4	0	1	1	8	1	0	0	6	0	1	1	10
97-98—Philadelphia	AHL	3	0	0	0	19	...	...	...	—	—	—	—	—
—Edmonton	NHL	4	0	0	0	10	0	0	0	—	—	—	—	—
—Hamilton	AHL	51	5	14	19	108	...	...	...	7	1	1	2	22
NHL Totals (6 years)		77	2	6	8	109	12	0	0					

BOYNTON, NICHOLAS — D — CAPITALS

PERSONAL: Born January 14, 1979, in Toronto. ... 6-2/210. ... Shoots right.
TRANSACTIONS/CAREER NOTES: Selected by Washington Capitals in first round (first Capitals pick, ninth overall) of NHL entry draft (June 21, 1997).
HONORS: Named to OHL All-Rookie team (1995-96). ... Won Can.HL Plus/Minus Award (1996-97).

Season Team	League	REGULAR SEASON								PLAYOFFS				
		Gms.	G	A	Pts.	PIM	+/-	PP	SH	Gms.	G	A	Pts.	PIM
94-95—Caledon	Jr. A	44	10	35	45	139	...	...	...	—	—	—	—	—
95-96—Ottawa	OHL	64	10	14	24	90	...	...	...	4	0	3	3	10
96-97—Ottawa	OHL	63	13	51	64	143	...	...	...	24	4	24	28	38
97-98—Ottawa	OHL	40	7	31	38	94	...	...	...	13	0	4	4	24

BRADLEY, BRIAN — C — LIGHTNING

PERSONAL: Born January 21, 1965, in Kitchener, Ont. ... 5-10/180. ... Shoots right. ... Full Name: Brian Walter Richard Bradley.
TRANSACTIONS/CAREER NOTES: Selected by Calgary Flames as underage junior in third round (second Flames pick, 51st overall) of NHL entry draft (June 8, 1983). ... Traded by Flames with RW Peter Bakovic and future considerations to Vancouver Canucks for C Craig Coxe (March 6, 1988); Canucks received D Kevan Guy to complete deal. ... Bruised knee (January 1989). ... Broke thumb knuckle (February 1, 1990); missed seven games. ... Traded by Canucks to Toronto Maple Leafs for D Tom Kurvers (January 12, 1991). ... Sprained ankle (November 10, 1991); missed six games. ... Suffered back spasms (December 10, 1991); missed two games. ... Selected by Tampa Bay Lightning in NHL expansion draft (June 18, 1992). ... Suffered injury (October 6, 1993); missed three games. ... Injured shoulder (October 22, 1993); missed one game. ... Suffered from the flu (January 4, 1994); missed one game. ... Suffered charley horse (February 17, 1995); missed two games. ... Bruised foot (October 15, 1995); missed one game. ... Bruised right knee (October 31, 1995); missed one game. ... Suffered hip pointer (January 6, 1996); missed one game. ... Bruised left knee (March 7, 1996); missed one game. ... Injured back (March 30, 1996); missed one game. ... Injured left knee (April 6, 1996); missed one game. ... Injured left knee (April 12, 1996); missed one game. ... Sprained left knee (October 31, 1996); missed one game. ... Reinjured knee (November 4, 1996); missed four games. ... Strained left knee (November 23, 1996); missed four games. ... Injured wrist (January 9, 1997); missed 37 games. ... Injured shoulder (October 26, 1997); missed one game. ... Suffered concussion (November 6, 1997); missed 13 games. ... Injured left wrist (December 10, 1997); missed remainder of season.
HONORS: Played in NHL All-Star Game (1993 and 1994).

MISCELLANEOUS: Captain of Tampa Bay Lightning (1994-95). ... Holds Tampa Bay Lightning all-time records for most goals (111), most assists (189), and most points (300). ... Failed to score on a penalty shot (vs. Felix Potvin, October 22, 1992; vs. Sean Burke, April 3, 1996).
STATISTICAL PLATEAUS: Three-goal games: 1992-93 (1).

Season Team	League	REGULAR SEASON								PLAYOFFS				
		Gms.	G	A	Pts.	PIM	+/-	PP	SH	Gms.	G	A	Pts.	PIM
81-82—London	OHL	62	34	44	78	34	...	...	...	—	—	—	—	—
82-83—London	OHL	67	37	82	119	37	...	...	...	3	1	0	1	0
83-84—London	OHL	49	40	60	100	24	...	...	...	4	2	4	6	0
84-85—London	OHL	32	27	49	76	22	...	...	...	8	5	10	15	4
85-86—Calgary	NHL	5	0	1	1	0	-3	0	0	1	0	0	0	0
—Moncton	AHL	59	23	42	65	40	...	...	...	10	6	9	15	4
86-87—Moncton	AHL	20	12	16	28	8	...	...	...	—	—	—	—	—
—Calgary	NHL	40	10	18	28	16	6	2	0	—	—	—	—	—
87-88—Canadian nat'l team	Int'l	47	18	19	37	42	...	...	...	—	—	—	—	—
—Can. Olympic Team	Int'l	7	0	4	4	0	...	...	...	—	—	—	—	—
—Vancouver	NHL	11	3	5	8	6	...	...	...	—	—	—	—	—
88-89—Vancouver	NHL	71	18	27	45	42	-5	6	0	7	3	4	7	10
89-90—Vancouver	NHL	67	19	29	48	65	5	2	0	—	—	—	—	—
90-91—Vancouver	NHL	44	11	20	31	42	-2	3	0	—	—	—	—	—
—Toronto	NHL	26	0	11	11	20	-7	0	0	—	—	—	—	—
91-92—Toronto	NHL	59	10	21	31	48	-3	4	0	—	—	—	—	—
92-93—Tampa Bay	NHL	80	42	44	86	92	-24	16	0	—	—	—	—	—
93-94—Tampa Bay	NHL	78	24	40	64	56	-8	6	0	—	—	—	—	—
94-95—Tampa Bay	NHL	46	13	27	40	42	-6	3	0	—	—	—	—	—
95-96—Tampa Bay	NHL	75	23	56	79	77	-11	9	0	5	0	3	3	6
96-97—Tampa Bay	NHL	35	7	17	24	16	2	1	2	—	—	—	—	—
97-98—Tampa Bay	NHL	14	2	5	7	6	-9	2	0	—	—	—	—	—
NHL Totals (13 years)		651	182	321	503	528	-65	54	2	13	3	7	10	16

BRADLEY, MATT   RW   SHARKS

PERSONAL: Born June 13, 1978, in Stittsville, Ont. ... 6-1/168. ... Shoots right.
TRANSACTIONS/CAREER NOTES: Selected by San Jose Sharks in fourth round (fourth Sharks pick, 102nd overall) of NHL entry draft (June 22, 1996).
HONORS: Won William Hanley Trophy (1997-98).

Season Team	League	REGULAR SEASON								PLAYOFFS				
		Gms.	G	A	Pts.	PIM	+/-	PP	SH	Gms.	G	A	Pts.	PIM
94-95—Cumberland	CJHL	49	13	20	33	18	...	...	...	—	—	—	—	—
95-96—Kingston	OHL	55	10	14	24	17	...	...	...	6	0	1	1	6
96-97—Kingston	OHL	65	24	24	48	41	...	...	...	5	0	4	4	2
—Kentucky	AHL	1	0	1	1	0	...	...	...	—	—	—	—	—
97-98—Kingston	OHL	55	33	50	83	24	...	...	...	8	3	4	7	7

BRASHEAR, DONALD   LW   CANUCKS

PERSONAL: Born January 7, 1972, in Bedford, Ind. ... 6-2/220. ... Shoots left. ... Name pronounced brah-SHEER.
TRANSACTIONS/CAREER NOTES: Signed as free agent by Montreal Canadiens (July 28, 1992). ... Bruised knee (November 23, 1993); missed one game. ... Injured shoulder (February 27, 1995); missed one game. ... Bruised hand (March 20, 1995); missed one game. ... Suffered cut to right thigh (December 30, 1995); missed seven games. ... Traded by Canadiens to Vancouver Canucks for D Jassen Cullimore (November 13, 1996). ... Strained back (February 8, 1997); missed three games. ... Suspended four games and fined $1,000 by NHL for fighting (February 25, 1997). ... Injured shoulder (March 11, 1998); missed two games.

Season Team	League	REGULAR SEASON								PLAYOFFS				
		Gms.	G	A	Pts.	PIM	+/-	PP	SH	Gms.	G	A	Pts.	PIM
89-90—Longueuil	QMJHL	64	12	14	26	169	...	...	...	7	0	0	0	11
90-91—Longueuil	QMJHL	68	12	26	38	195	...	...	...	8	0	3	3	33
91-92—Verdun	QMJHL	65	18	24	42	283	...	...	...	18	4	2	6	98
92-93—Fredericton	AHL	76	11	3	14	261	...	...	...	5	0	0	0	8
93-94—Fredericton	AHL	62	38	28	66	250	...	...	...	—	—	—	—	—
—Montreal	NHL	14	2	2	4	34	0	0	0	2	0	0	0	0
94-95—Montreal	NHL	20	1	1	2	63	-5	0	0	—	—	—	—	—
—Fredericton	AHL	29	10	9	19	182	...	...	...	17	7	5	12	77
95-96—Montreal	NHL	67	0	4	4	223	-10	0	0	6	0	0	0	2
96-97—Montreal	NHL	10	0	0	0	38	-2	0	0	—	—	—	—	—
—Vancouver	NHL	59	8	5	13	207	-6	0	0	—	—	—	—	—
97-98—Vancouver	NHL	77	9	9	18	*372	-9	0	0	—	—	—	—	—
NHL Totals (5 years)		247	20	21	41	937	-32	0	0	8	0	0	0	2

BRENNAN, RICH   D   RANGERS

PERSONAL: Born November 26, 1972, in Schenectady, N.Y. ... 6-2/200. ... Shoots right.
HIGH SCHOOL: Albany (N.Y.) Academy, then Tabor Academy (Marion, Mass.).
COLLEGE: Boston University.
TRANSACTIONS/CAREER NOTES: Selected by Quebec Nordiques in third round (third Nordiques pick, 56th overall) of NHL entry draft (June 22, 1991). ... Nordiques franchise moved to Colorado and renamed Avalanche for 1995-96 season (June 21, 1995). ... Signed as free agent by San Jose Sharks (July 9, 1997). ... Traded by Sharks to New York Rangers for G Jason Muzzatti (March 24, 1998).
HONORS: Named to Hockey East All-Star first team (1993-94).

Season Team	League	Gms.	G	A	Pts.	PIM	+/-	PP	SH	Gms.	G	A	Pts.	PIM
		REGULAR SEASON								**PLAYOFFS**				
88-89—Albany Academy	N.Y. H.S.	25	17	30	47	57	...	...	...	—	—	—	—	—
89-90—Tabor Academy	Mass. H.S.	33	12	14	26	68	...	...	...	—	—	—	—	—
90-91—Tabor Academy	Mass. H.S.	34	13	37	50	91	...	...	...	—	—	—	—	—
91-92—Boston University	Hockey East	31	4	13	17	54	...	...	...	—	—	—	—	—
92-93—Boston University	Hockey East	40	9	11	20	68	...	...	...	—	—	—	—	—
93-94—Boston University	Hockey East	41	8	27	35	82	...	...	...	—	—	—	—	—
94-95—Boston University	Hockey East	31	5	23	28	56	...	...	...	—	—	—	—	—
95-96—Brantford	Col.HL	5	1	2	3	2	...	...	...	23	2	†16	18	22
96-97—Hershey	AHL	74	11	45	56	88	...	...	...	—	—	—	—	—
—Colorado	NHL	2	0	0	0	0	0	0	0	—	—	—	—	—
97-98—Kentucky	AHL	42	11	17	28	71	...	...	...	—	—	—	—	—
—San Jose	NHL	11	1	2	3	2	-4	1	0	—	—	—	—	—
—Hartford	AHL	9	2	4	6	12	...	...	...	—	—	—	—	—
NHL Totals (2 years)		13	1	2	3	2	-4	1	0					

BREWER, ERIC — D — ISLANDERS

PERSONAL: Born April 17, 1979, in Vernon, B.C. ... 6-3/195. ... Shoots left.
TRANSACTIONS/CAREER NOTES: Selected by New York Islanders in first round (second Islanders pick, fifth overall) of NHL entry draft (June 21, 1997).
HONORS: Named to WHL (West) All-Star second team (1997-98).

Season Team	League	Gms.	G	A	Pts.	PIM	+/-	PP	SH	Gms.	G	A	Pts.	PIM
		REGULAR SEASON								**PLAYOFFS**				
95-96—Prince George	WHL	63	4	10	14	25	...	...	...	—	—	—	—	—
96-97—Prince George	WHL	71	5	24	29	81	...	...	...	15	2	4	6	16
97-98—Prince George	WHL	34	5	28	33	45	...	...	...	11	4	2	6	19

BRIERE, DANIEL — C — COYOTES

PERSONAL: Born October 6, 1977, in Gatineau, Que. ... 5-9/160. ... Shoots left.
TRANSACTIONS/CAREER NOTES: Selected by Phoenix Coyotes in first round (second Coyotes pick, 24th overall) of NHL entry draft (June 22, 1996). ... Separated shoulder (March 21, 1998); missed five games.
HONORS: Won Michel Bergeron Trophy (1994-95). ... Won Marcel Robert Trophy (1994-95). ... Won Jean Beliveau Trophy (1995-96). ... Named to QMJHL All-Star second team (1995-96). ... Won Frank J. Selke Trophy (1996-97). ... Named to Can.HL All-Star second team (1996-97). ... Named to AHL All-Star first team (1997-98). ... Won Dudley (Red) Garrett Trophy (1997-98).

Season Team	League	Gms.	G	A	Pts.	PIM	+/-	PP	SH	Gms.	G	A	Pts.	PIM
		REGULAR SEASON								**PLAYOFFS**				
94-95—Drummondville	QMJHL	72	51	72	123	54	...	...	...	—	—	—	—	—
95-96—Drummondville	QMJHL	67	*67	*96	*163	84	...	...	...	6	6	12	18	8
96-97—Drummondville	QMJHL	59	52	78	130	86	...	...	...	8	7	7	14	14
97-98—Springfield	AHL	68	36	56	92	42	...	...	...	4	1	2	3	4
—Phoenix.....................	NHL	5	1	0	1	2	1	0	0	—	—	—	—	—
NHL Totals (1 year)		5	1	0	1	2	1	0	0					

BRIGLEY, TRAVIS — LW — FLAMES

PERSONAL: Born June 16, 1977, in Coronation, Alta. ... 6-1/195. ... Shoots left.
TRANSACTIONS/CAREER NOTES: Selected by Calgary Flames in second round (second Flames pick, 39th overall) of NHL entry draft (June 22, 1996).

Season Team	League	Gms.	G	A	Pts.	PIM	+/-	PP	SH	Gms.	G	A	Pts.	PIM
		REGULAR SEASON								**PLAYOFFS**				
93-94—Lethbridge	WHL	1	0	0	0	0	...	...	...	—	—	—	—	—
94-95—Lethbridge	WHL	64	14	18	32	14	...	...	...	—	—	—	—	—
95-96—Lethbridge	WHL	69	34	43	77	94	...	...	...	4	2	3	5	8
96-97—Lethbridge	WHL	71	43	47	90	56	...	...	...	19	9	9	18	31
97-98—Saint John	AHL	79	17	15	32	28	...	...	...	8	0	0	0	0
—Calgary	NHL	2	0	0	0	2	0	0	0	—	—	—	—	—
NHL Totals (1 year)		2	0	0	0	2	0	0	0					

BRIND'AMOUR, ROD — LW/C — FLYERS

PERSONAL: Born August 9, 1970, in Ottawa. ... 6-1/198. ... Shoots left. ... Full Name: Rod Jean Brind'Amour. ... Name pronounced BRIHN-duh-MOHR.
COLLEGE: Michigan State.
TRANSACTIONS/CAREER NOTES: Broke wrist (November 1985). ... Selected by St. Louis Blues in first round (first Blues pick, ninth overall) of NHL entry draft (June 11, 1988). ... Traded by Blues with C Dan Quinn to Philadelphia Flyers for C Ron Sutter and D Murray Baron (September 22, 1991). ... Lacerated elbow (November 19, 1992); missed two games. ... Bruised right hand (February 20, 1993); missed one game.
HONORS: Named CCHA Rookie of the Year (1988-89). ... Named to CCHA All-Rookie team (1988-89). ... Named to NHL All-Rookie team (1989-90). ... Played in NHL All-Star Game (1992).
STATISTICAL PLATEAUS: Three-goal games: 1992-93 (1).

B

Season Team	League	REGULAR SEASON								PLAYOFFS				
		Gms.	G	A	Pts.	PIM	+/-	PP	SH	Gms.	G	A	Pts.	PIM
87-88—Notre Dame	SJHL	56	46	61	107	136	...	...	...	—	—	—	—	—
88-89—Michigan State	CCHA	42	27	32	59	63	...	...	...	—	—	—	—	—
—St. Louis	NHL	—	—	—	—	—	...	...	...	5	2	0	2	4
89-90—St. Louis	NHL	79	26	35	61	46	23	10	0	12	5	8	13	6
90-91—St. Louis	NHL	78	17	32	49	93	2	4	0	13	2	5	7	10
91-92—Philadelphia	NHL	80	33	44	77	100	-3	8	4	—	—	—	—	—
92-93—Philadelphia	NHL	81	37	49	86	89	-8	13	4	—	—	—	—	—
93-94—Philadelphia	NHL	84	35	62	97	85	-9	14	1	—	—	—	—	—
94-95—Philadelphia	NHL	48	12	27	39	33	-4	4	1	15	6	9	15	8
95-96—Philadelphia	NHL	82	26	61	87	110	20	4	4	12	2	5	7	6
96-97—Philadelphia	NHL	82	27	32	59	41	2	8	2	19	†13	8	21	10
97-98—Philadelphia	NHL	82	36	38	74	54	-2	10	2	5	2	2	4	7
—Can. Olympic Team	Int'l	6	1	2	3	0	...	...	...	—	—	—	—	—
NHL Totals (10 years)		696	249	380	629	651	21	75	18	81	32	37	69	51

BRISEBOIS, PATRICE D CANADIENS

PERSONAL: Born January 27, 1971, in Montreal. ... 6-2/204. ... Shoots right. ... Name pronounced pa-TREEZ BREES-bwah.

TRANSACTIONS/CAREER NOTES: Underwent surgery on fractured right thumb (February 1988). ... Tore ligaments in left knee (March 1988). ... Broke left thumb (August 1988). ... Selected by Montreal Canadiens in second round (second Canadiens pick, 30th overall) of NHL entry draft (June 17, 1989). ... Traded by Laval Titans with LW Allen Kerr to Drummondville Voltigeurs for second- and third-round picks in 1990 QMJHL draft (May 26, 1990). ... Sprained right ankle (October 10, 1992); missed two games. ... Suffered charley horse (December 16, 1992); missed two games. ... Injured knee (October 30, 1993); missed 10 games. ... Suffered hairline fracture of ankle (December 1, 1993); missed 14 games. ... Sprained ankle (February 21, 1994); missed seven games. ... Suffered acute herniated disc (April 3, 1995); missed 12 games. ... Injured rib cage (November 1, 1995). ... Sprained back (February 17, 1996); missed four games. ... Suffered mild disc irritation (March 25, 1996); missed last nine games of regular season. ... Separated shoulder (January 4, 1997); missed 27 games. ... Strained shoulder (March 22, 1997); missed four games. ... Injured rib (April 10, 1997); missed remainder of regular season and two playoff games. ... Sprained knee (April 15, 1998); missed three games.

HONORS: Won Michael Bossy Trophy (1988-89). ... Named to QMJHL All-Star second team (1989-90). ... Won Can.HL Defenseman of the Year Award (1990-91). ... Won Emile (Butch) Bouchard Trophy (1990-91). ... Named to QMJHL All-Star first team (1990-91). ... Named to Memorial Cup All-Star team (1990-91).

MISCELLANEOUS: Member of Stanley Cup championship team (1993).

Season Team	League	REGULAR SEASON								PLAYOFFS				
		Gms.	G	A	Pts.	PIM	+/-	PP	SH	Gms.	G	A	Pts.	PIM
87-88—Laval	QMJHL	48	10	34	44	95	...	...	...	6	0	2	2	2
88-89—Laval	QMJHL	50	20	45	65	95	...	...	...	17	8	14	22	45
89-90—Laval	QMJHL	56	18	70	88	108	...	...	...	13	7	9	16	26
90-91—Montreal	NHL	10	0	2	2	4	1	0	0	—	—	—	—	—
—Drummondville	QMJHL	54	17	44	61	72	...	...	...	14	6	18	24	49
91-92—Fredericton	AHL	53	12	27	39	51	...	...	...	—	—	—	—	—
—Montreal	NHL	26	2	8	10	20	9	0	0	11	2	4	6	6
92-93—Montreal	NHL	70	10	21	31	79	6	4	0	20	0	4	4	18
93-94—Montreal	NHL	53	2	21	23	63	5	1	0	7	0	4	4	6
94-95—Montreal	NHL	35	4	8	12	26	-2	0	0	—	—	—	—	—
95-96—Montreal	NHL	69	9	27	36	65	10	3	0	6	1	2	3	6
96-97—Montreal	NHL	49	2	13	15	24	-7	0	0	3	1	1	2	24
97-98—Montreal	NHL	79	10	27	37	67	16	5	0	10	1	0	1	0
NHL Totals (8 years)		391	39	127	166	348	38	13	0	57	5	15	20	60

BROCHU, MARTIN G CAPITALS

PERSONAL: Born March 10, 1973, in Anjou, Que. ... 5-10/200. ... Catches left. ... Name pronounced MAHR-tai broh-SHOO.

TRANSACTIONS/CAREER NOTES: Signed as free agent by Montreal Canadiens (September 22, 1992). ... Traded by Canadiens to Washington Capitals for future considerations (March 15, 1996).

Season Team	League	REGULAR SEASON							PLAYOFFS						
		Gms.	Min	W	L	T	GA	SO	Avg.	Gms.	Min.	W	L	GA	SO	Avg.
91-92—Granby	QMJHL	52	2772	15	29	2	218	0	4.72	—	—	—	—	—	—	—
92-93—Hull	QMJHL	29	1453	9	15	1	137	0	5.66	2	69	0	1	7	0	6.09
93-94—Fredericton	AHL	32	1506	10	11	3	76	2	3.03	—	—	—	—	—	—	—
94-95—Fredericton	AHL	44	2475	18	18	4	145	0	3.52	—	—	—	—	—	—	—
95-96—Fredericton	AHL	17	985	6	8	2	70	0	4.26	—	—	—	—	—	—	—
—Wheeling	ECHL	19	1060	10	6	‡2	51	1	2.89	—	—	—	—	—	—	—
—Portland	AHL	5	286	2	2	1	15	0	3.15	12	700	7	4	28	‡2	*2.40
96-97—Portland	AHL	55	2962	23	17	7	150	2	3.04	5	324	2	3	13	0	2.41
97-98—Portland	AHL	37	1926	16	14	1	96	2	2.99	6	297	3	2	16	0	3.23

BRODEUR, MARTIN G DEVILS

PERSONAL: Born May 6, 1972, in Montreal. ... 6-1/205. ... Catches left. ... Son of Denis Brodeur, goaltender with bronze medal-winning Canadian Olympic team (1956). ... Name pronounced MAHR-tan broh-DOOR.

TRANSACTIONS/CAREER NOTES: Suffered pinched nerve in elbow and slight concussion (March 9, 1990). ... Selected by New Jersey Devils in first round (first Devils pick, 20th overall) of NHL entry draft (June 16, 1990). ... Strained knee (February 24, 1994). ... Suffered from the flu (December 30, 1997); missed two games.

HONORS: Named to QMJHL All-Star second team (1991-92). ... Won Calder Memorial Trophy (1993-94). ... Named to NHL All-Rookie team (1993-94). ... Played in NHL All-Star Game (1996 through 1998). ... Shared William M. Jennings Trophy with Mike Dunham (1996-97). ... Named to NHL All-Star second team (1996-97). ... Won William M. Jennings Trophy (1997-98).

RECORDS: Holds NHL single-season record for most minutes played by goaltender—4,434 (1995-96). ... Shares NHL single-season playoff record for most wins by goaltender—16 (1995).
MISCELLANEOUS: Member of Stanley Cup championship team (1995). ... Holds New Jersey Devils franchise all-time records for most games played by a goalie (305), most wins (162), goals-against average (2.16) and most shutouts (32).

		REGULAR SEASON							PLAYOFFS					
Season Team	League	Gms.	Min	W	L	T	GA	SO	Avg.	Gms.	Min.	W	L	GA	SO	Avg.
89-90—St. Hyacinthe	QMJHL	42	2333	23	13	2	156	0	4.01	12	678	5	7	46	0	4.07
90-91—St. Hyacinthe	QMJHL	52	2946	22	24	4	162	2	3.30	4	232	0	4	16	0	4.14
91-92—St. Hyacinthe	QMJHL	48	2846	27	16	4	161	2	3.39	5	317	2	3	14	0	2.65
—New Jersey	NHL	4	179	2	1	0	10	0	3.35	1	32	0	1	3	0	5.63
92-93—Utica	AHL	32	1952	14	13	5	131	0	4.03	4	258	1	3	18	0	4.19
93-94—New Jersey	NHL	47	2625	27	11	8	105	3	2.40	17	1171	8	†9	38	1	1.95
94-95—New Jersey	NHL	40	2184	19	11	6	89	3	2.45	*20	*1222	*16	4	34	*3	*1.67
95-96—New Jersey	NHL	77	*4434	34	†30	12	173	6	2.34							
96-97—New Jersey	NHL	67	3838	37	14	13	120	*10	*1.88	10	659	5	5	19	2	*1.73
97-98—New Jersey	NHL	70	4128	*43	17	8	130	10	1.89	6	366	2	4	12	0	1.97
NHL Totals (6 years)		305	17388	162	84	47	627	32	2.16	54	3450	31	23	106	6	1.84

BROUSSEAU, PAUL　　　　RW　　　　PREDATORS

PERSONAL: Born September 18, 1973, in Pierrefonds, Que. ... 6-2/200. ... Shoots right. ... Name pronounced broo-SOH.
COLLEGE: Heritage College (Fla.).
TRANSACTIONS/CAREER NOTES: Selected by Quebec Nordiques in second round (second Nordiques pick, 28th overall) of NHL entry draft (June 20, 1992). ... Nordiques franchise moved to Colorado and renamed Colorado Avalanche for 1995-96 season (June 21, 1995). ... Signed as free agent by Tampa Bay Lightning (September 5, 1996). ... Selected by Nashville Predators in NHL expansion draft (June 26, 1998).
HONORS: Won Michael Bossy Trophy (1991-92). ... Named to AHL All-Star second team (1997-98).

		REGULAR SEASON							PLAYOFFS				
Season Team	League	Gms.	G	A	Pts.	PIM	+/-	PP	SH	Gms.	G	A	Pts.	PIM
89-90—Chicoutimi	QMJHL	57	17	24	41	32	...	...	...	7	0	3	3	0
90-91—Trois-Rivieres	QMJHL	67	30	66	96	48	...	...	...	6	3	2	5	2
91-92—Hull	QMJHL	57	35	61	96	54	...	...	...	6	3	5	8	10
92-93—Hull	QMJHL	59	27	48	75	49	...	...	...	10	7	8	15	6
93-94—Cornwall	AHL	69	18	26	44	35	...	...	...	1	0	0	0	0
94-95—Cornwall	AHL	57	19	17	36	29	...	...	...	7	2	1	3	10
95-96—Cornwall	AHL	63	21	22	43	60	...	...	...	8	4	0	4	2
—Colorado	NHL	8	1	1	2	2	1	0	0	—	—	—	—	—
96-97—Adirondack	AHL	66	35	31	66	25	...	...	...	4	1	2	3	0
—Tampa Bay	NHL	6	0	0	0	0	-4	0	0	—	—	—	—	—
97-98—Adirondack	AHL	67	45	20	65	18	...	...	...	3	1	1	2	0
—Tampa Bay	NHL	11	0	2	2	27	0	0	0	—	—	—	—	—
NHL Totals (3 years)		25	1	3	4	29	-3	0	0					

BROWN, BRAD　　　　D　　　　CANADIENS

PERSONAL: Born December 27, 1975, in Mississauga, Ont. ... 6-3/218. ... Shoots right.
HIGH SCHOOL: Chippewa (North Bay, Ont.).
TRANSACTIONS/CAREER NOTES: Selected by Montreal Canadiens in first round (first Canadiens pick, 18th overall) of NHL entry draft (June 28, 1994).

		REGULAR SEASON							PLAYOFFS				
Season Team	League	Gms.	G	A	Pts.	PIM	+/-	PP	SH	Gms.	G	A	Pts.	PIM
91-92—North Bay	OHL	49	2	9	11	170	...	...	...	18	0	6	6	43
92-93—North Bay	OHL	61	4	9	13	228	...	...	...	2	0	2	2	13
93-94—North Bay	OHL	66	8	24	32	196	...	...	...	18	3	12	15	33
94-95—North Bay	OHL	64	8	38	46	172	...	...	...	6	1	4	5	8
95-96—Regina	WHL	21	2	3	5	7	...	...	...	—	—	—	—	—
—Fredericton	AHL	38	0	3	3	148	...	...	...	10	2	1	3	6
96-97—Fredericton	AHL	64	3	7	10	368	...	...	...	—	—	—	—	—
—Montreal	NHL	8	0	0	0	22	-1	0	0	—	—	—	—	—
97-98—Fredericton	AHL	64	1	8	9	297	...	...	...	4	0	0	0	29
NHL Totals (1 year)		8	0	0	0	22	-1	0	0					

BROWN, CURTIS　　　　·　　　　LW/C　　　　SABRES

PERSONAL: Born February 12, 1976, in Unity, Sask. ... 6-0/190. ... Shoots left.
TRANSACTIONS/CAREER NOTES: Selected by Buffalo Sabres in second round (second Sabres pick, 43rd overall) of NHL entry draft (June 28, 1994). ... Injured ankle prior to 1995-96 season; missed two games.
HONORS: Named to Can.HL All-Star second team (1994-95). ... Named to WHL (East) All-Star first team (1994-95). ... Named to WHL (Central/East) All-Star second team (1995-96).

		REGULAR SEASON							PLAYOFFS				
Season Team	League	Gms.	G	A	Pts.	PIM	+/-	PP	SH	Gms.	G	A	Pts.	PIM
92-93—Moose Jaw	WHL	71	13	16	29	30	...	...	...	—	—	—	—	—
93-94—Moose Jaw	WHL	72	27	38	65	82	...	...	...	—	—	—	—	—
94-95—Moose Jaw	WHL	70	51	53	104	63	...	...	...	10	8	7	15	20
—Buffalo	NHL	1	1	1	2	2	0	0	0	—	—	—	—	—
95-96—Buffalo	NHL	4	0	0	0	0	0	0	0	—	—	—	—	—
—Moose Jaw	WHL	25	20	18	38	30	...	...	...	—	—	—	—	—
—Prince Albert	WHL	19	12	21	33	8	...	...	...	18	10	15	25	18
—Rochester	AHL	—	—	—	—	—	...	...	...	12	0	1	1	2

Season Team	League	REGULAR SEASON								PLAYOFFS				
		Gms.	G	A	Pts.	PIM	+/-	PP	SH	Gms.	G	A	Pts.	PIM
96-97—Buffalo	NHL	28	4	3	7	18	4	0	0	—	—	—	—	—
—Rochester	AHL	51	22	21	43	30	...	...	...	10	4	6	10	4
97-98—Buffalo	NHL	63	12	12	24	34	11	1	1	13	1	2	3	10
NHL Totals (4 years)		96	17	16	33	54	17	1	1	13	1	2	3	10

BROWN, DOUG   RW   RED WINGS

PERSONAL: Born June 12, 1964, in Southborough, Mass. ... 5-10/188. ... Shoots right. ... Full name: Douglas Allen Brown. ... Brother of Greg Brown, defenseman with Buffalo Sabres (1990-91and 1992-93), Pittsburgh Penguins (1993-94 and 1994-95) and Winnipeg Jets (1994-95).
HIGH SCHOOL: St. Mark's (Southborough, Mass.).
COLLEGE: Boston College.
TRANSACTIONS/CAREER NOTES: Signed as free agent by New Jersey Devils (August 6, 1986). ... Broke nose (October 1988). ... Injured back (November 25, 1989). ... Bruised right foot (February 13, 1991). ... Suspended by Devils for refusing to report to Utica (November 20, 1992). ... Reinstated by Devils (November 30, 1992). ... Signed as free agent by Pittsburgh Penguins (September 29, 1993). ... Injured leg (March 26, 1994); missed seven games. ... Selected by Detroit Red Wings from Penguins in waiver draft (January 18, 1995); Penguins claimed C Micah Aivazoff as compensation (who was then claimed by Edmonton Oilers). ... Suffered from the flu (December 2, 1995); missed one game. ... Selected by Nashville Predators in NHL expansion draft (June 26, 1998). ... Separated shoulder (April 18, 1998); missed 11 playoff games. ... Traded by Predators to Red Wings for C Petr Sykora, third-round pick in 1999 draft and future considerations (July 14, 1998).
HONORS: Named to NCAA All-America East second team (1984-85 and 1985-86). ... Named to Hockey East All-Star second team (1984-85 and 1985-86).
MISCELLANEOUS: Member of Stanley Cup championship team (1997 and 1998). ... Scored on a penalty shot (vs. Ken Wregget, November 23, 1991).

Season Team	League	REGULAR SEASON								PLAYOFFS				
		Gms.	G	A	Pts.	PIM	+/-	PP	SH	Gms.	G	A	Pts.	PIM
82-83—Boston College	ECAC	22	9	8	17	0	...	...	...	—	—	—	—	—
83-84—Boston College	ECAC	38	11	10	21	6	...	...	...	—	—	—	—	—
84-85—Boston College	Hockey East	45	37	31	68	10	...	...	...	—	—	—	—	—
85-86—Boston College	Hockey East	38	16	40	56	16	...	...	...	—	—	—	—	—
86-87—Maine	AHL	73	24	34	58	15	...	...	...	—	—	—	—	—
—New Jersey	NHL	4	0	1	1	0	-4	0	0	—	—	—	—	—
87-88—New Jersey	NHL	70	14	11	25	20	7	1	4	19	5	1	6	6
—Utica	AHL	2	0	2	2	2	...	...	...	—	—	—	—	—
88-89—New Jersey	NHL	63	15	10	25	15	-7	4	0	—	—	—	—	—
—Utica	AHL	4	1	4	5	0	...	...	...	—	—	—	—	—
89-90—New Jersey	NHL	69	14	20	34	16	7	1	3	6	0	1	1	2
90-91—New Jersey	NHL	58	14	16	30	4	18	0	2	7	2	2	4	2
91-92—New Jersey	NHL	71	11	17	28	27	17	1	2	—	—	—	—	—
92-93—New Jersey	NHL	15	0	5	5	2	3	0	0	—	—	—	—	—
—Utica	AHL	25	11	17	28	8	...	...	...	—	—	—	—	—
93-94—Pittsburgh	NHL	77	18	37	55	18	19	2	0	6	0	0	0	2
94-95—Detroit	NHL	45	9	12	21	16	14	1	1	18	4	8	12	2
95-96—Detroit	NHL	62	12	15	27	4	11	0	1	13	3	3	6	4
96-97—Detroit	NHL	49	6	7	13	8	-3	1	0	14	3	3	6	2
97-98—Detroit	NHL	80	19	23	42	12	17	6	1	9	4	2	6	0
NHL Totals (12 years)		663	132	174	306	142	99	17	14	92	21	20	41	20

BROWN, JEFF   D

PERSONAL: Born April 30, 1966, in Ottawa. ... 6-1/204. ... Shoots right. ... Full Name: Jeff Randall Brown.
HIGH SCHOOL: Sudbury (Ont.).
TRANSACTIONS/CAREER NOTES: Selected by Quebec Nordiques as underage junior in second round (second Nordiques pick, 36th overall) of NHL entry draft (June 9, 1984). ... Traded by Nordiques to St. Louis Blues for G Greg Millen and C Tony Hrkac (December 13, 1989). ... Broke left ankle (February 14, 1991); missed 13 games. ... Broke foot (January 14, 1993); missed 11 games. ... Suffered from sore foot (February 11, 1993); missed two games. ... Injured hand and foot (October 30, 1993); missed three games. ... Broke thumb (January 15, 1994); missed six games. ... Traded by Blues with D Brett Hedican and C Nathan LaFayette to Vancouver Canucks for C Craig Janney (March 21, 1994). ... Cracked bone in wrist (March 6, 1995); missed 12 games. ... Sprained shoulder (April 28, 1995); missed last two games of season. ... Traded by Canucks with third-round pick (traded to Dallas) in 1998 draft to Hartford Whalers for C Jim Dowd, D Frantisek Kucera and second-round pick (D Ryan Bonni) in 1997 draft (December 19, 1995). ... Underwent lower back surgery (October 23, 1996); missed final 81 games of regular season. ... Whalers franchise moved to North Carolina and renamed Carolina Hurricanes for 1997-98 season; NHL approved move on June 25, 1997. ... Traded by Hurricanes to Toronto Maple Leafs for conditional draft pick (January 2, 1998). ... Suffered ankle infection (January 10, 1998); missed nine games. ... Traded by Maple Leafs to Washington Capitals for D Sylvain Cote (March 24, 1998). ... Suffered from headaches (April 8, 1998); missed four games.
HONORS: Shared Max Kaminsky Trophy with Terry Carkner (1985-86). ... Named to OHL All-Star first team (1985-86).

Season Team	League	REGULAR SEASON								PLAYOFFS				
		Gms.	G	A	Pts.	PIM	+/-	PP	SH	Gms.	G	A	Pts.	PIM
81-82—Hawkesbury	COJHL	49	12	47	59	72	...	...	...	—	—	—	—	—
82-83—Sudbury	OHL	65	9	37	46	39	...	...	...	—	—	—	—	—
83-84—Sudbury	OHL	68	17	60	77	39	...	...	...	—	—	—	—	—
84-85—Sudbury	OHL	56	16	48	64	26	...	...	...	—	—	—	—	—
85-86—Sudbury	OHL	45	22	28	50	24	...	...	...	4	0	2	2	11
—Quebec	NHL	8	3	2	5	6	5	0	0	1	0	0	0	0
—Fredericton	AHL	—	—	—	—	—	...	...	...	1	0	1	1	0
86-87—Fredericton	AHL	26	2	14	16	16	...	...	...	—	—	—	—	—
—Quebec	NHL	44	7	22	29	16	11	3	0	13	3	3	6	2
87-88—Quebec	NHL	78	16	36	52	64	-25	9	0	—	—	—	—	—
88-89—Quebec	NHL	78	21	47	68	62	-22	13	1	—	—	—	—	—

Season Team	League	REGULAR SEASON								PLAYOFFS				
		Gms.	G	A	Pts.	PIM	+/-	PP	SH	Gms.	G	A	Pts.	PIM
89-90—Quebec	NHL	29	6	10	16	18	-14	2	0	—	—	—	—	—
—St. Louis	NHL	48	10	28	38	37	-12	6	1	12	2	10	12	4
90-91—St. Louis	NHL	67	12	47	59	39	4	6	1	13	3	9	12	6
91-92—St. Louis	NHL	80	20	39	59	38	8	10	0	6	2	1	3	2
92-93—St. Louis	NHL	71	25	53	78	58	-6	12	2	11	3	8	11	6
93-94—St. Louis	NHL	63	13	47	60	46	-13	7	0	—	—	—	—	—
—Vancouver.................	NHL	11	1	5	6	10	2	0	0	24	6	9	15	37
94-95—Vancouver.................	NHL	33	8	23	31	16	-2	3	0	5	1	3	4	2
95-96—Vancouver.................	NHL	28	1	16	17	18	6	0	0	—	—	—	—	—
—Hartford	NHL	48	7	31	38	38	2	5	0	—	—	—	—	—
96-97—Hartford	NHL	1	0	0	0	0	0	0	0	—	—	—	—	—
97-98—Carolina	NHL	32	3	10	13	16	-1	3	0	—	—	—	—	—
—Toronto	NHL	19	1	8	9	10	2	1	0	—	—	—	—	—
—Washington	NHL	9	0	6	6	6	4	0	0	2	0	2	2	0
NHL Totals (13 years).........		747	154	430	584	498	-51	80	5	87	20	45	65	59

B

BROWN, JEFF   D   RANGERS

PERSONAL: Born April 24, 1978, in Toronto. ... 6-1/190. ... Shoots right.
TRANSACTIONS/CAREER NOTES: Selected by New York Rangers in first round (first Rangers pick, 22nd overall) of NHL entry draft (June 22, 1996).

Season Team	League	REGULAR SEASON								PLAYOFFS				
		Gms.	G	A	Pts.	PIM	+/-	PP	SH	Gms.	G	A	Pts.	PIM
93-94—Thornhill	Jr. A	47	6	18	24	90	...	...	...	—	—	—	—	—
94-95—Sarnia	OHL	58	2	14	16	52	...	...	...	—	—	—	—	—
95-96—Sarnia	OHL	65	8	20	28	111	...	...	...	10	1	2	3	12
96-97—London	OHL	63	6	31	37	92	...	...	...	—	—	—	—	—
97-98—London	OHL	63	12	42	54	96	...	...	...	15	1	4	5	26

BROWN, KEVIN   RW

PERSONAL: Born May 11, 1974, in Birmingham, England. ... 6-1/212. ... Shoots right. ... Full Name: Kevin J. Brown.
HIGH SCHOOL: Quinte Secondary School (Belleville, Ont.).
TRANSACTIONS/CAREER NOTES: Selected by Los Angeles Kings in fourth round (third Kings pick, 87th overall) of NHL entry draft (June 20, 1992). ... Strained knee and hip (April 12, 1995); missed two games. ... Sprained right shoulder (April 19, 1995); missed last seven games of season. ... Traded by Kings to Ottawa Senators for D Jaroslav Modry (March 20, 1996). ... Traded by Senators to Mighty Ducks of Anaheim for LW Mike Maneluk (July 1, 1996). ... Traded by Mighty Ducks to Hartford Whalers for rights to C Espen Knutsen (October 1, 1996). ... Sprained shoulder (February 16, 1997); missed seven games. ... Whalers franchise moved to North Carolina and renamed Carolina Hurricanes for 1997-98 season; NHL approved move on June 25, 1997.
HONORS: Won Jim Mahon Memorial Trophy (1992-93 and 1993-94). ... Named to OHL All-Star second team (1992-93). ... Named to Can.HL All-Star second team (1993-94). ... Named to OHL All-Star first team (1993-94).

Season Team	League	REGULAR SEASON								PLAYOFFS				
		Gms.	G	A	Pts.	PIM	+/-	PP	SH	Gms.	G	A	Pts.	PIM
89-90—Georgetown Jr. B........	OHA	31	3	8	11	59	...	...	...	—	—	—	—	—
90-91—Waterloo Jr. B.............	OHA	46	25	33	58	116	...	...	...	—	—	—	—	—
91-92—Belleville	OHL	66	24	24	48	52	...	...	...	5	1	4	5	8
92-93—Belleville	OHL	6	2	5	7	4	...	...	...	—	—	—	—	—
—Detroit..........................	OHL	56	48	86	134	76	...	...	...	15	10	18	28	18
93-94—Detroit.......................	OHL	57	54	81	135	85	...	...	...	17	14	*26	*40	28
94-95—Phoenix.....................	IHL	48	19	31	50	64	...	...	...	—	—	—	—	—
—Los Angeles...............	NHL	23	2	3	5	18	-7	0	0	—	—	—	—	—
95-96—Los Angeles...............	NHL	7	1	0	1	4	-2	0	0	—	—	—	—	—
—Phoenix......................	IHL	45	10	16	26	39	...	...	...	—	—	—	—	—
—Prin. Edward Island	AHL	8	3	6	9	2	...	...	...	3	1	3	4	0
96-97—Springfield	AHL	48	32	16	48	45	...	...	...	17	†11	6	17	24
—Hartford	NHL	11	0	4	4	6	-6	0	0	—	—	—	—	—
97-98—Carolina	NHL	4	0	0	0	0	-2	0	0	—	—	—	—	—
—New Haven..................	AHL	67	28	44	72	65	...	...	...	3	0	2	2	0
NHL Totals (4 years)...........		45	3	7	10	28	-17	0	0					

BROWN, MIKE   C   PANTHERS

PERSONAL: Born April 27, 1979, in Surrey, B.C. ... 6-5/183. ... Shoots left.
TRANSACTIONS/CAREER NOTES: Selected by Florida Panthers in first round (first Panthers pick, 20th overall) of NHL entry draft (June 21, 1997).
HONORS: Won Jim Piggott Memorial Trophy (1995-96).

Season Team	League	REGULAR SEASON								PLAYOFFS				
		Gms.	G	A	Pts.	PIM	+/-	PP	SH	Gms.	G	A	Pts.	PIM
94-95—Merritt........................	BCJHL	45	3	4	7	128	...	...	...	—	—	—	—	—
95-96—Red Deer....................	WHL	62	4	5	9	125	...	...	...	10	0	0	0	18
96-97—Red Deer....................	WHL	70	19	13	32	243	...	...	...	16	1	2	3	47
97-98—Kamloops	WHL	72	23	33	56	305	...	...	...	7	2	1	3	22

BROWN, ROB   RW   PENGUINS

PERSONAL: Born April 10, 1968, in Kingston, Ont. ... 5-10/183. ... Shoots right. ... Full Name: Robert Brown.

TRANSACTIONS/CAREER NOTES: Selected by Pittsburgh Penguins as underage junior in fourth round (fourth Penguins pick, 67th overall) of NHL entry draft (June 21, 1986). ... Separated right shoulder (February 12, 1989); missed 12 games. ... Traded by Penguins to Hartford Whalers for RW Scott Young (December 21, 1990). ... Injured Adam's apple (April 5, 1991); missed one playoff game. ... Traded by Whalers to Chicago Blackhawks for D Steve Konroyd (January 24, 1992). ... Signed as free agent by Dallas Stars (August 6, 1993). ... Signed as free agent by Los Angeles Kings (June 14, 1994). ... Signed as free agent by Pittsburgh Penguins (October 1, 1997).

HONORS: Won WHL (West) Most Valuable Player Trophy (1985-86 and 1986-87). ... Won Bob Brownridge Memorial Trophy (1985-86). ... Named to WHL (West) All-Star first team (1985-86 and 1986-87). ... Won Can.HL Player of the Year Award (1986-87). ... Won Can.HL Plus/Minus Award (1986-87). ... Won WHL (West) Bob Brownridge Memorial Trophy (1986-87). ... Won WHL Player of the Year Award (1986-87). ... Played in NHL All-Star Game (1989). ... Won James Gatschene Memorial Trophy (1993-94). ... Won Leo P. Lamoureux Memorial Trophy (1993-94 and 1995-96). ... Named to IHL All-Star first team (1993-94, 1995-96 and 1996-97). ... Named to IHL All-Star second team (1994-95). ... Won Leo P. Lamoreux Memorial Trophy (1996-97).

STATISTICAL PLATEAUS: Three-goal games: 1988-89 (4), 1989-90 (3). Total: 7.

Season Team	League	REGULAR SEASON								PLAYOFFS				
		Gms.	G	A	Pts.	PIM	+/-	PP	SH	Gms.	G	A	Pts.	PIM
83-84—Kamloops	WHL	50	16	42	58	80	...	...	...	15	1	2	3	17
84-85—Kamloops	WHL	60	29	50	79	95	...	...	...	15	8	8	16	28
85-86—Kamloops	WHL	69	58	*115	*173	171	...	...	...	16	*18	*28	*46	14
86-87—Kamloops	WHL	63	*76	*136	*212	101	...	...	...	5	6	5	11	6
87-88—Pittsburgh	NHL	51	24	20	44	56	...	...	...	—	—	—	—	—
88-89—Pittsburgh	NHL	68	49	66	115	118	...	...	...	11	5	3	8	22
89-90—Pittsburgh	NHL	80	33	47	80	102	-10	12	0	—	—	—	—	—
90-91—Pittsburgh	NHL	25	6	10	16	31	...	...	...	—	—	—	—	—
—Hartford	NHL	44	18	24	42	101	...	...	...	5	1	0	1	7
91-92—Hartford	NHL	42	16	15	31	39	...	...	...	—	—	—	—	—
—Chicago	NHL	25	5	11	16	34	...	...	...	8	2	4	6	4
92-93—Chicago	NHL	15	1	6	7	33	6	0	0	—	—	—	—	—
—Indianapolis	IHL	19	14	19	33	32	...	...	...	2	0	1	1	2
93-94—Kalamazoo	IHL	79	42	*113	*155	188	...	...	...	5	1	3	4	6
—Dallas	NHL	1	0	0	0	0	-1	0	0	—	—	—	—	—
94-95—Phoenix	IHL	69	34	73	107	135	...	...	...	9	4	12	16	0
—Los Angeles	NHL	2	0	0	0	0	-2	0	0	—	—	—	—	—
95-96—Chicago	IHL	79	52	*91	*143	100	...	...	...	9	4	11	15	6
96-97—Chicago	IHL	76	37	*80	*117	98	...	...	...	4	2	4	6	16
97-98—Pittsburgh	NHL	82	15	25	40	59	-1	4	0	6	1	0	1	4
NHL Totals (9 years)		435	167	224	391	573	...	...	...	30	9	7	16	37

BROWN, SEAN   D   OILERS

PERSONAL: Born November 5, 1976, in Oshawa, Ont. ... 6-2/205. ... Shoots left.

HIGH SCHOOL: Quinte Secondary School (Belleville, Ont.).

TRANSACTIONS/CAREER NOTES: Selected by Boston Bruins in first round (second Bruins pick, 21st overall) of NHL entry draft (July 8, 1995). ... Traded by Boston Bruins with RW Mariusz Czerkawski and first-round pick (D Mattieu Descoteaux) in 1996 draft to Edmonton Oilers for G Bill Ranford (January 11, 1996).

HONORS: Named to OHL All-Star second team (1995-96).

Season Team	League	REGULAR SEASON								PLAYOFFS				
		Gms.	G	A	Pts.	PIM	+/-	PP	SH	Gms.	G	A	Pts.	PIM
92-93—Oshawa	Tier II Jr. A	15	0	1	1	9	...	...	...	—	—	—	—	—
93-94—Wellington	OJHL	32	5	14	19	165	...	...	...	—	—	—	—	—
—Belleville	OHL	28	1	2	3	53	...	...	...	8	0	0	0	17
94-95—Belleville	OHL	58	2	16	18	200	...	...	...	16	4	2	6	67
95-96—Belleville	OHL	37	10	23	33	150	...	...	...	—	—	—	—	—
—Sarnia	OHL	26	8	17	25	112	...	...	...	10	1	0	1	38
96-97—Hamilton	AHL	61	1	7	8	238	...	...	...	19	1	0	1	47
—Edmonton	NHL	5	0	0	0	4	-1	0	0	—	—	—	—	—
97-98—Edmonton	NHL	18	0	1	1	43	-1	0	0	—	—	—	—	—
—Hamilton	AHL	43	4	6	10	166	...	...	...	6	0	2	2	38
NHL Totals (2 years)		23	0	1	1	47	-2	0	0					

BRUNET, BENOIT   LW   CANADIENS

PERSONAL: Born August 24, 1968, in Montreal. ... 6-0/194. ... Shoots left. ... Name pronounced BEHN-wah broo-NAY.

TRANSACTIONS/CAREER NOTES: Selected by Montreal Canadiens as underage junior in second round (second Canadiens pick, 27th overall) of NHL entry draft (June 21, 1986). ... Injured ankle (September 1987). ... Tore left knee ligaments (September 24, 1990); missed 24 games. ... Fractured ankle (December 4, 1991). ... Sprained left knee (November 21, 1992); missed 10 games. ... Fractured thumb (January 22, 1993); missed 14 games. ... Bruised knee (November 17, 1993); missed four games. ... Suffered mild concussion (February 2, 1994); missed six games. ... Suffered sore throat (April 8, 1994); missed three games. ... Pulled hamstring (March 18, 1995); missed two games. ... Bruised right knee (May 3, 1995); missed one game. ... Sprained wrist (November 11, 1995); missed five games. ... Reinjured wrist (November 25, 1995); missed 18 games. ... Sprained back (January 11, 1996); missed 28 games. ... Bruised thigh (October 24, 1996); missed one game. ... Fractured left leg (November 2, 1996); missed 21 games. ... Suffered from tonsillitis (December 21, 1996); missed one game. ... Fractured hand (January 20, 1997); missed 19 games. ... Strained shoulder (October 23, 1997); missed three games. ... Suffered concussion (November 22, 1997); missed eight games. ... Suffered from the flu (December 22, 1997); missed one game. ... Strained rib (March 19, 1998); missed two games.

HONORS: Named to QMJHL All-Star second team (1986-87). ... Named to AHL All-Star first team (1988-89).

MISCELLANEOUS: Member of Stanley Cup championship team (1993).

Season Team	League	Gms.	G	A	Pts.	PIM	+/-	PP	SH	Gms.	G	A	Pts.	PIM
85-86—Hull	QMJHL	71	33	37	70	81	...	...	...	—	—	—	—	—
86-87—Hull	QMJHL	60	43	67	110	105	...	...	...	6	7	5	12	8
87-88—Hull	QMJHL	62	54	89	143	131	...	...	...	10	3	10	13	11
88-89—Montreal	NHL	2	0	1	1	0	0	0	0	—	—	—	—	—
—Sherbrooke	AHL	73	41	*76	117	95	...	...	...	6	2	0	2	4
89-90—Sherbrooke	AHL	72	32	35	67	82	...	...	...	12	8	7	15	20
90-91—Fredericton	AHL	24	13	18	31	16	...	...	...	6	5	6	11	2
—Montreal	NHL	17	1	3	4	0	-1	0	0	—	—	—	—	—
91-92—Fredericton	AHL	6	7	9	16	27	...	...	...	—	—	—	—	—
—Montreal	NHL	18	4	6	10	14	4	0	0	—	—	—	—	—
92-93—Montreal	NHL	47	10	15	25	19	13	0	0	20	2	8	10	8
93-94—Montreal	NHL	71	10	20	30	20	14	0	3	7	1	4	5	16
94-95—Montreal	NHL	45	7	18	25	16	7	1	1	—	—	—	—	—
95-96—Montreal	NHL	26	7	8	15	17	-4	3	1	3	0	2	2	0
—Fredericton	AHL	3	2	1	3	6	...	...	...	—	—	—	—	—
96-97—Montreal	NHL	39	10	13	23	14	6	2	0	4	1	3	4	4
97-98—Montreal	NHL	68	12	20	32	61	11	1	2	8	1	0	1	4
NHL Totals (9 years)		333	61	104	165	161	50	7	7	42	5	17	22	32

BRUNETTE, ANDREW   LW   PREDATORS

PERSONAL: Born August 24, 1973, in Sudbury, Ont. ... 6-0/212. ... Shoots left. ... Name pronounced broo-NEHT.
TRANSACTIONS/CAREER NOTES: Selected by Washington Capitals in sixth round (sixth Capitals pick, 174th overall) of NHL entry draft (June 26, 1993). ... Selected by Nashville Predators in NHL expansion draft (June 26, 1998).
HONORS: Won Eddie Powers Memorial Trophy (1992-93). ... Named to Can.HL All-Star second team (1992-93). ... Named to OHL All-Star first team (1992-93).

		REGULAR SEASON								PLAYOFFS				
Season Team	League	Gms.	G	A	Pts.	PIM	+/-	PP	SH	Gms.	G	A	Pts.	PIM
90-91—Owen Sound	OHL	63	15	20	35	15	...	...	...	—	—	—	—	—
91-92—Owen Sound	OHL	66	51	47	98	42	...	...	...	5	5	0	5	8
92-93—Owen Sound	OHL	66	*62	*100	*162	91	...	...	...	8	8	6	14	16
93-94—Portland	AHL	23	9	11	20	10	...	...	...	2	0	1	1	0
—Hampton	ECHL	20	12	18	30	32	...	...	...	7	7	6	13	18
—Providence	AHL	3	0	0	0	0	...	...	...	—	—	—	—	—
94-95—Portland	AHL	79	30	50	80	53	...	...	...	7	3	3	6	10
95-96—Portland	AHL	69	28	66	94	125	...	...	...	20	11	18	29	15
—Washington	NHL	11	3	3	6	5	0	0	0	6	1	3	4	0
96-97—Portland	AHL	50	22	51	73	48	...	...	...	5	1	2	3	0
—Washington	NHL	23	4	7	11	12	-3	2	0	—	—	—	—	—
97-98—Portland	AHL	43	21	46	67	64	...	...	...	10	1	11	12	12
—Washington	NHL	28	11	12	23	12	2	4	0	—	—	—	—	—
NHL Totals (3 years)		62	18	22	40	29	-1	6	0	6	1	3	4	0

BRYLIN, SERGEI   C   DEVILS

PERSONAL: Born January 13, 1974, in Moscow, U.S.S.R. ... 5-10/190. ... Shoots left. ... Name pronounced BREE-lihn.
TRANSACTIONS/CAREER NOTES: Selected by New Jersey Devils in second round (second Devils pick, 42nd overall) of NHL entry draft (June 20, 1992). ... Suffered from tonsillitis (May 3, 1995); missed last game of season. ... Broke hand (November 16, 1995); missed 13 games. ... Injured knee (September 19, 1997); missed 19 games.
MISCELLANEOUS: Member of Stanley Cup championship team (1995).

		REGULAR SEASON								PLAYOFFS				
Season Team	League	Gms.	G	A	Pts.	PIM	+/-	PP	SH	Gms.	G	A	Pts.	PIM
91-92—CSKA Moscow	CIS	44	1	6	7	4	...	...	...	—	—	—	—	—
92-93—CSKA Moscow	CIS	42	5	4	9	36	...	...	...	—	—	—	—	—
93-94—CSKA Moscow	CIS	39	4	6	10	36	...	...	...	3	0	1	1	0
—Russian Penguins	IHL	13	4	5	9	18	...	...	...	—	—	—	—	—
94-95—Albany	AHL	63	19	35	54	78	...	...	...	—	—	—	—	—
—New Jersey	NHL	26	6	8	14	8	12	0	0	12	1	2	3	4
95-96—New Jersey	NHL	50	4	5	9	26	-2	0	0	—	—	—	—	—
96-97—New Jersey	NHL	29	2	2	4	20	-13	0	0	—	—	—	—	—
—Albany	AHL	43	17	24	41	38	...	...	...	16	4	8	12	12
97-98—New Jersey	NHL	18	2	3	5	0	4	0	0	—	—	—	—	—
—Albany	AHL	44	21	22	43	60	...	...	...	—	—	—	—	—
NHL Totals (4 years)		123	14	18	32	54	1	0	0	12	1	2	3	4

BUCHBERGER, KELLY   RW/LW   OILERS

PERSONAL: Born December 12, 1966, in Langenburg, Sask. ... 6-2/205. ... Shoots left. ... Full Name: Kelly Michael Buchberger. ... Name pronounced BUK-buhr-guhr.
HIGH SCHOOL: Langenburg (Sask.).
TRANSACTIONS/CAREER NOTES: Selected by Edmonton Oilers as underage junior in ninth round (eighth Oilers pick, 188th overall) of NHL entry draft (June 15, 1985). ... Suspended six games by AHL for leaving bench to fight (March 30, 1988). ... Fractured right ankle (March 1989). ... Dislocated left shoulder (March 13, 1990). ... Reinjured shoulder (May 4, 1990). ... Strained shoulder (April 7, 1993); missed one game.
MISCELLANEOUS: Member of Stanley Cup championship team (1987 and 1990). ... Captain of Edmonton Oilers (1995-96 through 1997-98). ... Holds Edmonton Oilers all-time record for most penalty minutes (1,679).
STATISTICAL PLATEAUS: Three-goal games: 1992-93 (1).

Season Team	League	REGULAR SEASON								PLAYOFFS				
		Gms.	G	A	Pts.	PIM	+/-	PP	SH	Gms.	G	A	Pts.	PIM
83-84—Melville	SAJHL	60	14	11	25	139	...	...	...	—	—	—	—	—
84-85—Moose Jaw	WHL	51	12	17	29	114	...	...	...	—	—	—	—	—
85-86—Moose Jaw	WHL	72	14	22	36	206	...	...	...	13	11	4	15	37
86-87—Nova Scotia	AHL	70	12	20	32	257	...	...	...	5	0	1	1	23
—Edmonton	NHL	—	—	—	—	—	—	—	—	3	0	1	1	5
87-88—Edmonton	NHL	19	1	0	1	81	-1	0	0	—	—	—	—	—
—Nova Scotia	AHL	49	21	23	44	206	...	...	...	2	0	0	0	11
88-89—Edmonton	NHL	66	5	9	14	234	-14	1	0	—	—	—	—	—
89-90—Edmonton	NHL	55	2	6	8	168	-8	0	0	19	0	5	5	13
90-91—Edmonton	NHL	64	3	1	4	160	-6	0	0	12	2	1	3	25
91-92—Edmonton	NHL	79	20	24	44	157	9	0	4	16	1	4	5	32
92-93—Edmonton	NHL	83	12	18	30	133	-27	1	2	—	—	—	—	—
93-94—Edmonton	NHL	84	3	18	21	199	-20	0	0	—	—	—	—	—
94-95—Edmonton	NHL	48	7	17	24	82	0	2	1	—	—	—	—	—
95-96—Edmonton	NHL	82	11	14	25	184	-20	0	2	—	—	—	—	—
96-97—Edmonton	NHL	81	8	30	38	159	4	0	0	12	5	2	7	16
97-98—Edmonton	NHL	82	6	17	23	122	-10	1	1	12	1	2	3	25
NHL Totals (12 years)		743	78	154	232	1679	-93	5	10	74	9	15	24	116

BUCKBERGER, ASHLEY — RW

PERSONAL: Born February 19, 1975, in Esterhazy, Sask. ... 6-2/200. ... Shoots right. ... Name pronounced BUHK-buhr-guhr.
HIGH SCHOOL: Swift Current (Sask.) Comprehensive.
TRANSACTIONS/CAREER NOTES: Selected by Quebec Nordiques in second round (third Nordiques pick, 49th overall) of NHL entry draft (June 26, 1993). ... Signed as free agent by Florida Panthers (July 27, 1995).
HONORS: Won Jim Piggott Memorial Trophy (1991-92).

Season Team	League	REGULAR SEASON								PLAYOFFS				
		Gms.	G	A	Pts.	PIM	+/-	PP	SH	Gms.	G	A	Pts.	PIM
90-91—Swift Current	WHL	10	2	3	5	0	...	...	...	3	0	0	0	0
91-92—Swift Current	WHL	67	23	22	45	38	...	...	...	8	2	1	3	2
92-93—Swift Current	WHL	72	23	44	67	41	...	...	...	17	6	7	13	6
93-94—Swift Current	WHL	67	42	45	87	42	...	...	...	7	0	1	1	6
94-95—Swift Current	WHL	53	23	37	60	51	...	...	...	—	—	—	—	—
—Kamloops	WHL	21	9	13	22	13	...	...	...	19	7	11	18	22
95-96—Carolina	AHL	67	8	9	17	25	...	...	...	—	—	—	—	—
96-97—Carolina	AHL	69	8	10	18	24	...	...	...	—	—	—	—	—
97-98—New Haven	AHL	66	6	11	17	9	...	...	...	2	0	0	0	0

BULIS, JAN — C — CAPITALS

PERSONAL: Born March 18, 1978, in Pardubice, Czechoslovakia. ... 6-0/194. ... Shoots left. ... Name pronounced YAHN BOO-lihsh.
TRANSACTIONS/CAREER NOTES: Selected by Washington Capitals in second round (third Capitals pick, 43rd overall) of NHL entry draft (June 22, 1996). ... Suffered concussion (November 11, 1997); missed one game.

Season Team	League	REGULAR SEASON								PLAYOFFS				
		Gms.	G	A	Pts.	PIM	+/-	PP	SH	Gms.	G	A	Pts.	PIM
94-95—Kelowna	BCJHL	51	23	25	48	36	...	...	...	17	7	9	16	...
95-96—Barrie	OHL	59	29	30	59	22	...	...	...	7	2	3	5	2
96-97—Barrie	OHL	64	42	61	103	42	...	...	...	9	3	7	10	10
97-98—Washington	NHL	48	5	11	16	18	-5	0	0	—	—	—	—	—
—Portland	AHL	3	1	4	5	12	...	...	...	—	—	—	—	—
—Kingston	OHL	2	0	1	1	0	...	...	...	12	8	10	18	12
NHL Totals (1 year)		48	5	11	16	18	-5	0	0					

BURE, PAVEL — RW/LW — CANUCKS

PERSONAL: Born March 31, 1971, in Moscow, U.S.S.R. ... 5-10/189. ... Shoots left. ... Brother of Valeri Bure, right winger, Calgary Flames. ... Name pronounced BOOR-ay. ... Nickname: The Russian Rocket.
TRANSACTIONS/CAREER NOTES: Selected by Vancouver Canucks in sixth round (fourth Canucks pick, 113th overall) of NHL entry draft (June 17, 1989). ... Strained groin (October 24, 1993); missed eight games. ... Fined $500 by NHL for hitting another player with flagrant elbow (May 6, 1994). ... Played in Europe during 1994-95 NHL lockout. ... Suffered injury (March 17, 1995); missed two games. ... Tore knee ligament (November 9, 1995); missed remainder of season. ... Suspended one game and fined $1,000 by NHL for forearm blow (December 6, 1996). ... Suffered whiplash (March 3, 1997); missed remainder of season.
HONORS: Named Soviet League Rookie of the Year (1988-89). ... Won Calder Memorial Trophy (1991-92). ... Named to THE SPORTING NEWS All-Star second team (1993-94). ... Played in NHL All-Star Game (1993, 1994, 1997 and 1998). ... Named to NHL All-Star first team (1993-94). ... Named to play in NHL All-Star Game (1996); replaced due to injury.
MISCELLANEOUS: Scored on a penalty shot (vs. Rick Tabaracci, February 28, 1992; vs. Mike Vernon, November 12, 1997; vs. Nikolai Khabibulin, January 26, 1998; vs. Damian Rhodes, February 28, 1998). ... Failed to score on a penalty shot (vs. John Vanbiesbrouck, February 17, 1992; vs. Kelly Hrudey, October 6, 1993). ... Member of silver-medal-winning Russian Olympic team (1998).
STATISTICAL PLATEAUS: Three-goal games: 1992-93 (1), 1993-94 (3), 1994-95 (1), 1997-98 (3). Total: 8. ... Four-goal games: 1992-93 (1). ... Total hat tricks: 9.

Season Team	League	REGULAR SEASON								PLAYOFFS				
		Gms.	G	A	Pts.	PIM	+/-	PP	SH	Gms.	G	A	Pts.	PIM
87-88—CSKA Moscow	USSR	5	1	1	2	0	...	...	...	—	—	—	—	—
88-89—CSKA Moscow	USSR	32	17	9	26	8	...	...	...	—	—	—	—	—

B

Season Team	League	Gms.	G	A	Pts.	PIM	+/-	PP	SH	Gms.	G	A	Pts.	PIM
				REGULAR SEASON								PLAYOFFS		
89-90—CSKA Moscow	USSR	46	14	11	25	22	...	...	...	—	—	—	—	—
90-91—CSKA Moscow	USSR	46	35	12	47	24	...	...	...	—	—	—	—	—
91-92—Vancouver	NHL	65	34	26	60	30	0	7	3	13	6	4	10	14
92-93—Vancouver	NHL	83	60	50	110	69	35	13	†7	12	5	7	12	8
93-94—Vancouver	NHL	76	*60	47	107	86	1	†25	4	24	*16	15	31	40
94-95—Landshut	Germany	1	3	0	3	2	...	...	...	—	—	—	—	—
—Spartak Moscow	CIS	1	2	0	2	2	...	...	...	—	—	—	—	—
—Vancouver	NHL	44	20	23	43	47	-8	6	2	11	7	6	13	10
95-96—Vancouver	NHL	15	6	7	13	8	-2	1	1	—	—	—	—	—
96-97—Vancouver	NHL	63	23	32	55	40	-14	4	1	—	—	—	—	—
97-98—Vancouver	NHL	82	51	39	90	48	5	13	†6	—	—	—	—	—
—Russian Oly. team	Int'l	6	9	0	9	2	...	...	...	—	—	—	—	—
NHL Totals (7 years)		428	254	224	478	328	17	69	24	60	34	32	66	72

BURE, VALERI — RW — FLAMES

PERSONAL: Born June 13, 1974, in Moscow, U.S.S.R. ... 5-11/179. ... Shoots right. ... Brother of Pavel Bure, right/left winger, Vancouver Canucks. ... Name pronounced BOOR-ay.
TRANSACTIONS/CAREER NOTES: Selected by Montreal Canadiens in second round (second Canadiens pick, 33rd overall) of NHL entry draft (June 20, 1992). ... Bruised forearm (April 3, 1995); missed two games. ... Bruised kidney (October 19, 1996); missed 11 games. ... Bruised wrist (December 28, 1996); missed two games. ... Suffered concussion (January 4, 1997); missed five games. ... Bruised cheekbone (January 8, 1998); missed three games. ... Traded by Canadiens to Flames with fourth-round pick (C Shaun Sutter) in 1998 draft for D Zarley Zalapski and RW Jonas Hoglund (February 1, 1998). ... Suffered concussion (March 3, 1998); missed five games. ... Hyperextended shoulder (April 5, 1998); missed remainder of season.
HONORS: Named to WHL (West) All-Star first team (1992-93). ... Named to WHL (West) All-Star second team (1993-94).
MISCELLANEOUS: Member of silver-medal-winning Russian Olympic team (1998).
STATISTICAL PLATEAUS: Three-goal games: 1997-98 (1).

Season Team	League	Gms.	G	A	Pts.	PIM	+/-	PP	SH	Gms.	G	A	Pts.	PIM
				REGULAR SEASON								PLAYOFFS		
90-91—CSKA Moscow	USSR	3	0	0	0	0	...	...	...	—	—	—	—	—
91-92—Spokane	WHL	53	27	22	49	78	...	...	...	10	11	6	17	10
92-93—Spokane	WHL	66	68	79	147	49	...	...	...	9	6	11	17	14
93-94—Spokane	WHL	59	40	62	102	48	...	...	...	3	5	3	8	2
94-95—Fredericton	AHL	45	23	25	48	32	...	...	...	—	—	—	—	—
—Montreal	NHL	24	3	1	4	6	-1	0	0	—	—	—	—	—
95-96—Montreal	NHL	77	22	20	42	28	10	5	0	6	0	1	1	6
96-97—Montreal	NHL	64	14	21	35	6	4	4	0	5	0	1	1	2
97-98—Montreal	NHL	50	7	22	29	33	-5	2	0	—	—	—	—	—
—Calgary	NHL	16	5	4	9	2	0	0	0	—	—	—	—	—
—Russian Oly. team	Int'l	6	1	0	1	0	...	...	...	—	—	—	—	—
NHL Totals (4 years)		231	51	68	119	75	8	11	0	11	0	2	2	8

BUREAU, MARC — C/RW — FLYERS

PERSONAL: Born May 17, 1966, in Trois-Rivieres, Que. ... 6-1/202. ... Shoots right. ... Name pronounced BYOOR-oh.
TRANSACTIONS/CAREER NOTES: Traded by Chicoutimi Saguneens with C Stephane Roy, Lee Duhemee, Sylvain Demers and D Rene L'Ecuyer to Granby Bisons for LW Greg Choules and C Stephane Richer (January 1985). ... Signed as free agent by Calgary Flames (May 16, 1987). ... Suffered eye contusion (March 25, 1990); missed final two weeks of season. ... Traded by Flames to Minnesota North Stars for third-round pick (RW Sandy McCarthy) in 1991 draft (March 5, 1991). ... Injured shoulder (January 13, 1992); missed four games. ... Separated shoulder (February 15, 1992); missed five games. ... Separated shoulder (March 1, 1992); missed eight games. ... Claimed on waivers by Tampa Bay Lightning (October 16, 1992). ... Bruised shoulder (November 17, 1992); missed six games. ... Bruised right knee (April 3, 1993); missed remainder of season. ... Traded by Lightning to Montreal Canadiens for LW Brian Bellows (June 29, 1995). ... Broke foot (September 26, 1995); missed first eight games of season. ... Suffered sore neck (November 29, 1995); missed two games. ... Suspended five games and fined $1,000 by NHL for elbowing (February 3, 1996). ... Bruised foot (November 2, 1996); missed two games. ... Tore knee ligament (December 7, 1996); missed 26 games. ... Injured knee (February 10, 1997); missed five games. ... Suffered from the flu (April 1, 1997); missed one game. ... Broke finger (April 9, 1997); missed remainder of season. ... Bruised thigh (October 25, 1997); missed two games. ... Strained neck (February 28, 1998); missed one game. ... Signed as free agent by Philadelphia Flyers (July 6, 1998).
HONORS: Named to IHL All-Star second team (1989-90 and 1990-91).
MISCELLANEOUS: Failed to score on a penalty shot (vs. Don Beaupre, November 18, 1995; vs. Mike Richter, January 10, 1998).

Season Team	League	Gms.	G	A	Pts.	PIM	+/-	PP	SH	Gms.	G	A	Pts.	PIM
				REGULAR SEASON								PLAYOFFS		
83-84—Chicoutimi	QMJHL	56	6	16	22	14	...	...	...	—	—	—	—	—
84-85—Granby	QMJHL	68	50	70	120	29	...	...	...	—	—	—	—	—
85-86—Chicoutimi	QMJHL	63	36	62	98	69	...	...	...	9	3	7	10	10
86-87—Longueuil	QMJHL	66	54	58	112	68	...	...	...	20	17	20	37	12
87-88—Salt Lake City	IHL	69	7	20	27	86	...	...	...	7	0	3	3	8
88-89—Salt Lake City	IHL	76	28	36	64	119	...	...	...	14	7	5	12	31
89-90—Salt Lake City	IHL	67	43	48	91	173	...	...	...	11	4	8	12	0
—Calgary	NHL	5	0	0	0	4	-1	0	0	—	—	—	—	—
90-91—Calgary	NHL	5	0	0	0	2	-4	0	0	—	—	—	—	—
—Salt Lake City	IHL	54	40	48	88	101	...	...	...	—	—	—	—	—
—Minnesota	NHL	9	0	6	6	4	-3	0	0	23	3	2	5	20
91-92—Minnesota	NHL	46	6	4	10	50	-5	0	0	5	0	0	0	14
—Kalamazoo	IHL	7	2	8	10	2	...	...	...	—	—	—	—	—
92-93—Tampa Bay	NHL	63	10	21	31	111	-12	1	2	—	—	—	—	—
93-94—Tampa Bay	NHL	75	8	7	15	30	-9	0	1	—	—	—	—	—

Season Team	League	REGULAR SEASON								PLAYOFFS				
		Gms.	G	A	Pts.	PIM	+/-	PP	SH	Gms.	G	A	Pts.	PIM
94-95—Tampa Bay	NHL	48	2	12	14	30	-8	0	1	—	—	—	—	—
95-96—Montreal	NHL	65	3	7	10	46	-3	0	0	6	1	1	2	4
96-97—Montreal	NHL	43	6	9	15	16	4	1	1	—	—	—	—	—
97-98—Montreal	NHL	74	13	6	19	12	0	0	0	10	1	2	3	6
NHL Totals (9 years)		433	48	72	120	305	-41	2	5	44	5	5	10	44

BURKE, SEAN — G

PERSONAL: Born January 29, 1967, in Windsor, Ont. ... 6-4/210. ... Catches left. ... Name pronounced BUHRK.

TRANSACTIONS/CAREER NOTES: Selected by New Jersey Devils as underage junior in second round (second Devils pick, 24th overall) of NHL entry draft (June 15, 1985). ... Injured groin (December 1988). ... Underwent arthroscopic surgery to right knee (September 5, 1989). ... Traded by Devils with D Eric Weinrich to Hartford Whalers for RW Bobby Holik, second-round pick in 1993 draft (LW Jay Pandolfo) and future considerations (August 28, 1992). ... Sprained ankle (December 27, 1992); missed seven games. ... Suffered back spasms (March 13, 1993); missed remainder of season. ... Pulled hamstring (September 29, 1993); missed seven games. ... Reinjured hamstring (October 27, 1993); missed 14 games. ... Suffered back spasms (December 23, 1993); missed one game. ... Strained groin (February 28, 1995); missed two games. ... Suffered back spasms (November 19, 1995); missed two games. ... Suffered back spasms (February 7, 1996); missed three games. ... Dislocated thumb (November 30, 1996); missed 19 games. ... Strained hip flexor (February 26, 1997); missed one game. ... Whalers franchise moved to North Carolina and renamed Carolina Hurricanes for 1997-98 season; NHL approved move on June 25, 1997. ... Traded by Hurricanes to Canucks with LW Geoff Sanderson and D Enrico Ciccone for LW Martin Gelinas and G Kirk McLean (January 3, 1998). ... Traded by Canucks to Philadelphia Flyers for G Garth Snow (March 4, 1998). ... Suffered lower back spasms (March 8, 1998); missed six games.

HONORS: Played in NHL All-Star Game (1989).

MISCELLANEOUS: Member of silver-medal-winning Canadian Olympic team (1992). ... Holds Carolina Hurricanes franchise all-time record for most games played by a goaltender (281) and goals-against average (3.12). ... Stopped a penalty shot attempt (vs. Luc Robitaille, February 2, 1989; vs. Michal Pivonka, January 21, 1995; vs. Wayne Presley, March 8, 1996; vs. Brian Bradley, April 3, 1996; vs. Kevin Stevens, March 22, 1998).

Season Team	League	REGULAR SEASON								PLAYOFFS						
		Gms.	Min	W	L	T	GA	SO	Avg.	Gms.	Min.	W	L	GA	SO	Avg.
83-84—St. Michael's H.S.	MTHL	25	1482	...	...	...	120	0	4.86	—	—	—	—	—	—	—
84-85—Toronto	OHL	49	2987	25	21	3	211	0	4.24	5	266	1	3	25	0	5.64
85-86—Toronto	OHL	47	2840	16	27	3	†233	0	4.92	4	238	0	4	24	0	6.05
—Canadian nat'l team	Int'l	5	284	...	...	...	22	0	4.65	—	—	—	—	—	—	—
86-87—Canadian nat'l team	Int'l	46	2670	...	...	...	138	0	3.10	—	—	—	—	—	—	—
87-88—Canadian nat'l team	Int'l	37	1962	19	9	2	92	1	2.81	—	—	—	—	—	—	—
—Can. Olympic Team	Int'l	4	238	1	2	1	12	0	3.03	—	—	—	—	—	—	—
—New Jersey	NHL	13	689	10	1	0	35	1	3.05	17	1001	9	8	*57	†1	3.42
88-89—New Jersey	NHL	62	3590	22	31	9	†230	3	3.84	—	—	—	—	—	—	—
89-90—New Jersey	NHL	52	2914	22	22	6	175	0	3.60	2	125	0	2	8	0	3.84
90-91—New Jersey	NHL	35	1870	8	12	8	112	0	3.59	—	—	—	—	—	—	—
91-92—Int'l	Int'l	31	1721	18	6	4	75	1	2.61	—	—	—	—	—	—	—
—Can. Olympic Team	Int'l	7	429	5	2	0	17	0	2.38	—	—	—	—	—	—	—
—San Diego	IHL	7	424	4	2	‡1	17	0	2.41	3	160	0	3	13	0	4.88
92-93—Hartford	NHL	50	2656	16	27	3	184	0	4.16	—	—	—	—	—	—	—
93-94—Hartford	NHL	47	2750	17	24	5	137	2	2.99	—	—	—	—	—	—	—
94-95—Hartford	NHL	42	2418	17	19	4	108	0	2.68	—	—	—	—	—	—	—
95-96—Hartford	NHL	66	3669	28	28	6	190	4	3.11	—	—	—	—	—	—	—
96-97—Hartford	NHL	51	2985	22	22	6	134	4	2.69	—	—	—	—	—	—	—
97-98—Carolina	NHL	25	1415	7	11	5	66	1	2.80	—	—	—	—	—	—	—
—Vancouver	NHL	16	838	2	9	4	49	0	3.51	—	—	—	—	—	—	—
—Philadelphia	NHL	11	632	7	3	0	27	1	2.56	5	283	1	4	17	0	3.60
NHL Totals (10 years)		470	26426	178	209	56	1447	16	3.29	24	1409	10	14	82	1	3.49

BURNETT, GARRETT — D — SHARKS

PERSONAL: Born September 23, 1975, in Coquitlim, B.C. ... 6-3/220. ... Shoots left.

TRANSACTIONS/CAREER NOTES: Signed as free agent by San Jose Sharks (July 22, 1998).

Season Team	League	REGULAR SEASON								PLAYOFFS				
		Gms.	G	A	Pts.	PIM	+/-	PP	SH	Gms.	G	A	Pts.	PIM
95-96—Utica	Col.HL	15	0	1	1	85	...	...	...	—	—	—	—	—
—Nashville	ECHL	3	0	0	0	22	...	...	...	—	—	—	—	—
—Jacksonville	ECHL	8	0	1	1	38	...	...	...	1	0	0	0	0
96-97—Knoxville	ECHL	50	5	11	16	321	...	...	...	—	—	—	—	—
97-98—Johnstown	ECHL	12	1	1	2	2	...	...	...	—	—	—	—	—
—Philadelphia	AHL	14	1	2	3	129	...	...	...	—	—	—	—	—

BURR, SHAWN — LW/C — SHARKS

PERSONAL: Born July 1, 1966, in Sarnia, Ont. ... 6-1/205. ... Shoots left.

TRANSACTIONS/CAREER NOTES: Selected by Detroit Red Wings as underage junior in first round (first Red Wings pick, seventh overall) of NHL entry draft (June 9, 1984). ... Separated left shoulder (May 1988). ... Suffered lower back spasms (October 20, 1992); missed three games. ... Underwent wrist surgery (December 8, 1993); missed 18 games. ... Injured leg (January 25, 1994); missed seven games. ... Traded by Red Wings with third-round pick (traded to Boston) in 1996 draft to Tampa Bay Lightning for D Marc Bergevin and RW Ben Hankinson (August 17, 1995). ... Injured elbow (January 15, 1996); missed one game. ... Strained lower back (October 29, 1996); missed two games. ... Cut finger (December 19, 1996); missed six games. ... Traded by Lightning to San Jose Sharks for fifth-round pick (D Mark Thompson) in 1997 draft (June 21, 1997). ... Suffered knee injury (October 13, 1997); missed 40 games.

HONORS: Won Emms Family Award (1983-84). ... Named to OHL All-Star second team (1985-86).

STATISTICAL PLATEAUS: Three-goal games: 1986-87 (1), 1989-90 (1). Total: 2.

Season Team	League	REGULAR SEASON								PLAYOFFS				
		Gms.	G	A	Pts.	PIM	+/-	PP	SH	Gms.	G	A	Pts.	PIM
83-84—Kitchener	OHL	68	41	44	85	50	...	...	...	16	5	12	17	22
84-85—Kitchener	OHL	38	24	42	66	50	...	...	...	4	3	3	6	2
—Detroit	NHL	9	0	0	0	2	-4	0	0	—	—	—	—	—
—Adirondack	AHL	4	0	0	0	2	...	...	...	—	—	—	—	—
85-86—Kitchener	OHL	59	60	67	127	104	...	...	...	5	2	3	5	8
—Adirondack	AHL	3	2	2	4	2	...	...	...	17	5	7	12	32
—Detroit	NHL	5	1	0	1	4	1	0	1	—	—	—	—	—
86-87—Detroit	NHL	80	22	25	47	107	2	1	2	16	7	2	9	20
87-88—Detroit	NHL	78	17	23	40	97	7	5	3	9	3	1	4	14
88-89—Detroit	NHL	79	19	27	46	78	5	1	4	6	1	2	3	6
89-90—Adirondack	AHL	3	4	2	6	2	...	...	...	—	—	—	—	—
—Detroit	NHL	76	24	32	56	82	14	4	3	—	—	—	—	—
90-91—Detroit	NHL	80	20	30	50	112	14	6	0	7	0	4	4	15
91-92—Detroit	NHL	79	19	32	51	118	26	2	0	11	1	5	6	10
92-93—Detroit	NHL	80	10	25	35	74	18	1	1	7	2	1	3	2
93-94—Detroit	NHL	51	10	12	22	31	12	0	1	7	2	0	2	6
94-95—Detroit	NHL	42	6	8	14	60	13	0	0	16	0	2	2	6
95-96—Tampa Bay	NHL	81	13	15	28	119	4	1	0	6	0	2	2	8
96-97—Tampa Bay	NHL	74	14	21	35	106	5	1	0	—	—	—	—	—
97-98—San Jose	NHL	42	6	6	12	50	2	0	0	6	0	0	0	8
NHL Totals (14 years)		856	181	256	437	1040	119	22	15	91	16	19	35	95

BURRIDGE, RANDY   LW   SABRES

PERSONAL: Born January 7, 1966, in Fort Erie, Ont. ... 5-9/188. ... Shoots left. ... Full Name: Randy H. Burridge. ... Name pronounced BUHR-ihdj.
TRANSACTIONS/CAREER NOTES: Selected by Boston Bruins in eighth round (seventh Bruins pick, 157th overall) of NHL entry draft (June 15, 1985). ... Suspended by AHL during playoffs (April 1987). ... Sprained left knee ligament (February 6, 1990); missed 18 games. ... Tore right knee ligaments (February 7, 1991). ... Underwent surgery to right knee (February 13, 1991). ... Traded by Bruins to Washington Capitals for RW Stephen Leach (June 21, 1991). ... Partially tore left knee ligament (March 1, 1992); missed 14 games. ... Underwent knee surgery (September 5, 1992); missed first 71 games of season. ... Strained groin (October 6, 1993); missed three games. ... Traded by Capitals to Los Angeles Kings for LW Warren Rychel (February 10, 1995). ... Signed as free agent by Buffalo Sabres (October 4, 1995). ... Injured shoulder (October 7, 1995); missed two games. ... Injured left knee (February 28, 1996); missed five games. ... Underwent arthroscopic knee surgery (January 28, 1997); missed 27 games.
HONORS: Played in NHL All-Star Game (1992).
MISCELLANEOUS: Failed to score on a penalty shot (vs. Kay Whitmore, March 31, 1991; vs. Bill Ranford, February 3, 1996).
STATISTICAL PLATEAUS: Three-goal games: 1988-89 (2), 1993-94 (2). Total: 4.

Season Team	League	REGULAR SEASON								PLAYOFFS				
		Gms.	G	A	Pts.	PIM	+/-	PP	SH	Gms.	G	A	Pts.	PIM
82-83—Fort Erie Jr. B	OHA	42	32	56	88	32	...	...	...	—	—	—	—	—
83-84—Peterborough	OHL	55	6	7	13	44	...	...	...	8	3	2	5	7
84-85—Peterborough	OHL	66	49	57	106	88	...	...	...	17	9	16	25	18
85-86—Peterborough	OHL	17	15	11	26	23	...	...	...	3	1	3	4	2
—Boston	NHL	52	17	25	42	28	17	1	0	3	0	4	4	12
—Moncton	AHL	—	—	—	—	—	...	...	...	3	0	2	2	2
86-87—Moncton	AHL	47	26	41	67	139	...	...	...	3	1	2	3	30
—Boston	NHL	23	1	4	5	16	-6	0	0	2	1	0	1	2
87-88—Boston	NHL	79	27	28	55	105	0	5	3	23	2	10	12	16
88-89—Boston	NHL	80	31	30	61	39	19	6	2	10	5	2	7	8
89-90—Boston	NHL	63	17	15	32	47	9	7	0	21	4	11	15	14
90-91—Boston	NHL	62	15	13	28	40	17	1	0	19	0	3	3	39
91-92—Washington	NHL	66	23	44	67	50	-4	9	0	2	0	1	1	0
92-93—Baltimore	AHL	2	0	1	1	2	...	...	...	—	—	—	—	—
—Washington	NHL	4	0	0	0	0	1	0	0	4	1	0	1	0
93-94—Washington	NHL	78	25	17	42	73	-1	8	1	11	0	2	2	12
94-95—Washington	NHL	2	0	0	0	2	0	0	0	—	—	—	—	—
—Los Angeles	NHL	38	4	15	19	8	-4	2	0	—	—	—	—	—
95-96—Buffalo	NHL	74	25	33	58	30	0	6	0	—	—	—	—	—
96-97—Buffalo	NHL	55	10	21	31	20	17	1	3	12	5	1	6	2
97-98—Buffalo	NHL	30	4	6	10	0	0	1	0	—	—	—	—	—
—Rochester	AHL	6	0	1	1	19	...	...	...	1	0	1	1	0
NHL Totals (13 years)		706	199	251	450	458	65	47	9	107	18	34	52	105

BURT, ADAM   D   HURRICANES

PERSONAL: Born January 15, 1969, in Detroit. ... 6-1/208. ... Shoots left.
TRANSACTIONS/CAREER NOTES: Broke jaw (December 1985). ... Selected by Hartford Whalers as underage junior in second round (second Whalers pick, 39th overall) of NHL entry draft (June 13, 1987). ... Separated left shoulder (September 13, 1988). ... Bruised hip (December 1989). ... Dislocated left shoulder (January 19, 1989). ... Tore right knee ligaments (February 16, 1991); missed remainder of season. ... Sprained left wrist (January 11, 1992); missed six games. ... Broke bone in right foot (January 25, 1993); missed 13 games. ... Sprained shoulder (February 27, 1994); missed remainder of season. ... Strained groin (February 3, 1997); missed eight games. ... Sprained shoulder (March 5, 1997); missed three games. ... Whalers franchise moved to North Carolina and renamed Carolina Hurricanes for 1997-98 season; NHL approved move on June 25, 1997. ... Suffered back spasms (November 21, 1998); missed one game.
HONORS: Named to OHL All-Star second team (1987-88).
MISCELLANEOUS: Captain of Hartford Whalers (1994-95).

Season Team	League	REGULAR SEASON								PLAYOFFS				
		Gms.	G	A	Pts.	PIM	+/-	PP	SH	Gms.	G	A	Pts.	PIM
85-86—North Bay	OHL	49	0	11	11	81	...	...	...	10	0	0	0	24
86-87—North Bay	OHL	57	4	27	31	138	...	...	...	24	1	6	7	68
87-88—North Bay	OHL	66	17	54	71	176	...	...	...	2	0	3	3	6
—Binghamton	AHL	—	—	—	—	—	...	...	...	2	1	1	2	0
88-89—North Bay	OHL	23	4	11	15	45	...	...	...	12	2	12	14	12
—Binghamton	AHL	5	0	2	2	13	...	...	...	—	—	—	—	—
—Hartford	NHL	5	0	0	0	6	...	0	0	—	—	—	—	—
89-90—Hartford	NHL	63	4	8	12	105	3	1	0	2	0	0	0	0
90-91—Springfield	AHL	9	1	3	4	22	...	...	...	—	—	—	—	—
—Hartford	NHL	42	2	7	9	63	-4	1	0	—	—	—	—	—
91-92—Hartford	NHL	66	9	15	24	93	-16	4	0	2	0	0	0	0
92-93—Hartford	NHL	65	6	14	20	116	-11	0	0	—	—	—	—	—
93-94—Hartford	NHL	63	1	17	18	75	-4	0	0	—	—	—	—	—
94-95—Hartford	NHL	46	7	11	18	65	0	3	0	—	—	—	—	—
95-96—Hartford	NHL	78	4	9	13	121	-4	0	0	—	—	—	—	—
96-97—Hartford	NHL	71	2	11	13	79	-13	0	0	—	—	—	—	—
97-98—Carolina	NHL	76	1	11	12	106	-6	0	1	—	—	—	—	—
NHL Totals (10 years)		575	36	103	139	829	...	9	1	4	0	0	0	0

BUTENSCHON, SVEN D PENGUINS

PERSONAL: Born March 22, 1976, in Itzehoe, West Germany. ... 6-4/215. ... Shoots left. ... Name pronounced BOO-tihn-SHAHN.
HIGH SCHOOL: Crocus Plains (Brandon, Man.).
TRANSACTIONS/CAREER NOTES: Selected by Pittsburgh Penguins in third round (third Penguins pick, 57th overall) of NHL entry draft (June 29, 1994). ... Suffered from the flu (November 7, 1997); missed two games.

Season Team	League	REGULAR SEASON								PLAYOFFS				
		Gms.	G	A	Pts.	PIM	+/-	PP	SH	Gms.	G	A	Pts.	PIM
93-94—Brandon	WHL	70	3	19	22	51	...	...	...	4	0	0	0	6
94-95—Brandon	WHL	21	1	5	6	44	...	...	...	18	1	2	3	11
95-96—Brandon	WHL	70	4	37	41	99	...	...	...	19	1	12	13	18
96-97—Cleveland	IHL	75	3	12	15	68	...	...	...	10	0	1	1	4
97-98—Syracuse	AHL	65	14	23	37	66	...	...	...	5	1	2	3	0
—Pittsburgh	NHL	8	0	0	0	6	-1	0	0	—	—	—	—	—
NHL Totals (1 year)		8	0	0	0	6	-1	0	0					

BUTSAYEV, YURI C RED WINGS

PERSONAL: Born October 11, 1978, in Togliatti, U.S.S.R. ... 6-1/183. ... Shoots left.
TRANSACTIONS/CAREER NOTES: Selected by Detroit Red Wings in second round (first Red Wings pick, 49th overall) of NHL entry draft (June 21, 1997).

Season Team	League	REGULAR SEASON								PLAYOFFS				
		Gms.	G	A	Pts.	PIM	+/-	PP	SH	Gms.	G	A	Pts.	PIM
95-96—Lada Togliatti	CIS	1	0	0	0	0	...	...	...	—	—	—	—	—
—Lada-2 Togliatti	CIS Div. II	...	19	7	26	...	...	...	...	—	—	—	—	—
96-97—Lada Togliatti	Russian	42	13	11	24	38	...	...	...	11	2	2	4	8
97-98—Lada Togliatti	Russian	44	8	9	17	63	...	...	...	—	—	—	—	—

BUZAK, MIKE G DEVILS

PERSONAL: Born February 10, 1973, in Edson, Alta. ... 6-3/197. ... Catches left. ... Name pronounced BYOO-zak.
HIGH SCHOOL: Queen Elizabeth (Edmonton).
COLLEGE: Michigan State.
TRANSACTIONS/CAREER NOTES: Selected by St. Louis Blues in seventh round (fifth Blues pick, 167th overall) of NHL entry draft (June 26, 1993). ... Signed as free agent by Los Angeles Kings (March 24, 1998). ... Signed as free agent by New Jersey Devils (July 16, 1998).
HONORS: Named to CCHA All-Star second team (1993-94 and 1994-95). ... Shared James Norris Trophy with Kay Whitmore (1997-98).

Season Team	League	REGULAR SEASON							PLAYOFFS					
		Gms.	Min.	W	L	T	GA	SO	Avg.	Gms.	Min.	W	L	GA	SO	Avg.
91-92—Michigan State	CCHA	7	311	4	0	0	22	0	4.24	—	—	—	—	—	—	—
92-93—Michigan State	CCHA	38	2090	22	10	2	102	0	2.93	—	—	—	—	—	—	—
93-94—Michigan State	CCHA	39	2297	21	12	5	104	2	2.72	—	—	—	—	—	—	—
94-95—Michigan State	CCHA	31	1797	17	10	3	94	0	3.14	—	—	—	—	—	—	—
95-96—Worcester	AHL	30	1671	9	10	5	85	0	3.05	—	—	—	—	—	—	—
96-97—Worcester	AHL	19	973	9	4	3	41	1	2.53	1	59	0	1	3	0	3.05
—Baton Rouge	ECHL	3	108	0	2	‡0	7	0	3.89	—	—	—	—	—	—	—
97-98—Long Beach	IHL	31	1763	18	6	‡5	58	6	1.97	5	216	0	3	11	0	3.06

BUZEK, PETR D STARS

PERSONAL: Born April 26, 1977, in Jihlava, Czechoslovakia. ... 6-0/205. ... Shoots left. ... Name pronounced BOO-zihk.
TRANSACTIONS/CAREER NOTES: Selected by Dallas Stars in third round (third Stars pick, 63rd overall) of NHL entry draft (July 8, 1995).

Season Team	League	REGULAR SEASON								PLAYOFFS				
		Gms.	G	A	Pts.	PIM	+/-	PP	SH	Gms.	G	A	Pts.	PIM
93-94—Jihlava	Czech Rep.	29	6	16	22	...	...	...	...	—	—	—	—	—
—Dukla Jihlava	Czech Rep.	3	0	0	0	...	...	...	...	—	—	—	—	—
94-95—Dukla Jihlava	Czech Rep.	43	2	5	7	...	...	...	...	2	0	0	0	...
95-96—Jihlava	Czech Rep.	Did not play.												
96-97—Michigan	IHL	67	4	6	10	48	...	...	...	—	—	—	—	—
97-98—Michigan	IHL	60	10	15	25	58	...	...	...	2	0	1	1	17
—Dallas	NHL	2	0	0	0	2	1	0	0	—	—	—	—	—
NHL Totals (1 year)		2	0	0	0	2	1	0	0					

BYLSMA, DAN   RW   KINGS

PERSONAL: Born September 19, 1970, in Grand Rapids, Mich. ... 6-2/215. ... Shoots left. ... Full Name: Daniel Brian Bylsma. ... Name pronounced BIGHLS-muh.
COLLEGE: Bowling Green State.
TRANSACTIONS/CAREER NOTES: Selected by Winnipeg Jets in fourth round (sixth Jets pick, 69th overall) of NHL entry draft (June 17, 1989). ... Signed as free agent by Los Angeles Kings (July 14, 1994). ... Injured knee (March 19, 1997); missed one game. ... Strained groin (April 3, 1997); missed one game.

Season Team	League	REGULAR SEASON								PLAYOFFS				
		Gms.	G	A	Pts.	PIM	+/-	PP	SH	Gms.	G	A	Pts.	PIM
87-88—St. Mary's Jr. B	OHA	40	30	39	69	33	...	...	...	—	—	—	—	—
88-89—Bowling Green	CCHA	39	4	7	11	16	...	...	...	—	—	—	—	—
89-90—Bowling Green	CCHA	44	13	17	30	32	...	...	...	—	—	—	—	—
90-91—Bowling Green	CCHA	40	9	12	21	48	...	...	...	—	—	—	—	—
91-92—Bowling Green	CCHA	34	11	14	25	24	...	...	...	—	—	—	—	—
92-93—Rochester	AHL	2	0	1	1	0	...	...	...	—	—	—	—	—
93-94—Albany	AHL	3	0	1	1	2	...	...	...	—	—	—	—	—
—Moncton	AHL	50	12	16	28	25	...	...	...	21	3	4	7	31
—Greensboro	ECHL	25	14	16	30	52	...	...	...	—	—	—	—	—
94-95—Phoenix	IHL	81	19	23	42	41	...	...	...	—	—	—	—	—
95-96—Phoenix	IHL	78	22	20	42	48	...	...	...	4	1	0	1	2
—Los Angeles	NHL	4	0	0	0	0	0	0	0	—	—	—	—	—
96-97—Los Angeles	NHL	79	3	6	9	32	-15	0	0	—	—	—	—	—
97-98—Long Beach	IHL	8	2	3	5	0	...	...	...	—	—	—	—	—
—Los Angeles	NHL	65	3	9	12	33	9	0	0	2	0	0	0	0
NHL Totals (3 years)		148	6	15	21	65	-6	0	0	2	0	0	0	0

CABANA, CLINT   D   CANUCKS

PERSONAL: Born April 26, 1978, in Bonnyville, Alta. ... 6-2/192. ... Shoots right.
TRANSACTIONS/CAREER NOTES: Selected by Vancouver Canucks in seventh round (sixth Canucks pick, 175th overall) of NHL entry draft (June 22, 1996).

Season Team	League	REGULAR SEASON								PLAYOFFS				
		Gms.	G	A	Pts.	PIM	+/-	PP	SH	Gms.	G	A	Pts.	PIM
94-95—Medicine Hat	WHL	49	0	1	1	68	...	...	...	—	—	—	—	—
95-96—Medicine Hat	WHL	71	1	11	12	158	...	...	...	5	0	1	1	33
96-97—Medicine Hat	WHL	4	0	1	1	10	...	...	...	—	—	—	—	—
—Edmonton	WHL	67	3	12	15	302	...	...	...	—	—	—	—	—
97-98—Edmonton	WHL	17	1	5	6	60	...	...	...	—	—	—	—	—
—Regina	WHL	34	1	1	2	140	...	...	...	8	1	0	1	16

CAIRNS, ERIC   D   RANGERS

PERSONAL: Born June 27, 1974, in Oakville, Ont. ... 6-6/230. ... Shoots left. ... Name pronounced KAIR-ihns.
TRANSACTIONS/CAREER NOTES: Selected by New York Rangers in third round (third Rangers pick, 72nd overall) of NHL entry draft (June 20, 1992).

Season Team	League	REGULAR SEASON								PLAYOFFS				
		Gms.	G	A	Pts.	PIM	+/-	PP	SH	Gms.	G	A	Pts.	PIM
90-91—Burlington Jr. B	OHA	37	5	16	21	120	...	...	...	—	—	—	—	—
91-92—Detroit	OHL	64	1	11	12	237	...	...	...	7	0	0	0	31
92-93—Detroit	OHL	64	3	13	16	194	...	...	...	15	0	3	3	24
93-94—Detroit	OHL	59	7	35	42	204	...	...	...	17	0	4	4	46
94-95—Birmingham	ECHL	11	1	3	4	49	...	...	...	—	—	—	—	—
—Binghamton	AHL	27	0	3	3	134	...	...	...	9	1	1	2	28
95-96—Binghamton	AHL	46	1	13	14	192	...	...	...	4	0	0	0	37
—Charlotte	ECHL	6	0	1	1	34	...	...	...	—	—	—	—	—
96-97—New York Rangers	NHL	40	0	1	1	147	-7	0	0	3	0	0	0	0
—Binghamton	AHL	10	1	1	2	96	...	...	...	—	—	—	—	—
97-98—New York Rangers	NHL	39	0	3	3	92	-3	0	0	—	—	—	—	—
—Hartford	AHL	7	1	2	3	43	...	...	...	—	—	—	—	—
NHL Totals (2 years)		79	0	4	4	239	-10	0	0	3	0	0	0	0

CALDER, KYLE   C   BLACKHAWKS

PERSONAL: Born January 5, 1979, in Mannville, Alta. ... 5-11/180. ... Shoots left.
TRANSACTIONS/CAREER NOTES: Selected by Chicago Blackhawks in fifth round (seventh Blackhawks pick, 130th overall) of NHL entry draft (June 21, 1997).

Season Team	League	REGULAR SEASON									PLAYOFFS				
		Gms.	G	A	Pts.	PIM	+/-	PP	SH		Gms.	G	A	Pts.	PIM
95-96—Regina	WHL	27	1	8	9	10	...	...	...		11	0	0	0	0
96-97—Regina	WHL	62	25	34	59	17	...	...	...		5	3	0	3	6
97-98—Regina	WHL	62	27	50	77	58	...	...	...		2	0	1	1	0

CAMPBELL, JIM   RW   BLUES

PERSONAL: Born February 3, 1973, in Worcester, Mass. ... 6-3/205. ... Shoots right. ... Full name: James Campbell.
HIGH SCHOOL: Lawrence Academy (Groton, Mass.), then Northwood School (Lake Placid, N.Y.).
TRANSACTIONS/CAREER NOTES: Selected by Montreal Canadiens in second round (second Canadiens pick, 28th overall) of NHL entry draft (June 22, 1991). ... Loaned by Canadiens to U.S. Olympic Team (September 26, 1993). ... Traded by Canadiens to Mighty Ducks of Anaheim for D Robert Dirk (January 21, 1996). ... Signed as free agent by St. Louis Blues (July 3, 1996). ... Strained thumb (February 25, 1997); missed 10 games. ... Reinjured thumb (April 6, 1997); missed remainder of regular season. ... Strained groin (December 6, 1997); missed one game. ... Injured left heel (January 20, 1998); missed five games.
HONORS: Named to NHL All-Rookie team (1996-97).

Season Team	League	REGULAR SEASON									PLAYOFFS				
		Gms.	G	A	Pts.	PIM	+/-	PP	SH		Gms.	G	A	Pts.	PIM
88-89—Lawrence Academy	Mass. H.S.	12	12	8	20	6	...	...	...		—	—	—	—	—
89-90—Lawrence Academy	Mass. H.S.	8	14	7	21	8	...	...	...		—	—	—	—	—
90-91—Northwood School	N.Y. H.S.	26	36	47	83	36	...	...	...		—	—	—	—	—
91-92—Hull	QMJHL	64	41	44	85	51	...	...	...		6	7	3	10	8
92-93—Hull	QMJHL	50	42	29	71	66	...	...	...		8	11	4	15	43
93-94—U.S. national team	Int'l	56	24	33	57	59	...	...	...		—	—	—	—	—
—U.S. Olympic Team	Int'l	8	0	0	0	6	...	...	...		—	—	—	—	—
—Fredericton	AHL	19	6	17	23	6	...	...	...		—	—	—	—	—
94-95—Fredericton	AHL	77	27	24	51	103	...	...	...		12	0	7	7	8
95-96—Fredericton	AHL	44	28	23	51	24	...	...	...		—	—	—	—	—
—Baltimore	AHL	16	13	7	20	8	...	...	...		12	7	5	12	10
—Anaheim	NHL	16	2	3	5	36	0	1	0		—	—	—	—	—
96-97—St. Louis	NHL	68	23	20	43	68	3	5	0		4	1	0	1	6
97-98—St. Louis	NHL	76	22	19	41	55	0	7	0		10	7	3	10	12
NHL Totals (3 years)		160	47	42	89	159	3	13	0		14	8	3	11	18

CARBONNEAU, GUY   C   STARS

PERSONAL: Born March 18, 1960, in Sept-Iles, Que. ... 5-11/184. ... Shoots right. ... Name pronounced GEE KAHR-buh-noh.
TRANSACTIONS/CAREER NOTES: Selected by Montreal Canadiens as underage junior in third round (fourth Canadiens pick, 44th overall) of NHL entry draft (August 9, 1979). ... Strained right knee ligaments (October 7, 1989); missed nine games. ... Broke nose (October 28, 1989). ... Suffered concussion (October 8, 1990). ... Fractured rib (January 13, 1992); missed six games. ... Injured elbow (March 2, 1992); missed one game. ... Suffered right knee tendinitis (October 1, 1992); missed five games. ... Broke finger (November 14, 1992); missed three games. ... Suffered knee tendinitis (February 4, 1993); missed 15 games. ... Suffered from the flu (February 11, 1994); missed one game. ... Traded by Canadiens to St. Louis Blues for C Jim Montgomery (August 19, 1994). ... Underwent knee surgery (March 31, 1995); missed six games. ... Traded by Blues to Dallas Stars for RW Paul Broten (October 2, 1995). ... Injured groin (October 17, 1995); missed five games. ... Strained groin (December 8, 1996); missed one game. ... Bruised forearm (March 31, 1997); missed two games. ... Sprained neck (October 14, 1997); missed one game. ... Strained back (October 25, 1997); missed three games.
HONORS: Named to QMJHL All-Star second team (1979-80). ... Won Frank J. Selke Trophy (1987-88, 1988-89 and 1991-92).
MISCELLANEOUS: Member of Stanley Cup championship team (1986 and 1993). ... Co-captain of Montreal Canadiens (1989-90). ... Captain of Canadiens (1991-92 through 1993-1994).
STATISTICAL PLATEAUS: Three-goal games: 1982-83 (1), 1993-94 (1). Total: 2.

Season Team	League	REGULAR SEASON									PLAYOFFS				
		Gms.	G	A	Pts.	PIM	+/-	PP	SH		Gms.	G	A	Pts.	PIM
76-77—Chicoutimi	QMJHL	59	9	20	29	8	...	...	...		4	1	0	1	0
77-78—Chicoutimi	QMJHL	70	28	55	83	60	...	...	...		—	—	—	—	—
78-79—Chicoutimi	QMJHL	72	62	79	141	47	...	...	...		4	2	1	3	4
79-80—Chicoutimi	QMJHL	72	72	110	182	66	...	...	...		12	9	15	24	28
—Nova Scotia	AHL	—	—	—	—	—	...	...	...		2	1	1	2	2
80-81—Montreal	NHL	2	0	1	1	0	0	0	0		—	—	—	—	—
—Nova Scotia	AHL	78	35	53	88	87	...	...	...		6	1	3	4	9
81-82—Nova Scotia	AHL	77	27	67	94	124	...	...	...		9	2	7	9	8
82-83—Montreal	NHL	77	18	29	47	68	18	0	5		3	0	0	0	2
83-84—Montreal	NHL	78	24	30	54	75	5	3	7		15	4	3	7	12
84-85—Montreal	NHL	79	23	34	57	43	28	0	4		12	4	3	7	8
85-86—Montreal	NHL	80	20	36	56	57	18	1	2		20	7	5	12	35
86-87—Montreal	NHL	79	18	27	45	68	9	0	0		17	3	8	11	20
87-88—Montreal	NHL	80	17	21	38	61	14	0	3		11	0	4	4	2
88-89—Montreal	NHL	79	26	30	56	44	37	1	2		21	4	5	9	10
89-90—Montreal	NHL	68	19	36	55	37	21	1	1		11	2	3	5	6
90-91—Montreal	NHL	78	20	24	44	63	-1	4	1		13	1	5	6	10
91-92—Montreal	NHL	72	18	21	39	39	2	1	1		11	1	1	2	6
92-93—Montreal	NHL	61	4	13	17	20	-9	0	1		20	3	3	6	10
93-94—Montreal	NHL	79	14	24	38	48	16	0	0		7	1	3	4	4
94-95—St. Louis	NHL	42	5	11	16	16	11	1	0		7	1	2	3	6
95-96—Dallas	NHL	71	8	15	23	38	-2	0	2		—	—	—	—	—
96-97—Dallas	NHL	73	5	16	21	36	9	0	1		7	0	1	1	0
97-98—Dallas	NHL	77	7	17	24	40	3	0	1		16	3	1	4	6
NHL Totals (17 years)		1175	246	385	631	753	179	12	31		191	34	47	81	143

CAREY, JIM   G   BRUINS

PERSONAL: Born May 31, 1974, in Dorchester, Mass. ... 6-2/205. ... Catches left. ... Brother of Paul Carey, first baseman in Baltimore Orioles organization (1990-95).
HIGH SCHOOL: Catholic Memorial (Boston).
COLLEGE: Wisconsin.
TRANSACTIONS/CAREER NOTES: Selected by Washington Capitals in second round (second Capitals pick, 32nd overall) of NHL entry draft (June 20, 1992). ... Traded by Capitals with C Jason Allison, C Anson Carter and third-round pick (RW Lee Goren) in 1997 draft to Boston Bruins for C Adam Oates, RW Rick Tocchet and G Bill Ranford (March 1, 1997). ... Injured shoulder and underwent surgery (January 29, 1998); missed remainder of season.
HONORS: Won WCHA Rookie of the Year Award (1992-93). ... Named to WCHA All-Star second team (1992-93). ... Named to WCHA All-Rookie team (1992-93). ... Named to NHL All-Rookie team (1994-95). ... Won Dudley (Red) Garrett Memorial Trophy (1994-95). ... Won Aldege (Baz) Bastien Trophy (1994-95). ... Named to AHL All-Star first team (1994-95). ... Won Vezina Trophy (1995-96). ... Named to NHL All-Star first team (1995-96).
MISCELLANEOUS: Holds Washington Capitals all-time record for goals-against average (2.37) and shutouts (14). ... Stopped penalty shot attempt (vs. Todd Elik, November 19, 1996). ... Allowed penalty shot goal (vs. Jeff Friesen, December 2, 1995; vs. Sami Kapanen, March 12, 1997).

					REGULAR SEASON							PLAYOFFS					
Season Team	League	Gms.	Min	W	L	T	GA	SO	Avg.	Gms.	Min.	W	L	GA	SO	Avg.
89-90—Catholic Memorial	Mass. H.S.	12	...	12	0	0	...	...	...	—	—	—	—	—	—	—
90-91—Catholic Memorial	Mass. H.S.	14	...	13	0	0	...	6	...	—	—	—	—	—	—	—
91-92—Catholic Memorial	Mass. H.S.	21	1108	19	2	0	29	6	1.57	—	—	—	—	—	—	—
92-93—Univ. of Wisconsin	WCHA	26	1525	15	8	1	78	1	3.07	—	—	—	—	—	—	—
93-94—Univ. of Wisconsin	WCHA	39	*2247	*24	13	1	114	1	*3.04	—	—	—	—	—	—	—
94-95—Portland	AHL	55	3281	30	14	11	151	*6	2.76	—	—	—	—	—	—	—
—Washington	NHL	28	1604	18	6	3	57	4	2.13	7	358	2	4	25	0	4.19
95-96—Washington	NHL	71	4069	35	24	9	153	*9	2.26	3	97	0	1	10	0	6.19
96-97—Washington	NHL	40	2293	17	18	3	105	1	2.75	—	—	—	—	—	—	—
—Boston	NHL	19	1004	5	13	0	64	0	3.82	—	—	—	—	—	—	—
97-98—Boston	NHL	10	496	3	2	1	24	2	2.90	—	—	—	—	—	—	—
—Providence	AHL	10	605	2	7	1	40	0	3.97	—	—	—	—	—	—	—
NHL Totals (4 years)		168	9466	78	63	16	403	16	2.55	10	455	2	5	35	0	4.62

CARKNER, TERRY   D   PANTHERS

PERSONAL: Born March 7, 1966, in Smith Falls, Ont. ... 6-3/210. ... Shoots left.
TRANSACTIONS/CAREER NOTES: Selected by New York Rangers as underage junior in first round (first Rangers pick, 14th overall) of NHL entry draft (June 9, 1984). ... Traded by Rangers with LW Jeff Jackson to Quebec Nordiques for LW John Ogrodnick and D David Shaw (September 30, 1987). ... Suspended 10 games by NHL for leaving bench during fight (January 24, 1988). ... Traded by Nordiques to Philadelphia Flyers for D Greg Smyth and third-round pick (G John Tanner) in 1989 draft (July 25, 1988). ... Underwent surgery on left knee (September 23, 1989); missed 15 games. ... Bruised ankle (March 1990). ... Bruised foot (November 23, 1991); missed two games. ... Bruised wrist (November 19, 1992); missed one game. ... Traded by Flyers to Detroit Red Wings for D Yves Racine and fourth-round pick (LW Sebastien Vallee) in 1994 draft (October 5, 1993). ... Injured left shoulder (March 19, 1994); missed 11 games. ... Did not play due to contract dispute (February 24-March 15, 1995). ... Signed as free agent by Florida Panthers (August 17, 1995). ... Sprained ankle (November 7, 1996); missed eight games. ... Sprained right ankle (September 29, 1997); missed first two games of season.
HONORS: Named to OHL All-Star second team (1984-85). ... Shared Max Kaminsky Trophy with Jeff Brown (1985-86). ... Named to OHL All-Star first team (1985-86).

				REGULAR SEASON						PLAYOFFS				
Season Team	League	Gms.	G	A	Pts.	PIM	+/-	PP	SH	Gms.	G	A	Pts.	PIM
82-83—Brockville	COJHL	47	8	32	40	94	...	...	...	—	—	—	—	—
83-84—Peterborough	OHL	66	4	21	25	91	...	...	...	8	0	6	6	13
84-85—Peterborough	OHL	64	14	47	61	125	...	...	...	17	2	10	12	11
85-86—Peterborough	OHL	54	12	32	44	106	...	...	...	16	1	7	8	17
86-87—New Haven	AHL	12	2	6	8	56	...	...	...	3	1	0	1	0
—New York Rangers	NHL	52	2	13	15	120	-1	0	0	1	0	0	0	0
87-88—Quebec	NHL	63	3	24	27	159	-8	2	0	—	—	—	—	—
88-89—Philadelphia	NHL	78	11	32	43	149	-6	2	1	19	1	5	6	28
89-90—Philadelphia	NHL	63	4	18	22	167	-8	1	0	—	—	—	—	—
90-91—Philadelphia	NHL	79	7	25	32	204	-15	6	0	—	—	—	—	—
91-92—Philadelphia	NHL	73	4	12	16	195	-14	0	1	—	—	—	—	—
92-93—Philadelphia	NHL	83	3	16	19	150	18	0	0	—	—	—	—	—
93-94—Detroit	NHL	68	1	6	7	130	13	0	0	7	0	0	0	4
94-95—Detroit	NHL	20	1	2	3	21	7	0	0	—	—	—	—	—
95-96—Florida	NHL	73	3	10	13	80	10	1	0	22	0	4	4	10
96-97—Florida	NHL	70	0	14	14	96	-4	0	0	5	0	0	0	6
97-98—Florida	NHL	74	1	7	8	63	6	0	0	—	—	—	—	—
NHL Totals (12 years)		796	40	179	219	1534	-2	12	2	54	1	9	10	48

CARNEY, KEITH   D   COYOTES

PERSONAL: Born February 3, 1970, in Providence, R.I. ... 6-2/205. ... Shoots left. ... Full name: Keith Edward Carney.
COLLEGE: Maine.
TRANSACTIONS/CAREER NOTES: Selected by Buffalo Sabres in fourth round (third Sabres pick, 76th overall) of NHL entry draft (June 11, 1988). ... Traded by Sabres to Chicago Blackhawks for D Craig Muni (October 27, 1993). ... Traded by Blackhawks with RW Jim Cummins to Phoenix Coyotes for C Chad Kilger and D Jayson More (March 4, 1998).
HONORS: Named to Hockey East All-Rookie team (1988-89). ... Named to NCAA All-America East second team (1989-90). ... Named to Hockey East All-Star second team (1989-90). ... Named to NCAA All-America East first team (1990-91). ... Named to Hockey East All-Star first team (1990-91).

C

Season Team	League	Gms.	G	A	Pts.	PIM	+/-	PP	SH	Gms.	G	A	Pts.	PIM
		REGULAR SEASON								**PLAYOFFS**				
88-89—Univ. of Maine	Hockey East	40	4	22	26	24	...	...	...	—	—	—	—	—
89-90—Univ. of Maine	Hockey East	41	3	41	44	43	...	...	...	—	—	—	—	—
90-91—Univ. of Maine	Hockey East	40	7	49	56	38	...	...	...	—	—	—	—	—
91-92—U.S. national team	Int'l	49	2	17	19	16	...	...	...	—	—	—	—	—
—Rochester	AHL	24	1	10	11	2	...	...	...	2	0	2	2	0
—Buffalo	NHL	14	1	2	3	18	-3	1	0	7	0	3	3	0
92-93—Buffalo	NHL	30	2	4	6	55	3	0	0	8	0	3	3	6
—Rochester	AHL	41	5	21	26	32	...	...	...	—	—	—	—	—
93-94—Louisville	ECHL	15	1	4	5	14	...	...	...	—	—	—	—	—
—Buffalo	NHL	7	1	3	4	4	-1	0	0	—	—	—	—	—
—Indianapolis	IHL	28	0	14	14	20	...	...	...	—	—	—	—	—
—Chicago....................	NHL	30	3	5	8	35	15	0	0	6	0	1	1	4
94-95—Chicago.................	NHL	18	1	0	1	11	-1	0	0	4	0	1	1	0
95-96—Chicago.................	NHL	82	5	14	19	94	31	1	0	10	0	3	3	4
96-97—Chicago.................	NHL	81	3	15	18	62	26	0	0	6	1	1	2	2
97-98—Chicago.................	NHL	60	2	13	15	73	-7	0	1	—	—	—	—	—
—U.S. Olympic Team	Int'l	4	0	0	0	2	...	...	...	—	—	—	—	—
—Phoenix....................	NHL	20	1	6	7	18	5	1	0	6	0	0	0	4
NHL Totals (7 years)...........		342	19	62	81	370	68	3	1	47	1	12	13	20

C

CARPENTER, BOB   C   DEVILS

PERSONAL: Born July 13, 1963, in Beverly, Mass. ... 6-0/200. ... Shoots left. ... Full name: Robert E. Carpenter Jr.
HIGH SCHOOL: St. John's Prep (Danvers, Mass.).
TRANSACTIONS/CAREER NOTES: Selected by Washington Capitals as underage junior in first round (first Capitals pick, third overall) of NHL entry draft (June 10, 1981). ... Traded by Capitals with second-round pick in 1989 draft (RW Jason Prosofsky) to New York Rangers for C Mike Ridley, C Kelly Miller and RW Bobby Crawford (January 1, 1987). ... Traded by Rangers with D Tom Laidlaw to Los Angeles Kings for C Marcel Dionne, C Jeff Crossman and third-round pick in 1989 draft (March 10, 1987). ... Tore rotator cuff (January 1988). ... Broke right thumb and wrist (December 31, 1988). ... Traded by Kings to Boston Bruins for C Steve Kasper and LW Jay Miller (January 23, 1989). ... Tore ligaments of right wrist (April 1989). ... Injured left knee (October 1990). ... Suffered multiple fracture of left kneecap (December 8, 1990); missed remainder of season. ... Injured left wrist and suffered stiffness in knee (April 5, 1991). ... Strained calf (March 19, 1992). ... Signed as free agent by Capitals (June 30, 1992). ... Signed as free agent by New Jersey Devils (September 30, 1993). ... Sprained ankle (February 11, 1995); missed one game. ... Suffered charley horse (April 20, 1995); missed last five games of season and first three games of playoffs. ... Suffered cut to leg (September 28, 1995); missed two games. ... Reinjured cut to leg (October 14, 1995); missed five games. ... Reinjured cut to leg (October 31, 1995); missed 16 games. ... Suffered from the flu (December 6, 1995); missed two games. ... Bruised arm (March 2, 1996); missed one game. ... Suffered from the flu (December 10, 1996); missed two games. ... Bruised shoulder (December 20, 1996); missed eight games. ... Strained neck (February 15, 1997); missed five games. ... Suffered from the flu (April 8, 1997); missed two games. ... Bruised knee (November 22, 1997); missed one game. ... Fractured foot (January 22, 1998); missed eight games. ... Suffered stiff neck (March 10, 1998); missed two games.
HONORS: Played in NHL All-Star Game (1985).
MISCELLANEOUS: Member of Stanley Cup championship team (1995). ... Failed to score on a penalty shot (vs. Billy Smith, April 14, 1985).
STATISTICAL PLATEAUS: Three-goal games: 1987-88 (1), 1989-90 (1). Total: 2. ... Four-goal games: 1981-82 (1). ... Total hat tricks: 3.

Season Team	League	Gms.	G	A	Pts.	PIM	+/-	PP	SH	Gms.	G	A	Pts.	PIM
		REGULAR SEASON								**PLAYOFFS**				
79-80—St. John's Prep	Mass. H.S.	...	28	37	65	...	...	...	...	—	—	—	—	—
80-81—St. John's Prep	Mass. H.S.	18	14	24	38	...	...	...	...	—	—	—	—	—
81-82—Washington	NHL	80	32	35	67	69	-23	7	1	—	—	—	—	—
82-83—Washington	NHL	80	32	37	69	64	0	14	0	4	1	0	1	2
83-84—Washington	NHL	80	28	40	68	51	...	...	...	8	2	1	3	25
84-85—Washington	NHL	80	53	42	95	87	20	12	0	5	1	4	5	8
85-86—Washington	NHL	80	27	29	56	105	-12	7	0	9	5	4	9	12
86-87—Washington	NHL	22	5	7	12	21	-7	4	0	—	—	—	—	—
—New York Rangers......	NHL	28	2	8	10	20	-12	1	0	—	—	—	—	—
—Los Angeles................	NHL	10	2	3	5	6	-8	0	0	5	1	2	3	2
87-88—Los Angeles.............	NHL	71	19	33	52	84	-21	10	0	5	1	1	2	0
88-89—Los Angeles.............	NHL	39	11	15	26	16	3	3	0	—	—	—	—	—
—Boston	NHL	18	5	9	14	10	4	1	0	8	1	1	2	4
89-90—Boston	NHL	80	25	31	56	97	-3	5	0	21	4	6	10	39
90-91—Boston	NHL	29	8	8	16	22	2	2	0	1	0	1	1	2
91-92—Boston	NHL	60	25	23	48	46	-3	6	1	8	0	1	1	6
92-93—Washington	NHL	68	11	17	28	65	-16	2	0	6	1	4	5	6
93-94—New Jersey	NHL	76	10	23	33	51	7	0	2	20	1	7	8	20
94-95—New Jersey	NHL	41	5	11	16	19	-1	0	0	17	1	4	5	6
95-96—New Jersey	NHL	52	5	5	10	14	-10	0	0	—	—	—	—	—
96-97—New Jersey	NHL	62	4	15	19	14	6	0	1	10	1	2	3	2
97-98—New Jersey	NHL	66	9	9	18	22	-4	0	1	6	1	0	1	0
NHL Totals (17 years)..........		1122	318	400	718	883	-78	74	7	133	21	38	59	134

CARTER, ANSON   LW   BRUINS

PERSONAL: Born June 6, 1974, in Toronto. ... 6-1/185. ... Shoots right.
COLLEGE: Michigan State.
TRANSACTIONS/CAREER NOTES: Selected by Quebec Nordiques in 10th round (10th Nordiques pick, 220th overall) of NHL entry draft (June 20, 1992). ... Nordiques franchise moved to Colorado and renamed Avalanche for 1995-96 season (June 21, 1995). ... Traded by Avalanche to Washington Capitals for fourth-round pick (D Ben Storey) in 1996 entry draft (April 3, 1996). ... Signed as free agent by Washington Capitals (July 1, 1996). ... Sprained thumb (February 7, 1997); missed five games. ... Traded by Capitals with G Jim Carey, C Jason Allison and third-round pick (RW Lee Goren) in 1997 draft to Boston Bruins for C Adam Oates, RW Rick Tocchet and G Bill Ranford (March 1, 1997). ... Strained

hip flexor (October 7, 1997); missed two games. ... Suffered from upper respiratory infection (November 22, 1997); missed two games.
HONORS: Named to CCHA All-Star first team (1993-94 and 1994-95). ... Named to NCAA All-America West second team (1994-95). ... Named to CCHA All-Star second team (1995-96).

Season Team	League	REGULAR SEASON								PLAYOFFS				
		Gms.	G	A	Pts.	PIM	+/-	PP	SH	Gms.	G	A	Pts.	PIM
91-92—Wexford	OHA Jr. A	42	18	22	40	24	...	...	...	—	—	—	—	—
92-93—Michigan State	CCHA	36	19	11	30	20	...	...	...	—	—	—	—	—
93-94—Michigan State	CCHA	39	30	24	54	36	...	...	...	—	—	—	—	—
94-95—Michigan State	CCHA	39	34	17	51	40	...	...	...	—	—	—	—	—
95-96—Michigan State	CCHA	42	23	20	43	36	...	...	...	—	—	—	—	—
96-97—Washington	NHL	19	3	2	5	7	0	1	0	—	—	—	—	—
—Portland	AHL	27	19	19	38	11	...	...	...	—	—	—	—	—
—Boston	NHL	19	8	5	13	2	-7	1	1	—	—	—	—	—
97-98—Boston	NHL	78	16	27	43	31	7	6	0	6	1	1	2	0
NHL Totals (2 years)		116	27	34	61	40	0	8	1	6	1	1	2	0

CARTER, SHAWN — LW

PERSONAL: Born April 16, 1973, in Eagle River, Wis. ... 6-2/210. ... Shoots left.
COLLEGE: Wisconsin.
TRANSACTIONS/CAREER NOTES: Signed as free agent by Toronto Maple Leafs (February 10, 1997).

Season Team	League	REGULAR SEASON								PLAYOFFS				
		Gms.	G	A	Pts.	PIM	+/-	PP	SH	Gms.	G	A	Pts.	PIM
92-93—Univ. of Wisconsin	WCHA	5	1	0	1	4	...	...	...	—	—	—	—	—
93-94—Univ. of Wisconsin	WCHA	16	2	2	4	24	...	...	...	—	—	—	—	—
94-95—Univ. of Wisconsin	WCHA	43	15	13	28	98	...	...	...	—	—	—	—	—
95-96—Univ. of Wisconsin	WCHA	40	17	28	45	50	...	...	...	—	—	—	—	—
96-97—Orlando	IHL	53	22	25	47	40	...	...	...	—	—	—	—	—
—St. John's	AHL	18	5	6	11	15	...	...	...	7	1	2	3	6
97-98—St. John's	AHL	80	14	16	30	117	...	...	...	4	1	0	1	4

C

CASSELS, ANDREW — C — FLAMES

PERSONAL: Born July 23, 1969, in Mississauga, Ont. ... 6-1/185. ... Shoots left. ... Name pronounced KAS-uhls.
TRANSACTIONS/CAREER NOTES: Broke wrist (January 1986). ... Selected by Montreal Canadiens as underage junior in first round (first Canadiens pick, 17th overall) of NHL entry draft (June 13, 1987). ... Sprained left knee ligaments (September 1988). ... Separated right shoulder (November 22, 1989); missed 10 games. ... Traded by Canadiens to Hartford Whalers for second-round pick (RW Valeri Bure) in 1992 draft (September 17, 1991). ... Bruised kneecap (December 4, 1993); missed one game. ... Suffered facial injury (March 13, 1994); missed four games. ... Bruised forearm (December 2, 1995); missed one game. ... Suffered charley horse (March 6, 1997); missed one game. ... Whalers franchise moved to North Carolina and renamed Carolina Hurricanes for 1997-98 season; NHL approved move on June 25, 1997. ... Traded by Hurricanes with G Jean-Sebastien Giguere to Calgary Flames for LW Gary Roberts and G Trevor Kidd (August 25, 1997). ... Strained rib cage (October 9, 1997); missed one game.
HONORS: Won Emms Family Award (1986-87). ... Won Red Tilson Trophy (1987-88). ... Won Eddie Powers Memorial Trophy (1987-88). ... Won William Hanley Trophy (1987-88). ... Named to OHL All-Star first team (1987-88 and 1988-89).
MISCELLANEOUS: Captain of Hartford Whalers (1994-95). ... Scored on a penalty shot (vs. Ron Hextall, April 6, 1994).

Season Team	League	REGULAR SEASON								PLAYOFFS				
		Gms.	G	A	Pts.	PIM	+/-	PP	SH	Gms.	G	A	Pts.	PIM
85-86—Bramalea Jr. B	OHA	33	18	25	43	26	...	...	...	—	—	—	—	—
86-87—Ottawa	OHL	66	26	66	92	28	...	...	...	11	5	9	14	7
87-88—Ottawa	OHL	61	48	*103	*151	39	...	...	...	16	8	*24	†32	13
88-89—Ottawa	OHL	56	37	97	134	66	...	...	...	12	5	10	15	10
89-90—Sherbrooke	AHL	55	22	45	67	25	...	...	...	12	2	11	13	6
—Montreal	NHL	6	2	0	2	2	1	0	0	—	—	—	—	—
90-91—Montreal	NHL	54	6	19	25	20	2	1	0	8	0	2	2	2
91-92—Hartford	NHL	67	11	30	41	18	3	2	2	7	2	4	6	6
92-93—Hartford	NHL	84	21	64	85	62	-11	8	3	—	—	—	—	—
93-94—Hartford	NHL	79	16	42	58	37	-21	8	1	—	—	—	—	—
94-95—Hartford	NHL	46	7	30	37	18	-3	1	0	—	—	—	—	—
95-96—Hartford	NHL	81	20	43	63	39	8	6	0	—	—	—	—	—
96-97—Hartford	NHL	81	22	44	66	46	-16	8	0	—	—	—	—	—
97-98—Calgary	NHL	81	17	27	44	32	-7	6	1	—	—	—	—	—
NHL Totals (9 years)		579	122	299	421	274	-44	40	7	15	2	6	8	8

CASSIVI, FREDERIC — G — SENATORS

PERSONAL: Born June 12, 1975, in Sorel, Que. ... 6-4/205. ... Catches left. ... Name pronounced kuh-SIH-vee.
TRANSACTIONS/CAREER NOTES: Selected by Ottawa Senators in ninth round (seventh Senators pick, 210th overall) of NHL entry draft (June 29, 1994).

Season Team	League	REGULAR SEASON							PLAYOFFS					
		Gms.	Min	W	L	T	GA	SO	Avg.	Gms.	Min.	W	L	GA	SO	Avg.
93-94—St. Hyacinthe	QMJHL	35	1751	15	13	3	127	1	4.35	0	0	0	0	0	0	—
94-95—St. Jean	QMJHL	43	2383	21	18	1	160	1	4.03	5	258	2	3	18	0	4.19
95-96—Prin. Edward Island	AHL	41	2346	20	14	3	128	1	3.27	5	317	2	3	24	0	4.54
—Thunder Bay	Col.HL	12	714	6	4	2	51	0	4.29	—	—	—	—	—	—	—
96-97—Syracuse	AHL	55	3069	23	22	8	164	2	3.21	1	60	0	1	3	0	3.00
97-98—Worcester	AHL	45	2594	20	22	2	140	1	3.24	6	326	3	3	18	0	3.31

CECH, VRATISLAV D PANTHERS

PERSONAL: Born January 28, 1979, in Tabor, Czechoslovakia. ... 6-3/196. ... Shoots left. ... Name pronounced CHEHK.
TRANSACTIONS/CAREER NOTES: Selected by Florida Panthers in third round (third Panthers pick, 56th overall) of NHL entry draft (June 21, 1997).

		REGULAR SEASON								PLAYOFFS				
Season Team	League	Gms.	G	A	Pts.	PIM	+/-	PP	SH	Gms.	G	A	Pts.	PIM
95-96—Kometa Brno Jrs........	Czech Rep.	37	10	13	23	...	...	...	...	—	—	—	—	—
96-97—Kitchener..................	OHL	57	5	19	24	72	...	...	...	13	1	2	3	12
97-98—Kitchener..................	OHL	63	9	33	42	66	...	...	...	6	2	2	4	13

CERVEN, MARTIN C FLYERS

PERSONAL: Born March 7, 1977, in Trencin, Czechoslovakia. ... 6-4/200. ... Shoots left. ... Name pronounced SAIR-vihn.
TRANSACTIONS/CAREER NOTES: Selected by Edmonton Oilers in seventh round (sixth Oilers pick, 161st overall) of NHL entry draft (July 8, 1995). ... Rights traded by Oilers to Philadelphia Flyers for seventh-round pick (C Chad Hinz) in 1997 draft (May 28, 1997).

		REGULAR SEASON								PLAYOFFS				
Season Team	League	Gms.	G	A	Pts.	PIM	+/-	PP	SH	Gms.	G	A	Pts.	PIM
94-95—Dukla Trencin Jrs........	Slovakia	22	8	3	11	...	...	...	...	—	—	—	—	—
95-96—Spokane....................	WHL	40	9	9	18	42	...	...	...	—	—	—	—	—
—Seattle........................	WHL	27	6	14	20	10	...	...	...	5	1	2	3	0
96-97—Seattle....................	WHL	72	27	25	52	64	...	...	...	15	2	6	8	14
97-98—Philadelphia..............	AHL	50	7	11	18	27	...	...	...	8	1	2	3	2

CHABOT, FREDERIC G KINGS

PERSONAL: Born February 12, 1968, in Hebertville, Que. ... 5-11/175. ... Catches right. ... Name pronounced shuh-BAHT.
TRANSACTIONS/CAREER NOTES: Selected by New Jersey Devils in 10th round (10th Devils pick, 192nd overall) of NHL entry draft (June 21, 1986). ... Signed as free agent by Montreal Canadiens (January 16, 1990). ... Selected by Tampa Bay Lightning in NHL expansion draft (June 18, 1992). ... Traded by Lightning to Canadiens for G Jean-Claude Bergeron (June 18, 1992). ... Traded by Canadiens to Philadelphia Flyers for future considerations (February 21, 1994). ... Signed as free agent by Florida Panthers (August 15, 1994). ... Signed as free agent by Los Angeles Kings (September 5, 1997). ... Sprained right knee (March 10, 1998); missed seven games. ... Selected by Nashville Predators in NHL expansion draft (June 26, 1998). ... Claimed on waivers by Kings (July 20, 1998).
HONORS: Named to Memorial Cup All-Star team (1981-82). ... Named to WHL (East) All-Star first team (1988-89). ... Won Aldege (Baz) Bastien Trophy (1993-94). ... Named to IHL All-Star second team (1995-96). ... Won James Gatschene Memorial Trophy (1996-97). ... Named to IHL All-Star first team (1996-97).
STATISTICAL NOTES: Member of Stanley Cup championship team (1993).

		REGULAR SEASON								PLAYOFFS						
Season Team	League	Gms.	Min	W	L	T	GA	SO	Avg.	Gms.	Min.	W	L	GA	SO	Avg.
86-87—Drummondville	QMJHL	*62	*3508	31	29	0	293	1	5.01	8	481	2	6	40	0	4.99
87-88—Drummondville	QMJHL	58	3276	27	24	4	237	1	4.34	*16	1019	10	6	56	†1	*3.30
88-89—Moose Jaw..................	WHL	26	1385	...	...	...	114	1	4.94	—	—	—	—	—	—	—
—Prince Albert................	WHL	28	1572	...	...	...	88	1	3.36	4	199	1	1	16	0	4.82
89-90—Fort Wayne.................	IHL	23	1208	6	13	‡3	87	1	4.32	—	—	—	—	—	—	—
—Sherbrooke	AHL	2	119	1	1	0	8	0	4.03	—	—	—	—	—	—	—
90-91—Montreal....................	NHL	3	108	0	0	1	6	0	3.33	—	—	—	—	—	—	—
—Fredericton..................	AHL	35	1800	9	15	5	122	0	4.07	—	—	—	—	—	—	—
91-92—Winston-Salem	ECHL	25	1449	15	7	‡2	71	0	*2.94	—	—	—	—	—	—	—
—Fredericton..................	AHL	30	1761	17	9	4	79	2	*2.69	7	457	3	4	20	0	2.63
92-93—Fredericton................	AHL	45	2544	22	17	4	141	0	3.33	4	261	1	3	16	0	3.68
—Montreal.....................	NHL	1	40	0	0	0	1	0	1.50	—	—	—	—	—	—	—
93-94—Fredericton................	AHL	3	143	0	1	1	12	0	5.03	—	—	—	—	—	—	—
—Las Vegas...................	IHL	2	110	1	1	‡1	5	0	2.73	—	—	—	—	—	—	—
—Montreal.....................	NHL	1	60	0	1	0	5	0	5.00	—	—	—	—	—	—	—
—Hershey.....................	AHL	31	1607	13	6	7	75	2	*2.80	11	665	7	4	32	0	2.89
—Philadelphia.................	NHL	4	70	0	1	1	5	0	4.29	—	—	—	—	—	—	—
94-95—Cincinnati..................	IHL	48	2622	25	12	‡7	128	1	2.93	5	326	3	2	16	0	2.94
95-96—Cincinnati..................	IHL	38	2147	23	9	‡4	88	3	*2.46	14	854	9	5	37	1	2.60
96-97—Houston....................	IHL	*72	*4265	*39	26	‡7	*180	*7	2.53	13	777	8	5	34	†2	2.63
97-98—Los Angeles	NHL	12	554	3	3	2	29	0	3.14	—	—	—	—	—	—	—
—Houston	IHL	22	1237	12	7	‡2	46	1	2.23	4	239	1	3	11	0	2.76
NHL Totals (4 years)............		21	832	3	5	4	46	0	3.32							

CHAMBERS, SHAWN D STARS

PERSONAL: Born October 11, 1966, in Royal Oak, Mich. ... 6-2/200. ... Shoots left. ... Full name: Shawn Randall Chambers.
COLLEGE: Alaska-Fairbanks.
TRANSACTIONS/CAREER NOTES: Selected by Minnesota North Stars in NHL supplemental draft (June 13, 1987). ... Dislocated shoulder (February 1988). ... Separated right shoulder (September 1988). ... Injured left knee (September 11, 1990); missed first 11 games of season. ... Fractured left kneecap (December 5, 1990); missed three months. ... Underwent surgery to left knee to remove piece of loose cartilage (May 1991). ... Traded by North Stars to Washington Capitals for C Trent Klatt and LW Steve Maltais (June 21, 1991). ... Suffered sore knee (October 1991); missed first 47 games of season. ... Reinjured knee (January 26, 1992); missed remainder of season. ... Underwent arthroscopic knee surgery (February 4, 1992). ... Selected by Tampa Bay Lightning in NHL expansion draft (June 18, 1992). ... Underwent arthroscopic knee surgery (October 9, 1992); missed 14 games. ... Underwent arthroscopic knee surgery (October 21, 1993); missed 14 games. ... Injured shoulder (November 13, 1993); missed two games. ... Suffered facial cuts (January 2, 1994); missed one game. ... Suffered strep throat (February 7, 1995); missed one game. ... Traded by Lightning with RW Danton Cole to New Jersey Devils for C Alexander Semak and

RW Ben Hankinson (March 14, 1995). ... Suffered charley horse (November 14, 1995); missed one game. ... Bruised shoulder (December 6, 1995); missed three games. ... Broke right hand (March 13, 1996); missed 13 games. ... Bruised right knee (November 7, 1996); missed three games. ... Injured hip (March 19, 1997); missed one game. ... Signed as free agent by Dallas Stars (July 3, 1997). ... Fractured hand (October 1, 1997); missed eight games. ... Fractured thumb (November 5, 1997); missed nine games. ... Bruised hand (March 12, 1998); missed one game. ... Bruised hand (March 18, 1998); missed seven games.
MISCELLANEOUS: Member of Stanley Cup championship team (1995).

Season Team	League	REGULAR SEASON								PLAYOFFS				
		Gms.	G	A	Pts.	PIM	+/-	PP	SH	Gms.	G	A	Pts.	PIM
85-86—Alaska-Fairbanks	GWHC	25	15	21	36	34	...	...	...	—	—	—	—	—
86-87—Alaska-Fairbanks	GWHC	17	11	19	30	...	...	...	...	—	—	—	—	—
—Seattle	WHL	28	8	25	33	58	...	...	...	—	—	—	—	—
—Fort Wayne	IHL	12	2	6	8	0	...	...	...	10	1	4	5	5
87-88—Minnesota	NHL	19	1	7	8	21	-6	1	0	—	—	—	—	—
—Kalamazoo	IHL	19	1	6	7	22	...	...	...	—	—	—	—	—
88-89—Minnesota	NHL	72	5	19	24	80	-4	1	2	3	0	2	2	0
89-90—Minnesota	NHL	78	8	18	26	81	-2	0	1	7	2	1	3	10
90-91—Minnesota	NHL	29	1	3	4	24	2	0	0	23	0	7	7	16
—Kalamazoo	IHL	3	1	1	2	0	...	...	...	—	—	—	—	—
91-92—Baltimore	AHL	5	2	3	5	9	...	...	...	—	—	—	—	—
—Washington	NHL	2	0	0	0	2	-3	0	0	—	—	—	—	—
92-93—Atlanta	IHL	6	0	2	2	18	...	...	...	—	—	—	—	—
—Tampa Bay	NHL	55	10	29	39	36	-21	5	0	—	—	—	—	—
93-94—Tampa Bay	NHL	66	11	23	34	23	-6	6	1	—	—	—	—	—
94-95—Tampa Bay	NHL	24	2	12	14	6	0	1	0	—	—	—	—	—
—New Jersey	NHL	21	2	5	7	6	2	1	0	20	4	5	9	2
95-96—New Jersey	NHL	64	2	21	23	18	1	2	0	—	—	—	—	—
96-97—New Jersey	NHL	73	4	17	21	19	17	1	0	10	1	6	7	6
97-98—Dallas	NHL	57	2	22	24	26	11	1	1	14	0	3	3	20
NHL Totals (11 years)		560	48	176	224	342	-9	19	5	77	7	24	31	54

CHARA, ZDENO   D   ISLANDERS

PERSONAL: Born March 18, 1977, in Trencin, Czechoslovakia. ... 6-9/255. ... Shoots left. ... Name pronounced zuh-DAY-yoh CHAH-ruh.
TRANSACTIONS/CAREER NOTES: Selected by New York Islanders in third round (third Islanders pick, 56th overall) of NHL entry draft (June 22, 1996).

Season Team	League	REGULAR SEASON								PLAYOFFS				
		Gms.	G	A	Pts.	PIM	+/-	PP	SH	Gms.	G	A	Pts.	PIM
94-95—Dukla Trencin Jrs.	Slovakia	2	0	0	0	2	...	...	...	—	—	—	—	—
95-96—Dukla Trencin Jrs.	Slovakia	22	1	13	14	80	...	...	...	—	—	—	—	—
—HC Piestany	Slovakia Div. II	10	1	3	4	10	...	...	...	—	—	—	—	—
—Sparta Praha Jrs.	Czech Rep.	15	1	2	3	42	...	...	...	—	—	—	—	—
—Sparta Praha	Czech Rep.	1	0	0	0	0	...	...	...	—	—	—	—	—
96-97—Prince George	WHL	49	3	19	22	120	...	...	...	15	1	7	8	45
97-98—Kentucky	AHL	48	4	9	13	125	...	...	...	1	0	0	0	4
—New York Islanders	NHL	25	0	1	1	50	1	0	0	—	—	—	—	—
NHL Totals (1 year)		25	0	1	1	50	1	0	0					

CHARPENTIER, SEBASTIEN   G   CAPITALS

PERSONAL: Born April 18, 1977, in Drummondville, Que. ... 5-9/161. ... Catches left. ... Name pronounced SHAHR-pihnt-yay.
TRANSACTIONS/CAREER NOTES: Selected by Washington Capitals in fourth round (fourth Capitals pick, 93rd overall) of NHL entry draft (July 8, 1995).
HONORS: Won ECHL Playoff MVP Award (1997-98).

Season Team	League	REGULAR SEASON								PLAYOFFS						
		Gms.	Min.	W	L	T	GA	SO	Avg.	Gms.	Min.	W	L	GA	SO	Avg.
94-95—Laval	QMJHL	41	2152	25	12	1	99	2	2.76	16	886	9	4	45	0	3.05
95-96—Laval	QMJHL	18	938	4	10	0	97	0	6.20	—	—	—	—	—	—	—
—Val-d'Or	QMJHL	33	1906	21	9	1	87	1	2.74	13	778	7	5	47	0	3.62
96-97—Shawinigan	QMJHL	*62	*3474	*37	17	4	176	1	3.04	4	195	2	1	13	0	4.00
97-98—Hampton Roads	ECHL	43	2388	20	16	‡6	114	0	2.86	18	1183	14	4	38	1	1.93
—Portland	AHL	4	230	1	3	0	10	0	2.61	—	—	—	—	—	—	—

CHARRON, ERIC   D   FLAMES

PERSONAL: Born January 14, 1970, in Verdun, Que. ... 6-3/195. ... Shoots left. ... Name pronounced sha-ROH.
TRANSACTIONS/CAREER NOTES: Selected by Montreal Canadiens in first round (first Canadiens pick, 20th overall) of NHL entry draft (June 11, 1988). ... Traded by Canadiens with D Alain Cote and future considerations to Tampa Bay Lightning for D Rob Ramage (March 20, 1993); Canadiens sent D Donald Dufresne to Lightning to complete deal (June 18, 1993). ... Traded by Lightning to Washington Capitals for seventh-round pick (RW Eero Somervuori) in 1997 draft (November 17, 1995). ... Injured knee prior to 1996-97 season; missed first six games of season. ... Bruised ribs (December 13, 1996); missed one game. ... Traded by Capitals to Calgary Flames for future considerations (September 4, 1997).

Season Team	League	REGULAR SEASON								PLAYOFFS				
		Gms.	G	A	Pts.	PIM	+/-	PP	SH	Gms.	G	A	Pts.	PIM
87-88—Trois-Rivieres	QMJHL	67	3	13	16	135	...	...	...	—	—	—	—	—
88-89—Trois-Rivieres	QMJHL	38	2	16	18	111	...	...	...	—	—	—	—	—
—Verdun	QMJHL	28	2	15	17	66	...	...	...	—	—	—	—	—
—Sherbrooke	AHL	1	0	0	0	0	...	...	...	—	—	—	—	—
89-90—St. Hyacinthe	QMJHL	68	13	38	51	152	...	...	...	11	3	4	7	67
—Sherbrooke	AHL	—	—	—	—	—	...	...	...	2	0	0	0	0

Season Team	League	REGULAR SEASON								PLAYOFFS				
		Gms.	G	A	Pts.	PIM	+/-	PP	SH	Gms.	G	A	Pts.	PIM
90-91—Fredericton	AHL	71	1	11	12	108	...	...	...	2	1	0	1	29
91-92—Fredericton	AHL	59	2	11	13	98	...	...	...	6	1	0	1	4
92-93—Fredericton	AHL	54	3	13	16	93	...	...	...	—	—	—	—	—
—Montreal	NHL	3	0	0	0	2	0	0	0	—	—	—	—	—
—Atlanta	IHL	11	0	2	2	12	...	...	...	3	0	1	1	6
93-94—Atlanta	IHL	66	5	18	23	144	...	...	...	14	1	4	5	28
—Tampa Bay	NHL	4	0	0	0	2	0	0	0	—	—	—	—	—
94-95—Tampa Bay	NHL	45	1	4	5	26	1	0	0	—	—	—	—	—
95-96—Tampa Bay	NHL	14	0	0	0	18	-6	0	0	—	—	—	—	—
—Portland	AHL	45	0	8	8	88	...	...	...	20	1	1	2	33
—Washington	NHL	4	0	1	1	4	3	0	0	6	0	0	0	8
96-97—Washington	NHL	25	1	1	2	20	1	0	0	—	—	—	—	—
—Portland	AHL	29	6	8	14	55	...	...	...	5	0	3	3	0
97-98—Saint John	AHL	56	8	20	28	136	...	...	...	20	1	7	8	55
—Calgary	NHL	2	0	0	0	4	0	0	0	—	—	—	—	—
NHL Totals (6 years)		97	2	6	8	76	-1	0	0	6	0	0	0	8

CHASE, KELLY   RW   BLUES

C

PERSONAL: Born October 25, 1967, in Porcupine Plain, Sask. ... 5-11/193. ... Shoots right. ... Full name: Kelly Wayne Chase.

HIGH SCHOOL: Porcupine Plain (Sask.).

TRANSACTIONS/CAREER NOTES: Signed as free agent by St. Louis Blues (May 24, 1988). ... Bruised right foot (January 1990). ... Suffered back spasms (March 1990). ... Suspended 10 games by NHL for fighting (March 18, 1991). ... Injured knee (December 11, 1991); missed two games. ... Sprained left wrist (January 14, 1992); missed three games. ... Bruised thigh (February 2, 1992); missed five games. ... Injured hand (February 23, 1992); missed four games. ... Pulled groin (October 26, 1992); missed six games. ... Injured wrist (January 9, 1993); missed five games. ... Bruised lower leg (March 30, 1993); missed last six games of season. ... Suffered from the flu (December 4, 1993); missed one game. ... Injured leg (January 2, 1994); missed four games. ... Injured elbow (January 28, 1994); missed three games. ... Pulled groin (March 24, 1994); missed three games. ... Injured hand (April 5, 1994); missed one game. ... Selected by Hartford Whalers in 1994-95 waiver draft for cash (January 18, 1995). ... Suffered back spasms (February 24, 1995); missed 14 games. ... Suffered sore back (April 9, 1995); missed six games. ... Strained groin and injured neck (December 6, 1995); missed 10 games. ... Bruised hand (January 24, 1996); missed three games. ... Sprained knee (February 21, 1996); missed three games. ... Underwent arthroscopic knee surgery (December 13, 1996); missed 11 games. ... Traded by Whalers to Toronto Maple Leafs for eighth-round pick (RW Jaroslav Svoboda) in 1998 draft (March 18, 1997). ... Suffered from tendinitis in knee (March 19, 1997); missed 10 games. ... Traded by Maple Leafs to Blues for future considerations (September 30, 1997). ... Strained groin (November 6, 1997); missed two games. ... Injured thumb (December 4, 1997); missed three games. ... Strained knee (December 29, 1997); missed two games. ... Suffered sore leg (March 21, 1998); missed four games. ... Suspended one game by NHL for fighting (April 16, 1998).

HONORS: Won King Clancy Memorial Trophy (1997-98).

Season Team	League	REGULAR SEASON								PLAYOFFS				
		Gms.	G	A	Pts.	PIM	+/-	PP	SH	Gms.	G	A	Pts.	PIM
85-86—Saskatoon	WHL	57	7	18	25	172	...	...	...	10	3	4	7	37
86-87—Saskatoon	WHL	68	17	29	46	285	...	...	...	11	2	8	10	37
87-88—Saskatoon	WHL	70	21	34	55	*343	...	...	...	9	3	5	8	32
88-89—Peoria	IHL	38	14	7	21	278	...	...	...	—	—	—	—	—
89-90—Peoria	IHL	10	1	2	3	76	...	...	...	—	—	—	—	—
—St. Louis	NHL	43	1	3	4	244	-1	0	0	9	1	0	1	46
90-91—Peoria	IHL	61	20	34	54	406	...	...	...	10	4	3	7	61
—St. Louis	NHL	2	1	0	1	15	1	0	0	6	0	0	0	18
91-92—St. Louis	NHL	46	1	2	3	264	-6	0	0	1	0	0	0	7
92-93—St. Louis	NHL	49	2	5	7	204	-9	0	0	—	—	—	—	—
93-94—St. Louis	NHL	68	2	5	7	278	-5	0	0	4	0	1	1	6
94-95—Hartford	NHL	28	0	4	4	141	1	0	0	—	—	—	—	—
95-96—Hartford	NHL	55	2	4	6	230	-4	0	0	—	—	—	—	—
96-97—Hartford	NHL	28	1	2	3	122	2	0	0	—	—	—	—	—
—Toronto	NHL	2	0	0	0	27	0	0	0	—	—	—	—	—
97-98—St. Louis	NHL	67	4	3	7	231	10	0	0	7	0	0	0	23
NHL Totals (9 years)		388	14	28	42	1756	-11	0	0	27	1	1	2	100

CHEBATURKIN, VLADIMIR   D   ISLANDERS

PERSONAL: Born April 23, 1975, in Tyumen, U.S.S.R. ... 6-2/213. ... Shoots left. ... Name pronounced VLAD-ih-meer chuh-buh-TUHR-kihn.

TRANSACTIONS/CAREER NOTES: Selected by New York Islanders in third round (third Islanders pick, 66th overall) of NHL entry draft (June 26, 1993).

Season Team	League	REGULAR SEASON								PLAYOFFS				
		Gms.	G	A	Pts.	PIM	+/-	PP	SH	Gms.	G	A	Pts.	PIM
92-93—Kristall Elektrostal	CIS Div. II				Statistics unavailable.									
93-94—Kristall Elektrostal	CIS Div. II	42	4	4	8	38	...	...	...	—	—	—	—	—
94-95—Kristall Elektrostal	CIS	52	2	6	8	90	...	...	...	—	—	—	—	—
95-96—Kristall Elektrostal	CIS	44	1	6	7	30	...	...	...	1	0	0	0	0
96-97—Utah	IHL	68	0	4	4	34	...	...	...	—	—	—	—	—
97-98—Kentucky	AHL	54	6	8	14	52	...	...	...	2	0	0	0	4
—New York Islanders	NHL	2	0	2	2	0	-1	0	0	—	—	—	—	—
NHL Totals (1 year)		2	0	2	2	0	-1	0	0					

CHELIOS, CHRIS   D   BLACKHAWKS

PERSONAL: Born January 25, 1962, in Chicago. ... 6-1/190. ... Shoots right. ... Full name: Christos K. Chelios. ... Cousin of Nikos Tselios, defenseman, Carolina Hurricanes system. ... Name pronounced CHEH-lee-ohz.
COLLEGE: Wisconsin.
TRANSACTIONS/CAREER NOTES: Selected by Montreal Canadiens as underage junior in second round (fifth Canadiens pick, 40th overall) of NHL entry draft (June 10, 1981). ... Sprained right ankle (January 1985). ... Injured left knee (April 1985). ... Sprained knee (December 19, 1985). ... Reinjured knee (January 20, 1986). ... Suffered back spasms (October 1986). ... Broke finger on left hand (December 1987). ... Bruised tailbone (February 7, 1988). ... Strained left knee ligaments (February 1990). ... Underwent surgery to repair torn abdominal muscle (April 30, 1990). ... Traded by Canadiens with second-round pick in 1991 draft (C Michael Pomichter) to Chicago Blackhawks for C Denis Savard (June 29, 1990). ... Lacerated left temple (February 9, 1991). ... Suspended four games by NHL (October 15, 1993). ... Suspended four games without pay and fined $500 by NHL for eye-scratching incident (February 5, 1994). ... Played in Europe during 1994-95 NHL lockout. ... Sprained knee (March 1, 1997); missed eight games. ... Suffered sore back (April 6, 1997); missed one game.
HONORS: Named to NCAA All-Tournament team (1982-83). ... Named to WCHA All-Star second team (1982-83). ... Named to NHL All-Rookie team (1984-85). ... Played in NHL All-Star Game (1985, 1990-1994 and 1996-1998). ... Won James Norris Memorial Trophy (1988-89, 1992-93 and 1995-96). ... Named to THE SPORTING NEWS All-Star first team (1988-89, 1992-93 and 1995-96). ... Named to NHL All-Star first team (1988-89, 1992-93, 1994-95 and 1995-96). ... Named to THE SPORTING NEWS All-Star second team (1990-91 and 1991-92). ... Named to NHL All-Star second team (1990-91). ... Named to THE SPORTING NEWS All-Star team (1996-97).
MISCELLANEOUS: Member of Stanley Cup championship team (1986). ... Captain of Chicago Blackhawks (1996-97 and 1997-98).

Season Team	League	REGULAR SEASON								PLAYOFFS				
		Gms.	G	A	Pts.	PIM	+/-	PP	SH	Gms.	G	A	Pts.	PIM
79-80—Moose Jaw	SJHL	53	12	31	43	118	...	...	...	—	—	—	—	—
80-81—Moose Jaw	SJHL	54	23	64	87	175	...	...	...	—	—	—	—	—
81-82—Univ. of Wisconsin	WCHA	43	6	43	49	50	...	...	...	—	—	—	—	—
82-83—Univ. of Wisconsin	WCHA	45	16	32	48	62	...	...	...	—	—	—	—	—
83-84—U.S. national team	Int'l	60	14	35	49	58	...	...	...	—	—	—	—	—
—U.S. Olympic Team	Int'l	6	0	3	3	8	...	...	...	—	—	—	—	—
—Montreal	NHL	12	0	2	2	12	-5	0	0	15	1	9	10	17
84-85—Montreal	NHL	74	9	55	64	87	11	2	1	9	2	8	10	17
85-86—Montreal	NHL	41	8	26	34	67	4	2	0	20	2	9	11	49
86-87—Montreal	NHL	71	11	33	44	124	-5	6	0	17	4	9	13	38
87-88—Montreal	NHL	71	20	41	61	172	15	10	1	11	3	1	4	29
88-89—Montreal	NHL	80	15	58	73	185	35	8	0	21	4	15	19	28
89-90—Montreal	NHL	53	9	22	31	136	20	1	2	5	0	1	1	8
90-91—Chicago	NHL	77	12	52	64	192	23	5	2	6	1	7	8	46
91-92—Chicago	NHL	80	9	47	56	245	24	2	2	18	6	15	21	37
92-93—Chicago	NHL	84	15	58	73	282	14	8	0	4	0	2	2	14
93-94—Chicago	NHL	76	16	44	60	212	12	7	1	6	1	1	2	8
94-95—Biel-Bienne	Switzerland	3	0	3	3	4	...	...	...	—	—	—	—	—
—Chicago	NHL	48	5	33	38	72	17	3	1	16	4	7	11	12
95-96—Chicago	NHL	81	14	58	72	140	25	7	0	9	0	3	3	8
96-97—Chicago	NHL	72	10	38	48	112	16	2	0	6	0	1	1	8
97-98—Chicago	NHL	81	3	39	42	151	-7	1	0	—	—	—	—	—
—U.S. Olympic Team	Int'l	4	2	0	2	2	...	...	...	—	—	—	—	—
NHL Totals (15 years)		1001	156	606	762	2189	199	64	10	163	28	88	116	319

CHERNESKI, STEFAN   RW   RANGERS

PERSONAL: Born September 19, 1978, in Winnipeg. ... 6-0/195. ... Shoots left. ... Name pronounced chair-NEHZ-kee.
TRANSACTIONS/CAREER NOTES: Selected by New York Rangers in first round (first Rangers pick, 19th overall) of NHL entry draft (June 21, 1997).
HONORS: Won Can.HL Scholastic Player of the Year Award (1996-97).

Season Team	League	REGULAR SEASON								PLAYOFFS				
		Gms.	G	A	Pts.	PIM	+/-	PP	SH	Gms.	G	A	Pts.	PIM
95-96—Brandon	WHL	58	8	21	29	62	...	...	...	19	3	1	4	11
96-97—Brandon	WHL	56	39	29	68	83	...	...	...	0	0	0	0	0
97-98—Brandon	WHL	65	43	38	81	127	...	...	...	18	*15	8	23	21

CHERNOV, MIKHAIL   D   FLYERS

PERSONAL: Born November 11, 1978, in Prokopjevsk, U.S.S.R. ... 6-2/196. ... Shoots right.
TRANSACTIONS/CAREER NOTES: Selected by Philadelphia Flyers in fourth round (fourth Flyers pick, 103rd overall) of NHL entry draft (June 21, 1997).

Season Team	League	REGULAR SEASON								PLAYOFFS				
		Gms.	G	A	Pts.	PIM	+/-	PP	SH	Gms.	G	A	Pts.	PIM
94-95—Metal.-2 Novok.	CIS Div. II	12	0	3	3	0	...	...	...	—	—	—	—	—
95-96—Metal.-2 Novok.	CIS Div. II	40	2	7	9	10	...	...	...	—	—	—	—	—
96-97—Torpedo-2 Yaroslav.	Rus. Div. III	33	4	2	6	40	...	...	...	—	—	—	—	—
—Torpedo Yaroslavl	Russian	5	0	0	0	0	...	...	...	—	—	—	—	—
97-98—Torpedo Yaroslavl	Russian	7	0	0	0	4	...	...	...	—	—	—	—	—

CHIASSON, STEVE   D   HURRICANES

PERSONAL: Born April 14, 1967, in Barrie, Ont. ... 6-1/205. ... Shoots left. ... Name pronounced CHAY-sahn.
TRANSACTIONS/CAREER NOTES: Selected by Detroit Red Wings as underage junior in third round (third Red Wings pick, 50th overall) of NHL entry draft (June 15, 1985). ... Injured hand (October 1985). ... Separated right shoulder (February 1988). ... Injured foot (May 1988).

... Injured groin (October 1988). ... Bruised ribs (January 1989). ... Injured ankle (February 1989). ... Injured knee (November 29, 1990); missed three games. ... Broke right ankle (January 2, 1991). ... Reinjured right ankle (February 19, 1991); missed 26 games. ... Reinjured right ankle (March 9, 1991). ... Injured ankle (October 22, 1991); missed 14 games. ... Bruised thigh (October 25, 1992); missed three games. ... Pulled hamstring (January 21, 1993); missed one game. ... Suffered injuries (April 2, 1994); missed two games. ... Traded by Red Wings to Calgary Flames for G Mike Vernon (June 29, 1994). ... Bruised left foot (February 23, 1995); missed two games. ... Injured wrist (November 11, 1995); missed one game. ... Bruised knee (December 1, 1995); missed two games. ... Bruised hip (December 20, 1995); missed one game. ... Suffered concussion (February 8, 1996); missed two games. ... Sprained left medial collateral ligament (September 16, 1996); missed eight games. ... Reinjured left medial collateral ligament (December 3, 1996); missed 11 games. ... Traded by Flames with third-round pick (D Francis Lessard) in 1997 draft to Hartford Whalers for D Glen Featherstone, F Hnat Domenichelli, second-round pick (D Dimitri Kokorev) in 1997 draft and third-round pick (D Paul Manning) in 1998 draft (March 5, 1997). ... Whalers franchise moved to North Carolina and renamed Carolina Hurricanes for 1997-98 season; NHL approved move on June 25, 1997. ... Injured back (December 20, 1997); missed one game. ... Bruised shoulder (March 5, 1998); missed three games. ... Bruised shoulder (March 29, 1998); missed one game. ... Reinjured shoulder (April 4, 1998); missed eight games.

HONORS: Won Stafford Smythe Memorial Trophy (1985-86). ... Named to Memorial Cup All-Star team (1985-86). ... Played in NHL All-Star Game (1993).

MISCELLANEOUS: Scored on a penalty shot (vs. Byron Dafoe, December 11, 1995).

Season Team	League	REGULAR SEASON								PLAYOFFS				
		Gms.	G	A	Pts.	PIM	+/-	PP	SH	Gms.	G	A	Pts.	PIM
83-84—Guelph	OHL	55	1	9	10	112	...	...	...	—	—	—	—	—
84-85—Guelph	OHL	61	8	22	30	139	...	...	...	—	—	—	—	—
85-86—Guelph	OHL	54	12	29	41	126	...	...	...	18	10	10	20	37
86-87—Detroit	NHL	45	1	4	5	73	-7	0	0	2	0	0	0	19
87-88—Adirondack	AHL	23	6	11	17	58	...	...	...	—	—	—	—	—
—Detroit	NHL	29	2	9	11	57	15	0	0	9	2	2	4	31
88-89—Detroit	NHL	65	12	35	47	149	-6	5	2	5	2	1	3	6
89-90—Detroit	NHL	67	14	28	42	114	-16	4	0	—	—	—	—	—
90-91—Detroit	NHL	42	3	17	20	80	0	1	0	5	3	1	4	19
91-92—Detroit	NHL	62	10	24	34	136	22	5	0	11	1	5	6	12
92-93—Detroit	NHL	79	12	50	62	155	14	6	0	7	2	2	4	19
93-94—Detroit	NHL	82	13	33	46	122	17	4	1	7	2	3	5	2
94-95—Calgary	NHL	45	2	23	25	39	10	1	0	7	1	2	3	9
95-96—Calgary	NHL	76	8	25	33	62	3	5	0	4	2	1	3	0
96-97—Calgary	NHL	47	5	11	16	32	-11	1	2	—	—	—	—	—
—Hartford	NHL	18	3	11	14	7	-10	3	0	—	—	—	—	—
97-98—Carolina	NHL	66	7	27	34	65	-2	6	0	—	—	—	—	—
NHL Totals (12 years)		723	92	297	389	1091	29	41	5	57	15	17	32	117

CHORSKE, TOM   RW   ISLANDERS

PERSONAL: Born September 18, 1966, in Minneapolis. ... 6-1/212. ... Shoots right. ... Full name: Thomas Chorske. ... Name pronounced CHOHR-skee.
HIGH SCHOOL: Southwest (Minneapolis).
COLLEGE: Minnesota.
TRANSACTIONS/CAREER NOTES: Selected by Montreal Canadiens in first round (second Canadiens pick, 16th overall) of NHL entry draft (June 15, 1985). ... Separated shoulder (November 18, 1988); missed 11 games. ... Suffered hip pointer (October 26, 1989). ... Sprained right shoulder (March 14, 1991). ... Traded by Canadiens with RW Stephane Richer to New Jersey Devils for LW Kirk Muller and G Roland Melanson (September 20, 1991). ... Suffered charley horse (January 14, 1993); missed two games. ... Injured elbow (April 14, 1994); missed one game. ... Played in Europe during 1994-95 NHL lockout. ... Pulled groin (April 1, 1995); missed one game. ... Injured leg (April 20, 1995); missed two games. ... Claimed on waivers by Ottawa Senators (October 4, 1995). ... Injured back during 1995-96 season; missed two games. ... Suffered from the flu during 1995-96 season; missed one game. ... Bruised hip (October 9, 1996); missed four games. ... Strained hip flexor (October 28, 1996); missed three games. ... Underwent retinal surgery on left eye (December 15, 1996); missed six games. ... Claimed by New York Islanders from Senators in NHL waiver draft (September 27, 1997).
HONORS: Named to WCHA All-Star first team (1988-89).
MISCELLANEOUS: Member of Stanley Cup championship team (1995). ... Scored on a penalty shot (vs. Patrick Roy, March 7, 1998).

Season Team	League	REGULAR SEASON								PLAYOFFS				
		Gms.	G	A	Pts.	PIM	+/-	PP	SH	Gms.	G	A	Pts.	PIM
84-85—Minn. Southwest	Minn. H.S.	23	44	26	70	...	...	...	...	—	—	—	—	—
85-86—Univ. of Minnesota	WCHA	39	6	4	10	6	...	...	...	—	—	—	—	—
86-87—Univ. of Minnesota	WCHA	47	20	22	42	20	...	...	...	—	—	—	—	—
87-88—U.S. national team	Int'l	36	9	16	25	24	...	...	...	—	—	—	—	—
88-89—Univ. of Minnesota	WCHA	37	25	24	49	28	...	...	...	—	—	—	—	—
89-90—Montreal	NHL	14	3	1	4	2	2	0	0	—	—	—	—	—
—Sherbrooke	AHL	59	22	24	46	54	...	...	...	12	4	4	8	8
90-91—Montreal	NHL	57	9	11	20	32	-8	3	0	—	—	—	—	—
91-92—New Jersey	NHL	76	19	17	36	32	8	0	3	7	0	3	3	4
92-93—New Jersey	NHL	50	7	12	19	25	-1	0	0	1	0	0	0	0
—Utica	AHL	6	1	4	5	2	...	...	...	—	—	—	—	—
93-94—New Jersey	NHL	76	21	20	41	32	14	1	1	20	4	3	7	0
94-95—Milan	Italy	7	11	5	16	6	...	...	...	—	—	—	—	—
—New Jersey	NHL	42	10	8	18	16	-4	0	0	17	1	5	6	4
95-96—Ottawa	NHL	72	15	14	29	21	-9	0	2	—	—	—	—	—
96-97—Ottawa	NHL	68	18	8	26	16	-1	1	1	5	0	1	1	2
97-98—New York Islanders	NHL	82	12	23	35	39	7	1	4	—	—	—	—	—
NHL Totals (9 years)		537	114	114	228	215	8	6	11	50	5	12	17	10

CHRISTIAN, JEFF   LW   COYOTES

PERSONAL: Born July 30, 1970, in Burlington, Ont. ... 6-2/210. ... Shoots left. ... Full name: Jeffrey Christian.
TRANSACTIONS/CAREER NOTES: Selected by New Jersey Devils in second round (second Devils pick, 23rd overall) of NHL entry draft (June 11, 1988). ... Traded by London Knights to Owen Sound Platers for C Todd Hlushko and D David Noseworthy (November 27, 1989). ...

Suspended three games by OHL for high-sticking (March 28, 1990). ... Signed as free agent by Pittsburgh Penguins (August 2, 1994). ... Signed as free agent by Phoenix Coyotes (August 4, 1997).

Season Team	League	REGULAR SEASON								PLAYOFFS				
		Gms.	G	A	Pts.	PIM	+/-	PP	SH	Gms.	G	A	Pts.	PIM
86-87—Dundas Jr. C	OHA	29	20	34	54	42	...	...	...	—	—	—	—	—
87-88—London	OHL	64	15	29	44	154	...	...	...	9	1	5	6	27
88-89—London	OHL	60	27	30	57	221	...	...	...	20	3	4	7	56
89-90—London	OHL	18	14	7	21	64	...	...	...	—	—	—	—	—
—Owen Sound	OHL	37	19	26	45	145	...	...	...	10	6	7	13	43
90-91—Utica	AHL	80	24	42	66	165	...	...	...	—	—	—	—	—
91-92—Utica	AHL	76	27	24	51	198	...	...	...	4	0	0	0	16
—New Jersey	NHL	2	0	0	0	2	0	0	0	—	—	—	—	—
92-93—Utica	AHL	22	4	6	10	39	...	...	...	—	—	—	—	—
—Cincinnati	IHL	36	5	12	17	113	...	...	...	—	—	—	—	—
—Hamilton	AHL	11	2	5	7	35	...	...	...	—	—	—	—	—
93-94—Albany	AHL	76	34	43	77	227	...	...	...	5	1	2	3	19
94-95—Cleveland	IHL	56	13	24	37	126	...	...	...	2	0	1	1	8
—Pittsburgh	NHL	1	0	0	0	0	0	0	0	—	—	—	—	—
95-96—Cleveland	IHL	66	23	32	55	131	...	...	...	3	0	1	1	8
—Pittsburgh	NHL	3	0	0	0	2	0	0	0	—	—	—	—	—
96-97—Cleveland	IHL	69	40	40	80	262	...	...	...	12	6	8	14	44
—Pittsburgh	NHL	11	2	2	4	13	-3	0	0	—	—	—	—	—
97-98—Las Vegas	IHL	30	12	15	27	90	...	...	...	4	2	2	4	20
—Phoenix	NHL	1	0	0	0	0	-1	0	0	—	—	—	—	—
NHL Totals (5 years)		18	2	2	4	17	-4	0	0					

CHRISTIE, RYAN — LW — STARS

PERSONAL: Born July 3, 1978, in Beamsville, Ont. ... 6-2/175. ... Shoots left.
TRANSACTIONS/CAREER NOTES: Selected by Dallas Stars in fifth round (third Stars pick, 112th overall) of NHL entry draft (June 22, 1996).
HONORS: Named to OHL All-Star second team (1995-96).

Season Team	League	REGULAR SEASON								PLAYOFFS				
		Gms.	G	A	Pts.	PIM	+/-	PP	SH	Gms.	G	A	Pts.	PIM
95-96—Owen Sound	OHL	66	29	17	46	93	...	...	...	6	1	1	2	0
96-97—Owen Sound	OHL	66	23	29	52	136	...	...	...	4	1	1	2	8
97-98—Owen Sound	OHL	66	39	41	80	208	...	...	...	11	3	5	8	13

CHURCH, BRAD — LW — CAPITALS

PERSONAL: Born November 14, 1976, in Dauphin, Man. ... 6-1/215. ... Shoots left.
TRANSACTIONS/CAREER NOTES: Selected by Washington Capitals in first round (first Capitals pick, 17th overall) of NHL entry draft (July 8, 1995).

Season Team	League	REGULAR SEASON								PLAYOFFS				
		Gms.	G	A	Pts.	PIM	+/-	PP	SH	Gms.	G	A	Pts.	PIM
92-93—Dauphin	MJHL	45	15	23	38	80	...	...	...	—	—	—	—	—
93-94—Prince Albert	WHL	71	33	20	53	197	...	...	...	—	—	—	—	—
94-95—Prince Albert	WHL	62	26	24	50	184	...	...	...	15	6	9	15	32
95-96—Prince Albert	WHL	69	42	46	88	123	...	...	...	18	15	*20	*35	74
96-97—Portland	AHL	50	4	8	12	92	...	...	...	1	0	0	0	0
97-98—Portland	AHL	59	6	5	11	98	...	...	...	9	2	4	6	14
—Washington	NHL	2	0	0	0	0	0	0	0	—	—	—	—	—
NHL Totals (1 year)		2	0	0	0	0	0	0	0					

CHYNOWETH, DEAN — D — BRUINS

PERSONAL: Born October 30, 1968, in Saskatoon, Sask. ... 6-1/191. ... Shoots right. ... Son of Ed Chynoweth, former president of the Western Hockey League (1972-73 through 1978-79 and 1980-81 through 1995-96). ... Name pronounced shih-NOWTH.
TRANSACTIONS/CAREER NOTES: Broke hand (September 1985). ... Broke hand (April 1986). ... Broke hand (October 1986). ... Fractured rib and punctured lung (April 1987). ... Selected by New York Islanders as underage junior in first round (first Islanders pick, 13th overall) of NHL entry draft (June 13, 1987). ... Injured left eye (October 27, 1988); missed two months. ... Developed Osgood-Schlatter disease, an abnormal relationship between the muscles and the growing bones (December 1988); missed remainder of season. ... Injured ankle (October 31, 1989). ... Sprained ligaments in right thumb (November 1991). ... Strained shoulder (February 24, 1994); missed one game. ... Strained groin (March 15, 1994); missed 10 games. ... Bruised knee (February 20, 1995); missed three games. ... Injured groin (March 18, 1995); missed three games. ... Traded by Islanders to Boston Bruins for fifth-round pick (C Peter Sachl) in 1996 draft (December 9, 1995). ... Suffered pulled hamstring (March 18, 1996); missed remainder of regular season. ... Underwent offseason abdominal surgery (prior to 1996-97 season); missed first seven games of season. ... Strained groin (November 19, 1996); missed three games. ... Injured back (November 30, 1996); missed two games. ... Injured eye (February 1, 1997); missed one game. ... Suffered from the flu (April 10, 1997); missed three games. ... Injured groin (November 1, 1997); missed five games.
HONORS: Named to Memorial Cup All-Star team (1987-88).

Season Team	League	REGULAR SEASON								PLAYOFFS				
		Gms.	G	A	Pts.	PIM	+/-	PP	SH	Gms.	G	A	Pts.	PIM
85-86—Medicine Hat	WHL	69	3	12	15	208	...	...	...	17	3	2	5	52
86-87—Medicine Hat	WHL	67	3	18	21	285	...	...	...	13	4	2	6	28
87-88—Medicine Hat	WHL	64	1	21	22	274	...	...	...	16	0	6	6	*87
88-89—New York Islanders	NHL	6	0	0	0	48	-4	0	0	—	—	—	—	—
89-90—New York Islanders	NHL	20	0	2	2	39	0	0	0	—	—	—	—	—
—Springfield	AHL	40	0	7	7	98	...	...	...	17	0	4	4	36

Season Team	League	REGULAR SEASON								PLAYOFFS				
		Gms.	G	A	Pts.	PIM	+/-	PP	SH	Gms.	G	A	Pts.	PIM
90-91—New York Islanders.....	NHL	25	1	1	2	59	-6	0	0	—	—	—	—	—
—Capital District	AHL	44	1	5	6	176	...	...	...	—	—	—	—	—
91-92—Capital District	AHL	43	4	6	10	164	...	...	...	6	1	1	2	39
—New York Islanders.....	NHL	11	1	0	1	23	-3	0	0	—	—	—	—	—
92-93—Capital District	AHL	52	3	10	13	197	...	...	...	4	0	1	1	9
93-94—Salt Lake City..............	IHL	5	0	1	1	33	...	...	...	—	—	—	—	—
—New York Islanders.....	NHL	39	0	4	4	122	3	0	0	2	0	0	0	2
94-95—New York Islanders.....	NHL	32	0	2	2	77	9	0	0	—	—	—	—	—
95-96—New York Islanders.....	NHL	14	0	1	1	40	-4	0	0	—	—	—	—	—
—Boston	NHL	35	2	5	7	88	-1	0	0	4	0	0	0	24
96-97—Providence.................	AHL	2	0	0	0	13	...	...	...	—	—	—	—	—
—Boston	NHL	57	0	3	3	171	-12	0	0	—	—	—	—	—
97-98—Boston	NHL	2	0	0	0	0	-4	0	0	—	—	—	—	—
—Providence.................	AHL	28	2	2	4	123	...	...	...	—	—	—	—	—
—Quebec	IHL	15	2	2	4	39	...	...	...	—	—	—	—	—
NHL Totals (9 years)...........		241	4	18	22	667	-22	0	0	6	0	0	0	26

CICCARELLI, DINO   RW   PANTHERS

PERSONAL: Born February 8, 1960, in Sarnia, Ont. ... 5-10/180. ... Shoots right. ... Name pronounced DEE-noh sih-sih-REHL-ee.

TRANSACTIONS/CAREER NOTES: Fractured midshaft of right femur (spring 1978). ... Signed as free agent by Minnesota North Stars (September 1979). ... Injured shoulder (November 1984). ... Broke right wrist (December 1984). ... Suspended three games by NHL for making contact with linesman (October 5, 1987). ... Suspended 10 games by NHL for stick-swinging incident (January 6, 1988). ... Suspended by North Stars for failure to report to training camp (September 10, 1988). ... Traded by North Stars with D Bob Rouse to Washington Capitals for RW Mike Gartner and D Larry Murphy (March 7, 1989). ... Suffered concussion (March 8, 1989). ... Sprained left knee (April 23, 1990). ... Fractured right hand (October 20, 1990); missed 21 games. ... Injured groin (March 24, 1991); missed five games. ... Injured eye (December 4, 1991); missed one game. ... Traded by Capitals to Detroit Red Wings for RW Kevin Miller (June 20, 1992). ... Suffered from the flu (January 30, 1993); missed two games. ... Injured foot (January 15, 1994); missed 17 games. ... Lacerated face (February 8, 1995); missed one game. ... Strained right groin (April 2, 1995); missed one game. ... Suspended three games by NHL for punching another player (April 15, 1996). ... Traded by Red Wings to Tampa Bay Lightning for fourth-round pick (traded to Toronto) in 1998 draft (August 27, 1996). ... Injured back (December 21, 1996); missed one game. ... Suffered concussion (January 30, 1997); missed three games. ... Injured elbow (November 5, 1997); missed 10 games. ... Traded by Lightning with D Jeff Norton to Florida Panthers for G Mark Fitzpatrick and RW Jody Hull (January 15, 1998). ... Suffered concussion (March 4, 1998); missed two games. ... Suffered stiff neck (March 11, 1998); missed two games. ... Broke right ankle (April 14, 1998); missed remainder of season.

HONORS: Won Jim Mahon Memorial Trophy (1977-78). ... Named to OMJHL All-Star second team (1977-78). ... Played in NHL All-Star Game (1982, 1983, 1989 and 1997).

RECORDS: Holds NHL single-season playoff records for most points by rookie—21; and most goals by rookie—14 (1981). ... Shares NHL single-game playoff record for most power-play goals—3 (April 29, 1993).

STATISTICAL PLATEAUS: Three-goal games: 1981-82 (3), 1982-83 (1), 1983-84 (3), 1985-86 (3), 1986-87 (1), 1988-89 (2), 1990-91 (1), 1996-97 (1). Total: 15. ... Four-goal games: 1980-81 (1), 1988-89 (1), 1988-89 (1), 1989-90 (1), 1993-94 (1). Total: 5. ... Total hat tricks: 20.

MISCELLANEOUS: Failed to score on a penalty shot (vs. Denis Herron, March 16, 1983; vs. Allan Bester, November 26, 1988; vs. Nikolai Khabibulin, December 3, 1997).

Season Team	League	REGULAR SEASON								PLAYOFFS				
		Gms.	G	A	Pts.	PIM	+/-	PP	SH	Gms.	G	A	Pts.	PIM
76-77—London	OMJHL	66	39	43	82	45	...	...	...	—	—	—	—	—
77-78—London	OMJHL	68	*72	70	142	49	...	...	...	9	6	10	16	6
78-79—London	OMJHL	30	8	11	19	35	...	...	...	7	3	5	8	0
79-80—London	OMJHL	62	50	53	103	72	...	...	...	5	2	6	8	15
—Oklahoma City	CHL	6	3	2	5	0	...	...	...	—	—	—	—	—
80-81—Oklahoma City	CHL	48	32	25	57	45	...	...	...	—	—	—	—	—
—Minnesota..................	NHL	32	18	12	30	29	2	8	0	19	14	7	21	25
81-82—Minnesota..................	NHL	76	55	51	106	138	14	20	0	4	3	1	4	2
82-83—Minnesota..................	NHL	77	37	38	75	94	16	14	0	9	4	6	10	11
83-84—Minnesota..................	NHL	79	38	33	71	58	1	16	0	16	4	5	9	27
84-85—Minnesota..................	NHL	51	15	17	32	41	-10	5	0	9	3	3	6	8
85-86—Minnesota..................	NHL	75	44	45	89	51	12	19	0	5	0	1	1	6
86-87—Minnesota..................	NHL	80	52	51	103	88	10	22	0	—	—	—	—	—
87-88—Minnesota..................	NHL	67	41	45	86	79	-29	13	1	—	—	—	—	—
88-89—Minnesota..................	NHL	65	32	27	59	64	-16	13	0	—	—	—	—	—
—Washington...............	NHL	11	12	3	15	12	10	3	0	6	3	3	6	12
89-90—Washington...............	NHL	80	41	38	79	122	-5	10	0	8	8	3	11	6
90-91—Washington...............	NHL	54	21	18	39	66	-17	2	0	11	5	4	9	22
91-92—Washington...............	NHL	78	38	38	76	78	-10	13	0	7	5	4	9	14
92-93—Detroit......................	NHL	82	41	56	97	81	12	21	0	7	4	2	6	16
93-94—Detroit......................	NHL	66	28	29	57	73	10	12	0	7	5	2	7	14
94-95—Detroit......................	NHL	42	16	27	43	39	12	6	0	16	9	2	11	22
95-96—Detroit......................	NHL	64	22	21	43	99	14	13	0	17	6	2	8	26
96-97—Tampa Bay.................	NHL	77	35	25	60	116	-11	12	0	—	—	—	—	—
97-98—Tampa Bay.................	NHL	34	11	6	17	42	-14	3	0	—	—	—	—	—
—Florida........................	NHL	28	5	11	16	28	-2	2	0	—	—	—	—	—
NHL Totals (18 years).........		1218	602	591	1193	1398	28	227	1	141	73	45	118	211

CICCONE, ENRICO   D   LIGHTNING

PERSONAL: Born April 10, 1970, in Montreal. ... 6-5/220. ... Shoots left. ... Name pronounced en-REE-koh chih-KOH-nee.

TRANSACTIONS/CAREER NOTES: Selected by Minnesota North Stars in fifth round (fifth North Stars pick, 92nd overall) of NHL entry draft (June 16, 1990). ... North Stars franchise moved from Minnesota to Dallas and renamed Stars for 1993-94 season. ... Traded by Stars to Washington Capitals (June 25, 1993) to complete deal in which Capitals sent D Paul Cavallini to Stars for future considerations (June 20,

1993). ... Pulled groin (January 25, 1994); missed seven games. ... Traded by Capitals with third-round pick (traded to Mighty Ducks of Anaheim) in 1994 draft and conditional draft pick to Tampa Bay Lightning for D Joe Reekie (March 21, 1994). ... Suffered whiplash (February 5, 1995); missed one game. ... Injured neck (March 1, 1995); missed one game. ... Injured shoulder (April 26, 1995); missed two games. ... Tore ligament in right thumb (November 18, 1995); missed 10 games. ... Sprained right knee (January 30, 1996); missed one game. ... Traded by Lightning to Chicago Blackhawks for LW Patrick Poulin, D Igor Ulanov and second-round pick (traded to New Jersey) in 1996 draft (March 20, 1996). ... Bruised ribs (prior to 1996-97 season); missed first six games of season. ... Suffered hip flexor (March 20, 1997); missed one game. ... Traded by Blackhawks to Carolina Hurricanes for D Ryan Risidore and fifth-round pick (traded to Toronto) in 1998 draft (July 25, 1997). ... Strained groin (October 22, 1997); missed 20 games. ... Traded by Canucks to Hurricanes with G Sean Burke and LW Geoff Sanderson for LW Martin Gelinas and G Kirk McLean (January 3, 1998). ... Fractured tibia (January 8, 1998); missed 10 games. ... Traded by Canucks to Tampa Bay Lightning for D Jamie Huscroft (March 14, 1998). ... Strained groin (March 25, 1998); missed two games.
MISCELLANEOUS: Holds Tampa Bay Lightning all-time record for most penalty minutes (580).

		REGULAR SEASON								PLAYOFFS				
Season Team	League	Gms.	G	A	Pts.	PIM	+/-	PP	SH	Gms.	G	A	Pts.	PIM
87-88—Shawinigan	QMJHL	61	2	12	14	324	...	...	...	—	—	—	—	—
88-89—Shawinigan/T-Rivieres	QMJHL	58	7	19	26	289	...	...	...	—	—	—	—	—
89-90—Trois-Rivieres	QMJHL	40	4	24	28	227	...	...	...	3	0	0	0	15
90-91—Kalamazoo	IHL	57	4	9	13	384	...	...	...	4	0	1	1	32
91-92—Kalamazoo	IHL	53	4	16	20	406	...	...	...	10	0	1	1	58
—Minnesota	NHL	11	0	0	0	48	-2	0	0	—	—	—	—	—
92-93—Minnesota	NHL	31	0	1	1	115	2	0	0	—	—	—	—	—
—Kalamazoo	IHL	13	1	3	4	50	...	...	...	—	—	—	—	—
—Hamilton	AHL	6	1	3	4	44	...	...	...	—	—	—	—	—
93-94—Washington	NHL	46	1	1	2	174	-2	0	0	—	—	—	—	—
—Portland	AHL	6	0	0	0	27	...	...	...	—	—	—	—	—
—Tampa Bay	NHL	11	0	1	1	52	-2	0	0	—	—	—	—	—
94-95—Tampa Bay	NHL	41	2	4	6	225	3	0	0	—	—	—	—	—
95-96—Tampa Bay	NHL	55	2	3	5	258	-4	0	0	—	—	—	—	—
—Chicago	NHL	11	0	1	1	48	5	0	0	9	1	0	1	30
96-97—Chicago	NHL	67	2	2	4	233	-1	0	0	4	0	0	0	18
97-98—Carolina	NHL	14	0	3	3	83	3	0	0	—	—	—	—	—
—Vancouver	NHL	13	0	1	1	47	-2	0	0	—	—	—	—	—
—Tampa Bay	NHL	12	0	0	0	45	-3	0	0	—	—	—	—	—
NHL Totals (7 years)		312	7	17	24	1328	-3	0	0	13	1	0	1	48

CIERNIK, IVAN   RW   SENATORS

PERSONAL: Born October 30, 1977, in Levice, Czechoslovakia. ... 6-1/198. ... Shoots left. ... Name pronounced SEER-nihk.
TRANSACTIONS/CAREER NOTES: Selected by Ottawa Senators in ninth round (sixth Senators pick, 216th overall) of NHL entry draft (June 22, 1996).

		REGULAR SEASON								PLAYOFFS				
Season Team	League	Gms.	G	A	Pts.	PIM	+/-	PP	SH	Gms.	G	A	Pts.	PIM
94-95—HC Nitra Jrs.	Slovakia	30	22	15	37	36	...	...	...	—	—	—	—	—
—HC Nitra	Slovakia	7	1	0	1	2	...	...	...	—	—	—	—	—
95-96—HC Nitra	Slovakia	35	9	7	16	36	...	...	...	—	—	—	—	—
96-97—HC Nitra	Slovakia	41	11	19	30	...	...	...	...	—	—	—	—	—
97-98—Worcester	AHL	53	9	12	21	38	...	...	...	1	0	0	0	2
—Ottawa	NHL	2	0	0	0	0	0	0	0	—	—	—	—	—
NHL Totals (1 year)		2	0	0	0	0	0	0	0					

CLARK, BRETT   D   CANADIENS

PERSONAL: Born December 23, 1976, in Moosomin, Sask. ... 6-0/182. ... Shoots left.
COLLEGE: Maine.
TRANSACTIONS/CAREER NOTES: Selected by Montreal Canadiens in sixth round (seventh Canadiens pick, 154th overall) of NHL entry draft (June 22, 1996).
HONORS: Named to Hockey East All-Rookie team (1995-96).

		REGULAR SEASON								PLAYOFFS				
Season Team	League	Gms.	G	A	Pts.	PIM	+/-	PP	SH	Gms.	G	A	Pts.	PIM
94-95—Melville	SJHL	62	19	32	51	77	...	...	...	—	—	—	—	—
95-96—Univ. of Maine	Hockey East	39	7	31	38	22	...	...	...	—	—	—	—	—
96-97—Canadian nat'l team	Int'l	60	12	20	32	87	...	...	...	—	—	—	—	—
97-98—Montreal	NHL	41	1	0	1	20	-3	0	0	—	—	—	—	—
—Fredericton	AHL	20	0	6	6	6	...	...	...	4	0	1	1	17
NHL Totals (1 year)		41	1	0	1	20	-3	0	0					

CLARK, CHRIS   RW   FLAMES

PERSONAL: Born March 8, 1976, in South Windsor, Conn. ... 6-0/195. ... Shoots right.
HIGH SCHOOL: South Windsor (Conn.).
COLLEGE: Clarkson (N.Y.).
TRANSACTIONS/CAREER NOTES: Selected by Calgary Flames in third round (third Flames pick, 77th overall) of NHL entry draft (June 29, 1994).
HONORS: Named to ECAC All-Star second team (1997-98).

		REGULAR SEASON								PLAYOFFS				
Season Team	League	Gms.	G	A	Pts.	PIM	+/-	PP	SH	Gms.	G	A	Pts.	PIM
93-94—Springfield Jr. B	NEJHL	35	31	26	57	185	...	...	...	—	—	—	—	—
94-95—Clarkson	ECAC	32	12	11	23	92	...	...	...	—	—	—	—	—
95-96—Clarkson	ECAC	38	10	8	18	108	...	...	...	—	—	—	—	—
96-97—Clarkson	ECAC	37	23	25	48	86	...	...	...	—	—	—	—	—
97-98—Clarkson	ECAC	35	18	21	39	49	...	...	...	—	—	—	—	—

CLARK, JUSTIN   RW   AVALANCHE

PERSONAL: Born January 29, 1977, in Madison, Wis. ... 6-3/212. ... Shoots right.
HIGH SCHOOL: Forest Hills Central (Grand Rapids, Mich.), then Taft Prep (Watertown, Conn.).
COLLEGE: Michigan.
TRANSACTIONS/CAREER NOTES: Selected by Colorado Avalanche in ninth round (13th Avalanche pick, 240th overall) of NHL entry draft (June 22, 1996).

		REGULAR SEASON								PLAYOFFS				
Season Team	League	Gms.	G	A	Pts.	PIM	+/-	PP	SH	Gms.	G	A	Pts.	PIM
95-96—Univ. of Michigan........	CCHA	11	1	2	3	2	...	...	...	—	—	—	—	—
96-97—Univ. of Michigan........	CCHA	30	3	4	7	38	...	...	...	—	—	—	—	—
97-98—Univ. of Michigan........	CCHA	41	3	4	7	27	...	...	...	—	—	—	—	—

CLARK, WENDEL   LW   LIGHTNING

PERSONAL: Born October 25, 1966, in Kelvington, Sask. ... 5-10/194. ... Shoots left. ... Brother of Kerry Clark, right winger with New York Islanders and Calgary Flames organizations (1986-87 through 1991-92); and cousin of Joey Kocur, right winger, Detroit Red Wings.
TRANSACTIONS/CAREER NOTES: Selected by Toronto Maple Leafs as underage junior in first round (first Maple Leafs pick, first overall) of NHL entry draft (June 15, 1985). ... Suffered from virus (November 1985). ... Broke right foot (November 26, 1985); missed 14 games. ... Suffered back spasms (November 1987); missed 23 games. ... Suffered tendinitis in right shoulder (October 1987). ... Reinjured back (February 1988); missed 90 regular season games (March 1, 1989). ... Suffered recurrence of back problems (October 1989). ... Bruised muscle above left knee (November 4, 1989); missed seven games. ... Tore ligament in right knee (January 26, 1990); missed 29 games. ... Separated left shoulder (December 18, 1990). ... Pulled rib cage muscle (February 6, 1991); missed 12 games. ... Partially tore knee ligaments (October 7, 1991); missed 12 games. ... Strained knee ligaments (November 6, 1991); missed 24 games. ... Injured groin (October 24, 1992); missed four games. ... Strained rib muscle (January 17, 1993); missed 13 games. ... Strained knee (October 13, 1993); missed two games. ... Bruised foot (December 22, 1993); missed 17 games. ... Traded by Maple Leafs with D Sylvain Lefebvre, RW Landon Wilson and first-round pick in 1994 draft (D Jeffrey Kealty) to Quebec Nordiques for C Mats Sundin, D Garth Butcher, LW Todd Warriner and first-round pick (traded to Washington Capitals who selected D Nolan Baumgartner) in 1994 draft (June 28, 1994). ... Injured thigh (March 18, 1995); missed 11 games. ... Fined $1,000 by NHL for elbowing (May 10, 1995). ... Nordiques franchise moved to Colorado and renamed Avalanche for 1995-96 season (June 21, 1995). ... Traded by Avalanche to New York Islanders for RW Claude Lemieux (October 3, 1995). ... Suffered back spasms (January 30, 1996); missed eight games. ... Traded by Islanders with D Mathieu Schneider and D D.J. Smith to Toronto Maple Leafs for LW Sean Haggerty, C Darby Hendrickson, D Kenny Jonsson and first-round pick (G Roberto Luongo) in 1997 draft (March 13, 1996). ... Fractured thumb (December 10, 1996); missed 16 games. ... Bruised back (April 2, 1997); missed one game. ... Strained groin (January 10, 1998); missed 29 games. ... Reinjured groin and underwent surgery (April 7, 1998); missed remainder of season. ... Signed as free agent by Tampa Bay Lightning (July 16, 1998).
HONORS: Won Top Defenseman Trophy (1984-85). ... Named to WHL (East) All-Star first team (1984-85). ... Named NHL Rookie of the Year by THE SPORTING NEWS (1985-86). ... Named to NHL All-Rookie team (1985-86). ... Played in NHL All-Star Game (1986).
MISCELLANEOUS: Captain of Toronto Maple Leafs (1991-92 through 1993-94). ... Scored on a penalty shot (vs. Trevor Kidd, November 24, 1993). ... Failed to score on a penalty shot (vs. Darcy Wakaluk, December 21, 1995).
STATISTICAL PLATEAUS: Three-goal games: 1985-86 (1), 1989-90 (1), 1991-92 (2), 1993-94 (2), 1994-95 (1). Total: 7. ... Four-goal games: 1986-87 (1), 1996-97 (1). Total: 2. ... Total hat tricks: 9.

		REGULAR SEASON								PLAYOFFS				
Season Team	League	Gms.	G	A	Pts.	PIM	+/-	PP	SH	Gms.	G	A	Pts.	PIM
83-84—Saskatoon.................	WHL	72	23	45	68	225	...	...	...	—	—	—	—	—
84-85—Saskatoon.................	WHL	64	32	55	87	253	...	...	...	3	3	3	6	7
85-86—Toronto	NHL	66	34	11	45	227	-27	4	0	10	5	1	6	47
86-87—Toronto	NHL	80	37	23	60	271	-23	15	0	13	6	5	11	38
87-88—Toronto	NHL	28	12	11	23	80	-13	4	0	—	—	—	—	—
88-89—Toronto	NHL	15	7	4	11	66	-3	3	0	—	—	—	—	—
89-90—Toronto	NHL	38	18	8	26	116	2	7	0	5	1	1	2	19
90-91—Toronto	NHL	63	18	16	34	152	-5	4	0	—	—	—	—	—
91-92—Toronto	NHL	43	19	21	40	123	-14	7	0	—	—	—	—	—
92-93—Toronto	NHL	66	17	22	39	193	2	2	0	21	10	10	20	51
93-94—Toronto	NHL	64	46	30	76	115	10	21	0	18	9	7	16	24
94-95—Quebec	NHL	37	12	18	30	45	-1	5	0	6	1	2	3	6
95-96—New York Islanders.....	NHL	58	24	19	43	60	-12	6	0	—	—	—	—	—
—Toronto	NHL	13	8	7	15	16	7	2	0	6	2	2	4	2
96-97—Toronto	NHL	65	30	19	49	75	-2	6	0	—	—	—	—	—
97-98—Toronto	NHL	47	12	7	19	80	-21	4	0	—	—	—	—	—
NHL Totals (13 years).........		683	294	216	510	1619	-100	90	0	79	34	28	62	187

CLEARY, DAN   LW   BLACKHAWKS

PERSONAL: Born December 18, 1978, in Carbonear, Nfld. ... 6-0/203. ... Shoots left. ... Full name: Daniel Cleary.
TRANSACTIONS/CAREER NOTES: Selected by Chicago Blackhawks in first round (first Blackhawks pick, 13th overall) of NHL entry draft (June 21, 1997).
HONORS: Named to OHL All-Star first team (1995-96 and 1996-97).

		REGULAR SEASON								PLAYOFFS				
Season Team	League	Gms.	G	A	Pts.	PIM	+/-	PP	SH	Gms.	G	A	Pts.	PIM
93-94—Kingston	Tier II Jr. A	41	18	28	46	33	...	...	...	—	—	—	—	—
94-95—Belleville	OHL	62	26	55	81	62	...	...	...	16	7	10	17	23
95-96—Belleville	OHL	64	53	62	115	74	...	...	...	14	10	17	27	40
96-97—Belleville	OHL	64	32	48	80	88	...	...	...	6	3	4	7	6
97-98—Chicago.................	NHL	6	0	0	0	0	-2	0	0	—	—	—	—	—
—Indianapolis	IHL	4	2	1	3	6	...	...	...	—	—	—	—	—
—Belleville	OHL	30	16	31	47	14	...	...	...	10	6	*17	*23	10
NHL Totals (1 year)............		6	0	0	0	0	-2	0	0					

CLEMMENSEN, SCOTT — G — DEVILS

PERSONAL: Born July 23, 1977, in Des Moines, Iowa. ... 6-2/185. ... Catches left.
COLLEGE: Boston College.
TRANSACTIONS/CAREER NOTES: Selected by New Jersey Devils in eighth round (seventh Devils pick, 215th overall) of NHL entry draft (June 21, 1997).

		REGULAR SEASON								PLAYOFFS						
Season Team	League	Gms.	Min	W	L	T	GA	SO	Avg.	Gms.	Min.	W	L	GA	SO	Avg.
96-97—Des Moines	USHL	36	2042	...	...	...	111	1	3.26	—	—	—	—	—	—	—
97-98—Boston College	Hockey East	37	2205	24	9	4	102	4	2.78	—	—	—	—	—	—	—

CLOUTIER, DAN — G — RANGERS

PERSONAL: Born April 22, 1976, in Mont-Laurier, Que. ... 6-1/185. ... Catches left. ... Brother of Sylvain Cloutier, center, Detroit Red Wings system. ... Name pronounced KLOO-tee-yay.
HIGH SCHOOL: Notre-Dame-des-Grands-Lacs (Sault Ste. Marie, Ont.).
TRANSACTIONS/CAREER NOTES: Selected by New York Rangers in first round (first Rangers pick, 26th overall) of NHL entry draft (June 28, 1994).
HONORS: Named to OHL All-Star second team (1995-96). ... Won Dave Pinkney Trophy (1995-96). ... Named to AHL All-Rookie team (1996-97).

		REGULAR SEASON								PLAYOFFS						
Season Team	League	Gms.	Min	W	L	T	GA	SO	Avg.	Gms.	Min.	W	L	GA	SO	Avg.
91-92—St. Thomas	Jr. B	14	823	...	...	...	80	...	5.83	—	—	—	—	—	—	—
92-93—Sault Ste. Marie	OHL	12	572	4	6	0	44	0	4.62	4	231	1	2	12	0	3.12
93-94—Sault Ste. Marie	OHL	55	2934	28	14	6	174	†2	3.56	14	833	†10	4	52	0	3.75
94-95—Sault Ste. Marie	OHL	45	2517	15	25	2	184	1	4.39	—	—	—	—	—	—	—
95-96—Sault Ste. Marie	OHL	13	641	9	3	0	43	0	4.02	—	—	—	—	—	—	—
—Guelph	OHL	17	1004	12	2	2	35	2	2.09	16	993	11	5	52	*2	3.14
96-97—Binghamton	AHL	60	3367	23	†28	8	199	3	3.55	4	236	1	3	13	0	3.31
97-98—Hartford	AHL	24	1417	12	8	3	62	0	2.63	8	479	5	3	24	0	3.01
—New York Rangers	NHL	12	551	4	5	1	23	0	2.50	—	—	—	—	—	—	—
NHL Totals (1 year)		12	551	4	5	1	23	0	2.50							

CLOUTIER, SYLVAIN — C

PERSONAL: Born February 13, 1974, in Mont-Laurier, Que. ... 6-0/195. ... Shoots left. ... Brother of Dan Cloutier, goaltender, New York Rangers system. ... Name pronounced sihl-VAY CLOO-tee-yay.
HIGH SCHOOL: Bishop MacDonnell (Guelph, Ont.).
TRANSACTIONS/CAREER NOTES: Selected by Detroit Red Wings in third round (third Red Wings pick, 70th overall) of NHL entry draft (June 20, 1992).

		REGULAR SEASON							PLAYOFFS				
Season Team	League	Gms.	G	A	Pts.	PIM	+/-	PP	SH	Gms.	G	A	Pts.	PIM
91-92—Guelph	OHL	62	35	31	66	74	...	...	...	—	—	—	—	—
92-93—Guelph	OHL	44	26	29	55	78	...	...	...	5	0	5	5	14
93-94—Guelph	OHL	66	45	71	116	127	...	...	...	9	7	9	16	32
—Adirondack	AHL	2	0	2	2	2	...	...	...	—	—	—	—	—
94-95—Adirondack	AHL	71	7	26	33	144	...	...	...	—	—	—	—	—
95-96—Adirondack	AHL	65	11	17	28	118	...	...	...	3	0	0	0	4
—Toledo	ECHL	6	4	2	6	4	...	...	...	—	—	—	—	—
96-97—Adirondack	AHL	77	13	36	49	190	...	...	...	4	0	2	2	4
97-98—Adirondack	AHL	72	14	22	36	155	...	...	...	—	—	—	—	—
—Detroit	IHL	8	0	1	1	18	...	...	...	21	7	5	12	31

CLYMER, BEN — D — BRUINS

PERSONAL: Born April 11, 1978, in Edina, Mass. ... 6-1/195. ... Shoots right.
HIGH SCHOOL: Jefferson Senior (Alexandria, Minn.).
COLLEGE: Minnesota.
TRANSACTIONS/CAREER NOTES: Selected by Boston Bruins in second round (third Bruins pick, 27th overall) of NHL entry draft (June 21, 1997).
HONORS: Named to WCHA All-Rookie team (1996-97).

		REGULAR SEASON							PLAYOFFS				
Season Team	League	Gms.	G	A	Pts.	PIM	+/-	PP	SH	Gms.	G	A	Pts.	PIM
93-94—Thomas Jefferson	Minn. H.S.	23	3	7	10	6	...	...	...	—	—	—	—	—
94-95—Thomas Jefferson	Minn. H.S.	28	6	20	26	26	...	...	...	—	—	—	—	—
95-96—Thomas Jefferson	Minn. H.S.	19	12	28	40	38	...	...	...	—	—	—	—	—
96-97—Univ. of Minnesota	WCHA	29	7	13	20	64	...	...	...	—	—	—	—	—
97-98—Univ. of Minnesota	WCHA	1	0	0	0	2	...	...	...	—	—	—	—	—

COCKELL, MATT — G — CANUCKS

PERSONAL: Born May 4, 1979, in Calgary. ... 6-0/192. ... Catches left. ... Name pronounced KAH-kihl.
TRANSACTIONS/CAREER NOTES: Selected by Vancouver Canucks in fifth round (seventh Canucks pick, 117th overall) of NHL entry draft (June 21, 1997).

		REGULAR SEASON								PLAYOFFS					
Season Team	League	Gms.	Min	W	L	T	GA	SO	Avg.	Gms.	Min.	W	L	GA	SO	Avg.
95-96 —Winnipeg	MJHL	17	...	5	7	1	...	0	...	—	—	—	—	—	—	—
96-97 —Saskatoon	WHL	47	2609	14	26	4	175	0	4.02	—	—	—	—	—	—	—
97-98 —Saskatoon	WHL	22	1085	6	11	1	99	1	5.47	—	—	—	—	—	—	—
—Seattle	WHL	10	484	3	4	0	33	0	4.09	1	20	0	0	2	0	6.00

COFFEY, PAUL — D — BLACKHAWKS

PERSONAL: Born June 1, 1961, in Weston, Ont. ... 6-0/190. ... Shoots left. ... Full name: Paul Douglas Coffey.

TRANSACTIONS/CAREER NOTES: Selected by Edmonton Oilers in first round (first Oilers pick, sixth overall) of NHL entry draft (June 11, 1980). ... Suffered recurring back spasms (December 1986); missed 10 games. ... Traded by Oilers with LW Dave Hunter and RW Wayne Van Dorp to Pittsburgh Penguins for C Craig Simpson, C Dave Hannan, D Moe Mantha and D Chris Joseph (November 24, 1987). ... Tore knee cartilage (December 1987). ... Bruised right shoulder (November 16, 1988). ... Fractured finger (May 1990). ... Injured back (February 27, 1991). ... Injured hip muscle (March 9, 1991). ... Scratched left eye cornea (April 9, 1991). ... Broke jaw (April 1991). ... Pulled hip muscle (February 3, 1992); missed three games. ... Traded by Penguins to Los Angeles Kings for D Brian Benning, D Jeff Chychrun and first-round pick (LW Jason Bowen) in 1992 draft (February 19, 1992). ... Suffered back spasms (March 3, 1992); missed three games. ... Fractured wrist (March 17, 1992); missed five games. ... Traded by Kings with RW Jim Hiller and C/LW Sylain Couturier to Detroit Red Wings for C Jimmy Carson, RW Marc Potvin and C Gary Shuchuk (January 29, 1993). ... Injured groin (March 18, 1993); missed one game. ... Injured groin and left knee (October 18, 1993); missed four games. ... Injured back (January 28, 1995); missed two games. ... Injured back (November 4, 1995); missed two games. ... Sprained right thumb (January 6, 1996); missed two games. ... Suffered back spasms (April 7, 1996); missed one game. ... Traded by Red Wings with C Keith Primeau and first-round pick (traded to San Jose) in 1997 draft to Hartford Whalers for LW Brendan Shanahan and D Brian Glynn (October 9, 1996). ... Suffered hip flexor (October 17, 1996); missed three games. ... Suffered from the flu (November 8, 1996); missed two games. ... Injured groin (November 29, 1996); missed one game. ... Sore lower back (December 14, 1996); missed one game. ... Traded by Whalers with third-round pick (D Kris Mallette) in 1997 draft to Philadelphia Flyers for D Kevin Haller and first- (traded to San Jose) and seventh-round (C Andrew Merrick) picks in 1997 draft (December 15, 1996). ... Bruised left quadricep (December 21, 1996); missed one game. ... Suffered concussion (December 31, 1996); missed five games. ... Strained hamstring (February 4, 1997); missed two games. ... Separated left shoulder (March 25, 1997); missed three games. ... Twisted knee (April 12, 1997); missed final game of regular season. ... Strained rib muscle (January 11, 1998); missed two games. ... Suffered back spasms (March 16, 1998); missed one game. ... Traded by Flyers to Chicago Blackhawks for fifth-round pick (LW Francis Belanger) in 1998 draft (June 27, 1998).

HONORS: Named to OMJHL All-Star second team (1979-80). ... Named to NHL All-Star second team (1980-81 through 1983-84 and 1989-90). ... Named to The Sporting News All-Star second team (1981-82 through 1983-84, 1986-87 and 1989-90). ... Played in NHL All-Star Game (1982-1986, 1988-1994 and 1996-1997). ... Won James Norris Memorial Trophy (1984-85, 1985-86 and 1994-95). ... Named to The Sporting News All-Star first team (1984-85, 1985-86, 1988-89 and 1994-95). ... Named to NHL All-Star first team (1984-85, 1985-86, 1988-89 and 1994-95).

RECORDS: Holds NHL career records for most goals by a defenseman—383; most assists by a defenseman—1,090; and most points by a defenseman—1,473. ... Holds NHL single-season record for most goals by a defenseman—48 (1985-86). ... Shares NHL single-game records for most points by a defenseman—8 (March 14, 1986); and most assists by a defenseman—6 (March 14, 1986). ... Holds NHL record for most consecutive games scoring points by a defenseman—28 (1985-86). ... Holds NHL single-season playoff records for most goals by a defenseman—12; assists by a defenseman—25; and points by a defenseman—37 (1985). ... Holds NHL single-game playoff record for most points by a defenseman—6 (May 14, 1985).

STATISTICAL PLATEAUS: Three-goal games: 1982-83 (1), 1984-85 (1), 1985-86 (1), 1987-88 (1). Total: 4. ... Four-goal games: 1984-85 (1). ... Total hat tricks: 5.

MISCELLANEOUS: Member of Stanley Cup championship team (1984, 1985, 1987 and 1991).

		REGULAR SEASON								PLAYOFFS				
Season Team	League	Gms.	G	A	Pts.	PIM	+/-	PP	SH	Gms.	G	A	Pts.	PIM
77-78 —Kingston	OMJHL	8	2	2	4	11	...	...	...	—	—	—	—	—
—North York	MTHL	50	14	33	47	64	...	...	...	—	—	—	—	—
78-79 —Sault Ste. Marie	OMJHL	68	17	72	89	99	...	...	...	—	—	—	—	—
79-80 —Sault Ste. Marie	OMJHL	23	10	21	31	63	...	...	...	—	—	—	—	—
—Kitchener	OMJHL	52	19	52	71	130	...	...	...	—	—	—	—	—
80-81 —Edmonton	NHL	74	9	23	32	130	4	2	0	9	4	3	7	22
81-82 —Edmonton	NHL	80	29	60	89	106	35	13	0	5	1	1	2	6
82-83 —Edmonton	NHL	80	29	67	96	87	52	9	1	16	7	7	14	14
83-84 —Edmonton	NHL	80	40	86	126	104	52	14	1	19	8	14	22	21
84-85 —Edmonton	NHL	80	37	84	121	97	55	12	2	18	12	25	37	44
85-86 —Edmonton	NHL	79	48	90	138	120	61	9	*9	10	1	9	10	30
86-87 —Edmonton	NHL	59	17	50	67	49	12	10	2	17	3	8	11	30
87-88 —Pittsburgh	NHL	46	15	52	67	93	-1	6	2	—	—	—	—	—
88-89 —Pittsburgh	NHL	75	30	83	113	195	-10	11	0	11	2	13	15	31
89-90 —Pittsburgh	NHL	80	29	74	103	95	-25	10	0	—	—	—	—	—
90-91 —Pittsburgh	NHL	76	24	69	93	128	-18	8	0	12	2	9	11	6
91-92 —Pittsburgh	NHL	54	10	54	64	62	4	5	0	—	—	—	—	—
—Los Angeles	NHL	10	1	4	5	25	-3	0	0	6	4	3	7	2
92-93 —Los Angeles	NHL	50	8	49	57	50	9	2	0	—	—	—	—	—
—Detroit	NHL	30	4	26	30	27	7	3	0	7	2	9	11	2
93-94 —Detroit	NHL	80	14	63	77	106	28	5	0	7	1	6	7	8
94-95 —Detroit	NHL	45	14	44	58	72	18	4	1	18	6	12	18	10
95-96 —Detroit	NHL	76	14	60	74	90	19	3	1	17	5	9	14	30
96-97 —Hartford	NHL	20	3	5	8	18	0	1	0	—	—	—	—	—
—Philadelphia	NHL	37	6	20	26	20	11	0	1	17	1	8	9	6
97-98 —Philadelphia	NHL	57	2	27	29	30	3	1	0	—	—	—	—	—
NHL Totals (18 years)		1268	383	1090	1473	1704	313	128	20	189	59	136	195	262

COLAGIACOMO, ADAM — RW — SHARKS

PERSONAL: Born March 17, 1979, in Toronto. ... 6-2/206. ... Shoots right. ... Name pronounced koh-luh-JAH-kih-moh.

TRANSACTIONS/CAREER NOTES: Selected by San Jose Sharks in fourth round (third Sharks pick, 82nd overall) of NHL entry draft (June 21, 1997).

Season Team	League	REGULAR SEASON								PLAYOFFS				
		Gms.	G	A	Pts.	PIM	+/-	PP	SH	Gms.	G	A	Pts.	PIM
94-95—Royal York Royals	OPJHL	33	39	20	59	48	...	...	...	—	—	—	—	—
95-96—London	OHL	66	28	38	66	88	...	...	...	—	—	—	—	—
96-97—Oshawa....................	OHL	49	25	21	46	69	...	...	...	13	1	5	6	4
97-98—Oshawa....................	OHL	58	25	31	56	80	...	...	...	7	1	0	1	2

COLES, BRUCE   LW   FLYERS

PERSONAL: Born January 12, 1968, in Montreal ... 5-9/183. ... Shoots left.
COLLEGE: Rensselaer Polytechnic Institute (N.Y.).
TRANSACTIONS/CAREER NOTES: Selected by Montreal Canadiens in first round (23rd pick overall) of 1990 NHL supplemental draft. ... Signed as free agent by Philadelphia Flyers (May 31, 1995).

Season Team	League	REGULAR SEASON								PLAYOFFS				
		Gms.	G	A	Pts.	PIM	+/-	PP	SH	Gms.	G	A	Pts.	PIM
87-88—Rensselaer Poly. Inst..	ECAC	32	16	23	39	48	...	...	...	—	—	—	—	—
88-89—Rensselaer Poly. Inst..	ECAC	27	8	14	22	66	...	...	...	—	—	—	—	—
89-90—Rensselaer Poly. Inst..	ECAC	34	28	24	52	142	...	...	...	—	—	—	—	—
90-91—Rensselaer Poly. Inst..	ECAC	31	23	29	52	145	...	...	...	—	—	—	—	—
91-92—Winston-Salem	ECHL	16	2	6	8	37	...	...	...	—	—	—	—	—
—Johnstown................	ECHL	43	32	45	77	113	...	...	...	6	3	1	4	12
92-93—Johnstown................	ECHL	28	28	26	54	61	...	...	...	5	1	3	4	29
—Canadian nat'l team ...	Int'l	27	9	22	31	20	...	...	...	—	—	—	—	—
—Providence...............	AHL	2	0	0	0	0	...	...	...	—	—	—	—	—
93-94—Johnstown................	ECHL	24	23	20	43	56	...	...	...	3	0	1	1	10
94-95—Johnstown................	ECHL	29	20	25	45	56	...	...	...	—	—	—	—	—
—Hershey...................	AHL	51	16	25	41	73	...	...	...	6	1	5	6	14
95-96—Hershey	AHL	68	23	29	52	75	...	...	...	5	2	2	4	6
96-97—Philadelphia	AHL	79	31	49	80	152	...	...	...	10	2	5	7	28
97-98—Philadelphia	AHL	39	19	23	42	55	...	...	...	17	4	3	7	12

CONROY, CRAIG   C   BLUES

PERSONAL: Born September 4, 1971, in Potsdam, N.Y. ... 6-2/190. ... Shoots right.
HIGH SCHOOL: Northwood (Lake Placid, N.Y.).
COLLEGE: Clarkson (N.Y.).
TRANSACTIONS/CAREER NOTES: Selected by Montreal Canadiens in sixth round (seventh Canadiens pick, 123rd overall) of NHL entry draft (June 16, 1990). ... Traded by Canadiens with C Pierre Turgeon and D Rory Fitzpatrick to St. Louis Blues for LW Shayne Corson, D Murray Baron and fifth-round pick (D Gennady Razin) in 1997 draft (October 29, 1996).
HONORS: Named to NCAA All-America East first team (1993-94). ... Named to NCAA All-Tournament team (1993-94). ... Named to ECAC All-Star first team (1993-94).

Season Team	League	REGULAR SEASON								PLAYOFFS				
		Gms.	G	A	Pts.	PIM	+/-	PP	SH	Gms.	G	A	Pts.	PIM
90-91—Clarkson	ECAC	40	8	21	29	24	...	...	...	—	—	—	—	—
91-92—Clarkson	ECAC	31	19	17	36	36	...	...	...	—	—	—	—	—
92-93—Clarkson	ECAC	35	10	23	33	26	...	...	...	—	—	—	—	—
93-94—Clarkson	ECAC	34	26	40	66	66	...	...	...	—	—	—	—	—
94-95—Fredericton	AHL	55	26	18	44	29	...	...	...	11	7	3	10	6
—Montreal	NHL	6	1	0	1	0	-1	0	0	—	—	—	—	—
95-96—Fredericton	AHL	67	31	38	69	65	...	...	...	10	5	7	12	6
—Montreal	NHL	7	0	0	0	2	-4	0	0	—	—	—	—	—
96-97—Fredericton	AHL	9	10	6	16	10	...	...	...	—	—	—	—	—
—St. Louis..................	NHL	61	6	11	17	43	0	0	0	6	0	0	0	8
—Worcester	AHL	5	5	6	11	2	...	...	...	—	—	—	—	—
97-98—St. Louis....................	NHL	81	14	29	43	46	20	0	3	10	1	2	3	8
NHL Totals (4 years)...........		155	21	40	61	91	15	0	3	16	1	2	3	16

CONVERY, BRANDON   C   CANUCKS

PERSONAL: Born February 4, 1974, in Kingston, Ont. ... 6-1/182. ... Shoots right. ... Name pronounced KAHN-vuhr-ee.
HIGH SCHOOL: Lasalle Secondary School (Sudbury, Ont.).
TRANSACTIONS/CAREER NOTES: Selected by Toronto Maple Leafs in first round (first Maple Leafs pick, eighth overall) of NHL entry draft (June 20, 1992). ... Broke bone in wrist (March 2, 1996); missed four games. ... Traded by Maple Leafs to Vancouver Canucks for RW Lonny Bohonos (March 7, 1998).
HONORS: Won OHL Top Prospect Award (1991-92).

Season Team	League	REGULAR SEASON								PLAYOFFS				
		Gms.	G	A	Pts.	PIM	+/-	PP	SH	Gms.	G	A	Pts.	PIM
89-90—Kingston Jr. B.............	OHA	42	13	25	38	4	...	...	...	—	—	—	—	—
90-91—Sudbury.....................	OHL	56	26	22	48	18	...	...	...	5	1	1	2	2
91-92—Sudbury.....................	OHL	44	40	27	67	44	...	...	...	5	3	2	5	4
92-93—Sudbury.....................	OHL	7	7	9	16	6	...	...	...	—	—	—	—	—
—Niagara Falls..............	OHL	51	38	39	77	24	...	...	...	4	1	3	4	4
—St. John's..................	AHL	3	0	0	0	0	...	...	...	5	0	1	1	0
93-94—St. John's..................	AHL	—	—	—	—	—	...	...	...	1	0	0	0	0
—Niagara Falls..............	OHL	29	24	29	53	30	...	...	...	—	—	—	—	—
—Belleville	OHL	23	16	19	35	22	...	...	...	12	4	10	14	13

C

Season Team	League	REGULAR SEASON								PLAYOFFS				
		Gms.	G	A	Pts.	PIM	+/-	PP	SH	Gms.	G	A	Pts.	PIM
94-95—St. John's	AHL	76	34	37	71	43	...	...	...	5	2	2	4	4
95-96—St. John's	AHL	57	22	23	45	28	...	...	...	—	—	—	—	—
—Toronto	NHL	11	5	2	7	4	-7	3	0	5	0	0	0	2
96-97—Toronto	NHL	39	2	8	10	20	-9	0	0	—	—	—	—	—
—St. John's	AHL	25	14	14	28	15	...	...	...	—	—	—	—	—
97-98—St. John's	AHL	49	27	36	63	35	...	...	...	—	—	—	—	—
—Syracuse	AHL	2	1	2	3	5	...	...	...	—	—	—	—	—
—Vancouver	NHL	7	0	2	2	0	0	0	0	—	—	—	—	—
NHL Totals (3 years)		57	7	12	19	24	-16	3	0	5	0	0	0	2

COOKE, MATT LW CANUCKS

PERSONAL: Born September 7, 1978, in Belleville, Ont. ... 5-11/192. ... Shoots left.
TRANSACTIONS/CAREER NOTES: Selected by Vancouver Canucks in sixth round (eighth Canucks pick, 144th overall) of NHL entry draft (June 21, 1997).

Season Team	League	REGULAR SEASON								PLAYOFFS				
		Gms.	G	A	Pts.	PIM	+/-	PP	SH	Gms.	G	A	Pts.	PIM
95-96—Windsor	OHL	61	8	11	19	102	...	...	...	7	1	3	4	6
96-97—Windsor	OHL	65	45	50	95	146	...	...	...	5	5	5	10	4
97-98—Windsor	OHL	23	14	19	33	50	...	...	...	—	—	—	—	—
—Kingston	OHL	25	8	13	21	49	...	...	...	12	8	8	16	20

C

COOPER, DAVID D FLAMES

PERSONAL: Born November 2, 1973, in Ottawa. ... 6-2/204. ... Shoots left.
HIGH SCHOOL: Medicine Hat (Alta.).
TRANSACTIONS/CAREER NOTES: Selected by Buffalo Sabres in first round (first Sabres pick, 11th overall) of NHL entry draft (June 20, 1992). ... Signed as free agent by Toronto Maple Leafs (September 1996). ... Suffered from the flu (January 3, 1997); missed one game. ... Sprained knee (March 19, 1997); missed 11 games. ... Traded by Maple Leafs to Calgary Flames for RW Ladislov Kohn (July 2, 1998).
HONORS: Won WHL Top Prospect Award (1991-92). ... Named to WHL (East) All-Star first team (1991-92). ... Named to AHL All-Star second team (1997-98).

Season Team	League	REGULAR SEASON								PLAYOFFS				
		Gms.	G	A	Pts.	PIM	+/-	PP	SH	Gms.	G	A	Pts.	PIM
89-90—Medicine Hat	WHL	61	4	11	15	65	...	...	...	3	0	2	2	2
90-91—Medicine Hat	WHL	64	12	31	43	66	...	...	...	11	1	3	4	23
91-92—Medicine Hat	WHL	72	17	47	64	176	...	...	...	4	1	4	5	8
92-93—Medicine Hat	WHL	63	15	50	65	88	...	...	...	10	2	2	4	32
—Rochester	AHL	—	—	—	—	—	...	...	...	2	0	0	0	2
93-94—Rochester	AHL	68	10	25	35	82	...	...	...	4	1	1	2	2
94-95—Rochester	AHL	21	2	4	6	48	...	...	...	—	—	—	—	—
—South Carolina	ECHL	39	9	19	28	90	...	...	...	9	3	8	11	24
95-96—Rochester	AHL	67	9	18	27	79	...	...	...	8	0	1	1	12
96-97—St. John's	AHL	44	16	19	35	65	...	...	...	—	—	—	—	—
—Toronto	NHL	19	3	3	6	16	-3	2	0	—	—	—	—	—
97-98—Toronto	NHL	9	0	4	4	8	2	0	0	—	—	—	—	—
—St. John's	AHL	60	19	23	42	117	...	...	...	4	0	1	1	6
NHL Totals (2 years)		28	3	7	10	24	-1	2	0					

CORBET, RENE LW AVALANCHE

PERSONAL: Born June 25, 1973, in Victoriaville, Que. ... 6-0/187. ... Shoots left. ... Name pronounced ruh-NAY kohr-BAY.
TRANSACTIONS/CAREER NOTES: Selected by Quebec Nordiques in second round (second Nordiques pick, 24th overall) of NHL entry draft (June 22, 1991). ... Nordiques franchise moved to Colorado and renamed Avalanche for 1995-96 season (June 21, 1995). ... Injured shoulder (April 3, 1996); missed missed five games. ... Suffered concussion (December 17, 1996); missed three games. ... Suffered from the flu (October 24, 1997); missed two games. ... Strained hip muscle (November 21, 1997); missed two games. ... Injured wrist (January 3, 1998); missed three games. ... Injured shoulder (February 25, 1998); missed three games. ... Reinjured shoulder (March 14, 1998); missed four games.
HONORS: Won Michel Bergeron Trophy (1990-91). ... Named to QMJHL All-Rookie team (1990-91). ... Won Jean Beliveau Trophy (1992-93). ... Named to Can.HL All-Star first team (1992-93). ... Named to QMJHL All-Star first team (1992-93). ... Won Dudley (Red) Garrett Memorial Trophy (1993-94).
MISCELLANEOUS: Member of Stanley Cup championship team (1996).

Season Team	League	REGULAR SEASON								PLAYOFFS				
		Gms.	G	A	Pts.	PIM	+/-	PP	SH	Gms.	G	A	Pts.	PIM
90-91—Drummondville	QMJHL	45	25	40	65	34	...	...	...	14	11	6	17	15
91-92—Drummondville	QMJHL	56	46	50	96	90	...	...	...	4	1	2	3	17
92-93—Drummondville	QMJHL	63	*79	69	*148	143	...	...	...	10	7	13	20	16
93-94—Cornwall	AHL	68	37	40	77	56	...	...	...	13	7	2	9	18
—Quebec	NHL	9	1	1	2	0	1	0	0	—	—	—	—	—
94-95—Cornwall	AHL	65	33	24	57	79	...	...	...	12	2	8	10	27
—Quebec	NHL	8	0	3	3	2	3	0	0	2	0	1	1	0
95-96—Cornwall	AHL	9	5	6	11	10	...	...	...	—	—	—	—	—
—Colorado	NHL	33	3	6	9	33	10	0	0	8	3	2	5	2
96-97—Colorado	NHL	76	12	15	27	67	14	1	0	17	2	2	4	27
97-98—Colorado	NHL	68	16	12	28	133	8	4	0	2	0	0	0	2
NHL Totals (5 years)		194	32	37	69	235	36	5	0	29	5	5	10	31

CORKUM, BOB   C   COYOTES

PERSONAL: Born December 18, 1967, in Salisbury, Mass. ... 6-0/222. ... Shoots right. ... Full name: Robert Freeman Corkum.
HIGH SCHOOL: Triton Regional (Byfield, Mass.).
COLLEGE: Maine.
TRANSACTIONS/CAREER NOTES: Selected by Buffalo Sabres in third round (third Sabres pick, 47th overall) of NHL entry draft (June 21, 1986). ... Injured hip (March 19, 1992). ... Selected by Mighty Ducks of Anaheim in NHL expansion draft (June 24, 1993). ... Ruptured ankle tendon (March 27, 1994); missed remainder of season. ... Cut lower lip (November 24, 1995); missed two games. ... Traded by Mighty Ducks to Philadelphia Flyers for C Chris Herperger and seventh-round draft pick (LW Tony Mohagen) in 1997 draft (February 6, 1996). ... Strained right shoulder (February 17, 1996); missed three games. ... Selected by Phoenix Coyotes from Flyers in waiver draft for cash (September 30, 1996). ... Suffered from the flu (January 13, 1997); missed one game. ... Strained back (October 23, 1997); missed one game. ... Suffered mild concussion (March 16, 1998); missed five games.

		REGULAR SEASON								PLAYOFFS				
Season Team	League	Gms.	G	A	Pts.	PIM	+/-	PP	SH	Gms.	G	A	Pts.	PIM
84-85—Triton Regional	Mass. H.S.	18	35	36	71	...	...	...	...	—	—	—	—	—
85-86—Univ. of Maine	Hockey East	39	7	26	33	53	...	...	...	—	—	—	—	—
86-87—Univ. of Maine	Hockey East	35	18	11	29	24	...	...	...	—	—	—	—	—
87-88—Univ. of Maine	Hockey East	40	14	18	32	64	...	...	...	—	—	—	—	—
88-89—Univ. of Maine	Hockey East	45	17	31	48	64	...	...	...	—	—	—	—	—
89-90—Rochester	AHL	43	8	11	19	45	...	...	...	12	2	5	7	16
—Buffalo	NHL	8	2	0	2	4	2	0	0	5	1	0	1	4
90-91—Rochester	AHL	69	13	21	34	77	...	...	...	15	4	4	8	4
91-92—Rochester	AHL	52	16	12	28	47	...	...	...	8	0	6	6	8
—Buffalo	NHL	20	2	4	6	21	-9	0	0	4	1	0	1	0
92-93—Buffalo	NHL	68	6	4	10	38	-3	0	1	5	0	0	0	2
93-94—Anaheim	NHL	76	23	28	51	18	4	3	3	—	—	—	—	—
94-95—Anaheim	NHL	44	10	9	19	25	-7	0	0	—	—	—	—	—
95-96—Anaheim	NHL	48	5	7	12	26	0	0	0	—	—	—	—	—
—Philadelphia	NHL	28	4	3	7	8	3	0	0	12	1	2	3	6
96-97—Phoenix	NHL	80	9	11	20	40	-7	0	1	7	2	2	4	4
97-98—Phoenix	NHL	76	12	9	21	28	-7	0	5	6	1	0	1	4
NHL Totals (8 years)..........		**448**	**73**	**75**	**148**	**208**	**-24**	**3**	**10**	**39**	**6**	**4**	**10**	**20**

CORSO, DANIEL   RW   BLUES

PERSONAL: Born April 3, 1978, in St. Hubert, Que. ... 5-10/184.
TRANSACTIONS/CAREER NOTES: Selected by St. Louis Blues in seventh round (fifth Blues pick, 169th overall) of NHL entry draft (June 22, 1996).
HONORS: Won Michel Briere Trophy (1996-97). ... Named to Can.HL All-Star second team (1996-97). ... Named to QMJHL All-Star first team (1996-97).

		REGULAR SEASON								PLAYOFFS				
Season Team	League	Gms.	G	A	Pts.	PIM	+/-	PP	SH	Gms.	G	A	Pts.	PIM
94-95—Victoriaville	QMJHL	65	27	26	53	6	...	...	...	4	2	5	7	2
95-96—Victoriaville	QMJHL	65	49	65	114	77	...	...	...	12	6	7	13	4
96-97—Victoriaville	QMJHL	54	51	68	119	50	...	...	...	—	—	—	—	—
97-98—Victoriaville	QMJHL	35	24	51	75	20	...	...	...	3	1	1	2	2

CORSON, SHAYNE   LW   CANADIENS

PERSONAL: Born August 13, 1966, in Barrie, Ont. ... 6-1/199. ... Shoots left.
TRANSACTIONS/CAREER NOTES: Selected by Montreal Canadiens in first round (second Canadiens pick, eighth overall) of NHL entry draft (June 9, 1984). ... Broke jaw (January 24, 1987). ... Strained ligament in right knee (September 1987). ... Injured groin (March 1988). ... Injured knee (April 1988). ... Injured knee (April 1989). ... Bruised left shoulder (October 29, 1989). ... Broke toe on right foot (December 1989). ... Suffered hip pointer (November 10, 1990); missed seven games. ... Pulled groin (February 11, 1991). ... Traded by Canadiens with LW Vladimir Vujtek and C Brent Gilchrist to Edmonton Oilers for LW Vincent Damphousse and fourth-round pick (D Adam Wiesel) in 1993 draft (August 27, 1992). ... Fractured fibula (February 18, 1994); missed 12 games. ... Injured leg (March 23, 1994); missed remainder of season. ... Signed by St. Louis Blues to an offer sheet (July 28, 1995); Oilers received Blues first-round picks in 1996 and 1997 drafts as compensation; Oilers then traded picks to Blues for rights to G Curtis Joseph and RW Michael Grier (August 4, 1995). ... Suffered broken jaw (March 26, 1996); missed five games. ... Traded by Blues with D Murray Baron and fifth-round pick (D Gennady Razin) in 1997 draft to Canadiens for C Pierre Turgeon, C Craig Conroy and D Rory Fitzpatrick (October 29, 1996). ... Injured knee (November 25, 1996); missed 10 games. ... Underwent arthroscopic knee surgery (December 10, 1996). ... Sprained ankle (December 26, 1996); missed 10 games. ... Strained hip flexor (February 3, 1997); missed five games. ... Strained hip flexor (January 21, 1998); missed six games. ... Strained abdomen and groin (February 25, 1998); missed 13 games. ... Suffered charley horse (April 18, 1998); missed one game.
HONORS: Played in NHL All-Star Game (1990, 1994 and 1998).
MISCELLANEOUS: Captain of Edmonton Oilers (1994-95). ... Captain of St. Louis Blues (October 25, 1995 through February 24, 1996).
STATISTICAL PLATEAUS: Three-goal games: 1988-89 (2), 1993-94 (1). Total: 3.

		REGULAR SEASON								PLAYOFFS				
Season Team	League	Gms.	G	A	Pts.	PIM	+/-	PP	SH	Gms.	G	A	Pts.	PIM
82-83—Barrie	COJHL	23	13	29	42	87	...	...	...	—	—	—	—	—
83-84—Brantford	OHL	66	25	46	71	165	...	...	...	6	4	1	5	26
84-85—Hamilton	OHL	54	27	63	90	154	...	...	...	11	3	7	10	19
85-86—Hamilton	OHL	47	41	57	98	153	...	...	...	—	—	—	—	—
—Montreal	NHL	3	0	0	0	2	-3	0	0	—	—	—	—	—
86-87—Montreal	NHL	55	12	11	23	144	10	0	1	17	6	5	11	30
87-88—Montreal	NHL	71	12	27	39	152	22	2	0	3	1	0	1	12
88-89—Montreal	NHL	80	26	24	50	193	-1	10	0	21	4	5	9	65
89-90—Montreal	NHL	76	31	44	75	144	33	7	0	11	2	8	10	20
90-91—Montreal	NHL	71	23	24	47	138	9	7	0	13	9	6	15	36

Season Team	League	REGULAR SEASON								PLAYOFFS				
		Gms.	G	A	Pts.	PIM	+/-	PP	SH	Gms.	G	A	Pts.	PIM
91-92—Montreal	NHL	64	17	36	53	118	15	3	0	10	2	5	7	15
92-93—Edmonton	NHL	80	16	31	47	209	-19	9	2	—	—	—	—	—
93-94—Edmonton	NHL	64	25	29	54	118	-8	11	0	—	—	—	—	—
94-95—Edmonton	NHL	48	12	24	36	86	-17	2	0	—	—	—	—	—
95-96—St. Louis	NHL	77	18	28	46	192	3	13	0	13	8	6	14	22
96-97—St. Louis	NHL	11	2	1	3	24	-4	1	0	—	—	—	—	—
—Montreal	NHL	47	6	15	21	80	-5	2	0	5	1	0	1	4
97-98—Montreal	NHL	62	21	34	55	108	2	14	1	10	3	6	9	26
—Can. Olympic Team	Int'l	6	1	1	2	2	...	...	...	—	—	—	—	—
NHL Totals (13 years)		809	221	328	549	1708	37	81	4	103	36	41	77	230

CORVO, JOE — D — KINGS

PERSONAL: Born June 20, 1977, in Oak Park, Ill. ... 6-1/210. ... Shoots right. ... Full name: Joseph Corvo.
COLLEGE: Western Michigan.
TRANSACTIONS/CAREER NOTES: Selected by Los Angeles Kings in fourth round (fourth Kings pick, 83rd overall) of NHL entry draft (June 21, 1997).
HONORS: Named to CCHA All-Rookie team (1995-96). ... Named to CCHA All-Star second team (1996-97).

Season Team	League	REGULAR SEASON								PLAYOFFS				
		Gms.	G	A	Pts.	PIM	+/-	PP	SH	Gms.	G	A	Pts.	PIM
95-96—Western Michigan U.	CCHA	41	5	25	30	38	...	...	...	—	—	—	—	—
96-97—Western Michigan U.	CCHA	32	12	21	33	85	...	...	...	—	—	—	—	—
97-98—Western Michigan U.	CCHA	32	5	12	17	93	...	...	...	—	—	—	—	—

COTE, PATRICK — LW — PREDATORS

PERSONAL: Born January 24, 1975, in Lasalle, Que. ... 6-3/199. ... Shoots left. ... Name pronounced koh-TAY.
TRANSACTIONS/CAREER NOTES: Selected by Dallas Stars in second round (second Stars pick, 37th overall) of NHL entry draft (July 8, 1995). ... Separated shoulder (November 12, 1997); missed 61 games. ... Selected by Nashville Predators in NHL expansion draft (June 26, 1998).

Season Team	League	REGULAR SEASON								PLAYOFFS				
		Gms.	G	A	Pts.	PIM	+/-	PP	SH	Gms.	G	A	Pts.	PIM
93-94—Beauport	QMJHL	48	2	4	6	230	...	...	...	12	1	0	1	61
94-95—Beauport	QMJHL	56	20	20	40	314	...	...	...	17	8	8	16	115
95-96—Michigan	IHL	57	4	6	10	239	...	...	...	3	0	0	0	2
—Dallas	NHL	2	0	0	0	5	-2	0	0	—	—	—	—	—
96-97—Michigan	IHL	58	14	10	24	237	...	...	...	4	2	0	2	6
—Dallas	NHL	3	0	0	0	27	0	0	0	—	—	—	—	—
97-98—Dallas	NHL	3	0	0	0	15	-1	0	0	—	—	—	—	—
—Michigan	IHL	4	2	0	2	4	...	...	...	—	—	—	—	—
NHL Totals (3 years)		8	0	0	0	47	-3	0	0	—	—	—	—	—

COTE, SYLVAIN — D — MAPLE LEAFS

PERSONAL: Born January 19, 1966, in Quebec City. ... 6-0/190. ... Shoots right. ... Brother of Alain Cote, defenseman with five NHL teams (1985-86 through 1993-94). ... Name pronounced KOH-tay.
TRANSACTIONS/CAREER NOTES: Selected by Hartford Whalers as underage junior in first round (first Whalers pick, 11th overall) of NHL entry draft (June 9, 1984). ... Broke toe on left foot (October 28, 1989). ... Sprained left knee (December 1989). ... Fractured right foot (January 22, 1990). ... Traded by Whalers to Washington Capitals for second-round pick (LW Andrei Nikolishin) in 1992 draft (September 8, 1991). ... Broke wrist (September 25, 1992); missed six games. ... Suffered hip pointer (January 7, 1993); missed one game. ... Injured ankle (January 16, 1996); missed one game. ... Suffered MCL tear of right knee (October 18, 1996); missed 19 games. ... Strained knee (December 6, 1996); missed five games. ... Traded by Capitals to Toronto Maple Leafs for D Jeff Brown (March 24, 1998).
HONORS: Named to QMJHL All-Star second team (1983-84). ... Won Emile (Butch) Bouchard Trophy (1985-86). ... Shared Guy Lafleur Trophy with Luc Robitaille (1985-86). ... Named to QMJHL All-Star first team (1985-86).

Season Team	League	REGULAR SEASON								PLAYOFFS				
		Gms.	G	A	Pts.	PIM	+/-	PP	SH	Gms.	G	A	Pts.	PIM
82-83—Quebec	QMJHL	66	10	24	34	50	...	...	...	—	—	—	—	—
83-84—Quebec	QMJHL	66	15	50	65	89	...	...	...	5	1	1	2	0
84-85—Hartford	NHL	67	3	9	12	17	-30	1	0	—	—	—	—	—
85-86—Hartford	NHL	2	0	0	0	0	1	0	0	—	—	—	—	—
—Hull	QMJHL	26	10	33	43	14	...	...	...	13	6	*28	34	22
—Binghamton	AHL	12	2	6	8	0	...	...	...	—	—	—	—	—
86-87—Hartford	NHL	67	2	8	10	20	10	0	0	2	0	2	2	2
87-88—Hartford	NHL	67	7	21	28	30	-8	0	1	6	1	1	2	4
88-89—Hartford	NHL	78	8	9	17	49	-7	1	0	3	0	1	1	4
89-90—Hartford	NHL	28	4	2	6	14	2	1	0	5	0	0	0	0
90-91—Hartford	NHL	73	7	12	19	17	-17	1	0	6	0	2	2	2
91-92—Washington	NHL	78	11	29	40	31	7	6	0	7	1	2	3	4
92-93—Washington	NHL	77	21	29	50	34	28	8	2	6	1	1	2	4
93-94—Washington	NHL	84	16	35	51	66	30	3	2	9	1	8	9	6
94-95—Washington	NHL	47	5	14	19	53	2	1	0	7	1	3	4	2
95-96—Washington	NHL	81	5	33	38	40	5	3	0	6	2	0	2	12
96-97—Washington	NHL	57	6	18	24	28	11	2	0	—	—	—	—	—
97-98—Washington	NHL	59	1	15	16	36	-5	0	0	—	—	—	—	—
—Toronto	NHL	12	3	6	9	6	2	1	0	—	—	—	—	—
NHL Totals (14 years)		877	99	240	339	441	31	28	5	57	7	20	27	40

COURTNALL, GEOFF   LW   BLUES

PERSONAL: Born August 18, 1962, in Victoria, B.C. ... 6-0/195. ... Shoots left. ... Brother of Russ Courtnall, right winger, Los Angeles Kings.
TRANSACTIONS/CAREER NOTES: Signed as free agent by Boston Bruins (September 1983). ... Traded by Bruins with G Bill Ranford to Edmonton Oilers for G Andy Moog (March 8, 1988). ... Traded by Oilers to Washington Capitals for C Greg Adams (July 22, 1988). ... Traded by Capitals to St. Louis Blues for C Peter Zezel and D Mike Lalor (July 13, 1990). ... Traded by Blues with D Robert Dirk, C Cliff Ronning, LW Sergio Momesso and fifth-round pick in 1992 draft (RW Brian Loney) to Vancouver Canucks for C Dan Quinn and D Garth Butcher (March 5, 1991). ... Lacerated foot (February 28, 1992) and suffered from chronic fatigue (March 1992); missed nine games. ... Suspended two games by NHL (November 14, 1993). ... Suffered foot injury (April 20, 1995); missed three games. ... Signed as free agent by Blues (July 14, 1995). ... Broke thumb (February 18, 1996); missed 13 games. ... Suffered sore groin (January 3, 1998); missed two games.
MISCELLANEOUS: Member of Stanley Cup championship team (1988). ... Scored on a penalty shot (vs. Jeff Hackett, December 13, 1996). ... Failed to score on a penalty shot (vs. Alain Chevrier, February 7, 1988; vs. Damian Rhodes, March 21, 1995).
STATISTICAL NOTES: Tied for NHL lead with 11 game-winning goals (1992-93).
STATISTICAL PLATEAUS: Three-goal games: 1987-88 (1), 1988-89 (1), 1988-89 (1), 1989-90 (1), 1995-96 (1), 1997-98 (1). Total: 6.

		REGULAR SEASON								PLAYOFFS				
Season Team	League	Gms.	G	A	Pts.	PIM	+/-	PP	SH	Gms.	G	A	Pts.	PIM
80-81—Victoria	WHL	11	3	5	8	6	...	...	...	15	2	1	3	7
81-82—Victoria	WHL	72	35	57	92	100	...	...	...	4	1	0	1	2
82-83—Victoria	WHL	71	41	73	114	186	...	...	...	12	6	7	13	42
83-84—Hershey	AHL	74	14	12	26	51	...	...	...	—	—	—	—	—
—Boston	NHL	4	0	0	0	0	-1	0	0	—	—	—	—	—
84-85—Hershey	AHL	9	8	4	12	4	...	...	...	—	—	—	—	—
—Boston	NHL	64	12	16	28	82	-3	0	0	5	0	2	2	7
85-86—Moncton	AHL	12	8	8	16	6	...	...	...	—	—	—	—	—
—Boston	NHL	64	21	16	37	61	1	2	0	3	0	0	0	2
86-87—Boston	NHL	65	13	23	36	117	-4	2	0	1	0	0	0	0
87-88—Boston	NHL	62	32	26	58	108	24	8	0	—	—	—	—	—
—Edmonton	NHL	12	4	4	8	15	1	0	0	19	0	3	3	23
88-89—Washington	NHL	79	42	38	80	112	11	16	0	6	2	5	7	12
89-90—Washington	NHL	80	35	39	74	104	27	9	0	15	4	9	13	32
90-91—St. Louis	NHL	66	27	30	57	56	19	9	0	—	—	—	—	—
—Vancouver	NHL	11	6	2	8	8	-3	3	0	6	3	5	8	4
91-92—Vancouver	NHL	70	23	34	57	116	-6	12	0	12	6	8	14	20
92-93—Vancouver	NHL	84	31	46	77	167	27	9	0	12	4	10	14	12
93-94—Vancouver	NHL	82	26	44	70	123	15	12	1	24	9	10	19	51
94-95—Vancouver	NHL	45	16	18	34	81	2	7	0	11	4	2	6	34
95-96—St. Louis	NHL	69	24	16	40	101	-9	7	1	13	0	3	3	14
96-97—St. Louis	NHL	82	17	40	57	86	3	4	0	6	3	1	4	23
97-98—St. Louis	NHL	79	31	31	62	94	12	6	0	10	2	8	10	18
NHL Totals (15 years)		1018	360	423	783	1431	116	106	2	143	37	66	103	252

COURTNALL, RUSS   RW   KINGS

PERSONAL: Born June 2, 1965, in Victoria, B.C. ... 5-11/185. ... Shoots right. ... Brother of Geoff Courtnall, left winger, St. Louis Blues.
TRANSACTIONS/CAREER NOTES: Selected by Toronto Maple Leafs as underage junior in first round (first Maple Leafs pick, seventh overall) of NHL entry draft (June 8, 1983). ... Bruised knee (November 1987). ... Suffered from virus (February 1988). ... Suffered back spasms (March 1988). ... Traded by Maple Leafs to Montreal Canadiens for RW John Kordic and sixth-round pick (RW Michael Doers) in 1989 draft (November 7, 1988). ... Pulled muscle in right shoulder (October 8, 1991); missed 41 games. ... Injured hand (January 15, 1992); missed 12 games. ... Traded by Canadiens to Minnesota North Stars for LW Brian Bellows (August 31, 1992). ... North Stars franchise moved from Minnesota to Dallas and renamed Stars for 1993-94 season. ... Traded by Stars to Vancouver Canucks for LW Greg Adams, RW Dan Kesa and fifth-round pick (traded to Los Angeles) in 1995 draft (April 7, 1995). ... Injured groin (November 23, 1996); missed three games. ... Strained groin (December 3, 1996); missed 16 games. ... Traded by Canucks with LW Esa Tikkanen to Rangers for C Sergei Nemchinov and RW Brian Noonan (March 8, 1997). ... Signed as free agent by Los Angeles Kings (November 7, 1997). ... Strained hip flexor (February 26, 1998); missed two games.
HONORS: Played in NHL All-Star Game (1994).
MISCELLANEOUS: Scored on a penalty shot (vs. Tim Cheveldae, February 19, 1990).
STATISTICAL PLATEAUS: Three-goal games: 1985-86 (1), 1989-90 (1), 1992-93 (1), 1994-95 (1), 1995-96 (1). Total: 5.

		REGULAR SEASON								PLAYOFFS				
Season Team	League	Gms.	G	A	Pts.	PIM	+/-	PP	SH	Gms.	G	A	Pts.	PIM
82-83—Victoria	WHL	60	36	61	97	33	...	...	...	12	11	7	18	6
83-84—Victoria	WHL	32	29	37	66	63	...	...	...	—	—	—	—	—
—Can. Olympic Team	Int'l	16	4	7	11	10	...	...	...	—	—	—	—	—
—Toronto	NHL	14	3	9	12	6	0	1	0	—	—	—	—	—
84-85—Toronto	NHL	69	12	10	22	44	-23	0	2	—	—	—	—	—
85-86—Toronto	NHL	73	22	38	60	52	0	3	1	10	3	6	9	8
86-87—Toronto	NHL	79	29	44	73	90	-20	3	6	13	3	4	7	11
87-88—Toronto	NHL	65	23	26	49	47	-16	6	3	6	2	1	3	0
88-89—Toronto	NHL	9	1	1	2	4	-2	0	1	—	—	—	—	—
—Montreal	NHL	64	22	17	39	15	11	7	0	21	8	5	13	18
89-90—Montreal	NHL	80	27	32	59	27	14	3	0	11	5	1	6	10
90-91—Montreal	NHL	79	26	50	76	29	5	5	1	13	8	3	11	7
91-92—Montreal	NHL	27	7	14	21	6	6	0	1	10	1	1	2	4
92-93—Minnesota	NHL	84	36	43	79	49	1	14	2	—	—	—	—	—
93-94—Dallas	NHL	84	23	57	80	59	6	5	0	9	1	8	9	0
94-95—Dallas	NHL	32	7	10	17	13	-8	2	0	—	—	—	—	—
—Vancouver	NHL	13	4	14	18	4	10	0	2	11	4	8	12	21
95-96—Vancouver	NHL	81	26	39	65	40	25	6	4	6	1	3	4	2
96-97—Vancouver	NHL	47	9	19	28	24	4	1	0	—	—	—	—	—
—New York Rangers	NHL	14	2	5	7	2	-3	1	1	15	3	4	7	0
97-98—Los Angeles	NHL	58	12	6	18	27	-2	1	4	4	0	0	0	2
NHL Totals (15 years)		972	291	434	725	538	8	58	28	129	39	44	83	83

C

COURVILLE, LARRY   LW   CANUCKS

PERSONAL: Born April 2, 1975, in Timmins, Ont. ... 6-1/190. ... Shoots left.
HIGH SCHOOL: Huron Heights Secondary School (Newmarket, Ont.).
TRANSACTIONS/CAREER NOTES: Selected by Winnipeg Jets in fifth round (sixth Jets pick, 119th overall) of NHL entry draft (June 26, 1993). ... Returned to draft pool by Jets and selected by Vancouver Canucks in third round (second Canucks pick, 61st overall) of NHL entry draft (July 8, 1995).
HONORS: Named to OHL All-Star second team (1994-95).

		REGULAR SEASON								PLAYOFFS				
Season Team	League	Gms.	G	A	Pts.	PIM	+/-	PP	SH	Gms.	G	A	Pts.	PIM
90-91—Waterloo	USHL	48	20	18	38	144	...	...	...	—	—	—	—	—
91-92—Cornwall	OHL	60	8	12	20	80	...	...	...	6	0	0	0	8
92-93—Newmarket	OHL	64	21	18	39	181	...	...	...	7	0	6	6	14
93-94—Newmarket	OHL	39	20	19	39	134	...	...	...	—	—	—	—	—
—Moncton	AHL	8	2	0	2	37	...	...	...	10	2	2	4	27
94-95—Sarnia	OHL	16	9	9	18	58	...	...	...	—	—	—	—	—
—Oshawa	OHL	28	25	30	55	72	...	...	...	7	4	10	14	10
95-96—Syracuse	AHL	71	17	32	49	127	...	...	...	14	5	3	8	10
—Vancouver	NHL	3	1	0	1	0	1	0	0	—	—	—	—	—
96-97—Syracuse	AHL	54	20	24	44	103	...	...	...	3	0	1	1	20
—Vancouver	NHL	19	0	2	2	11	-4	0	0	—	—	—	—	—
97-98—Syracuse	AHL	29	6	12	18	84	...	...	...	—	—	—	—	—
—Vancouver	NHL	11	0	0	0	5	-7	0	0	—	—	—	—	—
NHL Totals (3 years)		33	1	2	3	16	-10	0	0					

COUSINEAU, MARCEL   G   ISLANDERS

PERSONAL: Born April 30, 1973, in Delson, Que. ... 5-9/180. ... Catches left. ... Name pronounced KOO-sih-noh.
TRANSACTIONS/CAREER NOTES: Selected by Boston Bruins in third round (third Bruins pick, 62nd overall) of NHL entry draft (June 22, 1991). ... Signed as free agent by Toronto Maple Leafs (November 13, 1993). ... Signed as free agent by New York Islanders (July 14, 1998).
HONORS: Named to QMJHL All-Rookie team (1990-91).

		REGULAR SEASON								PLAYOFFS						
Season Team	League	Gms.	Min	W	L	T	GA	SO	Avg.	Gms.	Min.	W	L	GA	SO	Avg.
90-91—Beauport	QMJHL	49	2739	13	29	3	196	1	4.29	—	—	—	—	—	—	—
91-92—Beauport	QMJHL	*67	*3673	26	*32	5	*241	0	3.94	—	—	—	—	—	—	—
92-93—Drummondville	QMJHL	60	3298	20	32	2	225	0	4.09	9	498	3	6	37	1	4.46
93-94—St. John's	AHL	37	2015	13	11	9	118	0	3.51	—	—	—	—	—	—	—
94-95—St. John's	AHL	58	3342	22	27	6	171	4	3.07	3	180	0	3	9	0	3.00
95-96—St. John's	AHL	62	3629	21	26	13	192	1	3.17	4	257	1	3	11	0	2.57
96-97—St. John's	AHL	19	1053	7	8	3	58	0	3.30	11	658	6	5	28	0	2.55
—Toronto	NHL	13	566	3	5	1	31	1	3.29	—	—	—	—	—	—	—
97-98—St. John's	AHL	57	3306	17	25	*13	167	1	3.03	4	254	1	3	10	0	2.36
—Toronto	NHL	2	17	0	0	0	0	0	0.00	—	—	—	—	—	—	—
NHL Totals (2 years)		15	583	3	5	1	31	1	3.19							

CRAVEN, MURRAY   LW

PERSONAL: Born July 20, 1964, in Medicine Hat, Alta. ... 6-3/190. ... Shoots left.
TRANSACTIONS/CAREER NOTES: Selected by Detroit Red Wings as underage junior in first round (first Red Wings pick, 17th overall) of NHL entry draft (June 9, 1982). ... Injured left knee cartilage (January 15, 1983). ... Traded by Red Wings with LW/C Joe Paterson to Philadelphia Flyers for C Darryl Sittler (October 1984). ... Broke foot (April 16, 1987). ... Hyperextended right knee and lacerated eye (November 1988). ... Bruised right foot (January 1989). ... Fractured left wrist (February 24, 1989). ... Fractured right wrist (April 5, 1989). ... Suffered back spasms (February 1990). ... Injured rotator cuff (March 24, 1990). ... Traded by Flyers with fourth-round pick (LW Kevin Smyth) in 1992 draft to Hartford Whalers for RW Kevin Dineen (November 13, 1991). ... Injured groin (January 21, 1992). ... Traded by Whalers with fifth-round pick in 1993 draft to Vancouver Canucks for LW Robert Kron, third-round pick (D Marek Malik) in 1993 draft and future considerations (March 22, 1993). ... Canucks sent RW Jim Sandlak to complete deal (May 17, 1993). ... Injured hip (November 2, 1993); missed three games. ... Strained groin (November 14, 1993); missed two games. ... Traded by Canucks to Chicago Blackhawks for C Christian Ruuttu (March 10, 1995). ... Suffered from sore back (1995); missed four games. ... Bruised foot (October 10, 1995); missed one game. ... Suffered charley horse (November 12, 1995); missed two games. ... Bruised knee (January 24, 1997); missed one game. ... Bruised shoulder (February 11, 1997); missed four games. ... Suffered stiff neck (March 5, 1997); missed one game. ... Injured thumb (October 22, 1997); missed six games. ... Suffered sore hand (November 25, 1997); missed one game. ... Strained neck (March 11, 1998); missed seven games.
MISCELLANEOUS: Scored on a penalty shot (vs. Don Beaupre, March 24, 1992; vs. Andre Racicot, December 23, 1990). ... Failed to score on a penalty shot (vs. Chris Terreri, October 13, 1991).
STATISTICAL PLATEAUS: Three-goal games: 1986-87 (1), 1987-88 (1), 1991-92 (1). Total: 3.

		REGULAR SEASON								PLAYOFFS				
Season Team	League	Gms.	G	A	Pts.	PIM	+/-	PP	SH	Gms.	G	A	Pts.	PIM
80-81—Medicine Hat	WHL	69	5	10	15	18	...	...	...	5	0	0	0	2
81-82—Medicine Hat	WHL	72	35	46	81	49	...	...	...	—	—	—	—	—
82-83—Medicine Hat	WHL	28	17	29	46	35	...	...	...	—	—	—	—	—
—Detroit	NHL	31	4	7	11	6	5	0	0	—	—	—	—	—
83-84—Medicine Hat	WHL	48	38	56	94	53	...	...	...	4	5	3	8	4
—Detroit	NHL	15	0	4	4	6	2	0	0	—	—	—	—	—
84-85—Philadelphia	NHL	80	26	35	61	30	45	2	2	19	4	6	10	11
85-86—Philadelphia	NHL	78	21	33	54	34	24	2	0	5	0	3	3	4
86-87—Philadelphia	NHL	77	19	30	49	38	1	5	3	12	3	1	4	9
87-88—Philadelphia	NHL	72	30	46	76	58	25	6	2	7	2	5	7	4
88-89—Philadelphia	NHL	51	9	28	37	52	4	0	0	1	0	0	0	0

Season Team	League	REGULAR SEASON								PLAYOFFS				
		Gms.	G	A	Pts.	PIM	+/-	PP	SH	Gms.	G	A	Pts.	PIM
89-90—Philadelphia	NHL	76	25	50	75	42	2	7	2	—	—	—	—	—
90-91—Philadelphia	NHL	77	19	47	66	53	-2	6	0	—	—	—	—	—
91-92—Philadelphia	NHL	12	3	3	6	8	2	1	0	—	—	—	—	—
—Hartford	NHL	61	24	30	54	38	-4	8	4	7	3	3	6	6
92-93—Hartford	NHL	67	25	42	67	20	-4	6	3	—	—	—	—	—
—Vancouver	NHL	10	0	10	10	12	3	0	0	12	4	6	10	4
93-94—Vancouver	NHL	78	15	40	55	30	5	2	1	22	4	9	13	18
94-95—Chicago	NHL	16	4	3	7	2	2	1	0	16	5	5	10	4
95-96—Chicago	NHL	66	18	29	47	36	20	5	1	9	1	4	5	2
96-97—Chicago	NHL	75	8	27	35	12	0	2	0	2	0	0	0	2
97-98—San Jose	NHL	67	12	17	29	25	4	2	3	6	1	1	2	0
NHL Totals (16 years)		1009	262	481	743	502	144	55	21	118	27	43	70	64

CROSS, CORY　　　　　D　　　　　LIGHTNING

PERSONAL: Born January 3, 1971, in Prince Albert, Sask. ... 6-5/230. ... Shoots left. ... Full name: Cory James Cross.
HIGH SCHOOL: Lloydminster (Alta.) Comprehensive.
COLLEGE: Alberta.
TRANSACTIONS/CAREER NOTES: Selected by Tampa Bay Lightning in NHL supplemental draft (June 19, 1992). ... Injured foot (November 3, 1995); missed one game. ... Bruised right foot (November 10, 1996); missed five games. ... Suffered from the flu (March 28, 1998); missed one game.
HONORS: Named to CWUAA All-Star second team (1992-93).

Season Team	League	REGULAR SEASON								PLAYOFFS				
		Gms.	G	A	Pts.	PIM	+/-	PP	SH	Gms.	G	A	Pts.	PIM
90-91—Univ. of Alberta	CWUAA	20	2	5	7	16	...	...	...	—	—	—	—	—
91-92—Univ. of Alberta	CWUAA	39	3	10	13	76	...	...	...	—	—	—	—	—
92-93—Univ. of Alberta	CWUAA	43	11	28	39	105	...	...	...	—	—	—	—	—
—Atlanta	IHL	7	0	1	1	2	...	...	...	4	0	0	0	6
93-94—Atlanta	IHL	70	4	14	18	72	...	...	...	9	1	2	3	14
—Tampa Bay	NHL	5	0	0	0	6	-3	0	0	—	—	—	—	—
94-95—Atlanta	IHL	41	5	10	15	67	...	...	...	—	—	—	—	—
—Tampa Bay	NHL	43	1	5	6	41	-6	0	0	—	—	—	—	—
95-96—Tampa Bay	NHL	75	2	14	16	66	4	0	0	6	0	0	0	22
96-97—Tampa Bay	NHL	72	4	5	9	95	6	0	0	—	—	—	—	—
97-98—Tampa Bay	NHL	74	3	6	9	77	-24	0	1	—	—	—	—	—
NHL Totals (5 years)		269	10	30	40	285	-23	0	1	6	0	0	0	22

CROWE, PHIL　　　　　LW　　　　　SENATORS

PERSONAL: Born April 14, 1970, in Red Deer, Alta. ... 6-2/215. ... Shoots left. ... Full name: Philip Crowe.
TRANSACTIONS/CAREER NOTES: Signed as free agent by Los Angeles Kings (November 8, 1993). ... Signed as free agent by Philadelphia Flyers (July 19, 1994). ... Suffered back spasms (October 29, 1995); missed five games. ... Signed as free agent by Ottawa Senators (July 4, 1996). ... Suffered charley horse (March 25, 1997); missed two games.

Season Team	League	REGULAR SEASON								PLAYOFFS				
		Gms.	G	A	Pts.	PIM	+/-	PP	SH	Gms.	G	A	Pts.	PIM
91-92—Adirondack	AHL	6	0	1	1	29	...	...	...	—	—	—	—	—
—Columbus	ECHL	32	4	7	11	145	...	...	...	—	—	—	—	—
92-93—Phoenix	IHL	53	3	3	6	190	...	...	...	—	—	—	—	—
93-94—Fort Wayne	IHL	5	0	1	1	26	...	...	...	—	—	—	—	—
—Phoenix	IHL	2	0	0	0	0	...	...	...	—	—	—	—	—
—Los Angeles	NHL	31	0	2	2	77	4	0	0	—	—	—	—	—
94-95—Hershey	AHL	46	11	6	17	132	...	...	...	6	0	1	1	19
95-96—Hershey	AHL	39	6	8	14	105	...	...	...	5	1	2	3	19
—Philadelphia	NHL	16	1	1	2	28	0	0	0	—	—	—	—	—
96-97—Detroit	IHL	41	7	7	14	83	...	...	...	—	—	—	—	—
—Ottawa	NHL	26	0	1	1	30	0	0	0	3	0	0	0	16
97-98—Detroit	IHL	55	6	13	19	160	...	...	...	20	5	2	7	48
—Ottawa	NHL	9	3	0	3	24	3	0	0	—	—	—	—	—
NHL Totals (4 years)		82	4	4	8	159	7	0	0	3	0	0	0	16

CROWLEY, MIKE　　　　　D　　　　　MIGHTY DUCKS

PERSONAL: Born July 4, 1975, in Bloomington, Minn. ... 5-11/190. ... Shoots left.
HIGH SCHOOL: Thomas Jefferson (Bloomington, Minn.).
COLLEGE: Minnesota.
TRANSACTIONS/CAREER NOTES: Selected by Philadelphia Flyers in sixth round (fifth Flyers pick, 140th overall) of NHL entry draft (June 26, 1993). ... Rights traded by Flyers with C Anatoli Semenov to Mighty Ducks of Anaheim for RW Brian Wesenberg (March 19, 1996).
HONORS: Named WCHA Rookie of the Year (1994-95). ... Named to NCAA All-America West first team (1995-96 and 1996-97). ... Named to WCHA All-Star first team (1995-96 and 1996-97). ... Named WCHA Player of the Year (1996-97).

Season Team	League	REGULAR SEASON								PLAYOFFS				
		Gms.	G	A	Pts.	PIM	+/-	PP	SH	Gms.	G	A	Pts.	PIM
90-91—Thomas Jefferson	Minn. H.S.	20	3	9	12	2	...	...	...	—	—	—	—	—
91-92—Thomas Jefferson	Minn. H.S.	28	5	18	23	8	...	...	...	—	—	—	—	—
92-93—Thomas Jefferson	Minn. H.S.	22	10	32	42	18	...	...	...	—	—	—	—	—

C

Season Team	League	Gms.	G	A	Pts.	PIM	+/-	PP	SH	Gms.	G	A	Pts.	PIM
93-94—Thomas Jefferson	Minn. H.S.	28	23	54	77	26	...	...	...	—	—	—	—	—
94-95—Univ. of Minnesota	WCHA	41	11	27	38	60	...	...	...	—	—	—	—	—
95-96—Univ. of Minnesota	WCHA	42	17	46	63	28	...	...	...	—	—	—	—	—
96-97—Univ. of Minnesota	WCHA	42	9	47	56	24	...	...	...	—	—	—	—	—
97-98—Cincinnati	AHL	76	12	26	38	91	...	...	...	—	—	—	—	—
—Anaheim	NHL	8	2	2	4	8	0	0	0	—	—	—	—	—
NHL Totals (1 year)		8	2	2	4	8	0	0	0					

CROZIER, GREG   LW   PENGUINS

PERSONAL: Born July 6, 1976, in Williamsville, N.Y. ... 6-3/199. ... Shoots left.
HIGH SCHOOL: Amherst (Mass.), then Lawrence Academy (Groton, Mass.).
COLLEGE: Michigan.
TRANSACTIONS/CAREER NOTES: Selected by Pittsburgh Penguins in third round (fourth Penguins pick, 73rd overall) of NHL entry draft (June 29, 1994).

Season Team	League	Gms.	G	A	Pts.	PIM	+/-	PP	SH	Gms.	G	A	Pts.	PIM
90-91—Amherst	Mass. H.S.	41	52	34	86	17	...	...	...	—	—	—	—	—
91-92—Amherst	Mass. H.S.	46	61	47	108	47	...	...	...	—	—	—	—	—
92-93—Lawrence Academy	Mass. H.S.	21	22	13	35	9	...	...	...	—	—	—	—	—
93-94—Lawrence Academy	Mass. H.S.	19	22	26	48	10	...	...	...	—	—	—	—	—
94-95—Lawrence Academy	Mass. H.S.	31	45	32	77	22	...	...	...	—	—	—	—	—
95-96—Univ. of Michigan	CCHA	42	14	10	24	46	...	...	...	—	—	—	—	—
96-97—Univ. of Michigan	CCHA	31	5	15	20	45	...	...	...	—	—	—	—	—
97-98—Univ. of Michigan	CCHA	43	12	9	21	24	...	...	...	—	—	—	—	—

CRUICKSHANK, CURTIS   G   CAPITALS

PERSONAL: Born March 21, 1979, in Ottawa. ... 6-2/209. ... Catches left. ... Name pronounced KRUK-shank.
TRANSACTIONS/CAREER NOTES: Selected by Washington Capitals in fourth round (third Capitals pick, 89th overall) of NHL entry draft (June 21, 1997).
HONORS: Named to OHL All-Rookie second team (1996-97).

Season Team	League	Gms.	Min	W	L	T	GA	SO	Avg.	Gms.	Min.	W	L	GA	SO	Avg.
95-96—Ottawa	Tier II Jr. A	24	...	12	4	0	...	0	...	—	—	—	—	—	—	—
96-97—Kingston	OHL	35	1792	13	16	1	118	2	3.95	1	26	0	1	4	0	9.23
97-98—Kingston	OHL	57	3166	30	20	4	207	2	3.92	12	702	5	6	45	0	3.85

CULLEN, MATT   C   MIGHTY DUCKS

PERSONAL: Born November 2, 1976, in Virginia, Minn. ... 6-1/195. ... Shoots left.
HIGH SCHOOL: Moorhead (Minn.) Senior.
COLLEGE: St. Cloud (Minn.) State.
TRANSACTIONS/CAREER NOTES: Selected by Mighty Ducks of Anaheim in second round (second Mighty Ducks pick, 35th overall) of NHL entry draft (June 22, 1996).
HONORS: Named to WCHA All-Rookie team (1995-96). ... Named to WCHA All-Star second team (1996-97).

Season Team	League	Gms.	G	A	Pts.	PIM	+/-	PP	SH	Gms.	G	A	Pts.	PIM
94-95—Moorhead Senior	Minn. H.S.	28	47	42	89	78	...	...	...	—	—	—	—	—
95-96—St. Cloud State	WCHA	39	12	29	41	28	...	...	...	—	—	—	—	—
96-97—St. Cloud State	WCHA	36	15	30	45	70	...	...	...	—	—	—	—	—
—Baltimore	AHL	6	3	3	6	7	...	...	...	3	0	2	2	0
97-98—Anaheim	NHL	61	6	21	27	23	-4	2	0	—	—	—	—	—
—Cincinnati	AHL	18	15	12	27	2	...	...	...	—	—	—	—	—
NHL Totals (1 year)		61	6	21	27	23	-4	2	0					

CULLIMORE, JASSEN   D   LIGHTNING

PERSONAL: Born December 4, 1972, in Simcoe, Ont. ... 6-5/234. ... Shoots left. ... Name pronounced KUHL-ih-MOHR.
TRANSACTIONS/CAREER NOTES: Selected by Vancouver Canucks in second round (second Canucks pick, 29th overall) of NHL entry draft (June 22, 1991). ... Suffered knee injury (March 31, 1995); missed three games. ... Traded by Canucks to Montreal Canadiens for LW Donald Brashear (November 13, 1996). ... Bruised eye (March 1, 1997); missed one game. ... Claimed on waivers by Tampa Bay Lightning (January 22, 1998). ... Sprained knee (April 4, 1998); missed remainder of season
HONORS: Named to OHL All-Star second team (1991-92).

Season Team	League	Gms.	G	A	Pts.	PIM	+/-	PP	SH	Gms.	G	A	Pts.	PIM
88-89—Peterborough	OHL	20	2	1	3	6	...	...	...	—	—	—	—	—
—Peterborough	Jr. B	29	11	17	28	88	...	...	...	—	—	—	—	—
89-90—Peterborough	OHL	59	2	6	8	61	...	...	...	11	0	2	2	8
90-91—Peterborough	OHL	62	8	16	24	74	...	...	...	4	1	0	1	7
91-92—Peterborough	OHL	54	9	37	46	65	...	...	...	10	3	6	9	8
92-93—Hamilton	AHL	56	5	7	12	60	...	...	...	—	—	—	—	—

Season Team	League	Gms.	G	A	Pts.	PIM	+/-	PP	SH	Gms.	G	A	Pts.	PIM
93-94—Hamilton	AHL	71	8	20	28	86	...	...	...	3	0	1	1	2
94-95—Syracuse	AHL	33	2	7	9	66	...	...	...	—	—	—	—	—
—Vancouver	NHL	34	1	2	3	39	-2	0	0	11	0	0	0	12
95-96—Vancouver	NHL	27	1	1	2	21	4	0	0	—	—	—	—	—
96-97—Vancouver	NHL	3	0	0	0	2	-2	0	0	—	—	—	—	—
—Montreal	NHL	49	2	6	8	42	4	0	1	2	0	0	0	2
97-98—Montreal	NHL	3	0	0	0	4	0	0	0	—	—	—	—	—
—Fredericton	AHL	5	1	0	1	8	...	...	...	—	—	—	—	—
—Tampa Bay	NHL	25	1	2	3	22	-4	1	0	—	—	—	—	—
NHL Totals (4 years)		141	5	11	16	130	0	1	1	13	0	0	0	14

CUMMINS, JIM   RW   COYOTES

PERSONAL: Born May 17, 1970, in Dearborn, Mich. ... 6-2/219. ... Shoots right. ... Full name: James Stephen Cummins. ... Name pronounced KUH-mihns.
COLLEGE: Michigan State.
TRANSACTIONS/CAREER NOTES: Selected by New York Rangers in fourth round (fifth Rangers pick, 67th overall) of NHL entry draft (June 17, 1989). ... Traded by Rangers with C Kevin Miller and D Dennis Vial to Detroit Red Wings for RW Joe Kocur and D Per Djoos (March 5, 1991). ... Suspended 11 games by NHL for leaving penalty box to join fight (January 23, 1993). ... Traded by Red Wings with fourth-round pick in 1993 draft (later traded to Boston which selected D Charles Paquette) to Philadelphia Flyers for rights to C Greg Johnson and future considerations (June 20, 1993). ... Suffered slightly separated shoulder during 1993-94 season. ... Traded by Flyers with fourth-round pick in 1995 draft to Tampa Bay Lightning for C Rob DiMaio (March 18, 1994). ... Traded by Lightning with D Jeff Buchanan and D Tom Tilley to Chicago Blackhawks for LW Paul Ysebaert and RW Rich Sutter (February 22, 1995). ... Sprained tricep (March 16, 1995); missed five games. ... Broke thumb (November 1, 1995); missed six games. ... Suspended eight games and fined $1,000 by NHL for cross checking and punching another player (March 14, 1996). ... Bruised clavicle (December 9, 1996); missed 11 games. ... Suspended one game by NHL for third game misconduct of season (January 23, 1997). ... Suffered from the flu (November 11, 1997); missed three games. ... Traded by Blackhawks with D Keith Carney to Phoenix Coyotes for C Chad Kilger and D Jayson More (March 4, 1998).
MISCELLANEOUS: Failed to score on a penalty shot (vs. Mike Vernon, April 7, 1996).

Season Team	League	Gms.	G	A	Pts.	PIM	+/-	PP	SH	Gms.	G	A	Pts.	PIM
87-88—Detroit Compuware	NAJHL	31	11	15	26	146	...	...	...	—	—	—	—	—
88-89—Michigan State	CCHA	36	3	9	12	100	...	...	...	—	—	—	—	—
89-90—Michigan State	CCHA	41	8	7	15	94	...	...	...	—	—	—	—	—
90-91—Michigan State	CCHA	34	9	6	15	110	...	...	...	—	—	—	—	—
91-92—Adirondack	AHL	65	7	13	20	338	...	...	...	5	0	0	0	19
—Detroit	NHL	1	0	0	0	7	0	0	0	—	—	—	—	—
92-93—Adirondack	AHL	43	16	4	20	179	...	...	...	9	3	1	4	4
—Detroit	NHL	7	1	1	2	58	0	0	0	—	—	—	—	—
93-94—Philadelphia	NHL	22	1	2	3	71	0	0	0	—	—	—	—	—
—Hershey	AHL	17	6	6	12	70	...	...	...	—	—	—	—	—
—Atlanta	IHL	7	4	5	9	14	...	...	...	13	1	2	3	90
—Tampa Bay	NHL	4	0	0	0	13	-1	0	0	—	—	—	—	—
94-95—Tampa Bay	NHL	10	1	0	1	41	-3	0	0	—	—	—	—	—
—Chicago	NHL	27	3	1	4	117	-3	0	0	14	1	1	2	4
95-96—Chicago	NHL	52	2	4	6	180	-1	0	0	10	0	0	0	2
96-97—Chicago	NHL	65	6	6	12	199	4	0	0	6	0	0	0	24
97-98—Chicago	NHL	55	0	2	2	178	-9	0	0	—	—	—	—	—
—Phoenix	NHL	20	0	0	0	47	-7	0	0	3	0	0	0	4
NHL Totals (7 years)		263	14	16	30	911	-20	0	0	33	1	1	2	34

CUNNEYWORTH, RANDY   LW

PERSONAL: Born May 10, 1961, in Etobicoke, Ont. ... 6-0/198. ... Shoots left. ... Full name: Randolph William Cunneyworth.
TRANSACTIONS/CAREER NOTES: Selected by Buffalo Sabres as underage junior in eighth round (ninth Sabres pick, 167th overall) of NHL entry draft (June 11, 1980). ... Attended Pittsburgh Penguins training camp as unsigned free agent (summer 1985); Sabres then traded his equalization rights with RW Mike Moller to Penguins for future considerations (October 4, 1985); Penguins sent RW Pat Hughes to Sabres to complete deal (October 1985). ... Suspended three games by NHL (January 1988). ... Suspended five games by NHL (January 1988). ... Fractured right foot (January 24, 1989). ... Traded by Penguins with G Richard Tabaracci and RW Dave McLlwain to Winnipeg Jets for RW Andrew McBain, D Jim Kyte and LW Randy Gilhen (June 17, 1989). ... Broke bone in right foot (October 1989). ... Traded by Jets to Hartford Whalers for C Paul MacDermid (December 13, 1989). ... Broke tibia bone in left leg (November 28, 1990); missed 38 games. ... Strained lower back (December 1991); missed one game. ... Strained ankle (December 21, 1991); missed two games. ... Strained left ankle (January 16, 1992); missed three games. ... Reinjured ankle (February 1, 1992); missed six games. ... Bruised ribs (November 15, 1992); missed four games. ... Suffered neck spasms (December 31, 1992); missed three games. ... Traded by Whalers with D Gary Suter and undisclosed draft pick to Chicago Blackhawks for D Frantisek Kucera and LW Jocelyn Lemieux (March 11, 1994). ... Signed as free agent by Ottawa Senators (June 30, 1994). ... Suffered back spasms during 1995-96 season; missed one game. ... Suffered back spasms (February 11, 1997); missed one game. ... Fractured cheekbone (February 28, 1997); missed five games. ... Injured groin (December 22, 1997); missed two games.
MISCELLANEOUS: Captain of Ottawa Senators (1994-95 and 1997-98).
STATISTICAL PLATEAUS: Three-goal games: 1986-87 (1). ... Four-goal games: 1986-87 (1). ... Total hat tricks: 2.

Season Team	League	Gms.	G	A	Pts.	PIM	+/-	PP	SH	Gms.	G	A	Pts.	PIM
79-80—Ottawa	OMJHL	63	16	25	41	145	...	...	...	11	0	1	1	13
80-81—Ottawa	OMJHL	67	54	74	128	240	...	...	...	15	5	8	13	35
—Rochester	AHL	1	0	1	1	2	...	...	...	—	—	—	—	—
—Buffalo	NHL	1	0	0	0	2	0	0	0	—	—	—	—	—
81-82—Rochester	AHL	57	12	15	27	86	...	...	...	9	4	0	4	30
—Buffalo	NHL	20	2	4	6	47	-3	0	0	—	—	—	—	—

Season Team	League	Gms.	G	A	Pts.	PIM	+/-	PP	SH	Gms.	G	A	Pts.	PIM
82-83—Rochester	AHL	78	23	33	56	111	...	...	...	16	4	4	8	35
83-84—Rochester	AHL	54	18	17	35	85	...	...	...	17	5	5	10	55
84-85—Rochester	AHL	72	30	38	68	148	...	...	...	5	2	1	3	16
85-86—Pittsburgh	NHL	75	15	30	45	74	12	2	2	—	—	—	—	—
86-87—Pittsburgh	NHL	79	26	27	53	142	14	3	2	—	—	—	—	—
87-88—Pittsburgh	NHL	71	35	39	74	141	13	14	0	—	—	—	—	—
88-89—Pittsburgh	NHL	70	25	19	44	156	-22	10	0	11	3	5	8	26
89-90—Winnipeg	NHL	28	5	6	11	34	-7	2	0	—	—	—	—	—
—Hartford	NHL	43	9	9	18	41	-4	2	0	4	0	0	0	2
90-91—Springfield	AHL	2	0	0	0	5	...	...	...	—	—	—	—	—
—Hartford	NHL	32	9	5	14	49	-6	0	0	1	0	0	0	0
91-92—Hartford	NHL	39	7	10	17	71	-5	0	0	7	3	0	3	9
92-93—Hartford	NHL	39	5	4	9	63	-1	0	0	—	—	—	—	—
93-94—Hartford	NHL	63	9	8	17	87	-2	0	1	—	—	—	—	—
—Chicago	NHL	16	4	3	7	13	1	0	0	6	0	0	0	8
94-95—Ottawa	NHL	48	5	5	10	68	-19	2	0	—	—	—	—	—
95-96—Ottawa	NHL	81	17	19	36	130	-31	4	0	—	—	—	—	—
96-97—Ottawa	NHL	76	12	24	36	99	-7	6	0	7	1	1	2	10
97-98—Ottawa	NHL	71	2	11	13	63	-14	1	0	6	0	1	1	6
NHL Totals (15 years)		852	187	223	410	1280	-82	46	5	42	7	7	14	61

CZERKAWSKI, MARIUSZ   RW   ISLANDERS

PERSONAL: Born April 13, 1972, in Radomski, Poland. ... 6-0/195. ... Shoots right. ... Name pronounced MAIR-ee-uhz chuhr-KAW-skee.
TRANSACTIONS/CAREER NOTES: Selected by Boston Bruins (fifth Bruins pick, 106th overall) of NHL entry draft (June 22, 1991). ... Played in Europe during 1994-95 NHL lockout. ... Traded by Bruins with D Sean Brown and first-round pick (D Matthieu Descoteaux) in 1996 draft to Edmonton Oilers for G Bill Ranford (January 11, 1996). ... Injured finger (March 23, 1996); missed two games. ... Suffered hip pointer (January 11, 1997); missed two games. ... Traded by Oilers to New York Islanders for LW Dan Lacouture (August 25, 1997).
STATISTICAL PLATEAUS: Three-goal games: 1996-97 (2).

Season Team	League	Gms.	G	A	Pts.	PIM	+/-	PP	SH	Gms.	G	A	Pts.	PIM
90-91—GKS Tychy	Poland	24	25	15	40		...	...	...	—	—	—	—	—
91-92—Djur. Stockholm	Sweden	39	8	5	13	4	...	...	...	3	0	0	0	2
—Polish Olympic Team	CIS	5	0	1	1	4	...	...	...	—	—	—	—	—
92-93—Hammarby	Swed. Dv.II	32	39	30	69	74	...	...	...	—	—	—	—	—
93-94—Djur. Stockholm	Sweden	39	13	21	34	20	...	...	...	—	—	—	—	—
—Boston	NHL	4	2	1	3	0	-2	1	0	13	3	3	6	4
94-95—Kiekko-Espoo	Finland	7	9	3	12	10	...	...	...	—	—	—	—	—
—Boston	NHL	47	12	14	26	31	4	1	0	5	1	0	1	0
95-96—Boston	NHL	33	5	6	11	10	-11	1	0	—	—	—	—	—
—Edmonton	NHL	37	12	17	29	8	7	2	0	—	—	—	—	—
96-97—Edmonton	NHL	76	26	21	47	16	0	4	0	12	2	1	3	10
97-98—New York Islanders	NHL	68	12	13	25	23	11	2	0	—	—	—	—	—
NHL Totals (5 years)		265	69	72	141	88	9	11	0	30	6	4	10	14

DACKELL, ANDREAS   RW   SENATORS

PERSONAL: Born December 29, 1972, in Gavle, Sweden. ... 5-11/191. ... Shoots right. ... Name pronounced AHN-dray-uhz DA-kuhl.
TRANSACTIONS/CAREER NOTES: Selected by Ottawa Senators in sixth round (third Senators pick, 136th overall) of NHL entry draft (June 22, 1996).

Season Team	League	Gms.	G	A	Pts.	PIM	+/-	PP	SH	Gms.	G	A	Pts.	PIM
90-91—Brynas Gavle	Sweden	3	0	1	1	2	...	...	...	—	—	—	—	—
91-92—Brynas Gavle	Sweden	4	0	0	0	2	...	...	...	2	0	1	1	4
92-93—Brynas Gavle	Sweden	40	12	15	27	12	...	...	...	10	4	5	9	2
93-94—Brynas Gavle	Sweden	38	12	17	29	47	...	...	...	7	2	2	4	8
94-95—Brynas Gavle	Sweden	39	17	16	33	34	...	...	...	14	3	3	6	14
95-96—Brynas Gavle	Sweden	22	6	6	12	8	...	...	...	—	—	—	—	—
96-97—Ottawa	NHL	79	12	19	31	8	-6	2	0	7	1	0	1	0
97-98—Ottawa	NHL	82	15	18	33	24	-11	3	2	11	1	1	2	2
NHL Totals (2 years)		161	27	37	64	32	-17	5	2	18	2	1	3	2

DAFOE, BYRON   G   BRUINS

PERSONAL: Born February 25, 1971, in Sussex, England. ... 5-11/190. ... Catches left. ... Full name: Byron Jaromir Dafoe.
TRANSACTIONS/CAREER NOTES: Selected by Washington Capitals in second round (second Capitals pick, 35th overall) of NHL entry draft (June 17, 1989). ... Underwent emergency appendectomy (December 1989). ... Traded by Capitals with LW/C Dimitri Khristich to Los Angeles Kings for first-(C Alexander Volchkov) and fourth-(RW Justin Davis) round picks in 1996 draft (July 8, 1995). ... Strained thumb (February 1, 1997); missed two games. ... Traded by Kings with LW Dimitri Khristich to Boston Bruins for C Jozef Stumpel, RW Sandy Moger and fourth-round pick (traded to New Jersey) in 1998 draft (August 29, 1997).
HONORS: Shared Harry (Hap) Holmes Memorial Trophy with Olaf Kolzig (1993-94). ... Named to AHL All-Star first team (1993-94).
MISCELLANEOUS: Allowed penalty shot goal (vs. Steve Chiasson, December 11, 1995).

Season Team	League	REGULAR SEASON								PLAYOFFS						
		Gms.	Min	W	L	T	GA	SO	Avg.	Gms.	Min.	W	L	GA	SO	Avg.
87-88—Juan de Fuca	BCJHL	32	1716	...	...	...	129	0	4.51	—	—	—	—	—	—	—
88-89—Portland	WHL	59	3279	29	24	3	*291	1	5.32	*18	*1091	10	8	*81	*1	4.45
89-90—Portland	WHL	40	2265	14	21	3	193	0	5.11	—	—	—	—	—	—	—
90-91—Portland	WHL	8	414	1	5	1	41	0	5.94	—	—	—	—	—	—	—
—Prince Albert	WHL	32	1839	13	12	4	124	0	4.05	—	—	—	—	—	—	—
91-92—New Haven	AHL	7	364	3	2	1	22	0	3.63	—	—	—	—	—	—	—
—Baltimore	AHL	33	1847	12	16	4	119	0	3.87	—	—	—	—	—	—	—
—Hampton Roads	ECHL	10	562	6	4	‡0	26	1	2.78	—	—	—	—	—	—	—
92-93—Baltimore	AHL	48	2617	16	*20	7	191	1	4.38	5	241	2	3	22	0	5.48
—Washington	NHL	1	1	0	0	0	0	0	...	—	—	—	—	—	—	—
93-94—Portland	AHL	47	2662	24	16	4	148	1	3.34	1	9	0	0	1	0	6.67
—Washington	NHL	5	230	2	2	0	13	0	3.39	2	118	0	2	5	0	2.54
94-95—Portland	AHL	6	330	5	0	0	16	0	2.91	7	417	3	4	29	0	4.17
—Phoenix	IHL	49	2744	25	16	‡6	169	2	3.70	—	—	—	—	—	—	—
—Washington	NHL	4	187	1	1	1	11	0	3.53	1	20	0	0	1	0	3.00
95-96—Los Angeles	NHL	47	2666	14	24	8	172	1	3.87	—	—	—	—	—	—	—
96-97—Los Angeles	NHL	40	2162	13	17	5	112	0	3.11	—	—	—	—	—	—	—
97-98—Boston	NHL	65	3693	30	25	9	138	6	2.24	6	422	2	4	14	1	1.99
NHL Totals (6 years)		162	8939	60	69	23	446	7	2.99	9	560	2	6	20	1	2.14

DAHL, KEVIN   D

PERSONAL: Born December 30, 1968, in Regina, Sask. ... 5-11/190. ... Shoots right.

COLLEGE: Bowling Green State (degree in physical education).

TRANSACTIONS/CAREER NOTES: Selected by Montreal Canadiens in 11th round (12th Canadiens pick, 230th overall) of NHL entry draft (June 11, 1988). ... Signed as free agent by Calgary Flames (August 1, 1991). ... Suffered charley horse (November 2, 1992); missed two games. ... Injured heel (November 28, 1992); missed one game. ... Strained left knee (December 15, 1992); missed 18 games. ... Fractured left foot (April 9, 1993); missed one game. ... Separated left shoulder (November 6, 1993); missed nine games. ... Strained left shoulder (December 7, 1993); missed 30 games. ... Separated left shoulder (February 16, 1995); missed two games. ... Injured rib cartilage (March 31, 1995); missed seven games. ... Injured knee (November 11, 1995); missed one game. ... Injured knee (December 19, 1995); missed three games. ... Signed as free agent by Phoenix Coyotes (August 26, 1996). ... Signed by Flames (August 29, 1997). ... Bruised hand (January 11, 1997); missed two games.

MISCELLANEOUS: Member of silver-medal-winning Canadian Olympic team (1992).

Season Team	League	REGULAR SEASON								PLAYOFFS				
		Gms.	G	A	Pts.	PIM	+/-	PP	SH	Gms.	G	A	Pts.	PIM
87-88—Bowling Green	CCHA	44	2	23	25	78	...	...	...	—	—	—	—	—
88-89—Bowling Green	CCHA	46	9	26	35	51	...	...	...	—	—	—	—	—
89-90—Bowling Green	CCHA	43	8	22	30	74	...	...	...	—	—	—	—	—
90-91—Fredericton	AHL	32	1	15	16	45	...	...	...	9	0	1	1	11
—Winston-Salem	ECHL	36	7	17	24	58	...	...	...	—	—	—	—	—
91-92—Canadian nat'l team	Int'l	45	2	15	17	44	...	...	...	—	—	—	—	—
—Can. Olympic Team	Int'l	8	2	0	2	6	...	...	...	—	—	—	—	—
—Salt Lake City	IHL	13	0	2	2	12	...	...	...	5	0	0	0	13
92-93—Calgary	NHL	61	2	9	11	56	9	1	0	6	0	2	2	8
93-94—Calgary	NHL	33	0	3	3	23	-2	0	0	6	0	0	0	4
—Saint John	AHL	2	0	0	0	0	...	...	...	—	—	—	—	—
94-95—Calgary	NHL	34	4	8	12	38	8	0	0	3	0	0	0	0
95-96—Calgary	NHL	32	1	1	2	26	-2	0	0	1	0	0	0	0
—Saint John	AHL	23	4	11	15	37	...	...	...	—	—	—	—	—
96-97—Las Vegas	IHL	73	10	21	31	101	...	...	...	3	0	0	0	2
—Phoenix	NHL	2	0	0	0	0	0	0	0	—	—	—	—	—
97-98—Calgary	NHL	19	0	1	1	6	-3	0	0	—	—	—	—	—
—Chicago	IHL	45	8	9	17	61	...	...	...	20	1	8	9	32
NHL Totals (6 years)		181	7	22	29	149	10	1	0	16	0	2	2	12

DAIGLE, ALEXANDRE   C/RW   FLYERS

PERSONAL: Born February 7, 1975, in Montreal. ... 6-0/202. ... Shoots left. ... Name pronounced DAYG.

TRANSACTIONS/CAREER NOTES: Selected by Ottawa Senators in first round (first Senators pick, first overall) of NHL entry draft (June 26, 1993). ... Fractured left forearm (February 3, 1996); missed remainder of season. ... Traded by Senators to Flyers for C Vaclav Prospal, RW Pat Falloon and second round pick (LW Chris Bala) in 1998 draft (January 17, 1998).

HONORS: Won Can.HL Rookie of the Year Award (1991-92). ... Named QMJHL Rookie of the Year (1991-92). ... Won Michel Bergeron Trophy (1991-92). ... Named to Can.HL All-Rookie team (1991-92). ... Named to QMJHL All-Star second team (1991-92). ... Won Can.HL Top Draft Prospect Award (1992-93). ... Won QMJHL Top Draft Prospect Award (1992-93). ... Named to QMJHL All-Star first team (1992-93).

MISCELLANEOUS: Failed to score on penalty shot attempt (vs. Guy Hebert, December 30, 1996).

STATISTICAL PLATEAUS: Three-goal games: 1994-95 (1), 1997-98 (1). Total: 2.

Season Team	League	REGULAR SEASON								PLAYOFFS				
		Gms.	G	A	Pts.	PIM	+/-	PP	SH	Gms.	G	A	Pts.	PIM
91-92—Victoriaville	QMJHL	66	35	75	110	63	...	...	...	—	—	—	—	—
92-93—Victoriaville	QMJHL	53	45	92	137	85	...	...	...	6	5	6	11	4
93-94—Ottawa	NHL	84	20	31	51	40	-45	4	0	—	—	—	—	—
94-95—Victoriaville	QMJHL	18	14	20	34	16	...	...	...	—	—	—	—	—
—Ottawa	NHL	47	16	21	37	14	-22	4	1	—	—	—	—	—
95-96—Ottawa	NHL	50	5	12	17	24	-30	1	0	—	—	—	—	—
96-97—Ottawa	NHL	82	26	25	51	33	-33	4	0	7	0	0	0	2
97-98—Ottawa	NHL	38	7	9	16	8	-7	4	0	—	—	—	—	—
—Philadelphia	NHL	37	9	17	26	6	-1	4	0	5	0	2	2	0
NHL Totals (5 years)		338	83	115	198	125	-138	21	1	12	0	2	2	2

DAIGLE, SYLVAIN   G   COYOTES

PERSONAL: Born October 20, 1976, in St. Hyacinthe, Que. ... 5-8/185. ... Catches right. ... Name pronounced DAYG.
TRANSACTIONS/CAREER NOTES: Selected by Winnipeg Jets in sixth round (seventh Jets pick, 136th overall) of NHL entry draft (July 8, 1995). ... Jets franchise moved to Phoenix and renamed Coyotes for 1996-97 season; NHL approved move on January 18, 1996.

Season Team	League	Gms.	Min	W	L	T	GA	SO	Avg.	Gms.	Min.	W	L	GA	SO	Avg.
93-94—Shawinigan	QMJHL	31	1645	14	11	3	113	0	4.12	—	—	—	—	—	—	—
94-95—Shawinigan	QMJHL	48	2831	27	17	3	159	3	3.37	14	824	7	6	57	0	4.15
95-96—Shawinigan	QMJHL	49	2705	23	14	5	159	†3	3.53	6	390	2	4	22	0	3.38
96-97—Springfield	AHL	13	691	8	3	0	23	1	2.00	6	312	1	4	18	0	3.46
—Mississippi	ECHL	34	1951	20	8	‡5	100	2	3.08	—	—	—	—	—	—	—
—Las Vegas	IHL	1	41	0	0	‡0	5	0	7.32	—	—	—	—	—	—	—
97-98—Springfield	AHL	21	1094	7	9	2	68	0	3.73	2	23	0	0	0	0	0.00

DAIGNEAULT, J.J.   D   PREDATORS

PERSONAL: Born October 12, 1965, in Montreal. ... 5-10/186. ... Shoots left. ... Full name: Jean-Jacques Daigneault. ... Name pronounced DAYN-yoh.
TRANSACTIONS/CAREER NOTES: Underwent knee surgery (March 1984). ... Selected by Vancouver Canucks as underage junior in first round (first Canucks pick, 10th overall) of NHL entry draft (June 1984). ... Broke finger (March 19, 1986). ... Traded by Canucks with second-round pick (C Kent Hawley) in 1986 draft and fifth-round pick in 1987 draft to Philadelphia Flyers for RW Rich Sutter, D Dave Richter and third-round pick (D Don Gibson) in 1986 draft (June 1986). ... Sprained ankle (April 12, 1987). ... Traded by Flyers to Montreal Canadiens for D Scott Sandelin (November 1988). ... Bruised shoulder (December 1990). ... Suffered left hip pointer (March 16, 1991). ... Injured knee (April 7, 1991). ... Bruised left knee (November 28, 1992); missed one game. ... Injured shoulder (December 23, 1992); missed two games. ... Sprained right ankle (March 1, 1993); missed 11 games. ... Suffered injury (December 22, 1993); missed three games and fined $500 by NHL for elbowing (January 7, 1994). ... Sprained wrist (January 10, 1994); missed six games. ... Suffered sore back (March 1, 1994); missed one game. ... Injured shoulder (February 4, 1995); missed one game. ... Suffered from cold (February 13, 1995); missed one game. ... Bruised ankle (April 12, 1995); missed one game. ... Traded by Canadiens to St. Louis Blues for G Pat Jablonski (November 7, 1995). ... Traded by Blues to Pittsburgh Penguins for sixth-round pick (C Stephen Wagner) in 1996 draft (March 20, 1996). ... Suffered back spasms (December 30, 1996); missed one game. ... Suffered back spasms (January 4, 1997); missed two games. ... Traded by Penguins to Anaheim Mighty Ducks for LW Garry Valk (February 21, 1997). ... Suspended 10 games and fined $1,000 by NHL for abusing an official (February 26, 1997). ... Traded by Mighty Ducks with C Mark Janssens and RW Joe Sacco to New York Islanders for C Travis Green, D Doug Houda and RW Tony Tuzzolino (February 6, 1998). ... Separated shoulder (March 12, 1998); missed six games. ... Reinjured shoulder (April 18, 1998); missed one game. ... Selected by Nashville Predators in NHL expansion draft (June 26, 1998).
HONORS: Won Emile (Butch) Bouchard Trophy (1982-83). ... Named to QMJHL All-Star first team (1982-83).
MISCELLANEOUS: Member of Stanley Cup championship team (1993).

Season Team	League	Gms.	G	A	Pts.	PIM	+/-	PP	SH	Gms.	G	A	Pts.	PIM
81-82—Laval	QMJHL	64	4	25	29	41	...	...	...	18	1	3	4	2
82-83—Longueuil	QMJHL	70	26	58	84	58	...	...	...	15	4	11	15	35
83-84—Can. Olympic Team	Int'l	62	6	15	21	40	...	...	...	—	—	—	—	—
—Longueuil	QMJHL	10	2	11	13	6	...	...	...	14	3	13	16	30
84-85—Vancouver	NHL	67	4	23	27	69	-14	2	0	—	—	—	—	—
85-86—Vancouver	NHL	64	5	23	28	45	-20	4	0	3	0	2	2	0
86-87—Philadelphia	NHL	77	6	16	22	56	12	0	0	9	1	0	1	0
87-88—Philadelphia	NHL	28	2	2	4	12	-8	2	0	—	—	—	—	—
—Hershey	AHL	10	1	5	6	8	...	...	...	—	—	—	—	—
88-89—Hershey	AHL	12	0	10	10	13	...	...	...	—	—	—	—	—
—Sherbrooke	AHL	63	10	33	43	48	...	...	...	6	1	3	4	2
89-90—Sherbrooke	AHL	28	8	19	27	18	...	...	...	—	—	—	—	—
—Montreal	NHL	36	2	10	12	14	11	0	0	9	0	0	0	2
90-91—Montreal	NHL	51	3	16	19	31	-2	2	0	5	0	1	1	0
91-92—Montreal	NHL	79	4	14	18	36	16	2	0	11	0	3	3	4
92-93—Montreal	NHL	66	8	10	18	57	25	0	0	20	1	3	4	22
93-94—Montreal	NHL	68	2	12	14	73	16	0	0	7	0	1	1	12
94-95—Montreal	NHL	45	3	5	8	40	2	0	0	—	—	—	—	—
95-96—Montreal	NHL	7	0	1	1	6	0	0	0	—	—	—	—	—
—St. Louis	NHL	37	1	3	4	24	-6	0	0	—	—	—	—	—
—Worcester	AHL	9	1	10	11	10	...	...	...	—	—	—	—	—
—Pittsburgh	NHL	13	3	3	6	23	0	2	0	17	1	9	10	36
96-97—Pittsburgh	NHL	53	3	14	17	36	-5	0	0	—	—	—	—	—
—Anaheim	NHL	13	2	9	11	22	5	0	0	11	2	7	9	16
97-98—Anaheim	NHL	53	2	15	17	28	-10	1	0	—	—	—	—	—
—New York Islanders	NHL	18	0	6	6	21	1	0	0	—	—	—	—	—
NHL Totals (13 years)		775	50	182	232	593	23	15	0	92	5	26	31	92

DALE, ANDREW   C   KINGS

PERSONAL: Born February 16, 1976, in Sudbury, Ont. ... 6-1/196. ... Shoots left.
TRANSACTIONS/CAREER NOTES: Selected by Los Angeles Kings in eighth round (sixth Kings pick, 189th overall) of NHL entry draft (June 29, 1994).

Season Team	League	Gms.	G	A	Pts.	PIM	+/-	PP	SH	Gms.	G	A	Pts.	PIM
93-94—Sudbury	OHL	53	8	13	21	21	...	...	...	9	0	3	3	4
94-95—Sudbury	OHL	65	21	30	51	99	...	...	...	18	2	9	11	37
95-96—Kitchener	OHL	64	44	45	89	75	...	...	...	12	5	5	10	25
96-97—Phoenix	IHL	32	7	6	13	19	...	...	...	—	—	—	—	—
—Mississippi	ECHL	19	6	9	15	16	...	...	...	2	0	1	1	0
97-98—Springfield	AHL	40	3	6	9	32	...	...	...	—	—	—	—	—
—Mississippi	ECHL	3	1	3	4	215	...	...	...	—	—	—	—	—

DAMPHOUSSE, J.F.   G   DEVILS

PERSONAL: Born July 21, 1979, in St. Alexis des Monts, Que. ... 6-0/165. ... Catches left. ... Full name: Jean-Francois Damphousse. ... Name pronounced dahm-FOOZ.
TRANSACTIONS/CAREER NOTES: Selected by New Jersey Devils in first round (first Devils pick, 24th overall) of NHL entry draft (June 21, 1997).

		REGULAR SEASON							PLAYOFFS					
Season Team	League	Gms.	Min	W	L	T	GA	SO	Avg.	Gms.	Min.	W	L	GA	SO	Avg.
96-97—Moncton	QMJHL	39	2061	6	25	2	190	0	5.53	—	—	—	—	—	—	—
97-98—Moncton	QMJHL	59	3400	24	26	*6	174	1	3.07	10	595	5	5	28	0	2.82

DAMPHOUSSE, VINCENT   C   CANADIENS

PERSONAL: Born December 17, 1967, in Montreal. ... 6-1/191. ... Shoots left. ... Name pronounced dahm-FOOZ.
TRANSACTIONS/CAREER NOTES: Selected by Toronto Maple Leafs as underage junior in first round (first Maple Leafs pick, sixth overall) of NHL entry draft (June 21, 1986). ... Traded by Maple Leafs with D Luke Richardson, G Peter Ing, C Scott Thornton and future considerations to Edmonton Oilers for G Grant Fuhr, LW/RW Glenn Anderson and LW Craig Berube (September 19, 1991). ... Traded by Oilers with fourth-round pick (D Adam Wiesel) in 1993 draft to Montreal Canadiens for LW Shayne Corson, LW Vladimir Vujtek and C Brent Gilchrist (August 27, 1992). ... Played in Europe during 1994-95 NHL lockout. ... Suspended two games and fined $1,000 by NHL for cross-checking incident (March 30, 1996). ... Partially dislocated shoulder (March 11, 1998); missed six games.
HONORS: Named to QMJHL All-Star second team (1985-86). ... Played in NHL All-Star Game (1991 and 1992). ... Named All-Star Game Most Valuable Player (1991).
RECORDS: Shares NHL All-Star single-game record for most goals—4 (1991).
STATISTICAL PLATEAUS: Three-goal games: 1988-89 (1), 1989-90 (2), 1992-93 (2), 1993-94 (2), 1996-97 (1), 1997-98 (2). Total: 10. ... Four-goal games: 1991-92 (1). ... Total hat tricks: 11.
MISCELLANEOUS: Member of Stanley Cup championship team (1993). ... Captain of Montreal Canadiens (October 29, 1996 through 1997-98). ... Failed to score on a penalty shot (vs. Dominik Hasek, March 8, 1997).

		REGULAR SEASON							PLAYOFFS				
Season Team	League	Gms.	G	A	Pts.	PIM	+/-	PP	SH	Gms.	G	A	Pts.	PIM
83-84—Laval	QMJHL	66	29	36	65	25	...	...	...	—	—	—	—	—
84-85—Laval	QMJHL	68	35	68	103	62	...	...	...	—	—	—	—	—
85-86—Laval	QMJHL	69	45	110	155	70	...	...	...	14	9	27	36	12
86-87—Toronto	NHL	80	21	25	46	26	-6	4	0	12	1	5	6	8
87-88—Toronto	NHL	75	12	36	48	40	2	1	0	6	0	1	1	10
88-89—Toronto	NHL	80	26	42	68	75	-8	6	0	—	—	—	—	—
89-90—Toronto	NHL	80	33	61	94	56	2	9	0	5	0	2	2	2
90-91—Toronto	NHL	79	26	47	73	65	-31	10	1	—	—	—	—	—
91-92—Edmonton	NHL	80	38	51	89	53	10	12	1	16	6	8	14	8
92-93—Montreal	NHL	84	39	58	97	98	5	9	3	20	11	12	23	16
93-94—Montreal	NHL	84	40	51	91	75	0	13	0	7	1	2	3	8
94-95—Ratingen	Germany	11	5	6	11	24	...	...	...	—	—	—	—	—
—Montreal	NHL	48	10	30	40	42	15	4	0	—	—	—	—	—
95-96—Montreal	NHL	80	38	56	94	158	5	11	4	6	4	4	8	0
96-97—Montreal	NHL	82	27	54	81	82	-6	7	2	5	0	0	0	2
97-98—Montreal	NHL	76	18	41	59	58	14	2	1	10	3	6	9	22
NHL Totals (12 years)		928	328	552	880	828	2	88	12	87	26	40	66	76

DANDENAULT, MATHIEU   D/RW   RED WINGS

PERSONAL: Born February 3, 1976, in Magog, Que. ... 6-1/200. ... Shoots right. ... Cousin of Eric Dandenault, defenseman in Philadelphia Flyers organization (1991-92 through 1993-94). ... Name pronounced DAN-dih-noh.
HIGH SCHOOL: CEGEP de Sherbrooke (Que.).
TRANSACTIONS/CAREER NOTES: Selected by Detroit Red Wings in second round (second Red Wings pick, 49th overall) of NHL entry draft (June 28, 1994). ... Suffered from the flu (November 11, 1995); missed one game. ... Bruised ribs (March 10, 1997); missed four games.
MISCELLANEOUS: Member of Stanley Cup championship team (1997 and 1998).

		REGULAR SEASON							PLAYOFFS				
Season Team	League	Gms.	G	A	Pts.	PIM	+/-	PP	SH	Gms.	G	A	Pts.	PIM
91-92—Gloucester	OPJHL	6	3	4	7	0	...	...	...	—	—	—	—	—
92-93—Gloucester	OPJHL	55	11	26	37	64	...	...	...	—	—	—	—	—
93-94—Sherbrooke	QMJHL	67	17	36	53	67	...	...	...	12	4	10	14	12
94-95—Sherbrooke	QMJHL	67	37	70	107	76	...	...	...	7	1	7	8	10
95-96—Detroit	NHL	34	5	7	12	6	6	1	0	—	—	—	—	—
—Adirondack	AHL	4	0	0	0	0	...	...	...	—	—	—	—	—
96-97—Detroit	NHL	65	3	9	12	28	-10	0	0	—	—	—	—	—
97-98—Detroit	NHL	68	5	12	17	43	5	0	0	3	1	0	1	0
NHL Totals (3 years)		167	13	28	41	77	1	1	0	3	1	0	1	0

DANEYKO, KEN   D   DEVILS

PERSONAL: Born April 17, 1964, in Windsor, Ont. ... 6-0/215. ... Shoots left. ... Full name: Kenneth Daneyko. ... Name pronounced DAN-ih-koh.
TRANSACTIONS/CAREER NOTES: Selected by Seattle Breakers from Spokane Flyers in WHL dispersal draft (December 1981). ... Selected by New Jersey Devils as underage junior in first round (second Devils pick, 18th overall) of NHL entry draft (June 1982). ... Fractured right fibula (November 2, 1983). ... Suspended one game and fined $500 by NHL for playing in West Germany without permission (October 1985). ... Injured wrist (February 25, 1987). ... Broke nose (February 24, 1988). ... Injured shoulder (March 29, 1994); missed six games. ... Injured knee (March 8, 1995); missed 23 games. ... Suffered from the flu (March 9, 1996); missed two games. ... Injured hip (October 12, 1996); missed one game. ... Suffered from the flu (January 31, 1997); missed one game. ... Voluntarily entered NHL/NHLPA substance abuse and behavioral health program (November 6, 1997); missed 45 games.
MISCELLANEOUS: Member of Stanley Cup championship team (1995). ... Holds New Jersey Devils franchise all-time record for most penalty minutes (2,175).

			REGULAR SEASON								PLAYOFFS				
Season Team	League	Gms.	G	A	Pts.	PIM	+/-	PP	SH		Gms.	G	A	Pts.	PIM
80-81—Spokane Flyers	WHL	62	6	13	19	140	...	...	...		4	0	0	0	6
81-82—Spokane Flyers	WHL	26	1	11	12	147	...	...	...		—	—	—	—	—
—Seattle	WHL	38	1	22	23	151	...	...	...		14	1	9	10	49
82-83—Seattle	WHL	69	17	43	60	150	...	...	...		4	1	3	4	14
83-84—Kamloops	WHL	19	6	28	34	52	...	...	...		17	4	9	13	28
—New Jersey	NHL	11	1	4	5	17	-1	0	0		—	—	—	—	—
84-85—New Jersey	NHL	1	0	0	0	10	-1	0	0		—	—	—	—	—
—Maine	AHL	80	4	9	13	206	...	...	...		11	1	3	4	36
85-86—Maine	AHL	21	3	2	5	75	...	...	...		—	—	—	—	—
—New Jersey	NHL	44	0	10	10	100	1	0	0		—	—	—	—	—
86-87—New Jersey	NHL	79	2	12	14	183	-13	0	0		—	—	—	—	—
87-88—New Jersey	NHL	80	5	7	12	239	-3	1	0		20	1	6	7	83
88-89—New Jersey	NHL	80	5	5	10	283	-22	1	0		—	—	—	—	—
89-90—New Jersey	NHL	74	6	15	21	216	15	0	1		6	2	0	2	21
90-91—New Jersey	NHL	80	4	16	20	249	-10	1	2		7	0	1	1	10
91-92—New Jersey	NHL	80	1	7	8	170	7	0	0		7	0	3	3	16
92-93—New Jersey	NHL	84	2	11	13	236	4	0	0		5	0	0	0	8
93-94—New Jersey	NHL	78	1	9	10	176	27	0	0		20	0	1	1	45
94-95—New Jersey	NHL	25	1	2	3	54	4	0	0		20	1	0	1	22
95-96—New Jersey	NHL	80	2	4	6	115	-10	0	0		—	—	—	—	—
96-97—New Jersey	NHL	77	2	7	9	70	24	0	0		10	0	0	0	28
97-98—New Jersey	NHL	37	0	1	1	57	3	0	0		6	0	1	1	10
NHL Totals (15 years)		910	32	110	142	2175	25	3	3		101	4	12	16	243

DANIELS, JEFF — LW — PREDATORS

PERSONAL: Born June 24, 1968, in Oshawa, Ont. ... 6-1/200. ... Shoots left.

TRANSACTIONS/CAREER NOTES: Selected by Pittsburgh Penguins as underage junior in sixth round (sixth Penguins pick, 109th overall) of NHL entry draft (June 21, 1986). ... Traded by Penguins to Florida Panthers for D Greg Hawgood (March 19, 1994). ... Loaned by Panthers to Detroit Vipers of IHL (February 14, 1995). ... Signed as free agent by Hartford Whalers (July 18, 1995). ... Tore knee ligament (December 20, 1996); missed 25 games. ... Whalers franchise moved to North Carolina and renamed Carolina Hurricanes for 1997-98 season; NHL approved move on June 25, 1997. ... Selected by Nashville Predators in NHL expansion draft (June 26, 1998).

MISCELLANEOUS: Member of Stanley Cup championship team (1992).

			REGULAR SEASON								PLAYOFFS				
Season Team	League	Gms.	G	A	Pts.	PIM	+/-	PP	SH		Gms.	G	A	Pts.	PIM
84-85—Oshawa	OHL	59	7	11	18	16	...	...	...		—	—	—	—	—
85-86—Oshawa	OHL	62	13	19	32	23	...	...	...		6	0	1	1	0
86-87—Oshawa	OHL	54	14	9	23	22	...	...	...		15	3	2	5	5
87-88—Oshawa	OHL	64	29	39	68	59	...	...	...		4	2	3	5	0
88-89—Muskegon	IHL	58	21	21	42	58	...	...	...		11	3	5	8	11
89-90—Muskegon	IHL	80	30	47	77	39	...	...	...		6	1	1	2	7
90-91—Pittsburgh	NHL	11	0	2	2	2	0	0	0		—	—	—	—	—
—Muskegon	IHL	62	23	29	52	18	...	...	...		5	1	3	4	2
91-92—Pittsburgh	NHL	2	0	0	0	0	0	0	0		—	—	—	—	—
—Muskegon	IHL	44	19	16	35	38	...	...	...		10	5	4	9	9
92-93—Pittsburgh	NHL	58	5	4	9	14	-5	0	0		12	3	2	5	0
—Cleveland	IHL	3	2	1	3	0	...	...	...		—	—	—	—	—
93-94—Pittsburgh	NHL	63	3	5	8	20	-1	0	0		—	—	—	—	—
—Florida	NHL	7	0	0	0	0	0	0	0		—	—	—	—	—
94-95—Florida	NHL	3	0	0	0	0	0	0	0		—	—	—	—	—
—Detroit	IHL	25	8	12	20	6	...	...	...		5	1	0	1	0
95-96—Springfield	AHL	72	22	20	42	32	...	...	...		10	3	0	3	2
96-97—Springfield	AHL	38	18	14	32	19	...	...	...		16	7	3	10	4
—Hartford	NHL	10	0	2	2	0	2	0	0		—	—	—	—	—
97-98—New Haven	AHL	71	24	27	51	34	...	...	...		3	0	1	1	0
—Carolina	NHL	2	0	0	0	0	0	0	0		—	—	—	—	—
NHL Totals (7 years)		156	8	13	21	36	-4	0	0		12	3	2	5	0

DANIELS, SCOTT — LW — DEVILS

PERSONAL: Born September 19, 1969, in Prince Albert, Sask. ... 6-3/210. ... Shoots left.

TRANSACTIONS/CAREER NOTES: Traded by Kamloops Blazers with C Mario Desjardins, Wayne MacDonald, Jason Bennings and future considerations to New Westminster Bruins for C Glenn Mulvenna and D Garth Premak (February 1987). ... Selected by Hartford Whalers in seventh round (sixth Whalers pick, 136th overall) of NHL entry draft (June 17, 1989). ... Injured knee (March 25, 1995); missed seven games. ... Suffered mild concussion (February 21, 1996); missed two games. ... Signed as free agent by Philadelphia Flyers (June 18, 1996). ... Fined $1,000 by NHL for fighting (November 13, 1996). ... Strained left buttock (November 4, 1996); missed two games. ... Bruised right quadricep (December 21, 1996); missed ten games. ... Bruised wrist (February 15, 1997); missed three games. ... Suffered from tonsillitis (March 1, 1997); missed two games. ... Strained rib muscle (March 22, 1997); missed seven games. ... Suffered charley horse (April 12, 1997); missed final game of regular season. ... Claimed by New Jersey Devils from Flyers in NHL waiver draft (September 28, 1997). ... Fractured left wrist (October 10, 1997); missed 37 games. ... Suspended two games and fined $1,000 by NHL for head-butting incident (January 28, 1998). ... Suffered charley horse (February 26, 1998); missed 17 games.

			REGULAR SEASON								PLAYOFFS				
Season Team	League	Gms.	G	A	Pts.	PIM	+/-	PP	SH		Gms.	G	A	Pts.	PIM
86-87—Kamloops	WHL	43	6	4	10	66	...	...	...		—	—	—	—	—
—New Westminster	WHL	19	4	7	11	30	...	...	...		—	—	—	—	—
87-88—New Westminster	WHL	37	6	11	17	157	...	...	...		—	—	—	—	—
—Regina	WHL	19	2	3	5	83	...	...	...		—	—	—	—	—
88-89—Regina	WHL	64	21	26	47	241	...	...	...		—	—	—	—	—

Season Team	League	REGULAR SEASON								PLAYOFFS				
		Gms.	G	A	Pts.	PIM	+/-	PP	SH	Gms.	G	A	Pts.	PIM
89-90—Regina	WHL	53	28	31	59	171	...	...	...	—	—	—	—	—
90-91—Springfield	AHL	40	2	6	8	121	...	...	...	—	—	—	—	—
—Louisville	ECHL	9	5	3	8	34	...	...	...	1	0	2	2	0
91-92—Springfield	AHL	54	7	15	22	213	...	...	...	10	0	0	0	32
92-93—Hartford	NHL	1	0	0	0	19	0	0	0	—	—	—	—	—
—Springfield	AHL	60	11	12	23	181	...	...	...	12	2	7	9	12
93-94—Springfield	AHL	52	9	11	20	185	...	...	...	6	0	1	1	53
94-95—Springfield	AHL	48	9	5	14	277	...	...	...	—	—	—	—	—
—Hartford	NHL	12	0	2	2	55	1	0	0	—	—	—	—	—
95-96—Hartford	NHL	53	3	4	7	254	-4	0	0	—	—	—	—	—
—Springfield	AHL	6	4	1	5	17	...	...	...	—	—	—	—	—
96-97—Philadelphia	NHL	56	5	3	8	237	2	0	0	—	—	—	—	—
97-98—New Jersey	NHL	26	0	3	3	102	1	0	0	1	0	0	0	0
NHL Totals (5 years)		148	8	12	20	667	0	0	0	1	0	0	0	0

DARBY, CRAIG   C   PREDATORS

PERSONAL: Born September 26, 1972, in Oneida, N.Y. ... 6-3/180. ... Shoots right.
HIGH SCHOOL: Albany (N.Y.) Academy.
COLLEGE: Providence.
TRANSACTIONS/CAREER NOTES: Selected by Montreal Canadiens in second round (third Canadiens pick, 43rd overall) of NHL entry draft (June 22, 1991). ... Traded by Canadiens with LW Kirk Muller and D Mathieu Schneider to New York Islanders for D Vladimir Malakhov and C Pierre Turgeon (April 5, 1995). ... Claimed on waivers by Philadelphia Flyers (June 4, 1996). ... Selected by Nashville Predators in NHL expansion draft (June 26, 1998).
HONORS: Named Hockey East co-Rookie of the Year with Ian Moran (1991-92). ... Named to Hockey East All-Rookie team (1991-92). ... Named to AHL All-Star first team (1997-98).

Season Team	League	REGULAR SEASON								PLAYOFFS				
		Gms.	G	A	Pts.	PIM	+/-	PP	SH	Gms.	G	A	Pts.	PIM
89-90—Albany Academy	N.Y. H.S.	29	32	53	85	...	...	...	...	—	—	—	—	—
90-91—Albany Academy	N.Y. H.S.	27	33	61	94	53	...	...	...	—	—	—	—	—
91-92—Providence College	Hockey East	35	17	24	41	47	...	...	...	—	—	—	—	—
92-93—Providence College	Hockey East	35	11	21	32	62	...	...	...	—	—	—	—	—
93-94—Fredericton	AHL	66	23	33	56	51	...	...	...	—	—	—	—	—
94-95—Fredericton	AHL	64	21	47	68	82	...	...	...	—	—	—	—	—
—Montreal	NHL	10	0	2	2	0	-5	0	0	—	—	—	—	—
—New York Islanders	NHL	3	0	0	0	0	-1	0	0	—	—	—	—	—
95-96—Worcester	AHL	68	22	28	50	47	...	...	...	4	1	1	2	2
—New York Islanders	NHL	10	0	2	2	0	-1	0	0	—	—	—	—	—
96-97—Philadelphia	AHL	59	26	33	59	24	...	...	...	10	3	6	9	0
—Philadelphia	NHL	9	1	4	5	2	2	0	1	—	—	—	—	—
97-98—Philadelphia	NHL	3	1	0	1	0	0	0	0	—	—	—	—	—
—Philadelphia	AHL	77	†42	45	87	34	...	...	...	20	5	9	14	4
NHL Totals (4 years)		35	2	8	10	2	-5	0	1					

DAUBENSPECK, KIRK   G   BLACKHAWKS

PERSONAL: Born July 16, 1974, in Madison, Wis. ... 6-0/190. ... Catches left. ... Full name: Kirk Alan Daubenspeck.
HIGH SCHOOL: Culver (Ind.) Military Academy.
COLLEGE: Wisconsin.
TRANSACTIONS/CAREER NOTES: Selected by Philadelphia Flyers in seventh round (seventh Flyers pick, 151st overall) of NHL entry draft (June 20, 1992). ... Traded by Flyers with LW Claude Boivin to Ottawa Senators for C Mark Lamb (March 5, 1994). ... Traded by Senators to Chicago Blackhawks for sixth-round pick (RW Christopher Neil) in 1998 draft (September 24, 1997).
HONORS: Named to NCAA All-America West second team (1996-97). ... Named to WCHA All-Star second team (1996-97).

Season Team	League	REGULAR SEASON								PLAYOFFS					
		Gms.	Min	W	L	T	GA	SO	Avg.	Gms.	Min.	W	L	GA	SO	Avg.
92-93—Sioux City	USHL	9	470	0	7	1	49	0	6.26	—	—	—	—	—	—
—Wisconsin	USHL	28	1542	5	20	1	123	...	4.79	—	—	—	—	—	—
93-94—Univ. of Wisconsin	WCHA	7	280	2	2	0	19	0	4.07	—	—	—	—	—	—
94-95—Univ. of Wisconsin	WCHA	42	2504	23	15	4	146	0	3.50	—	—	—	—	—	—
95-96—Univ. of Wisconsin	WCHA	39	2257	17	20	2	151	0	4.01	—	—	—	—	—	—
96-97—Univ. of Wisconsin	WCHA	33	1925	13	18	2	124	1	3.86	—	—	—	—	—	—
97-98—Indianapolis	IHL	18	953	6	9	‡0	58	0	3.65	—	—	—	—	—	—
—Jacksonville	ECHL	32	1865	20	9	‡2	92	1	2.96	—	—	—	—	—	—

DAVIDSON, MATT   LW   SABRES

PERSONAL: Born August 9, 1977, in Flin Flon, Man. ... 6-2/190. ... Shoots right.
HIGH SCHOOL: Beaverton (Ore.).
TRANSACTIONS/CAREER NOTES: Selected by Buffalo Sabres in fourth round (fifth Sabres pick, 94th overall) of NHL entry draft (July 8, 1995).

Season Team	League	REGULAR SEASON								PLAYOFFS				
		Gms.	G	A	Pts.	PIM	+/-	PP	SH	Gms.	G	A	Pts.	PIM
93-94—Portland	WHL	59	4	12	16	18	...	...	...	10	0	0	0	4
94-95—Portland	WHL	72	17	20	37	51	...	...	...	9	1	3	4	0
95-96—Portland	WHL	70	24	26	50	96	...	...	...	7	2	2	4	2
96-97—Portland	WHL	72	44	27	71	47	...	...	...	6	0	1	1	2
97-98—Rochester	AHL	72	15	12	27	12	...	...	...	3	1	0	1	2

DAW, JEFF   C   OILERS

PERSONAL: Born February 28, 1972, in Carlisle, Ont. ... 6-3/195. ... Shoots right.
COLLEGE: Massachusetts-Lowell.
TRANSACTIONS/CAREER NOTES: Signed as free agent by Edmonton Oilers (June 12, 1996).

Season Team	League	Gms.	G	A	Pts.	PIM	+/-	PP	SH	Gms.	G	A	Pts.	PIM
92-93—Mass.-Lowell	Hockey East	37	12	18	30	14	...	...	...	—	—	—	—	—
93-94—Mass.-Lowell	Hockey East	40	6	12	18	12	...	...	...	—	—	—	—	—
94-95—Mass.-Lowell	Hockey East	40	27	15	42	24	...	...	...	—	—	—	—	—
95-96—Mass.-Lowell	Hockey East	40	23	28	51	10	...	...	...	—	—	—	—	—
96-97—Wheeling	ECHL	13	3	8	11	26	...	...	...	—	—	—	—	—
—Hamilton	AHL	56	11	8	19	39	...	...	...	19	4	5	9	0
97-98—Hamilton	AHL	79	28	35	63	20	...	...	...	9	6	3	9	0

DAWE, JASON   LW   ISLANDERS

PERSONAL: Born May 29, 1973, in North York, Ont. ... 5-10/189. ... Shoots left. ... Name pronounced DAW.
TRANSACTIONS/CAREER NOTES: Tore ankle ligaments (September 1989). ... Selected by Buffalo Sabres in second round (second Sabres pick, 35th overall) of NHL entry draft (June 22, 1991). ... Slightly sprained knee (February 11, 1995); missed three games. ... Fractured ribs (February 21, 1996); missed six games. ... Traded by Sabres to New York Islanders for LW Paul Kruse and LW Jason Holland (March 24, 1998).
HONORS: Won George Parsons Trophy (1992-93). ... Named to Can.HL All-Star second team (1992-93). ... Named to OHL All-Star first team (1992-93).
STATISTICAL PLATEAUS: Three-goal games: 1995-96 (1), 1997-98 (1). Total: 2.

Season Team	League	Gms.	G	A	Pts.	PIM	+/-	PP	SH	Gms.	G	A	Pts.	PIM
89-90—Peterborough	OHL	50	15	18	33	19	...	...	...	12	4	7	11	4
90-91—Peterborough	OHL	66	43	27	70	43	...	...	...	4	3	1	4	0
91-92—Peterborough	OHL	66	53	55	108	55	...	...	...	4	5	0	5	0
92-93—Peterborough	OHL	59	58	68	126	80	...	...	...	21	18	33	51	18
—Rochester	AHL	0	0	0	0	0	—	—	—	3	1	0	1	0
93-94—Rochester	AHL	48	22	14	36	44	...	...	...	—	—	—	—	—
—Buffalo	NHL	32	6	7	13	12	1	3	0	6	0	1	1	6
94-95—Rochester	AHL	44	27	19	46	24	...	...	...	—	—	—	—	—
—Buffalo	NHL	42	7	4	11	19	-6	0	1	5	2	1	3	6
95-96—Buffalo	NHL	67	25	25	50	33	-8	8	1	—	—	—	—	—
—Rochester	AHL	7	5	4	9	2	...	...	...	—	—	—	—	—
96-97—Buffalo	NHL	81	22	26	48	32	14	4	1	11	2	1	3	6
97-98—Buffalo	NHL	68	19	17	36	36	10	4	1	—	—	—	—	—
—New York Islanders	NHL	13	1	2	3	6	-2	0	0	—	—	—	—	—
NHL Totals (5 years)		**303**	**80**	**81**	**161**	**138**	**9**	**19**	**4**	**22**	**4**	**3**	**7**	**18**

DAZE, ERIC   RW   BLACKHAWKS

PERSONAL: Born July 2, 1975, in Montreal. ... 6-6/222. ... Shoots left. ... Name pronounced dah-ZAY.
TRANSACTIONS/CAREER NOTES: Selected by Chicago Blackhawks in fourth round (fifth Blackhawks pick, 90th overall) of NHL entry draft (June 26, 1993). ... Sprained left ankle (preseason, 1996-97 season); missed eight games. ... Suffered from the flu (January 20, 1997); missed one game. ... Injured back (March 27, 1998); missed two games.
HONORS: Named to QMJHL All-Star first team (1993-94 and 1994-95). ... Won Can.HL Most Sportsmanlike Player of the Year Award (1994-95). ... Won Frank J. Selke Trophy (1994-95). ... Named NHL Rookie of the Year by THE SPORTING NEWS (1995-96). ... Named to NHL All-Rookie team (1995-96).
STATISTICAL PLATEAUS: Three-goal games: 1996-97 (1). ... Four-goal games: 1997-98 (1). ... Total hat tricks: 2.

Season Team	League	Gms.	G	A	Pts.	PIM	+/-	PP	SH	Gms.	G	A	Pts.	PIM
92-93—Beauport	QMJHL	68	19	36	55	24	...	...	...	—	—	—	—	—
93-94—Beauport	QMJHL	66	59	48	107	31	...	...	...	15	16	8	24	2
94-95—Beauport	QMJHL	57	54	45	99	20	...	...	...	16	9	12	21	23
—Chicago	NHL	4	1	1	2	2	2	0	0	16	0	1	1	4
95-96—Chicago	NHL	80	30	23	53	18	16	2	0	10	3	5	8	0
96-97—Chicago	NHL	71	22	19	41	16	-4	11	0	6	2	1	3	2
97-98—Chicago	NHL	80	31	11	42	22	4	10	0	—	—	—	—	—
NHL Totals (4 years)		**235**	**84**	**54**	**138**	**58**	**18**	**23**	**0**	**32**	**5**	**7**	**12**	**6**

DEADMARSH, ADAM   RW   AVALANCHE

PERSONAL: Born May 10, 1975, in Trail, B.C. ... 6-0/195. ... Shoots right. ... Cousin of Butch Deadmarsh, left winger with three NHL teams (1970-71 through 1974-75); and brother of Jake Deadmarsh, left winger in San Jose Sharks system.
HIGH SCHOOL: Lakeridge (Fruitvale, B.C.).
TRANSACTIONS/CAREER NOTES: Selected by Quebec Nordiques in first round (second Nordiques pick, 14th overall) of NHL entry draft (June 26, 1993). ... Nordiques franchise moved to Colorado and renamed Avalanche for 1995-96 season (June 21, 1995). ... Strained groin (April 3, 1996); missed four games. ... Injured shoulder (December 13, 1997); missed one game. ... Suffered from the flu (January 14, 1998); missed one game. ... Strained hip flexor (March 19, 1998); missed one game. ... Injured shoulder (April 1, 1998); missed two games. ... Bruised thigh (April 11, 1998); missed two games.
MISCELLANEOUS: Member of Stanley Cup championship team (1996). ... Scored on a penalty shot (vs. Jeff Hackett, March 1, 1997).
STATISTICAL NOTES: Tied for NHL lead with three game-tying goals (1997-98).

Season Team	League	REGULAR SEASON								PLAYOFFS				
		Gms.	G	A	Pts.	PIM	+/-	PP	SH	Gms.	G	A	Pts.	PIM
91-92—Portland	WHL	68	30	30	60	81	...	...	...	6	3	3	6	13
92-93—Portland	WHL	58	33	36	69	126	...	...	...	16	7	8	15	29
93-94—Portland	WHL	65	43	56	99	212	...	...	...	10	9	8	17	33
94-95—Portland	WHL	29	28	20	48	129	...	...	...	—	—	—	—	—
—Quebec	NHL	48	9	8	17	56	16	0	0	6	0	1	1	0
95-96—Colorado	NHL	78	21	27	48	142	20	3	0	22	5	12	17	25
96-97—Colorado	NHL	78	33	27	60	136	8	10	3	17	3	6	9	24
97-98—Colorado	NHL	73	22	21	43	125	0	10	0	7	2	0	2	4
—U.S. Olympic Team	Int'l	4	1	0	1	2	...	...	...					
NHL Totals (4 years)		277	85	83	168	459	44	23	3	52	10	19	29	53

DEAN, KEVIN　　　　　D　　　　　DEVILS

PERSONAL: Born April 1, 1969, in Madison, Wis. ... 6-3/205. ... Shoots left.
HIGH SCHOOL: Culver (Ind.) Military Academy.
COLLEGE: New Hampshire.
TRANSACTIONS/CAREER NOTES: Selected by New Jersey Devils in fourth round (fourth Devils pick, 86th overall) of NHL entry draft (June 13, 1987). ... Suffered rib injury (September 19, 1996); missed three games.
HONORS: Named to AHL All-Star first team (1994-95).
MISCELLANEOUS: Member of Stanley Cup championship team (1995).

Season Team	League	REGULAR SEASON								PLAYOFFS				
		Gms.	G	A	Pts.	PIM	+/-	PP	SH	Gms.	G	A	Pts.	PIM
85-86—Culver Military	Indiana H.S.	35	28	44	72	48	...	...	...	—	—	—	—	—
86-87—Culver Military	Indiana H.S.	25	19	25	44	30	...	...	...	—	—	—	—	—
87-88—New Hampshire	Hockey East	27	1	6	7	34	...	...	...	—	—	—	—	—
88-89—New Hampshire	Hockey East	34	1	12	13	28	...	...	...	—	—	—	—	—
89-90—New Hampshire	Hockey East	39	2	6	8	42	...	...	...	—	—	—	—	—
90-91—New Hampshire	Hockey East	31	10	12	22	22	...	...	...	—	—	—	—	—
—Utica	AHL	7	0	1	1	2	...	...	...	—	—	—	—	—
91-92—Utica	AHL	23	0	3	3	6	...	...	...	—	—	—	—	—
—Cincinnati	ECHL	30	3	22	25	43	...	...	...	9	1	6	7	8
92-93—Utica	AHL	57	2	16	18	76	...	...	...	5	1	0	1	8
—Cincinnati	IHL	13	2	1	3	15	...	...	...	—	—	—	—	—
93-94—Albany	AHL	70	9	33	42	92	...	...	...	5	0	2	2	7
94-95—Albany	AHL	68	5	37	42	66	...	...	...	8	0	4	4	4
—New Jersey	NHL	17	0	1	1	4	6	0	0	3	0	2	2	0
95-96—New Jersey	NHL	41	0	6	6	28	4	0	0	—	—	—	—	—
—Albany	AHL	1	1	0	1	2	...	...	...	—	—	—	—	—
96-97—New Jersey	NHL	28	2	4	6	6	2	0	0	1	1	0	1	0
—Albany	AHL	2	0	1	1	4	...	...	...	—	—	—	—	—
97-98—New Jersey	NHL	50	1	8	9	12	12	1	0	5	1	0	1	2
—Albany	AHL	2	0	1	1	2	...	...	...	—	—	—	—	—
NHL Totals (4 years)		136	3	19	22	50	24	1	0	9	2	2	4	2

DeBRUSK, LOUIE　　　　　LW　　　　　COYOTES

PERSONAL: Born March 19, 1971, in Cambridge, Ont. ... 6-2/215. ... Shoots left. ... Full name: Dennis Louis DeBrusk. ... Name pronounced dee-BRUHSK.
HIGH SCHOOL: Saugeen (Port Elgin, Ont.).
TRANSACTIONS/CAREER NOTES: Selected by New York Rangers in third round (fourth Rangers pick, 49th overall) of NHL entry draft (June 17, 1989). ... Traded by Rangers with C Bernie Nicholls, RW Steven Rice and future considerations to Edmonton Oilers for C Mark Messier and future considerations (October 4, 1991); Rangers traded D David Shaw to Oilers for D Jeff Beukeboom to complete deal (November 12, 1991). ... Separated shoulder (January 28, 1992); missed four games. ... Strained groin (January 1993); missed five games. ... Strained abdominal muscle (January 1993); missed 11 games. ... Underwent blood tests (April 17, 1995); missed one game. ... Suspended two games by NHL for headbutting an opponent (October 6, 1995). ... Injured elbow (November 26, 1995); missed 14 games. ... Suspended four games and fined $1,000 by NHL for slashing (October 9, 1996). ... Signed as free agent by Tampa Bay Lightning (August 26, 1997). ... Traded by Lightning with fifth-round pick (D Jay Leach) in 1998 draft to Phoenix Coyotes for C Craig Janney (June 11, 1998).

Season Team	League	REGULAR SEASON								PLAYOFFS				
		Gms.	G	A	Pts.	PIM	+/-	PP	SH	Gms.	G	A	Pts.	PIM
87-88—Stratford Jr. B	OHA	43	13	14	27	205	...	...	...	—	—	—	—	—
88-89—London	OHL	59	11	11	22	149	...	...	...	19	1	1	2	43
89-90—London	OHL	61	21	19	40	198	...	...	...	6	2	2	4	24
90-91—London	OHL	61	31	33	64	*223	...	...	...	7	2	2	4	14
—Binghamton	AHL	2	0	0	0	7	...	...	...	2	0	0	0	9
91-92—Edmonton	NHL	25	2	1	3	124	4	0	0	—	—	—	—	—
—Cape Breton	AHL	28	2	2	4	73	...	...	...	—	—	—	—	—
92-93—Edmonton	NHL	51	8	2	10	205	-16	0	0	—	—	—	—	—
93-94—Edmonton	NHL	48	4	6	10	185	-9	0	0	—	—	—	—	—
—Cape Breton	AHL	5	3	1	4	58	...	...	...	—	—	—	—	—
94-95—Edmonton	NHL	34	2	0	2	93	-4	0	0	—	—	—	—	—
95-96—Edmonton	NHL	38	1	3	4	96	-7	0	0	—	—	—	—	—
96-97—Edmonton	NHL	32	2	0	2	94	-6	0	0	6	0	0	0	4
97-98—Tampa Bay	NHL	54	1	2	3	166	-2	0	0	—	—	—	—	—
—San Antonio	IHL	17	7	4	11	130	...	...	...	—	—	—	—	—
NHL Totals (7 years)		282	20	14	34	963	-40	0	0	6	0	0	0	4

DEFAUW, BRAD — LW — HURRICANES

PERSONAL: Born November 10, 1977, in Edina, Minn. ... 6-2/210. ... Shoots left.
HIGH SCHOOL: Apple Valley (Minn.).
COLLEGE: North Dakota.
TRANSACTIONS/CAREER NOTES: Selected by Carolina Hurricanes in second round (second Hurricanes pick, 28th overall) of NHL entry draft (June 21, 1997).

Season Team	League	Gms.	G	A	Pts.	PIM	+/-	PP	SH	Gms.	G	A	Pts.	PIM
95-96—Apple Valley	Minn. H.S.	28	21	34	55	14	...			—	—	—	—	—
96-97—U. of North Dakota	WCHA	37	7	6	13	39	...			—	—	—	—	—
97-98—U. of North Dakota	WCHA	36	9	11	20	34	...			—	—	—	—	—

DELISLE, JONATHAN — RW — CANADIENS

PERSONAL: Born June 30, 1977, in Montreal. ... 5-10/193. ... Shoots right. ... Name pronounced duh-LIHL.
TRANSACTIONS/CAREER NOTES: Selected by Montreal Canadiens in fourth round (fourth Canadiens pick, 86th overall) of NHL entry draft (July 8, 1995).

Season Team	League	Gms.	G	A	Pts.	PIM	+/-	PP	SH	Gms.	G	A	Pts.	PIM
93-94—Verdun	QMJHL	61	16	17	33	130	...			4	0	1	1	14
94-95—Hull	QMJHL	60	21	38	59	218	...			19	11	8	19	43
95-96—Hull	QMJHL	62	31	57	88	193	...			18	6	13	19	64
96-97—Hull	QMJHL	61	35	53	88	210	...			14	11	13	24	48
97-98—Fredericton	AHL	78	15	21	36	138	...			4	0	1	1	7

DELMORE, ANDY — D — FLYERS

PERSONAL: Born December 26, 1976, in Windsor, Ont. ... 6-0/180. ... Shoots right.
TRANSACTIONS/CAREER NOTES: Signed as free agent by Philadelphia Flyers (June 9, 1997).
HONORS: Named to OHL All-Star first team (1996-97).

Season Team	League	Gms.	G	A	Pts.	PIM	+/-	PP	SH	Gms.	G	A	Pts.	PIM
92-93—Chatham Jr. B	OHA	47	4	21	25	38	...			—	—	—	—	—
93-94—North Bay	OHL	45	2	7	9	33	...			17	0	0	0	2
94-95—North Bay	OHL	40	2	14	16	21	...			—	—	—	—	—
—Sarnia	OHL	27	5	13	18	27	...			3	0	0	0	2
95-96—Sarnia	OHL	64	21	38	59	45	...			10	3	7	10	2
96-97—Sarnia	OHL	63	18	60	78	39	...			12	2	10	12	10
—Fredericton	AHL	4	0	1	1	0	...			—	—	—	—	—
97-98—Philadelphia	AHL	73	9	30	39	46	...			18	4	4	8	21

DEMITRA, PAVOL — LW/C — BLUES

PERSONAL: Born November 29, 1974, in Dubnica, Czechoslovakia. ... 5-11/193. ... Shoots left. ... Name pronounced PA-vuhl dih-MEE-truh.
TRANSACTIONS/CAREER NOTES: Selected by Ottawa Senators in ninth round (ninth Senators pick, 227th overall) of NHL entry draft (June 26,1993). ... Broke ankle (October 14, 1993); missed 23 games. ... Rights traded by Senators to St. Louis Blues for D Christer Olsson (November 27, 1996). ... Suffered back spasms and bruised tailbone (December 8, 1997); missed 10 games. ... Fractured jaw (March 7, 1998); missed 11 games.

Season Team	League	Gms.	G	A	Pts.	PIM	+/-	PP	SH	Gms.	G	A	Pts.	PIM
91-92—Sparta Dubnica	Czech Dv.II	28	13	10	23	12	...			—	—	—	—	—
92-93—Dukla Trencin	Czech.	46	11	17	28	0	...			—	—	—	—	—
—CAPEH Dubnica	Czech Dv.II	4	3	0	3		...			—	—	—	—	—
93-94—Ottawa	NHL	12	1	1	2	4	-7	1	0	—	—	—	—	—
—Prin. Edward Island	AHL	41	18	23	41	8	...			—	—	—	—	—
94-95—Prin. Edward Island	AHL	61	26	48	74	23	...			5	0	7	7	0
—Ottawa	NHL	16	4	3	7	0	-4	1	0	—	—	—	—	—
95-96—Prin. Edward Island	AHL	48	28	53	81	44	...			—	—	—	—	—
—Ottawa	NHL	31	7	10	17	6	-3	2	0	—	—	—	—	—
96-97—Las Vegas	IHL	22	8	13	21	10	...			—	—	—	—	—
—Grand Rapids	IHL	42	20	30	50	24	...			—	—	—	—	—
—St. Louis	NHL	8	3	0	3	2	0	2	0	6	1	3	4	6
97-98—St. Louis	NHL	61	22	30	52	22	11	4	4	10	3	3	6	2
NHL Totals (5 years)		128	37	44	81	34	-3	10	4	16	4	6	10	8

DENIS, MARC — G — AVALANCHE

PERSONAL: Born August 1, 1977, in Montreal. ... 6-0/188. ... Catches left. ... Name pronounced deh-NEE.
TRANSACTIONS/CAREER NOTES: Selected by Colorado Avalanche in first round (first Avalanche pick, 25th overall) of NHL entry draft (July 8, 1995).
HONORS: Won Marcel Robert Trophy (1995-96). ... Won Can.HL Goaltender of the Year Award (1996-97). ... Won Jacques Plante Trophy (1996-97). ... Named to Can.HL All-Star first team (1996-97). ... Named to QMJHL All-Star first team (1996-97).

		REGULAR SEASON								PLAYOFFS						
Season Team	League	Gms.	Min	W	L	T	GA	SO	Avg.	Gms.	Min.	W	L	GA	SO	Avg.
94-95—Chicoutimi	QMJHL	32	1688	17	9	1	98	0	3.48	6	374	4	2	19	1	3.05
95-96—Chicoutimi	QMJHL	51	2895	23	21	4	157	2	3.25	16	917	8	†8	66	0	4.32
96-97—Chicoutimi	QMJHL	41	2317	22	15	2	104	4	*2.69	*21	*1226	*11	*10	*70	*1	3.43
—Colorado	NHL	1	60	0	1	0	3	0	3.00	—						
—Hershey	AHL	—								4	56	1	0	1	0	*1.07
97-98—Hershey	AHL	47	2589	17	23	4	125	1	2.90	6	347	3	3	15	0	2.59
NHL Totals (1 year)		1	60	0	1	0	3	0	3.00							

DESCOTEAUX, MATHIEU   D   OILERS

PERSONAL: Born September 23, 1977, in Pierreville, Que. ... 6-3/200. ... Shoots left. ... Name pronounced day-koh-TOH.
TRANSACTIONS/CAREER NOTES: Selected by Edmonton Oilers in first round (second Oilers pick, 19th overall) of NHL entry draft (June 22, 1996).

		REGULAR SEASON							PLAYOFFS				
Season Team	League	Gms.	G	A	Pts.	PIM	+/-	PP	SH	Gms.	G	A	Pts.	PIM
94-95—Shawinigan	QMJHL	50	3	2	5	28	...	...	...	—				
95-96—Shawinigan	QMJHL	69	2	13	15	129	...	...	...	6	0	0	0	6
96-97—Shawinigan	QMJHL	38	6	18	24	103	...	...	...	—				
—Hull	QMJHL	32	6	19	25	34	...	...	...	14	2	5	7	20
97-98—Hamilton	AHL	67	2	8	10	70	...	...	...	2	0	0	0	0

DESJARDINS, ERIC   D   FLYERS

PERSONAL: Born June 14, 1969, in Rouyn, Que. ... 6-1/200. ... Shoots right. ... Name pronounced day-zhar-DAN.
TRANSACTIONS/CAREER NOTES: Selected by Montreal Canadiens as underage junior in second round (third Canadiens pick, 38th overall) of NHL entry draft (June 13, 1987). ... Suffered from the flu (January 1989). ... Pulled groin (November 2, 1989); missed seven games. ... Sprained left ankle (January 26, 1991); missed 16 games. ... Fractured right thumb (December 8, 1991); missed two games. ... Traded by Canadiens with LW Gilbert Dionne and C John LeClair to Philadelphia Flyers for RW Mark Recchi and third-round pick (C Martin Hohenberger) in 1995 draft (February 9, 1995). ... Slightly strained groin (March 28, 1995); missed one game. ... Reinjured groin (April 1, 1995); missed three games. ... Suffered from the flu (December 26, 1995); missed one game. ... Suffered inflamed pelvic bone (October 1, 1997); missed five games.
HONORS: Named to QMJHL All-Star second team (1986-87). ... Won Emile (Butch) Bouchard Trophy (1987-88). ... Named to QMJHL All-Star first team (1987-88). ... Played in NHL All-Star Game (1992 and 1996).
RECORDS: Shares NHL single-game playoff record for most goals by defensemen—3 (June 3, 1993).
MISCELLANEOUS: Member of Stanley Cup championship team (1993).

		REGULAR SEASON							PLAYOFFS				
Season Team	League	Gms.	G	A	Pts.	PIM	+/-	PP	SH	Gms.	G	A	Pts.	PIM
86-87—Granby	QMJHL	66	14	24	38	75	...	...	...	8	3	2	5	10
87-88—Granby	QMJHL	62	18	49	67	138	...	...	...	5	0	3	3	10
—Sherbrooke	AHL	3	0	0	0	6	...	...	...	4	0	2	2	2
88-89—Montreal	NHL	36	2	12	14	26	9	1	0	14	1	1	2	6
89-90—Montreal	NHL	55	3	13	16	51	1	1	0	6	0	0	0	10
90-91—Montreal	NHL	62	7	18	25	27	7	0	0	13	1	4	5	8
91-92—Montreal	NHL	77	6	32	38	50	17	4	0	11	3	3	6	4
92-93—Montreal	NHL	82	13	32	45	98	20	7	0	20	4	10	14	23
93-94—Montreal	NHL	84	12	23	35	97	-1	6	1	7	0	2	2	4
94-95—Montreal	NHL	9	0	6	6	2	2	0	0	—				
—Philadelphia	NHL	34	5	18	23	12	10	1	0	15	4	4	8	10
95-96—Philadelphia	NHL	80	7	40	47	45	19	5	0	12	0	6	6	2
96-97—Philadelphia	NHL	82	12	34	46	50	25	5	1	19	2	8	10	12
97-98—Philadelphia	NHL	77	6	27	33	36	11	2	1	5	0	1	1	0
—Can. Olympic Team	Int'l	6	0	0	0	2	...	...	...	—				
NHL Totals (10 years)		678	73	255	328	494	120	32	3	122	15	39	54	79

DEVEREAUX, BOYD   LW   OILERS

PERSONAL: Born April 16, 1978, in Seaforth, Ont. ... 6-2/195. ... Shoots left. ... Name pronounced DEH-vuh-roh.
TRANSACTIONS/CAREER NOTES: Selected by Edmonton Oilers in first round (first Oilers pick, sixth overall) of NHL entry draft (June 22, 1996).
HONORS: Won Can.HL Scholastic Player of the Year Award (1995-96). ... Named to OHL All-Rookie second team (1995-96). ... Won Bobby Smith Trophy (1995-96).

		REGULAR SEASON							PLAYOFFS				
Season Team	League	Gms.	G	A	Pts.	PIM	+/-	PP	SH	Gms.	G	A	Pts.	PIM
93-94—Stratford	OPJHL	46	12	27	39	8	...	...	...	—				
94-95—Stratford	OPJHL	45	31	74	105	21	...	...	...	—				
95-96—Kitchener	OHL	66	20	38	58	35	...	...	...	12	3	7	10	4
96-97—Kitchener	OHL	54	28	41	69	37	...	...	...	13	4	11	15	8
—Hamilton	AHL	—					...	...	...	1	0	1	1	0
97-98—Edmonton	NHL	38	1	4	5	6	-5	0	0	—				
—Hamilton	AHL	14	5	6	11	6	...	...	...	9	1	1	2	8
NHL Totals (1 year)		38	1	4	5	6	-5	0	0					

DE VRIES, GREG   D   OILERS

PERSONAL: Born January 4, 1973, in Sundridge, Ont. ... 6-3/218. ... Shoots left. ... Name pronounced duh-VREES.
COLLEGE: Bowling Green State.
TRANSACTIONS/CAREER NOTES: Signed as free agent by Edmonton Oilers (March 28, 1994). ... Sprained ankle (January 26, 1997); missed four games.

Season Team	League	Gms.	G	A	Pts.	PIM	+/-	PP	SH	Gms.	G	A	Pts.	PIM
				REGULAR SEASON								PLAYOFFS		
91-92—Bowling Green	CCHA	24	0	3	3	20	...	...	...	—	—	—	—	—
92-93—Niagara Falls	OHL	62	3	23	26	86	...	...	...	4	0	1	1	6
93-94—Niagara Falls	OHL	64	5	40	45	135	...	...	...	—	—	—	—	—
—Cape Breton	AHL	9	0	0	0	11	...	...	...	1	0	0	0	0
94-95—Cape Breton	AHL	77	5	19	24	68	...	...	...	—	—	—	—	—
95-96—Edmonton	NHL	13	1	1	2	12	-2	0	0	—	—	—	—	—
—Cape Breton	AHL	58	9	30	39	174	...	...	...	—	—	—	—	—
96-97—Hamilton	AHL	34	4	14	18	26	...	...	...	—	—	—	—	—
—Edmonton	NHL	37	0	4	4	52	-2	0	0	12	0	1	1	8
97-98—Edmonton	NHL	65	7	4	11	80	-17	1	0	7	0	0	0	21
NHL Totals (3 years)		115	8	9	17	144	-21	1	0	19	0	1	1	29

DeWOLF, JOSHUA   D   DEVILS

PERSONAL: Born July 25, 1977, in Bloomington, Minn. ... 6-2/190. ... Shoots left.
HIGH SCHOOL: Twin Cities (Bloomington, Minn.).
COLLEGE: St. Cloud (Minn.) State.
TRANSACTIONS/CAREER NOTES: Selected by New Jersey Devils in second round (third Devils pick, 41st overall) of NHL entry draft (June 22, 1996).

Season Team	League	Gms.	G	A	Pts.	PIM	+/-	PP	SH	Gms.	G	A	Pts.	PIM
				REGULAR SEASON								PLAYOFFS		
93-94—Bloom. Jefferson	USHL	25	1	14	15	32	...	...	...	—	—	—	—	—
94-95—Bloom. Jefferson	USHL	28	6	22	28	52	...	...	...	—	—	—	—	—
95-96—Twin Cities	Minn. H.S.	40	11	15	26	38	...	...	...	—	—	—	—	—
96-97—St. Cloud State	WCHA	31	3	11	14	62	...	...	...	—	—	—	—	—
97-98—St. Cloud State	WCHA	37	9	9	18	78	...	...	...	—	—	—	—	—
—Albany	AHL	2	0	0	0	0	...	...	...	—	—	—	—	—

DEYELL, MARK   C   MAPLE LEAFS

D

PERSONAL: Born March 26, 1976, in Regina, Sask. ... 6-0/180. ... Shoots right. ... Name pronounced day-EHL.
TRANSACTIONS/CAREER NOTES: Selected by Toronto Maple Leafs in fifth round (fourth Maple Leafs pick, 126th overall) of NHL entry draft (June 29, 1994).
HONORS: Won Bob Clarke Trophy (1995-96). ... Named to Can.HL All-Star second team (1995-96). ... Named to WHL (Central/East) All-Star first team (1995-96).

Season Team	League	Gms.	G	A	Pts.	PIM	+/-	PP	SH	Gms.	G	A	Pts.	PIM
				REGULAR SEASON								PLAYOFFS		
93-94—Saskatoon	WHL	66	17	36	53	52	...	...	...	16	5	2	7	20
94-95—Saskatoon	WHL	70	34	68	102	56	...	...	...	10	2	5	7	14
95-96—Saskatoon	WHL	69	61	*98	*159	122	...	...	...	4	0	5	5	8
96-97—St. John's	AHL	58	15	27	42	30	...	...	...	10	1	5	6	6
97-98—St. John's	AHL	72	20	45	65	75	...	...	...	4	1	1	2	4

DIDUCK, GERALD   D   COYOTES

PERSONAL: Born April 6, 1965, in Edmonton. ... 6-2/216. ... Shoots right. ... Name pronounced DIH-dihk.
TRANSACTIONS/CAREER NOTES: Selected by New York Islanders as underage junior in first round (second Islanders pick, 16th overall) of NHL entry draft (June 8, 1983). ... Fractured left foot (November 1987). ... Fractured right hand (November 1988). ... Injured knee (January 1989). ... Traded by Islanders to Montreal Canadiens for D Craig Ludwig (September 4, 1990). ... Traded by Canadiens to Vancouver Canucks for fourth-round pick (LW Vladimir Vujtek) in 1991 draft (January 12, 1991). ... Bruised knee (March 16, 1991). ... Strained groin (January 4, 1993); missed three games. ... Suffered stress fracture in ankle (January 1, 1994); missed 14 games. ... Bruised foot (February 17, 1994); missed six games. ... Suffered eye contusion (March 31, 1994); missed five games. ... Traded by Canucks to Chicago Blackhawks for RW Bogdan Savenko and third-round pick (LW Larry Courville) in 1995 draft (April 7, 1995). ... Signed as free agent by Hartford Whalers (August 1, 1995). ... Strained hamstring (November 4, 1996); missed four games. ... Suffered hernia (December 16, 1996); missed nine games. ... Traded by Whalers to Phoenix Coyotes for RW Chris Murray (March 18, 1997). ... Suffered back spasms (December 3, 1997); missed games. ... Injured hand (February 7, 1998); missed two games.

Season Team	League	Gms.	G	A	Pts.	PIM	+/-	PP	SH	Gms.	G	A	Pts.	PIM
				REGULAR SEASON								PLAYOFFS		
81-82—Lethbridge	WHL	71	1	15	16	81	...	...	...	12	0	3	3	27
82-83—Lethbridge	WHL	67	8	16	24	151	...	...	...	20	3	12	15	49
83-84—Lethbridge	WHL	65	10	24	34	133	...	...	...	5	1	4	5	27
—Indianapolis	IHL	—	—	—	—	—	...	...	...	10	1	6	7	19
84-85—New York Islanders	NHL	65	2	8	10	80	2	0	0	—	—	—	—	—
85-86—New York Islanders	NHL	10	1	2	3	2	5	0	0	—	—	—	—	—
—Springfield	AHL	61	6	14	20	175	...	...	...	—	—	—	—	—
86-87—Springfield	AHL	45	6	8	14	120	...	...	...	—	—	—	—	—
—New York Islanders	NHL	30	2	3	5	67	-3	0	0	14	0	1	1	35
87-88—New York Islanders	NHL	68	7	12	19	113	22	4	0	6	1	0	1	42
88-89—New York Islanders	NHL	65	11	21	32	155	9	6	0	—	—	—	—	—
89-90—New York Islanders	NHL	76	3	17	20	163	2	1	0	5	0	0	0	12
90-91—Montreal	NHL	32	1	2	3	39	3	0	0	—	—	—	—	—
—Vancouver	NHL	31	3	7	10	66	-8	0	0	6	1	0	1	11
91-92—Vancouver	NHL	77	6	21	27	229	-3	2	0	5	0	0	0	10
92-93—Vancouver	NHL	80	6	14	20	171	32	0	1	12	4	2	6	12
93-94—Vancouver	NHL	55	1	10	11	72	2	0	0	24	1	7	8	22

Season Team	League	REGULAR SEASON								PLAYOFFS				
		Gms.	G	A	Pts.	PIM	+/-	PP	SH	Gms.	G	A	Pts.	PIM
94-95—Vancouver..................	NHL	22	1	3	4	15	-8	1	0	—	—	—	—	—
—Chicago......................	NHL	13	1	0	1	48	3	0	0	16	1	3	4	22
95-96—Hartford	NHL	79	1	9	10	88	7	0	0	—	—	—	—	—
96-97—Hartford	NHL	56	1	10	11	40	-9	0	0	—	—	—	—	—
—Phoenix......................	NHL	11	1	2	3	23	2	1	0	7	0	0	0	10
97-98—Phoenix......................	NHL	78	8	10	18	118	14	1	0	6	0	2	2	20
NHL Totals (14 years).........		848	56	151	207	1489	72	16	1	101	8	15	23	196

DiMAIO, ROB   LW   BRUINS

PERSONAL: Born February 19, 1968, in Calgary. ... 5-10/190. ... Shoots right. ... Full name: Robert DiMaio. ... Name pronounced duh-MIGH-oh.

TRANSACTIONS/CAREER NOTES: Traded by Kamloops Blazers with LW Dave Mackey and C Kalvin Knibbs to Medicine Hat Tigers for LW Doug Pickel and LW Sean Pass (December 1985). ... Selected by New York Islanders in sixth round (sixth Islanders pick, 118th overall) of NHL entry draft (June 13, 1987). ... Suspended two games by WHL for leaving bench during fight (January 28, 1988). ... Bruised left hand (February 1989). ... Sprained clavicle (November 1989). ... Sprained wrist (February 20, 1992); missed four games. ... Reinjured wrist (February 29, 1992); missed final 17 games of season. ... Underwent surgery to repair torn ligaments in wrist (March 11, 1992). ... Selected by Tampa Bay Lightning in NHL expansion draft (June 18, 1992). ... Bruised wrist (November 28, 1992); missed four games. ... Sprained ankle (February 14, 1993); missed nine games. ... Reinjured right ankle (March 20, 1993); missed three games. ... Reinjured right ankle (April 1, 1993); missed remainder of season. ... Broke left leg (October 16, 1993); missed 27 games. ... Traded by Lightning to Philadelphia Flyers for RW Jim Cummins and fourth-round pick in 1995 draft (March 18, 1994). ... Bruised foot (February 28, 1995); missed two games. ... Suffered from the flu (April 16, 1995); missed one game. ... Suffered bone bruise in left leg (December 16, 1995); missed 14 games. ... Sprained right knee (March 29, 1996); missed final eight games of regular season. ... Selected by San Jose Sharks from Flyers in NHL waiver draft for cash (September 30, 1996). ... Traded by Sharks to Boston Bruins for fifth-round pick (RW Adam Nittel) in 1997 draft (September 30, 1996). ... Strained knee (November 6, 1996); missed five games. ... Suffered from the flu (December 17, 1996); missed one game. ... Sprained knee (March 8, 1997); missed two games. ... Injured hip (April 5, 1997); missed two games. ... Injured groin (January 12, 1998); missed one game. ... Suffered concussion (February 26, 1998); missed one game.

HONORS: Won Stafford Smythe Memorial Trophy (1987-88). ... Named to Memorial Cup All-Star team (1987-88).

MISCELLANEOUS: Failed to score on a penalty shot (vs. Andy Moog, October 4, 1997).

Season Team	League	REGULAR SEASON								PLAYOFFS				
		Gms.	G	A	Pts.	PIM	+/-	PP	SH	Gms.	G	A	Pts.	PIM
84-85—Kamloops	WHL	55	9	18	27	29	...	...	...	—	—	—	—	—
85-86—Kamloops	WHL	6	1	0	1	0	...	...	...	—	—	—	—	—
—Medicine Hat............	WHL	55	20	30	50	82	...	...	...	—	—	—	—	—
86-87—Medicine Hat..............	WHL	70	27	43	70	130	...	...	...	20	7	11	18	46
87-88—Medicine Hat..............	WHL	54	47	43	90	120	...	...	...	14	12	19	†31	59
88-89—New York Islanders......	NHL	16	1	0	1	30	-6	0	0	—	—	—	—	—
—Springfield	AHL	40	13	18	31	67	...	...	...	—	—	—	—	—
89-90—New York Islanders......	NHL	7	0	0	0	2	0	0	0	1	1	0	1	4
—Springfield	AHL	54	25	27	52	69	...	...	...	16	4	7	11	45
90-91—New York Islanders.....	NHL	1	0	0	0	0	0	0	0	—	—	—	—	—
—Capital District	AHL	12	3	4	7	22	...	...	...	—	—	—	—	—
91-92—New York Islanders......	NHL	50	5	2	7	43	-23	0	2	—	—	—	—	—
92-93—Tampa Bay	NHL	54	9	15	24	62	0	2	0	—	—	—	—	—
93-94—Tampa Bay	NHL	39	8	7	15	40	-5	2	0	—	—	—	—	—
—Philadelphia	NHL	14	3	5	8	6	1	0	0	—	—	—	—	—
94-95—Philadelphia	NHL	36	3	1	4	53	8	0	0	15	2	4	6	4
95-96—Philadelphia	NHL	59	6	15	21	58	0	1	1	3	0	0	0	0
96-97—Boston	NHL	72	13	15	28	82	-21	0	3	—	—	—	—	—
97-98—Boston	NHL	79	10	17	27	82	-13	0	0	6	1	0	1	8
NHL Totals (10 years).........		427	58	77	135	458	-59	5	6	25	4	4	8	16

DINEEN, KEVIN   RW   HURRICANES

PERSONAL: Born October 28, 1963, in Quebec City. ... 5-11/190. ... Shoots right. ... Full name: Kevin W. Dineen. ... Son of Bill Dineen, right winger with Detroit Red Wings and Chicago Blackhawks (1953-54 through 1957-58) and former head coach for Philadelphia Flyers (1992-93); brother of Gord Dineen, defenseman with four NHL teams (1982-83 through 1994-95); and brother of Peter Dineen, defenseman with Los Angeles Kings and Detroit Red Wings (1986-87 and 1989-90).

COLLEGE: Denver.

TRANSACTIONS/CAREER NOTES: Selected by Hartford Whalers as underage junior in third round (third Whalers pick, 56th overall) of NHL entry draft (June 9, 1982). ... Sprained left shoulder (October 24, 1985); missed nine games. ... Broke knuckle (January 12, 1986); missed seven games. ... Sprained knee (February 14, 1986). ... Suffered shoulder tendinitis (September 1988). ... Underwent surgery to right knee cartilage (August 1, 1990). ... Suffered hip pointer (November 28, 1990). ... Hospitalized due to complications caused by Crohn's disease (January 1, 1991); missed eight games. ... Injured groin (March 1991). ... Traded by Whalers to Philadelphia Flyers for C/LW Murray Craven and fourth-round pick (LW Kevin Smyth) in 1992 draft (November 13, 1991). ... Sprained wrist (February 4, 1992); missed one game. ... Strained right rotator cuff (December 3, 1992); missed one game. ... Suffered injury (October 9, 1993); missed one game. ... Bruised right shoulder (November 13, 1993); missed two games. ... Suffered recurrence of Crohn's disease (February 10, 1994); missed five games. ... Separated shoulder (March 8, 1994); missed three games. ... Strained left shoulder (January 31, 1995); missed three games. ... Reinjured left shoulder (February 11, 1995); missed three games. ... Traded by Flyers to Whalers for future considerations (December 28, 1995). ... Broke bone in wrist (February 9, 1996); missed 27 games. ... Strained abdominal muscle (March 13, 1997); missed one game. ... Whalers franchise moved to North Carolina and renamed Carolina Hurricanes for 1997-98 season; NHL approved move on June 25, 1997. ... Strained hamstring (October 4, 1997); missed five games. ... Pulled hamstring (November 21, 1997); missed six games. ... Pulled hamstring (December 26, 1997); missed seven games. ... Pulled hamstring (January 10, 1998); missed two games. ... Suffered charley horse (February 7, 1998); missed one game. ... Injured groin (March 23, 1998); missed four games. ... Reinjured groin (April 8, 1998); missed one game.

HONORS: Named to The SPORTING NEWS All-Star second team (1986-87). ... Played in NHL All-Star Game (1988 and 1989). ... Named Bud Light/NHL Man of the Year (1990-91).

MISCELLANEOUS: Captain of Philadelphia Flyers (1993-94). ... Captain of Hartford Whalers (1996-97). ... Captain of Carolina Hurricanes (1997-98). ... Failed to score on a penalty shot (vs. Mike Richter, October 19, 1998).

STATISTICAL PLATEAUS: Three-goal games: 1985-86 (1), 1986-87 (1), 1988-89 (1), 1989-90 (2), 1992-93 (3), 1993-94 (1). Total: 9. ... Four-goal games: 1993-94 (1). ... Total hat tricks: 10.

Season Team	League	REGULAR SEASON								PLAYOFFS				
		Gms.	G	A	Pts.	PIM	+/-	PP	SH	Gms.	G	A	Pts.	PIM
80-81—St. Michael's Jr. B	ODHA	40	15	28	43	167	...	...	...	—	—	—	—	—
81-82—Univ. of Denver	WCHA	38	12	22	34	105	...	...	...	—	—	—	—	—
82-83—Univ. of Denver	WCHA	36	16	13	29	108	...	...	...	—	—	—	—	—
83-84—Canadian nat'l team	Int'l	52	5	11	16	2	...	...	...	—	—	—	—	—
—Can. Olympic Team	Int'l	7	0	0	0	0	...	...	...	—	—	—	—	—
84-85—Binghamton	AHL	25	15	8	23	41	...	...	...	—	—	—	—	—
—Hartford	NHL	57	25	16	41	120	-6	8	4	—	—	—	—	—
85-86—Hartford	NHL	57	33	35	68	124	16	6	0	10	6	7	13	18
86-87—Hartford	NHL	78	40	39	79	110	7	11	0	6	2	1	3	31
87-88—Hartford	NHL	74	25	25	50	217	-14	5	0	6	4	4	8	8
88-89—Hartford	NHL	79	45	44	89	167	-6	20	1	4	1	0	1	10
89-90—Hartford	NHL	67	25	41	66	164	7	8	2	6	3	2	5	18
90-91—Hartford	NHL	61	17	30	47	104	-15	4	0	6	1	0	1	16
91-92—Hartford	NHL	16	4	2	6	23	-6	1	0	—	—	—	—	—
—Philadelphia	NHL	64	26	30	56	130	1	5	3	—	—	—	—	—
92-93—Philadelphia	NHL	83	35	28	63	201	14	6	3	—	—	—	—	—
93-94—Philadelphia	NHL	71	19	23	42	113	-9	5	1	—	—	—	—	—
94-95—Houston	IHL	17	6	4	10	42	...	...	...	—	—	—	—	—
—Philadelphia	NHL	40	8	5	13	39	-1	4	0	15	6	4	10	18
95-96—Philadelphia	NHL	26	0	2	2	50	-8	0	0	—	—	—	—	—
—Hartford	NHL	20	2	7	9	67	7	0	0	—	—	—	—	—
96-97—Hartford	NHL	78	19	29	48	141	-6	8	0	—	—	—	—	—
97-98—Carolina	NHL	54	7	16	23	105	-7	0	0	—	—	—	—	—
NHL Totals (14 years)		925	330	372	702	1875	-26	91	14	53	23	18	41	119

DINGMAN, CHRIS   LW   FLAMES

PERSONAL: Born July 6, 1976, in Edmonton. ... 6-4/245. ... Shoots left.
HIGH SCHOOL: Crocus Plains (Brandon, Man.).
TRANSACTIONS/CAREER NOTES: Selected by Calgary Flames in first round (first Flames pick, 19th overall) of NHL entry draft (June 28, 1994).

D

Season Team	League	REGULAR SEASON								PLAYOFFS				
		Gms.	G	A	Pts.	PIM	+/-	PP	SH	Gms.	G	A	Pts.	PIM
92-93—Brandon	WHL	50	10	17	27	64	...	...	...	4	0	0	0	0
93-94—Brandon	WHL	45	21	20	41	77	...	...	...	13	1	7	8	39
94-95—Brandon	WHL	66	40	43	83	201	...	...	...	3	1	0	1	9
95-96—Brandon	WHL	40	16	29	45	109	...	...	...	19	12	11	23	60
—Saint John	AHL	—	—	—	—	—	...	...	...	1	0	0	0	0
96-97—Saint John	AHL	71	5	6	11	195	...	...	...	—	—	—	—	—
97-98—Calgary	NHL	70	3	3	6	149	-11	1	0	—	—	—	—	—
NHL Totals (1 year)		70	3	3	6	149	-11	1	0					

DOAN, SHANE   RW   COYOTES

PERSONAL: Born October 10, 1976, in Eston, Sask. ... 6-2/217. ... Shoots right. ... Name pronounced DOHN.
TRANSACTIONS/CAREER NOTES: Selected by Winnipeg Jets in first round (first Jets pick, seventh overall) of NHL entry draft (July 8, 1995). ... Suffered from the flu (January 8, 1996); missed one game. ... Bruised ribs (January 14, 1996); missed two games. ... Strained back (February 23, 1996); missed two games. ... Jets franchise moved to Phoenix and renamed Coyotes for 1996-97 season; NHL approved move on January 18, 1996. ... Sprained ankle (October 14, 1996); missed two games. ... Strained ligament in foot (November 8, 1996); missed eight games. ... Bruised hand (February 22, 1997); missed four games.
HONORS: Won Stafford Smyth Memorial Trophy (1994-95). ... Named to Memorial Cup All-Star team (1994-95).

Season Team	League	REGULAR SEASON								PLAYOFFS				
		Gms.	G	A	Pts.	PIM	+/-	PP	SH	Gms.	G	A	Pts.	PIM
92-93—Kamloops	WHL	51	7	12	19	55	...	...	...	13	0	1	1	8
93-94—Kamloops	WHL	52	24	24	48	88	...	...	...	—	—	—	—	—
94-95—Kamloops	WHL	71	37	57	94	106	...	...	...	21	6	10	16	16
95-96—Winnipeg	NHL	74	7	10	17	101	-9	1	0	6	0	0	0	6
96-97—Phoenix	NHL	63	4	8	12	49	-3	0	0	4	0	0	0	2
97-98—Phoenix	NHL	33	5	6	11	35	-3	0	0	6	1	0	1	6
—Springfield	AHL	39	21	21	42	64	...	...	...	—	—	—	—	—
NHL Totals (3 years)		170	16	24	40	185	-15	1	0	16	1	0	1	14

DOIG, JASON   D   COYOTES

PERSONAL: Born January 29, 1977, in Montreal. ... 6-3/216. ... Shoots right. ... Name pronounced DOYG.
TRANSACTIONS/CAREER NOTES: Selected by Winnipeg Jets in second round (third Jets pick, 34th overall) of NHL entry draft (July 8, 1995). ... Suffered irregular heart beat (November 17, 1995); missed four games. ... Jets franchise moved to Phoenix and renamed Coyotes for 1996-97 season; NHL approved move on January 18, 1996. ... Hyperextended elbow prior to 1996-97 season; missed first five games of season. ... Sprained knee (November 20, 1997); missed 26 games.
HONORS: Won Guy Lafleur Trophy (1995-96). ... Named to Memorial Cup All-Star team (1995-96).

Season Team	League	REGULAR SEASON								PLAYOFFS				
		Gms.	G	A	Pts.	PIM	+/-	PP	SH	Gms.	G	A	Pts.	PIM
93-94—St. Jean	QMJHL	63	8	17	25	65	...	...	...	5	0	2	2	2
94-95—Laval	QMJHL	55	13	42	55	259	...	...	...	20	4	13	17	39
95-96—Winnipeg	NHL	15	1	1	2	28	-2	0	0	—	—	—	—	—
—Springfield	AHL	5	0	0	0	28	...	...	...	—	—	—	—	—
—Laval	QMJHL	2	1	1	2	6	...	...	...	—	—	—	—	—
—Granby	QMJHL	27	6	35	41	*105	...	...	...	20	10	22	32	110

Season Team	League	REGULAR SEASON Gms.	G	A	Pts.	PIM	+/-	PP	SH	PLAYOFFS Gms.	G	A	Pts.	PIM
96-97—Las Vegas	IHL	6	0	1	1	19	...	...	...	—	—	—	—	—
—Granby	QMJHL	39	14	33	47	197	...	...	...	5	0	4	4	27
—Springfield	AHL	5	0	3	3	2	...	...	...	17	1	4	5	37
97-98—Springfield	AHL	46	2	25	27	153	...	...	...	3	0	0	0	2
—Phoenix	NHL	4	0	1	1	12	-4	0	0	—	—	—	—	—
NHL Totals (2 years)		19	1	2	3	40	-6	0	0					

DOLLAS, BOBBY — D — PENGUINS

PERSONAL: Born January 31, 1965, in Montreal. ... 6-2/212. ... Shoots left. ... Name pronounced DAHL-ihz.
TRANSACTIONS/CAREER NOTES: Selected by Winnipeg Jets as underage junior in first round (second Jets pick, 14th overall) of NHL entry draft (June 8, 1983). ... Traded by Jets to Quebec Nordiques for RW Stu Kulak (December 17, 1987). ... Signed as free agent by Detroit Red Wings (October 18, 1990). ... Suffered from the flu (December 15, 1990); missed two games. ... Injured leg (January 9, 1991). ... Strained abdomen (November 7, 1991); missed 15 games. ... Selected by Mighty Ducks of Anaheim in NHL expansion draft (June 24, 1993). ... Sprained left thumb (October 1, 1993); missed five games. ... Suffered from chicken pox (March 30, 1997); missed three games. ... Tore tendon in left wrist (October 30, 1997); missed 16 games. ... Traded by Mighty Ducks to Edmonton Oilers for D Drew Bannister (January 9, 1998). ... Injured shoulder (March 9, 1998); missed seven games. ... Traded by Oilers with C Tony Hrkac to Pittsburgh Penguins for LW Josef Beranek (June 16, 1998).
HONORS: Won Raymond Lagace Trophy (1982-83). ... Named to QMJHL All-Star second team (1982-83). ... Won Eddie Shore Plaque (1992-93). ... Named to AHL All-Star first team (1992-93).

Season Team	League	REGULAR SEASON Gms.	G	A	Pts.	PIM	+/-	PP	SH	PLAYOFFS Gms.	G	A	Pts.	PIM
82-83—Laval	QMJHL	63	16	45	61	144	...	...	...	11	5	5	10	23
83-84—Laval	QMJHL	54	12	33	45	80	...	...	...	14	1	8	9	23
—Winnipeg	NHL	1	0	0	0	0	-2	0	0	—	—	—	—	—
84-85—Winnipeg	NHL	9	0	0	0	0	3	0	0	—	—	—	—	—
—Sherbrooke	AHL	8	1	3	4	4	...	...	...	17	3	6	9	17
85-86—Sherbrooke	AHL	25	4	7	11	29	...	...	...	—	—	—	—	—
—Winnipeg	NHL	46	0	5	5	66	-3	0	0	3	0	0	0	2
86-87—Sherbrooke	AHL	75	6	18	24	87	...	...	...	16	2	4	6	13
87-88—Quebec	NHL	9	0	0	0	2	-4	0	0	—	—	—	—	—
—Moncton	AHL	26	4	10	14	20	...	...	...	—	—	—	—	—
—Fredericton	AHL	33	4	8	12	27	...	...	...	15	2	2	4	24
88-89—Halifax	AHL	57	5	19	24	65	...	...	...	4	1	0	1	14
—Quebec	NHL	16	0	3	3	16	-11	0	0	—	—	—	—	—
89-90—Canadian nat'l team	Int'l	68	8	29	37	60	...	...	...	—	—	—	—	—
90-91—Detroit	NHL	56	3	5	8	20	6	0	0	7	1	0	1	13
91-92—Detroit	NHL	27	3	1	4	20	4	0	1	2	0	1	1	0
—Adirondack	AHL	19	1	6	7	33	...	...	...	18	7	4	11	22
92-93—Adirondack	AHL	64	7	36	43	54	...	...	...	11	3	8	11	8
—Detroit	NHL	6	0	0	0	2	-1	0	0	—	—	—	—	—
93-94—Anaheim	NHL	77	9	11	20	55	20	1	0	—	—	—	—	—
94-95—Anaheim	NHL	45	7	13	20	12	-3	3	1	—	—	—	—	—
95-96—Anaheim	NHL	82	8	22	30	64	9	0	1	—	—	—	—	—
96-97—Anaheim	NHL	79	4	14	18	55	17	1	0	11	0	0	0	4
97-98—Anaheim	NHL	22	0	1	1	27	-12	0	0	—	—	—	—	—
—Edmonton	NHL	30	2	5	7	22	6	0	0	11	0	0	0	16
NHL Totals (13 years)		505	36	80	116	361	29	5	3	34	1	1	2	35

DOME, ROBERT — C/LW — PENGUINS

PERSONAL: Born January 29, 1979, in Skalica, Czechoslovakia. ... 6-0/205. ... Shoots left. ... Name pronounced DEH-may.
TRANSACTIONS/CAREER NOTES: Selected by Pittsburgh Penguins in first round (first Penguins pick, 17th overall) of NHL entry draft (June 21, 1997).

Season Team	League	REGULAR SEASON Gms.	G	A	Pts.	PIM	+/-	PP	SH	PLAYOFFS Gms.	G	A	Pts.	PIM
94-95—Dukla Jrs.	Slov. Jr.	36	36	43	79	39	...	...	...	—	—	—	—	—
95-96—Utah	IHL	56	10	9	19	28	...	...	...	—	—	—	—	—
96-97—Long Beach	IHL	13	4	6	10	14	...	...	...	—	—	—	—	—
—Las Vegas	IHL	43	10	7	17	22	...	...	...	—	—	—	—	—
97-98—Pittsburgh	NHL	30	5	2	7	12	-1	1	0	—	—	—	—	—
—Syracuse	AHL	36	21	25	46	77	...	...	...	—	—	—	—	—
NHL Totals (1 year)		30	5	2	7	12	-1	1	0					

DOMENICHELLI, HNAT — C — FLAMES

PERSONAL: Born February 17, 1976, in Edmonton. ... 6-0/190. ... Shoots left. ... Name pronounced NAT dah-mih-KEHL-ee.
TRANSACTIONS/CAREER NOTES: Selected by Hartford Whalers in fourth round (second Whalers pick, 83rd overall) of NHL entry draft (June 29, 1994). ... Traded by Whalers with D Glen Featherstone, second-round pick (D Dimitri Kokorev) in 1997 draft and third-round pick (D Paul Manning) in 1998 draft to Calgary Flames for D Steve Chiasson and third-round pick (D Francis Lessard) in 1997 draft (March 5, 1997).
HONORS: Named to WHL (West) All-Star second team (1994-95). ... Won Brad Hornung Trophy (1995-96). ... Won Can.HL Most Sportsmanlike Player of the Year Award (1995-96). ... Named to Can.HL All-Star first team (1995-96). ... Named to WHL (West) All-Star first team (1995-96).
MISCELLANEOUS: Scored on a penalty shot (vs. Arturs Irbe, Febraury 27, 1998).

		REGULAR SEASON								PLAYOFFS				
Season Team	League	Gms.	G	A	Pts.	PIM	+/-	PP	SH	Gms.	G	A	Pts.	PIM
92-93—Kamloops	WHL	45	12	8	20	15	...	...	...	11	1	1	2	2
93-94—Kamloops	WHL	69	27	40	67	31	...	...	...	19	10	12	22	0
94-95—Kamloops	WHL	72	52	62	114	34	...	...	...	19	9	9	18	9
95-96—Kamloops	WHL	62	59	89	148	37	...	...	...	16	7	9	16	29
96-97—Hartford	NHL	13	2	1	3	7	-4	1	0	—	—	—	—	—
—Springfield	AHL	39	24	24	48	12	...	...	...	—	—	—	—	—
—Calgary	NHL	10	1	2	3	2	1	0	0	—	—	—	—	—
—Saint John	AHL	1	1	1	2	0	...	...	...	5	5	0	5	2
97-98—Saint John	AHL	48	33	13	46	24	...	...	...	19	7	8	15	14
—Calgary	NHL	31	9	7	16	6	4	1	0	—	—	—	—	—
NHL Totals (2 years)		54	12	10	22	15	1	2	0					

DOMI, TIE RW MAPLE LEAFS

PERSONAL: Born November 1, 1969, in Windsor, Ont. ... 5-10/200. ... Shoots right. ... Full name: Tahir Domi. ... Name pronounced TIGH DOH-mee. ... Nickname: The Albanian Agressor.

TRANSACTIONS/CAREER NOTES: Selected by Toronto Maple Leafs in second round (second Maple Leafs pick, 27th overall) of NHL entry draft (June 11, 1988). ... Traded by Maple Leafs with G Mark Laforest to New York Rangers for RW Greg Johnston (June 28, 1990). ... Suspended six games by AHL for pre-game fighting (November 25, 1990). ... Sprained right knee (March 11, 1992); missed eight games. ... Traded by Rangers with LW Kris King to Winnipeg Jets for C Ed Olczyk (December 28, 1992). ... Fined $500 by NHL for premeditated fight (January 4, 1993). ... Sprained knee (January 25, 1994); missed three games. ... Traded by Jets to Toronto Maple Leafs for C Mike Eastwood and third-round pick (RW Brad Isbister) in 1995 draft (April 7, 1995). ... Strained groin (April 8, 1995); missed two games. ... Suffered from the flu (April 19, 1995); missed one game. ... Suspended eight games by NHL for fighting (October 17, 1995). ... Sprained knee (December 2, 1995); missed two games. ... Fined $1,000 by NHL for fighting (November 13, 1996). ... Sprained ankle (April 2, 1997); missed two games. ... Strained abdomen (October 25, 1997); missed two games.

		REGULAR SEASON								PLAYOFFS				
Season Team	League	Gms.	G	A	Pts.	PIM	+/-	PP	SH	Gms.	G	A	Pts.	PIM
85-86—Windsor Jr. B	OHA	32	8	17	25	346	...	...	...	—	—	—	—	—
86-87—Peterborough	OHL	18	1	1	2	79	...	...	...	—	—	—	—	—
87-88—Peterborough	OHL	60	22	21	43	*292	...	...	...	12	3	9	12	24
88-89—Peterborough	OHL	43	14	16	30	175	...	...	...	17	10	9	19	*70
89-90—Newmarket	AHL	57	14	11	25	285	...	...	...	—	—	—	—	—
—Toronto	NHL	2	0	0	0	42	0	0	0	—	—	—	—	—
90-91—New York Rangers	NHL	28	1	0	1	185	-5	0	0	—	—	—	—	—
—Binghamton	AHL	25	11	6	17	219	...	...	...	7	3	2	5	16
91-92—New York Rangers	NHL	42	2	4	6	246	-4	0	0	6	1	1	2	32
92-93—New York Rangers	NHL	12	2	0	2	95	-1	0	0	—	—	—	—	—
—Winnipeg	NHL	49	3	10	13	249	2	0	0	6	1	0	1	23
93-94—Winnipeg	NHL	81	8	11	19	*347	-8	0	0	—	—	—	—	—
94-95—Winnipeg	NHL	31	4	4	8	128	-6	0	0	—	—	—	—	—
—Toronto	NHL	9	0	1	1	31	1	0	0	7	1	0	1	0
95-96—Toronto	NHL	72	7	6	13	297	-3	0	0	6	0	2	2	4
96-97—Toronto	NHL	80	11	17	28	275	-17	2	0	—	—	—	—	—
97-98—Toronto	NHL	80	4	10	14	365	-5	0	0	—	—	—	—	—
NHL Totals (9 years)		486	42	63	105	2260	-46	2	0	25	3	3	6	59

DONATO, TED LW BRUINS

PERSONAL: Born April 28, 1968, in Dedham, Mass. ... 5-10/181. ... Shoots left. ... Full name: Edward Paul Donato. ... Brother of Dan Donato, infielder in New York Yankees organization. ... Name pronounced duh-NAH-toh.

HIGH SCHOOL: Catholic Memorial (Boston).

COLLEGE: Harvard (degree in history).

TRANSACTIONS/CAREER NOTES: Selected by Boston Bruins in sixth round (sixth Bruins pick, 98th overall) of NHL entry draft (June 13, 1987). ... Broke collarbone (November 18, 1989). ... Played in Europe during 1994-95 NHL lockout. ... Injured groin (November 21, 1996); missed two games. ... Fractured finger (March 9, 1997); missed 13 games. ... Suspended three games by NHL and fined $1,000 for high-sticking (December 22, 1997).

HONORS: Named NCAA Tournament Most Valuable Player (1988-89). ... Named to NCAA All-Tournament team (1988-89). ... Named to ECAC All-Star first team (1990-91).

		REGULAR SEASON								PLAYOFFS				
Season Team	League	Gms.	G	A	Pts.	PIM	+/-	PP	SH	Gms.	G	A	Pts.	PIM
86-87—Catholic Memorial	Mass. H.S.	22	29	34	63	30	...	...	...	—	—	—	—	—
87-88—Harvard University	ECAC	28	12	14	26	24	...	...	...	—	—	—	—	—
88-89—Harvard University	ECAC	34	14	37	51	30	...	...	...	—	—	—	—	—
89-90—Harvard University	ECAC	16	5	6	11	34	...	...	...	—	—	—	—	—
90-91—Harvard University	ECAC	28	19	37	56	26	...	...	...	—	—	—	—	—
91-92—U.S. national team	Int'l	52	11	22	33	24	...	...	...	—	—	—	—	—
—U.S. Olympic Team	Int'l	8	4	3	7	8	...	...	...	—	—	—	—	—
—Boston	NHL	10	1	2	3	8	-1	0	0	15	3	4	7	4
92-93—Boston	NHL	82	15	20	35	61	2	3	2	4	0	1	1	0
93-94—Boston	NHL	84	22	32	54	59	0	9	2	13	4	2	6	10
94-95—TuTo Turku	Finland	14	5	5	10	47	...	...	...	—	—	—	—	—
—Boston	NHL	47	10	10	20	10	3	1	0	5	0	0	0	4
95-96—Boston	NHL	82	23	26	49	46	6	7	0	5	1	2	3	2
96-97—Boston	NHL	67	25	26	51	37	-9	6	2	—	—	—	—	—
97-98—Boston	NHL	79	16	23	39	54	6	3	0	5	0	0	0	2
NHL Totals (7 years)		451	112	139	251	275	7	29	6	47	8	9	17	22

DONOVAN, SHEAN — RW — AVALANCHE

PERSONAL: Born January 22, 1975, in Timmins, Ont. ... 6-3/210. ... Shoots right. ... Name pronounced SHAWN DAHN-ih-vihn.

TRANSACTIONS/CAREER NOTES: Selected by San Jose Sharks in second round (second Sharks pick, 28th overall) of NHL entry draft (June 26, 1993). ... Suffered a concussion (October 5, 1996); missed two games. ... Sore knee (December 21, 1996); missed two games. ... Traded by Sharks with first-round pick (C Alex Tanguay) in 1998 draft to Colorado Avalanche for C Mike Ricci and second-round pick (RW Jonathan Cheechoo) in 1998 draft (November 20, 1997). ... Bruised knee (January 3, 1998); missed one game. ... Bruised knee (January 21, 1998); missed three games.

		REGULAR SEASON							PLAYOFFS				
Season Team	League	Gms.	G	A	Pts.	PIM	+/-	PP	SH	Gms.	G	A	Pts.	PIM
91-92—Ottawa	OHL	58	11	8	19	14	...	...	...	11	1	0	1	5
92-93—Ottawa	OHL	66	29	23	52	33	...	...	...	—	—	—	—	—
93-94—Ottawa	OHL	62	35	49	84	63	...	...	...	17	10	11	21	14
94-95—Ottawa	OHL	29	22	19	41	41	...	...	...	—	—	—	—	—
—San Jose	NHL	14	0	0	0	6	-6	0	0	7	0	1	1	6
—Kansas City	IHL	5	0	2	2	7	...	...	...	14	5	3	8	23
95-96—Kansas City	IHL	4	0	0	0	8	...	...	...	5	0	0	0	8
—San Jose	NHL	74	13	8	21	39	-17	0	1	—	—	—	—	—
96-97—San Jose	NHL	73	9	6	15	42	-18	0	1	—	—	—	—	—
—Kentucky	AHL	3	1	3	4	18	...	...	...	—	—	—	—	—
97-98—San Jose	NHL	20	3	3	6	22	3	0	0	—	—	—	—	—
—Colorado	NHL	47	5	7	12	48	3	0	0	—	—	—	—	—
NHL Totals (4 years)		228	30	24	54	157	-35	0	2	7	0	1	1	6

DOURIS, PETER — RW

PERSONAL: Born February 19, 1966, in Toronto. ... 6-1/195. ... Shoots right. ... Name pronounced DOO-rihz.
COLLEGE: New Hampshire.
TRANSACTIONS/CAREER NOTES: Selected by Winnipeg Jets in second round (first Jets pick, 30th overall) of NHL entry draft (June 9, 1984). ... Traded by Jets to St. Louis Blues for LW/D Kent Carlson and 12th-round pick (RW Sergei Kharin) in 1989 draft (September 29, 1988). ... Signed as free agent by Boston Bruins (September 1989). ... Injured ankle (December 1990). ... Strained hip flexor (November 1991); missed three games. ... Signed as free agent by Mighty Ducks of Anaheim (July 22, 1993). ... Sprained left knee (September 16, 1993); missed eight games. ... Pulled groin (December 1, 1995); missed five games. ... Injured groin (December 27, 1995); missed remainder of season. ... Signed as free agent by Dallas Stars (July 16, 1997).

D

		REGULAR SEASON							PLAYOFFS				
Season Team	League	Gms.	G	A	Pts.	PIM	+/-	PP	SH	Gms.	G	A	Pts.	PIM
83-84—New Hampshire	ECAC	37	19	15	34	14	...	...	...	—	—	—	—	—
84-85—New Hampshire	Hockey East	42	27	24	51	34	...	...	...	—	—	—	—	—
85-86—Canadian nat'l team	Int'l	33	16	7	23	18	...	...	...	—	—	—	—	—
—Winnipeg	NHL	11	0	0	0	0	-1	0	0	—	—	—	—	—
86-87—Sherbrooke	AHL	62	14	28	42	24	...	...	...	17	7	*15	†22	16
—Winnipeg	NHL	6	0	0	0	0	-1	0	0	—	—	—	—	—
87-88—Moncton	AHL	73	42	37	79	53	...	...	...	—	—	—	—	—
—Winnipeg	NHL	4	0	2	2	0	-1	0	0	1	0	0	0	0
88-89—Peoria	IHL	81	28	41	69	32	...	...	...	4	1	2	3	0
89-90—Maine	AHL	38	17	20	37	14	...	...	...	—	—	—	—	—
—Boston	NHL	36	5	6	11	15	8	1	0	8	0	1	1	8
90-91—Maine	AHL	35	16	15	31	9	...	...	...	7	0	1	1	6
—Boston	NHL	39	5	2	7	9	-12	1	1	2	3	0	3	2
91-92—Boston	NHL	54	10	13	23	10	9	0	0	7	2	3	5	0
—Maine	AHL	12	4	3	7	2	...	...	...	—	—	—	—	—
92-93—Providence	AHL	50	29	26	55	12	...	...	...	—	—	—	—	—
—Boston	NHL	19	4	4	8	4	5	0	1	4	1	0	1	0
93-94—Anaheim	NHL	74	12	22	34	21	-5	1	0	—	—	—	—	—
94-95—Anaheim	NHL	46	10	11	21	12	4	0	0	—	—	—	—	—
95-96—Anaheim	NHL	31	8	7	15	9	-3	2	0	—	—	—	—	—
96-97—Milwaukee	IHL	80	36	36	72	14	...	...	...	3	2	2	4	2
97-98—Michigan	IHL	78	26	31	57	29	...	...	...	4	0	5	5	2
—Dallas	NHL	1	0	0	0	0	-1	0	0	—	—	—	—	—
NHL Totals (11 years)		321	54	67	121	80	-7	5	2	22	6	4	10	10

DOVIGI, PATRICK — G — OILERS

PERSONAL: Born July 2, 1979, in Sault Ste. Marie, Ont. ... 6-0/180. ... Catches left. ... Name pronounced duh-VEE-jee.
TRANSACTIONS/CAREER NOTES: Selected by Edmonton Oilers in second round (second Oilers pick, 41st overall) of NHL entry draft (June 21, 1997).

		REGULAR SEASON							PLAYOFFS				
Season Team	League	Gms.	Min	W	L	T	GA	SO	Avg.	Gms.	Min.	W	L	GA	SO	Avg.
95-96—Elmira	Jr. B	33		10	12	1		4		—	—					—
96-97—Erie	OHL	36	1764	11	14	4	114	3	3.88	5	303	1	4	18	0	3.56
97-98—Erie	OHL	41	2174	17	17	2	161	0	4.44	—	—					—

DOWD, JIM — C — PREDATORS

PERSONAL: Born December 25, 1968, in Brick, N.J. ... 6-1/190. ... Shoots right. ... Full name: James Dowd.
HIGH SCHOOL: Brick (N.J.) Township.

COLLEGE: Lake Superior State (Mich.).
TRANSACTIONS/CAREER NOTES: Selected by New Jersey Devils in eighth round (seventh Devils pick, 149th overall) of NHL entry draft (June 13, 1987). ... Injured shoulder (February 2, 1995) and underwent shoulder surgery (February 15, 1995); missed 35 games. ... Traded by Devils with second-round pick (traded to Calgary) in 1997 draft to Hartford Whalers for RW Jocelyn Lemieux and second-round pick (traded to Dallas) in 1998 draft (December 19, 1995). ... Traded by Whalers with D Frantisek Kucera and second-round pick (D Ryan Bonni) in 1997 draft to Vancouver Canucks for D Jeff Brown and fifth-round pick (traded to Dallas) in 1998 draft (December 19, 1995). ... Selected by New York Islanders from Canucks in waiver draft for cash (September 30, 1996). ... Signed as free agent by Calgary Flames (July 10, 1997). ... Traded by Flames to Nashville Predators for future considerations (June 27, 1998).
HONORS: Named to NCAA All-America West second team (1989-90). ... Named to CCHA All-Star second team (1989-90). ... Named to NCAA All-America West first team (1990-91). ... Named CCHA Player of the Year (1990-91). ... Named to CCHA All-Star first team (1990-91).
MISCELLANEOUS: Member of Stanley Cup championship team (1995).

Season Team	League	REGULAR SEASON								PLAYOFFS				
		Gms.	G	A	Pts.	PIM	+/-	PP	SH	Gms.	G	A	Pts.	PIM
83-84—Brick Township	N.J. H.S.	—	19	30	49	—	—	—	—	—	—	—	—	—
84-85—Brick Township	N.J. H.S.	—	58	55	113	—	—	—	—	—	—	—	—	—
85-86—Brick Township	N.J. H.S.	—	47	51	98	—	—	—	—	—	—	—	—	—
86-87—Brick Township	N.J. H.S.	20	62	53	115	—	...	...	...	—	—	—	—	—
87-88—Lake Superior	CCHA	45	18	27	45	16	...	...	...	—	—	—	—	—
88-89—Lake Superior	CCHA	46	24	35	59	40	...	...	...	—	—	—	—	—
89-90—Lake Superior	CCHA	46	25	67	92	30	...	...	...	—	—	—	—	—
90-91—Lake Superior	CCHA	44	24	54	78	53	...	...	...	—	—	—	—	—
91-92—Utica	AHL	78	17	42	59	47	...	...	...	4	2	2	4	4
—New Jersey	NHL	1	0	0	0	0	0	0	0	—	—	—	—	—
92-93—Utica	AHL	78	27	45	72	62	...	...	...	5	1	7	8	10
—New Jersey	NHL	1	0	0	0	0	-1	0	0	—	—	—	—	—
93-94—Albany	AHL	58	26	37	63	76	...	...	...	—	—	—	—	—
—New Jersey	NHL	15	5	10	15	0	8	2	0	19	2	6	8	8
94-95—New Jersey	NHL	10	1	4	5	0	-5	1	0	11	2	1	3	8
95-96—New Jersey	NHL	28	4	9	13	17	-1	0	0	—	—	—	—	—
—Vancouver	NHL	38	1	6	7	6	-8	0	0	1	0	0	0	0
96-97—New York Islanders	NHL	3	0	0	0	0	-1	0	0	—	—	—	—	—
—Utah	IHL	48	10	21	31	27	...	...	...	—	—	—	—	—
—Saint John	AHL	24	5	11	16	18	...	...	...	5	1	2	3	0
97-98—Saint John	AHL	35	8	30	38	20	...	...	...	19	3	13	16	10
—Calgary	NHL	48	6	8	14	12	10	0	1	—	—	—	—	—
NHL Totals (7 years)		144	17	37	54	35	2	3	1	31	4	7	11	16

DOWNEY, AARON — RW — BRUINS

PERSONAL: Born August 24, 1974, in Shelbourne, Ont. ... 6-0/210. ... Shoots right.
TRANSACTIONS/CAREER NOTES: Signed as free agent by Boston Bruins (January 20, 1998).

Season Team	League	REGULAR SEASON								PLAYOFFS				
		Gms.	G	A	Pts.	PIM	+/-	PP	SH	Gms.	G	A	Pts.	PIM
93-94—HC Vitkovice	Czech.	1	0	0	0					—	—	—	—	—
94-95—HC Vitkovice	Czech.	8	2	0	2	...	...	...	...	4	0	0	0	...
95-96—HC Vitkovice	Czech.	32	3	4	7	...	...	...	...	4	0	0	0	...
96-97—Moose Jaw	WHL	61	12	32	44	...	...	...	...	11	2	5	7	27
—HC Vitkovice	Czech.	1	0	0	0	...				—	—	—	—	—
97-98—Providence	AHL	78	5	10	15	*407	...	...	...	—	—	—	—	—

DOYLE, TREVOR — D

PERSONAL: Born January 1, 1974, in Ottawa. ... 6-3/204. ... Shoots right.
TRANSACTIONS/CAREER NOTES: Selected by Florida Panthers in seventh round (ninth Panthers pick, 161st overall) of NHL entry draft (June 26, 1993).

Season Team	League	REGULAR SEASON								PLAYOFFS				
		Gms.	G	A	Pts.	PIM	+/-	PP	SH	Gms.	G	A	Pts.	PIM
91-92—Smiths Falls-Nepean	Jr. A	34	5	13	18	64	...	...	...	—	—	—	—	—
—Kingston	OHL	26	0	1	1	19	...	...	...	—	—	—	—	—
92-93—Kingston	OHL	62	1	8	9	148	...	...	...	16	2	3	5	25
93-94—Kingston	OHL	53	2	12	14	246	...	...	...	3	0	0	0	4
94-95—Cincinnati	IHL	52	0	3	3	139	...	...	...	6	0	0	0	13
95-96—Carolina	AHL	48	1	2	3	117	...	...	...	—	—	—	—	—
96-97—Carolina	AHL	47	3	10	13	288	...	...	...	—	—	—	—	—
97-98—Fort Wayne	IHL	36	1	1	2	201	...	...	...	4	0	0	0	23

DRAKE, DALLAS — RW — COYOTES

PERSONAL: Born February 4, 1969, in Trail, B.C. ... 6-0/185. ... Shoots left. ... Full name: Dallas James Drake.
COLLEGE: Northern Michigan.
TRANSACTIONS/CAREER NOTES: Selected by Detroit Red Wings in sixth round (sixth Red Wings pick, 116th overall) of NHL entry draft (June 17, 1989). ... Bruised left leg (November 27, 1992); missed three games. ... Suffered back spasms (December 28, 1992); missed one game. ... Bruised kneecap (January 23, 1993); missed three games. ... Suffered concussion (February 13, 1993); missed one game. ... Injured right wrist (October 16, 1993); missed three games. ... Injured tendon in right hand (December 14, 1993); missed 16 games. ... Traded by Detroit Red Wings with G Tim Cheveldae to Winnipeg Jets for G Bob Essensa and D Sergei Bautin (March 8, 1994). ... Suffered back spasms (March 17, 1995); missed four games. ... Bruised right shoulder (October 22, 1995); missed seven games. ... Suffered ear infection (November 21, 1995); missed two games. ... Strained Achilles' tendon (December 28, 1995); missed two games. ... Jets franchise moved to

Phoenix and renamed Coyotes for 1996-97 season; NHL approved move on January 18, 1996. ... Sprained ankle (November 16, 1996); missed eight games. ... Sprained knee (January 29, 1997); missed 10 games. ... Suffered from the flu (October 19, 1997); missed one game. ... Injured knee (December 3, 1997); missed 12 games. ... Bruised knee (March 2, 1998); missed one game. ... Injured wrist (March 18, 1998); missed five games.

HONORS: Named to NCAA All-America West first team (1991-92). ... Won WCHA Player of the Year Award (1991-92). ... Named to WCHA All-Star first team (1991-92).

Season Team	League	REGULAR SEASON								PLAYOFFS				
		Gms.	G	A	Pts.	PIM	+/-	PP	SH	Gms.	G	A	Pts.	PIM
84-85—Rossland	KIJHL	30	13	37	50	...	...	...	...	—	—	—	—	—
85-86—Rossland	KIJHL	41	53	73	126	...	...	...	...	—	—	—	—	—
86-87—Rossland	KIJHL	40	55	80	135	...	...	...	...	—	—	—	—	—
87-88—Vernon	BCJHL	47	39	85	124	50	...	...	...	11	9	17	26	30
88-89—N. Michigan Univ.	WCHA	45	18	24	42	26	...	...	...	—	—	—	—	—
89-90—N. Michigan Univ.	WCHA	36	13	24	37	42	...	...	...	—	—	—	—	—
90-91—N. Michigan Univ.	WCHA	44	22	36	58	89	...	...	...	—	—	—	—	—
91-92—N. Michigan Univ.	WCHA	40	*39	44	83	58	...	...	...	—	—	—	—	—
92-93—Detroit	NHL	72	18	26	44	93	15	3	2	7	3	3	6	6
93-94—Detroit	NHL	47	10	22	32	37	5	0	1	—	—	—	—	—
—Adirondack	AHL	1	2	0	2	0	...	...	...	—	—	—	—	—
—Winnipeg	NHL	15	3	5	8	12	-6	1	1	—	—	—	—	—
94-95—Winnipeg	NHL	43	8	18	26	30	-6	0	0	—	—	—	—	—
95-96—Winnipeg	NHL	69	19	20	39	36	-7	4	4	3	0	0	0	0
96-97—Phoenix	NHL	63	17	19	36	52	-11	5	1	7	0	1	1	2
97-98—Phoenix	NHL	60	11	29	40	71	17	3	0	4	0	1	1	2
NHL Totals (6 years)		369	86	139	225	331	7	16	9	21	3	5	8	10

DRAPEAU, ETIENNE   C   CANADIENS

PERSONAL: Born January 10, 1978, in Quebec City. ... 6-1/180. ... Shoots left.
TRANSACTIONS/CAREER NOTES: Selected by Montreal Canadiens in fourth round (fifth Canadiens pick, 99th overall) of NHL entry draft (June 22, 1996).

Season Team	League	REGULAR SEASON								PLAYOFFS				
		Gms.	G	A	Pts.	PIM	+/-	PP	SH	Gms.	G	A	Pts.	PIM
94-95—Halifax	QMJHL	63	27	34	61	121	...	...	...	7	2	2	4	20
95-96—Beauport	QMJHL	70	18	37	55	135	...	...	...	20	8	7	15	66
96-97—Beauport	QMJHL	46	15	30	45	42	...	...	...	—	—	—	—	—
—Drummondville	QMJHL	21	10	15	25	42	...	...	...	8	3	6	9	9
97-98—Drummondville	QMJHL	32	18	19	37	30	...	...	...	—	—	—	—	—
—Victoriaville	QMJHL	30	14	30	44	43	...	...	...	6	1	3	4	20

D

DRAPER, KRIS   C   RED WINGS

PERSONAL: Born May 24, 1971, in Toronto. ... 5-11/190. ... Shoots left. ... Full name: Kris Bruce Draper.
TRANSACTIONS/CAREER NOTES: Selected by Winnipeg Jets in third round (fourth Jets pick, 62nd overall) of NHL entry draft (June 17, 1989). ... Traded by Jets to Detroit Red Wings for future considerations (June 30, 1993). ... Sprained right knee ligament (February 4, 1995); missed eight games. ... Suffered from the flu (January 5, 1996); missed one game. ... Injured right knee (February 15, 1996); missed 12 games. ... Reinjured right knee (March 25, 1996); missed three games. ... Dislocated thumb and underwent surgery (December 17, 1997); missed 18 games.
MISCELLANEOUS: Member of Stanley Cup championship team (1997 and 1998).

Season Team	League	REGULAR SEASON								PLAYOFFS				
		Gms.	G	A	Pts.	PIM	+/-	PP	SH	Gms.	G	A	Pts.	PIM
88-89—Canadian nat'l team	Int'l	60	11	15	26	16	...	...	...	—	—	—	—	—
89-90—Canadian nat'l team	Int'l	61	12	22	34	44	...	...	...	—	—	—	—	—
90-91—Winnipeg	NHL	3	1	0	1	5	0	0	0	—	—	—	—	—
—Moncton	AHL	7	2	1	3	2	...	...	...	—	—	—	—	—
—Ottawa	OHL	39	19	42	61	35	...	...	...	17	8	11	19	20
91-92—Moncton	AHL	61	11	18	29	113	...	...	...	4	0	1	1	6
—Winnipeg	NHL	10	2	0	2	2	0	0	0	2	0	0	0	0
92-93—Winnipeg	NHL	7	0	0	0	2	-6	0	0	—	—	—	—	—
—Moncton	AHL	67	12	23	35	40	...	...	...	5	2	2	4	18
93-94—Adirondack	AHL	46	20	23	43	49	...	...	...	—	—	—	—	—
—Detroit	NHL	39	5	8	13	31	11	0	1	7	2	2	4	4
94-95—Detroit	NHL	36	2	6	8	22	1	0	0	18	4	1	5	12
95-96—Detroit	NHL	52	7	9	16	32	2	0	0	18	4	2	6	18
96-97—Detroit	NHL	76	8	5	13	73	-11	1	0	20	2	4	6	12
97-98—Detroit	NHL	64	13	10	23	45	5	1	0	19	1	3	4	12
NHL Totals (8 years)		287	38	38	76	212	2	2	2	84	13	12	25	58

DRIVER, BRUCE   D

PERSONAL: Born April 29, 1962, in Toronto. ... 6-1/185. ... Shoots left. ... Full name: Bruce Douglas Driver.
COLLEGE: Wisconsin.
TRANSACTIONS/CAREER NOTES: Selected by Colorado Rockies as underage junior in sixth round (sixth Rockies pick, 108th overall) of NHL entry draft (June 10, 1981). ... Rockies franchise moved from Colorado to New Jersey and renamed Devils for 1982-83 season. ... Underwent surgery to left knee (February 1985). ... Reinjured knee (April 2, 1985). ... Bruised shoulder (March 9, 1986). ... Sprained ankle (February 1988). ... Broke right leg in three places (December 7, 1988). ... Broke rib (January 8, 1991); missed three games. ... Reinjured rib (January 22, 1991); missed four games. ... Injured shoulder (December 5, 1993); missed 14 games. ... Dislocated shoulder (February 20, 1995);

missed three games. ... Suffered stiff neck (April 16, 1995); missed one game. ... Signed as free agent by New York Rangers (August 24, 1995). ... Underwent shoulder surgery prior to 1995-96 season; missed first 13 games of season. ... Suffered from the flu (March 9, 1996); missed two games. ... Suffered from the flu (April 12, 1996); missed one game. ... Suffered from the flu (December 18, 1996); missed one game. ... Suffered from the flu (January 8, 1997); missed two games. ... Suffered from the flu (January 14, 1998); missed two games. ... Suffered from the flu (April 14, 1998); missed two games.

HONORS: Named to NCAA All-America West team (1981-82). ... Named to NCAA All-Tournament team (1981-82). ... Named to WCHA All-Star first team (1981-82). ... Named to WCHA All-Star second team (1982-83).

MISCELLANEOUS: Member of Stanley Cup championship team (1995). ... Captain of New Jersey Devils (1991-92).

		REGULAR SEASON								PLAYOFFS				
Season Team	League	Gms.	G	A	Pts.	PIM	+/-	PP	SH	Gms.	G	A	Pts.	PIM
78-79—Royal York Royals	OPJHL	45	13	36	49	...	...	...	...	—	—	—	—	—
79-80—Royal York Royals	OPJHL	43	13	57	70	102	...	...	...	—	—	—	—	—
80-81—Univ. of Wisconsin......	WCHA	42	5	15	20	42	...	...	...	—	—	—	—	—
81-82—Univ. of Wisconsin......	WCHA	46	7	37	44	84	...	...	...	—	—	—	—	—
82-83—Univ. of Wisconsin......	WCHA	39	16	34	50	50	...	...	...	—	—	—	—	—
83-84—Canadian nat'l team	Int'l	61	11	17	28	44	...	...	...	—	—	—	—	—
—Can. Olympic Team......	Int'l	7	3	1	4	10	...	...	...	—	—	—	—	—
—Maine........................	AHL	12	2	6	8	15	...	...	...	16	0	10	10	8
—New Jersey	NHL	4	0	2	2	0	-2	0	0	—	—	—	—	—
84-85—New Jersey...............	NHL	67	9	23	32	36	-22	3	1	—	—	—	—	—
85-86—Maine......................	AHL	15	4	7	11	16	...	...	...	—	—	—	—	—
—New Jersey	NHL	40	3	15	18	32	10	1	0	—	—	—	—	—
86-87—New Jersey...............	NHL	74	6	28	34	36	-26	0	0	—	—	—	—	—
87-88—New Jersey...............	NHL	74	15	40	55	68	7	7	0	20	3	7	10	14
88-89—New Jersey...............	NHL	27	1	15	16	24	0	1	0	—	—	—	—	—
89-90—New Jersey...............	NHL	75	7	46	53	63	6	1	0	6	1	5	6	6
90-91—New Jersey...............	NHL	73	9	36	45	62	11	7	0	7	1	2	3	12
91-92—New Jersey...............	NHL	78	7	35	42	66	5	3	1	7	0	4	4	2
92-93—New Jersey...............	NHL	83	14	40	54	66	-10	6	0	5	1	3	4	4
93-94—New Jersey...............	NHL	66	8	24	32	63	29	3	1	20	3	5	8	12
94-95—New Jersey...............	NHL	41	4	12	16	18	-1	1	0	17	1	6	7	8
95-96—New York Rangers......	NHL	66	3	34	37	42	2	3	0	11	0	7	7	4
96-97—New York Rangers......	NHL	79	5	25	30	48	8	2	1	15	0	1	1	2
97-98—New York Rangers......	NHL	75	5	15	20	46	-3	1	0	—	—	—	—	—
NHL Totals (15 years).........		922	96	390	486	670	4	39	4	108	10	40	50	64

DRUCE, JOHN   RW   FLYERS

PERSONAL: Born February 23, 1966, in Peterborough, Ont. ... 6-2/195. ... Shoots right. ... Full name: John W. Druce. ... Name pronounced DROOZ.

TRANSACTIONS/CAREER NOTES: Broke collarbone (October 1983). ... Tore ligaments in ankle (December 1984). ... Selected by Washington Capitals in second round (second Capitals pick, 40th overall) of NHL entry draft (June 15, 1985). ... Tore thumb ligaments (October 1985). ... Fractured wrist (October 18, 1992); missed 18 games. ... Traded by Capitals to Winnipeg Jets with conditional pick in 1993 draft for RW Pat Elynuik (October 1, 1992). ... Signed as free agent by Los Angeles Kings (August 2, 1992). ... Strained groin (April 7, 1995); missed two games. ... Traded by Kings with seventh-round pick (LW Todd Fedoruk) in 1997 draft to Philadelphia Flyers for fourth-round pick (C Mikael Simons) in 1996 draft (March 19, 1996). ... Sprained left knee (April 18, 1996); missed 10 playoff games. ... Strained neck (November 13, 1996); missed three games. ... Sprained shoulder (December 10, 1996); missed five games. ... Lacerated leg (March 2, 1997); missed seven games.

STATISTICAL PLATEAUS: Three-goal games: 1991-92 (1), 1993-94 (1). Total: 2.

		REGULAR SEASON								PLAYOFFS				
Season Team	League	Gms.	G	A	Pts.	PIM	+/-	PP	SH	Gms.	G	A	Pts.	PIM
83-84—Peterborough Jr. B	OHA	40	15	18	33	69	...	...	...	—	—	—	—	—
84-85—Peterborough.............	OHL	54	12	14	26	90	...	...	...	17	6	2	8	21
85-86—Peterborough.............	OHL	49	22	24	46	84	...	...	...	16	0	5	5	34
86-87—Binghamton	AHL	7	13	9	22	131	...	...	...	12	0	3	3	28
87-88—Binghamton	AHL	68	32	29	61	82	...	...	...	1	0	0	0	0
88-89—Washington	NHL	48	8	7	15	62	7	0	0	1	0	0	0	0
—Baltimore	AHL	16	2	11	13	10	...	...	...	—	—	—	—	—
89-90—Washington	NHL	45	8	3	11	52	-3	1	0	15	14	3	17	23
—Baltimore	AHL	26	15	16	31	38	...	...	...	—	—	—	—	—
90-91—Washington	NHL	80	22	36	58	46	4	7	1	11	1	1	2	7
91-92—Washington	NHL	67	19	18	37	39	14	1	0	7	1	0	1	2
92-93—Winnipeg...................	NHL	50	6	14	20	37	-4	0	0	2	0	0	0	0
93-94—Phoenix.....................	IHL	8	5	6	11	9	...	...	...	—	—	—	—	—
—Los Angeles	NHL	55	14	17	31	50	16	1	1	—	—	—	—	—
94-95—Los Angeles	NHL	43	15	5	20	20	-3	3	0	—	—	—	—	—
95-96—Los Angeles	NHL	64	9	12	21	14	-26	0	0	—	—	—	—	—
—Philadelphia	NHL	13	4	4	8	13	6	0	0	2	0	2	2	2
96-97—Philadelphia	NHL	43	7	8	15	12	-5	1	0	13	1	0	1	2
97-98—Philadelphia	AHL	39	21	28	49	45	...	...	...	—	—	—	—	—
—Philadelphia	NHL	23	1	2	3	2	0	0	0	2	0	0	0	2
NHL Totals (10 years).........		531	113	126	239	347	6	14	2	53	17	6	23	38

DRUKEN, HAROLD   LW   CANUCKS

PERSONAL: Born January 26, 1979, in St. John's, Nfld. ... 5-11/194. ... Shoots left. ... Name pronounced DROO-kihn.

HIGH SCHOOL: Noble & Greenough (Dedham, Mass.).

TRANSACTIONS/CAREER NOTES: Selected by Vancouver Canucks in second round (third Canucks pick, 36th overall) of NHL entry draft (June 21, 1997).

HONORS: Named to OHL All-Rookie team (1996-97).

Season Team	League	Gms.	G	A	Pts.	PIM	+/-	PP	SH	Gms.	G	A	Pts.	PIM
95-96—Noble & Greenough....	Mass. H.S.	30	37	28	65	28	...	...	...	—	—	—	—	—
96-97—Detroit.......................	OHL	63	27	31	58	14	...	...	...	5	3	2	5	0
97-98—Plymouth	OHL	64	38	44	82	12	...	...	...	15	9	11	20	4

DRURY, CHRIS C AVALANCHE

PERSONAL: Born August 20, 1976, in Trumbull, Conn. ... 5-10/180. ... Shoots right. ... Brother of Ted Drury, center/left winger, Mighty Ducks of Anaheim.
HIGH SCHOOL: Fairfield (Conn.) College Prep.
COLLEGE: Boston University.
TRANSACTIONS/CAREER NOTES: Selected by Quebec Nordiques in third round (fifth Nordiques pick, 72nd overall) of NHL entry draft (June 29, 1994). ... Nordiques franchise moved to Colorado and renamed Avalanche for 1995-96 season (June 21, 1995).
HONORS: Named to NCAA All-America East second team (1995-96). ... Named to Hockey East All-Star team (1995-96 and 1996-97). ... Named to NCAA All-America East first team (1996-97 and 1997-98). ... Named Hockey East Player of the Year (1996-97 and 1997-98). ... Named to NCAA All-Tournament team (1996-97). ... Won Hobey Baker Memorial Award (1997-98).

Season Team	League	Gms.	G	A	Pts.	PIM	+/-	PP	SH	Gms.	G	A	Pts.	PIM
92-93—Fairfield College Prep..	Conn. H.S.	24	25	32	57	15	...	...	...	—	—	—	—	—
93-94—Fairfield College Prep..	Conn. H.S.	24	37	18	55		...	...	...	—	—	—	—	—
94-95—Boston University	Hockey East	39	12	15	27	38	...	...	...	—	—	—	—	—
95-96—Boston University	Hockey East	37	35	33	68	46	...	...	...	—	—	—	—	—
96-97—Boston University	Hockey East	41	38	24	62	64	...	...	...	—	—	—	—	—
97-98—Boston University	Hockey East	38	28	29	57	88	...	...	...	—	—	—	—	—

DRURY, TED C/LW MIGHTY DUCKS

PERSONAL: Born September 13, 1971, in Boston. ... 6-0/208. ... Shoots left. ... Full name: Theodore Evans Drury. ... Brother of Chris Drury, center in Colorado Avalanche system. ... Name pronounced DROO-ree.
HIGH SCHOOL: Fairfield (Conn.) College Prep School.
COLLEGE: Harvard.
TRANSACTIONS/CAREER NOTES: Broke ankle (January 1988). ... Selected by Calgary Flames in second round (second Flames pick, 42nd overall) of NHL entry draft (June 17, 1989). ... Fractured kneecap (December 22, 1993); missed 15 games. ... Traded by Flames with D Gary Suter and LW Paul Ranheim to Hartford Whalers for C Mikael Nylander, D Zarley Zalapski and D James Patrick (March 10, 1994). ... Strained back (March 9, 1995); missed three games. ... Injured shoulder (November 4, 1995); missed three games. ... Suffered slight concussion (January 22, 1996); missed two games. ... Injured wrist (January 29, 1996). ... Signed as free agent by Ottawa Senators for 1995-96 season. ... Traded by Senators with rights to D Marc Moro to Mighty Ducks of Anaheim for C Shaun Van Allen and D Jason York (October 1, 1996). ... Fractured wrist (January 31, 1997); missed five games.
HONORS: Named to NCAA All-America East first team (1992-93). ... Named ECAC Player of the Year (1992-93). ... Named to ECAC All-Star first team (1992-93).

D

Season Team	League	Gms.	G	A	Pts.	PIM	+/-	PP	SH	Gms.	G	A	Pts.	PIM
87-88—Fairfield College Prep..	Conn. H.S.	—	21	28	49	—				—	—	—	—	—
88-89—Fairfield College Prep..	Conn. H.S.	—	35	31	66		...	...	...	—	—	—	—	—
89-90—Harvard University	ECAC	17	9	13	22	10	...	...	...	—	—	—	—	—
90-91—Harvard University	ECAC	26	18	18	36	22	...	...	...	—	—	—	—	—
91-92—U.S. national team	Int'l	53	11	23	34	30	...	...	...	—	—	—	—	—
—U.S. Olympic team	Int'l	7	1	1	2	0	...	...	...	—	—	—	—	—
92-93—Harvard University	ECAC	31	22	41	*63	26	...	...	...	—	—	—	—	—
93-94—Calgary	NHL	34	5	7	12	26	-5	0	1	—	—	—	—	—
—U.S. national team	Int'l	11	1	4	5	11	...	...	...	—	—	—	—	—
—U.S. Olympic team	Int'l	7	1	2	3	2	...	...	...	—	—	—	—	—
—Hartford	NHL	16	1	5	6	10	-10	0	0	—	—	—	—	—
94-95—Hartford	NHL	34	3	6	9	21	-3	0	0	—	—	—	—	—
—Springfield	AHL	2	0	1	1	0	...	...	...	—	—	—	—	—
95-96—Ottawa	NHL	42	9	7	16	54	-19	1	0	—	—	—	—	—
96-97—Anaheim	NHL	73	9	9	18	54	-9	1	0	10	1	0	1	4
97-98—Anaheim	NHL	73	6	10	16	82	-10	0	1	—	—	—	—	—
NHL Totals (5 years)...........		272	33	44	77	247	-56	2	2	10	1	0	1	4

DUBE, CHRISTIAN C RANGERS

PERSONAL: Born April 25, 1977, in Quebec City. ... 6-0/183. ... Shoots right. ... Son of Normand Dube, left winger with Kansas City Scouts (1974-75 and 1975-76). ... Name pronounced doo-BAY.
TRANSACTIONS/CAREER NOTES: Selected by New York Rangers in second round (first Rangers pick, 39th overall) of NHL entry draft (July 8, 1995). ... Injured right shoulder (September 28, 1996); missed two games.
HONORS: Won Michel Bergeron Trophy (1993-94). ... Won Can.HL Player of the Year Award (1995-96). ... Named to Can.HL All-Star first team (1995-96). ... Won Frank Selke Trophy (1995-96). ... Won Michel Briere Trophy (1995-96). ... Named to QMJHL All-Star first team (1995-96). ... Won Stafford Smythe Memorial Trophy (1996-97). ... Named to Memorial Cup All-Star Team (1996-97).

Season Team	League	Gms.	G	A	Pts.	PIM	+/-	PP	SH	Gms.	G	A	Pts.	PIM
93-94—Sherbrooke	QMJHL	72	31	41	72	22	...	...	...	11	3	2	5	6
94-95—Sherbrooke	QMJHL	71	36	65	101	43	...	...	...	7	1	7	8	8
95-96—Sherbrooke	QMJHL	62	52	93	145	105	...	...	...	7	5	5	10	6
96-97—New York Rangers	NHL	27	1	1	2	4	-4	1	0	3	0	0	0	0
—Hull	QMJHL	19	15	22	37	27	...	...	...	14	7	16	23	14
97-98—Hartford	AHL	79	11	46	57	46	...	...	...	9	0	4	4	6
NHL Totals (1 year)............		27	1	1	2					3	0	0	0	0

DUBINSKY, STEVE   C/LW   BLACKHAWKS

PERSONAL: Born July 9, 1970, in Montreal. ... 6-0/190. ... Shoots left. ... Name pronounced doo-BIHN-skee.
COLLEGE: Clarkson (N.Y.).
TRANSACTIONS/CAREER NOTES: Selected by Chicago Blackhawks in 11th round (11th Blackhawks pick, 226th overall) of NHL entry draft (June 16, 1990).

						REGULAR SEASON						PLAYOFFS			
Season Team	League	Gms.	G	A	Pts.	PIM	+/-	PP	SH		Gms.	G	A	Pts.	PIM
89-90—Clarkson	ECAC	35	7	10	17	24	...	...	...		—	—	—	—	—
90-91—Clarkson	ECAC	38	15	23	38	26	...	...	...		—	—	—	—	—
91-92—Clarkson	ECAC	33	21	34	55	40	...	...	...		—	—	—	—	—
92-93—Clarkson	ECAC	35	18	26	44	58	...	...	...		—	—	—	—	—
93-94—Chicago	NHL	27	2	6	8	16	1	0	0		6	0	0	0	10
—Indianapolis	IHL	54	15	25	40	63	...	...	...		—	—	—	—	—
94-95—Indianapolis	IHL	62	16	11	27	29	...	...	...		—	—	—	—	—
—Chicago	NHL	16	0	0	0	8	-5	0	0		—	—	—	—	—
95-96—Indianapolis	IHL	16	8	8	16	10	...	...	...		—	—	—	—	—
—Chicago	NHL	43	2	3	5	14	3	0	0		—	—	—	—	—
96-97—Indianapolis	IHL	77	32	40	72	53	...	...	...		1	3	1	4	0
—Chicago	NHL	5	0	0	0	0	2	0	0		4	1	0	1	4
97-98—Chicago	NHL	82	5	13	18	57	-6	0	1		—	—	—	—	—
NHL Totals (5 years)..........		173	9	22	31	95	-5	0	1		10	1	0	1	14

DUCHESNE, STEVE   D   KINGS

PERSONAL: Born June 30, 1965, in Sept-Iles, Que. ... 6-0/198. ... Shoots left. ... Name pronounced doo-SHAYN.
TRANSACTIONS/CAREER NOTES: Signed as free agent by Los Angeles Kings (October 1, 1984). ... Strained left knee (January 26, 1988). ... Separated left shoulder (November 1988). ... Traded by Kings with C Steve Kasper and fourth-round pick in 1991 draft (D Aris Brimanis) to Philadelphia Flyers for D Jeff Chychrun and rights to RW Jari Kurri (May 30, 1991). ... Traded by Flyers with G Ron Hextall, C Mike Ricci, C Peter Forsberg, D Kerry Huffman, first-round pick (G Jocelyn Thibault) in 1993 draft, cash and future considerations to Quebec Nordiques for C Eric Lindros (June 20, 1992). ... Flyers sent LW Chris Simon and first-round pick (traded to Toronto) in 1994 draft to Nordiques to complete deal (July 21, 1992). ... Suffered a concussion (January 2, 1993); missed one game. ... Suffered from the flu (March 20, 1993); missed one game. ... Refused to report to Nordiques in 1993-94 due to contract dispute. ... Traded by Nordiques with RW Denis Chasse to St. Louis Blues for C Ron Sutter, C Bob Bassen and D Garth Butcher (January 23, 1994). ... Injured back (March 30, 1994); missed one game. ... Injured shoulder (March 31, 1995); missed one game. ... Traded by Blues to Ottawa Senators for second-round pick (traded to Buffalo) in 1996 draft (August 4, 1995). ... Sprained ankle (November 18, 1995); missed 20 games. ... Bruised hand (October 9, 1996); missed two games. ... Suffered sore back (March 4, 1997); missed two games. ... Traded by Senators to Blues for D Igor Kravchuk (August 25, 1997). ... Suffered sore knee (April 7, 1998); missed one game. ... Signed as free agent by Los Angeles Kings (July 2, 1998).
HONORS: Named to QMJHL All-Star first team (1984-85). ... Named to NHL All-Rookie team (1986-87). ... Played in NHL All-Star Game (1989, 1990 and 1993).
STATISTICAL PLATEAUS: Three-goal games: 1988-89 (1), 1991-92 (1), 1993-94 (1). Total: 3.

						REGULAR SEASON						PLAYOFFS			
Season Team	League	Gms.	G	A	Pts.	PIM	+/-	PP	SH		Gms.	G	A	Pts.	PIM
83-84—Drummondville	QMJHL	67	1	34	35	79	...	...	...		—	—	—	—	—
84-85—Drummondville	QMJHL	65	22	54	76	94	...	...	...		5	4	7	11	8
85-86—New Haven	AHL	75	14	35	49	76	...	...	...		5	0	2	2	9
86-87—Los Angeles	NHL	75	13	25	38	74	8	5	0		5	2	2	4	4
87-88—Los Angeles	NHL	71	16	39	55	109	0	5	0		5	1	3	4	14
88-89—Los Angeles	NHL	79	25	50	75	92	31	8	5		11	4	4	8	12
89-90—Los Angeles	NHL	79	20	42	62	36	-3	6	0		10	2	9	11	6
90-91—Los Angeles	NHL	78	21	41	62	66	19	8	0		12	4	8	12	8
91-92—Philadelphia	NHL	78	18	38	56	86	-7	7	2		—	—	—	—	—
92-93—Quebec	NHL	82	20	62	82	57	15	8	0		6	0	5	5	6
93-94—St. Louis	NHL	36	12	19	31	14	1	8	0		4	0	2	2	2
94-95—St. Louis	NHL	47	12	26	38	36	29	1	0		7	0	4	4	2
95-96—Ottawa	NHL	62	12	24	36	42	-23	7	0		—	—	—	—	—
96-97—Ottawa	NHL	78	19	28	47	38	-9	10	2		7	1	4	5	0
97-98—St. Louis	NHL	80	14	42	56	32	9	5	1		10	0	4	4	6
NHL Totals (12 years).........		845	202	436	638	682	70	78	10		77	14	45	59	60

DUERDEN, DAVE   LW   PANTHERS

PERSONAL: Born April 11, 1977, in Oshawa, Ont. ... 6-2/182. ... Shoots left. ... Name pronounced DOOR-dihn.
HIGH SCHOOL: Thomas A. Stewart (Peterborough, Ont.).
TRANSACTIONS/CAREER NOTES: Selected by Florida Panthers in fourth round (fourth Panthers pick, 80th overall) of NHL entry draft (July 8, 1995).
HONORS: Named to OHL All-Star second team (1996-97).

						REGULAR SEASON						PLAYOFFS			
Season Team	League	Gms.	G	A	Pts.	PIM	+/-	PP	SH		Gms.	G	A	Pts.	PIM
93-94—Wexford	Tier II Jr. A	47	17	24	41	26	...	...	...		—	—	—	—	—
94-95—Peterborough.............	OHL	66	20	33	53	21	...	...	...		11	6	2	8	6
95-96—Peterborough.............	OHL	66	35	35	70	47	...	...	...		24	14	13	27	16
96-97—Peterborough.............	OHL	66	36	48	84	34	...	...	...		4	2	4	6	0
97-98—New Haven	AHL	36	6	7	13	10	...	...	...		—	—	—	—	—
—Fort Wayne	IHL	7	0	1	1	0	...	...	...		—	—	—	—	—
—Port Huron	UHL	7	0	4	4	10	...	...	...		—	—	—	—	—

DUMONT, JEAN-PIERRE — LW — BLACKHAWKS

PERSONAL: Born May 1, 1978, in Montreal. ... 6-1/187. ... Shoots left.
TRANSACTIONS/CAREER NOTES: Selected by New York Islanders in first round (first Islanders pick, third overall) of NHL entry draft (June 22, 1996). ... Traded by Islanders with fifth-round pick (traded to Philadelphia) in 1998 draft to Chicago Blackhawks for C/LW Dmitri Nabokov (May 30, 1998).
HONORS: Won Michael Bossy Trophy (1995-96). ... Named to QMJHL All-Star second team (1996-97). ... Won Guy Lafleur Trophy (1997-98).

Season Team	League	Gms.	G	A	Pts.	PIM	+/-	PP	SH	Gms.	G	A	Pts.	PIM
				REGULAR SEASON								PLAYOFFS		
93-94—Val-d'Or	QMJHL	25	9	11	20	10	...	...	...	—	—	—	—	—
94-95—Val-d'Or	QMJHL	48	5	14	19	24	...	...	...	—	—	—	—	—
95-96—Val-d'Or	QMJHL	66	48	57	105	109	...	...	...	13	12	8	20	22
96-97—Val-d'Or	QMJHL	62	44	64	108	88	...	...	...	13	9	7	16	12
97-98—Val-d'Or	QMJHL	55	57	42	99	63	...	...	...	19	*31	15	*46	18

DUNHAM, MIKE — G — PREDATORS

PERSONAL: Born June 1, 1972, in Johnson City, N.Y. ... 6-3/195. ... Catches left. ... Full name: Michael Francis Dunham.
HIGH SCHOOL: Canterbury (New Milford, Conn.).
COLLEGE: Maine.
TRANSACTIONS/CAREER NOTES: Selected by New Jersey Devils in third round (fourth Devils pick, 53rd overall) of NHL entry draft (June 16, 1990). ... Injured hand (January 1, 1998); missed three games. ... Pulled groin (March 21, 1998); missed one game. ... Injured knee and underwent surgery (March 5, 1998); missed 18 games. ... Selected by Nashville Predators in NHL expansion draft (June 26, 1998).
HONORS: Named to NCAA All-America East first team (1992-93). ... Named to Hockey East All-Star first team (1992-93). ... Shared Harry (Hap) Holmes Memorial Trophy with Corey Schwab (1994-95). ... Shared Jack Butterfield Trophy with Corey Schwab (1994-95). ... Named to AHL All-Star second team (1995-96). ... Shared William M. Jennings Trophy with Martin Brodeur (1996-97).

Season Team	League	Gms.	Min	W	L	T	GA	SO	Avg.	Gms.	Min.	W	L	GA	SO	Avg.
				REGULAR SEASON								PLAYOFFS				
87-88—Canterbury School	Conn. H.S.	29	...	...	...	...	...	4	...	—	—	—	—	—	—	—
88-89—Canterbury School	Conn. H.S.	25	...	...	...	...	63	2	...	—	—	—	—	—	—	—
89-90—Canterbury School	Conn. H.S.	32	1558	...	...	...	55	...	2.12	—	—	—	—	—	—	—
90-91—Univ. of Maine	Hockey East	23	1275	14	5	2	63	2	*2.96	—	—	—	—	—	—	—
91-92—Univ. of Maine	Hockey East	7	382	6	0	0	14	1	2.20	—	—	—	—	—	—	—
—U.S. national team	Int'l	3	157	0	1	1	10	0	3.82	—	—	—	—	—	—	—
92-93—Univ. of Maine	Hockey East	25	1429	21	1	1	63	...	2.65	—	—	—	—	—	—	—
—U.S. national team	Int'l	1	60	0	0	1	1	0	1.00	—	—	—	—	—	—	—
93-94—U.S. national team	Int'l	33	1983	22	9	2	125	2	3.78	—	—	—	—	—	—	—
—U.S. Olympic Team	Int'l	3	179	...	...	...	15	0	5.03	—	—	—	—	—	—	—
—Albany	AHL	5	305	2	2	1	26	0	5.11	—	—	—	—	—	—	—
94-95—Albany	AHL	35	2120	20	7	8	99	1	2.80	7	420	6	1	20	1	2.86
95-96—Albany	AHL	44	2591	30	10	2	109	1	2.52	3	181	1	2	5	1	1.66
96-97—Albany	AHL	3	184	1	1	1	12	0	3.91	—	—	—	—	—	—	—
—New Jersey	NHL	26	1013	8	7	1	43	2	2.55	—	—	—	—	—	—	—
97-98—New Jersey	NHL	15	773	5	5	3	29	1	2.25	—	—	—	—	—	—	—
NHL Totals (2 years)		41	1786	13	12	4	72	3	2.42							

DUSBABEK, JOE — RW — SHARKS

PERSONAL: Born May 1, 1978, in Fairbault, Minn. ... 6-1/200. ... Shoots right. ... Full name: Joe David Dusbabek.
HIGH SCHOOL: Minnetonka (Minn.).
COLLEGE: Notre Dame.
TRANSACTIONS/CAREER NOTES: Selected by San Jose Sharks in seventh round (fifth Sharks pick, 163rd overall) in NHL entry draft (June 21, 1997).

Season Team	League	Gms.	G	A	Pts.	PIM	+/-	PP	SH	Gms.	G	A	Pts.	PIM
				REGULAR SEASON								PLAYOFFS		
96-97—Notre Dame	CCHA	35	13	12	25	74	...	...	...	—	—	—	—	—
97-98—Notre Dame	CCHA	21	1	8	9	32	...	...	...	—	—	—	—	—

DUTIAUME, MARK — LW — SABRES

PERSONAL: Born January 31, 1977, in Winnipeg. ... 6-0/200. ... Shoots left. ... Name pronounced doo-tee-OHM.
TRANSACTIONS/CAREER NOTES: Selected by Buffalo Sabres in second round (third Sabres pick, 42nd overall) of NHL entry draft (July 8, 1995).

Season Team	League	Gms.	G	A	Pts.	PIM	+/-	PP	SH	Gms.	G	A	Pts.	PIM
				REGULAR SEASON								PLAYOFFS		
93-94—Tri-City	WHL	3	2	0	2	0	...	...	...	—	—	—	—	—
—Brandon	WHL	55	4	7	11	43	...	...	...	12	0	2	2	6
94-95—Brandon	WHL	62	23	21	44	80	...	...	...	17	1	2	3	33
95-96—Brandon	WHL	7	0	4	4	6	...	...	...	9	2	1	3	12
96-97—Brandon	WHL	48	12	1	13	73	...	...	...	6	2	2	4	13
—Rochester	AHL	6	1	1	2	0	...	...	...	—	—	—	—	—
97-98—Rochester	AHL	11	1	0	1	4	...	...	...	—	—	—	—	—
—South Carolina	ECHL	28	3	4	7	24	...	...	...	2	0	0	0	2

DVORAK, RADEK   C/RW   PANTHERS

PERSONAL: Born March 9, 1977, in Ceske Budejovice, Czechoslovakia. ... 6-2/185. ... Shoots right. ... Name pronounced RA-dihk duh-VOHR-ak.
TRANSACTIONS/CAREER NOTES: Selected by Florida Panthers in first round (first Panthers pick, 10th overall) of NHL entry draft (July 8, 1995). ... Fractured left wrist (October 30, 1997); missed 15 games.

		REGULAR SEASON								PLAYOFFS				
Season Team	League	Gms.	G	A	Pts.	PIM	+/-	PP	SH	Gms.	G	A	Pts.	PIM
92-93—Motor-Ceske Bude......	Czech.	35	44	46	90	...				—	—	—	—	—
93-94—HC Ceske Budejovice..	Czech Rep.	8	0	0	0	...				—	—	—	—	—
—Motor-Ceske Bude......	Czech Rep.	20	17	18	35	...				—	—	—	—	—
94-95—HC Ceske Budejovice..	Czech Rep.	10	3	5	8	...			...	9	5	1	6	...
95-96—Florida........................	NHL	77	13	14	27	20	5	0	0	16	1	3	4	0
96-97—Florida........................	NHL	78	18	21	39	30	-2	2	0	3	0	0	0	0
97-98—Florida........................	NHL	64	12	24	36	33	-1	2	3	—	—	—	—	—
NHL Totals (3 years)...........		219	43	59	102	83	2	4	3	19	1	3	4	0

DYKHUIS, KARL   D   LIGHTNING

PERSONAL: Born July 8, 1972, in Sept-Iles, Que. ... 6-3/214. ... Shoots left. ... Name pronounced DIGH-kowz.
TRANSACTIONS/CAREER NOTES: Selected by Chicago Blackhawks in first round (first Blackhawks pick, 16th overall) of NHL entry draft (June 16, 1990). ... QMJHL rights traded by Hull Olympiques to Longueuil College Francais for first- and sixth-round draft picks (January 10, 1991). ... Traded by Blackhawks to Philadelphia Flyers for D Bob Wilkie (February 16, 1995). ... Sprained knee (November 26, 1996); missed two games. ... Suffered facial lacerations (December 31, 1996); missed two games. ... Dislocated shoulder (January 28, 1997); missed 13 games. ... Traded by Flyers with F Mikael Renberg to Tampa Bay Lightning for C Chris Gratton (August 20, 1997). ... Suffered from the flu (November 14, 1997); missed one game. ... Suffered from the flu (January 31, 1998); missed one game.
HONORS: Won Raymond Lagace Trophy (1988-89). ... Won Michael Bossy Trophy (1989-90). ... Named to QMJHL All-Star first team (1989-90).

		REGULAR SEASON								PLAYOFFS				
Season Team	League	Gms.	G	A	Pts.	PIM	+/-	PP	SH	Gms.	G	A	Pts.	PIM
88-89—Hull............................	QMJHL	63	2	29	31	59	...	...	...	9	1	9	10	6
89-90—Hull............................	QMJHL	69	10	45	55	119	...	...	...	11	2	5	7	2
90-91—Longueuil..................	QMJHL	3	1	4	5	6	...	...	...	—	—	—	—	—
—Canadian nat'l team	Int'l	37	2	9	11	16	...	...	...	—	—	—	—	—
91-92—Longueuil..................	QMJHL	29	5	19	24	55	...	...	...	17	0	12	12	14
—Chicago....................	NHL	6	1	3	4	4	-1	1	0	—	—	—	—	—
92-93—Indianapolis................	IHL	59	5	18	23	76	...	...	...	5	1	1	2	8
—Chicago....................	NHL	12	0	5	5	0	2	0	0	—	—	—	—	—
93-94—Indianapolis................	IHL	73	7	25	32	132	...	...	...	—	—	—	—	—
94-95—Indianapolis................	IHL	52	2	21	23	63	...	...	...	—	—	—	—	—
—Hershey....................	AHL	1	0	0	0	0	...	...	...	—	—	—	—	—
—Philadelphia..............	NHL	33	2	6	8	37	7	1	0	15	4	4	8	14
95-96—Philadelphia..............	NHL	82	5	15	20	101	12	1	0	12	2	2	4	22
96-97—Philadelphia..............	NHL	62	4	15	19	35	6	2	0	18	0	3	3	2
97-98—Tampa Bay..................	NHL	78	5	9	14	110	-8	0	1	—	—	—	—	—
NHL Totals (6 years)...........		273	17	53	70	287	18	5	1	45	6	9	15	38

DZIEDZIC, JOE   LW

PERSONAL: Born December 18, 1971, in Minneapolis. ... 6-3/227. ... Shoots left. ... Full name: Joseph Walter Dziedzic. ... Name pronounced DEED-zihk.
HIGH SCHOOL: Edison (Minneapolis).
COLLEGE: Minnesota.
TRANSACTIONS/CAREER NOTES: Selected by Pittsburgh Penguins in third round (second Penguins pick, 61st overall) of NHL entry draft (June 16, 1990). ... Suffered stiff neck (November 8, 1995); missed four games. ... Suffered back spasms (October 11, 1996); missed three games. ... Separated shoulder (January 25, 1997); missed two games. ... Injured groin (March 18, 1997); missed two games.

		REGULAR SEASON								PLAYOFFS				
Season Team	League	Gms.	G	A	Pts.	PIM	+/-	PP	SH	Gms.	G	A	Pts.	PIM
88-89—Minneapolis Edison	Minn. H.S.	25	47	27	74	34	...	...	...	—	—	—	—	—
89-90—Minneapolis Edison	Minn. H.S.	17	29	19	48	0	...	...	...	—	—	—	—	—
90-91—Univ. of Minnesota......	WCHA	20	6	4	10	26	...	...	...	—	—	—	—	—
91-92—Univ. of Minnesota......	WCHA	37	9	10	19	68	...	...	...	—	—	—	—	—
92-93—Univ. of Minnesota......	WCHA	41	11	14	25	62	...	...	...	—	—	—	—	—
93-94—Univ. of Minnesota......	WCHA	18	7	10	17	48	...	...	...	—	—	—	—	—
94-95—Cleveland....................	IHL	68	15	15	30	74	...	...	...	4	1	0	1	10
95-96—Pittsburgh..................	NHL	69	5	5	10	68	-5	0	0	16	1	2	3	19
96-97—Pittsburgh..................	NHL	59	9	9	18	63	-4	0	0	5	0	1	1	4
97-98—Cleveland....................	IHL	65	21	20	41	176	...	...	...	10	3	4	7	28
NHL Totals (2 years)...........		128	14	14	28	131	-9	0	0	21	1	3	4	23

EAGLES, MIKE   C   CAPITALS

PERSONAL: Born March 7, 1963, in Sussex, N.B. ... 5-10/195. ... Shoots left. ... Full name: Michael Bryant Eagles.
TRANSACTIONS/CAREER NOTES: Selected by Quebec Nordiques as underage junior in sixth round (fifth Nordiques pick, 116th overall) of NHL entry draft (June 10, 1981). ... Broke hand (October 1984). ... Injured ribs (February 21, 1986). ... Traded by Nordiques to Chicago Blackhawks for G Bob Mason (July 1988). ... Broke left hand (February 1989). ... Bruised kidney (January 15, 1990); missed eight games. ... Traded by Blackhawks to Winnipeg Jets for fourth-round pick (D Igor Kravchuk) in 1991 draft (December 14, 1990). ... Fractured thumb (February 17, 1992); missed 14 games. ... Suffered concussion (November 30, 1993); missed one game. ... Strained shoulder (March 7, 1994); missed one game. ... Bruised kidneys (March 27, 1994); missed remainder of season. ... Traded by Jets with D Igor Ulanov to Washington Capitals for third-(traded to Dallas) and fifth-(G Brian Elder) round picks in 1995 draft (April 7, 1995). ... Suffered broken finger (January 1, 1996); missed 11 games. ... Injured wrist (November 9, 1997); missed 17 games. ... Injured foot (February 1, 1998); missed six games. ... Reinjured foot (March 3, 1998); missed seven games.
MISCELLANEOUS: Scored on a penalty shot (vs. Doug Keans, November 9, 1987).

Season Team	League	REGULAR SEASON								PLAYOFFS				
		Gms.	G	A	Pts.	PIM	+/-	PP	SH	Gms.	G	A	Pts.	PIM
79-80—Melville	SJHL	55	46	30	76	77	...	...	...	—	—	—	—	—
80-81—Kitchener	OMJHL	56	11	27	38	64	...	...	...	18	4	2	6	36
81-82—Kitchener	OHL	62	26	40	66	148	...	...	...	15	3	11	14	27
82-83—Kitchener	OHL	58	26	36	62	133	...	...	...	12	5	7	12	27
—Quebec	NHL	2	0	0	0	2	-1	0	0	—	—	—	—	—
83-84—Fredericton	AHL	68	13	29	42	85	...	...	...	4	0	0	0	5
84-85—Fredericton	AHL	36	4	20	24	80	...	...	...	3	0	0	0	2
85-86—Quebec	NHL	73	11	12	23	49	3	1	0	3	0	0	0	2
86-87—Quebec	NHL	73	13	19	32	55	-15	0	2	4	1	0	1	10
87-88—Quebec	NHL	76	10	10	20	74	-18	1	2	—	—	—	—	—
88-89—Chicago	NHL	47	5	11	16	44	-8	0	0	—	—	—	—	—
89-90—Indianapolis	IHL	24	11	13	24	47	...	...	...	13	*10	10	20	34
—Chicago	NHL	23	1	2	3	34	-4	0	0	—	—	—	—	—
90-91—Indianapolis	IHL	25	15	14	29	47	...	...	...	—	—	—	—	—
—Winnipeg	NHL	44	0	9	9	79	-10	0	0	—	—	—	—	—
91-92—Winnipeg	NHL	65	7	10	17	118	-17	0	1	7	0	0	0	8
92-93—Winnipeg	NHL	84	8	18	26	131	-1	1	0	5	0	1	1	6
93-94—Winnipeg	NHL	73	4	8	12	96	-20	0	1	—	—	—	—	—
94-95—Winnipeg	NHL	27	2	1	3	40	-13	0	0	—	—	—	—	—
—Washington	NHL	13	1	3	4	8	2	0	0	7	0	2	2	4
95-96—Washington	NHL	70	4	7	11	75	-1	0	0	6	1	1	2	2
96-97—Washington	NHL	70	1	7	8	42	-4	0	0	—	—	—	—	—
97-98—Washington	NHL	36	1	3	4	16	-2	0	0	12	0	2	2	2
NHL Totals (14 years)		776	68	120	188	863	-109	3	6	44	2	6	8	34

EAKINS, DALLAS   D   MAPLE LEAFS

PERSONAL: Born January 20, 1967, in Dade City, Fla. ... 6-2/195. ... Shoots left. ... Name pronounced AY-kihns.
TRANSACTIONS/CAREER NOTES: Selected by Washington Capitals as underage junior in 10th round (11th Capitals pick, 208th overall) of NHL entry draft (June 15, 1985). ... Injured back (October 1988). ... Signed as free agent by Winnipeg Jets (September 1989). ... Signed as free agent by Florida Panthers (July 14, 1993). ... Traded by Panthers to St. Louis Blues for fourth-round draft pick (RW Ivan Novoseltsev) in 1997 draft (September 28, 1995). ... Broke wrist (December 8, 1995); missed 29 games. ... Claimed on waivers by Winnipeg Jets (March 20, 1996). ... Jets franchise moved to Phoenix and renamed Coyotes for 1996-97 season; NHL approved move on January 18, 1996. ... Suffered back spasms (November 26, 1996); missed three games. ... Traded by Coyotes with C Mike Eastwood to New York Rangers for D Jay More (February 6, 1997). ... Signed as free agent by Florida Panthers (July 7, 1997). ... Sprained left knee prior to 1997-98 season; missed first 11 games. ... Signed as free agent by Toronto Maple Leafs (July 14, 1998).

Season Team	League	REGULAR SEASON								PLAYOFFS				
		Gms.	G	A	Pts.	PIM	+/-	PP	SH	Gms.	G	A	Pts.	PIM
84-85—Peterborough	OHL	48	0	8	8	96	...	...	...	7	0	0	0	18
85-86—Peterborough	OHL	60	6	16	22	134	...	...	...	16	0	1	1	30
86-87—Peterborough	OHL	54	3	11	14	145	...	...	...	12	1	4	5	37
87-88—Peterborough	OHL	64	11	27	38	129	...	...	...	12	3	12	15	16
88-89—Baltimore	AHL	62	0	10	10	139	...	...	...	—	—	—	—	—
89-90—Moncton	AHL	75	2	11	13	189	...	...	...	—	—	—	—	—
90-91—Moncton	AHL	75	1	12	13	132	...	...	...	9	0	1	1	44
91-92—Moncton	AHL	67	3	13	16	136	...	...	...	11	2	1	3	16
92-93—Moncton	AHL	55	4	6	10	132	...	...	...	—	—	—	—	—
—Winnipeg	NHL	14	0	2	2	38	2	0	0	—	—	—	—	—
93-94—Cincinnati	IHL	80	1	18	19	143	...	...	...	8	0	1	1	41
—Florida	NHL	1	0	0	0	0	0	0	0	—	—	—	—	—
94-95—Cincinnati	IHL	59	6	12	18	69	...	...	...	—	—	—	—	—
—Florida	NHL	17	0	1	1	35	2	0	0	—	—	—	—	—
95-96—St. Louis	NHL	16	0	1	1	34	-2	0	0	—	—	—	—	—
—Worcester	AHL	4	0	0	0	12	...	...	...	—	—	—	—	—
—Winnipeg	NHL	2	0	0	0	0	1	0	0	—	—	—	—	—
96-97—Springfield	AHL	38	6	7	13	63	...	...	...	—	—	—	—	—
—Phoenix	NHL	4	0	0	0	10	-3	0	0	—	—	—	—	—
—Binghamton	AHL	19	1	7	8	15	...	...	...	—	—	—	—	—
—New York Rangers	NHL	3	0	0	0	6	-1	0	0	4	0	0	0	4
97-98—Florida	NHL	23	0	1	1	44	1	0	0	—	—	—	—	—
—New Haven	AHL	4	0	1	1	7	...	...	...	—	—	—	—	—
NHL Totals (6 years)		80	0	5	5	167	0	0	0	4	0	0	0	4

EASTWOOD, MIKE   C   BLUES

PERSONAL: Born July 1, 1967, in Cornwall, Ont. ... 6-3/205. ... Shoots right. ... Full name: Michael B. Eastwood.
COLLEGE: Western Michigan.
TRANSACTIONS/CAREER NOTES: Selected by Toronto Maple Leafs in fifth round (fifth Maple Leafs pick, 91st overall) of NHL entry draft (June 13, 1987). ... Traded by Maple Leafs with third-round pick (RW Brad Isbister) in 1995 draft to Winnipeg Jets for RW Tie Domi (April 7, 1995). ... Jets franchise moved to Phoenix and renamed Coyotes for 1996-97 season; NHL approved move on January 18, 1996. ... Fractured wrist (October 28, 1996); missed eight games. ... Traded by Coyotes with D Dallas Eakins to New York Rangers for D Jay More (February 6, 1997). ... Traded by Rangers to St. Louis Blues for C Harry York (March 24, 1998). ... Suffered sore wrist (April 18, 1998); missed two games.
HONORS: Named to CCHA All-Star second team (1990-91).

Season Team	League	REGULAR SEASON								PLAYOFFS				
		Gms.	G	A	Pts.	PIM	+/-	PP	SH	Gms.	G	A	Pts.	PIM
86-87—Pembroke	COJHL	Statistics unavailable.												
87-88—Western Michigan U.	CCHA	42	5	8	13	14	...	...	...	—	—	—	—	—

Season Team	League	REGULAR SEASON								PLAYOFFS				
		Gms.	G	A	Pts.	PIM	+/-	PP	SH	Gms.	G	A	Pts.	PIM
88-89—Western Michigan U...	CCHA	40	10	13	23	87	...	...	...	—	—	—	—	—
89-90—Western Michigan U...	CCHA	40	25	27	52	36	...	...	...	—	—	—	—	—
90-91—Western Michigan U...	CCHA	42	29	32	61	84	...	...	...	—	—	—	—	—
91-92—St. John's..................	AHL	61	18	25	43	28	...	...	...	16	9	10	19	16
—Toronto......................	NHL	9	0	2	2	4	-4	0	0	—	—	—	—	—
92-93—St. John's..................	AHL	60	24	35	59	32	...	...	...	—	—	—	—	—
—Toronto......................	NHL	12	1	6	7	21	-2	0	0	10	1	2	3	8
93-94—Toronto......................	NHL	54	8	10	18	28	2	1	0	18	3	2	5	12
94-95—Toronto......................	NHL	36	5	5	10	32	-12	0	0	—	—	—	—	—
—Winnipeg..................	NHL	13	3	6	9	4	3	0	0	—	—	—	—	—
95-96—Winnipeg..................	NHL	80	14	14	28	20	-14	2	0	6	0	1	1	2
96-97—Phoenix......................	NHL	33	1	3	4	4	-3	0	0	—	—	—	—	—
—New York Rangers.....	NHL	27	1	7	8	10	2	0	0	15	1	2	3	22
97-98—New York Rangers......	NHL	48	5	5	10	16	-2	0	0	—	—	—	—	—
—St. Louis	NHL	10	1	0	1	6	0	0	0	3	1	0	1	0
NHL Totals (7 years)...........		322	39	58	97	145	-30	3	0	52	6	7	13	44

EATON, MARK — D — FLYERS

PERSONAL: Born May 6, 1977, in Washington, Det. ... 6-2/205. ... Shoots left. ... Full name: Mark Andrew Eaton.
HIGH SCHOOL: Dickinson (Wilmington, Del.).
COLLEGE: Notre Dame.
TRANSACTIONS/CAREER NOTES: Signed as free agent by Philadelphia Flyers (July 28, 1998).

Season Team	League	REGULAR SEASON								PLAYOFFS				
		Gms.	G	A	Pts.	PIM	+/-	PP	SH	Gms.	G	A	Pts.	PIM
97-98—Notre Dame	CCHA	41	12	17	29	32	...	...	...	—	—	—	—	—

EGELAND, ALLAN — C — LIGHTNING

PERSONAL: Born January 31, 1973, in Lethbridge, Alta. ... 6-0/175. ... Shoots left. ... Brother of Tracy Egeland, left winger with Chicago Blackhawks (1990-91 through 1992-93) and Philadelphia Flyers organizations (1993-94 and 1994-95). ... Name pronounced EHG-luhnd.
TRANSACTIONS/CAREER NOTES: Selected by Tampa Bay Lightning in third round (third Lightning pick, 55th overall) of NHL entry draft (June 26, 1993).
HONORS: Named to WHL (West) All-Star first team (1992-93). ... Named to WHL (West) All-Star second team (1993-94).

Season Team	League	REGULAR SEASON								PLAYOFFS				
		Gms.	G	A	Pts.	PIM	+/-	PP	SH	Gms.	G	A	Pts.	PIM
90-91—Lethbridge	WHL	67	2	16	18	57	...	...	...	9	0	0	0	0
91-92—Tacoma	WHL	72	35	39	74	115	...	...	...	4	0	1	1	18
92-93—Tacoma	WHL	71	56	57	113	119	...	...	...	7	9	7	16	18
93-94—Tacoma	WHL	70	47	76	123	204	...	...	...	8	5	3	8	26
94-95—Atlanta	IHL	60	8	16	24	112	...	...	...	5	0	1	1	16
95-96—Tampa Bay	NHL	5	0	0	0	2	0	0	0	—	—	—	—	—
—Atlanta	IHL	68	22	22	44	182	...	...	...	3	0	1	1	4
96-97—Adirondack	AHL	52	18	32	50	184	...	...	...	2	0	1	1	4
—Tampa Bay	NHL	4	0	0	0	5	-3	0	0	—	—	—	—	—
97-98—Adirondack	AHL	35	11	22	33	78	...	...	...	3	0	2	2	10
—Tampa Bay	NHL	8	0	0	0	9	0	0	0	—	—	—	—	—
NHL Totals (3 years)...........		17	0	0	0	16	-3	0	0	—	—	—	—	—

EKLUND, PER — LW

PERSONAL: Born July 9, 1970, in Stockholm, Sweden. ... 5-11/196. ... Shoots right.
TRANSACTIONS/CAREER NOTES: Selected by Detroit Red Wings in seventh round (eighth Red Wings pick, 182nd overall) of NHL entry draft (July 2, 1995).

Season Team	League	REGULAR SEASON								PLAYOFFS				
		Gms.	G	A	Pts.	PIM	+/-	PP	SH	Gms.	G	A	Pts.	PIM
91-92—Vasby.........................	Swed. Dv.II	29	13	24	37	26	...	...	...	—	—	—	—	—
92-93—Huddinge	Swed. Dv.II	36	22	23	45	14	...	...	...	—	—	—	—	—
93-94—Huddinge	Swed. Dv.II	35	20	11	31	40	...	...	...	—	—	—	—	—
94-95—Djur. Stockholm	Sweden	40	19	10	29	20	...	...	...	3	1	1	2	4
95-96—Djur. Stockholm	Sweden	39	17	10	27	10	...	...	...	1	0	0	0	0
96-97—Djur. Stockholm	Sweden	50	20	16	36	14	...	...	...	4	1	0	1	0
97-98—Adirondack	AHL	73	21	29	50	12	...	...	...	3	0	0	0	0

ELIAS, PATRIK — LW — DEVILS

PERSONAL: Born April 13, 1976, in Trebic, Czechoslovakia. ... 6-0/195. ... Shoots left. ... Name pronounced EH-lee-ahsh.
TRANSACTIONS/CAREER NOTES: Selected by New Jersey Devils in second round (second Devils pick, 51st overall) of NHL entry draft (June 28, 1994).
HONORS: Named to NHL All-Rookie team (1997-98).

Season Team	League	REGULAR SEASON								PLAYOFFS				
		Gms.	G	A	Pts.	PIM	+/-	PP	SH	Gms.	G	A	Pts.	PIM
92-93—HC Kladno.................	Czech.	2	0	0	0	0	...	...	...	—	—	—	—	—
93-94—HC Kladno.................	Czech Rep.	15	1	2	3	...	...	...	...	11	2	2	4	...
—Czech Rep. Olympic.....	Int'l	5	2	5	7	...	...	...	...	—	—	—	—	—

E

Season Team	League	REGULAR SEASON								PLAYOFFS				
		Gms.	G	A	Pts.	PIM	+/-	PP	SH	Gms.	G	A	Pts.	PIM
94-95—HC Kladno	Czech Rep.	28	4	3	7	...	...	...	...	7	1	2	3	...
95-96—Albany	AHL	74	27	36	63	83	...	...	...	4	1	1	2	2
—New Jersey	NHL	1	0	0	0	0	-1	0	0	—	—	—	—	—
96-97—Albany	AHL	57	24	43	67	76	...	...	...	6	1	2	3	8
—New Jersey	NHL	17	2	3	5	2	-4	0	0	8	2	3	5	4
97-98—New Jersey	NHL	74	18	19	37	28	18	5	0	4	0	1	1	0
—Albany	AHL	3	3	0	3	2	...	...	...	—	—	—	—	—
NHL Totals (3 years)		92	20	22	42	30	13	5	0	12	2	4	6	4

ELLETT, DAVE D BRUINS

PERSONAL: Born March 30, 1964, in Cleveland. ... 6-2/205. ... Shoots left. ... Name pronounced EHL-iht.
COLLEGE: Bowling Green State.
TRANSACTIONS/CAREER NOTES: Selected by Winnipeg Jets as underage junior in fourth round (third Jets pick, 75th overall) of NHL entry draft (June 9, 1982). ... Bruised thigh (March 6, 1988); missed 10 games. ... Sprained ankle (November 16, 1988). ... Traded by Jets with C Paul Fenton to Toronto Maple Leafs for C Ed Olczyk and LW Mark Osborne (November 10, 1990). ... Separated shoulder (March 2, 1993); missed 14 games. ... Suffered rib strain (December 11, 1993); missed 10 games. ... Separated shoulder (March 31, 1994); missed remainder of season. ... Cracked bone in foot (February 27, 1995); missed 15 games. ... Sprained knee (October 4, 1995); missed one game. ... Suffered from the flu (January 1, 1996). ... Scratched eye (December 27, 1996); missed one game. ... Bruised rib (January 31, 1997); missed four games. ... Traded by Maple Leafs with C Doug Gilmour and third-round pick in 1999 draft to New Jersey Devils for D Jason Smith, C Steve Sullivan and C Alyn McCauley (February 25, 1997). ... Signed as free agent by Boston Bruins (July 2, 1997).
HONORS: Named to NCAA All-Tournament team (1983-84). ... Named to CCHA All-Star second team (1983-84). ... Played in NHL All-Star Game (1989 and 1992).

Season Team	League	REGULAR SEASON								PLAYOFFS				
		Gms.	G	A	Pts.	PIM	+/-	PP	SH	Gms.	G	A	Pts.	PIM
81-82—Ottawa	COJHL	50	9	35	44	...	...	...	...	—	—	—	—	—
82-83—Bowling Green	CCHA	40	4	13	17	34	...	...	...	—	—	—	—	—
83-84—Bowling Green	CCHA	43	15	39	54	9	...	...	...	—	—	—	—	—
84-85—Winnipeg	NHL	80	11	27	38	85	20	3	0	8	1	5	6	4
85-86—Winnipeg	NHL	80	15	31	46	96	-38	2	0	3	0	1	1	0
86-87—Winnipeg	NHL	78	13	31	44	53	19	5	0	10	0	8	8	2
87-88—Winnipeg	NHL	68	13	45	58	106	-8	5	0	5	1	2	3	10
88-89—Winnipeg	NHL	75	22	34	56	62	-18	9	2	—	—	—	—	—
89-90—Winnipeg	NHL	77	17	29	46	96	-15	8	0	7	2	0	2	6
90-91—Winnipeg	NHL	17	4	7	11	6	-4	1	1	—	—	—	—	—
—Toronto	NHL	60	8	30	38	69	-4	5	0	—	—	—	—	—
91-92—Toronto	NHL	79	18	33	51	95	-13	9	1	—	—	—	—	—
92-93—Toronto	NHL	70	6	34	40	46	19	4	0	21	4	8	12	8
93-94—Toronto	NHL	68	7	36	43	42	6	5	0	18	3	15	18	31
94-95—Toronto	NHL	33	5	10	15	26	-6	3	0	7	0	2	2	0
95-96—Toronto	NHL	80	3	19	22	59	-10	1	1	6	0	0	0	4
96-97—Toronto	NHL	56	4	10	14	34	-8	0	0	—	—	—	—	—
—New Jersey	NHL	20	2	5	7	6	2	1	0	10	0	3	3	10
97-98—Boston	NHL	82	3	20	23	67	3	2	0	6	0	1	1	6
NHL Totals (14 years)		1023	151	401	552	948	-55	63	5	101	11	45	56	81

ELOMO, MIIKKA LW CAPITALS

PERSONAL: Born April 21, 1977, in Turku, Finland. ... 6-0/183. ... Shoots left. ... Name pronounced EHL-ih-moh. ... Brother of Teemu Elomo, left winger in Dallas Stars system.
TRANSACTIONS/CAREER NOTES: Selected by Washington Capitals in first round (second Capitals pick, 23rd overall) of NHL entry draft (July 8, 1995).

Season Team	League	REGULAR SEASON								PLAYOFFS				
		Gms.	G	A	Pts.	PIM	+/-	PP	SH	Gms.	G	A	Pts.	PIM
91-92—London	OHL	65	11	19	30	15	...	...	...	7	0	0	0	0
93-94—TPS Jr.	Finland	30	8	5	13	24	...	...	...	5	1	1	2	2
94-95—Kiekko-67	Finland Dv.II	14	9	2	11	39	...	...	...	—	—	—	—	—
—TPS Jr.	Finland	14	3	8	11	24	...	...	...	—	—	—	—	—
95-96—Kiekko-67	Finland Dv.II	21	9	6	15	100	...	...	...	—	—	—	—	—
—TPS Jr.	Finland	6	0	2	2	18	...	...	...	—	—	—	—	—
—TPS Turku	Finland	10	1	1	2	8	...	...	...	3	0	0	0	2
96-97—Portland	AHL	52	8	9	17	37	...	...	...	—	—	—	—	—
97-98—Portland	AHL	33	1	1	2	54	...	...	...	—	—	—	—	—

ELOMO, TEEMU LW STARS

PERSONAL: Born January 13, 1979, in Turku, Finland. ... 5-11/176. ... Shoots left. ... Brother of Miikka Elomo, left winger in Washington Capitals system.
TRANSACTIONS/CAREER NOTES: Selected by Dallas Stars in fifth round (fifth Stars pick, 132nd overall) of NHL entry draft (June 21, 1997).

Season Team	League	REGULAR SEASON								PLAYOFFS				
		Gms.	G	A	Pts.	PIM	+/-	PP	SH	Gms.	G	A	Pts.	PIM
95-96—Kiekko-67 Turku	Finland Dv.II	11	1	0	1	4	...	...	...	6	2	0	2	8
—TPS Turku Jrs.	Finland	2	0	0	0	0	...	...	...	—	—	—	—	—
96-97—TPS Turku	Finland	6	0	1	1	0	...	...	...	3	0	0	0	2
—Kiekko-67 Turku	Finland Dv.II	15	4	3	7	24	...	...	...	—	—	—	—	—
—TPS Turku Jrs.	Finland	9	6	2	8	16	...	...	...	—	—	—	—	—
97-98—TPS Turku Jrs.	Finland	26	3	3	6	14	...	...	...	3	1	0	1	2

E

EMERSON, NELSON   RW   HURRICANES

PERSONAL: Born August 17, 1967, in Hamilton, Ont. ... 5-11/175. ... Shoots right. ... Full name: Nelson Donald Emerson.
COLLEGE: Bowling Green State.
TRANSACTIONS/CAREER NOTES: Selected by St. Louis Blues in third round (second Blues pick, 44th overall) of NHL entry draft (June 15, 1985). ... Fractured bone under his eye (December 28, 1991). ... Injured leg (April 3, 1993); missed one game. ... Traded by Blues with D Stephane Quintal to Winnipeg Jets for D Phil Housley (September 24, 1993). ... Sprained neck (January 25, 1994); missed one game. ... Traded by Jets to Hartford Whalers for C Darren Turcotte (October 6, 1995). ... Suffered mild concussion (February 17, 1996); missed one game. ... Fractured ankle prior to 1996-97 season; missed five games. ... Fractured ankle (November 4, 1996); missed six games. ... Strained groin (January 1, 1997); missed three games. ... Whalers franchise moved to North Carolina and renamed Carolina Hurricanes for 1997-98 season; NHL approved move on June 25, 1997.
HONORS: Named CCHA Rookie of the Year (1986-87). ... Named to NCAA All-America West second team (1987-88). ... Named to CCHA All-Star first team (1987-88 and 1989-90). ... Named to NCAA All-America West first team (1989-90). ... Named to CCHA All-Star second team (1988-89). ... Won Garry F. Longman Memorial Trophy (1990-91). ... Named to IHL All-Star first team (1990-91).
STATISTICAL PLATEAUS: Three-goal games: 1994-95 (1).

Season Team	League	REGULAR SEASON								PLAYOFFS				
		Gms.	G	A	Pts.	PIM	+/-	PP	SH	Gms.	G	A	Pts.	PIM
84-85—Stratford Jr. B	OHA	40	23	38	61	70	...	...	...	—	—	—	—	—
85-86—Stratford Jr. B	OHA	39	54	58	112	91	...	...	...	—	—	—	—	—
86-87—Bowling Green	CCHA	45	26	35	61	28	...	...	...	—	—	—	—	—
87-88—Bowling Green	CCHA	45	34	49	83	54	...	...	...	—	—	—	—	—
88-89—Bowling Green	CCHA	44	22	46	68	46	...	...	...	—	—	—	—	—
89-90—Bowling Green	CCHA	44	30	52	82	42	...	...	...	—	—	—	—	—
—Peoria	IHL	3	1	1	2	0	...	...	...	—	—	—	—	—
90-91—St. Louis	NHL	4	0	3	3	2	-2	0	0	—	—	—	—	—
—Peoria	IHL	73	36	79	115	91	...	...	...	17	9	12	21	16
91-92—St. Louis	NHL	79	23	36	59	66	-5	3	0	6	3	3	6	21
92-93—St. Louis	NHL	82	22	51	73	62	2	5	2	11	1	6	7	6
93-94—Winnipeg	NHL	83	33	41	74	80	-38	4	5	—	—	—	—	—
94-95—Winnipeg	NHL	48	14	23	37	26	-12	4	1	—	—	—	—	—
95-96—Hartford	NHL	81	29	29	58	78	-7	12	2	—	—	—	—	—
96-97—Hartford	NHL	66	9	29	38	34	-21	2	1	—	—	—	—	—
97-98—Carolina	NHL	81	21	24	45	50	-17	6	0	—	—	—	—	—
NHL Totals (8 years)		524	151	236	387	398	-100	36	11	17	4	9	13	27

ERIKSSON, ANDERS   D   RED WINGS

PERSONAL: Born January 9, 1975, in Bollnas, Sweden. ... 6-3/218. ... Shoots left.
TRANSACTIONS/CAREER NOTES: Selected by Detroit Red Wings in first round (first Red Wings pick, 22nd overall) of NHL entry draft (June 26, 1993).
MISCELLANEOUS: Member of Stanley Cup championship team (1998).

Season Team	League	REGULAR SEASON								PLAYOFFS				
		Gms.	G	A	Pts.	PIM	+/-	PP	SH	Gms.	G	A	Pts.	PIM
92-93—MoDo Ornskoldvik	Sweden	20	0	2	2	2	...	...	...	—	—	—	—	—
93-94—MoDo Ornskoldvik	Sweden	38	2	8	10	42	...	...	...	11	0	0	0	8
94-95—MoDo Ornskoldvik	Sweden	39	3	6	9	54	...	...	...	—	—	—	—	—
95-96—Adirondack	AHL	75	6	36	42	64	...	...	...	3	0	0	0	0
—Detroit	NHL	1	0	0	0	2	1	0	0	3	0	0	0	0
96-97—Detroit	NHL	23	0	6	6	10	5	0	0	—	—	—	—	—
—Adirondack	AHL	44	3	25	28	36	...	...	...	4	0	1	1	4
97-98—Detroit	NHL	66	7	14	21	32	21	1	0	18	0	5	5	16
NHL Totals (3 years)		90	7	20	27	44	27	1	0	21	0	5	5	16

ERREY, BOB   RW   RANGERS

PERSONAL: Born September 21, 1964, in Montreal. ... 5-10/185. ... Shoots left. ... Cousin of Ted Lindsay, Hall of Fame left winger, Detroit Red Wings and Chicago Blackhawks (1944-45 through 1959-60 and 1964-65). ... Name pronounced AIR-ee.
TRANSACTIONS/CAREER NOTES: Selected by Pittsburgh Penguins as underage junior in first round (first Penguins pick, 15th overall) of NHL entry draft (June 8, 1983). ... Sprained right knee (March 18, 1987). ... Broke right wrist (October 1987). ... Injured shoulder (May 9, 1992). ... Sprained ankle (September 29, 1992); missed 14 games. ... Bruised tailbone (February 27, 1993); missed two games. ... Traded by Penguins to Buffalo Sabres for D Mike Ramsey (March 22, 1993). ... Sprained ankle (April 4, 1993); missed four games. ... Injured hip (April 18, 1993); missed two games. ... Signed as free agent by San Jose Sharks (August 17, 1993). ... Injured rib (October 10, 1993); missed three games. ... Suffered from the flu (October 26, 1993); missed three games. ... Suspended two games by NHL for checking from behind (December 31, 1993). ... Suffered hyperextended knee (February 1, 1994); missed two games. ... Sprained knee (March 22, 1994); missed five games. ... Injured ankle (February 6, 1995); missed two games. ... Reinjured ankle (February 17, 1995); missed two games. ... Traded by Sharks to Detroit Red Wings for fifth-round pick (C Michal Bros) in 1995 draft (February 27, 1995). ... Bruised sternum (January 30, 1996); missed two games. ... Injured right foot (March 12, 1996); missed two games. ... Broke foot (March 22, 1996); missed four games. ... Suspended two games and fined $1000 by NHL for slashing (April 14, 1996). ... Claimed on waivers by Sharks (February 8, 1997). ... Signed as free agent by Dallas Stars (July 17, 1997). ... Traded by Stars with RW Todd Harvey and fourth-round pick (LW Boyd Kane) in 1998 draft to New York Rangers for RW Mike Keane, C Brian Skrudland and sixth-round pick (RW Pavel Patera) in 1998 draft (March 24, 1998). ... Suffered concussion (March 13, 1998); missed one game.
HONORS: Named to OHL All-Star first team (1982-83).
MISCELLANEOUS: Member of Stanley Cup championship team (1991 and 1992). ... Captain of San Jose Sharks (1993-94). ... Scored on a penalty shot (vs. Chris Terreri, January 5, 1991; vs. Darcy Wakaluk, October 31, 1991). ... Failed to score on a penalty shot (vs. Nikolai Khabiblulin, March 22, 1995).
STATISTICAL PLATEAUS: Three-goal games: 1991-92 (1).

Season Team	League	REGULAR SEASON								PLAYOFFS				
		Gms.	G	A	Pts.	PIM	+/-	PP	SH	Gms.	G	A	Pts.	PIM
81-82—Peterborough	OHL	68	29	31	60	39	...	...	...	9	3	1	4	9
82-83—Peterborough	OHL	67	53	47	100	74	...	...	...	4	1	3	4	7
83-84—Pittsburgh	NHL	65	9	13	22	29	-20	1	0	—	—	—	—	—
84-85—Baltimore	AHL	59	17	24	41	14	...	...	...	8	3	4	7	11
—Pittsburgh	NHL	16	0	2	2	7	-8	0	0	—	—	—	—	—
85-86—Baltimore	AHL	18	8	7	15	28	...	...	...	—	—	—	—	—
—Pittsburgh	NHL	37	11	6	17	8	1	0	1	—	—	—	—	—
86-87—Pittsburgh	NHL	72	16	18	34	46	-5	2	1	—	—	—	—	—
87-88—Pittsburgh	NHL	17	3	6	9	18	6	0	0	—	—	—	—	—
88-89—Pittsburgh	NHL	76	26	32	58	124	40	0	3	11	1	2	3	12
89-90—Pittsburgh	NHL	78	20	19	39	109	3	0	1	—	—	—	—	—
90-91—Pittsburgh	NHL	79	20	22	42	115	11	0	1	24	5	2	7	29
91-92—Pittsburgh	NHL	78	19	16	35	119	1	0	3	14	3	0	3	10
92-93—Pittsburgh	NHL	54	8	6	14	76	-2	0	0	—	—	—	—	—
—Buffalo	NHL	8	1	3	4	4	2	0	0	4	0	1	1	10
93-94—San Jose	NHL	64	12	18	30	126	-11	5	0	14	3	2	5	10
94-95—San Jose	NHL	13	2	2	4	27	4	0	0	—	—	—	—	—
—Detroit	NHL	30	6	11	17	31	9	0	0	18	1	5	6	30
95-96—Detroit	NHL	71	11	21	32	66	30	2	2	14	0	4	4	8
96-97—Detroit	NHL	36	1	2	3	27	-3	0	0	—	—	—	—	—
—San Jose	NHL	30	3	6	9	20	-2	0	0	—	—	—	—	—
97-98—Dallas	NHL	59	2	9	11	46	7	0	0	—	—	—	—	—
—New York Rangers	NHL	12	0	0	0	7	-5	0	0	—	—	—	—	—
NHL Totals (15 years)		895	170	212	382	1005	58	10	12	99	13	16	29	109

ESAU, LEN   D   BLACKHAWKS

PERSONAL: Born March 16, 1968, in Meadow Lake, Sask. ... 6-3/190. ... Shoots right. ... Full name: Leonard Roy Esau. ... Name pronounced EE-sow.
COLLEGE: St. Cloud (Minn.) State.
TRANSACTIONS/CAREER NOTES: Selected by Toronto Maple Leafs in fifth round (fifth Maple Leafs pick, 86th overall) of NHL entry draft (June 11, 1988). ... Traded by Maple Leafs to Quebec Nordiques for C Ken McRae (July 21, 1992). ... Signed as free agent by Calgary Flames (September 6, 1993). ... Selected by Edmonton Oilers in 1994-95 waiver draft for cash (January 18, 1995). ... Claimed on waivers by Flames (March 7, 1995). ... Signed as free agent by Florida Panthers (July 27, 1995). ... Signed as free agent by Chicago Blackhawks (December 1997).

Season Team	League	REGULAR SEASON								PLAYOFFS				
		Gms.	G	A	Pts.	PIM	+/-	PP	SH	Gms.	G	A	Pts.	PIM
86-87—Humboldt	SJHL	57	4	26	30	278	...	...	...	—	—	—	—	—
87-88—Humboldt	SJHL	57	16	37	53	229	...	...	...	—	—	—	—	—
88-89—St. Cloud State	WCHA	35	12	27	39	69	...	...	...	—	—	—	—	—
89-90—St. Cloud State	WCHA	29	8	11	19	83	...	...	...	—	—	—	—	—
90-91—Newmarket	AHL	75	4	14	18	28	...	...	...	—	—	—	—	—
91-92—St. John's	AHL	78	9	29	38	68	...	...	...	13	0	2	2	14
—Toronto	NHL	2	0	0	0	0	0	0	0	—	—	—	—	—
92-93—Halifax	AHL	75	11	31	42	19	...	...	...	—	—	—	—	—
—Quebec	NHL	4	0	1	1	2	1	0	0	—	—	—	—	—
93-94—Saint John	AHL	75	12	36	48	129	...	...	...	7	2	2	4	6
—Calgary	NHL	6	0	3	3	7	-1	0	0	—	—	—	—	—
94-95—Saint John	AHL	54	13	27	40	73	...	...	...	5	0	2	2	0
—Edmonton	NHL	14	0	6	6	15	-8	0	0	—	—	—	—	—
—Calgary	NHL	1	0	0	0	0	-2	0	0	—	—	—	—	—
95-96—Cincinnati	IHL	82	15	21	36	150	...	...	...	17	5	6	11	26
96-97—Milwaukee	IHL	49	6	16	22	70	...	...	...	—	—	—	—	—
—Detroit	IHL	30	6	8	14	36	...	...	...	13	1	4	5	38
97-98—Milwaukee	IHL	26	3	9	12	32	...	...	...	—	—	—	—	—
—Indianapolis	IHL	55	6	33	39	28	...	...	...	5	0	0	0	4
NHL Totals (4 years)		27	0	10	10	24	-10	0	0					

ESCHE, ROBERT   G   COYOTES

PERSONAL: Born January 22, 1978, in Utica, N.Y. ... 6-0/188. ... Catches left. ... Name pronounced EHSH.
TRANSACTIONS/CAREER NOTES: Selected by Phoenix Coyotes in sixth round (fifth Coyotes pick, 139th overall) of NHL entry draft (June 22, 1996).
HONORS: Named to OHL All-Star second team (1997-98).

Season Team	League	REGULAR SEASON							PLAYOFFS					
		Gms.	Min	W	L	T	GA	SO	Avg.	Gms.	Min.	W	L	GA	SO	Avg.
95-96—Detroit	OHL	23	1219	13	6	0	76	1	3.74	3	105	0	2	4	0	2.29
96-97—Detroit	OHL	58	3241	24	28	2	206	2	3.81	5	317	1	4	19	0	3.60
97-98—Plymouth	OHL	48	2810	29	13	4	135	3	2.88	15	869	8	†7	45	0	3.11

ESSENSA, BOB   G   OILERS

PERSONAL: Born January 14, 1965, in Toronto. ... 6-0/185. ... Catches left. ... Full name: Robert Earle Essensa. ... Name pronounced EH-sihn-zuh.
HIGH SCHOOL: Henry Carr (Rexdale, Ont.).
COLLEGE: Michigan State.

TRANSACTIONS/CAREER NOTES: Selected by Winnipeg Jets in fourth round (fifth Jets pick, 69th overall) of NHL entry draft (June 8, 1983). ... Suffered severe lacerations to both hands and wrist (February 1985). ... Injured groin (September 1990); missed three weeks. ... Sprained knee (October 12, 1991); missed four games. ... Injured left hamstring (December 8, 1991); missed four games. ... Sprained knee (March 6, 1992); missed seven games. ... Strained knee (March 6, 1993); missed two games. ... Traded by Jets with D Sergei Bautin to Detroit Red Wings for G Tim Cheveldae and LW Dallas Drake (March 8, 1994). ... Loaned by Red Wings to San Diego Gulls of the IHL (January 27, 1995). ... Traded by Red Wings to Edmonton Oilers for future considerations (June 14, 1996).
HONORS: Named to CCHA All-Star first team (1984-85). ... Named to CCHA All-Star second team (1985-86). ... Named to NHL All-Rookie team (1989-90).
MISCELLANEOUS: Holds Poenix Coyotes franchise all-time records for games played by goaltender (281), most wins (116) and most shutouts (14). ... Stopped a penalty shot attempt (vs. Philippe Bozon, November 3, 1993; vs. Keith Tkachuk, January 24, 1998). ... Allowed a penalty shot goal (vs. Steve Yzerman, February 13, 1989; vs. Mike Craig, January 21, 1991; vs. Paul Ranheim, October 31, 1993).

Season Team	League	Gms.	Min	W	L	T	GA	SO	Avg.	Gms.	Min.	W	L	GA	SO	Avg.
				REGULAR SEASON								PLAYOFFS				
81-82—Henry Carr H.S.	MTHL	17	948	...	...	...	79	...	5.00	—	—	—	—	—	—	—
82-83—Henry Carr H.S.	MTHL	31	1840	...	...	...	98	2	3.20	—	—	—	—	—	—	—
83-84—Michigan State	CCHA	17	947	11	4	0	44	2	2.79	—	—	—	—	—	—	—
84-85—Michigan State	CCHA	18	1059	15	2	0	29	2	1.64	—	—	—	—	—	—	—
85-86—Michigan State	CCHA	23	1333	17	4	1	74	1	3.33	—	—	—	—	—	—	—
86-87—Michigan State	CCHA	25	1383	19	3	1	64	*2	*2.78	—	—	—	—	—	—	—
87-88—Moncton	AHL	27	1287	7	11	1	100	1	4.66	—	—	—	—	—	—	—
88-89—Winnipeg	NHL	20	1102	6	8	3	68	1	3.70	—	—	—	—	—	—	—
—Fort Wayne	IHL	22	1287	14	7	‡0	70	0	3.26	—	—	—	—	—	—	—
89-90—Moncton	AHL	6	358	3	3	0	15	0	2.51	—	—	—	—	—	—	—
—Winnipeg	NHL	36	2035	18	9	5	107	1	3.15	4	206	2	1	12	0	3.50
90-91—Moncton	AHL	2	125	1	0	1	6	0	2.88	—	—	—	—	—	—	—
—Winnipeg	NHL	55	2916	19	24	6	153	4	3.15	—	—	—	—	—	—	—
91-92—Winnipeg	NHL	47	2627	21	17	6	126	†5	2.88	1	33	0	0	3	0	5.45
92-93—Winnipeg	NHL	67	3855	33	26	6	227	2	3.53	6	367	2	4	20	0	3.27
93-94—Winnipeg	NHL	56	3136	19	30	6	201	1	3.85	—	—	—	—	—	—	—
—Detroit	NHL	13	778	4	7	2	34	1	2.62	2	109	0	2	9	0	4.95
94-95—San Diego	IHL	16	919	6	8	‡1	52	0	3.39	1	59	0	1	3	0	3.05
95-96—Adirondack	AHL	3	178	1	2	0	11	0	3.71	—	—	—	—	—	—	—
—Fort Wayne	IHL	45	2529	24	14	‡5	122	1	2.89	5	298	2	3	12	0	2.42
96-97—Edmonton	NHL	19	868	4	8	0	41	1	2.83	—	—	—	—	—	—	—
97-98—Edmonton	NHL	16	825	6	6	1	35	0	2.55	1	27	0	0	1	0	2.22
NHL Totals (8 years)		329	18142	130	135	35	992	16	3.28	14	742	4	7	45	0	3.64

EWEN, TODD   RW   SHARKS

PERSONAL: Born March 22, 1966, in Saskatoon, Sask. ... 6-3/230. ... Shoots right. ... Brother of Dean Ewen, left winger with New York Islanders (1987-88 through 1991-92) and San Jose Sharks organizations (1994-95). ... Name pronounced YOO-ihn.
TRANSACTIONS/CAREER NOTES: Selected by Edmonton Oilers as underage junior in eighth round (eighth Oilers pick, 168th overall) of NHL entry draft (June 9, 1984). ... Traded by Oilers to St. Louis Blues for D Shawn Evans (October 15, 1986). ... Sprained ankle (October 1987). ... Suspended one game by NHL for third game misconduct of season (January 1988). ... Pulled groin (October 1988). ... Tore right eye muscle (December 1988). ... Pulled left hamstring and bruised shoulder (February 1989). ... Suspended 10 games by NHL for coming off bench to instigate fight during playoff game (April 18, 1989); missed three playoff games and first seven games of 1989-90 season. ... Broke right hand (October 28, 1989). ... Traded by Blues to Montreal Canadiens for the return of a draft pick dealt to Montreal for D Mike Lalor (December 12, 1989). ... Strained knee ligaments and underwent surgery (November 19, 1990); missed 24 games. ... Fractured right hand at home (February 14, 1991); missed remainder of season. ... Separated shoulder (February 12, 1992); missed two games. ... Injured hand (January 10, 1993); missed two games. ... Pulled muscle in back (February 20, 1993); missed three games. ... Traded by Canadiens with C Patrik Carnback to Mighty Ducks of Anaheim for third-round pick (RW Chris Murray) in 1994 draft (August 10, 1993). ... Broke nose (October 19, 1993); missed one game. ... Sprained shoulder (April 2, 1994); missed five games. ... Suffered hip pointer (January 20, 1995); missed four games. ... Suffered slightly pulled groin (February 24, 1995); missed three games. ... Sprained thumb (March 31, 1995); missed five games. ... Suffered charley horse (April 21, 1995); missed six games. ... Injured left hand (November 7, 1995); missed 19 games. ... Lacerated right hand (March 10, 1996); missed two games. ... Signed as free agent by San Jose Sharks (July 25, 1996). ... Injured knee (October 8, 1996); missed 14 games. ... Injured groin (December 11, 1996); missed four games. ... Reinjured groin (December 26, 1996); missed four games. ... Injured hand (January 13, 1997); missed one game. ... Injured knee (February 23, 1997); missed four games. ... Reinjured knee (March 11, 1997); missed four games. ... Reinjured knee (October 16, 1997); missed entire 1997-98 season.
MISCELLANEOUS: Member of Stanley Cup championship team (1993).

Season Team	League	Gms.	G	A	Pts.	PIM	+/-	PP	SH	Gms.	G	A	Pts.	PIM
				REGULAR SEASON								PLAYOFFS		
82-83—Vernon	BCJHL	42	20	23	43	195	...	...	...	—	—	—	—	—
—Kamloops	WHL	3	0	0	0	2	...	...	...	2	0	0	0	0
83-84—New Westminster	WHL	68	11	13	24	176	...	...	...	7	2	1	3	15
84-85—New Westminster	WHL	56	11	20	31	304	...	...	...	10	1	8	9	60
85-86—New Westminster	WHL	60	28	24	52	289	...	...	...	—	—	—	—	—
—Maine	AHL	—	—	—	—	—	...	...	...	3	0	0	0	7
86-87—Peoria	IHL	16	3	3	6	110	...	...	...	—	—	—	—	—
—St. Louis	NHL	23	2	0	2	84	-1	0	0	4	0	0	0	23
87-88—St. Louis	NHL	64	4	2	6	227	-5	0	0	6	0	0	0	21
88-89—St. Louis	NHL	34	4	5	9	171	4	0	0	2	0	0	0	21
89-90—Peoria	IHL	2	0	0	0	12	...	...	...	—	—	—	—	—
—St. Louis	NHL	3	0	0	0	11	-2	0	0	—	—	—	—	—
—Montreal	NHL	41	4	6	10	158	1	0	0	10	0	0	0	4
90-91—Montreal	NHL	28	3	2	5	128	4	0	0	—	—	—	—	—
91-92—Montreal	NHL	46	1	2	3	130	3	0	0	3	0	0	0	18
92-93—Montreal	NHL	75	5	9	14	193	6	0	0	1	0	0	0	0
93-94—Anaheim	NHL	76	9	9	18	272	-7	0	0	—	—	—	—	—
94-95—Anaheim	NHL	24	0	0	0	90	-2	0	0	—	—	—	—	—
95-96—Anaheim	NHL	53	4	3	7	285	-5	0	0	—	—	—	—	—
96-97—San Jose	NHL	51	0	2	2	162	-5	0	0	—	—	—	—	—
97-98—					Did not play—injured.									
NHL Totals (11 years)		518	36	40	76	1911	-9	0	0	26	0	0	0	87

FALLOON, PAT   RW

PERSONAL: Born September 22, 1972, in Foxwarren, Man. ... 5-11/200. ... Shoots right. ... Full name: Patrick Falloon. ... Name pronounced fuh-LOON.

TRANSACTIONS/CAREER NOTES: WHL rights traded with future considerations by Regina Pats to Spokane Chiefs for RW Jamie Heward (October 1987). ... Tore right knee cartilage and underwent surgery (July 24, 1990). ... Selected by San Jose Sharks in first round (first Sharks pick, second overall) of NHL entry draft (June 22, 1991). ... Bruised shoulder (November 19, 1992); missed one game. ... Dislocated right shoulder (January 10, 1993) and underwent arthroscopic surgery (January 15, 1993); missed remainder of season. ... Injured hamstring (March 2, 1995); missed one game. ... Traded by Sharks to Philadelphia Flyers for LW Martin Spanhel and first-(traded to Winnipeg) and fourth-(traded to Buffalo) round picks in 1996 draft (November 16, 1995). ... Pulled left groin (December 21, 1996); missed seven games. ... Reinjured left groin (January 13, 1997); missed three games. ... Strained abdomen (January 9, 1998); missed four games. ... Traded by Flyers to Senators with C Vaclav Prospal and second round draft pick (LW Chris Bala) in 1998 draft for RW Alexandre Daigle (January 17, 1998).

HONORS: Named WHL (West) Division Rookie of the Year (1988-89). ... Named to WHL All-Star second team (1988-89). ... Won WHL (West) Division Most Sportsmanlike Player Award (1989-90). ... Named to WHL (West) All-Star first team (1989-90 and 1990-91). ... Won Can.HL Most Sportsmanlike Player of the Year Award (1990-91). ... Won Brad Hornung Trophy (1990-91). ... Won Stafford Smythe Memorial Trophy (1990-91). ... Named to Memorial Cup All-Star team (1990-91).

Season Team	League	Gms.	G	A	Pts.	PIM	+/-	PP	SH	Gms.	G	A	Pts.	PIM
87-88—Yellowbeard	TIER II	52	74	69	143	50	...	...	...	—	—	—	—	—
88-89—Spokane	WHL	72	22	56	78	41	...	...	...	5	5	8	13	4
89-90—Spokane	WHL	71	60	64	124	48	...	...	...	6	5	8	13	4
90-91—Spokane	WHL	61	64	74	138	33	...	...	...	15	10	14	24	10
91-92—San Jose	NHL	79	25	34	59	16	-32	5	0	—	—	—	—	—
92-93—San Jose	NHL	41	14	14	28	12	-25	5	1	—	—	—	—	—
93-94—San Jose	NHL	83	22	31	53	18	-3	6	0	14	1	2	3	6
94-95—San Jose	NHL	46	12	7	19	25	-4	0	0	11	3	1	4	0
95-96—San Jose	NHL	9	3	0	3	4	-1	0	0	—	—	—	—	—
—Philadelphia	NHL	62	22	26	48	6	15	9	0	12	3	2	5	2
96-97—Philadelphia	NHL	52	11	12	23	10	-8	2	0	14	3	1	4	2
97-98—Philadelphia	NHL	30	5	7	12	8	3	1	0	—	—	—	—	—
—Ottawa	NHL	28	3	3	6	8	-11	2	0	1	0	0	0	0
NHL Totals (7 years)		430	117	134	251	107	-66	30	1	52	10	6	16	10

FARKAS, JEFF   C   MAPLE LEAFS

PERSONAL: Born January 24, 1978, in Amherst, Mass. ... 6-0/174. ... Shoots left.
COLLEGE: Boston College.
TRANSACTIONS/CAREER NOTES: Selected by Toronto Maple Leafs in third round (first Maple Leafs pick, 57th overall) of NHL entry draft (June 21, 1997).

Season Team	League	Gms.	G	A	Pts.	PIM	+/-	PP	SH	Gms.	G	A	Pts.	PIM
94-95—Niagara	NAJHL	53	54	58	112	34	...	...	...	—	—	—	—	—
95-96—Niagara	NAJHL	74	64	107	171	95	...	...	...	—	—	—	—	—
96-97—Boston College	Hockey East	35	13	23	36	34	...	...	...	—	—	—	—	—
97-98—Boston College	Hockey East	40	11	28	39	42	...	...	...	—	—	—	—	—

FEDOROV, SERGEI   C   RED WINGS

PERSONAL: Born December 13, 1969, in Minsk, U.S.S.R. ... 6-1/200. ... Shoots left. ... Name pronounced SAIR-gay FEH-duh-rahf.
TRANSACTIONS/CAREER NOTES: Selected by Detroit Red Wings in fourth round (fourth Red Wings pick, 74th overall) of NHL entry draft (June 17, 1989). ... Bruised left shoulder (October 1990). ... Reinjured left shoulder (January 16, 1991). ... Sprained left shoulder (November 27, 1992); missed seven games. ... Suffered from the flu (January 30, 1993); missed two games. ... Suffered charley horse (February 11, 1993); missed one game. ... Suffered concussion (April 5, 1994); missed two games. ... Suspended four games without pay and fined $500 by NHL for high-sticking incident in playoff game (May 17, 1994); suspension reduced to three games due to abbreviated 1994-95 season. ... Suffered from the flu (February 7, 1995); missed one game. ... Bruised right hamstring (April 9, 1995); missed one game. ... Suffered from tonsillitis (October 6, 1995); missed three games. ... Sprained left wrist (December 15, 1995); missed one game. ... Strained groin (January 9, 1997); missed two games. ... Reinjured groin (January 20, 1997); missed six games. ... Missed first 59 games of 1997-98 season due to contract dispute. ... Tendered offer sheet by Carolina Hurricanes (February 19, 1998). ... Offer matched by Red Wings (February 26, 1998). ... Suspended two games and fined $1,000 by NHL for illegal check (March 31, 1998).

HONORS: Named to NHL All-Rookie team (1990-91). ... Played in NHL All-Star Game (1992, 1994 and 1996). ... Named NHL Player of the Year by THE SPORTING NEWS (1993-94). ... Named to THE SPORTING NEWS All-Star first team (1993-94). ... Won Hart Memorial Trophy (1993-94). ... Won Frank J. Selke Trophy (1993-94 and 1995-96). ... Won Lester B. Pearson Award (1993-94). ... Named to NHL All-Star first team (1993-94).

MISCELLANEOUS: Member of Stanley Cup championship team (1997 and 1998). ... Scored on a penalty shot (vs. Andy Moog, December 27, 1993). ... Failed to score on a penalty shot (vs. Kelly Hrudey, February 12, 1995).

STATISTICAL PLATEAUS: Three-goal games: 1993-94 (1). ... Four-goal games: 1994-95 (1). ... Five-goal games: 1996-97 (1). ... Total hat tricks: 3.

Season Team	League	Gms.	G	A	Pts.	PIM	+/-	PP	SH	Gms.	G	A	Pts.	PIM
85-86—Dynamo Minsk	USSR	15	6	1	7	10	...	...	...	—	—	—	—	—
86-87—CSKA Moscow	USSR	29	6	6	12	12	...	...	...	—	—	—	—	—
87-88—CSKA Moscow	USSR	48	7	9	16	20	...	...	...	—	—	—	—	—
88-89—CSKA Moscow	USSR	44	9	8	17	35	...	...	...	—	—	—	—	—
89-90—CSKA Moscow	USSR	48	19	10	29	20	...	...	...	—	—	—	—	—
90-91—Detroit	NHL	77	31	48	79	66	11	11	3	7	1	5	6	4
91-92—Detroit	NHL	80	32	54	86	72	26	7	2	11	5	5	10	8
92-93—Detroit	NHL	73	34	53	87	72	33	13	4	7	3	6	9	23

F

Season Team	League	REGULAR SEASON								PLAYOFFS				
		Gms.	G	A	Pts.	PIM	+/-	PP	SH	Gms.	G	A	Pts.	PIM
93-94—Detroit	NHL	82	56	64	120	34	48	13	4	7	1	7	8	6
94-95—Detroit	NHL	42	20	30	50	24	6	7	3	17	7	*17	*24	6
95-96—Detroit	NHL	78	39	68	107	48	49	11	3	19	2	*18	20	10
96-97—Detroit	NHL	74	30	33	63	30	29	9	2	20	8	12	20	12
97-98—Russian Oly. team	Int'l	6	1	5	6	8	...	...	...	—	—	—	—	—
—Detroit	NHL	21	6	11	17	25	10	2	0	22	*10	10	20	12
NHL Totals (8 years)		527	248	361	609	371	212	73	21	110	37	80	117	81

FEDOTOV, SERGEI   D   HURRICANES

PERSONAL: Born January 24, 1977, in Moscow, U.S.S.R. ... 6-2/180. ... Shoots left. ... Name pronounced fuh-DOH-tahf.
TRANSACTIONS/CAREER NOTES: Selected by Hartford Whalers in second round (second Whalers pick, 35th overall) of NHL entry draft (July 8, 1995). ... Whalers franchise moved to North Carolina and renamed Carolina Hurricanes for 1997-98 season; NHL approved move on June 25, 1997.

Season Team	League	REGULAR SEASON								PLAYOFFS				
		Gms.	G	A	Pts.	PIM	+/-	PP	SH	Gms.	G	A	Pts.	PIM
94-95—Dynamo Moscow	CIS	8	0	0	0	2	...	...	...	—	—	—	—	—
95-96—Dynamo Moscow	CIS	4	0	0	0	24	...	...	...	—	—	—	—	—
96-97—Detroit	OHL	52	10	27	37	60	...	...	...	5	0	2	2	9
97-98—New Haven	AHL	5	0	0	0	0	...	...	...	—	—	—	—	—
—Richmond	ECHL	5	1	1	2	4	...	...	...	—	—	—	—	—
—Plymouth	OHL	38	5	11	16	33	...	...	...	15	3	2	5	10

FELSNER, BRIAN   C/LW   BLACKHAWKS

PERSONAL: Born November 11, 1972, in Mt. Clemens, Mich. ... 5-11/189. ... Shoots left.
TRANSACTIONS/CAREER NOTES: Signed as free agent by Chicago Blackhawks (August 27, 1997).

Season Team	League	REGULAR SEASON								PLAYOFFS				
		Gms.	G	A	Pts.	PIM	+/-	PP	SH	Gms.	G	A	Pts.	PIM
93-94—Lake Superior	CCHA	6	1	1	2	6	...	...	...	—	—	—	—	—
94-95—Lake Superior	CCHA	41	24	28	52	51	...	...	...	—	—	—	—	—
95-96—Lake Superior	CCHA	38	16	36	52	40	...	...	...	—	—	—	—	—
96-97—Orlando	IHL	75	29	41	70	38	...	...	...	—	—	—	—	—
97-98—Indianapolis	IHL	53	17	36	53	36	...	...	...	—	—	—	—	—
—Chicago	NHL	12	1	3	4	12	0	0	0	—	—	—	—	—
—Milwaukee	IHL	15	7	8	15	20	...	...	...	10	3	9	12	12
NHL Totals (1 year)		12	1	3	4	12	0	0	0					

FERENCE, ANDREW   D   PENGUINS

PERSONAL: Born March 17, 1979, in Edmonton, Alta. ... 5-10/187. ... Shoots left.
TRANSACTIONS/CAREER NOTES: Selected by Pittsburgh Penguins in eighth round (eighth Penguins pick, 208th overall) of 1997 NHL entry draft.
HONORS: Named to WHL (West) All-Star first team (1997-98). ... Won Can.HL Plus/Minus Award (1997-98).

Season Team	League	REGULAR SEASON								PLAYOFFS				
		Gms.	G	A	Pts.	PIM	+/-	PP	SH	Gms.	G	A	Pts.	PIM
96-97—Portland	WHL	72	12	32	44	163	...	...	...	—	—	—	—	—
97-98—Portland	WHL	72	11	57	68	142	...	...	...	16	2	18	20	28

FERENCE, BRAD   D   CANUCKS

PERSONAL: Born April 2, 1979, in Calgary. ... 6-3/185. ... Shoots right. ... Name pronounced FAIR-intz.
TRANSACTIONS/CAREER NOTES: Selected by Vancouver Canucks in first round (first Canucks pick, 10th overall) of NHL entry draft (June 21, 1997).
HONORS: Named to Can.HL All-Rookie team (1996-97).

Season Team	League	REGULAR SEASON								PLAYOFFS				
		Gms.	G	A	Pts.	PIM	+/-	PP	SH	Gms.	G	A	Pts.	PIM
95-96—Spokane	WHL	5	0	2	2	18	...	...	...	—	—	—	—	—
96-97—Spokane	WHL	67	6	20	26	324	...	...	...	9	0	4	4	21
97-98—Spokane	WHL	54	9	29	38	213	...	...	...	18	0	7	7	59

FERGUSON, CRAIG   RW   PANTHERS

PERSONAL: Born April 8, 1970, in Castro Valley, Calif. ... 5-11/190. ... Shoots left.
COLLEGE: Yale.
TRANSACTIONS/CAREER NOTES: Selected by Montreal Canadiens in seventh round (seventh Canadiens pick, 146th overall) of NHL entry draft (June 22, 1991). ... Traded by Canadiens with LW Yves Sarault to Calgary Flames for eighth-round pick (D Petr Kubos) in 1997 draft (November 25, 1995). ... Traded by Flames to Los Angeles Kings for LW Pat Conacher (February 10, 1996). ... Signed as free agent by Florida Panthers (August 6, 1996).

Season Team	League	REGULAR SEASON								PLAYOFFS				
		Gms.	G	A	Pts.	PIM	+/-	PP	SH	Gms.	G	A	Pts.	PIM
88-89—Yale University	ECAC	24	11	6	17	20	...	...	...	—	—	—	—	—
89-90—Yale University	ECAC	35	6	15	21	38	...	...	...	—	—	—	—	—
90-91—Yale University	ECAC	29	11	10	21	34	...	...	...	—	—	—	—	—
91-92—Yale University	ECAC	27	9	16	25	28	...	...	...	—	—	—	—	—
92-93—Wheeling	ECHL	9	6	5	11	24	...	...	...	—	—	—	—	—
—Fredericton	AHL	55	15	13	28	20	...	...	...	5	0	1	1	2
93-94—Fredericton	AHL	57	29	32	61	60	...	...	...	—	—	—	—	—
—Montreal	NHL	2	0	1	1	0	1	0	0	—	—	—	—	—
94-95—Fredericton	AHL	80	27	35	62	62	...	...	...	17	6	2	8	6
—Montreal	NHL	1	0	0	0	0	0	0	0	—	—	—	—	—
95-96—Montreal	NHL	10	1	0	1	2	-5	0	0	—	—	—	—	—
—Calgary	NHL	8	0	0	0	4	-4	0	0	—	—	—	—	—
—Saint John	AHL	18	5	13	18	8	...	...	...	—	—	—	—	—
—Phoenix	IHL	31	6	9	15	25	...	...	...	4	0	2	2	6
96-97—Carolina	AHL	74	29	41	70	57	...	...	...	—	—	—	—	—
—Florida	NHL	3	0	0	0	0	-1	0	0	—	—	—	—	—
97-98—New Haven	AHL	64	24	28	52	41	...	...	...	3	2	1	3	2
NHL Totals (4 years)		24	1	1	2	6	-9	0	0					

FERGUSON, SCOTT — D — MIGHTY DUCKS

PERSONAL: Born January 6, 1973, in Camrose, Alta. ... 6-1/195. ... Shoots left.
TRANSACTIONS/CAREER NOTES: Signed as free agent by Edmonton Oilers (June 2, 1994). ... Traded by Oilers to Ottawa Senators for D Frank Musil (March 9, 1998). ... Signed as free agent by Mighty Ducks of Anaheim (July 22, 1998).

Season Team	League	REGULAR SEASON								PLAYOFFS				
		Gms.	G	A	Pts.	PIM	+/-	PP	SH	Gms.	G	A	Pts.	PIM
90-91—Kamloops	WHL	4	0	0	0	0	...	...	...	—	—	—	—	—
91-92—Kamloops	WHL	62	4	10	14	148	...	...	...	12	0	2	2	21
92-93—Kamloops	WHL	71	4	19	23	206	...	...	...	13	0	2	2	24
93-94—Kamloops	WHL	68	5	49	54	180	...	...	...	19	5	11	16	48
94-95—Wheeling	ECHL	5	1	5	6	16	...	...	...	—	—	—	—	—
—Cape Breton	AHL	58	4	6	10	103	...	...	...	—	—	—	—	—
95-96—Cape Breton	AHL	80	5	16	21	196	...	...	...	—	—	—	—	—
96-97—Hamilton	AHL	74	6	14	20	115	...	...	...	21	5	7	12	59
97-98—Hamilton	AHL	77	7	17	24	150	...	...	...	9	0	3	3	16
—Edmonton	NHL	1	0	0	0	0	1	0	0	—	—	—	—	—
NHL Totals (1 year)		1	0	0	0	0	1	0	0					

FERNANDEZ, MANNY — G — STARS

PERSONAL: Born August 27, 1974, in Etobicoke, Ont. ... 6-0/185. ... Catches left. ... Full name: Emmanuel Fernandez. ... Nephew of Jacques Lemaire, Hall of Fame center, Montreal Canadiens (1967-68 through 1978-79) and former head coach of New Jersey Devils.
TRANSACTIONS/CAREER NOTES: Selected by Quebec Nordiques in third round (fourth Nordiques pick, 52nd overall) of NHL entry draft (June 20, 1992). ... Traded by Nordiques to Dallas Stars for D Tommy Sjodin and undisclosed draft pick (February 13, 1994).
HONORS: Won Guy Lafleur Trophy (1992-93). ... Won Michel Briere Trophy (1993-94). ... Named to QMJHL All-Star first team (1993-94). ... Named to Can.HL All-Star second team (1993-94). ... Named to IHL All-Star second team (1994-95).

Season Team	League	REGULAR SEASON								PLAYOFFS						
		Gms.	Min	W	L	T	GA	SO	Avg.	Gms.	Min.	W	L	GA	SO	Avg.
91-92—Laval	QMJHL	31	1593	14	13	2	99	1	3.73	9	468	3	5	†39	0	5.00
92-93—Laval	QMJHL	43	2348	26	14	2	141	1	3.60	13	818	12	1	42	0	3.08
93-94—Laval	QMJHL	51	2776	29	14	1	143	*5	3.09	19	1116	14	5	49	†1	*2.63
94-95—Kalamazoo	IHL	46	2470	21	10	†9	115	2	2.79	12	655	9	1	†30	1	2.75
—Dallas	NHL	1	59	0	1	0	3	0	3.05	—	—	—	—	—	—	—
95-96—Michigan	IHL	47	2663	22	15	†9	133	†4	3.00	6	372	5	1	14	0	*2.26
—Dallas	NHL	5	249	0	1	1	19	0	4.58	—	—	—	—	—	—	—
96-97—Michigan	IHL	48	2721	20	24	‡2	142	2	3.13	4	277	1	3	15	0	3.25
97-98—Michigan	IHL	55	3023	27	17	‡5	139	5	2.76	2	89	0	2	7	0	4.72
—Dallas	NHL	2	69	1	0	0	2	0	1.74	1	2	0	0	0	0	0.00
NHL Totals (3 years)		8	377	1	2	1	24	0	3.82	1	2	0	0	0	0	0.00

FERRARO, CHRIS — C — OILERS

PERSONAL: Born January 24, 1973, in Port Jefferson, N.Y. ... 5-10/185. ... Shoots right. ... Twin brother of Peter Ferraro, center in New York Rangers system. ... Name pronounced fuh-RAH-roh.
COLLEGE: Maine.
TRANSACTIONS/CAREER NOTES: Selected by New York Rangers in fourth round (fourth Rangers pick, 85th overall) of NHL entry draft (June 20, 1992). ... Claimed on waivers by Pittsburgh Penguins (October 1, 1997). ... Signed as free agent by Edmonton Oilers (August 13, 1998).
HONORS: Named to Hockey East Rookie All-Star team (1992-93).

Season Team	League	REGULAR SEASON								PLAYOFFS				
		Gms.	G	A	Pts.	PIM	+/-	PP	SH	Gms.	G	A	Pts.	PIM
90-91—Dubuque	USHL	45	53	44	97		...	...	...	—	—	—	—	—
91-92—Waterloo	USHL	38	49	50	99	106	...	...	...	—	—	—	—	—
92-93—Univ. of Maine	Hockey East	39	25	26	51	46	...	...	...	—	—	—	—	—
93-94—U.S. national team	Int'l	48	8	34	42	58	...	...	...	—	—	—	—	—
—Univ. of Maine	Hockey East	4	0	1	1	8	...	...	...	—	—	—	—	—

F

Season Team	League	REGULAR SEASON								PLAYOFFS				
		Gms.	G	A	Pts.	PIM	+/-	PP	SH	Gms.	G	A	Pts.	PIM
94-95—Atlanta	IHL	54	13	14	27	72	...	...	...	—	—	—	—	—
—Binghamton	AHL	13	6	4	10	38	...	...	...	10	2	3	5	16
95-96—Binghamton	AHL	77	32	67	99	208	...	...	...	4	4	2	6	13
—New York Rangers	NHL	2	1	0	1	0	-3	1	0	—	—	—	—	—
96-97—Binghamton	AHL	53	29	34	63	94	...	...	...	—	—	—	—	—
—New York Rangers	NHL	12	1	1	2	6	1	0	0	—	—	—	—	—
97-98—Pittsburgh	NHL	46	3	4	7	43	-2	0	0	—	—	—	—	—
NHL Totals (3 years)		60	5	5	10	49	-4	1	0					

FERRARO, PETER · RW — BRUINS

PERSONAL: Born January 24, 1973, in Port Jefferson, N.Y. ... 5-10/180. ... Shoots right. ... Twin brother of Chris Ferraro, right winger, Pittsburgh Penguins. ... Name pronounced fuh-RAH-roh.
COLLEGE: Maine.
TRANSACTIONS/CAREER NOTES: Selected by New York Rangers in first round (first Rangers pick, 24th overall) of NHL entry draft (June 20, 1992). ... Claimed on waivers by Pittsburgh Penguins (October 1, 1997). ... Claimed on waivers by Rangers (January 14, 1998). ... Signed as free agent by Boston Bruins (July 21, 1998).
HONORS: Named to AHL All-Star first team (1995-96).

Season Team	League	REGULAR SEASON								PLAYOFFS				
		Gms.	G	A	Pts.	PIM	+/-	PP	SH	Gms.	G	A	Pts.	PIM
90-91—Dubuque	USHL	29	21	31	52	83	...	...	...	—	—	—	—	—
91-92—Waterloo	USHL	42	48	53	101	168	...	...	...	—	—	—	—	—
92-93—Univ. of Maine	Hockey East	36	18	32	50	106	...	...	...	—	—	—	—	—
93-94—U.S. national team	Int'l	59	28	39	67	48	...	...	...	—	—	—	—	—
—U.S. Olympic Team	Int'l	8	6	0	6	6	...	...	...	—	—	—	—	—
—Univ. of Maine	Hockey East	4	3	6	9	16	...	...	...	—	—	—	—	—
94-95—Atlanta	IHL	61	15	24	39	118	...	...	...	—	—	—	—	—
—Binghamton	AHL	12	2	6	8	67	...	...	...	11	4	3	7	51
95-96—Binghamton	AHL	68	48	53	101	157	...	...	...	4	1	6	7	22
—New York Rangers	NHL	5	0	1	1	0	-5	0	0	—	—	—	—	—
96-97—Binghamton	AHL	75	38	39	77	171	...	...	...	4	3	1	4	18
—New York Rangers	NHL	2	0	0	0	0	0	0	0	2	0	0	0	0
97-98—Pittsburgh	NHL	29	3	4	7	12	-2	0	0	—	—	—	—	—
—Hartford	AHL	36	17	23	40	54	...	...	...	15	8	6	14	59
—New York Rangers	NHL	1	0	0	0	2	-2	0	0	—	—	—	—	—
NHL Totals (3 years)		37	3	5	8	14	-9	0	0	2	0	0	0	0

FERRARO, RAY · C — KINGS

PERSONAL: Born August 23, 1964, in Trail, B.C. ... 5-10/192. ... Shoots left. ... Name pronounced fuh-RAH-roh.
TRANSACTIONS/CAREER NOTES: Selected by Hartford Whalers as underage junior in fifth round (fifth Whalers pick, 88th overall) of NHL entry draft (June 9, 1982). ... Traded by Whalers to New York Islanders for D Doug Crossman (November 13, 1990). ... Fractured right fibula (December 10, 1992); missed 36 games. ... Suffered from the flu (March 25, 1993); missed one game. ... Injured knee (March 9, 1995); missed one game. ... Signed as free agent by New York Rangers (July 19, 1995). ... Traded by Rangers with C Nathan Lafayette, C Ian Laperriere, D Mattias Norstrom and fourth-round pick (D Sean Blanchard) in 1997 draft to Los Angeles Kings for RW Shane Churla, LW Jari Kurri and D Marty McSorley (March 14, 1996). ... Strained neck (February 1, 1997); missed one game. ... Tore cartilage in left knee (October 5, 1997); missed 17 games. ... Underwent knee surgery (December 9, 1997); missed eight games. ... Strained lower back (January 20, 1998); missed two games. ... Suffered from the flu (March 2, 1998); missed one game. ... Strained left knee (March 21, 1998); missed three games. ... Strained left knee (April 11, 1998); missed three games.
HONORS: Won WHL Most Valuable Player Trophy (1983-84). ... Won Bob Brownridge Memorial Trophy (1983-84). ... Won WHL Player of the Year Award (1983-84). ... Named to WHL (East) All-Star first team (1983-84). ... Played in NHL All-Star Game (1992).
STATISTICAL PLATEAUS: Three-goal games: 1984-85 (2), 1986-87 (1), 1988-89 (1), 1989-90 (1), 1991-92 (1), 1995-96 (1). Total: 7. ... Four-goal games: 1991-92 (1). ... Total hat tricks: 8.

F

Season Team	League	REGULAR SEASON								PLAYOFFS				
		Gms.	G	A	Pts.	PIM	+/-	PP	SH	Gms.	G	A	Pts.	PIM
82-83—Portland	WHL	50	41	49	90	39	...	...	...	14	14	10	24	13
83-84—Brandon	WHL	72	*108	84	*192	84	...	...	...	11	13	15	28	20
84-85—Binghamton	AHL	37	20	13	33	29	...	...	...	—	—	—	—	—
—Hartford	NHL	44	11	17	28	40	-1	6	0	—	—	—	—	—
85-86—Hartford	NHL	76	30	47	77	57	12	14	0	10	3	6	9	4
86-87—Hartford	NHL	80	27	32	59	42	-9	14	0	6	1	1	2	8
87-88—Hartford	NHL	68	21	29	50	81	1	6	0	6	1	1	2	6
88-89—Hartford	NHL	80	41	35	76	86	1	11	0	4	2	0	2	4
89-90—Hartford	NHL	79	25	29	54	109	-15	7	0	7	0	3	3	2
90-91—Hartford	NHL	15	2	5	7	18	-1	1	0	—	—	—	—	—
—New York Islanders	NHL	61	19	16	35	52	-11	5	0	—	—	—	—	—
91-92—New York Islanders	NHL	80	40	40	80	92	25	7	0	—	—	—	—	—
92-93—New York Islanders	NHL	46	14	13	27	40	0	3	0	18	13	7	20	18
—Capital District	AHL	1	0	2	2	2	...	...	...	—	—	—	—	—
93-94—New York Islanders	NHL	82	21	32	53	83	1	5	0	4	1	0	1	6
94-95—New York Islanders	NHL	47	22	21	43	30	1	2	0	—	—	—	—	—
95-96—New York Rangers	NHL	65	25	29	54	82	13	8	0	—	—	—	—	—
—Los Angeles	NHL	11	4	2	6	10	-13	1	0	—	—	—	—	—
96-97—Los Angeles	NHL	81	25	21	46	112	-22	11	0	—	—	—	—	—
97-98—Los Angeles	NHL	40	6	9	15	42	-10	0	0	3	0	1	1	2
NHL Totals (14 years)		955	333	377	710	976	-28	101	0	58	21	19	40	50

FETISOV, SLAVA   D

PERSONAL: Born May 20, 1958, in Moscow, U.S.S.R. ... 6-1/215. ... Shoots left. ... Full name: Viacheslav Fetisov. ... Name pronounced SLAH-vuh fuh-TEE-sahf.
TRANSACTIONS/CAREER NOTES: Selected by Montreal Canadiens in 12th round (14th Canadiens pick, 201st overall) of NHL entry draft (June 15, 1978). ... Selected by New Jersey Devils in eighth round (sixth Devils pick, 150th overall) of NHL entry draft (June 8, 1983). ... Tore cartilage in left knee (November 22, 1989); missed six games. ... Suffered bronchial pneumonia and hospitalized twice (November 28, 1990); missed 10 games. ... Suffered from the flu (October 14, 1992); missed one game. ... Sprained knee (November 30, 1993); missed four games. ... Played in Europe during 1994-95 NHL lockout. ... Bruised leg (February 25, 1995); missed six games. ... Traded by Devils to Detroit Red Wings for third-round pick (RW David Gosselin) in 1995 draft (April 3, 1995). ... Injured groin (November 2, 1995); missed two games. ... Suspended two games by NHL for high-sticking (January 10, 1996). ... Underwent arthroscopic knee surgery (prior to 1996-97 season); missed first five games of season. ... Suffered from the flu (January 14, 1997); missed one game. ... Suffered injury (December 1, 1997); missed two games. ... Suffered injury (December 17, 1997); missed six games. ... Announced retirement and named assistant coach of Devils (July 28, 1998).
HONORS: Named to Soviet League All-Star team (1978-79, 1979-80, and 1981-82 through 1987-88). ... Won Soviet Player of the Year Award (1981-82, 1985-86 and 1987-88). ... Won Golden Stick Award (1983-84, 1987-88 and 1988-89). ... Played in NHL All-Star Game (1997 and 1998).
MISCELLANEOUS: Member of Stanley Cup championship team (1997 and 1998). ... Member of silver-medal-winning (1980) and gold-medal-winning U.S.S.R. Olympic teams (1984 and 1988).

Season Team	League	Gms.	G	A	Pts.	PIM	+/-	PP	SH	Gms.	G	A	Pts.	PIM
				REGULAR SEASON								PLAYOFFS		
74-75—CSKA Moscow	USSR	1	0	0	0	0	...	...	...	—	—	—	—	—
76-77—CSKA Moscow	USSR	28	3	4	7	14	...	...	...	—	—	—	—	—
77-78—CSKA Moscow	USSR	35	9	18	27	46	...	...	...	—	—	—	—	—
78-79—CSKA Moscow	USSR	29	10	19	29	40	...	...	...	—	—	—	—	—
79-80—CSKA Moscow	USSR	37	10	14	24	46	...	...	...	—	—	—	—	—
—Soviet Olympic Team..	WHL	7	5	4	9	10	...	...	...	—	—	—	—	—
80-81—CSKA Moscow	USSR	48	13	16	29	44	...	...	...	—	—	—	—	—
81-82—CSKA Moscow	USSR	46	15	26	41	20	...	...	...	—	—	—	—	—
82-83—CSKA Moscow	USSR	43	6	17	23	46	...	...	...	—	—	—	—	—
83-84—CSKA Moscow	USSR	44	19	30	49	38	...	...	...	—	—	—	—	—
—Soviet Olympic Team..	WHL	7	3	8	11	8	...	...	...	—	—	—	—	—
84-85—CSKA Moscow	USSR	20	13	12	25	6	...	...	...	—	—	—	—	—
85-86—CSKA Moscow	USSR	40	15	19	34	12	...	...	...	—	—	—	—	—
86-87—CSKA Moscow	USSR	39	13	20	33	18	...	...	...	—	—	—	—	—
87-88—CSKA Moscow	USSR	46	18	17	35	26	...	...	...	—	—	—	—	—
—Soviet Olympic Team..	WHL	8	4	9	13	6	...	...	...	—	—	—	—	—
88-89—CSKA Moscow	USSR	23	9	8	17	18	...	...	...	—	—	—	—	—
89-90—New Jersey	NHL	72	8	34	42	52	9	2	0	6	0	2	2	10
90-91—New Jersey	NHL	67	3	16	19	62	5	1	0	7	0	0	0	17
—Utica	AHL	1	1	1	2	0	...	...	...	—	—	—	—	—
91-92—New Jersey	NHL	70	3	23	26	108	11	0	0	6	0	3	3	8
92-93—New Jersey	NHL	76	4	23	27	158	7	1	1	5	0	2	2	4
93-94—New Jersey	NHL	52	1	14	15	30	14	0	0	14	1	0	1	8
94-95—Spartak Moscow	CIS	1	0	1	1	4	...	...	...	—	—	—	—	—
—New Jersey	NHL	4	0	1	1	0	-2	0	0	—	—	—	—	—
—Detroit	NHL	14	3	11	14	2	3	3	0	18	0	8	8	14
95-96—Detroit	NHL	69	7	35	42	96	37	1	1	19	1	4	5	34
96-97—Detroit	NHL	64	5	23	28	76	26	0	0	20	0	4	4	42
97-98—Detroit	NHL	58	2	12	14	72	4	0	0	21	0	3	3	10
NHL Totals (9 years)		546	36	192	228	656	114	8	2	116	2	26	28	147

FICHAUD, ERIC   G   OILERS

PERSONAL: Born November 4, 1975, in Montreal. ... 5-11/171. ... Catches left. ... Name pronounced FEE-shoh.
HIGH SCHOOL: CEGEP de Chicoutimi (Que.).
TRANSACTIONS/CAREER NOTES: Selected by Toronto Maple Leafs in first round (first Maple Leafs pick, 16th overall) of NHL entry draft (June 28, 1994). ... Traded by Maple Leafs to New York Islanders for C Benoit Hogue, third-round pick (RW Ryan Pepperall) in 1995 draft and fifth-round pick (D Brandon Sugden) in 1996 draft (April 6, 1995). ... Strained abdominal muscle (October 12, 1996); missed two games. ... Injured shoulder (December 2, 1997); missed seven games. ... Underwent shoulder surgery while assigned to Utah Grizzlies of IHL (January 20, 1998); missed remainder of season. ... Traded by Islanders to Edmonton Oilers for LW Mike Watt (June 18, 1998).
HONORS: Named to Memorial Cup All-Star team (1993-94). ... Won Hap Emms Memorial Trophy (1993-94). ... Won QMJHL Top Draft Prospect Award (1993-94). ... Won Guy Lafleur Award (1993-94). ... Named to QMJHL All-Star first team (1994-95).

Season Team	League	Gms.	Min	W	L	T	GA	SO	Avg.	Gms.	Min.	W	L	GA	SO	Avg.
				REGULAR SEASON								PLAYOFFS				
92-93—Chicoutimi	QMJHL	43	2040	18	13	1	149	0	4.38	—	—	—	—	—	—	—
93-94—Chicoutimi	QMJHL	63	3493	37	21	3	192	4	3.30	26	1560	16	10	86	†1	3.31
94-95—Chicoutimi	QMJHL	46	2637	21	19	4	151	4	3.44	7	430	2	5	20	0	2.79
95-96—Worcester	AHL	34	1988	13	15	6	97	1	2.93	2	127	1	1	7	0	3.31
—New York Islanders	NHL	24	1234	7	12	2	68	1	3.31	—	—	—	—	—	—	—
96-97—New York Islanders	NHL	34	1759	9	14	4	91	0	3.10	—	—	—	—	—	—	—
97-98—New York Islanders	NHL	17	807	3	8	3	40	0	2.97	—	—	—	—	—	—	—
—Utah	IHL	1	40	0	0	‡0	3	0	4.50	—	—	—	—	—	—	—
NHL Totals (3 years)		75	3800	19	34	9	199	1	3.14							

FINLEY, JEFF   D   RANGERS

PERSONAL: Born April 14, 1967, in Edmonton. ... 6-2/205. ... Shoots left.
TRANSACTIONS/CAREER NOTES: Selected by New York Islanders as underage junior in third round (fourth Islanders pick, 55th overall) of NHL entry draft (June 15, 1985). ... Suffered swollen left knee (September 1988). ... Traded by Islanders to Ottawa Senators for D Chris

Luongo (June 30, 1993). ... Signed as free agent by Philadelphia Flyers (August 2, 1993). ... Traded by Flyers to Winnipeg Jets for LW Russ Romaniuk (June 26, 1995). ... Separated shoulder (December 10, 1995); missed one game. ... Jets franchise moved to Phoenix and renamed Coyotes for 1996-97 season; NHL approved move on January 18, 1996. ... Suffered from the flu (December 7, 1996); missed two games. ... Strained hip flexor (December 30, 1996); missed one game. ... Sprained ankle (March 27, 1997); missed remainder of regular season and first six games of playoffs. ... Signed as free agent by New York Rangers (July 16, 1997).

		REGULAR SEASON								PLAYOFFS				
Season Team	League	Gms.	G	A	Pts.	PIM	+/-	PP	SH	Gms.	G	A	Pts.	PIM
83-84—Portland	WHL	5	0	0	0	0	...	...	...	5	0	1	1	4
—Summerland	BCJHL	49	0	21	21	14	...	...	...	—	—	—	—	—
84-85—Portland	WHL	69	6	44	50	57	...	...	...	6	1	2	3	2
85-86—Portland	WHL	70	11	59	70	83	...	...	...	15	1	7	8	16
86-87—Portland	WHL	72	13	53	66	113	...	...	...	20	1	†21	22	27
87-88—Springfield	AHL	52	5	18	23	50	...	...	...	—	—	—	—	—
—New York Islanders	NHL	10	0	5	5	15	5	0	0	1	0	0	0	2
88-89—New York Islanders	NHL	4	0	0	0	6	1	0	0	—	—	—	—	—
—Springfield	AHL	65	3	16	19	55	...	...	...	—	—	—	—	—
89-90—New York Islanders	NHL	11	0	1	1	0	0	0	0	5	0	2	2	2
—Springfield	AHL	57	1	15	16	41	...	...	...	13	1	4	5	23
90-91—Capital District	AHL	67	10	34	44	34	...	...	...	—	—	—	—	—
—New York Islanders	NHL	11	0	0	0	4	-1	0	0	—	—	—	—	—
91-92—Capital District	AHL	20	1	9	10	6	...	...	...	—	—	—	—	—
—New York Islanders	NHL	51	1	10	11	26	-6	0	0	—	—	—	—	—
92-93—Capital District	AHL	61	6	29	35	34	...	...	...	4	0	1	1	0
93-94—Philadelphia	NHL	55	1	8	9	24	16	0	0	—	—	—	—	—
94-95—Hershey	AHL	36	2	9	11	33	...	...	...	6	0	1	1	8
95-96—Springfield	AHL	14	3	12	15	22	...	...	...	—	—	—	—	—
—Winnipeg	NHL	65	1	5	6	8	-2	0	0	6	0	0	0	4
96-97—Phoenix	NHL	65	3	7	10	40	-8	1	0	1	0	0	0	2
97-98—New York Rangers	NHL	63	1	6	7	55	-3	0	0	—	—	—	—	—
NHL Totals (9 years)		335	7	42	49	251	2	1	0	13	0	2	2	10

FISET, STEPHANE G KINGS

PERSONAL: Born June 17, 1970, in Montreal. ... 6-1/197. ... Catches left. ... Name pronounced fih-SAY.
TRANSACTIONS/CAREER NOTES: Selected by Quebec Nordiques in second round (third Nordiques pick, 24th overall) of NHL entry draft (June 13, 1987). ... Underwent shoulder surgery (May 1989). ... Twisted knee (December 9, 1990). ... Sprained left knee (January 14, 1992); missed 12 games. ... Suffered slipped disc (November 4, 1993); missed 18 games. ... Injured groin (February 28, 1995); missed 18 games. ... Nordiques franchise moved to Colorado and renamed Avalanche for 1995-96 season (June 21, 1995). ... Traded by Avalanche with first-round pick (D Mathieu Biron) in 1998 draft to Los Angeles Kings for LW Eric Lacroix and first-round pick (D Martin Skoula) in 1998 draft (June 20, 1996). ... Strained abdominal muscle (December 3, 1996); missed one game. ... Strained groin and abdominal muscles (March 5, 1997); missed 13 games. ... Bruised thigh (January 24, 1998); missed one game. ... Strained groin (February 28, 1998); missed two games.
HONORS: Won Can.HL Goaltender of the Year Award (1988-89). ... Won Jacques Plante Trophy (1988-89). ... Named to QMJHL All-Star first team (1988-89).
MISCELLANEOUS: Member of Stanley Cup championship team (1996). ... Holds Colorado Avalanche franchise all-time record for most shutouts (6) and goals-against average (2.96). ... Stopped a penalty shot attempt (vs. Craig Janney, January 9, 1992; vs. Chris Dahlquist, March 21, 1992; vs. Peter Bondra, April 4, 1998). ... Allowed a penalty shot goal (vs. Kevin Miller, December 5, 1995).

		REGULAR SEASON							PLAYOFFS						
Season Team	League	Gms.	Min	W	L	T	GA	SO	Avg.	Gms.	Min.	W	L	GA	SO	Avg.
87-88—Victoriaville	QMJHL	40	2221	14	17	4	146	1	3.94	2	163	0	2	10	0	3.68
88-89—Victoriaville	QMJHL	43	2401	25	14	0	138	1	*3.45	12	711	9	2	33	0	*2.78
89-90—Victoriaville	QMJHL	24	1383	14	6	3	63	1	2.73	*14	*790	7	6	*49	0	3.72
—Quebec	NHL	6	342	0	5	1	34	0	5.96	—						
90-91—Quebec	NHL	3	186	0	2	1	12	0	3.87	—						
—Halifax	AHL	36	1902	10	15	8	131	0	4.13	—						
91-92—Halifax	AHL	29	1675	8	14	6	110	†3	3.94	—						
—Quebec	NHL	23	1133	7	10	2	71	1	3.76	—						
92-93—Quebec	NHL	37	1939	18	9	4	110	0	3.40	1	21	0	0	1	0	2.86
—Halifax	AHL	3	180	2	1	0	11	0	3.67	—						
93-94—Quebec	NHL	50	2798	20	25	4	158	2	3.39	—						
94-95—Quebec	NHL	32	1879	17	10	3	87	2	2.78	4	209	1	2	16	0	4.59
95-96—Colorado	NHL	37	2107	22	6	7	103	1	2.93	1	1	0	0	0	0	...
96-97—Los Angeles	NHL	44	2482	13	24	5	132	4	3.19	—						
97-98—Los Angeles	NHL	60	3497	26	25	8	158	2	2.71	2	93	0	2	7	0	4.52
NHL Totals (9 years)		292	16363	123	116	35	865	12	3.17	8	324	1	4	24	0	4.44

FITZGERALD, TOM RW/C PREDATORS

PERSONAL: Born August 28, 1968, in Melrose, Mass. ... 6-0/191. ... Shoots right. ... Full name: Thomas James Fitzgerald.
HIGH SCHOOL: Austin Prep (Reading, Mass.).
COLLEGE: Providence.
TRANSACTIONS/CAREER NOTES: Selected by New York Islanders in first round (first Islanders pick, 17th overall) of NHL entry draft (June 21, 1986). ... Bruised left knee (November 7, 1990). ... Strained abdominal muscle (October 22, 1991); missed 16 games. ... Tore rib cage muscle (October 24, 1992); missed four games. ... Selected by Florida Panthers in NHL expansion draft (June 24, 1993). ... Suffered sore hip (March 18, 1994); missed one game. ... Bruised eye (November 13, 1996); missed one game. ... Suffered from the flu (December 29, 1996); missed one game. ... Strained abdominal muscle (January 25, 1997); missed three games. ... Strained abdominal muscle (February 22, 1997); missed five games. ... Traded by Panthers to Colorado Avalanche for rights to LW Mark Parrish and third-round pick (D Lance Ward) in 1998 draft (March 24, 1998). ... Signed as free agent by Nashville Predators (July 6, 1998).
RECORDS: Shares NHL single-game playoff record for most shorthanded goals—2 (May 8, 1993).

MISCELLANEOUS: Holds Florida Panthers all-time record for most games played (213). ... Failed to score on a penalty shot (vs. Mark Fitzpatrick, January 31, 1998).

Season Team	League	REGULAR SEASON								PLAYOFFS				
		Gms.	G	A	Pts.	PIM	+/-	PP	SH	Gms.	G	A	Pts.	PIM
84-85—Austin Prep	Mass. H.S.	18	20	21	41	...	...	...	...	—	—	—	—	—
85-86—Austin Prep	Mass. H.S.	24	35	38	73	...	...	...	...	—	—	—	—	—
86-87—Providence College	Hockey East	27	8	14	22	22	...	...	...	—	—	—	—	—
87-88—Providence College	Hockey East	36	19	15	34	50	...	...	...	—	—	—	—	—
88-89—Springfield	AHL	61	24	18	42	43	...	...	...	—	—	—	—	—
—New York Islanders	NHL	23	3	5	8	10	1	0	0	—	—	—	—	—
89-90—Springfield	AHL	53	30	23	53	32	...	...	...	14	2	9	11	13
—New York Islanders	NHL	19	2	5	7	4	-3	0	0	4	1	0	1	4
90-91—New York Islanders	NHL	41	5	5	10	24	-9	0	0	—	—	—	—	—
—Capital District	AHL	27	7	7	14	50	...	...	...	—	—	—	—	—
91-92—New York Islanders	NHL	45	6	11	17	28	-3	0	2	—	—	—	—	—
—Capital District	AHL	4	1	1	2	4	...	...	...	—	—	—	—	—
92-93—New York Islanders	NHL	77	9	18	27	34	-2	0	3	18	2	5	7	18
93-94—Florida	NHL	83	18	14	32	54	-3	0	3	—	—	—	—	—
94-95—Florida	NHL	48	3	13	16	31	-3	0	0	—	—	—	—	—
95-96—Florida	NHL	82	13	21	34	75	-3	1	6	22	4	4	8	34
96-97—Florida	NHL	71	10	14	24	64	7	0	2	5	0	1	1	0
97-98—Florida	NHL	69	10	5	15	57	-4	0	1	—	—	—	—	—
—Colorado	NHL	11	2	1	3	22	0	0	1	7	0	1	1	20
NHL Totals (10 years)		569	81	112	193	403	-22	1	18	56	7	11	18	76

FITZPATRICK, MARK   G   BLACKHAWKS

PERSONAL: Born November 13, 1968, in Toronto. ... 6-2/198. ... Catches left.

TRANSACTIONS/CAREER NOTES: Injured knee (February 1987). ... Selected by Los Angeles Kings as underage junior in second round (second Kings pick, 27th overall) of NHL entry draft (June 13, 1987). ... Traded by Kings with D Wayne McBean and future considerations to New York Islanders for G Kelly Hrudey (February 22, 1989); Kings sent D Doug Crossman to Islanders to complete deal (May 23, 1989). ... Developed Eosinophilic Myalgia Syndrome (EMS) after a reaction to L-Trytophan, an ingredient in a vitamin supplement (September 1990); returned to play (March 1991). ... Suffered recurrence of EMS and underwent biopsy on right thigh (October 22, 1991); missed 10 games. ... Strained abdominal muscle (December 15, 1992); missed five games. ... Traded by Islanders with first-round pick (C Adam Deadmarsh) in 1993 draft to Quebec Nordiques for G Ron Hextall and first-round pick (C/RW Todd Bertuzzi) in 1993 draft (June 20, 1993). ... Selected by Florida Panthers in NHL expansion draft (June 24, 1993). ... Suspended two games without pay and fined $500 by NHL for high-sticking incident (February 16, 1994). ... Sprained lower back (April 22, 1995); missed one game. ... Suffered recurring back spasms (April 26, 1995); missed last four games of season. ... Traded by Panthers with RW Jody Hull to Tampa Bay Lightning for RW Dino Ciccarelli and D Jeff Norton (January 15, 1998). ... Traded by Lightning with fourth-round pick in 1998 draft to Chicago Blackhawks for D Michal Sykora (July 17, 1998).

HONORS: Won Top Goaltender Trophy (1985-86). ... Named to WHL All-Star second team (1985-86 and 1987-88). ... Named to Memorial Cup All-Star team (1986-87 and 1987-88). ... Won Bill Masterton Memorial Trophy (1991-92).

MISCELLANEOUS: Stopped a penalty shot attempt (vs. Doug Gilmour, October 7, 1989; vs. Dean McAmmond, January 5, 1996; vs. Jaromir Jagr, November 9, 1996; vs. Tom Fitzgerald, January 31, 1998). ... Allowed a penalty shot goal (vs. Mike Sillinger, January 14, 1997).

Season Team	League	REGULAR SEASON								PLAYOFFS						
		Gms.	Min	W	L	T	GA	SO	Avg.	Gms.	Min.	W	L	GA	SO	Avg.
83-84—Revelstoke	BCJHL	21	1019	...	...	...	90	0	5.30	—	—	—	—	—	—	—
84-85—Medicine Hat	WHL	3	180	...	...	...	9	0	3.00	—	—	—	—	—	—	—
85-86—Medicine Hat	WHL	41	2074	26	6	1	99	1	*2.86	*19	986	12	5	*58	0	3.53
86-87—Medicine Hat	WHL	50	2844	31	11	4	159	*4	3.35	*20	*1224	12	8	71	†1	3.48
87-88—Medicine Hat	WHL	63	3600	36	15	6	194	†2	*3.23	16	959	12	4	52	†1	*3.25
88-89—New Haven	AHL	18	980	10	5	1	54	1	3.31	—	—	—	—	—	—	—
—Los Angeles	NHL	17	957	6	7	3	64	0	4.01	—	—	—	—	—	—	—
—New York Islanders	NHL	11	627	3	5	2	41	0	3.92	—	—	—	—	—	—	—
89-90—New York Islanders	NHL	47	2653	19	19	5	150	3	3.39	4	152	0	2	13	0	5.13
90-91—Capital District	AHL	12	734	3	7	2	47	0	3.84	—	—	—	—	—	—	—
—New York Islanders	NHL	2	120	1	1	0	6	0	3.00	—	—	—	—	—	—	—
91-92—Capital District	AHL	14	782	6	5	1	39	0	2.99	—	—	—	—	—	—	—
—New York Islanders	NHL	30	1743	11	13	5	93	0	3.20	—	—	—	—	—	—	—
92-93—New York Islanders	NHL	39	2253	17	15	5	130	0	3.46	3	77	0	1	4	0	3.12
—Capital District	AHL	5	284	1	3	1	18	0	3.80	—	—	—	—	—	—	—
93-94—Florida	NHL	28	1603	12	8	6	73	1	2.73	—	—	—	—	—	—	—
94-95—Florida	NHL	15	819	6	7	2	36	2	2.64	—	—	—	—	—	—	—
95-96—Florida	NHL	34	1786	15	11	3	88	0	2.96	2	60	0	0	6	0	6.00
96-97—Florida	NHL	30	1680	8	9	9	66	0	2.36	—	—	—	—	—	—	—
97-98—Florida	NHL	12	640	2	7	2	32	1	3.00	—	—	—	—	—	—	—
—Fort Wayne	IHL	2	119	1	1	‡0	8	0	4.03	—	—	—	—	—	—	—
—Tampa Bay	NHL	34	1938	7	24	1	102	1	3.16	—	—	—	—	—	—	—
NHL Totals (10 years)		299	16819	107	126	43	881	8	3.14	9	289	0	3	23	0	4.78

F

FITZPATRICK, RORY   D   BLUES

PERSONAL: Born January 11, 1975, in Rochester, N.Y. ... 6-2/206. ... Shoots right.

TRANSACTIONS/CAREER NOTES: Selected by Montreal Canadiens in second round (second Canadiens pick, 47th overall) of NHL entry draft (June 26, 1993). ... Traded by Canadiens with C Pierre Turgeon and C Craig Conroy to St. Louis Blues for LW Shayne Corson, D Murray Baron and fifth-round pick (D Gennady Razin) in 1997 draft (October 29, 1996).

HONORS: Named to OHL All-Rookie team (1992-93).

Season Team	League	REGULAR SEASON								PLAYOFFS				
		Gms.	G	A	Pts.	PIM	+/-	PP	SH	Gms.	G	A	Pts.	PIM
90-91—Rochester Jr. B	OHA	40	0	5	5	...	...	...	...	—	—	—	—	—
91-92—Rochester Jr. B	OHA	28	8	28	36	141	...	...	...	—	—	—	—	—
92-93—Sudbury	OHL	58	4	20	24	68	...	...	...	14	0	0	0	17
93-94—Sudbury	OHL	65	12	34	46	112	...	...	...	10	2	5	7	10
94-95—Sudbury	OHL	56	12	36	48	72	...	...	...	18	3	15	18	21
—Fredericton	AHL	—	—	—	—	—	...	...	...	10	1	2	3	5
95-96—Fredericton	AHL	18	4	6	10	36	...	...	...	—	—	—	—	—
—Montreal	NHL	42	0	2	2	18	-7	0	0	6	1	1	2	0
96-97—Montreal	NHL	6	0	1	1	6	-2	0	0	—	—	—	—	—
—Worcester	AHL	49	4	13	17	78	...	...	...	5	1	2	3	0
—St. Louis	NHL	2	0	0	0	2	-2	0	0	—	—	—	—	—
97-98—Worcester	AHL	62	8	22	30	111	...	...	...	11	0	3	3	26
NHL Totals (2 years)		50	0	3	3	26	-11	0	0	6	1	1	2	0

FLAHERTY, WADE   G   ISLANDERS

PERSONAL: Born January 11, 1968, in Terrace, B.C. ... 6-0/170. ... Catches right.

TRANSACTIONS/CAREER NOTES: Selected by Buffalo Sabres in ninth round (10th Sabres pick, 181st overall) of NHL entry draft (June 11, 1988). ... Signed as free agent by San Jose Sharks (September 3, 1991). ... Injured ribs (February 28, 1995); missed three games. ... Strained groin (February 1, 1996); missed two games. ... Suffered back spasms (March 8, 1996); missed six games. ... Suffered back spasms (March 31, 1996); missed seven games. ... Broke collarbone (September 12, 1996); missed 23 games. ... Signed as free agent by New York Islanders (July 1, 1997).

HONORS: Named to WHL All-Star second team (1987-88). ... Won ECHL Playoff Most Valuable Player Award (1989-90). ... Shared James Norris Memorial Trophy with Arturs Irbe (1991-92). ... Named to IHL All-Star second team (1992-93 and 1993-94).

Season Team	League	REGULAR SEASON								PLAYOFFS						
		Gms.	Min	W	L	T	GA	SO	Avg.	Gms.	Min.	W	L	GA	SO	Avg.
84-85—Kelowna	WHL	1	55	0	0	0	5	0	5.45	—						
85-86—Seattle	WHL	9	271	1	3	0	36	0	7.97	—						
—Spokane	WHL	5	161	0	3	0	21	0	7.83	—						
86-87—Nanaimo	BCJHL	15	830	...	...	...	53	0	3.83	—						
—Victoria	WHL	3	127	0	2	0	16	0	7.56	—						
87-88—Victoria	WHL	36	2052	20	15	0	135	0	3.95	5	300	2	3	18	0	3.60
88-89—Victoria	WHL	42	2408	21	19	0	180	0	4.49	8	480	3	5	35	0	4.38
89-90—Kalamazoo	IHL	1	13	0	0	‡0	0	0	...	—						
—Greensboro	ECHL	27	1308	12	10	‡0	96	...	4.40	†9	567	*8	1	21	0	*2.22
90-91—Kansas City	IHL	†56	2990	16	31	‡4	*224	0	4.49	—						
91-92—Kansas City	IHL	43	2603	26	14	‡3	140	1	3.23	1	1	0	0	0	0	...
—San Jose	NHL	3	178	0	3	0	13	0	4.38	—						
92-93—Kansas City	IHL	61	*3642	*34	19	‡0	*195	2	3.21	12	*733	6	*5	†34	*1	2.78
—San Jose	NHL	1	60	0	1	0	5	0	5.00	—						
93-94—Kansas City	IHL	60	*3564	32	19	‡9	202	0	3.40	—						
94-95—San Jose	NHL	18	852	5	6	1	44	1	3.10	7	377	2	3	31	0	4.93
95-96—San Jose	NHL	24	1137	3	12	1	92	0	4.85	—						
96-97—Kentucky	AHL	19	1032	8	6	2	54	1	3.14	3	200	1	2	11	0	3.30
—San Jose	NHL	7	359	2	4	0	31	0	5.18	—						
97-98—Utah	IHL	24	1341	16	5	‡3	40	3	1.79	—						
—New York Islanders	NHL	16	694	4	4	3	23	3	1.99	—						
NHL Totals (6 years)		69	3280	14	30	5	208	4	3.80	7	377	2	3	31	0	4.93

FLEURY, THEO   RW   FLAMES

PERSONAL: Born June 29, 1968, in Oxbow, Sask. ... 5-6/180. ... Shoots right. ... Full name: Theoren Fleury. ... Name pronounced THAIR-ihn FLUH-ree.

TRANSACTIONS/CAREER NOTES: Selected by Calgary Flames in eighth round (ninth Flames pick, 166th overall) of NHL entry draft (June 13, 1987). ... Played in Europe during 1994-95 NHL lockout. ... Injured eye (April 6, 1996); missed two games. ... Injured knee (April 6, 1997); missed one game.

HONORS: Named to WHL (East) All-Star first team (1986-87). ... Shared Bob Clarke Trophy with Joe Sakic (1987-88). ... Named to WHL All-Star second team (1987-88). ... Shared Alka-Seltzer Plus Award with Marty McSorley (1990-91). ... Played in NHL All-Star Game (1991, 1992 and 1996-1998). ... Named to NHL All-Star second team (1994-95).

RECORDS: Holds NHL single-game record for highest plus-minus rating—9 (February 10, 1993).

STATISTICAL PLATEAUS: Three-goal games: 1990-91 (5), 1992-93 (1), 1993-94 (1), 1995-96 (3), 1996-97 (1). Total: 11.

MISCELLANEOUS: Member of Stanley Cup championship team (1989). ... Captain of Calgary Flames (1995-96 and 1996-97). ... Scored on a penalty shot (vs. Jacques Cloutier, February 23, 1991; vs. Rick Wamsley, December 11, 1992; vs. Patrick Roy, October 22, 1996). ... Holds Calgary Flames all-time record for most goals (334).

Season Team	League	REGULAR SEASON								PLAYOFFS				
		Gms.	G	A	Pts.	PIM	+/-	PP	SH	Gms.	G	A	Pts.	PIM
84-85—Moose Jaw	WHL	71	29	46	75	82	...	...	...	—	—	—	—	—
85-86—Moose Jaw	WHL	72	43	65	108	124	...	...	...	—	—	—	—	—
86-87—Moose Jaw	WHL	66	61	68	129	110	...	...	...	9	7	9	16	34
87-88—Moose Jaw	WHL	65	68	92	†160	235	...	...	...	—	—	—	—	—
—Salt Lake City	IHL	2	3	4	7	7	...	...	...	8	11	5	16	16
88-89—Salt Lake City	IHL	40	37	37	74	81	...	...	...	—	—	—	—	—
—Calgary	NHL	36	14	20	34	46	5	5	0	22	5	6	11	24
89-90—Calgary	NHL	80	31	35	66	157	22	9	3	6	2	3	5	10
90-91—Calgary	NHL	79	51	53	104	136	†48	9	7	7	2	5	7	14
91-92—Calgary	NHL	80	33	40	73	133	0	11	1	—	—	—	—	—
92-93—Calgary	NHL	83	34	66	100	88	14	12	2	6	5	7	12	27

Season Team	League	REGULAR SEASON								PLAYOFFS				
		Gms.	G	A	Pts.	PIM	+/-	PP	SH	Gms.	G	A	Pts.	PIM
93-94—Calgary	NHL	83	40	45	85	186	30	16	1	7	6	4	10	5
94-95—Tappara	Finland	10	8	9	17	22	...	...	...	—	—	—	—	—
—Calgary	NHL	47	29	29	58	112	6	9	2	7	7	7	14	2
95-96—Calgary	NHL	80	46	50	96	112	17	17	5	4	2	1	3	14
96-97—Calgary	NHL	81	29	38	67	104	-12	9	2	—	—	—	—	—
97-98—Calgary	NHL	82	27	51	78	197	0	3	2	—	—	—	—	—
—Can. Olympic Team	Int'l	6	1	3	4	2	...	...	...	—	—	—	—	—
NHL Totals (10 years)		731	334	427	761	1271	130	100	25	59	29	33	62	96

FOCHT, DAN   D   COYOTES

PERSONAL: Born December 31, 1977, in Reginan, Sask. ... 6-6/226. ... Shoots left. ... Name pronounced FOHKT.
TRANSACTIONS/CAREER NOTES: Selected by Phoenix Coyotes in first round (first Coyotes pick, 11th overall) of NHL entry draft (June 22, 1996).

Season Team	League	REGULAR SEASON								PLAYOFFS				
		Gms.	G	A	Pts.	PIM	+/-	PP	SH	Gms.	G	A	Pts.	PIM
95-96—Tri-City	WHL	63	6	12	18	161	...	...	...	11	1	1	2	23
96-97—Springfield	AHL	1	0	0	0	2	...	...	...	—	—	—	—	—
—Tri-City	WHL	28	0	5	5	92	...	...	...	—	—	—	—	—
—Regina	WHL	22	2	2	4	59	...	...	...	5	0	2	2	8
97-98—Springfield	AHL	61	2	5	7	125	...	...	...	3	0	0	0	4

FOOTE, ADAM   D   AVALANCHE

PERSONAL: Born July 10, 1971, in Toronto. ... 6-2/202. ... Shoots right. ... Full name: Adam David Vernon Foote. ... Name pronounced FUT.
TRANSACTIONS/CAREER NOTES: Selected by Quebec Nordiques in second round (second Nordiques pick, 22nd overall) of NHL entry draft (June 17, 1989). ... Fractured right thumb (February 1992); missed remainder of season. ... Injured knee (October 21, 1992); missed one game. ... Suffered from the flu (January 28, 1993); missed two games. ... Injured groin (January 18, 1994); missed eight games. ... Suffered herniated disc (February 11, 1994); underwent surgery and missed remainder of season. ... Injured back (February 9, 1995); missed two games. ... Injured groin (February 28, 1995); missed two games. ... Injured groin (March 26, 1995); missed four games. ... Reinjured groin (April 6, 1995); missed five games. ... Nordiques franchise moved to Colorado and renamed Avalanche for 1995-96 season (June 21, 1995). ... Broke wrist prior to 1995-96 season; missed first two games of season. ... Separated left shoulder (January 6, 1996); missed five games. ... Bruised left knee (February 8, 1997); missed two games. ... Bruised knee (January 2, 1998); missed one game. ... Bruised knee (January 10, 1998); missed three games.
HONORS: Named to OHL All-Star first team (1990-91).
MISCELLANEOUS: Member of Stanley Cup championship team (1996).

Season Team	League	REGULAR SEASON								PLAYOFFS				
		Gms.	G	A	Pts.	PIM	+/-	PP	SH	Gms.	G	A	Pts.	PIM
88-89—Sault Ste. Marie	OHL	66	7	32	39	120	...	...	...	—	—	—	—	—
89-90—Sault Ste. Marie	OHL	61	12	43	55	199	...	...	...	—	—	—	—	—
90-91—Sault Ste. Marie	OHL	59	18	51	69	93	...	...	...	14	5	12	17	28
91-92—Quebec	NHL	46	2	5	7	44	-4	0	0	—	—	—	—	—
—Halifax	AHL	6	0	1	1	2	...	...	...	—	—	—	—	—
92-93—Quebec	NHL	81	4	12	16	168	6	0	1	6	0	1	1	2
93-94—Quebec	NHL	45	2	6	8	67	3	0	0	—	—	—	—	—
94-95—Quebec	NHL	35	0	7	7	52	17	0	0	6	0	1	1	14
95-96—Colorado	NHL	73	5	11	16	88	27	1	0	22	1	3	4	36
96-97—Colorado	NHL	78	2	19	21	135	16	0	0	17	0	4	4	*62
97-98—Colorado	NHL	77	3	14	17	124	-3	0	0	7	0	0	0	23
—Can. Olympic Team	Int'l	6	0	1	1	4	...	...	...	—	—	—	—	—
NHL Totals (7 years)		435	18	74	92	678	62	1	1	58	1	9	10	137

FORBES, COLIN   LW   FLYERS

PERSONAL: Born February 16, 1976, in New Westminister, B.C. ... 6-3/205. ... Shoots left.
TRANSACTIONS/CAREER NOTES: Selected by Philadelphia Flyers in seventh round (fifth Flyers pick, 166th overall) of NHL entry draft (June 29, 1994).

Season Team	League	REGULAR SEASON								PLAYOFFS				
		Gms.	G	A	Pts.	PIM	+/-	PP	SH	Gms.	G	A	Pts.	PIM
93-94—Sherwood Park	AJHL	47	18	22	40	76	...	...	...	—	—	—	—	—
94-95—Portland	WHL	72	24	31	55	108	...	...	...	9	1	3	4	10
95-96—Portland	WHL	72	33	44	77	137	...	...	...	7	2	5	7	14
—Hershey	AHL	2	1	0	1	2	...	...	...	4	0	2	2	2
96-97—Philadelphia	AHL	74	21	28	49	108	...	...	...	10	5	5	10	33
—Philadelphia	NHL	3	1	0	1	0	0	0	0	3	0	0	0	0
97-98—Philadelphia	AHL	13	7	4	11	22	...	...	...	—	—	—	—	—
—Philadelphia	NHL	63	12	7	19	59	2	2	0	5	0	0	0	2
NHL Totals (2 years)		66	13	7	20	59	2	2	0	8	0	0	0	2

FORSBERG, PETER   C   AVALANCHE

PERSONAL: Born July 20, 1973, in Ornskoldsvik, Sweden. ... 6-0/190. ... Shoots left. ... Son of Kent Forsberg, head coach, Swedish Olympic team.
TRANSACTIONS/CAREER NOTES: Selected by Philadelphia Flyers in first round (first Flyers pick, sixth overall) of NHL entry draft (June 22, 1991). ... Traded by Flyers with G Ron Hextall, C Mike Ricci, D Steve Duchesne, D Kerry Huffman, first-round pick (G Jocelyn Thibault) in 1993 draft, cash and future considerations to Quebec Nordiques for C Eric Lindros (June 20, 1992); Flyers sent LW Chris Simon and first-

F

round pick (traded to Toronto) in 1994 draft to Nordiques to complete deal (July 21, 1992). ... Played in Europe during 1994-95 NHL lockout. ... Suffered from the flu (March 1, 1995); missed one game. ... Nordiques franchise moved to Colorado and renamed Avalanche for 1995-96 season (June 21, 1995). ... Bruised thigh (December 14, 1996); missed 17 games. ... Bruised shoulder (November 8, 1997); missed three games. ... Pulled groin (March 26, 1998); missed seven games. ... Suffered concussion (May 7, 1998); missed two playoff games. ... Suffered charley horse (May 22, 1998); missed one playoff game.

HONORS: Named to Swedish League All-Star team (1991-92). ... Named Swedish League Player of the Year (1993-94). ... Named NHL Rookie of the Year by THE SPORTING NEWS (1994-95). ... Won Calder Memorial Trophy (1994-95). ... Named to NHL All-Rookie team (1994-95). ... Played in NHL All-Star Game (1996 and 1998). ... Named to play in NHL All-Star Game (1997); replaced by LW Brendan Shanahan due to injury. ... Named to THE SPORTING NEWS All-Star team (1997-98). ... Named to NHL All-Star first team (1997-98).

MISCELLANEOUS: Member of Stanley Cup championship team (1996). ... Member of gold-medal-winning Swedish Olympic team (1994). ... Failed to score on a penalty shot (vs. Tim Cheveldae, February 1, 1996; vs. Grant Fuhr, December 6, 1996).

STATISTICAL PLATEAUS: Three-goal games: 1995-96 (2), 1996-97 (1). Total: 3.

Season Team	League	REGULAR SEASON								PLAYOFFS				
		Gms.	G	A	Pts.	PIM	+/-	PP	SH	Gms.	G	A	Pts.	PIM
89-90—MoDo Hockey Jrs.	Sweden Jr.	30	15	12	27	42	...	...	...	—	—	—	—	—
90-91—MoDo Ornskoldvik......	Sweden	23	7	10	17	22	...	...	...	—	—	—	—	—
91-92—MoDo Ornskoldvik......	Sweden	39	9	19	28	78	...	...	...	—	—	—	—	—
92-93—MoDo Ornskoldvik......	Sweden	39	23	24	47	92	...	...	...	3	4	1	5	...
93-94—MoDo Ornskoldvik......	Sweden	39	18	26	44	82	...	...	...	11	9	7	16	14
—Swedish Oly. team......	Int'l	8	2	6	8	6	...	...	...	—	—	—	—	—
94-95—MoDo Ornskoldvik......	Sweden	11	5	9	14	20	...	...	...	—	—	—	—	—
—Quebec	NHL	47	15	35	50	16	17	3	0	6	2	4	6	4
95-96—Colorado	NHL	82	30	86	116	47	26	7	3	22	10	11	21	18
96-97—Colorado	NHL	65	28	58	86	73	31	5	4	14	5	12	17	10
97-98—Colorado	NHL	72	25	66	91	94	6	7	3	7	6	5	11	12
—Swedish Oly. team......	Int'l	4	1	4	5	6	...	...	...	—	—	—	—	—
NHL Totals (4 years)...........		266	98	245	343	230	80	22	10	49	23	32	55	44

FORTIN, JEAN-FRANCOIS　　　D　　　CAPITALS

PERSONAL: Born March 15, 1979, in Laval, Que. ... 6-2/190. ... Shoots right.

TRANSACTIONS/CAREER NOTES: Selected by Washington Capitals in second round (second Capitals pick, 35th overall) of NHL entry draft (June 21, 1997).

Season Team	League	REGULAR SEASON								PLAYOFFS				
		Gms.	G	A	Pts.	PIM	+/-	PP	SH	Gms.	G	A	Pts.	PIM
95-96—Sherbrooke	QMJHL	69	7	15	22	40	...	...	...	7	2	6	8	2
96-97—Sherbrooke	QMJHL	59	7	30	37	89	...	...	...	2	0	1	1	14
97-98—Sherbrooke	QMJHL	55	12	25	37	37	...	...	...					

FOUNTAIN, MIKE　　　G　　　HURRICANES

PERSONAL: Born January 26, 1972, in Gravenhurst, Ont. ... 6-1/176. ... Catches left. ... Full name: Michael Fountain. ... Name pronounced FOWN-tihn.

COLLEGE: Trent (Ont.).

TRANSACTIONS/CAREER NOTES: Selected by Vancouver Canucks in second round (third Canucks pick, 45th overall) of NHL entry draft (June 20, 1992). ... Signed as free agent by Carolina Hurricanes (August 14, 1997).

HONORS: Named to Can.HL All-Star second team (1991-92). ... Named to OHL All-Star first team (1991-92). ... Named to AHL All-Star second team (1993-94).

Season Team	League	REGULAR SEASON							PLAYOFFS					
		Gms.	Min	W	L	T	GA	SO	Avg.	Gms.	Min.	W	L	GA	SO	Avg.
88-89—Huntsville Jr. C	OHA	22	1306	...	...	...	82	0	3.77	—	—	—	—	—	—	—
89-90—Chatham Jr. B	OHA	21	1249	...	...	...	76	0	3.65	—	—	—	—	—	—	—
90-91—Sault Ste. Marie	OHL	7	380	5	2	0	19	0	3.00	—	—	—	—	—	—	—
—Oshawa	OHL	30	1483	17	5	1	84	0	3.40	8	292	1	4	26	0	5.34
91-92—Oshawa	OHL	40	2260	18	13	6	149	1	3.96	7	428	3	4	26	0	3.64
92-93—Canadian nat'l team	Int'l	13	...	7	5	1	37	1	...	—	—	—	—	—	—	—
—Hamilton	AHL	12	618	2	8	0	46	0	4.47	—	—	—	—	—	—	—
93-94—Hamilton	AHL	70	*4005	*34	28	6	241	*4	3.61	3	146	0	2	12	0	4.93
94-95—Syracuse	AHL	61	*3618	25	*29	7	225	2	3.73	—	—	—	—	—	—	—
95-96—Syracuse	AHL	54	3060	21	27	3	184	1	3.61	15	915	8	*7	57	†2	3.74
96-97—Vancouver	NHL	6	245	2	2	0	14	1	3.43	—	—	—	—	—	—	—
—Syracuse........................	AHL	25	1462	8	14	2	78	1	3.20	2	120	0	2	12	0	6.00
97-98—New Haven	AHL	50	2923	25	19	5	139	3	2.85	—	—	—	—	—	—	—
—Carolina........................	NHL	3	163	0	3	0	10	0	3.68	—	—	—	—	—	—	—
NHL Totals (2 years).............		9	408	2	5	0	24	1	3.53							

FRANCIS, RON　　　C　　　HURRICANES

PERSONAL: Born March 1, 1963, in Sault Ste. Marie, Ont. ... 6-3/200. ... Shoots left. ... Full name: Ronald Francis. ... Cousin of Mike Liut, goaltender with three NHL teams (1979-80 through 1991-92) and Cincinnati Stingers of WHA (1977-78 and 1978-79).

TRANSACTIONS/CAREER NOTES: Selected by Hartford Whalers as underage junior in first round (first Whalers pick, fourth overall) of NHL entry draft (June 10, 1981). ... Injured eye (January 27, 1982); missed three weeks. ... Strained ligaments in right knee (November 30, 1983). ... Broke left ankle (January 18, 1986); missed 27 games. ... Broke left index finger (January 28, 1989); missed 11 games. ... Broke nose (November 24, 1990). ... Traded by Whalers with D Ulf Samuelsson and D Grant Jennings to Pittsburgh Penguins for C John Cullen, D Zarley Zalapski and RW Jeff Parker (March 4, 1991). ... Suffered from the flu (February 19, 1995); missed one game. ... Suffered back spasms (February 21, 1995); missed three games. ... Strained hip flexor (January 5, 1996); missed two games. ... Suspended two games and fined

F

$1000 by NHL for checking player from behind (February 27, 1996). ... Broke left foot (May 11, 1996); missed remainder of playoffs. ... Injured groin (February 22, 1997); missed one game. ... Pulled hamstring (April 16, 1998); missed one game. ... Signed as free agent by Carolina Hurricanes (July 13, 1998).
HONORS: Played in NHL All-Star Game (1983, 1985, 1990 and 1996). ... Won Lady Byng Memorial Trophy (1994-95 and 1997-98). ... Won Frank J. Selke Trophy (1994-95). ... Won NHL Alka-Seltzer Plus award (1994-95).
MISCELLANEOUS: Member of Stanley Cup championship team (1991 and 1992). ... Captain of Hartford Whalers (1984-85 through 1990-1991). ... Captain of Pittsburgh Penguins (1994-95, 1995-96 and 1997-98). ... Holds Carolina Hurricanes franchise all-time records for most games played (714), most goals (264), most assists (557) and most points (821).. ... Scored on a penalty shot (vs. Richard Sevigny, January 17, 1986).
STATISTICAL PLATEAUS: Three-goal games: 1982-83 (1), 1984-85 (1), 1985-86 (2), 1987-88 (1), 1988-89 (1), 1989-90 (1), 1990-91 (1), 1995-96 (1), 1997-98 (1). Total: 10. ... Four-goal games: 1983-84 (1). ... Total hat tricks: 11.

		REGULAR SEASON								PLAYOFFS				
Season Team	League	Gms.	G	A	Pts.	PIM	+/-	PP	SH	Gms.	G	A	Pts.	PIM
80-81—Sault Ste. Marie	OMJHL	64	26	43	69	33	...	...	...	19	7	8	15	34
81-82—Sault Ste. Marie	OHL	25	18	30	48	46	...	...	...	—	—	—	—	—
—Hartford	NHL	59	25	43	68	51	-13	12	0	—	—	—	—	—
82-83—Hartford	NHL	79	31	59	90	60	-25	4	2	—	—	—	—	—
83-84—Hartford	NHL	72	23	60	83	45	-10	5	0	—	—	—	—	—
84-85—Hartford	NHL	80	24	57	81	66	-23	4	0	—	—	—	—	—
85-86—Hartford	NHL	53	24	53	77	24	8	7	1	10	1	2	3	4
86-87—Hartford	NHL	75	30	63	93	45	10	7	0	6	2	2	4	6
87-88—Hartford	NHL	80	25	50	75	87	-8	11	1	6	2	5	7	2
88-89—Hartford	NHL	69	29	48	77	36	4	8	0	4	0	2	2	0
89-90—Hartford	NHL	80	32	69	101	73	13	15	1	7	3	3	6	8
90-91—Hartford	NHL	67	21	55	76	51	-2	10	1	—	—	—	—	—
—Pittsburgh	NHL	14	2	9	11	21	0	0	0	24	7	10	17	24
91-92—Pittsburgh	NHL	70	21	33	54	30	-7	5	1	21	8	*19	27	6
92-93—Pittsburgh	NHL	84	24	76	100	68	6	9	2	12	6	11	17	19
93-94—Pittsburgh	NHL	82	27	66	93	62	-3	8	0	6	0	2	2	6
94-95—Pittsburgh	NHL	44	11	*48	59	18	*30	3	0	12	6	13	19	4
95-96—Pittsburgh	NHL	77	27	92	119	56	25	12	1	11	3	6	9	4
96-97—Pittsburgh	NHL	81	27	63	90	20	7	10	1	5	1	2	3	2
97-98—Pittsburgh	NHL	81	25	62	87	20	12	7	0	6	1	5	6	2
NHL Totals (17 years)		1247	428	1006	1434	833	24	137	11	130	40	82	122	87

FRANEK, PETR   G   AVALANCHE

PERSONAL: Born April 6, 1975, in Most, Czechoslovakia. ... 5-11/187. ... Catches left. ... Name pronounced FRAN-ihk.
TRANSACTIONS/CAREER NOTES: Selected by Quebec Nordiques in eighth round (10th Nordiques pick, 205th overall) of NHL entry draft (June 29, 1993). ... Nordiques franchise moved to Colorado and renamed Avalanche for 1995-96 season (June 21, 1995).

		REGULAR SEASON								PLAYOFFS						
Season Team	League	Gms.	Min	W	L	T	GA	SO	Avg.	Gms.	Min.	W	L	GA	SO	Avg.
92-93—Litvinov	Czech.	5	273	...	...	...	15	...	3.30	—	—	—	—	—	—	—
93-94—Litvinov	Czech Rep.	11	535	...	...	...	34	...	3.81	2	61	...	...	10	...	9.84
94-95—Litvinov	Czech Rep.	12	657	...	...	...	47	...	4.29	1	16	...	...	0	...	—
95-96—Litvinov	Czech Rep.	36	2089	...	...	...	94	3	2.70	16	948	...	...	47	...	2.97
96-97—Hershey	AHL	15	457	4	1	0	23	3	3.02	—	—	—	—	—	—	—
—Brantford	Col.HL	6	321	4	1	0	14	0	2.62	—	—	—	—	—	—	—
—Quebec	IHL	6	357	3	3	‡0	18	0	3.03	1	40	0	1	4	0	6.00
97-98—Hershey	AHL	43	2169	19	14	2	98	2	2.71	1	60	0	1	4	0	4.00

FRASER, SCOTT   C   RANGERS

F

PERSONAL: Born May 3, 1972, in Moncton, New Brunswick. ... 6-1/178. ... Shoots right.
COLLEGE: Dartmouth.
TRANSACTIONS/CAREER NOTES: Selected by Montreal Canadiens in ninth round (12th Canadiens pick, 193rd overall) of NHL entry draft (June 22, 1991). ... Traded by Canadiens to Calgary Flames for RW David Ling and sixth-round pick (LW Gordie Dwyer) in 1998 draft (October 24, 1996). ... Signed as a free agent by Edmonton Oilers (July 23, 1997). ... Signed as free agent by New York Rangers (July 2, 1998).
HONORS: Named to ECAC All-Star second team (1992-93).

		REGULAR SEASON								PLAYOFFS				
Season Team	League	Gms.	G	A	Pts.	PIM	+/-	PP	SH	Gms.	G	A	Pts.	PIM
90-91—Dartmouth College	ECAC	24	10	10	20	30	...	...	...	—	—	—	—	—
91-92—Dartmouth College	ECAC	24	11	7	18	60	...	...	...	—	—	—	—	—
92-93—Canadian nat'l team	Int'l	5	1	0	1	0	...	...	...	—	—	—	—	—
—Dartmouth College	ECAC	26	21	23	44	13	...	...	...	—	—	—	—	—
93-94—Dartmouth College	ECAC	24	17	13	30	34	...	...	...	—	—	—	—	—
—Canadian nat'l team	Int'l	4	0	1	1	4	...	...	...	—	—	—	—	—
94-95—Wheeling	ECHL	8	4	2	6	8	...	...	...	—	—	—	—	—
—Fredericton	AHL	65	23	25	48	36	...	...	...	16	3	5	8	14
95-96—Fredericton	AHL	58	37	37	74	43	...	...	...	10	9	7	16	2
—Montreal	NHL	14	2	0	2	4	-1	0	0	—	—	—	—	—
96-97—Saint John	AHL	37	22	10	32	24	...	...	...	—	—	—	—	—
—Fredericton	AHL	7	3	8	11	0	...	...	...	—	—	—	—	—
—San Antonio	IHL	8	0	1	1	2	...	...	...	—	—	—	—	—
—Carolina	AHL	18	9	19	28	12	...	...	...	—	—	—	—	—
97-98—Hamilton	AHL	50	29	32	61	26	...	...	...	—	—	—	—	—
—Edmonton	NHL	29	12	11	23	6	6	6	0	11	1	1	2	0
NHL Totals (2 years)		43	14	11	25	10	5	6	0	11	1	1	2	0

FREADRICH, KYLE — LW — CANUCKS

PERSONAL: Born December 28, 1978, in Edmonton. ... 6-6/225. ... Shoots left. ... Name pronounced FREED-rihk.
TRANSACTIONS/CAREER NOTES: Selected by Vancouver Canucks in third round (fourth Canucks pick, 64th overall) of NHL entry draft (June 21, 1997).

Season Team	League	Gms.	G	A	Pts.	PIM	+/-	PP	SH	Gms.	G	A	Pts.	PIM
96-97—Prince George	WHL	12	0	0	0	12	...	...	...	—	—	—	—	—
—Regina	WHL	50	1	3	4	152	...	...	...	4	0	0	0	8
97-98—Regina	WHL	62	6	5	11	259	...	...	...	9	0	1	1	25

The header above the columns reads REGULAR SEASON (Gms. G A Pts. PIM +/- PP SH) and PLAYOFFS (Gms. G A Pts. PIM).

FRIEDMAN, DOUG — LW — PREDATORS

PERSONAL: Born September 1, 1971, in Cape Elizabeth, Me. ... 6-1/189. ... Shoots left.
HIGH SCHOOL: Lawrence Academy (Groton, Mass.).
COLLEGE: Boston University.
TRANSACTIONS/CAREER NOTES: Selected by Quebec Nordiques in 11th round (11th Nordiques pick, 222nd overall) of NHL entry draft (June 22, 1991). ... Nordiques franchise moved to Colorado and renamed Avalanche for 1995-96 season (June 21, 1995). ... Signed as free agent by Edmonton Oilers (July 3, 1997). ... Selected by Nashville Predators in NHL expansion draft (June 26, 1998).

Season Team	League	Gms.	G	A	Pts.	PIM	+/-	PP	SH	Gms.	G	A	Pts.	PIM
89-90—Lawrence Academy	Mass. H.S.	20	9	26	35	...	...	...	...	—	—	—	—	—
90-91—Boston University	Hockey East	36	6	6	12	37	...	...	...	—	—	—	—	—
91-92—Boston University	Hockey East	34	11	8	19	42	...	...	...	—	—	—	—	—
92-93—Boston University	Hockey East	38	17	24	41	62	...	...	...	—	—	—	—	—
93-94—Boston University	Hockey East	41	9	23	32	110	...	...	...	—	—	—	—	—
94-95—Cornwall	AHL	55	6	9	15	56	...	...	...	3	0	0	0	0
95-96—Cornwall	AHL	80	12	22	34	178	...	...	...	8	1	1	2	17
96-97—Hershey	AHL	61	12	21	33	245	...	...	...	23	6	9	15	49
97-98—Hamilton	AHL	55	19	27	46	235	...	...	...	9	4	4	8	40
—Edmonton	NHL	16	0	0	0	20	0	0	0	—	—	—	—	—
NHL Totals (1 year)		16	0	0	0	20	0	0	0					

FRIESEN, JEFF — LW — SHARKS

PERSONAL: Born August 5, 1976, in Meadow Lake, Sask. ... 6-1/200. ... Shoots left. ... Name pronounced FREE-sihn.
HIGH SCHOOL: Robert Usher (Regina, Sask.).
TRANSACTIONS/CAREER NOTES: Selected by San Jose Sharks in first round (first Sharks pick, 11th overall) of NHL entry draft (June 28, 1994). ... Injured hand (October 18, 1996); missed two games. ... Missed first three games of 1997-98 season due to contract holdout.
HONORS: Won Can.HL Rookie of the Year Award (1992-93). ... Won Jim Piggott Memorial Trophy (1992-93). ... Named to NHL All-Rookie team (1994-95).
MISCELLANEOUS: Scored on a penalty shot (vs. Jim Carey, December 2, 1995). ... Holds San Jose Sharks all-time records for most goals (89), most assists (107) and most points (196).
STATISTICAL PLATEAUS: Three-goal games: 1995-96 (1).

Season Team	League	Gms.	G	A	Pts.	PIM	+/-	PP	SH	Gms.	G	A	Pts.	PIM
91-92—Regina	WHL	4	3	1	4	2	...	...	...	—	—	—	—	—
92-93—Regina	WHL	70	45	38	83	23	...	...	...	13	7	10	17	8
93-94—Regina	WHL	66	51	67	118	48	...	...	...	4	3	2	5	2
94-95—Regina	WHL	25	21	23	44	22	...	...	...	—	—	—	—	—
—San Jose	NHL	48	15	10	25	14	-8	5	1	11	1	5	6	4
95-96—San Jose	NHL	79	15	31	46	42	-19	2	0	—	—	—	—	—
96-97—San Jose	NHL	82	28	34	62	75	-8	6	2	—	—	—	—	—
97-98—San Jose	NHL	79	31	32	63	40	8	7	†6	6	0	1	1	2
NHL Totals (4 years)		288	89	107	196	171	-27	20	9	17	1	6	7	6

FRIESEN, TERRY — G — SHARKS

PERSONAL: Born October 29, 1977, in Winkler, Man. ... 5-11/186. ... Catches left. ... Name pronounced FREE-sihn.
TRANSACTIONS/CAREER NOTES: Selected by San Jose Sharks in third round (third Sharks pick, 55th overall) of NHL entry draft (June 22, 1996).
HONORS: Named to WHL (Central/East) All-Star second team (1995-96). ... Named to WHL (East) All-Star first team (1997-98).

Season Team	League	Gms.	Min	W	L	T	GA	SO	Avg.	Gms.	Min.	W	L	GA	SO	Avg.
94-95—Winkler	MJHL	24	1164	...	...	...	72	1	3.71	—	—	—	—	—	—	—
95-96—Swift Current	WHL	42	2504	19	17	3	155	2	3.71	6	338	2	4	21	0	3.73
96-97—Swift Current	WHL	53	3090	28	19	3	170	1	3.30	10	592	6	4	27	0	2.74
97-98—Swift Current	WHL	44	2639	26	10	*7	124	1	2.82	12	754	7	5	28	1	*2.23

FUHR, GRANT — G — BLUES

PERSONAL: Born September 28, 1962, in Spruce Grove, Alta. ... 5-10/200. ... Catches right. ... Name pronounced FYOOR.
TRANSACTIONS/CAREER NOTES: Selected by Edmonton Oilers in first round (first Oilers pick, eighth overall) of NHL entry draft (June 10, 1981). ... Suffered partial separation of right shoulder (December 1981). ... Strained left knee ligaments and underwent surgery (December

13, 1983). ... Separated shoulder (February 1985). ... Bruised left shoulder (November 3, 1985); missed 10 games. ... Bruised left shoulder (November 1987). ... Injured right knee (November 1987). ... Suffered cervical neck strain (January 18, 1989). ... Underwent appendectomy (September 14, 1989); missed first six games of season. ... Underwent reconstructive surgery to left shoulder (December 27, 1989). ... Tore adhesions in left shoulder (March 13, 1990). ... Suspended six months by NHL for admitting to using drugs earlier in career (September 27, 1990). ... Traded by Oilers with RW/LW Glenn Anderson and LW Craig Berube to Toronto Maple Leafs for LW Vincent Damphousse, D Luke Richardson, G Peter Ing, C Scott Thornton and future considerations (September 19, 1991). ... Sprained thumb (October 17, 1991); missed two games. ... Pulled groin (November 12, 1991); missed three games. ... Sprained knee (February 11, 1992); missed four games. ... Sprained knee (October 20, 1992); missed 10 games. ... Strained shoulder (December 5, 1992); missed three games. ... Bruised shoulder muscle (January 17, 1993); missed four games. ... Traded by Maple Leafs with fifth-round pick (D Kevin Popp) in 1995 draft to Buffalo Sabres for LW Dave Andreychuk, G Daren Puppa and first-round pick (D Kenny Jonsson) in 1993 draft (February 2, 1993). ... Injured knee (November 24, 1993); missed 24 games. ... Traded by Sabres with D Philippe Boucher and D Denis Tsygurov to Los Angeles Kings for D Alexei Zhitnik, D Charlie Huddy, G Robb Stauber and fifth-round pick (D Marian Menhart) in 1995 draft (February 14, 1995). ... Signed as free agent by St. Louis Blues (July 11, 1995). ... Injured knee (March 31, 1996); missed three games. ... Underwent knee surgery due to injury suffered in playoffs (April 27, 1996); missed remainder of playoffs. ... Suffered sore arm (November 6, 1997); missed two games. ... Strained ligament and tore cartilage in right knee (February 26, 1998); missed eight games. ... Bruised knee (April 12, 1998); missed one game.

HONORS: Won Stewart (Butch) Paul Memorial Trophy (1979-80). ... Named to WHL All-Star first team (1979-80 and 1980-81). ... Won WHL Top Goaltender Trophy (1980-81). ... Named to THE SPORTING NEWS All-Star second team (1981-82 and 1985-86). ... Named to NHL All-Star second team (1981-82). ... Played in NHL All-Star Game (1982, 1984-1986, 1988 and 1989). ... Named All-Star Game Most Valuable Player (1986). ... Won Vezina Trophy (1987-88). ... Named to THE SPORTING NEWS All-Star first team (1987-88). ... Named to NHL All-Star first team (1987-88). ... Shared William M. Jennings Trophy with Dominik Hasek (1993-94).

RECORDS: Holds NHL single-season records for most points by a goaltender—14 (1983-84); most games by a goaltender—79 (1995-96); and most consecutive appearances—76 (1995-96). ... Shares NHL single-season playoff record for most wins by a goaltender—16 (1987-88).

MISCELLANEOUS: Member of Stanley Cup championship team (1984, 1985, 1987, 1988 and 1990). ... Scored goal against team (vs. Ron Duguay, January 9, 1984; vs. Brent Peterson, January 13, 1984; vs. Ron Sutter, May 28, 1985 (playoffs); vs. Dave Poulin, May 30, 1985 (playoffs); vs. Brendan Shanahan, December 27, 1992; vs. Dave Hannan, October 22, 1995; vs. Peter Forsberg, December 6, 1996). ... Allowed penalty shot goal (vs. Steve Yzerman, January 3, 1992; vs. Alexei Gusarov, March 10, 1993).

			REGULAR SEASON							PLAYOFFS						
Season Team	League	Gms.	Min	W	L	T	GA	SO	Avg.	Gms.	Min.	W	L	GA	SO	Avg.
79-80—Victoria	WHL	43	2488	30	12	0	130	2	3.14	8	465	5	3	22	0	2.84
80-81—Victoria	WHL	59	*3448	48	9	1	160	†4	*2.78	15	899	12	3	45	1	3.00
81-82—Edmonton	NHL	48	2847	28	5	14	157	0	3.31	5	309	2	3	26	0	5.05
82-83—Moncton	AHL	10	604	4	5	1	40	0	3.97	—	—	—	—	—	—	...
—Edmonton	NHL	32	1803	13	12	5	129	0	4.29	1	11	0	0	0	0	...
83-84—Edmonton	NHL	45	2625	30	10	4	171	1	3.91	16	883	11	4	44	1	2.99
84-85—Edmonton	NHL	46	2559	26	8	7	165	1	3.87	†18	*1064	*15	3	55	0	3.10
85-86—Edmonton	NHL	40	2184	29	8	0	143	0	3.93	9	541	5	4	28	0	3.11
86-87—Edmonton	NHL	44	2388	22	13	3	137	0	3.44	19	1148	14	5	47	0	2.46
87-88—Edmonton	NHL	*75	*4304	40	24	9	*246	†4	3.43	*19	*1136	*16	2	55	0	2.90
88-89—Edmonton	NHL	59	3341	23	26	6	213	1	3.83	7	417	3	4	24	1	3.45
89-90—Cape Breton	AHL	2	120	2	0	0	6	0	3.00	—	—	—	—	—	—	—
—Edmonton	NHL	21	1081	9	7	3	70	1	3.89	—	—	—	—	—	—	—
90-91—Cape Breton	AHL	4	240	2	2	0	17	0	4.25	—	—	—	—	—	—	—
—Edmonton	NHL	13	778	6	4	3	39	1	3.01	17	1019	8	7	51	0	3.00
91-92—Toronto	NHL	66	3774	25	*33	5	*230	2	3.66	—	—	—	—	—	—	—
92-93—Toronto	NHL	29	1665	13	9	4	87	1	3.14	—	—	—	—	—	—	—
—Buffalo	NHL	29	1694	11	15	2	98	0	3.47	8	474	3	4	27	1	3.42
93-94—Buffalo	NHL	32	1726	13	12	3	106	2	3.68	—	—	—	—	—	—	—
—Rochester	AHL	5	310	3	0	2	10	0	1.94	—	—	—	—	—	—	—
94-95—Buffalo	NHL	3	180	1	2	0	12	0	4.00	—	—	—	—	—	—	—
—Los Angeles	NHL	14	698	1	7	3	47	0	4.04	—	—	—	—	—	—	—
95-96—St. Louis	NHL	*79	4365	30	28	*16	*209	3	2.87	2	69	1	0	1	0	.87
96-97—St. Louis	NHL	73	4261	33	27	11	193	3	2.72	6	357	2	4	13	2	2.18
97-98—St. Louis	NHL	58	3274	29	21	6	138	3	2.53	10	616	6	4	28	0	2.73
NHL Totals (17 years)		806	45547	382	271	104	2590	23	3.41	137	8044	86	44	399	5	2.98

GAFFANEY, BRIAN   D   PENGUINS

PERSONAL: Born October 4, 1977, in Alexandria, Minn. ... 6-5/205. ... Shoots left.
COLLEGE: St. Cloud (Minn.) State.
TRANSACTIONS/CAREER NOTES: Selected by Pittsburgh Penguins in second round (second Penguins pick, 44th overall) of NHL entry draft (June 21, 1997).

		REGULAR SEASON							PLAYOFFS				
Season Team	League	Gms.	G	A	Pts.	PIM	+/-	PP	SH	Gms.	G	A	Pts.	PIM
96-97—North Iowa	USHL	48	8	13	21	49	...	...	...	—	—	—	—	—
97-98—St. Cloud State	WCHA	26	0	2	2	37	...	...	...	—	—	—	—	—

F

GAGNER, DAVE   C   PANTHERS   **G**

PERSONAL: Born December 11, 1964, in Chatham, Ont. ... 5-10/180. ... Shoots left. ... Name pronounced GAHN-yay.
TRANSACTIONS/CAREER NOTES: Selected by New York Rangers as underage junior in first round (first Rangers pick, 12th overall) of NHL entry draft (June 8, 1983). ... Fractured ankle (February 5, 1986). ... Underwent emergency appendectomy (December 1986). ... Traded by Rangers with RW Jay Caufield to Minnesota North Stars for D Jari Gronstrand and D Paul Boutilier (October 8, 1987). ... Broke kneecap (March 31, 1989). ... Underwent surgery to left knee cartilage (November 11, 1990). ... Underwent arthroscopic knee surgery (December 18, 1991); missed one game. ... Hyperextended knee (March 17, 1992); missed one game. ... North Stars franchise moved from Minnesota to Dallas and renamed Stars for 1993-94 season. ... Separated shoulder (November 1, 1993); missed seven games. ... Played in Europe during 1994-95 NHL lockout. ... Traded by Stars to Toronto Maple Leafs for LW Benoit Hogue and LW Randy Wood (January 28, 1996). ... Sprained shoulder (February 28, 1996); missed three games. ... Suffered concussion (March 30, 1996); missed three games. ... Traded by Maple Leafs to Calgary Flames for third-round pick (D Mike Lankshear) in 1996 draft (June 22, 1996). ... Signed as free agent by Florida Panthers (July 4, 1997). ... Strained abdomen (January 7, 1998); missed four games.

HONORS: Won Bobby Smith Trophy (1982-83). ... Named to OHL All-Star second team (1982-83). ... Played in NHL All-Star Game (1991).
RECORDS: Shares NHL single-game playoff record for most points in one period—4 (April 8, 1991, first period).
STATISTICAL PLATEAUS: Three-goal games: 1988-89 (2), 1990-91 (1), 1997-98 (1). Total: 4. ... Four-goal games: 1993-94 (1). ... Total hat tricks: 5.
MISCELLANEOUS: Failed to score on a penalty shot (vs. Bill Ranford, October 28, 1992; vs. Chris Osgood, April 1, 1995).

Season Team	League	REGULAR SEASON								PLAYOFFS				
		Gms.	G	A	Pts.	PIM	+/-	PP	SH	Gms.	G	A	Pts.	PIM
81-82—Brantford	OHL	68	30	46	76	31	...	...	...	11	3	6	9	6
82-83—Brantford	OHL	70	55	66	121	57	...	...	...	8	5	5	10	4
83-84—Can. Olympic Team	Int'l	50	19	18	37	26	...	...	...	—	—	—	—	—
—Brantford	OHL	12	7	13	20	4	...	...	...	6	0	4	4	6
84-85—New Haven	AHL	38	13	20	33	23	...	...	...	—	—	—	—	—
—New York Rangers	NHL	38	6	6	12	16	-16	0	1	—	—	—	—	—
85-86—New York Rangers	NHL	32	4	6	10	19	1	0	0	—	—	—	—	—
—New Haven	AHL	16	10	11	21	11	...	...	...	4	1	2	3	2
86-87—New York Rangers	NHL	10	1	4	5	12	-1	0	0	—	—	—	—	—
—New Haven	AHL	56	22	41	63	50	...	...	...	7	1	5	6	18
87-88—Kalamazoo	IHL	14	16	10	26	26	...	...	...	—	—	—	—	—
—Minnesota	NHL	51	8	11	19	55	-14	0	2	—	—	—	—	—
88-89—Minnesota	NHL	75	35	43	78	104	13	11	3	—	—	—	—	—
—Kalamazoo	IHL	1	0	1	1	4	...	...	...	—	—	—	—	—
89-90—Minnesota	NHL	79	40	38	78	54	-1	10	0	7	2	3	5	16
90-91—Minnesota	NHL	73	40	42	82	114	9	20	0	23	12	15	27	28
91-92—Minnesota	NHL	78	31	40	71	107	-4	17	0	7	2	4	6	8
92-93—Minnesota	NHL	84	33	43	76	143	-13	17	0	—	—	—	—	—
93-94—Dallas	NHL	76	32	29	61	83	13	10	0	9	5	1	6	2
94-95—Courmaosta	Italy	1	0	4	4	0	...	...	...	—	—	—	—	—
—Dallas	NHL	48	14	28	42	42	2	7	0	5	1	1	2	4
95-96—Dallas	NHL	45	14	13	27	44	-17	6	0	—	—	—	—	—
96-97—Calgary	NHL	82	27	33	60	48	2	9	0	—	—	—	—	—
—Toronto	NHL	28	7	15	22	59	-2	1	0	6	0	2	2	6
97-98—Florida	NHL	78	20	28	48	55	-21	5	1	—	—	—	—	—
NHL Totals (14 years)		877	312	379	691	955	-49	113	7	57	22	26	48	64

GAGNON, SEAN — D — COYOTES

PERSONAL: Born September 11, 1973, in Sault Ste. Marie, Ont. ... 6-2/210. ... Shoots left.
TRANSACTIONS/CAREER NOTES: Signed as free agent by Phoenix Coyotes (May 14, 1997). ... Bruised thigh (December 20, 1997); missed 11 games.

Season Team	League	REGULAR SEASON								PLAYOFFS				
		Gms.	G	A	Pts.	PIM	+/-	PP	SH	Gms.	G	A	Pts.	PIM
91-92—Sudbury	OHL	44	3	4	7	60	...	...	...	5	0	1	1	0
92-93—Sudbury	OHL	6	1	1	2	2	...	...	...	—	—	—	—	—
—Ottawa	OHL	33	2	10	12	68	...	...	...	—	—	—	—	—
—Sault Ste. Marie	OMJHL	24	1	5	6	65	...	...	...	15	2	2	4	25
93-94—Sault Ste. Marie	OMJHL	42	4	12	16	147	...	...	...	14	1	1	2	52
94-95—Dayton	ECHL	68	9	23	32	339	...	...	...	8	0	3	3	69
95-96—Dayton	ECHL	68	7	22	29	326	...	...	...	3	0	1	1	33
96-97—Fort Wayne	IHL	72	7	7	14	457	...	...	...	—	—	—	—	—
97-98—Springfield	AHL	54	4	13	17	330	...	...	...	2	0	1	1	17
—Phoenix	NHL	5	0	1	1	14	1	0	0	—	—	—	—	—
NHL Totals (1 year)		5	0	1	1	14	1	0	0					

GAINEY, STEVE — C — STARS

PERSONAL: Born January 26, 1979, in Montreal. ... 6-0/180. ... Shoots left. ... Son of Bob Gainey, general manager, Dallas Stars.
TRANSACTIONS/CAREER NOTES: Selected by Dallas Stars in third round (third Stars pick, 77th overall) of NHL entry draft (June 21, 1997).

Season Team	League	REGULAR SEASON								PLAYOFFS				
		Gms.	G	A	Pts.	PIM	+/-	PP	SH	Gms.	G	A	Pts.	PIM
95-96—Kamloops	WHL	49	1	4	5	40	...	...	...	3	0	0	0	0
96-97—Kamloops	WHL	60	9	18	27	60	...	...	...	2	0	0	0	9
97-98—Kamloops	WHL	68	21	34	55	93	...	...	...	7	1	7	8	15

G

GALANOV, MAXIM — D — RANGERS

PERSONAL: Born March 13, 1974, in Krasnoyarsk, U.S.S.R. ... 6-1/200. ... Shoots left. ... Name pronounced guh-LAH-nahf.
TRANSACTIONS/CAREER NOTES: Selected by New York Rangers in third round (third Rangers pick, 61st overall) of NHL entry draft (June 26, 1993).

Season Team	League	REGULAR SEASON								PLAYOFFS				
		Gms.	G	A	Pts.	PIM	+/-	PP	SH	Gms.	G	A	Pts.	PIM
92-93—Lada Togliatti	CIS	41	4	2	6	12	...	...	...	10	1	1	2	12
93-94—Lada Togliatti	CIS	7	1	0	1	4	...	...	...	12	1	0	1	8
94-95—Lada Togliatti	CIS	45	5	6	11	54	...	...	...	9	0	1	1	12
95-96—Binghamton	AHL	72	17	36	53	24	...	...	...	4	1	1	2	0
96-97—Binghamton	AHL	73	13	30	43	30	...	...	...	3	0	0	0	2
97-98—Hartford	AHL	61	6	24	30	22	...	...	...	13	3	6	9	2
—New York Rangers	NHL	6	0	1	1	2	1	0	0	—	—	—	—	—
NHL Totals (1 year)		6	0	1	1	2	1	0	0					

GALLEY, GARRY   D   KINGS

PERSONAL: Born April 16, 1963, in Ottawa. ... 6-0/204. ... Shoots left.
COLLEGE: Bowling Green State.
TRANSACTIONS/CAREER NOTES: Selected by Los Angeles Kings in fifth round (fourth Kings pick, 100th overall) of NHL entry draft (June 8, 1983). ... Injured knee (December 8, 1985). ... Traded by Kings to Washington Capitals for G Al Jensen (February 14, 1987). ... Signed as free agent by Boston Bruins; third-round pick in 1989 draft awarded to Capitals as compensation (July 8, 1988). ... Sprained left shoulder (September 30, 1989); missed first nine games of season. ... Suffered lacerations to cheek, both lips and part of neck (October 6, 1990). ... Dislocated right shoulder (December 22, 1990). ... Bruised left kneecap (March 23, 1991); missed two games. ... Pulled hamstring (April 17, 1991); missed three playoff games. ... Traded by Bruins with C Wes Walz and future considerations to Philadelphia Flyers for D Gord Murphy, RW Brian Dobbin and third-round pick (LW Sergei Zholtok) in 1992 draft (January 2, 1992). ... Bruised ribs (January 9, 1992); missed one game. ... Fractured foot (March 3, 1992); missed two games. ... Bruised jaw (February 24, 1993); missed one game. ... Strained shoulder (March 6, 1994); missed three games. ... Sprained wrist (February 13, 1995); missed three games. ... Traded by Flyers to Buffalo Sabres for D Petr Svoboda (April 7, 1995). ... Injured shoulder (November 12, 1995); missed three games. ... Injured knee (February 14, 1996); missed one game. ... Strained right shoulder (November 7, 1996); missed four games. ... Suffered concussion (December 4, 1996); missed two games. ... Tore abdominal muscle (February 9, 1997); missed one game. ... Fractured jaw (February 23, 1997); missed two games. ... Signed as free agent by Kings (July 5, 1997). ... Bruised left knee (February 24, 1998); missed three games.
HONORS: Named to CCHA All-Star first team (1982-83 and 1983-84). ... Named to NCAA All-Tournament team (1983-84). ... Played in NHL All-Star Game (1991 and 1994).

			REGULAR SEASON							PLAYOFFS				
Season Team	League	Gms.	G	A	Pts.	PIM	+/-	PP	SH	Gms.	G	A	Pts.	PIM
81-82—Bowling Green	CCHA	42	3	36	39	48	...	...	...	—	—	—	—	—
82-83—Bowling Green	CCHA	40	17	29	46	40	...	...	...	—	—	—	—	—
83-84—Bowling Green	CCHA	44	15	52	67	61	...	...	...	—	—	—	—	—
84-85—Los Angeles	NHL	78	8	30	38	82	3	1	1	3	1	0	1	2
85-86—Los Angeles	NHL	49	9	13	22	46	-9	1	0	—	—	—	—	—
—New Haven	AHL	4	2	6	8	6	...	...	...	—	—	—	—	—
86-87—Los Angeles	NHL	30	5	11	16	57	-9	2	0	—	—	—	—	—
—Washington	NHL	18	1	10	11	10	3	1	0	2	0	0	0	0
87-88—Washington	NHL	58	7	23	30	44	11	3	0	13	2	4	6	13
88-89—Boston	NHL	78	8	21	29	80	-7	2	1	9	0	1	1	33
89-90—Boston	NHL	71	8	27	35	75	2	1	0	21	3	3	6	34
90-91—Boston	NHL	70	6	21	27	84	0	1	0	16	1	5	6	17
91-92—Boston	NHL	38	2	12	14	83	-3	1	0	—	—	—	—	—
—Philadelphia	NHL	39	3	15	18	34	1	2	0	—	—	—	—	—
92-93—Philadelphia	NHL	83	13	49	62	115	18	4	1	—	—	—	—	—
93-94—Philadelphia	NHL	81	10	60	70	91	-11	5	1	—	—	—	—	—
94-95—Philadelphia	NHL	33	2	20	22	20	0	1	0	—	—	—	—	—
—Buffalo	NHL	14	1	9	10	10	4	1	0	5	0	3	3	4
95-96—Buffalo	NHL	78	10	44	54	81	-2	7	1	—	—	—	—	—
96-97—Buffalo	NHL	71	4	34	38	102	10	1	1	12	0	6	6	14
97-98—Los Angeles	NHL	74	9	28	37	63	-5	7	0	4	0	1	1	2
NHL Totals (14 years)		**963**	**106**	**427**	**533**	**1077**	**6**	**41**	**6**	**85**	**7**	**23**	**30**	**119**

GARDINER, BRUCE   RW   SENATORS

PERSONAL: Born February 11, 1971, in Barrie, Ont. ... 6-1/193. ... Shoots right.
COLLEGE: Colgate.
TRANSACTIONS/CAREER NOTES: Selected by St. Louis Blues in sixth round (sixth Blues pick, 131st overall) of NHL entry draft (June 22, 1991). ... Signed as free agent by Ottawa Senators (June 14, 1994). ... Suffered broken leg (September 23, 1995). ... Bruised left foot (November 27, 1996); missed two games. ... Separated left shoulder (February 1, 1997); missed 10 games. ... Bruised thigh (November 6, 1997); missed two games. ... Bruised thigh (November 15, 1997); missed three games. ... Tore medial collateral knee ligament (December 13, 1997); missed 21 games.
HONORS: Named to ECAC All-Star second team (1993-94).

			REGULAR SEASON							PLAYOFFS				
Season Team	League	Gms.	G	A	Pts.	PIM	+/-	PP	SH	Gms.	G	A	Pts.	PIM
90-91—Colgate University	ECAC	27	4	9	13	72	...	...	...	—	—	—	—	—
91-92—Colgate University	ECAC	23	7	8	15	77	...	...	...	—	—	—	—	—
92-93—Colgate University	ECAC	33	17	12	29	64	...	...	...	—	—	—	—	—
93-94—Colgate University	ECAC	33	23	23	46	68	...	...	...	—	—	—	—	—
—Peoria	IHL	3	0	0	0	0	...	...	...	—	—	—	—	—
94-95—Prin. Edward Island	AHL	72	17	20	37	132	...	...	...	7	4	1	5	4
95-96—Prin. Edward Island	AHL	38	11	13	24	87	...	...	...	5	2	4	6	4
96-97—Ottawa	NHL	67	11	10	21	49	4	0	1	7	0	1	1	2
97-98—Ottawa	NHL	55	7	11	18	50	2	0	0	11	1	3	4	2
NHL Totals (2 years)		**122**	**18**	**21**	**39**	**99**	**6**	**0**	**1**	**18**	**1**	**4**	**5**	**4**

G

GARNER, TYRONE   G   FLAMES

PERSONAL: Born July 27, 1978, in Stoney Creek, Ont. ... 6-1/170. ... Catches left.
TRANSACTIONS/CAREER NOTES: Selected by New York Islanders in fourth round (fourth Islanders pick, 83rd overall) of NHL entry draft (June 22, 1996). ... Traded by Islanders with LW Marty McInnis and sixth-round pick (D Ilja Demidov) in 1997 draft to Calgary Flames for C Robert Reichel (March 18, 1997).

			REGULAR SEASON							PLAYOFFS				
Season Team	League	Gms.	Min	W	L	T	GA	SO	Avg.	Gms.	Min.	W	L	GA	SO	Avg.
95-96—Oshawa	OHL	32	1697	11	15	4	112	0	3.96	3	88	1	0	6	0	4.09
96-97—Oshawa	OHL	9	434	6	1	0	20	0	2.76	3	88	1	0	6	0	4.09
97-98—Oshawa	OHL	54	2946	23	17	*8	162	1	3.30	7	450	3	4	25	0	3.33

GARON, MATHIEU   G   CANADIENS

PERSONAL: Born January 9, 1978, in Chandler, Que. ... 6-1/187. ... Catches right.
TRANSACTIONS/CAREER NOTES: Selected by Montreal Canadiens in second round (second Canadiens pick, 44th overall) of NHL entry draft (June 22, 1996).
HONORS: Won Raymond Lagace Trophy (1995-96). ... Named to QMJHL All-Rookie team (1995-96). ... Named to Can.HL All-Star first team (1997-98). ... Won Jacques Plante Trophy (1997-98). ... Named to QMJHL All-Star first team (1997-98). ... Won Can.HL Goaltender of the Year Award (1997-98).

			REGULAR SEASON							PLAYOFFS						
Season Team	League	Gms.	Min	W	L	T	GA	SO	Avg.	Gms.	Min.	W	L	GA	SO	Avg.
95-96—Victoriaville	QMJHL	51	2709	18	27	0	189	1	4.19	12	676	7	4	38	1	3.37
96-97—Victoriaville	QMJHL	53	3026	29	18	3	148	*6	2.93	6	330	2	4	23	0	4.18
97-98—Victoriaville	QMJHL	47	2802	27	18	2	125	5	2.68	6	345	2	4	22	0	3.83

GARPENLOV, JOHAN   LW   PANTHERS

PERSONAL: Born March 21, 1968, in Stockholm, Sweden. ... 5-11/184. ... Shoots left. ... Name pronounced YO-hahn GAHR-pihn-lahf.
TRANSACTIONS/CAREER NOTES: Selected by Detroit Red Wings in fifth round (fifth Red Wings pick, 85th overall) of NHL entry draft (June 9, 1984). ... Traded by Red Wings to San Jose Sharks for D Bob McGill and eighth-round pick (G C.J. Denomme) in 1992 draft (March 10, 1992). ... Strained back (October 20, 1992); missed three games. ... Suffered from the flu (March 25, 1993); missed one game. ... Injured thigh (October 10, 1993); missed one game. ... Sprained groin (January 30, 1995); missed six games. ... Traded by Sharks to Florida Panthers for fifth-round pick (traded back to Florida) in 1998 draft (March 3, 1995). ... Sprained knee ligament (November 18, 1996); missed 13 games. ... Sprained knee ligament (February 22, 1997); missed 16 games. ... Strained groin (December 5, 1997); missed 10 games.
STATISTICAL PLATEAUS: Three-goal games: 1990-91 (1), 1992-93 (1), 1995-96 (1). Total: 3. ... Four-goal games: 1990-91 (1). ... Total hat tricks: 4.

			REGULAR SEASON						PLAYOFFS				
Season Team	League	Gms.	G	A	Pts.	PIM	+/-	PP	SH	Gms.	G	A	Pts.	PIM
86-87—Djur. Stockholm	Sweden	29	5	8	13	20	...	...	...	—	—	—	—	—
87-88—Djur. Stockholm	Sweden	30	7	10	17	12	...	...	...	—	—	—	—	—
88-89—Djur. Stockholm	Sweden	36	12	19	31	20	...	...	...	—	—	—	—	—
89-90—Djur. Stockholm	Sweden	39	20	13	33	36	...	...	...	8	2	4	6	4
90-91—Detroit	NHL	71	18	22	40	18	-4	2	0	6	0	1	1	4
91-92—Detroit	NHL	16	1	1	2	4	2	0	0	—	—	—	—	—
—Adirondack	AHL	9	3	3	6	6	...	...	...	—	—	—	—	—
—San Jose	NHL	12	5	6	11	4	-2	1	0	—	—	—	—	—
92-93—San Jose	NHL	79	22	44	66	56	-26	14	0	—	—	—	—	—
93-94—San Jose	NHL	80	18	35	53	28	9	7	0	14	4	6	10	6
94-95—San Jose	NHL	13	1	1	2	2	-3	0	0	—	—	—	—	—
—Florida	NHL	27	3	9	12	0	4	0	0	—	—	—	—	—
95-96—Florida	NHL	82	23	28	51	36	-10	8	0	20	4	2	6	8
96-97—Florida	NHL	53	11	25	36	47	10	1	0	4	2	0	2	4
97-98—Florida	NHL	39	2	3	5	8	-6	0	0	—	—	—	—	—
NHL Totals (8 years)		472	104	174	278	203	-26	33	0	44	10	9	19	22

GARTNER, MIKE   RW

PERSONAL: Born October 29, 1959, in Ottawa. ... 6-0/190. ... Shoots right. ... Full name: Michael Alfred Gartner.
TRANSACTIONS/CAREER NOTES: Signed as underage junior by Cincinnati Stingers (August 1978). ... Selected by Washington Capitals in first round (first Capitals pick, fourth overall) of NHL entry draft (August 9, 1979). ... Injured eye (February 1983). ... Underwent arthroscopic surgery to repair torn cartilage in left knee (March 1988). ... Sprained right knee (November 1988). ... Traded by Capitals with D Larry Murphy to Minnesota North Stars for RW Dino Ciccarelli and D Bob Rouse (March 7, 1989). ... Underwent surgery to repair cartilage in left knee (April 14, 1989). ... Traded by North Stars to New York Rangers for C Ulf Dahlen, fourth-round pick (C Cal McGowan) in 1990 draft and future considerations (March 6, 1990). ... Underwent arthroscopic surgery to repair elbow (January 27, 1994); missed one game. ... Traded by Rangers to Toronto Maple Leafs for RW Glenn Anderson, rights to D Scott Malone and fourth-round pick (D Alexander Korobolin) in 1994 draft (March 21, 1994). ... Suffered partially collapsed lung (February 3, 1995); missed seven games. ... Suffered hairline fracture in foot (March 17, 1995); missed three games. ... Traded by Maple Leafs to Phoenix Coyotes for fourth-round pick (LW Vladimir Antipov) in 1996 draft (June 22, 1996). ... Tore medial collateral knee ligament (November 2, 1997); missed 15 games.
HONORS: Won Emms Family Award (1976-77). ... Named to OMJHL All-Star first team (1977-78). ... Played in NHL All-Star Game (1980, 1985, 1986, 1988, 1990, 1993 and 1996). ... Named All-Star Game Most Valuable Player (1993).
RECORDS: Holds NHL career record for most consecutive 30-goal seasons—15 (1979-80 through 1993-94); and most 30-or-more goal seasons—17. ... Holds NHL All-Star Game records for fastest two goals from start of game—3:37 (1993); and fastest two goals from start of period—3:37 (1993). ... Shares NHL All-Star Game record for most goals—4 (1991).
STATISTICAL PLATEAUS: Three-goal games: 1979-80 (2), 1980-81 (1), 1981-82 (1), 1982-83 (1), 1983-84 (1), 1984-85 (1), 1985-86 (3), 1987-88 (1), 1989-90 (2), 1991-92 (1), 1996-97 (1). Total: 15. ... Four-goal games: 1980-81 (1), 1986-87 (1). Total: 2. ... Total hat tricks: 17.
MISCELLANEOUS: Holds Washington Capitals all-time records for most goals (397) and most points (789). ... Scored on a penalty shot (vs. Wayne Thomas, December 20, 1980; vs. Mike Liut, January 17, 1987; vs. Glenn Resch, April 4, 1987).

			REGULAR SEASON						PLAYOFFS				
Season Team	League	Gms.	G	A	Pts.	PIM	+/-	PP	SH	Gms.	G	A	Pts.	PIM
75-76—St. Catharines	OHA Mj.Jr.A	3	1	3	4	0	...	...	...	—	—	—	—	—
76-77—Niagara Falls	OMJHL	62	33	42	75	125	...	...	...	—	—	—	—	—
77-78—Niagara Falls	OMJHL	64	41	49	90	56	...	...	...	—	—	—	—	—
78-79—Cincinnati	WHA	78	27	25	52	123	...	...	...	3	0	2	2	2
79-80—Washington	NHL	77	36	32	68	66	...	4	0	—	—	—	—	—
80-81—Washington	NHL	80	48	46	94	100	-5	13	0	—	—	—	—	—
81-82—Washington	NHL	80	35	45	80	121	-11	5	2	—	—	—	—	—
82-83—Washington	NHL	73	38	38	76	54	-2	10	1	4	0	0	0	4
83-84—Washington	NHL	80	40	45	85	90	22	8	0	8	3	7	10	16
84-85—Washington	NHL	80	50	52	102	71	17	17	0	5	4	3	7	9

G

Season Team	League	REGULAR SEASON								PLAYOFFS				
		Gms.	G	A	Pts.	PIM	+/-	PP	SH	Gms.	G	A	Pts.	PIM
85-86—Washington	NHL	74	35	40	75	63	-5	11	2	9	2	10	12	4
86-87—Washington	NHL	78	41	32	73	61	1	5	6	7	4	3	7	14
87-88—Washington	NHL	80	48	33	81	73	20	19	0	14	3	4	7	14
88-89—Washington	NHL	56	26	29	55	71	8	6	0	—	—	—	—	—
—Minnesota	NHL	13	7	7	14	6	3	3	0	5	0	0	0	0
89-90—Minnesota	NHL	67	34	36	70	32	-8	15	4	—	—	—	—	—
—New York Rangers	NHL	12	11	5	16	6	4	6	0	10	5	3	8	12
90-91—New York Rangers	NHL	79	49	20	69	53	-9	22	1	6	1	1	2	0
91-92—New York Rangers	NHL	76	40	41	81	55	11	15	0	13	8	8	16	4
92-93—New York Rangers	NHL	84	45	23	68	59	-4	13	0	—	—	—	—	—
93-94—New York Rangers	NHL	71	28	24	52	58	11	10	5	—	—	—	—	—
—Toronto	NHL	10	6	6	12	4	9	1	0	18	5	6	11	14
94-95—Toronto	NHL	38	12	8	20	6	0	2	1	5	2	2	4	2
95-96—Toronto	NHL	82	35	19	54	52	5	15	0	6	4	1	5	4
96-97—Phoenix	NHL	82	32	31	63	38	-11	13	1	7	1	2	3	4
97-98—Phoenix	NHL	60	12	15	27	24	-4	4	0	5	1	0	1	18
WHA Totals (1 year)		78	27	25	52	123	...	...	...	3	0	2	2	2
NHL Totals (19 years)		1432	708	627	1335	1163	...	217	23	122	43	50	93	119

GAUTHIER, DENIS　　　　D　　　　FLAMES

PERSONAL: Born October 1, 1976, in Montreal. ... 6-2/205. ... Shoots left. ... Full name: Denis Gauthier Jr.. ... Name pronounced GO-chay.
TRANSACTIONS/CAREER NOTES: Selected by Calgary Flames in first round (first Flames pick, 20th overall) of NHL entry draft (July 8, 1995). ... Suffered concussion (September 27, 1997); missed two games.
HONORS: Named to Can.HL All-Star first team (1995-96). ... Won Emile Bouchard Trophy (1995-96). ... Named to QMJHL All-Star first team (1995-96).

Season Team	League	REGULAR SEASON								PLAYOFFS				
		Gms.	G	A	Pts.	PIM	+/-	PP	SH	Gms.	G	A	Pts.	PIM
92-93—Drummondville	QMJHL	61	1	7	8	136	...	...	...	10	0	5	5	40
93-94—Drummondville	QMJHL	60	0	7	7	176	...	...	...	9	2	0	2	41
94-95—Drummondville	QMJHL	64	9	31	40	190	...	...	...	4	0	5	5	12
95-96—Drummondville	QMJHL	53	25	49	74	140	...	...	...	6	4	4	8	32
—Saint John	AHL	5	2	0	2	8	...	...	...	16	1	6	7	20
96-97—Saint John	AHL	73	3	28	31	74	...	...	...	5	0	0	0	6
97-98—Calgary	NHL	10	0	0	0	16	-5	0	0	—	—	—	—	—
—Saint John	AHL	68	4	20	24	154	...	...	...	21	0	4	4	83
NHL Totals (1 year)		10	0	0	0	16	-5	0	0					

GAVEY, AARON　　　　C　　　　STARS

PERSONAL: Born February 22, 1974, in Sudbury, Ont. ... 6-2/200. ... Shoots left. ... Name pronounced GAY-vee.
TRANSACTIONS/CAREER NOTES: Selected by Tampa Bay Lightning in fourth round (fourth Lightning pick, 74th overall) of NHL entry draft (June 20, 1992). ... Bruised left ankle (January 3, 1996); missed one game. ... Suffered facial laceration (February 4, 1996); missed eight games. ... Traded by Lightning to Calgary Flames for G Rick Tabaracci (November 19, 1996). ... Strained neck (February 28, 1997); missed 14 games. ... Strained abdomen (January 11, 1998); missed 37 games. ... Sprained thumb (April 15, 1998); missed two games. ... Traded by Flames to Dallas Stars for C Bob Bassen (July 14, 1998).

Season Team	League	REGULAR SEASON								PLAYOFFS				
		Gms.	G	A	Pts.	PIM	+/-	PP	SH	Gms.	G	A	Pts.	PIM
90-91—Peterborough Jr. B	OHA	42	26	30	56	68	...	...	...	—	—	—	—	—
91-92—Sault Ste. Marie	OHL	48	7	11	18	27	...	...	...	19	5	1	6	10
92-93—Sault Ste. Marie	OHL	62	45	39	84	114	...	...	...	18	5	9	14	36
93-94—Sault Ste. Marie	OHL	60	42	60	102	116	...	...	...	14	11	10	21	22
94-95—Atlanta	IHL	66	18	17	35	85	...	...	...	5	0	1	1	9
95-96—Tampa Bay	NHL	73	8	4	12	56	-6	1	1	6	0	0	0	4
96-97—Tampa Bay	NHL	16	1	2	3	12	-1	0	0	—	—	—	—	—
—Calgary	NHL	41	7	9	16	34	-11	3	0	—	—	—	—	—
97-98—Calgary	NHL	26	2	3	5	24	-5	0	0	—	—	—	—	—
—Saint John	AHL	8	4	3	7	28	...	...	...	—	—	—	—	—
NHL Totals (3 years)		156	18	18	36	126	-23	4	1	6	0	0	0	4

GELINAS, MARTIN　　　　LW　　　　HURRICANES

G

PERSONAL: Born June 5, 1970, in Shawinigan, Que. ... 5-11/195. ... Shoots left. ... Name pronounced MAHR-tai ZHEHL-ih-nuh.
HIGH SCHOOL: Polyvalente Val-Maurice (Shawinigan, Que.).
TRANSACTIONS/CAREER NOTES: Broke left clavicle (November 1983). ... Suffered hairline fracture of clavicle (July 1986). ... Selected by Los Angeles Kings in first round (first Kings pick, seventh overall) of NHL entry draft (June 11, 1988). ... Traded by Kings with C Jimmy Carson, first-round picks in 1989 (traded to New Jersey), 1991 (LW Martin Rucinsky) and 1993 (LW Martin Rucinsky) and 1993 (D Nick Stajduhar) drafts and cash to Edmonton Oilers for C Wayne Gretzky, RW‡ Marty McSorley and LW/C Mike Krushelnyski (August 9, 1988). ... Suspended five games by NHL (March 9, 1990). ... Underwent shoulder surgery (June 1990). ... Traded by Oilers with sixth-round pick (C Nicholas Checco) in 1993 draft to Quebec Nordiques for LW Scott Pearson (June 20, 1993). ... Injured thigh (October 20, 1993). ... Separated left shoulder (November 25, 1993); missed 10 games. ... Claimed on waivers by Vancouver Canucks (January 15, 1994). ... Suffered charley horse (March 27, 1994); missed six games. ... Injured knee (April 30, 1995); missed last game of season and eight playoff games. ... Fractured rib (November 2, 1996); missed eight games. ... Sprained knee (October 13, 1997); missed 16 games. ... Traded by Canucks to Carolina Hurricanes with G Kirk McLean for LW Geoff Sanderson, D Enrico Ciccone and G Sean Burke (January 3, 1998).
HONORS: Won Can.HL Rookie of the Year Award (1987-88). ... Won Michel Bergeron Trophy (1987-88). ... Named to QMJHL All-Star first team (1987-88).
MISCELLANEOUS: Member of Stanley Cup championship team (1990).
STATISTICAL PLATEAUS: Three-goal games: 1989-90 (1), 1996-97 (1). Total: 2. ... Four-goal games: 1996-97 (1). ... Total hat tricks: 3.

Season Team	League	REGULAR SEASON								PLAYOFFS				
		Gms.	G	A	Pts.	PIM	+/-	PP	SH	Gms.	G	A	Pts.	PIM
87-88—Hull	QMJHL	65	63	68	131	74	...	...	...	17	15	18	33	32
88-89—Edmonton	NHL	6	1	2	3	0	-1	0	0	—	—	—	—	—
—Hull	QMJHL	41	38	39	77	31	...	...	...	9	5	4	9	14
89-90—Edmonton	NHL	46	17	8	25	30	0	5	0	20	2	3	5	6
90-91—Edmonton	NHL	73	20	20	40	34	-7	4	0	18	3	6	9	25
91-92—Edmonton	NHL	68	11	18	29	62	14	1	0	15	1	3	4	10
92-93—Edmonton	NHL	65	11	12	23	30	3	0	0	—	—	—	—	—
93-94—Quebec	NHL	31	6	6	12	8	-2	0	0	—	—	—	—	—
—Vancouver	NHL	33	8	8	16	26	-6	3	0	24	5	4	9	14
94-95—Vancouver	NHL	46	13	10	23	36	8	1	0	3	0	1	1	0
95-96—Vancouver	NHL	81	30	26	56	59	8	3	4	6	1	1	2	12
96-97—Vancouver	NHL	74	35	33	68	42	6	6	1	—	—	—	—	—
97-98—Vancouver	NHL	24	4	4	8	10	-6	1	1	—	—	—	—	—
—Carolina	NHL	40	12	14	26	30	1	2	1	—	—	—	—	—
NHL Totals (10 years)		587	168	161	329	367	18	26	7	86	12	18	30	67

GENDRON, MARTIN   RW   CANADIENS

PERSONAL: Born February 15, 1974, in Valleyfield, Que. ... 5-9/190. ... Shoots right. ... Name pronounced MAHR-tai ZHEHND-rahn.
TRANSACTIONS/CAREER NOTES: Selected by Washington Capitals in third round (fourth Capitals pick, 71st overall) of NHL entry draft (June 20, 1992). ... Traded by Capitals with sixth-round pick (G Jonathan Pelletier) in 1998 draft to Chicago Blackhawks for fifth-round pick (C/LW Erik Wendell) in 1998 draft (October 10, 1997). ... Traded by Blackhawks to Montreal Canadiens for F David Ling (March 14, 1998).
HONORS: Named to QMJHL All-Rookie team (1990-91). ... Won Can.HL Most Sportsmanlike Player of the Year Award (1991-92). ... Won Shell Cup (1991-92). ... Won Frank J. Selke Trophy (1991-92 and 1992-93). ... Named to QMJHL All-Star first team (1991-92). ... Named to Can.HL All-Star first team (1992-93). ... Named to QMJHL All-Star second team (1992-93).

Season Team	League	REGULAR SEASON								PLAYOFFS				
		Gms.	G	A	Pts.	PIM	+/-	PP	SH	Gms.	G	A	Pts.	PIM
90-91—St. Hyacinthe	QMJHL	55	34	23	57	33	...	...	...	4	1	2	3	0
91-92—St. Hyacinthe	QMJHL	69	*71	66	137	45	...	...	...	6	7	4	11	14
92-93—St. Hyacinthe	QMJHL	63	73	61	134	44	...	...	...	—	—	—	—	—
—Baltimore	AHL	10	1	2	3	2	...	...	...	3	0	0	0	0
93-94—Canadian nat'l team	Int'l	19	4	5	9	2	...	...	...	—	—	—	—	—
—Hull	QMJHL	37	39	36	75	18	...	...	...	20	*21	17	38	8
94-95—Portland	AHL	72	36	32	68	54	...	...	...	4	5	1	6	2
—Washington	NHL	8	2	1	3	2	3	0	0	—	—	—	—	—
95-96—Washington	NHL	20	2	1	3	8	-5	0	0	—	—	—	—	—
—Portland	AHL	48	38	29	67	39	...	...	...	22	*15	18	33	8
96-97—Las Vegas	IHL	81	51	39	90	20	...	...	...	3	2	1	3	0
97-98—Indianapolis	IHL	17	8	6	14	16	...	...	...	—	—	—	—	—
—Chicago	NHL	2	0	0	0	0	-1	0	0	—	—	—	—	—
—Milwaukee	IHL	40	20	19	39	14	...	...	...	—	—	—	—	—
—Fredericton	AHL	10	5	10	15	4	...	...	...	2	0	0	0	4
NHL Totals (3 years)		30	4	2	6	10	-3	0	0					

GERIS, DAVE   D   PANTHERS

PERSONAL: Born June 7, 1976, in North Bay, Ont. ... 6-5/221. ... Shoots left. ... Name pronounced GAIR-ihs.
HIGH SCHOOL: W.F. Herman (Windsor, Ont.).
TRANSACTIONS/CAREER NOTES: Selected by Florida Panthers in fifth round (sixth Panthers pick, 105th overall) of NHL entry draft (June 29, 1994).

Season Team	League	REGULAR SEASON								PLAYOFFS				
		Gms.	G	A	Pts.	PIM	+/-	PP	SH	Gms.	G	A	Pts.	PIM
93-94—Windsor	OHL	63	0	6	6	121	...	...	...	3	0	0	0	6
94-95—Windsor	OHL	65	5	11	16	135	...	...	...	10	1	6	7	21
95-96—Windsor	OHL	64	8	20	28	205	...	...	...	7	1	0	1	20
96-97—Carolina	AHL	28	1	1	2	59	...	...	...	—	—	—	—	—
—Port Huron	Col.HL	42	1	7	8	117	...	...	...	5	0	1	1	0
97-98—Port Huron	UHL	25	2	2	4	67	...	...	...	—	—	—	—	—
—Tallahassee	ECHL	28	1	1	2	58	...	...	...					

GIGUERE, JEAN-SEBASTIEN   G   FLAMES

PERSONAL: Born May 16, 1977, in Montreal. ... 6-0/175. ... Catches left. ... Name pronounced zhee-GAIR.
TRANSACTIONS/CAREER NOTES: Selected by Hartford Whalers in first round (first Whalers pick, 13th overall) of NHL entry draft (July 8, 1995). ... Whalers franchise moved to North Carolina and renamed Carolina Hurricanes for 1997-98 season; NHL approved move on June 25, 1997. ... Traded by Hurricanes with C Andrew Cassels to Calgary Flames for LW Gary Roberts and G Trevor Kidd (August 25, 1997).
HONORS: Named to QMJHL All-Star second team (1996-97). ... Shared Harry (Hap) Holmes Trophy with Tyler Moss (1997-98).

Season Team	League	REGULAR SEASON							PLAYOFFS					
		Gms.	Min.	W	L	T	GA	SO	Avg.	Gms.	Min.	W	L	GA	SO	Avg.
93-94—Verdun	QMJHL	25	1234	13	5	2	66	0	3.21	—	—	—	—	—	—	—
94-95—Halifax	QMJHL	47	2755	14	27	5	181	2	3.94	7	417	3	4	17	1	2.45
95-96—Verdun	QMJHL	55	3228	26	23	2	185	1	3.44	6	356	1	5	24	0	4.04
96-97—Halifax	QMJHL	50	3009	28	19	3	169	2	3.37	16	954	9	7	58	0	3.65
—Hartford	NHL	8	394	1	4	0	24	0	3.65	—	—	—	—	—	—	—
97-98—Saint John	AHL	31	1758	16	10	3	72	2	2.46	10	537	5	3	27	0	3.02
NHL Totals (1 year)		8	394	1	4	0	24	0	3.65							

GILCHRIST, BRENT — LW — RED WINGS

PERSONAL: Born April 3, 1967, in Moose Jaw, Sask. ... 5-11/180. ... Shoots left.
TRANSACTIONS/CAREER NOTES: Strained medial collateral ligament (January 1985). ... Selected by Montreal Canadiens as underage junior in sixth round (sixth Canadiens pick, 79th overall) of NHL entry draft (June 15, 1985). ... Injured knee (January 1987). ... Broke right index finger (November 17, 1990); missed 19 games. ... Separated left shoulder (February 6, 1991); missed two games. ... Reinjured left shoulder (February 13, 1991); missed five games. ... Traded by Canadiens with LW Shayne Corson and LW Vladimir Vujtek to Edmonton Oilers for LW Vincent Damphousse and fourth-round pick (D Adam Wiesel) in 1993 draft (August 27, 1992). ... Suffered concussion (October 1992); missed two games. ... Fractured nose (December 21, 1992); missed two games. ... Traded by Oilers to Minnesota North Stars for C Todd Elik (March 5, 1993). ... Separated shoulder (March 18, 1993); missed remainder of season. ... North Stars franchise moved from Minnesota to Dallas and renamed Stars for 1993-94 season. ... Strained shoulder (October 27, 1993); missed four games. ... Pulled groin (November 21, 1993); missed four games. ... Underwent oral surgery (February 2, 1995); missed no games. ... Strained groin (February 20, 1995); missed two games. ... Strained groin and sprained wrist (February 26, 1995); missed 13 games. ... Suffered from sore wrist (April 11, 1995); missed one game. ... Injured groin (October 14, 1995); missed four games. ... Strained hip flexor (November 6, 1996); missed two games. ... Strained groin (December 21, 1996); missed three games. ... Strained groin (March 5, 1997); missed two games. ... Strained groin (March 16, 1997); missed seven games. ... Signed as free agent by Detroit Red Wings (July 8, 1997). ...Injured groin (March 4, 1998); missed 20 games.
MISCELLANEOUS: Failed to score on a penalty shot (vs. Kirk McLean, January 27, 1994). ... Member of Stanley Cup championship team (1998).
STATISTICAL PLATEAUS: Three-goal games: 1991-92 (1).

		REGULAR SEASON								PLAYOFFS				
Season Team	League	Gms.	G	A	Pts.	PIM	+/-	PP	SH	Gms.	G	A	Pts.	PIM
83-84—Kelowna	WHL	69	16	11	27	16	...	...	...	—	—	—	—	—
84-85—Kelowna	WHL	51	35	38	73	58	...	...	...	6	5	2	7	8
85-86—Spokane	WHL	52	45	45	90	57	...	...	...	9	6	7	13	19
86-87—Spokane	WHL	46	45	55	100	71	...	...	...	5	2	7	9	6
—Sherbrooke	AHL	—	—	—	—	—	—	—	—	10	2	7	9	2
87-88—Sherbrooke	AHL	77	26	48	74	83	...	...	...	6	1	3	4	6
88-89—Montreal	NHL	49	8	16	24	16	9	0	0	9	1	1	2	10
—Sherbrooke	AHL	7	6	5	11	7	...	...	...	—	—	—	—	—
89-90—Montreal	NHL	57	9	15	24	28	3	1	0	8	2	0	2	2
90-91—Montreal	NHL	51	6	9	15	10	-3	1	0	13	5	3	8	6
91-92—Montreal	NHL	79	23	27	50	57	29	2	0	11	2	4	6	6
92-93—Edmonton	NHL	60	10	10	20	47	-10	2	0	—	—	—	—	—
—Minnesota	NHL	8	0	1	1	2	-2	0	0	—	—	—	—	—
93-94—Dallas	NHL	76	17	14	31	31	0	3	1	9	3	1	4	2
94-95—Dallas	NHL	32	9	4	13	16	-3	1	3	5	0	1	1	2
95-96—Dallas	NHL	77	20	22	42	36	-11	6	1	—	—	—	—	—
96-97—Dallas	NHL	67	10	20	30	24	6	2	0	6	2	2	4	2
97-98—Detroit	NHL	61	13	14	27	40	4	5	0	15	2	1	3	12
NHL Totals (10 years)		617	125	152	277	307	22	23	5	76	17	13	30	42

GILL, HAL — D — BRUINS

PERSONAL: Born April 6, 1975, in Concord, Mass. ... 6-7/240. ... Shoots left.
HIGH SCHOOL: Nashoba Regional (Bolton, Mass.).
COLLEGE: Providence.
TRANSACTIONS/CAREER NOTES: Selected by Boston Bruins in eighth round (eighth Bruins pick, 207th overall) of NHL entry draft (June 26, 1993). ... Suffered from the flu (January 21, 1998); missed one game.

		REGULAR SEASON								PLAYOFFS				
Season Team	League	Gms.	G	A	Pts.	PIM	+/-	PP	SH	Gms.	G	A	Pts.	PIM
93-94—Providence College	Hockey East	31	1	2	3	26	...	...	...	—	—	—	—	—
94-95—Providence College	Hockey East	26	1	3	4	22	...	...	...	—	—	—	—	—
95-96—Providence College	Hockey East	39	5	12	17	54	...	...	...	—	—	—	—	—
96-97—Providence College	Hockey East	35	5	16	21	52	...	...	...	—	—	—	—	—
97-98—Boston	NHL	68	2	4	6	47	4	0	0	6	0	0	0	4
—Providence	AHL	4	1	0	1	23	...	...	...	—	—	—	—	—
NHL Totals (1 year)		68	2	4	6	47	4	0	0	6	0	0	0	4

GILL, TODD — D — BLUES

PERSONAL: Born November 9, 1965, in Brockville, Ont. ... 6-0/185. ... Shoots left.
TRANSACTIONS/CAREER NOTES: Selected by Toronto Maple Leafs as underage junior in second round (second Maple Leafs pick, 25th overall) of NHL entry draft (June 9, 1984). ... Broke bone in right foot (October 1987). ... Bruised shoulder (March 1989). ... Fractured finger (October 15, 1991); missed three games. ... Strained back (February 8, 1992); missed three games. ... Injured back prior to 1992-93 season; missed first two games of season. ... Bruised foot (November 14, 1992); missed 11 games. ... Strained groin (November 1, 1993); missed 26 games. ... Suffered back spasms (February 24, 1994); missed 13 games. ... Injured shoulder (March 17, 1995); missed one game. ... Pulled hamstring (November 10, 1995); missed four games. ... Suffered back spasms (February 7, 1996); missed four games. ... Traded by Maple Leafs to San Jose Sharks for C Jamie Baker and fifth-round pick (C Peter Cava) in 1996 draft (June 14, 1996). ... Suffered sore knee (April 9, 1997); missed three games. ... Traded by Sharks to St. Louis Blues for RW Joe Murphy (March 24, 1998).
MISCELLANEOUS: Captain of San Jose Sharks (1996-97 through March 2, 1998).

		REGULAR SEASON								PLAYOFFS				
Season Team	League	Gms.	G	A	Pts.	PIM	+/-	PP	SH	Gms.	G	A	Pts.	PIM
82-83—Windsor	OHL	70	12	24	36	108	...	...	...	3	0	0	0	11
83-84—Windsor	OHL	68	9	48	57	184	...	...	...	3	1	1	2	10
84-85—Toronto	NHL	10	1	0	1	13	-1	0	0	—	—	—	—	—
—Windsor	OHL	53	17	40	57	148	...	...	...	4	0	1	1	14
85-86—St. Catharines	AHL	58	8	25	33	90	...	...	...	10	1	6	7	17
—Toronto	NHL	15	1	2	3	28	0	0	0	1	0	0	0	0

G

Season Team	League	Gms.	G	A	Pts.	PIM	+/-	PP	SH	Gms.	G	A	Pts.	PIM
86-87—Newmarket	AHL	11	1	8	9	33	...	...	...	—	—	—	—	—
—Toronto	NHL	61	4	27	31	92	-3	1	0	13	2	2	4	42
87-88—Newmarket	AHL	2	0	1	1	2	...	...	...	—	—	—	—	—
—Toronto	NHL	65	8	17	25	131	-20	1	0	6	1	3	4	20
88-89—Toronto	NHL	59	11	14	25	72	-3	0	0	—	—	—	—	—
89-90—Toronto	NHL	48	1	14	15	92	-8	0	0	5	0	3	3	16
90-91—Toronto	NHL	72	2	22	24	113	-4	0	0	—	—	—	—	—
91-92—Toronto	NHL	74	2	15	17	91	-22	1	0	—	—	—	—	—
92-93—Toronto	NHL	69	11	32	43	66	4	5	0	21	1	10	11	26
93-94—Toronto	NHL	45	4	24	28	44	8	2	0	18	1	5	6	37
94-95—Toronto	NHL	47	7	25	32	64	-8	3	1	7	0	3	3	6
95-96—Toronto	NHL	74	7	18	25	116	-15	1	0	6	0	0	0	24
96-97—San Jose	NHL	79	0	21	21	101	-20	0	0	—	—	—	—	—
97-98—San Jose	NHL	64	8	13	21	31	-13	4	0	—	—	—	—	—
—St. Louis	NHL	11	5	4	9	10	2	3	0	10	2	2	4	10
NHL Totals (14 years)		793	72	248	320	1064	-103	21	1	87	7	28	35	181

GILLAM, SEAN — D — RED WINGS

PERSONAL: Born May 7, 1976, in Lethbridge, Alta. ... 6-2/187. ... Shoots right. ... Name pronounced GIHL-uhm.
HIGH SCHOOL: Spokane (Wash.).
TRANSACTIONS/CAREER NOTES: Selected by Detroit Red Wings in third round (third Red Wings pick, 75th overall) of NHL entry draft (June 29, 1994).
HONORS: Named to WHL (West) All-Star second team (1994-95 and 1995-96).

Season Team	League	Gms.	G	A	Pts.	PIM	+/-	PP	SH	Gms.	G	A	Pts.	PIM
92-93—Spokane	WHL	70	6	27	33	121	...	...	...	10	0	2	2	10
93-94—Spokane	WHL	70	7	17	24	106	...	...	...	3	0	0	0	6
94-95—Spokane	WHL	72	16	40	56	192	...	...	...	11	0	3	3	33
95-96—Spokane	WHL	69	11	58	69	123	...	...	...	18	2	12	14	26
96-97—Adirondack	AHL	64	1	7	8	50	...	...	...	—	—	—	—	—
97-98—Adirondack	AHL	73	1	9	10	60	...	...	...	3	1	0	1	0

GILLIS, NICK — RW — SENATORS

PERSONAL: Born February 20, 1978, in Cambridge, Mass. ... 6-0/188. ... Shoots right.
TRANSACTIONS/CAREER NOTES: Selected by Ottawa Senators in eighth round (seventh Senators pick, 203rd overall) of 1997 NHL entry draft.

Season Team	League	Gms.	G	A	Pts.	PIM	+/-	PP	SH	Gms.	G	A	Pts.	PIM
96-97—Cushing Academy	Mass. H.S.						Statistics unavailable.							
97-98—Cushing Academy	Mass. H.S.	32	30	54	84	27	...	...	...	—	—	—	—	—

GILMOUR, DOUG — C — BLACKHAWKS

PERSONAL: Born June 25, 1963, in Kingston, Ont. ... 5-11/175. ... Shoots left. ... Full name: Douglas Gilmour.
TRANSACTIONS/CAREER NOTES: Selected by St. Louis Blues as underage junior in seventh round (fourth Blues pick, 134th overall) of NHL entry draft (June 9, 1982). ... Sprained ankle (October 7, 1985); missed four games. ... Suffered concussion (January 1988). ... Bruised shoulder (March 1988). ... Traded by Blues with RW Mark Hunter, LW Steve Bozek and D/RW Michael Dark to Calgary Flames for C Mike Bullard, C Craig Coxe and D Tim Corkery (September 5, 1988). ... Suffered abscessed jaw (March 1989); missed six games. ... Broke bone in right foot (August 12, 1989). ... Traded by Flames with D Ric Nattress, D Jamie Macoun, LW Kent Manderville and G Rick Wamsley to Toronto Maple Leafs for LW Craig Berube, D Alexander Godynyuk, LW Gary Leeman, D Michel Petit and G Jeff Reese (January 2, 1992). ... Suspended eight off-days and fined $500 by NHL for slashing (November 27, 1992). ... Suspended one preseason game and fined $500 by NHL for headbutting (September 26, 1993). ... Played in Europe during 1994-95 NHL lockout. ... Pinched nerve in neck (February 8, 1995); missed one game. ... Broke nose (April 7, 1995); missed three games. ... Bruised ribs (March 19, 1996); missed one game. ... Traded by Maple Leafs with D Dave Ellett and third-round pick in 1999 draft to New Jersey Devils for D Jason Smith, C Steve Sullivan and C Alyn McCauley (February 25, 1997). ... Bruised eye (March 5, 1997); missed three games. ... Injured knee and underwent arthroscopic surgery (March 5, 1998); missed 18 games. ... Signed as free agent by Chicago Blackhawks (July 3, 1998).
HONORS: Won Red Tilson Trophy (1982-83). ... Won Eddie Powers Memorial Trophy (1982-83). ... Named to OHL All-Star first team (1982-83). ... Won Frank J. Selke Trophy (1992-93). ... Named to THE SPORTING NEWS All-Star second team (1992-93). ... Played in NHL All-Star Game (1993 and 1994).
MISCELLANEOUS: Member of Stanley Cup championship team (1989). ... Captain of Toronto Maple Leafs (1994-95 through February 25, 1997). ... Failed to score on a penalty shot (vs. Gilles Meloche, February 3, 1985; vs. Pat Riggin, March 1, 1987; vs. Mark Fitzpatrick, October 7, 1989).
STATISTICAL PLATEAUS: Three-goal games: 1985-86 (1), 1987-88 (1), 1993-94 (1). Total: 3.

Season Team	League	Gms.	G	A	Pts.	PIM	+/-	PP	SH	Gms.	G	A	Pts.	PIM
80-81—Cornwall	QMJHL	51	12	23	35	35	...	...	...	—	—	—	—	—
81-82—Cornwall	OHL	67	46	73	119	42	...	...	...	5	6	9	15	2
82-83—Cornwall	OHL	68	*70	*107	*177	62	...	...	...	8	8	10	18	16
83-84—St. Louis	NHL	80	25	28	53	57	6	3	1	11	2	9	11	10
84-85—St. Louis	NHL	78	21	36	57	49	3	3	1	3	1	1	2	2
85-86—St. Louis	NHL	74	25	28	53	41	-3	2	1	19	9	12	†21	25
86-87—St. Louis	NHL	80	42	63	105	58	-2	17	1	6	2	2	4	16
87-88—St. Louis	NHL	72	36	50	86	59	-13	19	2	10	3	14	17	18

G

Season Team	League	REGULAR SEASON								PLAYOFFS				
		Gms.	G	A	Pts.	PIM	+/-	PP	SH	Gms.	G	A	Pts.	PIM
88-89—Calgary	NHL	72	26	59	85	44	45	11	0	22	11	11	22	20
89-90—Calgary	NHL	78	24	67	91	54	20	12	1	6	3	1	4	8
90-91—Calgary	NHL	78	20	61	81	144	27	2	2	7	1	1	2	0
91-92—Calgary	NHL	38	11	27	38	46	12	4	1	—	—	—	—	—
—Toronto	NHL	40	15	34	49	32	13	6	0	—	—	—	—	—
92-93—Toronto	NHL	83	32	95	127	100	32	15	3	21	10	†25	35	30
93-94—Toronto	NHL	83	27	84	111	105	25	10	1	18	6	22	28	42
94-95—Rapperswil	Switz. Div. II	9	2	13	15	16	...			—	—	—	—	—
—Toronto	NHL	44	10	23	33	26	-5	3	0	7	0	6	6	6
95-96—Toronto	NHL	81	32	40	72	77	-5	10	2	6	1	7	8	12
96-97—Toronto	NHL	61	15	45	60	46	-5	2	1	—	—	—	—	—
—New Jersey	NHL	20	7	15	22	22	7	2	0	10	0	4	4	14
97-98—New Jersey	NHL	63	13	40	53	68	10	3	0	6	5	2	7	4
NHL Totals (15 years)		1125	381	795	1176	1028	167	124	17	152	54	117	171	207

GOC, SASCHA   D   DEVILS

PERSONAL: Born April 14, 1979, in Calw, West Germany. ... 6-2/196. ... Shoots right.
TRANSACTIONS/CAREER NOTES: Selected by New Jersey Devils in sixth round (fifth Devils pick, 159th overall) of NHL entry draft (June 21, 1997).

Season Team	League	REGULAR SEASON								PLAYOFFS				
		Gms.	G	A	Pts.	PIM	+/-	PP	SH	Gms.	G	A	Pts.	PIM
95-96—Schwenningen Jrs.	Germany	11	3	6	9	77	...	...	...	—	—	—	—	—
—Schwenningen	Germany	1	0	0	0	0	...	...	...	—	—	—	—	—
96-97—Schwenningen	Germany	41	3	1	4	28	...	...	...	5	0	0	0	0
97-98—Schwenningen	Germany	49	5	5	10	45	...	...	...	—	—	—	—	—

GODYNYUK, ALEXANDER   D

PERSONAL: Born January 27, 1970, in Kiev, U.S.S.R. ... 6-1/214. ... Shoots left. ... Name pronounced goh-DIHN-yuhk.
TRANSACTIONS/CAREER NOTES: Selected by Toronto Maple Leafs in sixth round (fifth Maple Leafs pick, 115th overall) of NHL entry draft (June 16, 1990). ... Traded by Maple Leafs with LW Craig Berube, RW Gary Leeman, D Michel Petit and G Jeff Reese to Calgary Flames for C Doug Gilmour, D Jamie Macoun, LW Kent Manderville, D Ric Nattress and G Rick Wamsley (January 2, 1992). ... Injured shoulder (February 23, 1993); missed one game. ... Selected by Florida Panthers in NHL expansion draft (June 24, 1993). ... Strained stomach muscle (November 14, 1993); missed two games. ... Traded by Panthers to Hartford Whalers for D Jim McKenzie (December 16, 1993). ... Bruised knee (December 28, 1993); missed one game. ... Injured knee (March 25, 1994); missed remainder of season. ... Injured groin (March 7, 1995); missed four games. ... Sore back (October 22, 1996); missed four games. ... Strained groin (November 23, 1996); missed five games. ... Whalers franchise moved to North Carolina and renamed Carolina Hurricanes for 1997-98 season; NHL approved move on June 25, 1997. ... Traded by Hurricanes with sixth-round pick (D Brad Voth) in 1998 draft to St. Louis Blues for RW Steve Leach (June 27, 1997). ... Strained knee (September 12, 1997); missed first seven games of 1997-98 season.

Season Team	League	REGULAR SEASON								PLAYOFFS				
		Gms.	G	A	Pts.	PIM	+/-	PP	SH	Gms.	G	A	Pts.	PIM
86-87—Sokol Kiev	USSR	9	0	1	1	2	...	...	...	—	—	—	—	—
87-88—Sokol Kiev	USSR	2	0	0	0	2	...	...	...	—	—	—	—	—
88-89—Sokol Kiev	USSR	30	3	3	6	12	...	...	...	—	—	—	—	—
89-90—Sokol Kiev	USSR	37	3	2	5	31	...	...	...	—	—	—	—	—
90-91—Sokol Kiev	USSR	19	3	1	4	20	...	...	...	—	—	—	—	—
—Toronto	NHL	18	0	3	3	16	-3	0	0	—	—	—	—	—
—Newmarket	AHL	11	0	1	1	29	...	...	...	—	—	—	—	—
91-92—Toronto	NHL	31	3	6	9	59	-12	1	0	—	—	—	—	—
—Calgary	NHL	6	0	1	1	4	-2	0	0	—	—	—	—	—
—Salt Lake City	IHL	17	2	1	3	24	...	...	...	—	—	—	—	—
92-93—Calgary	NHL	27	3	4	7	19	6	0	0	—	—	—	—	—
93-94—Florida	NHL	26	0	10	10	35	5	0	0	—	—	—	—	—
—Hartford	NHL	43	3	9	12	40	8	0	0	—	—	—	—	—
94-95—Hartford	NHL	14	0	0	0	8	1	0	0	—	—	—	—	—
95-96—Hartford	NHL	3	0	0	0	2	-1	0	0	—	—	—	—	—
—Detroit	IHL	7	0	3	3	12	...	...	...	—	—	—	—	—
—Minnesota	IHL	45	9	17	26	81	...	...	...	—	—	—	—	—
—Springfield	AHL	14	1	3	4	19	...	...	...	—	—	—	—	—
96-97—Hartford	NHL	55	1	6	7	41	-10	0	0	—	—	—	—	—
97-98—Chicago	IHL	50	5	11	16	85	...	...	...	1	0	0	0	0
NHL Totals (7 years)		223	10	39	49	224	-8	1	0	—	—	—	—	—

GOLDMANN, ERICH   D   SENATORS

PERSONAL: Born April 7, 1976, in Dingolfing, West Germany. ... 6-3/200. ... Shoots left. ... Name pronounced GOHLD-mahn.
TRANSACTIONS/CAREER NOTES: Selected by Ottawa Senators in eighth round (fifth Senators pick, 212th overall) of NHL entry draft (June 22, 1996).

Season Team	League	REGULAR SEASON								PLAYOFFS				
		Gms.	G	A	Pts.	PIM	+/-	PP	SH	Gms.	G	A	Pts.	PIM
95-96—Mannheim	Germany	47	0	3	3	40	...	...	...	8	0	0	0	2
96-97—Kaufbeuren	Germany	44	2	4	6	58	...	...	...	6	1	0	1	2
97-98—Worcester	AHL	31	0	2	2	40	...	...	...	—	—	—	—	—
—German Oly. team	Int'l	4	0	1	1	27	...	...	...	—	—	—	—	—
—Detroit	IHL	3	0	0	0	2	...	...	...	—	—	—	—	—
—Dayton	ECHL	3	0	2	2	5	...	...	...	5	0	0	0	8

G

GOLUBOVSKY, YAN   D   RED WINGS

PERSONAL: Born March 9, 1976, in Novosibirsk, U.S.S.R. ... 6-3/185. ... Shoots right. ... Name pronounced goh-loo-BAHV-skee.
TRANSACTIONS/CAREER NOTES: Selected by Detroit Red Wings in first round (first Red Wings pick, 23rd overall) of NHL entry draft (June 28, 1994).

		REGULAR SEASON								PLAYOFFS				
Season Team	League	Gms.	G	A	Pts.	PIM	+/-	PP	SH	Gms.	G	A	Pts.	PIM
93-94—Dynamo-2 Moscow	CIS Div. III	10	0	1	1	...	...	...	...	—	—	—	—	—
—Russian Penguins	IHL	8	0	0	0	23	...	...	...	—	—	—	—	—
94-95—Adirondack	AHL	57	4	2	6	39	...	...	...	—	—	—	—	—
95-96—Adirondack	AHL	71	5	16	21	97	...	...	...	3	0	0	0	2
96-97—Adirondack	AHL	62	2	11	13	67	...	...	...	4	0	0	0	0
97-98—Adirondack	AHL	52	1	15	16	57	...	...	...	3	0	0	0	2
—Detroit	NHL	12	0	2	2	6	1	0	0	—	—	—	—	—
NHL Totals (1 year)		12	0	2	2	6	1	0	0	—	—	—	—	—

GONCHAR, SERGEI   D   CAPITALS

PERSONAL: Born April 13, 1974, in Chelyabinsk, U.S.S.R. ... 6-2/210. ... Shoots left. ... Name pronounced GAHN-shahr.
TRANSACTIONS/CAREER NOTES: Selected by Washington Capitals in first round (first Capitals pick, 14th overall) of NHL entry draft (June 20, 1992). ... Injured groin (November 30, 1995); missed two games. ... Suffered from the flu (December 13, 1995); missed one game. ... Suffered from the flu (November 7, 1996); missed one game. ... Hyperextended elbow (November 18, 1996); missed one game. ... Suffered back spasms (December 28, 1996); missed eight games. ... Bruised knee (January 29, 1997); missed two games. ... Sprained knee (February 26, 1997); missed 12 games.

		REGULAR SEASON								PLAYOFFS				
Season Team	League	Gms.	G	A	Pts.	PIM	+/-	PP	SH	Gms.	G	A	Pts.	PIM
90-91—Mechel Chelyabinsk....	USSR	2	0	0	0	0	...	...	...	—	—	—	—	—
91-92—Traktor Chelyabinsk	CIS	31	1	0	1	6	...	...	...	—	—	—	—	—
92-93—Dynamo Moscow	CIS	31	1	3	4	70	...	...	...	10	0	0	0	12
93-94—Dynamo Moscow	CIS	44	4	5	9	36	...	...	...	10	0	3	3	14
—Portland	AHL	—	—	—	—	—	...	...	...	2	0	0	0	0
94-95—Portland	AHL	61	10	32	42	67	...	...	...	—	—	—	—	—
—Washington	NHL	31	2	5	7	22	4	0	0	7	2	2	4	2
95-96—Washington	NHL	78	15	26	41	60	25	4	0	6	2	4	6	4
96-97—Washington	NHL	57	13	17	30	36	-11	3	0	—	—	—	—	—
97-98—Washington	NHL	72	5	16	21	66	2	2	0	21	7	4	11	30
—Russian Oly. team	Int'l	6	0	2	2	0	...	...	...	—	—	—	—	—
NHL Totals (4 years)		238	35	64	99	184	20	9	0	34	11	10	21	36

GONEAU, DANIEL   RW   RANGERS

PERSONAL: Born January 16, 1976, in Lachine, Que. ... 6-0/195. ... Shoots left. ... Name pronounced guh-NOH.
TRANSACTIONS/CAREER NOTES: Selected by Boston Bruins in second round (second Bruins pick, 48th overall) of NHL entry draft (June 28, 1994). ... Returned to draft pool by Bruins and selected by New York Rangers in second round (second Rangers pick, 48th overall) of NHL entry draft (June 22, 1996).
HONORS: Won Can.HL Plus/Minus Award (1995-96). ... Named to QMJHL All-Star first team (1995-96).

		REGULAR SEASON								PLAYOFFS				
Season Team	League	Gms.	G	A	Pts.	PIM	+/-	PP	SH	Gms.	G	A	Pts.	PIM
92-93—Laval	QMJHL	62	16	25	41	44	...	...	...	13	0	4	4	4
93-94—Laval	QMJHL	68	29	57	86	81	...	...	...	19	8	21	29	45
94-95—Laval	QMJHL	56	16	31	47	78	...	...	...	20	5	10	15	33
95-96—Granby	QMJHL	67	54	51	105	115	...	...	...	21	11	22	33	40
96-97—New York Rangers	NHL	41	10	3	13	10	-5	3	0	—	—	—	—	—
—Binghamton	AHL	39	15	15	30	10	...	...	...	—	—	—	—	—
97-98—New York Rangers	NHL	11	2	0	2	4	-4	0	0	—	—	—	—	—
—Hartford	AHL	66	21	26	47	44	...	...	...	13	1	4	5	18
NHL Totals (2 years)		52	12	3	15	14	-9	3	0	—	—	—	—	—

GOREN, LEE   RW   BRUINS

PERSONAL: Born December 26, 1977, in Winnipeg. ... 6-3/190. ... Shoots right.
COLLEGE: North Dakota.
TRANSACTIONS/CAREER NOTES: Selected by Boston Bruins in third round (fifth Bruins pick, 63rd overall) of NHL entry draft (June 21, 1997).

		REGULAR SEASON								PLAYOFFS				
Season Team	League	Gms.	G	A	Pts.	PIM	+/-	PP	SH	Gms.	G	A	Pts.	PIM
95-96—Minote	Jr.A	64	31	55	86	—	...	...	...	—	—	—	—	—
96-97—Univ. of North Dakota .	WCHA			Did not play.										
97-98—Univ. of North Dakota .	WCHA	29	3	13	16	26	...	...	...	—	—	—	—	—

GRAHAME, JOHN   G   BRUINS

PERSONAL: Born August 31, 1975, in Denver. ... 6-2/210. ... Catches left. ... Name pronounced GRAY-ihm.
COLLEGE: Lake Superior State (Mich.).
TRANSACTIONS/CAREER NOTES: Selected by Boston Bruins in ninth round (seventh Bruins pick, 229th overall) of NHL entry draft (June 29, 1994).

Season Team	League	REGULAR SEASON								PLAYOFFS					
		Gms.	Min	W	L	T	GA	SO	Avg.	Gms.	Min.	W	L	GA	SO	Avg.
93-94—Sioux City	USHL	20	1136	...	...	...	72	0	3.80	—	—	—	—	—	—	—
94-95—Lake Superior	CCHA	28	1616	16	7	3	75	1	2.78	—	—	—	—	—	—	—
95-96—Lake Superior	CCHA	29	1658	21	4	2	67	2	2.42	—	—	—	—	—	—	—
96-97—Lake Superior	CCHA	37	2197	19	13	4	134	3	3.66	—	—	—	—	—	—	—
97-98—Providence	AHL	55	3054	15	*31	4	164	3	3.22	—	—	—	—	—	—	—

GRANATO, TONY   RW   SHARKS

PERSONAL: Born July 25, 1964, in Downers Grove, Ill. ... 5-10/185. ... Shoots right. ... Full name: Anthony Lewis Granato. ... Name pronounced gruh-NAH-toh.
HIGH SCHOOL: Northwood School (Lake Placid, N.Y.).
COLLEGE: Wisconsin.
TRANSACTIONS/CAREER NOTES: Selected by New York Rangers in sixth round (fifth Rangers pick, 120th overall) of NHL entry draft (June 9, 1982). ... Bruised foot (February 1989). ... Traded by Rangers with RW Tomas Sandstrom to Los Angeles Kings for C Bernie Nicholls (January 20, 1990). ... Pulled groin (January 25, 1990); missed 12 games. ... Injured knee (March 20, 1990). ... Tore rib cartilage (December 18, 1990); missed 10 games. ... Strained back (October 6, 1992); missed three games. ... Strained back (December 4, 1993); missed one game. ... Strained lower back (December 13, 1993); missed nine games. ... Suspended 15 games without pay and fined $500 by NHL for slashing incident (February 16, 1994). ... Strained back (April 3, 1994); missed remainder of season. ... Strained hip flexor (March 13, 1995); missed one game. ... Broke bone in foot (April 6, 1995); missed 13 games. ... Underwent brain surgery (February 14, 1996); missed remainder of season. ... Signed as free agent by San Jose Sharks (August 15, 1996). ... Sore back (December 21, 1996); missed one game. ... Sore back (January 29, 1997); missed two games. ... Suspended three games and fined $1,000 by NHL for cross-checking incident (February 5, 1997). ... Injured jaw (November 1, 1997); missed 19 games. ... Suspended two games and fined $1,000 by NHL for high-sticking incident (January 24, 1998).
HONORS: Named to NCAA All-America West second team (1984-85 and 1986-87). ... Named to WCHA All-Star second team (1986-87). ... Named to NHL All-Rookie team (1988-89). ... Played in NHL All-Star Game (1997). ... Won Bill Masterton Memorial Trophy (1996-97).
MISCELLANEOUS: Failed to score on a penalty shot (vs. Jocelyn Thibault, November 25, 1993).
STATISTICAL PLATEAUS: Three-goal games: 1988-89 (2), 1991-92 (1), 1994-95 (1), 1996-97 (2). Total: 6. ... Four-goal games: 1988-89 (1). ... Total hat tricks: 7.

Season Team	League	REGULAR SEASON							PLAYOFFS				
		Gms.	G	A	Pts.	PIM	+/-	PP	SH	Gms.	G	A	Pts.	PIM
81-82—Northwood School	N.Y. H.S.					Statistics unavailable.								
82-83—Northwood School	N.Y. H.S.					Statistics unavailable.								
83-84—Univ. of Wisconsin	WCHA	35	14	17	31	48	...	...	...	—	—	—	—	—
84-85—Univ. of Wisconsin	WCHA	42	33	34	67	94	...	...	...	—	—	—	—	—
85-86—Univ. of Wisconsin	WCHA	32	25	24	49	36	...	...	...	—	—	—	—	—
86-87—Univ. of Wisconsin	WCHA	42	28	45	73	64	...	...	...	—	—	—	—	—
87-88—U.S. national team	Int'l	49	40	31	71	55	...	...	...	—	—	—	—	—
—U.S. Olympic Team	Int'l	6	1	7	8	4	...	...	...	—	—	—	—	—
—Denver	IHL	22	13	14	27	36	...	...	...	8	9	4	13	16
88-89—New York Rangers	NHL	78	36	27	63	140	17	4	4	4	1	1	2	21
89-90—New York Rangers	NHL	37	7	18	25	77	1	1	0	—	—	—	—	—
—Los Angeles	NHL	19	5	6	11	45	-2	1	0	10	5	4	9	12
90-91—Los Angeles	NHL	68	30	34	64	154	22	11	1	12	1	4	5	28
91-92—Los Angeles	NHL	80	39	29	68	187	4	7	2	6	1	5	6	10
92-93—Los Angeles	NHL	81	37	45	82	171	-1	14	2	24	6	11	17	50
93-94—Los Angeles	NHL	50	7	14	21	150	-2	2	0	—	—	—	—	—
94-95—Los Angeles	NHL	33	13	11	24	68	9	2	0	—	—	—	—	—
95-96—Los Angeles	NHL	49	17	18	35	46	-5	5	0	—	—	—	—	—
96-97—San Jose	NHL	76	25	15	40	159	-7	5	1	—	—	—	—	—
97-98—San Jose	NHL	59	16	9	25	70	3	3	0	1	0	0	0	0
NHL Totals (10 years)		630	232	226	458	1267	39	55	10	57	14	25	39	121

GRAND-PIERRE, JEAN-LUC   D   SABRES

PERSONAL: Born February 2, 1977, in Montreal. ... 6-3/207. ... Shoots right. ... Name pronounced zhah-LOOK GRAHN-pee-AIR.
HIGH SCHOOL: CEGEP de Val d'Or (Que.).
TRANSACTIONS/CAREER NOTES: Selected by St. Louis Blues in seventh round (sixth Blues pick, 179th overall) of NHL entry draft (July 8, 1995). ... Traded by Blues with second-round pick (D Cory Sarich) in 1996 draft and third-round pick (RW Maxim Afinogenov) in 1997 draft to Buffalo Sabres for LW Yuri Khmylev and eighth-round pick (C Andrei Podkowicky) in 1996 draft (March 20, 1996).

G

Season Team	League	REGULAR SEASON							PLAYOFFS				
		Gms.	G	A	Pts.	PIM	+/-	PP	SH	Gms.	G	A	Pts.	PIM
93-94—Beauport	QMJHL	46	1	4	5	27	...	...	...	1	0	0	0	0
94-95—Val-d'Or	QMJHL	59	10	13	23	126	...	...	...	—	—	—	—	—
95-96—Val-d'Or	QMJHL	67	13	21	34	209	...	...	...	13	1	4	5	47
96-97—Val-d'Or	QMJHL	58	9	24	33	196	...	...	...	13	5	8	13	46
97-98—Rochester	AHL	75	4	6	10	211	...	...	...	4	0	0	0	2

GRATTON, BENOIT   C   CAPITALS

PERSONAL: Born December 28, 1976, in Montreal. ... 5-10/163. ... Shoots left. ... Name pronounced gruh-TAH.
TRANSACTIONS/CAREER NOTES: Selected by Washington Capitals in fifth round (sixth Capitals pick, 105th overall) of NHL entry draft (July 8, 1995). ... Injured groin (December 20, 1997); missed one game.

Season Team	League	REGULAR SEASON								PLAYOFFS				
		Gms.	G	A	Pts.	PIM	+/-	PP	SH	Gms.	G	A	Pts.	PIM
93-94—Laval	QMJHL	51	9	14	23	70	...	...	...	20	2	1	3	19
94-95—Laval	QMJHL	71	30	58	88	199	...	...	...	20	8	21	29	42
95-96—Granby	QMJHL	65	33	85	118	227	...	...	...	21	13	26	39	68
96-97—Portland	AHL	76	6	40	46	140	...	...	...	5	2	1	3	14
97-98—Portland	AHL	58	19	31	50	137	...	...	...	8	4	2	6	24
—Washington	NHL	6	0	1	1	6	1	0	0	—	—	—	—	—
NHL Totals (1 year)		6	0	1	1	6	1	0	0					

GRATTON, CHRIS   C   FLYERS

PERSONAL: Born July 5, 1975, in Brantford, Ont. ... 6-3/220. ... Shoots left. ... Name pronounced GRA-tuhn.
HIGH SCHOOL: Loyalist Collegiate (Brantford, Ont.).
TRANSACTIONS/CAREER NOTES: Selected by Tampa Bay Lightning in first round (first Lightning pick, third overall) of NHL entry draft (June 26, 1993). ... Bruised shoulder (April 2, 1995); missed two games. ... Traded by Lightning to Philadelphia Flyers for F Mikael Renberg and D Karl Dykhuis (August 20, 1997).
HONORS: Won Emms Family Award (1991-92). ... Named to OHL Rookie All-Star team (1991-92). ... Won OHL Top Draft Prospect Award (1992-93).
STATISTICAL PLATEAUS: Three-goal games: 1996-97 (1).

Season Team	League	REGULAR SEASON								PLAYOFFS				
		Gms.	G	A	Pts.	PIM	+/-	PP	SH	Gms.	G	A	Pts.	PIM
90-91—Brantford Jr. B	OHA	31	30	30	60	28	...	...	...	—	—	—	—	—
91-92—Kingston	OHL	62	27	39	66	35	...	...	...	—	—	—	—	—
92-93—Kingston	OHL	58	55	54	109	125	...	...	...	16	11	18	29	42
93-94—Tampa Bay	NHL	84	13	29	42	123	-25	5	1	—	—	—	—	—
94-95—Tampa Bay	NHL	46	7	20	27	89	-2	2	0	—	—	—	—	—
95-96—Tampa Bay	NHL	82	17	21	38	105	-13	7	0	6	0	2	2	27
96-97—Tampa Bay	NHL	82	30	32	62	201	-28	9	0	—	—	—	—	—
97-98—Philadelphia	NHL	82	22	40	62	159	11	5	0	5	2	0	2	10
NHL Totals (5 years)		376	89	142	231	677	-57	28	1	11	2	2	4	37

GRAVES, ADAM   LW   RANGERS

PERSONAL: Born April 12, 1968, in Toronto. ... 6-0/205. ... Shoots left.
TRANSACTIONS/CAREER NOTES: Bruised shoulder (February 1986). ... Selected by Detroit Red Wings as underage junior in second round (second Red Wings pick, 22nd overall) of NHL entry draft (June 21, 1986). ... Traded by Red Wings with C/RW Joe Murphy, LW Petr Klima and D Jeff Sharples to Edmonton Oilers for C Jimmy Carson, C Kevin McClelland and fifth-round pick (traded to Montreal Canadiens who selected D Brad Layzell) in 1991 draft (November 2, 1989). ... Signed as free agent by New York Rangers (September 2, 1991); Oilers received C/LW Troy Mallette as compensation (September 9, 1991). ... Suffered from infected elbow (February 11, 1995); missed one game. ... Sprained right knee (October 26, 1997); missed 10 games.
HONORS: Won King Clancy Memorial Trophy (1993-94). ... Named to THE SPORTING NEWS All-Star first team (1993-94). ... Named to NHL All-Star second team (1993-94). ... Played in NHL All-Star Game (1994).
MISCELLANEOUS: Member of Stanley Cup championship team (1990 and 1994). ... Captain of New York Rangers (1995-96).
STATISTICAL PLATEAUS: Three-goal games: 1989-90 (1), 1991-92 (1), 1992-93 (1), 1993-94 (1), 1994-95 (1), 1996-97 (1). Total: 6.

Season Team	League	REGULAR SEASON								PLAYOFFS				
		Gms.	G	A	Pts.	PIM	+/-	PP	SH	Gms.	G	A	Pts.	PIM
84-85—King City Jr. B	OHA	25	23	33	56	29	...	...	...	—	—	—	—	—
85-86—Windsor	OHL	62	27	37	64	35	...	...	...	16	5	11	16	10
86-87—Windsor	OHL	66	45	55	100	70	...	...	...	14	9	8	17	32
—Adirondack	AHL	—	—	—	—	—	...	...	...	5	0	1	1	0
87-88—Detroit	NHL	9	0	1	1	8	-2	0	0	—	—	—	—	—
—Windsor	OHL	37	28	32	60	107	...	...	...	12	14	18	†32	16
88-89—Detroit	NHL	56	7	5	12	60	-5	0	0	5	0	0	0	4
—Adirondack	AHL	14	10	11	21	28	...	...	...	14	11	7	18	17
89-90—Detroit	NHL	13	0	1	1	13	-5	0	0	—	—	—	—	—
—Edmonton	NHL	63	9	12	21	123	5	1	0	22	5	6	11	17
90-91—Edmonton	NHL	76	7	18	25	127	-21	2	0	18	2	4	6	22
91-92—New York Rangers	NHL	80	26	33	59	139	19	4	4	10	5	3	8	22
92-93—New York Rangers	NHL	84	36	29	65	148	-4	12	1	—	—	—	—	—
93-94—New York Rangers	NHL	84	52	27	79	127	27	20	4	23	10	7	17	24
94-95—New York Rangers	NHL	47	17	14	31	51	9	9	0	10	4	4	8	8
95-96—New York Rangers	NHL	82	22	36	58	100	18	9	1	10	7	1	8	4
96-97—New York Rangers	NHL	82	33	28	61	66	10	10	4	15	2	1	3	12
97-98—New York Rangers	NHL	72	23	12	35	41	-30	10	0	—	—	—	—	—
NHL Totals (11 years)		748	232	216	448	1003	21	77	14	113	35	26	61	113

G

GREEN, JOSH   LW   KINGS

PERSONAL: Born November 16, 1977, in Camrose, Alta. ... 6-3/180. ... Shoots left.
TRANSACTIONS/CAREER NOTES: Selected by Los Angeles Kings in second round (first Kings pick, 30th overall) of NHL entry draft (June 22, 1996).

Season Team	League	REGULAR SEASON								PLAYOFFS				
		Gms.	G	A	Pts.	PIM	+/-	PP	SH	Gms.	G	A	Pts.	PIM
93-94—Medicine Hat	WHL	63	22	22	44	43	...	...	...	3	0	0	0	4
94-95—Medicine Hat	WHL	68	32	23	55	64	...	...	...	5	5	1	6	2
95-96—Medicine Hat	WHL	46	18	25	43	55	...	...	...	5	2	2	4	4
96-97—Medicine Hat	WHL	51	25	32	57	61	...	...	...	—	—	—	—	—
—Swift Current	WHL	23	10	15	25	33	...	...	...	10	9	7	16	19
97-98—Portland	WHL	31	35	19	54	36	...	...	...	—	—	—	—	—
—Fredericton	AHL	43	16	15	31	14	...	...	...	4	1	3	4	6

GREEN, TRAVIS   C   MIGHTY DUCKS

PERSONAL: Born December 20, 1970, in Castlegar, B.C. ... 6-1/195. ... Shoots right.
TRANSACTIONS/CAREER NOTES: Selected by New York Islanders in second round (second Islanders pick, 23rd overall) of NHL entry draft (June 17, 1989). ... Traded by Spokane Chiefs to Medicine Hat Tigers for RW Mark Woolf, D/LW Chris Lafreniere and C Frank Esposito (January 26, 1990). ... Suffered sore groin (November 30, 1995); missed four games. ... Sprained knee (February 8, 1996); missed nine games. ... Traded by Islanders with D Doug Houda and RW Tony Tuzzolino to Mighty Ducks of Anaheim for D J.J. Daigneault, C Mark Janssens and RW Joe Sacco (February 6, 1998). ... Strained groin (February 7, 1998); missed five games.
STATISTICAL PLATEAUS: Three-goal games: 1993-94 (1).

Season Team	League	REGULAR SEASON								PLAYOFFS				
		Gms.	G	A	Pts.	PIM	+/-	PP	SH	Gms.	G	A	Pts.	PIM
85-86—Castlegar	KIJHL	35	30	40	70	41	...	...	...	—	—	—	—	—
86-87—Spokane	WHL	64	8	17	25	27	...	...	...	3	0	0	0	0
87-88—Spokane	WHL	72	33	53	86	42	...	...	...	15	10	10	20	13
88-89—Spokane	WHL	72	51	51	102	79	...	...	...	—	—	—	—	—
89-90—Spokane	WHL	50	45	44	89	80	...	...	...	—	—	—	—	—
—Medicine Hat	WHL	25	15	24	39	19	...	...	...	3	0	0	0	2
90-91—Capital District	AHL	73	21	34	55	26	...	...	...	—	—	—	—	—
91-92—Capital District	AHL	71	23	27	50	10	...	...	...	7	0	4	4	21
92-93—Capital District	AHL	20	12	11	23	39	...	...	...	—	—	—	—	—
—New York Islanders	NHL	61	7	18	25	43	4	1	0	12	3	1	4	6
93-94—New York Islanders	NHL	83	18	22	40	44	16	1	0	4	0	0	0	2
94-95—New York Islanders	NHL	42	5	7	12	25	-10	0	0	—	—	—	—	—
95-96—New York Islanders	NHL	69	25	45	70	42	-20	14	1	—	—	—	—	—
96-97—New York Islanders	NHL	79	23	41	64	38	-5	10	0	—	—	—	—	—
97-98—New York Islanders	NHL	54	14	12	26	66	-19	8	0	—	—	—	—	—
—Anaheim	NHL	22	5	11	16	16	-10	1	0	—	—	—	—	—
NHL Totals (6 years)		410	97	156	253	274	-44	35	1	16	3	1	4	8

GRETZKY, WAYNE   C   RANGERS

PERSONAL: Born January 26, 1961, in Brantford, Ont. ... 6-0/180. ... Shoots left. ... Full name: Wayne Douglas Gretzky. ... Brother of Brent Gretzky, center for Tampa Bay Lightning (1993-94 and 1994-95). ... Nickname: The Great One.
TRANSACTIONS/CAREER NOTES: Signed as underage junior by Indianapolis Racers to multi-year contract (May 1978). ... Traded by Racers with LW Peter Driscoll and G Ed Mio to Edmonton Oilers for cash and future considerations (November 1978). ... Bruised right shoulder (January 28, 1984). ... Underwent surgery on left ankle to remove benign growth (June 1984). ... Twisted right knee (December 30, 1987). ... Suffered corneal abrasion to left eye (February 19, 1988); missed three games. ... Traded by Oilers with RW‡ Marty McSorley and LW/C Mike Krushelnyski to Los Angeles Kings for C Jimmy Carson, LW Martin Gelinas, first-round picks in 1989 (traded to New Jersey), 1991 (LW Martin Rucinsky) and 1993 (D Nick Stajduhar) drafts and cash (August 9, 1988). ... Injured groin (March 17, 1990). ... Strained lower back (March 22, 1990); missed five regular-season games and two playoff games. ... Missed five games due to personal reasons (October 1991). ... Sprained knee (February 25, 1992); missed one game. ... Suffered herniated thoracic disc prior to 1992-93 season; missed first 39 games of season. ... Sprained left knee (April 9, 1994). ... Traded by Kings to St. Louis Blues for LW Craig Johnson, C Patrice Tardiff, C Roman Vopat, fifth-round pick (D Peter Hogan) in 1996 draft and first-round pick (LW Matt Zultek) in 1997 draft (February 27, 1996). ... Bruised lower back (April 4, 1996); missed three games. ... Signed as free agent by New York Rangers (July 21, 1996).
HONORS: Won William Hanley Trophy (1977-78). ... Won Emms Family Award (1977-78). ... Named to OMJHL All-Star second team (1977-78). ... Named WHA Rookie of the Year by The Sporting News (1978-79). ... Won WHA Rookie of the Year Award (1978-79). ... Named to WHA All-Star second team (1978-79). ... Won Hart Memorial Trophy (1979-80 through 1986-87 and 1988-89). ... Won Lady Byng Memorial Trophy (1979-80, 1990-91, 1991-92 and 1993-94). ... Named to The Sporting News All-Star second team (1979-80, 1987-88, 1988-89, 1991-92 and 1993-94). ... Named to NHL All-Star second team (1979-80, 1987-88 through 1989-90, 1993-94, 1996-97 and 1997-98). ... Named NHL Player of Year by The Sporting News (1980-81 through 1986-87). ... Won Art Ross Memorial Trophy (1980-81 through 1986-87, 1989-90, 1990-91 and 1993-94). ... Named to The Sporting News All-Star first team (1980-81 through 1986-87 and 1990-91) ... Named to NHL All-Star first team (1980-81 through 1986-87 and 1990-91). ... Played in NHL All-Star Game (1980-1986, 1988-1994 and 1996-1998). ... Named Man of the Year by The Sporting News (1981). ... Won Lester B. Pearson Award (1981-82 through 1984-85 and 1986-87). ... Won Emery Edge Award (1983-84, 1984-85 and 1986-87). ... Named All-Star Game Most Valuable Player (1983 and 1989). ... Named Canadian Athlete of the Year (1985). ... Won Conn Smythe Trophy (1984-85 and 1987-88). ... Won Dodge Performer of the Year Award (1984-85 through 1986-87). ... Won Dodge Performance of the Year Award (1988-89). ... Won Lester Patrick Trophy (1993-94).
RECORDS: Holds NHL career records for points—2,795; goals—885; assists—1,910; overtime assists—16; overtime points—18; points by a center—2,795; goals by a center—885; assists by a center—1,910; most points including playoffs—3,177; most goals including play-offs—1,007; most assists including playoffs—2,170; most games with three or more goals—50; most 40-or-more goal seasons—12; most consecutive 40-or-more goal seasons—12 (1979-80 through 1990-91); most consecutive 60-or-more goal seasons—4 (1981-82 through 1984-85); most 100-or-more point seasons—15; most consecutive 100-or-more point seasons—13 (1979-80 through 1991-92); highest assist-per-game average—1.348; and highest points-per-game average—1.972. ... Shares NHL career records for most 50-or-more goal sea-sons—9; and most 60-or-more goal seasons—5. ... Holds NHL single-season records for most goals—92 (1981-82); assists—163 (1985-86); points—215 (1985-86); games with three or more goals—10 (1981-82 and 1983-84); highest goals-per-game average—1.18 (1983-84); highest assists-per-game average—2.04 (1985-86); highest points-per-game average—2.77 (1983-84); most points including playoffs—255 (1984-85); most goals including playoffs—100 (1983-84); most assists including playoffs—174 (1985-86); most points by a center—215 (1985-86); most goals by a center—92 (1981-82); most assists by a center—163 (1985-86); and most goals, 50 games from start of season—61 (1981-82 and 1983-84). ... Shares NHL single-game records for most assists—7 (February 15, 1980; December 11, 1985; and February 14, 1986); most assists for road game—7(December 11, 1985); and most goals in one period—4 (February 18, 1981). ... Holds NHL records for most consecutive games scoring points—51 (October 5, 1983 through January 28, 1984); longest point-scoring streak from start of season—51 (1983-84); most consecutive games with an assist—23 (1990-91); and most assists in game by rookie—7 (February 15, 1980). ... Holds NHL career playoff records for most points—382; most goals—122; most assists—260; most games with three-or-more goals—10; and most game-winning goals—23. ... Holds NHL single-season playoff records for most assists—31 (1988); and most points—47 (1985). ... Shares NHL single-season playoff record for most shorthanded goals—3 (1983). ... Holds NHL final-series play-off records for most assists—10 (1988); and most points—13 (1988). ... Shares NHL single-series playoff record for most assists—14 (1985). ... Shares NHL single-game playoff records for most assists—6 (April 9, 1987); most shorthanded goals—2 (April 6, 1983); most assists in one period—3 (done five times); and most points in one period—4 (April 12, 1987). ... Holds NHL career All-Star Game record for most goals—12; and most points—21. ... Holds NHL All-Star Game records for most goals in one period—4 (1983); and most points in one period—4 (1983). ... Shares NHL All-Star Game record for most goals—4 (February 8, 1983).

G

STATISTICAL PLATEAUS: Three-goal games: 1979-80 (2), 1980-81 (2), 1981-82 (6), 1982-83 (2), 1983-84 (6), 1984-85 (5), 1985-86 (3), 1986-87 (3), 1987-88 (1), 1988-89 (2), 1989-90 (1), 1990-91 (2), 1991-92 (1), 1997-98 (1). Total: 37. ... Four-goal games: 1980-81 (1), 1981-82 (3), 1983-84 (4), 1986-87 (1). Total: 9. ... Five-goal games: 1980-81 (1), 1981-82 (1), 1984-85 (1), 1987-88 (1). Total: 4. ... Total hat tricks: 50.

MISCELLANEOUS: Member of Stanley Cup championship team (1984, 1985, 1987 and 1988). ... Captain of Edmonton Oilers (1983-84 through 1987-88). ... Captain of Los Angeles Kings (1989-90 through February 26, 1996). ... Captain of St. Louis Blues (February 27, 1996 through remainder of season). ... Holds Edmonton Oilers all-time records for most points (1,669), most goals (583) and most assists (1,086). ... Scored on a penalty shot (vs. Pierre Hamel, February 6, 1981; vs. Michel Larocque, January 16, 1982; vs. Pat Riggin, November 24, 1982; vs. Richard Brodeur, January 19, 1983; vs. Don Beaupre, April 28, 1984 (playoffs)). ... Failed to score on a penalty shot (vs. Pat Riggin, November 24, 1982; vs. Peter Ing, January 5, 1991).

			REGULAR SEASON								PLAYOFFS				
Season Team	League	Gms.	G	A	Pts.	PIM	+/-	PP	SH		Gms.	G	A	Pts.	PIM
76-77—Peterborough	OMJHL	3	0	3	3	0	...	...	...		—	—	—	—	—
77-78—Sault Ste. Marie	OMJHL	64	70	112	182	14	...	...	...		13	6	20	26	0
78-79—Indianapolis	WHA	8	3	3	6	0	...	...	...		—	—	—	—	—
—Edmonton	WHA	72	43	61	104	19	...	...	...		13	†10	10	*20	2
79-80—Edmonton	NHL	79	51	*86	†137	21	...	13	1		3	2	1	3	0
80-81—Edmonton	NHL	80	55	*109	*164	28	41	15	4		9	7	14	21	4
81-82—Edmonton	NHL	80	*92	*120	*212	26	*81	18	†6		5	5	7	12	8
82-83—Edmonton	NHL	80	*71	*125	*196	59	60	18	*6		16	12	*26	*38	4
83-84—Edmonton	NHL	74	*87	*118	*205	39	*76	*20	*12		19	13	*22	*35	12
84-85—Edmonton	NHL	80	*73	*135	*208	52	*98	8	*11		18	17	*30	*47	4
85-86—Edmonton	NHL	80	52	*163	*215	46	71	11	3		10	8	11	19	2
86-87—Edmonton	NHL	79	*62	*121	*183	28	*70	13	*7		21	5	*29	*34	6
87-88—Edmonton	NHL	64	40	*109	149	24	39	9	5		19	12	*31	*43	16
88-89—Los Angeles	NHL	78	54	†114	168	26	15	11	5		11	5	17	22	0
89-90—Los Angeles	NHL	73	40	*102	*142	42	8	10	4		7	3	7	10	0
90-91—Los Angeles	NHL	78	41	*122	*163	16	30	8	0		12	4	11	15	2
91-92—Los Angeles	NHL	74	31	*90	121	34	-12	12	2		6	2	5	7	2
92-93—Los Angeles	NHL	45	16	49	65	6	6	0	2		24	15	†25	*40	4
93-94—Los Angeles	NHL	81	38	*92	*130	20	-25	14	4		—	—	—	—	—
94-95—Los Angeles	NHL	48	11	37	48	6	-20	3	0		—	—	—	—	—
95-96—Los Angeles	NHL	62	15	66	81	32	-7	5	0		—	—	—	—	—
—St. Louis	NHL	18	8	13	21	2	-6	1	1		13	2	14	16	0
96-97—New York Rangers	NHL	82	25	†72	97	28	12	6	0		15	10	10	20	2
97-98—New York Rangers	NHL	82	23	67	90	28	-11	6	0		—	—	—	—	—
—Can. Olympic Team	Int'l	6	0	4	4	2	...	...	...		—	—	—	—	—
WHA Totals (1 year)		80	46	64	110	19	...	...	...		13	10	10	20	2
NHL Totals (19 years)		1417	885	1910	2795	563	526	201	73		208	122	260	382	66

GRIER, MIKE   RW   OILERS

PERSONAL: Born January 5, 1975, in Detroit. ... 6-1/225. ... Shoots right.
HIGH SCHOOL: St. Sebastian's Country Day (Needham, Mass.).
COLLEGE: Boston University.
TRANSACTIONS/CAREER NOTES: Selected by St. Louis Blues in ninth round (seventh Blues pick, 219th overall) of NHL entry draft (June 26, 1993). ... Rights traded by Blues with rights to G Curtis Joseph to Edmonton Oilers for first-round picks in 1996 (C Marty Reasoner) and 1997 (traded to Los Angeles) drafts (August 4, 1995); picks had been awarded earlier to Oilers as compensation for Blues signing free agent LW Shayne Corson (July 28, 1995). ... Strained medial collateral knee ligament (November 19, 1997); missed 14 games.
HONORS: Named to NCAA All-America East first team (1994-95). ... Named to Hockey East All-Star first team (1994-95).

			REGULAR SEASON								PLAYOFFS				
Season Team	League	Gms.	G	A	Pts.	PIM	+/-	PP	SH		Gms.	G	A	Pts.	PIM
92-93—St. Sebastian's	Mass. H.S.	22	16	27	43	32	...	...	...		—	—	—	—	—
93-94—Boston University	Hockey East	39	9	9	18	56	...	...	...		—	—	—	—	—
94-95—Boston University	Hockey East	37	29	26	55	85	...	...	...		—	—	—	—	—
95-96—Boston University	Hockey East	38	21	25	46	82	...	...	...		—	—	—	—	—
96-97—Edmonton	NHL	79	15	17	32	45	7	4	0		12	3	1	4	4
97-98—Edmonton	NHL	66	9	6	15	73	-3	1	0		12	2	2	4	13
NHL Totals (2 years)		145	24	23	47	118	4	5	0		24	5	3	8	17

GRIMES, JAKE   C   SENATORS

G

PERSONAL: Born September 13, 1972, in Montreal. ... 6-1/196. ... Shoots left. ... Full name: Jake Stephen Grimes.
TRANSACTIONS/CAREER NOTES: Selected by Ottawa Senators in 10th round (10th Senators pick, 217th overall) of NHL entry draft (June 20, 1992).

			REGULAR SEASON								PLAYOFFS				
Season Team	League	Gms.	G	A	Pts.	PIM	+/-	PP	SH		Gms.	G	A	Pts.	PIM
89-90—Belleville	OHL	66	9	12	21	11	...	...	...		11	0	5	5	14
90-91—Belleville	OHL	66	31	41	72	16	...	...	...		6	2	0	2	4
91-92—Belleville	OHL	66	44	69	113	18	...	...	...		5	4	0	4	0
92-93—New Haven	AHL	76	18	20	38	30	...	...	...		—	—	—	—	—
93-94—Thunder Bay	Col.HL	10	7	5	12	6	...	...	...		—	—	—	—	—
—Prin. Edward Island	AHL	42	12	13	25	24	...	...	...		—	—	—	—	—
94-95—Thunder Bay	Col.HL	15	10	12	22	4	...	...	...		—	—	—	—	—
95-96—					Statistics unavailable.										
96-97—					Statistics unavailable.										
97-98—					Statistics unavailable.										

GRIMES, KEVIN — D — AVALANCHE

PERSONAL: Born August 19, 1979, in Ottawa. ... 6-2/202. ... Shoots left. ... Related to Kris Draper, center, Detroit Red Wings.
TRANSACTIONS/CAREER NOTES: Selected by Colorado Avalanche in first round (first Avalanche pick, 26th overall) of NHL entry draft (June 21, 1997).
HONORS: Named to OHL All-Rookie second team (1996-97).

		REGULAR SEASON								PLAYOFFS				
Season Team	League	Gms.	G	A	Pts.	PIM	+/-	PP	SH	Gms.	G	A	Pts.	PIM
95-96—Cumberland	CJHL	51	2	10	12	220	...	...	...	—	—	—	—	—
96-97—Kingston	OHL	57	2	12	14	188	...	...	...	1	0	0	0	0
97-98—Kingston	OHL	62	1	27	28	179	...	...	...	12	0	1	1	16

GRIMSON, STU — LW — MIGHTY DUCKS

PERSONAL: Born May 20, 1965, in Kamloops, B.C. ... 6-6/226. ... Shoots left. ... Full name: Stuart Grimson. ... Nickname: The Grim Reaper.
COLLEGE: Manitoba.
TRANSACTIONS/CAREER NOTES: Fractured forearm (February 1983). ... Selected by Detroit Red Wings in 10th round (11th Red Wings pick, 186th overall) of NHL entry draft (June 8, 1983). ... Returned to draft pool and selected by Calgary Flames in seventh round (eighth Flames pick, 143rd overall) of NHL entry draft (June 15, 1985). ... Broke cheekbone (January 9, 1990). ... Claimed on waivers by Chicago Blackhawks (October 1, 1990). ... Injured eye (February 3, 1993). ... Selected by Mighty Ducks of Anaheim in NHL expansion draft (June 24, 1993). ... Lacerated hand (January 16, 1994); missed one game. ... Lacerated hand (March 9, 1994); missed one game. ... Lacerated hand (March 26, 1994); missed five games. ... Traded by Mighty Ducks with D Mark Ferner and sixth-round pick (LW Magnus Nilsson) in 1996 draft to Red Wings for C/RW Mike Sillinger and D Jason York (April 4, 1995). ... Signed by New York Rangers to offer sheet (August 18, 1995); Red Wings matched offer (August 24, 1995). ... Suffered from the flu (December 12, 1995); missed two games. ... Suspended two games and fined $1,000 by NHL for striking another player with a gloved hand (January 12, 1996). ... Claimed on waivers by Hartford Whalers (October 12, 1996). ... Whalers franchise moved to North Carolina and renamed Carolina Hurricanes for 1997-98 season; NHL approved move on June 25, 1997. ... Traded by Hurricanes with D Kevin Haller to Mighty Ducks of Anaheim for D Dave Karpa and 4th round pick in 2000 draft (August 11, 1998).

		REGULAR SEASON								PLAYOFFS				
Season Team	League	Gms.	G	A	Pts.	PIM	+/-	PP	SH	Gms.	G	A	Pts.	PIM
82-83—Regina	WHL	48	0	1	1	144	...	...	...	5	0	0	0	14
83-84—Regina	WHL	63	8	8	16	131	...	...	...	21	0	1	1	29
84-85—Regina	WHL	71	24	32	56	248	...	...	...	8	1	2	3	14
85-86—Univ.of Manitoba	CWUAA	12	7	4	11	113	...	...	...	3	1	1	2	20
86-87—Univ.of Manitoba	CWUAA	29	8	8	16	67	...	...	...	14	4	2	6	28
87-88—Salt Lake City	IHL	38	9	5	14	268	...	...	...	—	—	—	—	—
88-89—Calgary	NHL	1	0	0	0	5	0	0	0	—	—	—	—	—
—Salt Lake City	IHL	72	9	18	27	*397	...	...	...	15	2	3	5	*86
89-90—Salt Lake City	IHL	62	8	8	16	319	...	...	...	4	0	0	0	8
—Calgary	NHL	3	0	0	0	17	-1	0	0	—	—	—	—	—
90-91—Chicago	NHL	35	0	1	1	183	-3	0	0	5	0	0	0	46
91-92—Chicago	NHL	54	2	2	4	234	-2	0	0	14	0	1	1	10
—Indianapolis	IHL	5	1	1	2	17	...	...	...	—	—	—	—	—
92-93—Chicago	NHL	78	1	1	2	193	2	1	0	2	0	0	0	4
93-94—Anaheim	NHL	77	1	5	6	199	-6	0	0	—	—	—	—	—
94-95—Anaheim	NHL	31	0	1	1	110	-7	0	0	—	—	—	—	—
—Detroit	NHL	11	0	0	0	37	-4	0	0	11	1	0	1	26
95-96—Detroit	NHL	56	0	1	1	128	-10	0	0	2	0	0	0	0
96-97—Detroit	NHL	1	0	0	0	0	-1	0	0	—	—	—	—	—
—Hartford	NHL	75	2	2	4	218	-7	0	0	—	—	—	—	—
97-98—Carolina	NHL	82	3	4	7	204	0	0	0	—	—	—	—	—
NHL Totals (10 years)		504	9	17	26	1528	-39	1	0	34	1	1	2	86

GROLEAU, FRANCOIS — D — CANADIENS

PERSONAL: Born January 23, 1973, in Longueuil, Que. ... 6-0/200. ... Shoots left. ... Name pronounced FRAN-swah GROO-loh.
TRANSACTIONS/CAREER NOTES: Selected by Calgary Flames in second round (second Flames pick, 41st overall) of NHL entry draft (June 22, 1991). ... Traded by Flames to Quebec Nordiques for D Ed Ward (March 24, 1995). ... Signed as a free agent by Montreal Canadiens (March 14, 1996).
HONORS: Won Raymond Lagace Trophy (1989-90). ... Named to QMJHL All-Star second team (1989-90). ... Won Emile (Butch) Bouchard Trophy (1991-92). ... Named to QMJHL All-Star first team (1991-92).

		REGULAR SEASON								PLAYOFFS				
Season Team	League	Gms.	G	A	Pts.	PIM	+/-	PP	SH	Gms.	G	A	Pts.	PIM
89-90—Shawinigan	QMJHL	60	11	54	65	80	...	...	...	6	0	1	1	12
90-91—Shawinigan	QMJHL	70	9	60	69	70	...	...	...	6	0	3	3	2
91-92—Shawinigan	QMJHL	65	8	70	78	74	...	...	...	10	5	15	20	8
92-93—St. Jean	QMJHL	48	7	38	45	66	...	...	...	4	0	1	1	14
93-94—Saint John	AHL	73	8	14	22	49	...	...	...	7	0	1	1	2
94-95—Saint John	AHL	65	6	34	40	28	...	...	...	—	—	—	—	—
—Cornwall	AHL	8	1	2	3	7	...	...	...	14	2	7	9	16
95-96—San Francisco	IHL	63	6	26	32	60	...	...	...	—	—	—	—	—
—Fredericton	AHL	12	3	5	8	10	...	...	...	10	1	6	7	14
—Montreal	NHL	2	0	1	1	2	2	0	0	—	—	—	—	—
96-97—Fredericton	AHL	47	8	24	32	43	...	...	...	—	—	—	—	—
—Montreal	NHL	5	0	0	0	4	0	0	0	—	—	—	—	—
97-98—Montreal	NHL	1	0	0	0	0	1	0	0	—	—	—	—	—
—Fredericton	AHL	63	14	26	40	70	...	...	...	4	0	2	2	4
NHL Totals (3 years)		8	0	1	1	6	3	0	0					

G

GRON, STANISLAV   C   DEVILS

PERSONAL: Born October 28, 1978, in Bratislava, Czechoslovakia. ... 6-1/190. ... Shoots left.
TRANSACTIONS/CAREER NOTES: Selected by New Jersey Devils in second round (second Devils pick, 38th overall) of NHL entry draft (June 21, 1997).

Season Team	League	Gms.	G	A	Pts.	PIM	+/-	PP	SH	Gms.	G	A	Pts.	PIM
				REGULAR SEASON								**PLAYOFFS**		
94-95—Slov. Bratislava Jrs.	Slovakia	40	49	26	75	20	...	...	...	—	—	—	—	—
95-96—Slov. Bratislava Jrs.	Slovakia	43	33	25	58	14	...	...	...	—	—	—	—	—
—Slovan Bratislava	Slovakia	—	—	—	—	—	...	...	...	1	0	0	0	0
96-97—Slov. Bratislava Jrs.	Slovakia	22	20	15	35	...	...	...	...	—	—	—	—	—
—Slovan Bratislava	Slovakia	7	0	0	0	...	...	...	...	—	—	—	—	—
97-98—Seattle.......................	WHL	61	9	29	38	21	...	...	...	5	1	5	6	0

GRONMAN, TUOMAS   D   PENGUINS

PERSONAL: Born March 22, 1974, in Vitasaari, Finland. ... 6-3/219. ... Shoots left. ... Name pronounced GRAHN-muhn.
TRANSACTIONS/CAREER NOTES: Selected by Quebec Nordiques in second round (third Nordiques pick, 29th overall) of NHL entry draft (June 20, 1992). ... Nordiques franchise moved to Colorado and renamed Avalanche for 1995-96 season (June 21, 1995). ... Traded by Avalanche to Chicago Blackhawks for second-round pick (G Philippe Sauve) in 1998 draft (July 10, 1996). ... Dislocated elbow (October 15, 1996); missed 12 games. ... Traded by Blackhawks to Pittsburgh Penguins for C Greg Johnson (October 27, 1997). ... Suffered from the flu (November 12, 1997); missed one game.
MISCELLANEOUS: Member of bronze-medal-winning Finnish Olympic team (1998).

Season Team	League	Gms.	G	A	Pts.	PIM	+/-	PP	SH	Gms.	G	A	Pts.	PIM
				REGULAR SEASON								**PLAYOFFS**		
90-91—Rauman Lukko	Finland	40	15	20	35	60	...	...	...	—	—	—	—	—
91-92—Tacoma	WHL	61	5	18	23	102	...	...	...	4	0	1	1	2
—Finnish nat'l Jr. team ..	Finland	7	1	0	1	10	...	...	...	—	—	—	—	—
92-93—Rauman Lukko	Finland	45	2	11	13	46	...	...	...	—	—	—	—	—
93-94—Lukko..........................	Finland	44	4	12	16	40	...	...	...	9	0	1	1	14
94-95—TPS Turku	Finland	47	4	20	24	66	...	...	...	13	2	2	4	43
95-96—TPS Turku	Finland	32	5	7	12	85	...	...	...	11	1	4	5	16
96-97—Chicago......................	NHL	16	0	1	1	13	-4	0	0	—	—	—	—	—
—Indianapolis...............	IHL	51	5	16	21	89	...	...	...	4	1	1	2	6
97-98—Indianapolis...............	IHL	6	0	3	3	6	...	...	...	—	—	—	—	—
—Syracuse...................	AHL	33	6	14	20	45	...	...	...	—	—	—	—	—
—Pittsburgh.................	NHL	22	1	2	3	25	3	1	0	1	0	0	0	0
—Fin. Olympic Team	Int'l	4	0	0	0	2	...	...	...	—	—	—	—	—
NHL Totals (2 years)..........		38	1	3	4	38	-1	1	0	1	0	0	0	0

GROSEK, MICHAL   LW   SABRES

PERSONAL: Born June 1, 1975, in Gottwaldov, Czechoslovakia. ... 6-2/207. ... Shoots right. ... Name pronounced GROH-shehk.
TRANSACTIONS/CAREER NOTES: Selected by Winnipeg Jets in sixth round (seventh Jets pick, 145th overall) of NHL entry draft (June 26, 1993). ... Sprained knee ligaments (February 15, 1995); missed four games. ... Fractured foot (April 5, 1995); missed remainder of season. ... Traded by Jets with D Darryl Shannon to Buffalo Sabres for D Craig Muni (February 15, 1996).
STATISTICAL PLATEAUS: Three-goal games: 1996-97 (1).

Season Team	League	Gms.	G	A	Pts.	PIM	+/-	PP	SH	Gms.	G	A	Pts.	PIM
				REGULAR SEASON								**PLAYOFFS**		
92-93—ZPS Zlin	Czech.	17	1	3	4	0	...	...	...	—	—	—	—	—
93-94—Moncton	AHL	20	1	2	3	47	...	...	...	2	0	0	0	0
—Tacoma	WHL	30	25	20	45	106	...	...	...	7	2	2	4	30
—Winnipeg	NHL	3	1	0	1	0	-1	0	0	—	—	—	—	—
94-95—Springfield	AHL	45	10	22	32	98	...	...	...	—	—	—	—	—
—Winnipeg	NHL	24	2	2	4	21	-3	0	0	—	—	—	—	—
95-96—Springfield	AHL	39	16	19	35	68	...	...	...	—	—	—	—	—
—Winnipeg	NHL	1	0	0	0	0	-1	0	0	—	—	—	—	—
—Buffalo	NHL	22	6	4	10	31	0	2	0	—	—	—	—	—
96-97—Buffalo	NHL	82	15	21	36	71	25	1	0	12	3	3	6	8
97-98—Buffalo	NHL	67	10	20	30	60	9	2	0	15	6	4	10	28
NHL Totals (5 years)..........		199	34	47	81	183	29	5	0	27	9	7	16	36

GUERIN, BILL   RW/C   OILERS

PERSONAL: Born November 9, 1970, in Wilbraham, Mass. ... 6-2/210. ... Shoots right. ... Full name: William Robert Guerin. ... Name pronounced GAIR-ihn.
COLLEGE: Boston College.
TRANSACTIONS/CAREER NOTES: Selected by New Jersey Devils in first round (first Devils pick, fifth overall) of NHL entry draft (June 17, 1989). ... Suffered from the flu (February 1992); missed three games. ... Suffered from sore leg (March 19, 1994); missed two games. ... Suffered from the flu (December 6, 1995); missed two games. ... Missed first 21 games of 1997-98 season due to contract dispute. ... Traded by Devils with RW Valeri Zelepukin to Edmonton Oilers for C Jason Arnott and D Bryan Muir (January 4, 1998).
MISCELLANEOUS: Member of Stanley Cup championship team (1995).
STATISTICAL PLATEAUS: Three-goal games: 1996-97 (1).

G

Season Team	League	REGULAR SEASON								PLAYOFFS				
		Gms.	G	A	Pts.	PIM	+/-	PP	SH	Gms.	G	A	Pts.	PIM
85-86—Springfield Jr. B........	NEJHL	48	26	19	45	71	...	...	...	—	—	—	—	—
86-87—Springfield Jr. B........	NEJHL	32	34	20	54	40	...	...	...	—	—	—	—	—
87-88—Springfield Jr. B........	NEJHL	38	31	44	75	146	...	...	...	—	—	—	—	—
88-89—Springfield Jr. B........	NEJHL	31	32	37	69	90	...	...	...	—	—	—	—	—
89-90—Boston College	Hockey East	39	14	11	25	64	...	...	...	—	—	—	—	—
90-91—Boston College	Hockey East	38	26	19	45	102	...	...	...	—	—	—	—	—
91-92—U.S. national team	Int'l	46	12	15	27	67	...	...	...	—	—	—	—	—
—Utica	AHL	22	13	10	23	6	...	...	...	4	1	3	4	14
—New Jersey	NHL	5	0	1	1	9	1	0	0	6	3	0	3	4
92-93—New Jersey	NHL	65	14	20	34	63	14	0	0	5	1	1	2	4
—Utica	AHL	18	10	7	17	47	...	...	...	—	—	—	—	—
93-94—New Jersey	NHL	81	25	19	44	101	14	2	0	17	2	1	3	35
94-95—New Jersey	NHL	48	12	13	25	72	6	4	0	20	3	8	11	30
95-96—New Jersey	NHL	80	23	30	53	116	7	8	0	—	—	—	—	—
96-97—New Jersey	NHL	82	29	18	47	95	-2	7	0	8	2	1	3	18
97-98—New Jersey	NHL	19	5	5	10	13	0	1	0	—	—	—	—	—
—Edmonton	NHL	40	13	16	29	80	1	8	0	12	7	1	8	17
—U.S. Olympic Team	Int'l	4	0	3	3	2	...	...	...	—	—	—	—	—
NHL Totals (7 years)...........		420	121	122	243	549	41	30	0	68	18	12	30	108

GUOLLA, STEVE   LW   SHARKS

PERSONAL: Born March 15, 1973, in Scarborough, Ont. ... 6-0/190. ... Shoots left. ... Full name: Stephen Guolla. ... Name pronounced GWAH-luh.
HIGH SCHOOL: Stephen Leacock (Agincourt, Ont.).
COLLEGE: Michigan State.
TRANSACTIONS/CAREER NOTES: Sprained knee (December 1991); missed eight games. ... Selected by Ottawa Senators (first Senators pick, third overall) in NHL supplemental draft (June 28, 1994). ... Signed as free agent by San Jose Sharks (August 26, 1996).
HONORS: Named to NCCA All-America West second team (1993-94). ... Named to CCHA All-Star second team (1993-94). ... Named to AHL All-Star second team (1997-98). ... Won Les Cunningham Plaque (1997-98).

Season Team	League	REGULAR SEASON								PLAYOFFS				
		Gms.	G	A	Pts.	PIM	+/-	PP	SH	Gms.	G	A	Pts.	PIM
90-91—Wexford Jr. B.............	MTHL	—	37	42	79	—	...	...	...	—	—	—	—	—
91-92—Michigan State...........	CCHA	33	4	9	13	8	...	...	...	—	—	—	—	—
92-93—Michigan State...........	CCHA	39	19	35	54	6	...	...	...	—	—	—	—	—
93-94—Michigan State...........	CCHA	41	23	46	69	16	...	...	...	—	—	—	—	—
94-95—Michigan State...........	CCHA	40	16	35	51	16	...	...	...	—	—	—	—	—
95-96—Prin. Edward Island	AHL	72	32	48	80	28	...	...	...	3	0	0	0	0
96-97—Kentucky....................	AHL	34	22	22	44	10	...	...	...	4	2	1	3	0
—San Jose....................	NHL	43	13	8	21	14	-10	2	0	—	—	—	—	—
97-98—Kentucky....................	AHL	69	37	63	100	45	...	...	...	3	0	0	0	0
—San Jose....................	NHL	7	1	1	2	0	-2	0	0	—	—	—	—	—
NHL Totals (2 years)...........		50	14	9	23	14	-12	2	0					

GUREN, MIROSLAV   D   CANADIENS

PERSONAL: Born September 24, 1976, in Gottwaldov, Czechoslovakia. ... 6-2/210. ... Shoots left.
TRANSACTIONS/CAREER NOTES: Selected by Montreal Canadiens in third round (second Canadiens pick, 60th overall) of NHL entry draft (July 8, 1995).

Season Team	League	REGULAR SEASON								PLAYOFFS				
		Gms.	G	A	Pts.	PIM	+/-	PP	SH	Gms.	G	A	Pts.	PIM
93-94—ZPS Zlin	Czech Rep.	22	1	5	6	...	...	...	...	3	0	0	0	...
94-95—ZPS Zlin	Czech Rep.	32	3	7	10	...	...	...	...	12	1	0	1	...
95-96—ZPS Zlin	Czech Rep.	27	1	2	3	...	...	...	...	7	1	0	1	...
96-97—Fredericton	AHL	79	6	26	32	26	...	...	...	—	—	—	—	—
97-98—Fredericton	AHL	78	15	36	51	36	...	...	...	4	1	2	3	0

GUSAROV, ALEXEI   D   AVALANCHE   G

PERSONAL: Born July 8, 1964, in Leningrad, U.S.S.R. ... 6-3/185. ... Shoots left. ... Name pronounced GOO-sah-rahf.
TRANSACTIONS/CAREER NOTES: Selected by Quebec Nordiques in 11th round (11th Nordiques pick, 213th overall) in the NHL entry draft (June 11, 1988). ... Suffered hairline fracture of left ankle (December 15, 1990); missed seven games. ... Hyperextended right knee (February 28, 1991). ... Fractured finger (October 13, 1991); missed four games. ... Suffered from the flu (February 9, 1993); missed two games. ... Suffered concussion (March 31, 1993); missed two games. ... Bruised left thumb (November 13, 1993); missed one game. ... Suffered from the flu (January 11, 1994); missed two games. ... Suffered from inflammation of sinuses (March 30, 1994); missed two games. ... Injured foot (January 21, 1995); missed nine games. ... Reinjured foot (February 11, 1995); missed six games. ... Injured knee (March 26, 1995); missed last 17 games of season and entire playoffs. ... Nordiques franchise moved to Colorado and renamed Avalanche for 1995-96 season (June 21, 1995). ... Suffered concussion (December 13, 1995); missed two games. ... Suffered from the flu (November 11, 1996); missed three games. ... Scratched cornea (November 30, 1996); missed three games. ... Suffered concussion (December 17, 1996); missed 13 games. ... Suffered from the flu (January 28, 1998); missed one game. ... Injured finger (April 2, 1998); missed one game.
MISCELLANEOUS: Member of Stanley Cup championship team (1996). ... Member of gold-medal-winning U.S.S.R. Olympic team (1988). ... Scored on a penalty shot (vs. Grant Fuhr, March 10, 1993). ... Member of silver-medal-winning Russian Olympic team (1998).

Season Team	League	Gms.	G	A	Pts.	PIM	+/-	PP	SH	Gms.	G	A	Pts.	PIM
		REGULAR SEASON								**PLAYOFFS**				
81-82—SKA Leningrad............	USSR	20	1	2	3	16	...	...	...	—	—	—	—	—
82-83—SKA Leningrad............	USSR	42	2	1	3	32	...	...	...	—	—	—	—	—
83-84—SKA Leningrad............	USSR	43	2	3	5	32	...	...	...	—	—	—	—	—
84-85—CSKA Moscow.............	USSR	36	3	2	5	26	...	...	...	—	—	—	—	—
85-86—CSKA Moscow.............	USSR	40	3	5	8	30	...	...	...	—	—	—	—	—
86-87—CSKA Moscow.............	USSR	38	4	7	11	24	...	...	...	—	—	—	—	—
87-88—CSKA Moscow.............	USSR	39	3	2	5	28	...	...	...	—	—	—	—	—
88-89—CSKA Moscow.............	USSR	42	5	4	9	37	...	...	...	—	—	—	—	—
89-90—CSKA Moscow.............	USSR	42	4	7	11	42	...	...	...	—	—	—	—	—
90-91—CSKA Moscow.............	USSR	15	0	0	0	12	...	...	...	—	—	—	—	—
—Quebec	NHL	36	3	9	12	12	-4	1	0	—	—	—	—	—
—Halifax.....................	AHL	2	0	3	3	2	...	...	...	—	—	—	—	—
91-92—Quebec	NHL	68	5	18	23	22	-9	3	0	—	—	—	—	—
—Halifax.....................	AHL	3	0	0	0	0	...	...	...	—	—	—	—	—
92-93—Quebec	NHL	79	8	22	30	57	18	0	2	5	0	1	1	0
93-94—Quebec	NHL	76	5	20	25	38	3	0	1	—	—	—	—	—
94-95—Quebec	NHL	14	1	2	3	6	-1	0	0	—	—	—	—	—
95-96—Colorado	NHL	65	5	15	20	56	29	0	0	21	0	9	9	12
96-97—Colorado	NHL	58	2	12	14	28	4	0	0	17	0	3	3	14
97-98—Colorado	NHL	72	4	10	14	42	9	0	1	7	0	1	1	6
—Russian Oly. team.......	Int'l	6	0	1	1	8	...	...	...	—	—	—	—	—
NHL Totals (8 years)...........		468	33	108	141	261	49	4	4	50	0	14	14	32

GUSEV, SERGEY D STARS

PERSONAL: Born July 31, 1975, in Nizhny Tagil, U.S.S.R. ... 6-1/195. ... Shoots left. ... Name pronounced GOO-sehf.
TRANSACTIONS/CAREER NOTES: Selected by Dallas Stars in third round (fourth Stars pick, 69th overall) of NHL entry draft (July 8, 1995). ... Bruised thigh (October 18, 1997); missed two games.

Season Team	League	Gms.	G	A	Pts.	PIM	+/-	PP	SH	Gms.	G	A	Pts.	PIM
		REGULAR SEASON								**PLAYOFFS**				
94-95—CSK VVS Samara........	CIS	50	3	5	8	58	...	...	...	—	—	—	—	—
95-96—Michigan...................	IHL	73	11	17	28	76	...	...	...	—	—	—	—	—
96-97—Michigan...................	IHL	51	7	8	15	44	...	...	...	4	0	4	4	6
97-98—Dallas......................	NHL	9	0	0	0	2	-5	0	0	—	—	—	—	—
—Michigan...................	IHL	36	3	6	9	36	...	...	...	4	0	2	2	6
NHL Totals (1 year)..............		9	0	0	0	2	-5	0	0					

GUSTAFSSON, PER D

PERSONAL: Born April 6, 1970, in Jonkoping, Sweden. ... 6-2/195. ... Shoots left. ... Name pronounced PAIR GUZ-tuhv-suhn.
TRANSACTIONS/CAREER NOTES: Selected by Florida Panthers in 11th round (10th Panthers pick, 261st overall) of NHL entry draft (June 29, 1994). ... Traded by Panthers to Toronto Maple Leafs for D Mike Lankshear (June 12, 1997). ... Bruised ankle (December 6, 1997); missed two games. ... Traded by Maple Leafs to Ottawa Senators for eighth-round pick (D Dwight Wolfe) in 1998 draft (March 17, 1998).

Season Team	League	Gms.	G	A	Pts.	PIM	+/-	PP	SH	Gms.	G	A	Pts.	PIM
		REGULAR SEASON								**PLAYOFFS**				
93-94—HV 71 Jonkoping........	Sweden	34	9	7	16	10	...	...	...	—	—	—	—	—
94-95—HV 71 Jonkoping........	Sweden	38	10	6	16	14	...	...	...	13	7	5	12	8
95-96—HV 71 Jonkoping........	Sweden	34	8	13	21	12	...	...	...	4	3	1	4	2
—Vasteras....................	Sweden	16	2	1	3	4	...	...	...	—	—	—	—	—
96-97—Florida....................	NHL	58	7	22	29	22	11	2	0	—	—	—	—	—
97-98—Toronto	NHL	22	1	4	5	10	-5	0	0	—	—	—	—	—
—St. John's..................	AHL	25	7	17	24	10	...	...	...	—	—	—	—	—
—Ottawa.....................	NHL	9	0	1	1	6	3	0	0	1	0	0	0	0
NHL Totals (2 years)...........		89	8	27	35	38	9	2	0	1	0	0	0	0

HACKETT, JEFF G BLACKHAWKS

PERSONAL: Born June 1, 1968, in London, Ont. ... 6-1/195. ... Catches left.
TRANSACTIONS/CAREER NOTES: Selected by New York Islanders as underage junior in second round (second Islanders pick, 34th overall) of NHL entry draft (June 13, 1987). ... Strained groin (May 1, 1990). ... Selected by San Jose Sharks in NHL expansion draft (May 30, 1991). ... Injured groin and hamstring (December 3, 1991); missed nine games. ... Injured knee (March 23, 1992). ... Injured groin (October 30, 1992); missed 12 games. ... Suffered from the flu (February 20, 1993); missed five games. ... Traded by Sharks to Chicago Blackhawks for third-round pick (C Alexei Yegorov) in 1994 draft (July 13, 1993). ... Pulled groin (October 17, 1995); missed three games. ... Broke finger (March 22, 1996); missed three games. ... Broke finger (October 6, 1996); missed 12 games. ... Pulled groin (March 18, 1997); missed two games. ... Sprained ankle (October 9, 1997); missed 11 games.
HONORS: Won F.W. (Dinty) Moore Trophy (1986-87). ... Shared Dave Pinkney Trophy with Sean Evoy (1986-87). ... Won Jack Butterfield Trophy (1989-90).
MISCELLANEOUS: Stopped penalty shot attempt (vs. Brett Hull, January 4, 1996). ... Allowed penalty shot goal (vs. Randy Wood, January 11, 1994; vs. Geoff Courtnall, December 13, 1996; vs. Adam Deadmarsh, March 1, 1997).

Season Team	League	Gms.	Min	W	L	T	GA	SO	Avg.	Gms.	Min.	W	L	GA	SO	Avg.
		REGULAR SEASON								**PLAYOFFS**						
85-86—London Jr. B	OHA	19	1150				66	0	3.44	—	—	—	—	—	—	—
86-87—Oshawa	OHL	31	1672	18	9	2	85	2	3.05	15	895	8	7	40	0	2.68
87-88—Oshawa	OHL	53	3165	30	21	2	205	0	3.89	7	438	3	4	31	0	4.25
88-89—New York Islanders	NHL	13	662	4	7	0	39	0	3.53	—	—	—	—	—	—	—
—Springfield	AHL	29	1677	12	14	2	116	0	4.15	—	—	—	—	—	—	—

G
H

Season Team	League	REGULAR SEASON							PLAYOFFS					
		Gms.	Min	W	L	T	GA	SO	Avg.	Gms.	Min.	W	L	GA	SO	Avg.
89-90—Springfield	AHL	54	3045	24	25	3	187	1	3.68	†17	934	10	5	*60	0	3.85
90-91—New York Islanders	NHL	30	1508	5	18	1	91	0	3.62	—	—	—	—	—	—	—
91-92—San Jose	NHL	42	2314	11	27	1	148	0	3.84	—	—	—	—	—	—	—
92-93—San Jose	NHL	36	2000	2	30	1	176	0	5.28	—	—	—	—	—	—	—
93-94—Chicago	NHL	22	1084	2	12	3	62	0	3.43	—	—	—	—	—	—	—
94-95—Chicago	NHL	7	328	1	3	2	13	0	2.38	2	26	0	0	1	0	2.31
95-96—Chicago	NHL	35	2000	18	11	4	80	4	2.40	1	60	0	1	5	0	5.00
96-97—Chicago	NHL	41	2473	19	18	4	89	2	2.16	6	345	2	4	25	0	4.35
97-98—Chicago	NHL	58	3441	21	25	11	126	8	2.20	—	—	—	—	—	—	—
NHL Totals (9 years)		284	15810	83	151	27	824	14	3.13	9	431	2	5	31	0	4.32

HAGGERTY, SEAN LW ISLANDERS

PERSONAL: Born February 11, 1976, in Rye, N.Y. ... 6-1/186. ... Shoots left. ... Brother of Ryan Haggerty, center in Edmonton Oilers system.
HIGH SCHOOL: Westminster School (Simsbury, Conn.).
TRANSACTIONS/CAREER NOTES: Selected by Toronto Maple Leafs in second round (second Maple Leafs pick, 48th overall) of NHL entry draft (June 28, 1994). ... Traded by Maple Leafs with C Darby Hendrickson, D Kenny Jonsson and first-round pick (G Roberto Luongo) in 1997 draft to New York Islanders for LW Wendel Clark, D Mathieu Schneider and D D.J. Smith (March 13, 1996).
HONORS: Named to OHL All-Rookie team (1993-94). ... Named to Memorial Cup All-Star team (1994-95). ... Named to OHL All-Star second team (1995-96). ... Named to AHL All-Star second team (1997-98).

Season Team	League	REGULAR SEASON							PLAYOFFS				
		Gms.	G	A	Pts.	PIM	+/-	PP	SH	Gms.	G	A	Pts.	PIM
90-91—Westminster Prep	USHS (East)	25	20	22	42	...	...	...	...	—	—	—	—	—
91-92—Westminster Prep	USHS (East)	25	24	36	60	...	...	...	...	—	—	—	—	—
92-93—Boston	NEJHL	72	70	111	181	80	...	...	...	—	—	—	—	—
93-94—Detroit	OHL	60	31	32	63	21	...	...	...	17	9	10	19	11
94-95—Detroit	OHL	61	40	49	89	37	...	...	...	21	13	24	37	18
95-96—Detroit	OHL	66	*60	51	111	78	...	...	...	17	15	9	24	30
—Toronto	NHL	1	0	0	0	0	0	0	0	—	—	—	—	—
—Worcester	AHL	—	—	—	—	—	...	...	...	1	0	0	0	2
96-97—Kentucky	AHL	77	13	22	35	60	...	...	...	4	1	0	1	4
97-98—Kentucky	AHL	63	33	20	53	64	...	...	...	3	0	2	2	4
—New York Islanders	NHL	5	0	0	0	0	-3	0	0	—	—	—	—	—
NHL Totals (2 years)		6	0	0	0	0	-3	0	0					

HAJT, CHRIS D OILERS

PERSONAL: Born July 5, 1978, in Amherst, N.Y. ... 6-3/210. ... Shoots left. ... Son of Bill Hajt, defenseman with Buffalo Sabres (1973-74 through 1986-87). ... Name pronounced HIGHT.
TRANSACTIONS/CAREER NOTES: Selected by Edmonton Oilers in second round (third Oilers pick, 32nd overall) of NHL entry draft (June 22, 1996).
HONORS: Named to OHL All-Star second team (1997-98).

Season Team	League	REGULAR SEASON							PLAYOFFS				
		Gms.	G	A	Pts.	PIM	+/-	PP	SH	Gms.	G	A	Pts.	PIM
94-95—Guelph	OHL	57	1	7	8	35	...	...	...	14	0	2	2	9
95-96—Guelph	OHL	63	8	27	35	69	...	...	...	16	0	6	6	13
96-97—Guelph	OHL	58	11	15	26	62	...	...	...	18	0	8	8	25
97-98—Guelph	OHL	44	2	21	23	42	...	...	...	12	1	5	6	11

HALFNIGHT, ASHLIN D HURRICANES

PERSONAL: Born March 14, 1975, in Toronto. ... 6-1/195. ... Shoots left.
COLLEGE: Harvard.
TRANSACTIONS/CAREER NOTES: Selected by Hartford Whalers in ninth round (ninth Whalers pick, 213th overall) of NHL entry draft (June 29, 1994).

Season Team	League	REGULAR SEASON							PLAYOFFS				
		Gms.	G	A	Pts.	PIM	+/-	PP	SH	Gms.	G	A	Pts.	PIM
92-93—Canadian nat'l team	Int'l	3	1	0	1	2	...	...	...	—	—	—	—	—
93-94—Harvard University	ECAC	30	2	8	10	24	...	...	...	—	—	—	—	—
94-95—Harvard University	ECAC	24	5	15	20	42	...	...	...	—	—	—	—	—
95-96—Harvard University	ECAC	30	2	10	12	12	...	...	...	—	—	—	—	—
96-97—Harvard University	ECAC	31	6	6	12	50	...	...	...	—	—	—	—	—
97-98—New Haven	AHL	64	3	11	14	26	...	...	...	3	0	1	1	2

HALKO, STEVE D HURRICANES

PERSONAL: Born March 8, 1974, in Etobicoke, Ont. ... 6-1/190. ... Shoots right. ... Full name: Steven Halko. ... Name pronounced HAHL-koh.
HIGH SCHOOL: Notre Dame Secondary School (Brampton, Ont.).
COLLEGE: Michigan.
TRANSACTIONS/CAREER NOTES: Selected by Hartford Whalers in 10th round (10th Whalers pick, 225th overall) of NHL entry draft (June 20, 1992).
HONORS: Named to CCHA All-Star second team (1994-95). ... Named to NCAA All-Tournament team (1995-96). ... Named to CCHA All-Star second team (1995-96).

H

Season Team	League	REGULAR SEASON								PLAYOFFS				
		Gms.	G	A	Pts.	PIM	+/-	PP	SH	Gms.	G	A	Pts.	PIM
91-92—Thornhill	OHA Jr. A	44	15	46	61	43	...	...	...	—	—	—	—	—
92-93—Univ. of Michigan........	CCHA	39	1	12	13	12	...	...	...	—	—	—	—	—
93-94—Univ. of Michigan........	CCHA	41	2	13	15	32	...	...	...	—	—	—	—	—
94-95—Univ. of Michigan........	CCHA	39	2	14	16	20	...	...	...	—	—	—	—	—
95-96—Univ. of Michigan........	CCHA	43	4	16	20	32	...	...	...	—	—	—	—	—
96-97—Springfield	AHL	70	1	5	6	37	...	...	...	11	0	2	2	8
97-98—Carolina	NHL	18	0	2	2	10	-1	0	0	—	—	—	—	—
—New Haven	AHL	65	1	19	20	44	...	...	...	1	0	0	0	0
NHL Totals (1 year)............		18	0	2	2	10	-1	0	0					

HALLER, KEVIN   D   MIGHTY DUCKS

PERSONAL: Born December 5, 1970, in Trochu, Alta. ... 6-2/192. ... Shoots left. ... Name pronounced HAW-luhr.

TRANSACTIONS/CAREER NOTES: Broke leg (October 1986). ... Broke leg (May 1987). ... Selected by Buffalo Sabres in first round (first Sabres pick, 14th overall) of NHL entry draft (June 17, 1989). ... Separated shoulder (May 7, 1991); missed seven games. ... Traded by Sabres to Montreal Canadiens for D Petr Svoboda (March 10, 1992). ... Suspended four games and fined $500 by NHL for slashing (November 2, 1993). ... Traded by Canadiens to Philadelphia Flyers for D Yves Racine (June 29, 1994). ... Pulled right groin (January 26, 1995); missed four games. ... Suffered from the flu (March 2, 1995); missed two games. ... Strained groin (March 15, 1995); missed six games. ... Suffered sprain in chest (December 16, 1995); missed 13 games. ... Broke thumb (April 27, 1996); missed remainder of playoffs. ... Traded by Flyers with first- (traded to San Jose) and seventh-round (C Andrew Merrick) picks in 1997 draft to Hartford Whalers for D Paul Coffey and third-round pick (D Kris Mallette) in 1997 draft (December 15, 1996). ... Suffered from the flu (December 20, 1996); missed one game. ... Strained groin (January 1, 1997); missed 13 games. ... Sprained shoulder (March 5, 1997); missed six games. ... Whalers franchise moved to North Carolina and renamed Carolina Hurricanes for 1997-98 season; NHL approved move on June 25, 1997. ... Suffered infected ankle (March 15, 1998); missed one game. ... Injured groin (March 28, 1998); missed 11 games. ... Traded by Hurricanes with LW Stu Grimson to Mighty Ducks of Anaheim for D Dave Karpa and 4th round pick in 2000 draft (August 11, 1998).

HONORS: Won Bill Hunter Trophy (1989-90). ... Named to WHL (East) All-Star first team (1989-90).

MISCELLANEOUS: Member of Stanley Cup championship team (1993).

Season Team	League	REGULAR SEASON								PLAYOFFS				
		Gms.	G	A	Pts.	PIM	+/-	PP	SH	Gms.	G	A	Pts.	PIM
87-88—Olds	AJHL	54	13	31	44	58	...	...	...	—	—	—	—	—
88-89—Regina	WHL	72	10	31	41	99	...	...	...	—	—	—	—	—
89-90—Regina	WHL	58	16	37	53	93	...	...	...	11	2	9	11	16
—Buffalo	NHL	2	0	0	0	0	0	0	0	—	—	—	—	—
90-91—Rochester	AHL	52	2	8	10	53	...	...	...	10	2	1	3	6
—Buffalo	NHL	21	1	8	9	20	9	1	0	6	1	4	5	10
91-92—Buffalo	NHL	58	6	15	21	75	-13	2	0	—	—	—	—	—
—Rochester	AHL	4	0	0	0	18	...	...	...	—	—	—	—	—
—Montreal	NHL	8	2	2	4	17	4	1	0	9	0	0	0	6
92-93—Montreal	NHL	73	11	14	25	117	7	6	0	17	1	6	7	16
93-94—Montreal	NHL	68	4	9	13	118	3	0	0	7	1	1	2	19
94-95—Philadelphia	NHL	36	2	8	10	48	16	0	0	15	4	4	8	10
95-96—Philadelphia	NHL	69	5	9	14	92	18	0	2	6	0	1	1	8
96-97—Philadelphia	NHL	27	0	5	5	37	-1	0	0	—	—	—	—	—
—Hartford	NHL	35	2	6	8	48	-11	0	0	—	—	—	—	—
97-98—Carolina	NHL	65	3	5	8	94	-5	0	0	—	—	—	—	—
NHL Totals (9 years)...........		462	36	81	117	666	27	10	2	60	7	16	23	69

HAMEL, DENIS   LW   SABRES

PERSONAL: Born May 10, 1977, in Lachute, Que. ... 6-2/200. ... Shoots left. ... Name pronounced uh-MEHL.

TRANSACTIONS/CAREER NOTES: Selected by St. Louis Blues in sixth round (fifth Blues pick, 153rd overall) of NHL entry draft (July 8, 1995). ... Rights traded by Blues to Buffalo Sabres for D Charlie Huddy (March 19, 1996).

Season Team	League	REGULAR SEASON								PLAYOFFS				
		Gms.	G	A	Pts.	PIM	+/-	PP	SH	Gms.	G	A	Pts.	PIM
94-95—Chicoutimi	QMJHL	66	15	12	27	155	...	...	...	13	2	0	2	29
95-96—Chicoutimi	QMJHL	65	40	49	89	199	...	...	...	17	10	14	24	64
96-97—Chicoutimi	QMJHL	70	50	50	100	339	...	...	...	20	15	10	25	65
97-98—Rochester	AHL	74	10	15	25	98	...	...	...	4	1	2	3	0

HAMILTON, HUGH   D   HURRICANES

PERSONAL: Born February 11, 1977, in Saskatoon, Sask. ... 6-1/175. ... Shoots left.

HIGH SCHOOL: Joel E. Ferris (Spokane, Wash.).

TRANSACTIONS/CAREER NOTES: Selected by Hartford Whalers in fifth round (fifth Whalers pick, 113th overall) of NHL entry draft (July 8, 1995).

HONORS: Named to WHL (West) All-Star second team (1996-97).

Season Team	League	REGULAR SEASON								PLAYOFFS				
		Gms.	G	A	Pts.	PIM	+/-	PP	SH	Gms.	G	A	Pts.	PIM
93-94—Spokane......................	WHL	64	5	9	14	70	...	...	...	3	0	0	0	0
94-95—Spokane......................	WHL	60	5	28	33	102	...	...	...	11	3	5	8	16
95-96—Spokane......................	WHL	72	11	49	60	92	...	...	...	18	3	5	8	26
96-97—Spokane......................	WHL	57	8	37	45	69	...	...	...	9	1	6	7	14
97-98—New Haven	AHL	51	3	3	6	17	...	...	...	3	0	0	0	2

H

HAMRLIK, ROMAN — D — OILERS

PERSONAL: Born April 12, 1974, in Gottwaldov, Czechoslovakia. ... 6-2/202. ... Shoots left. ... Brother of Martin Hamrlik, defenseman in St. Louis Blues system. ... Name pronounced ROH-muhn HAM-uhr-lihk.
TRANSACTIONS/CAREER NOTES: Selected by Tampa Bay Lightning in first round (first Lightning pick, first overall) of NHL entry draft (June 20, 1992). ... Bruised shoulder (November 3, 1993); missed six games. ... Bruised shoulder (March 1, 1994); missed seven games. ... Played in Europe during 1994-95 NHL lockout. ... Suffered back spasms (January 9, 1997); missed two games. ... Traded by Lightning to Oilers with F Paul Comrie for C Steve Kelly, D Bryan Marchment and C Jason Bonsignore (December 30, 1997).
HONORS: Played in NHL All-Star Game (1996).
MISCELLANEOUS: Member of gold-medal-winning Czech Republic Olympic team (1998).

Season Team	League	REGULAR SEASON								PLAYOFFS				
		Gms.	G	A	Pts.	PIM	+/-	PP	SH	Gms.	G	A	Pts.	PIM
90-91—TJ Zlin	Czech.	14	2	2	4	18	...	...	...	—	—	—	—	—
91-92—ZPS Zlin	Czech.	34	5	5	10	34	...	...	...	—	—	—	—	—
92-93—Tampa Bay	NHL	67	6	15	21	71	-21	1	0	—	—	—	—	—
—Atlanta	IHL	2	1	1	2	2	...	...	...	—	—	—	—	—
93-94—Tampa Bay	NHL	64	3	18	21	135	-14	0	0	—	—	—	—	—
94-95—ZPS Zlin	Czech Rep.	2	1	0	1	10	...	...	...	—	—	—	—	—
—Tampa Bay	NHL	48	12	11	23	86	-18	7	1	—	—	—	—	—
95-96—Tampa Bay	NHL	82	16	49	65	103	-24	12	0	5	0	1	1	4
96-97—Tampa Bay	NHL	79	12	28	40	57	-29	6	0	—	—	—	—	—
97-98—Tampa Bay	NHL	37	3	12	15	22	-18	1	0	—	—	—	—	—
—Edmonton	NHL	41	6	20	26	48	3	4	1	12	0	6	6	12
—Czech Rep. Olympic....	Int'l	6	1	0	1	2	...	...	...	—	—	—	—	—
NHL Totals (6 years)		418	58	153	211	522	-121	31	2	17	0	7	7	16

HANDZUS, MICHAL — C — BLUES

PERSONAL: Born March 11, 1977, in Banska Bystrica, Czechoslovakia. ... 6-5/202. ... Shoots left. ... Name pronounced han-ZOOZ.
TRANSACTIONS/CAREER NOTES: Selected by St. Louis Blues in fourth round (third Blues pick, 101st overall) of NHL entry draft (July 8, 1995).

Season Team	League	REGULAR SEASON								PLAYOFFS				
		Gms.	G	A	Pts.	PIM	+/-	PP	SH	Gms.	G	A	Pts.	PIM
93-94—IS Banska Byst. Jrs. ...	Slovakia	40	23	36	59	...	...	...	...	—	—	—	—	—
94-95—IS Banska Bystrica	Slovakia Div. II	22	15	14	29	10	...	...	...	—	—	—	—	—
95-96—IS Banska Bystrica	Slovakia Div. II	19	3	1	4	8	...	...	...	—	—	—	—	—
96-97—Poprad	Slovakia	44	15	18	33	...	...	...	...	—	—	—	—	—
97-98—Worcester	AHL	69	27	36	63	54	...	...	...	11	2	6	8	10

HANKINSON, CASEY — LW — BLACKHAWKS

PERSONAL: Born May 8, 1976, in Edina, Minn. ... 6-1/187. ... Shoots left. ... Brother of Ben Hankinson, right winger in Pittsburgh Penguins system; and brother of Peter Hankinson, center with Winnipeg Jets organization (1989-90 through 1991-92).
HIGH SCHOOL: Edina (Minn.).
COLLEGE: Minnesota.
TRANSACTIONS/CAREER NOTES: Selected by Chicago Blackhawks in eighth round (ninth Blackhawks pick, 201st overall) of NHL entry draft (July 8, 1995).

Season Team	League	REGULAR SEASON								PLAYOFFS				
		Gms.	G	A	Pts.	PIM	+/-	PP	SH	Gms.	G	A	Pts.	PIM
92-93—Edina High School	Minn. H.S.	25	20	26	46	...	...	...	...	—	—	—	—	—
93-94—Edina High School	Minn. H.S.	24	21	20	41	50	...	...	...	—	—	—	—	—
94-95—Univ. of Minnesota	WCHA	33	7	1	8	86	...	...	...	—	—	—	—	—
95-96—Univ. of Minnesota	WCHA	39	16	19	35	101	...	...	...	—	—	—	—	—
96-97—Univ. of Minnesota	WCHA	42	17	24	41	79	...	...	...	—	—	—	—	—
97-98—Univ. of Minnesota	WCHA	35	10	12	22	81	...	...	...	—	—	—	—	—

HANNAN, SCOTT — D — SHARKS

PERSONAL: Born January 23, 1979, in Richmond, B.C. ... 6-1/210. ... Shoots left.
TRANSACTIONS/CAREER NOTES: Selected by San Jose Sharks in first round (second Sharks pick, 23rd overall) of NHL entry draft (June 21, 1997).

Season Team	League	REGULAR SEASON								PLAYOFFS				
		Gms.	G	A	Pts.	PIM	+/-	PP	SH	Gms.	G	A	Pts.	PIM
94-95—Tacoma	WHL	2	0	0	0	0	...	...	...	—	—	—	—	—
95-96—Kelowna	WHL	69	4	5	9	76	...	...	...	6	0	1	1	4
96-97—Kelowna	WHL	70	17	26	43	101	...	...	...	6	0	0	0	8
97-98—Kelowna	WHL	47	10	30	40	70	...	...	...	—	—	—	—	—

HANSEN, TAVIS — C/RW — COYOTES

H

PERSONAL: Born June 17, 1975, in Prince Albert, Sask. ... 6-1/180. ... Shoots right.
TRANSACTIONS/CAREER NOTES: Selected by Winnipeg Jets in third round (third Jets pick, 58th overall) of NHL entry draft (June 29, 1994). ... Jets franchise moved to Phoenix and renamed Coyotes for 1996-97 season; NHL approved move on January 18, 1996.

Season Team	League	REGULAR SEASON								PLAYOFFS				
		Gms.	G	A	Pts.	PIM	+/-	PP	SH	Gms.	G	A	Pts.	PIM
93-94—Tacoma	WHL	71	23	31	54	122	...	...	...	8	1	3	4	17
94-95—Tacoma	WHL	71	32	41	73	142	...	...	...	4	1	1	2	8
—Winnipeg	NHL	1	0	0	0	0	0	0	0	—	—	—	—	—
95-96—Springfield	AHL	67	6	16	22	85	...	...	...	5	1	2	3	2
96-97—Springfield	AHL	12	3	1	4	23	...	...	...	—	—	—	—	—
—Phoenix	NHL	1	0	0	0	0	0	0	0	—	—	—	—	—
97-98—Springfield	AHL	73	20	14	34	70	...	...	...	4	1	2	3	18
NHL Totals (2 years)		2	0	0	0	0	0	0	0					

HARDY, FRANCOIS — D — SENATORS

PERSONAL: Born July 6, 1978, in Les Saules, Que. ... 6-2/185. ... Shoots left.
TRANSACTIONS/CAREER NOTES: Selected by Ottawa Senators in seventh round (fourth Senators pick, 163rd overall) of NHL entry draft (June 22, 1996).

Season Team	League	REGULAR SEASON								PLAYOFFS				
		Gms.	G	A	Pts.	PIM	+/-	PP	SH	Gms.	G	A	Pts.	PIM
95-96—Val-d'Or	QMJHL	55	2	3	5	93	...	...	...	3	0	0	0	4
96-97—Val-d'Or	QMJHL	57	2	10	12	130	...	...	...	13	1	1	2	20
97-98—Val-d'Or	QMJHL	59	7	11	18	147	...	...	...	19	1	6	7	38

HARLOCK, DAVID — D — CAPITALS

PERSONAL: Born March 16, 1971, in Toronto. ... 6-2/205. ... Shoots left. ... Full name: David Alan Harlock.
COLLEGE: Michigan.
TRANSACTIONS/CAREER NOTES: Injured knee (October 1988). ... Selected by New Jersey Devils in second round (second Devils pick, 24th overall) of NHL entry draft (June 16, 1990). ... Signed as free agent by Toronto Maple Leafs (August 20, 1993). ... Loaned by Maple Leafs to Canadian national team (October 3, 1993). ... Signed as free agent by Washington Capitals (August 31, 1997).
MISCELLANEOUS: Member of silver-medal-winning Canadian Olympic team (1994).

Season Team	League	REGULAR SEASON								PLAYOFFS				
		Gms.	G	A	Pts.	PIM	+/-	PP	SH	Gms.	G	A	Pts.	PIM
86-87—Toronto Red Wings	MTHL	86	17	55	72	60	...	...	...	—	—	—	—	—
87-88—Toronto Red Wings	MTHL	70	16	56	72	100	...	...	...	—	—	—	—	—
88-89—St. Michael's Jr. B	ODHA	25	4	15	19	34	...	...	...	—	—	—	—	—
89-90—Univ. of Michigan	CCHA	42	2	13	15	44	...	...	...	—	—	—	—	—
90-91—Univ. of Michigan	CCHA	39	2	8	10	70	...	...	...	—	—	—	—	—
91-92—Univ. of Michigan	CCHA	44	1	6	7	80	...	...	...	—	—	—	—	—
92-93—Univ. of Michigan	CCHA	38	3	9	12	58	...	...	...	—	—	—	—	—
—Canadian nat'l team	Int'l	4	0	0	0	2	...	...	...	—	—	—	—	—
93-94—Canadian nat'l team	Int'l	41	0	3	3	28	...	...	...	—	—	—	—	—
—Can. Olympic Team	Int'l	8	0	0	0	8	...	...	...	—	—	—	—	—
—Toronto	NHL	6	0	0	0	0	-2	0	0	—	—	—	—	—
—St. John's	AHL	10	0	3	3	2	...	...	...	9	0	0	0	6
94-95—St. John's	AHL	58	0	6	6	44	...	...	...	5	0	0	0	0
—Toronto	NHL	1	0	0	0	0	-1	0	0	—	—	—	—	—
95-96—St. John's	AHL	77	0	12	12	92	...	...	...	4	0	1	1	2
—Toronto	NHL	1	0	0	0	0	0	0	0	—	—	—	—	—
—Portland	AHL	1	0	0	0	0	...	...	...	—	—	—	—	—
96-97—San Antonio	IHL	69	3	10	13	82	...	...	...	9	0	0	0	10
97-98—Portland	AHL	71	3	15	18	66	...	...	...	10	2	2	4	6
—Washington	NHL	6	0	0	0	4	2	0	0	—	—	—	—	—
NHL Totals (4 years)		14	0	0	0	4	-1	0	0					

HARLTON, TYLER — D — BLUES

PERSONAL: Born January 11, 1976, in Regina, Sask. ... 6-3/210. ... Shoots left.
COLLEGE: Michigan State.
TRANSACTIONS/CAREER NOTES: Selected by St. Louis Blues in fourth round (second Blues pick, 94th overall) of NHL entry draft (June 29, 1994).
HONORS: Named to NCAA All-America West second team (1997-98). ... Named to CCHA All-Star first team (1997-98).

Season Team	League	REGULAR SEASON								PLAYOFFS				
		Gms.	G	A	Pts.	PIM	+/-	PP	SH	Gms.	G	A	Pts.	PIM
93-94—Vernon	BCJHL	60	3	18	21	102	...	...	...	—	—	—	—	—
94-95—Michigan State	CCHA	39	1	4	5	55	...	...	...	—	—	—	—	—
95-96—Michigan State	CCHA	39	1	6	7	51	...	...	...	—	—	—	—	—
96-97—Michigan State	CCHA	39	2	9	11	75	...	...	...	—	—	—	—	—
97-98—Michigan State	CCHA	44	1	12	13	68	...	...	...	—	—	—	—	—

H

HARVEY, TODD — C — RANGERS

PERSONAL: Born February 17, 1975, in Hamilton, Ont. ... 6-0/200. ... Shoots right.
TRANSACTIONS/CAREER NOTES: Selected by Dallas Stars in first round (first Stars pick, ninth overall) of NHL entry draft (June 26, 1993). ... Strained back (March 13, 1995); missed one game. ... Sprained knee (October 30, 1995); missed two games. ... Pulled groin (November 3, 1996); missed one game. ... Sprained knee (November 19, 1996); missed five games. ... Suffered from the flu (December 29, 1996);

missed one game. ... Suspended two games and fined $1,000 by NHL for elbowing incident (February 2, 1997). ... Bruised hand (April 4, 1997); missed one game. ... Suffered concussion (November 16, 1997); missed one game. ... Strained hip flexor (December 20, 1997); missed one game. ... Sprained knee (January 7, 1998); missed five games. ... Injured hand (February 4, 1998); missed one game. ... Strained lower back (March 13, 1998); missed one game. ... Underwent right knee surgery (March 22, 1998); missed 12 games. ... Traded by Stars with LW Bob Errey and fourth-round pick (LW Boyd Kane) in 1998 draft to New York Rangers for RW Mike Keane, C Brian Skrudland and sixth-round pick (RW Pavel Patera) in 1998 draft (March 24, 1998).

HONORS: Named to Can.HL All-Rookie team (1991-92). ... Named to OHL Rookie All-Star team (1991-92).

STATISTICAL PLATEAUS: Three-goal games: 1994-95 (1).

		REGULAR SEASON								PLAYOFFS				
Season Team	League	Gms.	G	A	Pts.	PIM	+/-	PP	SH	Gms.	G	A	Pts.	PIM
89-90—Cambridge Jr. B.........	OHA	41	35	27	62	213	...	...	...	—	—	—	—	—
90-91—Cambridge Jr. B.........	OHA	35	32	39	71	174	...	...	...	—	—	—	—	—
91-92—Detroit......................	OHL	58	21	43	64	141	...	...	...	7	3	5	8	32
92-93—Detroit......................	OHL	55	50	50	100	83	...	...	...	15	9	12	21	39
93-94—Detroit......................	OHL	49	34	51	85	75	...	...	...	17	10	12	22	26
94-95—Detroit......................	OHL	11	8	14	22	12	...	...	...	—	—	—	—	—
—Dallas......................	NHL	40	11	9	20	67	-3	2	0	5	0	0	0	8
95-96—Dallas......................	NHL	69	9	20	29	136	-13	3	0	—	—	—	—	—
—Michigan..................	IHL	5	1	3	4	8	...	...	...	—	—	—	—	—
96-97—Dallas......................	NHL	71	9	22	31	142	19	1	0	7	0	1	1	10
97-98—Dallas......................	NHL	59	9	10	19	104	5	0	0	—	—	—	—	—
NHL Totals (4 years)..........		239	38	61	99	449	8	6	0	12	0	1	1	18

HASEK, DOMINIK   G   SABRES

PERSONAL: Born January 29, 1965, in Pardubice, Czechoslovakia. ... 5-11/168. ... Catches left. ... Name pronounced HA-shehk.

TRANSACTIONS/CAREER NOTES: Selected by Chicago Blackhawks in 10th round (11th Blackhawks pick, 199th overall) of NHL entry draft (June 8, 1983). ... Traded by Blackhawks to Buffalo Sabres for G Stephane Beauregard and future considerations (August 7, 1992). ... Injured groin (November 25, 1992); missed three games. ... Pulled stomach muscle (January 6, 1993); missed six games. ... Played in Europe during 1994-95 NHL lockout. ... Strained rotator cuff (March 16, 1995); missed three games. ... Injured abdominals (December 15, 1995); missed 10 games. ... Sprained left knee (April 6, 1996); missed last two games of season. ... Fractured rib (March 19, 1997); missed five games. ... Sprained knee ligament (April 21, 1997); missed six playoff games. ... Suspended three playoff games and fined $10,000 by NHL for grabbing a reporter who had written a critical column (May 1, 1997). ... Suffered ear infection (April 15, 1998); missed one game.

HONORS: Named Czechoslovakian League Player of the Year (1986-87, 1988-89 and 1989-90). ... Named to Czechoslovakian League All-Star team (1988-89 and 1989-90). ... Named to IHL All-Star first team (1990-91). ... Named to NHL All-Rookie team (1991-92). ... Won Vezina Trophy (1993-94, 1994-95, 1996-97 and 1997-98). ... Shared William M. Jennings Trophy with Grant Fuhr (1993-94). ... Named to THE SPORTING NEWS All-Star second team (1993-94). ... Named to NHL All-Star first team (1993-94, 1994-95, 1996-97 and 1997-98). ... Named to THE SPORTING NEWS All-Star first team (1994-95 and 1996-97). ... Played in NHL All-Star Game (1996-1998). ... Named NHL Player of the Year by THE SPORTING NEWS (1996-97 and 1997-98). ... Named to THE SPORTING NEWS All-Star team (1996-97 and 1997-98). ... Won Hart Memorial Trophy (1996-97 and 1997-98).

MISCELLANEOUS: Holds Buffalo Sabres all-time team records for most games played in by a goalie (325), most shutouts (32) and goals-against average (2.32). ... Stopped penalty shot attempt (vs. Mark Recchi, March 8, 1995; vs. Mario Lemieux, March 23, 1996; vs. Vincent Damphousse, March 8, 1997; vs. Jason Allison, April 10, 1997). ... Allowed penalty shot goal (vs. John MacLean, February 27, 1997; vs. Jere Lehtinen, October 7, 1997). ... Mermber of gold-medal-winning Czech Republic Olympic team (1998).

STATISTICAL NOTES: Led NHL in save percentage with .930 in 1993-94, .930 in 1994-95, .920 in 1995-96, .930 in 1996-97 and .932 in 1997-98.

		REGULAR SEASON								PLAYOFFS						
Season Team	League	Gms.	Min	W	L	T	GA	SO	Avg.	Gms.	Min.	W	L	GA	SO	Avg.
81-82—Pardubice.....................	Czech.	12	661	...	...	...	34	0	3.09	—	—	—	—	—	—	—
82-83—Pardubice.....................	Czech.	42	2358	...	...	...	105	0	2.67	—	—	—	—	—	—	—
83-84—Pardubice.....................	Czech.	40	2304	...	...	...	108	0	2.81	—	—	—	—	—	—	—
84-85—Pardubice.....................	Czech.	42	2419	...	...	...	131	0	3.25	—	—	—	—	—	—	—
85-86—Pardubice.....................	Czech.	45	2689	...	...	...	138	0	3.08	—	—	—	—	—	—	—
86-87—Pardubice.....................	Czech.	23	2515	...	...	...	103	0	2.46	—	—	—	—	—	—	—
87-88—Pardubice.....................	Czech.	31	2265	...	...	...	98	0	2.60	—	—	—	—	—	—	—
—Czech. Olympic Team....	Czech.	8	217	...	...	...	18	0	4.98	—	—	—	—	—	—	—
88-89—Pardubice.....................	Czech.	42	2507	...	...	...	114	0	2.73	—	—	—	—	—	—	—
89-90—Dukla Jihlava..............	Czech.	40	2251	...	...	...	80	0	2.13	—	—	—	—	—	—	—
90-91—Chicago......................	NHL	5	195	3	0	1	8	0	2.46	3	69	0	0	3	0	2.61
—Indianapolis	IHL	33	1903	20	11	‡4	80	*5	*2.52	1	60	1	0	3	0	3.00
91-92—Indianapolis	IHL	20	1162	7	10	‡3	69	1	3.56	—	—	—	—	—	—	—
—Chicago......................	NHL	20	1014	10	4	1	44	1	2.60	3	158	0	2	8	0	3.04
92-93—Buffalo	NHL	28	1429	11	10	4	75	0	3.15	1	45	1	0	1	0	1.33
93-94—Buffalo	NHL	58	3358	30	20	6	109	†7	*1.95	7	484	3	4	13	2	*1.61
94-95—HC Pardubice	Czech. Rep.	2	125	...	...	...	6	0	2.88	—	—	—	—	—	—	—
—Buffalo	NHL	41	2416	19	14	7	85	†5	*2.11	5	309	1	4	18	0	3.50
95-96—Buffalo	NHL	59	3417	22	†30	6	161	2	2.83	—	—	—	—	—	—	—
96-97—Buffalo	NHL	67	4037	37	20	10	153	5	2.27	3	153	1	1	5	0	1.96
97-98—Buffalo	NHL	*72	*4220	33	23	13	147	*13	2.09	15	948	10	5	32	1	2.03
—Czech Rep. Olympic....	Int'l	6	369	5	1	0	6	2	0.98	—	—	—	—	—	—	—
NHL Totals (8 years)..............		350	20086	165	121	48	782	33	2.34	37	2166	16	16	80	3	2.22

HATCHER, DERIAN   D   STARS   H

PERSONAL: Born June 4, 1972, in Sterling Heights, Mich. ... 6-5/225. ... Shoots left. ... Brother of Kevin Hatcher, defenseman, Pittsburgh Penguins.

TRANSACTIONS/CAREER NOTES: Underwent knee surgery (January 1989). ... Selected by Minnesota North Stars in first round (first North Stars pick, eighth overall) of NHL entry draft (June 16, 1990). ... Suspended 10 games by NHL (December 1991). ... Fractured ankle in off-ice incident (January 19, 1992); missed 21 games. ... Sprained knee (January 6, 1993); missed 14 games. ... Suspended one game by NHL for game misconduct penalties (March 9, 1993). ... North Stars franchise moved from Minnesota to Dallas and renamed Stars for 1993-94 season. ... Sprained ankle (February 2, 1995); missed one game. ... Suffered staph infection on little finger (February 14, 1995); missed four games. ... Injured right knee ligament (May 1, 1995); missed entire playoffs. ... Injured shoulder (November 14, 1995); missed three games. ... Strained knee (December 8, 1996); missed 14 games. ... Underwent arthroscopic knee surgery (March 19, 1997); missed five games. ... Injured knee (March 8, 1998); missed seven games.

HONORS: Played in NHL All-Star Game (1997).
MISCELLANEOUS: Captain of Dallas Stars (1995-96 through 1997-98).

Season Team	League	REGULAR SEASON								PLAYOFFS				
		Gms.	G	A	Pts.	PIM	+/-	PP	SH	Gms.	G	A	Pts.	PIM
88-89—Detroit G.P.D.	MNHL	51	19	35	54	100	...	...	...	—	—	—	—	—
89-90—North Bay	OHL	64	14	38	52	81	...	...	...	5	2	3	5	8
90-91—North Bay	OHL	64	13	50	63	163	...	...	...	10	2	10	12	28
91-92—Minnesota	NHL	43	8	4	12	88	7	0	0	5	0	2	2	8
92-93—Minnesota	NHL	67	4	15	19	178	-27	0	0	—	—	—	—	—
—Kalamazoo	IHL	2	1	2	3	21	...	...	...	—	—	—	—	—
93-94—Dallas	NHL	83	12	19	31	211	19	2	1	9	0	2	2	14
94-95—Dallas	NHL	43	5	11	16	105	3	2	0	—	—	—	—	—
95-96—Dallas	NHL	79	8	23	31	129	-12	2	0	—	—	—	—	—
96-97—Dallas	NHL	63	3	19	22	97	8	0	0	7	0	2	2	20
97-98—Dallas	NHL	70	6	25	31	132	9	3	0	17	3	3	6	39
—U.S. Olympic Team	Int'l	4	0	0	0	0	...	...	...	—	—	—	—	—
NHL Totals (7 years)		448	46	116	162	940	7	9	1	38	3	9	12	81

HATCHER, KEVIN — D — PENGUINS

PERSONAL: Born September 9, 1966, in Detroit. ... 6-3/232. ... Shoots right. ... Full name: Kevin John Hatcher. ... Brother of Derian Hatcher, defenseman, Dallas Stars.
TRANSACTIONS/CAREER NOTES: Selected by Washington Capitals as underage junior in first round (first Capitals pick, 17th overall) of NHL entry draft (June 9, 1984). ... Tore left knee cartilage (October 1987). ... Pulled groin (January 1989). ... Fractured two metatarsal bones in left foot (February 5, 1989); missed 15 games. ... Sprained left knee (April 27, 1990). ... Did not attend Capitals training camp due to contract dispute (September 1990). ... Injured right knee (November 10, 1990). ... Suspended one game by NHL for game misconduct penalties (February 2, 1993). ... Fractured right hand (December 23, 1993); missed 10 games. ... Suffered from the flu (March 29, 1994); missed one game. ... Pulled thigh (April 9, 1994); missed one game. ... Traded by Capitals to Dallas Stars for D Mark Tinordi and rights to D Rick Mrozik (January 18, 1995). ... Injured shoulder (October 17, 1995); missed three games. ... Suspended four games and fined $1,000 by NHL for slashing (December 5, 1995). ... Traded by Stars to Pittsburgh Penguins for D Sergei Zubov (June 22, 1996). ... Suffered stiff neck (February 5, 1997); missed two games. ... Bruised lower leg (November 8, 1997); missed six games. ... Suffered from the flu (April 16, 1998); missed one game.
HONORS: Named to OHL All-Star second team (1984-85). ... Played in NHL All-Star Game (1990-1992, 1996 and 1997).
STATISTICAL PLATEAUS: Three-goal games: 1992-93 (1), 1995-96 (1). Total: 2.

Season Team	League	REGULAR SEASON								PLAYOFFS				
		Gms.	G	A	Pts.	PIM	+/-	PP	SH	Gms.	G	A	Pts.	PIM
83-84—North Bay	OHL	67	10	39	49	61	...	...	...	4	2	2	4	11
84-85—North Bay	OHL	58	26	37	63	75	...	...	...	8	5	8	13	9
—Washington	NHL	2	1	0	1	0	1	0	1	1	0	0	0	0
85-86—Washington	NHL	79	9	10	19	119	6	1	0	9	1	1	2	19
86-87—Washington	NHL	78	8	16	24	144	-29	1	0	7	1	0	1	20
87-88—Washington	NHL	71	14	27	41	137	1	5	0	14	5	7	12	55
88-89—Washington	NHL	62	13	27	40	101	19	3	0	6	1	4	5	20
89-90—Washington	NHL	80	13	41	54	102	4	4	0	11	0	8	8	32
90-91—Washington	NHL	79	24	50	74	69	-10	9	2	11	3	3	6	8
91-92—Washington	NHL	79	17	37	54	105	18	8	1	7	2	4	6	19
92-93—Washington	NHL	83	34	45	79	114	-7	13	1	6	0	1	1	14
93-94—Washington	NHL	72	16	24	40	108	-13	6	0	11	3	4	7	37
94-95—Dallas	NHL	47	10	19	29	66	-4	3	0	5	2	1	3	2
95-96—Dallas	NHL	74	15	26	41	58	-24	7	0	—	—	—	—	—
96-97—Pittsburgh	NHL	80	15	39	54	103	11	9	0	5	1	1	2	4
97-98—Pittsburgh	NHL	74	19	29	48	66	-3	13	1	6	1	0	1	12
—U.S. Olympic Team	Int'l	3	0	2	2	0	...	...	...	—	—	—	—	—
NHL Totals (14 years)		960	208	390	598	1292	-30	82	6	99	20	34	54	242

HAY, DWAYNE — LW — PANTHERS

PERSONAL: Born February 11, 1977, in London, Ont. ... 6-1/183. ... Shoots left.
HIGH SCHOOL: Bishop MacDonnell (Guelph, Ont.).
TRANSACTIONS/CAREER NOTES: Selected by Washington Capitals in second round (third Capitals pick, 43rd overall) of NHL entry draft (July 8, 1995). ... Traded by Capitals with conditional pick in 1999 draft to Florida Panthers for F Esa Tikkanen (March 9, 1998).

Season Team	League	REGULAR SEASON								PLAYOFFS				
		Gms.	G	A	Pts.	PIM	+/-	PP	SH	Gms.	G	A	Pts.	PIM
93-94—Listowel Jr. B	OHA	48	10	24	34	56	...	...	...	—	—	—	—	—
94-95—Guelph	OHL	65	26	28	54	37	...	...	...	14	5	7	12	6
95-96—Guelph	OHL	60	28	30	58	49	...	...	...	16	4	9	13	18
96-97—Guelph	OHL	32	17	17	34	21	...	...	...	11	4	6	10	0
97-98—Portland	AHL	58	6	7	13	35	...	...	...	—	—	—	—	—
—Washington	NHL	2	0	0	0	2	0	0	0	—	—	—	—	—
—New Haven	AHL	10	3	2	5	4	...	...	...	2	0	0	0	0
NHL Totals (1 year)		2	0	0	0	2	0	0	0					

H

HEALEY, PAUL   RW   FLYERS

PERSONAL: Born March 20, 1975, in Edmonton. ... 6-2/185. ... Shoots right.
TRANSACTIONS/CAREER NOTES: Selected by Philadelphia Flyers in eighth round (seventh Flyers pick, 192nd overall) of NHL entry draft (June 26, 1993).
HONORS: Named to WHL (East) All-Star second team (1994-95).

		REGULAR SEASON								PLAYOFFS				
Season Team	League	Gms.	G	A	Pts.	PIM	+/-	PP	SH	Gms.	G	A	Pts.	PIM
92-93—Prince Albert	WHL	72	12	20	32	66	...	...	...	—	—	—	—	—
93-94—Prince Albert	WHL	63	23	26	49	70	...	...	...	—	—	—	—	—
94-95—Prince Albert	WHL	71	43	50	93	67	...	...	...	12	3	4	7	2
95-96—Hershey	AHL	61	7	15	22	35	...	...	...	—	—	—	—	—
96-97—Philadelphia	AHL	64	21	19	40	56	...	...	...	10	4	1	5	10
—Philadelphia	NHL	2	0	0	0	0	0	0	0	—	—	—	—	—
97-98—Philadelphia	AHL	71	34	18	52	48	...	...	...	20	6	2	8	4
—Philadelphia	NHL	4	0	0	0	12	0	0	0	—	—	—	—	—
NHL Totals (2 years)		6	0	0	0	12	0	0	0					

HEALY, GLENN   G   MAPLE LEAFS

PERSONAL: Born August 23, 1962, in Pickering, Ont. ... 5-10/185. ... Catches left. ... Full name: Glenn M. Healy.
COLLEGE: Western Michigan.
TRANSACTIONS/CAREER NOTES: Signed as free agent by Los Angeles Kings (June 13, 1985). ... Signed as free agent by New York Islanders (August 16, 1989); Kings received fourth-round pick (traded to Minnesota) in 1990 draft as compensation. ... Strained left ankle ligaments (October 13, 1990); missed eight games. ... Fractured right index finger (November 10, 1991); missed five games. ... Fractured right thumb (January 3, 1992); missed 10 games. ... Severed tip of finger in practice and underwent reconstructive surgery (March 2, 1992); missed 13 games. ... Suffered from tendinitis in right wrist (January 9, 1993); missed four games. ... Selected by Mighty Ducks of Anaheim in NHL expansion draft (June 24, 1993). ... Selected by Tampa Bay Lightning in Phase II of NHL expansion draft (June 25, 1993). ... Traded by Lightning to New York Rangers for third-round pick in 1993 draft; Lightning reacquired their original pick which they had traded away earlier (June 25, 1993). ... Signed as free agent by Toronto Maple Leafs (July 8, 1997). ... Strained groin (December 4, 1997); missed 10 games.
HONORS: Named to NCAA All-America West second team (1984-85). ... Named to CCHA All-Star second team (1984-85).
MISCELLANEOUS: Member of Stanley Cup championship team (1994).

		REGULAR SEASON								PLAYOFFS					
Season Team	League	Gms.	Min	W	L	T	GA	SO	Avg.	Gms.	Min.	W	L	GA	SO	Avg.
81-82—Western Michigan U.	CCHA	27	1569	7	19	1	116	0	4.44	—	—	—	—	—	—	—
82-83—Western Michigan U.	CCHA	30	1733	8	19	2	116	0	4.02	—	—	—	—	—	—	—
83-84—Western Michigan U.	CCHA	38	2242	19	16	3	146	0	3.91	—	—	—	—	—	—	—
84-85—Western Michigan U.	CCHA	37	2172	21	14	2	118	...	3.26	—	—	—	—	—	—	—
85-86—Toledo	IHL	7	402	...	...	...	28	0	4.18	—	—	—	—	—	—	—
—New Haven	AHL	43	2410	21	15	4	160	0	3.98	2	119	0	2	11	0	5.55
—Los Angeles	NHL	1	51	0	0	0	6	0	7.06	—	—	—	—	—	—	—
86-87—New Haven	AHL	47	2828	21	15	0	173	1	3.67	7	427	3	4	19	0	2.67
87-88—Los Angeles	NHL	34	1869	12	18	1	135	1	4.33	4	240	1	3	20	0	5.00
88-89—Los Angeles	NHL	48	2699	25	19	2	192	0	4.27	3	97	0	1	6	0	3.71
89-90—New York Islanders	NHL	39	2197	12	19	6	128	2	3.50	4	166	1	2	9	0	3.25
90-91—New York Islanders	NHL	53	2999	18	24	9	166	0	3.32	—	—	—	—	—	—	—
91-92—New York Islanders	NHL	37	1960	14	16	4	124	1	3.80	—	—	—	—	—	—	—
92-93—New York Islanders	NHL	47	2655	22	20	2	146	1	3.30	18	1109	9	8	59	0	3.19
93-94—New York Rangers	NHL	29	1368	10	12	2	69	2	3.03	2	68	0	0	1	0	.88
94-95—New York Rangers	NHL	17	888	8	6	1	35	1	2.36	5	230	2	1	13	0	3.39
95-96—New York Rangers	NHL	44	2564	17	14	11	124	2	2.90	—	—	—	—	—	—	—
96-97—New York Rangers	NHL	23	1357	5	12	4	59	1	2.61	—	—	—	—	—	—	—
97-98—Toronto	NHL	21	1068	4	10	2	53	0	2.98	—	—	—	—	—	—	—
NHL Totals (12 years)		393	21675	147	170	44	1237	11	3.42	36	1910	13	15	108	0	3.39

HEBERT, GUY   G   MIGHTY DUCKS

PERSONAL: Born January 7, 1967, in Troy, N.Y. ... 5-11/185. ... Catches left. ... Full name: Guy Andrew Hebert. ... Name pronounced GEE ay-BAIR.
HIGH SCHOOL: LaSalle Institute (Troy, N.Y.).
COLLEGE: Hamilton (N.Y.).
TRANSACTIONS/CAREER NOTES: Selected by St. Louis Blues in eighth round (eighth Blues pick, 159th overall) of NHL entry draft (June 13, 1987). ... Selected by Mighty Ducks of Anaheim in NHL expansion draft (June 24, 1993). ... Suffered concussion (April 30, 1995); missed one game. ... Suffered concussion (December 9, 1996); missed two games. ... Strained right shoulder (March 8, 1998); missed remainder of season.
HONORS: Shared James Norris Memorial Trophy with Pat Jablonski (1990-91). ... Named to IHL All-Star second team (1990-91). ... Played in NHL All-Star Game (1997).
MISCELLANEOUS: Holds Mighty Ducks of Anaheim all-time records for most games played by a goaltender (263), most wins (102), most shutouts (15) and goals-against average (2.85). ... Stopped a penalty shot attempt (vs. Alexandre Daigle, December 30, 1996; vs. Tony Amonte, February 1, 1998; vs. Glen Murray, February 7, 1998).

		REGULAR SEASON								PLAYOFFS					
Season Team	League	Gms.	Min	W	L	T	GA	SO	Avg.	Gms.	Min.	W	L	GA	SO	Avg.
85-86—Hamilton College	Div. II	18	1011	4	12	2	69	2	4.09	—	—	—	—	—	—	—
86-87—Hamilton College	Div. II	18	1070	12	5	0	40	0	2.24	—	—	—	—	—	—	—
87-88—Hamilton College	Div. II	8	450	5	3	0	19	0	2.53	—	—	—	—	—	—	—
88-89—Hamilton College	Div. II	25	1453	18	7	0	62	0	2.56	—	—	—	—	—	—	—
89-90—Peoria	IHL	30	1706	7	13	‡7	124	1	4.36	2	76	0	1	5	0	3.95
90-91—Peoria	IHL	36	2093	24	10	‡1	100	2	*2.87	8	458	3	4	32	0	4.19

H

Season Team	League	REGULAR SEASON								PLAYOFFS						
		Gms.	Min	W	L	T	GA	SO	Avg.	Gms.	Min.	W	L	GA	SO	Avg.
91-92—Peoria..........................	IHL	29	1731	20	9	‡0	98	0	3.40	4	239	3	1	9	0	*2.26
—St. Louis	NHL	13	738	5	5	1	36	0	2.93	—	—	—	—	—	—	—
92-93—St. Louis	NHL	24	1210	8	8	2	74	1	3.67	1	2	0	0	0	0	...
93-94—Anaheim................	NHL	52	2991	20	27	3	141	2	2.83	—	—	—	—	—	—	—
94-95—Anaheim................	NHL	39	2092	12	20	4	109	2	3.13	—	—	—	—	—	—	—
95-96—Anaheim................	NHL	59	3326	28	23	5	157	4	2.83	—	—	—	—	—	—	—
96-97—Anaheim................	NHL	67	3863	29	25	12	172	4	2.67	9	534	4	4	18	1	2.02
97-98—Anaheim................	NHL	46	2660	13	24	6	130	3	2.93	—	—	—	—	—	—	—
NHL Totals (7 years)............		300	16880	115	132	33	819	16	2.91	10	536	4	4	18	1	2.01

HECHT, JOCHEN　　　　C　　　　BLUES

PERSONAL: Born June 21, 1977, in Mannheim, West Germany. ... 6-1/191. ... Shoots left.
TRANSACTIONS/CAREER NOTES: Selected by St. Louis Blues in second round (first Blues pick, 49th overall) of NHL entry draft (July 8, 1995).

Season Team	League	REGULAR SEASON								PLAYOFFS				
		Gms.	G	A	Pts.	PIM	+/-	PP	SH	Gms.	G	A	Pts.	PIM
94-95—Mannheim..................	Germany	43	11	12	23	68	...	...	...	10	5	4	9	12
95-96—Mannheim..................	Germany	44	12	16	28	68	...	...	...	8	3	2	5	6
96-97—Mannheim..................	Germany	46	21	21	42	36	...	...	...	—	—	—	—	—
97-98—Mannheim..................	Germany	44	7	19	26	42	...	...	...	10	1	1	2	14
—German Oly. team	Int'l	4	1	0	1	6	...	...	...	—	—	—	—	—

HEDICAN, BRET　　　　D　　　　CANUCKS

PERSONAL: Born August 10, 1970, in St. Paul, Minn. ... 6-2/195. ... Shoots left. ... Full name: Bret Michael Hedican. ... Name pronounced HEHD-ih-kihn.
HIGH SCHOOL: North St. Paul (Minn.).
COLLEGE: St. Cloud (Minn.) State.
TRANSACTIONS/CAREER NOTES: Selected by St. Louis Blues in 10th round (10th Blues pick, 198th overall) of NHL entry draft (June 11, 1988). ... Sprained knee ligaments (September 27, 1992); missed first 15 games of season. ... Injured shoulder (October 24, 1993); missed three games. ... Injured groin (January 18, 1994); missed six games. ... Traded by Blues with D Jeff Brown and C Nathan LaFayette to Vancouver Canucks for C Craig Janney (March 21, 1994). ... Strained groin (March 27, 1994); missed three games. ... Injured back (February 1, 1996); missed three games. ... Strained back (October 5, 1996); missed six games. ... Strained groin (December 4, 1996); missed five games. ... Strained groin (December 26, 1996); missed four games. ... Missed one game for personal reasons (December 13, 1997). ... Strained back (January 21, 1998); missed one game. ... Strained abdominal muscle (February 17, 1998); missed six games.
HONORS: Named to WCHA All-Star first team (1990-91).

Season Team	League	REGULAR SEASON								PLAYOFFS				
		Gms.	G	A	Pts.	PIM	+/-	PP	SH	Gms.	G	A	Pts.	PIM
88-89—St. Cloud State...........	WCHA	28	5	3	8	28	...	...	...	—	—	—	—	—
89-90—St. Cloud State...........	WCHA	36	4	17	21	37	...	...	...	—	—	—	—	—
90-91—St. Cloud State...........	WCHA	41	18	30	48	52	...	...	...	—	—	—	—	—
91-92—U.S. national team	Int'l	54	1	8	9	59	...	...	...	—	—	—	—	—
—U.S. Olympic Team	Int'l	8	0	0	0	4	...	...	...	—	—	—	—	—
—St. Louis	NHL	4	1	0	1	0	1	0	0	5	0	0	0	0
92-93—Peoria	IHL	19	0	8	8	10	...	...	...	—	—	—	—	—
—St. Louis	NHL	42	0	8	8	30	-2	0	0	10	0	0	0	14
93-94—St. Louis	NHL	61	0	11	11	64	-8	0	0	—	—	—	—	—
—Vancouver..................	NHL	8	0	1	1	0	1	0	0	24	1	6	7	16
94-95—Vancouver..............	NHL	45	2	11	13	34	-3	0	0	11	0	2	2	6
95-96—Vancouver..............	NHL	77	6	23	29	83	8	1	0	6	0	1	1	10
96-97—Vancouver..............	NHL	67	4	15	19	51	-3	2	0	—	—	—	—	—
97-98—Vancouver..............	NHL	71	3	24	27	79	3	1	0	—	—	—	—	—
NHL Totals (7 years)............		375	16	93	109	341	-3	4	0	56	1	9	10	46

HEINS, SHAWN　　　　D　　　　SHARKS

PERSONAL: Born December 24, 1973 in Eganville, Ont. ... 6-4/215. ... Shoots left.
TRANSACTIONS: Signed as free agent by San Jose Sharks (January 5, 1998).

Season Team	League	REGULAR SEASON								PLAYOFFS				
		Gms.	G	A	Pts.	PIM	+/-	PP	SH	Gms.	G	A	Pts.	PIM
94-95—Renfrew	EOGHL	49	40	90	130	175	...	...	...	—	—	—	—	—
95-96—Cape Breton...............	AHL	1	0	0	0	0	...	...	...	—	—	—	—	—
—Mobile......................	ECHL	62	7	20	27	152	...	...	...	—	—	—	—	—
96-97—Kansas City................	IHL	6	0	0	0	9	...	...	...	—	—	—	—	—
—Mobile......................	ECHL	56	6	17	23	253	...	...	...	3	0	2	2	2
97-98—Kansas City................	IHL	82	22	28	50	303	...	...	...	11	1	0	1	49

HEINZE, STEVE　　　　RW　　　　BRUINS

PERSONAL: Born January 30, 1970, in Lawrence, Mass. ... 5-11/202. ... Shoots right. ... Full name: Stephen Herbert Heinze. ... Name pronounced HIGHNS.
HIGH SCHOOL: Lawrence Academy (Groton, Mass.).
COLLEGE: Boston College.
TRANSACTIONS/CAREER NOTES: Selected by Boston Bruins in second round (second Bruins pick, 60th overall) of NHL entry draft (June 11, 1988). ... Injured shoulder (May 1, 1992). ... Injured shoulder (March 20, 1993); missed 11 games. ... Injured knee (February 18, 1994); missed five games. ... Reinjured knee (March 26, 1994); missed two games. ... Strained abdominal muscle (December 5, 1996); missed one

H

game. ... Strained hip and groin and tore knee ligament (December 17, 1996); missed remainder of season. ... Sprained ankle (October 7, 1997); missed seven games. ... Broke foot (October 23, 1997); missed 14 games.
HONORS: Named to Hockey East All-Rookie team (1988-89). ... Named to NCAA All-America East first team (1989-90). ... Named to Hockey East All-Star first team (1989-90).
MISCELLANEOUS: Failed to score on a penalty shot (vs. Corey Schwab, December 17, 1997).
STATISTICAL PLATEAUS: Three-goal games: 1992-93 (1), 1995-96 (1), 1997-98 (2). Total: 4.

		REGULAR SEASON								PLAYOFFS				
Season Team	League	Gms.	G	A	Pts.	PIM	+/-	PP	SH	Gms.	G	A	Pts.	PIM
86-87—Lawrence Academy.....	Mass. H.S.	23	26	24	50	...	...	...	...	—	—	—	—	—
87-88—Lawrence Academy.....	Mass. H.S.	23	30	25	55	...	...	...	...	—	—	—	—	—
88-89—Boston College	Hockey East	36	26	23	49	26	...	...	...	—	—	—	—	—
89-90—Boston College	Hockey East	40	27	36	63	41	...	...	...	—	—	—	—	—
90-91—Boston College	Hockey East	35	21	26	47	35	...	...	...	—	—	—	—	—
91-92—U.S. national team	Int'l	49	18	15	33	38	...	...	...	—	—	—	—	—
—U.S. Olympic Team	Int'l	8	1	3	4	8	...	...	...	—	—	—	—	—
—Boston	NHL	14	3	4	7	6	-1	0	0	7	0	3	3	17
92-93—Boston	NHL	73	18	13	31	24	20	0	2	4	1	1	2	2
93-94—Boston	NHL	77	10	11	21	32	-2	0	2	13	2	3	5	7
94-95—Boston	NHL	36	7	9	16	23	0	0	1	5	0	0	0	0
95-96—Boston	NHL	76	16	12	28	43	-3	0	1	5	1	1	2	4
96-97—Boston	NHL	30	17	8	25	27	-8	4	2	—	—	—	—	—
97-98—Boston	NHL	61	26	20	46	54	8	9	0	6	0	0	0	6
NHL Totals (7 years)...........		367	97	77	174	209	14	13	8	40	4	8	12	36

HENDRICKSON, DARBY   C   MAPLE LEAFS

PERSONAL: Born August 28, 1972, in Richfield, Minn. ... 6-0/185. ... Shoots left.
HIGH SCHOOL: Richfield (Minn.).
COLLEGE: Minnesota.
TRANSACTIONS/CAREER NOTES: Selected by Toronto Maple Leafs in fourth round (third Maple Leafs pick, 73rd overall) of NHL entry draft (June 16, 1990). ... Suspended for three games by NHL for kneeing incident (October 26, 1995). ... Suffered from the flu (December 30, 1995); missed one game. ... Traded by Maple Leafs with LW Sean Haggerty, D Kenny Jonsson and first-round pick (G Roberto Luongo) in 1997 draft to New York Islanders for LW Wendel Clark, D Mathieu Schneider and D D.J. Smith (March 13, 1996). ... Traded by Islanders to Maple Leafs for fifth-round pick (C Jiri Dopita) in 1998 draft (October 11, 1996). ... Strained back (January 27, 1997); missed five games. ... Suffered back spasms (November 4, 1997); missed two games.
HONORS: Won WCHA Rookie of the Year Award (1991-92). ... Named to WCHA All-Rookie team (1991-92).

		REGULAR SEASON								PLAYOFFS				
Season Team	League	Gms.	G	A	Pts.	PIM	+/-	PP	SH	Gms.	G	A	Pts.	PIM
87-88—Richfield H.S..............	Minn. H.S.	22	12	9	21	10	...	...	...	—	—	—	—	—
88-89—Richfield H.S..............	Minn. H.S.	22	22	20	42	12	...	...	...	—	—	—	—	—
89-90—Richfield H.S..............	Minn. H.S.	24	23	27	50	49	...	...	...	—	—	—	—	—
90-91—Richfield H.S..............	Minn. H.S.	27	32	29	61	...	...	...	...	—	—	—	—	—
91-92—Univ. of Minnesota......	WCHA	41	25	28	53	61	...	...	...	—	—	—	—	—
92-93—Univ. of Minnesota......	WCHA	31	12	15	27	35	...	...	...	—	—	—	—	—
93-94—U.S. national team	Int'l	59	12	16	28	30	...	...	...	—	—	—	—	—
—U.S. Olympic Team	Int'l	8	0	0	0	6	...	...	...	—	—	—	—	—
—St. John's...................	AHL	6	4	1	5	4	...	...	...	3	1	1	2	0
—Toronto	NHL	—	—	—	—	—	—	—	—	2	0	0	0	0
94-95—St. John's...................	AHL	59	16	20	36	48	...	...	...	—	—	—	—	—
—Toronto	NHL	8	0	1	1	4	0	0	0	—	—	—	—	—
95-96—Toronto	NHL	46	6	6	12	47	-2	0	0	—	—	—	—	—
—New York Islanders.....	NHL	16	1	4	5	33	-6	0	0	—	—	—	—	—
96-97—St. John's...................	AHL	12	5	4	9	21	...	...	...	—	—	—	—	—
—Toronto	NHL	64	11	6	17	47	-20	0	1	—	—	—	—	—
—U.S. national team	Int'l	8	0	1	1	8	...	...	...	—	—	—	—	—
97-98—Toronto	NHL	80	8	4	12	67	-20	0	0	—	—	—	—	—
NHL Totals (5 years)...........		214	26	21	47	198	-48	0	1	2	0	0	0	0

HENRY, BURKE   D   RANGERS

PERSONAL: Born January 21, 1979, in Ste. Rose, Manitoba. ... 6-2/190. ... Shoots left. ... Full name: Larry Henry.
TRANSACTIONS/CAREER NOTES: Selected by New York Rangers in third round (third Rangers pick, 73rd overall) of NHL entry draft (June 21, 1997).
HONORS: Named to WHL (East) All-Star first team (1997-98).

		REGULAR SEASON								PLAYOFFS				
Season Team	League	Gms.	G	A	Pts.	PIM	+/-	PP	SH	Gms.	G	A	Pts.	PIM
95-96—Brandon....................	WHL	50	6	11	17	58	...	...	...	19	0	4	4	19
96-97—Brandon....................	WHL	55	6	25	31	81	...	...	...	6	1	3	4	4
97-98—Brandon....................	WHL	72	18	65	83	153	...	...	...	18	3	16	19	37

HERR, MATT   LW   CAPITALS

PERSONAL: Born May 26, 1976, in Hackensack, N.J. ... 6-1/180. ... Shoots left. ... Full name: Matthew Herr.
HIGH SCHOOL: Hotchkiss (Lakeville, Conn.).
COLLEGE: Michigan.
TRANSACTIONS/CAREER NOTES: Selected by Washington Capitals in fourth round (fourth Capitals pick, 93rd overall) of NHL entry draft (June 29, 1994).
MISCELLANEOUS: Selected by Atlanta Braves organization in 29th round of free-agent draft (June 2, 1994); did not sign.

Season Team	League	REGULAR SEASON								PLAYOFFS				
		Gms.	G	A	Pts.	PIM	+/-	PP	SH	Gms.	G	A	Pts.	PIM
90-91—Hotchkiss	Conn. H.S.	26	9	5	14	...	...	...	...	—	—	—	—	—
91-92—Hotchkiss	Conn. H.S.	25	17	16	33	...	...	...	...	—	—	—	—	—
92-93—Hotchkiss	Conn. H.S.	24	48	30	78	...	...	...	...	—	—	—	—	—
93-94—Hotchkiss	Conn. H.S.	20	28	19	47	...	...	...	...	—	—	—	—	—
94-95—Univ. of Michigan	CCHA	37	11	8	19	51	...	...	...	—	—	—	—	—
95-96—Univ. of Michigan	CCHA	40	18	13	31	55	...	...	...	—	—	—	—	—
96-97—Univ. of Michigan	CCHA	43	29	23	52	67	...	...	...	—	—	—	—	—
97-98—Univ. of Michigan	CCHA	29	13	17	30	60	...	...	...	—	—	—	—	—

HEWARD, JAMIE — D — PREDATORS

PERSONAL: Born March 30, 1971, in Regina, Sask. ... 6-2/207. ... Shoots right. ... Name pronounced HYOO-uhrd.

TRANSACTIONS/CAREER NOTES: Traded by Spokane Chiefs to Regina Pats for RW Pat Falloon and future considerations (October 1987). ... Broke jaw (November 1988). ... Selected by Pittsburgh Penguins in first round (first Penguins pick, 16th overall) of NHL entry draft (June 17, 1989). ... Suffered from mononucleosis (September 1989). ... Signed as free agent by Toronto Maple Leafs (May 4, 1995). ... Signed as free agent by Philadelphia Flyers (July 10, 1997). ... Signed as free agent by Nashville Predators (August 6, 1998).

HONORS: Named to WHL (East) All-Star first team (1990-91). ... Named to AHL All-Star first team (1995-96). ... Named to AHL All-Star first team (1997-98). ... Won Eddie Shore Plaque (1997-98).

Season Team	League	REGULAR SEASON								PLAYOFFS				
		Gms.	G	A	Pts.	PIM	+/-	PP	SH	Gms.	G	A	Pts.	PIM
87-88—Regina	WHL	68	10	17	27	17	...	...	...	4	1	1	2	2
88-89—Regina	WHL	52	31	28	59	29	...	...	...	—	—	—	—	—
89-90—Regina	WHL	72	14	44	58	42	...	...	...	11	2	2	4	10
90-91—Regina	WHL	71	23	61	84	41	...	...	...	8	2	9	11	6
91-92—Muskegon	IHL	54	6	21	27	37	...	...	...	14	1	4	5	4
92-93—Cleveland	IHL	58	9	18	27	64	...	...	...	—	—	—	—	—
93-94—Cleveland	IHL	73	8	16	24	72	...	...	...	—	—	—	—	—
94-95—Canadian nat'l team	Int'l	51	11	35	46	32	...	...	...	—	—	—	—	—
95-96—St. John's	AHL	73	22	34	56	33	...	...	...	3	1	1	2	6
—Toronto	NHL	5	0	0	0	0	-1	0	0	—	—	—	—	—
96-97—Toronto	NHL	20	1	4	5	6	-6	0	0	—	—	—	—	—
—St. John's	AHL	27	8	19	27	26	...	...	...	9	1	3	4	6
97-98—Philadelphia	AHL	72	17	48	65	54	...	...	...	20	3	16	19	10
NHL Totals (2 years)		25	1	4	5	6	-7	0	0					

HEXTALL, RON — G — FLYERS

PERSONAL: Born May 3, 1964, in Brandon, Man. ... 6-3/192. ... Catches left.

TRANSACTIONS/CAREER NOTES: Selected by Philadelphia Flyers as underage junior in sixth round (sixth Flyers pick, 119th overall) of NHL entry draft (June 9, 1982). ... Suspended eight games by NHL for slashing (May 1987). ... Pulled hamstring (March 7, 1989). ... Suspended first 12 games of 1989-90 season by NHL for attacking opposing player in final playoff game (May 11, 1989). ... Did not attend training camp due to a contract dispute (September 1989). ... Pulled groin (November 4, 1989). ... Pulled hamstring (November 15, 1989). ... Tore right groin muscle (December 13, 1989); missed 29 games. ... Injured left groin (March 8, 1990). ... Pulled groin (October 11, 1990); missed five games. ... Sprained left knee ligament (October 27, 1990); missed five weeks. ... Tore groin muscle (March 12, 1991); missed nine games. ... Suffered from the flu (November 14, 1991); missed one game. ... Developed shoulder tendinitis (November 27, 1991); missed nine games. ... Traded by Flyers with C Mike Ricci, C Peter Forsberg, D Steve Duchesne, D Kerry Huffman, first-round pick (Jocelyn Thibault) in 1993 draft, cash and future considerations to Quebec Nordiques for C Eric Lindros (June 20, 1992); Flyers sent LW Chris Simon and first-round pick in 1994 draft (traded to Toronto) to Nordiques to complete deal (July 21, 1992). ... Strained muscle in left thigh (February 20, 1993); missed 14 games. ... Traded by Nordiques with first-round pick (LW Todd Bertuzzi) in 1993 draft to New York Islanders for G Mark Fitzpatrick and first-round pick (C Adam Deadmarsh) in 1993 draft (June 20, 1993). ... Traded by Islanders with sixth-round pick (D Dimitri Tertyshny) in 1995 draft to Flyers for G Tommy Soderstrom (September 22, 1994). ... Injured groin (February 3, 1995); missed three games. ... Strained hamstring (October 20, 1995); missed nine games. ... Injured buttocks (November 20, 1995); missed two games. ... Suffered from the flu (October 10, 1996); missed one game. ... Strained hamstring (March 1, 1997); missed one game. ... Suffered from the flu (October 29, 1997); missed one game. ... Strained neck and back (November 3, 1997); missed one game. ... Strained left thigh muscle (November 29, 1997); missed four games. ... Suffered tendinitis in left hip (March 31, 1998); missed three games.

HONORS: Won Dudley (Red) Garrett Memorial Trophy (1985-86). ... Named to AHL All-Star first team (1985-86). ... Named NHL Rookie of the Year by THE SPORTING NEWS (1986-87). ... Won Vezina Trophy (1986-87). ... Won Conn Smythe Trophy (1986-87). ... Named to THE SPORTING NEWS All-Star second team (1986-87). ... Named to NHL All-Star first team (1986-87). ... Named to NHL All-Rookie team (1986-87). ... Played in NHL All-Star Game (1988).

MISCELLANEOUS: Allowed a penalty shot goal (vs. Dave Tippett, October 31, 1987; vs. Mark Johnson, March 12, 1988; vs. Andrew Cassels, April 6, 1994; vs. Benoit Hogue, January 24, 1995). ... Stopped a penalty shot attempt (vs. Stu Barnes, March 8, 1998). ... Scored a goal into Washington Capitals' empty net, becoming the first goaltender to score a goal in Stanley Cup playoffs (April 11, 1989).

Season Team	League	REGULAR SEASON							PLAYOFFS					
		Gms.	Min.	W	L	T	GA	SO	Avg.	Gms.	Min.	W	L	GA	SO	Avg.
80-81—Melville	SJHL	42	2127	...	...	...	254	0	7.17	—	—	—	—	—	—	—
81-82—Brandon	WHL	30	1398	12	11	0	133	0	5.71	3	103	0	2	16	0	9.32
82-83—Brandon	WHL	44	2589	13	30	0	249	0	5.77	—	—	—	—	—	—	—
83-84—Brandon	WHL	46	2670	29	13	2	190	0	4.27	10	592	5	5	37	0	3.75
84-85—Kalamazoo	IHL	19	1103	6	11	‡1	80	0	4.35	—	—	—	—	—	—	—
—Hershey	AHL	11	555	4	6	0	34	0	3.68	—	—	—	—	—	—	—
85-86—Hershey	AHL	*53	*3061	30	19	2	174	*5	3.41	13	780	5	7	42	*1	3.23
86-87—Philadelphia	NHL	*66	*3799	37	21	6	190	1	3.00	*26	*1540	15	11	*71	†2	2.77
87-88—Philadelphia	NHL	62	3561	30	22	7	208	0	3.50	7	379	2	4	30	0	4.75
88-89—Philadelphia	NHL	64	3756	30	28	6	202	0	3.23	15	886	8	7	49	0	3.32
89-90—Philadelphia	NHL	8	419	4	2	1	29	0	4.15	—	—	—	—	—	—	—
—Hershey	AHL	1	49	1	0	0	3	0	3.67	—	—	—	—	—	—	—
90-91—Philadelphia	NHL	36	2035	13	16	5	106	0	3.13	—	—	—	—	—	—	—

H

Season Team	League	REGULAR SEASON								PLAYOFFS						
		Gms.	Min	W	L	T	GA	SO	Avg.	Gms.	Min.	W	L	GA	SO	Avg.
91-92—Philadelphia	NHL	45	2668	16	21	6	151	3	3.40	—	—	—	—	—	—	—
92-93—Quebec	NHL	54	2988	29	16	5	172	0	3.45	6	372	2	4	18	0	2.90
93-94—New York Islanders	NHL	65	3581	27	26	6	184	5	3.08	3	158	0	3	16	0	6.08
94-95—Philadelphia	NHL	31	1824	17	9	4	88	1	2.89	15	897	10	5	*42	0	2.81
95-96—Philadelphia	NHL	53	3102	31	13	7	112	4	*2.17	12	760	6	6	27	0	2.13
96-97—Philadelphia	NHL	55	3094	31	16	5	132	5	2.56	8	444	4	3	22	0	2.97
97-98—Philadelphia	NHL	46	2688	21	17	7	97	4	2.17	1	20	0	0	1	0	3.00
NHL Totals (12 years)		585	33515	286	207	65	1671	23	2.99	93	5456	47	43	276	2	3.04

HICKS, ALEX   LW

PERSONAL: Born September 4, 1969, in Calgary. ... 6-0/195. ... Shoots left.
TRANSACTIONS/CAREER NOTES: Signed as free agent by Mighty Ducks of Anaheim (August 23, 1995). ... Traded by Mighty Ducks with D Fredrik Olausson to Pittsburgh Penguins for LW Shawn Antoski and D Dmitri Mironov (November 19, 1996). ... Suffered hip pointer (December 15, 1996); missed four games. ... Bruised leg (February 5, 1997); missed one game. ... Strained groin (February 18, 1997); missed two games. ... Strained groin (March 24, 1997); missed one game. ... Injured foot (October 15, 1997); missed one game. ... Fractured foot (December 1, 1997); missed 13 games. ... Separated shoulder (March 2, 1998); missed nine games. ... Suffered concussion (April 16, 1998); missed one game.

Season Team	League	REGULAR SEASON								PLAYOFFS				
		Gms.	G	A	Pts.	PIM	+/-	PP	SH	Gms.	G	A	Pts.	PIM
92-93—Toledo	ECHL	52	26	34	60	100	...	...	...	16	6	10	16	79
93-94—Toledo	ECHL	60	31	49	80	240	...	...	...	14	10	10	20	56
—Adirondack	AHL	8	1	3	4	2	...	...	...	—	—	—	—	—
94-95—Las Vegas	IHL	78	24	42	66	212	...	...	...	9	2	4	6	47
95-96—Baltimore	AHL	13	2	10	12	23	...	...	...	—	—	—	—	—
—Anaheim	NHL	64	10	11	21	37	11	0	0	—	—	—	—	—
96-97—Anaheim	NHL	18	2	6	8	14	1	0	0	—	—	—	—	—
—Pittsburgh	NHL	55	5	15	20	76	-6	0	0	5	0	1	1	2
97-98—Pittsburgh	NHL	58	7	13	20	54	4	0	0	6	0	0	0	2
NHL Totals (3 years)		195	24	45	69	181	10	0	0	11	0	1	1	4

HIGGINS, MATT   C   CANADIENS

PERSONAL: Born October 29, 1977, in Vernon, B.C. ... 6-2/182. ... Shoots left.
TRANSACTIONS/CAREER NOTES: Selected by Montreal Canadiens in first round (first Canadiens pick, 18th overall) of NHL entry draft (June 22, 1996).

Season Team	League	REGULAR SEASON								PLAYOFFS				
		Gms.	G	A	Pts.	PIM	+/-	PP	SH	Gms.	G	A	Pts.	PIM
93-94—Moose Jaw	WHL	64	6	10	16	10	...	...	...	—	—	—	—	—
94-95—Moose Jaw	WHL	72	36	34	70	26	...	...	...	10	1	2	3	2
95-96—Moose Jaw	WHL	67	30	33	63	43	...	...	...	—	—	—	—	—
96-97—Moose Jaw	WHL	71	33	57	90	51	...	...	...	12	3	5	8	2
97-98—Fredericton	AHL	50	5	22	27	12	...	...	...	4	1	2	3	2
—Montreal	NHL	1	0	0	0	0	-1	0	0	—	—	—	—	—
NHL Totals (1 year)		1	0	0	0	0	-1	0	0					

HILL, SEAN   D   HURRICANES

PERSONAL: Born February 14, 1970, in Duluth, Minn. ... 6-0/203. ... Shoots right. ... Full name: Sean Ronald Hill.
COLLEGE: Wisconsin.
TRANSACTIONS/CAREER NOTES: Selected by Montreal Canadiens in eighth round (ninth Canadiens pick, 167th overall) of NHL entry draft (June 11, 1988). ... Injured knee (December 29, 1990). ... Suspended two games by WCHA for elbowing (January 18, 1991). ... Strained abdominal muscle (October 13, 1992); missed 14 games. ... Selected by Mighty Ducks of Anaheim in NHL expansion draft (June 24, 1993). ... Sprained shoulder (January 6, 1994); missed nine games. ... Traded by Mighty Ducks with ninth-round pick (G Frederic Cassivi) in 1994 draft to Ottawa Senators for third-round pick in 1994 draft (June 29, 1994). ... Strained abdominal muscle during 1995-96 season; missed two games. ... Tore left knee ligament (October 18, 1996); missed remainder of season. ... Traded by Senators to Carolina Hurricanes for RW Chris Murray (November 18, 1997). ... Strained hip flexor (December 1, 1997); missed three games. ... Fractured fibula (March 26, 1998); missed final 13 games of season.
HONORS: Named to WCHA All-Star second team (1989-90 and 1990-91). ... Named to NCAA All-America West second team (1990-91).
MISCELLANEOUS: Member of Stanley Cup championship team (1993).

Season Team	League	REGULAR SEASON								PLAYOFFS				
		Gms.	G	A	Pts.	PIM	+/-	PP	SH	Gms.	G	A	Pts.	PIM
88-89—Univ. of Wisconsin	WCHA	45	2	23	25	69	...	...	...	—	—	—	—	—
89-90—Univ. of Wisconsin	WCHA	42	14	39	53	78	...	...	...	—	—	—	—	—
90-91—Univ. of Wisconsin	WCHA	37	19	32	51	122	...	...	...	—	—	—	—	—
—Fredericton	AHL	—	—	—	—	—	...	...	...	3	0	2	2	2
—Montreal	NHL	—	—	—	—	—	...	...	...	1	0	0	0	0
91-92—Fredericton	AHL	42	7	20	27	65	...	...	...	7	1	3	4	6
—U.S. national team	Int'l	12	4	3	7	16	...	...	...	—	—	—	—	—
—U.S. Olympic Team	Int'l	8	2	0	2	6	...	...	...	—	—	—	—	—
—Montreal	NHL	—	—	—	—	—	...	...	...	4	1	0	1	2
92-93—Montreal	NHL	31	2	6	8	54	-5	1	0	3	0	0	0	4
—Fredericton	AHL	6	1	3	4	10	...	...	...	—	—	—	—	—
93-94—Anaheim	NHL	68	7	20	27	78	-12	2	1	—	—	—	—	—

H

Season Team	League	REGULAR SEASON								PLAYOFFS						
		Gms.	Min	W	L	T	GA	SO	Avg.	Gms.	Min.	W	L	GA	SO	Avg.
94-95—Ottawa	NHL	45	1	14	15	30	-11	0	0	—	—	—	—	—	—	—
95-96—Ottawa	NHL	80	7	14	21	94	-26	2	0	—	—	—	—	—	—	—
96-97—Ottawa	NHL	5	0	0	0	4	1	0	0	—	—	—	—	—	—	—
97-98—Ottawa	NHL	13	1	1	2	6	-3	0	0	—	—	—	—	—	—	—
—Carolina	NHL	42	0	5	5	48	-2	0	0	—	—	—	—	—	—	—
NHL Totals (8 years)		284	18	60	78	314	-58	5	1	8		1	0		1	6

HILLIER, CRAIG — G — PENGUINS

PERSONAL: Born February 28, 1978, in Cole Harbour, Nova Scotia. ... 6-1/176. ... Catches left.
TRANSACTIONS/CAREER NOTES: Selected by Pittsburgh Penguins in first round (first Penguins pick, 23rd overall) of NHL entry draft (June 22, 1996).
HONORS: Named to OHL All-Star first team (1995-96). ... Shared Dave Pinkney Trophy with Seamus Kotyk (1997-98).

Season Team	League	REGULAR SEASON								PLAYOFFS						
		Gms.	Min	W	L	T	GA	SO	Avg.	Gms.	Min.	W	L	GA	SO	Avg.
94-95—Ottawa	OHL	24	1078	6	7	2	69	1	3.84	—	—	—	—	—	—	—
95-96—Ottawa	OHL	44	2439	24	14	3	117	2	2.88	3	130	0	2	12	0	5.54
96-97—Ottawa	OHL	36	2007	23	6	4	89	2	2.66	10	540	4	5	33	0	3.67
97-98—Ottawa	OHL	46	2587	27	12	4	108	*6	*2.50	9	447	6	2	20	1	2.68

HINOTE, DAN — RW — AVALANCHE

PERSONAL: Born January 30, 1977, in Leesburg, Fla. ... 6-0/187. ... Shoots right.
COLLEGE: Army.
TRANSACTIONS/CAREER NOTES: Selected by Colorado Avalanche in seventh round (ninth Avalanche pick, 167th overall) of NHL entry draft (June 22, 1996).

Season Team	League	REGULAR SEASON							PLAYOFFS				
		Gms.	G	A	Pts.	PIM	+/-	PP	SH	Gms.	G	A	Pts.	PIM
95-96—Army	Indep.	33	20	24	44	20	...	...	...	—	—	—	—	—
96-97—Oshawa	OHL	60	15	13	28	58	...	...	...	18	4	5	9	8
97-98—Hershey	AHL	24	1	4	5	25	...	...	...	—	—	—	—	—
—Oshawa	OHL	35	12	15	27	39	...	...	...	5	2	2	4	7

HIRSCH, COREY — G — CANUCKS

PERSONAL: Born July 1, 1972, in Medicine Hat, Alta. ... 5-10/160. ... Catches left.
TRANSACTIONS/CAREER NOTES: Selected by New York Rangers in eighth round (seventh Rangers pick, 169th overall) of NHL entry draft (June 22, 1991). ... Loaned by Rangers to Canadian national team (October 1, 1993). ... Returned to Rangers (March 8, 1994). ... Traded by Rangers to Vancouver Canucks for C Nathan LaFayette (April 7, 1995). ... Bruised ribs (October 6, 1996); missed five games.
HONORS: Named to WHL (West) All-Star second team (1989-90). ... Won Can.HL Goaltender of the Year Award (1991-92). ... Won Hap Emms Memorial Trophy (1991-92). ... Won Del Wilson Trophy (1991-92). ... Won WHL Player of the Year Award (1991-92). ... Named to Can.HL All-Star first team (1991-92). ... Named to Memorial Cup All-Star team (1991-92). ... Named to WHL (West) All-Star first team (1991-92). ... Won Aldege (Baz) Bastien Trophy (1992-93). ... Won Dudley (Red) Garrett Memorial Trophy (1992-93). ... Shared Harry (Hap) Holmes Memorial Trophy with Boris Rousson (1992-93). ... Named to AHL All-Star team (1992-93). ... Named to NHL All-Rookie team (1995-96).
MISCELLANEOUS: Member of silver-medal-winning Canadian Olympic team (1994).

Season Team	League	REGULAR SEASON								PLAYOFFS						
		Gms.	Min	W	L	T	GA	SO	Avg.	Gms.	Min.	W	L	GA	SO	Avg.
88-89—Kamloops	WHL	32	1516	11	12	2	106	2	4.20	5	245	3	2	19	0	4.65
89-90—Kamloops	WHL	63	3608	48	13	0	230	3	3.82	17	1043	14	3	60	0	3.45
90-91—Kamloops	WHL	38	1970	26	7	1	100	3	3.05	11	623	5	6	42	0	4.04
91-92—Kamloops	WHL	48	2732	35	10	2	124	*5	*2.72	*16	*954	*11	5	35	*2	*2.20
92-93—Binghamton	AHL	46	2692	*35	4	5	125	1	*2.79	14	831	7	7	46	0	3.32
—New York Rangers	NHL	4	224	1	2	1	14	0	3.75	—	—	—	—	—	—	—
93-94—Canadian nat'l team	Int'l	37	2158	19	15	2	107	0	2.97	—	—	—	—	—	—	—
—Can. Olympic Team	Int'l	8	495	5	2	1	17	0	2.06	—	—	—	—	—	—	—
—Binghamton	AHL	10	611	5	4	1	38	0	3.73	—	—	—	—	—	—	—
94-95—Binghamton	AHL	57	3371	31	20	5	175	0	3.11	—	—	—	—	—	—	—
95-96—Vancouver	NHL	41	2338	17	14	6	114	1	2.93	6	338	2	3	21	0	3.73
96-97—Vancouver	NHL	39	2127	12	20	4	116	2	3.27	—	—	—	—	—	—	—
97-98—Vancouver	NHL	1	50	0	0	0	5	0	6.00	—	—	—	—	—	—	—
—Syracuse	AHL	60	3513	30	22	6	187	1	3.19	5	297	2	3	10	1	*2.02
NHL Totals (4 years)		85	4739	30	36	11	249	3	3.15	6	338	2	3	21	0	3.73

HLAVAC, JAN — LW — FLAMES

PERSONAL: Born September 20, 1976, in Prague, Czechoslovakia. ... 6-0/183. ... Shoots left. ... Name pronounced YAHN luh-VAHCH.
TRANSACTIONS/CAREER NOTES: Selected by New York Islanders in second round (second Islanders pick, 28th overall) of NHL entry draft (July 8, 1995). ... Traded by Islanders to Calgary Flames for LW Jorgen Jonsson (July 14, 1998).

Season Team	League	REGULAR SEASON							PLAYOFFS				
		Gms.	G	A	Pts.	PIM	+/-	PP	SH	Gms.	G	A	Pts.	PIM
93-94—Sparta Prague Jr.	Czech Rep.	27	12	15	27	...	...	...	...	—	—	—	—	—
—Sparta Prague	Czech Rep.	9	1	1	2	...	...	...	...	—	—	—	—	—
94-95—Sparta Prague	Czech Rep.	38	7	6	13	...	...	...	...	5	0	2	2	...
95-96—Sparta Prague	Czech Rep.	34	8	5	13	...	...	...	...	12	1	2	3	...
96-97—Sparta Praha	Czech Rep.	38	8	13	21	24	...	...	...	10	5	2	7	2
97-98—Sparta Praha	Czech Rep.	48	17	30	47	40	...	...	...	5	1	0	1	2

H

HLUSHKO, TODD   LW/C   PENGUINS

PERSONAL: Born February 7, 1970, in Toronto. ... 5-11/185. ... Shoots left. ... Name pronounced huh-LOOSH-koh.
TRANSACTIONS/CAREER NOTES: Selected by Washington Capitals in 14th round (14th Capitals pick, 240th overall) of NHL entry draft (June 16, 1990). ... Signed as free agent by Philadelphia Flyers (March 6, 1994). ... Signed as free agent by Calgary Flames (June 27, 1994). ... Separated shoulder (February 11, 1995); missed 25 games. ... Suffered concussion (March 9, 1997); missed final 13 games of 1996-97 and first 17 games of 1997-98 season. ... Traded by Flames with C German Titov to Pittsburgh Penguins for G Ken Wregget and LW Dave Roche (June 17, 1998).

		REGULAR SEASON								PLAYOFFS				
Season Team	League	Gms.	G	A	Pts.	PIM	+/-	PP	SH	Gms.	G	A	Pts.	PIM
88-89—Guelph	OHL	66	28	18	46	71	...	...	...	7	5	3	8	18
89-90—Owen Sound	OHL	25	9	17	26	31	...	...	...	—	—	—	—	—
—London	OHL	40	27	17	44	39	...	...	...	6	2	4	6	10
90-91—Baltimore	AHL	66	9	14	23	55	...	...	...	—	—	—	—	—
91-92—Baltimore	AHL	74	16	35	51	113	...	...	...	—	—	—	—	—
92-93—Canadian nat'l team	Int'l	58	22	26	48	10	...	...	...	—	—	—	—	—
93-94—Canadian nat'l team	Int'l	55	22	6	28	61	...	...	...	—	—	—	—	—
—Can. Olympic Team	Int'l	8	5	0	5	6	...	...	...	—	—	—	—	—
—Philadelphia	NHL	2	1	0	1	0	1	0	0	—	—	—	—	—
—Hershey	AHL	9	6	0	6	4	...	...	...	6	2	1	3	4
94-95—Saint John	AHL	46	22	10	32	36	...	...	...	4	2	2	4	22
—Calgary	NHL	2	0	1	1	2	1	0	0	1	0	0	0	2
95-96—Saint John	AHL	35	14	13	27	70	...	...	...	16	8	1	9	26
—Calgary	NHL	4	0	0	0	6	0	0	0	—	—	—	—	—
96-97—Calgary	NHL	58	7	11	18	49	-2	0	0	—	—	—	—	—
97-98—Calgary	NHL	13	0	1	1	27	0	0	0	—	—	—	—	—
—Saint John	AHL	33	10	14	24	48	...	...	...	21	13	4	17	61
NHL Totals (5 years)		79	8	13	21	84	0	0	0	1	0	0	0	2

HOCKING, JUSTIN   D   SENATORS

PERSONAL: Born January 9, 1974, in Stettler, Alta. ... 6-4/215. ... Shoots right. ... Name pronounced HAH-kihng.
COLLEGE: Spokane (Wash.) Falls Community College.
TRANSACTIONS/CAREER NOTES: Selected by Los Angeles Kings in second round (first Kings pick, 39th overall) of NHL entry draft (June 20, 1992). ... Signed as free agent by Ottawa Senators (July 31, 1997).
HONORS: Named to WHL (East) All-Star second team (1993-94).

		REGULAR SEASON								PLAYOFFS				
Season Team	League	Gms.	G	A	Pts.	PIM	+/-	PP	SH	Gms.	G	A	Pts.	PIM
90-91—Fort Saskatchewan	AJHL	38	4	6	10	84	...	...	...	—	—	—	—	—
91-92—Spokane	WHL	71	4	6	10	309	...	...	...	10	0	3	3	28
92-93—Spokane	WHL	16	0	1	1	75	...	...	...	—	—	—	—	—
—Medicine Hat	WHL	54	1	9	10	119	...	...	...	10	0	1	1	75
93-94—Medicine Hat	WHL	68	7	26	33	236	...	...	...	3	0	0	0	6
—Phoenix	IHL	3	0	0	0	15	...	...	...	—	—	—	—	—
—Los Angeles	NHL	1	0	0	0	0	0	0	0	—	—	—	—	—
94-95—Phoenix	IHL	20	1	1	2	50	...	...	...	1	0	0	0	0
—Syracuse	AHL	7	0	0	0	24	...	...	...	—	—	—	—	—
—Portland	AHL	9	0	1	1	34	...	...	...	—	—	—	—	—
—Knoxville	ECHL	20	0	6	6	70	...	...	...	4	0	0	0	26
95-96—Prin. Edward Island	AHL	74	4	8	12	251	...	...	...	4	0	2	2	5
96-97—Worcester	AHL	68	1	10	11	198	...	...	...	5	0	3	3	2
97-98—Worcester	AHL	79	5	12	17	198	...	...	...	11	1	2	3	19
NHL Totals (1 year)		1	0	0	0	0	0	0	0					

HODSON, KEVIN   G   RED WINGS

PERSONAL: Born March 27, 1972, in Winnipeg. ... 6-0/182. ... Catches left.
TRANSACTIONS/CAREER NOTES: Signed as free agent by Chicago Blackhawks (August 27, 1992). ... Signed as free agent by Detroit Red Wings (May 3, 1993). ... Strained hip flexor (March 10, 1998); missed two games. ... Reinjured hip (March 17, 1998); missed one game.
HONORS: Won Hap Emms Memorial Trophy (1992-93).
MISCELLANEOUS: Member of Stanley Cup championship team (1998).

		REGULAR SEASON								PLAYOFFS						
Season Team	League	Gms.	Min.	W	L	T	GA	SO	Avg.	Gms.	Min.	W	L	GA	SO	Avg.
90-91—S.S. Marie	OHL	30	1638	18	11	0	88	2	*3.22	10	600	*9	1	28	0	2.80
91-92—S.S. Marie	OHL	50	2722	28	12	4	151	0	3.33	18	1116	12	6	59	1	3.17
92-93—S.S. Marie	OHL	26	1470	18	5	2	76	1	*3.10	8	448	8	0	17	0	2.28
—Indianapolis	IHL	14	777	5	9	‡0	53	0	4.09	—	—	—	—	—	—	—
93-94—Adirondack	AHL	37	2083	20	10	5	102	2	2.94	3	89	0	2	10	0	6.74
94-95—Adirondack	AHL	51	2731	19	22	8	161	1	3.54	4	238	0	4	14	0	3.53
95-96—Adirondack	AHL	32	1654	13	13	2	87	0	3.16	3	149	0	2	8	0	3.22
—Detroit	NHL	4	163	2	0	0	3	1	1.10	—	—	—	—	—	—	—
96-97—Detroit	NHL	6	294	2	2	1	8	1	1.63	—	—	—	—	—	—	—
—Quebec	IHL	2	118	1	1	‡0	7	0	3.56	—	—	—	—	—	—	—
97-98—Detroit	NHL	21	988	9	3	3	44	2	2.67	1	0	0	0	0	0	0.00
NHL Totals (3 years)		31	1445	13	5	4	55	4	2.28	1	0	0	0	0	0	0.00

H

HOGAN, PETER — D — KINGS

PERSONAL: Born January 10, 1978, in Scarborough, Ont. ... 6-2/167. ... Shoots right.
TRANSACTIONS/CAREER NOTES: Selected by Los Angeles Kings in fifth round (seventh Kings pick, 123rd overall) of NHL entry draft (June 22, 1996).

		REGULAR SEASON								PLAYOFFS				
Season Team	League	Gms.	G	A	Pts.	PIM	+/-	PP	SH	Gms.	G	A	Pts.	PIM
95-96—Oshawa	OHL	66	3	25	28	54	...	...	...	5	2	0	2	2
96-97—Oshawa	OHL	65	13	37	50	56	...	...	...	18	1	11	12	22
97-98—Oshawa	OHL	63	10	28	38	104	...	...	...	—	—	—	—	—

HOGLUND, JONAS — LW — CANADIENS

PERSONAL: Born August 29, 1972, in Hammaro, Sweden. ... 6-3/215. ... Shoots right. ... Name pronounced YOH-nuhz HOHG-luhnd.
TRANSACTIONS/CAREER NOTES: Selected by Calgary Flames in 10th round (11th Flames pick, 222nd overall) of NHL entry draft (June 20, 1992). ... Traded by Flames to Canadiens with D Zarley Zalapski for RW Valeri Bure and fourth-round draft pick (C Shaun Sutter) in 1998 draft (February 1, 1998).

		REGULAR SEASON								PLAYOFFS				
Season Team	League	Gms.	G	A	Pts.	PIM	+/-	PP	SH	Gms.	G	A	Pts.	PIM
88-89—Farjestad Karlstad	Sweden	1	0	0	0	0	...	...	...	—	—	—	—	—
89-90—Farjestad Karlstad	Sweden	1	0	0	0	0	...	...	...	—	—	—	—	—
90-91—Farjestad Karlstad	Sweden	40	5	5	10	4	...	...	...	8	1	0	1	0
91-92—Farjestad Karlstad	Sweden	40	14	11	25	6	...	...	...	6	2	4	6	2
92-93—Farjestad Karlstad	Sweden	40	13	13	26	14	...	...	...	3	1	0	1	0
93-94—Farjestad Karlstad	Sweden	22	7	2	9	10	...	...	...	—	—	—	—	—
94-95—Farjestad Karlstad	Sweden	40	14	12	26	16	...	...	...	4	3	2	5	0
95-96—Farjestad Karlstad	Sweden	40	32	11	43	18	...	...	...	8	2	1	3	6
96-97—Calgary	NHL	68	19	16	35	12	-4	3	0	—	—	—	—	—
97-98—Calgary	NHL	50	6	8	14	16	-9	0	0	—	—	—	—	—
—Montreal	NHL	28	6	5	11	6	2	4	0	10	2	0	2	0
NHL Totals (2 years)		146	31	29	60	34	-11	7	0	10	2	0	2	0

HOGUE, BENOIT — LW — LIGHTNING

PERSONAL: Born October 28, 1966, in Repentigny, Que. ... 5-10/194. ... Shoots left. ... Name pronounced BEHN-wah HOHG.
TRANSACTIONS/CAREER NOTES: Selected by Buffalo Sabres as underage junior in second round (second Sabres pick, 35th overall) of NHL entry draft (June 15, 1985). ... Suspended six games by AHL for fighting (October 1987). ... Suffered sore back (March 1988). ... Broke left cheekbone (October 11, 1989); missed 20 games. ... Sprained left ankle (March 14, 1990). ... Traded by Sabres with C Pierre Turgeon, D Uwe Krupp and C Dave McLlwain to New York Islanders for C Pat LaFontaine, LW Randy Wood, D Randy Hillier and future considerations; Sabres later received fourth-round pick (D Dean Melanson) in 1992 draft (October 25, 1991). ... Suffered stiff neck (December 7, 1992); missed five games. ... Suffered sore hand and foot (January 14, 1993); missed three games. ... Sprained knee ligament (March 14, 1993); missed six games. ... Injured shoulder (February 4, 1995); missed one game. ... Traded by Islanders with third-round pick (RW Ryan Pepperall) in 1995 draft and fifth-round pick (D Brandon Sugden) in 1996 draft to Toronto Maple Leafs for G Eric Fichaud (April 6, 1995). ... Sprained wrist (December 27, 1995); missed four games. ... Traded by Maple Leafs with LW Randy Wood to Dallas Stars for C Dave Gagner (January 28, 1996). ... Sprained neck (November 27, 1996); missed one game. ... Injured elbow (February 2, 1997); missed two games. ... Reinjured elbow (February 23, 1997); missed four games. ... Fractured ankle (December 3, 1997); missed 12 games. ... Fractured face (March 8, 1998); missed 13 games. ... Signed as free agent by Tampa Bay Lightning (July 29, 1998).
MISCELLANEOUS: Scored on a penalty shot (vs. Ron Tugnutt, February, 16, 1993; vs. Ron Hextall, January 24, 1995).
STATISTICAL PLATEAUS: Three-goal games: 1992-93 (1).

		REGULAR SEASON								PLAYOFFS				
Season Team	League	Gms.	G	A	Pts.	PIM	+/-	PP	SH	Gms.	G	A	Pts.	PIM
83-84—St. Jean	QMJHL	59	14	11	25	42	...	...	...	—	—	—	—	—
84-85—St. Jean	QMJHL	63	46	44	90	92	...	...	...	—	—	—	—	—
85-86—St. Jean	QMJHL	65	54	54	108	115	...	...	...	9	6	4	10	26
86-87—Rochester	AHL	52	14	20	34	52	...	...	...	12	5	4	9	8
87-88—Buffalo	NHL	3	1	1	2	0	3	0	0	—	—	—	—	—
—Rochester	AHL	62	24	31	55	141	...	...	...	7	6	1	7	46
88-89—Buffalo	NHL	69	14	30	44	120	-5	1	2	5	0	0	0	17
89-90—Buffalo	NHL	45	11	7	18	79	0	1	0	3	0	0	0	10
90-91—Buffalo	NHL	76	19	28	47	76	-8	1	0	5	3	1	4	10
91-92—Buffalo	NHL	3	0	1	1	0	0	0	0	—	—	—	—	—
—New York Islanders	NHL	72	30	45	75	67	30	8	0	—	—	—	—	—
92-93—New York Islanders	NHL	70	33	42	75	108	13	5	3	18	6	6	12	31
93-94—New York Islanders	NHL	83	36	33	69	73	-7	9	5	4	0	1	1	4
94-95—New York Islanders	NHL	33	6	4	10	34	0	1	0	—	—	—	—	—
—Toronto	NHL	12	3	3	6	0	0	1	0	7	0	0	0	6
95-96—Toronto	NHL	44	12	25	37	68	6	3	0	—	—	—	—	—
—Dallas	NHL	34	7	20	27	36	4	2	0	—	—	—	—	—
96-97—Dallas	NHL	73	19	24	43	54	8	5	0	7	2	2	4	6
97-98—Dallas	NHL	53	6	16	22	35	7	3	0	17	4	2	6	16
NHL Totals (11 years)		670	197	279	476	750	51	40	10	66	15	12	27	100

H

HOLDEN, JOSH — C — CANUCKS

PERSONAL: Born January 18, 1978, in Calgary. ... 5-11/187. ... Shoots left.
TRANSACTIONS/CAREER NOTES: Selected by Vancouver Canucks in first round (first Canucks pick, 12th overall) of NHL entry draft (June 22, 1996).
HONORS: Named to WHL (East) All-Star second team (1997-98).

Season Team	League	REGULAR SEASON								PLAYOFFS				
		Gms.	G	A	Pts.	PIM	+/-	PP	SH	Gms.	G	A	Pts.	PIM
94-95—Regina	WHL	62	20	23	43	45	...	...	...	4	3	1	4	0
95-96—Regina	WHL	70	57	55	112	105	...	...	...	11	4	5	9	23
96-97—Regina	WHL	58	49	49	98	148	...	...	...	5	3	2	5	10
97-98—Regina	WHL	56	41	58	99	134	...	...	...	2	2	2	4	10

HOLIK, BOBBY   C   DEVILS

PERSONAL: Born January 1, 1971, in Jihlava, Czechoslovakia. ... 6-3/225. ... Shoots right. ... Full name: Robert Holik. ... Name pronounced hoh-LEEK.
TRANSACTIONS/CAREER NOTES: Selected by Hartford Whalers in first round (first Whalers pick, 10th overall) of NHL entry draft (June 17, 1989). ... Broke right thumb (February 1990). ... Traded by Whalers with second-round pick (LW Jay Pandolfo) in 1993 draft and future considerations to New Jersey Devils for G Sean Burke and D Eric Weinrich (August 28, 1992). ... Fractured right thumb (January 22, 1993); missed 22 games. ... Bruised left shoulder (December 8, 1993); missed 11 games. ... Broke left index finger (October 7, 1995); missed 13 games. ... Sprained left ankle (February 28, 1996); missed six games.
HONORS: Played in NHL All-Star Game (1998).
MISCELLANEOUS: Member of Stanley Cup championship team (1995).
STATISTICAL PLATEAUS: Three-goal games: 1992-93 (2).

Season Team	League	REGULAR SEASON								PLAYOFFS				
		Gms.	G	A	Pts.	PIM	+/-	PP	SH	Gms.	G	A	Pts.	PIM
87-88—Dukla Jihlava	Czech.	31	5	9	14	...	...	...	...	—	—	—	—	—
88-89—Dukla Jihlava	Czech.	24	7	10	17	...	...	...	...	—	—	—	—	—
89-90—Dukla Jihlava	Czech.	42	15	26	41	...	...	...	...	—	—	—	—	—
—Czech. national team	Int'l	10	1	5	6	0	...	...	...	—	—	—	—	—
90-91—Hartford	NHL	78	21	22	43	113	-3	8	0	6	0	0	0	7
91-92—Hartford	NHL	76	21	24	45	44	4	1	0	7	0	1	1	6
92-93—Utica	AHL	1	0	0	0	2	...	...	...	—	—	—	—	—
—New Jersey	NHL	61	20	19	39	76	-6	7	0	5	1	1	2	6
93-94—New Jersey	NHL	70	13	20	33	72	28	2	0	20	0	3	3	6
94-95—New Jersey	NHL	48	10	10	20	18	9	0	0	20	4	4	8	22
95-96—New Jersey	NHL	63	13	17	30	58	9	1	0	—	—	—	—	—
96-97—New Jersey	NHL	82	23	39	62	54	24	5	0	10	2	3	5	4
97-98—New Jersey	NHL	82	29	36	65	100	23	8	0	5	0	0	0	8
NHL Totals (8 years)		560	150	187	337	535	88	32	0	73	7	12	19	59

HOLLAND, JASON   D   SABRES

PERSONAL: Born April 30, 1976, in Morinville, Alta. ... 6-2/193. ... Shoots right.
HIGH SCHOOL: Norkam (Kamloops, B.C.).
TRANSACTIONS/CAREER NOTES: Selected by New York Islanders in second round (second Islanders pick, 38th overall) of NHL entry draft (June 28, 1994). ... Traded by Islanders with LW Paul Kruse to Buffalo Sabres for RW Jason Dawe (March 24, 1998).
HONORS: Named to Can.HL All-Star second team (1995-96). ... Named to WHL (West) All-Star first team (1995-96). ... Named to AHL All-Rookie team (1996-97).

Season Team	League	REGULAR SEASON								PLAYOFFS				
		Gms.	G	A	Pts.	PIM	+/-	PP	SH	Gms.	G	A	Pts.	PIM
92-93—Kamloops	WHL	4	0	0	0	2	...	...	...	—	—	—	—	—
93-94—Kamloops	WHL	59	14	15	29	80	...	...	...	18	2	3	5	4
94-95—Kamloops	WHL	71	9	32	41	65	...	...	...	21	2	7	9	9
95-96—Kamloops	WHL	63	24	33	57	98	...	...	...	16	4	9	13	22
96-97—Kentucky	AHL	72	14	25	39	46	...	...	...	4	0	2	2	0
—New York Islanders	NHL	4	1	0	1	0	1	0	0	—	—	—	—	—
97-98—Kentucky	AHL	50	10	16	26	29	...	...	...	—	—	—	—	—
—New York Islanders	NHL	8	0	0	0	4	-4	0	0	—	—	—	—	—
—Rochester	AHL	9	0	4	4	10	...	...	...	4	0	3	3	4
NHL Totals (2 years)		12	1	0	1	4	-3	0	0					

HOLLINGER, TERRY   D   BLUES

PERSONAL: Born February 24, 1971, in Regina, Sask. ... 6-1/200. ... Shoots left. ... Name pronounced HAHL-ihn-juhr.
TRANSACTIONS/CAREER NOTES: Selected by St. Louis Blues in sixth round (sixth Blues pick, 153rd overall) of NHL entry draft (June 22, 1991).
HONORS: Named to AHL All-Star second team (1995-96). ... Named to AHL All-Star first team (1996-97).

Season Team	League	REGULAR SEASON								PLAYOFFS				
		Gms.	G	A	Pts.	PIM	+/-	PP	SH	Gms.	G	A	Pts.	PIM
87-88—Regina	WHL	7	1	1	2	4	...	...	...	—	—	—	—	—
88-89—Regina	WHL	65	2	27	29	49	...	...	...	—	—	—	—	—
89-90—Regina	WHL	70	14	43	57	40	...	...	...	11	1	3	4	10
90-91—Regina	WHL	8	1	6	7	6	...	...	...	—	—	—	—	—
—Lethbridge	WHL	62	9	32	41	113	...	...	...	16	3	14	17	22
91-92—Lethbridge	WHL	65	23	62	85	155	...	...	...	5	1	2	3	13
—Peoria	IHL	1	0	2	2	0	...	...	...	5	0	1	1	0
92-93—Peoria	IHL	72	2	28	30	67	...	...	...	4	1	1	2	0
93-94—Peoria	IHL	78	12	31	43	96	...	...	...	6	0	3	3	31
—St. Louis	NHL	2	0	0	0	0	1	0	0	—	—	—	—	—
94-95—Peoria	IHL	69	7	25	32	137	...	...	...	4	2	4	6	8
—St. Louis	NHL	5	0	0	0	2	-1	0	0	—	—	—	—	—

H

Season Team	League	REGULAR SEASON Gms.	G	A	Pts.	PIM	+/-	PP	SH	PLAYOFFS Gms.	G	A	Pts.	PIM
95-96—Rochester	AHL	62	5	50	55	71	...	...	...	19	3	11	14	12
96-97—Rochester	AHL	73	12	51	63	54	...	...	...	10	2	7	9	27
97-98—Worcester	AHL	55	8	24	32	34	...	...	...	—	—	—	—	—
—Houston	IHL	8	1	1	2	6	...	...	...	4	1	2	3	11
NHL Totals (2 years)...........		7	0	0	0	2	0	0	0					

HOLMQVIST, JOHAN   G   RANGERS

PERSONAL: Born May 24, 1978, in Tierp, Sweden. ... 6-1/200. ... Catches left.
TRANSACTIONS/CAREER NOTES: Selected by New York Rangers in seventh round (ninth pick, 182nd overall) of 1997 NHL entry draft.

Season Team	League	REGULAR SEASON Gms.	Min	W	L	T	GA	SO	Avg.	PLAYOFFS Gms.	Min.	W	L	GA	SO	Avg.
96-97—Brynas Gavle................	Sweden	2	...	...	...	...	...	...	3.00	—	—	—	—	—	—	—
97-98—Brynas Gavle................	Sweden	33	1897	...	...	...	82	...	2.59	3	180	...	...	14	...	4.67

HOLMSTROM, TOMAS   LW   RED WINGS

PERSONAL: Born January 23, 1973, in Pitea, Sweden. ... 6-0/210. ... Shoots left.
TRANSACTIONS/CAREER NOTES: Selected by Detroit Red Wings in 10th round (ninth Red Wings pick, 257th overall) of NHL entry draft (June 29, 1994). ... Sprained knee (October 30, 1996); missed seven games. ... Bruised shoulder (March 28, 1997); missed one game. ... Suffered injury (September 30, 1997); missed one game.
MISCELLANEOUS: Member of Stanley Cup championship team (1997 and 1998).

Season Team	League	REGULAR SEASON Gms.	G	A	Pts.	PIM	+/-	PP	SH	PLAYOFFS Gms.	G	A	Pts.	PIM
94-95—Lulea...........................	Sweden	40	14	14	28	56	...	...	...	8	1	2	3	20
95-96—Lulea...........................	Sweden	34	12	11	23	78	...	...	...	11	6	2	8	22
96-97—Detroit........................	NHL	47	6	3	9	33	-10	3	0	1	0	0	0	0
—Adirondack	AHL	6	3	1	4	7	...	...	...	—	—	—	—	—
97-98—Detroit........................	NHL	57	5	17	22	44	6	1	0	22	7	12	19	16
NHL Totals (2 years)...........		104	11	20	31	77	-4	4	0	23	7	12	19	16

HOLZINGER, BRIAN   C   SABRES

PERSONAL: Born October 10, 1972, in Parma, Ohio. ... 5-11/190. ... Shoots right. ... Full name: Brian Alan Holzinger. ... Name pronounced HOHL-zihng-uhr.
HIGH SCHOOL: Parma (Ohio).
COLLEGE: Bowling Green State.
TRANSACTIONS/CAREER NOTES: Selected by Buffalo Sabres in sixth round (seventh Sabres pick, 124th overall) of NHL entry draft (June 22, 1991). ... Bruised heel (November 10, 1997); missed three games. ... Sprained ankle (March 1, 1998); missed seven games.
HONORS: Named to CCHA All-Star second team (1993-94). ... Won Hobey Baker Memorial Award (1994-95). ... Named to NCAA All-America West first team (1994-95). ... Named CCHA Player of the Year (1994-95). ... Named to CCHA All-Star first team (1994-95).

Season Team	League	REGULAR SEASON Gms.	G	A	Pts.	PIM	+/-	PP	SH	PLAYOFFS Gms.	G	A	Pts.	PIM
90-91—Det. Jr. Red Wings......	NAJHL	37	45	41	86	16	...	...	...	—	—	—	—	—
91-92—Bowling Green	CCHA	30	14	8	22	36	...	...	...	—	—	—	—	—
92-93—Bowling Green	CCHA	41	31	26	57	44	...	...	...	—	—	—	—	—
93-94—Bowling Green	CCHA	38	22	15	37	24	...	...	...	—	—	—	—	—
94-95—Bowling Green	CCHA	38	35	34	69	42	...	...	...	—	—	—	—	—
—Buffalo	NHL	4	0	3	3	0	2	0	0	4	2	1	3	2
95-96—Buffalo	NHL	58	10	10	20	37	-21	5	0	—	—	—	—	—
—Rochester	AHL	17	10	11	21	14	...	...	...	19	10	14	24	10
96-97—Buffalo	NHL	81	22	29	51	54	9	2	2	12	2	5	7	8
97-98—Buffalo	NHL	69	14	21	35	36	-2	4	2	15	4	7	11	18
NHL Totals (4 years)...........		212	46	63	109	127	-12	11	4	31	8	13	21	28

HORACEK, JAN   D   BLUES

PERSONAL: Born May 22, 1979, in Benesov, Czechoslovakia. ... 6-4/206. ... Shoots right. ... Name pronounced HOHR-ih-chehk.
TRANSACTIONS/CAREER NOTES: Selected by St. Louis Blues in fourth round (third Blues pick, 98th overall) of NHL entry draft (June 21, 1997).

Season Team	League	REGULAR SEASON Gms.	G	A	Pts.	PIM	+/-	PP	SH	PLAYOFFS Gms.	G	A	Pts.	PIM
95-96—Slavia Praha................	Czech Rep.	8	0	1	1	4	...	...	...	—	—	—	—	—
—Slavia Praha Jrs.........	Czech Rep.	18	1	5	6	...	...	...	...	—	—	—	—	—
—HC Kralupy	Czech II	11	0	0	0	...	...	...	...	—	—	—	—	—
96-97—Slavia Praha Jrs.........	Czech Rep.	25	4	14	18	...	...	...	...	—	—	—	—	—
—Slavia Praha	Czech Rep.	9	0	0	0	6	...	...	...	3	0	0	0	...
—HC Beroun	Czech II	2	0	0	0	...	...	...	...	—	—	—	—	—
97-98—Moncton	QMJHL	54	3	18	21	146	...	...	...	10	1	5	6	20

HOSSA, MARIAN   LW   SENATORS

PERSONAL: Born January 12, 1979, in Stara Lubovna, Czechoslovakia. ... 6-1/194. ... Shoots left. ... Name pronounced HOH-suh.
TRANSACTIONS/CAREER NOTES: Selected by Ottawa Senators in first round (first Senators pick, 12th overall) of NHL entry draft (June 21, 1997).
HONORS: Won Jim Piggott Memorial Trophy (1997-98). ... Named to WHL (West) All-Star first team (1997-98). ... Named to Can.HL All-Star first team (1997-98).

Season Team	League	Gms.	G	REGULAR SEASON A	Pts.	PIM	+/-	PP	SH	Gms.	G	PLAYOFFS A	Pts.	PIM
95-96—Dukla Trencin Jrs.	Slovakia Jrs.	53	42	49	91	26	...	...	...	—	—	—	—	—
96-97—Dukla Trencin	Slovakia	46	25	19	44	33	...	...	...	7	5	5	10	...
97-98—Ottawa	NHL	7	0	1	1	0	-1	0	0	—	—	—	—	—
—Portland	WHL	53	45	40	85	50	...	...	...	16	13	6	19	6
NHL Totals (1 year)		7	0	1	1	0	-1	0	0					

HOUDA, DOUG   D   MIGHTY DUCKS

PERSONAL: Born June 3, 1966, in Blairmore, Alta. ... 6-2/190. ... Shoots right. ... Name pronounced HOO-duh.
TRANSACTIONS/CAREER NOTES: Selected by Detroit Red Wings as underage junior in second round (second Red Wings pick, 28th overall) of NHL entry draft (June 9, 1984). ... Fractured left cheekbone (September 23, 1988). ... Injured knee and underwent surgery (November 21, 1989). ... Traded by Red Wings to Hartford Whalers for D Doug Crossman (February 20, 1991). ... Separated shoulder (February 28, 1994); missed three games. ... Strained shoulder (March 15, 1994); missed two games. ... Traded by Whalers to Los Angeles Kings for RW Marc Potvin (November 3, 1993). ... Traded by Kings to Buffalo Sabres for D Sean O'Donnell (July 26, 1994). ... Severed tendon in hand (February 11, 1995); missed 12 games. ... Signed as free agent by New York Islanders (October 23, 1996). ... Traded by Islanders with C Travis Green and RW Tony Tuzzolino to Mighty Ducks of Anaheim for D J.J. Daigneault, C Mark Janssens and RW Joe Sacco (February 6, 1998).
HONORS: Named to WHL All-Star second team (1984-85). ... Named to AHL All-Star first team (1987-88).

Season Team	League	Gms.	G	REGULAR SEASON A	Pts.	PIM	+/-	PP	SH	Gms.	G	PLAYOFFS A	Pts.	PIM
81-82—Calgary	WHL	3	0	0	0	0	...	...	...	—	—	—	—	—
82-83—Calgary	WHL	71	5	23	28	99	...	...	...	16	1	3	4	44
83-84—Calgary	WHL	69	6	30	36	195	...	...	...	4	0	0	0	7
84-85—Calgary	WHL	65	20	54	74	182	...	...	...	8	3	4	7	29
—Kalamazoo	IHL	—	—	—	—	—	...	...	...	7	0	2	2	10
85-86—Calgary	WHL	16	4	10	14	60	...	...	...	—	—	—	—	—
—Medicine Hat	WHL	35	9	23	32	80	...	...	...	25	4	19	23	64
—Detroit	NHL	6	0	0	0	4	-7	0	0	—	—	—	—	—
86-87—Adirondack	AHL	77	6	23	29	142	...	...	...	11	1	8	9	50
87-88—Detroit	NHL	11	1	1	2	10	0	0	0	—	—	—	—	—
—Adirondack	AHL	71	10	32	42	169	...	...	...	11	0	3	3	44
88-89—Adirondack	AHL	7	0	3	3	8	...	...	...	—	—	—	—	—
—Detroit	NHL	57	2	11	13	67	17	0	0	6	0	1	1	0
89-90—Detroit	NHL	73	2	9	11	127	-5	0	0	—	—	—	—	—
90-91—Adirondack	AHL	38	9	17	26	67	...	...	...	—	—	—	—	—
—Detroit	NHL	22	0	4	4	43	-2	0	0	—	—	—	—	—
—Hartford	NHL	19	1	2	3	41	-3	0	0	6	0	0	0	8
91-92—Hartford	NHL	56	3	6	9	125	-2	1	0	6	0	2	2	13
92-93—Hartford	NHL	60	2	6	8	167	-19	0	0	—	—	—	—	—
93-94—Hartford	NHL	7	0	0	0	23	-4	0	0	—	—	—	—	—
—Los Angeles	NHL	54	2	6	8	165	-15	0	0	—	—	—	—	—
94-95—Buffalo	NHL	28	1	2	3	68	1	0	0	—	—	—	—	—
95-96—Buffalo	NHL	38	1	3	4	52	3	0	0	—	—	—	—	—
—Rochester	AHL	21	1	6	7	41	...	...	...	19	3	5	8	30
96-97—Utah	IHL	3	0	0	0	7	...	...	...	—	—	—	—	—
—New York Islanders	NHL	70	2	8	10	99	1	0	0	—	—	—	—	—
97-98—New York Islanders	NHL	31	1	2	3	47	-6	0	0	—	—	—	—	—
—Anaheim	NHL	24	1	2	3	52	-5	0	1	—	—	—	—	—
NHL Totals (12 years)		556	19	62	81	1090	-46	1	1	18	0	3	3	21

HOUDE, ERIC   C   CANADIENS

PERSONAL: Born December 9, 1976, in Montreal. ... 5-11/191. ... Shoots left. ... Name pronounced UHD.
COLLEGE: Saint Mary's (Halifax, Nova Scotia).
TRANSACTIONS/CAREER NOTES: Selected by Montreal Canadiens in ninth round (ninth Canadiens pick, 216th overall) of NHL entry draft (July 8, 1995).
HONORS: Named to AHL All-Rookie team (1996-97).

Season Team	League	Gms.	G	REGULAR SEASON A	Pts.	PIM	+/-	PP	SH	Gms.	G	PLAYOFFS A	Pts.	PIM
93-94—St. Jean	QMJHL	71	16	16	32	14	...	...	...	5	1	1	2	4
94-95—St. Jean	QMJHL	40	10	13	23	23	...	...	...	—	—	—	—	—
—Halifax	QMJHL	28	13	23	36	8	...	...	...	3	2	1	3	4
95-96—Halifax	QMJHL	69	40	48	88	35	...	...	...	6	3	4	7	2
96-97—Fredericton	AHL	66	30	36	66	20	...	...	...	—	—	—	—	—
—Montreal	NHL	13	0	2	2	2	1	0	0	—	—	—	—	—
97-98—Fredericton	AHL	71	28	42	70	24	...	...	...	4	5	2	7	4
—Montreal	NHL	9	1	0	1	0	-3	0	0	—	—	—	—	—
NHL Totals (2 years)		22	1	2	3	2	-2	0	0					

H

HOUGH, MIKE   LW   ISLANDERS

PERSONAL: Born February 6, 1963, in Montreal. ... 6-1/197. ... Shoots left. ... Full name: Mike L. Hough. ... Name pronounced HUHF.
TRANSACTIONS/CAREER NOTES: Selected by Quebec Nordiques as underage junior in ninth round (seventh Nordiques pick, 181st overall) of NHL entry draft (June 9, 1982). ... Sprained left shoulder and developed tendinitis (November 5, 1989); missed 14 games. ... Broke right thumb (January 23, 1990); missed 12 games. ... Injured back (November 8, 1990); missed nine games. ... Separated left shoulder (January 15, 1991); missed three games. ... Suffered concussion (February 10, 1991). ... Injured knee (December 28, 1991); missed three games. ... Fractured left thumb (February 15, 1992); missed 14 games. ... Suffered concussion prior to 1992-93 season; missed first two games of season. ... Sprained right shoulder (April 6, 1993); missed four games. ... Traded by Nordiques to Washington Capitals for RW Paul MacDermid and RW Reggie Savage (June 20, 1993). ... Selected by Florida Panthers in NHL expansion draft (June 24, 1993). ... Hyperextended left knee (October 30, 1993); missed five games. ... Broke finger (January 22, 1996); missed five games. ... Bruised thigh (April 8, 1996); missed three games. ... Sprained knee (February 6, 1997); missed five games. ... Signed as free agent by New York Islanders (July 1, 1997). ... Suffered from the flu (January 2, 1998); missed one game.
MISCELLANEOUS: Captain of Quebec Nordiques (1991-92). ... Failed to score on a penalty shot (vs. Olaf Kolzig, February 29, 1996).

Season Team	League	REGULAR SEASON Gms.	G	A	Pts.	PIM	+/-	PP	SH	PLAYOFFS Gms.	G	A	Pts.	PIM
80-81—Dixie	OPJHL	24	15	20	35	84	...	...	...	—	—	—	—	—
81-82—Kitchener	OHL	58	14	34	48	172	...	...	...	14	1	5	6	16
82-83—Kitchener	OHL	61	17	27	44	156	...	...	...	12	5	4	9	30
83-84—Fredericton	AHL	69	11	16	27	142	...	...	...	1	0	0	0	7
84-85—Fredericton	AHL	76	21	27	48	49	...	...	...	6	1	1	2	2
85-86—Fredericton	AHL	74	21	33	54	68	...	...	...	6	0	3	3	8
86-87—Quebec	NHL	56	6	8	14	79	-8	1	1	9	0	3	3	26
—Fredericton	AHL	10	1	3	4	20	...	...	...	—	—	—	—	—
87-88—Fredericton	AHL	46	16	25	41	133	...	...	...	15	4	8	12	55
—Quebec	NHL	17	3	2	5	2	-8	0	0	—	—	—	—	—
88-89—Halifax	AHL	22	11	10	21	87	...	...	...	—	—	—	—	—
—Quebec	NHL	46	9	10	19	39	-7	1	3	—	—	—	—	—
89-90—Quebec	NHL	43	13	13	26	84	-24	3	1	—	—	—	—	—
90-91—Quebec	NHL	63	13	20	33	111	-7	1	1	—	—	—	—	—
91-92—Quebec	NHL	61	16	22	38	77	-1	6	2	—	—	—	—	—
92-93—Quebec	NHL	77	8	22	30	69	-11	2	1	6	0	1	1	2
93-94—Florida	NHL	78	6	23	29	62	3	0	1	—	—	—	—	—
94-95—Florida	NHL	48	6	7	13	38	1	0	0	—	—	—	—	—
95-96—Florida	NHL	64	7	16	23	37	4	0	1	22	4	1	5	8
96-97—Florida	NHL	69	8	6	14	48	12	0	0	5	1	0	1	2
97-98—New York Islanders	NHL	74	5	7	12	27	-4	0	0	—	—	—	—	—
NHL Totals (12 years)		696	100	156	256	673	-50	14	11	42	5	5	10	38

HOULDER, BILL   D   SHARKS

PERSONAL: Born March 11, 1967, in Thunder Bay, Ont. ... 6-2/210. ... Shoots left. ... Full name: William Houlder.
TRANSACTIONS/CAREER NOTES: Selected by Washington Capitals as underage junior in fourth round (fourth Capitals pick, 82nd overall) of NHL entry draft (June 15, 1985). ... Pulled groin (January 1989). ... Traded by Capitals to Buffalo Sabres for D Shawn Anderson (September 30, 1990). ... Selected by Mighty Ducks of Anaheim in NHL expansion draft (June 24, 1993). ... Traded by Mighty Ducks to St. Louis Blues for D Jason Marshall (August 29, 1994). ... Signed as free agent by Tampa Bay Lightning (August 1, 1995). ... Pulled groin (October 7, 1995); missed two games. ... Injured ribs (November 8, 1995); missed four games. ... Pulled groin (February 3, 1996); missed three games. ... Reinjured groin (March 5, 1996); missed six games ... Reinjured groin (March 26, 1996); missed five games. ... Bruised wrist (November 4, 1996); missed three games. ... Signed as free agent by San Jose Sharks (July 9, 1997).
HONORS: Named to AHL All-Star first team (1990-91). ... Won Governors Trophy (1992-93). ... Named to IHL All-Star first team (1992-93).

Season Team	League	REGULAR SEASON Gms.	G	A	Pts.	PIM	+/-	PP	SH	PLAYOFFS Gms.	G	A	Pts.	PIM
83-84—Thunder Bay Beavers	TBAHA	23	4	18	22	37	...	...	...	—	—	—	—	—
84-85—North Bay	OHL	66	4	20	24	37	...	...	...	8	0	0	0	2
85-86—North Bay	OHL	59	5	30	35	97	...	...	...	10	1	6	7	12
86-87—North Bay	OHL	62	17	51	68	68	...	...	...	22	4	19	23	20
87-88—Washington	NHL	30	1	2	3	10	-2	0	0	—	—	—	—	—
—Fort Wayne	IHL	43	10	14	24	32	...	...	...	—	—	—	—	—
88-89—Baltimore	AHL	65	10	36	46	50	...	...	...	—	—	—	—	—
—Washington	NHL	8	0	3	3	4	7	0	0	—	—	—	—	—
89-90—Baltimore	AHL	26	3	7	10	12	...	...	...	7	0	2	2	2
—Washington	NHL	41	1	11	12	28	8	0	0	—	—	—	—	—
90-91—Rochester	AHL	69	13	53	66	28	...	...	...	15	5	13	18	4
—Buffalo	NHL	7	0	2	2	4	-2	0	0	—	—	—	—	—
91-92—Rochester	AHL	42	8	26	34	16	...	...	...	16	5	6	11	4
—Buffalo	NHL	10	1	0	1	8	-2	0	0	—	—	—	—	—
92-93—San Diego	IHL	64	24	48	72	39	...	...	...	—	—	—	—	—
—Buffalo	NHL	15	3	5	8	6	5	0	0	8	0	2	2	4
93-94—Anaheim	NHL	80	14	25	39	40	-18	3	0	—	—	—	—	—
94-95—St. Louis	NHL	41	5	13	18	20	16	1	0	4	1	1	2	0
95-96—Tampa Bay	NHL	61	5	23	28	22	1	3	0	6	0	1	1	4
96-97—Tampa Bay	NHL	79	4	21	25	30	16	0	0	—	—	—	—	—
97-98—San Jose	NHL	82	7	25	32	48	13	4	0	6	1	2	3	2
NHL Totals (11 years)		454	41	130	171	220	42	11	0	24	2	6	8	10

H

HOULE, JEAN-FRANCOIS   LW   CANADIENS

PERSONAL: Born January 14, 1975, in La Salle, Que. ... 5-9/185. ... Shoots left. ... Son of Rejean Houle, left winger/right winger with Montreal Canadiens (1969-70 through 1972-73 and 1976-77 through 1982-83) and Quebec Nordiques of WHA (1973-74 through 1975-76). ... Name pronounced OOL.

HIGH SCHOOL: Northwood (Lake Placid, N.Y.).
COLLEGE: Clarkson (N.Y.).
TRANSACTIONS/CAREER NOTES: Selected by Montreal Canadiens in fourth round (fifth Canadiens pick, 99th overall) of NHL entry draft (June 26, 1993).

Season Team	League	REGULAR SEASON								PLAYOFFS				
		Gms.	G	A	Pts.	PIM	+/-	PP	SH	Gms.	G	A	Pts.	PIM
92-93—Northwood School......	N.Y. H.S.	28	37	45	82	...	...	...	...	—	—	—	—	—
93-94—Clarkson	ECAC	34	6	19	25	18	...	...	...	—	—	—	—	—
94-95—Clarkson	ECAC	34	8	11	19	42	...	...	...	—	—	—	—	—
95-96—Clarkson	ECAC	38	14	15	29	46	...	...	...	—	—	—	—	—
96-97—Clarkson	ECAC	37	21	37	58	40	...	...	...	—	—	—	—	—
97-98—New Orleans	ECHL	53	25	37	62	119	...	...	...	4	1	1	2	16
—Fredericton	AHL	7	1	0	1	8	...	...	...	—	—	—	—	—

HOUSLEY, PHIL   D   FLAMES

PERSONAL: Born March 9, 1964, in St. Paul, Minn. ... 6-0/195. ... Shoots left. ... Full name: Phil F. Housley.
HIGH SCHOOL: South St. Paul (Minn.).
TRANSACTIONS/CAREER NOTES: Selected by Buffalo Sabres as underage player in first round (first Sabres pick, sixth overall) of NHL entry draft (June 9, 1982). ... Bruised shoulder (January 1984). ... Suspended three games by NHL (October 1984). ... Injured back (November 1987). ... Bruised back (January 12, 1989). ... Suffered hip pointer and bruised back (March 18, 1989). ... Pulled shoulder ligaments while playing at World Cup Tournament (April 1989). ... Traded by Sabres with LW Scott Arniel, RW Jeff Parker and first-round pick (C Keith Tkachuk) in 1990 draft to Winnipeg Jets for C Dale Hawerchuk and first-round pick (LW Brad May) in 1990 draft (June 16, 1990). ... Strained abdomen (February 26, 1992); missed five games. ... Strained groin (October 31, 1992); missed two games. ... Sprained wrist (January 19, 1993); missed two games. ... Traded by Jets to St. Louis Blues for RW Nelson Emerson and D Stephane Quintal (September 24, 1993). ... Suffered back spasms (October 26, 1993); missed five games. ... Suffered sore back (November 18, 1993). ... Underwent back surgery (January 4, 1994); missed 53 games. ... Traded by Blues with second-round picks in 1996 (C Steve Begin) and 1997 (RW John Tripp) drafts to Calgary Flames for free-agent rights to D Al MacInnis and fourth-round pick (D Didier Tremblay) in 1997 draft (July 4, 1994). ... Played in Europe during 1994-95 NHL lockout. ... Crushed right pinky (February 9, 1995); missed five games. ... Suffered from the flu (January 10, 1996); missed two games. ... Suffered from the flu (January 17, 1996); missed one game. ... Traded by Flames with D Dan Keczmer to New Jersey Devils for D Tommy Albelin, D Cale Hulse and LW Jocelyn Lemieux (February 26, 1996). ... Signed as free agent by Washington Capitals (July 22, 1996). ... Strained groin (March 16, 1997); missed five games. ... Broke finger (March 7, 1998); missed 10 games. ... Claimed on waivers by Calgary Flames (July 21, 1998).
HONORS: Named to NHL All-Rookie team (1982-83). ... Played in NHL All-Star Game (1984 and 1989-1993). ... Named to THE SPORTING NEWS All-Star second team (1991-92). ... Named to NHL All-Star second team (1991-92).
MISCELLANEOUS: Failed to score on a penalty shot (vs. Curtis Joseph, December 19, 1992). ... Member of Team U.S.A. at World Junior Championships and World Cup Tournament (1982).
STATISTICAL PLATEAUS: Three-goal games: 1982-83 (1), 1987-88 (1). Total: 2.

Season Team	League	REGULAR SEASON								PLAYOFFS				
		Gms.	G	A	Pts.	PIM	+/-	PP	SH	Gms.	G	A	Pts.	PIM
80-81—St. Paul	USHL	6	7	7	14	6	...	...	...	—	—	—	—	—
81-82—South St. Paul H.S.	Minn. H.S.	22	31	34	65	18	...	...	...	—	—	—	—	—
82-83—Buffalo	NHL	77	19	47	66	39	-4	11	0	10	3	4	7	2
83-84—Buffalo	NHL	75	31	46	77	33	4	13	2	3	0	0	0	6
84-85—Buffalo	NHL	73	16	53	69	28	15	3	0	5	3	2	5	2
85-86—Buffalo	NHL	79	15	47	62	54	-9	7	0	—	—	—	—	—
86-87—Buffalo	NHL	78	21	46	67	57	-2	8	1	—	—	—	—	—
87-88—Buffalo	NHL	74	29	37	66	96	-17	6	0	6	2	4	6	6
88-89—Buffalo	NHL	72	26	44	70	47	6	5	0	5	1	3	4	2
89-90—Buffalo	NHL	80	21	60	81	32	11	8	1	6	1	4	5	4
90-91—Winnipeg	NHL	78	23	53	76	24	-13	12	1	—	—	—	—	—
91-92—Winnipeg	NHL	74	23	63	86	92	-5	11	0	7	1	4	5	0
92-93—Winnipeg	NHL	80	18	79	97	52	-14	6	0	6	0	7	7	2
93-94—St. Louis	NHL	26	7	15	22	12	-5	4	0	4	2	1	3	4
94-95—Grasshoppers	Switz. Div. II	10	6	8	14	34	...	...	...	—	—	—	—	—
—Calgary	NHL	43	8	35	43	18	17	3	0	7	0	9	9	0
95-96—Calgary	NHL	59	16	36	52	22	-2	6	0	—	—	—	—	—
—New Jersey	NHL	22	1	15	16	8	-4	0	0	—	—	—	—	—
96-97—Washington	NHL	77	11	29	40	24	-10	3	1	—	—	—	—	—
97-98—Washington	NHL	64	6	25	31	24	-10	4	1	18	0	4	4	4
NHL Totals (16 years).........		1131	291	730	1021	662	-42	110	7	77	13	42	55	32

HRDINA, JAN   RW   PENGUINS

PERSONAL: Born February 5, 1976, in Hradec Kralove, Czechoslovakia. ... 6-0/197. ... Shoots right. ... Name pronounced YAHN huhr-DEE-nuh.
TRANSACTIONS/CAREER NOTES: Selected by Pittsburgh Penguins in fifth round (fourth Penguins pick, 128th overall) of NHL entry draft (July 8, 1995).

Season Team	League	REGULAR SEASON								PLAYOFFS				
		Gms.	G	A	Pts.	PIM	+/-	PP	SH	Gms.	G	A	Pts.	PIM
93-94—Std. Hradec Kralove....	Czech Rep.	21	1	5	6	...	...	...	...	—	—	—	—	—
94-95—Seattle........................	WHL	69	41	59	100	79	...	...	...	4	0	1	1	8
95-96—Seattle........................	WHL	30	19	28	47	37	...	...	...	—	—	—	—	—
—Spokane....................	WHL	18	10	16	26	25	...	...	...	18	5	14	19	49
96-97—Cleveland	IHL	68	23	31	54	82	...	...	...	13	1	2	3	8
97-98—Syracuse	AHL	72	20	24	44	82	...	...	...	5	1	3	4	10

H

HRKAC, TONY   C   STARS

PERSONAL: Born July 7, 1966, in Thunder Bay, Ont. ... 5-11/185. ... Shoots left. ... Full name: Anthony J. Hrkac. ... Name pronounced HUHR-kuhz.
COLLEGE: North Dakota.
TRANSACTIONS/CAREER NOTES: Selected by St. Louis Blues as underage junior in second round (second Blues pick, 32nd overall) of NHL entry draft (June 9, 1984). ... Suspended six games by coach for disciplinary reasons (January 1985). ... Bruised left leg (January 1987). ... Sprained shoulder (January 12, 1988). ... Lacerated ankle (March 1988). ... Bruised left shoulder (November 28, 1989). ... Traded by Blues with G Greg Millen to Quebec Nordiques for D Jeff Brown (December 13, 1989). ... Traded by Nordiques to San Jose Sharks for RW Greg Paslawski (May 30, 1991). ... Injured wrist during preseason (September 1991); missed first 27 games of season. ... Traded by Sharks to Chicago Blackhawks for conditional pick in 1993 draft (February 7, 1992). ... Signed as free agent by Blues (July 30, 1993). ... Signed as free agent by Dallas Stars (July 25, 1997). ... Claimed on waivers by Edmonton Oilers (January 6, 1998). ... Traded by Oilers with D Bobby Dollas to Pittsburgh Penguins for LW Josef Beranek (June 16, 1998). ... Selected by Nashville Predators in NHL expansion draft (June 26, 1998). ... Traded by Predators to Dallas Stars for future considerations (July 9, 1998).
HONORS: Won Hobey Baker Memorial Award (1986-87). ... Won WCHA Most Valuable Player Award (1986-87). ... Named NCAA Tournament Most Valuable Player (1986-87). ... Named to NCAA All-America West first team (1986-87). ... Named to WCHA All-Star first team (1986-87). ... Named to NCAA All-Tournament team (1986-87). ... Won James Gatschene Memorial Trophy (1992-93). ... Won Leo P. Lamoureux Memorial Trophy (1992-93). ... Named to IHL All-Star first team (1992-93).

		REGULAR SEASON								PLAYOFFS				
Season Team	League	Gms.	G	A	Pts.	PIM	+/-	PP	SH	Gms.	G	A	Pts.	PIM
83-84—Orillia	OHA	42	*52	54	*106	20	...	...	...	—	—	—	—	—
84-85—U. of North Dakota	WCHA	36	18	36	54	16	...	...	...	—	—	—	—	—
85-86—Canadian nat'l team	Int'l	62	19	30	49	36	...	...	...	—	—	—	—	—
86-87—U. of North Dakota	WCHA	48	46	*70	*116	48	...	...	...	—	—	—	—	—
—St. Louis	NHL	—	—	—	—	—	—	—	—	3	0	0	0	0
87-88—St. Louis	NHL	67	11	37	48	22	5	2	1	10	6	1	7	4
88-89—St. Louis	NHL	70	17	28	45	8	-10	5	0	4	1	1	2	0
89-90—St. Louis	NHL	28	5	12	17	8	1	1	0	—	—	—	—	—
—Quebec	NHL	22	4	8	12	2	-5	2	0	—	—	—	—	—
—Halifax	AHL	20	12	21	33	4	...	...	...	6	5	9	14	4
90-91—Halifax	AHL	3	4	1	5	2	...	...	...	—	—	—	—	—
—Quebec	NHL	70	16	32	48	16	-22	6	0	—	—	—	—	—
91-92—San Jose	NHL	22	2	10	12	4	-2	0	0	—	—	—	—	—
—Chicago	NHL	18	1	2	3	6	4	0	0	3	0	0	0	2
92-93—Indianapolis	IHL	80	45	*87	*132	70	...	...	...	5	0	2	2	2
93-94—St. Louis	NHL	36	6	5	11	8	-11	1	1	4	0	0	0	0
—Peoria	IHL	45	30	51	81	25	...	...	...	1	1	2	3	0
94-95—Milwaukee	IHL	71	24	67	91	26	...	...	...	15	4	9	13	16
95-96—Milwaukee	IHL	43	14	28	42	18	...	...	...	5	1	3	4	4
96-97—Milwaukee	IHL	81	27	61	88	20	...	...	...	3	1	1	2	2
97-98—Michigan	IHL	20	7	15	22	6	...	...	...	—	—	—	—	—
—Dallas	NHL	13	5	3	8	0	0	3	0	—	—	—	—	—
—Edmonton	NHL	36	8	11	19	10	3	4	0	12	0	3	3	2
NHL Totals (8 years)		382	75	148	223	84	-31	24	2	36	7	5	12	8

HRUDEY, KELLY   G

PERSONAL: Born January 13, 1961, in Edmonton. ... 5-10/190. ... Catches left. ... Full name: Kelly Stephen Hrudey. ... Name pronounced ROO-dee.
TRANSACTIONS/CAREER NOTES: Selected by New York Islanders as underage junior in second round (second Islanders pick, 38th overall) of NHL entry draft (June 11, 1980). ... Traded by Islanders to Los Angeles Kings for D Wayne McBean, G Mark Fitzpatrick and future considerations (February 27, 1989). ... Kings sent D Doug Crossman to Islanders to complete deal (May 23, 1989). ... Suffered from the flu (April 1989). ... Suffered from mononucleosis (February 1990); missed 14 games. ... Bruised ribs (April 20, 1990). ... Suffered from the flu (March 11, 1993); missed one game. ... Suffered from the flu (March 26, 1993); missed one game. ... Bruised right kneecap (January 22, 1995); missed four games. ... Sprained ankle prior to 1995-96 season; missed first 20 games of season. ... Signed as free agent by San Jose Sharks (July 18, 1996). ... Announced retirement (July 30, 1998).
HONORS: Named to WHL All-Star second team (1980-81). ... Shared Terry Sawchuk Trophy with Robert Holland (1981-82 and 1982-83). ... Won Max McNab Trophy (1981-82). ... Named to CHL All-Star first team (1981-82 and 1982-83). ... Won Tommy Ivan Trophy (1982-83).
MISCELLANEOUS: Stopped penalty shot attempt (vs. Ron Sutter, November 18, 1984; vs. Mats Sundin, February 2, 1993; vs. Pavel Bure, October 6, 1993; vs. Tony Amonte, January 27, 1994; vs. Sergei Fedorov, February 12, 1995; vs. Dirk Graham, March 9, 1995). ... Allowed penalty shot goal (vs. Michel Goulet, January 26, 1984; vs. Bill Gardner, October 13, 1984; vs. Joe Mullen, December 2, 1986; vs. Mario Lemieux, January 19, 1988 and March 7, 1989; vs. Al MacInnis, April 4, 1990 (playoffs); vs. Norman Lacombe, February 5, 1991).

		REGULAR SEASON								PLAYOFFS						
Season Team	League	Gms.	Min	W	L	T	GA	SO	Avg.	Gms.	Min.	W	L	GA	SO	Avg.
78-79—Medicine Hat	WHL	57	3093	12	34	7	*318	0	6.17	—	—	—	—	—	—	—
79-80—Medicine Hat	WHL	57	3049	25	23	4	212	1	4.17	13	638	6	6	48	0	4.51
80-81—Medicine Hat	WHL	55	3023	32	19	1	200	†4	3.97	4	244	...	...	17	0	4.18
—Indianapolis	CHL	—	—	—	—	—	—	—	—	2	135	...	...	8	0	3.56
81-82—Indianapolis	CHL	51	3033	27	19	4	149	1	*2.95	13	842	11	2	34	*1	*2.42
82-83—Indianapolis	CHL	47	2744	26	17	1	139	2	3.04	10	†637	*7	3	28	0	*2.64
83-84—Indianapolis	CHL	6	370	3	2	1	21	0	3.41	—	—	—	—	—	—	—
—New York Islanders	NHL	12	535	7	2	0	28	0	3.14	—	—	—	—	—	—	—
84-85—New York Islanders	NHL	41	2335	19	17	3	141	2	3.62	5	281	1	3	8	0	1.71
85-86—New York Islanders	NHL	45	2563	19	15	8	137	1	3.21	2	120	0	2	6	0	3.00
86-87—New York Islanders	NHL	46	2634	21	15	7	145	0	3.30	14	842	7	7	38	0	2.71
87-88—New York Islanders	NHL	47	2751	22	17	5	153	3	3.34	6	381	2	4	23	0	3.62
88-89—New York Islanders	NHL	50	2800	18	24	3	183	0	3.92	—	—	—	—	—	—	—
—Los Angeles	NHL	16	974	10	4	2	47	1	2.90	10	566	4	6	35	0	3.71
89-90—Los Angeles	NHL	52	2860	22	21	6	194	2	4.07	9	539	4	4	39	0	4.34
90-91—Los Angeles	NHL	47	2730	26	13	6	132	3	2.90	12	798	6	6	37	0	2.78

Season Team	League	REGULAR SEASON								PLAYOFFS						
		Gms.	Min	W	L	T	GA	SO	Avg.	Gms.	Min.	W	L	GA	SO	Avg.
91-92—Los Angeles	NHL	60	3509	26	17	*13	197	1	3.37	6	355	2	4	22	0	3.72
92-93—Los Angeles	NHL	50	2718	18	21	6	175	2	3.86	20	1261	10	10	74	0	3.52
93-94—Los Angeles	NHL	64	3713	22	31	7	228	1	3.68	—	—	—	—	—	—	—
94-95—Los Angeles	NHL	35	1894	14	13	5	99	0	3.14	—	—	—	—	—	—	—
95-96—Los Angeles	NHL	36	2077	7	15	10	113	0	3.26	—	—	—	—	—	—	—
—Phoenix	IHL	1	50	0	1	‡0	5	0	6.00	—	—	—	—	—	—	—
96-97—San Jose	NHL	48	2631	16	24	5	140	0	3.19	—	—	—	—	—	—	—
97-98—San Jose	NHL	28	1360	4	16	2	62	1	2.74	1	20	0	0	1	0	3.00
NHL Totals (15 years)		677	38084	271	265	88	2174	17	3.43	85	5163	36	46	283	0	3.29

HUARD, BILL   LW   OILERS

PERSONAL: Born June 24, 1967, in Alland, Ont. ... 6-1/215. ... Shoots left. ... Name pronounced HYOO-uhrd.

TRANSACTIONS/CAREER NOTES: Signed as free agent by New Jersey Devils (October 1, 1989). ... Signed as free agent by Boston Bruins (December 4, 1992). ... Signed as free agent by Ottawa Senators (July 20, 1993). ... Injured hip (December 9, 1993); missed three games. ... Strained back (February 23, 1994); missed nine games. ... Strained groin (March 29, 1995); missed five games. ... Traded by Senators to Quebec Nordiques for rights to D Mika Stromberg and fourth-round pick (LW Kevin Boyd) in 1995 draft (April 7, 1995). ... Nordiques franchise moved to Colorado and renamed Avalanche for 1995-96 season (June 21, 1995). ... Claimed by Dallas Stars from Nordiques in NHL waiver draft (October 2, 1995). ... Separated shoulder (October 10, 1996); missed 11 games. ... Strained shoulder (November 20, 1996); missed three games. ... Signed as free agent by Edmonton Oilers (July 3, 1997). ... Sprained medial collateral knee ligament (October 13, 1997); missed nine games. ... Fractured left hand (November 22, 1997); missed 24 games. ... Fractured right wrist (February 2, 1998); missed seven games.

Season Team	League	REGULAR SEASON								PLAYOFFS				
		Gms.	G	A	Pts.	PIM	+/-	PP	SH	Gms.	G	A	Pts.	PIM
86-87—Peterborough	OHL	61	14	11	25	61	...	...	...	12	5	2	7	19
87-88—Peterborough	OHL	66	28	33	61	132	...	...	...	12	7	8	15	33
88-89—Carolina	ECHL	40	27	21	48	177	...	...	...	10	7	2	9	70
89-90—Utica	AHL	27	1	7	8	67	...	...	...	5	0	1	1	33
—Nashville	ECHL	34	24	27	51	212	...	...	...	—	—	—	—	—
90-91—Utica	AHL	72	11	16	27	359	...	...	...	—	—	—	—	—
91-92—Utica	AHL	62	9	11	20	233	...	...	...	4	1	1	2	4
92-93—Providence	AHL	72	18	19	37	302	...	...	...	6	3	0	3	9
—Boston	NHL	2	0	0	0	0	0	0	0	—	—	—	—	—
93-94—Ottawa	NHL	63	2	2	4	162	-19	0	0	—	—	—	—	—
94-95—Ottawa	NHL	26	1	1	2	64	-2	0	0	—	—	—	—	—
—Quebec	NHL	7	2	2	4	13	2	0	0	1	0	0	0	0
95-96—Dallas	NHL	51	6	6	12	176	3	0	0	—	—	—	—	—
—Michigan	IHL	12	1	1	2	74	...	...	...	—	—	—	—	—
96-97—Dallas	NHL	40	5	6	11	105	5	0	0	—	—	—	—	—
97-98—Edmonton	NHL	30	0	1	1	72	-5	0	0	4	0	0	0	2
NHL Totals (6 years)		219	16	18	34	592	-16	0	0	5	0	0	0	2

HULBIG, JOE   LW   OILERS

PERSONAL: Born September 29, 1973, in Wrentham, Mass. ... 6-3/215. ... Shoots left. ... Name pronounced HUHL-bihg.

HIGH SCHOOL: St. Sebastian's Country Day (Needham, Mass.).

COLLEGE: Providence.

TRANSACTIONS/CAREER NOTES: Selected by Edmonton Oilers in first round (first Oilers pick, 13th overall) of NHL entry draft (June 20, 1992).

Season Team	League	REGULAR SEASON								PLAYOFFS				
		Gms.	G	A	Pts.	PIM	+/-	PP	SH	Gms.	G	A	Pts.	PIM
89-90—St. Sebastian's	Mass. H.S.	30	13	12	25	...	...	...	...	—	—	—	—	—
90-91—St. Sebastian's	Mass. H.S.	...	23	19	42	...	...	...	...	—	—	—	—	—
91-92—St. Sebastian's	Mass. H.S.	17	19	24	43	30	...	...	...	—	—	—	—	—
92-93—Providence College	Hockey East	26	3	13	16	22	...	...	...	—	—	—	—	—
93-94—Providence College	Hockey East	28	6	4	10	36	...	...	...	—	—	—	—	—
94-95—Providence College	Hockey East	37	14	21	35	36	...	...	...	—	—	—	—	—
95-96—Providence College	Hockey East	31	14	22	36	56	...	...	...	—	—	—	—	—
96-97—Hamilton	AHL	73	18	28	46	59	...	...	...	16	6	10	16	6
—Edmonton	NHL	6	0	0	0	0	-1	0	0	6	0	1	1	2
97-98—Edmonton	NHL	17	2	2	4	2	-1	0	0	—	—	—	—	—
—Hamilton	AHL	46	15	16	31	52	...	...	...	3	0	1	1	2
NHL Totals (2 years)		23	2	2	4	2	-2	0	0	6	0	1	1	2

HULL, BRETT   RW   STARS

PERSONAL: Born August 9, 1964, in Belleville, Ont. ... 5-11/204. ... Shoots right. ... Full name: Brett A. Hull. ... Son of Bobby Hull, Hall of Fame left winger with three NHL teams (1957-58 through 1971-72 and 1979-80) and Winnipeg Jets of WHA (1972-73 through 1978-79); and nephew of Dennis Hull, left winger with Chicago Blackhawks and Detroit Red Wings (1964-65 through 1977-78).

COLLEGE: Minnesota-Duluth.

TRANSACTIONS/CAREER NOTES: Selected by Calgary Flames in sixth round (sixth Flames pick, 117th overall) of NHL entry draft (June 9, 1984). ... Traded by Flames with LW Steve Bozek to St. Louis Blues for D Rob Ramage and G Rick Wamsley (March 7, 1988). ... Sprained left ankle (January 15, 1991); missed two regular-season games and All-Star Game. ... Suffered back spasms (March 12, 1992); missed seven games. ... Suffered sore wrist (March 20, 1993); missed four games. ... Injured abdominal muscle (October 7, 1993); missed three games. ... Pulled groin (November 1, 1995); missed two games. ... Pulled groin (November 10, 1995); missed five games. ... Pulled hamstring (March 28, 1996); missed four games. ... Strained groin (March 30, 1997); missed four games. ... Strained buttocks (December 8, 1997); missed

H

two games. ... Fractured left hand (December 27, 1997); missed 13 games. ... Signed as free agent by Dallas Stars (July 3, 1998).

HONORS: Won WCHA Freshman of the Year Award (1984-85). ... Named to WCHA All-Star first team (1985-86). ... Won Dudley (Red) Garrett Memorial Trophy (1986-87). ... Named to AHL All-Star first team (1986-87). ... Won Lady Byng Memorial Trophy (1989-90). ... Won Dodge Ram Tough Award (1989-90 and 1990-91). ... Named to THE SPORTING NEWS All-Star first team (1989-90 through 1991-92). ... Named to NHL All-Star first team (1989-90 through 1991-92). ... Played in NHL All-Star Game (1989, 1990, 1992-1994, 1996 and 1997). ... Named NHL Player of the Year by THE SPORTING NEWS (1990-91). ... Won Hart Memorial Trophy (1990-91). ... Won Lester B. Pearson Award (1990-91). ... Won Pro Set NHL Player of the Year Award (1990-91). ... Named All-Star Game Most Valuable Player (1992).

RECORDS: Holds NHL single-season record for most goals by a right winger—86 (1990-91).

STATISTICAL PLATEAUS: Three-goal games: 1987-88 (1), 1989-90 (5), 1990-91 (4), 1991-92 (8), 1993-94 (3), 1994-95 (1), 1995-96 (1), 1996-97 (2), 1997-98 (1). Total: 26. ... Four-goal games: 1994-95 (1), 1995-96 (1). Total: 2. ... Total hat tricks: 28.

MISCELLANEOUS: Captain of St. Louis Blues (1992-93 through October 22, 1995). ... Holds St. Louis Blues all-time record for most goals (527). ... Failed to score on a penalty shot (vs. Glen Healy, December 31, 1992; vs. Bill Ranford, March 26, 1995; vs. Jeff Hackett, January 4, 1996). ... Shares distinction with Bobby Hull of being the first father-son duo to win the same NHL trophy (both the Lady Byng Memorial and Hart Memorial trophies).

STATISTICAL NOTES: Became the first son of an NHL 50-goal scorer to score 50 goals in one season (1989-90). ... Tied for NHL lead with 12 game-winning goals (1989-90). ... Led NHL in game-winning goals with 11 (1990-91).

					REGULAR SEASON							PLAYOFFS			
Season Team	League	Gms.	G	A	Pts.	PIM	+/-	PP	SH		Gms.	G	A	Pts.	PIM
82-83—Penticton	BCJHL	50	48	56	104	27	...	...	...		—	—	—	—	—
83-84—Penticton	BCJHL	56	*105	83	*188	20	...	...	...		—	—	—	—	—
84-85—Minnesota-Duluth	WCHA	48	32	28	60	24	...	...	...		—	—	—	—	—
85-86—Minnesota-Duluth	WCHA	42	*52	32	84	46	...	...	...		—	—	—	—	—
—Calgary	NHL	—	—	—	—	—	—	—	—		2	0	0	0	0
86-87—Moncton	AHL	67	50	42	92	16	...	...	...		3	2	2	4	2
—Calgary	NHL	5	1	0	1	0	-1	0	0		4	2	1	3	0
87-88—Calgary	NHL	52	26	24	50	12	10	4	0		—	—	—	—	—
—St. Louis	NHL	13	6	8	14	4	4	2	0		10	7	2	9	4
88-89—St. Louis	NHL	78	41	43	84	33	-17	16	0		10	5	5	10	6
89-90—St. Louis	NHL	80	*72	41	113	24	-1	*27	0		12	13	8	21	17
90-91—St. Louis	NHL	78	*86	45	131	22	23	*29	0		13	11	8	19	4
91-92—St. Louis	NHL	73	*70	39	109	48	-2	20	5		6	4	4	8	4
92-93—St. Louis	NHL	80	54	47	101	41	-27	29	0		11	8	5	13	2
93-94—St. Louis	NHL	81	57	40	97	38	-3	†25	3		4	2	1	3	0
94-95—St. Louis	NHL	48	29	21	50	10	13	9	3		7	6	2	8	0
95-96—St. Louis	NHL	70	43	40	83	30	4	16	5		13	6	5	11	10
96-97—St. Louis	NHL	77	42	40	82	10	-9	12	2		6	2	7	9	2
97-98—St. Louis	NHL	66	27	45	72	26	-1	10	0		10	3	3	6	2
—U.S. Olympic Team	Int'l	4	2	1	3	0	...				—	—	—	—	—
NHL Totals (13 years)		801	554	433	987	298	-7	199	18		108	69	51	120	51

HULL, JODY   RW

PERSONAL: Born February 2, 1969, in Petrolia, Ont. ... 6-2/200. ... Shoots right.

HIGH SCHOOL: Thomas A. Stewart (Peterborough, Ont.).

TRANSACTIONS/CAREER NOTES: Strained ankle ligaments (September 1986). ... Pulled groin (February 1987). ... Selected by Hartford Whalers as underage junior in first round (first Whalers pick, 18th overall) of NHL entry draft (June 13, 1987). ... Pulled hamstring (March 1989). ... Traded by Whalers to New York Rangers for C Carey Wilson and third-round pick (C Mikael Nylander) in 1991 draft (July 9, 1990). ... Sprained muscle in right hand (October 6, 1990). ... Bruised left big toe (November 19, 1990); missed six games. ... Injured knee (March 13, 1991). ... Traded by Rangers to Ottawa Senators for future considerations (July 28, 1992). ... Injured groin (December 7, 1992); missed three games. ... Suffered concussion (January 10, 1993); missed one game. ... Sprained ankle (January 19, 1993); missed eight games. ... Sprained left ankle (April 1, 1993); missed two games. ... Signed as free agent by Florida Panthers (August 10, 1993). ... Bruised right shoulder (February 1, 1994); missed one game. ... Separated right shoulder (March 4, 1994); missed three games. ... Separated right shoulder (March 18, 1994); missed six games. ... Suffered viral illness (February 1, 1995); missed two games. ... Broke rib (October 28, 1995); missed four games. ... Suffered back spasms (May 5, 1996); missed four playoff games. ... Broke wrist (December 20, 1997); missed 13 games. ... Traded by Panthers with G Mark Fitzpatrick to Tampa Bay Lightning for RW Dino Ciccarelli and D Jeff Norton (January 15, 1998). ... Injured ankle (February 2, 1998); missed two games. ... Injured knee (April 2, 1998); missed three games.

HONORS: Named to OHL All-Star second team (1987-88).

STATISTICAL PLATEAUS: Three-goal games: 1988-89 (1).

					REGULAR SEASON							PLAYOFFS			
Season Team	League	Gms.	G	A	Pts.	PIM	+/-	PP	SH		Gms.	G	A	Pts.	PIM
84-85—Cambridge Jr. B	OHA	38	13	17	30	39	...	...	...		—	—	—	—	—
85-86—Peterborough	OHL	61	20	22	42	29	...	...	...		16	1	5	6	4
86-87—Peterborough	OHL	49	18	34	52	22	...	...	...		12	4	9	13	14
87-88—Peterborough	OHL	60	50	44	94	33	...	...	...		12	10	8	18	8
88-89—Hartford	NHL	60	16	18	34	10	6	6	0		1	0	0	0	2
89-90—Binghamton	AHL	21	7	10	17	6	...	...	...		—	—	—	—	—
—Hartford	NHL	38	7	10	17	21	-6	2	0		5	0	1	1	2
90-91—New York Rangers	NHL	47	5	8	13	10	2	0	0		—	—	—	—	—
91-92—New York Rangers	NHL	3	0	0	0	2	-4	0	0		—	—	—	—	—
—Binghamton	AHL	69	34	31	65	28	...	...	...		11	5	2	7	4
92-93—Ottawa	NHL	69	13	21	34	14	-24	5	1		—	—	—	—	—
93-94—Florida	NHL	69	13	13	26	8	6	0	1		—	—	—	—	—
94-95—Florida	NHL	46	11	8	19	8	-1	0	0		—	—	—	—	—
95-96—Florida	NHL	78	20	17	37	25	5	2	0		14	3	2	5	0
96-97—Florida	NHL	67	10	6	16	4	1	0	1		5	0	0	0	0
97-98—Florida	NHL	21	2	0	2	4	1	0	1		—	—	—	—	—
—Tampa Bay	NHL	28	2	4	6	4	2	0	0		—	—	—	—	—
NHL Totals (10 years)		526	99	105	204	110	-12	15	4		25	3	3	6	4

H

HULSE, CALE   D   FLAMES

PERSONAL: Born November 10, 1973, in Edmonton. ... 6-3/215. ... Shoots right. ... Name pronounced HUHLZ.
COLLEGE: Portland.
TRANSACTIONS/CAREER NOTES: Selected by New Jersey Devils in third round (third Devils pick, 66th overall) of NHL entry draft (June 20, 1992). ... Traded by Devils with D Tommy Albelin and RW Jocelyn Lemieux to Calgary Flames for D Phil Housley and D Dan Keczmer (February 26, 1996). ... Bruised ankle (February 28, 1997); missed four games. ... Reinjured ankle (March 7, 1997); missed one game. ... Reinjured ankle (March 21, 1997); missed one game.

		REGULAR SEASON								PLAYOFFS				
Season Team	League	Gms.	G	A	Pts.	PIM	+/-	PP	SH	Gms.	G	A	Pts.	PIM
90-91—Calgary Royals	AJHL	49	3	23	26	220	...	...	...	—	—	—	—	—
91-92—Portland	WHL	70	4	18	22	250	...	...	...	6	0	2	2	27
92-93—Portland	WHL	72	10	26	36	284	...	...	...	16	4	4	8	*65
93-94—Albany	AHL	79	7	14	21	186	...	...	...	5	0	3	3	11
94-95—Albany	AHL	77	5	13	18	215	...	...	...	12	1	1	2	17
95-96—Albany	AHL	42	4	23	27	107	...	...	...	—	—	—	—	—
—New Jersey	NHL	8	0	0	0	15	-2	0	0	—	—	—	—	—
—Saint John	AHL	13	2	7	9	39	...	...	...	—	—	—	—	—
—Calgary	NHL	3	0	0	0	5	3	0	0	1	0	0	0	0
96-97—Calgary	NHL	63	1	6	7	91	-2	0	1	—	—	—	—	—
97-98—Calgary	NHL	79	5	22	27	169	1	1	1	—	—	—	—	—
NHL Totals (3 years)		153	6	28	34	280	0	1	2	1	0	0	0	0

HUNTER, DALE   C   CAPITALS

PERSONAL: Born July 31, 1960, in Petrolia, Ont. ... 5-10/200. ... Shoots left. ... Full name: Dale Robert Hunter. ... Brother of Mark Hunter, right winger for four NHL teams (1981-82 through 1992-93); and brother of Dave Hunter, left winger with Edmonton Oilers of WHA (1978-79) and Edmonton Oilers, Pittsburgh Penguins and Winnipeg Jets (1979-80 through 1988-89).
TRANSACTIONS/CAREER NOTES: Selected by Quebec Nordiques as underage junior in second round (second Nordiques pick, 41st overall) of NHL entry draft (August 9, 1979). ... Suspended three games by NHL (March 1984). ... Suffered hand infection (April 21, 1985). ... Broke lower fibula of left leg (November 25, 1986). ... Traded by Nordiques with G Clint Malarchuk to Washington Capitals for C Alan Haworth, LW Gaetan Duchesne and first-round pick (C Joe Sakic) in 1987 draft (June 13, 1987). ... Broke thumb (September 1988). ... Suspended four games by NHL for elbowing D Gord Murphy (February 10, 1991). ... Suspended first 21 games of 1993-94 season by NHL for blindside check on player (May 4, 1993). ... Injured knee ligament (November 26, 1993); missed 10 games. ... Bruised left knee (February 13, 1995); missed three games.
HONORS: Played in NHL All-Star Game (1997).
RECORDS: Holds NHL career playoff record for most penalty minutes—691.
STATISTICAL PLATEAUS: Three-goal games: 1981-82 (2), 1983-84 (1), 1991-92 (1). Total: 4.
MISCELLANEOUS: Captain of Washington Capitals (1994-95 through 1997-98). ... Holds Colorado Avalanche franchise all-time record for most penalty minutes (1,545). ... Holds Washington Capitals all-time record for most penalty minutes (1,901). ... Scored on a penalty shot (vs. Rejean Lemelin, December 6, 1983). ... Failed to score on a penalty shot (vs. Wendell Young, December 6, 1989).

		REGULAR SEASON								PLAYOFFS				
Season Team	League	Gms.	G	A	Pts.	PIM	+/-	PP	SH	Gms.	G	A	Pts.	PIM
77-78—Kitchener	OMJHL	68	22	42	64	115	...	...	...	—	—	—	—	—
78-79—Sudbury	OMJHL	59	42	68	110	188	...	...	...	10	4	12	16	47
79-80—Sudbury	OMJHL	61	34	51	85	189	...	...	...	9	6	9	15	45
80-81—Quebec	NHL	80	19	44	63	226	5	2	0	5	4	2	6	34
81-82—Quebec	NHL	80	22	50	72	272	26	0	2	16	3	7	10	52
82-83—Quebec	NHL	80	17	46	63	206	10	1	2	4	2	1	3	24
83-84—Quebec	NHL	77	24	55	79	232	35	7	2	9	2	3	5	41
84-85—Quebec	NHL	80	20	52	72	209	23	3	3	17	4	6	10	*97
85-86—Quebec	NHL	80	28	42	70	265	37	0	0	3	0	0	0	15
86-87—Quebec	NHL	46	10	29	39	135	4	0	0	13	1	7	8	56
87-88—Washington	NHL	79	22	37	59	240	7	11	0	14	7	5	12	98
88-89—Washington	NHL	80	20	37	57	219	-3	9	0	6	0	4	4	29
89-90—Washington	NHL	80	23	39	62	233	17	9	1	15	4	8	12	61
90-91—Washington	NHL	76	16	30	46	234	-22	9	0	11	1	9	10	41
91-92—Washington	NHL	80	28	50	78	205	-2	13	0	7	1	4	5	16
92-93—Washington	NHL	84	20	59	79	198	3	10	0	6	7	1	8	35
93-94—Washington	NHL	52	9	29	38	131	-4	1	0	7	0	3	3	14
94-95—Washington	NHL	45	8	15	23	101	-4	3	0	7	4	4	8	24
95-96—Washington	NHL	82	13	24	37	112	5	4	0	6	1	5	6	24
96-97—Washington	NHL	82	14	32	46	125	-2	3	0	—	—	—	—	—
97-98—Washington	NHL	82	8	18	26	103	1	0	0	21	0	4	4	30
NHL Totals (18 years)		1345	321	688	1009	3446	136	85	10	167	41	73	114	691

HURLBUT, MIKE   D   SABRES

PERSONAL: Born July 10, 1966, in Massena, N.Y. ... 6-2/200. ... Shoots left. ... Full name: Michael Ray Hurlbut.
HIGH SCHOOL: Northwood (Lake Placid, N.Y.).
COLLEGE: St. Lawrence (N.Y.).
TRANSACTIONS/CAREER NOTES: Selected by New York Rangers in NHL supplemental draft (June 10, 1988). ... Sprained left knee (January 25, 1993); missed 13 games. ... Traded by Rangers to Quebec Nordiques for D Alexander Karpovtsev (September 9, 1993). ... Nordiques franchise moved to Colorado and renamed Avalanche for 1995-96 season (June 21, 1995). ... Signed as free agent by Buffalo Sabres (August 11, 1997).
HONORS: Named to NCAA All-America East first team (1988-89). ... Named to ECAC All-Star first team (1988-89). ... Named to AHL All-Star second team (1994-95).

H

Season Team	League	REGULAR SEASON								PLAYOFFS				
		Gms.	G	A	Pts.	PIM	+/-	PP	SH	Gms.	G	A	Pts.	PIM
84-85—Northwood School	N.Y. H.S.	34	20	27	47	30	...	...	...	—	—	—	—	—
85-86—St. Lawrence Univ.	ECAC	25	2	10	12	40	...	...	...	—	—	—	—	—
86-87—St. Lawrence Univ.	ECAC	35	8	15	23	44	...	...	...	—	—	—	—	—
87-88—St. Lawrence Univ.	ECAC	38	6	12	18	18	...	...	...	—	—	—	—	—
88-89—St. Lawrence Univ.	ECAC	36	8	25	33	30	...	...	...	—	—	—	—	—
—Flint	IHL	8	0	2	2	13	...	...	...	4	1	2	3	2
89-90—Flint	IHL	74	3	34	37	38	...	...	...	3	0	1	1	2
90-91—Binghamton	AHL	33	2	11	13	27	...	...	...	3	0	1	1	0
—San Diego	IHL	2	1	0	1	0	...	...	...	—	—	—	—	—
91-92—Binghamton	AHL	79	16	39	55	64	...	...	...	11	2	7	9	8
92-93—Binghamton	AHL	46	11	25	36	46	...	...	...	14	2	5	7	12
—New York Rangers	NHL	23	1	8	9	16	4	1	0	—	—	—	—	—
93-94—Cornwall	AHL	77	13	33	46	100	...	...	...	13	3	7	10	12
—Quebec	NHL	1	0	0	0	0	-1	0	0	—	—	—	—	—
94-95—Cornwall	AHL	74	11	49	60	69	...	...	...	3	1	0	1	15
95-96—Houston	IHL	38	3	12	15	33	...	...	...	—	—	—	—	—
—Minnesota	IHL	22	1	4	5	22	...	...	...	—	—	—	—	—
96-97—Houston	IHL	70	11	24	35	62	...	...	...	13	5	8	13	12
97-98—Buffalo	NHL	3	0	0	0	2	-1	0	0	—	—	—	—	—
—Rochester	AHL	45	10	20	30	48	...	...	...	4	1	1	2	2
NHL Totals (3 years)		27	1	8	9	18	2	1	0					

HURME, JANI G SENATORS

PERSONAL: Born January 18, 1975, in Turku, Finland. ... 6-0/187. ... Catches left. ... Name pronounced hoor-MAY.

TRANSACTIONS/CAREER NOTES: Selected by Ottawa Senators in third round (second Senators pick, 58th overall) of NHL entry draft (June 21, 1997).

Season Team	League	REGULAR SEASON								PLAYOFFS						
		Gms.	Min	W	L	T	GA	SO	Avg.	Gms.	Min.	W	L	GA	SO	Avg.
92-93—TPS Jr.	Finland	12	669	...	...	...	47	0	4.22	1	60	...	...	...	11	...
93-94—TPS Turku	Finland	1	2	...	...	...	0	0	...	—	—	—	—	—	—	—
—Kiekko-67 Turku	Fin. Div.II	3	190	...	...	...	7	0	2.21	—	—	—	—	—	—	—
—Kiekko-67 Turku Jrs.	Finland	18	...	...	...	...	...	...	...	—	—	—	—	—	—	—
94-95—Kiekko-67 Turku	Fin. Div.II	19	1049	...	...	...	53	...	3.03	3	180	...	...	6	...	2.00
—TPS Jr.	Finland	2	125	...	...	...	5	0	2.40	—	—	—	—	—	—	—
—Kiekko-67 Turku Jrs.	Finland	9	540	...	...	...	47	...	5.22	—	—	—	—	—	—	—
95-96—TPS Turku	Finland	16	945	...	...	...	34	2	2.16	10	545	...	...	22	2	2.42
—Kiekko-67 Turku	Fin. Div.II	16	968	...	...	...	39	1	2.42	—	—	—	—	—	—	—
—TPS Jr.	Finland	13	777	...	...	...	34	1	2.63	—	—	—	—	—	—	—
96-97—TPS Turku	Finland	48	2917	...	...	...	101	6	2.08	12	722	...	...	39	0	3.24
97-98—Detroit	IHL	6	291	2	2	‡2	20	0	4.12	—	—	—	—	—	—	—
—Indianapolis	IHL	29	1507	11	11	‡3	83	1	3.30	3	130	1	0	10	0	4.62

HUSCROFT, JAMIE D CANUCKS

PERSONAL: Born January 9, 1967, in Creston, B.C. ... 6-2/200. ... Shoots right. ... Full name: James Huscroft. ... Name pronounced HUZ-krawft.

TRANSACTIONS/CAREER NOTES: Selected by New Jersey Devils as underage junior in ninth round (ninth Devils pick, 171st overall) of NHL entry draft (June 15, 1985). ... Fractured arm (October 1986); missed eight weeks. ... Traded by Seattle Thunderbirds to Medicine Hat Tigers for C Mike Schwengler (February 1987). ... Fractured right wrist (October 1988). ... Injured groin (December 1988). ... Broke foot (January 1989); missed 19 games. ... Signed as free agent by Boston Bruins (July 16, 1992). ... Signed as free agent by Calgary Flames (July 27, 1995). ... Strained back prior to 1995-96 season; missed one game. ... Bruised foot (October 27, 1995); missed one game. ... Suffered from the flu (December 11, 1995); missed three games. ... Injured groin (April 1, 1996); missed three games. ... Cut forearm (March 4, 1997); missed three games. ... Traded by Flames to Tampa Bay Lightning for G Tyler Moss (March 18, 1997). ... Traded by Lightning to Vancouver Canucks for D Enrico Ciccone (March 14, 1998).

Season Team	League	REGULAR SEASON								PLAYOFFS				
		Gms.	G	A	Pts.	PIM	+/-	PP	SH	Gms.	G	A	Pts.	PIM
83-84—Portland	WHL	63	0	12	12	77	...	...	...	5	0	0	0	15
84-85—Seattle	WHL	69	3	13	16	273	...	...	...	—	—	—	—	—
85-86—Seattle	WHL	66	6	20	26	394	...	...	...	5	0	1	1	18
86-87—Seattle	WHL	21	1	18	19	99	...	...	...	20	0	3	3	0
—Medicine Hat	WHL	35	4	21	25	170	...	...	...	20	0	3	3	*125
87-88—Flint	IHL	3	1	0	1	2	...	...	...	16	0	1	1	110
—Utica	AHL	71	5	7	12	316	...	...	...	—	—	—	—	—
88-89—Utica	AHL	41	2	10	12	215	...	...	...	5	0	0	0	40
—New Jersey	NHL	15	0	2	2	51	-3	0	0	—	—	—	—	—
89-90—New Jersey	NHL	42	2	3	5	149	-2	0	0	5	0	0	0	16
—Utica	AHL	22	3	6	9	122	...	...	...	—	—	—	—	—
90-91—New Jersey	NHL	8	0	1	1	27	1	0	0	3	0	0	0	6
—Utica	AHL	59	5	15	18	339	...	...	...	—	—	—	—	—
91-92—Utica	AHL	50	4	7	11	224	...	...	...	—	—	—	—	—
92-93—Providence	AHL	69	2	15	17	257	...	...	...	2	0	1	1	6
93-94—Providence	AHL	32	1	10	11	157	...	...	...	—	—	—	—	—
—Boston	NHL	36	0	1	1	144	-2	0	0	4	0	0	0	9
94-95—Boston	NHL	34	0	6	6	103	-3	0	0	5	0	0	0	11
95-96—Calgary	NHL	70	3	9	12	162	14	0	0	4	0	1	1	4
96-97—Calgary	NHL	39	0	4	4	117	2	0	0	—	—	—	—	—
—Tampa Bay	NHL	13	0	1	1	34	-4	0	0	—	—	—	—	—
97-98—Tampa Bay	NHL	44	0	3	3	122	-4	0	0	—	—	—	—	—
—Vancouver	NHL	7	0	1	1	55	2	0	0	—	—	—	—	—
NHL Totals (8 years)		308	5	31	36	964	1	0	0	21	0	1	1	46

H

HUSKA, RYAN — LW — BLACKHAWKS

H
I

PERSONAL: Born July 2, 1975, in Cranbrook, B.C. ... 6-2/194. ... Shoots left. ... Name pronounced HUH-skuh.
HIGH SCHOOL: Norkam Secondary (Kamloops, B.C.).
TRANSACTIONS/CAREER NOTES: Selected by Chicago Blackhawks in third round (fourth Blackhawks pick, 76th overall) of NHL entry draft (June 26, 1993).

Season Team	League	Gms.	G	A	Pts.	PIM	+/-	PP	SH	Gms.	G	A	Pts.	PIM
				REGULAR SEASON								PLAYOFFS		
91-92—Kamloops	WHL	44	4	5	9	23	...	...	...	6	0	1	1	0
92-93—Kamloops	WHL	68	17	15	32	50	...	...	...	13	2	6	8	4
93-94—Kamloops	WHL	69	23	31	54	66	...	...	...	19	9	5	14	23
94-95—Kamloops	WHL	66	27	40	67	78	...	...	...	17	7	8	15	12
95-96—Indianapolis	IHL	28	2	3	5	15	...	...	...	5	1	1	2	27
96-97—Indianapolis	IHL	80	18	12	30	100	...	...	...	4	0	0	0	4
97-98—Indianapolis	IHL	80	19	16	35	115	...	...	...	5	0	3	3	10
—Chicago	NHL	1	0	0	0	0	0	0	0	—	—	—	—	—
NHL Totals (1 year)		1	0	0	0	0	0	0	0					

IAFRATE, AL — D — HURRICANES

PERSONAL: Born March 21, 1966, in Dearborn, Mich. ... 6-3/235. ... Shoots left. ... Full name: Al Anthony Iafrate. ... Name pronounced igh-uh-FRAY-tee. ... Nickname: Alley Cat.
TRANSACTIONS/CAREER NOTES: Selected by Toronto Maple Leafs as underage junior in first round (first Maple Leafs pick, fourth overall) of NHL entry draft (June 9, 1984). ... Bruised knee (February 1985). ... Broke nose (October 2, 1985); missed five games. ... Strained neck (January 29, 1986); missed six games. ... Suffered stiff back (January 1988). ... Broke back (October 22, 1988). ... Cut hand (December 9, 1988). ... Tore right knee ligament (March 24, 1990). ... Underwent knee surgery (April 9, 1990). ... Traded by Maple Leafs to Washington Capitals for D Bob Rouse and C Peter Zezel (January 16, 1991). ... Took a leave of absence due to mental exhaustion (March 30, 1991). ... Injured eye (February 19, 1992); missed one game. ... Pulled hamstring (April 10, 1993); missed three games. ... Sprained right knee (December 21, 1993); missed four games. ... Sore knee (January 2, 1994); missed one game. ... Traded by Capitals to Boston Bruins for LW Joe Juneau (March 21, 1994). ... Underwent offseason knee surgery; missed entire 1994-95 season. ... Missed entire 1995-96 season with knee injury. ... Traded by Bruins to San Jose Sharks for RW Jeff Odgers and fifth-round pick (D Elias Abrahamsson) in 1996 draft (June 21, 1996). ... Broke toe (November 12, 1996); missed eight games. ... Reinjured toe (December 7, 1996); missed four games. ... Sore back (January 24, 1997); missed two games. ... Underwent back surgery (March 5, 1997); missed remainder of season. ... Injured back (October 1, 1997); missed 29 games. ... Underwent knee surgery (December 28, 1997); missed 33 games. ... Selected by Nashville Predators in NHL expansion draft (June 26, 1998). ... Signed as free agent by Carolina Hurricanes (July 14, 1998).
HONORS: Played in NHL All-Star Game (1988, 1990, 1993 and 1994). ... Named to THE SPORTING NEWS All-Star second team (1992-93). ... Named to NHL All-Star second team (1992-93).
RECORDS: Shares NHL single-game playoff record for most goals by defenseman—3 (April 26, 1993).

Season Team	League	Gms.	G	A	Pts.	PIM	+/-	PP	SH	Gms.	G	A	Pts.	PIM
				REGULAR SEASON								PLAYOFFS		
83-84—U.S. national team	Int'l	55	4	17	21	26	...	...	...	—	—	—	—	—
—U.S. Olympic Team	Int'l	6	0	0	0	2	...	...	...	—	—	—	—	—
—Belleville	OHL	10	2	4	6	2	...	...	...	3	0	1	1	2
84-85—Toronto	NHL	68	5	16	21	51	-19	3	0	—	—	—	—	—
85-86—Toronto	NHL	65	8	25	33	40	-10	2	0	10	0	3	3	4
86-87—Toronto	NHL	80	9	21	30	55	-18	0	0	13	1	3	4	11
87-88—Toronto	NHL	77	22	30	52	80	-21	4	3	6	3	4	7	6
88-89—Toronto	NHL	65	13	20	33	72	3	1	2	—	—	—	—	—
89-90—Toronto	NHL	75	21	42	63	135	-4	6	1	—	—	—	—	—
90-91—Toronto	NHL	42	3	15	18	113	-15	2	0	—	—	—	—	—
—Washington	NHL	30	6	8	14	124	-1	0	1	10	1	3	4	22
91-92—Washington	NHL	78	17	34	51	180	1	6	0	7	4	2	6	14
92-93—Washington	NHL	81	25	41	66	169	15	11	1	6	6	0	6	4
93-94—Washington	NHL	67	10	35	45	143	10	4	0	—	—	—	—	—
—Boston	NHL	12	5	8	13	20	6	2	0	13	3	1	4	6
94-95—Boston	NHL				Did not play.					—	—	—	—	—
95-96—Boston	NHL				Did not play.					—	—	—	—	—
96-97—San Jose	NHL	38	6	9	15	91	-10	3	0	—	—	—	—	—
97-98—San Jose	NHL	21	2	7	9	28	-1	2	0	6	1	0	1	10
NHL Totals (14 years)		799	152	311	463	1301	-64	46	8	71	19	16	35	77

IGINLA, JAROME — C/RW — FLAMES

PERSONAL: Born July 1, 1977, in Edmonton. ... 6-1/202. ... Shoots right. ... Name pronounced ih-GIHN-luh.
TRANSACTIONS/CAREER NOTES: Selected by Dallas Stars in first round (first Stars pick, 11th overall) of NHL entry draft (July 8, 1995). ... Traded by Stars with C Corey Millen to Calgary Flames for C Joe Nieuwendyk (December 19, 1995). ... Fractured hand (January 21, 1998); missed 10 games.
HONORS: Won George Parsons Trophy (1994-95). ... Won Four Broncos Memorial Trophy (1995-96). ... Named to Can.HL All-Star first team (1995-96). ... Named to WHL (West) All-Star first team (1995-96). ... Named to NHL All-Rookie team (1996-97).

Season Team	League	Gms.	G	A	Pts.	PIM	+/-	PP	SH	Gms.	G	A	Pts.	PIM
				REGULAR SEASON								PLAYOFFS		
93-94—Kamloops	WHL	48	6	23	29	33	...	...	...	19	3	6	9	10
94-95—Kamloops	WHL	72	33	38	71	111	...	...	...	21	7	11	18	34
95-96—Kamloops	WHL	63	63	73	136	120	...	...	...	16	16	13	29	44
—Calgary	NHL	—	—	—	—	—	...	...	...	2	1	1	2	0
96-97—Calgary	NHL	82	21	29	50	37	-4	8	1	—	—	—	—	—
97-98—Calgary	NHL	70	13	19	32	29	-10	0	2	—	—	—	—	—
NHL Totals (3 years)		152	34	48	82	66	-14	8	3	2	1	1	2	0

IRBE, ARTURS   G

PERSONAL: Born February 2, 1967, in Riga, U.S.S.R. ... 5-8/175. ... Catches left. ... Name pronounced AHR-tuhrs UHR-bay.
TRANSACTIONS/CAREER NOTES: Selected by Minnesota North Stars in 10th round (11th North Stars pick, 196th overall) of NHL entry draft (June 17, 1989). ... Selected by San Jose Sharks in NHL dispersal draft (May 30, 1991). ... Sprained knee (November 27, 1992); missed 19 games. ... Injured foot (February 15, 1995); missed one game. ... Injured knee (January 17, 1996); remainder of season. ... Signed as free agent by Dallas Stars (July 22, 1996). ... Strained groin (November 8, 1996); missed six games. ... Signed as free agent by Vancouver Canucks (August 5, 1997).
HONORS: Named Soviet League Rookie of the Year (1987-88). ... Shared James Norris Memorial Trophy with Wade Flaherty (1991-92). ... Named to IHL All-Star first team (1991-92). ... Played in NHL All-Star Game (1994).
MISCELLANEOUS: Holds San Jose Sharks all-time records for most games played by goalie (183), most wins (57), most shutouts (8) and goals-against average (3.47). ... Allowed a penalty shot goal (vs. Mats Sundin, March 15, 1995; vs. Igor Larionov, November 22, 1995; vs. Hnat Domenichelli, February 27, 1998).

			REGULAR SEASON								PLAYOFFS						
Season Team	League	Gms.	Min	W	L	T	GA	SO	Avg.	Gms.	Min.	W	L	GA	SO	Avg.
86-87—Dynamo Riga	USSR	2	27	...	...	...	1	0	2.22	—	—	—	—	—	—	—
87-88—Dynamo Riga	USSR	34	1870	...	...	...	84	0	2.70	—	—	—	—	—	—	—
88-89—Dynamo Riga	USSR	41	2460	...	...	...	117	0	2.85	—	—	—	—	—	—	—
89-90—Dynamo Riga	USSR	48	2880	...	...	...	116	0	2.42	—	—	—	—	—	—	—
90-91—Dynamo Riga	USSR	46	2713	...	...	...	133	0	2.94	—	—	—	—	—	—	—
91-92—Kansas City	IHL	32	1955	24	7	‡1	80	0	*2.46	15	914	12	3	44	0	2.89
—San Jose	NHL	13	645	2	6	3	48	0	4.47	—	—	—	—	—	—	—
92-93—Kansas City	IHL	6	364	3	3	‡0	20	0	3.30	—	—	—	—	—	—	—
—San Jose	NHL	36	2074	7	26	0	142	1	4.11	—	—	—	—	—	—	—
93-94—San Jose	NHL	*74	*4412	30	28	*16	209	3	2.84	14	806	7	7	50	0	3.72
94-95—San Jose	NHL	38	2043	14	19	3	111	4	3.26	6	316	2	4	27	0	5.13
95-96—San Jose	NHL	22	1112	4	12	4	85	0	4.59	—	—	—	—	—	—	—
—Kansas City	IHL	4	226	1	2	‡1	16	0	4.25	—	—	—	—	—	—	—
96-97—Dallas	NHL	35	1965	17	12	3	88	3	2.69	1	13	0	0	0	0	...
97-98—Vancouver	NHL	41	1999	14	11	6	91	2	2.73	—	—	—	—	—	—	—
NHL Totals (7 years)		259	14250	88	114	35	774	13	3.26	21	1135	9	11	77	0	4.07

ISBISTER, BRAD   RW   COYOTES

PERSONAL: Born March 7, 1977, in Edmonton. ... 6-3/222. ... Shoots right. ... Name pronounced ihs-BIH-stuhr.
HIGH SCHOOL: Milwaukie (Ore.).
TRANSACTIONS/CAREER NOTES: Selected by Winnipeg Jets in third round (fourth Jets pick, 67th overall) of NHL entry draft (July 8, 1995). ... Jets franchise moved to Phoenix and renamed Coyotes for 1996-97 season; NHL approved move on January 18, 1996. ... Pulled abdominal muscle (November 22, 1997); missed six games.
HONORS: Named to WHL (West) All-Star second team (1996-97).

			REGULAR SEASON						PLAYOFFS				
Season Team	League	Gms.	G	A	Pts.	PIM	+/-	PP	SH	Gms.	G	A	Pts.	PIM
93-94—Portland	WHL	64	7	10	17	45	...	...	...	10	0	2	2	0
94-95—Portland	WHL	67	16	20	36	123	...	...	...	—	—	—	—	—
95-96—Portland	WHL	71	45	44	89	184	...	...	...	7	2	4	6	20
96-97—Springfield	AHL	7	3	1	4	14	...	...	...	9	1	2	3	10
—Portland	WHL	24	15	18	33	45	...	...	...	6	2	1	3	16
97-98—Phoenix	NHL	66	9	8	17	102	4	1	0	5	0	0	0	2
—Springfield	AHL	9	8	2	10	36	...	...	...	—	—	—	—	—
NHL Totals (1 year)		66	9	8	17	102	4	1	0	5	0	0	0	2

JABLONSKI, PAT   G   HURRICANES

PERSONAL: Born June 20, 1967, in Toledo, Ohio. ... 6-0/180. ... Catches right. ... Brother of Jeff Jablonski, left winger with New York Islanders organization (1986-87 through 1991-92).
TRANSACTIONS/CAREER NOTES: Selected by St. Louis Blues in seventh round (sixth Blues pick, 138th overall) of NHL entry draft (June 15, 1985). ... Pulled groin (December 7, 1991); missed 26 games. ... Traded by Blues with D Rob Robinson, RW Darin Kimble and RW Steve Tuttle to Tampa Bay Lightning for future considerations (June 19, 1992). ... Traded by Lightning to Toronto Maple Leafs for future considerations (February 21, 1994). ... Loaned by Maple Leafs to Chicago Wolves of IHL (February 17, 1995). ... Returned to Maple Leafs (March 6, 1995). ... Loaned by Maple Leafs to Houston Aeros of IHL (March 29, 1995). ... Returned to Maple Leafs (April 7, 1995). ... Signed as free agent by Blues (October 2, 1995). ... Traded by Blues to Montreal Canadiens for D J.J. Daigneault (November 7, 1995). ... Traded by Canadiens to Phoenix Coyotes for D Steve Cheredaryk (March 18, 1997). ... Signed as free agent by Carolina Hurricanes (August 11, 1997).
HONORS: Shared James Norris Memorial Trophy with Guy Hebert (1990-91).
MISCELLANEOUS: Stopped penalty shot attempt (vs. Michel Goulet, March 26, 1991; vs. Bryan Marchment, December 31, 1992). ... Allowed penalty shot goal (vs. Pierre Turgeon, November 7, 1992).

			REGULAR SEASON								PLAYOFFS						
Season Team	League	Gms.	Min	W	L	T	GA	SO	Avg.	Gms.	Min.	W	L	GA	SO	Avg.
84-85—Detroit Compuware	NAJHL	29	1483	...	...	...	95	0	3.84	—	—	—	—	—	—	—
85-86—Windsor	OHL	29	1600	6	16	4	119	1	4.46	6	263	0	3	20	0	4.56
86-87—Windsor	OHL	41	2328	22	14	2	128	†3	3.30	12	710	8	4	38	0	3.21
87-88—Windsor	OHL	18	994	14	3	0	48	2	*2.90	9	537	8	0	28	0	3.13
—Peoria	IHL	5	285	2	2	‡1	17	0	3.58	—	—	—	—	—	—	—
88-89—Peoria	IHL	35	2051	11	20	‡3	163	1	4.77	3	130	0	2	13	0	6.00
89-90—St. Louis	NHL	4	208	0	3	0	17	0	4.90	—	—	—	—	—	—	—
—Peoria	IHL	36	2043	14	17	‡4	165	0	4.85	4	223	1	3	19	0	5.11
90-91—St. Louis	NHL	8	492	2	3	3	25	0	3.05	3	90	0	0	5	0	3.33
—Peoria	IHL	29	1738	23	3	‡2	87	0	3.00	10	532	7	2	23	0	*2.59

Season Team	League	REGULAR SEASON								PLAYOFFS					
		Gms.	Min	W	L	T	GA	SO	Avg.	Gms.	Min.	W	L	GA	SO	Avg.
91-92—St. Louis	NHL	10	468	3	6	0	38	0	4.87	—	—	—	—	—	—	—
—Peoria	IHL	8	493	6	1	‡1	29	1	3.53	—	—	—	—	—	—	—
92-93—Tampa Bay	NHL	43	2268	8	24	4	150	1	3.97	—	—	—	—	—	—	—
93-94—Tampa Bay	NHL	15	834	5	6	3	54	0	3.88	—	—	—	—	—	—	—
—St. John's	AHL	16	963	12	3	1	49	1	3.05	—	—	—	—	—	—	—
94-95—Chicago	IHL	4	217	0	4	‡0	17	0	4.70	—	—	—	—	—	—	—
—Houston	IHL	3	179	1	1	‡1	9	0	3.02	—	—	—	—	—	—	—
95-96—St. Louis	NHL	1	8	0	0	0	1	0	7.50	—	—	—	—	—	—	—
—Montreal	NHL	23	1264	5	9	6	62	0	2.94	1	49	0	0	1	0	1.22
96-97—Montreal	NHL	17	754	4	6	2	50	0	3.98	—	—	—	—	—	—	—
—Phoenix	NHL	2	59	0	1	0	2	0	2.03	—	—	—	—	—	—	—
97-98—Cleveland	IHL	34	1951	13	13	‡6	98	0	3.01	—	—	—	—	—	—	—
—Carolina	NHL	5	279	1	4	0	14	0	3.01	—	—	—	—	—	—	—
—Quebec	IHL	7	368	3	3	‡0	21	0	3.42	—	—	—	—	—	—	—
NHL Totals (8 years)		128	6634	28	62	18	413	1	3.74	4	139	0	0	6	0	2.59

JACKMAN, RICHARD   D   STARS

PERSONAL: Born June 28, 1978, in Toronto. ... 6-2/180. ... Shoots right.
TRANSACTIONS/CAREER NOTES: Selected by Dallas Stars in first round (first Stars pick, fifth overall) of NHL entry draft (June 22, 1996).
HONORS: Named to Can.HL All-Rookie team (1995-96). ... Named to OHL All-Rookie first team (1995-96). ... Named to OHL All-Star second team (1997-98).

Season Team	League	REGULAR SEASON							PLAYOFFS				
		Gms.	G	A	Pts.	PIM	+/-	PP	SH	Gms.	G	A	Pts.	PIM
95-96—Sault Ste. Marie	OHL	66	13	29	42	97	...	...	...	4	1	0	1	15
96-97—Sault Ste. Marie	OHL	53	13	34	47	116	...	...	...	10	2	6	8	24
97-98—Sault Ste. Marie	OHL	60	33	40	73	111	...	...	...	—	—	—	—	—
—Michigan	IHL	14	1	5	6	10	...	...	...	4	0	0	0	10

JACKSON, DANE   RW   ISLANDERS

PERSONAL: Born May 17, 1970, in Winnipeg. ... 6-1/200. ... Shoots right. ... Full name: Dane K. Jackson.
COLLEGE: North Dakota.
TRANSACTIONS/CAREER NOTES: Selected by Vancouver Canucks in third round (third Canucks pick, 44th overall) of NHL entry draft (June 11, 1988). ... Bruised shoulder (January 9, 1994); missed two games. ... Signed as free agent by Buffalo Sabres (August 16, 1995). ... Signed as free agent by New York Islanders (July 21, 1997).

Season Team	League	REGULAR SEASON							PLAYOFFS				
		Gms.	G	A	Pts.	PIM	+/-	PP	SH	Gms.	G	A	Pts.	PIM
87-88—Vernon	BCJHL	50	28	32	60	99	...	...	...	13	7	10	17	49
88-89—U. of North Dakota	WCHA	30	4	5	9	33	...	...	...	—	—	—	—	—
89-90—U. of North Dakota	WCHA	44	15	11	26	56	...	...	...	—	—	—	—	—
90-91—U. of North Dakota	WCHA	37	17	9	26	79	...	...	...	—	—	—	—	—
91-92—U. of North Dakota	WCHA	39	23	19	42	81	...	...	...	—	—	—	—	—
92-93—Hamilton	AHL	68	23	20	43	59	...	...	...	—	—	—	—	—
93-94—Hamilton	AHL	60	25	35	60	75	...	...	...	4	2	2	4	16
—Vancouver	NHL	12	5	1	6	9	3	0	0	—	—	—	—	—
94-95—Syracuse	AHL	78	30	28	58	162	...	...	...	—	—	—	—	—
—Vancouver	NHL	3	1	0	1	4	0	0	0	6	0	0	0	10
95-96—Rochester	AHL	50	27	19	46	132	...	...	...	19	4	6	10	53
—Buffalo	NHL	22	5	4	9	41	3	0	0	—	—	—	—	—
96-97—Rochester	AHL	78	24	34	58	111	...	...	...	10	7	4	11	14
97-98—Rochester	AHL	28	10	13	23	55	...	...	...	3	2	2	4	4
—New York Islanders	NHL	8	1	1	2	4	1	0	0	—	—	—	—	—
NHL Totals (4 years)		45	12	6	18	58	7	0	0	6	0	0	0	10

JAGR, JAROMIR   RW   PENGUINS

PERSONAL: Born February 15, 1972, in Kladno, Czechoslovakia. ... 6-2/228. ... Shoots left. ... Name pronounced YAHR-oh-meer YAH-gihr.
TRANSACTIONS/CAREER NOTES: Selected by Pittsburgh Penguins in first round (first Penguins pick, fifth overall) of NHL entry draft (June 16, 1990). ... Separated shoulder (February 23, 1993); missed three games. ... Strained groin (January 21, 1994); missed four games. ... Played in Europe during 1994-95 NHL lockout. ... Suffered from the flu (January 11, 1997); missed one game. ... Strained groin (February 16, 1997); missed three games. ... Pulled groin (February 27, 1997); missed 13 games. ... Strained groin (April 10, 1997); missed two games. ... Strained hip flexor and groin (November 14, 1997); missed four games. ... Injured groin (April 16, 1998); missed one game.
HONORS: Named to Czechoslovakian League All-Star team (1989-90). ... Named to NHL All-Rookie team (1990-91). ... Played in NHL All-Star Game (1992, 1993 and 1996). ... Won Art Ross Trophy (1994-95 and 1997-98). ... Named to THE SPORTING NEWS All-Star first team (1994-95 and 1995-96). ... Named to NHL All-Star first team (1994-95, 1995-96 and 1997-98). ... Played in NHL All-Star Game (1988, 1990-1994 and 1998). ... Named to play in NHL All-Star Game (1997); replaced by C Adam Oates due to injury. ... Named to NHL All-Star second team (1996-97).
RECORDS: Holds NHL single-season records for most points by a right winger—149 (1995-96); and most assists by a right winger—87 (1995-96).
STATISTICAL PLATEAUS: Three-goal games: 1990-91 (1), 1994-95 (1), 1996-97 (2). Total: 4.
MISCELLANEOUS: Member of Stanley Cup championship team (1991 and 1992). ... Captain of Pittsburgh Penguins (1995-96). ... Failed to score on a penalty shot (vs. Don Beaupre, January 26, 1993; vs. Mark Fitzpatrick, November 9, 1996). ... Mermber of gold-medal-winning Czech Republic Olympic team (1998).
STATISTICAL NOTES: Led NHL with 12 game-winning goals (1995-96).

Season Team	League	REGULAR SEASON Gms.	G	A	Pts.	PIM	+/-	PP	SH	PLAYOFFS Gms.	G	A	Pts.	PIM
88-89—Poldi Kladno	Czech.	39	8	10	18	...	...	...	...	—	—	—	—	—
89-90—Poldi Kladno	Czech.	51	30	30	60	...	...	...	...	—	—	—	—	—
90-91—Pittsburgh	NHL	80	27	30	57	42	-4	7	0	24	3	10	13	6
91-92—Pittsburgh	NHL	70	32	37	69	34	12	4	0	21	11	13	24	6
92-93—Pittsburgh	NHL	81	34	60	94	61	30	10	1	12	5	4	9	23
93-94—Pittsburgh	NHL	80	32	67	99	61	15	9	0	6	2	4	6	16
94-95—HC Kladno	Czech Rep.	11	8	14	22	10	...	...	...	—	—	—	—	—
—HC Bolzano	Euro	5	8	8	16	4	...	...	...	—	—	—	—	—
—HC Bolzano	Italy	1	0	0	0	0	...	...	...	—	—	—	—	—
—Schalker Haie	Ger. Div. II	1	1	10	11	0	...	...	...	—	—	—	—	—
—Pittsburgh	NHL	48	32	38	†70	37	23	8	3	12	10	5	15	6
95-96—Pittsburgh	NHL	82	62	87	149	96	31	20	1	18	11	12	23	18
96-97—Pittsburgh	NHL	63	47	48	95	40	22	11	2	5	4	4	8	4
97-98—Pittsburgh	NHL	77	35	†67	102	64	17	7	0	6	4	5	9	2
—Czech Rep. Olympic	Int'l	6	1	4	5	2	...	...	...	—	—	—	—	—
NHL Totals (8 years)		581	301	434	735	435	146	76	7	104	50	57	107	81

JAKOPIN, JOHN   LW   PANTHERS

PERSONAL: Born May 16, 1975, in Toronto. ... 6-5/225. ... Shoots left. ... Name pronounced JAK-oh-pihn.
COLLEGE: Merrimack (Mass.).
TRANSACTIONS/CAREER NOTES: Selected by Detroit Red Wings in fourth round (fourth Red Wings pick, 97th overall) of NHL entry draft (June 26, 1993). ... Signed as free agent by Florida Panthers (June 4, 1997).
HONORS: Named to Hockey East All-Rookie team (1993-94).

Season Team	League	REGULAR SEASON Gms.	G	A	Pts.	PIM	+/-	PP	SH	PLAYOFFS Gms.	G	A	Pts.	PIM
92-93—St. Michael's	Tier II Jr. A	45	9	21	30	42	...	...	...	—	—	—	—	—
93-94—Merrimack College	Hockey East	36	2	8	10	64	...	...	...	—	—	—	—	—
94-95—Merrimack College	Hockey East	37	4	10	14	42	...	...	...	—	—	—	—	—
95-96—Merrimack College	Hockey East	32	10	15	25	68	...	...	...	—	—	—	—	—
96-97—Merrimack College	Hockey East	31	4	12	16	68	...	...	...	—	—	—	—	—
—Adirondack	AHL	3	0	0	0	9	...	...	...	—	—	—	—	—
97-98—New Haven	AHL	60	2	18	20	151	...	...	...	3	0	0	0	0
—Florida	NHL	2	0	0	0	4	-3	0	0	—	—	—	—	—
NHL Totals (1 year)		2	0	0	0	4	-3	0	0					

JANNEY, CRAIG   C   LIGHTNING

PERSONAL: Born September 26, 1967, in Hartford, Conn. ... 6-1/190. ... Shoots left. ... Full name: Craig Harlan Janney.
HIGH SCHOOL: Deerfield (Mass.) Academy.
COLLEGE: Boston College.
TRANSACTIONS/CAREER NOTES: Broke collarbone (December 1985). ... Selected by Boston Bruins in first round (first Bruins pick, 13th overall) of NHL entry draft (June 21, 1986). ... Suffered from mononucleosis (December 1986). ... Pulled right groin (December 1988); missed seven games. ... Tore right groin muscle (October 26, 1989); missed 21 games. ... Strained left shoulder (April 5, 1990). ... Sprained left shoulder (December 13, 1990). ... Sprained right ankle (March 30, 1991). ... Traded by Bruins with D Stephane Quintal to St. Louis Blues for C Adam Oates (February 7, 1992). ... Cut leg (December 1, 1993); missed one game. ... Strained knee (February 20, 1994); missed three games. ... Awarded to Vancouver Canucks with second-round pick (C Dave Scatchard) in 1994 draft as compensation for Blues signing free agent C Petr Nedved (March 14, 1994). ... Traded by Canucks to Blues for D Jeff Brown, D Bret Hedican and C Nathan LaFayette (March 21, 1994). ... Left Blues for personal reasons (February 17-March 6, 1995). ... Traded by Blues to San Jose Sharks for D Jeff Norton, third-round pick (traded to Colorado) in 1997 draft and future considerations (March 6, 1995). ... Traded by Sharks to Winnipeg Jets for C Darren Turcotte and second-round pick (traded to Chicago) in 1996 draft (March 18, 1996). ... Jets franchise moved to Phoenix and renamed Coyotes for 1996-97 season; NHL approved move on January 18, 1996. ... Sprained medial collateral knee ligament (March 14, 1998); missed 14 games. ... Traded by Coyotes to Tampa Bay Lightning for LW Louie Debrusk and fifth-round pick (D Jay Leach) in 1998 draft (June 11, 1998).
HONORS: Named to NCAA All-America East first team (1986-87). ... Named to Hockey East All-Star first team (1986-87). ... Named to Hockey East All-Decade team (1994).
MISCELLANEOUS: Failed to score on a penalty shot (vs. Stephane Fiset, January 9, 1992; vs. Robb Stauber, March 20, 1993).
STATISTICAL PLATEAUS: Three-goal games: 1987-88 (1), 1991-92 (1), 1992-93 (1). Total: 3.

Season Team	League	REGULAR SEASON Gms.	G	A	Pts.	PIM	+/-	PP	SH	PLAYOFFS Gms.	G	A	Pts.	PIM
84-85—Deerfield Academy	Mass. H.S.	17	33	35	68	6	...	...	...	—	—	—	—	—
85-86—Boston College	Hockey East	34	13	14	27	8	...	...	...	—	—	—	—	—
86-87—Boston College	Hockey East	37	28	*55	*83	6	...	...	...	—	—	—	—	—
87-88—U.S. national team	Int'l	52	26	44	70	6	...	...	...	—	—	—	—	—
—U.S. Olympic Team	Int'l	5	3	1	4	2	...	...	...	—	—	—	—	—
—Boston	NHL	15	7	9	16	0	6	1	0	23	6	10	16	11
88-89—Boston	NHL	62	16	46	62	12	20	2	0	10	4	9	13	21
89-90—Boston	NHL	55	24	38	62	4	3	11	0	18	3	19	22	2
90-91—Boston	NHL	77	26	66	92	8	15	9	1	18	4	18	22	11
91-92—Boston	NHL	53	12	39	51	20	1	3	0	—	—	—	—	—
—St. Louis	NHL	25	6	30	36	2	5	3	0	6	0	6	6	0
92-93—St. Louis	NHL	84	24	82	106	12	-4	8	0	11	2	9	11	0
93-94—St. Louis	NHL	69	16	68	84	24	-14	8	0	4	1	3	4	0
94-95—St. Louis	NHL	8	2	5	7	0	3	1	0	—	—	—	—	—
—San Jose	NHL	27	5	15	20	10	-4	2	0	11	3	4	7	4
95-96—San Jose	NHL	71	13	49	62	26	-35	5	0	—	—	—	—	—
—Winnipeg	NHL	13	7	13	20	0	2	2	0	6	1	2	3	0
96-97—Phoenix	NHL	77	15	38	53	26	-1	5	0	7	0	3	3	4
97-98—Phoenix	NHL	68	10	43	53	12	5	4	0	6	0	3	3	0
NHL Totals (11 years)		704	183	541	724	156	2	64	1	120	24	86	110	53

JANSSENS, MARK   C   BLACKHAWKS

PERSONAL: Born May 19, 1968, in Surrey, B.C. ... 6-3/212. ... Shoots left.
TRANSACTIONS/CAREER NOTES: Selected by New York Rangers as underage junior in fourth round (fourth Rangers pick, 72nd overall) of NHL entry draft (June 21, 1986). ... Fractured skull and suffered cerebral concussion (December 10, 1988). ... Traded by Rangers to Minnesota North Stars for C Mario Thyer and third-round pick (D Maxim Galanov) in 1993 draft (March 10, 1992). ... Traded by North Stars to Hartford Whalers for C James Black (September 3, 1992). ... Separated shoulder (December 26, 1992); missed five games. ... Fined $500 by Whalers for involvement in bar brawl (April 1, 1994). ... Suffered slight concussion (February 4, 1995); missed two games. ... Sprained knee (January 22, 1997); missed 14 games. ... Traded by Whalers to Mighty Ducks of Anaheim for LW Bates Battaglia and fourth-round pick (C Josef Vasicek) in 1998 draft (March 18, 1997). ... Traded by Mighty Ducks with D J.J. Daigneault and RW Joe Sacco to New York Islanders for C Travis Green, D Doug Houda and RW Tony Tuzzolino (February 6, 1998). ... Traded by Islanders to Phoenix Coyotes for ninth-round pick (RW Jason Doyle) in 1998 draft (March 24, 1998). ... Signed as free agent by Chicago Blackhawks (July 3, 1998).

		REGULAR SEASON								PLAYOFFS				
Season Team	League	Gms.	G	A	Pts.	PIM	+/-	PP	SH	Gms.	G	A	Pts.	PIM
84-85—Regina	WHL	70	8	22	30	51	...	...	...	5	1	1	2	0
85-86—Regina	WHL	71	25	38	63	146	...	...	...	9	0	2	2	17
86-87—Regina	WHL	68	24	38	62	209	...	...	...	3	0	1	1	14
87-88—Regina	WHL	71	39	51	90	202	...	...	...	4	3	4	7	6
—New York Rangers	NHL	1	0	0	0	0	0	0	0	—	—	—	—	—
—Colorado	IHL	6	2	2	4	24	...	...	...	12	3	2	5	20
88-89—New York Rangers	NHL	5	0	0	0	0	-4	0	0	—	—	—	—	—
—Denver	IHL	38	19	19	38	104	...	...	...	4	3	0	3	18
89-90—New York Rangers	NHL	80	5	8	13	161	-26	0	0	9	2	1	3	10
90-91—New York Rangers	NHL	67	9	7	16	172	-1	0	0	6	3	0	3	6
91-92—New York Rangers	NHL	4	0	0	0	5	-1	0	0	—	—	—	—	—
—Binghamton	AHL	55	10	23	33	109	...	...	...	—	—	—	—	—
—Minnesota	NHL	3	0	0	0	0	-1	0	0	—	—	—	—	—
—Kalamazoo	IHL	2	0	0	0	2	...	...	...	11	1	2	3	22
92-93—Hartford	NHL	76	12	17	29	237	-15	0	0	—	—	—	—	—
93-94—Hartford	NHL	84	2	10	12	137	-13	0	0	—	—	—	—	—
94-95—Hartford	NHL	46	2	5	7	93	-8	0	0	—	—	—	—	—
95-96—Hartford	NHL	81	2	7	9	155	-13	0	0	—	—	—	—	—
96-97—Hartford	NHL	54	2	4	6	90	-10	0	0	—	—	—	—	—
—Anaheim	NHL	12	0	2	2	47	-3	0	0	11	0	0	0	15
97-98—Anaheim	NHL	55	4	5	9	116	-22	0	0	—	—	—	—	—
—New York Islanders	NHL	12	0	0	0	34	-3	0	0	—	—	—	—	—
—Phoenix	NHL	7	1	2	3	4	4	0	0	1	0	0	0	2
NHL Totals (11 years)		587	39	67	106	1251	-116	0	0	27	5	1	6	33

JARVIS, WES   D   RANGERS

PERSONAL: Born April 16, 1979, in Toronto. ... 6-4/203. ... Shoots left.
TRANSACTIONS/CAREER NOTES: Selected by New York Rangers in second round (second Rangers pick, 46th overall) of NHL entry draft (June 21, 1997).

		REGULAR SEASON								PLAYOFFS				
Season Team	League	Gms.	G	A	Pts.	PIM	+/-	PP	SH	Gms.	G	A	Pts.	PIM
95-96—Gloucester	Tier II Jr. A	43	3	6	9	73	...	...	...	—	—	—	—	—
96-97—Kitchener	OHL	56	4	8	12	108	...	...	...	13	0	4	4	25
97-98—Kitchener	OHL	47	10	18	28	112	...	...	...	1	0	0	0	2

JOHANSSON, ANDREAS   C

PERSONAL: Born May 19, 1973, in Hofors, Sweden. ... 6-2/209. ... Shoots left. ... Name pronounced yoh-HAN-suhn.
TRANSACTIONS/CAREER NOTES: Selected by New York Islanders in seventh round (seventh Islanders pick, 136th overall) of NHL entry draft (June 22, 1991). ... Injured back (April 5, 1996); missed three games. ... Traded by Islanders with D Darius Kasparaitis to Pittsburgh Penguins for C Bryan Smolinski (November 17, 1996). ... Bruised shoulder (December 10, 1996); missed 12 games. ... Suffered from the flu (January 26, 1997); missed one game. ... Suffered back spasms (February 15, 1997); missed one game. ... Bruised ribs (November 15, 1997); missed six games. ... Sprained medial collateral knee ligament (March 8, 1998); missed 10 games.

		REGULAR SEASON								PLAYOFFS				
Season Team	League	Gms.	G	A	Pts.	PIM	+/-	PP	SH	Gms.	G	A	Pts.	PIM
90-91—Falun	Sweden	31	12	10	22	38	...	...	...	—	—	—	—	—
91-92—Farjestad Karlstad	Sweden	30	3	1	4	4	...	...	...	6	0	0	0	4
92-93—Farjestad Karlstad	Sweden	38	4	7	11	38	...	...	...	2	0	0	0	0
93-94—Farjestad Karlstad	Sweden	20	3	6	9	6	...	...	...	—	—	—	—	—
94-95—Farjestad Karlstad	Sweden	36	9	10	19	42	...	...	...	4	0	0	0	10
95-96—Worcester	AHL	29	5	5	10	32	...	...	...	—	—	—	—	—
—Utah	IHL	22	4	13	17	28	...	...	...	12	0	5	5	6
—New York Islanders	NHL	3	0	1	1	0	1	0	0	—	—	—	—	—
96-97—New York Islanders	NHL	15	2	2	4	0	-6	1	0	—	—	—	—	—
—Pittsburgh	NHL	27	2	7	9	20	-6	0	0	—	—	—	—	—
—Cleveland	IHL	10	2	4	6	42	...	...	...	11	1	5	6	8
97-98—Pittsburgh	NHL	50	5	10	15	20	4	0	1	1	0	0	0	0
—Swedish Oly. team	Int'l	3	0	0	0	2	...	...	...	—	—	—	—	—
NHL Totals (3 years)		95	9	20	29	40	-7	1	1	1	0	0	0	0

JOHANSSON, CALLE D CAPITALS

PERSONAL: Born February 14, 1967, in Goteborg, Sweden. ... 5-11/200. ... Shoots left. ... Name pronounced KAL-ee yoh-HAHN-suhn.
TRANSACTIONS/CAREER NOTES: Selected by Buffalo Sabres in first round (first Sabres pick, 14th overall) of NHL entry draft (June 15, 1985). ... Dislocated thumb (October 9, 1988). ... Traded by Sabres with second-round pick (G Byron Dafoe) in 1989 draft to Washington Capitals for D Grant Ledyard, G Clint Malarchuk and sixth-round pick (C Brian Holzinger) in 1991 draft (March 6, 1989). ... Injured back (October 7, 1989); missed 10 games. ... Bruised ribs (January 9, 1993); missed seven games. ... Played in Europe during 1994-95 NHL lockout. ... Suffered from the flu (March 25, 1995); missed two games. ... Broke hand (April 4, 1996); missed remainder of season. ... Broke jaw (November 12, 1996); missed 16 games. ... Bruised foot (February 14, 1997); missed one game. ... Injured knee (January 13, 1998); missed nine games.
HONORS: Named to NHL All-Rookie team (1987-88).

			REGULAR SEASON								PLAYOFFS			
Season Team	League	Gms.	G	A	Pts.	PIM	+/-	PP	SH	Gms.	G	A	Pts.	PIM
83-84—Vastra Frolunda	Sweden	34	5	10	15	20	...	...	...	—	—	—	—	—
84-85—Vastra Frolunda	Sweden	36	14	15	29	20	...	...	...	6	1	2	3	4
85-86—Bjorkloven	Sweden	17	1	1	2	14	...	...	...	—	—	—	—	—
86-87—Bjorkloven	Sweden	30	2	13	15	18	...	...	...	6	1	3	4	6
87-88—Buffalo	NHL	71	4	38	42	37	12	2	0	6	0	1	1	0
88-89—Buffalo	NHL	47	2	11	13	33	-7	0	0	—	—	—	—	—
—Washington	NHL	12	1	7	8	4	1	1	0	6	1	2	3	0
89-90—Washington	NHL	70	8	31	39	25	7	4	0	15	1	6	7	4
90-91—Washington	NHL	80	11	41	52	23	-2	2	1	10	2	7	9	8
91-92—Washington	NHL	80	14	42	56	49	2	5	2	7	0	5	5	4
92-93—Washington	NHL	77	7	38	45	56	3	6	0	6	0	5	5	4
93-94—Washington	NHL	84	9	33	42	59	3	4	0	6	1	3	4	4
94-95—Kloten	Switzerland	5	1	2	3	8	...	...	...	—	—	—	—	—
—Washington	NHL	46	5	26	31	35	-6	4	0	7	3	1	4	0
95-96—Washington	NHL	78	10	25	35	50	13	4	0	—	—	—	—	—
96-97—Washington	NHL	65	6	11	17	16	-2	2	0	—	—	—	—	—
97-98—Washington	NHL	73	15	20	35	30	-11	10	1	21	2	8	10	16
—Swedish Oly. team	Int'l	4	0	0	0	2	...	...	...	—	—	—	—	—
NHL Totals (11 years).........		783	92	323	415	417	13	44	4	84	10	38	48	40

JOHNSON, ANDY D BLACKHAWKS

PERSONAL: Born March 6, 1978, in Fredericton, N.B. ... 6-3/188. ... Shoots left.
TRANSACTIONS/CAREER NOTES: Selected by Chicago Blackhawks in fifth round (fourth Blackhawks pick, 130th overall) of NHL entry draft (June 22, 1996).

			REGULAR SEASON								PLAYOFFS			
Season Team	League	Gms.	G	A	Pts.	PIM	+/-	PP	SH	Gms.	G	A	Pts.	PIM
95-96—Peterborough.............	OHL	54	0	4	4	57	...	...	...	22	0	6	6	21
96-97—Peterborough.............	OHL	57	4	24	28	82	...	...	...	7	1	2	3	10
97-98—Peterborough.............	OHL	60	17	20	37	112	...	...	...	4	0	0	0	6

JOHNSON, BRENT G BLUES

PERSONAL: Born March 12, 1977, in Farmington, Mich. ... 6-4/191. ... Catches left.
TRANSACTIONS/CAREER NOTES: Selected by Colorado Avalanche in fifth round (fifth Avalanche pick, 129th overall) of NHL entry draft (July 8, 1995). ... Rights traded by Avalanche to St. Louis Blues for third-round pick (RW Ville Nieminen) in 1997 draft and conditional third-round pick in 2000 draft (May 30, 1997).

			REGULAR SEASON							PLAYOFFS				
Season Team	League	Gms.	Min.	W	L	T	GA	SO	Avg.	Gms.	Min.	W	L	GA	SO	Avg.
94-95—Owen Sound	OHL	18	904	3	9	1	75	0	4.98	4	253	0	4	24	0	5.69
95-96—Owen Sound	OHL	58	3211	24	28	1	243	1	4.54	6	371	2	4	29	0	4.69
96-97—Owen Sound	OHL	50	2798	20	28	1	201	1	4.31	4	253	0	4	24	0	5.69
97-98—Worcester	AHL	42	2241	14	15	7	119	0	3.19	6	332	3	2	19	0	3.43

JOHNSON, CRAIG LW KINGS

PERSONAL: Born March 18, 1972, in St. Paul, Minn. ... 6-2/198. ... Shoots left.
HIGH SCHOOL: Hill-Murray (St. Paul, Minn.).
COLLEGE: Minnesota.
TRANSACTIONS/CAREER NOTES: Suffered stress fracture of vertebrae (February 1987). ... Selected by St. Louis Blues in second round (first Blues pick, 33rd overall) of NHL entry draft (June 16, 1990). ... Separated shoulder (December 1990). ... Traded by Blues with C Patrice Tardiff, C Roman Vopat, fifth-round pick (D Peter Hogan) in 1996 draft and first-round pick (LW Matt Zultek) in 1997 draft to Los Angeles Kings for C Wayne Gretzky (February 27, 1996). ... Sprained left shoulder (March 13, 1996); missed seven games. ... Strained abdominal muscle prior to 1996-97 season; missed first seven games of season. ... Strained groin (November 2, 1996); missed one game. ... Strained abdominal muscle (November 30, 1996); missed 36 games. ... Strained groin (March 29, 1997); missed six games. ... Suffered from the flu (December 18, 1997); missed two games. ... Bruised abdomen (February 2, 1998); missed three games.
HONORS: Named to WCHA All-Rookie Team (1990-91).

			REGULAR SEASON								PLAYOFFS			
Season Team	League	Gms.	G	A	Pts.	PIM	+/-	PP	SH	Gms.	G	A	Pts.	PIM
87-88—Hill-Murray H.S.	Minn. H.S.	28	14	20	34	4	...	...	...	—	—	—	—	—
88-89—Hill-Murray H.S.	Minn. H.S.	24	22	30	52	10	...	...	...	—	—	—	—	—
89-90—Hill-Murray H.S.	Minn. H.S.	23	15	36	51	...	...	...	...	—	—	—	—	—

		REGULAR SEASON								PLAYOFFS				
Season Team	League	Gms.	G	A	Pts.	PIM	+/-	PP	SH	Gms.	G	A	Pts.	PIM
90-91—Univ. of Minnesota......	WCHA	33	13	18	31	34	...	...	...	—	—	—	—	—
91-92—Univ. of Minnesota......	WCHA	44	19	39	58	70	...	...	...	—	—	—	—	—
92-93—Univ. of Minnesota......	WCHA	42	22	24	46	70	...	...	...	—	—	—	—	—
93-94—U.S. national team	Int'l	54	25	26	51	64	...	...	...	—	—	—	—	—
—U.S. Olympic Team	Int'l	8	0	4	4	4	...	...	...	—	—	—	—	—
94-95—Peoria	IHL	16	2	6	8	25	...	...	...	9	0	4	4	10
—St. Louis	NHL	15	3	3	6	6	4	0	0	1	0	0	0	2
95-96—Worcester	AHL	5	3	0	3	2	...	...	...	—	—	—	—	—
—St. Louis	NHL	49	8	7	15	30	-4	1	0	—	—	—	—	—
—Los Angeles...............	NHL	11	5	4	9	6	-4	3	0	—	—	—	—	—
96-97—Mobile.......................	ECHL	4	0	0	0	74	...	...	...	—	—	—	—	—
—Los Angeles...............	NHL	31	4	3	7	26	-7	1	0	—	—	—	—	—
—Oklahoma City	CHL	36	6	11	17	134	...	...	...	—	—	—	—	—
—Michigan....................	IHL	2	0	0	0	2	...	...	...	—	—	—	—	—
—Manitoba....................	IHL	16	2	2	4	38	...	...	...	—	—	—	—	—
97-98—Los Angeles...............	NHL	74	17	21	38	42	9	6	0	4	1	0	1	4
NHL Totals (4 years)...........		180	37	38	75	110	-2	11	0	5	1	0	1	6

JOHNSON, GREG   C   PREDATORS

PERSONAL: Born March 16, 1971, in Thunder Bay, Ont. ... 5-10/185. ... Shoots left. ... Full name: Gregory Johnson. ... Brother of Ryan Johnson, center in Florida Panthers system.

COLLEGE: North Dakota.

TRANSACTIONS/CAREER NOTES: Selected by Philadelphia Flyers in second round (first Flyers pick, 33rd overall) of NHL entry draft (June 17, 1989). ... Separated right shoulder (November 24, 1990). ... Rights traded by Flyers with future considerations to Detroit Red Wings for RW Jim Cummins and fourth-round pick (traded to Boston) in 1993 draft (June 20, 1993). ... Loaned to Canadian Olympic Team (January 19, 1994). ... Returned to Red Wings (March 1, 1994). ... Sprained left ankle (April 14, 1995); missed last nine games of season. ... Injured left hand (October 8, 1995); missed two games. ... Injured knee (March 19, 1996); missed 12 games. ... Traded by Red Wings to Pittsburgh Penguins for RW Tomas Sandstrom (January 27, 1997). ... Bruised shoulder (April 3, 1997); missed one game. ... Strained groin (October 3, 1997); missed five games. ... Traded by Penguins to Chicago Blackhawks for D Tuomas Gronman (October 27, 1997). ... Strained groin (October 31, 1997); missed three games. ... Selected by Nashville Predators in NHL expansion draft (June 26, 1998).

HONORS: Named to USHL All-Star first team (1988-89). ... Named Canadian Junior A Player of the Year (1989). ... Named to Centennial Cup All-Star first team (1989). ... Named to NCAA All-America West first team (1990-91 and 1992-93). ... Named to WCHA All-Star first team (1990-91 through 1992-93). ... Named to NCAA West All-America second team (1991-92).

MISCELLANEOUS: Member of silver-medal-winning Canadian Olympic team (1994).

		REGULAR SEASON								PLAYOFFS				
Season Team	League	Gms.	G	A	Pts.	PIM	+/-	PP	SH	Gms.	G	A	Pts.	PIM
88-89—Thunder Bay Jrs.	USHL	47	32	64	96	4	...	...	...	12	5	13	18	...
89-90—U. of North Dakota......	WCHA	44	17	38	55	11	...	...	...	—	—	—	—	—
90-91—U. of North Dakota......	WCHA	38	18	*61	79	6	...	...	...	—	—	—	—	—
91-92—U. of North Dakota......	WCHA	39	20	54	74	8	...	...	...	—	—	—	—	—
92-93—Canadian nat'l team	Int'l	23	6	14	20	2	...	...	...	—	—	—	—	—
—U. of North Dakota......	WCHA	34	19	45	64	18	...	...	...	—	—	—	—	—
93-94—Detroit.......................	NHL	52	6	11	17	22	-7	1	1	7	2	2	4	2
—Canadian nat'l team	Int'l	6	2	6	8	4	...	...	...	—	—	—	—	—
—Can. Olympic Team.....	Int'l	8	0	3	3	0	...	...	...	—	—	—	—	—
—Adirondack	AHL	3	2	4	6	0	...	...	...	4	0	4	4	2
94-95—Detroit.......................	NHL	22	3	5	8	14	1	2	0	1	0	0	0	0
95-96—Detroit.......................	NHL	60	18	22	40	30	6	5	0	13	3	1	4	8
96-97—Detroit.......................	NHL	43	6	10	16	12	-5	0	0	—	—	—	—	—
—Pittsburgh.................	NHL	32	7	9	16	14	-13	1	0	5	1	0	1	2
97-98—Pittsburgh.................	NHL	5	1	0	1	2	0	0	0	—	—	—	—	—
—Chicago.....................	NHL	69	11	22	33	38	-2	4	0	—	—	—	—	—
NHL Totals (5 years)...........		283	52	79	131	132	-20	13	1	26	6	3	9	12

JOHNSON, JIM   D

PERSONAL: Born August 9, 1962, in New Hope, Minn. ... 6-1/191. ... Shoots left. ... Full name: James Erik Johnson.

HIGH SCHOOL: Cooper (New Hope, Minn.).

COLLEGE: Minnesota-Duluth.

TRANSACTIONS/CAREER NOTES: Signed as free agent by Pittsburgh Penguins (June 9, 1985). ... Tore cartilage in right knee (January 1988). ... Suffered back pain (October 1990). ... Injured neck (November 12, 1990); missed three games. ... Traded by Penguins with D Chris Dahlquist to Minnesota North Stars for D Peter Taglianetti and D Larry Murphy (December 11, 1990). ... Sprained back (February 12, 1991); missed five games. ... Bruised hip (April 1991). ... Injured groin (December 7, 1991); missed five games. ... Strained hamstring (March 10, 1992); missed two games. ... Cut face (November 14, 1992); missed two games. ... Broke finger (January 3, 1993); missed one game. ... Sprained knee (April 14, 1993); missed final two games of season. ... North Stars franchise moved from Minnesota to Dallas and renamed Stars for 1993-94 season. ... Sprained knee (October 23, 1993); missed three games. ... Injured neck (January 18, 1994); missed 14 games. ... Traded by Stars to Washington Capitals for LW Alan May and seventh-round pick (RW Jeff Dewar) in 1995 draft (March 21, 1994). ... Tore knee ligament (April 5, 1994); missed remainder of season. ... Bruised arm (February 13, 1995); missed one game. ... Suffered partial tear of ligament in left wrist (November 3, 1995); missed five games. ... Strained shoulder (January 1, 1996); missed five games. ... Signed as free agent by Phoenix Coyotes (July 15, 1996). ... Bruised heel (October 8, 1996); missed one game. ... Strained neck (November 16, 1996); missed six games. ... Suffered back spasms (February 26, 1997); missed two games. ... Sprained thumb (March 17, 1997); missed seven games. ... Suffered post-concussion syndrome (November 11, 1997); missed remainder of season. ... Announced retirement (July 21, 1998).

Season Team	League	REGULAR SEASON								PLAYOFFS				
		Gms.	G	A	Pts.	PIM	+/-	PP	SH	Gms.	G	A	Pts.	PIM
81-82—Minnesota-Duluth.......	WCHA	40	0	10	10	62	...	...	...	—	—	—	—	—
82-83—Minnesota-Duluth.......	WCHA	44	3	18	21	118	...	...	...	—	—	—	—	—
83-84—Minnesota-Duluth.......	WCHA	43	3	13	16	116	...	...	...	—	—	—	—	—
84-85—Minnesota-Duluth.......	WCHA	47	7	29	36	49	...	...	...	—	—	—	—	—
85-86—Pittsburgh.................	NHL	80	3	26	29	115	12	0	0	—	—	—	—	—
86-87—Pittsburgh.................	NHL	80	5	25	30	116	-6	0	0	—	—	—	—	—
87-88—Pittsburgh.................	NHL	55	1	12	13	87	-4	0	0	—	—	—	—	—
88-89—Pittsburgh.................	NHL	76	2	14	16	163	7	1	0	11	0	5	5	44
89-90—Pittsburgh.................	NHL	75	3	13	16	154	-20	1	0	—	—	—	—	—
90-91—Pittsburgh.................	NHL	24	0	5	5	23	-3	0	0	—	—	—	—	—
—Minnesota.................	NHL	44	1	9	10	100	9	0	0	14	0	1	1	52
91-92—Minnesota.................	NHL	71	4	10	14	102	11	0	0	7	1	3	4	18
92-93—Minnesota.................	NHL	79	3	20	23	105	9	1	0	—	—	—	—	—
93-94—Dallas.....................	NHL	53	0	7	7	51	-6	0	0	—	—	—	—	—
—Washington	NHL	8	0	0	0	12	-1	0	0	—	—	—	—	—
94-95—Washington	NHL	47	0	13	13	43	6	0	0	7	0	2	2	8
95-96—Washington	NHL	66	2	4	6	34	-3	0	0	6	0	0	0	6
96-97—Phoenix...................	NHL	55	3	7	10	74	5	0	0	6	0	0	0	4
97-98—Phoenix...................	NHL	16	2	1	3	18	0	0	0	—	—	—	—	—
NHL Totals (13 years).........		829	29	166	195	1197	16	3	0	51	1	11	12	132

JOHNSON, MATT   LW   KINGS

PERSONAL: Born November 23, 1975, in Pelham, Ont. ... 6-5/230. ... Shoots left.
TRANSACTIONS/CAREER NOTES: Selected by Los Angeles Kings in second round (second Kings pick, 33rd overall) of NHL entry draft (June 28, 1994). ... Suffered from the flu (February 25, 1995); missed one game. ... Bruised right hand (April 3, 1995); missed four games. ... Strained shoulder (December 18, 1996); missed six games. ... Suffered concussion (February 1, 1997); missed one game. ... Suspended four games and fined $1,000 by NHL for elbowing incident (February 5, 1997). ... Strained back (March 10, 1997); missed final 13 games of season. ... Suspended four games and fined $1,000 by NHL for slashing (September 29, 1997). ... Strained groin (December 23, 1997); missed one game. ... Strained left bicep (March 21, 1998); missed three games.

Season Team	League	REGULAR SEASON								PLAYOFFS				
		Gms.	G	A	Pts.	PIM	+/-	PP	SH	Gms.	G	A	Pts.	PIM
91-92—Welland....................	Jr. B	38	6	19	25	214	...	...	...	—	—	—	—	—
92-93—Peterborough.............	OHL	66	8	17	25	211	...	...	...	16	1	1	2	54
93-94—Peterborough.............	OHL	50	13	24	37	233	...	...	...	—	—	—	—	—
94-95—Peterborough.............	OHL	14	1	2	3	43	...	...	...	—	—	—	—	—
—Los Angeles...............	NHL	14	1	0	1	102	0	0	0	—	—	—	—	—
95-96—Los Angeles...............	NHL	1	0	0	0	5	0	0	0	—	—	—	—	—
—Phoenix...................	IHL	29	4	4	8	87	...	...	...	—	—	—	—	—
96-97—Los Angeles...............	NHL	52	1	3	4	194	-4	0	0	—	—	—	—	—
97-98—Los Angeles...............	NHL	66	2	4	6	249	-8	0	0	4	0	0	0	6
NHL Totals (4 years)...........		133	4	7	11	550	-12	0	0	4	0	0	0	6

JOHNSON, MIKE   RW   MAPLE LEAFS

PERSONAL: Born October 3, 1974, in Scarborough, Ont. ... 6-2/190. ... Shoots right. ... Full name: Michael Johnson.
HIGH SCHOOL: Sir John A. MacDonald (Toronto).
COLLEGE: Bowling Green State.
TRANSACTIONS/CAREER NOTES: Signed as a free agent by Toronto Maple Leafs (March 16, 1997).
HONORS: Named to NHL All-Rookie team (1997-98).

Season Team	League	REGULAR SEASON								PLAYOFFS				
		Gms.	G	A	Pts.	PIM	+/-	PP	SH	Gms.	G	A	Pts.	PIM
93-94—Bowling Green	CCHA	38	6	14	20	18	...	...	...	—	—	—	—	—
94-95—Bowling Green	CCHA	37	16	33	49	35	...	...	...	—	—	—	—	—
95-96—Bowling Green	CCHA	30	12	19	31	22	...	...	...	—	—	—	—	—
96-97—Bowling Green	CCHA	38	30	32	62	46	...	...	...	—	—	—	—	—
—Toronto......................	NHL	13	2	2	4	4	-2	0	1	—	—	—	—	—
97-98—Toronto......................	NHL	82	15	32	47	24	-4	5	0	—	—	—	—	—
NHL Totals (2 years)...........		95	17	34	51	28	-6	5	1					

JOHNSON, RYAN   C   PANTHERS

PERSONAL: Born June 14, 1976, in Thunder Bay, Ont. ... 6-2/180. ... Shoots left. ... Brother of Greg Johnson, center, Nashville Predators.
COLLEGE: North Dakota.
TRANSACTIONS/CAREER NOTES: Selected by Florida Panthers in second round (fourth Panthers pick, 36th overall) of NHL entry draft (June 28, 1994). ... Loaned to Canadian national team prior to 1995-96 season.

Season Team	League	REGULAR SEASON								PLAYOFFS				
		Gms.	G	A	Pts.	PIM	+/-	PP	SH	Gms.	G	A	Pts.	PIM
93-94—Thunder Bay Jrs.	USHL	48	14	36	50	28	...	...	...	—	—	—	—	—
94-95—U. of North Dakota......	WCHA	38	6	22	28	39	...	...	...	—	—	—	—	—
95-96—U. of North Dakota......	WCHA	21	2	17	19	14	...	...	...	—	—	—	—	—
—Canadian nat'l team	Int'l	28	5	12	17	14	...	...	...	—	—	—	—	—
96-97—Carolina	AHL	79	18	24	42	28	...	...	...	—	—	—	—	—
97-98—New Haven	AHL	64	19	48	67	12	...	...	...	3	0	1	1	0
—Florida.........................	NHL	10	0	2	2	0	-4	0	0	—	—	—	—	—
NHL Totals (1 year)............		10	0	2	2	0	-4	0	0					

JOKINEN, OLLI   C   KINGS

PERSONAL: Born December 5, 1978, in Kuopio, Finland ... 6-2/198. ... Shoots left. ... Name pronounced OH-lee YOH-kih-nehn.
TRANSACTIONS/CAREER NOTES: Selected by Los Angeles Kings in first round (first Kings pick, third overall) of NHL entry draft (June 21, 1997).

		REGULAR SEASON								PLAYOFFS				
Season Team	League	Gms.	G	A	Pts.	PIM	+/-	PP	SH	Gms.	G	A	Pts.	PIM
94-95—KalPa Kuopio Jrs.	Finland	6	0	1	1	6	...	...	...	—	—	—	—	—
95-96—KalPa Kuopio Jrs.	Finland	15	1	1	2	2	...	...	...	—	—	—	—	—
—KalPa Kuopio	Finland	15	1	1	2	2	...	...	...	—	—	—	—	—
96-97—HIFK Helsinki	Finland	50	14	27	41	88	...	...	...	—	—	—	—	—
97-98—Los Angeles	NHL	8	0	0	0	6	-5	0	0	—	—	—	—	—
—HIFK Helsinki	Finland	30	11	28	39	8	...	...	...	9	7	2	9	2
NHL Totals (1 year)		8	0	0	0	6	-5	0	0					

JOMPHE, J.F.   C   COYOTES

PERSONAL: Born December 28, 1972, in Harve St. Pierre, Que. ... 6-1/195. ... Shoots left. ... Full name: Jean-Francois Jomphe. ... Name pronounced ZHOHMF.
TRANSACTIONS/CAREER NOTES: Signed as free agent by Mighty Ducks of Anaheim (September 7, 1993). ... Loaned by Mighty Ducks to Canadian national team (September 28, 1994). ... Strained abdominal muscle (March 7, 1997); missed final 16 games of season. ... Traded by Mighty Ducks to Phoenix Coyotes for LW Jim McKenzie (June 18, 1998).
MISCELLANEOUS: Failed to score on a penalty shot (vs. Curtis Joseph, April 15, 1998).

		REGULAR SEASON								PLAYOFFS				
Season Team	League	Gms.	G	A	Pts.	PIM	+/-	PP	SH	Gms.	G	A	Pts.	PIM
90-91—Shawinigan	QMJHL	42	17	22	39	14	...	...	...	6	2	1	3	2
91-92—Shawinigan	QMJHL	44	28	33	61	69	...	...	...	10	6	10	16	10
92-93—Sherbrooke	QMJHL	60	43	43	86	86	...	...	...	15	10	13	23	18
93-94—San Diego	IHL	29	2	3	5	12	...	...	...	—	—	—	—	—
—Greensboro	ECHL	25	9	9	18	41	...	...	...	1	1	0	1	0
94-95—Canadian nat'l team	Int'l	52	33	25	58	85	...	...	...	—	—	—	—	—
95-96—Baltimore	AHL	47	21	34	55	75	...	...	...	—	—	—	—	—
—Anaheim	NHL	31	2	12	14	39	7	2	0	—	—	—	—	—
96-97—Anaheim	NHL	64	7	14	21	53	-9	0	1	—	—	—	—	—
97-98—Cincinnati	AHL	38	9	19	28	32	...	...	...	—	—	—	—	—
—Anaheim	NHL	9	1	3	4	8	1	0	0	—	—	—	—	—
—Quebec	IHL	17	6	4	10	24	...	...	...	—	—	—	—	—
NHL Totals (3 years)		104	10	29	39	100	-1	2	1					

JONES, KEITH   RW   AVALANCHE

PERSONAL: Born November 8, 1968, in Brantford, Ont. ... 6-2/200. ... Shoots left.
COLLEGE: Western Michigan.
TRANSACTIONS/CAREER NOTES: Selected by Washington Capitals in seventh round (seventh Capitals pick, 141st overall) of NHL entry draft (June 11, 1988). ... Suffered from the flu (January 21, 1993); missed two games. ... Sprained wrist (January 25, 1994); missed six games. ... Injured foot (March 16, 1995); missed one game. ... Separated ribs and bruised foot (March 29, 1995); missed six games. ... Pulled groin (March 12, 1996); missed seven games. ... Reinjured groin (March 29, 1996); missed seven games. ... Traded by Capitals with first- (D Scott Parker) and fourth-round (traded back to Washington) picks in 1998 draft to Colorado Avalanche for D Curtis Leschyshyn and LW Chris Simon (November 2, 1996). ... Injured knee (April 26, 1997); missed remainder of playoffs. ... Injured knee and underwent surgery (October 1, 1997); missed 58 games.
HONORS: Named to CCHA All-Star first team (1991-92).
MISCELLANEOUS: Failed to score on a penalty shot (vs. Patrick Labrecque, November 1, 1995).

		REGULAR SEASON								PLAYOFFS				
Season Team	League	Gms.	G	A	Pts.	PIM	+/-	PP	SH	Gms.	G	A	Pts.	PIM
87-88—Niagara Falls	OHA	40	50	80	130	...	...	...	...	—	—	—	—	—
88-89—Western Michigan U.	CCHA	37	9	12	21	51	...	...	...	—	—	—	—	—
89-90—Western Michigan U.	CCHA	40	19	18	37	82	...	...	...	—	—	—	—	—
90-91—Western Michigan U.	CCHA	41	30	19	49	106	...	...	...	—	—	—	—	—
91-92—Western Michigan U.	CCHA	35	25	31	56	77	...	...	...	—	—	—	—	—
—Baltimore	AHL	6	2	4	6	0	...	...	...	—	—	—	—	—
92-93—Baltimore	AHL	8	7	3	10	4	...	...	...	—	—	—	—	—
—Washington	NHL	71	12	14	26	124	18	0	0	6	0	0	0	10
93-94—Washington	NHL	68	16	19	35	149	4	5	0	11	0	1	1	36
—Portland	AHL	6	5	7	12	4	...	...	...	—	—	—	—	—
94-95—Washington	NHL	40	14	6	20	65	-2	1	0	7	4	4	8	22
95-96—Washington	NHL	68	18	23	41	103	8	5	0	2	0	0	0	7
96-97—Washington	NHL	11	2	3	5	13	-2	1	0	—	—	—	—	—
—Colorado	NHL	67	23	20	43	105	5	13	1	6	3	3	6	4
97-98—Colorado	NHL	23	3	7	10	22	-4	1	0	7	0	0	0	13
—Hershey	AHL	4	2	1	3	2	...	...	...	—	—	—	—	—
NHL Totals (6 years)		348	88	92	180	581	27	26	1	39	7	8	15	92

JONES, TY   RW   BLACKHAWKS

PERSONAL: Born February 22, 1979, in Richland, Wash. ... 6-3/218. ... Shoots right.
TRANSACTIONS/CAREER NOTES: Selected by Chicago Blackhawks in first round (second Blackhawks pick, 16th overall) of NHL entry draft (June 21, 1997).

J

Season Team	League	REGULAR SEASON								PLAYOFFS				
		Gms.	G	A	Pts.	PIM	+/-	PP	SH	Gms.	G	A	Pts.	PIM
95-96—Spokane	WHL	34	1	0	1	77	...	...	...	3	0	0	0	6
96-97—Spokane	WHL	67	20	34	54	202	...	...	...	9	2	4	6	...
97-98—Spokane	WHL	60	36	48	84	161	...	...	...	18	2	14	16	35

JONSSON, JORGEN   LW   ISLANDERS

PERSONAL: Born September 29, 1972, in Angelholm, Sweden. ... 6-0/185. ... Shoots left. ... Name pronounced YOHR-guhn YAHN-suhn.
TRANSACTIONS/CAREER NOTES: Selected by Calgary Flames in ninth round (11th Flames pick, 227th overall) of NHL entry draft (June 29, 1994). ... Rights traded by Flames to New York Islanders for C Jan Hlavac (July 14, 1998).

Season Team	League	REGULAR SEASON								PLAYOFFS				
		Gms.	G	A	Pts.	PIM	+/-	PP	SH	Gms.	G	A	Pts.	PIM
92-93—Rogle Angelholm	Sweden	40	17	11	28	28	...	...	...	—	—	—	—	—
93-94—Rogle Angelholm	Sweden	40	17	14	31	46	...	...	...	—	—	—	—	—
94-95—Rogle Angelholm	Sweden	22	4	6	10	18	...	...	...	—	—	—	—	—
95-96—Farjestad Karlstad	Sweden	39	11	15	26	36	...	...	...	8	0	4	4	6
96-97—Farjestad Karlstad	Sweden	49	12	21	33	58	...	...	...	14	9	5	14	14
97-98—Farjestad Karlstad	Sweden	45	22	25	47	53	...	...	...	12	2	9	11	12
—Swedish Oly. team	Int'l	1	0	0	0	0	...	...	...	—	—	—	—	—

JONSSON, KENNY   D   ISLANDERS

PERSONAL: Born October 5, 1974, in Angelholm, Sweden. ... 6-3/195. ... Shoots left. ... Name pronounced YAHN-suhn.
TRANSACTIONS/CAREER NOTES: Selected by Toronto Maple Leafs in first round (first Maple Leafs pick, 12th overall) of NHL entry draft (June 26, 1993). ... Played in Europe during 1994-95 NHL lockout. ... Suffered from the flu (February 13, 1995); missed two games. ... Strained hip flexor (February 27, 1995); missed one game. ... Suffered hip pointer (April 7, 1995); missed one game. ... Suffered from the flu (April 19, 1995); missed one game. ... Strained back (December 9, 1995); missed one game. ... Separated shoulder (January 30, 1996); missed 17 games. ... Traded by Maple Leafs with C Darby Hendrickson, LW Sean Haggerty and first-round pick (G Robert Luongo) in 1997 draft to New York Islanders for LW Wendel Clark, D Mathieu Schneider and D D.J. Smith (March 13, 1996). ... Suffered from the flu (December 23, 1996); missed one game. ... Injured knee (February 4, 1998); missed one game.
HONORS: Named Swedish League Rookie of the Year (1992-93). ... Named to NHL All-Rookie team (1994-95).

Season Team	League	REGULAR SEASON								PLAYOFFS				
		Gms.	G	A	Pts.	PIM	+/-	PP	SH	Gms.	G	A	Pts.	PIM
91-92—Rogle Angelholm	Sweden	30	4	11	15	24	...	...	...	—	—	—	—	—
92-93—Rogle Angelholm	Sweden	39	3	10	13	42	...	...	...	—	—	—	—	—
93-94—Rogle Angelholm	Sweden	36	4	13	17	40	...	...	...	3	1	1	2	...
—Swedish Oly. team	Int'l	3	1	0	1	0	...	...	...	—	—	—	—	—
94-95—Rogle Angelholm	Sweden	8	3	1	4	20	...	...	...	—	—	—	—	—
—St. John's	AHL	10	2	5	7	2	...	...	...	—	—	—	—	—
—Toronto	NHL	39	2	7	9	16	-8	0	0	4	0	0	0	0
95-96—Toronto	NHL	50	4	22	26	22	12	3	0	—	—	—	—	—
—New York Islanders	NHL	16	0	4	4	10	-5	0	0	—	—	—	—	—
96-97—New York Islanders	NHL	81	3	18	21	24	10	1	0	—	—	—	—	—
97-98—New York Islanders	NHL	81	14	26	40	58	-2	6	0	—	—	—	—	—
NHL Totals (4 years)		267	23	77	100	130	7	10	0	4	0	0	0	0

JOSEPH, CHRIS   D   FLYERS

PERSONAL: Born September 10, 1969, in Burnaby, B.C. ... 6-2/210. ... Shoots right. ... Full name: Robin Christopher Joseph.
HIGH SCHOOL: Alpha (Burnaby, B.C.).
TRANSACTIONS/CAREER NOTES: Selected by Pittsburgh Penguins in first round (first Penguins pick, fifth overall) of NHL entry draft (June 13, 1987). ... Traded by Penguins with C Craig Simpson, C Dave Hannan and D Moe Mantha to Edmonton Oilers for D Paul Coffey, LW Dave Hunter and RW Wayne Van Dorp (November 24, 1987). ... Strained knee ligaments (January 1989). ... Traded by Oilers to Tampa Bay Lightning for D Bob Beers (November 12, 1993). ... Selected by Pittsburgh Penguins in waiver draft for cash (January 18, 1995). ... Injured knee (March 2, 1995); missed 14 games. ... Injured knee (March 7, 1996); missed four games. ... Selected by Vancouver Canucks in NHL waiver draft for cash (September 30, 1996). ... Injured groin (December 18, 1996); missed seven games. ... Suffered from the flu (February 27, 1997); missed two games. ... Signed as free agent by Philadelphia Flyers (September 4, 1997).

Season Team	League	REGULAR SEASON								PLAYOFFS				
		Gms.	G	A	Pts.	PIM	+/-	PP	SH	Gms.	G	A	Pts.	PIM
85-86—Seattle	WHL	72	4	8	12	50	...	...	...	5	0	3	3	12
86-87—Seattle	WHL	67	13	45	58	155	...	...	...	—	—	—	—	—
87-88—Pittsburgh	NHL	17	0	4	4	12	2	0	0	—	—	—	—	—
—Edmonton	NHL	7	0	4	4	6	-3	0	0	—	—	—	—	—
—Nova Scotia	AHL	8	0	2	2	8	...	...	...	4	0	0	0	9
—Seattle	WHL	23	5	14	19	49	...	...	...	—	—	—	—	—
88-89—Cape Breton	AHL	5	1	1	2	18	...	...	...	—	—	—	—	—
—Edmonton	NHL	44	4	5	9	54	-9	0	0	—	—	—	—	—
89-90—Edmonton	NHL	4	0	2	2	2	-2	0	0	—	—	—	—	—
—Cape Breton	AHL	61	10	20	30	69	...	...	...	6	2	1	3	4
90-91—Edmonton	NHL	49	5	17	22	59	3	2	0	—	—	—	—	—
91-92—Edmonton	NHL	7	0	0	0	8	-1	0	0	5	1	3	4	2
—Cape Breton	AHL	63	14	29	43	72	...	...	...	5	0	2	2	8
92-93—Edmonton	NHL	33	2	10	12	48	-9	1	0	—	—	—	—	—
93-94—Edmonton	NHL	10	1	1	2	28	-8	1	0	—	—	—	—	—
—Tampa Bay	NHL	66	10	19	29	108	-13	7	0	—	—	—	—	—
94-95—Pittsburgh	NHL	33	5	10	15	46	3	3	0	10	1	1	2	12
95-96—Pittsburgh	NHL	70	5	14	19	71	6	0	0	15	1	0	1	8

Season Team	League	REGULAR SEASON								PLAYOFFS				
		Gms.	G	A	Pts.	PIM	+/-	PP	SH	Gms.	G	A	Pts.	PIM
96-97—Vancouver	NHL	63	3	13	16	62	-21	2	0	—	—	—	—	—
97-98—Philadelphia	NHL	15	1	0	1	19	1	0	0	1	0	0	0	2
—Philadelphia	AHL	6	2	3	5	2	...	...	...	—	—	—	—	—
NHL Totals (11 years)		418	36	99	135	523	-51	16	0	31	3	4	7	24

JOSEPH, CURTIS   G   MAPLE LEAFS

PERSONAL: Born April 29, 1967, in Keswick, Ont. ... 5-10/182. ... Catches left. ... Full name: Curtis Shayne Joseph. ... Nickname: Cujo.
HIGH SCHOOL: Huron Heights (Newmarket, Ont.).
COLLEGE: Wisconsin.
TRANSACTIONS/CAREER NOTES: Signed as free agent by St. Louis Blues (June 16, 1989). ... Dislocated left shoulder (April 11, 1990). ... Underwent surgery to left shoulder (May 10, 1990). ... Sprained right knee (February 26, 1991); missed remainder of season. ... Injured ankle (March 12, 1992); missed seven games. ... Suffered sore knee (January 2, 1993); missed three games. ... Suffered from the flu (February 9, 1993); missed one game. ... Slightly strained groin (January 26, 1995); missed three games. ... Pulled hamstring (April 16, 1995); missed four games. ... Rights traded by Blues with rights to RW Michael Grier to Edmonton Oilers for first-round picks in 1996 (C Marty Reasoner) and 1997 (traded to Los Angeles) drafts (August 4, 1995); picks had been awarded to Oilers as compensation for Blues signing free agent LW Shayne Corson (July 28, 1995). ... Injured right knee (March 30, 1996); missed three games. ... Strained groin (December 18, 1996); missed seven games. ... Signed as free agent by Toronto Maple Leafs (July 15, 1998).
HONORS: Named OHA Most Valuable Player (1986-87). ... Won WCHA Most Valuable Player Award (1988-89). ... Won WCHA Rookie of the Year Award (1988-89). ... Named to NCAA All-America West second team (1988-89). ... Named to WCHA All-Star first team (1988-89). ... Played in NHL All-Star Game (1994).
MISCELLANEOUS: Stopped a penalty shot attempt (vs. Greg Adams, January 25, 1992; vs. Todd Elik, April 16, 1992; vs. Phil Housley, December 19, 1992; vs. Mike Donnelly, April 7, 1994; vs. J.F. Jomphe, April 15, 1998). ... Allowed penalty shot goal (vs. Valeri Kamensky, October 26, 1996). ... Holds Edmonton Oilers all-time records for most shutouts (14) and goals-against average (2.90).
STATISTICAL NOTES: Led NHL with .911 save percentage (1992-93).

Season Team	League	REGULAR SEASON								PLAYOFFS						
		Gms.	Min.	W	L	T	GA	SO	Avg.	Gms.	Min.	W	L	GA	SO	Avg.
86-87—Richmond Hill	OHA										Statistics unavailable.					
87-88—Notre Dame	SCMHL	36	2174	25	4	7	94	1	2.59	—	—	—	—	—	—	—
88-89—Univ. of Wisconsin	WCHA	38	2267	21	11	5	94	1	2.49	—	—	—	—	—	—	—
89-90—Peoria	IHL	23	1241	10	8	‡2	80	0	3.87	—	—	—	—	—	—	—
—St. Louis	NHL	15	852	9	5	1	48	0	3.38	6	327	4	1	18	0	3.30
90-91—St. Louis	NHL	30	1710	16	10	2	89	0	3.12	—	—	—	—	—	—	—
91-92—St. Louis	NHL	60	3494	27	20	10	175	2	3.01	6	379	2	4	23	0	3.64
92-93—St. Louis	NHL	68	3890	29	28	9	196	1	3.02	11	715	7	4	27	2	2.27
93-94—St. Louis	NHL	71	4127	36	23	11	213	1	3.10	4	246	0	4	15	0	3.66
94-95—St. Louis	NHL	36	1914	20	10	1	89	1	2.79	7	392	3	3	24	0	3.67
95-96—Las Vegas	IHL	15	873	12	2	‡1	29	1	1.99	—	—	—	—	—	—	—
—Edmonton	NHL	34	1936	15	16	2	111	0	3.44	—	—	—	—	—	—	—
96-97—Edmonton	NHL	72	4100	32	29	9	200	6	2.93	12	767	5	†7	36	2	2.82
97-98—Edmonton	NHL	71	4132	29	31	9	181	8	2.63	12	716	5	7	23	3	1.93
NHL Totals (9 years)		457	26155	213	172	54	1302	19	2.99	58	3542	26	30	166	7	2.81

JOVANOVSKI, ED   D   PANTHERS

PERSONAL: Born June 26, 1976, in Windsor, Ont. ... 6-2/205. ... Shoots left. ... Name pronounced joh-vuh-NAHV-skee.
HIGH SCHOOL: Riverside Secondary (Windsor, Ont.).
TRANSACTIONS/CAREER NOTES: Selected by Florida Panthers in first round (first Panthers pick, first overall) of NHL entry draft (June 28, 1994). ... Broke right index finger (September 29, 1995); missed first 11 games of season. ... Sprained knee (January 15, 1997); missed 16 games.
HONORS: Named to Can.HL All-Rookie team (1993-94). ... Named to OHL All-Star second team (1993-94). ... Named to OHL All-Rookie team (1993-94). ... Named to Can.HL All-Star second team (1994-95). ... Named to OHL All-Star first team (1994-95). ... Named to NHL All-Rookie team (1995-96).

Season Team	League	REGULAR SEASON								PLAYOFFS				
		Gms.	G	A	Pts.	PIM	+/-	PP	SH	Gms.	G	A	Pts.	PIM
92-93—Windsor	OHL Jr. B	48	7	46	53	88	...	...	...	—	—	—	—	—
93-94—Windsor	OHL	62	15	35	50	221	...	...	...	4	0	0	0	15
94-95—Windsor	OHL	50	23	42	65	198	...	...	...	9	2	7	9	39
95-96—Florida	NHL	70	10	11	21	137	-3	2	0	22	1	8	9	52
96-97—Florida	NHL	61	7	16	23	137	-1	3	0	5	0	0	0	4
97-98—Florida	NHL	81	9	14	23	158	-12	2	1					
NHL Totals (3 years)		212	26	41	67	467	-16	7	1	27	1	8	9	56

JUNEAU, JOE   C   CAPITALS

PERSONAL: Born January 5, 1968, in Pont-Rouge, Que. ... 6-0/195. ... Shoots left. ... Name pronounced zhoh-AY ZHOO-noh.
COLLEGE: Rensselaer Polytechnic Institute (N.Y.).
TRANSACTIONS/CAREER NOTES: Selected by Boston Bruins in fourth round (third Bruins pick, 81st overall) of NHL entry draft (June 11, 1988). ... Suffered ligament problem in back (November 1990). ... Broke jaw (November 7, 1993); missed seven games. ... Reinjured jaw (February 18, 1994); missed two games. ... Traded by Bruins to Washington Capitals for D Al Iafrate (March 21, 1994). ... Strained hip flexor (January 29, 1995); missed one game. ... Strained back (February 15, 1995); missed one game. ... Bruised arm (April 11, 1995); missed one game. ... Injured leg (April 30, 1995); missed one game. ... Suffered from the flu (January 17, 1996); missed two games. ... Pulled hamstring (November 19, 1996); missed eight games. ... Bruised back and shoulder (January 1, 1997); missed two games. ... Sprained shoulder (February 7, 1997); missed four games. ... Sprained shoulder (February 18, 1997); missed five games. ... Strained hip (March 26, 1997); missed four games. ... Strained hip (April 12, 1997); missed one game. ... Injured groin (October 29, 1997); missed eight games. ... Injured knee (December 13, 1997); missed 16 games.

HONORS: Named to NCAA All-America East first team (1989-90). ... Named to ECAC All-Star first team (1989-90). ... Named to NCAA All-America East second team (1990-91). ... Named to ECAC All-Star second team (1990-91). ... Named to NHL All-Rookie team (1992-93).
RECORDS: Holds NHL single-season record for most assists by a left winger—70 (1992-93). ... Holds NHL single-season record for most assists by a rookie—70 (1992-93).
STATISTICAL PLATEAUS: Three-goal games: 1992-93 (1), 1996-97 (1). Total: 2.
MISCELLANEOUS: Member of silver-medal-winning Canadian Olympic team (1992).

Season Team	League	REGULAR SEASON								PLAYOFFS				
		Gms.	G	A	Pts.	PIM	+/-	PP	SH	Gms.	G	A	Pts.	PIM
87-88—R.P.I.	ECAC	31	16	29	45	18	...	...	...	—	—	—	—	—
88-89—R.P.I.	ECAC	30	12	23	35	40	...	...	...	—	—	—	—	—
89-90—R.P.I.	ECAC	34	18	*52	*70	31	...	...	...	—	—	—	—	—
—Canadian nat'l team	Int'l	3	0	2	2	4	...	...	...	—	—	—	—	—
90-91—R.P.I.	ECAC	29	23	40	63	70	...	...	...	—	—	—	—	—
—Canadian nat'l team	Int'l	7	2	3	5	0	...	...	...	—	—	—	—	—
91-92—Canadian nat'l team	Int'l	60	20	49	69	35	...	...	...	—	—	—	—	—
—Can. Olympic Team	Int'l	8	6	9	15	4	...	...	...	—	—	—	—	—
—Boston	NHL	14	5	14	19	4	6	2	0	15	4	8	12	21
92-93—Boston	NHL	84	32	70	102	33	23	9	0	4	2	4	6	6
93-94—Boston	NHL	63	14	58	72	35	11	4	0	—	—	—	—	—
—Washington	NHL	11	5	8	13	6	0	2	0	11	4	5	9	6
94-95—Washington	NHL	44	5	38	43	8	-1	3	0	7	2	6	8	2
95-96—Washington	NHL	80	14	50	64	30	-3	7	2	5	0	7	7	6
96-97—Washington	NHL	58	15	27	42	8	-11	9	1	—	—	—	—	—
97-98—Washington	NHL	56	9	22	31	26	-8	4	1	21	7	10	17	8
NHL Totals (7 years)		410	99	287	386	150	17	40	4	63	19	40	59	49

KABERLE, TOMAS   D   MAPLE LEAFS

PERSONAL: Born March 2, 1978, in Rakovnik, Czechoslovakia. ... 6-1/186. ... Shoots left.
TRANSACTIONS/CAREER NOTES: Selected by Toronto Maple Leafs in eighth round (13th Maple Leafs pick, 204th overall) of NHL entry draft (June 22, 1996).

Season Team	League	REGULAR SEASON								PLAYOFFS				
		Gms.	G	A	Pts.	PIM	+/-	PP	SH	Gms.	G	A	Pts.	PIM
95-96—Poldi Kladno Jrs.	Czech Rep.	23	6	13	19	19	...	...	...	—	—	—	—	—
—Poldi Kladno	Czech Rep.	23	0	1	1	2	...	...	...	2	0	0	0	0
96-97—Poldi Kladno	Czech Rep.	49	0	5	5	26	...	...	...	3	0	0	0	0
97-98—Poldi Kladno	Czech Rep.	47	4	19	23	12	...	...	...	—	—	—	—	—
—St. John's	AHL	2	0	0	0	0	...	...	...	—	—	—	—	—

KALLARSSON, TOMI   D   RANGERS

PERSONAL: Born March 15, 1979, in Lempaala, Finland. ... 6-3/194. ... Shoots left. ... Name pronounced TAH-mee CHEH-luhr-suhn.
TRANSACTIONS/CAREER NOTES: Selected by New York Rangers in fourth round (fourth Rangers pick, 93rd overall) of NHL entry draft (June 21, 1997).

Season Team	League	REGULAR SEASON								PLAYOFFS				
		Gms.	G	A	Pts.	PIM	+/-	PP	SH	Gms.	G	A	Pts.	PIM
95-96—Tappara Tampere Jrs.	Finland	31	3	5	8	24	...	...	...	6	0	3	3	0
96-97—HPK Hameenlinna	Finland	31	1	3	4	26	...	...	...	—	—	—	—	—
97-98—HPK Hameenlinna	Finland	12	0	0	0	2	...	...	...	—	—	—	—	—

KALMIKOV, KONSTANTIN   C   MAPLE LEAFS

PERSONAL: Born June 14, 1978, in Kharkov, U.S.S.R. ... 6-4/205. ... Shoots right. ... Name pronounced KAL-mih-kahv.
TRANSACTIONS/CAREER NOTES: Selected by Toronto Maple Leafs in third round (fourth Maple Leafs pick, 68th overall) of NHL entry draft (June 22, 1996).

Season Team	League	REGULAR SEASON								PLAYOFFS				
		Gms.	G	A	Pts.	PIM	+/-	PP	SH	Gms.	G	A	Pts.	PIM
95-96—Flint	Col.HL	38	4	12	16	16	...	...	...	—	—	—	—	—
—Detroit	Col.HL	5	0	1	1	0	...	...	...	—	—	—	—	—
96-97—Sudbury	OHL	66	22	34	56	25	...	...	...	—	—	—	—	—
—St. John's	AHL	2	0	0	0	0	...	...	...	—	—	—	—	—
97-98—Sudbury	OHL	66	32	32	64	21	...	...	...	10	7	2	9	2

KAMENSKY, VALERI   LW   AVALANCHE

PERSONAL: Born April 18, 1966, in Voskresensk, U.S.S.R. ... 6-2/198. ... Shoots right. ... Name pronounced kuh-MEHN-skee.
TRANSACTIONS/CAREER NOTES: Selected by Quebec Nordiques in seventh round (eighth Nordiques pick, 129th overall) of NHL entry draft (June 11, 1988). ... Fractured leg (October 1991); missed 57 games. ... Broke left thumb (October 17, 1992); missed three games. ... Broke right ankle (October 27, 1992); missed 47 games. ... Bruised left foot (October 21, 1993); missed two games. ... Bruised right foot (December 21, 1993); missed one game. ... Played in Europe during 1994-95 NHL lockout. ... Suffered kidney infection (February 26, 1995); missed eight games. ... Nordiques franchise moved to Colorado and renamed Avalanche for 1995-96 season (June 21, 1995). ... Bruised ribs (January 3, 1996); missed one game. ... Separated shoulder (December 31, 1996); missed six games. ... Injured shoulder (February 25, 1997); missed three games. ... Bruised shoulder (December 13, 1997); missed three games. ... Suffered from the flu (December 31, 1997); missed two games.
HONORS: Won Soviet Player of the Year Award (1990-91). ... Played in NHL All-Star Game (1998).
MISCELLANEOUS: Member of Stanley Cup championship team (1996). ... Member of gold-medal-winning U.S.S.R. Olympic team (1988). ... Scored on penalty shot (vs. Curtis Joseph, October 26, 1996). ... Member of silver-medal-winning Russian Olympic team (1998).
STATISTICAL PLATEAUS: Three-goal games: 1995-96 (2), 1996-97 (1), 1997-98 (1). Total: 4.

Season Team	League	REGULAR SEASON Gms.	G	A	Pts.	PIM	+/-	PP	SH	PLAYOFFS Gms.	G	A	Pts.	PIM
82-83—Khimik	USSR	5	0	0	0	0	...	...	...	—	—	—	—	—
83-84—Khimik	USSR	20	2	2	4	6	...	...	...	—	—	—	—	—
84-85—Khimik	USSR	45	9	3	12	24	...	...	...	—	—	—	—	—
85-86—CSKA Moscow	USSR	40	15	9	24	8	...	...	...	—	—	—	—	—
86-87—CSKA Moscow	USSR	37	13	8	21	16	...	...	...	—	—	—	—	—
87-88—CSKA Moscow	USSR	51	26	20	46	40	...	...	...	—	—	—	—	—
—Soviet Olympic Team	WHL	8	4	2	6	4	...	...	...	—	—	—	—	—
88-89—CSKA Moscow	USSR	40	18	10	28	30	...	...	...	—	—	—	—	—
89-90—CSKA Moscow	USSR	45	19	18	37	38	...	...	...	—	—	—	—	—
90-91—CSKA Moscow	USSR	46	20	26	46	66	...	...	...	—	—	—	—	—
91-92—Quebec	NHL	23	7	14	21	14	-1	2	0	—	—	—	—	—
92-93—Quebec	NHL	32	15	22	37	14	13	2	3	6	0	1	1	6
93-94—Quebec	NHL	76	28	37	65	42	12	6	0	—	—	—	—	—
94-95—Ambri Piotta	Switzerland	12	13	6	19	2	...	...	...	—	—	—	—	—
—Quebec	NHL	40	10	20	30	22	3	5	1	2	1	0	1	0
95-96—Colorado	NHL	81	38	47	85	85	14	18	1	22	10	12	22	28
96-97—Colorado	NHL	68	28	38	66	38	5	8	0	17	8	14	22	16
97-98—Colorado	NHL	75	26	40	66	60	-2	8	0	7	2	3	5	18
—Russian Oly. team	Int'l	6	1	2	3	0	...	...	...	—	—	—	—	—
NHL Totals (7 years)		395	152	218	370	275	44	49	5	54	21	30	51	68

KAPANEN, SAMI   LW   HURRICANES

K

PERSONAL: Born June 14, 1973, in Vantaa, Finland. ... 5-10/173. ... Shoots left. ... Name pronounced KAP-ih-nehn.

TRANSACTIONS/CAREER NOTES: Selected by Hartford Whalers in fourth round (fourth Whalers pick, 87th overall) of NHL entry draft (July 8, 1995). ... Suffered from the flu (October 20, 1996); missed two games. ... Sprained knee (November 30, 1996); missed 16 games. ... Sprained knee (January 10, 1997); missed nine games. ... Sprained knee (February 26, 1997); missed three games. ... Sprained knee (March 15, 1997); missed six games. ... Suffered from the flu (April 5, 1997); missed one game. ... Whalers franchise moved to North Carolina and renamed Carolina Hurricanes for 1997-98 season; NHL approved move on June 25, 1997. ... Suffered from the flu (March 12, 1998); missed one game.

MISCELLANEOUS: Scored on a penalty shot (vs. Jim Carey, March 12, 1997). ... Member of bronze-medal-winning Finnish Olympic team (1998).

STATISTICAL PLATEAUS: Three-goal games: 1997-98 (2).

Season Team	League	REGULAR SEASON Gms.	G	A	Pts.	PIM	+/-	PP	SH	PLAYOFFS Gms.	G	A	Pts.	PIM
90-91—KalPa Kuopio	Finland	14	1	2	3	2	...	...	...	8	2	1	3	2
91-92—KalPa Kuopio	Finland	42	15	10	25	8	...	...	...	—	—	—	—	—
92-93—KalPa Kuopio	Finland	37	4	17	21	12	...	...	...	—	—	—	—	—
93-94—KalPa Kuopio	Finland	48	23	32	55	16	...	...	...	—	—	—	—	—
94-95—HIFK Helsinki	Finland	49	14	28	42	42	...	...	...	3	0	0	0	0
95-96—Springfield	AHL	28	14	17	31	4	...	...	...	3	1	2	3	0
—Hartford	NHL	35	5	4	9	6	0	0	0	—	—	—	—	—
96-97—Hartford	NHL	45	13	12	25	2	6	3	0	—	—	—	—	—
97-98—Carolina	NHL	81	26	37	63	16	9	4	0	—	—	—	—	—
—Fin. Olympic Team	Int'l	6	0	1	1	0	...	...	...	—	—	—	—	—
NHL Totals (3 years)		161	44	53	97	24	15	7	0					

KARALAHTI, JERE   D   KINGS

PERSONAL: Born March 25, 1975, in Helsinki, Finland. ... 6-2/185. ... Shoots right. ... Name pronounced YAIR-ee KAIR-uh-LAH-tee.

TRANSACTIONS/CAREER NOTES: Selected by Los Angeles Kings in sixth round (seventh Kings pick, 146th overall) of NHL entry draft (June 26, 1993).

Season Team	League	REGULAR SEASON Gms.	G	A	Pts.	PIM	+/-	PP	SH	PLAYOFFS Gms.	G	A	Pts.	PIM
91-92—HIFK Juniors	Finland Jrs.	30	12	5	17	36	...	...	...	—	—	—	—	—
92-93—HIFK Juniors	Finland Jrs.	30	2	13	15	49	...	...	...	—	—	—	—	—
93-94—HIFK Helsinki	Finland	46	1	10	11	36	...	...	...	3	0	0	0	6
94-95—HIFK Helsinki	Finland	37	1	7	8	42	...	...	...	3	0	0	0	0
95-96—HIFK Helsinki	Finland	36	4	6	10	102	...	...	...	3	0	0	0	4
96-97—HIFK Helsinki	Finland	18	3	5	8	20	...	...	...	—	—	—	—	—
97-98—HIFK Helsinki	Finland	43	14	16	30	32	...	...	...	9	2	0	2	8

KARIYA, PAUL   LW   MIGHTY DUCKS

PERSONAL: Born October 16, 1974, in Vancouver. ... 5-11/180. ... Shoots left. ... Name pronounced kuh-REE-uh.

COLLEGE: Maine.

TRANSACTIONS/CAREER NOTES: Selected by Mighty Ducks of Anaheim in first round (first Mighty Ducks pick, fourth overall) of NHL entry draft (June 26, 1993). ... Suffered lower back spasms (February 12, 1995); missed one game. ... Strained abdominal muscle prior to 1996 season; missed first 11 games of season. ... Suffered mild concussion (November 13, 1996); missed two games. ... Missed first 32 games of 1997-98 season due to contract dispute. ... Suffered concussion (February 1, 1998); missed remainder of season.

HONORS: Won Hobey Baker Memorial Award (1992-93). ... Named Hockey East Player of the Year (1992-93). ... Named Hockey East Rookie of the Year (1992-93). ... Named to NCAA All-America East first team (1992-93). ... Named to NCAA All-Tournament team (1992-93). ... Named to Hockey East All-Star first team (1992-93). ... Named to Hockey East All-Rookie team (1992-93). ... Named to Hockey East All-Decade team (1994). ... Named to NHL All-Rookie team (1994-95). ... Played in NHL All-Star Game (1996 and 1997). ... Won Lady Byng Memorial Trophy (1995-96 and 1996-97). ... Named to NHL All-Star first team (1995-96 and 1996-97).

MISCELLANEOUS: Member of silver-medal-winning Canadian Olympic team (1994). ... Captain of Mighty Ducks of Anaheim (1996-97 and December 11, 1997 through February 4, 1998). ... Holds Mighty Ducks of Anaheim all-time records for most goals (129), most assists (148) and most points (277). ... Scored on a penalty shot (vs. Kevin Weekes, January 21, 1998).

STATISTICAL NOTES: Led NHL with 10 game-winning goals (1996-97).
STATISTICAL PLATEAUS: Three-goal games: 1996-97 (2), 1997-98 (1). Total: 3.

Season Team	League	REGULAR SEASON								PLAYOFFS				
		Gms.	G	A	Pts.	PIM	+/-	PP	SH	Gms.	G	A	Pts.	PIM
90-91—Penticton	BCJHL	54	45	67	112	8	...	...	...	—	—	—	—	—
91-92—Penticton	BCJHL	40	46	86	132	16	...	...	...	—	—	—	—	—
92-93—Univ. of Maine	Hockey East	39	25	*75	*100	12	...	...	...	—	—	—	—	—
93-94—Canadian nat'l team ...	Int'l	23	7	34	41	2	...	...	...	—	—	—	—	—
—Can. Olympic Team ...	Int'l	8	3	4	7	2	...	...	...	—	—	—	—	—
—Univ. of Maine	Hockey East	12	8	16	24	4	...	...	...	—	—	—	—	—
94-95—Anaheim	NHL	47	18	21	39	4	-17	7	1	—	—	—	—	—
95-96—Anaheim	NHL	82	50	58	108	20	9	20	3	—	—	—	—	—
96-97—Anaheim	NHL	69	44	55	99	6	36	15	3	11	7	6	13	4
97-98—Anaheim	NHL	22	17	14	31	23	12	3	0	—	—	—	—	—
NHL Totals (4 years)...........		220	129	148	277	53	40	45	7	11	7	6	13	4

KARLIN, MATTIAS   C   BRUINS

PERSONAL: Born July 4, 1979, in Ornskoldsvik, Sweden. ... 5-11/183. ... Shoots left.
TRANSACTIONS/CAREER NOTES: Selected by Boston Bruins in third round (fourth Bruins pick, 54th overall) of NHL entry draft (June 21, 1997).

Season Team	League	REGULAR SEASON								PLAYOFFS				
		Gms.	G	A	Pts.	PIM	+/-	PP	SH	Gms.	G	A	Pts.	PIM
95-96—MoDo Ornsk. Jrs.	Sweden	30	12	23	35	16	...	...	...	—	—	—	—	—
96-97—MoDo Ornskoldvik......	Sweden	6	0	0	0	0	...	...	...	—	—	—	—	—
97-98—MoDo Ornskoldvik......	Sweden	32	0	2	2	8	...	...	...	1	0	0	0	0

KARPA, DAVE   D   HURRICANES

PERSONAL: Born May 7, 1971, in Regina, Sask. ... 6-1/210. ... Shoots right. ... Full name: David James Karpa.
COLLEGE: Ferris State (Mich.).
TRANSACTIONS/CAREER NOTES: Selected by Quebec Nordiques in fourth round (fourth Nordiques pick, 68th overall) of NHL entry draft (June 22, 1991). ... Broke right wrist (January 26, 1994); missed 18 games. ... Traded by Nordiques to Los Angeles Kings for fourth-round pick in 1995 or 1996 draft (February 28, 1995); trade invalidated by NHL because Karpa failed his physical examination (March 3, 1995). ... Traded by Nordiques to Mighty Ducks of Anaheim for fourth-round pick (traded to St. Louis) in 1997 draft (March 8, 1995). ... Underwent right wrist surgery (May 9, 1995). ... Bruised right knee (November 24, 1995); missed eight games. ... Fractured right hand (February 4, 1997); missed 13 games. ... Pulled hamstring (December 6, 1997); missed two games. ... Traded by Mighty Ducks with 4th round pick in 2000 draft to Carolina Hurricanes for LW Stu Grimson and D Kevin Haller (August 11, 1998).
MISCELLANEOUS: Holds Mighty Ducks of Anaheim all-time record for most penalty minutes (788).

Season Team	League	REGULAR SEASON								PLAYOFFS				
		Gms.	G	A	Pts.	PIM	+/-	PP	SH	Gms.	G	A	Pts.	PIM
88-89—Notre Dame	SCMHL	—	16	37	53	—	—	—	—	—	—	—	—	—
89-90—Notre Dame	SCMHL	43	9	19	28	271	...	...	...	—	—	—	—	—
90-91—Ferris State	CCHA	41	6	19	25	109	...	...	...	—	—	—	—	—
91-92—Ferris State	CCHA	34	7	12	19	124	...	...	...	—	—	—	—	—
—Halifax......................	AHL	2	0	0	0	4	...	...	...	—	—	—	—	—
—Quebec	NHL	4	0	0	0	14	2	0	0	—	—	—	—	—
92-93—Halifax	AHL	71	4	27	31	167	...	...	...	—	—	—	—	—
—Quebec	NHL	12	0	1	1	13	-6	0	0	3	0	0	0	0
93-94—Quebec	NHL	60	5	12	17	148	0	2	0	—	—	—	—	—
—Cornwall	AHL	1	0	0	0	0	...	...	...	12	2	2	4	27
94-95—Cornwall	AHL	6	0	2	2	19	...	...	...	—	—	—	—	—
—Quebec	NHL	2	0	0	0	0	-1	0	0	—	—	—	—	—
—Anaheim	NHL	26	1	5	6	91	0	0	0	—	—	—	—	—
95-96—Anaheim	NHL	72	3	16	19	270	-3	0	1	—	—	—	—	—
96-97—Anaheim	NHL	69	2	11	13	210	11	0	0	8	1	1	2	20
97-98—Anaheim	NHL	78	1	11	12	217	-3	0	0	—	—	—	—	—
NHL Totals (7 years)...........		323	12	56	68	963	0	2	1	11	1	1	2	20

KARPOVTSEV, ALEXANDER   D   RANGERS

PERSONAL: Born April 7, 1970, in Moscow, U.S.S.R. ... 6-3/215. ... Shoots right. ... Name pronounced KAHR-puht-sehf.
TRANSACTIONS/CAREER NOTES: Selected by Quebec Nordiques in seventh round (seventh Nordiques pick, 158th overall) of NHL entry draft (June 16, 1990). ... Traded by Nordiques to New York Rangers for D Mike Hurlbut (September 9, 1993). ... Bruised buttocks (October 9, 1993); missed one game. ... Bruised hip (November 3, 1993); missed six games. ... Reinjured hip (November 23, 1993); missed one game. ... Injured face (February 28, 1994); missed two games. ... Suffered injury (March 14, 1994); missed two games. ... Played in Europe during 1994-95 NHL lockout. ... Suffered sore ankle (April 14, 1995); missed one game. ... Hyperextended elbow (October 29, 1995); missed one game. ... Suffered back spasms (February 10, 1996); missed one game. ... Suffered back spasms (February 18, 1996); missed one game. ... Bruised thumb (March 13, 1996); missed two games. ... Suffered back spasms (March 27, 1996); missed six games. ... Bruised toe (April 3, 1997); missed one game. ... Hyperextended elbow (April 10, 1997); missed one game. ... Suffered throat infection (October 10, 1997); missed one game. ... Sprained right wrist (January 19, 1998); missed one game. ... Underwent wrist surgery (February 2, 1998); missed 28 games.
MISCELLANEOUS: Member of Stanley Cup championship team (1994). ... Member of silver-medal-winning Russian Olympic team (1998).

Season Team	League	REGULAR SEASON								PLAYOFFS				
		Gms.	G	A	Pts.	PIM	+/-	PP	SH	Gms.	G	A	Pts.	PIM
89-90—Dynamo Moscow........	USSR	35	1	1	2	27	...	...	...	—	—	—	—	—
90-91—Dynamo Moscow........	USSR	40	0	5	5	15	...	...	...	—	—	—	—	—
91-92—Dynamo Moscow........	CIS	28	3	2	5	22	...	...	...	—	—	—	—	—
92-93—Dynamo Moscow........	CIS	40	3	11	14	100	...	...	...	—	—	—	—	—

		REGULAR SEASON							PLAYOFFS				
Season Team	League	Gms.	G	A	Pts.	PIM	+/-	PP	SH	Gms.	G	A	Pts.	PIM
93-94—New York Rangers......	NHL	67	3	15	18	58	12	1	0	17	0	4	4	12
94-95—Dynamo Moscow........	CIS	13	0	2	2	10	...	...	...	—	—	—	—	—
—New York Rangers......	NHL	47	4	8	12	30	-4	1	0	8	1	0	1	0
95-96—New York Rangers......	NHL	40	2	16	18	26	12	1	0	6	0	1	1	4
96-97—New York Rangers......	NHL	77	9	29	38	59	1	6	1	13	1	3	4	20
97-98—New York Rangers......	NHL	47	3	7	10	38	-1	1	0	—	—	—	—	—
NHL Totals (5 years)............		**278**	**21**	**75**	**96**	**211**	**20**	**10**	**1**	**44**	**2**	**8**	**10**	**36**

KASPARAITIS, DARIUS   D   PENGUINS

PERSONAL: Born October 16, 1972, in Elektrenai, U.S.S.R. ... 5-11/209. ... Shoots left. ... Name pronounced kas-puhr-IGH-tihz.

TRANSACTIONS/CAREER NOTES: Selected by New York Islanders in first round (first Islanders pick, fifth overall) of NHL entry draft (June 20, 1992). ... Suffered back spasms (February 12, 1993); missed two games. ... Strained back (April 15, 1993); missed one game. ... Strained lower back (November 10, 1993); missed two games. ... Jammed wrist (March 5, 1994); missed four games. ... Tore knee ligament (February 20, 1995); missed remainder of season and first 15 games of 1995-96 season. ... Suffered from the flu (December 2, 1995); missed two games. ... Severed two tendons in right hand (December 9, 1995); missed 16 games. ... Injured groin (February 8, 1996); missed two games. ... Traded by Islanders with C Andreas Johansson to Pittsburgh Penguins for C Bryan Smolinski (November 17, 1996). ... Suffered concussion (December 23, 1996); missed two games. ... Suffered facial laceration (January 2, 1997); missed one game. ... Twisted ankle (January 23, 1997); missed one game. ... Suffered concussion (March 18, 1997); missed three games. ... Suffered from the flu (March 29, 1998); missed one game.

MISCELLANEOUS: Member of gold-medal-winning Unified Olympic team (1992). ... Member of silver-medal-winning Russian Olympic team (1998).

		REGULAR SEASON							PLAYOFFS				
Season Team	League	Gms.	G	A	Pts.	PIM	+/-	PP	SH	Gms.	G	A	Pts.	PIM
88-89—Dynamo Moscow........	USSR	3	0	0	0	0	...	...	...	—	—	—	—	—
89-90—Dynamo Moscow........	USSR	1	0	0	0	0	...	...	...	—	—	—	—	—
90-91—Dynamo Moscow........	USSR	17	0	1	1	10	...	...	...	—	—	—	—	—
91-92—Dynamo Moscow........	CIS	31	2	10	12	14	...	...	...	—	—	—	—	—
—Unif. Olympic Team	Sweden	8	0	2	2	2	...	...	...	—	—	—	—	—
92-93—Dynamo Moscow........	CIS	7	1	3	4	8	...	...	...	—	—	—	—	—
—New York Islanders.....	NHL	79	4	17	21	166	15	0	0	18	0	5	5	31
93-94—New York Islanders.....	NHL	76	1	10	11	142	-6	0	0	4	0	0	0	8
94-95—New York Islanders.....	NHL	13	0	1	1	22	-11	0	0	—	—	—	—	—
95-96—New York Islanders.....	NHL	46	1	7	8	93	-12	0	0	—	—	—	—	—
96-97—New York Islanders.....	NHL	18	0	5	5	16	-7	0	0	—	—	—	—	—
—Pittsburgh................	NHL	57	2	16	18	84	24	0	0	5	0	0	0	6
97-98—Pittsburgh................	NHL	81	4	8	12	127	3	0	2	5	0	0	0	8
—Russian Oly. team.......	Int'l	6	0	2	2	6	...	...	...	—	—	—	—	—
NHL Totals (6 years)............		**370**	**12**	**64**	**76**	**650**	**6**	**0**	**2**	**32**	**0**	**5**	**5**	**53**

KAVANAGH, PAT   RW   FLYERS

PERSONAL: Born March 14, 1979, in Ottawa. ... 6-3/192. ... Shoots right.

TRANSACTIONS/CAREER NOTES: Selected by Philadelphia Flyers in second round (second Flyers pick, 50th overall) of NHL entry draft (June 21, 1997).

		REGULAR SEASON							PLAYOFFS				
Season Team	League	Gms.	G	A	Pts.	PIM	+/-	PP	SH	Gms.	G	A	Pts.	PIM
96-97—Peterborough..............	OHL	43	6	8	14	53	...	...	...	11	1	1	2	12
97-98—Peterborough..............	OHL	66	10	16	26	85	...	...	...	4	1	0	1	6

KEALTY, JEFF   D   AVALANCHE

PERSONAL: Born April 9, 1976, in Framingham, Mass. ... 6-4/175. ... Shoots left. ... Full name: Jeffrey Kealty.

HIGH SCHOOL: Catholic Memorial (Boston).

COLLEGE: Boston University.

TRANSACTIONS/CAREER NOTES: Selected by Quebec Nordiques in first round (second Nordiques pick, 22nd overall) of NHL entry draft (June 28, 1994). ... Nordiques franchise moved to Colorado and renamed Avalanche for 1995-96 season (June 21, 1995).

		REGULAR SEASON							PLAYOFFS				
Season Team	League	Gms.	G	A	Pts.	PIM	+/-	PP	SH	Gms.	G	A	Pts.	PIM
90-91—Catholic Memorial.......	Mass. H.S.	5	0	2	2	0	...	...	...	—	—	—	—	—
91-92—Catholic Memorial.......	Mass. H.S.	25	2	13	15	8	...	...	...	—	—	—	—	—
92-93—Catholic Memorial.......	Mass. H.S.	24	3	22	25	10	...	...	...	—	—	—	—	—
93-94—Catholic Memorial.......	Mass. H.S.	25	10	22	32	...	...	...	...	—	—	—	—	—
94-95—Boston University	Hockey East	25	0	5	5	29	...	...	...	—	—	—	—	—
95-96—Boston University	Hockey East	35	4	14	18	38	...	...	...	—	—	—	—	—
96-97—Boston University	Hockey East	40	4	9	13	42	...	...	...	—	—	—	—	—
97-98—Boston University	Hockey East	38	11	15	26	53	...	...	...	—	—	—	—	—

KEANE, MIKE   RW   STARS

PERSONAL: Born May 29, 1967, in Winnipeg. ... 5-10/185. ... Shoots right. ... Name pronounced KEEN.

TRANSACTIONS/CAREER NOTES: Signed as free agent by Montreal Canadiens (March 1987). ... Separated right shoulder (December 21, 1988). ... Cut left kneecap (October 31, 1990); missed seven games. ... Injured neck (March 1991). ... Sprained ankle (January 16, 1992);

missed four games. ... Re-sprained ankle (February 1, 1992); missed 10 games. ... Bruised ankle (March 11, 1992); missed one game. ... Suspended four off-days and fined $500 by NHL for swinging stick in preseason game (October 13, 1992). ... Suffered wrist tendinitis (January 26, 1993); missed three games. ... Suffered back spasms (February 12, 1993); missed two games. ... Fractured toe (February 27, 1993); missed two games. ... Suffered back spasms (October 16, 1993); missed one game. ... Suffered back spasms (January 12, 1994); missed three games. ... Injured groin (November 1, 1995); missed one game. ... Injured neck (November 18, 1995); missed three games. ... Injured groin (November 25, 1995); missed two games. ... Traded by Canadiens with G Patrick Roy to Colorado Avalanche for G Jocelyn Thibault, LW Martin Rucinsky and RW Andrei Kovalenko (December 6, 1995). ... Signed as free agent by New York Rangers (July 7, 1997). ... Traded by Rangers with C Brian Skrudland and sixth-round pick (RW Pavel Patera) in 1998 draft to Dallas Stars for LW Bob Errey, RW Todd Harvey and fourth-round pick (LW Boyd Kane) in 1998 draft (March 24, 1998).

MISCELLANEOUS: Member of Stanley Cup championship team (1993 and 1996). ... Captain of Montreal Canadiens (1994-95 through December 6, 1995). ... Scored on a penalty shot (vs. Corey Schwab, October 24, 1997).

Season Team	League	REGULAR SEASON								PLAYOFFS				
		Gms.	G	A	Pts.	PIM	+/-	PP	SH	Gms.	G	A	Pts.	PIM
83-84—Winnipeg	WHL	1	0	0	0	0	...	...	...	—	—	—	—	—
84-85—Moose Jaw	WHL	65	17	26	43	141	...	...	...	—	—	—	—	—
85-86—Moose Jaw	WHL	67	34	49	83	162	...	...	...	13	6	8	14	9
86-87—Moose Jaw	WHL	53	25	45	70	107	...	...	...	9	3	9	12	11
—Sherbrooke	AHL	—	—	—	—	—				9	2	2	4	16
87-88—Sherbrooke	AHL	78	25	43	68	70	...	...	...	6	1	1	2	18
88-89—Montreal	NHL	69	16	19	35	69	9	5	0	21	4	3	7	17
89-90—Montreal	NHL	74	9	15	24	78	0	1	0	11	0	1	1	8
90-91—Montreal	NHL	73	13	23	36	50	6	2	1	12	3	2	5	6
91-92—Montreal	NHL	67	11	30	41	64	16	2	0	8	1	1	2	16
92-93—Montreal	NHL	77	15	45	60	95	29	0	0	19	2	13	15	6
93-94—Montreal	NHL	80	16	30	46	119	6	6	2	6	3	1	4	4
94-95—Montreal	NHL	48	10	10	20	15	5	1	0	—	—	—	—	—
95-96—Montreal	NHL	18	0	7	7	6	-6	0	0	—	—	—	—	—
—Colorado	NHL	55	10	10	20	40	1	0	2	22	3	2	5	16
96-97—Colorado	NHL	81	10	17	27	63	2	0	1	17	3	1	4	24
97-98—New York Rangers	NHL	70	8	10	18	47	-12	2	0	—	—	—	—	—
—Dallas	NHL	13	2	3	5	5	0	0	0	17	4	4	8	0
NHL Totals (10 years)		725	120	219	339	651	56	19	6	133	23	28	51	97

KECZMER, DAN   D   STARS

PERSONAL: Born May 25, 1968, in Mt. Clemens, Mich. ... 6-1/190. ... Shoots left. ... Full name: Daniel Leonard Keczmer. ... Name pronounced KEHZ-muhr.

COLLEGE: Lake Superior State (Mich.).

TRANSACTIONS/CAREER NOTES: Selected by Minnesota North Stars in 10th round (11th North Stars pick, 201st overall) of NHL entry draft (June 21, 1986). ... Injured shoulder (February 2, 1990). ... Claimed by San Jose Sharks as part of ownership change with North Stars (October 1990). ... Traded by Sharks to Hartford Whalers for C Dean Evason (October 2, 1991). ... Released by U.S. National team prior to Olympics (January 1992). ... Bruised right leg (February 8, 1993); missed three games. ... Traded by Whalers to Calgary Flames for G Jeff Reese and future considerations (November 19, 1993). ... Separated right shoulder (February 16, 1995); missed 10 games. ... Traded by Flames with D Phil Housley to New Jersey Devils for D Tommy Albelin, D Cale Hulse and RW Jocelyn Lemieux (February 26, 1996). ... Signed as free agent by Dallas Stars (August 7, 1996).

HONORS: Named to CCHA All-Star second team (1989-90).

Season Team	League	REGULAR SEASON								PLAYOFFS				
		Gms.	G	A	Pts.	PIM	+/-	PP	SH	Gms.	G	A	Pts.	PIM
86-87—Lake Superior	CCHA	38	3	5	8	28	...	...	...	—	—	—	—	—
87-88—Lake Superior	CCHA	41	2	15	17	34	...	...	...	—	—	—	—	—
88-89—Lake Superior	CCHA	46	3	26	29	70	...	...	...	—	—	—	—	—
89-90—Lake Superior	CCHA	43	13	23	36	48	...	...	...	—	—	—	—	—
90-91—Minnesota	NHL	9	0	1	1	6	0	0	0	—	—	—	—	—
—Kalamazoo	IHL	60	4	20	24	60	...	...	...	9	1	2	3	10
91-92—U.S. national team	Int'l	51	3	11	14	56	...	...	...	—	—	—	—	—
—Springfield	AHL	18	3	4	7	10	...	...	...	4	0	0	0	6
—Hartford	NHL	1	0	0	0	0	-1	0	0	—	—	—	—	—
92-93—Springfield	AHL	37	1	13	14	38	...	...	...	12	0	4	4	14
—Hartford	NHL	23	4	4	8	28	-3	2	0	—	—	—	—	—
93-94—Hartford	NHL	12	0	1	1	12	-6	0	0	—	—	—	—	—
—Springfield	AHL	7	0	1	1	4	...	...	...	—	—	—	—	—
—Calgary	NHL	57	1	20	21	48	-2	0	0	3	0	0	0	4
94-95—Calgary	NHL	28	2	3	5	10	7	0	0	7	0	1	1	2
95-96—Saint John	AHL	22	3	11	14	14	...	...	...	—	—	—	—	—
—Calgary	NHL	13	0	0	0	14	-6	0	0	—	—	—	—	—
—Albany	AHL	17	0	4	4	4	...	...	...	1	0	0	0	0
96-97—Michigan	IHL	42	3	17	20	24	...	...	...	—	—	—	—	—
—Dallas	NHL	13	0	1	1	6	3	0	0	—	—	—	—	—
97-98—Dallas	NHL	17	1	2	3	26	5	0	0	2	0	0	0	2
—Michigan	IHL	44	1	11	12	29	...	...	...	—	—	—	—	—
NHL Totals (8 years)		173	8	32	40	150	-3	2	0	12	0	1	1	8

KELLEHER, CHRIS   D   PENGUINS

PERSONAL: Born March 23, 1975, in Cambridge, Mass. ... 6-2/220. ... Shoots left.

HIGH SCHOOL: Belmont (Mass.) Hill, then St. Sebastian's Country Day (Needham, Mass.).

COLLEGE: Boston University.

TRANSACTIONS/CAREER NOTES: Selected by Pittsburgh Penguins in fifth round (fifth Penguins pick, 130th overall) of NHL entry draft (June 26, 1993).

HONORS: Named to NCAA All-America East second team (1996-97 and 1997-98). ... Named to Hockey East All-Star second team (1997-98).

K

Season Team	League	REGULAR SEASON								PLAYOFFS				
		Gms.	G	A	Pts.	PIM	+/-	PP	SH	Gms.	G	A	Pts.	PIM
90-91—Belmont Hill...............	Mass. H.S.	20	4	23	27	14	...	...	...	—	—	—	—	—
91-92—St. Sebastian's...........	Mass. H.S.	28	7	27	34	12	...	...	...	—	—	—	—	—
92-93—St. Sebastian's...........	Mass. H.S.	25	8	30	38	16	...	...	...	—	—	—	—	—
93-94—St. Sebastian's...........	Mass. H.S.	24	10	21	31	...	...	...	...	—	—	—	—	—
94-95—Boston University	Hockey East	35	3	17	20	62	...	...	...	—	—	—	—	—
95-96—Boston University	Hockey East	37	7	18	25	43	...	...	...	—	—	—	—	—
96-97—Boston University	Hockey East	39	10	24	34	54	...	...	...	—	—	—	—	—
97-98—Boston University	Hockey East	37	4	26	30	40	...	...	...	—	—	—	—	—

KELLY, STEVE — C — LIGHTNING

PERSONAL: Born October 26, 1976, in Vancouver. ... 6-1/190. ... Shoots left.
TRANSACTIONS/CAREER NOTES: Selected by Edmonton Oilers in first round (first Oilers pick, sixth overall) of NHL entry draft (July 8, 1995). ... Traded by Oilers to Tampa Bay Lightning with C Jason Bonsignore and D Bryan Marchment for D Roman Hamrlik and F Paul Comrie (December 30, 1997). ... Suffered from the flu (January 21, 1998); missed two games. ... Suffered from the flu (January 31, 1998); missed one game.

Season Team	League	REGULAR SEASON								PLAYOFFS				
		Gms.	G	A	Pts.	PIM	+/-	PP	SH	Gms.	G	A	Pts.	PIM
92-93—Prince Albert..............	WHL	65	11	9	20	75	...	...	...	—	—	—	—	—
93-94—Prince Albert..............	WHL	65	19	42	61	106	...	...	...	—	—	—	—	—
94-95—Prince Albert..............	WHL	68	31	41	72	153	...	...	...	15	7	9	16	35
95-96—Prince Albert..............	WHL	70	27	74	101	203	...	...	...	18	13	18	31	47
96-97—Hamilton	AHL	48	9	29	38	111	...	...	...	11	3	3	6	24
—Edmonton	NHL	8	1	0	1	6	-1	0	0	6	0	0	0	2
97-98—Edmonton	NHL	19	0	2	2	8	-4	0	0	—	—	—	—	—
—Hamilton	AHL	11	2	8	10	18	...	...	...	—	—	—	—	—
—Tampa Bay	NHL	24	2	1	3	15	-9	1	0	—	—	—	—	—
—Milwaukee..................	IHL	5	0	1	1	19	...	...	...	—	—	—	—	—
—Cleveland	IHL	5	1	1	2	29	...	...	...	1	0	1	1	0
NHL Totals (2 years)...........		51	3	3	6	29	-14	1	0	6	0	0	0	2

KENADY, CHRIS — RW — BLUES

PERSONAL: Born April 10, 1973, in Mound, Minn. ... 6-2/208. ... Shoots left. ... Name pronounced KEHN-ih-dee.
HIGH SCHOOL: Mound (Minn.) Westonka.
COLLEGE: Denver.
TRANSACTIONS/CAREER NOTES: Selected by St. Louis Blues in eighth round (eighth Blues pick, 175th overall) of NHL entry draft (June 22, 1991).

Season Team	League	REGULAR SEASON								PLAYOFFS				
		Gms.	G	A	Pts.	PIM	+/-	PP	SH	Gms.	G	A	Pts.	PIM
90-91—St. Paul	USHL	45	16	20	36	57	...	...	...	—	—	—	—	—
91-92—Univ. of Denver	WCHA	36	8	5	13	56	...	...	...	—	—	—	—	—
92-93—Univ. of Denver	WCHA	38	8	16	24	95	...	...	...	—	—	—	—	—
93-94—Univ. of Denver	WCHA	37	14	11	25	125	...	...	...	—	—	—	—	—
94-95—Univ. of Denver	WCHA	39	21	17	38	113	...	...	...	—	—	—	—	—
95-96—Worcester	AHL	43	9	10	19	58	...	...	...	2	0	0	0	0
96-97—Worcester	AHL	73	23	26	49	131	...	...	...	5	0	1	1	2
97-98—Worcester	AHL	63	23	22	45	84	...	...	...	11	1	5	6	26
—St. Louis	NHL	5	0	2	2	0	1	0	0	—	—	—	—	—
NHL Totals (1 year).............		5	0	2	2	0	1	0	0					

KENNEDY, MIKE — RW

PERSONAL: Born April 3, 1972, in Vancouver. ... 6-1/204. ... Shoots right.
COLLEGE: British Columbia.
TRANSACTIONS/CAREER NOTES: Selected by Minnesota North Stars in fifth round (third North Stars pick, 97th overall) of NHL entry draft (June 22, 1991). ... North Stars franchise moved from Minnesota to Dallas and renamed Stars for 1993-94 season. ... Signed as free agent by Toronto Maple Leafs (July 3, 1997). ... Traded by Maple Leafs to Dallas Stars for eighth-round pick (LW Mihail Travnicek) in 1998 draft (March 24, 1998).

Season Team	League	REGULAR SEASON								PLAYOFFS				
		Gms.	G	A	Pts.	PIM	+/-	PP	SH	Gms.	G	A	Pts.	PIM
89-90—British Columbia	CWUAA	9	5	7	12	0	...	...	...	—	—	—	—	—
90-91—British Columbia	CWUAA	28	17	17	34	18	...	...	...	—	—	—	—	—
91-92—Seattle.......................	WHL	71	42	47	89	134	...	...	...	15	11	6	17	20
92-93—Kalamazoo	IHL	77	21	30	51	39	...	...	...	—	—	—	—	—
93-94—Kalamazoo	IHL	63	20	18	38	42	...	...	...	—	—	—	—	—
94-95—Kalamazoo	IHL	42	20	28	48	29	...	...	...	—	—	—	—	—
—Dallas.........................	NHL	44	6	12	18	33	4	2	0	5	0	0	0	9
95-96—Dallas.........................	NHL	61	9	17	26	48	-7	4	0	—	—	—	—	—
96-97—Dallas.........................	NHL	24	1	6	7	13	3	0	0	—	—	—	—	—
—Michigan.....................	IHL	2	0	1	1	2	...	...	...	—	—	—	—	—
97-98—St. John's...................	AHL	49	11	17	28	86	...	...	...	—	—	—	—	—
—Toronto	NHL	13	0	1	1	14	-2	0	0	—	—	—	—	—
—Dallas.........................	NHL	2	0	0	0	2	1	0	0	—	—	—	—	—
NHL Totals (4 years)...........		144	16	36	52	110	-1	6	0	5	0	0	0	9

K

KEYES, TIM   G   CANUCKS

PERSONAL: Born May 28, 1976, in Grananoque, Ont. ... 5-11/185. ... Catches left.
TRANSACTIONS/CAREER NOTES: Signed as free agent by Vancouver Canucks (August 14, 1997).

Season Team	League	REGULAR SEASON								PLAYOFFS						
		Gms.	Min	W	L	T	GA	SO	Avg.	Gms.	Min.	W	L	GA	SO	Avg.
93-94—Kingston	OHL	6	171	0	2	0	16	0	5.61	—	—	—	—	—	—	—
94-95—Kingston	OHL	16	750	7	2	2	56	0	4.48	1	27	0	0	5	0	11.11
95-96—Ottawa	OHL	27	1497	15	7	2	73	1	2.93	3	110	0	2	12	0	6.55
96-97—Ottawa	OHL	37	1990	26	5	2	87	2	2.62	17	929	10	5	50	0	3.23
97-98—Syracuse	AHL	15	831	2	7	4	59	0	4.26	—	—	—	—	—	—	—
—Raleigh	ECHL	1	60	0	1	‡0	4	0	4.00	—	—	—	—	—	—	—
—Dayton	ECHL	9	534	1	6	‡2	33	0	3.71	—	—	—	—	—	—	—

KHABIBULIN, NIKOLAI   G   COYOTES

PERSONAL: Born January 13, 1973, in Sverdlovsk, U.S.S.R. ... 6-1/196. ... Catches left. ... Name pronounced hah-bee-BOO-lihn.
TRANSACTIONS/CAREER NOTES: Selected by Winnipeg Jets in ninth round (eighth Jets pick, 204th overall) of NHL entry draft (June 20, 1992). ... Sprained knee (November 30, 1995); missed 20 games. ... Jets franchise moved to Phoenix and renamed Coyotes for 1996-97 season; NHL approved move on January 18, 1996.
HONORS: Played in NHL All-Star Game (1998).
MISCELLANEOUS: Stopped a penalty shot attempt (vs. Bob Errey, March 22, 1995; vs. Kevin Stevens, February 26, 1996; vs. Dino Ciccarelli, December 3, 1997). ... Allowed a penalty shot goal (vs. Pavel Bure, January 26, 1998). ... Holds Phoenix Coyotes franchise all-time record for goals-against average (2.93).

Season Team	League	REGULAR SEASON								PLAYOFFS						
		Gms.	Min	W	L	T	GA	SO	Avg.	Gms.	Min.	W	L	GA	SO	Avg.
88-89—Avtomo. Sverdlovsk	USSR	1	3	0	0	0	0	0	...	—	—	—	—	—	—	—
89-90—Avtomo. Sverd. Jr.	USSR						Statistics unavailable.									
90-91—Sputnik Nizhny Tagil	USSR Dv.III						Statistics unavailable.									
91-92—CSKA Moscow	CIS	2	34	...	...	...	2	...	3.53	—	—	—	—	—	—	—
92-93—CSKA Moscow	CIS	13	491	...	...	...	27	...	3.30	—	—	—	—	—	—	—
93-94—Russian Penguins	IHL	12	639	2	7	‡2	47	0	4.41	—	—	—	—	—	—	—
—CSKA Moscow	CIS	46	2625	...	...	...	116	5	2.65	3	193	1	2	11	0	3.42
94-95—Springfield	AHL	23	1240	9	9	3	80	0	3.87	—	—	—	—	—	—	—
—Winnipeg	NHL	26	1339	8	9	4	76	0	3.41	—	—	—	—	—	—	—
95-96—Winnipeg	NHL	53	2914	26	20	3	152	2	3.13	6	359	2	4	19	0	3.18
96-97—Phoenix	NHL	72	4091	30	33	6	193	7	2.83	7	426	3	4	15	1	2.11
97-98—Phoenix	NHL	70	4026	30	28	10	†184	4	2.74	4	185	2	1	13	0	4.22
NHL Totals (4 years)		221	12370	94	90	23	605	13	2.93	17	970	7	9	47	1	2.91

KHRISTICH, DIMITRI   RW   BRUINS

PERSONAL: Born July 23, 1969, in Kiev, U.S.S.R. ... 6-2/195. ... Shoots right. ... Name pronounced KHRIHZ-tihch.
TRANSACTIONS/CAREER NOTES: Selected by Washington Capitals in sixth round (sixth Capitals pick, 120th overall) of NHL entry draft (June 11, 1988). ... Injured hip (February 16, 1990); missed six games. ... Broke foot (October 3, 1992); missed 20 games. ... Traded by Capitals with G Byron Dafoe to Los Angeles Kings for first-(C Alexander Volchkov) and fourth-(RW Justin Davis) round picks in 1996 draft (July 8, 1995). ... Suffered concussion (December 22, 1995); missed three games. ... Sprained right knee (February 23, 1996); missed three games. ... Suffered cut near right eye (February 1, 1997); missed seven games. ... Traded by Kings with G Byron Dafoe to Boston Bruins for C Jozef Stumpel, RW Sandy Moger and fourth-round pick (traded to New Jersey) in 1998 draft (August 29, 1997).
HONORS: Played in NHL All-Star Game (1997).
MISCELLANEOUS: Scored on a penalty shot (vs. Darcy Wakaluk, January 7, 1992).
STATISTICAL PLATEAUS: Three-goal games: 1992-93 (2).

Season Team	League	REGULAR SEASON								PLAYOFFS				
		Gms.	G	A	Pts.	PIM	+/-	PP	SH	Gms.	G	A	Pts.	PIM
88-89—Sokol Kiev	USSR	42	17	8	25	15	...	...	...	—	—	—	—	—
89-90—Sokol Kiev	USSR	47	14	22	36	32	...	...	...	—	—	—	—	—
90-91—Sokol Kiev	USSR	28	10	12	22	20	...	...	...	—	—	—	—	—
—Baltimore	AHL	3	0	0	0	0	...	...	...	—	—	—	—	—
—Washington	NHL	40	13	14	27	21	-1	1	0	11	1	3	4	6
91-92—Washington	NHL	80	36	37	73	35	24	14	1	7	3	2	5	15
92-93—Washington	NHL	64	31	35	66	28	29	9	1	6	2	5	7	2
93-94—Washington	NHL	83	29	29	58	73	-2	10	0	11	2	3	5	10
94-95—Washington	NHL	48	12	14	26	41	0	8	0	7	1	4	5	0
95-96—Los Angeles	NHL	76	27	37	64	44	0	12	0	—	—	—	—	—
96-97—Los Angeles	NHL	75	19	37	56	38	8	3	0	—	—	—	—	—
97-98—Boston	NHL	82	29	37	66	42	25	13	2	6	2	2	4	2
NHL Totals (8 years)		548	196	240	436	322	83	70	4	48	11	19	30	35

KIDD, TREVOR   G   HURRICANES

PERSONAL: Born March 29, 1972, in St. Boniface, Man. ... 6-2/190. ... Catches left.
TRANSACTIONS/CAREER NOTES: Broke finger (December 1987). ... Selected by Calgary Flames in first round (first Flames pick, 11th overall) of NHL entry draft (June 16, 1990). ... Traded by Brandon Wheat Kings with D Bart Cote to Spokane Chiefs for RW Bobby House, C Marty Murray and G Don Blishen (January 21, 1991). ... Sprained left ankle (October 18, 1993); missed one game. ... Traded by Flames with LW Gary Roberts to Carolina Hurricanes for G Jean-Sebastien Giguere C Andrew Cassels (August 25, 1997). ... Strained groin (November 9, 1997); missed seven games. ... Fractured finger on right hand (December 20, 1997); missed seven games. ... Injured groin (April 16, 1998); missed three games.

HONORS: Won Del Wilson Trophy (1989-90). ... Named to WHL (West) All-Star first team (1989-90).
MISCELLANEOUS: Member of silver-medal-winning Canadian Olympic team (1992). ... Holds Calgary Flames all-time record for goals-against average (2.83). ... Stopped a penalty shot attempt (vs. Teemu Selanne, February 6, 1995; vs. Brendan Shanahan, November 5, 1997). ... Allowed a penalty shot goal (vs. Wendel Clark, November 24, 1993; vs. Joe Sakic, January 14, 1996).

				REGULAR SEASON								PLAYOFFS					
Season Team	League	Gms.	Min	W	L	T	GA	SO	Avg.	Gms.	Min.	W	L	GA	SO	Avg.
88-89—Brandon	WHL	32	1509	...	...	...	102	0	4.06	—	—	—	—	—	—	—
89-90—Brandon	WHL	*63	*3676	24	32	2	254	2	4.15	—	—	—	—	—	—	—
90-91—Brandon	WHL	30	1730	10	19	1	117	0	4.06	—	—	—	—	—	—	—
—Spokane	WHL	14	749	8	3	0	44	0	3.52	15	926	*14	1	32	*2	*2.07
91-92—Canadian nat'l team	Int'l	28	1349	18	4	4	79	2	3.51	—	—	—	—	—	—	—
—Can. Olympic Team	Int'l	1	60	1	0	0	0	1	...	—	—	—	—	—	—	—
—Calgary	NHL	2	120	1	1	0	8	0	4.00	—	—	—	—	—	—	—
92-93—Salt Lake City	IHL	30	1696	10	16	‡0	111	1	3.93	—	—	—	—	—	—	—
93-94—Calgary	NHL	31	1614	13	7	6	85	0	3.16	—	—	—	—	—	—	—
94-95—Calgary	NHL	†43	2463	22	14	6	107	3	2.61	7	434	3	4	26	1	3.59
95-96—Calgary	NHL	47	2570	15	21	8	119	3	2.78	2	83	0	1	9	0	6.51
96-97—Calgary	NHL	55	2979	21	23	6	141	4	2.84	—	—	—	—	—	—	—
97-98—Carolina	NHL	47	2685	21	21	3	97	3	2.17	—	—	—	—	—	—	—
NHL Totals (6 years)		225	12431	93	87	29	557	13	2.69	9	517	3	5	35	1	4.06

KILGER, CHAD   C   BLACKHAWKS

K

PERSONAL: Born November 27, 1976, in Cornwall, Ont. ... 6-3/204. ... Shoots left. ... Son of Bob Kilger, former NHL referee (1970-71 through 1979-80) and current deputy speaker in House of Commons in Canadian Parliament.
TRANSACTIONS/CAREER NOTES: Selected by Mighty Ducks of Anaheim in first round (first Mighty Ducks pick, fourth overall) of NHL entry draft (July 8, 1995). ... Traded by Mighty Ducks with D Oleg Tverdovsky and third-round pick (D Per-Anton Lundstrom) in 1996 draft to Winnipeg Jets for C Marc Chouinard, RW Teemu Selanne and fourth-round pick (traded to Toronto) in 1996 draft (February 7, 1996). ... Suffered from the flu (February 21, 1996); missed one game. ... Jets franchise moved to Phoenix and renamed Coyotes for 1996-97 season; NHL approved move on January 18, 1996. ... Bruised thigh (October 7, 1996); missed one game. ... Traded by Coyotes with D Jayson More to Chicago Blackhawks for D Keith Carney and RW Jim Cummins (March 4, 1998).

				REGULAR SEASON						PLAYOFFS				
Season Team	League	Gms.	G	A	Pts.	PIM	+/-	PP	SH	Gms.	G	A	Pts.	PIM
92-93—Cornwall	CJHL	55	30	36	66	26	...	...	...	6	0	0	0	0
93-94—Kingston	OHL	66	17	35	52	23	...	...	...	6	7	2	9	8
94-95—Kingston	OHL	65	42	53	95	95	...	...	...	6	5	2	7	10
95-96—Anaheim	NHL	45	5	7	12	22	-2	0	0	—	—	—	—	—
—Winnipeg	NHL	29	2	3	5	12	-2	0	0	4	1	0	1	0
96-97—Phoenix	NHL	24	4	3	7	13	-5	1	0	—	—	—	—	—
—Springfield	AHL	52	17	28	45	36	...	...	...	16	5	7	12	56
97-98—Springfield	AHL	35	14	14	28	33	...	...	...	—	—	—	—	—
—Phoenix	NHL	10	0	1	1	4	-2	0	0	—	—	—	—	—
—Chicago	NHL	22	3	8	11	6	2	2	0	—	—	—	—	—
NHL Totals (3 years)		130	14	22	36	57	-9	3	0	4	1	0	1	0

KING, DEREK   LW   MAPLE LEAFS

PERSONAL: Born February 11, 1967, in Hamilton, Ont. ... 6-0/212. ... Shoots left.
TRANSACTIONS/CAREER NOTES: Selected by New York Islanders as underage junior in first round (second Islanders pick, 13th overall) of NHL entry draft (June 15, 1985). ... Sprained right knee (September 1985). ... Fractured left wrist (December 12, 1987). ... Separated shoulder (November 23, 1988). ... Suffered concussion (November 2, 1990). ... Separated right shoulder (February 14, 1991). ... Bruised hip (November 27, 1992); missed two games. ... Suffered hip pointer (December 26, 1992); missed four games. ... Broke finger on left hand (April 3, 1993); missed one game. ... Suffered hip pointer (January 8, 1994); missed two games. ... Injured knee (March 9, 1995); missed one game. ... Injured elbow (April 28, 1995); missed two games. ... Injured foot (November 24, 1995); missed one game. ... Broke jaw and suffered mild concussion (March 3, 1996); missed remainder of season. ... Traded by Islanders to Hartford Whalers for fifth-round pick (C Adam Ediger) in 1997 draft (March 18, 1997). ... Signed as free agent by Toronto Maple Leafs (July 3, 1997). ... Sprained ankle (October 7, 1997); missed five games.
HONORS: Won Emms Family Award (1984-85). ... Named to OHL All-Star first team (1986-87).
MISCELLANEOUS: Scored on a penalty shot (vs. John Vanbiesbrouck, February 7, 1998).
STATISTICAL PLATEAUS: Three-goal games: 1989-90 (1), 1991-92 (2), 1993-94 (1), 1996-97 (1), 1997-98 (1). Total: 6. ... Four-goal games: 1990-91 (1). ... Total hat tricks: 7.

				REGULAR SEASON						PLAYOFFS				
Season Team	League	Gms.	G	A	Pts.	PIM	+/-	PP	SH	Gms.	G	A	Pts.	PIM
83-84—Hamilton Jr. A	OHA	37	10	14	24	142	...	...	...	—	—	—	—	—
84-85—Sault Ste. Marie	OHL	63	35	38	73	106	...	...	...	16	3	13	16	11
85-86—Sault Ste. Marie	OHL	25	12	17	29	33	...	...	...	—	—	—	—	—
—Oshawa	OHL	19	8	13	21	15	...	...	...	6	3	2	5	13
86-87—Oshawa	OHL	57	53	53	106	74	...	...	...	17	14	10	24	40
—New York Islanders	NHL	2	0	0	0	0	0	0	0	—	—	—	—	—
87-88—New York Islanders	NHL	55	12	24	36	30	7	1	0	5	0	2	2	2
—Springfield	AHL	10	7	6	13	6	...	...	...	—	—	—	—	—
88-89—Springfield	AHL	4	4	0	4	0	...	...	...	—	—	—	—	—
—New York Islanders	NHL	60	14	29	43	14	10	4	0	—	—	—	—	—
89-90—Springfield	AHL	21	11	12	23	33	...	...	...	—	—	—	—	—
—New York Islanders	NHL	46	13	27	40	20	2	5	0	4	0	0	0	4
90-91—New York Islanders	NHL	66	19	26	45	44	1	2	0	—	—	—	—	—
91-92—New York Islanders	NHL	80	40	38	78	46	-10	21	0	—	—	—	—	—
92-93—New York Islanders	NHL	77	38	38	76	47	-4	21	0	18	3	11	14	14

Season Team	League	REGULAR SEASON								PLAYOFFS				
		Gms.	G	A	Pts.	PIM	+/-	PP	SH	Gms.	G	A	Pts.	PIM
93-94—New York Islanders.....	NHL	78	30	40	70	59	18	10	0	4	0	1	1	0
94-95—New York Islanders.....	NHL	43	10	16	26	41	-5	7	0	—	—	—	—	—
95-96—New York Islanders.....	NHL	61	12	20	32	23	-10	5	1	—	—	—	—	—
96-97—New York Islanders.....	NHL	70	23	30	53	20	-6	5	0	—	—	—	—	—
—Hartford.....................	NHL	12	3	3	6	2	0	1	0	—	—	—	—	—
97-98—Toronto..................	NHL	77	21	25	46	43	-7	4	0	—	—	—	—	—
NHL Totals (12 years).........		727	235	316	551	389	-4	86	1	31	3	14	17	20

KING, KRIS — LW — MAPLE LEAFS

PERSONAL: Born February 18, 1966, in Bracebridge, Ont. ... 5-11/208. ... Shoots left.

TRANSACTIONS/CAREER NOTES: Selected by Washington Capitals as underage junior in fourth round (fourth Capitals pick, 80th overall) of NHL entry draft (June 9, 1984). ... Signed as free agent by Detroit Red Wings (June 1987). ... Traded by Red Wings to New York Rangers for LW Chris McRae and fifth-round pick (D Tony Burns) in 1990 draft (September 7, 1989). ... Sprained knee (January 7, 1991); missed six games. ... Traded by Rangers with RW Tie Domi to Winnipeg Jets for C Ed Olczyk (December 28, 1992). ... Suffered abdominal injury (February 13, 1996); missed one game. ... Jets franchise moved to Phoenix and renamed Coyotes for 1996-97 season; NHL approved move on January 18, 1996. ... Signed as free agent by Toronto Maple Leafs (July 7, 1997).

HONORS: Won King Clancy Trophy (1995-96).

K

Season Team	League	REGULAR SEASON								PLAYOFFS				
		Gms.	G	A	Pts.	PIM	+/-	PP	SH	Gms.	G	A	Pts.	PIM
82-83—Gravenhurst..............	SOJHL	32	72	53	125	115	...	...	...	—	—	—	—	—
83-84—Peterborough.............	OHL	62	13	18	31	168	...	...	...	8	3	3	6	14
84-85—Peterborough.............	OHL	61	18	35	53	222	...	...	...	16	2	8	10	28
85-86—Peterborough.............	OHL	58	19	40	59	254	...	...	...	8	4	0	4	21
86-87—Peterborough.............	OHL	46	23	33	56	160	...	...	...	12	5	8	13	41
—Binghamton..............	AHL	7	0	0	0	18	...	...	...	—	—	—	—	—
87-88—Adirondack	AHL	78	21	32	53	337	...	...	...	10	4	4	8	53
—Detroit.................	NHL	3	1	0	1	2	1	0	0	—	—	—	—	—
88-89—Detroit..................	NHL	55	2	3	5	168	-7	0	0	2	0	0	0	2
89-90—New York Rangers......	NHL	68	6	7	13	286	2	0	0	10	0	1	1	38
90-91—New York Rangers......	NHL	72	11	14	25	154	-1	0	0	6	2	0	2	36
91-92—New York Rangers......	NHL	79	10	9	19	224	13	0	0	13	4	1	5	14
92-93—New York Rangers......	NHL	30	0	3	3	67	-1	0	0	—	—	—	—	—
—Winnipeg...............	NHL	48	8	8	16	136	5	0	0	6	1	1	2	4
93-94—Winnipeg...............	NHL	83	4	8	12	205	-22	0	0	—	—	—	—	—
94-95—Winnipeg...............	NHL	48	4	2	6	85	0	0	0	—	—	—	—	—
95-96—Winnipeg...............	NHL	81	9	11	20	151	-7	0	1	5	0	1	1	4
96-97—Phoenix.................	NHL	81	3	11	14	185	-7	0	0	7	0	0	0	17
97-98—Toronto.................	NHL	82	3	3	6	199	-13	0	0	—	—	—	—	—
NHL Totals (11 years).........		730	61	79	140	1862	-37	0	1	49	7	4	11	115

KIPRUSOFF, MIIKKA — G — SHARKS

PERSONAL: Born October 26, 1976, in Turku, Finland. ... 6-0/176. ... Catches left. ... Brother of Marko Kiprusoff, defenseman in Montreal Canadiens system.

TRANSACTIONS/CAREER NOTES: Selected by San Jose Sharks in fifth round (fifth Sharks pick, 115th overall) of NHL entry draft (July 8, 1995).

Season Team	League	REGULAR SEASON								PLAYOFFS						
		Gms.	Min	W	L	T	GA	SO	Avg.	Gms.	Min.	W	L	GA	SO	Avg.
93-94—TPS Jr.	Finland	35	...	...	...	...	...	...	...	6	—	—	—	—	—	—
94-95—TPS Jr.	Finland	31	1880	...	...	...	93	...	2.97	—	—	—	—	—	—	—
—TPS Turku	Finland	4	240	...	...	...	12	0	3.00	2	120	...	...	7	...	3.50
95-96—TPS Turku	Finland	12	550	...	...	...	38	...	4.15	—	—	—	—	—	—	—
—Kiekko................	Finland	5	300	...	...	...	7	...	1.40	—	—	—	—	—	—	—
96-97—AIK	Sweden	42	2466	...	...	...	104	3	2.53	7	420	...	...	23	0	3.29
97-98—AIK Solna..............	Sweden	42	2457	...	...	...	110	...	2.69							

KLATT, TRENT — RW — FLYERS

PERSONAL: Born January 30, 1971, in Robbinsdale, Minn. ... 6-1/210. ... Shoots right. ... Full name: Trent Thomas Klatt. ... Name pronounced KLAT.

HIGH SCHOOL: Osseo (Minn.).

COLLEGE: Minnesota.

TRANSACTIONS/CAREER NOTES: Selected by Washington Capitals in fourth round (fifth Capitals pick, 82nd overall) of NHL entry draft (June 17, 1989). ... Rights traded by Capitals with LW Steve Maltais to Minnesota North Stars for D Sean Chambers (June 21, 1991). ... Injured finger (January 7, 1993); missed three games. ... North Stars franchise moved from Minnesota to Dallas and renamed Stars for 1993-94 season. ... Strained back (November 9, 1993); missed one game. ... Sprained knee (November 11, 1993); missed two games. ... Sprained knee (February 6, 1994); missed three games. ... Traded by Stars to Philadelphia Flyers for LW Brent Fedyk (December 13, 1995). ... Suffered concussion (March 9, 1997); missed two games.

MISCELLANEOUS: Failed to score on a penalty shot (vs. John Vanbiesbrouck, October 1, 1997).

STATISTICAL PLATEAUS: Three-goal games: 1996-97 (1).

Season Team	League	REGULAR SEASON								PLAYOFFS				
		Gms.	G	A	Pts.	PIM	+/-	PP	SH	Gms.	G	A	Pts.	PIM
87-88—Osseo H.S................	Minn. H.S.	22	19	17	36	...	...	...	...	—	—	—	—	—
88-89—Osseo H.S................	Minn. H.S.	22	24	39	63	...	...	...	...	—	—	—	—	—
89-90—Univ. of Minnesota......	WCHA	38	22	14	36	16	...	...	...	—	—	—	—	—
90-91—Univ. of Minnesota......	WCHA	39	16	28	44	58	...	...	...	—	—	—	—	—

		REGULAR SEASON									PLAYOFFS				
Season Team	League	Gms.	G	A	Pts.	PIM	+/-	PP	SH		Gms.	G	A	Pts.	PIM
91-92—Univ. of Minnesota	WCHA	44	30	36	66	78	...				—	—	—	—	—
—Minnesota	NHL	1	0	0	0	0	0	0	0		6	0	0	0	2
92-93—Kalamazoo	IHL	31	8	11	19	18	...				—	—	—	—	—
—Minnesota	NHL	47	4	19	23	38	2	1	0		—	—	—	—	—
93-94—Dallas	NHL	61	14	24	38	30	13	3	0		9	2	1	3	4
—Kalamazoo	IHL	6	3	2	5	4	...				—	—	—	—	—
94-95—Dallas	NHL	47	12	10	22	26	-2	5	0		5	1	0	1	0
95-96—Dallas	NHL	22	4	4	8	23	0	0	0		—	—	—	—	—
—Michigan	IHL	2	1	2	3	5	...				—	—	—	—	—
—Philadelphia	NHL	49	3	8	11	21	2	0	0		12	4	1	5	0
96-97—Philadelphia	NHL	76	24	21	45	20	9	5	5		19	4	3	7	12
97-98—Philadelphia	NHL	82	14	28	42	16	2	5	0		5	0	0	0	0
NHL Totals (7 years)		385	75	114	189	174	26	19	5		56	11	5	16	18

KLEE, KEN   D   CAPITALS

PERSONAL: Born April 24, 1971, in Indianapolis. ... 6-1/205. ... Shoots right. ... Full name: Kenneth William Klee.

HIGH SCHOOL: Rockhurst (Kansas City, Mo.).

COLLEGE: St. Michael's College (Vt.), then Bowling Green State.

TRANSACTIONS/CAREER NOTES: Selected by Washington Capitals in ninth round (11th Capitals pick, 177th overall) of NHL entry draft (June 16, 1990). ... Injured foot (January 27, 1995); missed six games. ... Pulled groin (March 12, 1996); missed 13 games. ... Sprained knee (April 10, 1996); missed two games. ... Fractured facial bones (March 28, 1998); missed eight games.

MISCELLANEOUS: Failed to score on penalty shot (vs. Mike Richter, March 12, 1997).

		REGULAR SEASON									PLAYOFFS				
Season Team	League	Gms.	G	A	Pts.	PIM	+/-	PP	SH		Gms.	G	A	Pts.	PIM
89-90—Bowling Green	CCHA	39	0	5	5	52	...	...	...		—	—	—	—	—
90-91—Bowling Green	CCHA	37	7	28	35	50	...	...	...		—	—	—	—	—
91-92—Bowling Green	CCHA	10	0	1	1	14	...	...	...		—	—	—	—	—
92-93—Baltimore	AHL	77	4	14	18	68	...	...	...		7	0	1	1	15
93-94—Portland	AHL	65	2	9	11	87	...	...	...		17	1	2	3	14
94-95—Portland	AHL	49	5	7	12	89	...	...	...		—	—	—	—	—
—Washington	NHL	23	3	1	4	41	2	0	0		7	0	0	0	4
95-96—Washington	NHL	66	8	3	11	60	-1	0	1		1	0	0	0	0
96-97—Washington	NHL	80	3	8	11	115	-5	0	0		—	—	—	—	—
97-98—Washington	NHL	51	4	2	6	46	-3	0	0		9	1	0	1	10
NHL Totals (4 years)		220	18	14	32	262	-7	0	1		17	1	0	1	14

KLEMM, JON   D   AVALANCHE

PERSONAL: Born January 8, 1970, in Cranbrook, B.C. ... 6-3/200. ... Shoots right. ... Full name: Jonathan Darryl Klemm.

TRANSACTIONS/CAREER NOTES: Injured abdomen (March 28, 1995); missed five games. ... Reinjured abdomen (April 8, 1995); missed remainder of season. ... Nordiques franchise moved to Colorado and renamed Avalanche for 1995-96 season (June 21, 1995). ... Injured groin (January 27, 1996); missed one game. ... Sprained left thumb (October 30, 1997); missed 11 games. ... Strained groin (December 27, 1997); missed one game.

HONORS: Named to WHL (West) All-Star second team (1990-91).

MISCELLANEOUS: Member of Stanley Cup championship team (1996).

		REGULAR SEASON									PLAYOFFS				
Season Team	League	Gms.	G	A	Pts.	PIM	+/-	PP	SH		Gms.	G	A	Pts.	PIM
87-88—Seattle	WHL	68	6	7	13	24	...	...	...		—	—	—	—	—
88-89—Seattle	WHL	2	1	1	2	0	...	...	...		—	—	—	—	—
—Spokane	WHL	66	6	34	40	42	...	...	...		—	—	—	—	—
89-90—Spokane	WHL	66	3	28	31	100	...	...	...		6	1	1	2	5
90-91—Spokane	WHL	72	7	58	65	65	...	...	...		15	3	6	9	8
91-92—Halifax	AHL	70	6	13	19	40	...	...	...		—	—	—	—	—
—Quebec	NHL	4	0	1	1	0	2	0	0		—	—	—	—	—
92-93—Halifax	AHL	80	3	20	23	32	...	...	...		—	—	—	—	—
93-94—Cornwall	AHL	66	4	26	30	78	...	...	...		13	1	2	3	6
—Quebec	NHL	7	0	0	0	4	-1	0	0		—	—	—	—	—
94-95—Cornwall	AHL	65	6	13	19	84	...	...	...		—	—	—	—	—
—Quebec	NHL	4	1	0	1	2	3	0	0		—	—	—	—	—
95-96—Colorado	NHL	56	3	12	15	20	12	0	1		15	2	1	3	0
96-97—Colorado	NHL	80	9	15	24	37	12	1	2		17	1	1	2	6
97-98—Colorado	NHL	67	6	8	14	30	-3	0	0		4	0	0	0	0
NHL Totals (6 years)		218	19	36	55	93	25	1	3		36	3	2	5	6

KNUBLE, MIKE   RW   RED WINGS

PERSONAL: Born July 4, 1972, in Toronto. ... 6-3/225. ... Shoots right. ... Full name: Michael Knuble. ... Name pronounced kuh-NOO-buhl.

HIGH SCHOOL: East Kentwood (Mich.).

COLLEGE: Michigan.

TRANSACTIONS/CAREER NOTES: Selected by Detroit Red Wings in fourth round (fourth Red Wings pick, 76th overall) of NHL entry draft (June 22, 1991). ... Strained groin (October 8, 1997); missed two games.

HONORS: Named to CCHA All-Star second team (1993-94 and 1994-95). ... Named to NCAA All-America West second team (1994-95).

MISCELLANEOUS: Member of Stanley Cup championship team (1998).

Season Team	League	REGULAR SEASON									PLAYOFFS				
		Gms.	G	A	Pts.	PIM	+/-	PP	SH		Gms.	G	A	Pts.	PIM
88-89—East Kentwood H.S.	Mich. H.S.	28	52	37	89	60	...	...	...		—	—	—	—	—
89-90—East Kentwood H.S.	Mich. H.S.	29	63	40	103	40	...	...	...		—	—	—	—	—
90-91—Kalamazoo	NAJHL	36	18	24	42	30	...	...	...		—	—	—	—	—
91-92—Univ. of Michigan	CCHA	43	7	8	15	48	...	...	...		—	—	—	—	—
92-93—Univ. of Michigan	CCHA	39	26	16	42	57	...	...	...		—	—	—	—	—
93-94—Univ. of Michigan	CCHA	41	32	26	58	71	...	...	...		—	—	—	—	—
94-95—Univ. of Michigan	CCHA	34	38	22	60	62	...	...	...		—	—	—	—	—
95-96—Adirondack	AHL	—	—	—	—	—	...	...	...		3	0	0	0	0
96-97—Adirondack	AHL	68	28	35	63	54	...	...	...		—	—	—	—	—
—Detroit	NHL	9	1	0	1	0	-1	0	0		—	—	—	—	—
97-98—Detroit	NHL	53	7	6	13	16	2	0	0		3	0	1	1	0
NHL Totals (2 years)		62	8	6	14	16	1	0	0		3	0	1	1	0

KNUTSEN, ESPEN — C — MIGHTY DUCKS

PERSONAL: Born January 12, 1972, in Oslo, Norway. ... 5-11/172. ... Shoots left. ... Name pronounced kuh-NOOT-sihn.

TRANSACTIONS/CAREER NOTES: Selected by Hartford Whalers in 10th round (ninth Whalers pick, 204th overall) of NHL entry draft (June 16, 1990). ... Rights traded by Whalers to Mighty Ducks of Anaheim for RW Kevin Brown (October 1, 1996).

Season Team	League	REGULAR SEASON									PLAYOFFS				
		Gms.	G	A	Pts.	PIM	+/-	PP	SH		Gms.	G	A	Pts.	PIM
89-90—Valerengen	Knutsen	34	22	26	48	...	...	...	...		—	—	—	—	—
90-91—Valerengen	Knutsen	31	30	24	54	42	...	...	...		5	3	4	7	...
91-92—Valerengen	Knutsen	30	28	26	54	37	...	...	...		8	7	8	15	15
92-93—Valerengen	Knutsen	13	11	13	24	4	...	...	...		—	—	—	—	—
93-94—Valerengen	Knutsen	38	32	26	58	20	...	...	...		—	—	—	—	—
94-95—Djur. Stockholm	Sweden	30	6	14	20	18	...	...	...		3	0	1	1	0
95-96—Djur. Stockholm	Sweden	32	10	23	33	50	...	...	...		4	1	0	1	2
96-97—Djur. Stockholm	Sweden	39	16	33	49	20	...	...	...		4	2	4	6	6
97-98—Anaheim	NHL	19	3	0	3	6	-10	1	0		—	—	—	—	—
—Cincinnati	AHL	41	4	13	17	18	...	...	...		—	—	—	—	—
NHL Totals (1 year)		19	3	0	3	6	-10	1	0		—	—	—	—	—

KOCUR, JOEY — RW — RED WINGS

PERSONAL: Born December 21, 1964, in Calgary. ... 6-0/220. ... Shoots right. ... Full name: Joe Kocur. ... Cousin of Wendel Clark, left winger, Tampa Bay Lightning; cousin of Kory Kocur with Detroit Red Wings organization (1988-89 through 1992-93). ... Name pronounced KOH-suhr.

TRANSACTIONS/CAREER NOTES: Stretched knee ligaments (December 1981). ... Selected by Detroit Red Wings as underage junior in fifth round (sixth Red Wings pick, 88th overall) of NHL entry draft (June 8, 1983). ... Cut right hand (January 1985). ... Sprained thumb (December 11, 1985). ... Strained ligaments (March 26, 1986). ... Suffered sore right elbow (October 1987). ... Strained sternum and collarbone (November 1987). ... Injured shoulder (December 1987). ... Separated shoulder (May 1988). ... Injured knee (November 1988). ... Injured back (February 1989). ... Bruised right foot (February 16, 1990). ... Strained right knee ligaments (March 1990). ... Injured right hand and arm (December 1, 1990); missed three weeks. ... Traded by Red Wings with D Per Djoos to New York Rangers for C Kevin Miller, D Dennis Vial and RW Jim Cummins (March 5, 1991). ... Suspended four games by NHL for high-sticking (March 10, 1991). ... Suspended additional four games by NHL for high-sticking during appeal of March 10 incident (March 14, 1991); missed final seven games of 1990-91 season and first game of 1991-92 season. ... Underwent surgery to middle knuckle of right hand (May 10, 1991). ... Strained hip flexor (October 1991); missed first five games of season. ... Separated shoulder (January 28, 1992); missed 13 games. ... Slightly sprained right knee (March 5, 1992); missed six games. ... Sprained leg (November 21, 1992); missed one game. ... Injured back (February 10, 1993); missed two games. ... Injured back (February 20, 1993); missed two games. ... Pulled groin (April 9, 1993); missed three games. ... Bruised hand (January 28, 1994); missed three games. ... Reinjured hand (February 9, 1994); missed four games. ... Suffered back spasms (April 4, 1994); missed two games. ... Traded by Rangers to Vancouver Canucks for G Kay Whitmore (March 20, 1996). ... Suffered back spasms (April 1, 1996); missed three games. ... Signed as free agent by Red Wings (December 26, 1996). ... Strained hip flexor (January 9, 1997); missed two games. ... Suffered from the flu (March 26, 1997); missed one game. ... Strained lower back (April 9, 1997); missed two games. ... Injured shoulder (October 1, 1997); missed two games. ... Injured hand (October 31, 1997); missed two games. ... Bruised knee (November 19, 1997); missed three games. ... Suffered injury (January 2, 1998); missed two games. ... Suffered injury (March 18, 1998); missed three games.

MISCELLANEOUS: Member of Stanley Cup championship team (1994, 1997 and 1998). ... Scored on a penalty shot (vs. Jacques Cloutier, November 29, 1990).

Season Team	League	REGULAR SEASON									PLAYOFFS				
		Gms.	G	A	Pts.	PIM	+/-	PP	SH		Gms.	G	A	Pts.	PIM
80-81—Yorkton	SJHL	48	6	9	15	307	...	...	...		—	—	—	—	—
81-82—Yorkton	SJHL	47	20	21	41	199	...	...	...		—	—	—	—	—
82-83—Saskatoon	WHL	62	23	17	40	289	...	...	...		6	2	3	5	25
83-84—Saskatoon	WHL	69	40	41	81	258	...	...	...		—	—	—	—	—
—Adirondack	AHL	—	—	—	—	—	...	...	...		5	0	0	0	20
84-85—Detroit	NHL	17	1	0	1	64	-4	0	0		3	1	0	1	5
—Adirondack	AHL	47	12	7	19	171	...	...	...		—	—	—	—	—
85-86—Adirondack	AHL	9	6	2	8	34	...	...	...		—	—	—	—	—
—Detroit	NHL	59	9	6	15	*377	-24	2	0		—	—	—	—	—
86-87—Detroit	NHL	77	9	9	18	276	-10	2	0		16	2	3	5	71
87-88—Detroit	NHL	64	7	7	14	263	-11	0	0		10	0	1	1	13
88-89—Detroit	NHL	60	9	9	18	213	-4	1	0		3	0	1	1	6
89-90—Detroit	NHL	71	16	20	36	268	-4	1	0		—	—	—	—	—
90-91—Detroit	NHL	52	5	4	9	253	-6	0	0		—	—	—	—	—
—New York Rangers	NHL	5	0	0	0	36	-1	0	0		6	0	2	2	21
91-92—New York Rangers	NHL	51	7	4	11	121	-4	0	0		12	1	1	2	38
92-93—New York Rangers	NHL	65	3	6	9	131	-9	2	0		—	—	—	—	—
93-94—New York Rangers	NHL	71	2	1	3	129	-9	0	0		20	1	1	2	17
94-95—New York Rangers	NHL	48	1	2	3	71	-4	0	0		10	0	0	0	8

Season Team	League	REGULAR SEASON								PLAYOFFS				
		Gms.	G	A	Pts.	PIM	+/-	PP	SH	Gms.	G	A	Pts.	PIM
95-96—New York Rangers	NHL	38	1	2	3	49	-4	0	0	—	—	—	—	—
—Vancouver..................	NHL	7	0	1	1	19	-3	0	0	1	0	0	0	0
96-97—San Antonio..............	IHL	5	1	1	2	24	...	...	...	—	—	—	—	—
—Detroit........................	NHL	34	2	1	3	70	-7	0	0	19	1	3	4	22
97-98—Detroit.......................	NHL	63	6	5	11	92	7	0	0	18	4	0	4	30
NHL Totals (14 years).........		782	78	77	155	2432	-97	8	0	118	10	12	22	231

KOHN, LADISLAV   RW   MAPLE LEAFS

PERSONAL: Born March 4, 1975, in Uherske Hradiste, Czechoslovakia. ... 5-10/180. ... Shoots left. ... Name pronounced KOHN.
TRANSACTIONS/CAREER NOTES: Selected by Calgary Flames in seventh round (ninth Flames pick, 175th overall) in NHL entry draft (June 29, 1994). ... Suffered concussion (November 26, 1997); missed 12 games. ... Traded by Flames to Toronto Maple Leafs for D David Cooper (July 2, 1998).

Season Team	League	REGULAR SEASON								PLAYOFFS				
		Gms.	G	A	Pts.	PIM	+/-	PP	SH	Gms.	G	A	Pts.	PIM
93-94—Brandon......................	WHL	2	0	0	0	0	...	...	...	—	—	—	—	—
—Swift Current	WHL	69	33	35	68	68	...	...	...	7	5	4	9	8
94-95—Swift Current	WHL	65	32	60	92	122	...	...	...	6	2	6	8	14
—Saint John	AHL	1	0	0	0	0	...	...	...	—	—	—	—	—
95-96—Saint John	AHL	73	28	45	73	97	...	...	...	16	6	5	11	12
—Calgary	NHL	5	1	0	1	2	-1	0	0	—	—	—	—	—
96-97—Saint John	AHL	76	28	29	57	81	...	...	...	5	0	0	0	0
97-98—Saint John	AHL	65	25	31	56	90	...	...	...	21	*14	6	20	20
—Calgary	NHL	4	0	1	1	0	2	0	0	—	—	—	—	—
NHL Totals (2 years)...........		9	1	1	2	2	1	0	0					

KOIVU, SAKU   C   CANADIENS

PERSONAL: Born November 23, 1974, in Turku, Finland. ... 5-10/183. ... Shoots left. ... Name pronounced SAK-oo KOY-voo.
TRANSACTIONS/CAREER NOTES: Selected by Montreal Canadiens in first round (first Canadiens pick, 21st overall) of NHL entry draft (June 26, 1993). ... Tore knee ligament (December 7, 1996); missed 26 games. ... Sprained shoulder (March 10, 1997); missed five games. ... Suffered from tonsillitis (March 29, 1997); missed one game. ... Injured ribcage (January 8, 1998); missed seven games. ... Fractured hand (April 7, 1998); missed six games.
HONORS: Played in NHL All-Star Game (1998).
MISCELLANEOUS: Member of bronze-medal-winning Finnish Olympic team (1994 and 1998).

Season Team	League	REGULAR SEASON								PLAYOFFS				
		Gms.	G	A	Pts.	PIM	+/-	PP	SH	Gms.	G	A	Pts.	PIM
91-92—TPS Jr.	Finland	42	30	37	67	63	...	...	...	—	—	—	—	—
92-93—TPS Turku	Finland	46	3	7	10	28	...	...	...	—	—	—	—	—
93-94—TPS Turku	Finland	47	23	30	53	42	...	...	...	11	4	8	12	16
—Fin. Olympic Team	Int'l	8	4	3	7	12	...	...	...	—	—	—	—	—
94-95—TPS Turku	Finland	45	27	47	74	73	...	...	...	13	7	10	17	16
95-96—Montreal	NHL	82	20	25	45	40	-7	8	3	6	3	1	4	8
96-97—Montreal	NHL	50	17	39	56	38	7	5	0	5	1	3	4	10
97-98—Montreal	NHL	69	14	43	57	48	8	2	2	6	2	3	5	2
—Fin. Olympic Team	Int'l	6	2	8	10	4	...	...	...	—	—	—	—	—
NHL Totals (3 years)...........		201	51	107	158	126	8	15	5	17	6	7	13	20

KOKOREV, DMITRI   D   FLAMES

PERSONAL: Born January 9, 1979, in Moscow, U.S.S.R. ... 6-3/198. ... Shoots left.
TRANSACTIONS/CAREER NOTES: Selected by Calgary Flames in second round (fourth Flames pick, 51st overall) of NHL entry draft (June 21, 1997).

Season Team	League	REGULAR SEASON								PLAYOFFS				
		Gms.	G	A	Pts.	PIM	+/-	PP	SH	Gms.	G	A	Pts.	PIM
94-95—Dynamo Moscow........	CIS Div. II	10	0	1	1	8	...	...	...	—	—	—	—	—
95-96—Dynamo Moscow........	CIS Div. II	4	0	4	4	...	...	...	...	—	—	—	—	—
96-97—Dynamo-2 Moscow	Rus. Div. III	27	2	4	6	24	...	...	...	—	—	—	—	—
—Dynamo Moscow........	Russian	1	0	0	0	0	...	...	...	—	—	—	—	—
97-98—Dynamo Moscow	Russian				Statistics unavailable.									

KOLKUNOV, ALEXEI   C   PENGUINS

PERSONAL: Born February 3, 1977, in Belgorod, U.S.S.R. ... 6-2/190. ... Shoots left.
TRANSACTIONS/CAREER NOTES: Selected by Pittsburgh Penguins in sixth round (fifth Penguins pick, 154th overall) of NHL entry draft (July 8, 1995).

Season Team	League	REGULAR SEASON								PLAYOFFS				
		Gms.	G	A	Pts.	PIM	+/-	PP	SH	Gms.	G	A	Pts.	PIM
94-95—Krylja Sov. Moscow....	Russian	44	9	16	25	36	...	...	...	2	0	0	0	4
—Soviet Wings	CIS	7	0	0	0	0	...	...	...	4	1	0	1	0
95-96—Soviet Wings	CIS	43	9	3	12	35	...	...	...	—	—	—	—	—
96-97—Krylja Sov. Moscow....	Russian	44	9	16	25	36	...	...	...	2	0	0	0	4
97-98—Krylja Sov. Moscow....	Russian	20	6	4	10	22	...	...	...	—	—	—	—	—

K

KOLZIG, OLAF   G   CAPITALS

PERSONAL: Born April 6, 1970, in Johannesburg, South Africa. ... 6-3/225. ... Catches left. ... Name pronounced OH-lahf KOHL-zihg.
TRANSACTIONS/CAREER NOTES: Underwent surgery to right knee (November 1988). ... Selected by Washington Capitals in first round (first Capitals pick, 19th overall) of NHL entry draft (June 17, 1989). ... Loaned by Capitals to Rochester Americans (October 2, 1992). ... Dislocated kneecap (October 13, 1993); missed 14 games. ... Suffered from mononucleosis (October 8, 1996); missed three games.
HONORS: Shared Harry (Hap) Holmes Memorial Trophy with Byron Dafoe (1993-94). ... Won Jack Butterfield Trophy (1993-94). ... Played in NHL All-Star Game (1998).
MISCELLANEOUS: Stopped penalty shot attempt (vs. Mike Hough, February 29, 1996; vs. Todd Marchant, January, 26, 1997).

Season Team	League	|REGULAR SEASON|								|PLAYOFFS|						
		Gms.	Min	W	L	T	GA	SO	Avg.	Gms.	Min.	W	L	GA	SO	Avg.
87-88—New Westminster.........	WHL	15	650	6	5	0	48	1	4.43	3	149	0	0	11	0	4.43
88-89—Tri-City	WHL	30	1671	16	10	2	97	1	*3.48	—	—	—	—	—	—	—
89-90—Washington..................	NHL	2	120	0	2	0	12	0	6.00	—	—	—	—	—	—	—
—Tri-City	WHL	48	2504	27	27	3	187	1	4.48	6	318	4	0	27	0	5.09
90-91—Baltimore	AHL	26	1367	10	12	1	72	0	3.16	—	—	—	—	—	—	—
—Hampton Roads	ECHL	21	1248	11	9	‡1	71	2	3.41	3	180	1	2	14	0	4.67
91-92—Baltimore	AHL	28	1503	5	17	2	105	1	4.19	—	—	—	—	—	—	—
—Hampton Roads	ECHL	14	847	11	3	‡0	41	0	2.90	—	—	—	—	—	—	—
92-93—Rochester	AHL	49	2737	25	16	4	168	0	3.68	17	*1040	9	*8	61	0	3.52
—Washington	NHL	1	20	0	0	0	2	0	6.00	—	—	—	—	—	—	—
93-94—Portland	AHL	29	1726	16	8	5	88	3	3.06	17	1035	†12	5	44	0	*2.55
—Washington	NHL	7	224	0	3	0	20	0	5.36	—	—	—	—	—	—	—
94-95—Washington..................	NHL	14	724	2	8	2	30	0	2.49	2	44	1	0	1	0	1.36
—Portland	AHL	2	125	1	0	1	3	0	1.44	—	—	—	—	—	—	—
95-96—Washington..................	NHL	18	897	4	8	2	46	0	3.08	5	341	2	3	11	0	1.94
—Portland	AHL	5	300	5	0	0	7	1	1.40	—	—	—	—	—	—	—
96-97—Washington	NHL	29	1644	8	15	4	71	2	2.59	—	—	—	—	—	—	—
97-98—Washington	NHL	64	3788	33	18	10	139	5	2.20	21	1351	12	*9	44	*4	1.95
—German Olympic team ..	Int'l	2	120	2	0	0	2	1	1.00	—	—	—	—	—	—	—
NHL Totals (7 years).............		**135**	**7417**	**47**	**54**	**18**	**320**	**.7**	**2.59**	**28**	**1736**	**15**	**12**	**56**	**4**	**1.94**

KOMARNISKI, ZENITH   D   CANUCKS

PERSONAL: Born August 13, 1978, in Edmonton. ... 6-0/192. ... Shoots left. ... Name pronounced ZEH-nihth koh-mahr-NIH-skee.
TRANSACTIONS/CAREER NOTES: Selected by Vancouver Canucks in third round (second Canucks pick, 75th overall) of NHL entry draft (June 22, 1996).
HONORS: Named to WHL (West) All-Star first team (1996-97).

Season Team	League	|REGULAR SEASON|							|PLAYOFFS|				
		Gms.	G	A	Pts.	PIM	+/-	PP	SH	Gms.	G	A	Pts.	PIM
94-95—Tri-City	WHL	66	5	19	24	110	...	...	...	17	1	2	3	47
95-96—Tri-City	WHL	42	5	21	26	85	...	...	...	—	—	—	—	—
96-97—Tri-City	WHL	58	12	44	56	112	...	...	...	—	—	—	—	—
97-98—Tri-City	WHL	3	0	4	4	18	...	...	...	—	—	—	—	—
—Spokane.....................	WHL	43	7	20	27	90	...	...	...	18	4	6	10	49

KOMAROV, ALEXEI   D   STARS

PERSONAL: Born June 11, 1978, in Moscow, U.S.S.R. ... 6-4/194. ... Shoots left.
TRANSACTIONS/CAREER NOTES: Selected by Dallas Stars in eighth round (eighth Stars pick, 216th overall) of NHL entry draft (June 21, 1997).

Season Team	League	|REGULAR SEASON|							|PLAYOFFS|				
		Gms.	G	A	Pts.	PIM	+/-	PP	SH	Gms.	G	A	Pts.	PIM
97-98—Dyn.-Energiya Yekat....	Russian	19	0	0	0	6	...	...	...	—	—	—	—	—

KONOWALCHUK, STEVE   LW   CAPITALS

PERSONAL: Born November 11, 1972, in Salt Lake City. ... 6-1/205. ... Shoots left. ... Full name: Steven Reed Konowalchuk. ... Name pronounced kah-nah-WAHL-chuhk.
TRANSACTIONS/CAREER NOTES: Selected by Washington Capitals in third round (fifth Capitals pick, 58th overall) of NHL entry draft (June 22, 1991). ... Separated shoulder (October 13, 1995); missed four games. ... Injured left hand (March 26, 1996); missed eight games. ... Separated rib cartilage prior to 1996-97 season; missed four games. ... Injured groin (January 28, 1998); missed two games.
HONORS: Won Four Broncos Memorial Trophy (1991-92). ... Named to Can.HL All-Star second team (1991-92). ... Named to WHL (West) All-Star first team (1991-92).
MISCELLANEOUS: Failed to score on a penalty shot (vs. Mike Richter, March 5, 1995).
STATISTICAL PLATEAUS: Three-goal games: 1995-96 (2).

Season Team	League	|REGULAR SEASON|							|PLAYOFFS|				
		Gms.	G	A	Pts.	PIM	+/-	PP	SH	Gms.	G	A	Pts.	PIM
90-91—Portland	WHL	72	43	49	92	78	...	...	...	—	—	—	—	—
91-92—Portland	WHL	64	51	53	104	95	...	...	...	6	3	6	9	12
—Baltimore	AHL	3	1	1	2	0	...	...	...	—	—	—	—	—
—Washington	NHL	1	0	0	0	0	0	0	0	—	—	—	—	—
92-93—Baltimore	AHL	37	18	28	46	74	...	...	...	—	—	—	—	—
—Washington	NHL	36	4	7	11	16	4	1	0	2	0	1	1	0
93-94—Portland	AHL	8	11	4	15	4	...	...	...	—	—	—	—	—
—Washington	NHL	62	12	14	26	33	9	0	0	11	0	1	1	10
94-95—Washington	NHL	46	11	14	25	44	7	3	3	7	2	5	7	12
95-96—Washington	NHL	70	23	22	45	92	13	7	1	2	0	2	2	0
96-97—Washington	NHL	78	17	25	42	67	-3	2	1	—	—	—	—	—
97-98—Washington	NHL	80	10	24	34	80	9	2	0	—	—	—	—	—
NHL Totals (7 years)...........		**373**	**77**	**106**	**183**	**332**	**39**	**15**	**5**	**22**	**2**	**9**	**11**	**22**

K

KORDIC, DAN   LW   FLYERS

PERSONAL: Born April 18, 1971, in Edmonton. ... 6-5/227. ... Shoots left. ... Brother of John Kordic, right winger for four NHL teams (1985-86 through 1991-92). ... Name pronounced KOHR-dihk.
TRANSACTIONS/CAREER NOTES: Selected by Philadelphia Flyers in fifth round (eighth Flyers pick, 88th overall) of NHL entry draft (June 16, 1990). ... Suffered from the flu (January 1992); missed five games. ... Underwent knee surgery prior to 1992-93 season; missed 63 games. ... Sprained left knee (February 26, 1997); missed two games. ... Strained lower back (November 13, 1997); missed 10 games.

		REGULAR SEASON								PLAYOFFS				
Season Team	League	Gms.	G	A	Pts.	PIM	+/-	PP	SH	Gms.	G	A	Pts.	PIM
87-88—Medicine Hat..............	WHL	63	1	5	6	75	...	...	...	—	—	—	—	—
88-89—Medicine Hat..............	WHL	70	1	13	14	190	...	...	...	—	—	—	—	—
89-90—Medicine Hat..............	WHL	59	4	12	16	182	...	...	...	3	0	0	0	9
90-91—Medicine Hat..............	WHL	67	8	15	23	150	...	...	...	12	2	6	8	42
91-92—Philadelphia	NHL	46	1	3	4	126	1	0	0	—	—	—	—	—
92-93—Hershey	AHL	14	0	2	2	17	...	...	...	—	—	—	—	—
93-94—Hershey	AHL	64	0	4	4	164	...	...	...	11	0	3	3	26
—Philadelphia	NHL	4	0	0	0	5	0	0	0	—	—	—	—	—
94-95—Hershey	AHL	37	0	2	2	121	...	...	...	6	0	1	1	21
95-96—Hershey	AHL	52	2	6	8	101	...	...	...	—	—	—	—	—
—Philadelphia	NHL	9	1	0	1	31	1	0	0	—	—	—	—	—
96-97—Philadelphia	NHL	75	1	4	5	210	-1	0	0	12	1	0	1	22
97-98—Philadelphia	NHL	61	1	1	2	210	-4	0	0	—	—	—	—	—
NHL Totals (5 years)............		**195**	**4**	**8**	**12**	**582**	**-3**	**0**	**0**	**12**	**1**	**0**	**1**	**22**

KOROLEV, EVGENY   D   ISLANDERS

PERSONAL: Born July 24, 1978, in Moscow, U.S.S.R. ... 6-1/208. ... Shoots left.
TRANSACTIONS/CAREER NOTES: Selected by New York Islanders in sixth round (seventh Islanders pick, 138th overall) of NHL entry draft (June 22, 1996).

		REGULAR SEASON								PLAYOFFS				
Season Team	League	Gms.	G	A	Pts.	PIM	+/-	PP	SH	Gms.	G	A	Pts.	PIM
95-96—Peterborough..............	OHL	60	2	12	14	60	...	...	...	6	0	0	0	2
96-97—Peterborough..............	OHL	64	5	17	22	60	...	...	...	11	1	1	2	8
97-98—Peterborough..............	OHL	37	5	21	26	39	...	...	...	—	—	—	—	—
—London	OHL	27	4	10	14	36	...	...	...	15	2	7	9	29

KOROLEV, IGOR   C/LW   MAPLE LEAFS

PERSONAL: Born September 6, 1970, in Moscow, U.S.S.R. ... 6-1/187. ... Shoots left. ... Name pronounced EE-gohr KOHR-ih-lehv.
TRANSACTIONS/CAREER NOTES: Selected by St. Louis Blues in second round (first Blues pick, 38th overall) of NHL entry draft (June 20, 1992). ... Suffered from the flu (March 3, 1994); missed one game. ... Injured March (March 12, 1994); missed three games. ... Selected by Winnipeg Jets in 1994-95 waiver draft for cash (January 18, 1995). ... Played in Europe during 1994-95 NHL lockout. ... Broke wrist (December 10, 1995); missed two games. ... Suffered hip pointer (February 1, 1996); missed three games. ... Jets franchise moved to Phoenix and renamed Coyotes for 1996-97 season; NHL approved move on January 18, 1996. ... Signed as free agent by Toronto Maple Leafs (September 28, 1997). ... Sprained shoulder (October 28, 1997); missed one game. ... Strained back (January 6, 1998); missed one game.
STATISTICAL PLATEAUS: Three-goal games: 1995-96 (1).

		REGULAR SEASON								PLAYOFFS				
Season Team	League	Gms.	G	A	Pts.	PIM	+/-	PP	SH	Gms.	G	A	Pts.	PIM
88-89—Dynamo Moscow........	USSR	1	0	0	0	2	...	...	...	—	—	—	—	—
89-90—Dynamo Moscow........	USSR	17	3	2	5	2	...	...	...	—	—	—	—	—
90-91—Dynamo Moscow........	USSR	38	12	4	16	12	...	...	...	—	—	—	—	—
91-92—Dynamo Moscow........	CIS	39	15	12	27	16	...	...	...	—	—	—	—	—
92-93—Dynamo Moscow........	CIS	5	1	2	3	4	...	...	...	—	—	—	—	—
—St. Louis	NHL	74	4	23	27	20	-1	2	0	3	0	0	0	0
93-94—St. Louis	NHL	73	6	10	16	40	-12	0	0	2	0	0	0	0
94-95—Dynamo Moscow........	CIS	13	4	6	10	18	...	...	...	—	—	—	—	—
—Winnipeg	NHL	45	8	22	30	10	1	1	0	—	—	—	—	—
95-96—Winnipeg	NHL	73	22	29	51	42	1	8	0	6	0	3	3	0
96-97—Michigan.....................	IHL	4	2	2	4	0	...	...	...	—	—	—	—	—
—Phoenix.....................	IHL	4	2	6	8	4	...	...	...	—	—	—	—	—
—Phoenix.....................	NHL	41	3	7	10	28	-5	2	0	1	0	0	0	0
97-98—Toronto	NHL	78	17	22	39	22	-18	6	3	—	—	—	—	—
NHL Totals (6 years)............		**384**	**60**	**113**	**173**	**162**	**-34**	**19**	**3**	**12**	**0**	**3**	**3**	**0**

KOROLYUK, ALEXANDER   RW   SHARKS

PERSONAL: Born January 15, 1976, in Moscow, U.S.S.R. ... 5-9/165. ... Shoots left. ... Name pronounced KOH-rohl-yook.
TRANSACTIONS/CAREER NOTES: Selected by San Jose Sharks in sixth round (sixth Sharks pick, 141st overall) of NHL entry draft (June 29, 1994).

		REGULAR SEASON								PLAYOFFS				
Season Team	League	Gms.	G	A	Pts.	PIM	+/-	PP	SH	Gms.	G	A	Pts.	PIM
93-94—Soviet Wings	CIS	22	4	4	8	20	...	...	...	3	1	0	1	4
94-95—Soviet Wings	CIS	52	16	13	29	62	...	...	...	4	1	2	3	4
95-96—Soviet Wings	CIS	50	30	19	49	77	...	...	...	—	—	—	—	—
96-97—Manitoba.....................	IHL	42	20	16	36	71	...	...	...	—	—	—	—	—
97-98—San Jose	NHL	19	2	3	5	6	-5	1	0	—	—	—	—	—
—Kentucky.....................	AHL	44	16	23	39	96	...	...	...	3	0	0	0	0
NHL Totals (1 year).............		**19**	**2**	**3**	**5**	**6**	**-5**	**1**	**0**					

KOVALENKO, ANDREI RW OILERS

PERSONAL: Born July 7, 1970, in Gorky, U.S.S.R. ... 5-10/215. ... Shoots left. ... Name pronounced koh-vuh-LEHN-koh.

TRANSACTIONS/CAREER NOTES: Selected by Quebec Nordiques in eighth round (sixth Nordiques pick, 148th overall) of NHL entry draft (June 16, 1990). ... Suffered from tonsillitis (December 22, 1992); missed two games. ... Suffered from the flu (March 15, 1993); missed one game. ... Suffered concussion (November 4, 1993); missed five games. ... Bruised ribs (January 11, 1994); missed two games. ... Injured shoulder (January 25, 1994); missed 14 games. ... Suffered from tonsillitis (April 3, 1994); missed two games. ... Played in Europe during 1994-95 NHL lockout. ... Pulled groin (March 9, 1995); missed one game. ... Injured neck (April 5, 1995); missed one game. ... Injured thumb (April 20, 1995); missed one game. ... Nordiques franchise moved to Colorado and renamed Avalanche for 1995-96 season (June 21, 1995). ... Traded by Avalanche with G Jocelyn Thibault and LW Martin Rucinsky to Montreal Canadiens for G Patrick Roy and RW Mike Keane (December 6, 1995). ... Broke nose (December 16, 1995); missed five games. ... Strained left rotator cuff (February 15, 1996); missed two games. ... Traded by Canadiens to Edmonton Oilers for C Scott Thornton (September 6, 1996). ... Suffered back spasms (February 17, 1997); missed two games. ... Suffered hip pointer (March 1, 1997); missed five games. ... Suffered back spasms (October 13, 1997); missed one game. ... Suffered rib injury (December 30, 1997); missed one game. ... Suffered from the flu (March 4, 1998); missed one game. ... Suffered back spasms (March 11, 1998); missed three games. ... Suffered back spasms (March 30, 1998); missed final eight games of regular season and 11 playoff games.

MISCELLANEOUS: Member of gold-medal-winning Unified Olympic team (1992). ... Scored on a penalty shot (vs. Kirk McLean, December 4, 1993). ... Member of silver-medal-winning Russian Olympic team (1998).

STATISTICAL PLATEAUS: Three-goal games: 1992-93 (1).

			REGULAR SEASON								PLAYOFFS				
Season Team	League	Gms.	G	A	Pts.	PIM	+/-	PP	SH		Gms.	G	A	Pts.	PIM
88-89—CSKA Moscow	USSR	10	1	0	1	0	...	...	...		—	—	—	—	—
89-90—CSKA Moscow	USSR	48	8	5	13	18	...	...	...		—	—	—	—	—
90-91—CSKA Moscow	USSR	45	13	8	21	26	...	...	...		—	—	—	—	—
91-92—CSKA Moscow	CIS	44	19	13	32	32	...	...	...		—	—	—	—	—
—Unif. Olympic Team	Int'l	8	1	1	2	2	...	...	...		—	—	—	—	—
92-93—CSKA Moscow	CIS	3	3	1	4	4	...	...	...		—	—	—	—	—
—Quebec	NHL	81	27	41	68	57	13	8	1		4	1	0	1	2
93-94—Quebec	NHL	58	16	17	33	46	-5	5	0		—	—	—	—	—
94-95—Lada Togliatti	CIS	11	9	2	11	14	...	...	...		—	—	—	—	—
—Quebec	NHL	45	14	10	24	31	-4	1	0		6	0	1	1	2
95-96—Colorado	NHL	26	11	11	22	16	11	3	0		—	—	—	—	—
—Montreal	NHL	51	17	17	34	33	9	3	0		6	0	0	0	6
96-97—Edmonton	NHL	74	32	27	59	81	-5	14	0		12	4	3	7	6
97-98—Edmonton	NHL	59	6	17	23	28	-14	1	0		1	0	0	0	2
—Russian Oly. team	Int'l	6	4	1	5	14	...	...	...		—	—	—	—	—
NHL Totals (6 years)		394	123	140	263	292	5	35	1		29	5	4	9	18

KOVALEV, ALEXEI RW RANGERS

PERSONAL: Born February 24, 1973, in Moscow, U.S.S.R. ... 6-2/210. ... Shoots left. ... Name pronounced KOH-vuh-lahf.

TRANSACTIONS/CAREER NOTES: Selected by New York Rangers in first round (first Rangers pick, 15th overall) of NHL entry draft (June 22, 1991). ... Suffered back spasms (January 16, 1993); missed one game. ... Suspended one game by NHL (November 10, 1993). ... Suspended five games by NHL for tripping (November 30, 1993). ... Suspended two games by NHL (February 12, 1994). ... Played in Europe during 1994-95 NHL lockout. ... Suffered from the flu (December 2, 1995); missed one game. ... Tore knee ligament (January 8, 1997); missed remainder of season. ... Sprained knee and underwent athroscopic surgery (January 22, 1998); missed eight games.

MISCELLANEOUS: Member of Stanley Cup championship team (1994). ... Member of gold-medal-winning Unified Olympic team (1992). ... Failed to score on a penalty shot (vs. Jon Casey, October 5, 1993). ... Member of silver-medal-winning Russian Olympic team (1998).

STATISTICAL PLATEAUS: Three-goal games: 1992-93 (1), 1996-97 (1). Total: 2.

			REGULAR SEASON								PLAYOFFS				
Season Team	League	Gms.	G	A	Pts.	PIM	+/-	PP	SH		Gms.	G	A	Pts.	PIM
89-90—Dynamo Moscow	USSR	1	0	0	0	0	...	...	...		—	—	—	—	—
90-91—Dynamo Moscow	USSR	18	1	2	3	4	...	...	...		—	—	—	—	—
91-92—Dynamo Moscow	CIS	33	16	9	25	20	...	...	...		—	—	—	—	—
—Unif. Olympic Team	Int'l	8	1	2	3	14	...	...	...		—	—	—	—	—
92-93—New York Rangers	NHL	65	20	18	38	79	-10	3	0		—	—	—	—	—
—Binghamton	AHL	13	13	11	24	35	...	...	...		9	3	5	8	14
93-94—New York Rangers	NHL	76	23	33	56	154	18	7	0		23	9	12	21	18
94-95—Lada Togliatti	CIS	12	8	8	16	49	...	...	...		—	—	—	—	—
—New York Rangers	NHL	48	13	15	28	30	-6	1	1		10	4	7	11	10
95-96—New York Rangers	NHL	81	24	34	58	98	5	8	1		11	3	4	7	14
96-97—New York Rangers	NHL	45	13	22	35	42	11	1	0		—	—	—	—	—
97-98—New York Rangers	NHL	73	23	30	53	44	-22	8	0		—	—	—	—	—
NHL Totals (6 years)		388	116	152	268	447	-4	28	2		44	16	23	39	42

KOZLOV, SLAVA LW RED WINGS

PERSONAL: Born May 3, 1972, in Voskresensk, U.S.S.R. ... 5-10/185. ... Shoots left. ... Full name: Vyacheslav Kozlov. ... Name pronounced VYACH-ih-slav KAHZ-lahf.

TRANSACTIONS/CAREER NOTES: Selected by Detroit Red Wings in third round (second Red Wings pick, 45th overall) of NHL entry draft (June 16, 1990). ... Played in Europe during 1994-95 NHL lockout. ... Bruised left foot (April 16, 1995); missed one game. ... Sprained knee (April 15, 1998); missed final two games of regular season.

HONORS: Named Soviet League Rookie of the Year (1989-90).

MISCELLANEOUS: Member of Stanley Cup championship team (1997 and 1998).

STATISTICAL PLATEAUS: Three-goal games: 1993-94 (1). ... Four-goal games: 1995-96 (1). ... Total hat tricks: 2.

Season Team	League	REGULAR SEASON								PLAYOFFS				
		Gms.	G	A	Pts.	PIM	+/-	PP	SH	Gms.	G	A	Pts.	PIM
87-88—Khimik	USSR	2	0	1	1	0	...	...	...	—	—	—	—	—
88-89—Khimik	USSR	13	0	1	1	2	...	...	...	—	—	—	—	—
89-90—Khimik	USSR	45	14	12	26	38	...	...	...	—	—	—	—	—
90-91—Khimik	USSR	45	11	13	24	46	...	...	...	—	—	—	—	—
91-92—Khimik	USSR	11	6	5	11	12	...	...	...	—	—	—	—	—
—Detroit	NHL	7	0	2	2	2	-2	0	0	—	—	—	—	—
92-93—Detroit	NHL	17	4	1	5	14	-1	0	0	4	0	2	2	2
—Adirondack	AHL	45	23	36	59	54	...	...	...	4	1	1	2	4
93-94—Detroit	NHL	77	34	39	73	50	27	8	2	7	2	5	7	12
—Adirondack	AHL	3	0	1	1	15	...	...	...	—	—	—	—	—
94-95—CSKA Moscow	CIS	10	3	4	7	14	...	...	...	—	—	—	—	—
—Detroit	NHL	46	13	20	33	45	12	5	0	18	9	7	16	10
95-96—Detroit	NHL	82	36	37	70	73	33	9	0	19	5	7	12	10
96-97—Detroit	NHL	75	23	22	45	46	21	3	0	20	8	5	13	14
97-98—Detroit	NHL	80	25	27	52	46	14	6	0	22	6	8	14	10
NHL Totals (7 years)		384	135	148	283	273	104	31	2	90	30	34	64	58

KOZLOV, VIKTOR — LW — PANTHERS

PERSONAL: Born February 14, 1975, in Togliatti, U.S.S.R. ... 6-5/225. ... Shoots right. ... Name pronounced KAHZ-lahf.
TRANSACTIONS/CAREER NOTES: Selected by San Jose Sharks in first round (first Sharks pick, sixth overall) of NHL entry draft (June 26, 1993). ... Suffered displaced ankle fracture (November 27, 1994); missed 13 games. ... Played in Europe during 1994-95 NHL lockout. ... Bruised ankle (March 26, 1997); missed four games. ... Traded by Sharks with fifth-round pick (D Jaroslav Spacek) in 1998 draft to Florida Panthers for LW Dave Lowry and first-round pick (traded to Tampa Bay) in 1998 draft (November 13, 1997). ... Separated right shoulder (November 18, 1997); missed 16 games. ... Suffered concussion (April 1, 1998); missed three games.

K

Season Team	League	REGULAR SEASON								PLAYOFFS				
		Gms.	G	A	Pts.	PIM	+/-	PP	SH	Gms.	G	A	Pts.	PIM
90-91—Lada Togliatti	USSR Div. II	2	2	0	2	0	...	...	...	—	—	—	—	—
91-92—Lada Togliatti	CIS	3	0	0	0	0	...	...	...	—	—	—	—	—
92-93—Dynamo Moscow	CIS	30	6	5	11	4	...	...	...	10	3	0	3	0
93-94—Dynamo Moscow	CIS	42	16	9	25	14	...	...	...	7	3	2	5	0
94-95—Dynamo Moscow	CIS	3	1	1	2	2	...	...	...	—	—	—	—	—
—San Jose	NHL	16	2	0	2	2	-5	0	0	—	—	—	—	—
—Kansas City	IHL	—	—	—	—	—	...	...	...	13	4	5	9	12
95-96—Kansas City	IHL	15	4	7	11	12	...	...	...	—	—	—	—	—
—San Jose	NHL	62	6	13	19	6	-15	1	0	—	—	—	—	—
96-97—San Jose	NHL	78	16	25	41	40	-16	4	0	—	—	—	—	—
97-98—San Jose	NHL	18	5	2	7	2	-2	2	0	—	—	—	—	—
—Florida	NHL	46	12	11	23	14	-1	3	2	—	—	—	—	—
NHL Totals (4 years)		220	41	51	92	64	-39	10	2					

KRAVCHUK, IGOR — D — SENATORS

PERSONAL: Born September 13, 1966, in Ufa, U.S.S.R. ... 6-0/200. ... Shoots left. ... Name pronounced EE-gohr KRAV-chuk.
TRANSACTIONS/CAREER NOTES: Selected by Chicago Blackhawks in fourth round (fifth Blackhawks pick, 71st overall) of NHL entry draft (June 22, 1991). ... Sprained knee (October 25, 1992); missed four games. ... Sprained left ankle (December 29, 1992); missed 18 games. ... Traded by Blackhawks with C Dean McAmmond to Edmonton Oilers for RW Joe Murphy (February 25, 1993). ... Sprained left knee (April 6, 1993); missed remainder of season. ... Strained groin (November 15, 1993); missed three games. ... Injured left knee (January 30, 1995) and underwent surgery (February 6, 1995); missed 12 games. ... Suffered deep bone bruise to left leg (October 21, 1995); missed six games. ... Injured knee (November 20, 1995); missed four games. ... Traded by Oilers with D Ken Sutton to St. Louis Blues for D Donald Dufresne and D Jeff Norton (January 4, 1996). ... Traded by Blues to Ottawa Senators for D Steve Duchesne (August 25, 1997). ... Injured hip (March 20, 1998); missed one game.
HONORS: Played in NHL All-Star Game (1998).
MISCELLANEOUS: Member of gold-medal-winning U.S.S.R. Olympic team (1988) and gold-medal-winning Unified Olympic team (1992). ... Member of silver-medal-winning Russian Olympic team (1998).

Season Team	League	REGULAR SEASON								PLAYOFFS				
		Gms.	G	A	Pts.	PIM	+/-	PP	SH	Gms.	G	A	Pts.	PIM
87-88—CSKA Moscow	USSR	47	1	8	9	12	...	...	...	—	—	—	—	—
88-89—CSKA Moscow	USSR	27	3	4	7	2	...	...	...	—	—	—	—	—
89-90—CSKA Moscow	USSR	48	1	3	4	16	...	...	...	—	—	—	—	—
90-91—CSKA Moscow	USSR	41	6	5	11	16	...	...	...	—	—	—	—	—
91-92—CSKA Moscow	CIS	30	3	7	10	2	...	...	...	—	—	—	—	—
—Unif. Olympic Team	Int'l	8	3	2	5	...	...	...	...	—	—	—	—	—
—Chicago	NHL	18	1	8	9	4	-3	0	0	18	2	6	8	8
92-93—Chicago	NHL	38	6	9	15	30	11	3	0	—	—	—	—	—
—Edmonton	NHL	17	4	8	12	2	-8	1	0	—	—	—	—	—
93-94—Edmonton	NHL	81	12	38	50	16	-12	5	0	—	—	—	—	—
94-95—Edmonton	NHL	36	7	11	18	29	-15	3	1	—	—	—	—	—
95-96—Edmonton	NHL	26	4	4	8	10	-13	3	0	—	—	—	—	—
—St. Louis	NHL	40	3	12	15	24	-6	0	0	10	1	5	6	4
96-97—St. Louis	NHL	82	4	24	28	35	7	1	0	2	0	0	0	2
97-98—Ottawa	NHL	81	8	27	35	8	-19	3	1	11	2	3	5	4
—Russian Oly. team	Int'l	6	0	2	2	2	...	...	...	—	—	—	—	—
NHL Totals (7 years)		419	49	141	190	158	-58	19	2	41	5	14	19	18

KRISTOFFERSON, MARCUS   RW   STARS

PERSONAL: Born January 22, 1979, in Ostersund, Sweden. ... 6-3/200. ... Shoots left.
TRANSACTIONS/CAREER NOTES: Selected by Dallas Stars in fourth round (fourth Stars pick, 105th overall) of NHL entry draft (June 21, 1997).

		REGULAR SEASON								PLAYOFFS				
Season Team	League	Gms.	G	A	Pts.	PIM	+/-	PP	SH	Gms.	G	A	Pts.	PIM
95-96—Mora Jrs.	Sweden	16	2	2	4	28	...	...	...	—	—	—	—	—
—Mora	Swed. Dv.II	26	1	0	1	20	...	...	...	5	0	0	0	2
96-97—Mora	Swed. Dv.II	33	1	5	6	26	...	...	...	—	—	—	—	—
97-98—Mora	Swed. Dv.II	13	5	3	8	16	...	...	...	—	—	—	—	—

KRIVOKRASOV, SERGEI   RW   PREDATORS

PERSONAL: Born April 15, 1974, in Angarsk, U.S.S.R. ... 5-10/185. ... Shoots left. ... Name pronounced SAIR-gay KREE-voh-KRAS-ahf.
TRANSACTIONS/CAREER NOTES: Selected by Chicago Blackhawks in first round (first Blackhawks pick, 12th overall) of NHL entry draft (June 20, 1992). ... Sprained knee (January 31, 1996); missed 14 games. ... Sprained knee (March 14, 1996); missed 13 games. ... Sprained left knee (December 17, 1997); missed 16 games. ... Lacerated elbow (March 9, 1998); missed five games. ... Traded by Blackhawks to Nashville Predators for future considerations (June 27, 1998).
MISCELLANEOUS: Member of silver-medal-winning Russian Olympic team (1998).

		REGULAR SEASON								PLAYOFFS				
Season Team	League	Gms.	G	A	Pts.	PIM	+/-	PP	SH	Gms.	G	A	Pts.	PIM
90-91—CSKA Moscow	USSR	41	4	0	4	8	...	...	...	—	—	—	—	—
91-92—CSKA Moscow	CIS	42	10	8	18	35	...	...	...	—	—	—	—	—
92-93—Chicago	NHL	4	0	0	0	2	-2	0	0	—	—	—	—	—
—Indianapolis	IHL	78	36	33	69	157	...	...	...	5	3	1	4	2
93-94—Indianapolis	IHL	53	19	26	45	145	...	...	...	—	—	—	—	—
—Chicago	NHL	9	1	0	1	4	-2	0	0	—	—	—	—	—
94-95—Indianapolis	IHL	29	12	15	27	41	...	...	...	—	—	—	—	—
—Chicago	NHL	41	12	7	19	33	9	6	0	10	0	0	0	8
95-96—Indianapolis	IHL	9	4	5	9	28	...	...	...	—	—	—	—	—
—Chicago	NHL	46	6	10	16	32	10	0	0	5	1	0	1	2
96-97—Chicago	NHL	67	13	11	24	42	-1	2	0	6	1	0	1	4
97-98—Chicago	NHL	58	10	13	23	33	-1	1	0	—	—	—	—	—
—Russian Oly. team	Int'l	6	0	0	0	4	...	...	...	—	—	—	—	—
NHL Totals (6 years)		225	42	41	83	146	13	9	0	21	2	0	2	14

KRIZ, PAVEL   D   BLACKHAWKS

PERSONAL: Born January 2, 1977, in Kladno, Czechoslovakia. ... 6-2/205. ... Shoots right.
TRANSACTIONS/CAREER NOTES: Selected by Chicago Blackhawks in fourth round (fifth Blackhawks pick, 97th overall) of NHL entry draft (July 8, 1995).

		REGULAR SEASON								PLAYOFFS				
Season Team	League	Gms.	G	A	Pts.	PIM	+/-	PP	SH	Gms.	G	A	Pts.	PIM
92-93—Kladno	Czech. Jrs.	30	10	14	24	50	...	...	...	—	—	—	—	—
93-94—Kladno	Czech. Jrs.	45	20	25	45	52	...	...	...	—	—	—	—	—
94-95—Tri-City	WHL	68	6	34	40	47	...	...	...	17	5	12	17	6
95-96—Saskatoon	WHL	71	11	52	63	96	...	...	...	4	0	2	2	0
96-97—Pardubice	Czech Rep.	37	0	7	7	63	...	...	...	8	0	1	1	8
97-98—Pojistovna Pardubice	Czech Rep.	42	4	6	10	52	...	...	...	3	1	0	1	14

KRON, ROBERT   RW   HURRICANES

PERSONAL: Born February 27, 1967, in Brno, Czechoslovakia. ... 5-11/182. ... Shoots right. ... Name pronounced KRAHN.
TRANSACTIONS/CAREER NOTES: Selected by Vancouver Canucks in fourth round (fifth Canucks pick, 88th overall) of NHL entry draft (June 15, 1985). ... Played entire season with a broken bone in left wrist (1990-91). ... Underwent surgery to repair torn knee ligaments and wrist fracture (March 22, 1991). ... Fractured ankle (January 28, 1992); missed 22 games. ... Traded by Canucks with third-round pick (D Marek Malik) in 1993 draft and future considerations to Hartford Whalers for C/LW Murray Craven and fifth-round pick (D Scott Walker) in 1993 draft (March 22, 1993); Canucks sent RW Jim Sandlak to Whalers to complete deal (May 17, 1993). ... Sprained shoulder (February 26, 1994); missed seven games. ... Broke thumb (March 29, 1995); missed 11 games. ... Injured groin (March 27, 1996); missed one game. ... Strained abdominal muscle (April 8, 1996); missed three games. ... Sprained knee (January 25, 1997); missed 12 games. ... Whalers franchise moved to North Carolina and renamed Carolina Hurricanes for 1997-98 season; NHL approved move on June 25, 1997.

		REGULAR SEASON								PLAYOFFS				
Season Team	League	Gms.	G	A	Pts.	PIM	+/-	PP	SH	Gms.	G	A	Pts.	PIM
86-87—Zetor Brno	Czech.	28	14	11	25		...	...	...	—	—	—	—	—
87-88—Zetor Brno	Czech.	32	12	6	18		...	...	...	—	—	—	—	—
88-89—Zetor Brno	Czech.	43	28	19	47		...	...	...	—	—	—	—	—
89-90—Dukla Trencin	Czech.	39	22	22	44		...	...	...	—	—	—	—	—
90-91—Vancouver	NHL	76	12	20	32	21	-11	2	3	—	—	—	—	—
91-92—Vancouver	NHL	36	2	2	4	2	-9	0	0	11	1	2	3	2
92-93—Vancouver	NHL	32	10	11	21	14	10	2	2	—	—	—	—	—
—Hartford	NHL	13	4	2	6	4	-5	2	0	—	—	—	—	—
93-94—Hartford	NHL	77	24	26	50	8	0	2	1	—	—	—	—	—
94-95—Hartford	NHL	37	10	8	18	10	-3	3	1	—	—	—	—	—
95-96—Hartford	NHL	77	22	28	50	6	-1	8	1	—	—	—	—	—
96-97—Hartford	NHL	68	10	12	22	10	-18	2	0	—	—	—	—	—
97-98—Carolina	NHL	81	16	20	36	12	-8	4	0	—	—	—	—	—
NHL Totals (8 years)		497	110	129	239	87	-45	25	8	11	1	2	3	2

KROUPA, VLASTIMIL   D   DEVILS

PERSONAL: Born April 27, 1975, in Most, Czechoslovakia. ... 6-3/210. ... Shoots left. ... Name pronounced VLAS-tih-mihl KROO-puh.
TRANSACTIONS/CAREER NOTES: Selected by San Jose Sharks in second round (third Sharks pick, 45th overall) of NHL entry draft (June 26, 1993). ... Injured back (November 17, 1995); missed two games. ... Traded by Sharks to New Jersey Devils for third-round pick (traded to Nashville) in 1998 draft (August 22, 1997).

		REGULAR SEASON							PLAYOFFS				
Season Team	League	Gms.	G	A	Pts.	PIM	+/-	PP	SH	Gms.	G	A	Pts.	PIM
91-92—Litvinov	Czech. Jrs.	37	9	16	25	...	...	...	...	—	—	—	—	—
92-93—Chemo. Litvinov	Czech.	9	0	1	1	...	...	...	...	—	—	—	—	—
93-94—San Jose	NHL	27	1	3	4	20	-6	0	0	14	1	2	3	21
—Kansas City	IHL	39	3	12	15	12	...	...	...	—	—	—	—	—
94-95—Kansas City	IHL	51	4	8	12	49	...	...	...	12	2	4	6	22
—San Jose	NHL	14	0	2	2	16	-7	0	0	6	0	0	0	4
95-96—Kansas City	IHL	39	5	22	27	44	...	...	...	5	0	1	1	6
—San Jose	NHL	27	1	7	8	18	-17	0	0	—	—	—	—	—
96-97—Kentucky	AHL	5	0	3	3	0	...	...	...	—	—	—	—	—
—San Jose	NHL	35	2	6	8	12	-17	2	0	—	—	—	—	—
97-98—New Jersey	NHL	2	0	1	1	0	1	0	0	—	—	—	—	—
—Albany	AHL	71	5	29	34	48	...	...	...	12	0	3	3	6
NHL Totals (5 years)		105	4	19	23	66	-46	2	0	20	1	2	3	25

KRUPP, UWE   D   RED WINGS

K

PERSONAL: Born June 24, 1965, in Cologne, West Germany. ... 6-6/235. ... Shoots right. ... Name pronounced YOO-ee KROOP.
TRANSACTIONS/CAREER NOTES: Selected by Buffalo Sabres in 11th round (13th Sabres pick, 214th overall) of NHL entry draft (June 8, 1983). ... Bruised hip (November 1987). ... Injured head (April 1988). ... Broke rib (January 6, 1989). ... Banned from international competition for 18 months by IIHF after failing random substance test (April 20, 1990). ... Suffered from cyst on foot (January 2, 1991). ... Traded by Sabres with C Pierre Turgeon, RW Benoit Hogue and C Dave McLlwain to New York Islanders for C Pat LaFontaine, LW Randy Wood, D Randy Hillier and future considerations; Sabres received fourth-round pick (D Dean Melanson) in 1992 draft to complete deal (October 25, 1991). ... Sprained left knee (December 28, 1991); missed five games. ... Bruised thigh (February 7, 1992). ... Suffered from the flu (March 2, 1993); missed one game. ... Suffered sore shoulder (April 10, 1993); missed three games. ... Broke toe (October 10, 1993); missed three games. ... Fractured sinus bone (October 26, 1993); missed 17 games. ... Suffered severely sprained hamstring (December 19, 1993); missed nine games. ... Suffered from the flu, bruised jaw and sprained wrist (February 27, 1994); missed four games. ... Sprained wrist (March 5, 1994); missed nine games. ... Traded by Islanders with first-round pick (D Wade Belak) in 1994 draft to Quebec Nordiques for C Ron Sutter and first-round pick (RW Brett Lindros) in 1994 draft (June 28, 1994). ... Played in Europe during 1994-95 NHL lockout. ... Injured hip (February 23, 1995); missed two games. ... Injured hip flexor (April 18, 1995); missed two games. ... Nordiques franchise moved to Colorado and renamed Avalanche for 1995-96 season (June 21, 1995). ... Tore knee ligaments (October 6, 1995); missed first 76 games of season. ... Separated shoulder (November 8, 1996); missed five games. ... Suffered tendinitis in elbow (February 18, 1997); missed eight games. ... Suffered sore back (March 26, 1997); missed remainder of season. ... Injured back (January 31, 1998); missed two games. ... Suffered sore back (March 11, 1998); missed one game. ... Selected by Nashville Predators in NHL expansion draft (June 26, 1998). ... Signed as free agent by Detroit Red Wings (July 6, 1998).
HONORS: Played in NHL All-Star Game (1991).
MISCELLANEOUS: Member of Stanley Cup championship team (1996).
STATISTICAL PLATEAUS: Three-goal games: 1994-95 (1).

		REGULAR SEASON							PLAYOFFS				
Season Team	League	Gms.	G	A	Pts.	PIM	+/-	PP	SH	Gms.	G	A	Pts.	PIM
83-84—KEC	W. Germ.	40	0	4	4	22	...	...	...	—	—	—	—	—
84-85—KEC	W. Germ.	39	11	8	19	36	...	...	...	—	—	—	—	—
85-86—KEC	W. Germ.	45	10	21	31	83	...	...	...	—	—	—	—	—
86-87—Rochester	AHL	42	3	19	22	50	...	...	...	17	1	11	12	16
—Buffalo	NHL	26	1	4	5	23	-9	0	0	—	—	—	—	—
87-88—Buffalo	NHL	75	2	9	11	151	-1	0	0	6	0	0	0	15
88-89—Buffalo	NHL	70	5	13	18	55	0	0	1	5	0	1	1	4
89-90—Buffalo	NHL	74	3	20	23	85	15	0	1	6	0	0	0	4
90-91—Buffalo	NHL	74	12	32	44	66	14	6	0	6	1	1	2	6
91-92—Buffalo	NHL	8	2	0	2	6	0	0	0	—	—	—	—	—
—New York Islanders	NHL	59	6	29	35	43	13	2	0	—	—	—	—	—
92-93—New York Islanders	NHL	80	9	29	38	67	6	2	0	18	1	5	6	12
93-94—New York Islanders	NHL	41	7	14	21	30	11	3	0	4	0	1	1	4
94-95—Landshut	Germany	5	1	2	3	6	...	...	...	—	—	—	—	—
—Quebec	NHL	44	6	17	23	20	14	3	0	5	0	2	2	2
95-96—Colorado	NHL	6	0	3	3	4	4	0	0	22	4	12	16	33
96-97—Colorado	NHL	60	4	17	21	48	12	2	0	—	—	—	—	—
97-98—Colorado	NHL	78	9	22	31	38	21	5	0	7	0	1	1	4
—German Oly. team	Int'l	2	0	2	2	4	...	...	...	—	—	—	—	—
NHL Totals (12 years)		695	66	209	275	636	100	23	2	79	6	23	29	84

KRUSE, PAUL   LW   SABRES

PERSONAL: Born March 15, 1970, in Merritt, B.C. ... 6-0/202. ... Shoots left. ... Name pronounced KROOS.
TRANSACTIONS/CAREER NOTES: Selected by Calgary Flames in fourth round (sixth Flames pick, 83rd overall) of NHL entry draft (June 16, 1990). ... Injured eye (March 8, 1992); missed four games. ... Suffered hip pointer (March 21, 1993); missed one game. ... Broke toe on right foot (September 27, 1993); missed 12 games. ... Bruised left foot (March 2, 1995); missed one game. ... Bruised left knee (April 29, 1995); missed one game. ... Bruised ribs (February 13, 1996); missed three games. ... Cut wrist (April 9, 1996); missed two games. ... Traded by Flames to New York Islanders for third-round pick (traded to Hartford) in 1997 draft (November 27, 1996). ... Strained abdominal muscle (March 16, 1997); missed 12 games. ... Traded by Islanders with LW Jason Holland to Buffalo Sabres for RW Jason Dawe (March 24, 1998). ... Strained hip flexor (February 4, 1998); missed one game. ... Bruised hand (March 6, 1998); missed one game. ... Sprained knee (April 15, 1998); missed final two games of regular season and nine playoff games.

Season Team	League	REGULAR SEASON								PLAYOFFS				
		Gms.	G	A	Pts.	PIM	+/-	PP	SH	Gms.	G	A	Pts.	PIM
86-87—Merritt	BCJHL	35	8	15	23	120	...	...	...	—	—	—	—	—
87-88—Merritt	BCJHL	44	12	32	44	227	...	...	...	4	1	4	5	18
—Moose Jaw	WHL	1	0	0	0	0	...	...	...	—	—	—	—	—
88-89—Kamloops	WHL	68	8	15	23	209	...	...	...	—	—	—	—	—
89-90—Kamloops	WHL	67	22	23	45	291	...	...	...	17	3	5	8	†79
90-91—Salt Lake City	IHL	83	24	20	44	313	...	...	...	4	1	1	2	4
—Calgary	NHL	1	0	0	0	7	-1	0	0	—	—	—	—	—
91-92—Salt Lake City	IHL	57	14	15	29	267	...	...	...	5	1	2	3	19
—Calgary	NHL	16	3	1	4	65	1	0	0	—	—	—	—	—
92-93—Salt Lake City	IHL	35	1	4	5	206	...	...	...	—	—	—	—	—
—Calgary	NHL	27	2	3	5	41	2	0	0	—	—	—	—	—
93-94—Calgary	NHL	68	3	8	11	185	-6	0	0	7	0	0	0	14
94-95—Calgary	NHL	45	11	5	16	141	13	0	0	7	4	2	6	10
95-96—Calgary	NHL	75	3	12	15	145	-5	0	0	3	0	0	0	4
96-97—Calgary	NHL	14	2	0	2	30	-4	0	0	—	—	—	—	—
—New York Islanders	NHL	48	4	2	6	111	-5	0	0	—	—	—	—	—
97-98—New York Islanders	NHL	62	6	1	7	138	-12	0	0	—	—	—	—	—
—Buffalo	NHL	12	1	1	2	49	1	0	0	1	1	0	1	4
NHL Totals (8 years)		368	35	33	68	912	-16	0	0	18	5	2	7	32

KRYGIER, TODD — LW

PERSONAL: Born October 12, 1965, in Northville, Mich. ... 6-0/193. ... Shoots left. ... Full name: Todd Andrew Krygier. ... Name pronounced KREE-guhr.
COLLEGE: Connecticut.
TRANSACTIONS/CAREER NOTES: Selected by Hartford Whalers in NHL supplemental draft (June 10, 1988). ... Bruised heel (March 13, 1990). ... Traded by Whalers to Washington Capitals for fourth-round pick (traded to Calgary) in 1993 draft (October 3, 1991). ... Separated right shoulder (December 28, 1993); missed seven games. ... Traded by Capitals to Mighty Ducks of Anaheim for fourth-round pick (traded to Dallas) in 1996 draft (February 2, 1995). ... Slightly strained groin (March 11, 1995); missed three games. ... Strained groin (March 30, 1995); missed three games. ... Traded by Mighty Ducks to Washington Capitals for G Mike Torchia (March 8, 1996). ... Suffered from the flu (April 11, 1996); missed one game. ... Injured wrist (November 6, 1996); missed one game. ... Sprained left wrist (December 20, 1996); missed 17 games. ... Reinjured left wrist (March 10, 1997); missed six games. ... Injured sternum (December 10, 1997); missed eight games.
STATISTICAL PLATEAUS: Three-goal games: 1993-94 (1).

Season Team	League	REGULAR SEASON								PLAYOFFS				
		Gms.	G	A	Pts.	PIM	+/-	PP	SH	Gms.	G	A	Pts.	PIM
84-85—Univ. of Connecticut	ECAC-II	14	14	11	25	12	...	...	...	—	—	—	—	—
85-86—Univ. of Connecticut	ECAC-II	32	29	27	56	46	...	...	...	—	—	—	—	—
86-87—Univ. of Connecticut	ECAC-II	28	24	24	48	44	...	...	...	—	—	—	—	—
87-88—Univ. of Connecticut	ECAC-II	27	32	39	71	38	...	...	...	—	—	—	—	—
—New Haven	AHL	13	1	5	6	34	...	...	...	—	—	—	—	—
88-89—Binghamton	AHL	76	26	42	68	77	...	...	...	—	—	—	—	—
89-90—Binghamton	AHL	12	1	9	10	16	...	...	...	—	—	—	—	—
—Hartford	NHL	58	18	12	30	52	4	5	1	7	2	1	3	4
90-91—Hartford	NHL	72	13	17	30	95	1	3	0	6	0	2	2	0
91-92—Washington	NHL	67	13	17	30	107	-1	1	0	5	2	1	3	4
92-93—Washington	NHL	77	11	12	23	60	-13	0	2	6	1	1	2	4
93-94—Washington	NHL	66	12	18	30	60	-4	0	1	5	2	0	2	10
94-95—Anaheim	NHL	35	11	11	22	10	1	1	0	—	—	—	—	—
95-96—Anaheim	NHL	60	9	28	37	70	-9	2	1	—	—	—	—	—
—Washington	NHL	16	6	5	11	12	8	1	0	6	2	0	2	12
96-97—Washington	NHL	47	5	11	16	37	-10	1	0	—	—	—	—	—
97-98—Washington	NHL	45	2	12	14	30	-3	0	0	13	1	2	3	6
—Portland	AHL	6	3	4	7	6	...	...	...	—	—	—	—	—
NHL Totals (9 years)		543	100	143	243	533	-26	14	5	48	10	7	17	40

KUBA, FILIP — D — PANTHERS

PERSONAL: Born December 29, 1976, in Ostrava, Czechoslovakia. ... 6-3/202. ... Shoots left. ... Name pronounced KOO-buh.
TRANSACTIONS/CAREER NOTES: Selected by Florida Panthers in eighth round (eighth Panthers pick, 192nd overall) of NHL entry draft (July 8, 1995).

Season Team	League	REGULAR SEASON								PLAYOFFS				
		Gms.	G	A	Pts.	PIM	+/-	PP	SH	Gms.	G	A	Pts.	PIM
94-95—Vitkovice Jr.	Czech Rep.	35	10	15	25	...	...	...	...	—	—	—	—	—
—Vitkovice	Czech Rep.	—	—	—	—	...	...	...	...	4	0	0	0	2
95-96—Vitkovice	Czech Rep.	19	0	1	1	...	...	...	...	—	—	—	—	—
96-97—Carolina	AHL	51	0	12	12	38	...	...	...	—	—	—	—	—
97-98—New Haven	AHL	77	4	13	17	58	...	...	...	3	1	1	2	0

KUBINA, PAVEL — D — LIGHTNING

PERSONAL: Born April 15, 1977, in Caledna, Czechoslovakia ... 6-3/225. ... Shoots left. ... Name pronounced koo-BEE-nuh.
TRANSACTIONS/CAREER NOTES: Selected by Tampa Bay Lightning in seventh round (sixth Lightning pick, 179th overall) of NHL entry draft (June 22, 1996).

Season Team	League	REGULAR SEASON Gms.	G	A	Pts.	PIM	+/-	PP	SH	PLAYOFFS Gms.	G	A	Pts.	PIM
93-94—HC Vitkovice	Czech Rep.	1	0	0	0	0	...	...	...	—	—	—	—	—
94-95—HC Vitkovice	Czech Rep.	8	2	0	2	0	...	...	...	4	0	0	0	0
95-96—HC Vitkovice	Czech Rep.	32	3	4	7	0	...	...	...	4	0	0	0	0
96-97—Moose Jaw	WHL	61	12	32	44	116	...	...	...	11	2	5	7	27
—HC Vitkovice	Czech.	1	0	0	0	0	...	...	...	—	—	—	—	—
97-98—Adirondack	AHL	55	4	8	12	86	...	...	...	1	1	0	1	14
—Tampa Bay	NHL	10	1	2	3	22	-1	0	0	—	—	—	—	—
NHL Totals (1 year)		10	1	2	3	22	-1	0	0					

KURRI, JARI   C/RW

PERSONAL: Born May 18, 1960, in Helsinki, Finland. ... 6-1/195. ... Shoots right. ... Name pronounced YAH-ree KOOR-ee.

TRANSACTIONS/CAREER NOTES: Selected by Edmonton Oilers in fourth round (third Oilers pick, 69th overall) of NHL entry draft (June 11, 1980). ... Pulled groin (November 24, 1981). ... Pulled groin (January 1980); missed 16 games. ... Sprained left knee ligament (February 12, 1989). ... Signed two-year contract with Milan Devils of Italian Hockey League (July 30, 1990). ... Injured knee (January 1991). ... Rights traded by Oilers with RW Dave Brown and D Corey Foster to Philadelphia Flyers for RW Scott Mellanby, LW Craig Berube and C Craig Fisher (May 30, 1991). ... Rights traded by Flyers to Los Angeles Kings for D Steve Duchesne, C Steve Kasper and fourth-round pick (D Aris Brimanis) in 1991 draft (May 30, 1991). ... Sprained shoulder (November 12, 1991); missed three games. ... Suffered from the flu (January 1992); missed two games. ... Bruised knee (November 6, 1993); missed two games. ... Played in Europe during 1994-95 NHL lockout. ... Strained hip flexor (March 11, 1995); missed two games. ... Strained groin (March 20, 1995); missed two games. ... Strained groin (March 26, 1995); missed five games. ... Strained groin (April 7, 1995); missed one game. ... Broke right thumb (December 21, 1995); missed 11 games. ... Traded by Kings with RW Shane Churla and D Marty McSorley to New York Rangers for C Ray Ferraro, C Ian Laperriere, C Nathan Lafayette, D Mattias Norstrom and fourth-round pick (D Sean Blanchard) in 1997 draft (March 14, 1996). ... Signed as free agent by Mighty Ducks of Anaheim (August 14, 1996). ... Signed as free agent by Colorado Avalanche (July 11, 1997). ... Injured back (November 16, 1997); missed one game.

HONORS: Named to NHL All-Star second team (1983-84, 1985-86 and 1988-89). ... Played in NHL All-Star Game (1983, 1985, 1986, 1988-1990, 1993 and 1998). ... Won Lady Byng Memorial Trophy (1984-85). ... Named to THE SPORTING NEWS All-Star first team (1984-85). ... Named to NHL All-Star first team (1984-85 and 1986-87). ... Named to THE SPORTING NEWS All-Star second team (1985-86 and 1988-89).

RECORDS: Holds NHL single-season playoff record for most three-or-more-goal games—4 (1985). ... Shares NHL single-season playoff records for most goals—19 (1985); and most game-winning goals—5 (1987). ... Holds NHL single-series playoff record for most goals—12 (1985); and most three-or-more-goal games—3 (1985). ... Shares NHL single-game playoff records for most shorthanded goals—2 (April 24, 1983); most shorthanded goals in one period—2 (April 24, 1983); and most power-play goals—3 (April 9, 1987).

STATISTICAL PLATEAUS: Three-goal games: 1980-81 (3), 1982-83 (2), 1983-84 (3), 1984-85 (5), 1985-86 (2), 1986-87 (1), 1988-89 (2), 1991-92 (1), 1992-93 (1), 1995-96 (1). Total: 21. ... Four-goal games: 1985-86 (1). ... Five-goal games: 1983-84 (1). ... Total hat tricks: 23.

MISCELLANEOUS: Member of Stanley Cup championship team (1984, 1985, 1987, 1988 and 1990). ... Member of bronze-medal-winning Finnish Olympic team (1998).

STATISTICAL NOTES: Tied for NHL lead with nine game-winning goals (1985-86).

Season Team	League	REGULAR SEASON Gms.	G	A	Pts.	PIM	+/-	PP	SH	PLAYOFFS Gms.	G	A	Pts.	PIM
77-78—Jokerit	Finland	29	2	9	11	12	...	...	...	—	—	—	—	—
78-79—Jokerit	Finland	33	16	14	30	12	...	...	...	—	—	—	—	—
79-80—Jokerit	Finland	33	23	16	39	22	...	...	...	6	7	2	9	13
—Fin. Olympic Team	Int'l	7	2	1	3	6	...	...	...	—	—	—	—	—
80-81—Edmonton	NHL	75	32	43	75	40	26	9	0	9	5	7	12	4
81-82—Edmonton	NHL	71	32	54	86	32	38	6	1	5	2	5	7	10
82-83—Edmonton	NHL	80	45	59	104	22	47	10	1	16	8	15	23	8
83-84—Edmonton	NHL	64	52	61	113	14	38	10	5	19	*14	14	28	13
84-85—Edmonton	NHL	73	71	64	135	30	76	14	3	18	*19	12	31	6
85-86—Edmonton	NHL	78	*68	63	131	22	45	16	6	10	2	10	12	4
86-87—Edmonton	NHL	79	54	54	108	41	-9	0	0	21	*15	10	25	20
87-88—Edmonton	NHL	80	43	53	96	30	25	10	3	19	*14	17	31	12
88-89—Edmonton	NHL	76	44	58	102	69	19	10	5	7	3	5	8	6
89-90—Edmonton	NHL	78	33	60	93	48	18	10	2	22	10	15	25	18
90-91—Milan	Italy	40	37	60	97	8	...	...	...	10	10	12	22	2
91-92—Los Angeles	NHL	73	23	37	60	24	-24	10	1	4	1	2	3	4
92-93—Los Angeles	NHL	82	27	60	87	38	19	12	2	24	9	8	17	12
93-94—Los Angeles	NHL	81	31	46	77	48	-24	14	4	—	—	—	—	—
94-95—Jokerit Helsinki	Finland	20	10	9	19	10	...	...	...	—	—	—	—	—
—Los Angeles	NHL	38	10	19	29	24	-17	2	0	—	—	—	—	—
95-96—Los Angeles	NHL	57	17	23	40	37	-12	5	1	—	—	—	—	—
—New York Rangers	NHL	14	1	4	5	2	-4	0	0	11	3	5	8	2
96-97—Anaheim	NHL	82	13	22	35	12	-13	3	0	11	1	2	3	4
97-98—Colorado	NHL	70	5	17	22	12	6	2	0	4	0	0	0	0
—Fin. Olympic Team	Int'l	6	1	4	5	2	...	...	...	—	—	—	—	—
NHL Totals (17 years)		1251	601	797	1398	545	254	143	34	200	106	127	233	123

KUZNETSOV, MAXIM   D   RED WINGS

PERSONAL: Born March 24, 1977, in Pavlodar, U.S.S.R. ... 6-5/198. ... Shoots left. ... Name pronounced koos-NEHT-sahf.

TRANSACTIONS/CAREER NOTES: Selected by Detroit Red Wings in first round (first Red Wings pick, 26th overall) of NHL entry draft (July 8, 1995).

Season Team	League	REGULAR SEASON Gms.	G	A	Pts.	PIM	+/-	PP	SH	PLAYOFFS Gms.	G	A	Pts.	PIM
94-95—Dynamo Moscow	CIS	11	0	0	0	8	...	...	...	—	—	—	—	—
95-96—Dynamo Moscow	CIS	9	1	1	2	22	...	...	...	4	0	0	0	0
96-97—Dynamo Moscow	CIS	23	0	2	2	16	...	...	...	—	—	—	—	—
—Adirondack	AHL	2	0	1	1	6	...	...	...	2	0	0	0	0
97-98—Adirondack	AHL	51	5	5	10	43	...	...	...	3	0	1	1	4

K

KVASHA, OLEG   LW   PANTHERS

PERSONAL: Born July 26, 1978, in Moscow, U.S.S.R. ... 6-5/205. ... Shoots right. ... Name pronounced kuh-VA-shuh.
TRANSACTIONS/CAREER NOTES: Selected by Florida Panthers in third round (third Panthers pick, 65th overall) of NHL entry draft (June 22, 1996).

		REGULAR SEASON								PLAYOFFS				
Season Team	League	Gms.	G	A	Pts.	PIM	+/-	PP	SH	Gms.	G	A	Pts.	PIM
95-96—CSKA Moscow	CIS	38	2	3	5	14	...	...	...	2	0	0	0	0
96-97—CSKA Moscow	USSR	44	20	22	42	115	...	...	...	—	—	—	—	—
97-98—New Haven	AHL	57	13	16	29	46	...	...	...	3	2	1	3	0

KYPREOS, NICK   LW

PERSONAL: Born June 4, 1966, in Toronto. ... 6-0/207. ... Shoots left. ... Full name: Nicholas George Kypreos. ... Name pronounced KIHP-ree-ohz.
TRANSACTIONS/CAREER NOTES: Signed as free agent by Philadelphia Flyers (September 30, 1984). ... Underwent surgery to right knee (summer 1988); missed first 52 games of 1988-89 season. ... Selected by Washington Capitals in NHL waiver draft for $20,000 (October 2, 1989). ... Underwent surgery to right knee (February 8, 1990). ... Traded by Capitals to Hartford Whalers for RW Mark Hunter and future considerations (June 15, 1992); Whalers sent LW Yvon Corriveau to Capitals to complete deal (August 20, 1992). ... Suspended two games by NHL for game misconduct penalties (February 3,1993). ... Injured abdominal muscle (April 3, 1993); missed remainder of season. ... Traded by Whalers with RW Steve Larmer, D Barry Richter and sixth-round pick (C Yuri Litvinov) in 1994 draft to New York Rangers for D James Patrick and C Darren Turcotte (November 2, 1993). ... Suspended five games and fined $500 by NHL for deliberately injuring player with late hit (November 2, 1993). ... Underwent root canal surgery (April 1, 1994); missed one game. ... Traded by Rangers with RW Wayne Presley to Toronto Maple Leafs for LW Bill Berg and LW Sergio Momesso (February 29, 1996). ... Suspended one playoff game by NHL for interfering with opposing goaltender (April 21, 1996). ... Fractured ankle (November 19, 1996); missed 35 games. ... Suffered post-concussion syndrome; missed entire 1997-98 season.
HONORS: Named to OHL All-Star first team (1985-86). ... Named to OHL All-Star second team (1986-87).
MISCELLANEOUS: Member of Stanley Cup championship team (1994).

		REGULAR SEASON								PLAYOFFS				
Season Team	League	Gms.	G	A	Pts.	PIM	+/-	PP	SH	Gms.	G	A	Pts.	PIM
83-84—North Bay	OHL	51	12	11	23	36	...	...	...	4	3	2	5	9
84-85—North Bay	OHL	64	41	36	77	71	...	...	...	8	2	2	4	15
85-86—North Bay	OHL	64	62	35	97	112	...	...	...	—	—	—	—	—
86-87—North Bay	OHL	46	49	41	90	54	...	...	...	24	11	5	16	78
—Hershey	AHL	10	0	1	1	4	...	...	...	12	0	2	2	17
87-88—Hershey	AHL	71	24	20	44	101	...	...	...	12	0	2	2	17
88-89—Hershey	AHL	28	12	15	27	19	...	...	...	12	4	5	9	11
89-90—Washington	NHL	31	5	4	9	82	2	0	0	7	1	0	1	15
—Baltimore	AHL	14	6	5	11	6	...	...	...	7	4	1	5	17
90-91—Washington	NHL	79	9	9	18	196	-4	0	0	9	0	1	1	38
91-92—Washington	NHL	65	4	6	10	206	-3	0	0	—	—	—	—	—
92-93—Hartford	NHL	75	17	10	27	325	-5	0	0	—	—	—	—	—
93-94—Hartford	NHL	10	0	0	0	37	-8	0	0	—	—	—	—	—
—New York Rangers	NHL	46	3	5	8	102	-8	0	0	3	0	0	0	2
94-95—New York Rangers	NHL	40	1	3	4	93	0	0	0	10	0	2	2	6
95-96—New York Rangers	NHL	42	3	4	7	77	1	0	0	—	—	—	—	—
—Toronto	NHL	19	1	1	2	30	0	0	0	5	0	0	0	4
96-97—Toronto	NHL	35	3	2	5	62	1	0	0	—	—	—	—	—
—St. John's	AHL	4	0	0	0	4	...	...	...	—	—	—	—	—
97-98—Toronto	NHL					Did not play—injured.								
NHL Totals (8 years)		442	46	44	90	1210	-24	0	0	34	1	3	4	65

LAAKSONEN, ANTTI   LW   BRUINS

PERSONAL: Born October 3, 1973, in Tammela, Finland ... 6-0/180. ... Shoots left.
COLLEGE: Denver.
TRANSACTIONS/CAREER NOTES: Selected by Boston Bruins in eighth round (10th Bruins pick, 191st overall) of NHL entry draft (July 21, 1997).

		REGULAR SEASON								PLAYOFFS				
Season Team	League	Gms.	G	A	Pts.	PIM	+/-	PP	SH	Gms.	G	A	Pts.	PIM
93-94—Univ. of Denver	WCHA	36	12	9	21	38	...	...	...	—	—	—	—	—
94-95—Univ. of Denver	WCHA	40	17	18	35	42	...	...	...	—	—	—	—	—
95-96—Univ. of Denver	WCHA	39	25	28	53	71	...	...	...	—	—	—	—	—
96-97—Univ. of Denver	WCHA	39	21	17	38	63	...	...	...	—	—	—	—	—
97-98—Providence	AHL	38	3	2	5	14	...	...	...	—	—	—	—	—
—Charlotte	ECHL	15	4	3	7	12	...	...	...	6	0	3	3	0

LACHANCE, BOB   RW   BLUES

PERSONAL: Born February 1, 1974, in Northampton, Mass. ... 6-0/194. ... Shoots right. ... Brother of Scott Lachance, defenseman, New York Islanders.
COLLEGE: Boston University.
TRANSACTIONS/CAREER NOTES: Selected by St. Louis Blues in sixth round (fifth Blues pick, 134th overall) of NHL entry draft (June 20, 1992).

		REGULAR SEASON								PLAYOFFS				
Season Team	League	Gms.	G	A	Pts.	PIM	+/-	PP	SH	Gms.	G	A	Pts.	PIM
91-92—Springfield Jr. B	NEJHL	46	40	98	138	87	...	...	...	—	—	—	—	—
92-93—Boston University	Hockey East	33	4	10	14	24	...	...	...	—	—	—	—	—
93-94—Boston University	Hockey East	32	13	19	32	42	...	...	...	—	—	—	—	—
94-95—Boston University	Hockey East	37	12	29	41	51	...	...	...	—	—	—	—	—

Season Team	League	REGULAR SEASON								PLAYOFFS				
		Gms.	G	A	Pts.	PIM	+/-	PP	SH	Gms.	G	A	Pts.	PIM
95-96—Boston University	Hockey East	39	15	37	52	67	...	...	...	—	—	—	—	—
—Worcester	AHL	7	1	0	1	6	...	...	...	—	—	—	—	—
96-97—Worcester	AHL	74	21	35	56	66	...	...	...	5	0	2	2	4
97-98—Worcester	AHL	70	15	33	48	56	...	...	...	11	6	10	16	12

LACHANCE, SCOTT   D   ISLANDERS

PERSONAL: Born October 22, 1972, in Charlottesville, Va. ... 6-1/196. ... Shoots left. ... Full name: Scott Joseph Lachance. ... Brother of Bob Lachance, right winger, St. Louis Blues system.
COLLEGE: Boston University.
TRANSACTIONS/CAREER NOTES: Selected by New York Islanders in first round (first Islanders pick, fourth overall) of NHL entry draft (June 22, 1991). ... Sprained wrist (April 13, 1993); missed remainder of season. ... Underwent wrist surgery (April 30, 1993). ... Suffered mild separation of right shoulder (October 8, 1993); missed four games. ... Broke ankle (February 25, 1995); missed 22 games. ... Injured groin (October 31, 1995); missed 27 games. ... Suffered broken finger (November 1, 1997); missed two games. ... Strained abdomen (March 14, 1998); missed five games. ... Reinjured abdomen (March 28, 1998); missed 11 games.
HONORS: Named to Hockey East All-Rookie team (1990-91). ... Played in NHL All-Star Game (1997).

Season Team	League	REGULAR SEASON								PLAYOFFS				
		Gms.	G	A	Pts.	PIM	+/-	PP	SH	Gms.	G	A	Pts.	PIM
88-89—Springfield Jr. B	NEJHL	36	8	28	36	20	...	...	...	—	—	—	—	—
89-90—Springfield Jr. B	NEJHL	34	25	41	66	62	...	...	...	—	—	—	—	—
90-91—Boston University	Hockey East	31	5	19	24	48	...	...	...	—	—	—	—	—
91-92—U.S. national team	Int'l	36	1	10	11	34	...	...	...	—	—	—	—	—
—U.S. Olympic Team	Int'l	8	0	1	1	6	...	...	...	—	—	—	—	—
—New York Islanders	NHL	17	1	4	5	9	13	0	0	—	—	—	—	—
92-93—New York Islanders.....	NHL	75	7	17	24	67	-1	0	1	—	—	—	—	—
93-94—New York Islanders.....	NHL	74	3	11	14	70	-5	0	0	3	0	0	0	0
94-95—New York Islanders.....	NHL	26	6	7	13	26	2	3	0	—	—	—	—	—
95-96—New York Islanders.....	NHL	55	3	10	13	54	-19	1	0	—	—	—	—	—
96-97—New York Islanders.....	NHL	81	3	11	14	47	-7	1	0	—	—	—	—	—
97-98—New York Islanders.....	NHL	63	2	11	13	45	-11	1	0	—	—	—	—	—
NHL Totals (7 years)...........		391	25	71	96	318	-28	6	1	3	0	0	0	0

LACOUTURE, DAN   LW   OILERS

PERSONAL: Born April 13, 1977, in Hyannis, Mass. ... 6-2/201. ... Shoots left. ... Name pronounced LA-kuh-toor.
COLLEGE: Boston University.
TRANSACTIONS/CAREER NOTES: Selected by New York Islanders in second round (second Islanders pick, 29th overall) of NHL entry draft (June 22, 1996). ... Traded by Islanders to Edmonton Oilers for RW Mariusz Czerkawski (August 25, 1997).

Season Team	League	REGULAR SEASON								PLAYOFFS				
		Gms.	G	A	Pts.	PIM	+/-	PP	SH	Gms.	G	A	Pts.	PIM
94-95—Springfield Jr. B	EJHL	49	37	39	76	100	...	...	...	—	—	—	—	—
95-96—Jr. Whalers	EJHL	42	36	48	84	102	...	...	...	—	—	—	—	—
96-97—Boston University	Hockey East	31	13	12	25	18	...	...	...	—	—	—	—	—
97-98—Hamilton	AHL	77	15	10	25	31	...	...	...	5	1	0	1	0

LACROIX, DAN   C   FLYERS

PERSONAL: Born March 11, 1969, in Montreal. ... 6-2/205. ... Shoots left. ... Full name: Daniel Lacroix. ... Name pronounced luh-KWAH.
TRANSACTIONS/CAREER NOTES: Selected as underage junior by New York Rangers in second round (second Rangers pick, 31st overall) of NHL entry draft (June 13, 1987). ... Traded by Rangers to Boston Bruins for D Glen Featherstone (August 19, 1994). ... Claimed on waivers by Rangers (March 23, 1995). ... Signed as free agent by Philadelphia Flyers (July 15, 1996). ... Bruised ribs (September 25, 1996); missed first five games of season. ... Suspended two games and fined $1,000 by NHL for throwing flagrant elbow (October 17, 1996). ... Suspended three games and fined $1,000 by NHL for cross-checking incident (March 5, 1998). ... Sprained left knee (March 26, 1998); missed four games. ... Cut left eye (April 9, 1998); missed four games.
HONORS: Won Marcel Robert Trophy (1988-89).

Season Team	League	REGULAR SEASON								PLAYOFFS				
		Gms.	G	A	Pts.	PIM	+/-	PP	SH	Gms.	G	A	Pts.	PIM
86-87—Granby	QMJHL	54	9	16	25	311	...	...	...	8	1	2	3	22
87-88—Granby	QMJHL	58	24	50	74	468	...	...	...	5	0	4	4	12
88-89—Granby	QMJHL	70	45	49	94	320	...	...	...	4	1	1	2	57
—Denver	IHL	2	0	1	1	0	...	...	...	2	0	1	1	0
89-90—Flint..........................	IHL	61	12	16	28	128	...	...	...	4	2	0	2	24
90-91—Binghamton	AHL	54	7	12	19	237	...	...	...	5	1	0	1	24
91-92—Binghamton	AHL	52	12	20	32	149	...	...	...	11	2	4	6	28
92-93—Binghamton	AHL	73	21	22	43	255	...	...	...	—	—	—	—	—
93-94—New York Rangers	NHL	4	0	0	0	0	0	0	0	—	—	—	—	—
—Binghamton	AHL	59	20	23	43	278	...	...	...	—	—	—	—	—
94-95—Providence.................	AHL	40	15	11	26	266	...	...	...	—	—	—	—	—
—Boston	NHL	23	1	0	1	38	-2	0	0	—	—	—	—	—
—New York Rangers	NHL	1	0	0	0	0	0	0	0	—	—	—	—	—
95-96—Binghamton	AHL	26	12	15	27	155	...	...	...	—	—	—	—	—
—New York Rangers	NHL	25	2	2	4	30	-1	0	0	—	—	—	—	—
96-97—Philadelphia	NHL	74	7	1	8	163	-1	1	0	12	0	1	1	22
97-98—Philadelphia	NHL	56	1	4	5	135	0	0	0	4	0	0	0	4
NHL Totals (5 years)...........		183	11	7	18	366	-4	1	0	16	0	1	1	26

L

LACROIX, ERIC   LW   AVALANCHE

PERSONAL: Born July 15, 1971, in Montreal. ... 6-1/205. ... Shoots left. ... Name pronounced luh-KWAH.
HIGH SCHOOL: Governor Dummer (Byfield, Mass.).
COLLEGE: St. Lawrence (N.Y.).
TRANSACTIONS/CAREER NOTES: Selected by Toronto Maple Leafs in seventh round (sixth Maple Leafs pick, 136th overall) of NHL entry draft (June 16, 1990). ... Separated shoulder (November 27, 1993); missed eight games. ... Traded by Maple Leafs with D Chris Snell and fourth-round pick (C Eric Belanger) in 1996 draft to Los Angeles Kings for RW Dixon Ward, C Guy Leveque, RW Shayne Toporowski and C Kelly Fairchild (October 3, 1994). ... Sprained knee (February 4, 1995); missed one game. ... Sprained knee (February 23, 1995); missed two games. ... Suspended three games by NHL for unnecessary contact with an official (October 16, 1995). ... Suspended five games by NHL for checking from behind (November 22, 1995). ... Traded by Kings with first-round pick (D Martin Skoula) in 1998 draft to Colorado Avalanche for G Stephane Fiset and first-round pick (D Mathieu Biron) in 1998 draft (June 20, 1996).
STATISTICAL PLATEAUS: Three-goal games: 1996-97 (1).

Season Team	League	Gms.	G	A	Pts.	PIM	+/-	PP	SH	Gms.	G	A	Pts.	PIM
89-90—Governor Dummer	Mass. H.S.	—	23	18	41	—				—	—	—	—	—
90-91—St. Lawrence Univ.	ECAC	35	13	11	24	35	...	...	...	—	—	—	—	—
91-92—St. Lawrence Univ.	ECAC	34	11	20	31	40	...	...	...	—	—	—	—	—
92-93—St. John's	AHL	76	15	19	34	59	...	...	...	9	5	3	8	4
93-94—St. John's	AHL	59	17	22	39	69	...	...	...	11	5	3	8	6
—Toronto	NHL	3	0	0	0	2	0	0	0	2	0	0	0	0
94-95—St. John's	AHL	1	0	0	0	2	...	...	...	—	—	—	—	—
—Phoenix	IHL	25	7	1	8	31	...	...	...	—	—	—	—	—
—Los Angeles	NHL	45	9	7	16	54	2	2	1	—	—	—	—	—
95-96—Los Angeles	NHL	72	16	16	32	110	-11	3	0	—	—	—	—	—
96-97—Colorado	NHL	81	18	18	36	26	16	2	0	17	1	4	5	19
97-98—Colorado	NHL	82	16	15	31	84	0	5	0	7	0	0	0	6
NHL Totals (5 years)		283	59	56	115	276	7	12	1	26	1	4	5	25

LaFAYETTE, NATHAN   C   KINGS

PERSONAL: Born February 17, 1973, in New Westminster, B.C. ... 6-1/200. ... Shoots right. ... Name pronounced LAH-fay-eht.
TRANSACTIONS/CAREER NOTES: Traded by Kingston Frontenacs with Joel Sandie and Shawn Caplice (January 6, 1991). ... Selected by St. Louis Blues in third round (third Blues pick, 65th overall) of NHL entry draft (June 22, 1991). ... Traded by Blues with D Jeff Brown and D Bret Hedican to Vancouver Canucks for C Craig Janney (March 21, 1994). ... Traded by Canucks to New York Rangers for G Corey Hirsch (April 7, 1995). ... Traded by Rangers with C Ray Ferraro, C Ian Lapierre, D Mattis Norstrom and fourth-round pick (D Sean Blanchard) in 1997 draft to Los Angeles Kings for RW Shane Churla, LW Jari Kurri and D/RW Marty McSorley (March 14, 1996). ... Loaned by Kings to Syracuse of the AHL (December 27, 1996). ... Suffered concussion (March 5, 1998); missed 18 games.
HONORS: Won Bobby Smith Trophy (1990-91 and 1991-92). ... Won Can.HL Scholastic Player of the Year Award (1991-92).

Season Team	League	Gms.	G	A	Pts.	PIM	+/-	PP	SH	Gms.	G	A	Pts.	PIM
89-90—Kingston	OHL	53	6	8	14	14	...	...	...	7	0	1	1	0
90-91—Kingston	OHL	35	13	13	26	10	...	...	...	—	—	—	—	—
—Cornwall	OHL	28	16	22	38	25	...	...	...	—	—	—	—	—
91-92—Cornwall	OHL	66	28	45	73	26	...	...	...	6	2	5	7	16
92-93—Newmarket	OHL	58	49	38	87	26	...	...	...	7	4	6	10	19
93-94—Peoria	IHL	27	13	11	24	20	...	...	...	—	—	—	—	—
—St. Louis	NHL	38	2	3	5	14	-9	0	0	—	—	—	—	—
—Vancouver	NHL	11	1	1	2	4	2	0	0	20	2	7	9	4
94-95—Syracuse	AHL	27	9	9	18	10	...	...	...	—	—	—	—	—
—Vancouver	NHL	27	4	4	8	2	2	0	1	—	—	—	—	—
—New York Rangers	NHL	12	0	0	0	0	1	0	0	—	—	—	—	—
95-96—Binghamton	AHL	57	21	27	48	32	...	...	...	—	—	—	—	—
—New York Rangers	NHL	5	0	0	0	2	-1	0	0	—	—	—	—	—
—Los Angeles	NHL	12	2	4	6	6	-3	1	0	—	—	—	—	—
96-97—Phoenix	IHL	31	2	5	7	16	...	...	...	—	—	—	—	—
—Syracuse	AHL	26	14	11	25	18	...	...	...	3	1	0	1	2
—Los Angeles	NHL	15	1	3	4	8	-8	0	1	—	—	—	—	—
97-98—Fredericton	AHL	28	7	8	15	36	...	...	...	4	0	0	0	2
—Los Angeles	NHL	34	5	3	8	32	2	1	0	—	—	—	—	—
NHL Totals (5 years)		154	15	18	33	68	-14	2	2	24	2	7	9	4

LAFLAMME, CHRISTIAN   D   BLACKHAWKS

PERSONAL: Born November 24, 1976, in St. Charles, Que. ... 6-1/202. ... Shoots right. ... Name pronounced lah-FLAHM.
TRANSACTIONS/CAREER NOTES: Selected by Chicago Blackhawks in second round (second Blackhawks pick, 45th overall) of NHL entry draft (July 8, 1995). ... Fractured left foot (October 1, 1997); missed six games. ... Fractured right cheekbone (January 24, 1998); missed four games.
HONORS: Named to QMJHL All-Rookie team (1992-93). ... Named to QMJHL All-Star second team (1994-95).

Season Team	League	Gms.	G	A	Pts.	PIM	+/-	PP	SH	Gms.	G	A	Pts.	PIM
92-93—Verdun	QMJHL	69	2	17	19	70	...	...	...	3	0	2	2	6
93-94—Verdun	QMJHL	72	4	34	38	85	...	...	...	4	0	3	3	4
94-95—Beauport	QMJHL	67	6	41	47	82	...	...	...	8	1	4	5	6
95-96—Beauport	QMJHL	41	13	23	36	63	...	...	...	20	7	17	24	32
96-97—Indianapolis	IHL	62	5	15	20	60	...	...	...	4	1	1	2	16
—Chicago	NHL	4	0	1	1	2	3	0	0	—	—	—	—	—
97-98—Chicago	NHL	72	0	11	11	59	14	0	0	—	—	—	—	—
NHL Totals (2 years)		76	0	12	12	61	17	0	0	—	—	—	—	—

LaFONTAINE, PAT   C

PERSONAL: Born February 22, 1965, in St. Louis. ... 5-10/185. ... Shoots right. ... Name pronounced luh-FAHN-tayn.
TRANSACTIONS/CAREER NOTES: Selected by New York Islanders as underage junior in first round (first Islanders pick, third overall) of NHL entry draft (June 8, 1983). ... Damaged ligaments in left knee (August 16, 1984). ... Suffered from mononucleosis (January 1985). ... Separated right shoulder (January 25, 1986). ... Bruised knee (March 1988). ... Broke nose (October 7, 1988); played entire season with injury. ... Sprained ligaments in right wrist (November 5, 1988). ... Strained left hamstring (October 13, 1990); missed three games. ... Traded by Islanders with LW Randy Wood, D Randy Hillier and future considerations to Buffalo Sabres for C Pierre Turgeon, RW Benoit Hogue, D Uwe Krupp and C Dave McLlwain; Sabres later received fourth-round pick (D Dean Melanson) in 1992 draft (October 25, 1991). ... Fractured jaw (November 16, 1991); missed 13 games. ... Injured knee (November 13, 1993); missed remainder of season and first 24 games of 1994-95 season. ... Suffered mild concussion (December 27, 1995); missed two games. ... Suffered concussion (October 17, 1996); missed remainder of season. ... Traded by Sabres to New York Rangers for second-round pick (LW Andrew Peters) in 1998 draft and future considerations (September 29, 1997). ... Suffered head injury (March 16, 1998); missed 15 games. ... Announced retirement (August 11, 1998).
HONORS: Won Can.HL Player of the Year Award (1982-83). ... Won Michel Briere Trophy (1982-83). ... Won Jean Beliveau Trophy (1982-83). ... Won Frank J. Selke Trophy (1982-83). ... Won Des Instructeurs Trophy (1982-83). ... Won Guy Lafleur Trophy (1982-83). ... Named to QMJHL All-Star first team (1982-83). ... Played in NHL All-Star Game (1988-1991 and 1993). ... Won Dodge Performer of the Year Award (1989-90). ... Named to THE SPORTING NEWS All-Star second team (1989-90). ... Named to NHL All-Star second team (1992-93). ... Won Bill Masterton Memorial Trophy (1994-95).
RECORDS: Holds NHL playoff record for fastest two goals from the start of a period—35 seconds (May 19, 1984).
STATISTICAL PLATEAUS: Three-goal games: 1983-84 (1), 1987-88 (1), 1988-89 (2), 1989-90 (2), 1990-91 (1), 1991-92 (4), 1992-93 (1), 1995-96 (1). Total: 13.
MISCELLANEOUS: Captain of Buffalo Sabres (1992-93 through 1996-97). ... Scored on a penalty shot (vs. Peter Sidorkiewicz, November 29, 1992).
STATISTICAL NOTES: Tied for league lead with three game-tying goals in 1997-98.

		REGULAR SEASON								PLAYOFFS				
Season Team	League	Gms.	G	A	Pts.	PIM	+/-	PP	SH	Gms.	G	A	Pts.	PIM
82-83—Verdun	QMJHL	70	*104	*130	*234	10	...	...	...	15	11	*24	*35	4
83-84—U.S. national team	Int'l	58	56	55	111	22	...	...	...	—	—	—	—	—
—U.S. Olympic Team	Int'l	6	5	3	8	0	...	...	...	—	—	—	—	—
—New York Islanders	NHL	15	13	6	19	6	9	1	0	16	3	6	9	8
84-85—New York Islanders	NHL	67	19	35	54	32	9	1	0	9	1	2	3	4
85-86—New York Islanders	NHL	65	30	23	53	43	16	2	0	3	1	0	1	0
86-87—New York Islanders	NHL	80	38	32	70	70	-10	19	1	14	5	7	12	10
87-88—New York Islanders	NHL	75	47	45	92	52	12	15	0	6	4	5	9	8
88-89—New York Islanders	NHL	79	45	43	88	26	-8	16	0	—	—	—	—	—
89-90—New York Islanders	NHL	74	54	51	105	38	-13	13	2	2	0	1	1	0
90-91—New York Islanders	NHL	75	41	44	85	42	-6	12	2	—	—	—	—	—
91-92—Buffalo	NHL	57	46	47	93	98	10	23	0	7	8	3	11	4
92-93—Buffalo	NHL	84	53	95	148	63	11	20	2	7	2	10	12	0
93-94—Buffalo	NHL	16	5	13	18	2	-4	1	0	—	—	—	—	—
94-95—Buffalo	NHL	22	12	15	27	4	2	6	1	5	2	2	4	2
95-96—Buffalo	NHL	76	40	51	91	36	-8	15	3	—	—	—	—	—
96-97—Buffalo	NHL	13	2	6	8	4	-8	1	0	—	—	—	—	—
97-98—New York Rangers	NHL	67	23	39	62	36	-16	11	0	—	—	—	—	—
—U.S. Olympic Team	Int'l	4	1	1	2	0	...	...	...	—	—	—	—	—
NHL Totals (15 years)		865	468	545	1013	552	-4	156	11	69	26	36	62	36

LAKOVIC, SASHA   LW   DEVILS

PERSONAL: Born September 7, 1971, in Vancouver. ... 6-0/207. ... Shoots left.
TRANSACTIONS/CAREER NOTES: Traded by Saginaw of the IHL with RW Jamie Allen to Brantford of the IHL for C Jamey Hicks (July 27, 1994). ... Signed as free agent by Calgary Flames (October 15, 1996). ... Suspended two games by NHL for attacking a fan (November 26, 1996). ... Signed as free agent by Calgary Flames (October 15, 1996). ... Signed as free agent by New Jersey Devils (September 1, 1997).

		REGULAR SEASON								PLAYOFFS				
Season Team	League	Gms.	G	A	Pts.	PIM	+/-	PP	SH	Gms.	G	A	Pts.	PIM
95-96—Las Vegas	IHL	49	1	2	3	416	...	...	...	13	1	1	2	57
96-97—Las Vegas	IHL	10	0	0	0	81	...	...	...	2	0	0	0	14
—Saint John	AHL	18	1	8	9	182	...	...	...	—	—	—	—	—
—Calgary	NHL	19	0	1	1	54	-1	0	0	—	—	—	—	—
97-98—Albany	AHL	30	7	6	13	158	...	...	...	13	3	4	7	*84
—New Jersey	NHL	2	0	0	0	5	0	0	0	—	—	—	—	—
NHL Totals (2 years)		21	0	1	1	59	-1	0	0					

LAMBERT, DENNY   LW   PREDATORS

PERSONAL: Born January 7, 1970, in Wawa, Ont. ... 5-11/200. ... Shoots left. ... Name pronounced lam-BAIR.
TRANSACTIONS/CAREER NOTES: Signed as free agent by Mighty Ducks of Anaheim (August 16, 1993). ... Signed as free agent by Ottawa Senators (July 8, 1996). ... Selected by Nashville Predators in NHL expansion draft (June 26, 1998).

		REGULAR SEASON								PLAYOFFS				
Season Team	League	Gms.	G	A	Pts.	PIM	+/-	PP	SH	Gms.	G	A	Pts.	PIM
88-89—Sault Ste. Marie	OHL	61	14	15	29	203	...	...	...	—	—	—	—	—
89-90—Sault Ste. Marie	OHL	61	23	29	52	*276	...	...	...	—	—	—	—	—
90-91—Sault Ste. Marie	OHL	59	28	39	67	169	...	...	...	14	7	9	16	48
91-92—San Diego	IHL	71	17	14	31	229	...	...	...	3	0	0	0	10
92-93—St. Thomas	Col.HL	5	2	6	8	9	...	...	...	—	—	—	—	—
—San Diego	IHL	56	18	12	30	277	...	...	...	14	1	1	2	44
93-94—San Diego	IHL	79	13	14	27	314	...	...	...	6	1	0	1	45

Season Team	League	Gms.	G	A	Pts.	PIM	+/-	PP	SH	Gms.	G	A	Pts.	PIM
94-95—San Diego	IHL	75	25	35	60	222	...	...	...	—	—	—	—	—
—Anaheim	NHL	13	1	3	4	4	3	0	0	—	—	—	—	—
95-96—Anaheim	NHL	33	0	8	8	55	-2	0	0	—	—	—	—	—
—Baltimore	AHL	44	14	28	42	126	...	...	...	12	3	9	12	39
96-97—Ottawa	NHL	80	4	16	20	217	-4	0	0	6	0	1	1	9
97-98—Ottawa	NHL	72	9	10	19	250	4	0	0	11	0	0	0	19
NHL Totals (4 years)		198	14	37	51	526	1	0	0	17	0	1	1	28

LAMOTHE, MARC — G — BLACKHAWKS

PERSONAL: Born February 27, 1974, in New Liskeard, Ont. ... 6-1/204. ... Catches left. ... Name pronounced luh-MAHTh.

TRANSACTIONS/CAREER NOTES: Selected by Montreal Canadiens in fourth round (sixth Canadiens pick, 92nd overall) of NHL entry draft (June 20, 1992). ... Signed as free agent by Chicago Blackhawks (August 21, 1996).

Season Team	League	Gms.	Min	W	L	T	GA	SO	Avg.	Gms.	Min.	W	L	GA	SO	Avg.
90-91—Ottawa	OHA Mj.Jr A	25	1220	...	...	...	82	1	4.03	—	—	—	—	—	—	—
91-92—Kingston	OHL	42	2378	10	25	2	189	1	4.77	—	—	—	—	—	—	—
92-93—Kingston	OHL	45	2489	23	12	6	162	†1	3.91	15	733	8	5	46	†1	3.77
93-94—Kingston	OHL	48	2828	23	20	5	177	†2	3.76	6	224	2	2	12	0	3.21
94-95—Fredericton	AHL	9	428	2	5	0	32	0	4.49	—	—	—	—	—	—	—
—Wheeling	ECHL	13	737	9	2	‡1	38	0	3.09	—	—	—	—	—	—	—
95-96—Fredericton	AHL	23	1165	5	9	3	73	1	3.76	3	160	1	2	9	0	3.38
96-97—Indianapolis	IHL	38	2271	20	14	‡4	100	1	2.64	1	20	0	0	1	0	3.00
97-98—Indianapolis	IHL	31	1773	18	10	‡2	72	3	2.44	4	178	1	3	10	0	3.37

LANDRY, ERIC — C — FLAMES

PERSONAL: Born January 29, 1976, in Montreal. ... 5-11/190. ... Shoots left.

TRANSACTIONS/CAREER NOTES: Selected by San Jose Sharks in eighth round (eighth Sharks pick, 193rd overall) of NHL entry draft (June 29, 1994). ... Signed as free agent by Calgary Flames (August 6, 1997). ... Suffered concussion (November 22, 1997); missed one game.

Season Team	League	Gms.	G	A	Pts.	PIM	+/-	PP	SH	Gms.	G	A	Pts.	PIM
93-94—Guelph	OHL	57	7	15	22	96	...	...	...	9	0	0	0	10
94-95—Guelph	OHL	13	1	4	5	20	...	...	...	—	—	—	—	—
—Sault Ste. Marie	OHL	44	7	8	15	88	...	...	...	—	—	—	—	—
—St. Hyacinthe	QMJHL	68	38	36	74	249	...	...	...	5	2	1	3	10
95-96—Peterborough	OHL	58	11	11	22	116	...	...	...	24	1	5	6	46
96-97—Roanoke	ECHL	46	13	19	32	130	...	...	...	—	—	—	—	—
97-98—Saint John	AHL	61	17	21	38	194	...	...	...	20	4	6	10	58
—Calgary	NHL	12	1	0	1	4	-2	0	0	—	—	—	—	—
NHL Totals (1 year)		12	1	0	1	4	-2	0	0	—	—	—	—	—

LANG, ROBERT — C — PENGUINS

PERSONAL: Born December 19, 1970, in Teplice, Czechoslovakia. ... 6-2/216. ... Shoots right.

TRANSACTIONS/CAREER NOTES: Selected by Los Angeles Kings in seventh round (sixth Kings pick, 133rd overall) of NHL entry draft (June 16, 1990). ... Dislocated shoulder (April 3, 1994); missed remainder of season. ... Played in Europe during 1994-95 NHL lockout. ... Strained left shoulder (March 26, 1995); missed one game. ... Strained back (November 20, 1995); missed seven games. ... Signed as free agent by Edmonton Oilers (October 19, 1996). ... Loaned by Oilers to Sparta Praha of Czech Republic League (October 19, 1996). ... Signed as free agent by Pittsburgh Penguins (September 2, 1997). ... Fractured thumb (March 21, 1998); missed nine games.

Season Team	League	Gms.	G	A	Pts.	PIM	+/-	PP	SH	Gms.	G	A	Pts.	PIM
88-89—Litvinov	Czech.	7	3	2	5	0	...	...	...	—	—	—	—	—
89-90—Litvinov	Czech.	39	11	10	21	20	...	...	...	—	—	—	—	—
90-91—Litvinov	Czech.	56	26	26	52	38	...	...	...	—	—	—	—	—
91-92—Litvinov	Czech.	43	12	31	43	34	...	...	...	—	—	—	—	—
—Czech. national team	Int'l	8	5	8	13	8	...	...	...	—	—	—	—	—
—Czech. Oly. Team	Int'l	8	5	8	13	8	...	...	...	—	—	—	—	—
92-93—Los Angeles	NHL	11	0	5	5	2	-3	0	0	—	—	—	—	—
—Phoenix	IHL	38	9	21	30	20	...	...	...	—	—	—	—	—
93-94—Phoenix	IHL	44	11	24	35	34	...	...	...	—	—	—	—	—
—Los Angeles	NHL	32	9	10	19	10	7	0	0	—	—	—	—	—
94-95—Chemo. Litvinov	Czech Rep.	16	4	19	23	28	...	...	...	—	—	—	—	—
—Los Angeles	NHL	36	4	8	12	4	-7	0	0	—	—	—	—	—
95-96—Los Angeles	NHL	68	6	16	22	10	-15	0	2	—	—	—	—	—
96-97—Sparta Praha	Czech Rep.	38	14	27	41	30	...	...	...	5	1	2	3	4
97-98—Boston	NHL	3	0	0	0	2	1	0	0	—	—	—	—	—
—Houston	IHL	9	1	7	8	4	...	...	...	—	—	—	—	—
—Pittsburgh	NHL	51	9	13	22	14	6	1	1	6	0	3	3	2
—Czech Rep. Olympic	Int'l	6	0	3	3	0	...	...	...	—	—	—	—	—
NHL Totals (5 years)		201	28	52	80	42	-11	1	3	6	0	3	3	2

LANGDON, DARREN   LW   RANGERS

PERSONAL: Born January 8, 1971, in Deer Lake, Nfld. ... 6-1/205. ... Shoots left.
TRANSACTIONS/CAREER NOTES: Signed as free agent by New York Rangers (August 16, 1993). ... Suspended three games by NHL for abuse of an official in preseason game (September 23, 1995). ... Sprained right knee (December 13, 1996); missed 13 games. ... Suspended two games by NHL for initiating an altercation (March 7, 1997). ... Sprained knee (November 21, 1997); missed six games. ... Bruised sternum (March 4, 1998); missed three games.

		REGULAR SEASON							PLAYOFFS				
Season Team	League	Gms.	G	A	Pts.	PIM	+/-	PP	SH	Gms.	G	A	Pts.	PIM
91-92—Summerside	MJHL	44	34	49	83	441	...	...	...	—	—	—	—	—
92-93—Binghamton	AHL	18	3	4	7	115	...	...	...	8	0	1	1	14
—Dayton	ECHL	54	23	22	45	429	...	...	...	3	0	1	1	40
93-94—Binghamton	AHL	54	2	7	9	327	...	...	...	11	1	3	4	*84
94-95—Binghamton	AHL	55	6	14	20	296	...	...	...	11	1	3	4	84
—New York Rangers	NHL	18	1	1	2	62	0	0	0	—	—	—	—	—
95-96—New York Rangers	NHL	64	7	4	11	175	2	0	0	2	0	0	0	0
—Binghamton	AHL	1	0	0	0	12	...	...	...	—	—	—	—	—
96-97—New York Rangers	NHL	60	3	6	9	195	-1	0	0	10	0	0	0	2
97-98—New York Rangers	NHL	70	3	3	6	197	0	0	0	—	—	—	—	—
NHL Totals (4 years)		212	14	14	28	629	1	0	0	12	0	0	0	2

LANGENBRUNNER, JAMIE   C   STARS

PERSONAL: Born April 21, 1975, in Edmonton. ... 5-11/185. ... Shoots right. ... Name pronounced LANG-ihn-BRUH-nuhr.
HIGH SCHOOL: Cloquet (Minn.).
TRANSACTIONS/CAREER NOTES: Selected by Dallas Stars in second round (second Stars pick, 35th overall) of NHL entry draft (June 26, 1993). ... Suffered back spasms (February 21, 1997); missed one game. ... Suffered whiplash (January 12, 1998); missed one game.

		REGULAR SEASON							PLAYOFFS				
Season Team	League	Gms.	G	A	Pts.	PIM	+/-	PP	SH	Gms.	G	A	Pts.	PIM
90-91—Cloquet H.S.	Minn. H.S.	20	6	16	22	8	...	...	...	—	—	—	—	—
91-92—Cloquet H.S.	Minn. H.S.	23	16	23	39	24	...	...	...	—	—	—	—	—
92-93—Cloquet H.S.	Minn. H.S.	27	27	62	89	18	...	...	...	—	—	—	—	—
93-94—Peterborough	OHL	62	33	58	91	53	...	...	...	7	4	6	10	2
94-95—Peterborough	OHL	62	42	57	99	84	...	...	...	11	8	14	22	12
—Dallas	NHL	2	0	0	0	2	0	0	0	—	—	—	—	—
—Kalamazoo	IHL	—	—	—	—	—	...	...	...	11	1	3	4	2
95-96—Michigan	IHL	59	25	40	65	129	...	...	...	10	3	10	13	8
—Dallas	NHL	12	2	2	4	6	-2	1	0	—	—	—	—	—
96-97—Dallas	NHL	76	13	26	39	51	-2	3	0	5	1	1	2	14
97-98—Dallas	NHL	81	23	29	52	61	9	8	0	16	1	4	5	14
—U.S. Olympic Team	Int'l	3	0	0	0	4	...	...	...	—	—	—	—	—
NHL Totals (4 years)		171	38	57	95	120	5	12	0	21	2	5	7	28

LANGFELD, JOSH   RW   SENATORS

PERSONAL: Born July 17, 1977, in Fridley, Minn. ... 6-3/205. ... Shoots right.
COLLEGE: Michigan.
TRANSACTIONS/CAREER NOTES: Selected by Ottawa Senators in third round (third Senators pick, 66th overall) of NHL entry draft (June 21, 1997).
HONORS: Named to NCAA All-Tournament team (1997-98).

		REGULAR SEASON							PLAYOFFS				
Season Team	League	Gms.	G	A	Pts.	PIM	+/-	PP	SH	Gms.	G	A	Pts.	PIM
96-97—Lincoln	Jr. A	38	35	23	58	100	...	...	...	—	—	—	—	—
97-98—Univ. of Michigan	CCHA	46	19	17	36	66	...	...	...	—	—	—	—	—

LANGKOW, DAYMOND   C   LIGHTNING

PERSONAL: Born September 27, 1976, in Edmonton. ... 5-11/180. ... Shoots left. ... Name pronounced LANG-kow.
TRANSACTIONS/CAREER NOTES: Selected by Tampa Bay Lightning in first round (first Lightning pick, fifth overall) of NHL entry draft (July 8, 1995). ... Suffered from the flu (October 1, 1997); missed one game. ... Suffered from concussion (January 7, 1998); missed two games. ... Suffered from the flu (January 31, 1998); missed three games
HONORS: Won Bob Clarke Trophy (1994-95). ... Named to Can.HL All-Star first team (1994-95). ... Named to WHL (West) All-Star first team (1994-95). ... Named to WHL (West) All-Star second team (1995-96).

		REGULAR SEASON							PLAYOFFS				
Season Team	League	Gms.	G	A	Pts.	PIM	+/-	PP	SH	Gms.	G	A	Pts.	PIM
91-92—Tri-City	WHL	1	0	0	0	0	...	...	...	4	2	2	4	15
92-93—Tri-City	WHL	65	22	42	64	96	...	...	...	4	1	0	1	4
93-94—Tri-City	WHL	61	40	43	83	174	...	...	...	4	2	2	4	15
94-95—Tri-City	WHL	72	67	73	140	142	...	...	...	17	12	15	27	52
95-96—Tampa Bay	NHL	4	0	1	1	0	-1	0	0	—	—	—	—	—
—Tri-City	WHL	48	30	61	91	103	...	...	...	11	14	13	27	20
96-97—Adirondack	AHL	2	1	1	2	0	...	...	...	—	—	—	—	—
—Tampa Bay	NHL	79	15	13	28	35	1	3	1	—	—	—	—	—
97-98—Tampa Bay	NHL	68	8	14	22	62	-9	2	0	—	—	—	—	—
NHL Totals (3 years)		151	23	28	51	97	-9	5	1					

LANGKOW, SCOTT   G   COYOTES

PERSONAL: Born April 21, 1975, in Edmonton. ... 5-11/190. ... Catches left. ... Name pronounced LANG-koh.
HIGH SCHOOL: Aloha (Beaverton, Ore.).
TRANSACTIONS/CAREER NOTES: Selected by Winnipeg Jets in second round (second Jets pick, 31st overall) of NHL entry draft (June 26, 1993). ... Jets franchise moved to Phoenix and renamed Coyotes for 1996-97 season; NHL approved move on January 18, 1996.
HONORS: Named to WHL (West) All-Star second team (1993-94 and 1994-95). ... Won Harry (Hap) Holmes Memorial Trophy (1995-96). ... Named to AHL All-Star first team (1997-98). ... Won Baz Bastien Trophy (1997-98).

| | | REGULAR SEASON | | | | | | | | PLAYOFFS | | | | | | |
Season Team	League	Gms.	Min	W	L	T	GA	SO	Avg.	Gms.	Min.	W	L	GA	SO	Avg.
91-92—Portland	WHL	1	33	0	0	0	2	0	3.64	—	—	—	—	—	—	—
92-93—Portland	WHL	34	2064	24	8	2	119	2	3.46	9	535	6	3	31	0	3.48
93-94—Portland	WHL	39	2302	27	9	1	121	2	3.15	10	600	6	4	34	0	3.40
94-95—Portland	WHL	63	3638	20	36	5	240	1	3.96	8	510	3	5	30	0	3.53
95-96—Springfield	AHL	39	2329	18	15	6	116	3	2.99	7	392	4	2	23	0	3.52
—Winnipeg	NHL	1	6	0	0	0	0	0	...	—	—	—	—	—	—	—
96-97—Springfield	AHL	33	1929	15	9	7	85	0	2.64	—	—	—	—	—	—	—
97-98—Springfield	AHL	51	2875	30	13	5	128	3	2.67	4	216	1	3	14	0	3.89
—Phoenix	NHL	3	137	0	1	1	10	0	4.38	—	—	—	—	—	—	—
NHL Totals (2 years)		4	143	0	1	1	10	0	4.20							

LANK, JEFF   D   FLYERS

PERSONAL: Born March 1, 1975, in Indianhead, Sask. ... 6-3/185. ... Shoots left.
HIGH SCHOOL: Carlton Comprehensive (Prince Albert, Sask.).
TRANSACTIONS/CAREER NOTES: Selected by Montreal Canadiens in fifth round (sixth Canadiens pick, 113th overall) of NHL entry draft (June 26, 1993). ... Returned to draft pool by Canadiens and selected by Philadelphia Flyers in ninth round (ninth Flyers pick, 230th overall) of NHL entry draft (July 8, 1995).

| | | REGULAR SEASON | | | | | | | | PLAYOFFS | | | | |
Season Team	League	Gms.	G	A	Pts.	PIM	+/-	PP	SH	Gms.	G	A	Pts.	PIM
90-91—Columbia Valley	KIJHL	36	4	28	32	40	...	...	...	—	—	—	—	—
91-92—Prince Albert	WHL	56	2	8	10	26	...	...	...	9	0	0	0	2
92-93—Prince Albert	WHL	63	1	11	12	60	...	...	...	—	—	—	—	—
93-94—Prince Albert	WHL	72	9	38	47	62	...	...	...	—	—	—	—	—
94-95—Prince Albert	WHL	68	12	25	37	60	...	...	...	13	2	10	12	8
95-96—Hershey	AHL	72	7	13	20	70	...	...	...	5	0	0	0	8
96-97—Philadelphia	AHL	44	2	12	14	49	...	...	...	7	2	1	3	4
97-98—Philadelphia	AHL	69	7	9	16	59	...	...	...	20	1	4	5	22

L

LAPERRIERE, IAN   C   KINGS

PERSONAL: Born January 19, 1974, in Montreal. ... 6-1/195. ... Shoots left. ... Name pronounced EE-ihn luh-PAIR-ee-AIR.
TRANSACTIONS/CAREER NOTES: Selected by St. Louis Blues in seventh round (sixth Blues pick, 158th overall) of NHL entry draft (June 20, 1992). ... Suffered concussion (March 26, 1995); missed three games. ... Traded by Blues to New York Rangers for LW Stephane Matteau (December 28, 1995). ... Traded by Rangers with C Ray Ferraro, C Nathan Lafayette, D Matis Norstrom and fourth-round pick (D Sean Blanchard) in 1997 draft to Los Angeles Kings for RW Shane Churla, LW Jari Kurri and D/RW Marty McSorley (March 14, 1996). ... Sprained left shoulder (March 16, 1996); missed two games. ... Strained shoulder (October 29, 1996); missed three games. ... Strained hip flexor (February 1, 1997); missed three games. ... Suffered concussion (February 25, 1997); missed two games. ... Underwent shoulder surgery (March 17, 1997); missed final 11 games of regular season. ... Suffered blurred vision (December 31, 1997); missed three games.
HONORS: Named to QMJHL All-Star second team (1992-93).

| | | REGULAR SEASON | | | | | | | | PLAYOFFS | | | | |
Season Team	League	Gms.	G	A	Pts.	PIM	+/-	PP	SH	Gms.	G	A	Pts.	PIM
90-91—Drummondville	QMJHL	65	19	29	48	117	...	...	...	—	—	—	—	—
91-92—Drummondville	QMJHL	70	28	49	77	160	...	...	...	—	—	—	—	—
92-93—Drummondville	QMJHL	60	44	†96	140	188	...	...	...	10	6	13	19	20
93-94—Drummondville	QMJHL	62	41	72	113	150	...	...	...	9	4	6	10	35
—St. Louis	NHL	1	0	0	0	0	0	0	0	—	—	—	—	—
—Peoria	IHL	—								5	1	3	4	2
94-95—Peoria	IHL	51	16	32	48	111	...	...	...	—	—	—	—	—
—St. Louis	NHL	37	13	14	27	85	12	1	0	7	0	4	4	21
95-96—St. Louis	NHL	33	3	6	9	87	-4	1	0	—	—	—	—	—
—Worcester	AHL	3	2	1	3	22	...			—	—	—	—	—
—New York Rangers	NHL	28	1	2	3	53	-5	0	0	—	—	—	—	—
—Los Angeles	NHL	10	2	3	5	15	-2	0	0	—	—	—	—	—
96-97—Los Angeles	NHL	62	8	15	23	102	-25	0	1	—	—	—	—	—
97-98—Los Angeles	NHL	77	6	15	21	131	0	0	1	4	1	0	1	6
NHL Totals (5 years)		248	33	55	88	473	-24	2	2	11	1	4	5	27

LAPLANTE, DARRYL   C   RED WINGS

PERSONAL: Born March 28, 1977, in Calgary. ... 6-1/177. ... Shoots right. ... Name pronounced luh-PLANT.
COLLEGE: Vanier (Edson, Alta.).
TRANSACTIONS/CAREER NOTES: Selected by Detroit Red Wings in third round (third Red Wings pick, 58th overall) of NHL entry draft (July 8, 1995).

Season Team	League	Gms.	G	A	Pts.	PIM	+/-	PP	SH	Gms.	G	A	Pts.	PIM
				REGULAR SEASON								PLAYOFFS		
94-95—Moose Jaw	WHL	71	22	24	46	66	...	...	...	10	2	2	4	7
95-96—Moose Jaw	WHL	72	42	40	82	76	...	...	...	—	—	—	—	—
96-97—Moose Jaw	WHL	69	38	42	80	79	...	...	...	12	2	4	6	15
97-98—Adirondack	AHL	77	15	10	25	51	...	...	...	3	0	1	1	4
—Detroit	NHL	2	0	0	0	0	0	0	0	—	—	—	—	—
NHL Totals (1 year)		2	0	0	0	0	0	0	0					

LAPOINTE, CLAUDE　　　　C　　　　ISLANDERS

PERSONAL: Born October 11, 1968, in Lachine, Que. ... 5-9/181. ... Shoots left. ... Name pronounced KLOHD luh-pwah.

TRANSACTIONS/CAREER NOTES: Traded by Trois-Rivieres Draveurs with G Alain Dubeau and third-round pick (D Patrice Brisebois) in QMJHL draft to Laval Titans for D Raymond Saumier, LW Mike Gober, D Eric Gobeil and second-round pick (D Eric Charron) in QMJHL draft (May 1987). ... Selected by Quebec Nordiques in 12th round (12th Nordiques pick, 234th overall) of NHL entry draft (June 11, 1988). ... Tore groin muscle (February 9, 1991). ... Injured groin (October 23, 1991); missed one game. ... Injured back in training camp (September 1992); missed five games. ... Bruised hip (April 6, 1993); missed two games. ... Sprained left knee (October 18, 1993); missed 13 games. ... Sprained back (February 1, 1994); missed nine games. ... Injured back (March 19, 1994); missed three games. ... Suffered lower back pain (January 21, 1995); missed 16 games. ... Suffered from the flu (April 16, 1995); missed one game. ... Injured hip (April 30, 1995); missed one game. ... Nordiques franchise moved to Colorado and renamed Avalanche for 1995-96 season (June 21, 1995). ... Traded by Avalanche to Calgary Flames for seventh-round pick (C Samuel Pahlsson) in 1996 draft (November 1, 1995). ... Pulled groin (December 20, 1995); missed one game. ... Reinjured groin (December 27, 1995); missed three games. ... Reinjured groin (January 5, 1996); missed three games. ... Injured hip (January 26, 1996); missed 17 games. ... Signed as free agent by New York Islanders (August 22, 1996). ... Hyperextended ankle (January 2, 1997); missed one game. ... Suffered sore ankle (January 25, 1997); missed one game. ... Bruised foot (January 22, 1998); missed one game. ... Broke toe (February 1, 1998); missed three games.

Season Team	League	Gms.	G	A	Pts.	PIM	+/-	PP	SH	Gms.	G	A	Pts.	PIM
				REGULAR SEASON								PLAYOFFS		
85-86—Trois-Rivieres	QMJHL	72	19	38	57	74	...	...	...	—	—	—	—	—
86-87—Trois-Rivieres	QMJHL	70	47	57	104	123	...	...	...	—	—	—	—	—
87-88—Laval	QMJHL	69	37	83	120	143	...	...	...	13	2	17	19	53
88-89—Laval	QMJHL	63	32	72	104	158	...	...	...	17	5	14	19	66
89-90—Halifax	AHL	63	18	19	37	51	...	...	...	6	1	1	2	34
90-91—Quebec	NHL	13	2	2	4	4	3	0	0	—	—	—	—	—
—Halifax	AHL	43	17	17	34	46	...	...	...	—	—	—	—	—
91-92—Quebec	NHL	78	13	20	33	86	-8	0	2	—	—	—	—	—
92-93—Quebec	NHL	74	10	26	36	98	5	0	0	6	2	4	6	8
93-94—Quebec	NHL	59	11	17	28	70	2	1	1	—	—	—	—	—
94-95—Quebec	NHL	29	4	8	12	41	5	0	0	5	0	0	0	8
95-96—Colorado	NHL	3	0	0	0	0	-1	0	0	—	—	—	—	—
—Calgary	NHL	32	4	5	9	20	2	0	2	2	0	0	0	0
—Saint John	AHL	12	5	3	8	10	...	...	...	—	—	—	—	—
96-97—Utah	IHL	9	7	6	13	14	...	...	...	—	—	—	—	—
—New York Islanders	NHL	73	13	5	18	49	-12	0	3	—	—	—	—	—
97-98—New York Islanders	NHL	78	10	10	20	47	-9	0	1	—	—	—	—	—
NHL Totals (8 years)		439	67	93	160	415	-13	1	9	13	2	4	6	16

LAPOINTE, MARTIN　　　　RW　　　　RED WINGS

PERSONAL: Born September 12, 1973, in Lachine, Que. ... 5-11/215. ... Shoots right. ... Name pronounced MAHR-tai luh-POYNT.

TRANSACTIONS/CAREER NOTES: Selected by Detroit Red Wings in first round (first Red Wings pick, 10th overall) of NHL entry draft (June 22, 1991). ... Fractured wrist (October 9, 1991); missed 22 games. ... Injured left knee (February 29, 1996); missed eight games. ... Injured leg (April 10, 1996); missed two games. ... Fractured finger (December 1, 1996); missed four games. ... Strained hamstring (February 25, 1998); missed one game. ... Suspended two games and fined $1,000 by NHL for cross-checking incident (March 18, 1998).

HONORS: Won Michel Bergeron Trophy (1989-90). ... Named to QMJHL All-Star first team (1989-90 and 1992-93). ... Named to QMJHL All-Star second team (1990-91).

MISCELLANEOUS: Member of Stanley Cup championship team (1997 and 1998).

Season Team	League	Gms.	G	A	Pts.	PIM	+/-	PP	SH	Gms.	G	A	Pts.	PIM
				REGULAR SEASON								PLAYOFFS		
89-90—Laval	QMJHL	65	42	54	96	77	...	...	...	14	8	17	25	54
90-91—Laval	QMJHL	64	44	54	98	66	...	...	...	13	7	14	21	26
91-92—Detroit	NHL	4	0	1	1	5	2	0	0	3	0	1	1	4
—Laval	QMJHL	31	25	30	55	84	...	...	...	10	4	10	14	32
—Adirondack	AHL	—	—	—	—	—	...	...	...	8	2	2	4	4
92-93—Adirondack	AHL	8	1	2	3	9	...	...	...	—	—	—	—	—
—Detroit	NHL	3	0	0	0	0	-2	0	0	—	—	—	—	—
—Laval	QMJHL	35	38	51	89	41	...	...	...	13	*13	*17	*30	22
93-94—Adirondack	AHL	28	25	21	46	47	...	...	...	4	1	1	2	8
—Detroit	NHL	50	8	8	16	55	7	2	0	4	0	0	0	6
94-95—Adirondack	AHL	39	29	16	45	80	...	...	...	—	—	—	—	—
—Detroit	NHL	39	4	6	10	73	1	0	0	2	0	1	1	8
95-96—Detroit	NHL	58	6	3	9	93	0	1	0	11	1	2	3	12
96-97—Detroit	NHL	78	16	17	33	167	-14	5	1	20	4	8	12	60
97-98—Detroit	NHL	79	15	19	34	106	0	4	0	21	9	6	15	20
NHL Totals (7 years)		311	49	54	103	499	-6	12	1	61	14	18	32	110

LARAQUE, GEORGES   RW   OILERS

PERSONAL: Born December 7, 1976, in Montreal. ... 6-3/235. ... Shoots right. ... Name pronounced la-RAHK.
TRANSACTIONS/CAREER NOTES: Selected by Edmonton Oilers in second round (second Oilers pick, 31st overall) of NHL entry draft (July 8, 1995). ... Fractured left foot (November 17, 1997); missed five games. ... Tore cartilige in right knee (December 5, 1997); missed seven games.

		REGULAR SEASON								PLAYOFFS				
Season Team	League	Gms.	G	A	Pts.	PIM	+/-	PP	SH	Gms.	G	A	Pts.	PIM
93-94—St. Jean	QMJHL	70	11	11	22	142	...	...	...	4	0	0	0	7
94-95—St. Jean	QMJHL	62	19	22	41	259	...	...	...	7	1	1	2	42
95-96—Laval	QMJHL	11	8	13	21	76	...	...	...	—	—	—	—	—
—St. Hyacinthe	QMJHL	8	3	4	7	59	...	...	...	—	—	—	—	—
—Granby	QMJHL	22	9	7	16	125	...	...	...	18	7	6	13	104
96-97—Hamilton	AHL	73	14	20	34	179	...	...	...	15	1	3	4	12
97-98—Hamilton	AHL	46	10	20	30	154	...	...	...	3	0	0	0	11
—Edmonton	NHL	11	0	0	0	59	-4	0	0	—	—	—	—	—
NHL Totals (1 year)		11	0	0	0	59	-4	0	0					

LARIONOV, IGOR   C   RED WINGS

PERSONAL: Born December 3, 1960, in Voskresensk, U.S.S.R. ... 5-9/170. ... Shoots left. ... Name pronounced EE-gohr LAIR-ee-AH-nahf.
TRANSACTIONS/CAREER NOTES: Selected by Vancouver Canucks in 11th round (11th Canucks pick, 214th overall) of NHL entry draft (June 15, 1985). ... Injured groin (October 25, 1990); missed four games. ... Sprained ankle (January 8, 1991). ... Reinjured ankle (January 30, 1991); missed seven games. ... Signed to play with Lugano of Switzerland (July 14, 1992). ... Selected by San Jose Sharks in NHL waiver draft (October 4, 1992). ... Injured shoulder (September 30, 1993); missed four games. ... Reinjured shoulder (October 16, 1993); missed four games. ... Suffered from the flu (November 7, 1993); missed two games. ... Sprained knee (December 12, 1993); missed 10 games. ... Suffered from respiratory infection (February 11, 1994); missed one game. ... Suffered from the flu (February 26, 1994); missed two games. ... Injured groin (February 15, 1995); missed three games. ... Injured foot (February 26, 1995); missed 12 games. ... Traded by Sharks with second-round pick (traded to St. Louis) in 1998 draft to Detroit Red Wings for RW Ray Sheppard (October 25, 1995). ... Suffered from the flu (December 29, 1995); missed two games. ... Pulled groin (October 15, 1996); missed four games. ... Bruised wrist (October 30, 1996); missed seven games. ... Suffered from the flu (March 21, 1997); missed one game. ... Bruised back (April 8, 1997); missed three games. ... Strained groin (December 26, 1997); missed one game. ... Reinjured groin (December 29, 1997); missed one game. ... Reinjured groin (March 18, 1998); missed two games. ... Reinjured groin (March 26, 1998); missed three games. ... Injured elbow (April 9, 1998); missed four games.
HONORS: Named to Soviet League All-Star team (1982-83 and 1985-86 through 1987-88). ... Won Soviet Player of the Year Award (1987-88). ... Played in NHL All-Star Game (1998).
MISCELLANEOUS: Member of Stanley Cup championship team (1997 and 1998). ... Member of gold-medal-winning U.S.S.R. Olympic teams (1984 and 1988). ... Scored on a penalty shot (vs. Arturs Irbe, November 22, 1995).
STATISTICAL PLATEAUS: Three-goal games: 1991-92 (2), 1993-94 (2). Total: 4.

		REGULAR SEASON								PLAYOFFS				
Season Team	League	Gms.	G	A	Pts.	PIM	+/-	PP	SH	Gms.	G	A	Pts.	PIM
77-78—Khimik Voskresensk	USSR	6	3	0	3	4	...			—	—	—	—	—
78-79—Khimik Voskresensk	USSR	25	3	4	7	12	...			—	—	—	—	—
79-80—Khimik Voskresensk	USSR	42	11	7	18	24	...			—	—	—	—	—
80-81—Khimik Voskresensk	USSR	56	22	23	45	36	...			—	—	—	—	—
81-82—CSKA Moscow	USSR	46	31	22	53	6	...			—	—	—	—	—
82-83—CSKA Moscow	USSR	44	20	19	39	20	...			—	—	—	—	—
83-84—CSKA Moscow	USSR	43	15	26	41	30	...			—	—	—	—	—
—Soviet Olympic Team	Int'l	7	1	4	5	6	...			—	—	—	—	—
84-85—CSKA Moscow	USSR	40	18	28	46	20	...			—	—	—	—	—
85-86—CSKA Moscow	USSR	40	21	31	52	33	...			—	—	—	—	—
86-87—CSKA Moscow	USSR	39	20	26	46	34	...			—	—	—	—	—
87-88—CSKA Moscow	USSR	51	25	32	57	54	...			—	—	—	—	—
—Soviet Olympic Team	Int'l	8	4	9	13	4	...			—	—	—	—	—
88-89—CSKA Moscow	USSR	31	15	12	27	22	...			—	—	—	—	—
89-90—Vancouver	NHL	74	17	27	44	20	-5	8	0	—	—	—	—	—
90-91—Vancouver	NHL	64	13	21	34	14	-3	1	1	6	1	0	1	6
91-92—Vancouver	NHL	72	21	44	65	54	7	10	3	13	3	7	10	4
92-93—Lugano	Switzerland	24	10	19	29	44	...			—	—	—	—	—
93-94—San Jose	NHL	60	18	38	56	40	20	3	2	14	5	13	18	10
94-95—San Jose	NHL	33	4	20	24	14	-3	0	0	11	1	8	9	2
95-96—San Jose	NHL	4	1	1	2	0	-6	1	0	—	—	—	—	—
—Detroit	NHL	69	21	50	71	34	37	9	1	19	6	7	13	6
96-97—Detroit	NHL	64	12	42	54	26	31	2	1	20	4	8	12	8
97-98—Detroit	NHL	69	8	39	47	40	14	3	0	22	3	10	13	12
NHL Totals (8 years)		509	115	282	397	242	92	37	8	105	23	53	76	48

LARIVEE, FRANCIS   G   MAPLE LEAFS

PERSONAL: Born November 8, 1977, in Verdun, Que. ... 6-2/198. ... Catches left.
TRANSACTIONS/CAREER NOTES: Selected by Toronto Maple Leafs in second round (second Maple Leafs pick, 50th overall) of NHL entry draft (June 22, 1996).

		REGULAR SEASON								PLAYOFFS						
Season Team	League	Gms.	Min	W	L	T	GA	SO	Avg.	Gms.	Min.	W	L	GA	SO	Avg.
93-94—Val-d'Or	QMJHL	36	1706	5	20	1	162	3	5.70	—	—	—	—	—	—	—
94-95—Val-d'Or	QMJHL	38	1795	9	21	1	132	0	4.41	—	—	—	—	—	—	—
95-96—Val-d'Or	QMJHL	22	1162	12	4	2	73	0	3.77	—	—	—	—	—	—	—
—Laval	QMJHL	39	2085	9	24	1	178	0	5.12	—	—	—	—	—	—	—
96-97—Laval	QMJHL	21	1069	6	11	1	79	1	4.43	—	—	—	—	—	—	—
—Granby	QMJHL	3	135	2	0	0	7	0	3.11	1	1	0	0	1	0	60.00
—St. John's	AHL	4	244	3	1	0	9	0	2.21	2	1	0	0	0	0	0.00
97-98—St. John's	AHL	30	1461	6	12	5	79	0	3.24	—	—	—	—	—	—	—

LAROCQUE, MARIO   D   LIGHTNING

PERSONAL: Born April 24, 1978, in Montreal. ... 6-3/172. ... Shoots left. ... Name pronounced luh-RAHK.
TRANSACTIONS/CAREER NOTES: Selected by Tampa Bay Lightning in first round (first Lightning pick, 16th overall) of NHL entry draft (June 22, 1996).
HONORS: Named to QMJHL All-Rookie team (1995-96).

		REGULAR SEASON								PLAYOFFS				
Season Team	League	Gms.	G	A	Pts.	PIM	+/-	PP	SH	Gms.	G	A	Pts.	PIM
95-96—Hull	QMJHL	68	7	19	26	196	...	...	...	14	2	5	7	16
96-97—Hull	QMJHL	64	13	37	50	160	...	...	...	14	2	5	7	34
97-98—Sherbrooke	QMJHL	28	6	10	16	125	...	...	...	—	—	—	—	—

LAROCQUE, MICHEL   G   SHARKS

PERSONAL: Born October 3, 1976, in Lahr, West Germany. ... 5-11/192. ... Catches left.
COLLEGE: Boston University.
TRANSACTIONS/CAREER NOTES: Selected by San Jose Sharks in sixth round (fifth Sharks pick, 137th overall) of NHL entry draft (June 22, 1996).
HONORS: Named to Hockey East All-Rookie team (1995-96). ... Named Hockey East Tournament Most Valuable Player (1996-97). ... Named to Hockey East All-Star second team (1997-98).

		REGULAR SEASON								PLAYOFFS						
Season Team	League	Gms.	Min	W	L	T	GA	SO	Avg.	Gms.	Min.	W	L	GA	SO	Avg.
95-96—Boston University	Hockey East	14	735	10	1	1	42	0	3.43	—	—	—	—	—	—	—
96-97—Boston University	Hockey East	24	1466	16	4	4	58	0	2.37	—	—	—	—	—	—	—
97-98—Boston University	Hockey East	24	1370	17	4	1	50	1	2.19	—	—	—	—	—	—	—

LARSEN, BRAD   LW   AVALANCHE

PERSONAL: Born June 28, 1977, in Nakusp, B.C. ... 6-0/207. ... Shoots left.
TRANSACTIONS/CAREER NOTES: Selected by Ottawa Senators in third round (third Senators pick, 53rd overall) of NHL entry draft (July 8, 1995). ... Rights traded by Senators to Colorado Avalanche for D Janne Laukkanen (January 25, 1996); did not sign. ... Returned to draft pool by Avalanche and selected by Avalanche in fourth round (fifth Avalanche pick, 87th overall) of NHL entry draft (June 21, 1997).
HONORS: Named to WHL (East) All-Star second team (1996-97).

		REGULAR SEASON								PLAYOFFS				
Season Team	League	Gms.	G	A	Pts.	PIM	+/-	PP	SH	Gms.	G	A	Pts.	PIM
92-93—Nelson	Tier II Jr. A	42	31	37	68	164	...	...	...	—	—	—	—	—
93-94—Swift Current	WHL	64	15	18	33	37	...	...	...	7	1	2	3	4
94-95—Swift Current	WHL	62	24	33	57	73	...	...	...	6	0	1	1	2
95-96—Swift Current	WHL	51	30	47	77	67	...	...	...	6	3	2	5	13
96-97—Swift Current	WHL	61	36	46	82	61	...	...	...	—	—	—	—	—
97-98—Hershey	AHL	65	12	10	22	80	...	...	...	7	3	2	5	2
—Colorado	NHL	1	0	0	0	0	0	0	0	—	—	—	—	—
NHL Totals (1 year)		1	0	0	0	0	0	0	0					

LAUKKANEN, JANNE   D   SENATORS

PERSONAL: Born March 19, 1970, in Lahti, Finland. ... 6-0/180. ... Shoots left. ... Name pronounced YAH-nee LOW-kih-nihn.
TRANSACTIONS/CAREER NOTES: Selected by Quebec Nordiques in eighth round (eighth Nordiques pick, 156th overall) of NHL entry draft (June 22, 1991). ... Injured groin (April 14, 1995); missed four games. ... Reinjured groin (April 30, 1995); missed last game of season. ... Nordiques franchise moved to Colorado and renamed Avalanche for 1995-96 season (June 21, 1995). ... Traded by Avalanche to Ottawa Senators for LW Brad Larsen (January 25, 1996). ... Suffered hip flexor during 1995-96 season; missed five games. ... Sprained left knee (March 25, 1996); missed two games. ... Bruised finger (November 15, 1996); missed one game. ... Suffered from the flu (December 10, 1996); missed two games. ... Suffered from the flu (March 17, 1997); missed one game. ... Injured knee (March 25, 1997); missed two games. ... Suffered concussion (October 19, 1997); missed two games. ... Strained groin (November 20, 1997); missed five games. ... Suffered from the flu (February 2, 1998); missed one game. ... Bruised foot (March 1, 1998); missed one game. ... Strained groin (March 13, 1998); missed five games. ... Reinjured groin (March 25, 1998); missed eight games.
MISCELLANEOUS: Member of bronze-medal-winning Finnish Olympic team (1994 and 1998).

		REGULAR SEASON								PLAYOFFS				
Season Team	League	Gms.	G	A	Pts.	PIM	+/-	PP	SH	Gms.	G	A	Pts.	PIM
89-90—Ilves Tampere	Finland	39	5	6	11	10	...	...	...	—	—	—	—	—
90-91—Reipas	Finland	44	8	14	22	56	...	...	...	—	—	—	—	—
91-92—Helsinki HPK	Finland	43	5	14	19	62	...	...	...	—	—	—	—	—
—Fin. Olympic Team	Int'l	8	0	1	1	6	...	...	...	—	—	—	—	—
92-93—HPK Hameenlinna	Finland	47	8	21	29	76	...	...	...	12	1	4	5	10
93-94—HPK Hameenlinna	Finland	48	5	24	29	46	...	...	...	—	—	—	—	—
—Fin. Olympic Team	Int'l	8	0	2	2	12	...	...	...	—	—	—	—	—
94-95—Cornwall	AHL	55	8	26	34	41	...	...	...	—	—	—	—	—
—Quebec	NHL	11	0	3	3	4	3	0	0	6	1	0	1	2
95-96—Cornwall	AHL	35	7	20	27	60	...	...	...	—	—	—	—	—
—Colorado	NHL	3	1	0	1	0	-1	1	0	—	—	—	—	—
—Ottawa	NHL	20	0	2	2	14	0	0	0	—	—	—	—	—
96-97—Ottawa	NHL	76	3	18	21	76	-14	2	0	7	0	1	1	6
97-98—Ottawa	NHL	60	4	17	21	64	-15	2	0	11	2	2	4	8
—Fin. Olympic Team	Int'l	6	0	0	0	4	...	...	...	—	—	—	—	—
NHL Totals (4 years)		170	8	40	48	158	-27	5	0	24	3	3	6	16

LAUS, PAUL D PANTHERS

PERSONAL: Born September 26, 1970, in Beamsville, Ont. ... 6-1/216. ... Shoots right. ... Name pronounced LAWS.
TRANSACTIONS/CAREER NOTES: Suffered inflamed knuckles (September 1988). ... Suspended three playoff games by OHL for spearing (April 28, 1989). ... Selected by Pittsburgh Penguins in second round (second Penguins pick, 37th overall) of NHL entry draft (June 17, 1989). ... Selected by Florida Panthers in NHL expansion draft (June 24, 1993). ... Strained groin (February 19, 1995); missed six games. ... Separated left shoulder (April 16, 1995); missed two games. ... Bruised left ankle (October 16, 1996); missed two games. ... Sprained ankle (March 5, 1997); missed one game. ... Bruised hand (March 19, 1997); missed two games. ... Sprained back (March 11, 1998); missed four games.
MISCELLANEOUS: Holds Florida Panthers all-time record for most penalty minutes (1,089).

		REGULAR SEASON							PLAYOFFS				
Season Team	League	Gms.	G	A	Pts.	PIM	+/-	PP	SH	Gms.	G	A	Pts.	PIM
86-87—St. Catharines Jr. B	OHA	40	1	8	9	56	...	...	...	—	—	—	—	—
87-88—Hamilton	OHL	56	1	9	10	171	...	...	...	14	0	0	0	28
88-89—Niagara Falls	OHL	49	1	10	11	225	...	...	...	15	0	5	5	56
89-90—Niagara Falls	OHL	60	13	35	48	231	...	...	...	16	6	16	22	71
90-91—Muskegon	IHL	35	3	4	7	103	...	...	...	4	0	0	0	13
—Albany	IHL	7	0	0	0	7	...	...	...	—	—	—	—	—
—Knoxville	ECHL	20	6	12	18	83	...	...	...	—	—	—	—	—
91-92—Muskegon	IHL	75	0	21	21	248	...	...	...	14	2	5	7	70
92-93—Cleveland	IHL	76	8	18	26	427	...	...	...	4	1	0	1	27
93-94—Florida	NHL	39	2	0	2	109	9	0	0	—	—	—	—	—
94-95—Florida	NHL	37	0	7	7	138	12	0	0	—	—	—	—	—
95-96—Florida	NHL	78	3	6	9	236	-2	0	0	21	2	6	8	*62
96-97—Florida	NHL	77	0	12	12	313	13	0	0	5	0	1	1	4
97-98—Florida	NHL	77	0	11	11	293	-5	0	0	—	—	—	—	—
NHL Totals (5 years)		308	5	36	41	1089	27	0	0	26	2	7	9	66

LAWRENCE, MARK RW ISLANDERS

PERSONAL: Born January 27, 1972, in Burlington, Ont. ... 6-4/215. ... Shoots right.
TRANSACTIONS/CAREER NOTES: Selected by Dallas Stars in sixth round (fourth Stars pick, 118th overall) of NHL entry draft (June 22, 1991). ... Signed as free agent by New York Islanders (July 29, 1997).

		REGULAR SEASON							PLAYOFFS				
Season Team	League	Gms.	G	A	Pts.	PIM	+/-	PP	SH	Gms.	G	A	Pts.	PIM
87-88—Burlington Jr. B	OHA	40	11	12	23	90	...	...	...	—	—	—	—	—
88-89—Niagara Falls	OHL	63	9	27	36	142	...	...	...	—	—	—	—	—
89-90—Niagara Falls	OHL	54	15	18	33	123	...	...	...	16	2	5	7	42
90-91—Detroit	OHL	66	27	38	65	53	...	...	...	—	—	—	—	—
91-92—Detroit	OHL	28	19	26	45	54	...	...	...	—	—	—	—	—
—North Bay	OHL	24	13	14	27	21	...	...	...	21	*23	12	35	36
92-93—Dayton	ECHL	20	8	14	22	46	...	...	...	—	—	—	—	—
—Kalamazoo	IHL	57	22	13	35	47	...	...	...	—	—	—	—	—
93-94—Kalamazoo	IHL	64	17	20	37	90	...	...	...	—	—	—	—	—
94-95—Kalamazoo	IHL	77	21	29	50	92	...	...	...	16	3	7	10	28
—Dallas	NHL	2	0	0	0	0	0	0	0	—	—	—	—	—
95-96—Michigan	IHL	55	15	14	29	92	...	...	...	10	3	4	7	30
—Dallas	NHL	13	0	1	1	17	0	0	0	—	—	—	—	—
96-97—Michigan	IHL	68	15	21	36	141	...	...	...	4	0	0	0	18
97-98—Utah	IHL	80	36	28	64	102	...	...	...	4	1	1	2	4
—New York Islanders	NHL	2	0	0	0	2	0	0	0	—	—	—	—	—
NHL Totals (3 years)		17	0	1	1	19	0	0	0	—	—	—	—	—

LEACH, STEVE RW HURRICANES

PERSONAL: Born January 16, 1966, in Cambridge, Mass. ... 5-11/197. ... Shoots right. ... Full name: Stephen Morgan Leach. ... Uncle of Jay Leach, defenseman in Phoenix Coyotes system.
HIGH SCHOOL: Matignon (Cambridge, Mass.).
COLLEGE: New Hampshire.
TRANSACTIONS/CAREER NOTES: Selected by Washington Capitals in second round (second Capitals pick, 34th overall) of NHL entry draft (June 9, 1984). ... Strained left knee (February 1989). ... Injured thumb (March 1990). ... Suffered concussion (October 10, 1990). ... Separated right shoulder (February 2, 1991); missed four games. ... Traded by Capitals to Boston Bruins for LW Randy Burridge (June 21, 1991). ... Injured thigh (October 1992); missed one game. ... Injured ribs (January 1993); missed four games. ... Injured knee (January 8, 1994); missed 25 games. ... Reinjured knee (March 7, 1994); missed 15 games. ... Broke foot (April 8, 1995). ... Traded by Bruins to St. Louis Blues for F Kevin Sawyer and D Steve Staios (March 7, 1996). ... Injured ankle (November 3, 1996); missed 59 games. ... Traded by Blues to Carolina Hurricanes for D Alexander Godynyuk and sixth-round pick (D Brad Voth) in 1998 draft (June 27, 1997). ... Strained neck (December 12, 1998); missed two games. ... Reinjured neck (January 24, 1998); missed remainder of season.
HONORS: Named to Hockey East All-Freshman team (1984-85).

		REGULAR SEASON							PLAYOFFS				
Season Team	League	Gms.	G	A	Pts.	PIM	+/-	PP	SH	Gms.	G	A	Pts.	PIM
83-84—Matignon	Mass. H.S.	21	27	22	49	49	...	...	...	—	—	—	—	—
84-85—New Hampshire	Hockey East	41	12	25	37	53	...	...	...	—	—	—	—	—
85-86—New Hampshire	Hockey East	25	22	6	28	30	...	...	...	—	—	—	—	—
—Washington	NHL	11	1	1	2	2	0	0	0	6	0	1	1	0
86-87—Binghamton	AHL	54	18	21	39	39	...	...	...	13	3	1	4	6
—Washington	NHL	15	1	0	1	6	-4	0	0	—	—	—	—	—

Season Team	League	REGULAR SEASON								PLAYOFFS				
		Gms.	G	A	Pts.	PIM	+/-	PP	SH	Gms.	G	A	Pts.	PIM
87-88—U.S. national team	Int'l	53	26	20	46	...	...	...	...	—	—	—	—	—
—U.S. Olympic Team	Int'l	6	1	2	3	0	...	...	...	—	—	—	—	—
—Washington	NHL	8	1	1	2	17	2	0	0	9	2	1	3	0
88-89—Washington	NHL	74	11	19	30	94	-4	4	0	6	1	0	1	12
89-90—Washington	NHL	70	18	14	32	104	10	0	0	14	2	2	4	6
90-91—Washington	NHL	68	11	19	30	99	-9	4	0	9	1	2	3	8
91-92—Boston	NHL	78	31	29	60	147	-8	12	0	15	4	0	4	10
92-93—Boston	NHL	79	26	25	51	126	-6	9	0	4	1	1	2	2
93-94—Boston	NHL	42	5	10	15	74	-10	1	0	5	0	1	1	2
94-95—Boston	NHL	35	5	6	11	68	-3	1	0	—	—	—	—	—
95-96—Boston	NHL	59	9	13	22	86	-4	1	0	—	—	—	—	—
—St. Louis	NHL	14	2	4	6	22	-3	0	0	11	3	2	5	10
96-97—St. Louis	NHL	17	2	1	3	24	-2	0	0	6	0	0	0	33
97-98—Carolina	NHL	45	4	5	9	42	-19	1	1	—	—	—	—	—
NHL Totals (13 years).........		615	127	147	274	911	-60	33	1	85	14	10	24	83

LeBOUTILLIER, PETER   RW   MIGHTY DUCKS

PERSONAL: Born January 11, 1975, in Minnedosa, Man. ... 6-1/198. ... Shoots right. ... Name pronounced lay-boo-TIHL-ee-yay.

HIGH SCHOOL: Lindsay Thurber (Red Deer, Alta.).

TRANSACTIONS/CAREER NOTES: Selected by New York Islanders in sixth round (sixth Islanders pick, 144th overall) of NHL entry draft (June 26, 1993). ... Returned to draft pool by Islanders and selected by Mighty Ducks of Anaheim in sixth round (fifth Mighty Ducks pick, 133rd overall) of entry draft (July 8, 1995). ... Strained knee (March 14, 1997); missed five games. ... Strained knee (March 26, 1997); missed final seven games of season.

Season Team	League	REGULAR SEASON								PLAYOFFS				
		Gms.	G	A	Pts.	PIM	+/-	PP	SH	Gms.	G	A	Pts.	PIM
91-92—Neepawa	Jr. A	35	11	14	25	99	...	...	...	—	—	—	—	—
92-93—Red Deer....................	WHL	67	8	26	34	284	...	...	...	2	0	1	1	5
93-94—Red Deer....................	WHL	66	19	20	39	300	...	...	...	2	0	1	1	4
94-95—Red Deer....................	WHL	59	27	16	43	159	...	...	...	—	—	—	—	—
95-96—Baltimore	AHL	68	7	9	16	228	...	...	...	11	0	0	0	33
96-97—Baltimore	AHL	47	6	12	18	175	...	...	...	—	—	—	—	—
—Anaheim	NHL	23	1	0	1	121	0	0	0	—	—	—	—	—
97-98—Cincinnati...................	AHL	51	9	11	20	143	...	...	...	—	—	—	—	—
—Anaheim	NHL	12	1	1	2	55	-1	0	0	—	—	—	—	—
NHL Totals (2 years)...........		35	2	1	3	176	-1	0	0					

LeCLAIR, JOHN   LW   FLYERS

PERSONAL: Born July 5, 1969, in St. Albans, Vt. ... 6-2/220. ... Shoots left. ... Full name: John Clark LeClair.

HIGH SCHOOL: Bellows Free Academy (St. Albans, Vt.).

COLLEGE: Vermont.

TRANSACTIONS/CAREER NOTES: Selected by Montreal Canadiens in second round (second Canadiens pick, 33rd overall) of NHL entry draft (June 13, 1987). ... Injured thigh; missed 16 games during 1988-89 season. ... Injured knee and underwent surgery (January 20, 1990); missed remainder of season. ... Injured shoulder (January 15, 1992); missed four games. ... Suffered charley horse (January 20, 1993); missed four games. ... Sprained knee (October 2, 1993); missed eight games. ... Bruised sternum (March 28, 1994); missed two games. ... Traded by Canadiens with LW Gilbert Dionne and D Eric Desjardins to Philadelphia Flyers for RW Mark Recchi and third-round pick (C Martin Hohenberger) in 1995 draft (February 9, 1995). ... Strained right hip (April 18, 1995); missed one playoff game.

HONORS: Named to ECAC All-Star second team (1990-91). ... Named to The Sporting News All-Star first team (1994-95). ... Named to NHL All-Star first team (1994-95 and 1997-98). ... Played in NHL All-Star Game (1996-1998). ... Named to NHL All-Star second team (1995-96 and 1996-97). ... Named to The Sporting News All-Star team (1996-97 and 1997-98).

MISCELLANEOUS: Member of Stanley Cup championship team (1993).

STATISTICAL PLATEAUS: Three-goal games: 1994-95 (2), 1995-96 (2), 1996-97 (1), 1997-98 (1). Total: 6. ... Four-goal games: 1996-97 (1). ... Total hat tricks: 7.

Season Team	League	REGULAR SEASON								PLAYOFFS				
		Gms.	G	A	Pts.	PIM	+/-	PP	SH	Gms.	G	A	Pts.	PIM
85-86—Bellows Free Acad.	VT. H.S.	22	41	28	69	14	...	...	...	—	—	—	—	—
86-87—Bellows Free Acad.	VT. H.S.	23	44	40	84	25	...	...	...	—	—	—	—	—
87-88—Univ. of Vermont........	ECAC	31	12	22	34	62	...	...	...	—	—	—	—	—
88-89—Univ. of Vermont........	ECAC	19	9	12	21	40	...	...	...	—	—	—	—	—
89-90—Univ. of Vermont........	ECAC	10	10	6	16	38	...	...	...	—	—	—	—	—
90-91—Univ. of Vermont........	ECAC	33	25	20	45	58	...	...	...	—	—	—	—	—
—Montreal	NHL	10	2	5	7	2	1	0	0	3	0	0	0	0
91-92—Montreal	NHL	59	8	11	19	14	5	3	0	8	1	1	2	4
—Fredericton	AHL	8	7	7	14	10	...	...	...	2	0	0	0	4
92-93—Montreal	NHL	72	19	25	44	33	11	2	0	20	4	6	10	14
93-94—Montreal	NHL	74	19	24	43	32	17	1	0	7	2	1	3	8
94-95—Montreal	NHL	9	1	4	5	10	-1	1	0	—	—	—	—	—
—Philadelphia	NHL	37	25	24	49	20	21	5	0	15	5	7	12	4
95-96—Philadelphia	NHL	82	51	46	97	64	21	19	0	11	6	5	11	6
96-97—Philadelphia	NHL	82	50	47	97	58	*44	10	0	19	9	12	21	10
97-98—Philadelphia	NHL	82	51	36	87	32	30	16	0	5	1	1	2	8
—U.S. Olympic Team	Int'l	4	0	1	1	0	...	...	...	—	—	—	—	—
NHL Totals (8 years)...........		507	226	222	448	265	149	57	0	88	28	33	61	54

LECLERC, MIKE LW MIGHTY DUCKS

PERSONAL: Born November 10, 1976, in Winnipeg. ... 6-1/205. ... Shoots left. ... Name pronounced luh-KLAIR.
TRANSACTIONS/CAREER NOTES: Selected by Mighty Ducks of Anaheim in third round (third Mighty Ducks pick, 55th overall) of NHL entry draft (July 8, 1995).
HONORS: Named to WHL (Central/East) All-Star second team (1995-96). ... Named to AHL All-Rookie team (1996-97).

Season Team	League	REGULAR SEASON								PLAYOFFS				
		Gms.	G	A	Pts.	PIM	+/-	PP	SH	Gms.	G	A	Pts.	PIM
91-92—St. Boniface	Tier II Jr. A	43	16	12	28	25	...	...	...	—	—	—	—	—
—Victoria	WHL	2	0	0	0	0	...	...	...	—	—	—	—	—
92-93—Victoria	WHL	70	4	11	15	118	...	...	...	—	—	—	—	—
93-94—Victoria	WHL	68	29	11	40	112	...	...	...	—	—	—	—	—
94-95—Prince George	WHL	43	20	36	56	78	...	...	...	—	—	—	—	—
—Brandon	WHL	23	5	8	13	50	...	...	...	18	10	6	16	33
95-96—Brandon	WHL	71	58	53	111	161	...	...	...	19	6	19	25	25
96-97—Baltimore	AHL	71	29	27	56	134	...	...	...	—	—	—	—	—
—Anaheim	NHL	5	1	1	2	0	2	0	0	1	0	0	0	0
97-98—Cincinnati	AHL	48	18	22	40	83	...	...	...	—	—	—	—	—
—Anaheim	NHL	7	0	0	0	6	-6	0	0	—	—	—	—	—
NHL Totals (2 years)		12	1	1	2	6	-4	0	0	1	0	0	0	0

LEDYARD, GRANT D BRUINS

PERSONAL: Born November 19, 1961, in Winnipeg. ... 6-2/195. ... Shoots left.
TRANSACTIONS/CAREER NOTES: Signed as free agent by New York Rangers (July 7, 1982). ... Injured hip (October 1984). ... Traded by Rangers to Los Angeles Kings for LW Brian MacLellan and fourth-round pick (C Michael Sullivan) in 1987 draft; Rangers also sent second-round pick (D Neil Wilkinson) in 1986 draft and fourth-round pick (RW John Weisbrod) in 1987 draft to Minnesota North Stars and the North Stars sent G Roland Melanson to the Kings as part of the same deal (December 1986). ... Sprained ankle (October 1987). ... Traded by Kings to Washington Capitals for RW Craig Laughlin (February 9, 1988). ... Traded by Capitals with G Clint Malarchuk and sixth-round pick (C Brian Holzinger) in 1991 draft to Buffalo Sabres for D Calle Johansson and second-round pick (G Byron Dafoe) in 1989 draft (March 6, 1989). ... Injured knee (February 12, 1991). ... Injured shoulder (March 2, 1991). ... Bruised ankle (March 14, 1992); missed four games. ... Broke finger (October 28, 1992); missed 25 games. ... Injured eye (March 7, 1993); missed three games. ... Signed as free agent by Dallas Stars (August 13, 1993). ... Sprained ankle (February 13, 1995); missed two games. ... Fractured ankle (April 16, 1995); missed last eight games of season and first game of playoffs. ... Suffered from the flu (May 14, 1995); missed one game. ... Fractured orbital bone prior to 1996-97 season; missed first game of season. ... Suspended two games and fined $1,000 by NHL for kneeing incident (November 26, 1996). ... Suffered from the flu (February 2, 1997); missed two games. ... Signed as free agent by Vancouver Canucks (July 14, 1997). ... Suffered concussion (October 30, 1997); missed one game. ... Traded by Canucks to Boston Bruins for eighth-round pick (LW Curtis Valentine) in 1998 draft (March 3, 1998).
HONORS: Named MJHL Most Valuable Player (1981-82). ... Named to MJHL All-Star first team (1981-82). ... Won Bob Gassoff Award (1983-84). ... Won Max McNab Trophy (1983-84).

Season Team	League	REGULAR SEASON								PLAYOFFS				
		Gms.	G	A	Pts.	PIM	+/-	PP	SH	Gms.	G	A	Pts.	PIM
79-80—Fort Garry	MJHL	49	13	24	37	90	...	...	...	—	—	—	—	—
80-81—Saskatoon	WHL	71	9	28	37	148	...	...	...	—	—	—	—	—
81-82—Fort Garry	MJHL	63	25	45	70	150	...	...	...	—	—	—	—	—
82-83—Tulsa	CHL	80	13	29	42	115	...	...	...	—	—	—	—	—
83-84—Tulsa	CHL	58	9	17	26	71	...	...	...	9	5	4	9	10
84-85—New Haven	AHL	36	6	20	26	18	...	...	...	—	—	—	—	—
—New York Rangers	NHL	42	8	12	20	53	8	1	0	3	0	2	2	4
85-86—New York Rangers	NHL	27	2	9	11	20	-7	0	0	—	—	—	—	—
—Los Angeles	NHL	52	7	18	25	78	-22	4	0	—	—	—	—	—
86-87—Los Angeles	NHL	67	14	23	37	93	-40	5	0	5	0	0	0	10
87-88—New Haven	AHL	3	2	1	3	4	...	...	...	—	—	—	—	—
—Los Angeles	NHL	23	1	7	8	52	-7	1	0	—	—	—	—	—
—Washington	NHL	21	4	3	7	14	-4	1	0	14	1	0	1	30
88-89—Washington	NHL	61	3	11	14	43	1	1	0	—	—	—	—	—
—Buffalo	NHL	13	1	5	6	8	1	0	0	5	1	2	3	2
89-90—Buffalo	NHL	67	2	13	15	37	2	0	0	—	—	—	—	—
90-91—Buffalo	NHL	60	8	23	31	46	13	2	1	6	3	3	6	10
91-92—Buffalo	NHL	50	5	16	21	45	-4	0	0	—	—	—	—	—
92-93—Buffalo	NHL	50	2	14	16	45	-2	1	0	8	0	0	0	8
—Rochester	AHL	5	0	2	2	8	...	...	...	—	—	—	—	—
93-94—Dallas	NHL	84	9	37	46	42	7	6	0	9	1	2	3	6
94-95—Dallas	NHL	38	5	13	18	20	6	4	0	3	0	0	0	2
95-96—Dallas	NHL	73	5	19	24	20	-15	2	0	—	—	—	—	—
96-97—Dallas	NHL	67	1	15	16	61	31	0	0	7	0	2	2	0
97-98—Vancouver	NHL	49	2	13	15	14	-2	1	0	—	—	—	—	—
—Boston	NHL	22	2	7	9	6	-2	1	0	6	0	0	0	2
NHL Totals (14 years)		866	81	258	339	697	-36	30	1	66	6	11	17	74

LEETCH, BRIAN D RANGERS

PERSONAL: Born March 3, 1968, in Corpus Christi, Texas. ... 6-1/190. ... Shoots left. ... Full name: Brian Joseph Leetch.
HIGH SCHOOL: Avon (Conn.) Old Farms School for Boys.
COLLEGE: Boston College.
TRANSACTIONS/CAREER NOTES: Selected by New York Rangers in first round (first Rangers pick, ninth overall) of NHL entry draft (June 21, 1986). ... Sprained ligaments in left knee at U.S. Olympic Festival (July 1987). ... Fractured bone in left foot (December 1988). ... Suffered

hip pointer (March 15, 1989). ... Fractured left ankle (March 14, 1990). ... Injured ankle (November 21, 1992); missed one game. ... Suffered stretched nerve in neck (December 17, 1992); missed 34 games. ... Broke ankle (March 19, 1993) and underwent ankle surgery (March 31, 1993); missed remainder of season. ... Suffered nerve compression in right leg (January 4, 1998); missed two games. ... Suffered head injury (April 5, 1998); missed four games.

HONORS: Named Hockey East Player of the Year (1986-87). ... Named Hockey East Rookie of the Year (1986-87). ... Named Hockey East Tournament Most Valuable Player (1986-87). ... Named to NCAA All-America East first team (1986-87). ... Named to Hockey East All-Star first team (1986-87). ... Named to Hockey East All-Freshman team (1986-87). ... Named NHL Rookie of the Year by THE SPORTING NEWS (1988-89). ... Won Calder Memorial Trophy (1988-89). ... Named to NHL All-Rookie team (1988-89). ... Named to THE SPORTING NEWS All-Star second team (1990-91 and 1993-94). ... Named to NHL All-Star second team (1990-91, 1993-94 and 1995-96). ... Played in NHL All-Star Game (1990-1992, 1994 and 1996-1998). ... Won James Norris Memorial Trophy (1991-92 and 1996-97). ... Named to THE SPORTING NEWS All-Star first team (1991-92). ... Named to NHL All-Star first team (1991-92 and 1996-97). ... Won Conn Smythe Trophy (1993-94). ... Named to Hockey East All-Decade team (1994). ... Named to THE SPORTING NEWS All-Star team (1996-97).

RECORDS: Holds NHL single-season record for most goals by a rookie defenseman—23 (1988-89).

MISCELLANEOUS: Member of Stanley Cup championship team (1994). ... Captain of New York Rangers (1997-98).

Season Team	League	REGULAR SEASON								PLAYOFFS				
		Gms.	G	A	Pts.	PIM	+/-	PP	SH	Gms.	G	A	Pts.	PIM
84-85—Avon Old Farms H.S.	Conn. H.S.	26	30	46	76	15	...	...	...	—	—	—	—	—
85-86—Avon Old Farms H.S.	Conn. H.S.	28	40	44	84	18	...	...	...	—	—	—	—	—
86-87—Boston College	Hockey East	37	9	38	47	10	...	...	...	—	—	—	—	—
87-88—U.S. national team	Int'l	60	13	61	74	38	...	...	...	—	—	—	—	—
—U.S. Olympic Team	Int'l	6	1	5	6	4	...	...	...	—	—	—	—	—
—New York Rangers	NHL	17	2	12	14	0	5	1	0	—	—	—	—	—
88-89—New York Rangers	NHL	68	23	48	71	50	8	8	3	4	3	2	5	2
89-90—New York Rangers	NHL	72	11	45	56	26	-18	5	0	—	—	—	—	—
90-91—New York Rangers	NHL	80	16	72	88	42	2	6	0	6	1	3	4	0
91-92—New York Rangers	NHL	80	22	80	102	26	25	10	1	13	4	11	15	4
92-93—New York Rangers	NHL	36	6	30	36	26	2	2	1	—	—	—	—	—
93-94—New York Rangers	NHL	84	23	56	79	67	28	17	1	23	11	*23	*34	6
94-95—New York Rangers	NHL	48	9	32	41	18	0	3	0	10	6	8	14	8
95-96—New York Rangers	NHL	82	15	70	85	30	12	7	0	11	1	6	7	4
96-97—New York Rangers	NHL	82	20	58	78	40	31	9	0	15	2	8	10	6
97-98—New York Rangers	NHL	76	17	33	50	32	-36	11	0	—	—	—	—	—
—U.S. Olympic Team	Int'l	4	1	1	2	0	...	...	...	—	—	—	—	—
NHL Totals (11 years)		725	164	536	700	357	59	79	6	82	28	61	89	30

L

LEFEBVRE, SYLVAIN   D   AVALANCHE

PERSONAL: Born October 14, 1967, in Richmond, Que. ... 6-2/205. ... Shoots left. ... Name pronounced luh-FAYV.

TRANSACTIONS/CAREER NOTES: Signed as free agent by Montreal Canadiens (September 24, 1986). ... Traded by Canadiens to Toronto Maple Leafs for third-round pick (D Martin Belanger) in 1994 draft (August 20, 1992). ... Traded by Maple Leafs with LW Wendel Clark, RW Landon Wilson and first-round pick (D Jeffrey Kealty) in 1994 draft to Quebec Nordiques for C Mats Sundin, D Garth Butcher, LW Todd Warriner and first-round pick (traded to Washington Capitals who selected D Nolan Baumgartner) in 1994 draft (June 28, 1994). ... Nordiques franchise moved to Colorado and renamed Avalanche for 1995-96 season (June 21, 1995). ... Sprained right ankle (November 29, 1995); missed six games. ... Fractured forearm (December 18, 1996); missed 10 games. ... Suffered sore hip (December 12, 1997); missed one game.

HONORS: Named to AHL All-Star second team (1988-89).

MISCELLANEOUS: Member of Stanley Cup championship team (1996).

Season Team	League	REGULAR SEASON								PLAYOFFS				
		Gms.	G	A	Pts.	PIM	+/-	PP	SH	Gms.	G	A	Pts.	PIM
84-85—Laval	QMJHL	66	7	5	12	31	...	...	...	—	—	—	—	—
85-86—Laval	QMJHL	71	8	17	25	48	...	...	...	14	1	0	1	25
86-87—Laval	QMJHL	70	10	36	46	44	...	...	...	15	1	6	7	12
87-88—Sherbrooke	AHL	79	3	24	27	73	...	...	...	6	2	3	5	4
88-89—Sherbrooke	AHL	77	15	32	47	119	...	...	...	6	1	3	4	4
89-90—Montreal	NHL	68	3	10	13	61	18	0	0	6	0	0	0	2
90-91—Montreal	NHL	63	5	18	23	30	-11	1	0	11	1	0	1	6
91-92—Montreal	NHL	69	3	14	17	91	9	0	0	2	0	0	0	2
92-93—Toronto	NHL	81	2	12	14	90	8	0	0	21	3	3	6	20
93-94—Toronto	NHL	84	2	9	11	79	33	0	0	18	0	3	3	16
94-95—Quebec	NHL	48	2	11	13	17	13	0	0	6	0	2	2	2
95-96—Colorado	NHL	75	5	11	16	49	26	2	0	22	0	5	5	12
96-97—Colorado	NHL	71	2	11	13	30	12	1	0	17	0	0	0	25
97-98—Colorado	NHL	81	0	10	10	48	2	0	0	7	0	0	0	4
NHL Totals (9 years)		640	24	106	130	495	110	4	0	110	4	13	17	89

LEHTINEN, JERE   RW   STARS

PERSONAL: Born June 24, 1973, in Espoo, Finland. ... 6-0/185. ... Shoots right. ... Name pronounced YAIR-ee LEH-tih-nehn.

TRANSACTIONS/CAREER NOTES: Selected by Minnesota North Stars in fourth round (third North Stars pick, 88th overall) of NHL entry draft (June 20, 1992). ... North Stars franchise moved from Minnesota to Dallas and renamed Stars for 1993-94 season. ... Strained groin (December 21, 1995); missed six games. ... Reaggravated groin (January 10, 1996); missed one game. ... Sprained ankle (March 20, 1996); missed remainder of season. ... Sprained knee (January 31, 1997); missed 13 games. ... Sprained knee (March 5, 1997); missed five games. ... Separated shoulder (October 19, 1997); missed 10 games.

HONORS: Played in NHL All-Star Game (1998). ... Won Frank J. Selke Trophy (1997-98).

MISCELLANEOUS: Member of bronze-medal-winning Finnish Olympic team (1994 and 1998). ... Scored on a penalty shot (vs. Dominik Hasek, October 7, 1997).

		REGULAR SEASON								PLAYOFFS				
Season Team	League	Gms.	G	A	Pts.	PIM	+/-	PP	SH	Gms.	G	A	Pts.	PIM
90-91—Kiekko-Espoo	Finland	32	15	9	24	12	...	...	...	—	—	—	—	—
91-92—Kiekko-Espoo	Finland	43	32	17	49	6	...	...	...	—	—	—	—	—
92-93—Kiekko-Espoo	Finland	45	13	14	27	6	...	...	...	—	—	—	—	—
93-94—TPS Turku	Finland	42	19	20	39	6	...	...	...	11	11	2	13	2
—Fin. Olympic Team	Int'l	8	3	0	3	11	...	...	...	—	—	—	—	—
94-95—TPS Turku	Finland	39	19	23	42	33	...	...	...	13	8	6	14	4
95-96—Dallas	NHL	57	6	22	28	16	5	0	0	—	—	—	—	—
—Michigan	IHL	1	1	0	1	0	...	...	...	—	—	—	—	—
96-97—Dallas	NHL	63	16	27	43	2	26	3	1	7	2	2	4	0
97-98—Dallas	NHL	72	23	19	42	20	19	7	2	12	3	5	8	2
—Fin. Olympic Team	Int'l	6	4	2	6	2	...	...	...	—	—	—	—	—
NHL Totals (3 years)		192	45	68	113	38	50	10	3	19	5	7	12	2

LEMANOWICZ, DAVID   G   PANTHERS

PERSONAL: Born March 8, 1976, in Edmonton. ... 6-2/190. ... Catches left. ... Name pronounced luh-MAN-oh-wihts.
TRANSACTIONS/CAREER NOTES: Selected by Florida Panthers in ninth round (ninth Panthers pick, 218th overall) of NHL entry draft (July 8, 1995).

		REGULAR SEASON							PLAYOFFS						
Season Team	League	Gms.	Min	W	L	T	GA	SO	Avg.	Gms.	Min.	W	L	GA	SO	Avg.
92-93—Spokane	WHL	16	738	3	11	0	61	1	4.96	—	—	—	—	—	—	—
93-94—Spokane	WHL	6	256	1	2	0	21	0	4.92	—	—	—	—	—	—	—
94-95—Spokane	WHL	16	761	5	5	1	41	2	3.23	1	1	0	0	0	0	0.00
95-96—Spokane	WHL	62	3362	42	10	2	162	*4	*2.89	18	1036	9	†6	59	†2	3.42
96-97—Carolina	AHL	33	1796	11	18	0	117	2	3.91	—	—	—	—	—	—	—
—Port Huron	Col.HL	3	167	1	2	0	11	0	3.95	—	—	—	—	—	—	—
97-98—New Haven	AHL	16	880	5	9	0	49	0	3.34	—	—	—	—	—	—	—
—Tallahassee	ECHL	25	1330	6	16	‡0	119	0	5.37	—	—	—	—	—	—	—

LEMIEUX, CLAUDE   RW   AVALANCHE

PERSONAL: Born July 16, 1965, in Buckingham, Que. ... 6-1/215. ... Shoots right. ... Brother of Jocelyn Lemieux, right winger, Phoenix Coyotes. ... Name pronounced luh-MYOO.
TRANSACTIONS/CAREER NOTES: Selected by Montreal Canadiens as underage junior in second round (second Canadiens pick, 26th overall) of NHL entry draft (June 8, 1983). ... Tore ankle ligaments (October 1987). ... Fractured orbital bone above right eye (January 14, 1988). ... Pulled groin (March 1989). ... Underwent surgery to repair torn stomach muscle (November 1, 1989); missed 41 games. ... Traded by Canadiens to New Jersey Devils for LW Sylvain Turgeon (September 4, 1990). ... Bruised right eye retina (February 25, 1991). ... Suffered sore back (November 27, 1991); missed four games. ... Injured ankle (March 11, 1992); missed two games. ... Suffered back spasms (October 24, 1992); missed three games. ... Injured right elbow (March 21, 1993); missed one game. ... Suspended three games and fined $500 by NHL for altercation with opponent's bench (March 28, 1995). ... Traded by Devils to New York Islanders for RW Steve Thomas (October 3, 1995). ... Traded by Islanders to Colorado Avalanche for LW Wendel Clark (October 3, 1995). ... Broke finger (December 3, 1995); missed two games. ... Suspended one playoff game and fined $1,000 by NHL for punching another player (May 24, 1996). ... Suspended two games in Stanley Cup finals and fined $1,000 by NHL for checking from behind (June 2, 1996). ... Tore abdominal muscle (October 5, 1996); missed 37 games. ... Injured back (March 2, 1998); missed two games.
HONORS: Named to QMJHL All-Star second team (1983-84). ... Won Guy Lafleur Trophy (1984-85). ... Named to QMJHL All-Star first team (1984-85). ... Won Conn Smythe Trophy (1994-95).
MISCELLANEOUS: Member of Stanley Cup championship team (1986, 1995 and 1996).
STATISTICAL PLATEAUS: Three-goal games: 1988-89 (1), 1990-91 (2), 1992-93 (1), 1995-96 (2), 1997-98 (1). Total: 7.

		REGULAR SEASON								PLAYOFFS				
Season Team	League	Gms.	G	A	Pts.	PIM	+/-	PP	SH	Gms.	G	A	Pts.	PIM
82-83—Trois-Rivieres	QMJHL	62	28	38	66	187	...	...	...	4	1	0	1	30
83-84—Verdun	QMJHL	51	41	45	86	225	...	...	...	9	8	12	20	63
—Montreal	NHL	8	1	1	2	12	-2	0	0	—	—	—	—	—
—Nova Scotia	AHL	—	—	—	—	—	...	...	...	2	1	0	1	0
84-85—Verdun	QMJHL	52	58	66	124	152	...	...	...	14	*23	17	*40	38
—Montreal	NHL	1	0	1	1	7	1	0	0	—	—	—	—	—
85-86—Sherbrooke	AHL	58	21	32	53	145	...	...	...	—	—	—	—	—
—Montreal	NHL	10	1	2	3	22	-6	1	0	20	10	6	16	68
86-87—Montreal	NHL	76	27	26	53	156	0	5	0	17	4	9	13	41
87-88—Montreal	NHL	78	31	30	61	137	16	6	0	11	3	2	5	20
88-89—Montreal	NHL	69	29	22	51	136	14	7	0	18	4	3	7	58
89-90—Montreal	NHL	39	8	10	18	106	-8	3	0	11	1	3	4	38
90-91—New Jersey	NHL	78	30	17	47	105	-8	10	0	7	4	0	4	34
91-92—New Jersey	NHL	74	41	27	68	109	9	13	1	7	4	3	7	26
92-93—New Jersey	NHL	77	30	51	81	155	3	13	0	5	2	0	2	19
93-94—New Jersey	NHL	79	18	26	44	86	13	5	0	20	7	11	18	44
94-95—New Jersey	NHL	45	6	13	19	86	2	1	0	20	*13	3	16	20
95-96—Colorado	NHL	79	39	32	71	117	14	9	2	19	5	7	12	55
96-97—Colorado	NHL	45	11	17	28	43	-4	5	0	17	†13	10	23	32
97-98—Colorado	NHL	78	26	27	53	115	-7	11	1	7	3	3	6	8
NHL Totals (15 years)		836	298	302	600	1392	37	89	4	179	73	60	133	463

LEMIEUX, JOCELYN   RW   COYOTES

PERSONAL: Born November 18, 1967, in Mont-Laurier, Que. ... 5-10/200. ... Shoots left. ... Brother of Claude Lemieux, right winger, Colorado Avalanche. ... Name pronounced luh-MYOO.

TRANSACTIONS/CAREER NOTES: Selected by St. Louis Blues as underage junior in first round (first Blues pick, 10th overall) of NHL entry draft (June 21, 1986). ... Severed tendon in left pinkie (December 1986). ... Broke left leg and tore ligaments (January 1988). ... Traded by Blues with G Darrell May and second-round pick (D Patrice Brisebois) in 1989 draft to Montreal Canadiens for LW Sergio Momesso and G Vincent Riendeau (August 9, 1988). ... Traded by Canadiens to Chicago Blackhawks for third-round pick (D Charles Poulin) in 1990 draft (January 5, 1990). ... Suffered concussion and cracked orbital bone above right eye (February 26, 1991); missed a month. ... Traded by Blackhawks with D Frantisek Kucera to Hartford Whalers for LW Randy Cunneyworth and D Gary Suter (March 11, 1994). ... Injured shoulder (March 14, 1995); missed seven games. ... Traded by Whalers with second-round pick (traded to Dallas) in 1998 draft to New Jersey Devils for C Jim Dowd and second-round pick (traded to Calgary) in 1997 draft (December 19, 1995). ... Injured shoulder (December 26, 1995); missed two games. ... Traded by Devils with D Tommy Albelin and D Cal Hulse to Calgary Flames for D Phil Housley and D Dan Keczmer (February 26, 1996). ... Signed as free agent by Phoenix Coyotes (March 17, 1997). ... Fractured arm (March 22, 1997); missed remainder of regular season. ... Bruised ribs (November 5, 1997); missed four games.

HONORS: Named to QMJHL All-Star first team (1985-86).
STATISTICAL PLATEAUS: Three-goal games: 1989-90 (1), 1993-94 (1). Total: 2.

Season Team	League	REGULAR SEASON								PLAYOFFS				
		Gms.	G	A	Pts.	PIM	+/-	PP	SH	Gms.	G	A	Pts.	PIM
84-85—Laval	QMJHL	68	13	19	32	92	...	...	...	—	—	—	—	—
85-86—Laval	QMJHL	71	57	68	125	131	...	...	...	14	9	15	24	37
86-87—St. Louis	NHL	53	10	8	18	94	1	1	0	5	0	1	1	6
87-88—Peoria	IHL	8	0	5	5	35	...	...	...	—	—	—	—	—
—St. Louis	NHL	23	1	0	1	42	-5	0	0	5	0	0	0	0
88-89—Montreal	NHL	1	0	1	1	0	-1	0	0	—	—	—	—	—
—Sherbrooke	AHL	73	25	28	53	134	...	...	...	4	3	1	4	6
89-90—Montreal	NHL	34	4	2	6	61	-1	0	0	—	—	—	—	—
—Chicago	NHL	39	10	11	21	47	0	1	0	18	1	8	9	28
90-91—Chicago	NHL	67	6	7	13	119	-7	1	1	4	0	0	0	0
91-92—Chicago	NHL	78	6	10	16	80	-2	0	0	18	3	1	4	33
92-93—Chicago	NHL	81	10	21	31	111	5	1	0	4	1	0	1	2
93-94—Chicago	NHL	66	12	8	20	63	5	0	0	—	—	—	—	—
—Hartford	NHL	16	6	1	7	19	-8	0	0	—	—	—	—	—
94-95—Hartford	NHL	41	6	5	11	32	-7	0	0	—	—	—	—	—
95-96—Hartford	NHL	29	1	2	3	31	-11	0	0	—	—	—	—	—
—New Jersey	NHL	18	0	1	1	4	-7	0	0	—	—	—	—	—
—Calgary	NHL	20	4	4	8	10	-1	0	0	4	0	0	0	0
96-97—Long Beach	IHL	28	4	10	14	54	...	...	...	—	—	—	—	—
—Phoenix	NHL	2	1	0	1	0	0	0	0	2	0	0	0	4
97-98—Phoenix	NHL	30	3	3	6	27	0	1	0	—	—	—	—	—
—Long Beach	IHL	10	3	5	8	24	...	...	...	—	—	—	—	—
—Springfield	AHL	6	3	1	4	0	...	...	...	4	2	2	4	2
NHL Totals (12 years)		598	80	84	164	740	-39	5	1	60	5	10	15	73

LEROUX, FRANCOIS   D

PERSONAL: Born April 18, 1970, in St. Adele, Que. ... 6-6/237. ... Shoots left. ... Name pronounced FRAN-swah luh-ROO.
TRANSACTIONS/CAREER NOTES: Selected by Edmonton Oilers in first round (first Oilers pick, 19th overall) of NHL entry draft (June 11, 1988). ... Separated shoulder (March 20, 1989). ... Traded by St. Jean Lynx with LW Patrick Lebeau and LW Jean Blouin to Victoriaville Tigres for RW Trevor Duhaime, second- and third-round draft picks and future considerations (February 15, 1990). ... Tore left knee ligaments (March 18, 1990). ... Underwent surgery to left knee (March 22, 1990). ... Claimed on waivers by Ottawa Senators (October 6, 1993). ... Fractured left thumb (December 6, 1993); missed 16 games. ... Selected by Pittsburgh Penguins from Senators in waiver draft for cash (January 18, 1995). ... Suffered from the flu (February 16, 1995); missed one game. ... Twisted knee (March 9, 1995); missed two games. ... Suffered back spasms (April 23, 1995); missed one game. ... Suffered back spasms (October 12, 1995); missed one game. ... Suffered back spasms (December 30, 1995); missed eight games. ... Cracked thumb (February 12, 1996); missed one game. ... Suffered hip pointer (December 15, 1996); missed two games. ... Suffered back spasms (January 7, 1997); missed three games. ... Suffered from the flu (February 1, 1997); missed one game. ... Suffered from the flu (March 14, 1997); missed two games. ... Traded by Penguins to Colorado Avalanche for third-round pick (C David Cameron) in 1998 draft (September 28, 1997). ... Suffered back spasms (November 26, 1997); missed four games. ... Injured thumb (January 12, 1998); missed three games. ... Reinjured back (January 26, 1998); missed one game. ... Dislocated left shoulder (February 26, 1998); missed 11 games. ... Reinjured shoulder (April 4, 1998); missed four games.

Season Team	League	REGULAR SEASON								PLAYOFFS				
		Gms.	G	A	Pts.	PIM	+/-	PP	SH	Gms.	G	A	Pts.	PIM
87-88—St. Jean	QMJHL	58	3	8	11	143	...	...	...	7	2	0	2	21
88-89—Edmonton	NHL	2	0	0	0	0	1	0	0	—	—	—	—	—
—St. Jean	QMJHL	57	8	34	42	185	...	...	...	—	—	—	—	—
89-90—Edmonton	NHL	3	0	1	1	0	-2	0	0	—	—	—	—	—
—St. Jean/Victoriaville	QMJHL	54	4	33	37	160	...	...	...	—	—	—	—	—
90-91—Cape Breton	AHL	71	2	7	9	124	...	...	...	4	0	1	1	19
—Edmonton	NHL	1	0	2	2	0	1	0	0	—	—	—	—	—
91-92—Cape Breton	AHL	61	7	22	29	114	...	...	...	5	0	0	0	8
—Edmonton	NHL	4	0	0	0	7	-1	0	0	—	—	—	—	—
92-93—Cape Breton	AHL	55	10	24	34	139	...	...	...	16	0	5	5	29
—Edmonton	NHL	1	0	0	0	4	0	0	0	—	—	—	—	—
93-94—Ottawa	NHL	23	0	1	1	70	-4	0	0	—	—	—	—	—
—Prin. Edward Island	AHL	25	4	6	10	52	...	...	...	—	—	—	—	—
94-95—Prin. Edward Island	AHL	45	4	14	18	137	...	...	...	—	—	—	—	—
—Pittsburgh	NHL	40	0	2	2	114	7	0	0	12	0	2	2	14
95-96—Pittsburgh	NHL	66	2	9	11	161	2	0	0	18	1	1	2	20
96-97—Pittsburgh	NHL	59	0	3	3	81	-3	0	0	3	0	0	0	0
97-98—Colorado	NHL	50	1	2	3	140	-3	0	0	—	—	—	—	—
NHL Totals (10 years)		249	3	20	23	577	-2	0	0	33	1	3	4	34

LEROUX, JEAN-YVES   LW   BLACKHAWKS

PERSONAL: Born June 24, 1976, in Montreal. ... 6-2/211. ... Shoots left. ... Name pronounced zhahn-eev luh-ROO.
TRANSACTIONS/CAREER NOTES: Selected by Chicago Blackhawks in second round (second Blackhawks pick, 40th overall) of NHL entry draft (June 28, 1994). ... Pulled abdominal muscle (October 29, 1997); missed two games. ... Injured shoulder (November 20, 1997); missed one game. ... Injured shoulder (December 4, 1997); missed one game. ... Injured back (February 3, 1998); missed three games. ... Suffered concussion (March 29, 1998); missed four games.

		REGULAR SEASON							PLAYOFFS				
Season Team	League	Gms.	G	A	Pts.	PIM	+/-	PP	SH	Gms.	G	A	Pts.	PIM
92-93—Beauport	QMJHL	62	20	25	45	33	...	...	...	—	—	—	—	—
93-94—Beauport	QMJHL	45	14	25	39	43	...	...	...	15	7	6	13	33
94-95—Beauport	QMJHL	59	19	33	52	125	...	...	...	17	4	6	10	39
95-96—Beauport	QMJHL	54	41	41	82	176	...	...	...	20	5	18	23	20
96-97—Indianapolis	IHL	69	14	17	31	112	...	...	...	4	1	0	1	2
—Chicago	NHL	1	0	1	1	5	1	0	0	—	—	—	—	—
97-98—Chicago	NHL	66	6	7	13	55	-2	0	0	—	—	—	—	—
NHL Totals (2 years)		67	6	8	14	60	-1	0	0					

LESCHYSHYN, CURTIS   D   HURRICANES

PERSONAL: Born September 21, 1969, in Thompson, Man. ... 6-1/205. ... Shoots left. ... Full name: Curtis Michael Leschyshyn. ... Name pronounced luh-SIH-shihn.
TRANSACTIONS/CAREER NOTES: Selected by Quebec Nordiques in first round (first Nordiques pick, third overall) of NHL entry draft (June 11, 1988). ... Separated shoulder (January 10, 1989). ... Sprained left knee (November 1989). ... Damaged knee ligaments (February 18, 1991) and underwent surgery (February 20, 1991); missed final 19 games of 1990-91 season and first 30 games of 1991-92 season. ... Strained back (October 13, 1992); missed two games. ... Strained right collarbone (December 30, 1994); missed two games. ... Pulled thigh muscle (March 19, 1994); missed two games. ... Injured groin (March 31, 1994); missed remainder of season. ... Lacerated groin (April 22, 1995); missed last four games of season. ... Nordiques franchise moved to Colorado and renamed Avalanche for 1995-96 season (June 21, 1995). ... Injured hip flexor (January 17, 1996); missed three games. ... Traded by Avalanche with LW Chris Simon to Washington Capitals for RW Keith Jones and first- (D Scott Parker) and fourth-round (traded back to Washington) picks in 1998 draft (November 2, 1996). ... Traded by Capitals to Hartford Whalers for C Andrei Nikolishin (November 9, 1996). ... Injured abdominal muscle (March 7, 1997); missed five games. ... Whalers franchise moved to North Carolina and renamed Carolina Hurricanes for 1997-98 season; NHL approved move on June 25, 1997. ... Strained groin (September 25, 1997); missed four games. ... Strained groin (November 13, 1997); missed one game. ... Suffered back spasms (February 28, 1998); missed one game.
HONORS: Named to WHL (East) All-Star first team (1987-88).
MISCELLANEOUS: Member of Stanley Cup championship team (1996).

		REGULAR SEASON							PLAYOFFS				
Season Team	League	Gms.	G	A	Pts.	PIM	+/-	PP	SH	Gms.	G	A	Pts.	PIM
85-86—Saskatoon	WHL	1	0	0	0	0	...	...	...	—	—	—	—	—
86-87—Saskatoon	WHL	70	14	26	40	107	...	...	...	11	1	5	6	14
87-88—Saskatoon	WHL	56	14	41	55	86	...	...	...	10	2	5	7	16
88-89—Quebec	NHL	71	4	9	13	71	-32	1	1	—	—	—	—	—
89-90—Quebec	NHL	68	2	6	8	44	-41	1	0	—	—	—	—	—
90-91—Quebec	NHL	55	3	7	10	49	-19	2	0	—	—	—	—	—
91-92—Quebec	NHL	42	5	12	17	42	-28	3	0	—	—	—	—	—
—Halifax	AHL	6	0	2	2	4	...	...	...	—	—	—	—	—
92-93—Quebec	NHL	82	9	23	32	61	25	4	0	6	1	1	2	6
93-94—Quebec	NHL	72	5	17	22	65	-2	3	0	—	—	—	—	—
94-95—Quebec	NHL	44	2	13	15	20	29	0	0	3	0	1	1	4
95-96—Colorado	NHL	77	4	15	19	73	32	0	0	17	1	2	3	8
96-97—Colorado	NHL	11	0	5	5	6	1	0	0	—	—	—	—	—
—Washington	NHL	2	0	0	0	2	0	0	0	—	—	—	—	—
—Hartford	NHL	64	4	13	17	30	-19	1	1	—	—	—	—	—
97-98—Carolina	NHL	73	2	10	12	45	-2	1	0	—	—	—	—	—
NHL Totals (10 years)		661	40	130	170	508	-56	16	2	26	2	4	6	18

LESSARD, FRANCIS   D   HURRICANES

PERSONAL: Born May 30, 1979, in Montreal. ... 6-2/184. ... Shoots right. ... Name pronounced luh-SAHRD.
TRANSACTIONS/CAREER NOTES: Selected by Carolina Hurricanes in third round (third Hurricanes pick, 80th overall) of NHL entry draft (June 21, 1997).

		REGULAR SEASON							PLAYOFFS				
Season Team	League	Gms.	G	A	Pts.	PIM	+/-	PP	SH	Gms.	G	A	Pts.	PIM
96-97—Val-d'Or	QMJHL	66	1	9	10	287	...	...	...	—	—	—	—	—
97-98—Val-d'Or	QMJHL	63	3	20	23	338	...	...	...	19	1	6	7	*101

LETOWSKI, TREVOR   C   COYOTES

PERSONAL: Born April 5, 1977, in Thunder Bay, Ont. ... 5-10/170. ... Shoots right.
TRANSACTIONS/CAREER NOTES: Selected by Phoenix Coyotes in seventh round (sixth Coyotes pick, 174th overall) of NHL entry draft (June 22, 1996).

		REGULAR SEASON							PLAYOFFS				
Season Team	League	Gms.	G	A	Pts.	PIM	+/-	PP	SH	Gms.	G	A	Pts.	PIM
94-95—Sarnia	OHL	66	22	19	41	33	...	...	...	4	0	1	1	9
95-96—Sarnia	OHL	66	36	63	99	66	...	...	...	10	9	5	14	10
96-97—Sarnia	OHL	55	35	73	108	51	...	...	...	12	9	12	21	20
97-98—Springfield	AHL	75	11	20	31	26	...	...	...	4	1	2	3	18

LEVINS, SCOTT   C/RW

PERSONAL: Born January 30, 1970, in Portland, Ore. ... 6-4/210. ... Shoots right. ... Name pronounced LEH-vihns.
TRANSACTIONS/CAREER NOTES: Selected by Winnipeg Jets in fourth round (fourth Jets pick, 75th overall) of NHL entry draft (June 16, 1990). ... Bruised shoulder (November 17, 1992); missed four games. ... Selected by Florida Panthers in NHL expansion draft (June 24, 1993). ... Fractured hip bone (October 17, 1993); missed eight games. ... Traded by Panthers with LW Evgeny Davydov and sixth-round pick (D Mike Gaffney) in 1994 draft to Ottawa Senators for RW Bob Kudelski (January 6, 1994). ... Injured eye (January 10, 1994); missed one game. ... Injured left knee (February 12, 1994); missed one game. ... Injured back (March 15, 1994); missed four games. ... Suffered ear infection (April 12, 1995); missed two games. ... Suffered concussion during 1995-96 season; missed three games. ... Signed as free agent by Phoenix Coyotes (July 31, 1997).
HONORS: Named to WHL All-Star second team (1989-90).

		REGULAR SEASON								PLAYOFFS				
Season Team	League	Gms.	G	A	Pts.	PIM	+/-	PP	SH	Gms.	G	A	Pts.	PIM
88-89—Penticton	BCJHL	50	27	58	85	154	...	...	...	—	—	—	—	—
89-90—Tri-City	WHL	71	25	37	62	132	...	...	...	6	2	3	5	18
90-91—Moncton	AHL	74	12	26	38	133	...	...	...	4	0	0	0	4
91-92—Moncton	AHL	69	15	18	33	271	...	...	...	11	3	4	7	30
92-93—Moncton	AHL	54	22	26	48	158	...	...	...	5	1	3	4	14
—Winnipeg	NHL	9	0	1	1	18	-2	0	0	—	—	—	—	—
93-94—Florida	NHL	29	5	6	11	69	0	2	0	—	—	—	—	—
—Ottawa	NHL	33	3	5	8	93	-26	2	0	—	—	—	—	—
94-95—Ottawa	NHL	24	5	6	11	51	4	0	0	—	—	—	—	—
—Prin. Edward Island	AHL	6	0	4	4	14	...	...	...	—	—	—	—	—
95-96—Ottawa	NHL	27	0	2	2	80	-3	0	0	—	—	—	—	—
—Detroit	IHL	9	0	0	0	9	...	...	...	—	—	—	—	—
96-97—Springfield	AHL	68	24	23	47	267	...	...	...	11	5	4	9	37
97-98—Springfield	AHL	79	28	39	67	177	...	...	...	4	2	0	2	24
—Phoenix	NHL	2	0	0	0	5	-1	0	0	—	—	—	—	—
NHL Totals (5 years)		124	13	20	33	316	-28	4	0					

LIBBY, JEFF   D   ISLANDERS

PERSONAL: Born March 1, 1974, in Nurnberg, West Germany. ... 6-3/215. ... Shoots left.
COLLEGE: Maine.
TRANSACTIONS/CAREER NOTES: Signed as free agent by New York Islanders (April 14, 1997).

		REGULAR SEASON								PLAYOFFS				
Season Team	League	Gms.	G	A	Pts.	PIM	+/-	PP	SH	Gms.	G	A	Pts.	PIM
94-95—Univ. of Maine	Hockey East	22	2	4	6	6	...	...	...	—	—	—	—	—
95-96—Univ. of Maine	Hockey East	39	0	9	9	42	...	...	...	—	—	—	—	—
96-97—Univ. of Maine	Hockey East	34	6	25	31	41	...	...	...	—	—	—	—	—
97-98—Utah	IHL	47	1	5	6	25	...	...	...	1	0	0	0	0
—New York Islanders	NHL	1	0	0	0	0	0	0	0	—	—	—	—	—
—Kentucky	AHL	8	0	3	3	4	...	...	...	3	0	0	0	4
NHL Totals (1 year)		1	0	0	0	0	0	0	0					

LIDSTER, DOUG   D

PERSONAL: Born October 18, 1960, in Kamloops, B.C. ... 6-1/195. ... Shoots right. ... Full name: John Douglas Andrew Lidster.
COLLEGE: Colorado College.
TRANSACTIONS/CAREER NOTES: Selected by Vancouver Canucks in seventh round (sixth Canucks pick, 133rd overall) of NHL entry draft (June 11, 1980). ... Strained left knee (January 1988). ... Hyperextended elbow (October 1988). ... Broke hand (November 13, 1988). ... Fractured cheekbone (March 1989). ... Separated shoulder (March 1, 1992); missed 13 games. ... Sprained knee (December 13, 1992); missed nine games. ... Suffered from the flu (February 24, 1993); missed one game. ... Traded by Canucks to New York Rangers (June 25, 1993) to complete deal in which Rangers sent G John Vanbiesbrouck to Canucks for future considerations (June 20, 1993). ... Traded by Rangers with LW Esa Tikkanen to St. Louis Blues for C Petr Nedved (July 24, 1994); trade arranged as compensation for Blues signing coach Mike Keenan. ... Broke nose (April 27, 1995); missed two games. ... Traded by Blues to Rangers for D Jay Wells (July 31, 1995). ... Suffered from the flu (December 30, 1995); missed one game. ... Suffered facial fracture (January 5, 1996); missed 12 games. ... Suffered back spasms (October 24, 1996); missed two games.
HONORS: Named to WCHA All-Star first team (1981-82 and 1982-83). ... Named to NCAA All-America West team (1982-83).
MISCELLANEOUS: Member of Stanley Cup championship team (1994). ... Captain of Vancouver Canucks (1990-91).

		REGULAR SEASON								PLAYOFFS				
Season Team	League	Gms.	G	A	Pts.	PIM	+/-	PP	SH	Gms.	G	A	Pts.	PIM
77-78—Seattle	WHL	2	0	0	0	0	...	...	...	—	—	—	—	—
78-79—Kamloops	BCJHL	59	36	47	83	50	...	...	...	—	—	—	—	—
79-80—Colorado College	WCHA	39	18	25	43	52	...	...	...	—	—	—	—	—
80-81—Colorado College	WCHA	36	10	30	40	54	...	...	...	—	—	—	—	—
81-82—Colorado College	WCHA	36	13	22	35	32	...	...	...	—	—	—	—	—
82-83—Colorado College	WCHA	34	15	41	56	30	...	...	...	—	—	—	—	—
83-84—Canadian nat'l team	Int'l	59	6	20	26	28	...	...	...	—	—	—	—	—
—Can. Olympic Team	Int'l	7	0	2	2	2	...	...	...	—	—	—	—	—
—Vancouver	NHL	8	0	0	0	4	-7	0	0	2	0	1	1	0
84-85—Vancouver	NHL	78	6	24	30	55	-11	2	0	—	—	—	—	—
85-86—Vancouver	NHL	78	12	16	28	56	-12	1	1	3	0	1	1	2
86-87—Vancouver	NHL	80	12	51	63	40	-35	3	0	—	—	—	—	—
87-88—Vancouver	NHL	64	4	32	36	105	-19	2	1	—	—	—	—	—
88-89—Vancouver	NHL	63	5	17	22	78	-4	3	0	7	1	1	2	9
89-90—Vancouver	NHL	80	8	28	36	36	-16	1	0	—	—	—	—	—

Season Team	League	REGULAR SEASON Gms.	G	A	Pts.	PIM	+/-	PP	SH	PLAYOFFS Gms.	G	A	Pts.	PIM
90-91—Vancouver	NHL	78	6	32	38	77	-6	4	0	6	0	2	2	6
91-92—Vancouver	NHL	66	6	23	29	39	9	3	0	11	1	2	3	11
92-93—Vancouver	NHL	71	6	19	25	36	9	3	0	12	0	3	3	8
93-94—New York Rangers	NHL	34	0	2	2	33	-12	0	0	9	2	0	2	10
94-95—St. Louis	NHL	37	2	7	9	12	9	1	0	4	0	0	0	2
95-96—New York Rangers	NHL	59	5	9	14	50	11	0	0	7	1	0	1	6
96-97—New York Rangers	NHL	48	3	4	7	24	10	0	0	15	1	5	6	8
97-98—New York Rangers	NHL	36	0	4	4	24	2	0	0	—	—	—	—	—
NHL Totals (15 years)		880	75	268	343	669	-72	23	2	76	6	15	21	62

LIDSTROM, NICKLAS   D   RED WINGS

PERSONAL: Born April 28, 1970, in Vasteras, Sweden. ... 6-2/190. ... Shoots left. ... Name pronounced NIHK-luhs LIHD-struhm.

TRANSACTIONS/CAREER NOTES: Selected by Detroit Red Wings in third round (third Red Wings pick, 53rd overall) of NHL entry draft (June 17, 1989). ... Played in Europe during 1994-95 NHL lockout. ... Suffered back spasms (April 9, 1995); missed five games. ... Suffered from the flu (April 14, 1996); missed one game. ... Suffered from the flu (January 20, 1997); missed one game. ... Suffered injury (November 11, 1997); missed one game.

HONORS: Named to Swedish League All-Star team (1990-91). ... Named to NHL All-Rookie team (1991-92). ... Played in NHL All-Star Game (1996 and 1998). ... Named to The Sporting News All-Star team (1997-98). ... Named to NHL All-Star first team (1997-98).

MISCELLANEOUS: Member of Stanley Cup championship team (1997 and 1998).

Season Team	League	REGULAR SEASON Gms.	G	A	Pts.	PIM	+/-	PP	SH	PLAYOFFS Gms.	G	A	Pts.	PIM
88-89—Vasteras	Sweden	19	0	2	2	4	...	...	...	—	—	—	—	—
89-90—Vasteras	Sweden	39	8	8	16	14	...	...	...	—	—	—	—	—
90-91—Vasteras	Sweden	20	2	12	14	14	...	...	...	—	—	—	—	—
91-92—Detroit	NHL	80	11	49	60	22	36	5	0	11	1	2	3	0
92-93—Detroit	NHL	84	7	34	41	28	7	3	0	7	1	0	1	0
93-94—Detroit	NHL	84	10	46	56	26	43	4	0	7	3	2	5	0
94-95—Vasteras	Sweden	13	2	10	12	4	...	...	...	—	—	—	—	—
—Detroit	NHL	43	10	16	26	6	15	7	0	18	4	12	16	8
95-96—Detroit	NHL	81	17	50	67	20	29	8	1	19	5	9	14	10
96-97—Detroit	NHL	79	15	42	57	30	11	8	0	20	2	6	8	2
97-98—Detroit	NHL	80	17	42	59	18	22	7	1	22	6	13	19	8
—Swedish Oly. Team	Int'l	4	1	1	2	2	...	...	...	—	—	—	—	—
NHL Totals (7 years)		531	87	279	366	150	163	42	2	104	22	44	66	28

LIND, JUHA   LW   STARS

PERSONAL: Born January 2, 1974, in Helsinki, Finland. ... 5-11/180. ... Shoots left. ... Name pronounced YOO-hah LIHND.

TRANSACTIONS/CAREER NOTES: Selected by Minnesota North Stars in eighth round (sixth North Stars pick, 178th overall) of NHL entry draft (June 26, 1992). ... North Stars franchise moved from Minnesota to Dallas and renamed Stars for 1993-94 season. ... Bruised thigh (March 29, 1998); missed nine games.

MISCELLANEOUS: Member of bronze-medal-winning Finnish Olympic team (1998).

Season Team	League	REGULAR SEASON Gms.	G	A	Pts.	PIM	+/-	PP	SH	PLAYOFFS Gms.	G	A	Pts.	PIM
91-92—Jokerit Helsinki Jrs.	Finland	28	16	24	40	10	...	...	...	—	—	—	—	—
92-93—Vantaa HT	Finland Dv.II	25	8	12	20	8	...	...	...	—	—	—	—	—
—Jokerit Helsinki	Finland	6	0	0	0	2	...	...	...	1	0	0	0	0
93-94—Jokerit Helsinki	Finland	47	17	11	28	37	...	...	...	11	2	5	7	4
94-95—Jokerit Helsinki	Finland	50	10	8	18	12	...	...	...	11	1	2	3	6
95-96—Jokerit Helsinki	Finland	50	15	22	37	32	...	...	...	11	4	5	9	4
96-97—Jokerit	Finland	50	16	22	38	28	...	...	...	9	5	3	8	0
97-98—Michigan	IHL	8	2	2	4	2	...	...	...	—	—	—	—	—
—Dallas	NHL	39	2	3	5	6	4	0	0	15	2	2	4	8
—Fin. Olympic Team	Int'l	6	0	1	1	6	...	...	...	—	—	—	—	—
NHL Totals (1 year)		39	2	3	5	6	4	0	0	15	2	2	4	8

LINDBOM, JOHAN   RW   RANGERS

PERSONAL: Born July 8, 1971, in Alvesta, Sweden. ... 6-3/210. ... Shoots left. ... Name pronounced YOH-hahn LIHND-buhm.

TRANSACTIONS/CAREER NOTES: Selected by New York Rangers in fifth round (sixth Rangers pick, 134th overall) of NHL entry draft (June 21, 1997). ... Partially dislocated left shoulder (October 7, 1997); missed 13 games. ... Bruised shoulder (November 19, 1997); missed two games. ... Suffered back spasms (January 3, 1998); missed two games.

Season Team	League	REGULAR SEASON Gms.	G	A	Pts.	PIM	+/-	PP	SH	PLAYOFFS Gms.	G	A	Pts.	PIM
91-92—Tyringe	Swed. Dv.II	30	10	11	21	68	...	...	...	—	—	—	—	—
92-93—Troja-Ljungby	Swed. Dv.II	30	10	16	26	20	...	...	...	10	6	3	9	18
93-94—Troja-Ljungby	Swed. Dv.II	33	16	11	27	30	...	...	...	11	6	6	12	2
94-95—HV 71 Jonkoping	Sweden	39	9	7	16	30	...	...	...	13	2	5	7	12
95-96—HV 71 Jonkoping	Sweden	37	12	14	26	30	...	...	...	4	0	0	0	4
96-97—HV 71 Jonkoping	Sweden	49	20	14	34	26	...	...	...	5	1	0	1	0
97-98—New York Rangers	NHL	38	1	3	4	28	4	0	0	—	—	—	—	—
—Hartford	AHL	7	1	5	6	6	...	...	...	—	—	—	—	—
NHL Totals (1 year)		38	1	3	4	28	4	0	0					

LINDEN, TREVOR　　　　　　　C/RW　　　　　　　ISLANDERS

PERSONAL: Born April 11, 1970, in Medicine Hat, Alta. ... 6-4/210. ... Shoots right. ... Brother of Jamie Linden, right winger in Florida Panthers system.
TRANSACTIONS/CAREER NOTES: Selected by Vancouver Canucks in first round (first Canucks pick, second overall) of NHL entry draft (June 11, 1988). ... Hyperextended elbow (October 1989). ... Separated shoulder (March 17, 1990). ... Sprained knee ligament (December 1, 1996); missed 24 games. ... Bruised ribs (March 8, 1997); missed eight games. ... Injured knee (April 5, 1997); missed one game. ... Strained groin (November 16, 1997); missed eight games. ... Sprained knee (January 26, 1998); missed six games. ... Traded by Canucks to New York Islanders for D Bryan McCabe, LW Todd Bertuzzi and third-round pick (LW Jarkko Ruutu) in 1998 draft (February 6, 1998).
HONORS: Named to WHL All-Star second team (1987-88). ... Named to Memorial Cup All-Star team (1987-88). ... Named to NHL All-Rookie team (1988-89). ... Played in NHL All-Star Game (1991 and 1992). ... Won King Clancy Memorial Trophy (1996-97).
MISCELLANEOUS: Captain of Vancouver Canucks (1990-91 through 1996-97). ... Captain of New York Islanders (March 3, 1998 through remainder of season).
STATISTICAL PLATEAUS: Three-goal games: 1988-89 (2), 1990-91 (1), 1995-96 (1). Total: 4.

		REGULAR SEASON								PLAYOFFS				
Season Team	League	Gms.	G	A	Pts.	PIM	+/-	PP	SH	Gms.	G	A	Pts.	PIM
85-86—Medicine Hat..............	WHL	5	2	0	2	0	...	...	...	—	—	—	—	—
86-87—Medicine Hat..............	WHL	72	14	22	36	59	...	...	...	20	5	4	9	17
87-88—Medicine Hat..............	WHL	67	46	64	110	76	...	...	...	16	†13	12	25	19
88-89—Vancouver................	NHL	80	30	29	59	41	-10	10	1	7	3	4	7	8
89-90—Vancouver................	NHL	73	21	30	51	43	-17	6	2	—	—	—	—	—
90-91—Vancouver................	NHL	80	33	37	70	65	-25	16	2	6	0	7	7	2
91-92—Vancouver................	NHL	80	31	44	75	101	3	6	1	13	4	8	12	6
92-93—Vancouver................	NHL	84	33	39	72	64	19	8	0	12	5	8	13	16
93-94—Vancouver................	NHL	84	32	29	61	73	6	10	2	24	12	13	25	18
94-95—Vancouver................	NHL	48	18	22	40	40	-5	9	0	11	2	6	8	12
95-96—Vancouver................	NHL	82	33	47	80	42	6	12	1	6	4	4	8	6
96-97—Vancouver................	NHL	49	9	31	40	27	5	2	2	—	—	—	—	—
97-98—Vancouver................	NHL	42	7	14	21	49	-13	2	0	—	—	—	—	—
—New York Islanders.....	NHL	25	10	7	17	33	-1	3	2	—	—	—	—	—
—Can. Olympic Team.....	Int'l	6	1	0	1	10	...	...	...	—	—	—	—	—
NHL Totals (10 years).........		727	257	329	586	578	-32	84	13	79	30	50	80	68

LINDGREN, MATS　　　　　　　LW　　　　　　　OILERS

PERSONAL: Born October 1, 1974, in Skelleftea, Sweden. ... 6-2/200. ... Shoots left.
HIGH SCHOOL: Lindsay Thurber (Red Deer, Alta.).
TRANSACTIONS/CAREER NOTES: Selected by Winnipeg Jets in first round (first Jets pick, 15th overall) of NHL entry draft (June 26, 1993). ... Traded by Jets with D Boris Mironov and first-(C Jason Bonsignore) and fourth-(RW Adam Copeland) round picks in 1994 draft to Edmonton Oilers for D Dave Manson and sixth-round pick (traded to New Jersey) in 1994 draft (March 15, 1994). ... Strained lower back (March 17, 1995); missed 23 games.
HONORS: Named Swedish League Rookie of the Year (1993-94).

		REGULAR SEASON								PLAYOFFS				
Season Team	League	Gms.	G	A	Pts.	PIM	+/-	PP	SH	Gms.	G	A	Pts.	PIM
90-91—Skelleftea	Swed. Dv.II	1	0	0	0	0	...	...	...	—	—	—	—	—
91-92—Skelleftea	Swed. Dv.II	29	14	8	22	14	...	...	...	—	—	—	—	—
92-93—Skelleftea	Swed. Dv.II	32	20	14	34	18	...	...	...	—	—	—	—	—
93-94—Farjestad Karlstad	Sweden	22	11	6	17	26	...	...	...	—	—	—	—	—
94-95—Farjestad Karlstad	Sweden	37	17	15	32	20	...	...	...	3	0	0	0	4
95-96—Cape Breton..............	AHL	13	7	5	12	6	...	...	...	—	—	—	—	—
96-97—Hamilton	AHL	9	6	7	13	6	...	...	...	—	—	—	—	—
—Edmonton..................	NHL	69	11	14	25	12	-7	2	3	12	0	4	4	0
97-98—Edmonton	NHL	82	13	13	26	42	0	1	3	12	1	1	2	10
—Swedish Oly. team......	Int'l	4	0	0	0	2	...	...	...	—	—	—	—	—
NHL Totals (2 years)...........		151	24	27	51	54	-7	3	6	24	1	5	6	10

LINDQUIST, FREDRIK　　　　　　　C　　　　　　　OILERS

PERSONAL: Born June 21, 1973, in Sodertalje, Sweden. ... 5-11/176. ... Shoots left.
TRANSACTIONS/CAREER NOTES: Selected by New Jersey Devils in third round (fourth Devils pick, 55th overall) of NHL entry draft (June 22, 1994). ... Signed as free agent by Edmonton Oilers (July 16, 1998).

		REGULAR SEASON								PLAYOFFS				
Season Team	League	Gms.	G	A	Pts.	PIM	+/-	PP	SH	Gms.	G	A	Pts.	PIM
89-90—Huddinge	Swed. Dv.II	2	0	0	0	0	...	...	...	—	—	—	—	—
90-91—Djur. Stockholm..........	Sweden	28	6	4	10	0	...	...	...	7	1	0	1	2
91-92—Djur. Stockholm..........	Sweden	39	9	6	15	14	...	...	...	10	1	1	2	2
92-93—Djur. Stockholm..........	Sweden	39	9	11	20	8	...	...	...	4	1	2	3	2
93-94—Djur. Stockholm..........	Sweden	25	5	8	13	8	...	...	...	6	2	1	3	2
94-95—Djur. Stockholm..........	Sweden	40	11	16	27	14	...	...	...	3	0	0	0	2
95-96—Djur. Stockholm..........	Sweden	33	12	19	31	16	...	...	...	1	0	0	0	0
96-97—Djur. Stockholm..........	Sweden	44	19	28	47	20	...	...	...	4	0	3	3	2
97-98—Djur. Stockholm..........	Sweden	42	10	32	42	30	...	...	...	13	3	6	9	4

LINDROS, ERIC   C   FLYERS

PERSONAL: Born February 28, 1973, in London, Ont. ... 6-4/229. ... Shoots right. ... Brother of Brett Lindros, right winger, New York Islanders (1994-95 and 1995-96). ... Name pronounced LIHND-rahz.

TRANSACTIONS/CAREER NOTES: Selected by Sault Ste. Marie Greyhounds in OHL priority draft; refused to report (August 30, 1989); played for Detroit Compuware. ... Rights traded by Greyhounds to Oshawa Generals for RW Mike DeCoff, RW Jason Denomme, G Mike Lenarduzzi, second-round picks in 1991 and 1992 drafts and cash (December 17, 1989). ... Suspended two games by OHL for fighting (February 7, 1990). ... Selected by Quebec Nordiques in first round (first Nordiques pick, first overall) of NHL entry draft (June 22, 1991); refused to report. ... Traded by Nordiques to Philadelphia Flyers for G Ron Hextall, C Mike Ricci, C Peter Forsberg, D Steve Duchesne, D Kerry Huffman, first-round pick (G Jocelyn Thibault) in 1993 draft, cash and future considerations (June 20, 1992); Flyers sent LW Chris Simon and first-round pick (traded to Toronto Maple Leafs) in 1994 draft to Nordiques to complete deal (July 21, 1992). ... Sprained knee ligament (November 22, 1992); missed nine games. ... Injured knee (December 29, 1992); missed two games. ... Reinjured knee (January 10, 1993); missed 12 games. ... Tore ligament in right knee (November 12, 1993); missed 14 games. ... Suffered back spasms (March 6, 1994); missed one game. ... Sprained shoulder (April 4, 1994); missed remainder of season. ... Suffered from the flu (January 29, 1995); missed one game. ... Bruised eye (April 30, 1995); missed last game of season and first three playoff games. ... Bruised left knee (November 2, 1995); missed seven games. ... Injured knee (April 5, 1996); missed two games. ... Pulled right groin (October 1, 1996); missed 23 games. ... Bruised bone in back (February 13, 1997); missed two games. ... Suffered charley horse (March 2, 1997); missed one game. ... Bruised calf (March 22, 1997); missed two games. ... Suspended two games and fined $2,000 by NHL for two high-sticking incidents (April 9, 1997). ... Bruised ribs (November 6, 1997); missed one game. ... Suffered concussion (March 8, 1998); missed 18 games.

HONORS: Named to Memorial Cup All-Star Team (1989-90). ... Won Can.HL Player of the Year Award (1990-91). ... Won Can.HL Plus/Minus Award (1990-91). ... Won Can.HL Top Draft Prospect Award (1990-91). ... Won Red Tilson Trophy (1990-91). ... Won Eddie Powers Memorial Trophy (1990-91). ... Named to OHL All-Star first team (1990-91). ... Named to NHL All-Rookie team (1992-93). ... Played in NHL All-Star Game (1994 and 1996-1998). ... Named NHL Player of the Year by THE SPORTING NEWS (1994-95). ... Won Hart Memorial Trophy (1994-95). ... Named to THE SPORTING NEWS All-Star first team (1994-95). ... Named to NHL All-Star first team (1994-95). ... Named to NHL All-Star second team (1995-96).

MISCELLANEOUS: Member of silver-medal-winning Canadian Olympic team (1992). ... Captain of Philadelphia Flyers (1994-95 through 1997-98). ... Scored on a penalty shot (vs. Don Beaupre, December 26, 1992; vs. Steve Shields, May 11, 1997 (playoffs)).

STATISTICAL PLATEAUS: Three-goal games: 1992-93 (3), 1993-94 (1), 1994-95 (3), 1995-96 (1), 1997-98 (1). Total: 9. ... Four-goal games: 1996-97 (1). ... Total hat tricks: 10.

Season Team	League	REGULAR SEASON								PLAYOFFS				
		Gms.	G	A	Pts.	PIM	+/-	PP	SH	Gms.	G	A	Pts.	PIM
88-89—St. Michaels	MTHL	37	24	43	67	193	...	...	...	—	—	—	—	—
89-90—Detroit Compuware	NAJHL	14	23	29	52	123	...	...	...	—	—	—	—	—
—Oshawa	OHL	25	17	19	36	61	...	...	...	17	*18	18	36	*76
90-91—Oshawa	OHL	57	*71	78	*149	189	...	...	...	16	*18	20	*38	*93
91-92—Oshawa	OHL	13	9	22	31	54	...	...	...	—	—	—	—	—
—Canadian nat'l team	Int'l	24	19	16	35	34	...	...	...	—	—	—	—	—
—Can. Olympic Team	Int'l	8	5	6	11	6	...	...	...	—	—	—	—	—
92-93—Philadelphia	NHL	61	41	34	75	147	28	8	1	—	—	—	—	—
93-94—Philadelphia	NHL	65	44	53	97	103	16	13	2	—	—	—	—	—
94-95—Philadelphia	NHL	46	29	41	†70	60	27	7	0	12	4	11	15	18
95-96—Philadelphia	NHL	73	47	68	115	163	26	15	0	12	6	6	12	43
96-97—Philadelphia	NHL	52	32	47	79	136	31	9	0	19	12	14	*26	40
97-98—Philadelphia	NHL	63	30	41	71	136	14	10	1	5	1	2	3	17
—Can. Olympic Team	Int'l	6	2	3	5	2	...	...	...	—	—	—	—	—
NHL Totals (6 years)		360	223	284	507	743	142	62	4	48	23	33	56	118

LINDSAY, BILL   LW   PANTHERS

PERSONAL: Born May 17, 1971, in Big Fork, Mont. ... 6-0/190. ... Shoots left. ... Full name: William Hamilton Lindsay.

TRANSACTIONS/CAREER NOTES: Selected by Quebec Nordiques in fifth round (sixth Nordiques pick, 103rd overall) of NHL entry draft (June 22, 1991). ... Separated right shoulder (December 26, 1992); missed four games. ... Selected by Florida Panthers in NHL expansion draft (June 24, 1993). ... Cut left hand (February 22, 1996); missed seven games. ... Strained hip flexor (April 1, 1996); missed three games.

HONORS: Named to WHL (West) All-Star second team (1991-92).

MISCELLANEOUS: Tied for Florida Panthers all-time record for most games played (368).

Season Team	League	REGULAR SEASON								PLAYOFFS				
		Gms.	G	A	Pts.	PIM	+/-	PP	SH	Gms.	G	A	Pts.	PIM
89-90—Tri-City	WHL	72	40	45	85	84	...	...	...	—	—	—	—	—
90-91—Tri-City	WHL	63	46	47	93	151	...	...	...	—	—	—	—	—
91-92—Tri-City	WHL	42	34	59	93	111	...	...	...	3	2	3	5	16
—Quebec	NHL	23	2	4	6	14	-6	0	0	—	—	—	—	—
92-93—Quebec	NHL	44	4	9	13	16	0	0	0	—	—	—	—	—
—Halifax	AHL	20	11	13	24	18	...	...	...	—	—	—	—	—
93-94—Florida	NHL	84	6	6	12	97	-2	0	0	—	—	—	—	—
94-95—Florida	NHL	48	10	9	19	46	1	0	1	—	—	—	—	—
95-96—Florida	NHL	73	12	22	34	57	13	0	3	22	5	5	10	18
96-97—Florida	NHL	81	11	23	34	120	1	0	1	3	0	1	1	8
97-98—Florida	NHL	82	12	16	28	80	-2	0	2	—	—	—	—	—
NHL Totals (7 years)		435	57	89	146	430	5	0	7	25	5	6	11	26

LINDSAY, EVAN   G   FLAMES

PERSONAL: Born May 15, 1979, in Calgary. ... 6-1/180. ... Catches left.

TRANSACTIONS/CAREER NOTES: Selected by Calgary Flames in second round (second Flames pick, 32nd overall) of NHL entry draft (June 21, 1997).

HONORS: Named to WHL (East) All-Star second team (1997-98).

Season Team	League	REGULAR SEASON							PLAYOFFS						
		Gms.	Min	W	L	T	GA	SO	Avg.	Gms.	Min.	W	L	GA	SO	Avg.
95-96—Olds	AJHL	11	—	4	5	0	—	—	—	—	—	—	—	—	—	—
96-97—Prince Albert	WHL	44	2651	20	17	6	153	1	3.46	4	240	0	4	16	0	4.00
97-98—Prince Albert	WHL	52	3005	14	30	4	193	1	3.85	—	—	—	—	—	—	—

LING, DAVID   RW   BLACKHAWKS

PERSONAL: Born January 9, 1975, in Halifax, Nova Scotia. ... 5-9/185. ... Shoots right.
TRANSACTIONS/CAREER NOTES: Selected by Quebec Nordiques in seventh round (ninth Nordiques pick, 179th overall) of NHL entry draft (June 29, 1993). ... Nordiques franchise moved to Colorado and renamed Avalanche for 1995-96 season (June 21, 1995). ... Traded by Avalanche with ninth-round pick (D Steve Shirreffs) to Calgary Flames for ninth-round pick (RW Chris George) in 1995 draft (July 7, 1995). ... Traded by Flames with sixth-round pick (LW Gordie Dwyer) in 1998 draft to Montreal Canadiens for C Scott Fraser (October 24, 1996). ... Traded by Canadiens to Chicago Blackhawks for F Martin Gendron (March 14, 1998).
HONORS: Won Can.HL Player of the Year Award (1994-95). ... Won Jim Mahon Memorial Trophy (1994-95). ... Won Red Tilson Trophy (1994-95). ... Named to Can.HL All-Star first team (1994-95). ... Named to OHL All-Star first team (1994-95).

Season Team	League	REGULAR SEASON							PLAYOFFS				
		Gms.	G	A	Pts.	PIM	+/-	PP	SH	Gms.	G	A	Pts.	PIM
92-93—Kingston	OHL	64	17	46	63	275	...	...	...	16	3	12	15	72
93-94—Kingston	OHL	61	37	40	77	254	...	...	...	6	4	2	6	16
94-95—Kingston	OHL	62	*61	74	135	136	...	...	...	6	7	8	15	12
95-96—Saint John	AHL	75	24	32	56	179	...	...	...	9	0	5	5	12
96-97—Fredericton	AHL	48	22	36	58	229	...	...	...	—	—	—	—	—
—Montreal	NHL	2	0	0	0	0	0	0	0	—	—	—	—	—
—Saint John	AHL	5	0	2	2	19	...	...	...	—	—	—	—	—
97-98—Fredericton	AHL	67	25	41	66	148	...	...	...	—	—	—	—	—
—Montreal	NHL	1	0	0	0	0	-1	0	0	—	—	—	—	—
—Indianapolis	IHL	12	8	6	14	30	...	...	...	5	4	1	5	31
NHL Totals (2 years)		3	0	0	0	0	-1	0	0					

LINTNER, RICHARD   D   COYOTES

PERSONAL: Born November 15, 1977, in Trencin, Czechoslovakia. ... 6-3/194. ... Shoots right.
TRANSACTIONS/CAREER NOTES: Selected by Phoenix Coyotes in fifth round (fourth Coyotes pick, 119th overall) of NHL entry draft (June 22, 1996).

Season Team	League	REGULAR SEASON							PLAYOFFS				
		Gms.	G	A	Pts.	PIM	+/-	PP	SH	Gms.	G	A	Pts.	PIM
94-95—Dukla Trencin Jrs.	Slovakia	42	12	13	25	25	...	...	...	—	—	—	—	—
95-96—Dukla Trencin Jrs.	Slovakia	30	15	17	32	210	...	...	...	—	—	—	—	—
—Dukla Trencin	Slovakia	2	0	0	0	0	...	...	...	—	—	—	—	—
96-97—Spisska Nova Ves	Slovakia	35	2	1	3	—	...	...	...	—	—	—	—	—
97-98—Springfield	AHL	71	6	9	15	61	...	...	...	3	1	1	2	4

LITTLE, NEIL   G   FLYERS

PERSONAL: Born December 18, 1971, in Medicine Hat, Alta. ... 6-1/180. ... Catches left.
COLLEGE: Rensselaer Polytechnic Institute (N.Y.).
TRANSACTIONS/CAREER NOTES: Selected by Philadelphia Flyers in 11th round (10th Flyers pick, 226th overall) of NHL entry draft (June 22, 1991).
HONORS: Named SJHL Rookie of the Year (1989-90). ... Named to SJHL All-Star first team (1989-90). ... Named NCAA All-America East second team (1992-93). ... Named to ECAC All-Star first team (1992-93).

Season Team	League	REGULAR SEASON							PLAYOFFS						
		Gms.	Min	W	L	T	GA	SO	Avg.	Gms.	Min.	W	L	GA	SO	Avg.
89-90—Estevan	SJHL	46	2707	21	19	4	150	1	3.32	—	—	—	—	—	—	—
90-91—Rensselaer Poly. Inst.	ECAC	18	1032	9	8	0	71	0	4.13	—	—	—	—	—	—	—
91-92—Rensselaer Poly. Inst.	ECAC	28	1532	11	11	3	96	0	3.76	—	—	—	—	—	—	—
92-93—Rensselaer Poly. Inst.	ECAC	31	1801	19	9	3	88	0	2.93	—	—	—	—	—	—	—
93-94—Rensselaer Poly. Inst.	ECAC	27	1570	16	7	4	88	0	3.36	—	—	—	—	—	—	—
—Hershey	AHL	1	18	0	0	0	1	0	3.33	—	—	—	—	—	—	—
94-95—Hershey	AHL	19	919	5	7	3	60	0	3.92	—	—	—	—	—	—	—
—Johnstown	ECHL	16	897	7	6	‡1	55	0	3.68	3	145	0	2	11	0	4.55
95-96—Hershey	AHL	48	2679	21	18	6	149	0	3.34	1	59	0	1	4	0	4.07
96-97—Philadelphia	AHL	54	3007	31	12	7	145	0	2.89	10	620	6	4	20	1	1.94
97-98—Philadelphia	AHL	51	2961	*31	11	7	145	0	2.94	*20	*1193	*15	†5	*48	*3	2.41

LOJKIN, ALEXEI   LW   CANADIENS

PERSONAL: Born February 21, 1974, in Minsk, U.S.S.R. ... 5-9/176. ... Shoots left.
TRANSACTIONS/CAREER NOTES: Signed as free agent by Montreal Canadiens (October 21, 1995).
HONORS: Won Michel Bergeron Trophy (1993-94).

Season Team	League	REGULAR SEASON							PLAYOFFS				
		Gms.	G	A	Pts.	PIM	+/-	PP	SH	Gms.	G	A	Pts.	PIM
93-94—Chicoutimi	QMJHL	66	40	67	107	68	...	...	...	27	9	34	43	15
94-95—Chicoutimi	QMJHL	57	43	58	101	26	...	...	...	11	6	5	11	2
95-96—Fredericton	AHL	73	24	33	57	16	...	...	...	7	1	3	4	0
96-97—Fredericton	AHL	79	33	56	89	41	...	...	...	—	—	—	—	—
97-98—Fredericton	AHL	61	13	22	35	18	...	...	...	2	0	1	1	0

LONG, ANDREW   RW   PANTHERS

PERSONAL: Born August 10, 1978, in Toronto. ... 6-2/181. ... Shoots right.
TRANSACTIONS/CAREER NOTES: Selected by Florida Panthers in fifth round (fifth Panthers pick, 129th overall) of NHL entry draft (June 22, 1996).

		REGULAR SEASON								PLAYOFFS				
Season Team	League	Gms.	G	A	Pts.	PIM	+/-	PP	SH	Gms.	G	A	Pts.	PIM
94-95—Guelph	OHL	36	1	6	7	9	...	...	...	—	—	—	—	—
95-96—Guelph	OHL	49	8	10	18	16	...	...	...	10	0	1	1	4
96-97—Guelph	OHL	42	10	36	46	30	...	...	...	13	2	10	12	6
97-98—Guelph	OHL	62	29	40	69	41	...	...	...	8	3	3	6	10

LOW, REED   RW   BLUES

PERSONAL: Born June 26, 1976, in Moose Jaw, Sask. ... 6-5/228. ... Shoots right. ... Name pronounced LOH.
TRANSACTIONS/CAREER NOTES: Selected by St. Louis Blues in seventh round (seventh Blues pick, 177th overall) of NHL entry draft (June 22, 1996).

		REGULAR SEASON								PLAYOFFS				
Season Team	League	Gms.	G	A	Pts.	PIM	+/-	PP	SH	Gms.	G	A	Pts.	PIM
94-95—Regina	WHL	2	0	0	0	5	...	...	...	—	—	—	—	—
95-96—Moose Jaw	WHL	61	12	7	19	221	...	...	...	—	—	—	—	—
96-97—Moose Jaw	WHL	62	16	11	27	228	...	...	...	12	2	1	3	50
97-98—Baton Rouge	ECHL	39	4	2	6	145	...	...	...	—	—	—	—	—
—Worcester	AHL	17	1	1	2	75	...	...	...	3	0	0	0	0

LOWE, KEVIN   D

PERSONAL: Born April 15, 1959, in Lachute, Que. ... 6-2/200. ... Shoots left. ... Full name: Kevin Hugh Lowe. ... Husband of Karen Percy, Canadian Olympic bronze-medal-winning downhill skier (1988); and brother of Ken Lowe, trainer for Edmonton Oilers. ... Name pronounced LOH.
TRANSACTIONS/CAREER NOTES: Selected by Edmonton Oilers in first round (first Oilers pick, 21st overall) of NHL entry draft (August 9, 1979). ... Broke index finger (March 7, 1986); missed six games. ... Broke left wrist (March 9, 1988). ... Pulled rib muscle (September 1988). ... Suffered concussion (October 14, 1988). ... Suffered back spasms (April 8, 1990). ... Bruised back (December 28, 1991); missed one game. ... Strained rotator cuff (January 28, 1992); missed three games. ... Re-strained rotator cuff (February 5, 1992); missed 21 games. ... Strained groin (April 12, 1992); missed playoffs. ... Did not report to Oilers in 1992-93 season because of contract dispute; missed 30 games. ... Traded by Oilers to New York Rangers for RW Roman Oksiuta and third-round pick (RW Alexander Kerch) in 1993 draft (December 11, 1992). ... Suffered stiff neck (December 19, 1992); missed one game. ... Suffered from the flu (December 23, 1992); missed one game. ... Injured back (February 15, 1993); missed one game. ... Injured back (February 24, 1993); missed one game. ... Suspended three preseason games and fined $500 by NHL for high-sticking incident (September 28, 1993). ... Bruised right foot (October 9, 1993); missed two games. ... Bruised thigh (October 15, 1993); missed one game. ... Suffered from the flu (December 31, 1993); missed one game. ... Injured back (February 28, 1994); missed one game. ... Reinjured back (March 10, 1994); missed one game. ... Reinjured back (March 14, 1994); missed two games. ... Sprained wrist (April 2, 1994); missed five games. ... Suffered from the flu (March 18, 1995); missed one game. ... Pinched nerve in neck (April 23, 1995); missed two games. ... Suffered sore hand (October 11, 1995); missed one game. ... Suffered from the flu (October 21, 1995); missed two games. ... Bruised foot (January 24, 1996); missed one game. ... Strained groin (February 27, 1996); missed 17 games. ... Signed as free agent by Oilers (September 19, 1996). ... Strained neck (October 4, 1996); missed six games. ... Strained neck (October 22, 1996); missed two games. ... Strained neck (January 21, 1997); missed one game. ... Suffered from the flu (February 12, 1997); missed one game. ... Injured ankle (April 11, 1997); missed last game of regular season and 11 playoff games. ... Suspended three games and fined $1,000 by NHL for high-sticking incident (October 15, 1997). ... Suffered inner ear infection (October 21, 1997); missed 67 games. ... Announced retirement and named assistant coach of Oilers (July 30, 1998).
HONORS: Named to QMJHL All-Star second team (1977-78 and 1978-79). ... Played in NHL All-Star Game (1984-1986, 1988-1990 and 1993). ... Won King Clancy Memorial Trophy (1989-90). ... Named Budweiser/NHL Man of the Year (1989-90).
MISCELLANEOUS: Member of Stanley Cup championship team (1984, 1985, 1987, 1988, 1990 and 1994). ... Captain of Edmonton Oilers (1991-92). ... Holds Edmonton Oilers record for most games played (1,037).

		REGULAR SEASON								PLAYOFFS				
Season Team	League	Gms.	G	A	Pts.	PIM	+/-	PP	SH	Gms.	G	A	Pts.	PIM
76-77—Quebec	QMJHL	69	3	19	22	39	...	...	...	—	—	—	—	—
77-78—Quebec	QMJHL	64	13	52	65	86	...	...	...	4	1	2	3	6
78-79—Quebec	QMJHL	68	26	60	86	120	...	...	...	6	1	7	8	36
79-80—Edmonton	NHL	64	2	19	21	70	...	2	0	3	0	1	1	0
80-81—Edmonton	NHL	79	10	24	34	94	-7	4	0	9	0	2	2	11
81-82—Edmonton	NHL	80	9	31	40	63	46	1	1	5	0	3	3	0
82-83—Edmonton	NHL	80	6	34	40	43	39	1	0	16	1	8	9	10
83-84—Edmonton	NHL	80	4	42	46	59	37	1	0	19	3	7	10	16
84-85—Edmonton	NHL	80	4	22	26	104	9	1	0	16	0	5	5	8
85-86—Edmonton	NHL	74	2	16	18	90	24	0	0	10	1	3	4	15
86-87—Edmonton	NHL	77	8	29	37	94	41	2	2	21	2	4	6	22
87-88—Edmonton	NHL	70	9	15	24	89	18	2	1	19	0	2	2	26
88-89—Edmonton	NHL	76	7	18	25	98	26	0	0	7	1	2	3	4
89-90—Edmonton	NHL	78	7	26	33	140	18	2	1	20	0	2	2	10
90-91—Edmonton	NHL	73	3	13	16	113	-9	0	0	14	1	1	2	14
91-92—Edmonton	NHL	55	2	8	10	107	-4	0	0	11	0	3	3	16
92-93—New York Rangers	NHL	49	3	12	15	58	-2	0	0	—	—	—	—	—
93-94—New York Rangers	NHL	71	5	14	19	70	4	0	0	22	1	0	1	20
94-95—New York Rangers	NHL	44	1	7	8	58	-2	1	0	10	0	1	1	12
95-96—New York Rangers	NHL	53	1	5	6	76	20	0	0	10	0	4	4	4
96-97—Edmonton	NHL	64	1	13	14	50	-1	0	0	1	0	0	0	0
97-98—Edmonton	NHL	7	0	0	0	22	-3	0	0	1	0	0	0	4
NHL Totals (19 years)		1254	84	348	432	1498	...	17	5	214	10	48	58	192

LOWRY, DAVE   LW

PERSONAL: Born January 14, 1965, in Sudbury, Ont. ... 6-1/200. ... Shoots left. ... Name pronounced LOW-ree.
HIGH SCHOOL: Sir Wilfrid Laurier (London, Ont.).
TRANSACTIONS/CAREER NOTES: Underwent arthroscopic knee surgery (December 1982). ... Selected as underage junior by Vancouver Canucks in sixth round (fourth Canucks pick, 110th overall) of NHL entry draft (June 8, 1983). ... Traded by Canucks to St. Louis Blues for C Ernie Vargas (September 29, 1988). ... Injured groin (March 1990). ... Sprained shoulder (October 1991); missed two games. ... Injured knee (October 26, 1992); missed 26 games. ... Selected by Florida Panthers in NHL expansion draft (June 24, 1993). ... Fractured cheekbone (November 26, 1993); missed three games. ... Injured knee (December 12, 1993); missed one game. ... Suffered abrasion to right cornea (April 28, 1995); missed three games. ... Sprained left knee (October 24, 1995); missed 18 games. ... Sprained knee ligament (February 9, 1997); missed three games. ... Traded by Panthers with first-round pick (traded to Tampa Bay) in 1998 draft to San Jose Sharks for LW Viktor Kozlov and fifth-round pick (D Jaroslav Spacek) in 1998 draft (November 13, 1997).
HONORS: Named to OHL All-Star first team (1984-85).

		REGULAR SEASON								PLAYOFFS				
Season Team	League	Gms.	G	A	Pts.	PIM	+/-	PP	SH	Gms.	G	A	Pts.	PIM
82-83—London	OHL	42	11	16	27	48	...	...	...	3	0	0	0	14
83-84—London	OHL	66	29	47	76	125	...	...	...	8	6	6	12	41
84-85—London	OHL	61	60	60	120	94	...	...	...	8	6	5	11	10
85-86—Vancouver	NHL	73	10	8	18	143	-21	1	0	3	0	0	0	0
86-87—Vancouver	NHL	70	8	10	18	176	-23	0	0	—	—	—	—	—
87-88—Fredericton	AHL	46	18	27	45	59	...	...	...	14	7	3	10	72
—Vancouver	NHL	22	1	3	4	38	-2	0	0	—	—	—	—	—
88-89—Peoria	IHL	58	31	35	66	45	...	...	...	—	—	—	—	—
—St. Louis	NHL	21	3	3	6	11	1	0	1	10	0	5	5	4
89-90—St. Louis	NHL	78	19	6	25	75	1	0	2	12	2	1	3	39
90-91—St. Louis	NHL	79	19	21	40	168	19	0	2	13	1	4	5	35
91-92—St. Louis	NHL	75	7	13	20	77	-11	0	0	6	0	1	1	20
92-93—St. Louis	NHL	58	5	8	13	101	-18	0	0	11	2	0	2	14
93-94—Florida	NHL	80	15	22	37	64	-4	3	0	—	—	—	—	—
94-95—Florida	NHL	45	10	10	20	25	-3	2	0	—	—	—	—	—
95-96—Florida	NHL	63	10	14	24	36	-2	0	0	22	10	7	17	39
96-97—Florida	NHL	77	15	14	29	51	2	2	0	5	0	0	0	0
97-98—Florida	NHL	7	0	0	0	2	-1	0	0	—	—	—	—	—
—San Jose	NHL	50	4	4	8	51	0	0	0	6	0	0	0	18
NHL Totals (13 years)		798	126	136	262	1018	-62	8	5	88	15	18	33	169

LUDWIG, CRAIG   D   STARS

PERSONAL: Born March 15, 1961, in Rhinelander, Wis. ... 6-3/217. ... Shoots left. ... Full name: Craig Lee Ludwig. ... Name pronounced LUHD-wihg.
COLLEGE: North Dakota.
TRANSACTIONS/CAREER NOTES: Selected by Montreal Canadiens in third round (fifth Canadiens pick, 61st overall) of NHL entry draft (June 11, 1980). ... Fractured knuckle in left hand (October 1984). ... Broke hand (December 2, 1985); missed nine games. ... Broke right facial bone (January 1988); missed five games. ... Suspended five games by NHL for elbowing (November 19, 1988). ... Separated right shoulder (March 21, 1990). ... Traded by Canadiens to New York Islanders for D Gerald Diduck (September 4, 1990). ... Traded by Islanders to Minnesota North Stars as part of a three-way deal in which North Stars sent D Dave Babych to Vancouver Canucks and Canucks sent D Tom Kurvers to Islanders (June 22, 1991). ... Injured foot (December 8, 1991); missed six games. ... Injured foot (January 30, 1993); missed two games. ... Pinched nerve in neck (March 18, 1993); missed two games. ... North Stars franchise moved from Minnesota to Dallas and renamed Stars for 1993-94 season. ... Suffered sore back (April 2, 1995); missed one game. ... Broke finger (December 23, 1995); missed 12 games. ... Sprained knee (February 4, 1996); missed four games. ... Strained hip flexor (February 23, 1997); missed three games. ... Suspended two games and fined $1,000 by NHL for elbowing incident (March 18, 1998).
HONORS: Named to WCHA All-Star second team (1981-82).
MISCELLANEOUS: Member of Stanley Cup championship team (1986).

		REGULAR SEASON								PLAYOFFS				
Season Team	League	Gms.	G	A	Pts.	PIM	+/-	PP	SH	Gms.	G	A	Pts.	PIM
79-80—U. of North Dakota	WCHA	33	1	8	9	32	...	...	...	—	—	—	—	—
80-81—U. of North Dakota	WCHA	34	4	8	12	48	...	...	...	—	—	—	—	—
81-82—U. of North Dakota	WCHA	47	5	26	31	70	...	...	...	—	—	—	—	—
82-83—Montreal	NHL	80	0	25	25	59	4	0	0	3	0	0	0	2
83-84—Montreal	NHL	80	7	18	25	52	-10	0	0	15	0	3	3	23
84-85—Montreal	NHL	72	5	14	19	90	5	1	0	12	0	2	2	6
85-86—Montreal	NHL	69	2	4	6	63	7	0	0	20	0	1	1	48
86-87—Montreal	NHL	75	4	12	16	105	3	0	0	17	2	3	5	30
87-88—Montreal	NHL	74	4	10	14	69	17	0	0	11	1	1	2	6
88-89—Montreal	NHL	74	3	13	16	73	33	0	1	21	0	2	2	24
89-90—Montreal	NHL	73	1	15	16	108	24	0	0	11	0	1	1	16
90-91—New York Islanders	NHL	75	1	8	9	77	-24	0	0	—	—	—	—	—
91-92—Minnesota	NHL	73	2	9	11	54	0	0	0	7	0	1	1	19
92-93—Minnesota	NHL	78	1	10	11	153	1	0	0	—	—	—	—	—
93-94—Dallas	NHL	84	1	13	14	123	-1	1	0	9	0	3	3	8
94-95—Dallas	NHL	47	2	7	9	61	-6	0	0	4	0	1	1	2
95-96—Dallas	NHL	65	1	2	3	70	-17	0	0	—	—	—	—	—
96-97—Dallas	NHL	77	2	11	13	62	17	0	0	7	0	2	2	18
97-98—Dallas	NHL	80	0	7	7	131	21	0	0	17	0	1	1	22
NHL Totals (16 years)		1176	36	178	214	1350	74	2	1	154	3	21	24	224

L

LUHNING, WARREN — RW — ISLANDERS

PERSONAL: Born July 3, 1975, in Edmonton. ... 6-2/185. ... Shoots right. ... Name pronounced LOO-nihng.
COLLEGE: Michigan.
TRANSACTIONS/CAREER NOTES: Selected by New York Islanders in fourth round (fourth Islanders pick, 92nd overall) of NHL entry draft (June 26, 1993).

Season Team	League	Gms.	G	A	Pts.	PIM	+/-	PP	SH	Gms.	G	A	Pts.	PIM
92-93—Calgary Royals............	AJHL	46	18	25	43	287	...	...	...	—	—	—	—	—
93-94—Univ. of Michigan.......	CCHA	38	13	6	19	83	...	...	...	—	—	—	—	—
94-95—Univ. of Michigan.......	CCHA	36	17	24	41	80	...	...	...	—	—	—	—	—
95-96—Univ. of Michigan.......	CCHA	40	20	32	52	123	...	...	...	—	—	—	—	—
96-97—Univ. of Michigan.......	CCHA	43	22	23	45	106	...	...	...	—	—	—	—	—
97-98—New York Islanders.....	NHL	8	0	0	0	0	-4	0	0	—	—	—	—	—
—Kentucky....................	AHL	51	6	7	13	82	...	...	...	—	—	—	—	—
NHL Totals (1 year).............		8	0	0	0	0	-4	0	0	—	—	—	—	—

LUKOWICH, BRAD — D — STARS

PERSONAL: Born August 12, 1976, in Surrey, B.C. ... 6-1/170. ... Shoots left. ... Name pronounced LOO-kih-wihch.
HIGH SCHOOL: Norkam Secondary (Kamloops, B.C.).
TRANSACTIONS/CAREER NOTES: Selected by New York Islanders in fourth round (fourth Islanders pick, 90th overall) of NHL entry draft (June 29, 1994). ... Traded by Islanders to Dallas Stars for third-round pick (D Robert Schnabel) in 1997 draft (June 1, 1996).

Season Team	League	Gms.	G	A	Pts.	PIM	+/-	PP	SH	Gms.	G	A	Pts.	PIM
92-93—Cranbook	Tier II Jr. A	54	21	41	62	162	...	...	...	—	—	—	—	—
—Kamloops	WHL	1	0	0	0	0	...	...	...	—	—	—	—	—
93-94—Kamloops	WHL	42	5	11	16	166	...	...	...	16	0	1	1	35
94-95—Kamloops	WHL	63	10	35	45	125	...	...	...	18	0	7	7	21
95-96—Kamloops	WHL	65	14	55	69	114	...	...	...	13	2	10	12	29
96-97—Michigan....................	IHL	69	2	6	8	77	...	...	...	4	0	1	1	2
97-98—Michigan....................	IHL	60	6	27	33	104	...	...	...	4	0	4	4	14
—Dallas........................	NHL	4	0	1	1	2	-2	0	0	—	—	—	—	—
NHL Totals (1 year).............		4	0	1	1	2	-2	0	0	—	—	—	—	—

LUMME, JYRKI — D — COYOTES

PERSONAL: Born July 16, 1966, in Tampere, Finland. ... 6-1/205. ... Shoots left. ... Name pronounced YUHR-kee LOO-mee.
TRANSACTIONS/CAREER NOTES: Selected by Montreal Canadiens in third round (third Canadiens pick, 57th overall) of NHL entry draft (June 21, 1986). ... Strained left knee ligaments (December 1988). ... Stretched knee ligaments (February 21, 1989). ... Bruised right foot (November 1989). ... Traded by Canadiens to Vancouver Canucks for second-round pick (C Craig Darby) in 1991 draft (March 6, 1990). ... Cut eye (November 19, 1991); missed three games. ... Sprained knee (January 19, 1993); missed nine games. ... Played in Europe during 1994-95 NHL lockout. ... Injured knee (February 15, 1995); missed six games. ... Bruised ribs (March 1, 1995); missed five games. ... Sprained ankle (November 13, 1996); missed two games. ... Strained shoulder (December 23, 1996); missed 11 games. ... Suffered charley horse (March 13, 1997); missed three games. ... Injured groin (October 11, 1997); missed two games. ... Strained groin (October 26, 1997); missed five games. ... Signed as free agent by Phoenix Coyotes (July 3, 1998).
MISCELLANEOUS: Member of silver-medal-winning Finnish Olympic team (1988). ... Member of bronze-medal-winning Finnish Olympic team (1998).

Season Team	League	Gms.	G	A	Pts.	PIM	+/-	PP	SH	Gms.	G	A	Pts.	PIM
84-85—Koo Vee	Finland	30	6	4	10	44	...	...	...	—	—	—	—	—
85-86—Ilves Tampere	Finland	31	1	5	6	4	...	...	...	—	—	—	—	—
86-87—Ilves Tampere	Finland	43	12	12	24	52	...	...	...	4	0	1	1	0
87-88—Ilves Tampere	Finland	43	8	22	30	75	...	...	...	—	—	—	—	—
—Fin. Olympic Team	Int'l	6	0	1	1	2	...	...	...	—	—	—	—	—
88-89—Montreal....................	NHL	21	1	3	4	10	3	1	0	—	—	—	—	—
—Sherbrooke................	AHL	26	4	11	15	10	...	...	...	6	1	3	4	4
89-90—Montreal....................	NHL	54	1	19	20	41	17	0	0	—	—	—	—	—
—Vancouver.................	NHL	11	3	7	10	8	0	0	0	—	—	—	—	—
90-91—Vancouver.................	NHL	80	5	27	32	59	-15	1	0	6	2	3	5	0
91-92—Vancouver.................	NHL	75	12	32	44	65	25	3	1	13	2	3	5	4
92-93—Vancouver.................	NHL	74	8	36	44	55	30	3	2	12	0	5	5	6
93-94—Vancouver.................	NHL	83	13	42	55	50	3	1	3	24	2	11	13	16
94-95—Ilves Tampere	Finland	12	4	4	8	24	...	...	...	—	—	—	—	—
—Vancouver.................	NHL	36	5	12	17	26	4	3	0	11	2	6	8	8
95-96—Vancouver.................	NHL	80	17	37	54	50	-9	8	0	6	1	3	4	2
96-97—Vancouver.................	NHL	66	11	24	35	32	8	5	0	—	—	—	—	—
97-98—Vancouver.................	NHL	74	9	21	30	34	-25	4	0	—	—	—	—	—
—Fin. Olympic Team	Int'l	6	1	0	1	16	...	...	...	—	—	—	—	—
NHL Totals (10 years).........		654	85	260	345	430	41	29	6	72	9	31	40	36

LUONGO, ROBERTO — G — ISLANDERS

PERSONAL: Born April 4, 1979, in St. Leonard, Que. ... 6-2/175. ... Catches left. ... Name pronounced luh-WAHN-goh.
TRANSACTIONS/CAREER NOTES: Selected by New York Islanders in first round (first Islanders pick, fourth overall) of NHL entry draft (June 21, 1997).
HONORS: Won Michael Bossy Trophy (1996-97).

Season Team	League	Gms.	Min	W	L	T	GA	SO	Avg.	Gms.	Min.	W	L	GA	SO	Avg.
95-96—Val-d'Or........................	QMJHL	23	1199	6	11	4	74	0	3.70	3	68	0	1	5	0	4.41
96-97—Val-d'Or........................	QMJHL	60	3305	32	21	2	171	2	3.10	13	777	8	5	44	0	3.40
97-98—Val-d'Or........................	QMJHL	54	3046	27	20	5	157	*7	3.09	*17	*1019	*14	3	37	*2	*2.18

LYASHENKO, ROMAN   C   STARS

PERSONAL: Born May 2, 1979, in Murmansk, U.S.S.R. ... 6-0/176. ... Shoots right.
TRANSACTIONS/CAREER NOTES: Selected by Dallas Stars in second round (second Stars pick, 52nd overall) of NHL entry draft (June 21, 1997).

Season Team	League	Gms.	G	A	Pts.	PIM	+/-	PP	SH	Gms.	G	A	Pts.	PIM
95-96—Torpedo-2 Yaroslavl....	CIS Div. II	60	7	10	17	12	...	...	...	—	—	—	—	—
96-97—Torpedo Yaroslavl.......	Russian	42	5	7	12	16	...	...	...	9	3	0	3	6
—Torpedo-2 Yaroslav....	Rus. Div. III	2	1	1	2	8	...	...	...	—	—	—	—	—
97-98—Torpedo Yaroslavl.......	Russian	46	7	6	13	28	...	...	...	—	—	—	—	—

MacDONALD, AARON   G   PANTHERS

PERSONAL: Born August 29, 1977, in Grande Prairie, Alta. ... 6-1/186. ... Catches left.
TRANSACTIONS/CAREER NOTES: Selected by Florida Panthers in second round (second Panthers pick, 36th overall) of NHL entry draft (July 8, 1995).

Season Team	League	Gms.	Min	W	L	T	GA	SO	Avg.	Gms.	Min.	W	L	GA	SO	Avg.
93-94—Swift Current................	WHL	18	710	6	6	0	48	0	4.06	1	1	0	0	0	0	0.00
94-95—Swift Current................	WHL	53	2957	24	20	6	177	4	3.59	6	393	2	4	18	0	2.75
95-96—Swift Current................	WHL	29	1657	14	12	2	98	0	3.55	—	—	—	—	—	—	—
—Calgary........................	WHL	19	1025	2	14	1	84	0	4.92	—	—	—	—	—	—	—
96-97—Calgary........................	WHL	30	1679	6	19	3	112	0	4.00	—	—	—	—	—	—	—
—Kelowna........................	WHL	23	1364	17	6	0	76	0	3.34	6	360	2	4	24	0	4.00
97-98—Tallahassee...................	ECHL	37	1832	11	19	‡2	127	0	4.16	—	—	—	—	—	—	—

MacDONALD, CRAIG   LW   HURRICANES

PERSONAL: Born April 7, 1977, in Antigonish, Nova Scotia. ... 6-2/185. ... Shoots left.
HIGH SCHOOL: Lawrence Academy (Groten, Mass.).
COLLEGE: Harvard.
TRANSACTIONS/CAREER NOTES: Selected by Hartford Whalers in fourth round (third Whalers pick, 88th overall) of NHL entry draft (June 22, 1996). ... Whalers franchise moved to North Carolina and renamed Carolina Hurricanes for 1997-98 season; NHL approved move on June 25, 1997.
HONORS: Named to ECAC All-Rookie team (1995-96).

Season Team	League	Gms.	G	A	Pts.	PIM	+/-	PP	SH	Gms.	G	A	Pts.	PIM
94-95—Lawrence Academy.....	Mass. H.S.	30	25	52	77	10	...	...	...	—	—	—	—	—
95-96—Harvard University......	ECAC	34	7	10	17	10	...	...	...	—	—	—	—	—
96-97—Harvard University......	ECAC	32	6	10	16	20	...	...	...	—	—	—	—	—
97-98—Canadian nat'l team	Int'l	51	15	20	35	133	...	...	...	—	—	—	—	—

L
M

MacDONALD, TODD   G   PANTHERS

PERSONAL: Born July 5, 1975, in Charlottetown, P.E.I. ... 6-0/155. ... Catches left.
TRANSACTIONS/CAREER NOTES: Selected by Florida Panthers in fifth round (seventh Panthers pick, 109th overall) of NHL entry draft (June 26, 1993).
HONORS: Named to WHL (West) All-Star first team (1994-95).

Season Team	League	Gms.	Min	W	L	T	GA	SO	Avg.	Gms.	Min.	W	L	GA	SO	Avg.
91-92—Kingston........................	OHA Mj.Jr.A	28	1680	...	...	...	84	0	3.00	—	—	—	—	—	—	—
92-93—Tacoma	WHL	19	823	6	6	0	59	0	4.30	—	—	—	—	—	—	—
93-94—Tacoma	WHL	29	1606	13	10	2	109	1	4.07	—	—	—	—	—	—	—
94-95—Tacoma	WHL	60	3433	35	21	2	179	3	3.13	4	255	1	3	13	0	3.06
95-96—Carolina........................	AHL	18	979	3	12	2	78	0	4.78	—	—	—	—	—	—	—
—Detroit..........................	Col.HL	2	119	1	1	0	8	0	4.03	2	132	1	1	3	0	1.36
96-97—Carolina........................	AHL	1	58	0	1	0	4	0	4.14	—	—	—	—	—	—	—
—Cincinnati......................	IHL	31	1616	11	9	‡5	73	2	2.71	1	20	0	0	1	0	3.00
97-98—Cincinnati......................	IHL	15	797	4	6	‡3	46	0	3.46	—	—	—	—	—	—	—
—Birmingham	ECHL	3	180	1	1	‡1	8	0	2.67	—	—	—	—	—	—	—
—New Haven..................	AHL	13	790	8	3	2	30	1	2.28	3	177	0	3	15	0	5.08

MacINNIS, AL   D   BLUES

PERSONAL: Born July 11, 1963, in Inverness, Nova Scotia ... 6-1/202. ... Shoots right. ... Full name: Allan MacInnis. ... Name pronounced muh-KIHN-ihz.
TRANSACTIONS/CAREER NOTES: Selected by Calgary Flames as underage junior in first round (first Flames pick, 15th overall) of NHL entry draft (June 10, 1981). ... Twisted knee (February 1985). ... Lacerated hand (March 23, 1986). ... Stretched ligaments of knee (April 8, 1990).

... Separated shoulder (November 22, 1991); missed eight games. ... Dislocated left hip (November 12, 1992); missed 34 games. ... Strained shoulder (December 22, 1993); missed one game. ... Strained shoulder (January 2, 1994); missed four games. ... Bruised knee (February 24, 1994); missed four games. ... Traded by Flames with fourth-round pick (D Didier Tremblay) in 1997 draft to St. Louis Blues for D Phil Housley and second-round pick in 1996 (C Steve Begin) and 1997 (RW John Tripp) drafts (July 4, 1994). ... Injured shoulder (January 31, 1995); missed eight games. ... Suffered from the flu (April 9, 1995); missed three games. ... Injured shoulder (April 25, 1995); missed last five games of season. ... Dislocated shoulder (February 4, 1997); missed nine games. ... Dislocated shoulder (December 13, 1997); missed nine games. ... Suffered laceration around left eye (April 12, 1998); missed one game.

HONORS: Named to OHL All-Star first team (1981-82 and 1982-83). ... Named to Memorial Cup All-Star team (1981-82). ... Won Max Kaminsky Trophy (1982-83). ... Played in NHL All-Star Game (1985, 1988, 1990-1992, 1994 and 1996-1998). ... Named to NHL All-Star second team (1986-87, 1988-89 and 1993-94). ... Won Conn Smythe Trophy (1988-89). ... Named to THE SPORTING NEWS All-Star first team (1989-90 and 1990-91). ... Named to THE SPORTING NEWS All-Star second team (1993-94). ... Named to NHL All-Star first team (1989-90 and 1990-91).

MISCELLANEOUS: Member of Stanley Cup championship team (1989). ... Holds Calgary Flames all-time records for most games played (803), most assists (609) and most points (822). ... Scored on a penalty shot (vs. Kelly Hrudey, April 4, 1990 (playoffs)).

STATISTICAL PLATEAUS: Three-goal games: 1991-92 (1), 1996-97 (1). Total: 2.

			REGULAR SEASON							PLAYOFFS				
Season Team	League	Gms.	G	A	Pts.	PIM	+/-	PP	SH	Gms.	G	A	Pts.	PIM
79-80—Regina Blues	SJHL	59	20	28	48	110	...	...	...	—	—	—	—	—
80-81—Kitchener	OMJHL	47	11	28	39	59	...	...	...	18	4	12	16	20
81-82—Kitchener	OHL	59	25	50	75	145	...	...	...	15	5	10	15	44
—Calgary	NHL	2	0	0	0	0	...	...	...	—	—	—	—	—
82-83—Kitchener	OHL	51	38	46	84	67	...	...	...	8	3	8	11	9
—Calgary	NHL	14	1	3	4	9	0	0	0	—	—	—	—	—
83-84—Colorado	CHL	19	5	14	19	22	...	...	...	—	—	—	—	—
—Calgary	NHL	51	11	34	45	42	...	...	...	11	2	12	14	13
84-85—Calgary	NHL	67	14	52	66	75	7	8	0	4	1	2	3	8
85-86—Calgary	NHL	77	11	57	68	76	39	4	0	21	4	*15	19	30
86-87—Calgary	NHL	79	20	56	76	97	20	7	0	4	1	0	1	0
87-88—Calgary	NHL	80	25	58	83	114	13	7	2	7	3	6	9	18
88-89—Calgary	NHL	79	16	58	74	126	38	8	0	22	7	*24	*31	46
89-90—Calgary	NHL	79	28	62	90	82	20	14	1	6	2	3	5	8
90-91—Calgary	NHL	78	28	75	103	90	42	17	0	7	2	3	5	8
91-92—Calgary	NHL	72	20	57	77	83	13	11	0	—	—	—	—	—
92-93—Calgary	NHL	50	11	43	54	61	15	7	0	6	1	6	7	10
93-94—Calgary	NHL	75	28	54	82	95	35	12	1	7	2	6	8	12
94-95—St. Louis	NHL	32	8	20	28	43	19	2	0	7	1	5	6	10
95-96—St. Louis	NHL	82	17	44	61	88	5	9	1	13	3	4	7	20
96-97—St. Louis	NHL	72	13	30	43	65	2	6	1	6	1	2	3	4
97-98—St. Louis	NHL	71	19	30	49	80	6	9	1	8	2	6	8	12
—Can. Olympic Team	Int'l	6	2	0	2	2	...	...	...	—	—	—	—	—
NHL Totals (17 years)		1060	270	733	1003	1226	...	...	...	129	32	94	126	199

M

MacISAAC, DAVE   D   FLYERS

PERSONAL: Born April 23, 1972, in Arlington, Mass. ... 6-2/225. ... Shoots left.
COLLEGE: Maine.
TRANSACTIONS/CAREER NOTES: Signed as free agent by Philadelphia Flyers (July 30, 1996).

			REGULAR SEASON							PLAYOFFS				
Season Team	League	Gms.	G	A	Pts.	PIM	+/-	PP	SH	Gms.	G	A	Pts.	PIM
92-93—Univ. of Maine	Hockey East	35	5	32	37	14	...	...	...	—	—	—	—	—
93-94—Univ. of Maine	Hockey East	31	4	20	24	22	...	...	...	—	—	—	—	—
94-95—Univ. of Maine	Hockey East	44	5	13	18	44	...	...	...	—	—	—	—	—
—Milwaukee	IHL	2	0	0	0	5	...	...	...	9	0	2	2	2
95-96—Milwaukee	IHL	71	7	16	23	165	...	...	...	—	—	—	—	—
96-97—Philadelphia	AHL	61	3	15	18	187	...	...	...	10	0	1	1	31
97-98—Philadelphia	AHL	80	7	21	28	241	...	...	...	18	5	13	18	20

MacIVER, NORM   D

PERSONAL: Born September 8, 1964, in Thunder Bay, Ont. ... 5-10/173. ... Shoots left. ... Full name: Norman Steven Maciver.
HIGH SCHOOL: Sir Winston Churchill (Thunder Bay, Ont.).
COLLEGE: Minnesota-Duluth.
TRANSACTIONS/CAREER NOTES: Signed as free agent by New York Rangers (September 8, 1986). ... Dislocated right shoulder (March 1988). ... Suffered hip pointer (November 1988). ... Traded by Rangers with LW Don Maloney and C Brian Lawton to Hartford Whalers for C Carey Wilson and fifth-round pick (C Lubos Rob) in 1990 draft (December 26, 1988). ... Traded by Whalers to Edmonton Oilers for D Jim Ennis (October 9, 1989). ... Selected by Ottawa Senators in NHL waiver draft (October 4, 1992). ... Suffered sore back (December 9, 1992); missed one game. ... Injured back (January 19, 1993); missed one game. ... Injured wrist (January 28, 1993); missed two games. ... Suffered chest contusion (October 26, 1993); missed 10 games. ... Injured left knee (January 13, 1994); missed three games. ... Injured ankle (March 2, 1994); missed 15 games. ... Broke leg (April 10, 1994); missed three games. ... Pulled groin (1995); missed one game. ... Bruised ribs (1995); missed three games. ... Suffered slight concussion (March 29, 1995); missed one game. ... Traded by Senators with C Troy Murray to Pittsburgh Penguins for C Martin Straka (April 7, 1995). ... Traded by Penguins to Winnipeg Jets for D Neil Wilkinson (December 28, 1995). ... Pulled groin (March 3, 1996); missed seven games. ... Pulled groin (March 23, 1996); missed one game. ... Jets franchise moved to Phoenix and renamed Coyotes for 1996-97 season; NHL approved move on January 18, 1996. ... Sprained neck (October 22, 1996); missed seven games. ... Underwent neck surgery (November 22, 1996); missed 27 games. ... Bruised foot (March 10, 1997); missed seven games. ... Sprained thumb (April 1, 1997); missed remainder of season. ... Fractured hand (October 13, 1997); missed nine games. ... Suffered sore hand (December 8, 1997); missed 14 games. ... Reinjured hand (February 7, 1998); missed 11 games.
HONORS: Named to WCHA All-Star second team (1983-84). ... Named to NCAA All-America West first team (1984-85 and 1985-86). ... Named to WCHA All-Star first team (1984-85 and 1985-86). ... Won Eddie Shore Plaque (1990-91). ... Named to AHL All-Star first team (1990-91).

Season Team	League	REGULAR SEASON								PLAYOFFS				
		Gms.	G	A	Pts.	PIM	+/-	PP	SH	Gms.	G	A	Pts.	PIM
82-83—Minnesota-Duluth	WCHA	45	1	26	27	40	...	...	...	6	0	2	2	2
83-84—Minnesota-Duluth	WCHA	31	13	28	41	28	...	...	...	8	1	10	11	8
84-85—Minnesota-Duluth	WCHA	47	14	47	61	63	...	...	...	10	3	3	6	6
85-86—Minnesota-Duluth	WCHA	42	11	51	62	36	...	...	...	4	2	3	5	2
86-87—New Haven	AHL	71	6	30	36	73	...	...	...	7	0	0	0	9
—New York Rangers	NHL	3	0	1	1	0	-5	0	0	—	—	—	—	—
87-88—Colorado	IHL	27	6	20	26	22	...	...	...	—	—	—	—	—
—New York Rangers	NHL	37	9	15	24	14	10	4	0	—	—	—	—	—
88-89—New York Rangers	NHL	26	0	10	10	14	-3	0	0	—	—	—	—	—
—Hartford	NHL	37	1	22	23	24	0	1	0	1	0	0	0	2
89-90—Binghamton	AHL	2	0	0	0	0	...	...	...	—	—	—	—	—
—Cape Breton	AHL	68	13	37	50	55	...	...	...	6	0	7	7	10
—Edmonton	NHL	1	0	0	0	0	-1	0	0	—	—	—	—	—
90-91—Cape Breton	AHL	56	13	46	59	60	...	...	...	—	—	—	—	—
—Edmonton	NHL	21	2	5	7	14	1	1	0	18	0	4	4	8
91-92—Edmonton	NHL	57	6	34	40	38	20	2	0	13	1	2	3	10
92-93—Ottawa	NHL	80	17	46	63	84	-46	7	1	—	—	—	—	—
93-94—Ottawa	NHL	53	3	20	23	26	-26	0	0	—	—	—	—	—
94-95—Ottawa	NHL	28	4	7	11	10	-9	2	0	—	—	—	—	—
—Pittsburgh	NHL	13	0	9	9	6	7	0	0	12	1	4	5	8
95-96—Pittsburgh	NHL	32	2	21	23	32	12	1	0	—	—	—	—	—
—Winnipeg	NHL	39	5	25	30	26	-6	2	0	6	1	0	1	2
96-97—Phoenix	NHL	32	4	9	13	24	-11	1	0	—	—	—	—	—
97-98—Phoenix	NHL	41	2	6	8	38	-11	0	1	6	0	1	1	2
NHL Totals (12 years)		500	55	230	285	350	-68	21	2	56	3	11	14	32

MacLEAN, DONALD   C   KINGS

PERSONAL: Born January 14, 1977, in Sydney, Nova Scotia. ... 6-2/174. ... Shoots left.
TRANSACTIONS/CAREER NOTES: Selected by Los Angeles Kings in second round (second Kings pick, 33rd overall) of NHL entry draft (July 8, 1995).

Season Team	League	REGULAR SEASON								PLAYOFFS				
		Gms.	G	A	Pts.	PIM	+/-	PP	SH	Gms.	G	A	Pts.	PIM
94-95—Beauport	QMJHL	64	15	27	42	37	...	...	...	17	4	4	8	6
95-96—Beauport	QMJHL	1	0	1	1	0	...	...	...	—	—	—	—	—
—Laval	QMJHL	21	17	11	28	29	...	...	...	—	—	—	—	—
—Hull	QMJHL	39	26	34	60	44	...	...	...	17	6	7	13	14
96-97—Hull	QMJHL	69	34	47	81	67	...	...	...	14	11	10	21	29
97-98—Los Angeles	NHL	22	5	2	7	4	-1	2	0	—	—	—	—	—
—Fredericton	AHL	39	9	5	14	32	...	...	...	4	1	3	4	2
NHL Totals (1 year)		22	5	2	7	4	-1	2	0					

MacLEAN, JOHN   RW   RANGERS

M

PERSONAL: Born November 20, 1964, in Oshawa, Ont. ... 6-0/200. ... Shoots right. ... Name pronounced muh-KLAYN.
TRANSACTIONS/CAREER NOTES: Selected by New Jersey Devils as underage junior in first round (first Devils pick, sixth overall) of NHL entry draft (June 8, 1983). ... Bruised shoulder (November 1984). ... Injured right knee (January 25, 1985). ... Reinjured knee and underwent arthroscopic surgery (January 31, 1985). ... Bruised ankle (November 2, 1986). ... Sprained right elbow (December 1988). ... Bruised ribs (March 1, 1989). ... Suffered concussion and stomach contusions (October 1990). ... Suffered concussion (December 11, 1990). ... Tore ligament in right knee (September 30, 1991); missed entire 1991-92 season. ... Underwent surgery to right knee (November 23, 1991). ... Injured forearm (November 3, 1993); missed two games. ... Lacerated eye (February 24, 1994); missed one game. ... Bruised foot (April 9, 1995); missed one game. ... Injured knee (March 10, 1996); missed six games. ... Traded by Devils with D Ken Sutton to San Jose Sharks in exchange for D Doug Bodger and LW Dody Wood (December 7, 1997). ... Signed as free agent by New York Rangers (July 9, 1998).
HONORS: Named to Memorial Cup All-Star team (1982-83). ... Played in NHL All-Star Game (1989 and 1991).
MISCELLANEOUS: Member of Stanley Cup championship team (1995). ... Scored on a penalty shot attempt (vs. Dominik Hasek, February 27, 1997). ... Holds New Jersey Devils franchise all-time records for most games played (934), most goals (347), most assists (354) and most points (701).
STATISTICAL PLATEAUS: Three-goal games: 1987-88 (1), 1988-89 (3), 1990-91 (2). Total: 6.

Season Team	League	REGULAR SEASON								PLAYOFFS				
		Gms.	G	A	Pts.	PIM	+/-	PP	SH	Gms.	G	A	Pts.	PIM
81-82—Oshawa	OHL	67	17	22	39	197	...	...	...	12	3	6	9	63
82-83—Oshawa	OHL	66	47	51	98	138	...	...	...	17	*18	20	†38	35
83-84—New Jersey	NHL	23	1	0	1	10	-7	0	0	—	—	—	—	—
—Oshawa	OHL	30	23	36	59	58	...	...	...	7	2	5	7	18
84-85—New Jersey	NHL	61	13	20	33	44	-11	1	0	—	—	—	—	—
85-86—New Jersey	NHL	74	21	36	57	112	-2	1	0	—	—	—	—	—
86-87—New Jersey	NHL	80	31	36	67	120	-23	9	0	—	—	—	—	—
87-88—New Jersey	NHL	76	23	16	39	147	-10	12	0	20	7	11	18	60
88-89—New Jersey	NHL	74	42	45	87	122	26	14	0	—	—	—	—	—
89-90—New Jersey	NHL	80	41	38	79	80	17	10	3	6	4	1	5	12
90-91—New Jersey	NHL	78	45	33	78	150	8	19	2	7	5	3	8	20
91-92—New Jersey	NHL							Did not play.						
92-93—New Jersey	NHL	80	24	24	48	102	-6	7	1	5	0	1	1	10
93-94—New Jersey	NHL	80	37	33	70	95	30	8	0	20	6	10	16	22
94-95—New Jersey	NHL	46	17	12	29	32	13	2	1	20	5	13	18	14
95-96—New Jersey	NHL	76	20	28	48	91	3	3	3	—	—	—	—	—
96-97—New Jersey	NHL	80	29	25	54	49	11	5	0	10	4	5	9	4
97-98—New Jersey	NHL	26	3	8	11	14	-6	1	0	—	—	—	—	—
—San Jose	NHL	51	13	19	32	28	0	5	0	6	2	3	5	4
NHL Totals (15 years)		985	360	373	733	1196	43	97	10	94	33	47	80	146

MacNEIL, IAN   C   HURRICANES

PERSONAL: Born April 27, 1977, in Halifax, Nova Scotia ... 6-2/178. ... Shoots left.
TRANSACTIONS/CAREER NOTES: Selected by Hartford Whalers in fourth round (third Whalers pick, 85th overall) of NHL entry draft (July 8, 1995).

Season Team	League	REGULAR SEASON								PLAYOFFS				
		Gms.	G	A	Pts.	PIM	+/-	PP	SH	Gms.	G	A	Pts.	PIM
94-95—Oshawa	OHL	60	7	21	28	57	...	...	...	7	0	2	2	0
95-96—Oshawa	OHL	49	15	17	32	54	...	...	...	5	1	2	3	8
96-97—Oshawa	OHL	64	23	20	43	96	...	...	...	18	2	3	5	37
97-98—New Haven	AHL	68	12	21	33	67	...	...	...	3	1	0	1	10

MACOUN, JAMIE   D   RED WINGS

PERSONAL: Born August 17, 1961, in Newmarket, Ont. ... 6-2/196. ... Shoots left. ... Name pronounced muh-KOW-ihn.
COLLEGE: Ohio State.
TRANSACTIONS/CAREER NOTES: Signed as free agent by Calgary Flames (January 30, 1983). ... Fractured cheekbone (December 26, 1984). ... Suffered nerve damage to left arm in automobile accident (May 1987). ... Suffered concussion (January 23, 1989). ... Traded by Flames with C Doug Gilmour, LW Kent Manderville, D Ric Nattress and G Rick Wamsley to Toronto Maple Leafs for LW Craig Berube, D Alexander Godynyuk, LW Gary Leeman, D Michel Petit and G Jeff Reese (January 2, 1992). ... Pulled groin (February 27, 1993); missed four games. ... Suspended for one game for two stick-related game misconducts (March 9, 1994). ... Suffered from the flu (March 10, 1994); missed one game. ... Strained hip muscle (April 2, 1995); missed two games. ... Injured rib (December 3, 1996); missed seven games. ... Strained rib (January 3, 1997); missed two games. ... Injured rib (March 18, 1998); missed two games. ... Traded by Maple Leafs to Detroit Red Wings for fourth-round pick (RW Alexei Ponikarovsky) in 1998 draft (March 24, 1998).
HONORS: Named to NHL All-Rookie team (1983-84).
MISCELLANEOUS: Member of Stanley Cup championship team (1989 and 1998).

Season Team	League	REGULAR SEASON								PLAYOFFS				
		Gms.	G	A	Pts.	PIM	+/-	PP	SH	Gms.	G	A	Pts.	PIM
80-81—Ohio State	CCHA	38	9	20	29	83	...	...	...	—	—	—	—	—
81-82—Ohio State	CCHA	25	2	18	20	89	...	...	...	—	—	—	—	—
82-83—Ohio State	CCHA	19	6	21	27	54	...	...	...	—	—	—	—	—
—Calgary	NHL	22	1	4	5	25	3	0	0	9	0	2	2	8
83-84—Calgary	NHL	72	9	23	32	97	3	0	1	11	1	0	1	0
84-85—Calgary	NHL	70	9	30	39	67	44	0	0	4	1	0	1	4
85-86—Calgary	NHL	77	11	21	32	81	14	0	2	22	1	6	7	23
86-87—Calgary	NHL	79	7	33	40	111	33	1	0	3	0	1	1	8
87-88—Calgary	NHL				Did not play.									
88-89—Calgary	NHL	72	8	19	27	76	40	0	0	22	3	6	9	30
89-90—Calgary	NHL	78	8	27	35	70	34	1	0	6	0	3	3	10
90-91—Calgary	NHL	79	7	15	22	84	29	1	1	7	0	1	1	4
91-92—Calgary	NHL	37	2	12	14	53	10	1	0	—	—	—	—	—
—Toronto	NHL	39	3	13	16	18	0	2	0	—	—	—	—	—
92-93—Toronto	NHL	77	4	15	19	55	3	2	0	21	0	6	6	36
93-94—Toronto	NHL	82	3	27	30	115	-5	1	0	18	1	1	2	12
94-95—Toronto	NHL	46	2	8	10	75	-6	1	0	7	1	2	3	8
95-96—Toronto	NHL	82	0	8	8	87	2	0	0	6	0	2	2	8
96-97—Toronto	NHL	73	1	10	11	93	-14	0	0	—	—	—	—	—
97-98—Toronto	NHL	67	0	7	7	63	-17	0	0	—	—	—	—	—
—Detroit	NHL	7	0	0	0	2	0	0	0	22	2	2	4	18
NHL Totals (16 years)		1059	75	272	347	1172	173	10	4	158	10	32	42	169

MADDEN, JOHN   C   DEVILS

PERSONAL: Born May 4, 1973, in Barrie, Ont. ... 5-11/185. ... Shoots left.
COLLEGE: Michigan.
TRANSACTIONS/CAREER NOTES: Signed as free agent by New Jersey Devils (June 26, 1997).
HONORS: Named CCHA Tournament Most Valuable Player (1995-96). ... Named to NCAA All-America West first team (1996-97). ... Named to CCHA First All-Star Team (1996-97).

Season Team	League	REGULAR SEASON								PLAYOFFS				
		Gms.	G	A	Pts.	PIM	+/-	PP	SH	Gms.	G	A	Pts.	PIM
92-93—Barrie	COJHL	62	...	...	162	...	...	...	...	18	...	...	38	...
93-94—Univ. of Michigan	CCHA	36	6	11	17	14	...	...	...	—	—	—	—	—
94-95—Univ. of Michigan	CCHA	39	21	22	43	8	...	...	...	—	—	—	—	—
95-96—Univ. of Michigan	CCHA	43	27	30	57	45	...	...	...	—	—	—	—	—
96-97—Univ. of Michigan	CCHA	42	26	37	63	56	...	...	...	—	—	—	—	—
97-98—Albany	AHL	74	20	36	56	40	...	...	...	13	3	13	16	14

MAIR, ADAM   C   MAPLE LEAFS

PERSONAL: Born February 15, 1979, in Hamilton, Ont. ... 6-0/189. ... Shoots right.
TRANSACTIONS/CAREER NOTES: Selected by Toronto Maple Leafs in fourth round (second Maple Leafs pick, 84th overall) of NHL entry draft (June 21, 1997).

Season Team	League	REGULAR SEASON								PLAYOFFS				
		Gms.	G	A	Pts.	PIM	+/-	PP	SH	Gms.	G	A	Pts.	PIM
94-95—Ohsweken	Jr. B	39	21	23	44	91	...	...	...	—	—	—	—	—
95-96—Owen Sound	OHL	62	12	15	27	63	...	...	...	6	0	0	0	2
96-97—Owen Sound	OHL	65	16	35	51	113	...	...	...	4	1	0	1	2
97-98—Owen Sound	OHL	56	25	27	52	179	...	...	...	11	6	3	9	31

MALAKHOV, VLADIMIR — D — CANADIENS

PERSONAL: Born August 30, 1968, in Sverdlovsk, U.S.S.R. ... 6-4/227. ... Shoots left. ... Name pronounced MAL-uh-kahf.

TRANSACTIONS/CAREER NOTES: Selected by New York Islanders in 10th round (12th Islanders pick, 191st overall) of NHL entry draft (June 17, 1989). ... Suffered sore groin prior to 1992-93 season; missed first two games of season. ... Injured right shoulder (January 16, 1993); missed eight games. ... Sprained shoulder (March 14, 1993); missed five games. ... Suffered concussion (December 7, 1993); missed one game. ... Strained lower back (December 28, 1993); missed six games. ... Strained hip flexor (February 9, 1995); missed five games. ... Suffered charley horse (March 14, 1995); missed two games. ... Traded by Islanders with C Pierre Turgeon to Montreal Canadiens for LW Kirk Muller, D Mathieu Schneider and C Craig Darby (April 5, 1995). ... Strained hip flexor (April 24, 1995); missed one game. ... Suffered from stomach flu (October 25, 1995); missed two games. ... Strained right leg (December 12, 1995); missed two games. ... Bruised ribs (October 24, 1996); missed one game. ... Fractured thumb (December 23, 1996); missed 16 games. ... Bruised lower back (October 29, 1997); missed one game. ... Sprained knee (December 10, 1997); missed four games. ... Suffered shoulder tendinitis (February 28, 1998); missed three games.

HONORS: Named to NHL All-Rookie team (1992-93).

MISCELLANEOUS: Member of gold-medal-winning Unified Olympic team (1992).

STATISTICAL PLATEAUS: Three-goal games: 1997-98 (1).

Season Team	League	REGULAR SEASON								PLAYOFFS				
		Gms.	G	A	Pts.	PIM	+/-	PP	SH	Gms.	G	A	Pts.	PIM
86-87—Spartak Moscow	USSR	22	0	1	1	12	...	...	...	—	—	—	—	—
87-88—Spartak Moscow	USSR	28	2	2	4	26	...	...	...	—	—	—	—	—
88-89—CSKA Moscow	USSR	34	6	2	8	16	...	...	...	—	—	—	—	—
89-90—CSKA Moscow	USSR	48	2	10	12	34	...	...	...	—	—	—	—	—
90-91—CSKA Moscow	USSR	46	5	13	18	22	...	...	...	—	—	—	—	—
91-92—CSKA Moscow	CIS	40	1	9	10	12	...	...	...	—	—	—	—	—
—Unif. Olympic Team	Int'l	8	3	0	3	4	...	...	...	—	—	—	—	—
92-93—Capital District	AHL	3	2	1	3	11	...	...	...	—	—	—	—	—
—New York Islanders	NHL	64	14	38	52	59	14	7	0	17	3	6	9	12
93-94—New York Islanders	NHL	76	10	47	57	80	29	4	0	4	0	0	0	6
94-95—New York Islanders	NHL	26	3	13	16	32	-1	1	0	—	—	—	—	—
—Montreal	NHL	14	1	4	5	14	-2	0	0	—	—	—	—	—
95-96—Montreal	NHL	61	5	23	28	79	7	2	0	—	—	—	—	—
96-97—Montreal	NHL	65	10	20	30	43	3	5	0	5	0	0	0	6
97-98—Montreal	NHL	74	13	31	44	70	16	8	0	9	3	4	7	10
NHL Totals (6 years)		380	56	176	232	377	66	27	0	35	6	10	16	34

MALGUNAS, STEWART — D — CAPITALS

PERSONAL: Born April 21, 1970, in Prince George, B.C. ... 6-0/200. ... Shoots left. ... Name pronounced mal-GOO-nuhz.

TRANSACTIONS/CAREER NOTES: Selected by Detroit Red Wings in fourth round (third Red Wings pick, 66th overall) of NHL entry draft (June 16, 1990). ... Injured knee (September 26, 1992); missed first 10 games of season. ... Traded by Red Wings to Philadelphia Flyers for fifth-round pick (G Frederic Deschenes) in 1994 draft (September 8, 1993). ... Sprained medial collateral ligament in left knee (February 5, 1994); missed 12 games. ... Signed as free agent by Winnipeg Jets (August 8, 1995). ... Traded by Jets to Washington Capitals for RW Denis Chasse (February 15, 1996). ... Injured shoulder (April 6, 1996); missed three games.

HONORS: Named to WHL (West) All-Star first team (1989-90).

Season Team	League	REGULAR SEASON								PLAYOFFS				
		Gms.	G	A	Pts.	PIM	+/-	PP	SH	Gms.	G	A	Pts.	PIM
87-88—Prince George	BCJHL	54	12	34	46	99	...	...	...	—	—	—	—	—
—New Westminster	WHL	6	0	0	0	0	...	...	...	—	—	—	—	—
88-89—Seattle	WHL	72	11	41	52	51	...	...	...	—	—	—	—	—
89-90—Seattle	WHL	63	15	48	63	116	...	...	...	13	2	9	11	32
90-91—Adirondack	AHL	78	5	19	24	70	...	...	...	2	0	0	0	4
91-92—Adirondack	AHL	69	4	28	32	82	...	...	...	18	2	6	8	28
92-93—Adirondack	AHL	45	3	12	15	39	...	...	...	11	3	3	6	8
93-94—Philadelphia	NHL	67	1	3	4	86	2	0	0	—	—	—	—	—
94-95—Hershey	AHL	32	3	5	8	28	...	...	...	6	2	1	3	31
—Philadelphia	NHL	4	0	0	0	4	-1	0	0	—	—	—	—	—
95-96—Winnipeg	NHL	29	0	1	1	32	-10	0	0	—	—	—	—	—
—Portland	AHL	16	2	5	7	18	...	...	...	13	1	3	4	19
—Washington	NHL	1	0	0	0	0	0	0	0	—	—	—	—	—
96-97—Portland	AHL	68	6	12	18	59	...	...	...	5	0	0	0	8
—Washington	NHL	6	0	0	0	2	2	0	0	—	—	—	—	—
97-98—Portland	AHL	69	14	25	39	73	...	...	...	9	1	1	2	19
—Washington	NHL	8	0	0	0	12	1	0	0	—	—	—	—	—
NHL Totals (5 years)		115	1	4	5	136	-6	0	0					

MALKOC, DEAN — D

PERSONAL: Born January 26, 1970, in Vancouver. ... 6-3/200. ... Shoots left. ... Name pronounced MAL-kahk.

TRANSACTIONS/CAREER NOTES: Selected by New Jersey Devils in fifth round (seventh Devils pick, 95th overall) of NHL entry draft (June 16, 1990). ... Traded by Kamloops Blazers with LW Todd Esselmont to Swift Current Broncos for RW Eddie Patterson (October 17, 1990). ... Signed as free agent by Vancouver Canucks (August 9, 1995). ... Selected by Boston Bruins from Canucks in waiver draft for cash (September 30, 1996). ... Injured left wrist and underwent arthroscopic surgery (October 5, 1996); missed 35 games. ... Suffered from the flu (April 6, 1998); missed one game.

Season Team	League	REGULAR SEASON								PLAYOFFS				
		Gms.	G	A	Pts.	PIM	+/-	PP	SH	Gms.	G	A	Pts.	PIM
87-88—Williams Lake	PCJHL	—	6	32	38	215	—	—	—	—	—	—	—	—
88-89—Powell River	BCJHL	55	10	32	42	370	...	...	...	—	—	—	—	—
89-90—Kamloops	WHL	48	3	18	21	209	...	...	...	17	0	3	3	56

M

Season Team	League	REGULAR SEASON								PLAYOFFS				
		Gms.	G	A	Pts.	PIM	+/-	PP	SH	Gms.	G	A	Pts.	PIM
90-91 —Kamloops	WHL	8	1	4	5	47	...	...	...	—	—	—	—	—
—Swift Current	WHL	56	10	23	33	248	...	...	...	3	0	2	2	5
—Utica	AHL	1	0	0	0	0	...	...	...	—	—	—	—	—
91-92 —Utica	AHL	66	1	11	12	274	...	...	...	4	0	2	2	6
92-93 —Utica	AHL	73	5	19	24	255	...	...	...	5	0	1	1	8
93-94 —Albany	AHL	79	0	9	9	296	...	...	...	5	0	0	0	21
94-95 —Albany	AHL	9	0	1	1	52	...	...	...	—	—	—	—	—
—Indianapolis	IHL	62	1	3	4	193	...	...	...	—	—	—	—	—
95-96 —Vancouver.................	NHL	41	0	2	2	136	-10	0	0	—	—	—	—	—
96-97 —Boston	NHL	33	0	0	0	70	-14	0	0	—	—	—	—	—
—Providence.................	AHL	4	0	2	2	28	...	...	...	—	—	—	—	—
97-98 —Boston	NHL	40	1	0	1	86	-12	0	0	—	—	—	—	—
NHL Totals (3 years)..........		114	1	2	3	292	-36	0	0					

MALLETTE, TROY   LW

PERSONAL: Born February 25, 1970, in Sudbury, Ont. ... 6-3/219. ... Shoots left. ... Full name: Troy Matthew Mallette. ... Name pronounced muh-LEHT.

TRANSACTIONS/CAREER NOTES: Selected by New York Rangers in second round (first Rangers pick, 22nd overall) of NHL entry draft (June 11, 1988). ... Fined $500 by NHL for head-butting (March 19, 1990). ... Sprained left knee ligaments (September 1990). ... Fined $500 by NHL for attempting to injure another player (October 28, 1990). ... Reinjured knee (October 29, 1990). ... Injured shoulder (January 13, 1991). ... Awarded to Edmonton Oilers as compensation for Rangers signing free agent C/LW Adam Graves (September 9, 1991). ... Strained knee ligament (November 1991); missed two games. ... Traded by Oilers to New Jersey Devils for LW David Maley (January 12, 1992). ... Sprained right ankle (January 24, 1992); missed four games. ... Suffered pinched nerve in neck (January 2, 1993); missed one game. ... Traded by Devils with G Craig Billington and fourth-round pick (C Cosmo Dupaul) in 1993 draft to Ottawa Senators for G Peter Sidorkiewicz and future considerations (June 20, 1993); Senators sent LW Mike Peluso to Devils to complete deal (June 26, 1993). ... Bruised ribs (February 24, 1995); missed five games. ... Injured hip flexor (November 4, 1995); missed 11 games. ... Reinjured hip flexor (December 2, 1995); missed three games. ... Signed as free agent by Boston Bruins (July 17, 1996). ... Injured hip (preseason, 1996-97 season); missed two games. ... Suffered back spasms (October 24, 1996); missed one game. ... Suffered back spasms (November 26, 1996); missed four games. ... Suspended two games and fined $1,000 by NHL for elbowing incident (January 7, 1997). ... Injured neck (March 22, 1997); missed two games. ... Signed as free agent by Tampa Bay Lightning (October 1, 1997). ... Strained hip flexor (October 1, 1997); missed two games. ... Injured neck (October 23, 1997); missed 72 games.

Season Team	League	REGULAR SEASON								PLAYOFFS				
		Gms.	G	A	Pts.	PIM	+/-	PP	SH	Gms.	G	A	Pts.	PIM
86-87 —Sault Ste. Marie	OHL	65	20	25	45	157	...	...	...	4	0	2	2	2
87-88 —Sault Ste. Marie	OHL	62	18	30	48	186	...	...	...	6	1	3	4	12
88-89 —Sault Ste. Marie	OHL	64	39	37	76	172	...	...	...	—	—	—	—	—
89-90 —New York Rangers	NHL	79	13	16	29	305	-8	4	0	10	2	2	4	81
90-91 —New York Rangers......	NHL	71	12	10	22	252	-8	0	0	5	0	0	0	18
91-92 —Edmonton	NHL	15	1	3	4	36	-1	0	0	—	—	—	—	—
—New Jersey	NHL	17	3	4	7	43	7	0	0	—	—	—	—	—
92-93 —New Jersey	NHL	34	4	3	7	56	3	0	0	—	—	—	—	—
—Utica	AHL	5	3	3	6	17	...	...	...	—	—	—	—	—
93-94 —Ottawa	NHL	82	7	16	23	166	-33	0	0	—	—	—	—	—
94-95 —Ottawa	NHL	23	3	5	8	35	6	0	0	—	—	—	—	—
—Prin. Edward Island	AHL	5	1	5	6	9	...	...	...	—	—	—	—	—
95-96 —Ottawa	NHL	64	2	3	5	171	-7	0	0	—	—	—	—	—
96-97 —Boston	NHL	68	6	8	14	155	-8	0	0	—	—	—	—	—
97-98 —Tampa Bay	NHL	3	0	0	0	7	0	0	0	—	—	—	—	—
NHL Totals (9 years)..........		456	51	68	119	1226	-49	4	0	15	2	2	4	99

MALTBY, KIRK   LW   RED WINGS

PERSONAL: Born December 22, 1972, in Guelph, Ont. ... 6-0/200. ... Shoots right.

COLLEGE: Georgian (Ont.).

TRANSACTIONS/CAREER NOTES: Selected by Edmonton Oilers in third round (fourth Oilers pick, 65th overall) of NHL entry draft (June 20, 1992). ... Suffered chip fracture of ankle bone (February 2, 1994); missed 13 games. ... Lacerated right eye (March 1, 1995); missed last game of season. ... Scratched left cornea (February 1, 1996); missed 16 games. ... Traded by Oilers to Detroit Red Wings for D Dan McGillis (March 20, 1996). ... Separated shoulder (September 24, 1997); missed 16 games.

MISCELLANEOUS: Member of Stanley Cup championship team (1997 and 1998).

Season Team	League	REGULAR SEASON								PLAYOFFS				
		Gms.	G	A	Pts.	PIM	+/-	PP	SH	Gms.	G	A	Pts.	PIM
88-89 —Cambridge Jr. B.........	OHA	48	28	18	46	138	...	...	...	—	—	—	—	—
89-90 —Owen Sound	OHL	61	12	15	27	90	...	...	...	12	1	6	7	15
90-91 —Owen Sound	OHL	66	34	32	66	100	...	...	...	—	—	—	—	—
91-92 —Owen Sound	OHL	64	50	41	91	99	...	...	...	5	3	3	6	18
92-93 —Cape Breton	AHL	73	22	23	45	130	...	...	...	16	3	3	6	45
93-94 —Edmonton	NHL	68	11	8	19	74	-2	0	1	—	—	—	—	—
94-95 —Edmonton	NHL	47	8	3	11	49	-11	0	2	—	—	—	—	—
95-96 —Edmonton	NHL	49	2	6	8	61	-16	0	0	—	—	—	—	—
—Cape Breton..............	AHL	4	1	2	3	6	...	...	...	—	—	—	—	—
—Detroit.......................	NHL	6	1	0	1	6	0	0	0	8	0	1	1	4
96-97 —Detroit.......................	NHL	66	3	5	8	75	3	0	0	20	5	2	7	24
97-98 —Detroit.......................	NHL	65	14	9	23	89	11	2	1	22	3	1	4	30
NHL Totals (5 years)..........		301	39	31	70	354	-15	2	1	50	8	4	12	58

M

MANDERVILLE, KENT   C   HURRICANES

PERSONAL: Born April 12, 1971, in Edmonton. ... 6-3/200. ... Shoots left. ... Full name: Kent Stephen Manderville.
COLLEGE: Cornell.
TRANSACTIONS/CAREER NOTES: Selected by Calgary Flames in second round (first Flames pick, 24th overall) of NHL entry draft (June 17, 1989). ... Traded by Flames with C Doug Gilmour, D Jamie Macoun, D Ric Nattress and G Rick Wamsley to Toronto Maple Leafs for LW Craig Berube, D Alexander Godynyuk, RW Gary Leeman, D Michel Petit and G Jeff Reese (January 2, 1992). ... Bruised hand (October 5, 1993); missed one game. ... Suffered from the flu (December 17, 1993); missed two games. ... Sprained ankle (January 30, 1995); missed one game. ... Traded by Maple Leafs to Edmonton Oilers for C Peter White and fourth-round pick (RW Jason Sessa) in 1996 draft (December 4, 1995). ... Sprained left wrist (February 18, 1996); missed nine games. ... Signed as free agent by Hartford Whalers (October 1, 1996). ... Whalers franchise moved to North Carolina and renamed Carolina Hurricanes for 1997-98 season; NHL approved move on June 25, 1997. ... Strained abdomen (March 12, 1998); missed four games.
HONORS: Named ECAC Rookie of the Year (1989-90). ... Named to ECAC All-Rookie team (1989-90).
MISCELLANEOUS: Member of silver-medal-winning Canadian Olympic team (1992).
STATISTICAL PLATEAUS: Three-goal games: 1996-97 (1).

		REGULAR SEASON								PLAYOFFS				
Season Team	League	Gms.	G	A	Pts.	PIM	+/-	PP	SH	Gms.	G	A	Pts.	PIM
88-89—Notre Dame	SJHL	58	39	36	75	165	...	...	...	—	—	—	—	—
89-90—Cornell University	ECAC	26	11	15	26	28	...	...	...	—	—	—	—	—
90-91—Cornell University	ECAC	28	17	14	31	60	...	...	...	—	—	—	—	—
—Canadian nat'l team	Int'l	3	1	2	3	0	...	...	...	—	—	—	—	—
91-92—Canadian nat'l team ...	Int'l	63	16	23	39	75	...	...	...	—	—	—	—	—
—Can. Olympic Team	Int'l	8	1	2	3	0	...	...	...	—	—	—	—	—
—Toronto	NHL	15	0	4	4	0	1	0	0	—	—	—	—	—
—St. John's..................	AHL	—	—	—	—	—	...	...	...	12	5	9	14	14
92-93—Toronto	NHL	18	1	1	2	17	-9	0	0	18	1	0	1	8
—St. John's..................	AHL	56	19	28	47	86	...	...	...	2	0	2	2	0
93-94—Toronto	NHL	67	7	9	16	63	5	0	0	12	1	0	1	4
94-95—Toronto	NHL	36	0	1	1	22	-2	0	0	7	0	0	0	6
95-96—St. John's..................	AHL	27	16	12	28	26	...	...	...	—	—	—	—	—
—Edmonton	NHL	37	3	5	8	38	-5	0	2	—	—	—	—	—
96-97—Springfield	AHL	23	5	20	25	18	...	...	...	—	—	—	—	—
—Hartford	NHL	44	6	5	11	18	3	0	0	—	—	—	—	—
97-98—Carolina	NHL	77	4	4	8	31	-6	0	0	—	—	—	—	—
NHL Totals (7 years)..........		294	21	29	50	189	-13	0	2	37	2	0	2	18

MANELUK, MIKE   LW   FLYERS

PERSONAL: Born October 1, 1973, in Winnipeg. ... 5-11/188. ... Shoots right. ... Name pronounced MAN-ih-luhk.
TRANSACTIONS/CAREER NOTES: Signed as free agent by Mighty Ducks of Anaheim (January 28, 1994). ... Traded by Mighty Ducks to Ottawa Senators for RW Kevin Brown (July 1, 1996). ... Traded by Ottawa Senators to Philadelphia Flyers for cash (October 21, 1997).
HONORS: Won Jack Butterfield Trophy (1997-98).

		REGULAR SEASON								PLAYOFFS				
Season Team	League	Gms.	G	A	Pts.	PIM	+/-	PP	SH	Gms.	G	A	Pts.	PIM
90-91—St. Boniface	MJHL	45	29	41	70	199	...	...	...	—	—	—	—	—
91-92—Brandon	WHL	68	23	30	53	102	...	...	...	—	—	—	—	—
92-93—Brandon	WHL	72	36	51	87	75	...	...	...	4	2	1	3	2
93-94—Brandon	WHL	63	50	47	97	112	...	...	...	13	11	3	14	23
—San Diego	IHL	—	—	—	—	—	...	...	...	1	0	0	0	0
94-95—San Diego	IHL	10	0	1	1	4	...	...	...	—	—	—	—	—
—Canadian nat'l team ...	Int'l	44	36	24	60	34	...	...	...	—	—	—	—	—
95-96—Baltimore	AHL	74	33	38	71	73	...	...	...	6	4	3	7	14
96-97—Worcester	AHL	70	27	27	54	89	...	...	...	5	1	2	3	14
97-98—Worcester	AHL	5	3	3	6	4	...	...	...	—	—	—	—	—
—Philadelphia	AHL	66	27	35	62	62	...	...	...	20	13	*21	*34	30

MANN, CAMERON   RW   BRUINS

PERSONAL: Born April 20, 1977, in Thompson, Man. ... 6-0/194. ... Shoots right. ... Name pronounced MAN.
HIGH SCHOOL: Thomas A. Stewart (Peterborough, Ont.).
TRANSACTIONS/CAREER NOTES: Selected by Boston Bruins in fourth round (fifth Bruins pick, 99th overall) of NHL entry draft (July 8, 1995).
HONORS: Named to OHL All-Star first team (1995-96 and 1996-97). ... Won Jim Mahon Memorial Trophy (1995-96). ... Won Stafford Smythe Memorial Trophy (May 1996). ... Named to Memorial Cup All-Star team (1995-96). ... Named to OHL All-Star first team (1996-97).

		REGULAR SEASON								PLAYOFFS				
Season Team	League	Gms.	G	A	Pts.	PIM	+/-	PP	SH	Gms.	G	A	Pts.	PIM
93-94—Peterborough.............	Tier II Jr. A	16	3	14	17	23	...	...	...	—	—	—	—	—
—Peterborough.............	OHL	49	8	17	25	18	...	...	...	7	1	1	2	2
94-95—Peterborough.............	OHL	64	18	25	43	40	...	...	...	11	3	8	11	4
95-96—Peterborough.............	OHL	66	42	60	102	108	...	...	...	24	*27	16	*43	33
96-97—Peterborough.............	OHL	51	33	50	83	91	...	...	...	11	10	18	28	16
97-98—Providence................	AHL	71	21	26	47	99	...	...	...	—	—	—	—	—
—Boston	NHL	9	0	1	1	4	1	0	0	—	—	—	—	—
NHL Totals (1 year)..........		9	0	1	1	4	1	0	0					

M

PERSONAL: Born January 27, 1967, in Prince Albert, Sask. ... 6-2/219. ... Shoots left. ... Full name: David Manson.
HIGH SCHOOL: Carleton (Prince Albert, Sask.).
TRANSACTIONS/CAREER NOTES: Selected by Chicago Blackhawks as underage junior in first round (first Blackhawks pick, 11th overall) of NHL entry draft (June 15, 1985). ... Suspended three games by NHL for pushing linesman (October 8, 1989). ... Bruised right thigh (December 8, 1989). ... Suspended 13 games by NHL for abusing linesman and returning to ice to fight (December 23, 1989). ... Suspended three games by NHL for biting (February 27, 1990). ... Suspended four games by NHL for attempting to injure another player (October 20, 1990). ... Traded by Blackhawks with third-round pick (RW Kirk Maltby) in 1992 draft to Edmonton Oilers for D Steve Smith (October 2, 1991). ... Suspended five off-days and fined $500 by NHL for spearing (October 19, 1992). ... Strained ligaments in left knee (December 7, 1992); missed one game. ... Separated shoulder (October 22, 1993); missed 13 games. ... Traded by Oilers with sixth-round pick in 1994 draft to Winnipeg Jets for C Mats Lindgren, D Boris Mironov and first-(C Jason Bonsignore) and fourth-(RW Adam Copeland) round picks in 1994 draft (March 15, 1994). ... Bruised kidneys (January 21, 1995); missed one game. ... Bruised hand (April 19, 1995); missed two games. ... Jets franchise moved to Phoenix and renamed Coyotes for 1996-97 season; NHL approved move on January 18, 1996. ... Broke toe (November 8, 1996); missed five games. ... Traded by Coyotes to Montreal Canadiens for D Murray Baron and RW Chris Murray (March 18, 1997). ... Fined $1,000 by NHL for criticizing a referee (April 21, 1997). ... Strained hip flexor (February 7, 1998); missed one game.
HONORS: Named to WHL All-Star second team (1985-86). ... Played in NHL All-Star Game (1989 and 1993).
MISCELLANEOUS: Failed to score on a penalty shot (vs. Darcy Wakaluk, January 24, 1991).

					REGULAR SEASON							PLAYOFFS			
Season Team	League	Gms.	G	A	Pts.	PIM	+/-	PP	SH		Gms.	G	A	Pts.	PIM
83-84—Prince Albert	WHL	70	2	7	9	233	...	...	...		5	0	0	0	4
84-85—Prince Albert	WHL	72	8	30	38	247	...	...	...		13	1	0	1	34
85-86—Prince Albert	WHL	70	14	34	48	177	...	...	...		20	1	8	9	63
86-87—Chicago	NHL	63	1	8	9	146	-2	0	0		3	0	0	0	10
87-88—Saginaw	IHL	6	0	3	3	37	...	...	...		—	—	—	—	—
—Chicago	NHL	54	1	6	7	185	-12	0	0		5	0	0	0	27
88-89—Chicago	NHL	79	18	36	54	352	5	8	1		16	0	8	8	*84
89-90—Chicago	NHL	59	5	23	28	301	4	1	0		20	2	4	6	46
90-91—Chicago	NHL	75	14	15	29	191	20	6	1		6	0	1	1	36
91-92—Edmonton	NHL	79	15	32	47	220	9	7	0		16	3	9	12	44
92-93—Edmonton	NHL	83	15	30	45	210	-28	9	1		—	—	—	—	—
93-94—Edmonton	NHL	57	3	13	16	140	-4	0	0		—	—	—	—	—
—Winnipeg	NHL	13	1	4	5	51	-10	1	0		—	—	—	—	—
94-95—Winnipeg	NHL	44	3	15	18	139	-20	2	0		—	—	—	—	—
95-96—Winnipeg	NHL	82	7	23	30	205	8	3	0		6	2	1	3	30
96-97—Phoenix	NHL	66	3	17	20	164	-25	2	0		—	—	—	—	—
—Montreal	NHL	9	1	1	2	23	-1	0	0		—	—	—	—	—
97-98—Montreal	NHL	81	4	30	34	122	22	2	0		10	0	1	1	14
NHL Totals (12 years)		844	91	253	344	2449	-34	41	3		82	7	24	31	291

M

PERSONAL: Born September 7, 1979, in Ridgewood, N.J. ... 6-4/185. ... Shoots left.
HIGH SCHOOL: Belmont Hill (Mass.).
TRANSACTIONS/CAREER NOTES: Selected by Tampa Bay Lightning in first round (first Lightning pick, seventh overall) of NHL entry draft (June 21, 1997).
HONORS: Named to OHL All-Rookie team (1996-97).

					REGULAR SEASON							PLAYOFFS			
Season Team	League	Gms.	G	A	Pts.	PIM	+/-	PP	SH		Gms.	G	A	Pts.	PIM
94-95—Belmont Hill	Mass. H.S.	29	19	24	43	24	...	...	...		—	—	—	—	—
95-96—Belmont Hill	Mass. H.S.	28	18	20	38	40	...	...	...		—	—	—	—	—
96-97—Sudbury	OHL	44	9	34	43	61	...	...	...		—	—	—	—	—
97-98—Sudbury	OHL	25	8	18	26	79	...	...	...		15	3	14	17	30
—Plymouth	OHL	25	8	15	23	30	...	...	...		—	—	—	—	—

PERSONAL: Born October 2, 1974, in Belleville, Ont. ... 5-9/175. ... Catches left. ... Name pronounced MAIR-ih-kuhl.
HIGH SCHOOL: Marion Graham (Regina, Sask.).
TRANSACTIONS/CAREER NOTES: Selected by Detroit Red Wings in fifth round (sixth Red Wings pick, 126th overall) of NHL entry draft (June 26, 1993).
HONORS: Named to Can.HL All-Rookie team (1991-92). ... Named to WHL (East) All-Star second team (1992-93). ... Won Can.HL Goaltender-of-the-Year Award (1993-94). ... Won Del Wilson Trophy (1993-94). ... Named to Can.HL All-Star first team (1993-94). ... Named to WHL (East) All-Star first team (1993-94). ... Named to AHL All-Star second team (1996-97). ... Named to AHL All-Star second team (1997-98).

						REGULAR SEASON						PLAYOFFS				
Season Team	League	Gms.	Min	W	L	T	GA	SO	Avg.		Gms.	Min.	W	L	GA	SO	Avg.
91-92—Saskatoon	WHL	29	1529	13	6	3	87	1	3.41		15	860	9	5	37	0	2.58
92-93—Saskatoon	WHL	53	2939	27	18	3	160	1	3.27		9	569	4	5	33	0	3.48
93-94—Saskatoon	WHL	56	3219	*41	13	1	148	2	2.76		16	939	†11	5	48	†1	3.07
94-95—Adirondack	AHL	39	1997	12	15	2	119	0	3.58		—	—	—	—	—	—	—
95-96—Adirondack	AHL	54	2949	24	18	6	135	2	2.75		1	29	0	1	4	0	8.28
96-97—Adirondack	AHL	*68	*3843	†34	22	9	*173	2	2.70		4	192	1	3	10	1	3.13
97-98—Adirondack	AHL	*66	*3710	27	29	8	*190	1	3.07		3	180	0	3	10	0	3.33
—Detroit	NHL	4	178	2	0	1	6	0	2.02		—	—	—	—	—	—	—
NHL Totals (1 year)		4	178	2	0	1	6	0	2.02								

MARCHANT, TERRY — LW — OILERS

PERSONAL: Born February 24, 1976, in Buffalo, N.Y. ... 6-2/205. ... Shoots left. ... Brother of Todd Marchant, center, Edmonton Oilers.
COLLEGE: Lake Superior State (Mich.).
TRANSACTIONS/CAREER NOTES: Selected by Edmonton Oilers in sixth round (ninth Oilers pick, 136th overall) of NHL entry draft (June 29, 1994).
HONORS: Named to CCHA All-Star second team (1997-98).

Season Team	League	REGULAR SEASON								PLAYOFFS				
		Gms.	G	A	Pts.	PIM	+/-	PP	SH	Gms.	G	A	Pts.	PIM
93-94—Niagara	NAJHL	42	27	40	67	43	...	...	...	—	—	—	—	—
94-95—Lake Superior State	CCHA	23	2	5	7	12	...	...	...	—	—	—	—	—
95-96—Lake Superior State	CCHA	36	8	5	13	15	...	...	...	—	—	—	—	—
96-97—Lake Superior State	CCHA	38	12	14	26	26	...	...	...	—	—	—	—	—
97-98—Lake Superior State	CCHA	36	17	22	39	24	...	...	...	—	—	—	—	—

MARCHANT, TODD — C — OILERS

PERSONAL: Born August 12, 1973, in Buffalo, N.Y. ... 5-10/180. ... Shoots left. ... Brother of Terry Marchant, left winger in Edmonton Oilers system. ... Name pronounced MAHR-shahnt.
COLLEGE: Clarkson (N.Y.).
TRANSACTIONS/CAREER NOTES: Selected by New York Rangers in seventh round (eighth Rangers pick, 164th overall) of NHL entry draft (June 26, 1991). ... Traded by Rangers to Edmonton Oilers for C Craig MacTavish (March 21, 1994). ... Suffered concussion (March 9, 1997); missed three games. ... Strained groin (November 10, 1997); missed four games. ... Scratched left eye (February 4, 1998); missed two games.
MISCELLANEOUS: Failed to score on a penalty shot (vs. Damian Rhodes, November 13, 1996; vs. Olaf Kolzig, January 26, 1997).

Season Team	League	REGULAR SEASON								PLAYOFFS				
		Gms.	G	A	Pts.	PIM	+/-	PP	SH	Gms.	G	A	Pts.	PIM
91-92—Clarkson	ECAC	33	20	12	32	32	...	...	...	—	—	—	—	—
92-93—Clarkson	ECAC	33	18	28	46	38	...	...	...	—	—	—	—	—
93-94—U.S. national team	Int'l	59	28	39	67	48	...	...	...	—	—	—	—	—
—U.S. Olympic team	Int'l	8	1	1	2	6	...	...	...	—	—	—	—	—
—Binghamton	AHL	8	2	7	9	6	...	...	...	—	—	—	—	—
—New York Rangers	NHL	1	0	0	0	0	-1	0	0	—	—	—	—	—
—Edmonton	NHL	3	0	1	1	2	-1	0	0	—	—	—	—	—
—Cape Breton	AHL	3	1	4	5	2	...	...	...	5	1	1	2	0
94-95—Cape Breton	AHL	38	22	25	47	25	...	...	...	—	—	—	—	—
—Edmonton	NHL	45	13	14	27	32	-3	3	2	—	—	—	—	—
95-96—Edmonton	NHL	81	19	19	38	66	-19	2	3	—	—	—	—	—
96-97—Edmonton	NHL	79	14	19	33	44	11	0	4	12	4	2	6	12
97-98—Edmonton	NHL	76	14	21	35	71	9	2	1	12	1	1	2	10
NHL Totals (5 years)		285	60	74	134	215	-4	7	10	24	5	3	8	22

MARCHMENT, BRYAN — D — SHARKS

M

PERSONAL: Born May 1, 1969, in Scarborough, Ont. ... 6-1/205. ... Shoots left.
TRANSACTIONS/CAREER NOTES: Suspended three games by OHL (October 1, 1986). ... Selected by Winnipeg Jets as underage junior in first round (first Jets pick, 16th overall) of NHL entry draft (June 13, 1987). ... Suspended six games by AHL for fighting (December 10, 1989). ... Sprained shoulder (March 1990). ... Suffered back spasms (March 13, 1991). ... Traded by Jets with D Chris Norton to Chicago Blackhawks for C Troy Murray and LW Warren Rychel (July 22, 1991). ... Fractured cheekbone (December 12, 1991); missed 12 games. ... Suspended one preseason game and fined $500 by NHL for headbutting (September 30, 1993). ... Traded with RW Steve Larmer by Blackhawks to Hartford Whalers for LW Patrick Poulin and D Eric Weinrich (November 2, 1993). ... Suspended two games and fined $500 by NHL for illegal check (December 21, 1993). ... Sprained ankle (January 14, 1994); missed three games. ... Sprained ankle (February 19, 1994); missed remainder of season. ... Awarded to Edmonton Oilers as compensation for Whalers signing free agent RW Steven Rice (August 30, 1994). ... Suspended one game by NHL for game misconduct penalties (March 22, 1995). ... Suspended two games by NHL for game misconduct penalties (March 27, 1995). ... Strained lower back (April 15, 1995); missed two games. ... Suspended three games and fined $500 by NHL for leaving bench to fight (April 29, 1995). ... Suspended five games by NHL for kneeing player in preseason game (September 25, 1995). ... Injured ribs (October 22, 1996); missed two games. ... Suffered from the flu (January 28, 1997); missed one game. ... Cracked ribs (February 13, 1997); missed eight games. ... Suffered concussion (April 18, 1997); missed remainder of season. ... Suspended three games and fined $1,000 by NHL for hitting another player (December 5, 1997). ... Traded by Oilers to Tampa Bay Lightning with C Steve Kelly and C Jason Bonsignore for D Roman Hamrlik and F Paul Comrie (December 30, 1997). ... Suspended three games by NHL for kneeing incident (February 6, 1998). ... Suspended eight games and fined $1,000 by NHL for kneeing incident (February 25, 1998). ... Traded by Lightning with D David Shaw and first-round pick (traded to Nashville) in 1998 draft to San Jose Sharks for LW Andrei Nazarov, first-round pick (C Vincent Lecavalier) in 1998 draft and future considerations (March 24, 1998).
HONORS: Named to OHL All-Star second team (1988-89).
MISCELLANEOUS: Failed to score on a penalty shot (vs. Pat Jablonski, December 31, 1992).

Season Team	League	REGULAR SEASON								PLAYOFFS				
		Gms.	G	A	Pts.	PIM	+/-	PP	SH	Gms.	G	A	Pts.	PIM
84-85—Toronto Nationals	MTHL	...	14	35	49	229	...	...	...	—	—	—	—	—
85-86—Belleville	OHL	57	5	15	20	225	...	...	...	21	0	7	7	*83
86-87—Belleville	OHL	52	6	38	44	238	...	...	...	6	0	4	4	17
87-88—Belleville	OHL	56	7	51	58	200	...	...	...	6	1	3	4	19
88-89—Belleville	OHL	43	14	36	50	198	...	...	...	5	0	1	1	12
—Winnipeg	NHL	2	0	0	0	2	0	0	0	—	—	—	—	—
89-90—Winnipeg	NHL	7	0	2	2	28	0	0	0	—	—	—	—	—
—Moncton	AHL	56	4	19	23	217	...	...	...	—	—	—	—	—
90-91—Winnipeg	NHL	28	2	2	4	91	-5	0	0	—	—	—	—	—
—Moncton	AHL	33	2	11	13	101	...	...	...	—	—	—	—	—
91-92—Chicago	NHL	58	5	10	15	168	-4	2	0	16	1	0	1	36
92-93—Chicago	NHL	78	5	15	20	313	15	1	0	4	0	0	0	12

Season Team	League	REGULAR SEASON									PLAYOFFS				
		Gms.	G	A	Pts.	PIM	+/-	PP	SH		Gms.	G	A	Pts.	PIM
93-94—Chicago	NHL	13	1	4	5	42	-2	0	0		—	—	—	—	—
—Hartford	NHL	42	3	7	10	124	-12	0	1		—	—	—	—	—
94-95—Edmonton	NHL	40	1	5	6	184	-11	0	0		—	—	—	—	—
95-96—Edmonton	NHL	78	3	15	18	202	-7	0	0		—	—	—	—	—
96-97—Edmonton	NHL	71	3	13	16	132	13	1	0		3	0	0	0	4
97-98—Edmonton	NHL	27	0	4	4	58	-2	0	0		—	—	—	—	—
—Tampa Bay	NHL	22	2	4	6	43	-3	0	0		—	—	—	—	—
—San Jose	NHL	12	0	3	3	43	2	0	0		6	0	0	0	10
NHL Totals (10 years)		478	25	84	109	1430	-16	4	1		29	1	0	1	62

MARHA, JOSEF   C   MIGHTY DUCKS

PERSONAL: Born June 2, 1976, in Havlickov Brod, Czechoslovakia. ... 6-0/176. ... Shoots left. ... Name pronounced MAHR-hah.
TRANSACTIONS/CAREER NOTES: Selected by Quebec Nordiques in second round (third Nordiques pick, 35th overall) of NHL entry draft (June 28, 1994). ... Nordiques franchise moved to Colorado and renamed Avalanche for 1995-96 season (June 21, 1995). ... Traded by Avalanche to Mighty Ducks of Anaheim for LW Warren Rychel and conditional pick in 1999 draft (March 24, 1998).

Season Team	League	REGULAR SEASON									PLAYOFFS				
		Gms.	G	A	Pts.	PIM	+/-	PP	SH		Gms.	G	A	Pts.	PIM
91-92—Jihlava	Czech.	25	12	13	25	0	...	...	...		—	—	—	—	—
92-93—Dukla Jihlava	Czech.	7	2	2	4	4	...	...	...		—	—	—	—	—
93-94—Dukla Jihlava	Czech Rep.	41	7	2	9	...	...	...	...		3	0	1	1	...
94-95—Dukla Jihlava	Czech Rep.	35	3	7	10	...	...	...	...		—	—	—	—	—
95-96—Cornwall	AHL	74	18	30	48	30	...	...	...		8	1	2	3	10
—Colorado	NHL	2	0	1	1	0	1	0	0		—	—	—	—	—
96-97—Hershey	AHL	67	23	49	72	44	...	...	...		19	6	†16	*22	10
—Colorado	NHL	6	0	1	1	0	0	0	0		—	—	—	—	—
97-98—Hershey	AHL	55	6	46	52	30	...	...	...		—	—	—	—	—
—Colorado	NHL	11	2	5	7	4	0	0	0		—	—	—	—	—
—Anaheim	NHL	12	7	4	11	0	4	3	0		—	—	—	—	—
NHL Totals (3 years)		31	9	11	20	4	5	3	0						

MARKOV, DANIIL   D   MAPLE LEAFS

PERSONAL: Born July 11, 1976, in Moscow, U.S.S.R. ... 6-1/196. ... Shoots left.
TRANSACTIONS/CAREER NOTES: Selected by Toronto Maple Leafs in ninth round (seventh Maple Leafs pick, 223rd overall) of NHL entry draft (July 8, 1995).

Season Team	League	REGULAR SEASON									PLAYOFFS				
		Gms.	G	A	Pts.	PIM	+/-	PP	SH		Gms.	G	A	Pts.	PIM
93-94—Spartak Moscow	CIS	13	1	0	1	6	...	...	...		1	0	0	0	0
94-95—Spartak Moscow	CIS	39	0	1	1	36	...	...	...		—	—	—	—	—
95-96—Spartak Moscow	CIS	38	2	0	2	12	...	...	...		2	0	0	0	2
96-97—Spartak Moscow	Russian	36	3	6	9	41	...	...	...		—	—	—	—	—
—St. John's	AHL	10	2	4	6	18	...	...	...		11	2	6	8	14
97-98—St. John's	AHL	52	3	23	26	124	...	...	...		2	0	1	1	0
—Toronto	NHL	25	2	5	7	28	0	1	0		—	—	—	—	—
NHL Totals (1 year)		25	2	5	7	28	0	1	0						

MARLEAU, PATRICK   C   SHARKS

PERSONAL: Born September 15, 1979, in Swift Current, Sask. ... 6-2/200. ... Shoots left. ... Name pronounced MAHR-loh.
TRANSACTIONS/CAREER NOTES: Selected by San Jose Sharks in first round (first Sharks pick, second overall) of NHL entry draft (June 21, 1997).
HONORS: Named to Can.HL All-Star second team (1996-97). ... Named to WHL (West) All-Star first team (1996-97).

Season Team	League	REGULAR SEASON									PLAYOFFS				
		Gms.	G	A	Pts.	PIM	+/-	PP	SH		Gms.	G	A	Pts.	PIM
94-95—Swift Current	Jr. A	30	30	22	52	20	...	...	...		—	—	—	—	—
95-96—Seattle	WHL	72	32	42	74	22	...	...	...		5	3	4	7	4
96-97—Seattle	WHL	71	51	74	125	37	...	...	...		15	7	16	23	12
97-98—San Jose	NHL	74	13	19	32	14	5	1	0		5	0	1	1	0
NHL Totals (1 year)		74	13	19	32	14	5	1	0		5	0	1	1	0

MARSHALL, GRANT   RW   STARS

PERSONAL: Born June 9, 1973, in Toronto. ... 6-1/185. ... Shoots right.
HIGH SCHOOL: Hillcrest (Thunder Bay, Ont.).
TRANSACTIONS/CAREER NOTES: Selected by Toronto Maple Leafs in first round (second Maple Leafs pick, 23rd overall) of NHL entry draft (June 20, 1992). ... Awarded to Dallas Stars with C Peter Zezel as compensation for Maple Leafs signing free-agent RW Mike Craig (August 10, 1994). ... Strained muscle (November 15, 1996); missed four games. ... Sprained shoulder (December 8, 1996); missed four games. ... Suffered concussion (January 4, 1997); missed two games. ... Strained groin (November 21, 1997); missed five games. ... Strained groin (April 16, 1998); missed one game. ... Fined $1,000 by NHL for elbowing incident (May 8, 1998).

Season Team	League	REGULAR SEASON								PLAYOFFS				
		Gms.	G	A	Pts.	PIM	+/-	PP	SH	Gms.	G	A	Pts.	PIM
90-91—Ottawa	OHL	26	6	11	17	25	...	...	...	1	0	0	0	0
91-92—Ottawa	OHL	61	32	51	83	132	...	...	...	11	6	11	17	11
92-93—Newmarket	OHL	31	12	25	37	85	...	...	...	7	4	7	11	20
—Ottawa	OHL	30	14	28	42	83	...	...	...	—	—	—	—	—
—St. John's	AHL	2	0	0	0	0	...	...	...	2	0	0	0	2
93-94—St. John's	AHL	67	11	29	40	155	...	...	...	11	1	5	6	17
94-95—Kalamazoo	IHL	61	17	29	46	96	...	...	...	16	9	3	12	27
—Dallas	NHL	2	0	1	1	0	1	0	0	—	—	—	—	—
95-96—Dallas	NHL	70	9	19	28	111	0	0	0	—	—	—	—	—
96-97—Dallas	NHL	56	6	4	10	98	5	0	0	5	0	2	2	8
97-98—Dallas	NHL	72	9	10	19	96	-2	3	0	17	0	2	2	*47
NHL Totals (4 years)		200	24	34	58	305	4	3	0	22	0	4	4	55

MARSHALL, JASON — D — MIGHTY DUCKS

PERSONAL: Born February 22, 1971, in Cranbrook, B.C. ... 6-2/200. ... Shoots right.

TRANSACTIONS/CAREER NOTES: WHL rights traded by Regina Pats with RW Devin Derksen to Tri-City Americans for RW Mark Cipriano (August 1988). ... Selected by St. Louis Blues in first round (first Blues pick, ninth overall) of NHL entry draft (June 17, 1989). ... Traded by Blues to Mighty Ducks of Anaheim for D Bill Houlder (August 29, 1994). ... Cut finger (November 24, 1996); missed two games. ... Bruised hand (March 19, 1997); missed five games. ... Separated right shoulder (December 19, 1997); missed eight games.

Season Team	League	REGULAR SEASON								PLAYOFFS				
		Gms.	G	A	Pts.	PIM	+/-	PP	SH	Gms.	G	A	Pts.	PIM
87-88—Columbia Valley	KIJHL	40	4	28	32	150	...	...	...	—	—	—	—	—
88-89—Vernon	BCJHL	48	10	30	40	197	...	...	...	31	6	6	12	141
—Canadian nat'l team	Int'l	2	0	1	1	0	...	...	...	—	—	—	—	—
89-90—Canadian nat'l team	Int'l	72	1	11	12	57	...	...	...	—	—	—	—	—
90-91—Tri-City	WHL	59	10	34	44	236	...	...	...	7	1	2	3	20
—Peoria	IHL	—	—	—	—	—	...	...	...	18	0	1	1	48
91-92—Peoria	IHL	78	4	18	22	178	...	...	...	10	0	1	1	16
—St. Louis	NHL	2	1	0	1	4	0	0	0	—	—	—	—	—
92-93—Peoria	IHL	77	4	16	20	229	...	...	...	4	0	0	0	20
93-94—Peoria	IHL	20	1	1	2	72	...	...	...	3	2	0	2	2
—Canadian nat'l team	Int'l	41	3	10	13	60	...	...	...	—	—	—	—	—
94-95—San Diego	IHL	80	7	18	25	218	...	...	...	5	0	1	1	8
—Anaheim	NHL	1	0	0	0	0	-2	0	0	—	—	—	—	—
95-96—Baltimore	AHL	57	1	13	14	150	...	...	...	—	—	—	—	—
—Anaheim	NHL	24	0	1	1	42	3	0	0	—	—	—	—	—
96-97—Anaheim	NHL	73	1	9	10	140	6	0	0	7	0	1	1	4
97-98—Anaheim	NHL	72	3	6	9	189	-8	1	0	—	—	—	—	—
NHL Totals (5 years)		172	5	16	21	375	-1	1	0	7	0	1	1	4

MARTIN, JEFF — C — SABRES

M

PERSONAL: Born April 26, 1979, in Stratford, Ont. ... 6-1/177. ... Shoots left.

TRANSACTIONS/CAREER NOTES: Selected by Buffalo Sabres in third round (fourth Sabres pick, 75th overall) of NHL entry draft (June 21, 1997).

Season Team	League	REGULAR SEASON								PLAYOFFS				
		Gms.	G	A	Pts.	PIM	+/-	PP	SH	Gms.	G	A	Pts.	PIM
95-96—Windsor	OHL	63	9	5	14	8	...	...	...	7	1	1	2	4
96-97—Windsor	OHL	65	24	23	47	37	...	...	...	5	2	0	2	2
97-98—Windsor	OHL	65	40	54	94	48	...	...	...	—	—	—	—	—

MARTINS, STEVE — C — SENATORS

PERSONAL: Born April 13, 1972, in Gatineau, Que. ... 5-9/175. ... Shoots left.

HIGH SCHOOL: Choate Rosemary Hall (Wallingford, Conn.).

COLLEGE: Harvard.

TRANSACTIONS/CAREER NOTES: Injured ankle (1992); missed first 11 games of 1992-93 season. ... Selected by Hartford Whalers in first round (first Whalers pick, fifth overall) of NHL supplemental draft (June 24, 1994). ... Whalers franchise moved to North Carolina and renamed Carolina Hurricanes for 1997-98 season; NHL approved move on June 25, 1997. ... Signed as free agent by Ottawa Senators (July 22, 1998).

HONORS: Named to NCAA All-America East first team (1993-94). ... Named ECAC Player of the Year (1993-94). ... Named to NCAA All-Tournament team (1993-94). ... Named to ECAC All-Star first team (1993-94).

Season Team	League	REGULAR SEASON								PLAYOFFS				
		Gms.	G	A	Pts.	PIM	+/-	PP	SH	Gms.	G	A	Pts.	PIM
91-92—Harvard University	ECAC	20	13	14	27	26	...	...	...	—	—	—	—	—
92-93—Harvard University	ECAC	18	6	8	14	40	...	...	...	—	—	—	—	—
93-94—Harvard University	ECAC	32	25	35	60	93	...	...	...	—	—	—	—	—
94-95—Harvard University	ECAC	28	15	23	38	93	...	...	...	—	—	—	—	—
95-96—Springfield	AHL	30	9	20	29	10	...	...	...	—	—	—	—	—
—Hartford	NHL	23	1	3	4	8	-3	0	0	—	—	—	—	—
96-97—Springfield	AHL	63	12	31	43	78	...	...	...	17	1	3	4	26
—Hartford	NHL	2	0	1	1	0	0	0	0	—	—	—	—	—
97-98—Chicago	IHL	78	20	41	61	122	...	...	...	21	6	14	20	28
—Carolina	NHL	3	0	0	0	0	0	0	0	—	—	—	—	—
NHL Totals (3 years)		28	1	4	5	8	-3	0	0					

MATHIEU, ALEXANDRE   C   PENGUINS

PERSONAL: Born February 12, 1979, in Repentigny, Que. ... 6-2/180. ... Shoots left.
TRANSACTIONS/CAREER NOTES: Selected by Pittsburgh Penguins in fourth round (fourth Penguins pick, 97th overall) of NHL entry draft (June 21, 1997).

Season Team	League	REGULAR SEASON								PLAYOFFS				
		Gms.	G	A	Pts.	PIM	+/-	PP	SH	Gms.	G	A	Pts.	PIM
96-97—Halifax	QMJHL	70	12	22	34	18	...	...	...	18	2	5	7	2
97-98—Halifax	QMJHL	68	35	41	76	52	...	...	...	5	1	1	2	4

MATTE, CHRISTIAN   RW   AVALANCHE

PERSONAL: Born January 20, 1975, in Hull, Que. ... 6-0/180. ... Shoots right. ... Name pronounced MAT.
TRANSACTIONS/CAREER NOTES: Selected by Quebec Nordiques in sixth round (eighth Nordiques pick, 153rd overall) of NHL entry draft (June 26, 1993). ... Nordiques franchise moved to Colorado and renamed Avalanche for 1995-96 season (June 21, 1995). ... Broke hand (January 2, 1997); missed six games.
HONORS: Named to QMJHL All-Star second team (1993-94).

Season Team	League	REGULAR SEASON								PLAYOFFS				
		Gms.	G	A	Pts.	PIM	+/-	PP	SH	Gms.	G	A	Pts.	PIM
92-93—Granby	QMJHL	68	17	36	53	56	...	...	...	—	—	—	—	—
93-94—Granby	QMJHL	59	50	47	97	103	...	...	...	7	5	5	10	12
—Cornwall	AHL	1	0	0	0	0	...	...	...	—	—	—	—	—
94-95—Granby	QMJHL	66	50	66	116	86	...	...	...	13	11	7	18	12
—Cornwall	AHL	—	—	—	—	—				3	0	1	1	2
95-96—Cornwall	AHL	64	20	32	52	51	...	...	...	7	1	1	2	6
96-97—Hershey	AHL	49	18	18	36	78	...	...	...	22	8	3	11	25
—Colorado	NHL	5	1	1	2	0	1	0	0	—	—	—	—	—
97-98—Hershey	AHL	71	33	40	73	109	...	...	...	7	3	2	5	4
—Colorado	NHL	5	0	0	0	6	0	0	0	—	—	—	—	—
NHL Totals (2 years)		10	1	1	2	6	1	0	0					

MATTEAU, STEPHANE   LW   SHARKS

PERSONAL: Born September 2, 1969, in Rouyn, Que. ... 6-4/220. ... Shoots left. ... Name pronounced muh-TOH.
TRANSACTIONS/CAREER NOTES: Selected by Calgary Flames as underage junior in second round (second Flames pick, 25th overall) of NHL entry draft (June 13, 1987). ... Bruised thigh (October 10, 1991); missed 43 games. ... Traded by Flames to Chicago Blackhawks for D Trent Yawney (December 16, 1991). ... Fractured left foot (January 27, 1992); missed 12 games. ... Suffered tonsillitis (September 1992); missed first three games of 1992-93 season. ... Pulled groin (December 17, 1993); missed three games. ... Traded by Blackhawks with RW Brian Noonan to New York Rangers for RW Tony Amonte and rights to LW Matt Oates (March 21, 1994). ... Suffered from the flu (February 1, 1995); missed one game. ... Suffered back spasms (April 24, 1995); missed two games. ... Broke hand (September 24, 1995); missed six games. ... Traded by Rangers to St. Louis Blues for C Ian Laperriere (December 28, 1995). ... Traded by Blues to San Jose Sharks for C Darren Turcotte (July 25, 1997). ... Injured back (October 9, 1997); missed three games. ... Injured neck (December 16, 1998); missed two games. ... Injured hand (March 12, 1998); missed four games.
MISCELLANEOUS: Member of Stanley Cup championship team (1994).

Season Team	League	REGULAR SEASON								PLAYOFFS				
		Gms.	G	A	Pts.	PIM	+/-	PP	SH	Gms.	G	A	Pts.	PIM
85-86—Hull	QMJHL	60	6	8	14	19	...	...	...	4	0	0	0	0
86-87—Hull	QMJHL	69	27	48	75	115	...	...	...	8	3	7	10	8
87-88—Hull	QMJHL	57	17	40	57	179	...	...	...	18	5	14	19	84
88-89—Hull	QMJHL	59	44	45	89	202	...	...	...	9	8	6	14	30
—Salt Lake City	IHL	—	—	—	—	—				9	0	4	4	13
89-90—Salt Lake City	IHL	81	23	35	58	130	...	...	...	10	6	3	9	38
90-91—Calgary	NHL	78	15	19	34	93	17	0	1	5	0	1	1	0
91-92—Calgary	NHL	4	1	0	1	19	2	0	0	—	—	—	—	—
—Chicago	NHL	20	5	8	13	45	3	1	0	18	4	6	10	24
92-93—Chicago	NHL	79	15	18	33	98	6	2	0	3	0	1	1	2
93-94—Chicago	NHL	65	15	16	31	55	10	2	0					
—New York Rangers	NHL	12	4	3	7	2	5	1	0	23	6	3	9	20
94-95—New York Rangers	NHL	41	3	5	8	25	-8	0	0	9	0	1	1	10
95-96—New York Rangers	NHL	32	4	2	6	22	-4	1	0	—	—	—	—	—
—St. Louis	NHL	46	7	13	20	65	-4	3	0	11	0	2	2	8
96-97—St. Louis	NHL	74	16	20	36	50	11	1	2	5	0	0	0	0
97-98—San Jose	NHL	73	15	14	29	60	4	1	0	4	0	1	1	0
NHL Totals (8 years)		524	100	118	218	534	42	12	3	78	10	15	25	64

MATVICHUK, RICHARD   D   STARS

PERSONAL: Born February 5, 1973, in Edmonton. ... 6-2/190. ... Shoots left. ... Name pronounced MAT-vih-chuck.
TRANSACTIONS/CAREER NOTES: Selected by Minnesota North Stars in first round (first North Stars pick, eighth overall) of 1991 NHL entry draft (June 22, 1991). ... Strained lower back (November 9, 1992); missed two games. ... Sprained ankle (December 27, 1992); missed 10 games. ... North Stars franchise moved from Minnesota to Dallas and renamed Stars for 1993-94 season. ... Bruised shoulder (April 5, 1994); missed one game. ... Tore knee ligaments and underwent knee surgery (September 20, 1994); missed first 16 games of season. ... Suffered concussion (March 13, 1996); missed five games. ... Bruised shoulder (October 26, 1996); missed two games. ... Strained groin (February 18, 1997); missed 19 games. ... Tore anterior cruciate knee ligament (January 21, 1998); missed eight games.
HONORS: Won Bill Hunter Trophy (1991-92). ... Named to Can.HL All-Star second team (1991-92). ... Named to WHL (East) All-Star first team (1991-92).

Season Team	League	REGULAR SEASON								PLAYOFFS				
		Gms.	G	A	Pts.	PIM	+/-	PP	SH	Gms.	G	A	Pts.	PIM
88-89—Fort Saskatchewan	AJHL	58	7	36	43	147	...	...	...	—	—	—	—	—
89-90—Saskatoon..................	WHL	56	8	24	32	126	...	...	...	10	2	8	10	16
90-91—Saskatoon..................	WHL	68	13	36	49	117	...	...	...	—	—	—	—	—
91-92—Saskatoon..................	WHL	58	14	40	54	126	...	...	...	22	1	9	10	61
92-93—Minnesota..................	NHL	53	2	3	5	26	-8	1	0	—	—	—	—	—
—Kalamazoo.................	IHL	3	0	1	1	6	...	...	...	—	—	—	—	—
93-94—Kalamazoo.................	IHL	43	8	17	25	84	...	...	...	—	—	—	—	—
—Dallas.......................	NHL	25	0	3	3	22	1	0	0	7	1	1	2	12
94-95—Dallas.......................	NHL	14	0	2	2	14	-7	0	0	5	0	2	2	4
—Kalamazoo.................	IHL	17	0	6	6	16	...	...	...	—	—	—	—	—
95-96—Dallas.......................	NHL	73	6	16	22	71	4	0	0	—	—	—	—	—
96-97—Dallas.......................	NHL	57	5	7	12	87	1	0	2	7	0	1	1	20
97-98—Dallas.......................	NHL	74	3	15	18	63	7	0	0	16	1	1	2	14
NHL Totals (6 years)............		296	16	46	62	283	-2	1	2	35	2	5	7	50

MAY, BRAD   LW   CANUCKS

PERSONAL: Born November 29, 1971, in Toronto. ... 6-1/206. ... Shoots left.
TRANSACTIONS/CAREER NOTES: Selected by Buffalo Sabres in first round (first Sabres pick, 14th overall) of NHL entry draft (June 16, 1990). ... Injured knee (August 1990). ... Injured left knee ligaments (November 1990). ... Broke bone in hand (March 11, 1995); missed 15 games. ... Injured left arm (March 3, 1996); missed one game. ... Suspended one game for accumulating three game misconduct penalties (March 31, 1996). ... Underwent right shoulder surgery (October 14, 1996); missed 27 games. ... Broken right hand (December 20, 1996); missed nine games. ... Fractured thumb (March 1, 1997); missed four games. ... Strained shoulder (September 27, 1997); missed first six games of season. ... Sprained knee (December 29, 1997); missed 11 games. ... Traded by Sabres with third-round pick in 1999 draft to Vancouver Canucks for LW Geoff Sanderson (February 4, 1998).
HONORS: Named to OHL All-Star second team (1989-90 and 1990-91).
MISCELLANEOUS: Scored on a penalty shot (vs. Andy Moog, November, 11, 1992).

Season Team	League	REGULAR SEASON								PLAYOFFS				
		Gms.	G	A	Pts.	PIM	+/-	PP	SH	Gms.	G	A	Pts.	PIM
87-88—Markham Jr. B	OHA	6	1	1	2	21	...	...	...	—	—	—	—	—
88-89—Niagara Falls	OHL	65	8	14	22	304	...	...	...	17	0	1	1	55
89-90—Niagara Falls	OHL	61	33	58	91	223	...	...	...	16	9	13	22	64
90-91—Niagara Falls	OHL	34	37	32	69	93	...	...	...	14	11	14	25	53
91-92—Buffalo	NHL	69	11	6	17	309	-12	1	0	7	1	4	5	2
92-93—Buffalo	NHL	82	13	13	26	242	3	0	0	8	1	1	2	14
93-94—Buffalo	NHL	84	18	27	45	171	-6	3	0	7	0	2	2	9
94-95—Buffalo	NHL	33	3	3	6	87	5	1	0	4	0	0	0	2
95-96—Buffalo	NHL	79	15	29	44	295	6	3	0	—	—	—	—	—
96-97—Buffalo	NHL	42	3	4	7	106	-8	1	0	10	1	1	2	32
97-98—Buffalo	NHL	36	4	7	11	113	2	0	0	—	—	—	—	—
—Vancouver.................	NHL	27	9	3	12	41	0	4	0	—	—	—	—	—
NHL Totals (7 years)............		452	76	92	168	1364	-10	13	0	36	3	8	11	59

MAYERS, JAMAL   C   BLUES   **M**

PERSONAL: Born October 24, 1974, in Toronto. ... 6-1/207. ... Shoots right. ... Name pronounced MIGHRS.
HIGH SCHOOL: Erindale Secondary (Mississauga, Ont.).
COLLEGE: Western Michigan.
TRANSACTIONS/CAREER NOTES: Selected by St. Louis Blues in fourth round (third Blues pick, 89th overall) of NHL entry draft (June 26, 1993).

Season Team	League	REGULAR SEASON								PLAYOFFS				
		Gms.	G	A	Pts.	PIM	+/-	PP	SH	Gms.	G	A	Pts.	PIM
90-91—Thornhill	Jr. A	44	12	24	36	78	...	...	...	—	—	—	—	—
91-92—Thornhill	Jr. A	56	38	69	107	36	...	...	...	—	—	—	—	—
92-93—Western Michigan U. ...	CCHA	38	8	17	25	26	...	...	...	—	—	—	—	—
93-94—Western Michigan U. ...	CCHA	40	17	32	49	40	...	...	...	—	—	—	—	—
94-95—Western Michigan U. ...	CCHA	39	13	33	46	40	...	...	...	—	—	—	—	—
95-96—Western Michigan U. ...	CCHA	38	17	22	39	75	...	...	...	—	—	—	—	—
96-97—Worcester	AHL	62	12	14	26	104	...	...	...	5	4	4	8	4
—St. Louis	NHL	6	0	1	1	2	-3	0	0	—	—	—	—	—
97-98—Worcester	AHL	61	19	24	43	117	...	...	...	11	3	4	7	10
NHL Totals (1 year).............		6	0	1	1	2	-3	0	0					

McALLISTER, CHRIS   D   CANUCKS

PERSONAL: Born June 16, 1975, in Saskatoon, Sask. ... 6-7/225. ... Shoots left.
TRANSACTIONS/CAREER NOTES: Selected by Vancouver Canucks in second round (first Canucks pick, 40th overall) of NHL entry draft (July 8, 1995). ... Suffered from heel spur (December 13, 1997); missed three games.

Season Team	League	REGULAR SEASON								PLAYOFFS				
		Gms.	G	A	Pts.	PIM	+/-	PP	SH	Gms.	G	A	Pts.	PIM
93-94—Humboldt....................	SJHL	50	3	5	8	150	...	...	...	—	—	—	—	—
—Saskatoon..................	WHL	2	0	0	0	5	...	...	...	—	—	—	—	—
94-95—Saskatoon..................	WHL	65	2	8	10	134	...	...	...	10	0	0	0	28
95-96—Syracuse....................	AHL	68	0	2	2	142	...	...	...	16	0	0	0	34
96-97—Syracuse....................	AHL	43	3	1	4	108	...	...	...	3	0	0	0	6
97-98—Syracuse....................	AHL	23	0	1	1	71	...	...	...	5	0	0	0	21
—Vancouver.................	NHL	36	1	2	3	106	-12	0	0	—	—	—	—	—
NHL Totals (1 year).............		36	1	2	3	106	-12	0	0					

McALPINE, CHRIS   D   BLUES

PERSONAL: Born December 1, 1971, in Roseville, Minn. ... 6-0/204. ... Shoots right. ... Name pronounced muh-KAL-pighn.
HIGH SCHOOL: Roseville (Minn.).
COLLEGE: Minnesota.
TRANSACTIONS/CAREER NOTES: Selected by New Jersey Devils in seventh round (seventh Devils pick, 137th overall) of NHL entry draft (June 16, 1990). ... Injured thumb (March 26, 1995); missed four games. ... Traded by Devils with ninth-round pick in 1999 draft to St. Louis Blues for C Peter Zezel (February 11, 1997). ... Suffered from the flu (March 14, 1998); missed one game.
HONORS: Named to NCCA All-America West second team (1993-94). ... Named to WCHA All-Star first team (1993-94).
MISCELLANEOUS: Member of Stanley Cup championship team (1995).

		REGULAR SEASON								PLAYOFFS				
Season Team	League	Gms.	G	A	Pts.	PIM	+/-	PP	SH	Gms.	G	A	Pts.	PIM
89-90—Roseville H.S.	Minn. H.S.	25	15	13	28	...	...	...	...	—	—	—	—	—
90-91—Univ. of Minnesota......	WCHA	38	7	9	16	112	...	...	...	—	—	—	—	—
91-92—Univ. of Minnesota......	WCHA	39	3	9	12	126	...	...	...	—	—	—	—	—
92-93—Univ. of Minnesota......	WCHA	41	14	9	23	82	...	...	...	—	—	—	—	—
93-94—Univ. of Minnesota......	WCHA	36	12	18	30	121	...	...	...	—	—	—	—	—
94-95—Albany	AHL	48	4	18	22	49	...	...	...	—	—	—	—	—
—New Jersey	NHL	24	0	3	3	17	4	0	0	—	—	—	—	—
95-96—Albany	AHL	57	5	14	19	72	...	...	...	4	0	0	0	13
96-97—Albany	AHL	44	1	9	10	48	...	...	...	—	—	—	—	—
—St. Louis	NHL	15	0	0	0	24	-2	0	0	4	0	1	1	0
97-98—St. Louis	NHL	54	3	7	10	36	14	0	0	10	0	0	0	16
NHL Totals (3 years)...........		93	3	10	13	77	16	0	0	14	0	1	1	16

McAMMOND, DEAN   LW   OILERS

PERSONAL: Born June 15, 1973, in Grand Cache, Alta. ... 5-11/195. ... Shoots left.
TRANSACTIONS/CAREER NOTES: Selected by Chicago Blackhawks in first round (first Blackhawks pick, 22nd overall) of NHL entry draft (June 22, 1991). ... Traded by Blackhawks with D Igor Kravchuk to Edmonton Oilers for RW Joe Murphy (February 25, 1993). ... Severed left Achilles' tendon (February 1, 1995); missed last 41 games of season. ... Fractured nose (November 11, 1996); missed two games. ... Suffered from the flu (January 21, 1997); missed two games. ... Suffered back spasms (March 1, 1997); missed remainder of season.
HONORS: Won Can.HL Plus/Minus Award (1991-92).
MISCELLANEOUS: Failed to score on a penalty shot (vs. Mark Fitzpatrick, January 5, 1996).

		REGULAR SEASON								PLAYOFFS				
Season Team	League	Gms.	G	A	Pts.	PIM	+/-	PP	SH	Gms.	G	A	Pts.	PIM
89-90—Prince Albert..............	WHL	53	11	11	22	49	...	...	...	14	2	3	5	18
90-91—Prince Albert..............	WHL	71	33	35	68	108	...	...	...	2	0	1	1	6
91-92—Prince Albert..............	WHL	63	37	54	91	189	...	...	...	10	12	11	23	26
—Chicago...................	NHL	5	0	2	2	0	-2	0	0	3	0	0	0	2
92-93—Prince Albert..............	WHL	30	19	29	48	44	...	...	...	—	—	—	—	—
—Swift Current	WHL	18	10	13	23	29	...	...	...	17	*16	19	35	20
93-94—Edmonton	NHL	45	6	21	27	16	12	2	0	—	—	—	—	—
—Cape Breton	AHL	28	9	12	21	38	...	...	...	—	—	—	—	—
94-95—Edmonton	NHL	6	0	0	0	0	-1	0	0	—	—	—	—	—
95-96—Edmonton	NHL	53	15	15	30	23	6	4	0	—	—	—	—	—
—Cape Breton	AHL	22	9	15	24	55	...	...	...	—	—	—	—	—
96-97—Edmonton	NHL	57	12	17	29	28	-15	4	0	12	1	4	5	12
97-98—Edmonton	NHL	77	19	31	50	46	9	8	0	15	1	4	5	14
NHL Totals (6 years)...........		243	52	86	138	113	9	18	0	15	1	4	5	14

McARTHUR, MARK   G   ISLANDERS

PERSONAL: Born November 16, 1975, in East York, Ont. ... 5-10/175. ... Catches left.
HIGH SCHOOL: Bishop MacDonnell (Guelph, Ont.).
TRANSACTIONS/CAREER NOTES: Selected by New York Islanders in fifth round (fifth Islanders pick, 112th overall) of NHL entry draft (June 29, 1994).
HONORS: Shared Dave Pinkney Trophy with Andy Adams (1994-95). ... Named to OHL All-Star second team (1994-95). ... Won James Norris Memorial Trophy (1995-96).

		REGULAR SEASON							PLAYOFFS					
Season Team	League	Gms.	Min	W	L	T	GA	SO	Avg.	Gms.	Min.	W	L	GA	SO	Avg.
91-92—Peterborough	Jr. B	25	1198	...	...	...	98	0	4.91	—	—	—	—	—	—	—
92-93—Guelph	OHL	35	1853	14	14	3	180	0	5.83	—	—	—	—	—	—	—
93-94—Guelph	OHL	51	2936	25	18	5	201	0	4.11	9	561	4	5	38	0	4.06
94-95—Guelph	OHL	48	2776	34	8	4	130	1	*2.81	13	797	9	4	44	0	3.31
95-96—Utah	IHL	26	1482	12	12	‡0	77	0	3.12	—	—	—	—	—	—	—
96-97—Utah	IHL	56	3111	28	20	‡6	155	3	2.99	—	—	—	—	—	—	—
97-98—Utah	IHL	20	1060	7	7	‡2	60	0	3.40	1	63	0	1	4	0	3.81

McBAIN, JASON   D

PERSONAL: Born April 12, 1974, in Ilion, N.Y. ... 6-2/178. ... Shoots left. ... Brother of Mike McBain, defenseman, Tampa Bay Lightning.
TRANSACTIONS/CAREER NOTES: Selected by Hartford Whalers in fourth round (fifth Whalers pick, 81st overall) of NHL entry draft (June 20, 1992). ... Whalers franchise moved to North Carolina and renamed Carolina Hurricanes for 1997-98 season; NHL approved move on June 25, 1997.

Season Team	League	REGULAR SEASON								PLAYOFFS				
		Gms.	G	A	Pts.	PIM	+/-	PP	SH	Gms.	G	A	Pts.	PIM
90-91—Lethbridge	WHL	52	2	7	9	39	...	...	...	1	0	0	0	0
91-92—Lethbridge	WHL	13	0	1	1	12	...	...	...	—	—	—	—	—
—Portland	WHL	54	9	23	32	95	...	...	...	6	1	0	1	13
92-93—Portland	WHL	71	9	35	44	76	...	...	...	16	2	12	14	14
93-94—Portland	WHL	63	15	51	66	86	...	...	...	10	2	7	9	14
94-95—Springfield	AHL	77	16	28	44	92	...	...	...	—	—	—	—	—
95-96—Springfield	AHL	73	11	33	44	43	...	...	...	8	1	1	2	2
—Hartford	NHL	3	0	0	0	0	-1	0	0	—	—	—	—	—
96-97—Springfield	AHL	58	8	26	34	40	...	...	...	16	0	8	8	12
—Hartford	NHL	6	0	0	0	0	-4	0	0	—	—	—	—	—
97-98—Cleveland	IHL	65	8	22	30	62	...	...	...	3	0	2	2	2
NHL Totals (2 years)		9	0	0	0	0	-5	0	0					

McBAIN, MIKE — D — LIGHTNING

PERSONAL: Born January 12, 1977, in Kimberley, B.C. ... 6-2/195. ... Shoots left. ... Brother of Jason McBain, defenseman in Carolina Hurricanes system.
TRANSACTIONS/CAREER NOTES: Selected by Tampa Bay Lightning in second round (second Lightning pick, 30th overall) of NHL entry draft (July 8, 1995).

Season Team	League	REGULAR SEASON								PLAYOFFS				
		Gms.	G	A	Pts.	PIM	+/-	PP	SH	Gms.	G	A	Pts.	PIM
92-93—Kimberley	RMJHL	35	0	4	4	38	...	...	...	—	—	—	—	—
93-94—Red Deer	WHL	58	4	13	17	41	...	...	...	4	0	0	0	0
94-95—Red Deer	WHL	68	6	28	34	55	...	...	...	—	—	—	—	—
95-96—Red Deer	WHL	68	7	34	41	68	...	...	...	10	1	7	8	10
96-97—Red Deer	WHL	59	14	35	49	55	...	...	...	15	1	6	7	9
97-98—Adirondack	AHL	42	2	13	15	28	...	...	...	—	—	—	—	—
—Tampa Bay	NHL	27	0	1	1	8	-10	0	0	—	—	—	—	—
NHL Totals (1 year)		27	0	1	1	8	-10	0	0					

McCABE, BRYAN — D — CANUCKS

PERSONAL: Born June 8, 1975, in St. Catharines, Ont. ... 6-1/204. ... Shoots left.
HIGH SCHOOL: Joel E. Ferris (Spokane, Wash.).
TRANSACTIONS/CAREER NOTES: Selected by New York Islanders in second round (second Islanders pick, 40th overall) of NHL entry draft (June 26, 1993). ... Traded by Islanders with LW Todd Bertuzzi and third-round pick (LW Jarkko Ruutu) in 1998 draft to Vancouver Canucks for C Trevor Linden (February 6, 1998).
HONORS: Named to WHL (West) All-Star second team (1992-93). ... Named to WHL (West) All-Star first team (1993-94). ... Named to WHL (East) All-Star first team (1994-95). ... Named to Memorial Cup All-Star team (1994-95).
MISCELLANEOUS: Captain of New York Islanders (1997 through February 7, 1998).

M

Season Team	League	REGULAR SEASON								PLAYOFFS				
		Gms.	G	A	Pts.	PIM	+/-	PP	SH	Gms.	G	A	Pts.	PIM
91-92—Medicine Hat	WHL	68	6	24	30	157	...	...	...	4	0	0	0	6
92-93—Medicine Hat	WHL	14	0	13	13	83	...	...	...	—	—	—	—	—
—Spokane	WHL	46	3	44	47	134	...	...	...	10	1	5	6	28
93-94—Spokane	WHL	64	22	62	84	218	...	...	...	3	0	4	4	4
94-95—Spokane	WHL	42	14	39	53	115	...	...	...	—	—	—	—	—
—Brandon	WHL	20	6	10	16	38	...	...	...	18	4	13	17	59
95-96—New York Islanders	NHL	82	7	16	23	156	-24	3	0	—	—	—	—	—
96-97—New York Islanders	NHL	82	8	20	28	165	-2	2	1	—	—	—	—	—
97-98—New York Islanders	NHL	56	3	9	12	145	9	1	0	—	—	—	—	—
—Vancouver	NHL	26	1	11	12	64	10	0	1	—	—	—	—	—
NHL Totals (3 years)		246	19	56	75	530	-7	6	2					

McCARTHY, SANDY — RW — LIGHTNING

PERSONAL: Born June 15, 1972, in Toronto. ... 6-3/225. ... Shoots right.
TRANSACTIONS/CAREER NOTES: Suspended one game by QMJHL for attempting to injure another player (October 2, 1989). ... Suspended one playoff game by QMJHL for pre-game fight (March 19, 1990). ... Selected by Calgary Flames in third round (third Flames pick, 52nd overall) of NHL entry draft (June 22, 1991). ... Strained right shoulder (December 18, 1993); missed two games. ... Strained shoulder (December 27, 1993); missed one game. ... Strained right knee (January 20, 1995); missed five games. ... Suffered hernia (February 3, 1995); missed six games. ... Injured ribs (December 16, 1995); missed seven games. ... Fractured ankle (October 9, 1996); missed 25 games. ... Reinjured left ankle (January 9, 1997); underwent ankle surgery (January 24, 1997) and missed 23 games. ... Bruised shoulder (November 13, 1997); missed six games. ... Injured groin (December 9, 1997); missed two games. ... Suffered hip pointer (December 22, 1997); missed four games. ... Suffered charley horse (January 24, 1998); missed one game. ... Traded by Flames with third- (LW Brad Richards) and fifth-round (D Curtis Rich) picks in 1998 draft to Tampa Bay Lightning for C Jason Wiemer (March 24, 1998).

Season Team	League	REGULAR SEASON								PLAYOFFS				
		Gms.	G	A	Pts.	PIM	+/-	PP	SH	Gms.	G	A	Pts.	PIM
89-90—Laval	QMJHL	65	10	11	21	269	...	...	...	—	—	—	—	—
90-91—Laval	QMJHL	68	21	19	40	297	...	...	...	—	—	—	—	—
91-92—Laval	QMJHL	62	39	51	90	326	...	...	...	8	4	5	9	81
92-93—Salt Lake City	IHL	77	18	20	38	220	...	...	...	—	—	—	—	—
93-94—Calgary	NHL	79	5	5	10	173	-3	0	0	7	0	0	0	34
94-95—Calgary	NHL	37	5	3	8	101	1	0	0	6	0	1	1	17

			REGULAR SEASON							PLAYOFFS				
Season Team	League	Gms.	G	A	Pts.	PIM	+/-	PP	SH	Gms.	G	A	Pts.	PIM
95-96—Calgary	NHL	75	9	7	16	173	-8	3	0	4	0	0	0	10
96-97—Calgary	NHL	33	3	5	8	113	-8	1	0	—	—	—	—	—
97-98—Calgary	NHL	52	8	5	13	170	-18	1	0	—	—	—	—	—
—Tampa Bay	NHL	14	0	5	5	71	-1	0	0	—	—	—	—	—
NHL Totals (5 years)		290	30	30	60	801	-37	5	0	17	0	1	1	61

McCARTY, DARREN   RW   RED WINGS

PERSONAL: Born April 1, 1972, in Burnaby, B.C. ... 6-1/215. ... Shoots right.
HIGH SCHOOL: Quinte Secondary School (Belleville, Ont.).
TRANSACTIONS/CAREER NOTES: Selected by Detroit Red Wings in second round (second Red Wings pick, 46th overall) of NHL entry draft (June 20, 1992). ... Injured groin (January 29, 1994); missed five games. ... Injured shoulder (March 23, 1994); missed five games. ... Separated right shoulder (February 7, 1995); missed eight games. ... Injured right hand (March 30, 1995); missed two games. ... Injured left knee (April 9, 1995); missed five games. ... Injured right heel (November 7, 1995); missed one game ... Separated shoulder (December 2, 1995); missed six games. ... Lacerated right forearm (January 12, 1996); missed three games. ... Injured left hand (February 15, 1996); missed seven games. ... Injured hand (January 3, 1997); missed seven games. ... Bruised thigh (January 29, 1997); missed four games. ... Injured groin (April 5, 1997); missed two games. ... Fractured foot (January 11, 1998); missed eight games. ... Suffered from vertigo (April 4, 1998); missed three games.
HONORS: Won Jim Mahon Memorial Trophy (1991-92). ... Named to Can.HL All-Star first team (1991-92). ... Named to OHL All-Star first team (1991-92).
MISCELLANEOUS: Member of Stanley Cup championship team (1997 and 1998).

			REGULAR SEASON							PLAYOFFS				
Season Team	League	Gms.	G	A	Pts.	PIM	+/-	PP	SH	Gms.	G	A	Pts.	PIM
88-89—Peterborough Jr. B	OHA	34	18	17	35	135	...	...	...	—	—	—	—	—
89-90—Belleville	OHL	63	12	15	27	142	...	...	...	11	1	1	2	21
90-91—Belleville	OHL	60	30	37	67	151	...	...	...	6	2	2	4	13
91-92—Belleville	OHL	65	*55	72	127	177	...	...	...	5	1	4	5	13
92-93—Adirondack	AHL	73	17	19	36	278	...	...	...	11	0	1	1	33
93-94—Detroit	NHL	67	9	17	26	181	12	0	0	7	2	2	4	8
94-95—Detroit	NHL	31	5	8	13	88	5	1	0	18	3	2	5	14
95-96—Detroit	NHL	63	15	14	29	158	14	8	0	19	3	2	5	20
96-97—Detroit	NHL	68	19	30	49	126	14	5	0	20	3	4	7	34
97-98—Detroit	NHL	71	15	22	37	157	0	5	1	22	3	8	11	34
NHL Totals (5 years)		300	63	91	154	710	45	19	1	86	14	18	32	110

McCAULEY, ALYN   C   MAPLE LEAFS

PERSONAL: Born May 29, 1977, in Brockville, Ont. ... 5-11/185. ... Shoots left.
HIGH SCHOOL: Canterbury (Ottawa, Ont.).
TRANSACTIONS/CAREER NOTES: Selected by New Jersey Devils in fourth round (fifth Devils pick, 79th overall) of NHL entry draft (July 8, 1995). ... Traded by Devils with D Jason Smith and C Steve Sullivan to Toronto Maple Leafs for C Doug Gilmour, D Dave Ellett and third-round pick in 1999 draft (February 25, 1997). ... Fractured ankle (December 31, 1997); missed 17 games. ... Strained shoulder (February 26, 1998); missed three games.
HONORS: Named to OHL All-Star first team (1995-96 and 1996-97). ... Won Red Tilson Trophy (1995-96 and 1996-97). ... Won Can.HL Player of the Year Award (1996-97). ... Won William Hanley Trophy (1996-97). ... Named to Can.HL All-Star first team (1996-97).

			REGULAR SEASON							PLAYOFFS				
Season Team	League	Gms.	G	A	Pts.	PIM	+/-	PP	SH	Gms.	G	A	Pts.	PIM
92-93—Kingston Jr. A	MTHL	38	31	29	60	18	...	...	...	—	—	—	—	—
93-94—Ottawa	OHL	38	13	23	36	10	...	...	...	13	5	14	19	4
94-95—Ottawa	OHL	65	16	38	54	20	...	...	...	—	—	—	—	—
95-96—Ottawa	OHL	55	34	48	82	24	...	...	...	2	0	0	0	0
96-97—Ottawa	OHL	50	†56	56	112	16	...	...	...	22	14	22	36	14
—St. John's	AHL	—	—	—	—	—	...	...	...	3	0	1	1	0
97-98—Toronto	NHL	60	6	10	16	6	-7	0	0	—	—	—	—	—
NHL Totals (1 year)		60	6	10	16	6	-7	0	0					

McCOSH, SHAWN   C   FLYERS

PERSONAL: Born June 5, 1969, in Oshawa, Ont. ... 6-0/188. ... Shoots right.
TRANSACTIONS/CAREER NOTES: Selected by Detroit Red Wings in fifth round (fifth Red Wings pick, 95th overall) of NHL entry draft (June 17, 1989). ... Traded by Red Wings to Los Angeles Kings for eighth-round pick (D Justin Krall) in 1992 draft (August 15, 1990). ... Traded by Kings with RW Bob Kudelski to Ottawa Senators for RW Jim Thomson and C Marc Fortier (December 20, 1992). ... Signed as free agent by New York Rangers (August 17, 1993). ... Signed as free agent by Philadelphia Flyers (July 31, 1995).

			REGULAR SEASON							PLAYOFFS				
Season Team	League	Gms.	G	A	Pts.	PIM	+/-	PP	SH	Gms.	G	A	Pts.	PIM
86-87—Hamilton	OHL	50	11	17	28	49	...	...	...	6	1	0	1	2
87-88—Hamilton	OHL	64	17	36	53	96	...	...	...	14	6	8	14	14
88-89—Niagara Falls	OHL	56	41	62	103	75	...	...	...	14	4	13	17	23
89-90—Niagara Falls	OHL	9	6	10	16	24	...	...	...	—	—	—	—	—
—Dukes of Hamilton	OHL	39	24	28	52	65	...	...	...	—	—	—	—	—
90-91—New Haven	AHL	66	16	21	37	104	...	...	...	—	—	—	—	—
91-92—Los Angeles	NHL	4	0	0	0	4	0	0	0	—	—	—	—	—
—Phoenix	IHL	71	21	32	53	118	...	...	...	—	—	—	—	—
—New Haven	AHL	—	—	—	—	—	...	...	...	5	0	1	1	0
92-93—Phoenix	IHL	22	9	8	17	36	...	...	...	—	—	—	—	—
—New Haven	AHL	46	22	32	54	54	...	...	...					

Season Team	League	REGULAR SEASON								PLAYOFFS				
		Gms.	G	A	Pts.	PIM	+/-	PP	SH	Gms.	G	A	Pts.	PIM
93-94—Binghamton	AHL	75	31	44	75	68	...	...	...	—	—	—	—	—
94-95—Binghamton	AHL	67	23	60	83	73	...	...	...	8	3	9	12	6
—New York Rangers	NHL	5	1	0	1	2	1	0	0	—	—	—	—	—
95-96—Hershey	AHL	71	31	52	83	82	...	...	...	5	1	5	6	8
96-97—Philadelphia	AHL	79	30	51	81	110	...	...	...	10	3	9	12	23
97-98—Philadelphia	AHL	80	24	54	78	102	...	...	...	20	6	13	19	14
NHL Totals (2 years)		9	1	0	1	6	1	0	0					

McDONELL, KENT   RW   HURRICANES

PERSONAL: Born March 1, 1979, in Cornwall, Ont. ... 6-0/175. ... Shoots right.
TRANSACTIONS/CAREER NOTES: Selected by Carolina Hurricanes in ninth round (ninth Hurricanes pick, 225th overall) of NHL entry draft (June 21, 1997).

Season Team	League	REGULAR SEASON								PLAYOFFS				
		Gms.	G	A	Pts.	PIM	+/-	PP	SH	Gms.	G	A	Pts.	PIM
96-97—Guelph	OHL	56	7	5	12	57	...	...	...	16	0	2	2	4
97-98—Guelph	OHL	57	28	23	51	76	...	...	...	12	7	4	11	18

McEACHERN, SHAWN   LW   SENATORS

PERSONAL: Born February 28, 1969, in Waltham, Mass. ... 5-11/195. ... Shoots left. ... Full name: Shawn K. McEachern. ... Name pronounced muh-KEH-kuhrn.
HIGH SCHOOL: Matignon (Cambridge, Mass.).
COLLEGE: Boston University.
TRANSACTIONS/CAREER NOTES: Selected by Pittsburgh Penguins in sixth round (sixth Penguins pick, 110th overall) of NHL entry draft (June 13, 1987). ... Traded by Penguins to Los Angeles Kings for D Marty McSorley (August 27, 1993). ... Traded by Kings to Penguins for D Marty McSorley and D Jim Paek (February 15, 1994). ... Played in Europe during 1994-95 NHL lockout. ... Suspended for first three games of 1994-95 season and fined $500 by NHL for slashing (September 21, 1994); suspension reduced to two games due to abbreviated 1994-95 season. ... Traded by Penguins with LW Kevin Stevens to Boston Bruins for C Bryan Smolinski and RW Glen Murray (August 2, 1995). ... Traded by Bruins to Ottawa Senators for RW Trent McCleary and third-round pick (LW Eric Naud) in 1996 draft (June 22, 1996). ... Fractured jaw (December 6, 1996); missed 17 games. ... Suffered back spasms (February 7, 1998); missed one game.
HONORS: Named to Hockey East All-Star second team (1989-90). ... Named Hockey East Tournament Most Valuable Player (1990-91). ... Named to NCAA All-America East first team (1990-91). ... Named to Hockey East All-Star first team (1990-91).
MISCELLANEOUS: Member of Stanley Cup championship team (1992).
STATISTICAL PLATEAUS: Three-goal games: 1997-98 (1).

Season Team	League	REGULAR SEASON								PLAYOFFS				
		Gms.	G	A	Pts.	PIM	+/-	PP	SH	Gms.	G	A	Pts.	PIM
85-86—Matignon	Mass. H.S.	20	32	20	52	...	...	...	...	—	—	—	—	—
86-87—Matignon	Mass. H.S.	16	29	28	57	...	...	...	...	—	—	—	—	—
87-88—Matignon	Mass. H.S.	...	52	40	92	...	...	...	...	—	—	—	—	—
88-89—Boston University	Hockey East	36	20	28	48	32	...	...	...	—	—	—	—	—
89-90—Boston University	Hockey East	43	25	31	56	78	...	...	...	—	—	—	—	—
90-91—Boston University	Hockey East	41	34	48	82	43	...	...	...	—	—	—	—	—
91-92—U.S. national team	Int'l	57	26	23	49	38	...	...	...	—	—	—	—	—
—U.S. Olympic Team	Int'l	8	1	0	1	10	...	...	...	—	—	—	—	—
—Pittsburgh	NHL	15	0	4	4	0	1	0	0	19	2	7	9	4
92-93—Pittsburgh	NHL	84	28	33	61	46	21	7	0	12	3	2	5	10
93-94—Los Angeles	NHL	49	8	13	21	24	1	0	3	—	—	—	—	—
—Pittsburgh	NHL	27	12	9	21	10	13	0	2	6	1	0	1	2
94-95—Kiekko-Espoo	Finland	8	1	3	4	6	...	...	...	—	—	—	—	—
—Pittsburgh	NHL	44	13	13	26	22	4	1	2	11	0	2	2	8
95-96—Boston	NHL	82	24	29	53	34	-5	3	2	5	2	1	3	8
96-97—Ottawa	NHL	65	11	20	31	18	-5	0	1	7	2	0	2	8
97-98—Ottawa	NHL	81	24	24	48	42	1	8	2	11	0	4	4	8
NHL Totals (7 years)		447	120	145	265	196	31	19	12	71	10	16	26	48

McGILLIS, DAN   D   FLYERS

PERSONAL: Born July 1, 1972, in Hawkesbury, Ont. ... 6-2/225. ... Shoots left. ... Full name: Daniel McGillis.
COLLEGE: Northeastern.
TRANSACTIONS/CAREER NOTES: Selected by Detroit Red Wings in 10th round (10th Red Wings pick, 238th overall) of NHL entry draft (June 20, 1992). ... Signed as free agent by Edmonton Oilers (September 6, 1996). ... Traded by Oilers with second-round pick (D Jason Beckett) in 1998 draft to Philadelphia Flyers for D Janne Niinimaa (March 24, 1998).
HONORS: Named to Hockey East All-Star first team (1994-95). ... Named to NCAA All-America East first team (1995-96). ... Named to Hockey East All-Star team (1995-96).

Season Team	League	REGULAR SEASON								PLAYOFFS				
		Gms.	G	A	Pts.	PIM	+/-	PP	SH	Gms.	G	A	Pts.	PIM
91-92—Hawkesbury	Tier II Jr. A	36	5	19	24	106	...	...	...	—	—	—	—	—
92-93—Northeastern Univ.	Hockey East	35	5	12	17	42	...	...	...	—	—	—	—	—
93-94—Northeastern Univ.	Hockey East	38	4	25	29	82	...	...	...	—	—	—	—	—
94-95—Northeastern Univ.	Hockey East	34	9	22	31	70	...	...	...	—	—	—	—	—
95-96—Northeastern Univ.	Hockey East	34	12	24	36	50	...	...	...	—	—	—	—	—
96-97—Edmonton	NHL	73	6	16	22	52	2	2	1	12	0	5	5	24
97-98—Edmonton	NHL	67	10	15	25	74	-17	5	0	—	—	—	—	—
—Philadelphia	NHL	13	1	5	6	35	-4	1	0	5	1	2	3	10
NHL Totals (2 years)		153	17	36	53	161	-19	8	1	17	1	7	8	34

M

McINNIS, MARTY — C/LW — FLAMES

PERSONAL: Born June 2, 1970, in Weymouth, Mass. ... 5-11/190. ... Shoots right. ... Full name: Martin Edward McInnis. ... Name pronounced muh-KIH-nihz.

HIGH SCHOOL: Milton (Mass.) Academy.

COLLEGE: Boston College.

TRANSACTIONS/CAREER NOTES: Selected by New York Islanders in eighth round (10th Islanders pick, 163rd overall) of NHL entry draft (June 11, 1988). ... Injured eye (March 9, 1993); missed two games. ... Fractured patella (March 27, 1993); missed remainder of regular season and 14 playoff games. ... Sprained wrist (April 18, 1995); missed one game. ... Injured ribs (March 7, 1996); missed one game. ... Injured ribs (March 16, 1996); missed six games. ... Traded by Islanders with G Tyrone Garner and sixth-round pick (D Ilja Demidov) in 1997 draft to Calgary Flames for C Robert Reichel (March 18, 1997). ... Injured shoulder (December 23, 1997); missed six games.

MISCELLANEOUS: Scored on a penalty shot (vs. Kelly Hrudey, April 4, 1990). ... Failed to score on a penalty shot (vs. Tom Draper, March 8, 1992).

STATISTICAL PLATEAUS: Three-goal games: 1997-98 (1).

		REGULAR SEASON								PLAYOFFS				
Season Team	League	Gms.	G	A	Pts.	PIM	+/-	PP	SH	Gms.	G	A	Pts.	PIM
86-87—Milton Academy	Mass. H.S.	—	21	19	40	—	—	—	—	—	—	—	—	—
87-88—Milton Academy	Mass. H.S.	—	26	25	51	—	—	—	—	—	—	—	—	—
88-89—Boston College	Hockey East	39	13	19	32	8	...	...	...	—	—	—	—	—
89-90—Boston College	Hockey East	41	24	29	53	43	...	...	...	—	—	—	—	—
90-91—Boston College	Hockey East	38	21	36	57	40	...	...	...	—	—	—	—	—
91-92—U.S. national team	Int'l	54	15	19	34	20	...	...	...	—	—	—	—	—
—U.S. Olympic Team	Int'l	8	5	2	7	4	...	...	...	—	—	—	—	—
—New York Islanders	NHL	15	3	5	8	0	6	0	0	—	—	—	—	—
92-93—New York Islanders	NHL	56	10	20	30	24	7	0	1	3	0	1	1	0
—Capital District	AHL	10	4	12	16	2	...	...	...	—	—	—	—	—
93-94—New York Islanders	NHL	81	25	31	56	24	31	3	5	4	0	0	0	0
94-95—New York Islanders	NHL	41	9	7	16	8	-1	0	0	—	—	—	—	—
95-96—New York Islanders	NHL	74	12	34	46	39	-11	2	0	—	—	—	—	—
96-97—New York Islanders	NHL	70	20	22	42	20	-7	4	1	—	—	—	—	—
—Calgary	NHL	10	3	4	7	2	-1	1	0	—	—	—	—	—
97-98—Calgary	NHL	75	19	25	44	34	1	5	4	—	—	—	—	—
NHL Totals (7 years)		422	101	148	249	151	25	15	11	7	0	1	1	0

McKAY, RANDY — RW — DEVILS

PERSONAL: Born January 25, 1967, in Montreal. ... 6-2/210. ... Shoots right. ... Full name: Hugh Randall McKay.

COLLEGE: Michigan Tech.

TRANSACTIONS/CAREER NOTES: Selected by Detroit Red Wings in sixth round (sixth Red Wings pick, 113th overall) of NHL entry draft (June 15, 1985). ... Injured knee (February 1989). ... Lacerated forearm (February 23, 1991). ... Sent by Red Wings with C Dave Barr to New Jersey Devils as compensation for Red Wings signing free agent RW Troy Crowder (September 9,1991). ... Sprained knee (January 16, 1993); missed nine games. ... Bruised shoulder (November 3, 1993); missed three games. ... Bruised shoulder (January 24, 1994); missed three games. ... Injured groin (February 24, 1995); missed nine games. ... Reinjured groin (March 18, 1995); missed six games. ... Suffered charley horse (May 26, 1995); missed one playoff game. ... Suffered concussion (December 31, 1995); missed five games. ... Bruised eye (February 27, 1997); missed five games. ... Sprained left knee (March 26, 1998); missed eight games.

MISCELLANEOUS: Member of Stanley Cup championship team (1995).

STATISTICAL PLATEAUS: Three-goal games: 1996-97 (1), 1997-98 (1). Total: 2.

		REGULAR SEASON								PLAYOFFS				
Season Team	League	Gms.	G	A	Pts.	PIM	+/-	PP	SH	Gms.	G	A	Pts.	PIM
84-85—Michigan Tech	WCHA	25	4	5	9	32	...	...	...	—	—	—	—	—
85-86—Michigan Tech	WCHA	40	12	22	34	46	...	...	...	—	—	—	—	—
86-87—Michigan Tech	WCHA	39	5	11	16	46	...	...	...	—	—	—	—	—
87-88—Michigan Tech	WCHA	41	17	24	41	70	...	...	...	—	—	—	—	—
—Adirondack	AHL	10	0	3	3	12	...	...	...	6	0	4	4	0
88-89—Adirondack	AHL	58	29	34	63	170	...	...	...	14	4	7	11	60
—Detroit	NHL	3	0	0	0	0	-1	0	0	2	0	0	0	2
89-90—Detroit	NHL	33	3	6	9	51	1	0	0	—	—	—	—	—
—Adirondack	AHL	36	16	23	39	99	...	...	...	6	3	0	3	35
90-91—Detroit	NHL	47	1	7	8	183	-15	0	0	5	0	1	1	41
91-92—New Jersey	NHL	80	17	16	33	246	6	2	0	7	1	3	4	10
92-93—New Jersey	NHL	73	11	11	22	206	0	1	0	5	0	0	0	16
93-94—New Jersey	NHL	78	12	15	27	244	24	0	0	20	1	2	3	24
94-95—New Jersey	NHL	33	5	7	12	44	10	0	0	19	8	4	12	11
95-96—New Jersey	NHL	76	11	10	21	145	7	3	0	—	—	—	—	—
96-97—New Jersey	NHL	77	9	18	27	109	15	0	0	10	1	1	2	0
97-98—New Jersey	NHL	74	24	24	48	86	30	8	0	6	0	1	1	0
NHL Totals (10 years)		574	93	114	207	1314	77	14	0	74	11	12	23	104

McKEE, JAY — D — SABRES

PERSONAL: Born September 8, 1977, in Kingston, Ont. ... 6-3/195. ... Shoots left.

HIGH SCHOOL: Stamford (Niagara Falls, Ont.).

TRANSACTIONS/CAREER NOTES: Selected by Buffalo Sabres in first round (first Sabres pick, 14th overall) of NHL entry draft (July 8, 1995). ... Bruised stomach (March 29, 1998); missed two games.

HONORS: Named to OHL All-Star second team (1995-96).

M

Season Team	League	REGULAR SEASON								PLAYOFFS				
		Gms.	G	A	Pts.	PIM	+/-	PP	SH	Gms.	G	A	Pts.	PIM
92-93—Ernestown	Jr. C	36	0	17	17	37	...	...	...	—	—	—	—	—
93-94—Sudbury	OHL	51	0	1	1	51	...	...	...	3	0	0	0	0
94-95—Sudbury	OHL	39	6	6	12	91	...	...	...	—	—	—	—	—
—Niagara Falls	OHL	26	3	13	16	60	...	...	...	6	2	3	5	10
95-96—Niagara Falls	OHL	64	5	41	46	129	...	...	...	10	1	5	6	16
—Rochester	AHL	4	0	1	1	15	...	...	...	—	—	—	—	—
—Buffalo	NHL	1	0	1	1	2	1	0	0	—	—	—	—	—
96-97—Buffalo	NHL	43	1	9	10	35	3	0	0	3	0	0	0	0
—Rochester	AHL	7	2	5	7	4	...	...	...	—	—	—	—	—
97-98—Buffalo	NHL	56	1	13	14	42	-1	0	0	1	0	0	0	0
—Rochester	AHL	13	1	7	8	11	...	...	...	—	—	—	—	—
NHL Totals (3 years)		100	2	23	25	79	3	0	0	4	0	0	0	0

McKENNA, STEVE — LW — KINGS

PERSONAL: Born August 21, 1973, in Hespeler, Ont. ... 6-8/247. ... Shoots left.
COLLEGE: Merrimack (Mass.).
TRANSACTIONS/CAREER NOTES: Signed as free agent by Los Angeles Kings (May 17, 1996).

Season Team	League	REGULAR SEASON								PLAYOFFS				
		Gms.	G	A	Pts.	PIM	+/-	PP	SH	Gms.	G	A	Pts.	PIM
93-94—Merrimack College	Hockey East	37	1	2	3	74	...	...	...	—	—	—	—	—
94-95—Merrimack College	Hockey East	37	1	9	10	74	...	...	...	—	—	—	—	—
95-96—Merrimack College	Hockey East	33	3	11	14	67	...	...	...	—	—	—	—	—
96-97—Phoenix	IHL	66	6	5	11	187	...	...	...	—	—	—	—	—
—Los Angeles	NHL	9	0	0	0	37	1	0	0	—	—	—	—	—
97-98—Fredericton	AHL	6	2	1	3	48	...	...	...	—	—	—	—	—
—Los Angeles	NHL	62	4	4	8	150	-9	1	0	3	0	1	1	8
NHL Totals (2 years)		71	4	4	8	187	-8	1	0	3	0	1	1	8

McKENZIE, JIM — LW — MIGHTY DUCKS

PERSONAL: Born November 3, 1969, in Gull Lake, Sask. ... 6-3/205. ... Shoots left.
TRANSACTIONS/CAREER NOTES: Selected by Hartford Whalers in fourth round (third Whalers pick, 73rd overall) of NHL entry draft (June 17, 1989). ... Injured elbow (January 31, 1992); missed two games. ... Suffered hip flexor (November 11, 1992); missed three games. ... Suffered hip flexor (December 5, 1992); missed four games. ... Suffered back spasms (January 24, 1993); missed three games. ... Suspended two games by NHL for game misconduct penalties (April 3, 1993). ... Suspended three games by NHL for game misconduct penalties (April 10, 1993). ... Traded by Whalers to Florida Panthers for D Alexander Godynyuk (December 16, 1993). ... Traded by Panthers to Dallas Stars for fourth-round pick (LW Jamie Wright) in 1994 draft (December 16, 1993). ... Traded by Stars to Pittsburgh Penguins for RW Mike Needham (March 21, 1994). ... Broke toe (November 24, 1993); missed four games. ... Bruised hand (March 11, 1995); missed one game. ... Sprained wrist (April 5, 1995); missed seven games. ... Signed as free agent by New York Islanders (July 31, 1995). ... Claimed by Winnipeg Jets in NHL waiver draft (October 2, 1995). ... Jets franchise moved to Phoenix and renamed Coyotes for 1996-97 season; NHL approved move on January 18, 1996. ... Fractured leg (November 8, 1996); missed five games. ... Suffered from the flu (January 27, 1997); missed one game. ... Fractured leg (December 23, 1997); missed 11 games. ... Traded by Coyotes to Mighty Ducks of Anaheim for C J.F. Jomphe (June 18, 1998).
STATISTICAL PLATEAUS: Three-goal games: 1996-97 (1).

Season Team	League	REGULAR SEASON								PLAYOFFS				
		Gms.	G	A	Pts.	PIM	+/-	PP	SH	Gms.	G	A	Pts.	PIM
85-86—Moose Jaw	WHL	3	0	2	2	0	...	...	...	—	—	—	—	—
86-87—Moose Jaw	WHL	65	5	3	8	125	...	...	...	9	0	0	0	7
87-88—Moose Jaw	WHL	62	1	17	18	134	...	...	...	—	—	—	—	—
88-89—Victoria	WHL	67	15	27	42	176	...	...	...	8	1	4	5	30
89-90—Binghamton	AHL	56	4	12	16	149	...	...	...	—	—	—	—	—
—Hartford	NHL	5	0	0	0	4	0	0	0	—	—	—	—	—
90-91—Springfield	AHL	24	3	4	7	102	...	...	...	—	—	—	—	—
—Hartford	NHL	41	4	3	7	108	-7	0	0	6	0	0	0	8
91-92—Hartford	NHL	67	5	1	6	87	-6	0	0	—	—	—	—	—
92-93—Hartford	NHL	64	3	6	9	202	-10	0	0	—	—	—	—	—
93-94—Hartford	NHL	26	1	2	3	67	-6	0	0	—	—	—	—	—
—Dallas	NHL	34	2	3	5	63	4	0	0	—	—	—	—	—
—Pittsburgh	NHL	11	0	0	0	16	-5	0	0	3	0	0	0	0
94-95—Pittsburgh	NHL	39	2	1	3	63	-7	0	0	5	0	0	0	4
95-96—Winnipeg	NHL	73	4	2	6	202	-4	0	0	1	0	0	0	2
96-97—Phoenix	NHL	65	5	3	8	200	-5	0	0	7	0	0	0	2
97-98—Phoenix	NHL	64	3	4	7	146	-7	0	0	1	0	0	0	0
NHL Totals (9 years)		489	29	25	54	1158	-53	0	0	23	0	0	0	16

McKERCHER, JEFF — D — STARS

PERSONAL: Born January 14, 1979, in Cornwall, Ont. ... 6-2/196. ... Shoots right.
TRANSACTIONS/CAREER NOTES: Selected by Dallas Stars in seventh round (seventh Stars pick, 189th overall) of NHL entry draft (June 21, 1997).

Season Team	League	REGULAR SEASON								PLAYOFFS				
		Gms.	G	A	Pts.	PIM	+/-	PP	SH	Gms.	G	A	Pts.	PIM
95-96—Cornwall	Jr. A	53	1	17	18	40	...	...	...	—	—	—	—	—
96-97—Barrie	OHL	60	1	4	5	32	...	...	...	9	0	1	1	13
97-98—Barrie	OHL	51	0	2	2	21	...	...	...	6	0	0	0	2

McLAREN, KYLE　　　　　　　　D　　　　　　　　BRUINS

PERSONAL: Born June 18, 1977, in Humboldt, Sask. ... 6-4/219. ... Shoots left.

TRANSACTIONS/CAREER NOTES: Selected by Boston Bruins in first round (first Bruins pick, ninth overall) of NHL entry draft (July 8, 1995). ... Injured back (November 21, 1995); missed one game. ... Injured knee (November 25, 1995); missed five games. ... Suffered from the flu (January 3, 1996); missed one game. ... Suffered concussion (March 10, 1996); missed one game. ... Suffered from charley horse (October 26, 1996); missed two games. ... Strained shoulder (February 2, 1997); missed 13 games. ... Injured foot (March 15, 1997); missed one game. ... Sprained thumb (March 27, 1997); missed final seven games of season. ... Suffered hip pointer (November 1, 1997); missed five games. ... Injured knee (December 17, 1997); missed one game. ... Fractured foot (March 19, 1998); missed seven games. ... Strained groin (April 7, 1998); missed three games.

HONORS: Named to NHL All-Rookie team (1995-96).

		REGULAR SEASON								PLAYOFFS				
Season Team	League	Gms.	G	A	Pts.	PIM	+/-	PP	SH	Gms.	G	A	Pts.	PIM
93-94—Tacoma	WHL	62	1	9	10	53	...	...	...	6	1	4	5	6
94-95—Tacoma	WHL	47	13	19	32	68	...	...	...	4	1	1	2	4
95-96—Boston	NHL	74	5	12	17	73	16	0	0	5	0	0	0	14
96-97—Boston	NHL	58	5	9	14	54	-9	0	0	—	—	—	—	—
97-98—Boston	NHL	66	5	20	25	56	13	2	0	6	1	0	1	4
NHL Totals (3 years)		198	15	41	56	183	20	2	0	11	1	0	1	18

McLEAN, KIRK　　　　　　　　G　　　　　　　　PANTHERS

PERSONAL: Born June 26, 1966, in Willowdale, Ont. ... 6-0/180. ... Catches left. ... Name pronounced muh-KLAYN.

TRANSACTIONS/CAREER NOTES: Selected by New Jersey Devils as underage junior in sixth round (sixth Devils pick, 107th overall) of NHL entry draft (June 9, 1984). ... Traded by Devils with C Greg Adams and second-round pick (D Leif Rohlin) in 1988 draft to Vancouver Canucks for C Patrik Sundstrom, second- (LW Jeff Christian) and fourth- (LW Matt Ruchty) round picks in 1988 draft (September 15, 1987). ... Suffered tendinitis in left wrist (February 25, 1991). ... Injured knee (January 13, 1996); missed 18 games. ... Injured knee (November 11, 1996); missed 19 games. ... Injured finger (March 5, 1997); missed nine games. ... Traded by Canucks to Hurricanes with LW Martin Gelinas for LW Geoff Sanderson, D Enrico Ciccone and G Sean Burke (January 3, 1998). ... Traded by Hurricanes to Florida Panthers for RW Ray Sheppard (March 24, 1998).

HONORS: Played in NHL All-Star Game (1990 and 1992). ... Named to THE SPORTING NEWS All-Star second team (1991-92). ... Named to NHL All-Star second team (1991-92).

RECORDS: Holds NHL single-season playoff record for most minutes played by a goaltender—1,544 (1994).

MISCELLANEOUS: Holds Vancouver Canucks all-time record for most games played by goalie (516), most wins (211), goals-against average (3.17) and most shutouts (20). ... Stopped penalty shot attempt (vs. Brent Gilchrist, January 27, 1994). ... Allowed penalty shot goal (vs. Brent Ashton, December 11, 1988; vs. Mike Donnelly, November 12, 1992; vs. Andrei Kovalenko, December 4, 1993).

		REGULAR SEASON								PLAYOFFS						
Season Team	League	Gms.	Min	W	L	T	GA	SO	Avg.	Gms.	Min.	W	L	GA	SO	Avg.
83-84—Oshawa	OHL	17	940	5	9	0	67	0	4.28	—	—	—	—	—	—	—
84-85—Oshawa	OHL	47	2581	23	17	2	143	1	*3.32	5	271	1	3	21	0	4.65
85-86—Oshawa	OHL	51	2830	24	21	2	169	1	3.58	4	201	1	2	18	0	5.37
—New Jersey	NHL	2	111	1	1	0	11	0	5.95	—	—	—	—	—	—	—
86-87—New Jersey	NHL	4	160	1	1	0	10	0	3.75	—	—	—	—	—	—	—
—Maine	AHL	45	2606	15	23	4	140	1	3.22	—	—	—	—	—	—	—
87-88—Vancouver	NHL	41	2380	11	27	3	147	1	3.71	—	—	—	—	—	—	—
88-89—Vancouver	NHL	42	2477	20	17	3	127	4	3.08	5	302	2	3	18	0	3.58
89-90—Vancouver	NHL	*63	*3739	21	30	10	*216	0	3.47	—	—	—	—	—	—	—
90-91—Vancouver	NHL	41	1969	10	22	3	131	0	3.99	2	123	1	1	7	0	3.41
91-92—Vancouver	NHL	65	3852	†38	17	9	176	†5	2.74	13	785	6	7	33	†2	2.52
92-93—Vancouver	NHL	54	3261	28	21	5	184	3	3.39	12	754	6	6	42	0	3.34
93-94—Vancouver	NHL	52	3128	23	26	3	156	3	2.99	24	*1544	15	†9	59	†4	2.29
94-95—Vancouver	NHL	40	2374	18	12	10	109	1	2.75	11	660	4	†7	36	0	3.27
95-96—Vancouver	NHL	45	2645	15	21	9	156	2	3.54	1	21	0	1	3	0	8.57
96-97—Vancouver	NHL	44	2581	21	18	3	138	0	3.21	—	—	—	—	—	—	—
97-98—Vancouver	NHL	29	1583	6	17	4	97	1	3.68	—	—	—	—	—	—	—
—Carolina	NHL	8	401	4	2	0	22	0	3.29	—	—	—	—	—	—	—
—Florida	NHL	7	406	4	2	1	22	0	3.25	—	—	—	—	—	—	—
NHL Totals (13 years)		537	31067	221	234	63	1702	20	3.29	68	4189	34	34	198	6	2.84

McLENNAN, JAMIE　　　　　　　　G　　　　　　　　BLUES

PERSONAL: Born June 30, 1971, in Edmonton. ... 6-0/192. ... Catches left.

TRANSACTIONS/CAREER NOTES: Selected by New York Islanders in third round (third Islanders pick, 48th overall) of NHL entry draft (June 22, 1991). ... Signed as free agent by St. Louis Blues (July 3, 1996). ... Strained groin (October 29, 1997); missed two games. ... Strained groin (March 22, 1998); missed one game.

HONORS: Won Del Wilson Trophy (1990-91). ... Named to WHL (East) All-Star first team (1990-91). ... Won Bill Masterton Memorial Trophy (1997-98).

		REGULAR SEASON								PLAYOFFS						
Season Team	League	Gms.	Min	W	L	T	GA	SO	Avg.	Gms.	Min.	W	L	GA	SO	Avg.
88-89—Spokane	WHL	11	578	...	...	...	63	0	6.54	—	—	—	—	—	—	—
—Lethbridge	WHL	7	368	...	...	...	22	0	3.59	—	—	—	—	—	—	—
89-90—Lethbridge	WHL	34	1690	20	4	2	110	1	3.91	13	677	6	5	44	0	3.90
90-91—Lethbridge	WHL	56	3230	32	18	4	205	0	3.81	*16	*970	8	8	*56	0	3.46
91-92—Capital District	AHL	18	952	4	10	2	60	1	3.78	—	—	—	—	—	—	—
—Richmond	ECHL	32	1837	16	12	†2	114	0	3.72	—	—	—	—	—	—	—
92-93—Capital District	AHL	38	2171	17	14	6	117	1	3.23	1	20	0	1	5	0	15.00
93-94—Salt Lake City	IHL	24	1320	8	12	†2	80	0	3.64	—	—	—	—	—	—	—
—New York Islanders	NHL	22	1287	8	7	6	61	0	2.84	2	82	0	1	6	0	4.39

M

Season Team	League	REGULAR SEASON								PLAYOFFS						
		Gms.	Min	W	L	T	GA	SO	Avg.	Gms.	Min.	W	L	GA	SO	Avg.
94-95—New York Islanders	NHL	21	1185	6	11	2	67	0	3.39	—	—	—	—	—	—	—
—Denver	IHL	4	240	3	0	‡1	12	0	3.00	11	641	8	2	23	1	*2.15
95-96—Utah	IHL	14	728	9	2	2	29	0	2.39	—	—	—	—	—	—	—
—New York Islanders	NHL	13	636	3	9	1	39	0	3.68	—	—	—	—	—	—	—
—Worcester	AHL	22	1215	14	7	1	57	0	2.81	2	118	0	2	8	0	4.07
96-97—Worcester	AHL	39	2152	18	13	4	100	2	2.79	4	262	2	2	16	0	3.66
97-98—St. Louis	NHL	30	1658	16	8	2	60	2	2.17	1	14	0	0	1	0	4.29
NHL Totals (4 years)		86	4766	33	35	11	227	2	2.86	3	96	0	1	7	0	4.38

McMAHON, MARK · D · HURRICANES

PERSONAL: Born February 10, 1978, in Geraldton, Ont. ... 6-2/186. ... Shoots left.
TRANSACTIONS/CAREER NOTES: Selected by Hartford Whalers in fifth round (fifth Whalers pick, 116th overall) of NHL entry draft (June 22, 1996). ... Whalers franchise moved to North Carolina and renamed Carolina Hurricanes for 1997-98 season; NHL approved move on June 25, 1997.

Season Team	League	REGULAR SEASON								PLAYOFFS				
		Gms.	G	A	Pts.	PIM	+/-	PP	SH	Gms.	G	A	Pts.	PIM
94-95—Elmira Jr. B	OHA	41	3	10	13	91	...	...	...	—	—	—	—	—
95-96—Kitchener	OHL	55	1	8	9	105	...	...	...	5	0	1	1	17
96-97—Kitchener	OHL	63	4	18	22	155	...	...	...	13	0	6	6	31
97-98—Kitchener	OHL	61	12	38	50	175	...	...	...	6	1	5	6	27
—New Haven	AHL	4	0	1	1	6	...	...	...	2	0	0	0	16

McSORLEY, MARTY · D

PERSONAL: Born May 18, 1963, in Hamilton, Ont. ... 6-2/230. ... Shoots right. ... Full name: Martin James McSorley.
TRANSACTIONS/CAREER NOTES: Signed as free agent by Pittsburgh Penguins (April 1983). ... Traded by Penguins with C Tim Hrynewich to Edmonton Oilers for G Gilles Meloche (August 1985). ... Suspended by NHL for AHL incident (March 1987). ... Sprained knee (November 1987). ... Suspended three playoff games by NHL for spearing (April 23, 1988). ... Traded by Oilers with C Wayne Gretzky and LW/C Mike Krushelnyski to Los Angeles Kings for C Jimmy Carson, LW Martin Gelinas, first-round picks in 1989 (traded to New Jersey), 1991 (LW Martin Rucinsky) and 1993 (D Nick Stajduhar) drafts and cash (August 9, 1988). ... Injured shoulder (December 31, 1988). ... Sprained knee (February 1989). ... Suspended four games by NHL for game-misconduct penalties (1989-90). ... Twisted right knee (October 14, 1990); missed four games. ... Twisted ankle (February 9, 1991). ... Suspended three games by NHL for striking another player with a gloved hand (March 2, 1991). ... Suffered from throat virus (November 23, 1991); missed six games. ... Sprained shoulder (February 19, 1992); missed three games. ... Suspended six off-days and fined $500 by NHL for cross-checking (October 31, 1992). ... Suspended one game by NHL for game-misconduct penalties (November 27, 1992). ... Traded by Kings to Pittsburgh Penguins for C Shawn McEachern (August 27, 1993). ... Sprained ankle (November 16, 1993); missed eight games. ... Traded by Penguins with D Jim Paek to Los Angeles Kings for RW Thomas Sandstrom and C Shawn McEachern (February 15, 1993). ... Suspended four games without pay and fined $500 for eye-gouging incident (February 23, 1994). ... Sprained abdomen (April 7, 1994); missed remainder of season. ... Strained groin (February 12, 1995); missed seven games. ... Strained groin (January 5, 1996); missed six games. ... Bruised left thigh (February 28, 1996); missed 11 games. ... Traded by Kings with RW Shane Churla and LW Jari Kurri to New York Rangers for C Ray Ferraro, C Nathan Lafayette, C Ian Laperriere, D Mattias Norstrom and fourth-round pick (D Sean Blanchard) in 1997 draft (March 14, 1996). ... Injured groin (April 4, 1996); missed four games. ... Injured groin (April 12, 1996); missed one game. ... Traded by Rangers to San Jose Sharks for D Jayson More, C Brian Swanson and fourth-round pick (D Tomi Kallarsson) in 1997 draft (August 20, 1996). ... Underwent hip surgery (September 10, 1996); missed 17 games. ... Injured groin (November 16, 1996); missed five games. ... Reinjured groin (January 2, 1997); missed three games. ... Strained knee (October 9, 1997); missed three games. ... Strained groin (October 29, 1997); missed three games.
HONORS: Shared Alka-Seltzer Plus Award with Theoren Fleury (1990-91).
MISCELLANEOUS: Member of Stanley Cup championship team (1987 and 1988). ... Holds Los Angeles Kings all-time record for penalty minutes (1,846).

M

Season Team	League	REGULAR SEASON								PLAYOFFS				
		Gms.	G	A	Pts.	PIM	+/-	PP	SH	Gms.	G	A	Pts.	PIM
81-82—Belleville	OHL	58	6	13	19	234	...	...	...	—	—	—	—	—
82-83—Belleville	OHL	70	10	41	51	183	...	...	...	4	0	0	0	7
—Baltimore	AHL	2	0	0	0	22	...	...	...	—	—	—	—	—
83-84—Pittsburgh	NHL	72	2	7	9	224	-39	0	0	—	—	—	—	—
84-85—Baltimore	AHL	58	6	24	30	154	...	...	...	14	0	7	7	47
—Pittsburgh	NHL	15	0	0	0	15	-3	0	0	—	—	—	—	—
85-86—Edmonton	NHL	59	11	12	23	265	9	0	0	8	0	2	2	50
—Nova Scotia	AHL	9	2	4	6	34	...	...	...	—	—	—	—	—
86-87—Edmonton	NHL	41	2	4	6	159	-4	0	0	21	4	3	7	65
—Nova Scotia	AHL	7	2	2	4	48	...	...	...	—	—	—	—	—
87-88—Edmonton	NHL	60	9	17	26	223	23	0	0	16	0	3	3	67
88-89—Los Angeles	NHL	66	10	17	27	350	3	2	0	11	0	2	2	33
89-90—Los Angeles	NHL	75	15	21	36	322	2	2	1	10	1	3	4	18
90-91—Los Angeles	NHL	61	7	32	39	221	†48	1	1	12	0	0	0	58
91-92—Los Angeles	NHL	71	7	22	29	268	-13	2	1	6	1	0	1	21
92-93—Los Angeles	NHL	81	15	26	41	*399	1	3	3	24	4	6	10	60
93-94—Pittsburgh	NHL	47	3	18	21	139	-9	0	0	—	—	—	—	—
—Los Angeles	NHL	18	4	6	10	55	-3	1	0	—	—	—	—	—
94-95—Los Angeles	NHL	41	3	18	21	83	-14	1	0	—	—	—	—	—
95-96—Los Angeles	NHL	59	10	21	31	148	-14	1	1	—	—	—	—	—
—New York Rangers	NHL	9	0	2	2	21	-6	0	0	4	0	0	0	0
96-97—San Jose	NHL	57	4	12	16	186	-6	0	1	—	—	—	—	—
97-98—San Jose	NHL	56	2	10	12	140	10	0	0	—	—	—	—	—
NHL Totals (15 years)		888	104	245	349	3218	-15	13	8	112	10	19	29	372

MELICHAR, JOSEF — D — PENGUINS

PERSONAL: Born January 20, 1979, in Ceske Budejovice, Czechoslovakia. ... 6-3/198. ... Shoots left.
TRANSACTIONS/CAREER NOTES: Selected by Pittsburgh Penguins in third round (third Penguins pick, 71st overall) of NHL entry draft (June 21, 1997).

		REGULAR SEASON								PLAYOFFS				
Season Team	League	Gms.	G	A	Pts.	PIM	+/-	PP	SH	Gms.	G	A	Pts.	PIM
95-96—Ceske Budejovice........	Czech Rep.	38	3	4	7	...	...	...	...	—	—	—	—	—
96-97—Ceske Budejovice........	Czech Rep.	41	2	3	5	10	...	...	...	—	—	—	—	—
97-98—Tri-City	WHL	67	9	24	33	152	...	...	...	—	—	—	—	—

MELLANBY, SCOTT — RW — PANTHERS

PERSONAL: Born June 11, 1966, in Montreal. ... 6-1/199. ... Shoots right. ... Full name: Scott Edgar Mellanby.
HIGH SCHOOL: Henry Carr (Rexdale, Ont.).
COLLEGE: Wisconsin.
TRANSACTIONS/CAREER NOTES: Selected by Philadelphia Flyers as underage junior in second round (first Flyers pick, 27th overall) of NHL entry draft (June 9, 1984). ... Lacerated right index finger (October 1987). ... Severed nerve and damaged tendon in left forearm (August 1989); missed first 20 games of season. ... Suffered viral infection (November 1989). ... Traded by Flyers with LW Craig Berube and C Craig Fisher to Edmonton Oilers for RW Dave Brown, D Corey Foster and rights to RW Jari Kurri (May 30, 1991). ... Injured shoulder (February 14, 1993); missed 15 games. ... Selected by Florida Panthers in NHL expansion draft (June 24, 1993). ... Fractured nose and lacerated face (February 1, 1994); missed four games. ... Fractured finger (March 7, 1996); missed three games. ... Sprained left knee (January 9, 1998); missed three games.
HONORS: Played in NHL All-Star Game (1996).
MISCELLANEOUS: Holds Florida Panthers all-time records for most goals (117), most assists (133) and most points (250), and tied for most games played (289). ... Captain of Florida Panthers (1997-98).

		REGULAR SEASON								PLAYOFFS				
Season Team	League	Gms.	G	A	Pts.	PIM	+/-	PP	SH	Gms.	G	A	Pts.	PIM
83-84—Henry Carr H.S.	MTHL	39	37	37	74	97	...	...	...	—	—	—	—	—
84-85—Univ. of Wisconsin......	WCHA	40	14	24	38	60	...	...	...	—	—	—	—	—
85-86—Univ. of Wisconsin......	WCHA	32	21	23	44	89	...	...	...	—	—	—	—	—
—Philadelphia	NHL	2	0	0	0	0	-1	0	0	—	—	—	—	—
86-87—Philadelphia	NHL	71	11	21	32	94	8	1	0	24	5	5	10	46
87-88—Philadelphia	NHL	75	25	26	51	185	-7	7	0	7	0	1	1	16
88-89—Philadelphia	NHL	76	21	29	50	183	-13	11	0	19	4	5	9	28
89-90—Philadelphia	NHL	57	6	17	23	77	-4	0	0	—	—	—	—	—
90-91—Philadelphia	NHL	74	20	21	41	155	8	5	0	—	—	—	—	—
91-92—Edmonton	NHL	80	23	27	50	197	5	7	0	16	2	1	3	29
92-93—Edmonton	NHL	69	15	17	32	147	-4	6	0	—	—	—	—	—
93-94—Florida........................	NHL	80	30	30	60	149	0	17	0	—	—	—	—	—
94-95—Florida........................	NHL	48	13	12	25	90	-16	4	0	—	—	—	—	—
95-96—Florida........................	NHL	79	32	38	70	160	4	19	0	22	3	6	9	44
96-97—Florida........................	NHL	82	27	29	56	170	7	9	1	5	0	2	2	4
97-98—Florida........................	NHL	79	15	24	39	127	-14	6	0	—	—	—	—	—
NHL Totals (13 years).........		872	238	291	529	1734	-27	92	1	93	14	20	34	167

MELOCHE, ERIC — RW — PENGUINS

PERSONAL: Born May 1, 1976, in Montreal. ... 5-11/195. ... Shoots right.
COLLEGE: Ohio State.
TRANSACTIONS/CAREER NOTES: Selected by Pittsburgh Penguins in seventh round (seventh Penguins pick, 186th overall) of 1996 NHL entry draft.

		REGULAR SEASON								PLAYOFFS				
Season Team	League	Gms.	G	A	Pts.	PIM	+/-	PP	SH	Gms.	G	A	Pts.	PIM
95-96—Cornwall	Tier II	64	68	53	121	162	...	...	...	—	—	—	—	—
96-97—Ohio State..................	CCHA	39	12	11	23	78	...	...	...	—	—	—	—	—
97-98—Ohio State..................	CCHA	42	26	22	48	86	...	...	...	—	—	—	—	—

MESSIER, ERIC — D — AVALANCHE

PERSONAL: Born October 29, 1973, in Drummondville, Que. ... 6-2/200. ... Shoots left. ... Name pronounced MEHZ-yay.
TRANSACTIONS/CAREER NOTES: Signed as free agent by Colorado Avalanche (October 1, 1995). ... Sprained ankle (October 28, 1997); missed three games.

		REGULAR SEASON								PLAYOFFS				
Season Team	League	Gms.	G	A	Pts.	PIM	+/-	PP	SH	Gms.	G	A	Pts.	PIM
91-92—Troise Rivieres	QMJHL	58	2	10	12	28	...	...	...	15	2	2	4	13
92-93—Sherbrooke	QMJHL	51	4	17	21	82	...	...	...	15	0	4	4	18
93-94—Sherbrooke	QMJHL	67	4	24	28	69	...	...	...	12	1	7	8	14
94-95—					Statistics unavailable.									
95-96—Cornwall	AHL	72	5	9	14	111	...	...	...	8	1	1	2	20
96-97—Hershey	AHL	55	16	26	42	69	...	...	...	9	3	8	11	14
—Colorado	NHL	21	0	0	0	4	7	0	0	—	—	—	—	—
97-98—Colorado	NHL	62	4	12	16	20	4	0	0	—	—	—	—	—
NHL Totals (2 years)...........		83	4	12	16	24	11	0	0					

PERSONAL: Born January 18, 1961, in Edmonton. ... 6-1/205. ... Shoots left. ... Full name: Mark Douglas Messier. ... Brother of Paul Messier, center with Colorado Rockies (1978-79); cousin of Mitch Messier, center/right winger, Dallas Stars system; cousin of Joby Messier, defenseman with New York Rangers (1992-93 through 1994-95); and brother-in-law of John Blum, defenseman with four NHL teams (1982-83 through 1989-90). ... Name pronounced MEHZ-yay.

TRANSACTIONS/CAREER NOTES: Given five-game trial by Indianapolis Racers (November 1978). ... Signed as free agent by Cincinnati Stingers of WHA (January 1979). ... Selected by Edmonton Oilers in third round (second Oilers pick, 48th overall) of NHL entry draft (August 9, 1979). ... Injured ankle (November 7, 1981). ... Chipped bone in wrist (March 1983). ... Suspended six games by NHL for hitting another player with stick (January 18, 1984). ... Sprained knee ligaments (November 1984). ... Suspended 10 games by NHL for injuring another player (December 26, 1984). ... Bruised left foot (December 3, 1985); missed 17 games. ... Suspended and fined by Oilers after refusing to report to training camp (October 1987); missed three weeks of camp. ... Suspended six games by NHL for injuring another player with his stick (October 23, 1988). ... Twisted left knee (January 28, 1989). ... Strained right knee (February 3, 1989). ... Bruised left knee (February 12, 1989). ... Sprained left knee ligaments (October 16, 1990); missed 10 games. ... Reinjured left knee (December 12, 1990); missed three games. ... Reinjured knee (December 22, 1990); missed nine games. ... Broke left thumb (February 11, 1991); missed eight games. ... Missed one game due to contract dispute (October 1991). ... Traded by Oilers with future considerations to New York Rangers for C Bernie Nicholls, LW Louie DeBrusk, RW Steven Rice and future considerations (October 4, 1991); Oilers traded C Jeff Beukeboom to Rangers for D David Shaw to complete deal (November 12, 1991). ... Sprained ligament in wrist (January 19, 1993); missed six games. ... Strained rib cage muscle (February 27, 1993); missed two games. ... Strained rib cage muscle (March 11, 1993); missed one game. ... Suspended three off-days and fined $500 by NHL for stick-swinging incident (March 18, 1993). ... Sprained wrist (December 22, 1993); missed six games. ... Bruised thigh (March 16, 1994); missed two games. ... Suffered back spasms (April 30, 1995); missed two games. ... Bruised shoulder (February 27, 1996); missed two games. ... Bruised ribs (April 4, 1996); missed six games. ... Suspended two games and fined $1,000 by NHL for checking opponent from behind (October 8, 1996). ... Hyperextended elbow (December 7, 1996); missed four games. ... Suffered back spasms (February 23, 1997); missed two games. ... Suffered charley horse (March 27, 1997); missed two games. ... Signed as free agent by Vancouver Canucks (July 28, 1997).

HONORS: Named to THE SPORTING NEWS All-Star first team (1981-82, 1982-83, 1989-90 and 1991-92). ... Named to NHL All-Star first team (1981-82, 1982-83, 1989-90 and 1991-92). ... Played in NHL All-Star Game (1982-1984, 1986, 1988-1992, 1994 and 1996-1998). ... Won Conn Smythe Trophy (1983-84). ... Named to NHL All-Star second team (1983-84). ... Named to THE SPORTING NEWS All-Star second team (1986-87). ... Named NHL Player of the Year by THE SPORTING NEWS (1989-90 and 1991-92). ... Won Hart Memorial Trophy (1989-90 and 1991-92). ... Won Lester B. Pearson Award (1989-90 and 1991-92).

RECORDS: Holds NHL career playoff record for most shorthanded goals—11; and most games—236.. ... Shares NHL single-game playoff record for most shorthanded goals—2 (April 21, 1992).

STATISTICAL PLATEAUS: Three-goal games: 1980-81 (1), 1981-82 (2), 1982-83 (1), 1983-84 (2), 1985-86 (1), 1987-88 (1), 1989-90 (2), 1991-92 (2), 1995-96 (1), 1996-97 (2). Total: 15. ... Four-goal games: 1982-83 (1), 1988-89 (1), 1989-90 (1), 1991-92 (1). Total: 4. ... Total hat tricks: 19.

MISCELLANEOUS: Member of Stanley Cup championship team (1984, 1985, 1987, 1988, 1990 and 1994). ... Captain of Edmonton Oilers (1988-89 through 1990-91). ... Captain of New York Rangers (1991-92 through 1996-97). ... Captain of Vancouver Canucks (1997-98).

		REGULAR SEASON								PLAYOFFS				
Season Team	League	Gms.	G	A	Pts.	PIM	+/-	PP	SH	Gms.	G	A	Pts.	PIM
76-77—Spruce Grove	AJHL	57	27	39	66	91	...	...	...	—	—	—	—	—
77-78—St. Albert	AJHL					Statistics unavailable.								
—Portland	WHL	—	—	—	—	—	...	...	...	7	4	1	5	2
78-79—Indianapolis	WHA	5	0	0	0	0	...	...	...	—	—	—	—	—
—Cincinnati	WHA	47	1	10	11	58	...	...	...	—	—	—	—	—
79-80—Houston	CHL	4	0	3	3	4	...	...	...	—	—	—	—	—
—Edmonton	NHL	75	12	21	33	120	...	1	1	3	1	2	3	2
80-81—Edmonton	NHL	72	23	40	63	102	-12	4	0	9	2	5	7	13
81-82—Edmonton	NHL	78	50	38	88	119	21	10	0	5	1	2	3	8
82-83—Edmonton	NHL	77	48	58	106	72	19	12	1	15	15	6	21	14
83-84—Edmonton	NHL	73	37	64	101	165	40	7	4	19	8	18	26	19
84-85—Edmonton	NHL	55	23	31	54	57	8	4	5	18	12	13	25	12
85-86—Edmonton	NHL	63	35	49	84	68	36	10	5	10	4	6	10	18
86-87—Edmonton	NHL	77	37	70	107	73	21	7	4	21	12	16	28	16
87-88—Edmonton	NHL	77	37	74	111	103	21	12	3	19	11	23	34	29
88-89—Edmonton	NHL	72	33	61	94	130	-5	6	6	7	1	11	12	8
89-90—Edmonton	NHL	79	45	84	129	79	19	13	6	22	9	*22	†31	20
90-91—Edmonton	NHL	53	12	52	64	34	15	3	1	18	4	11	15	16
91-92—New York Rangers	NHL	79	35	72	107	76	31	12	4	11	7	7	14	6
92-93—New York Rangers	NHL	75	25	66	91	72	-6	7	2	—	—	—	—	—
93-94—New York Rangers	NHL	76	26	58	84	76	25	6	2	23	12	18	30	33
94-95—New York Rangers	NHL	46	14	39	53	40	8	3	3	10	3	10	13	8
95-96—New York Rangers	NHL	74	47	52	99	122	29	14	1	11	4	7	11	16
96-97—New York Rangers	NHL	71	36	48	84	88	12	7	5	15	3	9	12	6
97-98—Vancouver	NHL	82	22	38	60	58	-10	8	2	—	—	—	—	—
WHA Totals (1 year)		52	1	10	11	58	...	...	...					
NHL Totals (19 years)		1354	597	1015	1612	1654	...	146	55	236	109	186	295	244

M

PERSONAL: Born April 26, 1978, in Montreal. ... 6-0/175. ... Shoots right. ... Name pronounced meh-TOH.

TRANSACTIONS/CAREER NOTES: Selected by Buffalo Sabres in third round (fourth Sabres pick, 54th overall) of NHL entry draft (June 22, 1996).

		REGULAR SEASON								PLAYOFFS				
Season Team	League	Gms.	G	A	Pts.	PIM	+/-	PP	SH	Gms.	G	A	Pts.	PIM
94-95—St. Hyacinthe	QMJHL	60	14	38	52	22	...	...	...	5	0	1	1	0
95-96—St. Hyacinthe	QMJHL	68	32	62	94	22	...	...	...	12	6	6	12	4
96-97—Rouyn-Noranda	QMJHL	47	21	30	51	22	...	...	...	—	—	—	—	—
—Shawinigan	QMJHL	18	9	17	26	2	...	...	...	7	2	6	8	2
97-98—Shawinigan	QMJHL	36	23	42	65	10	...	...	...	6	1	3	4	5

MIKA, PETR   LW   ISLANDERS

PERSONAL: Born February 12, 1979, in Prague, Czechoslovakia. ... 6-4/194. ... Shoots right. ... Name pronounced MEE-kuh.
TRANSACTIONS/CAREER NOTES: Selected by New York Islanders in fourth round (sixth Islanders pick, 85th overall) of NHL entry draft (June 21, 1997).

		REGULAR SEASON								PLAYOFFS				
Season Team	League	Gms.	G	A	Pts.	PIM	+/-	PP	SH	Gms.	G	A	Pts.	PIM
95-96—Slavia Praha Jrs..........	Czech. Jrs.	26	5	12	17	...	...	...	...	—	—	—	—	—
—Slavia Praha...............	Czech Rep.	1	0	0	0	...	...	...	...	—	—	—	—	—
96-97—Slavia Praha Jrs..........	Czech. Jrs.	15	8	0	8	...	...	...	...	—	—	—	—	—
—HC Beroun	Czech II	9	1	0	1	...	...	...	...	—	—	—	—	—
—Slavia Praha...............	Czech Rep.	20	1	2	3	6	...	...	...	—	—	—	—	—
97-98—Ottawa	OHL	41	10	8	18	28	...	...	...	—	—	—	—	—

MIKKOLA, ILKKA   D   CANADIENS

PERSONAL: Born January 18, 1979, in Oulu, Finland. ... 6-0/189. ... Shoots left.
TRANSACTIONS/CAREER NOTES: Selected by Montreal Canadiens in third round (third Canadiens pick, 65th overall) of NHL entry draft (June 21, 1997).

		REGULAR SEASON								PLAYOFFS				
Season Team	League	Gms.	G	A	Pts.	PIM	+/-	PP	SH	Gms.	G	A	Pts.	PIM
95-96—Karpat Oulu.................	Finland Dv.II	10	0	4	4	29	...	...	...	2	0	0	0	2
—Karpat Oulu Jrs............	Finland	21	2	3	5	20	...	...	...	—	—	—	—	—
96-97—Karpat Oulu.................	Finland Dv.II	40	7	12	19	32	...	...	...	6	0	0	0	4
97-98—Karpat........................	Finland	28	7	2	9	34	...	...	...	—	—	—	—	—
—Karpat Jrs.	Finland	12	7	6	13	16	...	...	...	—	—	—	—	—

MILLAR, CRAIG   D   OILERS

PERSONAL: Born July 12, 1976, in Winnipeg, Man. ... 6-2/200. ... Shoots left.
TRANSACTIONS/CAREER NOTES: Selected by Buffalo Sabres in ninth round (10th Sabres pick, 225th overall) of NHL entry draft (June 29, 1994). ... Traded by Sabres with LW Barrie Moore to Edmonton Oilers for F Miroslav Satan (March 18, 1997).
HONORS: Named to WHL (Central/East) All-Star first team (1995-96). ... Named to AHL All-Rookie team (1996-97).

		REGULAR SEASON								PLAYOFFS				
Season Team	League	Gms.	G	A	Pts.	PIM	+/-	PP	SH	Gms.	G	A	Pts.	PIM
92-93—Swift Current	WHL	43	2	1	3	8	...	...	...	—	—	—	—	—
93-94—Swift Current	WHL	66	2	9	11	53	...	...	...	—	—	—	—	—
94-95—Swift Current	WHL	72	8	42	50	80	...	...	...	6	1	1	2	10
95-96—Swift Current	WHL	72	31	46	77	151	...	...	...	6	1	0	1	22
96-97—Rochester	AHL	64	7	18	25	65	...	...	...	—	—	—	—	—
—Edmonton..................	NHL	1	0	0	0	2	0	0	0	—	—	—	—	—
—Hamilton....................	AHL	10	1	3	4	10	...	...	...	22	4	4	8	21
97-98—Hamilton....................	AHL	60	10	22	32	113	...	...	...	9	3	1	4	22
—Edmonton..................	NHL	11	4	0	4	8	-3	1	0	—	—	—	—	—
NHL Totals (2 years)...........		12	4	0	4	10	-3	1	0					

MILLER, AARON   D   AVALANCHE

PERSONAL: Born August 11, 1971, in Buffalo. ... 6-3/205. ... Shoots right. ... Full name: Aaron Michael Miller.
COLLEGE: Vermont.
TRANSACTIONS/CAREER NOTES: Selected by New York Rangers in fifth round (sixth Rangers pick, 88th overall) of NHL entry draft (June 17, 1989). ... Traded by Rangers with fifth-round pick (LW Bill Lindsay) in 1991 draft to Quebec Nordiques for D Joe Cirella (January 17, 1991). ... Nordiques franchise moved to Colorado and renamed Avalanche for 1995-96 season (June 21, 1995).
HONORS: Named to ECAC All-Rookie team (1989-90). ... Named to NCAA All-America East second team (1992-93). ... Named to ECAC All-Star first team (1992-93).

		REGULAR SEASON								PLAYOFFS				
Season Team	League	Gms.	G	A	Pts.	PIM	+/-	PP	SH	Gms.	G	A	Pts.	PIM
87-88—Niagara	NAJHL	30	4	9	13	2	...	...	...	—	—	—	—	—
88-89—Niagara	NAJHL	59	24	38	62	60	...	...	...	—	—	—	—	—
89-90—Univ. of Vermont........	ECAC	31	1	15	16	24	...	...	...	—	—	—	—	—
90-91—Univ. of Vermont........	ECAC	30	3	7	10	22	...	...	...	—	—	—	—	—
91-92—Univ. of Vermont........	ECAC	31	3	16	19	36	...	...	...	—	—	—	—	—
92-93—Univ. of Vermont........	ECAC	30	4	13	17	16	...	...	...	—	—	—	—	—
93-94—Cornwall	AHL	64	4	10	14	49	...	...	...	13	0	2	2	10
—Quebec	NHL	1	0	0	0	0	-1	0	0	—	—	—	—	—
94-95—Cornwall	AHL	76	4	18	22	69	...	...	...	—	—	—	—	—
—Quebec	NHL	9	0	3	3	6	2	0	0	—	—	—	—	—
95-96—Cornwall	AHL	62	4	23	27	77	...	...	...	8	0	1	1	6
—Colorado	NHL	5	0	0	0	0	0	0	0	—	—	—	—	—
96-97—Colorado	NHL	56	5	12	17	15	15	0	0	17	1	2	3	10
97-98—Colorado	NHL	55	2	2	4	51	0	0	0	7	0	0	0	8
NHL Totals (5 years)...........		126	7	17	24	72	16	0	0	24	1	2	3	18

MILLER, KELLY   RW   CAPITALS

PERSONAL: Born March 3, 1963, in Lansing, Mich. ... 5-11/195. ... Shoots left. ... Full name: Kelly David Miller. ... Brother of Kevin Miller, left winger, Chicago Blackhawks; and brother of Kip Miller, center, New York Islanders.
HIGH SCHOOL: Eastern (Lansing, Mich.).
COLLEGE: Michigan State.
TRANSACTIONS/CAREER NOTES: Selected by New York Rangers in ninth round (ninth Rangers pick, 183rd overall) of NHL entry draft (June 9, 1982). ... Injured ankle (September 1985). ... Sprained knee (January 27, 1986); missed five games. ... Traded by Rangers with C Mike Ridley and RW Bobby Crawford to Washington Capitals for C Bobby Carpenter and second-round pick (RW Jason Prosofsky) in 1989 draft (January 1, 1987). ... Pulled groin (November 1988). ... Sprained knee (September 22, 1990). ... Strained abdominal muscle and groin (December 14, 1995); missed eight games. ... Sprained knee (March 6, 1997); missed one game. ... Sprained shoulder (March 11, 1997); missed three games. ... Injured knee and shoulder (April 12, 1997); missed one game. ... Injured back (October 1, 1997); missed six games.
HONORS: Named to NCAA All-America West first team (1984-85). ... Named to CCHA All-Star first team (1984-85).
MISCELLANEOUS: Holds Washington Capitals all-time record for most games played (878).

		REGULAR SEASON								PLAYOFFS				
Season Team	League	Gms.	G	A	Pts.	PIM	+/-	PP	SH	Gms.	G	A	Pts.	PIM
81-82—Michigan State...........	CCHA	40	11	19	30	21	...	...	...	—	—	—	—	—
82-83—Michigan State...........	CCHA	36	16	19	35	12	...	...	...	—	—	—	—	—
83-84—Michigan State...........	CCHA	46	28	21	49	12	...	...	...	—	—	—	—	—
84-85—Michigan State...........	CCHA	43	27	23	50	21	...	...	...	—	—	—	—	—
—New York Rangers......	NHL	5	0	2	2	2	-2	0	0	3	0	0	0	2
85-86—New York Rangers......	NHL	74	13	20	33	52	3	0	1	16	3	4	7	4
86-87—New York Rangers......	NHL	38	6	14	20	22	-5	2	0	—	—	—	—	—
—Washington	NHL	39	10	12	22	26	10	3	1	7	2	2	4	0
87-88—Washington	NHL	80	9	23	32	35	9	0	1	14	4	4	8	10
88-89—Washington	NHL	78	19	21	40	45	13	2	1	6	1	0	1	2
89-90—Washington	NHL	80	18	22	40	49	-2	3	2	15	3	5	8	23
90-91—Washington	NHL	80	24	26	50	29	10	4	2	11	4	2	6	6
91-92—Washington	NHL	78	14	38	52	49	20	0	1	7	1	2	3	4
92-93—Washington	NHL	84	18	27	45	32	-2	3	0	6	0	3	3	2
93-94—Washington	NHL	84	14	25	39	32	8	0	1	11	2	7	9	0
94-95—Washington	NHL	48	10	13	23	6	5	2	0	7	0	3	3	4
95-96—Washington	NHL	74	7	13	20	30	7	0	2	6	0	1	1	4
96-97—Washington	NHL	77	10	14	24	33	4	0	1	—	—	—	—	—
97-98—Washington	NHL	76	7	7	14	41	-2	0	3	10	0	1	1	4
NHL Totals (14 years).........		995	179	277	456	483	76	19	16	119	20	34	54	65

MILLER, KEVIN   LW   BLACKHAWKS

PERSONAL: Born August 9, 1965, in Lansing, Mich. ... 5-11/190. ... Shoots right. ... Full name: Kevin Bradley Miller. ... Brother of Kelly Miller, left winger, Washington Capitals; and brother of Kip Miller, center, New York Islanders.
HIGH SCHOOL: Eastern (Lansing, Mich.).
COLLEGE: Michigan State.
TRANSACTIONS/CAREER NOTES: Selected by New York Rangers in 10th round (10th Rangers pick, 202nd overall) of NHL entry draft (June 9, 1984). ... Pulled groin (September 1990). ... Sprained shoulder (December 1990). ... Traded by Rangers with D Dennis Vial and RW Jim Cummings to Detroit Red Wings for RW Joe Kocur and D Per Djoos (March 5, 1991). ... Traded by Red Wings to Washington Capitals for RW Dino Ciccarelli (June 20, 1992). ... Traded by Capitals to St. Louis Blues for D Paul Cavallini (November 1, 1992). ... Suffered sore knee (November 3, 1993); missed two games. ... Injured knee (November 24, 1993); missed two games. ... Injured hip (March 30, 1994); missed one game. ... Suffered sore groin (April 8, 1994); missed three games. ... Traded by Blues to San Jose Sharks for C Todd Elik (March 23, 1995). ... Injured knee (March 15, 1996); missed two games. ... Traded by Sharks to Pittsburgh Penguins for fifth-round pick in 1996 draft (March 20, 1996). ... Signed as free agent by Chicago Blackhawks (July 17, 1996). ... Suffered the flu (November 22, 1996); missed one game. ... Pulled groin (January 10, 1997); missed two games. ... Strained groin (December 20, 1997); missed one game.
MISCELLANEOUS: Scored on a penalty shot (vs. Patrick Roy, October 30, 1991; vs. Stephane Fiset, December 5, 1995). ... Failed to score on a penalty shot (vs. Mike Vernon, December 17, 1993).
STATISTICAL PLATEAUS: Three-goal games: 1991-92 (1), 1992-93 (1), 1993-94 (1), 1995-96 (1). Total: 4.

		REGULAR SEASON								PLAYOFFS				
Season Team	League	Gms.	G	A	Pts.	PIM	+/-	PP	SH	Gms.	G	A	Pts.	PIM
84-85—Michigan State...........	CCHA	44	11	29	40	84	...	...	...	—	—	—	—	—
85-86—Michigan State...........	CCHA	45	19	52	71	112	...	...	...	—	—	—	—	—
86-87—Michigan State...........	CCHA	42	25	56	81	63	...	...	...	—	—	—	—	—
87-88—Michigan State...........	CCHA	9	6	3	9	18	...	...	...	—	—	—	—	—
—U.S. Olympic Team	Int'l	50	32	34	66	...	...	...	...	—	—	—	—	—
88-89—New York Rangers......	NHL	24	3	5	8	2	-1	0	0	—	—	—	—	—
—Denver	IHL	55	29	47	76	19	...	...	...	4	2	1	3	2
89-90—New York Rangers......	NHL	16	0	5	5	2	-1	0	0	1	0	0	0	0
—Flint	IHL	48	19	23	42	41	...	...	...	—	—	—	—	—
90-91—New York Rangers......	NHL	63	17	27	44	63	1	1	2	—	—	—	—	—
—Detroit	NHL	11	5	2	7	4	-4	0	1	7	3	2	5	20
91-92—Detroit	NHL	80	20	26	46	53	6	3	1	9	0	2	2	4
92-93—Washington	NHL	10	0	3	3	35	-4	0	0	—	—	—	—	—
—St. Louis	NHL	72	24	22	46	65	6	8	3	10	0	3	3	11
93-94—St. Louis	NHL	75	23	25	48	83	6	6	3	3	1	0	1	4
94-95—St. Louis	NHL	15	2	5	7	4	0	0	0	—	—	—	—	—
—San Jose...................	NHL	21	6	7	13	13	0	1	1	6	0	0	0	2
95-96—San Jose...................	NHL	68	22	20	42	41	-8	2	2	—	—	—	—	—
—Pittsburgh..................	NHL	13	6	5	11	4	4	1	0	18	3	2	5	8
96-97—Chicago...................	NHL	69	14	17	31	41	-10	5	1	6	0	1	1	0
97-98—Indianapolis	IHL	26	11	11	22	41	...	...	...	2	1	1	2	0
—Chicago...................	NHL	37	4	7	11	8	-4	0	0	—	—	—	—	—
NHL Totals (10 years).........		574	146	176	322	414	-5	27	14	60	7	10	17	49

M

MILLER, KIP   C   ISLANDERS

PERSONAL: Born June 11, 1969, in Lansing, Mich. ... 5-10/190. ... Shoots left. ... Full name: Kip Charles Miller. ... Brother of Kelly Miller, left winger, Washington Capitals; and brother of Kevin Miller, left winger, Chicago Blackhawks.
HIGH SCHOOL: Eastern (Lansing, Mich.).
COLLEGE: Michigan State.
TRANSACTIONS/CAREER NOTES: Selected by Quebec Nordiques in fourth round (fourth Nordiques pick, 72nd overall) of NHL entry draft (June 13, 1987). ... Injured hand and forearm in off-ice accident (November 1987). ... Traded by Nordiques to Minnesota North Stars for LW Steve Maltais (March 8, 1992). ... North Stars franchise moved from Minnesota to Dallas and renamed Stars for 1993-94 season. ... Signed as free agent by San Jose Sharks (August 10, 1993). ... Signed as free agent by New York Islanders (August 2, 1994). ... Signed as free agent by Chicago Blackhawks (August 10, 1995). ... Loaned by Blackhawks to Chicago Wolves of the IHL (September 17, 1996).
HONORS: Named to NCAA All-America West first team (1988-89 and 1989-90). ... Named to CCHA All-Star first team (1988-89 and 1989-90). ... Won Hobey Baker Memorial Award (1989-90). ... Named CCHA Player of the Year (1989-90). ... Won N.R. (Bud) Poile Trophy (1994-95).

		REGULAR SEASON								PLAYOFFS				
Season Team	League	Gms.	G	A	Pts.	PIM	+/-	PP	SH		Gms.	G	A	Pts.	PIM
86-87—Michigan State	CCHA	41	20	19	39	92	...	...	...	—	—	—	—	—
87-88—Michigan State	CCHA	39	16	25	41	51	...	...	...	—	—	—	—	—
88-89—Michigan State	CCHA	47	32	45	77	94	...	...	...	—	—	—	—	—
89-90—Michigan State	CCHA	45	*48	53	*101	60	...	...	...	—	—	—	—	—
90-91—Quebec	NHL	13	4	3	7	7	-1	0	0	—	—	—	—	—
—Halifax	AHL	66	36	33	69	40	...	...	...	—	—	—	—	—
91-92—Quebec	NHL	36	5	10	15	12	-21	1	0	—	—	—	—	—
—Halifax	AHL	24	9	17	26	8	...	...	...	—	—	—	—	—
—Minnesota	NHL	3	1	2	3	2	-1	1	0	—	—	—	—	—
—Kalamazoo	IHL	6	1	8	9	4	...	...	...	12	3	9	12	12
92-93—Kalamazoo	IHL	61	17	39	56	59	...	...	...	—	—	—	—	—
93-94—San Jose	NHL	11	2	2	4	6	-1	0	0	—	—	—	—	—
—Kansas City	IHL	71	38	54	92	51	...	...	...	—	—	—	—	—
94-95—Denver	IHL	71	46	60	106	54	...	...	...	17	*15	14	29	8
—New York Islanders	NHL	8	0	1	1	0	1	0	0	—	—	—	—	—
95-96—Indianapolis	IHL	73	32	59	91	46	...	...	...	5	2	6	8	2
—Chicago	NHL	10	1	4	5	2	1	0	0	—	—	—	—	—
96-97—Chicago	IHL	43	11	41	52	32	...	...	...	—	—	—	—	—
—Indianapolis	IHL	37	17	24	41	18	...	...	...	4	2	2	4	2
97-98—Utah	IHL	72	38	59	97	30	...	...	...	4	3	2	5	10
—New York Islanders	NHL	9	1	3	4	2	-2	0	0	—	—	—	—	—
NHL Totals (6 years)		90	14	25	39	31	-24	2	0					

MILLS, CRAIG   RW   BLACKHAWKS

PERSONAL: Born August 27, 1976, in Toronto. ... 6-0/190. ... Shoots right.
TRANSACTIONS/CAREER NOTES: Selected by Winnipeg Jets in fifth round (fifth Jets pick, 108th overall) of NHL entry draft (June 29, 1994). ... Jets franchise moved to Phoenix and renamed Coyotes for 1996-97 season; NHL approved move on January 18, 1996. ... Traded by Coyotes with C Alexei Zhamnov and first-round pick (RW Ty Jones) in 1997 draft to Chicago Blackhawks for C Jeremy Roenick (August 16, 1996).
HONORS: Won Can.HL Humanitarian Award (1995-96).

		REGULAR SEASON								PLAYOFFS				
Season Team	League	Gms.	G	A	Pts.	PIM	+/-	PP	SH		Gms.	G	A	Pts.	PIM
92-93—St. Michael's	Tier II Jr. A	44	8	12	20	51	...	...	...	—	—	—	—	—
93-94—Belleville	OHL	63	15	18	33	88	...	...	...	12	2	1	3	11
94-95—Belleville	OHL	62	39	41	80	104	...	...	...	13	7	9	16	8
95-96—Belleville	OHL	48	10	19	29	113	...	...	...	14	4	5	9	32
—Winnipeg	NHL	4	0	2	2	0	0	0	0	1	0	0	0	0
—Springfield	AHL	—	—	—	—	—	...	...	...	2	0	0	0	0
96-97—Indianapolis	IHL	80	12	7	19	199	...	...	...	4	0	0	0	4
97-98—Chicago	NHL	20	0	3	3	34	1	0	0	—	—	—	—	—
—Indianapolis	IHL	42	8	11	19	119	...	...	...	5	0	0	0	27
NHL Totals (2 years)		24	0	5	5	34	1	0	0	1	0	0	0	0

MINARD, MIKE   G   OILERS

PERSONAL: Born January 11, 1976, in Owen Sound, Ont. ... 6-3/205. ... Catches left. ... Name pronounced mih-NAHRD.
TRANSACTIONS/CAREER NOTES: Selected by Edmonton Oilers in fourth round (fourth Oilers pick, 83rd overall) of NHL entry draft (July 8, 1995).

		REGULAR SEASON							PLAYOFFS					
Season Team	League	Gms.	Min	W	L	T	GA	SO	Avg.	Gms.	Min.	W	L	GA	SO	Avg.
94-95—Chilliwack	BCJHL	40	2330	...	...	...	136	0	3.50	—	—	—	—	—	—	—
95-96—Barrie	OHL	1	52	0	1	0	8	0	9.23	—	—	—	—	—	—	—
—Detroit	OHL	42	2314	25	10	4	128	2	3.32	17	922	9	6	55	1	3.58
96-97—Hamilton	AHL	3	100	1	1	0	7	0	4.20	—	—	—	—	—	—	—
—Wheeling	ECHL	23	899	3	7	‡1	69	0	4.61	3	148	0	2	16	0	6.49
97-98—Hamilton	AHL	2	80	1	0	0	2	0	1.50	—	—	—	—	—	—	—
—New Orleans	ECHL	11	429	6	2	‡0	30	0	4.20	—	—	—	—	—	—	—
—Milwaukee	IHL	8	362	2	2	‡0	19	0	3.15	—	—	—	—	—	—	—

MIRONOV, BORIS   D   OILERS

PERSONAL: Born March 21, 1972, in Moscow, U.S.S.R. ... 6-3/215. ... Shoots right. ... Brother of Dmitri Mironov, defenseman, Washington Capitals. ... Name pronounced MEER-ih-nahf.

M

TRANSACTIONS/CAREER NOTES: Selected by Winnipeg Jets in second round (second Jets pick, 27th overall) of NHL entry draft (June 20, 1992). ... Bruised back (February 2, 1994); missed three games. ... Traded by Jets with C Mats Lindgren and first- (C Jason Bonsignore) and fourth- (RW Adam Copeland) round picks in 1994 draft to Edmonton Oilers for D Dave Manson and sixth-round pick (March 15, 1994). ... Bruised ankle (April 3, 1995); missed one game. ... Strained lower back (April 13, 1995); missed 10 games. ... Strained abdominal muscle (January 21, 1997); missed 12 games. ... Strained groin (February 19, 1997); missed five games. ... Strained groin (March 7, 1997); missed five games.

HONORS: Named to NHL All-Rookie team (1993-94).

MISCELLANEOUS: Member of silver-medal-winning Russian Olympic team (1998).

Season Team	League	REGULAR SEASON								PLAYOFFS				
		Gms.	G	A	Pts.	PIM	+/-	PP	SH	Gms.	G	A	Pts.	PIM
88-89—CSKA Moscow	USSR	1	0	0	0	0	...	...	...	—	—	—	—	—
89-90—CSKA Moscow	USSR	7	0	0	0	0	...	...	...	—	—	—	—	—
90-91—CSKA Moscow	USSR	36	1	5	6	16	...	...	...	—	—	—	—	—
91-92—CSKA Moscow	CIS	36	2	1	3	22	...	...	...	—	—	—	—	—
92-93—CSKA Moscow	CIS	19	0	5	5	20	...	...	...	—	—	—	—	—
93-94—Winnipeg	NHL	65	7	22	29	96	-29	5	0	—	—	—	—	—
—Edmonton	NHL	14	0	2	2	14	-4	0	0	—	—	—	—	—
94-95—Cape Breton	AHL	4	2	5	7	23	...	...	...	—	—	—	—	—
—Edmonton	NHL	29	1	7	8	40	-9	0	0	—	—	—	—	—
95-96—Edmonton	NHL	78	8	24	32	101	-23	7	0	—	—	—	—	—
96-97—Edmonton	NHL	55	6	26	32	85	2	2	0	12	2	8	10	16
97-98—Edmonton	NHL	81	16	30	46	100	-8	10	1	12	3	3	6	27
—Russian Oly. team	Int'l	6	0	2	2	2	...	...	...	—	—	—	—	—
NHL Totals (5 years)		322	38	111	149	436	-71	24	1	24	5	11	16	43

MIRONOV, DMITRI   D   CAPITALS

PERSONAL: Born December 25, 1965, in Moscow, U.S.S.R. ... 6-3/215. ... Shoots right. ... Brother of Boris Mironov, defenseman, Edmonton Oilers. ... Name pronounced MEER-ih-nahf.

TRANSACTIONS/CAREER NOTES: Selected by Toronto Maple Leafs in eighth round (seventh Maple Leafs pick, 160th overall) of NHL entry draft (June 22, 1991). ... Broke nose (March 23, 1992). ... Suffered infected tooth (March 18, 1993); missed 10 games. ... Suffered quad contusion (December 28, 1993); missed one game. ... Lacerated lip (March 7, 1994); missed two games. ... Suffered rib and muscle strain (April 2, 1994); missed remainder of season. ... Bruised thigh (February 18, 1995); missed one game. ... Separated shoulder (March 27, 1995); missed 14 games. ... Traded by Maple Leafs with second-round pick (traded to New Jersey) in 1996 draft to Pittsburgh Penguins for D Larry Murphy (July 8, 1995). ... Bruised shoulder (March 14, 1996); missed eight games. ... Traded by Penguins with LW Shawn Antoski to Mighty Ducks of Anaheim for C Alex Hicks and D Fredrik Olausson (November 19, 1996). ... Traded by Mighty Ducks to Detroit Red Wings for D Jamie Pushor and fourth-round pick (C Viktor Wallin) in 1998 draft (March 24, 1998). ... Signed as free agent by Washington Capitals (July 14, 1998).

HONORS: Played in NHL All-Star Game (1998).

MISCELLANEOUS: Member of gold-medal-winning Unified Olympic team (1992). ... Member of silver-medal-winning Russian Olympic team (1998). ... Member of Stanley Cup championship team (1998).

Season Team	League	REGULAR SEASON								PLAYOFFS				
		Gms.	G	A	Pts.	PIM	+/-	PP	SH	Gms.	G	A	Pts.	PIM
90-91—Soviet Wings	USSR	45	16	12	28	22	...	...	...	—	—	—	—	—
91-92—Soviet Wings	USSR	35	15	16	31	62	...	...	...	—	—	—	—	—
—Unif. Olympic Team	Int'l	8	3	1	4	4	...	...	...	—	—	—	—	—
—Toronto	NHL	7	1	0	1	0	-4	0	0	—	—	—	—	—
92-93—Toronto	NHL	59	7	24	31	40	-1	4	0	14	1	2	3	2
93-94—Toronto	NHL	76	9	27	36	78	5	3	0	18	6	9	15	6
94-95—Toronto	NHL	33	5	12	17	28	6	2	0	6	2	1	3	2
95-96—Pittsburgh	NHL	72	3	31	34	88	19	1	0	15	0	1	1	10
96-97—Pittsburgh	NHL	15	1	5	6	24	-4	0	0	—	—	—	—	—
—Anaheim	NHL	62	12	34	46	77	20	3	1	11	1	10	11	10
97-98—Anaheim	NHL	66	6	30	36	115	-7	2	0	—	—	—	—	—
—Russian Oly. team	Int'l	6	0	3	3	0	...	...	...	—	—	—	—	—
—Detroit	NHL	11	2	5	7	4	0	1	0	7	0	3	3	14
NHL Totals (7 years)		401	46	168	214	454	34	16	1	71	10	26	36	44

MITCHELL, JEFF   RW   STARS

PERSONAL: Born May 16, 1975, in Wayne, Ind. ... 6-1/175. ... Shoots right.

TRANSACTIONS/CAREER NOTES: Selected by Los Angeles Kings in third round (third Kings pick, 68th overall) of NHL entry draft (June 26, 1993). ... Traded by Kings to Dallas Stars for fifth-round pick (C Jason Morgan) in 1995 draft (June 6, 1995).

Season Team	League	REGULAR SEASON								PLAYOFFS				
		Gms.	G	A	Pts.	PIM	+/-	PP	SH	Gms.	G	A	Pts.	PIM
92-93—Detroit	OHL	62	10	15	25	25	...	...	...	15	3	3	6	16
93-94—Detroit	OHL	59	25	18	43	99	...	...	...	17	3	5	8	22
94-95—Detroit	OHL	61	30	30	60	121	...	...	...	21	9	12	21	48
95-96—Michigan	IHL	50	5	4	9	119	...	...	...	—	—	—	—	—
96-97—Michigan	IHL	24	0	3	3	40	...	...	...	—	—	—	—	—
—Philadelphia	AHL	31	7	5	12	103	...	...	...	10	1	1	2	20
97-98—Michigan	IHL	62	9	8	17	206	...	...	...	4	0	0	0	30
—Dallas	NHL	7	0	0	0	7	0	0	0	—	—	—	—	—
NHL Totals (1 year)		7	0	0	0	7	0	0	0					

MITCHELL, WILLIE — D — DEVILS

PERSONAL: Born April 23, 1977, in Port McNeill, B.C. ... 6-3/210. ... Shoots left.
COLLEGE: Clarkson (N.Y.).
TRANSACTIONS/CAREER NOTES: Selected by New Jersey Devils in eighth round (12th Devils pick, 199th overall) of NHL entry draft (June 22, 1996).

Season Team	League	REGULAR SEASON								PLAYOFFS				
		Gms.	G	A	Pts.	PIM	+/-	PP	SH	Gms.	G	A	Pts.	PIM
95-96—Melfort	Jr. A	19	2	6	8	0	...	...	...	14	0	2	2	12
96-97—Melfort	Jr. A	64	14	42	56	227	...	...	...	4	0	1	1	23
97-98—Clarkson	ECAC	34	9	17	26	105	...	...	...	—	—	—	—	—

MODANO, MIKE — C — STARS

PERSONAL: Born June 7, 1970, in Livonia, Mich. ... 6-3/200. ... Shoots left. ... Full name: Michael Modano. ... Name pronounced muh-DAH-noh.
TRANSACTIONS/CAREER NOTES: Selected by Minnesota North Stars in first round (first North Stars pick, first overall) of NHL entry draft (June 11, 1988). ... Fractured scaphoid bone in left wrist (January 24, 1989). ... Broke nose (March 4, 1990). ... Pulled groin (November 30, 1992); missed two games. ... North Stars franchise moved from Minnesota to Dallas and renamed Stars for 1993-94 season. ... Strained medial collateral knee ligament (January 6, 1994); missed six games. ... Suffered concussion (February 26, 1994); missed two games. ... Bruised ankle (March 12, 1995); missed four games. ... Ruptured tendons in ankle (April 4, 1995) and underwent surgery (April 11, 1995); missed last 14 games of season and entire playoffs. ... Injured stomach muscle (November 9, 1995); missed four games. ... Suffered from the flu (February 9, 1997); missed one game. ... Bruised ankle (November 12, 1997); missed one game. ... Tore medial collateral knee ligament (December 5, 1997); missed 10 games. ... Injured knee (January 2, 1998); missed two games. ... Separated shoulder (March 13, 1998); missed 17 games.
HONORS: Named to WHL (East) All-Star first team (1988-89). ... Named to NHL All-Rookie team (1989-90). ... Played in NHL All-Star Game (1993 and 1998). ... Named to play in NHL All-Star Game (1997); replaced by LW Keith Tkachuk due to injury.
STATISTICAL PLATEAUS: Three-goal games: 1989-90 (1), 1993-94 (1), 1997-98 (1). Total: 3. ... Four-goal games: 1995-96 (1). ... Total hat tricks: 4.

Season Team	League	REGULAR SEASON								PLAYOFFS				
		Gms.	G	A	Pts.	PIM	+/-	PP	SH	Gms.	G	A	Pts.	PIM
86-87—Prince Albert	WHL	70	32	30	62	96	...	...	...	8	1	4	5	4
87-88—Prince Albert	WHL	65	47	80	127	80	...	...	...	9	7	11	18	18
88-89—Prince Albert	WHL	41	39	66	105	74	...	...	...	—	—	—	—	—
—Minnesota	NHL	—	—	—	—	—	...	...	...	2	0	0	0	0
89-90—Minnesota	NHL	80	29	46	75	63	-7	12	0	7	1	1	2	12
90-91—Minnesota	NHL	79	28	36	64	61	2	9	0	23	8	12	20	16
91-92—Minnesota	NHL	76	33	44	77	46	-9	5	0	7	3	2	5	4
92-93—Minnesota	NHL	82	33	60	93	83	-7	9	0	—	—	—	—	—
93-94—Dallas	NHL	76	50	43	93	54	-8	18	0	9	7	3	10	16
94-95—Dallas	NHL	30	12	17	29	8	7	4	1	—	—	—	—	—
95-96—Dallas	NHL	78	36	45	81	63	-12	8	4	—	—	—	—	—
96-97—Dallas	NHL	80	35	48	83	42	43	9	5	7	4	1	5	0
97-98—Dallas	NHL	52	21	38	59	32	25	7	5	17	4	10	14	12
—U.S. Olympic Team	Int'l	4	2	0	2	0	...	...	...	—	—	—	—	—
NHL Totals (10 years)		633	277	377	654	452	34	81	15	72	27	29	56	60

MODIN, FREDRIK — RW — MAPLE LEAFS

PERSONAL: Born October 8, 1974, in Jonkoping, Sweden. ... 6-3/222. ... Shoots left. ... Name pronounced moh-DEEN.
TRANSACTIONS/CAREER NOTES: Selected by Toronto Maple Leafs in third round (third Maple Leafs pick, 64th overall) of NHL entry draft (June 29, 1994). ... Suffered concussion (October 22, 1996); missed three games. ... Suffered from the flu (March 10, 1997); missed one game. ... Strained groin (December 2, 1997); missed two games.

Season Team	League	REGULAR SEASON								PLAYOFFS				
		Gms.	G	A	Pts.	PIM	+/-	PP	SH	Gms.	G	A	Pts.	PIM
91-92—Sundsvall Timra	Swed. Dv.II	11	1	0	1	0	...	...	...	—	—	—	—	—
92-93—Sundsvall Timra	Swed. Dv.II	30	5	7	12	12	...	...	...	—	—	—	—	—
93-94—Sundsvall Timra	Swed. Dv.II	30	16	15	31	36	...	...	...	—	—	—	—	—
94-95—Brynas Gavle	Sweden	38	9	10	19	33	...	...	...	14	4	4	8	6
95-96—Brynas Gavle	Sweden	22	4	8	12	22	...	...	...	—	—	—	—	—
96-97—Toronto	NHL	76	6	7	13	24	-14	0	0	—	—	—	—	—
97-98—Toronto	NHL	74	16	16	32	32	-5	1	0	—	—	—	—	—
NHL Totals (2 years)		150	22	23	45	56	-19	1	0					

MOGER, SANDY — RW — KINGS

PERSONAL: Born March 21, 1969, in 100 Mile House, B.C. ... 6-3/218. ... Shoots right. ... Full name: Alexander Sandy Moger. ... Name pronounced MOH-guhr.
COLLEGE: Lake Superior State (Mich.).
TRANSACTIONS/CAREER NOTES: Broke wrist (September 1988). ... Selected by Vancouver Canucks in ninth round (seventh Canucks pick, 176th overall) of NHL entry draft (June 17, 1989). ... Signed as free agent by Boston Bruins (July 6, 1994). ... Broke arm (April 28, 1995); missed remainder of season and entire playoffs. ... Broke foot (preseason, 1996-97 season); missed first seven games of season. ... Fractured elbow (December 14, 1996); missed 25 games. ... Fractured finger (March 12, 1997); missed remainder of season. ... Traded by Bruins with C Jozef Stumpel and fourth-round pick (traded to New Jersey) in 1998 draft to Los Angeles Kings for LW Dimitri Khristich and G Byron Dafoe (August 29, 1997). ... Suffered sore ribs (November 23, 1997); missed two games. ... Sprained left knee (March 26, 1998); missed final 12 games of regular season and entire playoffs.
HONORS: Named to CCHA All-Star second team (1991-92).

Season Team	League	Gms.	G	A	Pts.	PIM	+/-	PP	SH	Gms.	G	A	Pts.	PIM
86-87—Vernon	BCJHL	13	5	4	9	10	...	...	...	—	—	—	—	—
87-88—Yorkton	SJHL	60	39	41	80	144	...	...	...	—	—	—	—	—
88-89—Lake Superior	CCHA	31	4	6	10	28	...	...	...	—	—	—	—	—
89-90—Lake Superior	CCHA	46	17	15	32	76	...	...	...	—	—	—	—	—
90-91—Lake Superior	CCHA	45	27	21	48	*172	...	...	...	—	—	—	—	—
91-92—Lake Superior	CCHA	42	26	25	51	111	...	...	...	—	—	—	—	—
92-93—Hamilton	AHL	78	23	26	49	57	...	...	...	—	—	—	—	—
93-94—Hamilton	AHL	29	9	8	17	41	...	...	...	—	—	—	—	—
94-95—Providence	AHL	63	32	29	61	105	...	...	...	—	—	—	—	—
—Boston	NHL	18	2	6	8	6	-1	2	0	—	—	—	—	—
95-96—Boston	NHL	80	15	14	29	65	-9	4	0	5	2	2	4	12
96-97—Providence	AHL	3	0	2	2	19	...	...	...	—	—	—	—	—
—Boston	NHL	34	10	3	13	45	-12	3	0	—	—	—	—	—
97-98—Los Angeles	NHL	62	11	13	24	70	4	1	0	—	—	—	—	—
NHL Totals (4 years)		194	38	36	74	186	-18	10	0	5	2	2	4	12

MOGILNY, ALEXANDER   RW   CANUCKS

PERSONAL: Born February 18, 1969, in Khabarovsk, U.S.S.R. ... 5-11/187. ... Shoots left. ... Name pronounced moh-GIHL-nee.

TRANSACTIONS/CAREER NOTES: Selected by Buffalo Sabres in fifth round (fourth Sabres pick, 89th overall) of NHL entry draft (June 11, 1988). ... Suffered from the flu (November 26, 1989). ... Missed games due to fear of flying (January 22, 1990); spent remainder of season traveling on ground. ... Separated shoulder (February 8, 1991); missed six games. ... Suffered from the flu (November 1991); missed two games. ... Suffered from the flu (December 18, 1991); missed one game. ... Bruised shoulder (October 10, 1992); missed six games. ... Broke fibula and tore ankle ligaments (May 6, 1993); missed remainder of 1992-93 playoffs and first nine games of 1993-94 season. ... Suffered sore ankle (February 2, 1994); missed four games. ... Suffered inflamed tendon in ankle (February 15, 1994); missed four games. ... Played in Europe during 1994-95 NHL lockout. ... Pinched nerve in neck (April 9, 1995); missed three games. ... Traded by Sabres with fifth-round pick (LW Todd Norman) in 1995 draft to Vancouver Canucks for RW Mike Peca, D Mike Wilson and first-round pick (D Jay McKee) in 1995 draft (July 8, 1995). ... Pulled hamstring (October 28, 1995); missed three games. ... Suffered from the flu (December 3, 1996); missed two games. ... Strained groin (April 4, 1997); missed remainder of season. ... Missed first 16 games of regular season due to contract dispute. ... Injured groin (December 15, 1997); missed 11 games. ... Strained back (February 24, 1998); missed four games.

HONORS: Played in NHL All-Star Game (1992-1994 and 1996). ... Named to THE SPORTING NEWS All-Star second team (1992-93). ... Named to NHL All-Star second team (1992-93 and 1995-96).

RECORDS: Shares NHL record for fastest goal from start of a game—5 seconds (December 21, 1991).

STATISTICAL PLATEAUS: Three-goal games: 1990-91 (1), 1991-92 (1), 1992-93 (5), 1993-94 (1), 1995-96 (3), 1996-97 (1). Total: 12. ... Four-goal games: 1992-93 (2). ... Total hat tricks: 14.

MISCELLANEOUS: Member of gold-medal-winning U.S.S.R. Olympic team (1988). ... Captain of Buffalo Sabres (1993-94 and 1994-95). ... Failed to score on a penalty shot (vs. Bill Ranford, January 10, 1992; vs. Robb Stauber, December 17, 1993). ... Scored on a penalty shot (vs. Chris Osgood, December 1, 1997).

STATISTICAL NOTES: Led NHL with 11 game-winning goals (1992-93).

Season Team	League	Gms.	G	A	Pts.	PIM	+/-	PP	SH	Gms.	G	A	Pts.	PIM
86-87—CSKA Moscow	USSR	28	15	1	16	4	...	...	...	—	—	—	—	—
87-88—CSKA Moscow	USSR	39	12	8	20	20	...	...	...	—	—	—	—	—
88-89—CSKA Moscow	USSR	31	11	11	22	24	...	...	...	—	—	—	—	—
89-90—Buffalo	NHL	65	15	28	43	16	8	4	0	4	0	1	1	2
90-91—Buffalo	NHL	62	30	34	64	16	14	3	3	6	0	6	6	2
91-92—Buffalo	NHL	67	39	45	84	73	7	15	0	2	0	2	2	0
92-93—Buffalo	NHL	77	†76	51	127	40	7	27	0	7	7	3	10	6
93-94—Buffalo	NHL	66	32	47	79	22	8	17	0	7	4	2	6	6
94-95—Spartak Moscow	CIS	1	0	1	1	0	...	...	...	—	—	—	—	—
—Buffalo	NHL	44	19	28	47	36	0	12	0	5	3	2	5	2
95-96—Vancouver	NHL	79	55	52	107	16	14	10	5	6	1	8	9	8
96-97—Vancouver	NHL	76	31	42	73	18	9	7	1	—	—	—	—	—
97-98—Vancouver	NHL	51	18	27	45	36	-6	5	4	—	—	—	—	—
NHL Totals (9 years)		587	315	354	669	273	61	100	13	37	15	24	39	26

MONTGOMERY, JIM   C   FLYERS

PERSONAL: Born June 30, 1969, in Montreal. ... 5-9/180. ... Shoots right.

COLLEGE: Maine.

TRANSACTIONS/CAREER NOTES: Signed as free agent by St. Louis Blues (June 2, 1993). ... Suspended four games and fined $500 by NHL for high-sticking incident (October 4, 1993). ... Traded by Blues to Montreal Canadiens for C Guy Carbonneau (August 19, 1994). ... Claimed on waivers by Philadelphia Flyers (February 10, 1995).

HONORS: Named to NCAA All-America East second team (1990-91 and 1992-93). ... Named to Hockey East All-Star second team (1990-91 and 1991-92). ... Named NCAA Tournament Most Valuable Player (1992-93). ... Named Hockey East Tournament Most Valuable Player (1992-93). ... Named to NCAA All-Tournament team (1992-93). ... Named to Hockey East All-Star first team (1992-93). ... Named to Hockey East All-Decade team (1994). ... Named to AHL All-Star second team (1995-96).

Season Team	League	Gms.	G	A	Pts.	PIM	+/-	PP	SH	Gms.	G	A	Pts.	PIM
89-90—Univ. of Maine	Hockey East	45	26	34	60	35	...	...	...	—	—	—	—	—
90-91—Univ. of Maine	Hockey East	43	24	57	81	44	...	...	...	—	—	—	—	—
91-92—Univ. of Maine	Hockey East	37	21	44	65	46	...	...	...	—	—	—	—	—
92-93—Univ. of Maine	Hockey East	45	32	63	95	40	...	...	...	—	—	—	—	—
93-94—St. Louis	NHL	67	6	14	20	44	-1	0	0	—	—	—	—	—
—Peoria	IHL	12	7	8	15	10	...	...	...	—	—	—	—	—

		REGULAR SEASON								PLAYOFFS				
Season Team	**League**	**Gms.**	**G**	**A**	**Pts.**	**PIM**	**+/-**	**PP**	**SH**	**Gms.**	**G**	**A**	**Pts.**	**PIM**
94-95—Montreal	NHL	5	0	0	0	2	-2	0	0	—	—	—	—	—
—Philadelphia	NHL	8	1	1	2	6	-2	0	0	7	1	0	1	2
—Hershey	AHL	16	8	6	14	14	...	...	...	6	3	2	5	25
95-96—Hershey	AHL	78	34	†71	105	95	...	...	...	4	3	2	5	6
—Philadelphia	NHL	5	1	2	3	9	1	0	0	1	0	0	0	0
96-97—Kolner Haie	Germany	50	12	35	47	11	...	...	...	—	—	—	—	—
97-98—Philadelphia	AHL	68	19	43	62	75	...	...	...	20	13	16	29	55
NHL Totals (3 years)		85	8	17	25	61	-4	0	0	8	1	0	1	2

MOOG, ANDY G

PERSONAL: Born February 18, 1960, in Penticton, B.C. ... 5-8/177. ... Catches left. ... Full name: Donald Andrew Moog. ... Name pronounced MOHG.

TRANSACTIONS/CAREER NOTES: Selected by Edmonton Oilers in seventh round (sixth Oilers pick, 132nd overall) of NHL entry draft (June 11, 1980). ... Suffered viral infection (December 1983). ... Injured ligaments in both knees (March 1, 1985). ... Traded by Oilers to Boston Bruins for LW Geoff Courtnall and G Bill Ranford (March 1988). ... Hyperextended right knee (January 31, 1991); missed three weeks. ... Injured back (January 1993); missed three games. ... Injured hamstring (February 1993); missed four games. ... Traded by Bruins to Dallas Stars for G Jon Casey (June 25, 1993) to complete deal in which Bruins sent D Gord Murphy to Stars for future considerations (June 20, 1993). ... Strained groin (November 24, 1993); missed five games. ... Strained hip muscle (March 30, 1995); missed two games. ... Strained hamstring (April 11, 1995); missed one game. ... Reinjured hamstring (April 19, 1995); missed five games. ... Bruised knee (January 3, 1996); missed 18 games. ... Sprained knee (December 30, 1996); missed three games. ... Strained back and ankle (March 7, 1997); missed eight games. ... Signed as free agent by Montreal Canadiens (July 17, 1997). ... Sprained knee (November 12, 1997); missed five games. ... Announced retirement (June 22, 1998).

HONORS: Named to WHL All-Star second team (1979-80). ... Named to CHL All-Star second team (1981-82). ... Named to The Sporting News All-Star second team (1982-83). ... Played in NHL All-Star Game (1985, 1986, 1991 and 1997). ... Shared William M. Jennings Trophy with Rejean Lemelin (1989-90).

MISCELLANEOUS: Member of Stanley Cup championship team (1984, 1985 and 1987). ... Stopped a penalty shot attempt (vs. John Cullen, January 16, 1992; vs. Rob DiMaio, October 4, 1997). ... Allowed a penalty shot goal (vs. Rocky Trottier, December 17, 1984; vs. John Tucker, April 9, 1988; vs. Brad May, November, 11, 1992; Sergei Fedorov, December 27, 1993).

		REGULAR SEASON								PLAYOFFS						
Season Team	**League**	**Gms.**	**Min**	**W**	**L**	**T**	**GA**	**SO**	**Avg.**	**Gms.**	**Min.**	**W**	**L**	**GA**	**SO**	**Avg.**
76-77—Kamloops	BCJHL	44	2735	...	...	...	173	0	*3.80	—	—	—	—	—	—	—
—Kamloops	WCHL	1	35	...	...	...	6	0	10.29	—	—	—	—	—	—	—
77-78—Penticton	BCJHL	39	2243	...	...	...	191	0	5.11	—	—	—	—	—	—	—
78-79—Billings	WHL	26	1306	13	5	4	90	*3	4.13	5	229	1	3	21	0	5.50
79-80—Billings	WHL	46	2435	23	14	1	149	1	3.67	3	190	2	1	10	0	3.16
80-81—Wichita	CHL	29	1602	14	13	1	89	0	3.33	5	300	3	2	16	0	3.20
—Edmonton	NHL	7	313	3	3	0	20	0	3.83	9	526	5	4	32	0	3.65
81-82—Edmonton	NHL	8	399	3	5	0	32	0	4.81	—	—	—	—	—	—	—
—Wichita	CHL	40	2391	23	13	3	119	1	2.99	7	434	3	4	23	0	3.18
82-83—Edmonton	NHL	50	2833	33	8	7	167	1	3.54	16	949	11	5	48	0	3.03
83-84—Edmonton	NHL	38	2212	27	8	1	139	1	3.77	7	263	4	0	12	0	2.74
84-85—Edmonton	NHL	39	2019	22	9	3	111	1	3.30	2	20	0	0	0	0	...
85-86—Edmonton	NHL	47	2664	27	9	7	164	1	3.69	1	60	1	0	1	0	1.00
86-87—Edmonton	NHL	46	2461	28	11	3	144	0	3.51	2	120	2	0	8	0	4.00
87-88—Canadian nat'l team	Int'l	27	1438	10	7	5	86	0	3.59	—	—	—	—	—	—	—
—Can. Olympic Team	Int'l	4	240	4	0	0	9	1	2.25	—	—	—	—	—	—	—
—Boston	NHL	6	360	4	2	0	17	1	2.83	7	354	1	4	25	0	4.24
88-89—Boston	NHL	41	2482	18	14	8	133	1	3.22	6	359	4	2	14	0	2.34
89-90—Boston	NHL	46	2536	24	10	7	122	3	2.89	20	1195	13	7	44	*2	*2.21
90-91—Boston	NHL	51	2844	25	13	9	136	4	2.87	19	1133	10	9	60	0	3.18
91-92—Boston	NHL	62	3640	28	22	9	196	1	3.23	15	866	8	7	46	1	3.19
92-93—Boston	NHL	55	3194	37	14	3	168	3	3.16	3	161	0	3	14	0	5.22
93-94—Dallas	NHL	55	3121	24	20	7	170	2	3.27	4	246	1	3	12	0	2.93
94-95—Dallas	NHL	31	1770	10	12	7	72	2	2.44	5	277	1	4	16	0	3.47
95-96—Dallas	NHL	41	2228	13	19	7	111	1	2.99	—	—	—	—	—	—	—
96-97—Dallas	NHL	48	2738	28	13	5	98	3	2.15	7	449	3	4	21	0	2.81
97-98—Montreal	NHL	42	2337	18	17	5	97	3	2.49	9	474	4	5	24	1	3.04
NHL Totals (18 years)		713	40151	372	209	88	2097	28	3.13	132	7452	68	57	377	4	3.04

MORAN, IAN RW PENGUINS

PERSONAL: Born August 24, 1972, in Cleveland. ... 6-0/206. ... Shoots right. ... Name pronounced muh-RAN.

HIGH SCHOOL: Belmont Hill (Mass.).

COLLEGE: Boston College.

TRANSACTIONS/CAREER NOTES: Underwent knee surgery (June 1988). ... Separated shoulder (March 1989). ... Selected by Pittsburgh Penguins in sixth round (fifth Penguins pick, 107th overall) of NHL entry draft (June 16, 1990). ... Bruised shoulder (November 22, 1995); missed nine games. ... Injured shoulder (February 21, 1996); missed one game. ... Underwent shoulder surgery (March 21, 1996); missed remainder of season. ... Injured back and neck (April 10, 1997); missed two games. ... Bruised kneecap and underwent surgery (September 30, 1997); missed 34 games. ... Suffered concussion (February 2, 1998); missed four games. ... Injured knee (March 21, 1998); missed five games.

HONORS: Named Hockey East co-Rookie of the Year with Craig Darby (1991-92). ... Named to Hockey East All-Rookie team (1991-92).

		REGULAR SEASON								PLAYOFFS				
Season Team	**League**	**Gms.**	**G**	**A**	**Pts.**	**PIM**	**+/-**	**PP**	**SH**	**Gms.**	**G**	**A**	**Pts.**	**PIM**
87-88—Belmont Hill	Mass. H.S.	25	3	13	16	15	...	...	...	—	—	—	—	—
88-89—Belmont Hill	Mass. H.S.	23	7	25	32	8	...	...	...	—	—	—	—	—
89-90—Belmont Hill	Mass. H.S.	—	10	36	46	0	—	—	—	—	—	—	—	—

Season Team	League	REGULAR SEASON								PLAYOFFS				
		Gms.	G	A	Pts.	PIM	+/-	PP	SH	Gms.	G	A	Pts.	PIM
90-91—Belmont Hill	Mass. H.S.	23	7	44	51	12	...	...	...	—	—	—	—	—
91-92—Boston College	Hockey East	30	2	16	18	44	...	...	...	—	—	—	—	—
92-93—Boston College	Hockey East	31	8	12	20	32	...	...	...	—	—	—	—	—
93-94—U.S. national team	Int'l	50	8	15	23	69	...	...	...	—	—	—	—	—
—Cleveland	IHL	33	5	13	18	39	...	...	...	—	—	—	—	—
94-95—Cleveland	IHL	64	7	31	38	94	...	...	...	4	0	1	1	2
—Pittsburgh	NHL	—	—	—	—	—	...	...	...	8	0	0	0	0
95-96—Pittsburgh	NHL	51	1	1	2	47	-1	0	0	—	—	—	—	—
96-97—Cleveland	IHL	36	6	23	29	26	...	...	...	—	—	—	—	—
—Pittsburgh	NHL	36	4	5	9	22	-11	0	0	5	1	2	3	4
97-98—Pittsburgh	NHL	37	1	6	7	19	0	0	0	6	0	0	0	2
NHL Totals (4 years)		124	6	12	18	88	-12	0	0	19	1	2	3	6

MORE, JAY   D   PREDATORS

PERSONAL: Born January 12, 1969, in Souris, Man. ... 6-3/215. ... Shoots right. ... Full name: Jayson More. ... Name pronounced MOHR.

TRANSACTIONS/CAREER NOTES: Selected by New York Rangers as underage junior in first round (first Rangers pick, 10th overall) of NHL entry draft (June 13, 1987). ... Traded by Rangers to Minnesota North Stars for C Dave Archibald (November 1, 1989). ... Traded by North Stars to Montreal Canadiens for G Brian Hayward (November 7, 1990). ... Selected by San Jose Sharks in NHL expansion draft (May 30, 1991). ... Injured foot during preseason (September 1991); missed 16 games. ... Injured knee (March 1992). ... Pulled groin (December 9, 1992); missed four games. ... Reaggravated groin injury (December 23, 1992); missed four games. ... Suspended one game by NHL for accumulating three game misconduct penalties (January 27, 1993). ... Strained hip (March 7, 1993); missed one game. ... Suspended for last game of season and first game of 1993-94 season for accumulating four game misconduct penalties (April 11, 1993). ... Fractured wrist (October 23, 1993); missed 25 games. ... Bruised hand (February 18, 1995); missed two games. ... Injured leg (April 7, 1995); missed one game. ... Injured jaw (November 7, 1995); missed one game. ... Injured groin (November 21, 1995); missed one game. ... Injured abdomen (January 5, 1996); missed two games. ... Injured hand (March 20, 1996); missed one game. ... Injured back (April 4, 1996); missed three games. ... Traded by Sharks with C Brian Swanson and fourth-round pick (D Tomi Kallarsson) in 1997 draft to New York Rangers for D Marty McSorley (August 20, 1996). ... Traded by Rangers to Phoenix Coyotes for C Mike Eastwood and D Dallas Eakins (February 6, 1997). ... Suffered concussion (February 10, 1997); missed two games. ... Strained groin (November 6, 1997); missed four games. ... Bruised thigh (November 23, 1997); missed one game. ... Suffered from the flu (December 17, 1997); missed two games. ... Traded by Coyotes with C Chad Kilger to Chicago Blackhawks for D Keith Carney and RW Jim Cummins (March 4, 1998). ... Signed as free agent by Nashville Predators (June 4, 1998).

HONORS: Named to WHL (West) All-Star first team (1987-88).

Season Team	League	REGULAR SEASON								PLAYOFFS				
		Gms.	G	A	Pts.	PIM	+/-	PP	SH	Gms.	G	A	Pts.	PIM
84-85—Lethbridge	WHL	71	3	9	12	101	...	...	...	4	1	0	1	7
85-86—Lethbridge	WHL	61	7	18	25	155	...	...	...	9	0	2	2	36
86-87—New Westminster	WHL	64	8	29	37	217	...	...	...	—	—	—	—	—
87-88—New Westminster	WHL	70	13	47	60	270	...	...	...	5	0	2	2	26
88-89—Denver	IHL	62	7	15	22	138	...	...	...	3	0	1	1	26
—New York Rangers	NHL	1	0	0	0	0	-1	0	0	—	—	—	—	—
89-90—Flint	IHL	9	1	5	6	41	...	...	...	—	—	—	—	—
—Kalamazoo	IHL	64	9	25	34	216	...	...	...	10	0	3	3	13
—Minnesota	NHL	5	0	0	0	16	1	0	0	—	—	—	—	—
90-91—Kalamazoo	IHL	10	0	5	5	46	...	...	...	—	—	—	—	—
—Fredericton	AHL	57	7	17	24	152	...	...	...	9	1	1	2	34
91-92—San Jose	NHL	46	4	13	17	85	-32	1	0	—	—	—	—	—
—Kansas City	IHL	2	0	2	2	4	...	...	...	—	—	—	—	—
92-93—San Jose	NHL	73	5	6	11	179	-35	0	1	—	—	—	—	—
93-94—San Jose	NHL	49	1	6	7	63	-5	0	0	13	0	2	2	32
—Kansas City	IHL	2	1	0	1	25	...	...	...	—	—	—	—	—
94-95—San Jose	NHL	45	0	6	6	71	7	0	0	11	0	4	4	6
95-96—San Jose	NHL	74	2	7	9	147	-32	0	0	—	—	—	—	—
96-97—New York Rangers	NHL	14	0	1	1	25	0	0	0	—	—	—	—	—
—Phoenix	NHL	23	1	6	7	37	10	0	0	7	0	0	0	7
97-98—Phoenix	NHL	41	5	5	10	53	0	0	1	—	—	—	—	—
—Chicago	NHL	17	0	2	2	8	7	0	0	—	—	—	—	—
NHL Totals (9 years)		388	18	52	70	684	-80	1	2	31	0	6	6	45

MOREAU, ETHAN   LW   BLACKHAWKS

PERSONAL: Born September 22, 1975, in Orillia, Ont. ... 6-2/205. ... Shoots left. ... Name pronounced MOHR-oh.

TRANSACTIONS/CAREER NOTES: Selected by Chicago Blackhawks in first round (first Blackhawks pick, 14th overall) of NHL entry draft (June 28, 1994). ... Fractured knuckle (November 16, 1997); missed seven games. ... Fractured ankle (December 14, 1997); missed 20 games.

HONORS: Won Bobby Smith Trophy (1993-94).

Season Team	League	REGULAR SEASON								PLAYOFFS				
		Gms.	G	A	Pts.	PIM	+/-	PP	SH	Gms.	G	A	Pts.	PIM
90-91—Orillia	OHA	42	17	22	39	26	...	...	...	—	—	—	—	—
91-92—Niagara Falls	OHL	62	20	35	55	39	...	...	...	17	4	6	10	4
92-93—Niagara Falls	OHL	65	32	41	73	69	...	...	...	4	0	3	3	4
93-94—Niagara Falls	OHL	59	44	54	98	100	...	...	...	—	—	—	—	—
94-95—Niagara Falls	OHL	39	25	41	66	69	...	...	...	—	—	—	—	—
—Sudbury	OHL	23	13	17	30	22	...	...	...	18	6	12	18	26
95-96—Indianapolis	IHL	71	21	20	41	126	...	...	...	5	4	0	4	8
—Chicago	NHL	8	0	1	1	4	1	0	0	—	—	—	—	—
96-97—Chicago	NHL	82	15	16	31	123	13	0	0	6	1	0	1	9
97-98—Chicago	NHL	54	9	9	18	73	0	2	0	—	—	—	—	—
NHL Totals (3 years)		144	24	26	50	200	14	2	0	6	1	0	1	9

M

MORGAN, JASON   C   KINGS

PERSONAL: Born October 9, 1976, in Kitchener, Ont. ... 6-1/200. ... Shoots left.
HIGH SCHOOL: Loyalist C & VI (Kingston, Ont.).
TRANSACTIONS/CAREER NOTES: Selected by Los Angeles Kings in fifth round (fifth Kings pick, 118th overall) of NHL entry draft (July 8, 1995).

		REGULAR SEASON								PLAYOFFS				
Season Team	League	Gms.	G	A	Pts.	PIM	+/-	PP	SH		Gms.	G	A	Pts.	PIM
93-94—Kitchener	OHL	65	6	15	21	16	...	...	...		5	1	0	1	0
94-95—Kitchener	OHL	35	3	15	18	25	...	...	...		—	—	—	—	—
—Kingston	OHL	20	0	3	3	14	...	...	...		6	0	2	2	0
95-96—Kingston	OHL	66	16	38	54	50	...	...	...		6	1	2	3	0
96-97—Phoenix	IHL	57	3	6	9	29	...	...	...		—	—	—	—	—
—Mississippi	ECHL	6	3	0	3	0	...	...	...		3	1	1	2	6
—Los Angeles	NHL	3	0	0	0	0	-3	0	0		—	—	—	—	—
97-98—Springfield	AHL	58	13	22	35	66	...	...	...		3	1	0	1	18
—Los Angeles	NHL	11	1	0	1	4	-7	0	0		—	—	—	—	—
NHL Totals (2 years)		14	1	0	1	4	-10	0	0						

MORO, MARC   D   MIGHTY DUCKS

PERSONAL: Born July 17, 1977, in Toronto. ... 6-1/220. ... Shoots left. ... Name pronounced muh-ROH.
HIGH SCHOOL: Loyalist C & VI (Kingston, Ont.).
TRANSACTIONS/CAREER NOTES: Selected by Ottawa Senators in second round (second Senators pick, 27th overall) of NHL entry draft (July 8, 1995). ... Rights traded by Senators with C Ted Drury to Mighty Ducks of Anaheim for C Shaun Van Allen and D Jason York (October 1, 1996).

		REGULAR SEASON								PLAYOFFS				
Season Team	League	Gms.	G	A	Pts.	PIM	+/-	PP	SH		Gms.	G	A	Pts.	PIM
92-93—Mississauga	Jr. A	2	0	0	0	0	...	...	...		—	—	—	—	—
93-94—Kingston	Tier II Jr. A	12	0	2	2	20	...	...	...		—	—	—	—	—
—Kingston	OHL	43	0	3	3	81	...	...	...		—	—	—	—	—
94-95—Kingston	OHL	64	4	12	16	255	...	...	...		6	0	0	0	23
95-96—Kingston	OHL	66	4	17	21	261	...	...	...		6	0	0	0	12
—Prin. Edward Island	AHL	2	0	0	0	7	...	...	...		2	0	0	0	4
96-97—Sault Ste. Marie	OHL	63	4	13	17	171	...	...	...		11	1	6	7	38
97-98—Cincinnati	AHL	74	1	6	7	181	...	...	...		—	—	—	—	—
—Anaheim	NHL	1	0	0	0	0	0	0	0		—	—	—	—	—
NHL Totals (1 year)		1	0	0	0	0	0	0	0						

MOROZOV, ALEXEI   RW   PENGUINS

PERSONAL: Born February 16, 1977, in Moscow, U.S.S.R. ... 6-1/195. ... Shoots left. ... Name pronounced muh-ROH-sahf.
TRANSACTIONS/CAREER NOTES: Selected by Pittsburgh Penguins in first round (first Penguins pick, 24th overall) of NHL entry draft (July 8, 1995). ... Chipped bone in toe (December 27, 1997); missed one game.
MISCELLANEOUS: Member of silver-medal-winning Russian Olympic team (1998).

		REGULAR SEASON								PLAYOFFS				
Season Team	League	Gms.	G	A	Pts.	PIM	+/-	PP	SH		Gms.	G	A	Pts.	PIM
93-94—Soviet Wings	CIS	7	0	0	0	0	...	...	...		3	0	0	0	2
94-95—Soviet Wings	CIS	48	15	12	27	53	...	...	...		4	0	3	3	0
95-96—Soviet Wings	CIS	47	12	9	21	26	...	...	...		—	—	—	—	—
96-97—Krylja Sov. Moscow	Russian	44	21	11	32	32	...	...	...		2	0	1	1	2
97-98—Pittsburgh	NHL	76	13	13	26	8	-4	2	0		6	0	1	1	2
—Russian Oly. team	Int'l	6	2	2	4	0	...	...	...		—	—	—	—	—
NHL Totals (1 year)		76	13	13	26	8	-4	2	0		6	0	1	1	2

MORRIS, DEREK   D   FLAMES

PERSONAL: Born August 24, 1978, in Edmonton. ... 6-0/200. ... Shoots right.
TRANSACTIONS/CAREER NOTES: Selected by Calgary Flames in first round (first Flames pick, 13th overall) of NHL entry draft (June 22, 1996).
HONORS: Named to Can.HL All-Star second team (1996-97). ... Named to WHL (East) All-Star first team (1996-97). ... Named to NHL All-Rookie team (1997-98).

		REGULAR SEASON								PLAYOFFS				
Season Team	League	Gms.	G	A	Pts.	PIM	+/-	PP	SH		Gms.	G	A	Pts.	PIM
95-96—Regina	WHL	67	8	44	52	70	...	...	...		11	1	7	8	26
96-97—Regina	WHL	67	18	57	75	180	...	...	...		5	0	3	3	9
—Saint John	AHL	7	0	3	3	7	...	...	...		5	0	3	3	7
97-98—Calgary	NHL	82	9	20	29	88	1	5	1		—	—	—	—	—
NHL Totals (1 year)		82	9	20	29	88	1	5	1						

MORRISON, BRENDAN   C   DEVILS

PERSONAL: Born August 12, 1975, in North Vancouver. ... 5-11/180. ... Shoots left.
HIGH SCHOOL: Pitt Meadows (B.C.) Secondary.
COLLEGE: Michigan.
TRANSACTIONS/CAREER NOTES: Selected by New Jersey Devils in second round (third Devils pick, 39th overall) of NHL entry draft (June 26, 1993).

HONORS: Won CCHA Rookie of the Year Award (1993-94). ... Named to CCHA All-Rookie team (1993-94). ... Named to NCAA All-America West first team (1994-95, 1995-96 and 1996-97). ... Named to CCHA All-Star first team (1994-95, 1995-96 and 1996-97). ... Named CCHA Player of the Year (1995-96 and 1996-97). ... Named NCAA Tournament Most Valuable Player (1995-96). ... Named to NCAA All-Tournament team (1995-96). ... Won Hobey Baker Memorial Award (1996-97). ... Named CCHA Tournament Most Valuable Player (1996-97).

		REGULAR SEASON								PLAYOFFS				
Season Team	League	Gms.	G	A	Pts.	PIM	+/-	PP	SH	Gms.	G	A	Pts.	PIM
92-93—Penticton	BCJHL	56	35	59	94	45	...	...	...	—	—	—	—	—
93-94—Univ. of Michigan.......	CCHA	38	20	28	48	24	...	...	...	—	—	—	—	—
94-95—Univ. of Michigan.......	CCHA	39	23	53	76	42	...	...	...	—	—	—	—	—
95-96—Univ. of Michigan.......	CCHA	35	28	44	72	41	...	...	...	—	—	—	—	—
96-97—Univ. of Michigan.......	CCHA	43	31	57	88	52	...	...	...	—	—	—	—	—
97-98—Albany	AHL	72	35	49	84	44	...	...	...	8	3	4	7	19
—New Jersey	NHL	11	5	4	9	0	3	0	0	3	0	1	1	0
NHL Totals (1 year)............		11	5	4	9	0	3	0	0	3	0	1	1	0

MORROW, BRENDEN   LW   STARS

PERSONAL: Born January 16, 1979, in Carlyle, Sask. ... 5-11/195. ... Shoots left.
TRANSACTIONS/CAREER NOTES: Selected by Dallas Stars in first round (first Stars pick, 25th overall) of NHL entry draft (June 21, 1997).

		REGULAR SEASON								PLAYOFFS				
Season Team	League	Gms.	G	A	Pts.	PIM	+/-	PP	SH	Gms.	G	A	Pts.	PIM
95-96—Portland.....................	WHL	65	13	12	25	61	...	...	...	7	0	0	0	8
96-97—Portland.....................	WHL	71	39	49	88	178	...	...	...	6	2	1	3	4
97-98—Portland.....................	WHL	68	34	52	86	184	...	...	...	16	10	8	18	65

MOSS, TYLER   G   FLAMES

PERSONAL: Born June 29, 1975, in Ottawa. ... 6-0/184. ... Catches right.
TRANSACTIONS/CAREER NOTES: Selected by Tampa Bay Lightning in second round (second Lightning pick, 29th overall) of NHL entry draft (June 26, 1993). ... Traded by Lightning to Calgary Flames for D Jamie Huscroft (March 18, 1997).
HONORS: Named to OHL All-Rookie team (1992-93). ... Named to OHL All-Star first team (1994-95). ... Shared Happy (Hap) Holmes Trophy with Jean-Sebastien Giguere (1997-98).
MISCELLANEOUS: Allowed a penalty shot goal (vs. Joe Sakic, November 1, 1997).

		REGULAR SEASON							PLAYOFFS					
Season Team	League	Gms.	Min	W	L	T	GA	SO	Avg.	Gms.	Min.	W	L	GA	SO	Avg.
91-92—Nepean........................	COJHL	26	1335	...	...	...	109	0	4.90	—	—	—	—	—	—	—
92-93—Kingston......................	OHL	31	1537	13	7	5	97	0	3.79	6	228	1	2	19	0	5.00
93-94—Kingston......................	OHL	13	795	6	4	3	42	1	3.17	3	136	0	2	8	0	3.53
94-95—Kingston......................	OHL	57	3249	33	17	5	164	1	3.03	6	333	2	4	27	0	4.86
95-96—Atlanta.......................	IHL	40	2030	11	19	‡4	138	1	4.08	3	213	0	3	11	0	3.10
96-97—Adirondack..................	AHL	11	507	1	5	2	42	1	4.97	—	—	—	—	—	—	—
—Grand Rapids..............	IHL	15	715	5	6	‡1	35	0	2.94	—	—	—	—	—	—	—
—Saint John.................	AHL	9	534	6	1	1	17	0	1.91	5	242	2	3	15	0	3.72
—Muskegon	Col.HL	2	119	1	1	0	5	0	2.52	—	—	—	—	—	—	—
97-98—Saint John..................	AHL	39	2194	19	10	7	91	0	2.49	15	762	8	†5	37	0	2.91
—Calgary......................	NHL	6	367	2	3	1	20	0	3.27	—	—	—	—	—	—	—
NHL Totals (1 year)............		6	367	2	3	1	20	0	3.27							

MOTTAU, MIKE   D   RANGERS

PERSONAL: Born March 19, 1978, in Quincy, Mass. ... 6-0/188. ... Shoots left.
COLLEGE: Boston College.
TRANSACTIONS/CAREER NOTES: Selected by New York Rangers in seventh round (10th pick, 182nd overall) of 1997 NHL entry draft.
HONORS: Named to NCAA All-America East second team (1997-98). ... Named to NCAA All-Tournament team (1997-98). ... Named to Hockey East All-Star first team (1997-98).

		REGULAR SEASON								PLAYOFFS				
Season Team	League	Gms.	G	A	Pts.	PIM	+/-	PP	SH	Gms.	G	A	Pts.	PIM
96-97—Boston College	Hockey East	38	5	18	23	77	...	...	...	—	—	—	—	—
97-98—Boston College	Hockey East	40	13	36	49	50	...	...	...	—	—	—	—	—

MRAZEK, FRANTISEK   LW   MAPLE LEAFS

PERSONAL: Born May 16, 1979, in Ceske Budejovice, Czechoslovakia. ... 6-4/211. ... Shoots left. ... Name pronounced muh-RA-zihk.
TRANSACTIONS/CAREER NOTES: Selected by Toronto Maple Leafs in fifth round (third Maple Leafs pick, 111th overall) of NHL entry draft (June 21, 1997).

		REGULAR SEASON								PLAYOFFS				
Season Team	League	Gms.	G	A	Pts.	PIM	+/-	PP	SH	Gms.	G	A	Pts.	PIM
95-96—Ceske Budejovice Jrs..	Czech Rep.	19	8	3	11	...	...	...	...	—	—	—	—	—
96-97—Ceske Budejovice Jrs..	Czech Rep.	41	18	15	33	...	...	...	...	—	—	—	—	—
97-98—Red Deer.....................	WHL	65	30	24	54	71	...	...	...	5	1	0	1	2

M

MROZIK, RICK   D   CAPITALS

PERSONAL: Born January 2, 1975, in Duluth, Minn. ... 6-2/218. ... Shoots left. ... Full name: Richard Donald Mrozik. ... Name pronounced MROH-zihk.
HIGH SCHOOL: Cloquet (Minn.).
COLLEGE: Minnesota-Duluth.
TRANSACTIONS/CAREER NOTES: Selected by Dallas Stars in sixth round (fourth Stars pick, 136th overall) of NHL entry draft (June 26, 1993). ... Rights traded by Stars with D Mark Tinordi to Washington Capitals for D Kevin Hatcher (January 18, 1995).
HONORS: Named to WCHA All-Star second team (1996-97).

		REGULAR SEASON								PLAYOFFS				
Season Team	League	Gms.	G	A	Pts.	PIM	+/-	PP	SH	Gms.	G	A	Pts.	PIM
92-93—Cloquet H.S.	Minn. H.S.	28	9	38	47	12	...	...	...	—	—	—	—	—
93-94—Minnesota-Duluth	WCHA	38	2	9	11	38	...	...	...	—	—	—	—	—
94-95—Minnesota-Duluth	WCHA	3	0	0	0	2	...	...	...	—	—	—	—	—
95-96—Minnesota-Duluth	WCHA	33	3	19	22	63	...	...	...	—	—	—	—	—
96-97—Minnesota-Duluth	WCHA	38	11	23	34	56	...	...	...	—	—	—	—	—
97-98—Portland	AHL	75	2	15	17	52	...	...	...	10	1	3	4	2

MUCKALT, BILL   RW   CANUCKS

PERSONAL: Born July 15, 1974, in Williams Lake, B.C. ... 6-0/195. ... Shoots right.
HIGH SCHOOL: Kelowna (B.C.) Christian.
COLLEGE: Michigan.
TRANSACTIONS/CAREER NOTES: Selected by Vancouver Canucks in ninth round (seventh Canucks pick, 221st overall) of NHL entry draft (June 29, 1994).
HONORS: Named to NCAA All-America West first team (1997-98). ... Named to CCHA All-Star first team (1997-98).

		REGULAR SEASON								PLAYOFFS				
Season Team	League	Gms.	G	A	Pts.	PIM	+/-	PP	SH	Gms.	G	A	Pts.	PIM
91-92—Merritt........................	BCJHL	55	14	11	25	75	...	...	...	—	—	—	—	—
92-93—Merritt........................	BCJHL	59	31	43	74	80	...	...	...	5	5	2	7	11
93-94—Merritt........................	BCJHL	43	58	51	109	99	...	...	...	—	—	—	—	—
—Kelowna......................	BCJHL	15	12	10	22	20	...	...	...	28	19	19	38	25
94-95—Univ. of Michigan........	CCHA	39	19	18	37	42	...	...	...	—	—	—	—	—
95-96—Univ. of Michigan........	CCHA	41	28	30	58	34	...	...	...	—	—	—	—	—
96-97—Univ. of Michigan........	CCHA	36	26	38	64	69	...	...	...	—	—	—	—	—
97-98—Univ. of Michigan........	CCHA	44	32	33	65	94	...	...	...	—	—	—	—	—

MUIR, BRYAN   D   DEVILS

PERSONAL: Born June 8, 1973, in Winnipeg. ... 6-4/220. ... Shoots left. ... Name pronounced MYOOR.
COLLEGE: New Hampshire.
TRANSACTIONS/CAREER NOTES: Signed to five-game amateur tryout from the Canadian national team (February 29, 1996). ... Signed as free agent by Edmonton Oilers (April 1996). ... Traded by Oilers with C Jason Arnott to New Jersey Devils for RW Bill Guerin and RW Valeri Zelepukin (January 4, 1998).

		REGULAR SEASON								PLAYOFFS				
Season Team	League	Gms.	G	A	Pts.	PIM	+/-	PP	SH	Gms.	G	A	Pts.	PIM
92-93—New Hampshire	Hockey East	26	1	2	3	24	...	...	...	—	—	—	—	—
93-94—New Hampshire	Hockey East	36	0	4	4	48	...	...	...	—	—	—	—	—
94-95—New Hampshire	Hockey East	28	9	9	18	48	...	...	...	—	—	—	—	—
95-96—Canadian nat'l team ...	Int'l	42	6	12	18	36	...	...	...	—	—	—	—	—
—Edmonton..................	NHL	5	0	0	0	6	-4	0	0	—	—	—	—	—
96-97—Hamilton	AHL	75	8	16	24	80	...	...	...	14	0	5	5	12
—Edmonton..................	NHL	—	—	—	—	—	—	—	—	5	0	0	0	4
97-98—Hamilton	AHL	28	3	10	13	62	...	...	...	—	—	—	—	—
—Edmonton..................	NHL	7	0	0	0	17	0	0	0	—	—	—	—	—
—Albany.......................	AHL	41	3	10	13	67	...	...	...	13	3	0	3	12
NHL Totals (3 years)............		12	0	0	0	23	-4	0	0	5	0	0	0	4

MULHERN, RYAN   RW   CAPITALS

PERSONAL: Born January 11, 1973, in Philadelphia, Pa. ... 6-1/200. ... Shoots right. ... Full name: Ryan Patrick Mulhern.
HIGH SCHOOL: Malvern Prep (Pa.), then St. George's School (Newport, R.I.), then Canterbury (New Milford, Conn.).
COLLEGE: Brown.
TRANSACTIONS/CAREER NOTES: Selected by Calgary Flames in eighth round (eighth Flames pick, 174th overall) in NHL entry draft (June 6, 1994). ... Signed as free agent by Washington Capitals (March 17, 1997).
HONORS: Named to AHL All-Star first team (1997-98).

		REGULAR SEASON								PLAYOFFS				
Season Team	League	Gms.	G	A	Pts.	PIM	+/-	PP	SH	Gms.	G	A	Pts.	PIM
91-92—Canterbury School......	Conn. H.S.	37	51	27	78	50	...	...	...	—	—	—	—	—
92-93—Brown University	ECAC	31	15	9	24	46	...	...	...	—	—	—	—	—
93-94—Brown University	ECAC	27	18	17	35	48	...	...	...	—	—	—	—	—
94-95—Brown University	ECAC	30	18	16	34	108	...	...	...	—	—	—	—	—
95-96—Brown University	ECAC	32	10	15	25	78	...	...	...	—	—	—	—	—
96-97—Hampton Roads.........	ECHL	40	22	16	38	52	...	...	...	—	—	—	—	—
—Portland....................	AHL	38	19	15	34	16	...	...	...	5	1	1	2	2
97-98—Portland....................	AHL	71	25	40	65	85	...	...	...	6	1	0	1	12
—Washington	NHL	3	0	0	0	0	0	0	0	—	—	—	—	—
NHL Totals (1 year).............		3	0	0	0	0	0	0	0					

MULLER, KIRK   C/LW   PANTHERS

PERSONAL: Born February 8, 1966, in Kingston, Ont. ... 6-0/205. ... Shoots left. ... Name pronounced MUH-luhr.
TRANSACTIONS/CAREER NOTES: Selected by New Jersey Devils as underage junior in first round (first Devils pick, second overall) of NHL entry draft (June 9, 1984). ... Strained knee (January 13, 1986). ... Fractured ribs (April 1986). ... Traded by Devils with G Roland Melanson to Montreal Canadiens for RW Stephane Richer and RW Tom Chorske (September 1991). ... Injured eye (January 21, 1992); missed one game. ... Bruised ribs (November 7, 1992); missed one game. ... Sprained wrist (March 6, 1993); missed two games. ... Injured shoulder (October 11, 1993); missed eight games. ... Traded by Canadiens with D Mathieu Schneider and C Craig Darby to New York Islanders for C Pierre Turgeon and D Vladimir Malakhov (April 5, 1995). ... Traded by Islanders to Toronto Maple Leafs for LW Ken Belanger and G Damian Rhodes (January 23, 1996). ... Separated shoulder (January 3, 1997); missed two games. ... Bruised ankle (March 8, 1997); missed two games. ... Traded by Maple Leafs to Florida Panthers for RW Jason Podollan (March 18, 1997). ... Suspended two games and fined $1,000 by NHL for high-sticking incident (December 1, 1997). ... Sprained left knee (December 20, 1997); missed eight games.
HONORS: Won William Hanley Trophy (1982-83). ... Played in NHL All-Star Game (1985, 1986, 1988, 1990, 1992 and 1993).
MISCELLANEOUS: Member of Stanley Cup championship team (1993). ... Captain of New Jersey Devils (1987-88 through 1990-91). ... Captain of Montreal Canadiens (1994-95). ... Holds New Jersey Devils all-time record for most assists (335). ... Scored on a penalty shot (vs. Greg Millen, March 21, 1987). ... Failed to score on a penalty shot (vs. Mike Vernon, March 14, 1989).
STATISTICAL PLATEAUS: Three-goal games: 1986-87 (1), 1987-88 (3), 1991-92 (2), 1995-96 (1). Total: 7.

Season Team	League	REGULAR SEASON								PLAYOFFS				
		Gms.	G	A	Pts.	PIM	+/-	PP	SH	Gms.	G	A	Pts.	PIM
80-81—Kingston	OMJHL	2	0	0	0	0	...	...	...	—	—	—	—	—
81-82—Kingston	OHL	67	12	39	51	27	...	...	...	4	5	1	6	4
82-83—Guelph	OHL	66	52	60	112	41	...	...	...	—	—	—	—	—
83-84—Can. Olympic Team	Int'l	15	2	2	4	6	...	...	...	—	—	—	—	—
—Guelph	OHL	49	31	63	94	27	...	...	...	—	—	—	—	—
84-85—New Jersey	NHL	80	17	37	54	69	-31	9	1	—	—	—	—	—
85-86—New Jersey	NHL	77	25	41	66	45	-19	5	1	—	—	—	—	—
86-87—New Jersey	NHL	79	26	50	76	75	-7	10	1	—	—	—	—	—
87-88—New Jersey	NHL	80	37	57	94	114	19	17	2	20	4	8	12	37
88-89—New Jersey	NHL	80	31	43	74	119	-23	12	1	—	—	—	—	—
89-90—New Jersey	NHL	80	30	56	86	74	-1	9	0	6	1	3	4	11
90-91—New Jersey	NHL	80	19	51	70	76	1	7	0	7	0	2	2	10
91-92—Montreal	NHL	78	36	41	77	86	15	15	1	11	4	3	7	31
92-93—Montreal	NHL	80	37	57	94	77	8	12	0	20	10	7	17	18
93-94—Montreal	NHL	76	23	34	57	96	-1	9	2	7	6	2	8	4
94-95—Montreal	NHL	33	8	11	19	33	-21	3	0	—	—	—	—	—
—New York Islanders	NHL	12	3	5	8	14	3	1	1	—	—	—	—	—
95-96—New York Islanders	NHL	15	4	3	7	15	-10	0	0	—	—	—	—	—
—Toronto	NHL	36	9	16	25	42	-3	7	0	6	3	2	5	0
96-97—Toronto	NHL	66	20	17	37	85	-23	9	1	—	—	—	—	—
—Florida	NHL	10	1	2	3	4	-2	1	0	5	1	2	5	4
97-98—Florida	NHL	70	8	21	29	54	-14	1	0	—	—	—	—	—
NHL Totals (14 years)		1032	334	542	876	1078	-109	127	11	82	29	29	58	115

MUNI, CRAIG   D

M

PERSONAL: Born July 19, 1962, in Toronto. ... 6-3/208. ... Shoots left. ... Full name: Craig Douglas Muni. ... Name pronounced MYOO-nee.
TRANSACTIONS/CAREER NOTES: Selected by Toronto Maple Leafs as underage junior in second round (first Maple Leafs pick, 25th overall) of NHL entry draft (June 11, 1980). ... Tore left knee ligaments (September 1981). ... Broke ankle (January 1983). ... Signed as free agent by Edmonton Oilers (August 18, 1986). ... Traded by Oilers to Buffalo Sabres for cash (October 2, 1986). ... Traded by Sabres to Pittsburgh Penguins for future considerations (October 3, 1986). ... Traded by Penguins to Oilers to complete earlier trade for G Gilles Meloche (October 6, 1986). ... Bruised kidney (May 1987). ... Bruised ankle (January 1988). ... Bruised ankle (December 17, 1988). ... Strained right shoulder (January 1989). ... Broke little finger of right hand (January 27, 1990); missed eight games. ... Suffered pinched nerve (January 15, 1992); missed 17 games. ... Injured knee (March 19, 1992); missed eight games. ... Suspended two games by NHL during playoffs for kneeing (May 22, 1992); missed final 1992 playoff game and first game of 1992-93 regular season. ... Suffered from the flu (December 1992); missed one game. ... Injured eye (February 18, 1993); missed two games. ... Traded by Oilers to Chicago Blackhawks for C Mike Hudson (March 22, 1993). ... Traded by Blackhawks to Buffalo Sabres for D Keith Carney (October 27, 1993). ... Pulled left hamstring (February 15, 1995); missed six games. ... Injured left knee (March 16, 1995); missed two games. ... Traded by Sabres to Winnipeg Jets for LW Michael Grosek and D Darryl Shannon (February 15, 1996). ... Strained groin (March 13, 1996); missed three games. ... Signed as free agent by Penguins (October 1, 1996). ... Bruised leg (December 10, 1996); missed three games. ... Suffered from the flu (January 14, 1997); missed two games. ... Injured jaw (February 8, 1997); missed six games. ... Signed as free agent by Dallas Stars (October 2, 1997). ... Strained groin (February 25, 1998); missed three games. ... Strained groin (March 26, 1998); missed nine games.
MISCELLANEOUS: Member of Stanley Cup championship team (1987, 1988 and 1990).

Season Team	League	REGULAR SEASON								PLAYOFFS				
		Gms.	G	A	Pts.	PIM	+/-	PP	SH	Gms.	G	A	Pts.	PIM
79-80—Kingston	OMJHL	66	6	28	34	114	...	...	...	—	—	—	—	—
80-81—Kingston	OMJHL	38	2	14	16	65	...	...	...	—	—	—	—	—
—Windsor	OMJHL	25	5	11	16	41	...	...	...	11	1	4	5	14
—New Brunswick	AHL	—	—	—	—	—	...	...	...	2	0	1	1	10
81-82—Toronto	NHL	3	0	0	0	2	-4	0	0	—	—	—	—	—
—Windsor	OHL	49	5	32	37	92	...	...	...	9	2	3	5	16
—Cincinnati	CHL	—	—	—	—	—	...	...	...	3	0	2	2	2
82-83—Toronto	NHL	2	0	1	1	0	-3	0	0	—	—	—	—	—
—St. Catharines	AHL	64	6	32	38	52	...	...	...	—	—	—	—	—
83-84—St. Catharines	AHL	64	4	16	20	79	...	...	...	7	0	1	1	0
84-85—St. Catharines	AHL	68	7	17	24	54	...	...	...	—	—	—	—	—
—Toronto	NHL	8	0	0	0	0	0	0	0	—	—	—	—	—
85-86—Toronto	NHL	6	0	1	1	4	-3	0	0	—	—	—	—	—
—St. Catharines	AHL	73	3	34	37	91	...	...	...	13	0	5	5	16
86-87—Edmonton	NHL	79	7	22	29	85	45	0	0	14	0	2	2	17

Season Team	League	REGULAR SEASON								PLAYOFFS				
		Gms.	G	A	Pts.	PIM	+/-	PP	SH	Gms.	G	A	Pts.	PIM
87-88—Edmonton	NHL	72	4	15	19	77	32	0	1	19	0	4	4	31
88-89—Edmonton	NHL	69	5	13	18	71	43	0	0	7	0	3	3	8
89-90—Edmonton	NHL	71	5	12	17	81	22	0	2	22	0	3	3	16
90-91—Edmonton	NHL	76	1	9	10	77	10	0	0	18	0	3	3	20
91-92—Edmonton	NHL	54	2	5	7	34	11	0	0	3	0	0	0	2
92-93—Edmonton	NHL	72	0	11	11	67	-15	0	0	—	—	—	—	—
—Chicago.....................	NHL	9	0	0	0	8	1	0	0	4	0	0	0	2
93-94—Chicago.....................	NHL	9	0	4	4	4	3	0	0	—	—	—	—	—
—Buffalo	NHL	73	2	8	10	62	28	0	1	7	0	0	0	4
94-95—Buffalo	NHL	40	0	6	6	36	-4	0	0	5	0	1	1	2
95-96—Buffalo	NHL	47	0	4	4	69	-12	0	0	—	—	—	—	—
—Winnipeg	NHL	25	1	3	4	37	6	0	0	6	0	1	1	2
96-97—Pittsburgh	NHL	64	0	4	4	36	-6	0	0	3	0	0	0	0
97-98—Dallas........................	NHL	40	1	1	2	25	0	0	0	5	0	0	0	4
NHL Totals (16 years)..........		819	28	119	147	775	154	0	4	113	0	17	17	108

MURPHY, GORD   D   PANTHERS

PERSONAL: Born February 23, 1967, in Willowdale, Ont. ... 6-2/198. ... Shoots right. ... Full name: Gordon Murphy.

TRANSACTIONS/CAREER NOTES: Injured clavicle (January 1985). ... Selected by Philadelphia Flyers as underage junior in ninth round (10th Flyers pick, 189th overall) of NHL entry draft (June 15, 1985). ... Injured left foot and suffered hip pointer (March 24, 1990). ... Traded by Flyers with RW Brian Dobbin and third-round pick (LW Sergei Zholtok) in 1992 draft to Boston Bruins for D Garry Galley, C Wes Walz and future considerations (January 2, 1992). ... Injured ankle (January 1993); missed 16 games. ... Traded by Bruins to Dallas Stars for future considerations (June 20, 1993); Bruins sent G Andy Moog to Stars for G Jon Casey to complete deal (June 25, 1993). ... Selected by Florida Panthers in NHL expansion draft (June 24, 1993). ... Suffered illness (March 26, 1995); missed one game. ... Sprained left ankle (April 5, 1995); missed one game. ... Sprained right ankle (January 29, 1996); missed nine games. ... Injured toe (April 8, 1996); missed three games. ... Suffered from the flu (January 27, 1998); missed three games.

HONORS: Named to Memorial Cup All-Star team (1986-87).

Season Team	League	REGULAR SEASON								PLAYOFFS				
		Gms.	G	A	Pts.	PIM	+/-	PP	SH	Gms.	G	A	Pts.	PIM
83-84—Don Mills Flyers..........	MTHL	65	24	42	66	130	...	...	...	—	—	—	—	—
84-85—Oshawa.....................	OHL	59	3	12	15	25	...	...	...	—	—	—	—	—
85-86—Oshawa.....................	OHL	64	7	15	22	56	...	...	...	6	1	1	2	6
86-87—Oshawa.....................	OHL	56	7	30	37	95	...	...	...	24	6	16	22	22
87-88—Hershey	AHL	62	8	20	28	44	...	...	...	12	0	8	8	12
88-89—Philadelphia	NHL	75	4	31	35	68	-3	3	0	19	2	7	9	13
89-90—Philadelphia	NHL	75	14	27	41	95	-7	4	0	—	—	—	—	—
90-91—Philadelphia	NHL	80	11	31	42	58	-7	6	0	—	—	—	—	—
91-92—Philadelphia	NHL	31	2	8	10	33	-4	0	0	—	—	—	—	—
—Boston	NHL	42	3	6	9	51	2	0	0	15	1	0	1	12
92-93—Boston	NHL	49	5	12	17	62	-13	3	0	—	—	—	—	—
—Providence................	AHL	2	1	3	4	2	...	...	...	—	—	—	—	—
93-94—Florida.......................	NHL	84	14	29	43	71	-11	9	0	—	—	—	—	—
94-95—Florida.......................	NHL	46	6	16	22	24	-14	5	0	—	—	—	—	—
95-96—Florida.......................	NHL	70	8	22	30	30	5	4	0	14	0	4	4	6
96-97—Florida.......................	NHL	80	8	15	23	51	3	2	0	5	0	5	5	4
97-98—Florida.......................	NHL	79	6	11	17	46	-3	3	0	—	—	—	—	—
NHL Totals (10 years)..........		711	81	208	289	589	-52	39	0	53	3	16	19	35

MURPHY, JOE   RW   SHARKS

PERSONAL: Born October 16, 1967, in London, Ont. ... 6-0/194. ... Shoots left. ... Full name: Joseph Patrick Murphy.

COLLEGE: Michigan State.

TRANSACTIONS/CAREER NOTES: Selected by Detroit Red Wings in first round (first Red Wings pick, first overall) of NHL entry draft (June 21, 1986). ... Sprained right ankle (January 1988). ... Traded by Red Wings with C/LW Adam Graves, LW Petr Klima and D Jeff Sharples to Edmonton Oilers for C Jimmy Carson, C Kevin McClelland and fifth-round pick (traded to Montreal Canadiens who selected D Brad Layzell) in 1991 draft (November 2, 1989). ... Bruised both thighs (March 1990). ... Did not report to Oilers in 1992-93 season because of contract dispute; missed 63 games. ... Traded by Oilers to Chicago Blackhawks for D Igor Kravchuk and C Dean McAmmond (February 25, 1993). ... Pulled groin (February 3, 1995); missed three games. ... Reinjured groin (March 6, 1995); missed four games. ... Sprained knee (March 21, 1995); missed one game. ... Suspended 10 games by NHL for being third man in fight (September 20, 1995). ... Strained back (December 28, 1995); missed four games. ... Strained back (January 6, 1996). ... Signed as free agent by St. Louis Blues (July 3, 1996). ... Suffered from a virus (October 31, 1996); missed five games. ... Strained groin (January 30, 1997); missed one game. ... Tore ligament in left wrist (November 6, 1997); missed 42 games. ... Strained groin (March 3, 1998); missed one game. ... Traded by Blues to San Jose Sharks for D Todd Gill (March 24, 1998). ... Suspended two games and fined $1,000 by NHL for slashing incident (March 31, 1998).

HONORS: Named BCJHL Rookie of the Year (1984-85). ... Named CCHA Rookie of the Year (1985-86).

MISCELLANEOUS: Member of Stanley Cup championship team (1990).

Season Team	League	REGULAR SEASON								PLAYOFFS				
		Gms.	G	A	Pts.	PIM	+/-	PP	SH	Gms.	G	A	Pts.	PIM
84-85—Penticton	BCJHL	51	68	84	*152	92	...	...	...	—	—	—	—	—
85-86—Michigan State............	CCHA	35	24	37	61	50	...	...	...	—	—	—	—	—
—Canadian nat'l team	Int'l	8	3	3	6	2	...	...	...	—	—	—	—	—
86-87—Adirondack	AHL	71	21	38	59	61	...	...	...	10	2	1	3	33
—Detroit.......................	NHL	5	0	1	1	2	0	0	0	—	—	—	—	—
87-88—Adirondack	AHL	6	5	6	11	4	...	...	...	—	—	—	—	—
—Detroit.......................	NHL	50	10	9	19	37	-4	1	0	8	0	1	1	6
88-89—Detroit.......................	NHL	26	1	7	8	28	-7	0	0	—	—	—	—	—
—Adirondack	AHL	47	31	35	66	66	...	...	...	16	6	11	17	17

M

Season Team	League	Gms.	G	A	Pts.	PIM	+/-	PP	SH	Gms.	G	A	Pts.	PIM
89-90—Detroit........................	NHL	9	3	1	4	4	4	0	0	—	—	—	—	—
—Edmonton..................	NHL	62	7	18	25	56	1	2	0	22	6	8	14	16
90-91—Edmonton..................	NHL	80	27	35	62	35	2	4	1	15	2	5	7	14
91-92—Edmonton..................	NHL	80	35	47	82	52	17	10	2	16	8	16	24	12
92-93—Chicago..................	NHL	19	7	10	17	18	-3	5	0	4	0	0	0	8
93-94—Chicago..................	NHL	81	31	39	70	111	1	7	4	6	1	3	4	25
94-95—Chicago..................	NHL	40	23	18	41	89	7	7	0	16	9	3	12	29
95-96—Chicago..................	NHL	70	22	29	51	86	-3	8	0	10	6	2	8	33
96-97—St. Louis	NHL	75	20	25	45	69	-1	4	1	6	1	1	2	10
97-98—St. Louis	NHL	27	4	9	13	22	8	2	0	—	—	—	—	—
—San Jose..................	NHL	10	5	4	9	14	1	2	0	6	1	1	2	20
NHL Totals (12 years).........		**634**	**195**	**252**	**447**	**623**	**23**	**52**	**8**	**109**	**34**	**40**	**74**	**173**

MURPHY, LARRY   D   RED WINGS

PERSONAL: Born March 8, 1961, in Scarborough, Ont. ... 6-2/218. ... Shoots right. ... Full name: Lawrence Thomas Murphy.

TRANSACTIONS/CAREER NOTES: Selected by Los Angeles Kings as underage junior in first round (first Kings pick, fourth overall) of NHL entry draft (June 11, 1980). ... Traded by Kings to Washington Capitals for D Brian Engblom and RW Ken Houston (October 18, 1983). ... Injured foot (October 29, 1985). ... Broke ankle (May 1988). ... Traded by Capitals with RW Mike Gartner to Minnesota North Stars for RW Dino Ciccarelli and D Bob Rouse (March 7, 1989). ... Traded by North Stars with D Peter Taglianetti to Pittsburgh Penguins for D Jim Johnson and D Chris Dahlquist (December 11, 1990). ... Fractured right foot (February 22, 1991); played until March 5 then missed five games. ... Suffered back spasms (March 28, 1993); missed one game. ... Traded by Penguins to Toronto Maple Leafs for D Dmitri Mironov and second-round pick (traded to New Jersey) in 1996 draft (July 8, 1995). ... Traded by Maple Leafs to Detroit Red Wings for future considerations (March 18, 1997).

HONORS: Won Max Kaminsky Trophy (1979-80). ... Named to OMJHL All-Star first team (1979-80). ... Named to Memorial Cup All-Star team (1979-80). ... Named to THE SPORTING NEWS All-Star second team (1986-87 and 1992-93). ... Named to NHL All-Star second team (1986-87, 1992-93 and 1994-95). ... Played in NHL All-Star Game (1994 and 1996).

RECORDS: Holds NHL rookie-season records for most points by a defenseman—76; and most assists by a defenseman—60 (1980-81).

MISCELLANEOUS: Member of Stanley Cup championship team (1991, 1992, 1997 and 1998).

Season Team	League	Gms.	G	A	Pts.	PIM	+/-	PP	SH	Gms.	G	A	Pts.	PIM
78-79—Peterborough.............	OMJHL	66	6	21	27	82	...	...	...	19	1	9	10	42
79-80—Peterborough.............	OMJHL	68	21	68	89	88	...	...	...	14	4	13	17	20
80-81—Los Angeles...............	NHL	80	16	60	76	79	17	5	1	4	3	0	3	2
81-82—Los Angeles...............	NHL	79	22	44	66	95	-13	8	1	10	2	8	10	12
82-83—Los Angeles...............	NHL	77	14	48	62	81	2	9	0	—	—	—	—	—
83-84—Los Angeles...............	NHL	6	0	3	3	0	-4	0	0	—	—	—	—	—
—Washington...............	NHL	72	13	33	46	50	12	2	0	8	0	3	3	6
84-85—Washington...............	NHL	79	13	42	55	51	21	3	0	5	2	3	5	0
85-86—Washington...............	NHL	78	21	44	65	50	3	8	1	9	1	5	6	6
86-87—Washington...............	NHL	80	23	58	81	39	25	8	0	7	2	2	4	6
87-88—Washington...............	NHL	79	8	53	61	72	2	7	0	13	4	4	8	33
88-89—Washington...............	NHL	65	7	29	36	70	-5	3	0	—	—	—	—	—
—Minnesota...............	NHL	13	4	6	10	12	5	3	0	5	0	2	2	8
89-90—Minnesota...............	NHL	77	10	58	68	44	-13	4	0	7	1	2	3	31
90-91—Minnesota...............	NHL	31	4	11	15	38	-8	1	0	—	—	—	—	—
—Pittsburgh...............	NHL	44	5	23	28	30	2	2	0	23	5	18	23	44
91-92—Pittsburgh...............	NHL	77	21	56	77	48	33	7	2	21	6	10	16	19
92-93—Pittsburgh...............	NHL	83	22	63	85	73	45	6	2	12	2	11	13	10
93-94—Pittsburgh...............	NHL	84	17	56	73	44	10	7	0	6	0	5	5	0
94-95—Pittsburgh...............	NHL	48	13	25	38	18	12	4	0	12	2	13	15	0
95-96—Toronto...............	NHL	82	12	49	61	34	-2	8	0	6	0	2	2	4
96-97—Toronto...............	NHL	69	7	32	39	20	1	4	0	—	—	—	—	—
—Detroit...............	NHL	12	2	4	6	0	2	1	0	20	2	9	11	8
97-98—Detroit........................	NHL	82	11	41	52	37	35	2	1	22	3	12	15	2
NHL Totals (18 years).........		**1397**	**265**	**838**	**1103**	**985**	**182**	**102**	**8**	**190**	**35**	**109**	**144**	**191**

MURRAY, CHRIS   RW   SENATORS

PERSONAL: Born October 25, 1974, in Port Hardy, B.C. ... 6-2/209. ... Shoots right.

TRANSACTIONS/CAREER NOTES: Selected by Montreal Canadiens in third round (third Canadiens pick, 54th overall) of NHL entry draft (June 29, 1994). ... Suspended three games without pay and fined $1000 by NHL for cross-checking (April 3, 1996). ... Fractured hand (October 3, 1996); missed 10 games. ... Traded by Canadiens with D Murray Baron to Phoenix Coyotes for D Dave Manson (March 18, 1997). ... Traded by Coyotes to Hartford Whalers for D Gerald Diduck (March 18, 1997). ... Suffered from the flu (March 27, 1997); missed two games. ... Whalers franchise moved to North Carolina and renamed Carolina Hurricanes for 1997-98 season; NHL approved move on June 25, 1997. ... Sprained knee (October 18, 1997); missed 11 games. ... Traded by Hurricanes to Ottawa Senators for D Sean Hill (November 18, 1997). ... Injured shoulder (November 27, 1997); missed nine games.

Season Team	League	Gms.	G	A	Pts.	PIM	+/-	PP	SH	Gms.	G	A	Pts.	PIM
90-91—Bellingham Jr. A	BCJHL	54	5	8	13	150	...	...	...	—	—	—	—	—
91-92—Kamloops	WHL	33	1	1	2	168	...	...	...	5	0	0	0	10
92-93—Kamloops	WHL	62	6	10	16	217	...	...	...	13	0	4	4	34
93-94—Kamloops	WHL	59	14	16	30	260	...	...	...	15	4	2	6	107
94-95—Fredericton	AHL	55	6	12	18	234	...	...	...	12	1	1	2	50
—Montreal...............	NHL	3	0	0	0	4	0	0	0	—	—	—	—	—
95-96—Fredericton	AHL	30	13	13	26	217	...	...	...	—	—	—	—	—
—Montreal...............	NHL	48	3	4	7	163	5	0	0	4	0	0	0	4

M

Season Team	League	REGULAR SEASON								PLAYOFFS				
		Gms.	G	A	Pts.	PIM	+/-	PP	SH	Gms.	G	A	Pts.	PIM
96-97—Montreal	NHL	56	4	2	6	114	-8	0	0	—	—	—	—	—
—Hartford	NHL	8	1	1	2	10	1	0	0	—	—	—	—	—
97-98—Carolina	NHL	7	0	1	1	22	2	0	0	—	—	—	—	—
—Ottawa	NHL	46	5	3	8	96	1	0	0	11	1	0	1	8
NHL Totals (4 years)		168	13	11	24	409	1	0	0	15	1	0	1	12

MURRAY, GLEN   RW   KINGS

PERSONAL: Born November 1, 1972, in Halifax, Nova Scotia. ... 6-2/221. ... Shoots right.

TRANSACTIONS/CAREER NOTES: Selected by Boston Bruins in first round (first Bruins pick, 18th overall) of NHL entry draft (June 22, 1991). ... Injured elbow (December 15, 1993); missed two games. ... Traded by Bruins with C Bryan Smolinski to Pittsburgh Penguins for LW Kevin Stevens and C Shawn McEachern (August 2, 1995). ... Separated shoulder (January 1, 1996); missed 10 games. ... Suffered concussion (April 11, 1996); missed one game. ... Traded by Penguins to Los Angeles Kings for C Ed Olczyk (March 18, 1997). ... Suffered from the flu (November 13, 1997); missed one game.

MISCELLANEOUS: Failed to score on a penalty shot (vs. Guy Hebert, February 7, 1998).

STATISTICAL PLATEAUS: Three-goal games: 1997-98 (1).

Season Team	League	REGULAR SEASON								PLAYOFFS				
		Gms.	G	A	Pts.	PIM	+/-	PP	SH	Gms.	G	A	Pts.	PIM
89-90—Sudbury	OHL	62	8	28	36	17	...	...	...	7	0	0	0	4
90-91—Sudbury	OHL	66	27	38	65	82	...	...	...	5	8	4	12	10
91-92—Sudbury	OHL	54	37	47	84	93	...	...	...	11	7	4	11	18
—Boston	NHL	5	3	1	4	0	2	1	0	15	4	2	6	10
92-93—Providence	AHL	48	30	26	56	42	...	...	...	6	1	4	5	4
—Boston	NHL	27	3	4	7	8	-6	2	0	—	—	—	—	—
93-94—Boston	NHL	81	18	13	31	48	-1	0	0	13	4	5	9	14
94-95—Boston	NHL	35	5	2	7	46	-11	0	0	2	0	0	0	2
95-96—Pittsburgh	NHL	69	14	15	29	57	4	0	0	18	2	6	8	10
96-97—Pittsburgh	NHL	66	11	11	22	24	-19	3	0	—	—	—	—	—
—Los Angeles	NHL	11	5	3	8	8	-2	0	0	—	—	—	—	—
97-98—Los Angeles	NHL	81	29	31	60	54	6	7	3	4	2	0	2	6
NHL Totals (7 years)		375	88	80	168	245	-27	13	3	52	12	13	25	42

MURRAY, MARTY   C   FLAMES

PERSONAL: Born February 16, 1975, in Deloraine, Man. ... 5-9/178. ... Shoots left.

TRANSACTIONS/CAREER NOTES: Selected by Calgary Flames in fourth round (fifth Flames pick, 96th overall) of NHL entry draft (June 26, 1993). ... Bruised foot (April 8, 1996); missed three games.

HONORS: Named to Can.HL All-Star second team (1993-94). ... Named to WHL (East) All-Star first team (1993-94 and 1994-95). ... Won Four Broncos Memorial Trophy (1994-95).

Season Team	League	REGULAR SEASON								PLAYOFFS				
		Gms.	G	A	Pts.	PIM	+/-	PP	SH	Gms.	G	A	Pts.	PIM
91-92—Brandon	WHL	68	20	36	56	12	...	...	...	—	—	—	—	—
92-93—Brandon	WHL	67	29	65	94	50	...	...	...	4	1	3	4	0
93-94—Brandon	WHL	64	43	71	114	33	...	...	...	14	6	14	20	14
94-95—Brandon	WHL	65	40	88	128	53	...	...	...	18	9	20	29	16
95-96—Calgary	NHL	15	3	3	6	0	-4	2	0	—	—	—	—	—
—Saint John	AHL	58	25	31	56	20	...	...	...	14	2	4	6	4
96-97—Saint John	AHL	67	19	39	58	40	...	...	...	5	2	3	5	4
—Calgary	NHL	2	0	0	0	4	0	0	0	—	—	—	—	—
97-98—Calgary	NHL	2	0	0	0	2	1	0	0	—	—	—	—	—
—Saint John	AHL	41	10	30	40	16	...	...	...	21	10	10	20	12
NHL Totals (3 years)		19	3	3	6	6	-3	2	0					

MURRAY, REM   C/LW   OILERS

PERSONAL: Born October 9, 1972, in Stratford, Ont. ... 6-2/195. ... Shoots left. ... Full name: Raymond Murray.

COLLEGE: Michigan State.

TRANSACTIONS/CAREER NOTES: Selected by Los Angeles Kings in sixth round (fifth Kings pick, 135th overall) of NHL entry draft (June 20, 1992). ... Signed as free agent by Edmonton Oilers (August 17, 1995). ... Missed first five games of 1997-98 season recovering from wrist injury and off-season appendectomy. ... Strained neck (March 17, 1998); missed one game. ... Suffered from the flu (April 6, 1998); missed three games.

HONORS: Named to CCHA All-Star second team (1994-95).

STATISTICAL PLATEAUS: Three-goal games: 1996-97 (1).

Season Team	League	REGULAR SEASON								PLAYOFFS				
		Gms.	G	A	Pts.	PIM	+/-	PP	SH	Gms.	G	A	Pts.	PIM
90-91—Stratford Jr. B	OHA	48	39	59	98	22	...	...	...	—	—	—	—	—
91-92—Michigan State	CCHA	44	12	36	48	16	...	...	...	—	—	—	—	—
92-93—Michigan State	CCHA	40	22	35	57	24	...	...	...	—	—	—	—	—
93-94—Michigan State	CCHA	41	16	38	54	18	...	...	...	—	—	—	—	—
94-95—Michigan State	CCHA	40	20	36	56	21	...	...	...	—	—	—	—	—
95-96—Cape Breton	AHL	79	31	59	90	40	...	...	...	—	—	—	—	—
96-97—Edmonton	NHL	82	11	20	31	16	9	1	0	12	1	2	3	4
97-98—Edmonton	NHL	61	9	9	18	39	-9	2	2	11	1	4	5	2
NHL Totals (2 years)		143	20	29	49	55	0	3	2	23	2	6	8	6

PERSONAL: Born April 4, 1967, in Toronto. ... 6-1/180. ... Shoots right. ... Full name: Robert Murray.
TRANSACTIONS/CAREER NOTES: Selected by Washington Capitals as underage junior in third round (third Capitals pick, 61st overall) of NHL entry draft (June 15, 1985). ... Suspended two games by OHL (November 2, 1986). ... Injured right hip (December 21, 1989); missed 10 games. ... Selected by Minnesota North Stars in NHL expansion draft (May 30, 1991). ... Traded by North Stars with future considerations to Winnipeg Jets for seventh-round pick (G Geoff Finch) in 1991 draft and future considerations (May 30, 1991). ... Strained groin (November 2, 1992); missed three games. ... Suffered back spasms (December 15, 1992); missed six games. ... Jets franchise moved to Phoenix and renamed Coyotes for 1996-97; NHL approved move on January 18, 1996.

		REGULAR SEASON								PLAYOFFS				
Season Team	League	Gms.	G	A	Pts.	PIM	+/-	PP	SH	Gms.	G	A	Pts.	PIM
83-84—Mississauga	OHA	35	18	36	54	32	...	...	...	—	—	—	—	—
84-85—Peterborough	OHL	63	12	9	21	155	...	...	...	17	2	7	9	45
85-86—Peterborough	OHL	52	14	18	32	125	...	...	...	16	1	2	3	50
86-87—Peterborough	OHL	62	17	37	54	204	...	...	...	3	1	4	5	8
87-88—Fort Wayne	IHL	80	12	21	33	139	...	...	...	6	0	2	2	16
88-89—Baltimore	AHL	80	11	23	34	235	...	...	...	—	—	—	—	—
89-90—Baltimore	AHL	23	5	4	9	63	...	...	...	—	—	—	—	—
—Washington	NHL	41	2	7	9	58	-10	0	0	9	0	0	0	18
90-91—Baltimore	AHL	48	6	20	26	177	...	...	...	4	0	0	0	12
—Washington	NHL	17	0	3	3	19	0	0	0	—	—	—	—	—
91-92—Moncton	AHL	60	16	15	31	247	...	...	...	8	0	1	1	56
—Winnipeg	NHL	9	0	1	1	18	-2	0	0	—	—	—	—	—
92-93—Moncton	AHL	56	16	21	37	147	...	...	...	3	0	0	0	6
—Winnipeg	NHL	10	1	0	1	6	0	0	0	—	—	—	—	—
93-94—Moncton	AHL	69	25	32	57	280	...	...	...	21	2	3	5	60
—Winnipeg	NHL	6	0	0	0	2	0	0	0	—	—	—	—	—
94-95—Springfield	AHL	78	16	38	54	373	...	...	...	—	—	—	—	—
—Winnipeg	NHL	10	0	2	2	2	1	0	0	—	—	—	—	—
95-96—Springfield	AHL	74	10	28	38	263	...	...	...	10	1	6	7	32
—Winnipeg	NHL	1	0	0	0	2	-1	0	0	—	—	—	—	—
96-97—Springfield	AHL	78	16	27	43	234	...	...	...	17	2	3	5	66
97-98—Springfield	AHL	80	7	30	37	255	...	...	...	4	0	2	2	2
NHL Totals (7 years)		94	3	13	16	107	-12	0	0	9	0	0	0	18

PERSONAL: Born December 9, 1966, in Regina, Sask. ... 6-2/200. ... Shoots left. ... Name pronounced MUHR-zihn.
TRANSACTIONS/CAREER NOTES: Selected by Hartford Whalers as underage junior in first round (first Whalers pick, fifth overall) of NHL entry draft (June 15, 1985). ... Traded by Whalers with RW Shane Churla to Calgary Flames for C Carey Wilson, D Neil Sheehy and LW Lane MacDonald (January 3, 1988). ... Strained knee (March 13, 1989). ... Pulled groin (February 4, 1990). ... Bruised hip (October 25, 1990); missed 11 games. ... Separated shoulder (December 1, 1990); missed 34 games. ... Traded by Flames to Vancouver Canucks for RW Ron Stern, D Kevan Guy and option to switch fourth-round picks in 1992 draft; Flames did not exercise option (March 5, 1991). ... Suffered from the flu (February 26, 1993); missed two games. ... Underwent minor knee surgery (January 21, 1995); missed five games. ... Sprained knee (April 30, 1995); missed last game of season. ... Underwent knee surgery (November 8, 1995); missed 12 games. ... Sprained wrist (October 17, 1996); missed 14 games. ... Injured shoulder (December 1, 1996); missed four games. ... Injured knee (December 27, 1997); missed remainder of season.
HONORS: Named to WHL (East) All-Star first team (1984-85). ... Named to NHL All-Rookie team (1985-86).
MISCELLANEOUS: Member of Stanley Cup championship team (1989).
STATISTICAL PLATEAUS: Three-goal games: 1989-90 (1).

		REGULAR SEASON								PLAYOFFS				
Season Team	League	Gms.	G	A	Pts.	PIM	+/-	PP	SH	Gms.	G	A	Pts.	PIM
83-84—Calgary	WHL	65	11	20	31	135	...	...	...	2	0	0	0	0
84-85—Calgary	WHL	72	32	60	92	233	...	...	...	8	1	11	12	16
85-86—Hartford	NHL	78	3	23	26	125	1	0	0	4	0	0	0	10
86-87—Hartford	NHL	74	9	19	28	95	18	1	0	6	2	1	3	29
87-88—Hartford	NHL	33	1	6	7	45	-8	1	0	—	—	—	—	—
—Calgary	NHL	41	6	5	11	94	9	0	0	5	2	0	2	13
88-89—Calgary	NHL	63	3	19	22	142	26	0	1	21	0	3	3	20
89-90—Calgary	NHL	78	7	13	20	140	19	1	0	6	2	2	4	2
90-91—Calgary	NHL	19	0	2	2	30	-4	0	0	—	—	—	—	—
—Vancouver	NHL	10	1	0	1	8	-3	0	0	6	0	1	1	8
91-92—Vancouver	NHL	70	3	11	14	147	15	0	1	1	0	0	0	15
92-93—Vancouver	NHL	79	5	11	16	196	34	0	0	12	3	2	5	18
93-94—Vancouver	NHL	80	6	14	20	109	4	0	1	7	0	0	0	4
94-95—Vancouver	NHL	40	0	8	8	129	14	0	0	8	0	1	1	22
95-96—Vancouver	NHL	69	2	10	12	130	9	0	0	6	0	0	0	25
96-97—Vancouver	NHL	61	1	7	8	118	7	0	0	—	—	—	—	—
97-98—Vancouver	NHL	31	5	2	7	42	-3	0	0	—	—	—	—	—
NHL Totals (13 years)		826	52	150	202	1550	138	3	3	82	9	10	19	166

PERSONAL: Born December 17, 1964, in Pardubice, Czechoslovakia. ... 6-3/215. ... Shoots left. ... Full name: Frantisek Musil. ... Name pronounced MYOO-sihl.
TRANSACTIONS/CAREER NOTES: Selected by Minnesota North Stars in second round (third North Stars pick, 38th overall) of NHL entry draft (June 8, 1983). ... Separated shoulder (December 9, 1986). ... Fractured foot (December 17, 1988). ... Suffered concussion (February

M

9, 1989). ... Strained lower back muscles (February 18, 1989). ... Suffered back spasms (November 2, 1989); missed 10 games. ... Separated right shoulder (April 1990). ... Traded by North Stars to Calgary Flames for D Brian Glynn (October 26, 1990). ... Suffered back spasms (November 8, 1993); missed one game. ... Strained neck (December 28, 1993); missed four games. ... Hyperextended elbow (March 22, 1994); missed four games. ... Played in Europe during 1994-95 NHL lockout. ... Bruised right knee (January 24, 1995); missed one game. ... Sprained right knee (February 9, 1995); missed three games. ... Suffered back spasms (February 28, 1995); missed one game. ... Sprained right knee (April 7, 1995); missed seven games. ... Traded by Flames to Ottawa Senators for fourth-round pick (D Chris St. Croix) in 1997 draft (October 7, 1995). ... Suffered concussion during 1995-96 season; missed one game. ... Lacerated neck (January 21, 1996); missed six games. ... Bruised right foot (February 3, 1996); missed seven games. ... Traded by Senators to Edmonton Oilers for D Scott Ferguson (March 9, 1998).

			REGULAR SEASON								PLAYOFFS				
Season Team	League	Gms.	G	A	Pts.	PIM	+/-	PP	SH		Gms.	G	A	Pts.	PIM
85-86—Dukla Jihlava	Czech.	35	3	7	10	85	...	...	...		—	—	—	—	—
86-87—Minnesota..................	NHL	72	2	9	11	148	0	0	0		—	—	—	—	—
87-88—Minnesota..................	NHL	80	9	8	17	213	-2	1	1		—	—	—	—	—
88-89—Minnesota..................	NHL	55	1	19	20	54	4	0	0		5	1	1	2	4
89-90—Minnesota..................	NHL	56	2	8	10	109	0	0	0		4	0	0	0	14
90-91—Minnesota..................	NHL	8	0	2	2	23	0	0	0		—	—	—	—	—
—Calgary	NHL	67	7	14	21	160	12	2	0		7	0	0	0	10
91-92—Calgary	NHL	78	4	8	12	103	12	1	1		—	—	—	—	—
92-93—Calgary	NHL	80	6	10	16	131	28	0	0		6	1	1	2	7
93-94—Calgary	NHL	75	1	8	9	50	38	0	0		7	0	1	1	4
94-95—Sparta Prague............	Czech Rep.	19	1	4	5	30	...	...	...		—	—	—	—	—
—Sachsen......................	Germany	1	0	0	0	2	...	...	...		—	—	—	—	—
—Calgary	NHL	35	0	5	5	61	6	0	0		5	0	1	1	0
95-96—Ottawa	NHL	65	1	3	4	85	-10	0	0		—	—	—	—	—
96-97—Ottawa	NHL	57	0	5	5	58	6	0	0		—	—	—	—	—
97-98—Detroit......................	IHL	9	0	0	0	6	...	...	...		—	—	—	—	—
—Indianapolis	IHL	52	5	8	13	122	...	...	...		—	—	—	—	—
—Edmonton..................	NHL	17	1	2	3	8	1	0	1		7	0	0	0	6
NHL Totals (12 years).........		745	34	101	135	1203	95	4	3		41	2	4	6	45

MUZZATTI, JASON G SHARKS

PERSONAL: Born February 3, 1970, in Toronto. ... 6-2/195. ... Catches left. ... Full name: Jason Mark Muzzatti. ... Name pronounced muh-ZAH-tee.

COLLEGE: Michigan State.

TRANSACTIONS/CAREER NOTES: Selected by Calgary Flames in first round (first Flames pick, 21st overall) of NHL entry draft (June 11, 1988). ... Loaned to Indianapolis Ice of IHL (January 11, 1993). ... Suffered from the flu (November 4, 1993); missed four games. ... Claimed on waivers by Hartford Whalers (June 1995). ... Whalers franchise moved to North Carolina and renamed Carolina Hurricanes for 1997-98 season; NHL approved move on June 25, 1997. ... Traded by Hurricanes to New York Rangers for fourth-round pick (LW Tommy Westlund) in 1998 draft (August 8, 1997). ... Traded by Rangers to San Jose Sharks for D Rich Brennan (March 24, 1998).

HONORS: Named to CCHA All-Star second team (1987-88). ... Named to NCAA All-America West second team (1989-90). ... Named to CCHA All-Star first team (1989-90). ... Named to CCHA All-Tournament team (1989-90).

			REGULAR SEASON							PLAYOFFS					
Season Team	League	Gms.	Min	W	L	T	GA	SO	Avg.	Gms.	Min.	W	L	GA	SO	Avg.
86-87—St. Mikes Jr. B..............	MTHL	20	1054	...	...	...	69	1	3.93	—	—	—	—	—	—	—
87-88—Michigan State.............	CCHA	33	1916	19	9	3	109	1	3.41	—	—	—	—	—	—	—
88-89—Michigan State.............	CCHA	42	2515	32	9	1	127	3	3.03	—	—	—	—	—	—	—
89-90—Michigan State.............	CCHA	33	1976	24	6	0	99	0	3.01	—	—	—	—	—	—	—
90-91—Michigan State.............	CCHA	22	1204	8	10	2	75	0	3.74	—	—	—	—	—	—	—
91-92—Salt Lake City..............	IHL	52	3033	24	22	‡5	167	2	3.30	4	247	1	3	18	0	4.37
92-93—Salt Lake City..............	IHL	13	747	5	6	‡0	52	0	4.18	—	—	—	—	—	—	—
—Canadian nat'l team	Int'l	16	880	6	9	0	53	0	3.61	—	—	—	—	—	—	—
—Indianapolis	IHL	12	707	5	6	‡0	48	0	4.07	—	—	—	—	—	—	—
93-94—Calgary	NHL	1	60	0	1	0	8	0	8.00	—	—	—	—	—	—	—
—Saint John.....................	AHL	51	2939	26	21	3	183	2	3.74	7	415	3	4	19	0	2.75
94-95—Saint John..................	AHL	31	1741	10	14	4	101	2	3.48	—	—	—	—	—	—	—
—Calgary	NHL	1	10	0	0	0	0	0	...	—	—	—	—	—	—	—
95-96—Springfield	AHL	5	300	4	0	1	12	1	2.40	—	—	—	—	—	—	—
—Hartford	NHL	22	1013	4	8	3	49	1	2.90	—	—	—	—	—	—	—
96-97—Hartford	NHL	31	1591	9	13	5	91	0	3.43	—	—	—	—	—	—	—
97-98—New York Rangers	NHL	6	313	0	3	2	17	0	3.26	—	—	—	—	—	—	—
—Hartford	AHL	17	1000	11	5	1	57	0	3.42	—	—	—	—	—	—	—
—Kentucky	AHL	7	430	2	3	2	25	0	3.49	3	154	0	3	13	0	5.06
—San Jose...................	NHL	1	27	0	0	0	2	0	4.44	—	—	—	—	—	—	—
NHL Totals (5 years).............		62	3014	13	25	10	167	1	3.32							

MYHRES, BRANTT RW

PERSONAL: Born March 18, 1974, in Edmonton. ... 6-3/220. ... Shoots right. ... Name pronounced MIGH-urhs.

HIGH SCHOOL: Sir Winston Churchill (Calgary).

TRANSACTIONS/CAREER NOTES: Selected by Tampa Bay Lightning in fifth round (fifth Lightning pick, 97th overall) of NHL entry draft (June 20, 1992). ... Injured shoulder (April 11, 1995); missed one game. ... Injured hip (February 1, 1997); missed one game. ... Sprained ankle (February 23, 1997); missed three games. ... Suffered from the flu (April 4, 1997); missed three games. ... Traded by Lightning with conditional draft pick to Edmonton Oilers for C Vladimir Vujtek (July 16, 1997). ... Traded by Oilers to Philadelphia Flyers for F Jason Bowen (October 15, 1997). ... Bruised left hand (November 26, 1997); missed two games.

Season Team	League	REGULAR SEASON								PLAYOFFS				
		Gms.	G	A	Pts.	PIM	+/-	PP	SH	Gms.	G	A	Pts.	PIM
90-91—Portland	WHL	59	2	7	9	125	...	...	...	—	—	—	—	—
91-92—Portland	WHL	4	0	2	2	22	...	...	...	—	—	—	—	—
—Lethbridge	WHL	53	4	11	15	359	...	...	...	5	0	0	0	36
92-93—Lethbridge	WHL	64	13	35	48	277	...	...	...	3	0	0	0	11
93-94—Atlanta	IHL	2	0	0	0	17	...	...	...	—	—	—	—	—
—Lethbridge	WHL	34	10	21	31	103	...	...	...	—	—	—	—	—
—Spokane	WHL	27	10	22	32	139	...	...	...	3	1	4	5	7
94-95—Atlanta	IHL	40	5	5	10	213	...	...	...	—	—	—	—	—
—Tampa Bay	NHL	15	2	0	2	81	-2	0	0	—	—	—	—	—
95-96—Atlanta	IHL	12	0	2	2	58	...	...	...	—	—	—	—	—
96-97—San Antonio	IHL	12	0	0	0	98	...	...	...	—	—	—	—	—
—Tampa Bay	NHL	47	3	1	4	136	1	0	0	—	—	—	—	—
97-98—Philadelphia	AHL	18	4	4	8	67	...	...	...	—	—	—	—	—
—Philadelphia	NHL	23	0	0	0	169	-1	0	0	—	—	—	—	—
NHL Totals (3 years)		125	10	6	16	599	-2	0	0					

MYRVOLD, ANDERS   D

PERSONAL: Born August 12, 1975, in Lorenskog, Norway. ... 6-2/200. ... Shoots left. ... Name pronounced MUHR-vohld.
TRANSACTIONS/CAREER NOTES: Selected by Quebec Nordiques in fifth round (sixth Nordiques pick, 127th overall) of NHL entry draft (June 26, 1993). ... Nordiques franchise moved to Colorado and renamed Avalanche for 1995-96 season (June 21, 1995). ... Traded by Avalanche with RW Landon Wilson to Boston Bruins for first-round pick (D Robyn Regehr) in 1998 draft (November 22, 1996).
HONORS: Named to Can.HL All-Rookie team (1994-95).

Season Team	League	REGULAR SEASON								PLAYOFFS				
		Gms.	G	A	Pts.	PIM	+/-	PP	SH	Gms.	G	A	Pts.	PIM
92-93—Farjestad Karlstad	Sweden	2	0	0	0	0	...	...	...	—	—	—	—	—
93-94—Grums	Swed. Dv.II	24	1	0	1	59	...	...	...	—	—	—	—	—
94-95—Laval	QMJHL	64	14	50	64	173	...	...	...	20	4	10	14	68
—Cornwall	AHL	—	—	—	—	—	...	...	...	3	0	1	1	2
95-96—Colorado	NHL	4	0	1	1	6	-2	0	0	—	—	—	—	—
—Cornwall	AHL	70	5	24	29	125	...	...	...	5	1	0	1	19
96-97—Hershey	AHL	20	0	3	3	16	...	...	...	—	—	—	—	—
—Providence	AHL	53	6	15	21	107	...	...	...	10	0	1	1	6
—Boston	NHL	9	0	2	2	4	-1	0	0	—	—	—	—	—
97-98—Providence	AHL	75	4	21	25	91	...	...	...	—	—	—	—	—
NHL Totals (2 years)		13	0	3	3	10	-3	0	0					

NABOKOV, DIMITRI   C/LW   ISLANDERS

PERSONAL: Born January 4, 1977, in Novosibirsk, U.S.S.R. ... 6-2/216. ... Shoots right.
TRANSACTIONS/CAREER NOTES: Selected by Chicago Blackhawks in first round (first Blackhawks pick, 19th overall) of NHL entry draft (July 8, 1995). ... Traded by Blackhawks to New York Islanders for LW Jean-Pierre Dumont and fifth-round pick (traded to Philadelphia) in 1998 draft (May 30, 1998).
HONORS: Named to WHL (East) All-Star second team (1996-97).

Season Team	League	REGULAR SEASON								PLAYOFFS				
		Gms.	G	A	Pts.	PIM	+/-	PP	SH	Gms.	G	A	Pts.	PIM
93-94—Soviet Wings	CIS	17	0	2	2	6	...	...	...	3	0	0	0	0
94-95—Soviet Wings	CIS	49	15	12	27	32	...	...	...	4	5	0	5	6
95-96—Soviet Wings	CIS	50	12	14	26	51	...	...	...	—	—	—	—	—
96-97—Soviet Wings	USSR	1	0	0	0	0	...	...	...	—	—	—	—	—
—Regina	WHL	50	39	56	95	61	...	...	...	5	2	3	5	2
—Indianapolis	IHL	2	0	0	0	0	...	...	...	—	—	—	—	—
97-98—Indianapolis	IHL	46	6	15	21	16	...	...	...	5	2	1	3	0
—Chicago	NHL	25	7	4	11	10	-1	3	0	—	—	—	—	—
NHL Totals (1 year)		25	7	4	11	10	-1	3	0					

NABOKOV, JOHN   G   SHARKS

PERSONAL: Born July 25, 1975, in Ust-Kamenogorsk, U.S.S.R. ... 6-0/180. ... Catches left. ... Full name: Yevgeny Nabokov. ... Name pronounced nuh-BAH-kahf.
TRANSACTIONS/CAREER NOTES: Selected by San Jose Sharks in ninth round (ninth Sharks pick, 219th overall) of NHL entry draft (June 29, 1994).

Season Team	League	REGULAR SEASON							PLAYOFFS					
		Gms.	Min	W	L	T	GA	SO	Avg.	Gms.	Min.	W	L	GA	SO	Avg.
92-93—Torpedo Ust-Kam.	CIS	4	109	...	...	...	5	...	2.75	—	—	—	—	—	—	—
93-94—Torpedo Ust-Kam.	CIS	11	539	...	...	...	29	0	3.23	—	—	—	—	—	—	—
94-95—Dynamo Moscow	CIS	37	2075	...	...	...	70	...	2.02	—	—	—	—	—	—	—
95-96—Dynamo Moscow	CIS	37	1948	...	...	...	70	...	2.16	6	298	...	...	7	...	1.41
96-97—Dynamo Moscow	Russian	27	1588	...	...	...	56	2	2.12	4	255	...	...	12	0	2.82
97-98—Kentucky	AHL	33	1867	10	21	2	122	0	3.92	1	23	0	0	1	0	2.61

NAGY, LADISLAV   C   BLUES

PERSONAL: Born June 1, 1979, in Presov, Yugoslavia. ... 5-11/183. ... Shoots left.
TRANSACTIONS/CAREER NOTES: Selected by St. Louis Blues in seventh round (sixth Blues pick, 177th overall) of 1997 NHL entry draft.

		REGULAR SEASON								PLAYOFFS				
Season Team	League	Gms.	G	A	Pts.	PIM	+/-	PP	SH	Gms.	G	A	Pts.	PIM
95-96—Kosice Jr.	Czech Rep.	45	29	30	59	105	...	...	...	—	—	—	—	—
96-97—Kosice Jr.	Czech Rep.	45	29	30	59	105	...	...	...	—	—	—	—	—
97-98—Kosice Jr.	Czech Rep.	25	14	13	27	8	...	...	...	—	—	—	—	—

NAMESTNIKOV, JOHN   D   ISLANDERS

PERSONAL: Born October 9, 1971, in Norvgrood, U.S.S.R. ... 5-11/190. ... Shoots right. ... Full name: Yevgeny Namestnikov. ... Name pronounced ehv-GEH-nee nuh-MEHST-nih-kahf.
TRANSACTIONS/CAREER NOTES: Selected by Vancouver Canucks in sixth round (fifth Canucks pick, 117th overall) of NHL entry draft (June 22, 1991). ... Sprained ankle (May 7, 1995); missed 10 playoff games. ... Signed as free agent by New York Islanders (July 16, 1997).

		REGULAR SEASON								PLAYOFFS				
Season Team	League	Gms.	G	A	Pts.	PIM	+/-	PP	SH	Gms.	G	A	Pts.	PIM
88-89—Torpedo Gorky	USSR	2	0	0	0	2	...	...	...	—	—	—	—	—
89-90—Torpedo Gorky	USSR	23	0	0	0	25	...	...	...	—	—	—	—	—
90-91—Tor. Nizhny Nov.	USSR	45	1	2	3	49	...	...	...	—	—	—	—	—
91-92—CSKA Moscow	CIS	42	1	1	2	47	...	...	...	—	—	—	—	—
92-93—CSKA Moscow	CIS	42	5	5	10	68	...	...	...	—	—	—	—	—
93-94—Hamilton	AHL	59	7	27	34	97	...	...	...	4	0	2	2	19
—Vancouver	NHL	17	0	5	5	10	-2	0	0	—	—	—	—	—
94-95—Syracuse	AHL	59	11	22	33	59	...	...	...	—	—	—	—	—
—Vancouver	NHL	16	0	3	3	4	2	0	0	1	0	0	0	2
95-96—Syracuse	AHL	59	13	34	47	85	...	...	...	15	1	8	9	16
—Vancouver	NHL	—	—	—	—	—				1	0	0	0	0
96-97—Syracuse	AHL	55	9	37	46	73	...	...	...	3	2	0	2	0
—Vancouver	NHL	2	0	0	0	4	-1	0	0	—	—	—	—	—
97-98—Utah	IHL	62	6	19	25	48	...	...	...	4	1	0	1	2
—New York Islanders	NHL	6	0	1	1	4	-1	0	0	—	—	—	—	—
NHL Totals (5 years)		41	0	9	9	22	-2	0	0	2	0	0	0	2

NASLUND, MARKUS   LW   CANUCKS

PERSONAL: Born July 30, 1973, in Harnosand, Sweden. ... 6-0/186. ... Shoots left. ... Name pronounced NAZ-luhnd.
TRANSACTIONS/CAREER NOTES: Selected by Pittsburgh Penguins in first round (first Penguins pick, 16th overall) of NHL entry draft (June 22, 1991). ... Traded by Penguins to Vancouver Canucks for LW Alex Stojanov (March 20, 1996). ... Suffered from the flu (November 26, 1996); missed one game.
STATISTICAL PLATEAUS: Three-goal games: 1995-96 (1).

		REGULAR SEASON								PLAYOFFS				
Season Team	League	Gms.	G	A	Pts.	PIM	+/-	PP	SH	Gms.	G	A	Pts.	PIM
89-90—MoDo Hockey Jrs.	Sweden Jr.	33	43	35	78	20	...	...	...	—	—	—	—	—
90-91—MoDo Ornskoldvik	Sweden	32	10	9	19	14	...	...	...	—	—	—	—	—
91-92—MoDo Ornskoldvik	Sweden	39	22	18	40	54	...	...	...	—	—	—	—	—
92-93—MoDo Ornskoldvik	Sweden	39	22	17	39	67	...	...	...	3	3	2	5	...
93-94—Pittsburgh	NHL	71	4	7	11	27	-3	1	0	—	—	—	—	—
—Cleveland	IHL	5	1	6	7	4	...	...	...	—	—	—	—	—
94-95—Pittsburgh	NHL	14	2	2	4	2	0	0	0	—	—	—	—	—
—Cleveland	IHL	7	3	4	7	6	...	...	...	4	1	3	4	8
95-96—Pittsburgh	NHL	66	19	33	52	36	17	3	0	—	—	—	—	—
—Vancouver	NHL	10	3	0	3	6	3	1	0	6	1	2	3	8
96-97—Vancouver	NHL	78	21	20	41	30	-15	4	0	—	—	—	—	—
97-98—Vancouver	NHL	76	14	20	34	56	5	2	1	—	—	—	—	—
NHL Totals (5 years)		315	63	82	145	157	7	11	1	6	1	2	3	8

NASREDDINE, ALAIN   D   BLACKHAWKS

PERSONAL: Born July 10, 1975, in Montreal. ... 6-1/201. ... Shoots left. ... Name pronounced AL-ai NAS-rih-DEEN.
TRANSACTIONS/CAREER NOTES: Selected by Florida Panthers in sixth round (eighth Panthers pick, 135th overall) of NHL entry draft (June 26, 1993). ... Traded by Panthers with conditional pick in 1999 draft to Chicago Blackhawks for D Ivan Droppa (December 8, 1996).
HONORS: Named to QMJHL All-Star second team (1994-95).

		REGULAR SEASON								PLAYOFFS				
Season Team	League	Gms.	G	A	Pts.	PIM	+/-	PP	SH	Gms.	G	A	Pts.	PIM
91-92—Drummondville	QMJHL	61	1	9	10	78	...	...	...	4	0	0	0	17
92-93—Drummondville	QMJHL	64	0	14	14	137	...	...	...	10	0	1	1	36
93-94—Chicoutimi	QMJHL	60	3	24	27	218	...	...	...	26	2	10	12	118
94-95—Chicoutimi	QMJHL	67	8	31	39	342	...	...	...	13	3	5	8	40
95-96—Carolina	AHL	63	0	5	5	245	...	...	...	—	—	—	—	—
96-97—Carolina	AHL	26	0	4	4	109	...	...	...	—	—	—	—	—
—Indianapolis	IHL	49	0	2	2	248	...	...	...	4	1	1	2	27
97-98—Indianapolis	IHL	75	1	12	13	258	...	...	...	5	0	2	2	12

N

NAUMENKO, NICK   D

PERSONAL: Born July 7, 1974, in Chicago. ... 5-11/197. ... Shoots right. ... Name pronounced nah-MEHN-koh.
COLLEGE: North Dakota.
TRANSACTIONS/CAREER NOTES: Selected by St. Louis Blues in eighth round (ninth Blues pick, 182nd overall) of NHL entry draft (June 20, 1992).
HONORS: Named to WCHA All-Star first team (1994-95). ... Named to WCHA All-Star first team (1995-96).

		REGULAR SEASON								PLAYOFFS				
Season Team	League	Gms.	G	A	Pts.	PIM	+/-	PP	SH	Gms.	G	A	Pts.	PIM
91-92—Dubuque	USHL	24	6	19	25	4	...	...	...	—	—	—	—	—
92-93—Univ. of North Dakota	WCHA	38	10	24	34	26	...	...	...	—	—	—	—	—
93-94—Univ. of North Dakota	WCHA	32	4	22	26	22	...	...	...	—	—	—	—	—
94-95—Univ. of North Dakota	WCHA	39	13	26	39	78	...	...	...	—	—	—	—	—
95-96—Univ. of North Dakota	WCHA	37	11	30	41	52	...	...	...	—	—	—	—	—
96-97—Worcester	AHL	54	6	22	28	72	...	...	...	1	0	0	0	0
97-98—Worcester	AHL	71	12	34	46	63	...	...	...	11	1	7	8	8

NAZAROV, ANDREI   RW   LIGHTNING

PERSONAL: Born March 21, 1972, in Chelyabinsk, U.S.S.R. ... 6-5/230. ... Shoots right. ... Name pronounced nuh-ZAH-rahf.
TRANSACTIONS/CAREER NOTES: Selected by San Jose Sharks in first round (second Sharks pick, 10th overall) of NHL entry draft (June 20, 1992). ... Suspended four games and fined $500 by NHL for head-butting (March 8, 1995). ... Suffered facial fracture (February 5, 1997); missed 14 games. ... Suspended 13 games by NHL for physical abuse of officials (March 25, 1997). ... Injured knee (October 13, 1997); missed seven games. ... Traded by Sharks with first-round pick (C Vincent Lecavalier) in 1998 draft and future considerations to Tampa Bay Lightning for D Bryan Marchment, D David Shaw and first-round pick (traded to Nashville) in 1998 draft (March 24, 1998).

		REGULAR SEASON								PLAYOFFS				
Season Team	League	Gms.	G	A	Pts.	PIM	+/-	PP	SH	Gms.	G	A	Pts.	PIM
90-91—Mechel Chelyabinsk	USSR	2	0	0	0	0	...	...	...	—	—	—	—	—
91-92—Dynamo Moscow	CIS	2	1	0	1	2	...	...	...	—	—	—	—	—
92-93—Dynamo Moscow	CIS	42	8	2	10	79	...	...	...	10	1	1	2	8
93-94—Kansas City	IHL	71	15	18	33	64	...	...	...	—	—	—	—	—
—San Jose	NHL	1	0	0	0	0	0	0	0	—	—	—	—	—
94-95—Kansas City	IHL	43	15	10	25	55	...	...	...	—	—	—	—	—
—San Jose	NHL	26	3	5	8	94	-1	0	0	6	0	0	0	9
95-96—San Jose	NHL	42	7	7	14	62	-15	2	0	—	—	—	—	—
—Kansas City	IHL	27	4	6	10	118	...	...	...	2	0	0	0	2
96-97—San Jose	NHL	60	12	15	27	222	-4	1	0	—	—	—	—	—
—Kentucky	AHL	3	1	2	3	4	...	...	...	—	—	—	—	—
97-98—San Jose	NHL	40	1	1	2	112	-4	0	0	—	—	—	—	—
—Tampa Bay	NHL	14	1	1	2	58	-9	0	0	—	—	—	—	—
NHL Totals (5 years)		183	24	29	53	548	-33	3	0	6	0	0	0	9

NDUR, RUMUN   D   SABRES

PERSONAL: Born July 7, 1975, in Zaria, Nigeria. ... 6-2/200. ... Shoots left. ... Name pronounced ruh-MOHN EHN-duhr.
HIGH SCHOOL: Bishop MacDonnell (Guelph, Ont.).
TRANSACTIONS/CAREER NOTES: Selected by Buffalo Sabres in third round (third Sabres pick, 69th overall) of NHL entry draft (June 29, 1994).

		REGULAR SEASON								PLAYOFFS				
Season Team	League	Gms.	G	A	Pts.	PIM	+/-	PP	SH	Gms.	G	A	Pts.	PIM
91-92—Clearwater	Jr. C	4	0	4	4	4	...	...	...	—	—	—	—	—
—Sarnia	Jr. B	30	2	5	7	46	...	...	...	—	—	—	—	—
92-93—Guelph	Jr. B	24	7	8	15	202	...	...	...	—	—	—	—	—
—Guelph	OHL	22	1	3	4	30	...	...	...	4	0	1	1	4
93-94—Guelph	OHL	61	6	33	39	176	...	...	...	9	4	1	5	24
94-95—Guelph	OHL	63	10	21	31	187	...	...	...	14	0	4	4	28
95-96—Rochester	AHL	73	2	12	14	306	...	...	...	17	1	2	3	33
96-97—Rochester	AHL	68	5	11	16	282	...	...	...	10	3	1	4	21
—Buffalo	NHL	2	0	0	0	2	1	0	0	—	—	—	—	—
97-98—Rochester	AHL	50	1	12	13	207	...	...	...	4	0	2	2	16
—Buffalo	NHL	1	0	0	0	2	-1	0	0	—	—	—	—	—
NHL Totals (2 years)		3	0	0	0	4	0	0	0					

NECKAR, STANISLAV   D   SENATORS

PERSONAL: Born December 22, 1975, in Ceske Budejovice, Czechoslovakia. ... 6-1/212. ... Shoots left. ... Name pronounced NEHTS-kash.
TRANSACTIONS/CAREER NOTES: Selected by Ottawa Senators in second round (second Senators pick, 29th overall) of NHL entry draft (June 28, 1994). ... Suffered partially torn knee ligament (October 18, 1996); missed remainder of the season. ... Injured right knee (January 24, 1998); missed two games. ... Reinjured knee and underwent surgery (April 3, 1998); missed final nine games of season.

		REGULAR SEASON								PLAYOFFS				
Season Team	League	Gms.	G	A	Pts.	PIM	+/-	PP	SH	Gms.	G	A	Pts.	PIM
91-92—Budejovice	Czech Dv.II	18	1	3	4		...	...	...	—	—	—	—	—
92-93—Motor-Ceske Bude.	Czech.	42	2	9	11	12	...	...	...	—	—	—	—	—
93-94—HC Ceske Budejovice	Czech Rep.	12	3	2	5	2	...	...	...	3	0	0	0	0
94-95—Detroit	IHL	15	2	2	4	15	...	...	...	—	—	—	—	—
—Ottawa	NHL	48	1	3	4	37	-20	0	0	—	—	—	—	—
95-96—Ottawa	NHL	82	3	9	12	54	-16	1	0	—	—	—	—	—
96-97—Ottawa	NHL	5	0	0	0	2	0	0	0	—	—	—	—	—
97-98—Ottawa	NHL	60	2	2	4	31	-14	0	0	9	0	0	0	2
NHL Totals (4 years)		195	6	14	20	124	-48	1	0	9	0	0	0	2

NEHRLING, LUCAS   D   DEVILS

PERSONAL: Born September 14, 1979, in Peterborough, Ont. ... 6-4/195. ... Shoots right.
TRANSACTIONS/CAREER NOTES: Selected by New Jersey Devils in fourth round (third Devils pick, 104th overall) of NHL entry draft (June 21, 1997).

		REGULAR SEASON								PLAYOFFS				
Season Team	League	Gms.	G	A	Pts.	PIM	+/-	PP	SH	Gms.	G	A	Pts.	PIM
96-97—Sarnia	OHL	63	3	12	15	74	...	...	...	12	0	2	2	23
97-98—Sarnia	OHL	22	0	2	2	46	...	...	...	—	—	—	—	—
—Kingston	OHL	39	1	8	9	83	...	...	...	120	0	1	1	19

NEMCHINOV, SERGEI   C   ISLANDERS

PERSONAL: Born January 14, 1964, in Moscow, U.S.S.R. ... 6-0/200. ... Shoots left. ... Name pronounced SAIR-gay nehm-CHEE-nahf.
TRANSACTIONS/CAREER NOTES: Selected by New York Rangers in 12th round (14th Rangers pick, 244th overall) of NHL entry draft (June 16, 1990). ... Sprained knee (November 4, 1991); missed seven games. ... Strained buttocks (April 4, 1993); missed three games. ... Suspended eight games and fined $500 by NHL for hitting another player (March 16, 1994). ... Bruised Achilles' tendon (January 30, 1995); missed one game. ... Suffered mild concussion (December 13, 1995); missed one game. ... Bruised elbow (April 7, 1996); missed two games. ... Traded by Rangers with RW Brian Noonan to Vancouver Canucks for LW Esa Tikkanen and RW Russ Courtnall (March 8, 1997). ... Strained rib muscle (February 28, 1997); missed 11 games. ... Injured foot (April 4, 1997); missed three games. ... Signed as free agent by New York Islanders (July 2, 1997). ... Suffered back spasms (November 28, 1997); missed two games. ... Suffered back spasms (December 17, 1997); missed one game. ... Injured back (April 6, 1998); missed one game. ... Suffered concussion (April 11, 1998); missed two games. ... Strained neck (April 16, 1998); missed final two games of season.
MISCELLANEOUS: Member of Stanley Cup championship team (1994). ... Member of silver-medal-winning Russian Olympic team (1998).
STATISTICAL PLATEAUS: Three-goal games: 1992-93 (1).

		REGULAR SEASON								PLAYOFFS				
Season Team	League	Gms.	G	A	Pts.	PIM	+/-	PP	SH	Gms.	G	A	Pts.	PIM
81-82—Soviet Wings	USSR	15	1	0	1	0	...	...	...	—	—	—	—	—
82-83—CSKA Moscow	USSR	11	0	0	0	2	...	...	...	—	—	—	—	—
83-84—CSKA Moscow	USSR	20	6	5	11	4	...	...	...	—	—	—	—	—
84-85—CSKA Moscow	USSR	31	2	4	6	4	...	...	...	—	—	—	—	—
85-86—Soviet Wings	USSR	39	7	12	19	28	...	...	...	—	—	—	—	—
86-87—Soviet Wings	USSR	40	13	9	22	24	...	...	...	—	—	—	—	—
87-88—Soviet Wings	USSR	48	17	11	28	26	...	...	...	—	—	—	—	—
88-89—Soviet Wings	USSR	43	15	14	29	28	...	...	...	—	—	—	—	—
89-90—Soviet Wings	USSR	48	17	16	33	34	...	...	...	—	—	—	—	—
90-91—Soviet Wings	USSR	46	21	24	45	30	...	...	...	—	—	—	—	—
91-92—New York Rangers	NHL	73	30	28	58	15	19	2	0	13	1	4	5	8
92-93—New York Rangers	NHL	81	23	31	54	34	15	0	1	—	—	—	—	—
93-94—New York Rangers	NHL	76	22	27	49	36	13	4	0	23	2	5	7	6
94-95—New York Rangers	NHL	47	7	6	13	16	-6	0	0	10	4	5	9	2
95-96—New York Rangers	NHL	78	17	15	32	38	9	0	0	6	0	1	1	2
96-97—New York Rangers	NHL	63	6	13	19	12	5	1	0	—	—	—	—	—
—Vancouver	NHL	6	2	3	5	4	4	0	0	—	—	—	—	—
97-98—New York Islanders	NHL	74	10	19	29	24	3	2	1	—	—	—	—	—
—Russian Olympic team	Int'l	6	1	0	1	0	...	...	...	—	—	—	—	—
NHL Totals (7 years)		498	117	142	259	179	62	9	2	52	7	15	22	18

NEMECEK, JAN   D   KINGS

N

PERSONAL: Born February 14, 1976, in Pisek, Czechoslovakia. ... 6-1/194. ... Shoots right. ... Name pronounced YAHN NEHM-ih-chehk.
TRANSACTIONS/CAREER NOTES: Selected by Los Angeles Kings in ninth round (seventh Kings pick, 215th overall) of NHL entry draft (June 29, 1994).
HONORS: Named to QMJHL All-Star second team (1995-96).

		REGULAR SEASON								PLAYOFFS				
Season Team	League	Gms.	G	A	Pts.	PIM	+/-	PP	SH	Gms.	G	A	Pts.	PIM
92-93—Budejovice	Czech.	15	0	0	0	...	...	...	...	—	—	—	—	—
93-94—Budejovice	Czech Rep.	16	0	1	1	16	...	...	...	—	—	—	—	—
94-95—Hull	QMJHL	49	10	16	26	48	...	...	...	21	5	9	14	10
95-96—Hull	QMJHL	57	17	49	66	58	...	...	...	17	2	13	15	10
96-97—Phoenix	IHL	24	1	1	2	2	...	...	...	—	—	—	—	—
—Mississippi	ECHL	20	3	9	12	16	...	...	...	3	0	0	0	4
97-98—Fredericton	AHL	65	7	24	31	43	...	...	...	2	0	0	0	0

NEMIROVSKY, DAVID   RW   PANTHERS

PERSONAL: Born August 1, 1976, in Toronto. ... 6-1/192. ... Shoots right. ... Name pronounced nehm-uh-RAHV-skee.
TRANSACTIONS/CAREER NOTES: Selected by Florida Panthers in fourth round (fifth Panthers pick, 84th overall) of NHL entry draft (June 29, 1994).

		REGULAR SEASON								PLAYOFFS				
Season Team	League	Gms.	G	A	Pts.	PIM	+/-	PP	SH	Gms.	G	A	Pts.	PIM
91-92—Pickering-Weston	Jr. A	38	27	23	50	70	...	...	...	—	—	—	—	—
92-93—Weston-North York	MTHL	40	19	23	42	27	...	...	...	—	—	—	—	—
93-94—Ottawa	OHL	64	21	31	52	18	...	...	...	17	10	10	20	2
94-95—Ottawa	OHL	59	27	29	56	25	...	...	...	—	—	—	—	—

Season Team	League	REGULAR SEASON								PLAYOFFS				
		Gms.	G	A	Pts.	PIM	+/-	PP	SH	Gms.	G	A	Pts.	PIM
95-96—Florida	NHL	9	0	2	2	2	-1	0	0	—	—	—	—	—
—Sarnia	OHL	26	18	27	45	14	...	...	...	10	8	8	16	6
—Carolina	AHL	5	1	2	3	0	...	...	...	—	—	—	—	—
96-97—Carolina	AHL	34	21	21	42	18	...	...	...	—	—	—	—	—
—Florida	NHL	39	7	7	14	32	1	1	0	3	1	0	1	0
97-98—Florida	NHL	41	9	12	21	8	-3	2	0	—	—	—	—	—
—New Haven	AHL	29	10	15	25	10	...	...	...	1	1	0	1	0
NHL Totals (3 years)		89	16	21	37	42	-3	3	0	3	1	0	1	0

NICHOL, SCOTT   C   SABRES

PERSONAL: Born December 31, 1974, in Calgary. ... 5-8/160. ... Shoots right.
TRANSACTIONS/CAREER NOTES: Selected by Buffalo Sabres in 11th round (ninth Sabres pick, 272nd overall) of NHL entry draft (June 26, 1993).

Season Team	League	REGULAR SEASON								PLAYOFFS				
		Gms.	G	A	Pts.	PIM	+/-	PP	SH	Gms.	G	A	Pts.	PIM
92-93—Portland	WHL	67	31	33	64	146	...	...	...	—	—	—	—	—
93-94—Portland	WHL	65	40	53	93	144	...	...	...	—	—	—	—	—
94-95—Rochester	AHL	71	11	16	27	136	...	...	...	5	0	3	3	14
95-96—Rochester	AHL	62	14	17	31	170	...	...	...	19	7	6	13	36
—Buffalo	NHL	2	0	0	0	10	0	0	0	—	—	—	—	—
96-97—Rochester	AHL	68	22	21	43	133	...	...	...	10	2	1	3	26
97-98—Rochester	AHL	35	13	7	20	113	...	...	...	—	—	—	—	—
—Buffalo	NHL	3	0	0	0	4	0	0	0	—	—	—	—	—
NHL Totals (2 years)		5	0	0	0	14	0	0	0					

NICHOLLS, BERNIE   C

PERSONAL: Born June 24, 1961, in Haliburton, Ont. ... 6-0/190. ... Shoots right. ... Full name: Bernard Irvine Nicholls.
TRANSACTIONS/CAREER NOTES: Selected by Los Angeles Kings as underage junior in fourth round (fourth Kings pick, 73rd overall) of NHL entry draft (June 11, 1980). ... Partially tore right knee ligament (November 18, 1982). ... Broke jaw (February 1984); missed two games. ... Fractured left index finger in three places (October 8, 1987). ... Traded by Kings to New York Rangers for RW Tomas Sandstrom and LW Tony Granato (January 20, 1990). ... Separated left shoulder (January 22, 1991); missed five games. ... Suspended three games by NHL for stick-swinging incident (February 14, 1991). ... Traded by Rangers with LW Louie DeBrusk, RW Steven Rice and future considerations to Edmonton Oilers for C Mark Messier and future considerations (October 4, 1991); Rangers traded D David Shaw to Oilers for D Jeff Beukeboom to complete the deal (November 12, 1991). ... Did not report to Oilers to be with his wife for the birth of their child (October 4, 1991); missed 27 games. ... Reported to Oilers (December 6, 1991). ... Strained abdominal muscle (February 16, 1992); missed two games. ... Suspended seven off-days and fined $500 by NHL for swinging stick in preseason game (October 13, 1992). ... Traded by Oilers to New Jersey Devils for C Kevin Todd and LW Zdeno Ciger (January 13, 1993). ... Fractured left foot (February 27, 1993); missed 13 games. ... Sprained left knee (December 4, 1993); missed nine games. ... Injured hand (April 10, 1994); missed one game. ... Suspended one game by NHL for cross-check to neck (May 21, 1994). ... Signed as free agent by Chicago Blackhawks (July 14, 1994). ... Bruised spleen (November 5, 1995); missed 23 games. ... Signed as free agent by San Jose Sharks (July 30, 1996). ... Suspended two games and fined $1,000 by NHL for deliberate-injury penalty (February 28, 1997). ... Underwent hernia surgery (March 11, 1997); missed final 15 games of season. ... Suffered hand injury (November 10, 1997); missed 13 games.
HONORS: Played in NHL All-Star Game (1984, 1989 and 1990).
STATISTICAL PLATEAUS: Three-goal games: 1981-82 (1), 1983-84 (1), 1984-85 (1), 1985-86 (1), 1986-87 (1), 1987-88 (1), 1988-89 (4), 1993-94 (1), 1994-95 (1). Total: 14. ... Four-goal games: 1983-84 (1), 1984-85 (1), 1994-95 (2). Total: 4. ... Total hat tricks: 18.

Season Team	League	REGULAR SEASON								PLAYOFFS				
		Gms.	G	A	Pts.	PIM	+/-	PP	SH	Gms.	G	A	Pts.	PIM
78-79—Kingston	OMJHL	2	0	1	1	0	...	...	...	—	—	—	—	—
79-80—Kingston	OMJHL	68	36	43	79	85	...	...	...	3	1	0	1	10
80-81—Kingston	OMJHL	65	63	89	152	109	...	...	...	14	8	10	18	17
81-82—New Haven	AHL	55	41	30	71	31	...	...	...	—	—	—	—	—
—Los Angeles	NHL	22	14	18	32	27	2	8	1	10	4	0	4	23
82-83—Los Angeles	NHL	71	28	22	50	124	-23	12	0	—	—	—	—	—
83-84—Los Angeles	NHL	78	41	54	95	83	-21	8	4	—	—	—	—	—
84-85—Los Angeles	NHL	80	46	54	100	76	-4	15	0	3	1	1	2	9
85-86—Los Angeles	NHL	80	36	61	97	78	-5	10	4	—	—	—	—	—
86-87—Los Angeles	NHL	80	33	48	81	101	-16	10	1	5	2	5	7	6
87-88—Los Angeles	NHL	65	32	46	78	114	2	8	7	5	2	6	8	11
88-89—Los Angeles	NHL	79	70	80	150	96	30	21	8	11	7	9	16	12
89-90—Los Angeles	NHL	47	27	48	75	66	-6	8	0	—	—	—	—	—
—New York Rangers	NHL	32	12	25	37	20	-3	7	0	10	7	5	12	16
90-91—New York Rangers	NHL	71	25	48	73	96	5	8	0	5	4	3	7	8
91-92—New York Rangers	NHL	1	0	0	0	0	-1	0	0	—	—	—	—	—
—Edmonton	NHL	49	20	29	49	60	5	7	0	16	8	11	19	25
92-93—Edmonton	NHL	46	8	32	40	40	-16	4	0	—	—	—	—	—
—New Jersey	NHL	23	5	15	20	40	3	1	0	5	0	0	0	6
93-94—New Jersey	NHL	61	19	27	46	86	24	3	0	16	4	9	13	28
94-95—Chicago	NHL	48	22	29	51	32	4	11	2	16	1	11	12	8
95-96—Chicago	NHL	59	19	41	60	60	11	6	0	10	2	7	9	4
96-97—San Jose	NHL	65	12	33	45	63	-21	2	1	—	—	—	—	—
97-98—San Jose	NHL	60	6	22	28	26	-4	3	0	6	0	5	5	8
NHL Totals (17 years)		1117	475	732	1207	1288	-34	152	28	118	42	72	114	164

NIECKAR, BARRY   LW   COYOTES

PERSONAL: Born December 16, 1967, in Rama, Sask. ... 6-3/210. ... Shoots left. ... Name pronounced NIGH-kahr.
TRANSACTIONS/CAREER NOTES: Signed as free agent by Hartford Whalers (September 1992). ... Signed as free agent by Calgary Flames (February 10, 1995). ... Signed as free agent by New York Islanders (July 25, 1995). ... Signed as free agent by Mighty Ducks of Anaheim (October 2, 1996). ... Signed as free agent by Phoenix Coyotes (August 12, 1998).

				REGULAR SEASON								PLAYOFFS			
Season Team	League	Gms.	G	A	Pts.	PIM	+/-	PP	SH		Gms.	G	A	Pts.	PIM
91-92—Phoenix	IHL	5	0	0	0	9	...	...	...		—	—	—	—	—
—Raleigh	ECHL	46	10	18	28	229	...	...	...		4	4	0	4	22
92-93—Springfield	AHL	21	2	4	6	65	...	...	...		6	1	0	1	14
—Hartford	NHL	2	0	0	0	2	-2	0	0		—	—	—	—	—
93-94—Springfield	AHL	30	0	2	2	67	...	...	...		—	—	—	—	—
94-95—Saint John	AHL	65	8	7	15	*491	...	...	...		4	0	0	0	22
—Calgary	NHL	3	0	0	0	12	0	0	0		—	—	—	—	—
95-96—Utah	IHL	53	9	15	24	194	...	...	...		—	—	—	—	—
—Peoria	IHL	10	3	3	6	72	...	...	...		12	4	6	10	48
96-97—Long Beach	IHL	63	3	10	13	386	...	...	...		5	0	0	0	22
—Anaheim	NHL	2	0	0	0	5	0	0	0		—	—	—	—	—
97-98—Cincinnati	AHL	75	10	14	24	295	...	...	...		—	—	—	—	—
—Anaheim	NHL	1	0	0	0	2	0	0	0		—	—	—	—	—
NHL Totals (4 years)		8	0	0	0	21	-2	0	0		—	—	—	—	—

NIEDERMAYER, ROB   C   PANTHERS

PERSONAL: Born December 28, 1974, in Cassiar, B.C. ... 6-2/201. ... Shoots left. ... Brother of Scott Niedermayer, defenseman, New Jersey Devils. ... Name pronounced NEE-duhr-MIGH-uhr.
COLLEGE: Medicine Hat.
TRANSACTIONS/CAREER NOTES: Selected by Florida Panthers in first round (first Panthers pick, fifth overall) of NHL entry draft (June 26, 1993). ... Separated right shoulder (November 18, 1993); missed 17 games. ... Sprained knee ligament (November 22, 1996); missed 17 games. ... Strained groin (March 5, 1997); missed two games. ... Sprained wrist (March 20, 1997); missed three games. ... Suffered concussion (October 1, 1997); missed 10 games. ... Dislocated right thumb (November 18, 1997); missed 15 games. ... Underwent knee surgery during 1997-98 all-star break; missed eight games. ... Suffered post-concussion syndrome (March 19, 1998); missed remainder of season.
HONORS: Won WHL Top Draft Prospect Award (1992-93). ... Named to WHL (East) All-Star first team (1992-93).
MISCELLANEOUS: Failed to score on a penalty shot (vs. Corey Hirsch, March 13, 1997).

				REGULAR SEASON								PLAYOFFS			
Season Team	League	Gms.	G	A	Pts.	PIM	+/-	PP	SH		Gms.	G	A	Pts.	PIM
90-91—Medicine Hat	WHL	71	24	26	50	8	...	...	...		12	3	7	10	2
91-92—Medicine Hat	WHL	71	32	46	78	77	...	...	...		4	2	3	5	2
92-93—Medicine Hat	WHL	52	43	34	77	67	...	...	...		—	—	—	—	—
93-94—Florida	NHL	65	9	17	26	51	-11	3	0		—	—	—	—	—
94-95—Medicine Hat	WHL	13	9	15	24	14	...	...	...		—	—	—	—	—
—Florida	NHL	48	4	6	10	36	-13	1	0		—	—	—	—	—
95-96—Florida	NHL	82	26	35	61	107	1	11	0		22	5	3	8	12
96-97—Florida	NHL	60	14	24	38	54	4	3	0		5	2	1	3	6
97-98—Florida	NHL	33	8	7	15	41	-9	5	0		—	—	—	—	—
NHL Totals (5 years)		288	61	89	150	289	-28	23	0		27	7	4	11	18

NIEDERMAYER, SCOTT   D   DEVILS

N

PERSONAL: Born August 31, 1973, in Edmonton. ... 6-0/205. ... Shoots left. ... Brother of Rob Niedermayer, center, Florida Panthers. ... Name pronounced NEE-duhr-MIGH-uhr.
TRANSACTIONS/CAREER NOTES: Stretched left knee ligaments (March 12, 1991); missed nine games. ... Selected by New Jersey Devils in first round (first Devils pick, third overall) of NHL entry draft (June 22, 1991). ... Suffered sore back (December 9, 1992); missed four games. ... Injured knee (December 19, 1995); missed three games. ... Strained groin (February 12, 1997); missed one game. ... Suffered from the flu (February 4, 1998); missed one game.
HONORS: Won Can.HL Scholastic Player of the Year Award (1990-91). ... Named WHL Scholastic Player of the Year (1990-91). ... Named to WHL (West) All-Star first team (1990-91 and 1991-92). ... Won Stafford Smythe Memorial Trophy (1991-92). ... Named to Can.HL All-Star first team (1991-92). ... Named to Memorial Cup All-Star team (1991-92). ... Named to NHL All-Rookie team (1992-93). ... Played in NHL All-Star Game (1998). ... Named to NHL All-Star second team (1997-98).
MISCELLANEOUS: Member of Stanley Cup championship team (1995). ... Failed to score on a penalty shot (vs. Ken Wregget, February 7, 1996).

				REGULAR SEASON								PLAYOFFS			
Season Team	League	Gms.	G	A	Pts.	PIM	+/-	PP	SH		Gms.	G	A	Pts.	PIM
89-90—Kamloops	WHL	64	14	55	69	64	...	...	...		17	2	14	16	35
90-91—Kamloops	WHL	57	26	56	82	52	...	...	...		—	—	—	—	—
91-92—New Jersey	NHL	4	0	1	1	2	1	0	0		—	—	—	—	—
—Kamloops	WHL	35	7	32	39	61	...	...	...		17	9	14	23	28
92-93—New Jersey	NHL	80	11	29	40	47	8	5	0		5	0	3	3	2
93-94—New Jersey	NHL	81	10	36	46	42	34	5	0		20	2	2	4	8
94-95—New Jersey	NHL	48	4	15	19	18	19	4	0		20	4	7	11	10
95-96—New Jersey	NHL	79	8	25	33	46	5	6	0		—	—	—	—	—
96-97—New Jersey	NHL	81	5	30	35	64	-4	3	0		10	2	4	6	6
97-98—New Jersey	NHL	81	14	43	57	27	5	11	0		6	0	2	2	4
NHL Totals (7 years)		454	52	179	231	246	68	34	0		61	8	18	26	30

NIELSEN, JEFF — RW — MIGHTY DUCKS

PERSONAL: Born September 20, 1971, in Grand Rapids, Minn. ... 6-0/200. ... Shoots left. ... Full name: Jeffrey Michael Nielsen.
HIGH SCHOOL: Grand Rapids (Minn.).
COLLEGE: Minnesota.
TRANSACTIONS/CAREER NOTES: Selected by New York Rangers in fourth round (fourth Rangers pick, 69th overall) of NHL entry draft (June 16, 1990). ... Signed as free agent by Mighty Ducks of Anaheim (August 11, 1997). ... Fractured left ankle (January 27, 1998); missed 15 games.
HONORS: Named to WCHA All-Star second team (1993-94).

		REGULAR SEASON								PLAYOFFS				
Season Team	League	Gms.	G	A	Pts.	PIM	+/-	PP	SH	Gms.	G	A	Pts.	PIM
87-88—Grand Rapids H.S.	Minn. H.S.	21	9	11	20	14	...	...	...	—	—	—	—	—
88-89—Grand Rapids H.S.	Minn. H.S.	25	13	17	30	26	...	...	...	—	—	—	—	—
89-90—Grand Rapids H.S.	Minn. H.S.	28	32	25	57	...	...	...	...	—	—	—	—	—
90-91—Univ. of Minnesota	WCHA	45	11	14	25	50	...	...	...	—	—	—	—	—
91-92—Univ. of Minnesota	WCHA	44	15	15	30	74	...	...	...	—	—	—	—	—
92-93—Univ. of Minnesota	WCHA	42	21	20	41	80	...	...	...	—	—	—	—	—
93-94—Univ. of Minnesota	WCHA	41	29	16	45	94	...	...	...	—	—	—	—	—
94-95—Binghamton	AHL	76	24	13	37	139	...	...	...	7	0	0	0	22
95-96—Binghamton	AHL	64	22	20	42	56	...	...	...	4	1	1	2	4
96-97—Binghamton	AHL	76	27	26	53	71	...	...	...	4	0	0	0	7
—New York Rangers	NHL	2	0	0	0	2	-1	0	0	—	—	—	—	—
97-98—Cincinnati	AHL	18	4	8	12	37	...	...	...	—	—	—	—	—
—Anaheim	NHL	32	4	5	9	16	-1	0	0	—	—	—	—	—
NHL Totals (2 years)		34	4	5	9	18	-2	0	0					

NIELSEN, KIRK — RW

PERSONAL: Born October 19, 1973, in Grand Rapids, Minn. ... 6-1/205. ... Shoots right.
COLLEGE: Harvard.
TRANSACTIONS/CAREER NOTES: Signed as free agent by Boston Bruins (June 7, 1996).

		REGULAR SEASON								PLAYOFFS				
Season Team	League	Gms.	G	A	Pts.	PIM	+/-	PP	SH	Gms.	G	A	Pts.	PIM
92-93—Harvard University	ECAC	30	2	2	4	38	...	...	...	—	—	—	—	—
93-94—Harvard University	ECAC	32	6	9	15	41	...	...	...	—	—	—	—	—
94-95—Harvard University	ECAC	30	13	8	21	24	...	...	...	—	—	—	—	—
95-96—Harvard University	ECAC	31	12	16	28	66	...	...	...	—	—	—	—	—
96-97—Providence	AHL	68	12	23	35	30	...	...	...	9	2	1	3	2
97-98—Providence	AHL	72	19	29	48	40	...	...	...	—	—	—	—	—
—Boston	NHL	6	0	0	0	0	-1	0	0	—	—	—	—	—
NHL Totals (1 year)		6	0	0	0	0	-1	0	0					

NIEMI, ANTTI-JUSSI — C — SENATORS

PERSONAL: Born September 22, 1977, in Vantaa, Finland. ... 6-1/183. ... Shoots left.
TRANSACTIONS/CAREER NOTES: Selected by Ottawa Senators in fourth round (second Senators pick, 81st overall) of NHL entry draft (June 22, 1996).

		REGULAR SEASON								PLAYOFFS				
Season Team	League	Gms.	G	A	Pts.	PIM	+/-	PP	SH	Gms.	G	A	Pts.	PIM
93-94—Jokerit Helsinki Jrs.	Finland	33	0	3	3	26	...	...	...	—	—	—	—	—
94-95—Jokerit Helsinki Jrs.	Finland	24	4	8	12	74	...	...	...	—	—	—	—	—
95-96—Jokerit Helsinki Jrs.	Finland	34	11	18	29	56	...	...	...	6	0	4	4	33
—Jokerit Helsinki	Finland	6	0	2	2	6	...	...	...	3	0	1	1	0
96-97—Jokerit Helsinki	Finland	44	2	9	11	38	...	...	...	9	0	2	2	2
97-98—Jokerit Helsinki	Finland	46	2	6	8	24	...	...	...	8	0	1	1	...

N

NIEMINEN, VILLE — RW — AVALANCHE

PERSONAL: Born April 6, 1977, in Tampere, Finland. ... 5-11/205. ... Shoots left.
TRANSACTIONS/CAREER NOTES: Selected by Colorado Avalanche in third round (fourth Avalanche pick, 78th overall) of NHL entry draft (June 21, 1997).

		REGULAR SEASON								PLAYOFFS				
Season Team	League	Gms.	G	A	Pts.	PIM	+/-	PP	SH	Gms.	G	A	Pts.	PIM
94-95—Tappara Tampere Jrs.	Finland	16	11	21	32	47	...	...	...	—	—	—	—	—
—Tappara Tampere	Finland	16	0	0	0	0	...	...	...	—	—	—	—	—
95-96—Tappara Tampere Jrs.	Finland	20	20	23	43	63	...	...	...	—	—	—	—	—
—Tappara Tampere	Finland	4	0	1	1	8	...	...	...	—	—	—	—	—
—KooVee Tampere	Finland	7	2	1	3	4	...	...	...	—	—	—	—	—
96-97—Tappara Tampere	Finland	49	10	13	23	120	...	...	...	3	1	0	1	8
97-98—Hershey	AHL	74	14	22	36	85	...	...	...	—	—	—	—	—

NIEUWENDYK, JOE — C — STARS

PERSONAL: Born September 10, 1966, in Oshawa, Ont. ... 6-1/195. ... Shoots left. ... Full name: Joe T. Nieuwendyk. ... Cousin of Jeff Beukeboom, defenseman, New York Rangers. ... Name pronounced NOO-ihn-dighk.
COLLEGE: Cornell.

TRANSACTIONS/CAREER NOTES: Selected by Calgary Flames in second round (second Flames pick, 27th overall) of NHL entry draft (June 15, 1985). ... Suffered concussion (November 1987). ... Bruised ribs (May 25, 1989). ... Tore left knee ligament (April 17, 1990). ... Underwent arthroscopic knee surgery (September 28, 1991); missed 12 games. ... Suffered from the flu (November 19, 1992); missed one game. ... Strained right knee (March 26, 1993); missed four games. ... Suffered from charley horse (November 13, 1993); missed three games. ... Strained right knee ligaments (February 24, 1994); missed 17 games. ... Strained back (April 29, 1995); missed two games. ... Traded by Flames to Dallas Stars for C Corey Millen and rights to C/RW Jarome Iginla (December 19, 1995). ... Bruised chest (October 5, 1996); missed 12 games. ... Sprained knee (December 18, 1997); missed eight games. ... Reinjured knee (January 9, 1998); missed one game.

HONORS: Won Ivy League Rookie of the Year Trophy (1984-85). ... Named to NCAA All-America East first team (1985-86 and 1986-87). ... Named to ECAC All-Star first team (1985-86 and 1986-87). ... Named ECAC Player of the Year (1986-87). ... Named NHL Rookie of the Year by THE SPORTING NEWS (1987-88). ... Won Calder Memorial Trophy (1987-88). ... Won Dodge Ram Tough Award (1987-88). ... Named to NHL All-Rookie team (1987-88). ... Played in NHL All-Star Game (1988-1990 and 1994). ... Won King Clancy Trophy (1994-95).

RECORDS: Shares NHL single-game record for most goals in one period—4 (January 11, 1989).

STATISTICAL PLATEAUS: Three-goal games: 1987-88 (2), 1988-89 (1), 1989-90 (1), 1992-93 (1), 1993-94 (1), 1994-95 (1), 1997-98 (1). Total: 8. ... Four-goal games: 1987-88 (2), 1997-98 (1). Total: 3. ... Five-goal games: 1988-89 (1). ... Total hat tricks: 12.

MISCELLANEOUS: Member of Stanley Cup championship team (1989). ... Captain of Calgary Flames (1991-92 through 1994-95). ... Scored on a penalty shot (vs. Steve Weeks, December 16, 1988). ... Failed to score on a penalty shot (vs. Jeff Reese, December 12, 1988; vs. Ken Wregget, January 23, 1993).

STATISTICAL NOTES: Third player in NHL history to score 50 goals in each of his first two seasons. ... Led NHL with 11 game-winning goals (1988-89).

					REGULAR SEASON						PLAYOFFS				
Season Team	League	Gms.	G	A	Pts.	PIM	+/-	PP	SH	Gms.	G	A	Pts.	PIM
83-84—Pickering Jr. B	MTHL	38	30	28	58	35	...	...	...	—	—	—	—	—
84-85—Cornell University	ECAC	23	18	21	39	20	...	...	...	—	—	—	—	—
85-86—Cornell University	ECAC	21	21	21	42	45	...	...	...	—	—	—	—	—
86-87—Cornell University	ECAC	23	26	26	52	26	...	...	...	—	—	—	—	—
—Calgary	NHL	9	5	1	6	0	0	2	0	6	2	2	4	0
87-88—Calgary	NHL	75	51	41	92	23	20	*31	3	8	3	4	7	2
88-89—Calgary	NHL	77	51	31	82	40	26	19	3	22	10	4	14	10
89-90—Calgary	NHL	79	45	50	95	40	32	18	0	6	4	6	10	4
90-91—Calgary	NHL	79	45	40	85	36	19	22	4	7	4	1	5	10
91-92—Calgary	NHL	69	22	34	56	55	-1	7	0	—	—	—	—	—
92-93—Calgary	NHL	79	38	37	75	52	9	14	0	6	3	6	9	10
93-94—Calgary	NHL	64	36	39	75	51	19	14	1	6	2	2	4	0
94-95—Calgary	NHL	46	21	29	50	33	11	3	0	5	4	3	7	0
95-96—Dallas	NHL	52	14	18	32	41	-17	8	0	—	—	—	—	—
96-97—Dallas	NHL	66	30	21	51	32	-5	8	0	7	2	2	4	6
97-98—Dallas	NHL	73	39	30	69	30	16	14	0	1	1	0	1	0
—Can. Olympic Team	Int'l	6	2	3	5	2	...	...	...	—	—	—	—	—
NHL Totals (12 years)		768	397	371	768	433	129	160	11	74	35	30	65	42

NIINIMAA, JANNE — D — OILERS

N

PERSONAL: Born May 22, 1975, in Raahe, Finland. ... 6-1/200. ... Shoots left. ... Name pronounced YAH-nee NEE-nuh-muh.

TRANSACTIONS/CAREER NOTES: Selected by Philadelphia Flyers in second round (first Flyers pick, 36th overall) of NHL entry draft (June 26, 1993). ... Traded by Flyers to Edmonton Oilers for D Dan McGillis and second-round pick (D Jason Beckett) in 1998 draft (March 24, 1998).

HONORS: Named to NHL All-Rookie team (1996-97).

MISCELLANEOUS: Member of bronze-medal-winning Finnish Olympic team (1998).

					REGULAR SEASON						PLAYOFFS				
Season Team	League	Gms.	G	A	Pts.	PIM	+/-	PP	SH	Gms.	G	A	Pts.	PIM
91-92—Karpat Oulu	Finland Dv.II	41	2	11	13	49	...	...	...	—	—	—	—	—
92-93—Karpat Oulu	Finland Dv.II	29	2	3	5	14	...	...	...	—	—	—	—	—
—Karpat Jr.	Finland	10	3	9	12	16	...	...	...	—	—	—	—	—
93-94—Jokerit Helsinki	Finland	45	3	8	11	24	...	...	...	12	1	1	2	4
94-95—Jokerit Helsinki	Finland	42	7	10	17	36	...	...	...	10	1	4	5	35
95-96—Jokerit Helsinki	Finland	49	5	15	20	79	...	...	...	11	0	2	2	12
96-97—Philadelphia	NHL	77	4	40	44	58	12	1	0	19	1	12	13	16
97-98—Philadelphia	NHL	66	3	31	34	56	6	2	0	—	—	—	—	—
—Fin. Olympic Team	Int'l	6	0	3	3	8	...	...	...	—	—	—	—	—
—Edmonton	NHL	11	1	8	9	6	7	1	0	11	1	1	2	12
NHL Totals (2 years)		154	8	79	87	120	25	4	0	30	2	13	15	28

NIKOLISHIN, ANDREI — C — CAPITALS

PERSONAL: Born March 25, 1973, in Vorkuta, U.S.S.R. ... 5-11/205. ... Shoots left. ... Name pronounced nih-koh-LEE-shihn.

TRANSACTIONS/CAREER NOTES: Selected by Hartford Whalers in second round (second Whalers pick, 47th overall) of NHL entry draft (June 20, 1992). ... Played in Europe during 1994-95 NHL lockout. ... Sprained ankle (October 21, 1995); missed one game. ... Injured back (November 15, 1995); missed five games. ... Strained back (December 2, 1995); missed 15 games. ... Traded by Whalers to Washington Capitals for D Curtis Leschyshyn (November 9, 1996). ... Suffered bulging disc in back (February 2, 1997); missed eight games. ... Injured knee prior to 1997-98 season; missed first 42 games.

HONORS: Named to CIS All-Star team (1993-94). ... Named CIS Player of the Year (1993-94).

MISCELLANEOUS: Member of gold-medal-winning Russian Olympic team (1994).

					REGULAR SEASON						PLAYOFFS				
Season Team	League	Gms.	G	A	Pts.	PIM	+/-	PP	SH	Gms.	G	A	Pts.	PIM
90-91—Dynamo Moscow	USSR	2	0	0	0	0	...	...	...	—	—	—	—	—
91-92—Dynamo Moscow	CIS	18	1	0	1	4	...	...	...	—	—	—	—	—
92-93—Dynamo Moscow	CIS	42	5	7	12	30	...	...	...	10	2	1	3	8
93-94—Dynamo Moscow	CIS	41	8	12	20	30	...	...	...	9	1	3	4	4
—Russian Oly. team	Int'l	8	2	5	7	6	...	...	...	—	—	—	—	—

Season Team	League	REGULAR SEASON								PLAYOFFS				
		Gms.	G	A	Pts.	PIM	+/-	PP	SH	Gms.	G	A	Pts.	PIM
94-95—Dynamo Moscow........	CIS	12	7	2	9	6	...	—	—	—	—	—	—	—
—Hartford	NHL	39	8	10	18	10	7	1	1	—	—	—	—	—
95-96—Hartford	NHL	61	14	37	51	34	-2	4	1	—	—	—	—	—
96-97—Hartford	NHL	12	2	5	7	2	-2	0	0	—	—	—	—	—
—Washington	NHL	59	7	14	21	30	5	1	0	—	—	—	—	—
97-98—Portland	AHL	2	0	0	0	2	...	...	...	—	—	—	—	—
—Washington	NHL	38	6	10	16	14	1	1	0	21	1	13	14	12
NHL Totals (4 years)..........		209	37	76	113	90	9	7	2	21	1	13	14	12

NILSON, MARCUS   C   PANTHERS

PERSONAL: Born March 1, 1978, in Stockholm, Sweden. ... 6-1/183. ... Shoots right.
TRANSACTIONS/CAREER NOTES: Selected by Florida Panthers in first round (first Panthers pick, 20th overall) of NHL entry draft (June 22, 1996).

Season Team	League	REGULAR SEASON								PLAYOFFS				
		Gms.	G	A	Pts.	PIM	+/-	PP	SH	Gms.	G	A	Pts.	PIM
94-95—Djurgarden Jrs............	Sweden	24	7	8	15	22	...	...	...	—	—	—	—	—
95-96—Djurgarden Jrs............	Sweden	25	19	17	36	46	...	...	...	2	1	1	2	12
—Djur. Stockholm.........	Sweden	12	0	0	0	0	...	...	...	1	0	0	0	0
96-97—Djur. Stockholm.........	Sweden	37	0	3	3	33	...	...	...	4	0	0	0	0
97-98—Djur. Stockholm.........	Sweden	41	4	7	11	18	...	...	...	15	2	1	3	16

NITTEL, ADAM   RW   SHARKS

PERSONAL: Born July 17, 1978, in Kitchener, Ont. ... 6-1/206. ... Shoots right. ... Name pronounced NIH-tehl.
TRANSACTIONS/CAREER NOTES: Selected by San Jose Sharks in fifth round (fourth Sharks pick, 107th overall) of NHL entry draft (June 21, 1997).

Season Team	League	REGULAR SEASON								PLAYOFFS				
		Gms.	G	A	Pts.	PIM	+/-	PP	SH	Gms.	G	A	Pts.	PIM
95-96—Niagara Falls	OHL	39	3	3	6	74	...	...	...	10	0	3	3	39
96-97—Erie	OHL	46	8	11	19	194	...	...	...	—	—	—	—	—
97-98—Erie	OHL	48	11	17	28	309	...	...	...	—	—	—	—	—

NOLAN, OWEN   RW   SHARKS

PERSONAL: Born February 12, 1972, in Belfast, Northern Ireland. ... 6-1/215. ... Shoots right.
TRANSACTIONS/CAREER NOTES: Separated shoulder (February 22, 1990); missed eight games. ... Selected by Quebec Nordiques in first round (first Nordiques pick, first overall) of NHL entry draft (June 16, 1990). ... Suffered concussion, sore knee and sore back (October 1990). ... Suspended four off-days by NHL for cross-checking (December 7, 1992). ... Bruised hand (March 2, 1993); missed three games. ... Bruised shoulder (March 15, 1993); eight games. ... Injured right shoulder (October 19, 1993); missed 11 games. ... Dislocated left shoulder (November 12, 1993); missed remainder of season. ... Bruised shoulder (April 16, 1995); missed two games. ... Nordiques franchise moved to Colorado and renamed Avalanche for 1995-96 season (June 21, 1995). ... Traded by Avalanche to San Jose Sharks for D Sandis Ozolinsh (October 26, 1995). ... Suffered from the flu (March 5, 1996); missed two games. ... Suffered from an illness (November 27, 1996); missed one game. ... Bruised shoulder (January 9, 1997); missed two games. ... Suffered sore ankle (March 20, 1997); missed four games. ... Strained groin (April 7, 1997); missed three games. ... Strained shoulder (March 26, 1998); missed six games.
HONORS: Won Emms Family Award (1988-89). ... Won Jim Mahon Memorial Trophy (1989-90). ... Named to OHL All-Star first team (1989-90). ... Played in NHL All-Star Game (1992, 1996 and 1997).
STATISTICAL NOTES: Led NHL with eight game-winning goals (1994-95).
STATISTICAL PLATEAUS: Three-goal games: 1991-92 (2), 1992-93 (2), 1994-95 (3), 1996-97 (1). Total: 8. ... Four-goal games: 1995-96 (1). ... Total hat tricks: 9.

Season Team	League	REGULAR SEASON								PLAYOFFS				
		Gms.	G	A	Pts.	PIM	+/-	PP	SH	Gms.	G	A	Pts.	PIM
88-89—Cornwall	OHL	62	34	25	59	213	...	...	...	18	5	11	16	41
89-90—Cornwall	OHL	58	51	59	110	240	...	...	...	6	7	5	12	26
90-91—Quebec	NHL	59	3	10	13	109	-19	0	0	—	—	—	—	—
—Halifax	AHL	6	4	4	8	11	...	...	...	—	—	—	—	—
91-92—Quebec	NHL	75	42	31	73	183	-9	17	0	—	—	—	—	—
92-93—Quebec	NHL	73	36	41	77	185	-1	15	0	5	1	0	1	2
93-94—Quebec	NHL	6	2	2	4	8	2	0	0	—	—	—	—	—
94-95—Quebec	NHL	46	30	19	49	46	21	13	2	6	2	3	5	6
95-96—Colorado	NHL	9	4	4	8	9	-3	4	0	—	—	—	—	—
—San Jose..................	NHL	72	29	32	61	137	-30	12	1	—	—	—	—	—
96-97—San Jose..................	NHL	72	31	32	63	155	-19	10	0	—	—	—	—	—
97-98—San Jose..................	NHL	75	14	27	41	144	-2	3	1	6	2	2	4	26
NHL Totals (8 years)..........		487	191	198	389	976	-60	74	4	17	5	5	10	34

NOONAN, BRIAN   RW

PERSONAL: Born May 29, 1965, in Boston. ... 6-1/200. ... Shoots right.
HIGH SCHOOL: Archbishop Williams (Braintree, Mass.).
TRANSACTIONS/CAREER NOTES: Selected by Chicago Blackhawks in ninth round (10th Blackhawks pick, 179th overall) of NHL entry draft (June 8, 1983). ... Separated shoulder (April 3, 1988). ... Refused to report to Indianapolis (October 18, 1990); suspended without pay by Blackhawks. ... Suffered death in family (February 28, 1991); missed six games. ... Damaged left knee ligaments (January 30, 1992); missed 12 games. ... Bruised shoulder (October 31, 1992); missed four games. ... Suspended one game by NHL for accumulating three game mis-

conduct penalties (January 21, 1993). ... Suffered from the flu (February 25, 1993); missed three games. ... Traded by Blackhawks with LW Stephane Matteau to New York Rangers for RW Tony Amonte and rights to LW Matt Oates (March 21, 1994). ... Sprained right knee (April 2, 1995); missed three games. ... Strained groin (May 6, 1995); missed five playoff games. ... Signed as free agent by St. Louis Blues (July 11, 1995). ... Injured knee (November 3, 1996); missed four games. ... Traded by Blues to Rangers for LW Sergio Momesso (November 13, 1996). ... Traded by Rangers with C Sergei Nemchinov to Vancouver Canucks for LW Esa Tikkanen and RW Russ Courtnall (March 8, 1997).
HONORS: Won Ken McKenzie Trophy (1985-86). ... Named to IHL All-Star second team (1989-90). ... Named to IHL All-Star first team (1990-91).
MISCELLANEOUS: Member of Stanley Cup championship team (1994).
STATISTICAL PLATEAUS: Three-goal games: 1991-92 (2), 1994-95 (1). Total: 3. ... Four-goal games: 1991-92 (1). ... Total hat tricks: 4.

					REGULAR SEASON								PLAYOFFS			
Season Team	League	Gms.	G	A	Pts.	PIM	+/-	PP	SH		Gms.	G	A	Pts.	PIM
82-83—Archbishop Williams...	Mass. H.S.	21	26	17	43	...	...	...	...		—	—	—	—	—
83-84—Archbishop Williams...	Mass. H.S.	17	14	23	37	...	...	...	...		—	—	—	—	—
84-85—New Westminster	WHL	72	50	66	116	76	...	...	...		11	8	7	15	4
85-86—Saginaw....................	IHL	76	39	39	78	69	...	...	...		11	6	3	9	6
—Nova Scotia	AHL	2	0	0	0	0	...	...	...		—	—	—	—	—
86-87—Nova Scotia	AHL	70	25	26	51	30	...	...	...		5	3	1	4	4
87-88—Chicago....................	NHL	77	10	20	30	44	-27	3	0		3	0	0	0	4
88-89—Chicago....................	NHL	45	4	12	16	28	-2	2	0		1	0	0	0	0
—Saginaw....................	IHL	19	18	13	31	36	...	...	...		1	0	0	0	0
89-90—Chicago....................	NHL	8	0	2	2	6	0	0	0		—	—	—	—	—
—Indianapolis..............	IHL	56	40	36	76	85	...	...	...		14	6	9	15	20
90-91—Indianapolis............	IHL	59	38	53	91	67	...	...	...		7	6	4	10	18
—Chicago....................	NHL	7	0	4	4	2	-1	0	0		—	—	—	—	—
91-92—Chicago....................	NHL	65	19	12	31	81	9	4	0		18	6	9	15	30
92-93—Chicago....................	NHL	63	16	14	30	82	3	5	0		4	3	0	3	4
93-94—Chicago....................	NHL	64	14	21	35	57	2	8	0		—	—	—	—	—
—New York Rangers......	NHL	12	4	2	6	12	5	2	0		22	4	7	11	17
94-95—New York Rangers......	NHL	45	14	13	27	26	-3	7	0		5	0	0	0	8
95-96—St. Louis..................	NHL	81	13	22	35	84	2	3	1		13	4	1	5	10
96-97—St. Louis..................	NHL	13	2	5	7	0	2	0	0		—	—	—	—	—
—New York Rangers......	NHL	44	6	9	15	28	-7	3	0		—	—	—	—	—
—Vancouver..................	NHL	16	4	8	12	6	2	0	1		—	—	—	—	—
97-98—Vancouver..................	NHL	82	10	15	25	62	-19	1	0		—	—	—	—	—
NHL Totals (11 years).........		622	116	159	275	518	-34	38	2		66	17	17	34	73

NORONEN, MIKA　　　　　　　　G　　　　　　　　SABRES

PERSONAL: Born June 17, 1979, in Tampere, Finland. ... 6-0/190. ... Catches left.
TRANSACTIONS/CAREER NOTES: Selected by Buffalo Sabres in first round (first Sabres pick, 21st overall) of NHL entry draft (June 21, 1997).

				REGULAR SEASON								PLAYOFFS					
Season Team	League	Gms.	Min	W	L	T	GA	SO	Avg.		Gms.	Min.	W	L	GA	SO	Avg.
95-96—Tappara Tampere Jrs.....	Finland	16	962	...	...	...	37	2	2.31		—	—	—	—	—	—	—
96-97—Tappara Tampere..........	Finland	5	215	...	...	...	17	0	4.74		—	—	—	—	—	—	—
97-98—Tappara Tampere..........	Finland	31	1703	14	12	3	83	1	2.92		4	196	1	2	12	0	3.67

NORSTROM, MATTIAS　　　　　　　　D　　　　　　　　KINGS

PERSONAL: Born January 2, 1972, in Stockholm, Sweden. ... 6-1/205. ... Shoots left. ... Name pronounced muh-TEE-uhz NOHR-struhm.
TRANSACTIONS/CAREER NOTES: Selected by New York Rangers in second round (second Rangers pick, 48th overall) of NHL entry draft (June 20, 1992). ... Suffered from the flu (April 28, 1995); missed two games. ... Separated shoulder (December 30, 1995); missed six games. ... Traded by Rangers with C Ray Ferraro, C Ian Laperriere, C Nathan Lafayette and fourth-round pick (D Sean Blanchard) in 1997 draft to Los Angeles Kings for RW Shane Churla, LW Jari Kurri and D Marty McSorley (March 14, 1996). ... Bruised left wrist (November 7, 1996); missed one game. ... Suspended one game by NHL for illegal check (January 12, 1998).
MISCELLANEOUS: Member of Stanley Cup championship team (1994).

					REGULAR SEASON								PLAYOFFS			
Season Team	League	Gms.	G	A	Pts.	PIM	+/-	PP	SH		Gms.	G	A	Pts.	PIM
91-92—AIK Solna...................	Sweden	39	4	4	8	28	...	...	...		—	—	—	—	—
92-93—AIK Solna...................	Sweden	22	0	1	1	16	...	...	...		—	—	—	—	—
93-94—New York Rangers.......	NHL	9	0	2	2	6	0	0	0		—	—	—	—	—
—Binghamton	AHL	55	1	9	10	70	...	...	...		—	—	—	—	—
94-95—Binghamton	AHL	63	9	10	19	91	...	...	...		—	—	—	—	—
—New York Rangers......	NHL	9	0	3	3	2	2	0	0		3	0	0	0	0
95-96—New York Rangers......	NHL	25	2	1	3	22	5	0	0		—	—	—	—	—
—Los Angeles..............	NHL	11	0	1	1	18	-8	0	0		—	—	—	—	—
96-97—Los Angeles..............	NHL	80	1	21	22	84	-4	0	0		—	—	—	—	—
97-98—Los Angeles..............	NHL	73	1	12	13	90	14	0	0		4	0	0	0	2
—Swedish Oly. team	Int'l	4	0	1	1	2	...	...	...		—	—	—	—	—
NHL Totals (5 years)..........		207	4	40	44	222	9	0	0		7	0	0	0	2

NORTON, BRAD　　　　　　　　D　　　　　　　　OILERS

PERSONAL: Born February 13, 1975, in Cambridge, Mass. ... 6-5/235. ... Shoots left. ... Full name: Brad Joseph Norton.
HIGH SCHOOL: Cushing Academy (Ashburnham, Mass.).
COLLEGE: Massachusetts.
TRANSACTIONS/CAREER NOTES: Selected by Edmonton Oilers in ninth round (ninth Oilers pick, 215th overall) of NHL entry draft (June 26, 1993).

Season Team	League	REGULAR SEASON Gms.	G	A	Pts.	PIM	+/-	PP	SH	PLAYOFFS Gms.	G	A	Pts.	PIM
92-93—Cushing Academy	Mass. H.S.	31	10	26	36	36	...	...	...	—	—	—	—	—
93-94—Cushing Academy	Mass. H.S.						Statistics unavailable.			—	—	—	—	—
94-95—Univ. of Mass.	Hockey East	30	0	6	6	89	...	...	...	—	—	—	—	—
95-96—Univ. of Mass.	Hockey East	34	4	12	16	99	...	...	...	—	—	—	—	—
96-97—Univ. of Mass.	Hockey East	35	2	16	18	88	...	...	...	—	—	—	—	—
97-98—Univ. of Mass.	Hockey East	20	2	13	15	28	...	...	...	—	—	—	—	—

NORTON, JEFF — D — PANTHERS

PERSONAL: Born November 25, 1965, in Acton, Mass. ... 6-2/200. ... Shoots left. ... Full name: Jeffrey Zaccari Norton.

HIGH SCHOOL: Cushing Academy (Ashburnham, Mass.).

COLLEGE: Michigan.

TRANSACTIONS/CAREER NOTES: Selected by New York Islanders in third round (third Islanders pick, 62nd overall) of NHL entry draft (June 9, 1984). ... Bruised ribs (November 16, 1988). ... Injured groin (February 1990). ... Strained groin and abdominal muscles (March 2, 1990); missed games. ... Suffered concussion (April 9, 1990). ... Suspended eight games by NHL for intentionally injuring another player in preseason game (September 30, 1990). ... Dislocated right shoulder (November 3, 1990); missed four games. ... Reinjured shoulder (December 27, 1990); missed five games. ... Reinjured shoulder and underwent surgery (February 23, 1991); missed remainder of season. ... Suffered concussion (October 26, 1991); missed one game. ... Tore ligaments in left wrist (January 3, 1992); missed final 42 games of season. ... Underwent surgery to left wrist (January 8, 1992). ... Suffered hip flexor (October 23, 1992); missed five games. ... Suffered sore shoulder (December 31, 1992); missed one game. ... Pulled groin (February 25, 1993); missed two games. ... Traded by Islanders to San Jose Sharks for third-round pick (D Jason Strudwick) in 1994 draft (June 20, 1993). ... Sprained ankle (December 11, 1993); missed nine games. ... Reinjured ankle (January 4, 1994); missed five games. ... Sprained ankle (February 19, 1994); missed five games. ... Suffered from the flu (January 28, 1995); missed one game. ... Traded by Sharks with third-round pick (traded to Colorado) in 1997 draft and future considerations to St. Louis Blues for C Craig Janney (March 6, 1995). ... Injured hand (March 7, 1995); missed one game. ... Traded by Blues with D Donald Dufresne to Edmonton Oilers for D Igor Kravchuck and D Ken Sutton (January 4, 1996). ... Fractured thumb (February 9, 1996); missed two games. ... Suffered back spasms (March 17, 1996); missed one game. ... Sprained left knee (March 24, 1996); missed nine games. ... Sprained ankle (October 15, 1996); missed six games. ... Injured right ankle (November 7, 1996); missed one game. ... Strained groin (January 7, 1997); missed one game. ... Traded by Oilers to Tampa Bay Lightning for D Drew Bannister and sixth-round draft pick in 1997 (March 18, 1997). ... Strained groin (October 5, 1997); missed three games. ... Traded by Lightning with RW Dino Ciccarelli to Florida Panthers for G Mark Fitzpatrick and RW Jody Hull (January 15, 1998). ... Suffered cracked sternum and bruised chest (March 21, 1998); missed remainder of season.

HONORS: Named to CCHA All-Star second team (1986-87).

Season Team	League	REGULAR SEASON Gms.	G	A	Pts.	PIM	+/-	PP	SH	PLAYOFFS Gms.	G	A	Pts.	PIM
83-84—Cushing Academy	Mass. H.S.	21	22	33	55	...	...	...	...	—	—	—	—	—
84-85—Univ. of Michigan	CCHA	37	8	16	24	103	...	...	...	—	—	—	—	—
85-86—Univ. of Michigan	CCHA	37	15	30	45	99	...	...	...	—	—	—	—	—
86-87—Univ. of Michigan	CCHA	39	12	37	49	92	...	...	...	—	—	—	—	—
87-88—U.S. national team	Int'l	57	7	25	32	...	...	...	...	—	—	—	—	—
—U.S. Olympic Team	Int'l	6	0	4	4	4	...	...	...	—	—	—	—	—
—New York Islanders	NHL	15	1	6	7	14	3	1	0	3	0	2	2	13
88-89—New York Islanders	NHL	69	1	30	31	74	-24	1	0	—	—	—	—	—
89-90—New York Islanders	NHL	60	4	49	53	65	-9	4	0	4	1	3	4	17
90-91—New York Islanders	NHL	44	3	25	28	16	-13	2	1	—	—	—	—	—
91-92—New York Islanders	NHL	28	1	18	19	18	2	0	1	—	—	—	—	—
92-93—New York Islanders	NHL	66	12	38	50	45	-3	5	0	10	1	1	2	4
93-94—San Jose	NHL	64	7	33	40	36	16	1	0	14	1	5	6	20
94-95—San Jose	NHL	20	1	9	10	39	1	0	0	—	—	—	—	—
—St. Louis	NHL	28	2	18	20	33	21	0	0	7	1	1	2	11
95-96—St. Louis	NHL	36	4	7	11	26	4	0	0	—	—	—	—	—
—Edmonton	NHL	30	4	16	20	16	5	1	0	—	—	—	—	—
96-97—Edmonton	NHL	62	2	11	13	42	-7	0	0	—	—	—	—	—
—Tampa Bay	NHL	13	0	5	5	16	0	0	0	—	—	—	—	—
97-98—Tampa Bay	NHL	37	4	6	10	26	-25	4	0	—	—	—	—	—
—Florida	NHL	19	0	7	7	18	-7	0	0	—	—	—	—	—
NHL Totals (11 years)		591	46	278	324	484	-36	19	2	38	4	12	16	65

NOVOSELTSEV, IVAN — RW — PANTHERS

PERSONAL: Born January 23, 1979, in Golitsino, U.S.S.R. ... 6-1/200. ... Shoots left. ... Name pronounced noh-vuh-SEHLT-sehf.

TRANSACTIONS/CAREER NOTES: Selected by Florida Panthers in fourth round (fifth Panthers pick, 95th overall) of NHL entry draft (June 21, 1997).

Season Team	League	REGULAR SEASON Gms.	G	A	Pts.	PIM	+/-	PP	SH	PLAYOFFS Gms.	G	A	Pts.	PIM
95-96—Krylja Sov. Moscow	CIS	1	0	0	0	0	...	...	...	—	—	—	—	—
96-97—Krylja Sov. Moscow	Russian	30	0	3	3	18	...	...	...	2	0	0	0	4
—Krylja Sov. Moscow	Rus. Div. III	19	5	3	8	39	...	...	...	—	—	—	—	—
97-98—Sarnia	OHL	53	26	22	48	41	...	...	...	5	1	1	2	8

NUMMINEN, TEPPO — D — COYOTES

PERSONAL: Born July 3, 1968, in Tampere, Finland. ... 6-1/195. ... Shoots right. ... Full name: Teppo Kalevi Numminen. ... Name pronounced TEH-poh NOO-mih-nehn.

TRANSACTIONS/CAREER NOTES: Selected by Winnipeg Jets in second round (second Jets pick, 29th overall) of NHL entry draft (June 21, 1986). ... Separated shoulder (March 5, 1989). ... Broke thumb (April 14, 1990). ... Fractured foot (January 28, 1993); missed 17 games. ...

N

Dislocated thumb (February 9, 1994); missed remainder of season. ... Played in Europe during 1994-95 NHL lockout. ... Suffered from stomach flu (January 23, 1995); missed one game. ... Suffered surface stress fracture in right knee (February 22, 1995); missed five games. ... Separated shoulder (November 28, 1995); missed eight games. ... Jets franchise moved to Phoenix and renamed Coyotes for 1996-97 season; NHL approved move on January 18, 1996.
MISCELLANEOUS: Member of silver-medal-winning Finnish Olympic team (1988). ... Member of bronze-medal-winning Finnish Olympic team (1998).

Season Team	League	REGULAR SEASON									PLAYOFFS				
		Gms.	G	A	Pts.	PIM	+/-	PP	SH		Gms.	G	A	Pts.	PIM
84-85—Tappara	Finland	30	14	17	31	10	...	...	...		—	—	—	—	—
85-86—Tappara	Finland	39	2	4	6	6	...	...	...		8	0	0	0	0
86-87—Tappara	Finland	44	9	9	18	16	...	...	...		9	4	1	5	4
87-88—Tappara	Finland	44	10	10	20	29	...	...	...		10	6	6	12	6
—Fin. Olympic Team	Int'l	6	1	4	5	0	...	...	...		—	—	—	—	—
88-89—Winnipeg	NHL	69	1	14	15	36	-11	0	1		—	—	—	—	—
89-90—Winnipeg	NHL	79	11	32	43	20	-4	1	0		7	1	2	3	10
90-91—Winnipeg	NHL	80	8	25	33	28	-15	3	0		—	—	—	—	—
91-92—Winnipeg	NHL	80	5	34	39	32	15	4	0		7	0	0	0	0
92-93—Winnipeg	NHL	66	7	30	37	33	4	3	1		6	1	1	2	2
93-94—Winnipeg	NHL	57	5	18	23	28	-23	4	0		—	—	—	—	—
94-95—TuTo Turku	Finland	12	3	8	11	4	...	...	...		—	—	—	—	—
—Winnipeg	NHL	42	5	16	21	16	12	2	0		—	—	—	—	—
95-96—Winnipeg	NHL	74	11	43	54	22	-4	6	0		6	0	0	0	2
96-97—Phoenix	NHL	82	2	25	27	28	-3	0	0		7	3	3	6	0
97-98—Phoenix	NHL	82	11	40	51	30	25	6	0		1	0	0	0	0
—Fin. Olympic Team	Int'l	6	1	1	2	2	...	...	...		—	—	—	—	—
NHL Totals (10 years)		711	66	277	343	273	-4	29	2		34	5	6	11	14

NYLANDER, MICHAEL   C   FLAMES

PERSONAL: Born October 3, 1972, in Stockholm, Sweden. ... 5-11/195. ... Shoots left. ... Name pronounced NEE-lan-duhr.
TRANSACTIONS/CAREER NOTES: Selected by Hartford Whalers in third round (fourth Whalers pick, 59th overall) of NHL entry draft (June 22, 1991). ... Broke jaw (January 23, 1993); missed 15 games. ... Traded by Whalers with D Zarley Zalapski and D James Patrick to Calgary Flames for D Gary Suter, LW Paul Ranheim and C Ted Drury (March 10, 1994). ... Played in Europe during 1994-95 NHL lockout. ... Broke left wrist and forearm (January 24, 1995); missed 42 games. ... Injured wrist (January 16, 1996); missed three games. ... Injured left knee (March 26, 1998); missed 11 games.
HONORS: Named Swedish League Rookie of the Year (1991-92).
STATISTICAL PLATEAUS: Three-goal games: 1992-93 (1).

Season Team	League	REGULAR SEASON									PLAYOFFS				
		Gms.	G	A	Pts.	PIM	+/-	PP	SH		Gms.	G	A	Pts.	PIM
89-90—Huddinge	Sweden	31	7	15	22	4	...	...	...		—	—	—	—	—
90-91—Huddinge	Sweden	33	14	20	34	10	...	...	...		—	—	—	—	—
91-92—AIK Solna	Sweden	40	11	17	28	30	...	...	...		—	—	—	—	—
—Swedish nat'l team	Int'l	6	0	1	1	0	...	...	...		—	—	—	—	—
92-93—Hartford	NHL	59	11	22	33	36	-7	3	0		—	—	—	—	—
93-94—Hartford	NHL	58	11	33	44	24	-2	4	0		—	—	—	—	—
—Springfield	AHL	4	0	9	9	0	...	...	...		—	—	—	—	—
—Calgary	NHL	15	2	9	11	6	10	0	0		3	0	0	0	0
94-95—JyP HT	Finland	16	11	19	30	63	...	...	...		—	—	—	—	—
—Calgary	NHL	6	0	1	1	2	1	0	0		6	0	6	6	2
95-96—Calgary	NHL	73	17	38	55	20	0	4	0		4	0	0	0	0
96-97—Lugano	Switzerland	36	12	43	55	...	...	...	...		—	—	—	—	—
97-98—Calgary	NHL	65	13	23	36	24	10	0	0		—	—	—	—	—
—Swedish Oly. team	Int'l	4	0	0	0	6	...	...	...		—	—	—	—	—
NHL Totals (5 years)		276	54	126	180	112	12	11	0		13	0	6	6	2

OATES, ADAM   C   CAPITALS

PERSONAL: Born August 27, 1962, in Weston, Ont. ... 5-11/185. ... Shoots right. ... Full name: Adam R. Oates. ... Name pronounced OHTS.
COLLEGE: Rensselaer Polytechnic Institute (N.Y.).
TRANSACTIONS/CAREER NOTES: Signed as free agent by Detroit Red Wings (June 28, 1985). ... Pulled abdominal muscle (October 1987). ... Suffered from chicken pox (November 1988). ... Bruised thigh (December 1988). ... Traded by Red Wings with RW Paul MacLean to St. Louis Blues for LW Tony McKegney and C Bernie Federko (June 15, 1989). ... Tore rib and abdominal muscles (November 5, 1990); missed 18 games. ... Traded by Blues to Boston Bruins for C Craig Janney and D Stephane Quintal (February 7, 1992). ... Injured groin (January 6, 1994); missed seven games. ... Injured knee (October 28, 1995); missed 12 games. ... Traded by Bruins with RW Rick Tocchet and G Bill Ranford to Washington Capitals for G Jim Carey, C Jason Allison, C Anson Carter and third-round pick (RW Lee Goren) in 1997 draft (March 1, 1997). ... Injured back (April 10, 1997); missed two games.
HONORS: Named to ECAC All-Star second team (1983-84). ... Named to NCAA All-America East first team (1984-85). ... Named to NCAA All-Tournament team (1984-85). ... Named to ECAC All-Star first team (1984-85). ... Named to THE SPORTING NEWS All-Star second team (1990-91). ... Named to NHL All-Star second team (1990-91). ... Played in NHL All-Star Game (1991-1994 and 1997).
RECORDS: Holds NHL All-Star Game record for most assists in one period—4 (first period, 1993).
STATISTICAL PLATEAUS: Three-goal games: 1992-93 (3), 1993-94 (2), 1997-98 (1). Total: 6. ... Four-goal games: 1995-96 (1). ... Total hat tricks: 7.
STATISTICAL NOTES: Tied for NHL lead with 11 game-winning goals (1992-93).

Season Team	League	REGULAR SEASON									PLAYOFFS				
		Gms.	G	A	Pts.	PIM	+/-	PP	SH		Gms.	G	A	Pts.	PIM
82-83—R.P.I.	ECAC	22	9	33	42	8	...	...	...		—	—	—	—	—
83-84—R.P.I.	ECAC	38	26	57	83	15	...	...	...		—	—	—	—	—
84-85—R.P.I.	ECAC	38	31	60	91	29	...	...	...		—	—	—	—	—

N
O

Season Team	League	Gms.	G	A	Pts.	PIM	+/-	PP	SH	Gms.	G	A	Pts.	PIM
85-86—Adirondack	AHL	34	18	28	46	4	...	...	...	17	7	14	21	4
—Detroit	NHL	38	9	11	20	10	1	0	-24	—	—	—	—	—
86-87—Detroit	NHL	76	15	32	47	21	0	4	0	16	4	7	11	6
87-88—Detroit	NHL	63	14	40	54	20	16	3	0	16	8	12	20	6
88-89—Detroit	NHL	69	16	62	78	14	-1	2	0	6	0	8	8	2
89-90—St. Louis	NHL	80	23	79	102	30	9	6	2	12	2	12	14	4
90-91—St. Louis	NHL	61	25	90	115	29	15	3	1	13	7	13	20	10
91-92—St. Louis	NHL	54	10	59	69	12	-4	3	0	—	—	—	—	—
—Boston	NHL	26	10	20	30	10	-5	3	0	15	5	14	19	4
92-93—Boston	NHL	84	45	*97	142	32	24	1		4	0	9	9	4
93-94—Boston	NHL	77	32	80	112	45	10	16	2	13	3	9	12	8
94-95—Boston	NHL	48	12	41	53	8	-11	4	1	5	1	0	1	2
95-96—Boston	NHL	70	25	67	92	18	16	7	1	5	2	5	7	2
96-97—Boston	NHL	63	18	52	70	10	-3	2	2	—	—	—	—	—
—Washington	NHL	17	4	8	12	4	-2	1	0	—	—	—	—	—
97-98—Washington	NHL	82	18	58	76	36	6	3	2	21	6	11	17	8
NHL Totals (13 years)		908	276	796	1072	299	62	81	-12	126	38	100	138	56

ODELEIN, LYLE — D — DEVILS

PERSONAL: Born July 21, 1968, in Quill Lake, Sask. ... 5-11/210. ... Shoots right. ... Name pronounced OH-duh-lighn.
TRANSACTIONS/CAREER NOTES: Selected by Montreal Canadiens as underage junior in seventh round (eighth Canadiens pick, 141st overall) of NHL entry draft (June 21, 1986). ... Bruised right ankle (January 22, 1991); missed five games. ... Twisted right ankle (February 9, 1991). ... Suspended one game by NHL for game misconduct penalties (March 1, 1993). ... Bruised shoulder (January 24, 1994); missed three games. ... Suspended two games without pay and fined $1,000 by NHL for shooting puck into the opposing team's bench (April 3, 1996). ... Traded by Canadiens to New Jersey Devils for RW Stephane Richer (August 22, 1996). ... Bruised knee (January 21, 1997); missed three games. ... Bruised shoulder (November 12, 1997); missed one game.
MISCELLANEOUS: Member of Stanley Cup championship team (1993).
STATISTICAL PLATEAUS: Three-goal games: 1993-94 (1).

Season Team	League	Gms.	G	A	Pts.	PIM	+/-	PP	SH	Gms.	G	A	Pts.	PIM
85-86—Moose Jaw	WHL	67	9	37	46	117	...	...	...	13	1	6	7	34
86-87—Moose Jaw	WHL	59	9	50	59	70	...	...	...	9	2	5	7	26
87-88—Moose Jaw	WHL	63	15	43	58	166	...	...	...	—	—	—	—	—
88-89—Sherbrooke	AHL	33	3	4	7	120	...	...	...	3	0	2	2	5
—Peoria	IHL	36	2	8	10	116	...	...	...	—	—	—	—	—
89-90—Sherbrooke	AHL	68	7	24	31	265	...	...	...	12	6	5	11	79
—Montreal	NHL	8	0	2	2	33	...	0	0	—	—	—	—	—
90-91—Montreal	NHL	52	0	2	2	259	7	0	0	12	0	0	0	54
91-92—Montreal	NHL	71	1	7	8	212	15	0	0	7	0	0	0	11
92-93—Montreal	NHL	83	2	14	16	205	35	0	0	20	1	5	6	30
93-94—Montreal	NHL	79	11	29	40	276	8	6	0	7	0	0	0	17
94-95—Montreal	NHL	48	3	7	10	152	-13	0	0	—	—	—	—	—
95-96—Montreal	NHL	79	3	14	17	230	8	0	1	6	1	1	2	6
96-97—New Jersey	NHL	79	3	13	16	110	16	1	0	10	2	2	4	19
97-98—New Jersey	NHL	79	4	19	23	171	11	1	0	6	1	1	2	21
NHL Totals (9 years)		578	27	107	134	1648	...	8	1	68	5	9	14	158

O'DETTE, MATT — D — PANTHERS

PERSONAL: Born November 9, 1975, in East York, Ont. ... 6-4/205. ... Shoots right. ... Name pronounced oh-DEHT.
TRANSACTIONS/CAREER NOTES: Selected by Florida Panthers in sixth round (seventh Panthers pick, 151st overall) of NHL entry draft (June 29, 1994).

Season Team	League	Gms.	G	A	Pts.	PIM	+/-	PP	SH	Gms.	G	A	Pts.	PIM
92-93—Kitchener	OHL	28	0	0	0	6	...	...	...	—	—	—	—	—
93-94—Kitchener	OHL	46	1	3	4	107	...	...	...	—	—	—	—	—
94-95—Kitchener	OHL	10	1	2	3	29	...	...	...	—	—	—	—	—
—Sault Ste. Marie	OHL	42	3	12	15	94	...	...	...	—	—	—	—	—
95-96—Kitchener	OHL	57	6	7	13	146	...	...	...	4	0	0	0	2
96-97—Roanoke	ECHL	69	6	16	22	139	...	...	...	4	0	0	0	10
97-98—Saint John	AHL	58	0	5	5	92	...	...	...	15	0	1	1	10
—Roanoke	ECHL	5	0	0	0	29	...	...	...	—	—	—	—	—

ODGERS, JEFF — RW — AVALANCHE

PERSONAL: Born May 31, 1969, in Spy Hill, Sask. ... 6-0/195. ... Shoots right. ... Name pronounced AH-juhrs.
TRANSACTIONS/CAREER NOTES: Signed as free agent by San Jose Sharks (September 3, 1991). ... Injured hand (December 21, 1991); missed four games. ... Broke hand (November 5, 1992); missed 15 games. ... Suspended one game by NHL for accumulating three game misconduct penalties (January 29, 1993). ... Suspended two games by NHL for accumulating four game misconduct penalties (February 19, 1993). ... Traded by Sharks with fifth-round pick (D Elias Abrahamsson) in 1996 draft to Boston Bruins for D Al Iafrate (June 21, 1996). ... Injured neck (January 9, 1997); missed one game. ... Signed as free agent by Colorado Avalanche (October 24, 1997). ... Suffered from the flu (January 26, 1998); missed one game.
MISCELLANEOUS: Captain of San Jose Sharks (1994-95 and 1995-96). ... Holds San Jose Sharks all-time records for most games played (334) and most penalty minutes (1,001).

Season Team	League	REGULAR SEASON								PLAYOFFS				
		Gms.	G	A	Pts.	PIM	+/-	PP	SH	Gms.	G	A	Pts.	PIM
86-87—Brandon	WHL	70	7	14	21	150	...	...	...	—	—	—	—	—
87-88—Brandon	WHL	70	17	18	35	202	...	...	...	4	1	1	2	14
88-89—Brandon	WHL	71	31	29	60	277	...	...	...	—	—	—	—	—
89-90—Brandon	WHL	64	37	28	65	209	...	...	...	—	—	—	—	—
90-91—Kansas City	IHL	77	12	19	31	*318	...	...	...	—	—	—	—	—
91-92—Kansas City	IHL	12	2	2	4	56	...	...	...	9	3	0	3	13
—San Jose	NHL	61	7	4	11	217	-21	0	0	—	—	—	—	—
92-93—San Jose	NHL	66	12	15	27	253	-26	6	0	—	—	—	—	—
93-94—San Jose	NHL	81	13	8	21	222	-13	7	0	11	0	0	0	11
94-95—San Jose	NHL	48	4	3	7	117	-8	0	0	11	1	1	2	23
95-96—San Jose	NHL	78	12	4	16	192	-4	0	0	—	—	—	—	—
96-97—Boston	NHL	80	7	8	15	197	-15	1	0	—	—	—	—	—
97-98—Providence	AHL	4	0	0	0	31	...	...	...	—	—	—	—	—
—Colorado	NHL	68	5	8	13	213	5	0	0	6	0	0	0	25
NHL Totals (7 years)		482	60	50	110	1411	-82	14	0	28	1	1	2	59

ODJICK, GINO   LW   ISLANDERS

PERSONAL: Born September 7, 1970, in Maniwaki, Que. ... 6-3/210. ... Shoots left. ... Name pronounced OH-jihk.

TRANSACTIONS/CAREER NOTES: Suspended five games by QMJHL for attempting to attack another player (May 1, 1989). ... Suspended one game by QMJHL for fighting (March 19, 1990). ... Suspended one game by QMJHL for fighting (April 14, 1990). ... Selected by Vancouver Canucks in fifth round (fifth Canucks pick, 86th overall) of NHL entry draft (June 16, 1990). ... Broke cheekbone (February 27, 1991). ... Suspended six games by NHL for stick foul (November 26, 1991). ... Underwent arthroscopic knee surgery (February 11, 1993); missed five games. ... Suspended one game by NHL for accumulating three game misconduct penalties (January 27, 1993). ... Suspended one game by NHL for accumulating four game misconduct penalties (March 26, 1993). ... Suspended two games by NHL for stick incident (April 8, 1993). ... Separated shoulder (November 27, 1993); missed two games. ... Suspended by NHL for 10 games (September 1994); NHL reduced suspension to six games due to abbreviated 1994-95 season (January 19, 1995). ... Strained groin (March 10, 1995); missed six games. ... Strained abdomen (April 7, 1995); missed last 13 games of season. ... Injured knee (October 10, 1995); missed one game. ... Strained abdominal muscle (November 22, 1995); missed 24 games. ... Suspended four games and fined $1,000 by NHL for striking opposing player (November 29, 1995). ... Strained groin (January 20, 1997); missed five games. ... Fractured finger (April 4, 1997); missed remainder of season. ... Injured groin (November 8, 1997); missed nine games. ... Injured knee (January 24, 1998); missed seven games. ... Traded by Canucks to New York Islanders for D Jason Strudwick (March 23, 1998).

MISCELLANEOUS: Scored on a penalty shot (vs. Mike Vernon, October 19, 1991). ... Holds Vancouver Canucks all-time record for most penalty minutes (2,127).

Season Team	League	REGULAR SEASON								PLAYOFFS				
		Gms.	G	A	Pts.	PIM	+/-	PP	SH	Gms.	G	A	Pts.	PIM
88-89—Laval	QMJHL	50	9	15	24	278	...	...	...	16	0	9	9	*129
89-90—Laval	QMJHL	51	12	26	38	280	...	...	...	13	6	5	11	*110
90-91—Milwaukee	IHL	17	7	3	10	102	...	...	...	—	—	—	—	—
—Vancouver	NHL	45	7	1	8	296	-6	0	0	6	0	0	0	18
91-92—Vancouver	NHL	65	4	6	10	348	-1	0	0	4	0	0	0	6
92-93—Vancouver	NHL	75	4	13	17	370	3	0	0	1	0	0	0	0
93-94—Vancouver	NHL	76	16	13	29	271	13	4	0	10	0	0	0	18
94-95—Vancouver	NHL	23	4	5	9	109	-3	0	0	5	0	0	0	47
95-96—Vancouver	NHL	55	3	4	7	181	-16	0	0	6	3	1	4	6
96-97—Vancouver	NHL	70	5	8	13	371	-5	1	0	—	—	—	—	—
97-98—Vancouver	NHL	35	3	2	5	181	-3	0	0	—	—	—	—	—
—New York Islanders	NHL	13	0	0	0	31	1	0	0	—	—	—	—	—
NHL Totals (8 years)		457	46	52	98	2158	-17	5	0	32	3	1	4	95

O'DONNELL, SEAN   D   KINGS

PERSONAL: Born September 13, 1971, in Ottawa. ... 6-3/228. ... Shoots left.

TRANSACTIONS/CAREER NOTES: Selected by Buffalo Sabres in sixth round (sixth Sabres pick, 123rd overall) of NHL entry draft (June 22, 1991). ... Traded by Sabres to Los Angeles Kings for D Doug Houda (July 26, 1994). ... Bruised sternum (February 4, 1995); missed two games. ... Sprained left wrist (January 27, 1996); missed eight games. ... Sprained wrist (December 26, 1996); missed nine games. ... Suspended one game by NHL for an altercation while on the bench (January 30, 1997). ... Strained back (March 1, 1997); missed two games.

Season Team	League	REGULAR SEASON								PLAYOFFS				
		Gms.	G	A	Pts.	PIM	+/-	PP	SH	Gms.	G	A	Pts.	PIM
90-91—Sudbury	OHL	66	8	23	31	114	...	...	...	5	1	4	5	10
91-92—Rochester	AHL	73	4	9	13	193	...	...	...	16	1	2	3	21
92-93—Rochester	AHL	74	3	18	21	203	...	...	...	17	1	6	7	38
93-94—Rochester	AHL	64	2	10	12	242	...	...	...	4	0	1	1	21
94-95—Phoenix	IHL	61	2	18	20	132	...	...	...	9	0	1	1	21
—Los Angeles	NHL	15	0	2	2	49	-2	0	0	—	—	—	—	—
95-96—Los Angeles	NHL	71	2	5	7	127	3	0	0	—	—	—	—	—
96-97—Los Angeles	NHL	55	5	12	17	144	-13	2	0	—	—	—	—	—
97-98—Los Angeles	NHL	80	2	15	17	179	7	0	0	4	1	0	1	36
NHL Totals (4 years)		221	9	34	43	499	-5	2	0	4	1	0	1	36

ODUYA, FREDRIK   D   SHARKS

PERSONAL: Born May 31, 1975, in Stockholm, Sweden. ... 6-2/185. ... Shoots left. ... Name pronounced oh-DOO-yuh.

TRANSACTIONS/CAREER NOTES: Selected by San Jose Sharks in sixth round (eighth Sharks pick, 154th overall) of NHL entry draft (June 26, 1993).

O

Season Team	League	REGULAR SEASON Gms.	G	A	Pts.	PIM	+/-	PP	SH	PLAYOFFS Gms.	G	A	Pts.	PIM
91-92—Windsor	OHL Jr. B	43	2	8	10	24	...	...	...	—	—	—	—	—
92-93—Guelph	OHL	23	2	4	6	29	...	...	...	—	—	—	—	—
—Ottawa	OHL	17	0	3	3	70	...	...	...	—	—	—	—	—
93-94—Ottawa	OHL	51	11	12	23	181	...	...	...	17	0	3	3	22
94-95—Ottawa	OHL	61	2	13	15	175	...	...	...	—	—	—	—	—
95-96—Kansas City	IHL	56	2	6	8	235	...	...	...	3	0	0	0	2
96-97—Kentucky	AHL	69	2	9	11	241	...	...	...	—	—	—	—	—
97-98—Kentucky	AHL	72	6	10	16	300	...	...	...	—	—	—	—	—

O'GRADY, MIKE · D · PANTHERS

PERSONAL: Born March 22, 1977, in Neilburg, Sask. ... 6-3/200. ... Shoots left.
TRANSACTIONS/CAREER NOTES: Selected by Florida Panthers in third round (third Panthers pick, 62nd overall) of NHL entry draft (July 8, 1995).

Season Team	League	REGULAR SEASON Gms.	G	A	Pts.	PIM	+/-	PP	SH	PLAYOFFS Gms.	G	A	Pts.	PIM
93-94—Saskatoon	WHL	13	0	1	1	29	...	...	...	—	—	—	—	—
94-95—Saskatoon	WHL	39	0	7	7	157	...	...	...	—	—	—	—	—
—Lethbridge	WHL	21	1	2	3	124	...	...	...	—	—	—	—	—
95-96—Lethbridge	WHL	61	2	9	11	242	...	...	...	4	1	0	1	8
96-97—Lethbridge	WHL	61	8	25	33	262	...	...	...	18	1	5	6	41
97-98—New Haven	AHL	32	1	4	5	58	...	...	...	2	0	0	0	0
—Tallahassee	ECHL	4	0	0	0	18	...	...	...	—	—	—	—	—
—Port Huron	UHL	12	2	3	5	30	...	...	...	—	—	—	—	—

OHLUND, MATTIAS · D · CANUCKS

PERSONAL: Born September 9, 1976, in Pitea, Sweden. ... 6-3/217. ... Shoots left. ... Name pronounced muh-TEE-uhz OH-luhnd.
TRANSACTIONS/CAREER NOTES: Selected by Vancouver Canucks in first round (first Canucks pick, 13th overall) of NHL entry draft (June 28, 1994). ... Suffered concussion (March 26, 1998); missed four games.
HONORS: Named to NHL All-Rookie team (1997-98).

Season Team	League	REGULAR SEASON Gms.	G	A	Pts.	PIM	+/-	PP	SH	PLAYOFFS Gms.	G	A	Pts.	PIM
92-93—Pitea	Swed. Dv.II	22	0	6	6	16	...	...	...	—	—	—	—	—
93-94—Pitea	Swed. Dv.II	28	7	10	17	62	...	...	...	—	—	—	—	—
94-95—Lulea	Sweden	34	6	10	16	34	...	...	...	9	4	0	4	16
95-96—Lulea	Sweden	38	4	10	14	26	...	...	...	13	0	1	1	47
96-97—Lulea	Sweden	47	7	9	16	38	...	...	...	10	1	2	3	8
—Kentucky	AHL	69	2	9	11	241	...	...	...	—	—	—	—	—
97-98—Vancouver	NHL	77	7	23	30	76	3	1	0	—	—	—	—	—
—Swedish Oly. team	Int'l	4	0	1	1	4	...	...	...	—	—	—	—	—
NHL Totals (1 year)		77	7	23	30	76	3	1	0					

OLAUSSON, FREDRIK · D

PERSONAL: Born October 5, 1966, in Vaxsjo, Sweden. ... 6-0/198. ... Shoots right. ... Name pronounced OHL-ih-suhn.
TRANSACTIONS/CAREER NOTES: Selected by Winnipeg Jets in fourth round (fourth Jets pick, 81st overall) of NHL entry draft (June 15, 1985). ... Dislocated shoulder (August 1987). ... Underwent shoulder surgery (November 1987). ... Signed five-year contract with Farjestad, Sweden (June 19, 1989); Farjestad agreed to allow Olausson to remain in Winnipeg. ... Sprained knee (January 22, 1993); missed 11 games. ... Lacerated ankle (November 8, 1993); missed two games. ... Suffered from the flu (January 18, 1993); missed one game. ... Sprained knee (January 23, 1993); missed 11 games. ... Suffered from the flu (March 4, 1993); missed one game. ... Traded by Jets with seventh-round pick (LW Curtis Sheptak) in 1994 draft to Edmonton Oilers for third-round pick (C Tavis Hansen) in 1994 draft (December 5, 1993). ... Strained knee (January 11, 1994). ... Played in Europe during 1994-95 NHL lockout. ... Suffered from the flu (February 17, 1995); missed one game. ... Suffered colitis (March 3, 1995); missed 10 games. ... Cracked ribs (November 4, 1995); missed 14 games. ... Suffered irregular heart beat (December 6, 1995); missed five games. ... Claimed on waivers by Mighty Ducks of Anaheim (January 16, 1996) ... Traded by Mighty Ducks with C Alex Hicks to Pittsburgh Penguins for LW Shawn Antoski and D Dmitri Mironov (November 19, 1996). ... Fractured cheekbone (January 26, 1997); missed nine games. ... Strained groin (February 27, 1997); missed three games. ... Bruised foot (November 2, 1997); missed three games. ... Bruised wrist (December 9, 1997); missed two games.
HONORS: Named to Swedish League All-Star team (1985-86).

Season Team	League	REGULAR SEASON Gms.	G	A	Pts.	PIM	+/-	PP	SH	PLAYOFFS Gms.	G	A	Pts.	PIM
83-84—Nybro	Sweden	28	8	14	22	32	...	...	...	—	—	—	—	—
84-85—Farjestad Karlstad	Sweden	34	6	12	18	24	...	...	...	3	1	0	1	0
85-86—Farjestad Karlstad	Sweden	33	5	12	17	14	...	...	...	8	3	2	5	6
86-87—Winnipeg	NHL	72	7	29	36	24	-3	1	0	10	2	3	5	4
87-88—Winnipeg	NHL	38	5	10	15	18	3	2	0	5	1	1	2	0
88-89—Winnipeg	NHL	75	15	47	62	32	6	4	0	—	—	—	—	—
89-90—Winnipeg	NHL	77	9	46	55	32	-1	3	0	7	0	2	2	2
90-91—Winnipeg	NHL	71	12	29	41	24	-22	5	0	—	—	—	—	—
91-92—Winnipeg	NHL	77	20	42	62	34	-31	13	1	7	1	5	6	4
92-93—Winnipeg	NHL	68	16	41	57	22	-4	11	0	6	0	2	2	2
93-94—Winnipeg	NHL	18	2	5	7	10	-3	1	0	—	—	—	—	—
—Edmonton	NHL	55	9	19	28	20	-4	6	0	—	—	—	—	—
94-95—Ehrwald	Austria	10	4	3	7	8	...	...	...	—	—	—	—	—
—Edmonton	NHL	33	0	10	10	20	-4	0	0	—	—	—	—	—
95-96—Edmonton	NHL	20	0	6	6	14	-14	0	0	—	—	—	—	—
—Anaheim	NHL	36	2	16	18	24	7	1	0	—	—	—	—	—
96-97—Anaheim	NHL	20	2	9	11	8	-5	1	0	—	—	—	—	—
—Pittsburgh	NHL	51	7	20	27	24	21	2	0	4	0	1	1	0
97-98—Pittsburgh	NHL	76	6	27	33	42	13	2	0	6	0	3	3	2
NHL Totals (12 years)		787	112	356	468	348	-41	52	1	45	4	17	21	14

OLCZYK, EDDIE — C/RW

PERSONAL: Born August 16, 1966, in Chicago. ... 6-1/207. ... Shoots left. ... Full name: Ed Olczyk. ... Name pronounced OHL-chehk.

TRANSACTIONS/CAREER NOTES: Selected by Chicago Blackhawks in first round (first Blackhawks pick, third overall) of NHL entry draft (June 9, 1984). ... Hyperextended knee (September 3, 1984). ... Broke bone in left foot (December 16, 1984). ... Traded by Blackhawks with LW Al Secord to Toronto Maple Leafs for RW Rick Vaive, LW Steve Thomas and D Bob McGill (September 1987). ... Pinched nerve in left knee (January 3, 1990). ... Traded by Maple Leafs with LW Mark Osborne to Winnipeg Jets for D Dave Ellett and LW Paul Fenton (November 10, 1990). ... Dislocated elbow and sprained ankle (January 8, 1992); missed 15 games. ... Sprained knee (November 24, 1992); missed nine games. ... Traded by Jets to New York Rangers for LW Kris King and RW Tie Domi (December 28, 1992). ... Fractured right thumb (January 31, 1994); missed 24 games. ... Suffered from kidney stones (January 24, 1995); missed six games. ... Suffered back spasms (March 3, 1995); missed three games. ... Traded by Rangers to Jets for fifth-round pick (D Alexei Vasiljev) in 1995 draft (April 7, 1995). ... Strained rib cage (October 28, 1995); missed four games. ... Strained back (January 3, 1996); missed four games. ... Sprained knee (March 7, 1996); missed 13 games. ... Signed as free agent by Los Angeles Kings (July 8, 1996). ... Suffered from the flu (December 12, 1996); missed two games. ... Traded by Kings to Pittsburgh Penguins for RW Glen Murray (March 18, 1997). ... Suffered concussion (October 4, 1997); missed five games. ... Suffered depressed fracture of zygomatic arch in neck (December 1, 1997); missed 18 games. ... Suffered back spasms (March 8, 1998); missed two games.

MISCELLANEOUS: Member of Stanley Cup championship team (1994).

STATISTICAL PLATEAUS: Three-goal games: 1988-89 (1), 1989-90 (1), 1992-93 (1), 1995-96 (1), 1996-97 (1). Total: 5.

Season Team	League	REGULAR SEASON								PLAYOFFS				
		Gms.	G	A	Pts.	PIM	+/-	PP	SH	Gms.	G	A	Pts.	PIM
83-84—U.S. national team	Int'l	56	19	40	59	36	...	...	...	—	—	—	—	—
—U.S. Olympic Team	Int'l	6	2	6	8	0	...	...	...					
84-85—Chicago	NHL	70	20	30	50	67	11	1	1	15	6	5	11	11
85-86—Chicago	NHL	79	29	50	79	47	2	8	1	3	0	0	0	0
86-87—Chicago	NHL	79	16	35	51	119	-4	2	1	4	1	1	2	4
87-88—Toronto	NHL	80	42	33	75	55	-22	14	4	6	5	4	9	2
88-89—Toronto	NHL	80	38	52	90	75	0	11	2	—				
89-90—Toronto	NHL	79	32	56	88	78	0	6	0	5	1	2	3	14
90-91—Toronto	NHL	18	4	10	14	13	-7	0	0	—				
—Winnipeg	NHL	61	26	31	57	69	-20	14	0	—				
91-92—Winnipeg	NHL	64	32	33	65	67	11	12	0	6	2	1	3	4
92-93—Winnipeg	NHL	25	8	12	20	26	-11	2	0	—				
—New York Rangers	NHL	46	13	16	29	26	9	0	0	—				
93-94—New York Rangers	NHL	37	3	5	8	28	-1	0	0	1	0	0	0	0
94-95—New York Rangers	NHL	20	2	1	3	4	-2	1	0	—				
—Winnipeg	NHL	13	2	8	10	8	1	1	0	—				
95-96—Winnipeg	NHL	51	27	22	49	65	0	16	0	6	1	2	3	6
96-97—Los Angeles	NHL	67	21	23	44	45	-22	5	1	—				
—Pittsburgh	NHL	12	4	7	11	6	8	0	0	5	1	0	1	12
97-98—Pittsburgh	NHL	56	11	11	22	35	-9	5	1	6	2	0	2	4
NHL Totals (14 years)		937	330	435	765	833	-56	98	11	57	19	15	34	57

OLIWA, KRZYSZTOF — RW — DEVILS

PERSONAL: Born April 12, 1973, in Tychy, Poland. ... 6-5/235. ... Shoots left. ... Name pronounced KRIH-stahf OH-lee-vuh.

TRANSACTIONS/CAREER NOTES: Selected by New Jersey Devils in third round (fourth Devils pick, 65th overall) of NHL entry draft (June 26, 1993). ... Loaned by Devils to Detroit Vipers of IHL (January 31, 1995). ... Returned by Vipers to Albany (February 9, 1995). ... Loaned by Devils to Saint John of the AHL (February 17, 1995). ... Injured foot (November 10, 1997); missed two games.

Season Team	League	REGULAR SEASON								PLAYOFFS				
		Gms.	G	A	Pts.	PIM	+/-	PP	SH	Gms.	G	A	Pts.	PIM
90-91—GKS Katowice	Poland Jrs.	5	4	4	8	10	...	...	...	—				
91-92—GKS Tychy	Poland	10	3	7	10	6	...	...	...	—				
92-93—Welland Jr. B	OHA	30	13	21	34	127	...	...	...	—				
93-94—Albany	AHL	33	2	4	6	151	...	...	...	—				
—Raleigh	ECHL	15	0	2	2	65	...	...	...	9	0	0	0	35
94-95—Albany	AHL	20	1	1	2	77	...	...	...	—				
—Detroit	IHL	4	0	1	1	24	...	...	...	—				
—Saint John	AHL	14	1	4	5	79	...	...	...	—				
—Raleigh	ECHL	5	0	2	2	32	...	...	...	—				
95-96—Albany	AHL	51	5	11	16	217	...	...	...	—				
—Raleigh	ECHL	9	1	0	1	53	...	...	...	—				
96-97—Albany	AHL	60	13	14	27	322	...	...	...	15	7	1	8	49
—New Jersey	NHL	1	0	0	0	5	-1	0	0	—				
97-98—New Jersey	NHL	73	2	3	5	295	3	0	0	6	0	0	0	23
NHL Totals (2 years)		74	2	3	5	300	2	0	0	6	0	0	0	23

O'NEILL, JEFF — C — HURRICANES

PERSONAL: Born February 23, 1976, in Richmond Hill, Ont. ... 6-0/195. ... Shoots right.

HIGH SCHOOL: Bishop MacDonnell (Guelph, Ont.).

TRANSACTIONS/CAREER NOTES: Selected by Hartford Whalers in first round (first Whalers pick, fifth overall) of NHL entry draft (June 28, 1994). ... Bruised foot (December 30, 1995); missed four games. ... Reinjured foot (January 10, 1996); missed four games. ... Injured shoulder (February 17, 1996); missed four games. ... Injured groin (January 2, 1997); missed one game. ... Sprained wrist (April 2, 1997); missed four games. ... Whalers franchise moved to North Carolina and renamed Carolina Hurricanes for 1997-98 season; NHL approved move on June 25, 1997. ... Suffered concussion (December 20, 1997); missed one game. ... Fractured kneecap (April 13, 1998); missed three games.

HONORS: Won Emms Family Award (1992-93). ... Named to Can.HL All-Rookie team (1992-93). ... Named to OHL All-Rookie team (1992-93). ... Won Can.HL Top Draft Prospect Award (1993-94). ... Named to Can.HL All-Star second team (1994-95). ... Named to OHL All-Star first team (1994-95).

STATISTICAL PLATEAUS: Three-goal games: 1996-97 (1).

O

Season Team	League	Gms.	G	A	Pts.	PIM	+/-	PP	SH	Gms.	G	A	Pts.	PIM
		REGULAR SEASON								PLAYOFFS				
91-92—Thornhill	Tier II Jr. A	43	27	53	80	48	...	...	...	—	—	—	—	—
92-93—Guelph	OHL	65	32	47	79	88	...	...	...	5	2	2	4	6
93-94—Guelph	OHL	66	45	81	126	95	...	...	...	9	2	11	13	31
94-95—Guelph	OHL	57	43	81	124	56	...	...	...	14	8	18	26	34
95-96—Hartford	NHL	65	8	19	27	40	-3	1	0	—	—	—	—	—
96-97—Hartford	NHL	72	14	16	30	40	-24	2	1	—	—	—	—	—
—Springfield	AHL	1	0	0	0	0	...	...	...	—	—	—	—	—
97-98—Carolina	NHL	74	19	20	39	67	-8	7	1	—	—	—	—	—
NHL Totals (3 years)...........		211	41	55	96	147	-35	10	2					

ORSZAGH, VLADIMIR — LW — ISLANDERS

PERSONAL: Born May 24, 1977, in Banska Bystrica, Czechoslovakia. ... 5-11/173. ... Shoots left. ... Name pronounced OHR-sahg.
TRANSACTIONS/CAREER NOTES: Selected by New York Islanders in fifth round (fourth Islanders pick, 106th overall) of NHL entry draft (July 8, 1995).

Season Team	League	Gms.	G	A	Pts.	PIM	+/-	PP	SH	Gms.	G	A	Pts.	PIM
		REGULAR SEASON								PLAYOFFS				
93-94—IS Banska Byst. Jrs. ...	Slovakia	—	38	27	65	—	—	—	—	—	—	—	—	—
94-95—Banska Bystrica	Slovakia Div. II	38	18	12	30	—	...	...	...	—	—	—	—	—
—Martimex ZTS Martin..	Slovakia	1	0	0	0	0	...	...	...	—	—	—	—	—
95-96—Banska Bystrica	Slovakia	31	9	5	14	22	...	...	...	—	—	—	—	—
96-97—Utah	IHL	68	12	15	27	30	...	...	...	3	0	1	1	4
97-98—Utah	IHL	62	13	10	23	60	...	...	...	4	2	0	2	0
—New York Islanders.....	NHL	11	0	1	1	2	-3	0	0	—	—	—	—	—
NHL Totals (1 year).............		11	0	1	1	2	-3	0	0					

OSGOOD, CHRIS — G — RED WINGS

PERSONAL: Born November 26, 1972, in Peace River, Alta. ... 5-10/178. ... Catches left.
TRANSACTIONS/CAREER NOTES: Selected by Detroit Red Wings in third round (third Red Wings pick, 54th overall) of NHL entry draft (June 22, 1991). ... Strained hamstring (January 14, 1997); missed five games. ... Strained groin (March 14, 1998); missed four games.
HONORS: Named to WHL (East) All-Star second team (1990-91). ... Played in NHL All-Star Game (1996). ... Named to THE SPORTING NEWS All-Star first team (1995-96). ... Shared William M. Jennings Trophy with Mike Vernon (1995-96). ... Named to NHL All-Star second team (1995-96). ... Named to play in NHL All-Star Game (1997); replaced by G Guy Hebert due to injury.
RECORDS: Shares NHL single-season playoff record for most wins by goaltender—16 (1998).
MISCELLANEOUS: Member of Stanley Cup championship team (1997 and 1998). ... Stopped a penalty shot attempt (vs. Peter Zezel, March 4, 1994; vs. Dave Gagner, April 1, 1995; vs. Mike Hudson, November 18, 1996). ... Allowed a penalty shot goal (vs. Alexander Mogilny, December 1, 1997). ... Holds Detroit Red Wings all-time record for goals-against average (2.32).

Season Team	League	Gms.	Min	W	L	T	GA	SO	Avg.	Gms.	Min.	W	L	GA	SO	Avg.
		REGULAR SEASON								PLAYOFFS						
89-90—Medicine Hat................	WHL	57	3094	24	28	2	228	0	4.42	3	173	3	4	17	0	5.90
90-91—Medicine Hat................	WHL	46	2630	23	18	3	173	2	3.95	12	714	7	5	42	0	3.53
91-92—Medicine Hat................	WHL	15	819	10	3	0	44	0	3.22	—	—	—	—	—	—	—
—Brandon......................	WHL	16	890	3	10	1	60	1	4.04	—	—	—	—	—	—	—
—Seattle.........................	WHL	21	1217	12	7	1	65	1	3.20	15	904	9	6	51	0	3.38
92-93—Adirondack.................	AHL	45	2438	19	19	2	159	0	3.91	1	59	0	1	2	0	2.03
93-94—Adirondack.................	AHL	4	240	3	1	0	13	0	3.25	—	—	—	—	—	—	—
—Detroit..........................	NHL	41	2286	23	8	5	105	2	2.76	6	307	3	2	12	1	2.35
94-95—Adirondack.................	AHL	2	120	1	1	0	6	0	3.00	—	—	—	—	—	—	—
—Detroit..........................	NHL	19	1087	14	5	0	41	1	2.26	2	68	0	0	2	0	1.76
95-96—Detroit.......................	NHL	50	2933	*39	6	5	106	5	2.17	15	936	8	7	33	2	2.12
96-97—Detroit.......................	NHL	47	2769	23	13	9	106	6	2.30	2	47	0	0	2	0	2.55
97-98—Detroit.......................	NHL	64	3807	33	20	11	140	6	2.21	22	*1361	*16	6	*48	2	2.12
NHL Totals (5 years).............		221	12882	132	52	30	498	20	2.32	47	2719	27	15	97	5	2.14

O'SULLIVAN, CHRIS — D — FLAMES

PERSONAL: Born May 15, 1974, in Dorchester, Mass. ... 6-2/205. ... Shoots left.
HIGH SCHOOL: Catholic Memorial (Boston).
COLLEGE: Boston University.
TRANSACTIONS/CAREER NOTES: Selected by Calgary Flames in second round (second Flames pick, 30th overall) of NHL entry draft (June 20, 1992). ... Suffered concussion (December 20, 1997); missed three games.
HONORS: Named NCAA Tournament Most Valuable Player (1994-95). ... Named to NCAA All-Tournament team (1994-95). ... Named to NCAA All-America second team (1994-95).

Season Team	League	Gms.	G	A	Pts.	PIM	+/-	PP	SH	Gms.	G	A	Pts.	PIM
		REGULAR SEASON								PLAYOFFS				
91-92—Catholic Memorial.......	Mass. H.S.	26	26	23	49	65	...	...	...	—	—	—	—	—
92-93—Boston University	Hockey East	5	0	2	2	4	...	...	...	—	—	—	—	—
93-94—Boston University	Hockey East	32	5	18	23	25	...	...	...	—	—	—	—	—
94-95—Boston University	Hockey East	40	23	33	56	48	...	...	...	—	—	—	—	—
95-96—Boston University	Hockey East	37	12	35	47	50	...	...	...	—	—	—	—	—
96-97—Calgary	NHL	27	2	8	10	2	0	1	0	—	—	—	—	—
—Saint John	AHL	29	3	8	11	17	...	...	...	5	0	4	4	0
97-98—Saint John	AHL	32	4	10	14	2	...	...	...	21	2	17	19	18
—Calgary	NHL	12	0	2	2	10	4	0	0	—	—	—	—	—
NHL Totals (2 years)...........		39	2	10	12	12	4	1	0					

PERSONAL: Born October 29, 1961, in Elk River, Minn. ... 6-4/225. ... Shoots right. ... Full name: Joel Stuart Otto.
COLLEGE: Bemidji (Minn.) State.
TRANSACTIONS/CAREER NOTES: Signed as free agent by Calgary Flames (September 11, 1984). ... Tore right knee cartilage (March 10, 1987). ... Strained right knee ligaments (October 8, 1987). ... Bruised ribs (November 1989). ... Hospitalized after being crosschecked from behind (January 13, 1990). ... Injured ankle (March 10, 1992); missed two games. ... Injured rib (January 5, 1993); missed eight games. ... Bruised foot (February 2, 1993); missed one game. ... Signed as free agent by Philadelphia Flyers (July 20, 1995). ... Sprained right knee (November 2, 1995); missed two games. ... Sprained left knee (February 14, 1996); missed six games. ... Sprained left knee (March 8, 1996); missed two games. ... Reinjured left knee (March 19, 1996); missed five games. ... Bruised ribs (October 10, 1996); missed four games. ... Hyperextended right elbow (November 6, 1997); missed six games. ... Sprained left wrist and suffered sore right elbow (December 27, 1997); missed four games. ... Suffered from the flu (March 28, 1998); missed two games. ... Suffered back spasms (March 19, 1998); missed one game.
MISCELLANEOUS: Member of Stanley Cup championship team (1989).
STATISTICAL PLATEAUS: Three-goal games: 1986-87 (1), 1993-94 (1). Total: 2.

			REGULAR SEASON								PLAYOFFS				
Season Team	League	Gms.	G	A	Pts.	PIM	+/-	PP	SH		Gms.	G	A	Pts.	PIM
80-81—Bemidji State	NCAA-II	23	5	11	16	10	...	...	...		—	—	—	—	—
81-82—Bemidji State	NCAA-II	31	19	33	52	24	...	...	...		—	—	—	—	—
82-83—Bemidji State	NCAA-II	37	33	28	61	68	...	...	...		—	—	—	—	—
83-84—Bemidji State	NCAA-II	31	32	43	75	32	...	...	...		—	—	—	—	—
84-85—Moncton	AHL	56	27	36	63	89	...	...	...		—	—	—	—	—
—Calgary	NHL	17	4	8	12	30	3	1	0		3	2	1	3	10
85-86—Calgary	NHL	79	25	34	59	188	22	9	1		22	5	10	15	80
86-87—Calgary	NHL	68	19	31	50	185	8	5	0		2	0	2	2	6
87-88—Calgary	NHL	62	13	39	52	194	16	4	1		9	3	2	5	26
88-89—Calgary	NHL	72	23	30	53	213	12	10	2		22	6	13	19	46
89-90—Calgary	NHL	75	13	20	33	116	4	7	0		6	2	2	4	2
90-91—Calgary	NHL	76	19	20	39	183	-4	7	1		7	1	2	3	8
91-92—Calgary	NHL	78	13	21	34	161	-10	5	1		—	—	—	—	—
92-93—Calgary	NHL	75	19	33	52	150	2	6	1		6	4	2	6	4
93-94—Calgary	NHL	81	11	12	23	92	-17	3	1		3	0	1	1	4
94-95—Calgary	NHL	47	8	13	21	130	8	0	2		7	0	3	3	2
95-96—Philadelphia	NHL	67	12	29	41	115	11	6	1		12	3	4	7	11
96-97—Philadelphia	NHL	78	13	19	32	99	12	0	1		18	1	5	6	8
97-98—Philadelphia	NHL	68	3	4	7	78	-2	0	0		5	0	0	0	0
—U.S. Olympic Team	Int'l	4	0	0	0	0	...	...	...		—	—	—	—	—
NHL Totals (14 years)		943	195	313	508	1934	65	63	12		122	27	47	74	207

PERSONAL: Born August 3, 1972, in Riga, U.S.S.R. ... 6-3/205. ... Shoots left. ... Name pronounced SAN-diz OH-zoh-lihnsh.
TRANSACTIONS/CAREER NOTES: Selected by San Jose Sharks in second round (third Sharks pick, 30th overall) of NHL entry draft (June 22, 1991). ... Strained back (November 7, 1992); missed one game. ... Tore knee ligaments (December 30, 1992) and underwent surgery to repair anterior cruciate ligament; missed remainder of season. ... Injured knee (December 11, 1993); missed one game. ... Traded by Sharks to Colorado Avalanche for RW Owen Nolan (October 26, 1995). ... Separated left shoulder (December 7, 1995); missed four games. ... Broke finger (February 23, 1996); missed two games. ... Suffered back spasms (March 9, 1997); missed two games. ... Separated shoulder (October 7, 1997); missed two games. ... Injured knee and underwent arthroscopic surgery (October 17, 1997); missed 13 games.
HONORS: Played in NHL All-Star Game (1994, 1997 and 1998). ... Named to NHL All-Star first team (1996-97).
MISCELLANEOUS: Member of Stanley Cup championship team (1996).

			REGULAR SEASON								PLAYOFFS				
Season Team	League	Gms.	G	A	Pts.	PIM	+/-	PP	SH		Gms.	G	A	Pts.	PIM
90-91—Dynamo Riga	USSR	44	0	3	3	49	...	...	...		—	—	—	—	—
91-92—HC Riga	CIS	30	5	0	5	42	...	...	...		—	—	—	—	—
—Kansas City	IHL	34	6	9	15	20	...	...	...		15	2	5	7	22
92-93—San Jose	NHL	37	7	16	23	40	-9	2	0		—	—	—	—	—
93-94—San Jose	NHL	81	26	38	64	24	16	4	0		14	0	10	10	8
94-95—San Jose	NHL	48	9	16	25	30	-6	3	1		11	3	2	5	6
95-96—San Francisco	IHL	2	1	0	1	0	...	...	...		—	—	—	—	—
—San Jose	NHL	7	1	3	4	4	2	1	0		—	—	—	—	—
—Colorado	NHL	66	13	37	50	50	0	7	1		22	5	14	19	16
96-97—Colorado	NHL	80	23	45	68	88	4	13	0		17	4	13	17	24
97-98—Colorado	NHL	66	13	38	51	65	-12	9	0		7	0	7	7	14
NHL Totals (6 years)		385	92	193	285	301	-5	39	2		71	12	46	58	68

O
P

PERSONAL: Born May 5, 1972, in Skalica, Czechoslovakia. ... 5-10/183. ... Shoots left. ... Name pronounced PAL-fee.
TRANSACTIONS/CAREER NOTES: Selected by New York Islanders in second round (second Islanders pick, 26th overall) of NHL entry draft (June 22, 1991). ... Loaned to Slovak Olympic team (January 31, 1994). ... Suffered concussion (February 17, 1996); missed one game. ... Sprained shoulder (January 13, 1997); missed two games.
HONORS: Named Czechoslovakian League Rookie of the Year (1990-91). ... Named to Czechoslovakian League All-Star team (1991-92). ... Named to play in NHL All-Star Game (1997); replaced by D Scott Lachance due to injury. ... Played in NHL All-Star Game (1998).
STATISTICAL PLATEAUS: Three-goal games: 1995-96 (2), 1996-97 (1), 1997-98 (2). Total: 5.

Season Team	League	REGULAR SEASON								PLAYOFFS				
		Gms.	G	A	Pts.	PIM	+/-	PP	SH	Gms.	G	A	Pts.	PIM
90-91—Nitra	Czech.	50	34	16	50	18	...	...	...	—	—	—	—	—
91-92—Dukla Trencin	Czech.	32	23	25	*48		...	...	...	—	—	—	—	—
92-93—Dukla Trencin	Czech.	43	38	41	79		...	...	...	—	—	—	—	—
93-94—Salt Lake City	IHL	57	25	32	57	83	...	...	...	—	—	—	—	—
—Slov. Olympic team	Int'l	8	3	7	10	8	...	...	...	—	—	—	—	—
—New York Islanders	NHL	5	0	0	0	0	-6	0	0	—	—	—	—	—
94-95—Denver	IHL	33	20	23	43	40	...	...	...	—	—	—	—	—
—New York Islanders	NHL	33	10	7	17	6	3	1	0	—	—	—	—	—
95-96—New York Islanders	NHL	81	43	44	87	56	-17	17	1	—	—	—	—	—
96-97—New York Islanders	NHL	80	48	42	90	43	21	6	4	—	—	—	—	—
97-98—New York Islanders	NHL	82	45	42	87	34	-2	*17	2	—	—	—	—	—
NHL Totals (5 years)		281	146	135	281	139	-1	41	7					

PANDOLFO, JAY　　　LW　　　DEVILS

PERSONAL: Born December 27, 1974, in Winchester, Mass. ... 6-1/200. ... Shoots left.
HIGH SCHOOL: Burlington (Mass.).
COLLEGE: Boston University.
TRANSACTIONS/CAREER NOTES: Selected by New Jersey Devils in second round (second Devils pick, 32nd overall) of NHL entry draft (June 26, 1993).
HONORS: Named to NCAA All-America East first team (1995-96). ... Named Hockey East Player of the Year (1995-96). ... Named to Hockey East All-Star team (1995-96).

Season Team	League	REGULAR SEASON								PLAYOFFS				
		Gms.	G	A	Pts.	PIM	+/-	PP	SH	Gms.	G	A	Pts.	PIM
90-91—Burlington H.S.	Mass. H.S.	20	19	27	46	10	...	...	...	—	—	—	—	—
91-92—Burlington H.S.	Mass. H.S.	20	35	34	69	14	...	...	...	—	—	—	—	—
92-93—Boston University	Hockey East	37	16	22	38	16	...	...	...	—	—	—	—	—
93-94—Boston University	Hockey East	37	17	25	42	27	...	...	...	—	—	—	—	—
94-95—Boston University	Hockey East	20	7	13	20	6	...	...	...	—	—	—	—	—
95-96—Boston University	Hockey East	39	38	29	67	6	...	...	...	—	—	—	—	—
—Albany	AHL	5	3	1	4	0	...	...	...	3	0	0	0	0
96-97—Albany	AHL	12	3	9	12	0	...	...	...	—	—	—	—	—
—New Jersey	NHL	46	6	8	14	6	-1	0	0	6	0	1	1	0
97-98—New Jersey	NHL	23	1	3	4	4	-4	0	0	3	0	2	2	0
—Albany	AHL	51	18	19	37	24	...	...	...	—	—	—	—	—
NHL Totals (2 years)		69	7	11	18	10	-5	0	0	9	0	3	3	0

PARENT, RICH　　　G　　　BLUES

PERSONAL: Born January 12, 1973, in Montreal. ... 6-3/195. ... Catches left.
TRANSACTIONS/CAREER NOTES: Signed as free agent by St. Louis Blues (July 17, 1997). ... Strained groin (October 1, 1997); missed three games.
HONORS: Won Norris Trophy (1996-97). ... Named Colonial Hockey League Goaltender of the year (1994-95 and 1995-96).

Season Team	League	REGULAR SEASON								PLAYOFFS						
		Gms.	Min	W	L	T	GA	SO	Avg.	Gms.	Min	W	L	GA	SO	Avg.
94-95—Muskegon	Col.HL	35	1867	17	11	3	112	1	3.60	13	725	7	3	47	1	3.89
95-96—Muskegon	Col.HL	36	2086	23	7	4	85	2	2.44	—	—	—	—	—	—	—
—Detroit	IHL	19	1040	16	0	‡1	48	2	2.77	7	362	3	3	22	0	3.65
96-97—Detroit	IHL	53	2815	31	13	‡4	104	4	2.22	15	786	8	3	21	1	*1.60
97-98—Manitoba	IHL	26	1334	8	12	‡2	69	3	3.10	—	—	—	—	—	—	—
—St. Louis	NHL	1	12	0	0	0	0	0	0.00	—	—	—	—	—	—	—
—Detroit	IHL	7	418	4	0	‡3	15	0	2.15	5	157	1	0	6	0	2.29
NHL Totals (1 year)		1	12	0	0	0	0	0	0.00							

PARK, RICHARD　　　C

PERSONAL: Born May 27, 1976, in Seoul, South Korea. ... 5-11/190. ... Shoots right.
TRANSACTIONS/CAREER NOTES: Selected by Pittsburgh Penguins in second round (second Penguins pick, 50th overall) of NHL entry draft (June 28, 1994). ... Traded by Penguins to Mighty Ducks of Anaheim for RW Roman Oksiuta (March 18, 1997).

Season Team	League	REGULAR SEASON								PLAYOFFS				
		Gms.	G	A	Pts.	PIM	+/-	PP	SH	Gms.	G	A	Pts.	PIM
91-92—Williams Lake	PCJHL	76	49	58	107	91	...	...	...	—	—	—	—	—
92-93—Belleville	OHL	66	23	38	61	38	...	...	...	5	0	0	0	14
93-94—Belleville	OHL	59	27	49	76	70	...	...	...	12	3	5	8	18
94-95—Belleville	OHL	45	28	51	79	35	...	...	...	16	9	18	27	12
—Pittsburgh	NHL	1	0	1	1	2	1	0	0	3	0	0	0	2
95-96—Belleville	OHL	6	7	6	13	2	...	...	...	14	18	12	30	10
—Pittsburgh	NHL	56	4	6	10	36	3	0	1	1	0	0	0	0
96-97—Cleveland	IHL	50	12	15	27	30	...	...	...	—	—	—	—	—
—Pittsburgh	NHL	1	0	0	0	0	-1	0	0	—	—	—	—	—
—Anaheim	NHL	11	1	1	2	10	0	0	0	11	0	1	1	2
97-98—Cincinnati	AHL	56	17	26	43	36	...	...	...	—	—	—	—	—
—Anaheim	NHL	15	0	2	2	8	-3	0	0	—	—	—	—	—
NHL Totals (4 years)		84	5	10	15	56	0	0	1	15	0	1	1	4

P

PARRISH, MARK   C   PANTHERS

PERSONAL: Born February 2, 1977, in Edina, Minn. ... 6-0/185. ... Shoots right.
HIGH SCHOOL: Thomas Jefferson Senior (Alexandria, Minn.).
COLLEGE: St. Cloud (Minn.) State.
TRANSACTIONS/CAREER NOTES: Selected by Colorado Avalanche in third round (third Avalanche pick, 79th overall) of NHL entry draft (June 22, 1996). ... Rights traded by Avalanche with third-round pick (D Lance Ward) in 1998 draft to Florida Panthers for RW Tom Fitzgerald (March 24, 1998).
HONORS: Named to NCAA All-America West second team (1996-97). ... Named to Can.HL All-Star second team (1997-98). ... Named to WHL (West) All-Star first team (1997-98).

		REGULAR SEASON								PLAYOFFS				
Season Team	League	Gms.	G	A	Pts.	PIM	+/-	PP	SH	Gms.	G	A	Pts.	PIM
94-95—Thomas Jefferson.......	Minn. H.S.	27	40	20	60	42	...	...	...	—	—	—	—	—
95-96—St. Cloud State...........	WCHA	38	15	14	29	28	...	...	...	—	—	—	—	—
96-97—St. Cloud State...........	WCHA	35	27	15	42	60	...	...	...	—	—	—	—	—
97-98—Seattle........................	WHL	54	54	38	92	29	...	...	...	5	2	3	5	2
—New Haven	AHL	1	1	0	1	2	...	...	...	—	—	—	—	—

PARTHENAIS, PAT   D   PANTHERS

PERSONAL: Born July 17, 1979, in Rochester, N.Y. ... 6-3/212. ... Shoots left. ... Name pronounced PAHR-thuh-nay.
TRANSACTIONS/CAREER NOTES: Selected by Florida Panthers in fifth round (sixth Panthers pick, 127th overall) of NHL entry draft (June 21, 1997).

		REGULAR SEASON								PLAYOFFS				
Season Team	League	Gms.	G	A	Pts.	PIM	+/-	PP	SH	Gms.	G	A	Pts.	PIM
96-97—Detroit......................	OHL	58	0	4	4	88	...	...	...	5	0	0	0	5
97-98—Plymouth	OHL	63	2	7	9	155	...	...	...	1	0	0	0	0

PASSMORE, STEVE   G   OILERS

PERSONAL: Born January 29, 1973, in Thunder Bay, Ont. ... 5-9/165. ... Catches left.
TRANSACTIONS/CAREER NOTES: Selected by Quebec Nordiques in ninth round (10th Nordiques pick, 196th overall) of NHL entry draft (June 20, 1992). ... Traded by Nordiques to Edmonton Oilers for D Brad Werenka (March 21, 1994).
HONORS: Named to WHL (West) All-Star first team (1992-93 and 1993-94). ... Won Fred Hunt Memorial Award (1996-97).

		REGULAR SEASON								PLAYOFFS						
Season Team	League	Gms.	Min	W	L	T	GA	SO	Avg.	Gms.	Min.	W	L	GA	SO	Avg.
88-89—Tri-City	WHL	1	60	...	...	...	6	0	6.00	—	—	—	—	—	—	—
89-90—Tri-City	WHL	4	215	...	...	...	17	0	4.74	—	—	—	—	—	—	—
90-91—Victoria........................	WHL	35	1838	3	25	1	190	0	6.20	—	—	—	—	—	—	—
91-92—Victoria........................	WHL	*71	*4228	15	50	7	347	0	4.92	—	—	—	—	—	—	—
92-93—Victoria........................	WHL	43	2402	14	24	2	150	1	3.75	—	—	—	—	—	—	—
—Kamloops..................	WHL	25	1479	19	6	0	69	1	2.80	7	401	4	2	22	1	3.29
93-94—Kamloops..................	WHL	36	1927	22	9	2	88	1	*2.74	18	1099	†11	7	60	0	3.28
94-95—Cape Breton	AHL	25	1455	8	13	3	93	0	3.84	—	—	—	—	—	—	—
95-96—Cape Breton	AHL	2	90	1	0	0	2	0	1.33	—	—	—	—	—	—	—
96-97—Raleigh......................	ECHL	2	118	1	1	‡0	13	0	6.61	—	—	—	—	—	—	—
—Hamilton..................	AHL	27	1568	12	12	3	70	1	2.68	22	1325	12	*10	*61	†2	2.76
97-98—Hamilton..................	AHL	27	1656	11	10	6	87	2	3.15	3	133	0	2	14	0	6.32
—San Antonio	IHL	14	737	3	8	‡2	56	0	4.56	—	—	—	—	—	—	—

PATRICK, JAMES   D

PERSONAL: Born June 14, 1963, in Winnipeg. ... 6-2/200. ... Shoots right. ... Full name: James A. Patrick. ... Brother of Steve Patrick, right winger for three NHL teams (1980-81 through 1985-86).
COLLEGE: North Dakota.
TRANSACTIONS/CAREER NOTES: Selected by New York Rangers as underage junior in first round (first Rangers pick, ninth overall) of NHL entry draft (June 10, 1981). ... Injured groin (October 1984). ... Pinched nerve (December 15, 1985). ... Strained left knee ligaments (March 1988). ... Bruised shoulder and chest (December 1988). ... Pulled groin (March 13, 1989). ... Sprained shoulder (November 4, 1992); missed three games. ... Bruised right shoulder (November 27, 1992); missed three games. ... Sprained left knee (January 27, 1993); missed four games. ... Suffered herniated disc (February 24, 1993); missed two games. ... Suffered herniated disc (March 28, 1993); missed remainder of season. ... Traded by Rangers with C Darren Turcotte to Hartford Whalers for RW Steve Larmer, LW Nick Kypreos and sixth-round pick (C Yuri Litvinov) in 1994 draft (November 2, 1993). ... Suffered herniated disc (December 7, 1993); missed five games. ... Traded by Whalers with C Michael Nylander and D Zarley Zalapski to Calgary Flames for D Gary Suter, LW Paul Ranheim and C Ted Drury (March 10, 1994). ... Strained left hip (March 10, 1995); missed five games. ... Suffered concussion (April 9, 1996); missed two games. ... Sore back (October 16, 1996); missed one game. ... Strained knee (October 24, 1996); missed five games. ... Suffered concussion (November 20, 1996); missed two games. ... Underwent knee surgery (December 12, 1996); missed remainder of season. ... Strained neck (October 22, 1997); missed six games. ... Reinjured neck (November 13, 1997); missed nine games. ... Suffered charley horse (January 5, 1998); missed one game.
HONORS: Named SJHL Player of the Year (1980-81). ... Named to SJHL All-Star first team (1980-81). ... Won WCHA Rookie of the Year Award (1981-82). ... Named to WCHA All-Star second team (1981-82). ... Named to NCAA All-Tournament team (1981-82). ... Named to NCAA All-America West team (1982-83). ... Named to WCHA All-Star first team (1982-83).

		REGULAR SEASON								PLAYOFFS				
Season Team	League	Gms.	G	A	Pts.	PIM	+/-	PP	SH	Gms.	G	A	Pts.	PIM
80-81—Prince Albert..............	SJHL	59	21	61	82	162	...	...	...	4	1	6	7	0
81-82—U. of North Dakota......	WCHA	42	5	24	29	26	...	...	...	—	—	—	—	—
82-83—U. of North Dakota......	WCHA	36	12	36	48	29	...	...	...	—	—	—	—	—

P

Season Team	League	Gms.	G	A	Pts.	PIM	+/-	PP	SH	Gms.	G	A	Pts.	PIM
						REGULAR SEASON						PLAYOFFS		
83-84—Can. Olympic Team.....	Int'l	63	7	24	31	52	...	...	...	—	—	—	—	—
—New York Rangers......	NHL	12	1	7	8	2	6	0	0	5	0	3	3	2
84-85—New York Rangers......	NHL	75	8	28	36	71	-17	4	1	3	0	0	0	4
85-86—New York Rangers......	NHL	75	14	29	43	88	14	2	1	16	1	5	6	34
86-87—New York Rangers......	NHL	78	10	45	55	62	13	5	0	6	1	2	3	2
87-88—New York Rangers......	NHL	70	17	45	62	52	16	9	0	—	—	—	—	—
88-89—New York Rangers......	NHL	68	11	36	47	41	3	6	0	4	0	1	1	2
89-90—New York Rangers......	NHL	73	14	43	57	50	4	9	0	10	3	8	11	0
90-91—New York Rangers......	NHL	74	10	49	59	58	-5	6	0	6	0	0	0	6
91-92—New York Rangers......	NHL	80	14	57	71	54	34	6	0	13	0	7	7	12
92-93—New York Rangers......	NHL	60	5	21	26	61	1	3	0	—	—	—	—	—
93-94—New York Rangers......	NHL	6	0	3	3	2	1	0	0	—	—	—	—	—
—Hartford......	NHL	47	8	20	28	32	-12	4	1	—	—	—	—	—
—Calgary......	NHL	15	2	2	4	6	6	1	0	7	0	1	1	6
94-95—Calgary......	NHL	43	0	10	10	14	-3	0	0	5	0	1	1	0
95-96—Calgary......	NHL	80	3	32	35	30	3	1	0	4	0	0	0	2
96-97—Calgary......	NHL	19	3	1	4	6	2	1	0	—	—	—	—	—
97-98—Calgary......	NHL	60	6	11	17	26	-2	1	0	—	—	—	—	—
NHL Totals (15 years).........		935	126	439	565	655	64	58	3	79	5	28	33	70

PAUL, JEFF   RW   BLACKHAWKS

PERSONAL: Born March 1, 1978, in London, Ont. ... 6-3/196. ... Shoots right.
TRANSACTIONS/CAREER NOTES: Selected by Chicago Blackhawks in second round (second Blackhawks pick, 42nd overall) of NHL entry draft (June 22, 1996).

Season Team	League	Gms.	G	A	Pts.	PIM	+/-	PP	SH	Gms.	G	A	Pts.	PIM
						REGULAR SEASON						PLAYOFFS		
94-95—Niagara Falls..............	OHL	57	3	10	13	64	...	...	...	6	0	2	2	0
95-96—Niagara Falls..............	OHL	48	1	7	8	81	...	...	...	10	0	4	4	37
96-97—Erie	OHL	60	4	23	27	152	...	...	...	5	2	0	2	12
97-98—Erie	OHL	48	3	17	20	108	...	...	...	7	0	2	2	13

PAYETTE, ANDRE   C   FLYERS

PERSONAL: Born July 29, 1976, in Cornwall, Ont. ... 6-2/182. ... Shoots left. ... Name pronounced pigh-EHT.
TRANSACTIONS/CAREER NOTES: Selected by Philadelphia Flyers in 10th round (ninth Flyers pick, 244th overall) of NHL entry draft (June 29, 1994).

Season Team	League	Gms.	G	A	Pts.	PIM	+/-	PP	SH	Gms.	G	A	Pts.	PIM
						REGULAR SEASON						PLAYOFFS		
93-94—Sault Ste. Marie.........	OHL	40	2	3	5	98	...	...	...	—	—	—	—	—
94-95—Sault Ste. Marie.........	OHL	50	15	15	30	177	...	...	...	—	—	—	—	—
95-96—Sault Ste. Marie.........	OHL	57	20	19	39	257	...	...	...	4	0	0	0	5
96-97—Kingston....................	OHL	33	13	13	26	162	...	...	...	2	0	0	0	2
97-98—Philadelphia................	AHL	56	5	5	10	209	...	...	...	4	0	0	0	9

PEAKE, PAT   RW

PERSONAL: Born May 28, 1973, in Detroit. ... 6-1/195. ... Shoots right. ... Full name: Patrick Michael Peake. ... Name pronounced PEEK.
TRANSACTIONS/CAREER NOTES: Injured wrist (August 31, 1990). ... Selected by Washington Capitals in first round (first Capitals pick, 14th overall) of NHL entry draft (June 22, 1991). ... Suffered sore ankle (October 30, 1993); missed two games. ... Suffered sore shoulder (December 23, 1993); missed six games. ... Suffered from the flu (February 2, 1994); missed two games. ... Bruised ribs (February 21, 1994); missed 14 games. ... Suffered from the flu (February 15, 1995); missed one game. ... Suffered from mononeucleosis (March 2, 1995); missed nine games. ... Broke thyroid cartilage (October 29, 1995); missed 10 games. ... Injured shoulder (January 28, 1996); missed three games. ... Injured kidney (March 9, 1996); missed one game. ... Bruised knee (April 3, 1996); missed five games. ... Fractured heel (April 26, 1996); missed one playoff game and first 67 games of 1996-97 season. ... Suffered concussion (April 10, 1997); missed three games. ... Suffered from the flu (October 1, 1997); missed eight games. ... Injured heel (October 18, 1997); missed eight games. ... Reinjured heel (November 8, 1997); missed remainder of season.
HONORS: Won Can.HL Player of the Year Award (1992-93). ... Won Red Tilson Trophy (1992-93). ... Won William Hanley Trophy (1992-93). ... Named to Can.HL All-Star first team (1992-93). ... Named to OHL All-Star first team (1992-93).

Season Team	League	Gms.	G	A	Pts.	PIM	+/-	PP	SH	Gms.	G	A	Pts.	PIM
						REGULAR SEASON						PLAYOFFS		
89-90—Detroit Compuware.....	NAJHL	40	36	37	73	57	...	...	...	—	—	—	—	—
90-91—Detroit.......................	OHL	63	39	51	90	54	...	...	...	—	—	—	—	—
91-92—Detroit.......................	OHL	53	41	52	93	44	...	...	...	7	8	9	17	10
—Baltimore..................	AHL	3	1	0	1	4	...	...	...	—	—	—	—	—
92-93—Detroit.......................	OHL	46	58	78	136	64	...	...	...	2	1	3	4	2
93-94—Portland....................	AHL	4	0	5	5	2	...	...	...	—	—	—	—	—
—Washington	NHL	49	11	18	29	39	1	3	0	8	0	1	1	8
94-95—Washington	NHL	18	0	4	4	12	-6	0	0	—	—	—	—	—
—Portland....................	AHL	5	1	3	4	2	...	...	...	4	0	3	3	6
95-96—Washington	NHL	62	17	19	36	46	7	8	0	5	2	1	3	12
96-97—Portland....................	AHL	3	0	2	2	0	...	...	...	—	—	—	—	—
—Washington	NHL	4	0	0	0	4	1	0	0	—	—	—	—	—
97-98—Washington	NHL	1	0	0	0	4	0	0	0	—	—	—	—	—
NHL Totals (5 years).........		134	28	41	69	105	3	11	0	13	2	2	4	20

P

PECA, MICHAEL   C   SABRES

PERSONAL: Born March 26, 1974, in Toronto. ... 5-11/181. ... Shoots right. ... Name pronounced PEH-kuh.
HIGH SCHOOL: LaSalle Secondary (Kinston, Ont.).
TRANSACTIONS/CAREER NOTES: Selected by Vancouver Canucks in second round (second Canucks pick, 40th overall) of NHL entry draft (June 20, 1992). ... Cracked cheek bone (February 9, 1995); missed 12 games. ... Injured wrist (April 26, 1995); missed one game. ... Traded by Canucks with D Mike Wilson and first-round pick (D Jay McKee) in 1995 draft to Buffalo Sabres for RW Alexander Mogilny and fifth-round pick (LW Todd Norman) in 1995 draft (July 8, 1995). ... Strained back (October 29, 1995); missed six games. ... Bruised sternum (December 2, 1995); missed one game. ... Sprained right knee (March 18, 1996); missed seven games. ... Injured shoulder (November 27, 1996); missed three games. ... Missed first 11 games of 1997-98 season due to contract dispute. ... Injured hip (November 6, 1997); missed three games. ... Suspended three games and fined $1,000 by NHL for elbowing incident (March 27, 1998). ... Reinjured hip (April 8, 1998); missed two games. ... Sprained knee (April 15, 1998); missed final two games of regular season and two playoff games.
HONORS: Won Frank J. Selke Trophy (1996-97).
MISCELLANEOUS: Captain of Buffalo Sabres (1997-98).

Season Team	League	REGULAR SEASON								PLAYOFFS				
		Gms.	G	A	Pts.	PIM	+/-	PP	SH	Gms.	G	A	Pts.	PIM
90-91—Sudbury	OHL	62	14	27	41	24	...	...	...	5	1	0	1	7
91-92—Sudbury	OHL	39	16	34	50	61	...	...	...	—	—	—	—	—
—Ottawa	OHL	27	8	17	25	32	...	...	...	11	6	10	16	6
92-93—Ottawa	OHL	55	38	64	102	80	...	...	...	—	—	—	—	—
—Hamilton	AHL	9	6	3	9	11	...	...	...	—	—	—	—	—
93-94—Ottawa	OHL	55	50	63	113	101	...	...	...	17	7	22	29	30
—Vancouver	NHL	4	0	0	0	2	-1	0	0	—	—	—	—	—
94-95—Syracuse	AHL	35	10	24	34	75	...	...	...	—	—	—	—	—
—Vancouver	NHL	33	6	6	12	30	-6	2	0	5	0	1	1	8
95-96—Buffalo	NHL	68	11	20	31	67	-1	4	3	—	—	—	—	—
96-97—Buffalo	NHL	79	20	29	49	80	26	5	*6	10	0	2	2	8
97-98—Buffalo	NHL	61	18	22	40	57	12	6	5	13	3	2	5	8
NHL Totals (5 years)		245	55	77	132	236	30	17	14	28	3	5	8	24

PEDERSON, DENIS   C   DEVILS

PERSONAL: Born September 10, 1975, in Prince Albert, Sask. ... 6-2/205. ... Shoots right. ... Name pronounced PEE-duhr-suhn.
HIGH SCHOOL: Carlton Comprehensive (Prince Albert, Sask.).
TRANSACTIONS/CAREER NOTES: Selected by New Jersey Devils in first round (first Devils pick, 13th overall) of NHL entry draft (June 26, 1993). ... Bruised thigh (December 31, 1996); missed one game. ... Suffered head injury (February 19, 1997); missed one game. ... Suffered from the flu (March 11, 1997); missed one game.
HONORS: Named to WHL All-Rookie team (1992-93). ... Named to WHL (East) All-Star second team (1993-94).

Season Team	League	REGULAR SEASON								PLAYOFFS				
		Gms.	G	A	Pts.	PIM	+/-	PP	SH	Gms.	G	A	Pts.	PIM
91-92—Prince Albert	WHL	10	0	0	0	6	...	...	...	7	0	1	1	13
92-93—Prince Albert	WHL	72	33	40	73	134	...	...	...	—	—	—	—	—
93-94—Prince Albert	WHL	71	53	45	98	157	...	...	...	—	—	—	—	—
94-95—Prince Albert	WHL	63	30	38	68	122	...	...	...	15	11	14	25	14
—Albany	AHL	—	—	—	—	—	...	...	...	3	0	0	0	2
95-96—Albany	AHL	68	28	43	71	104	...	...	...	4	1	2	3	0
—New Jersey	NHL	10	3	1	4	0	-1	1	0	—	—	—	—	—
96-97—Albany	AHL	3	1	3	4	7	...	...	...	—	—	—	—	—
—New Jersey	NHL	70	12	20	32	62	7	3	0	9	0	0	0	2
97-98—New Jersey	NHL	80	15	13	28	97	-6	7	0	6	1	1	2	2
NHL Totals (3 years)		160	30	34	64	159	0	11	0	15	1	1	2	4

PELLERIN, SCOTT   LW   BLUES

PERSONAL: Born January 9, 1970, in Shediac, N.B. ... 5-10/193. ... Shoots left. ... Full name: Jaque-Frederick Scott Pellerin. ... Name pronounced PEHL-ih-rihn.
COLLEGE: Maine.
TRANSACTIONS/CAREER NOTES: Selected by New Jersey Devils in third round (fourth Devils pick, 47th overall) of NHL entry draft (June 17, 1989). ... Signed as free agent by St. Louis Blues (July 3, 1996). ... Suffered sore ankle (March 9, 1998); missed one game.
HONORS: Named Hockey East co-Rookie of the Year with Rob Gaudreau (1988-89). ... Named to Hockey East All-Rookie team (1988-89). ... Won Hobey Baker Memorial Award (1991-92). ... Named to NCAA All-America East first team (1991-92). ... Named Hockey East Player of the Year (1991-92). ... Named Hockey East Tournament Most Valuable Player (1991-92). ... Named Hockey East All-Star first team (1991-92). ... Named to Hockey East All-Decade team (1994).

Season Team	League	REGULAR SEASON								PLAYOFFS				
		Gms.	G	A	Pts.	PIM	+/-	PP	SH	Gms.	G	A	Pts.	PIM
87-88—Notre Dame	SJHL	57	37	49	86	139	...	...	...	—	—	—	—	—
88-89—Univ. of Maine	Hockey East	45	29	33	62	92	...	...	...	—	—	—	—	—
89-90—Univ. of Maine	Hockey East	42	22	34	56	68	...	...	...	—	—	—	—	—
90-91—Univ. of Maine	Hockey East	43	23	25	48	60	...	...	...	—	—	—	—	—
91-92—Univ. of Maine	Hockey East	37	32	25	57	54	...	...	...	—	—	—	—	—
—Utica	AHL	—	—	—	—	—	...	...	...	3	1	0	1	0
92-93—Utica	AHL	27	15	18	33	33	...	...	...	2	0	1	1	0
—New Jersey	NHL	45	10	11	21	41	-1	1	2	—	—	—	—	—
93-94—Albany	IHL	73	28	46	74	84	...	...	...	5	2	1	3	11
—New Jersey	NHL	1	0	0	0	2	0	0	0	—	—	—	—	—
94-95—Albany	AHL	74	23	33	56	95	...	...	...	14	6	4	10	8

P

Season Team	League	REGULAR SEASON Gms.	G	A	Pts.	PIM	+/-	PP	SH	PLAYOFFS Gms.	G	A	Pts.	PIM
95-96—Albany	AHL	75	35	47	82	142	...	...	...	4	0	3	3	10
—New Jersey	NHL	6	2	1	3	0	1	0	0	—	—	—	—	—
96-97—Worcester	AHL	24	10	16	26	37	...	...	...	—	—	—	—	—
—St. Louis	NHL	54	8	10	18	35	12	0	2	6	0	0	0	6
97-98—St. Louis	NHL	80	8	21	29	62	14	1	1	10	0	2	2	10
NHL Totals (5 years)		186	28	43	71	140	26	2	5	16	0	2	2	16

PELLETIER, JEAN-MARC   G   FLYERS

PERSONAL: Born March 4, 1978, in Atlanta. ... 6-3/195. ... Catches left.
COLLEGE: Cornell.
TRANSACTIONS/CAREER NOTES: Selected by Philadelphia Flyers in second round (first Flyers pick, 30th overall) of NHL entry draft (June 21, 1997).
HONORS: Named to QMJHL All-Rookie Team (1997-98).

Season Team	League	REGULAR SEASON Gms.	Min	W	L	T	GA	SO	Avg.	PLAYOFFS Gms.	Min.	W	L	GA	SO	Avg.
95-96—Cornell University	ECAC	5	179	1	2	0	15	0	5.03	—	—	—	—	—	—	—
96-97—Cornell University	ECAC	11	678	5	2	3	28	1	2.48	—	—	—	—	—	—	—
97-98—Rimouski	QMJHL	34	1913	17	11	3	118	0	3.70	16	895	11	3	†51	1	3.42

PELTONEN, VILLE   LW   PREDATORS

PERSONAL: Born May 24, 1973, in Vantaa, Finland. ... 5-10/180. ... Shoots left. ... Name pronounced VIHL-lay PEHL-tuh-nehn.
TRANSACTIONS/CAREER NOTES: Selected by San Jose Sharks in third round (fourth Sharks pick, 58th overall) of NHL entry draft (June 26, 1993). ... Injured knee (October 15, 1996); missed 10 games. ... Signed as free agent by Nashville Predators (June 29, 1998).
MISCELLANEOUS: Member of bronze-medal-winning Finnish Olympic team (1994 and 1998). ... Failed to score on a penalty shot (vs. Patrick Roy, March 5, 1996).

Season Team	League	REGULAR SEASON Gms.	G	A	Pts.	PIM	+/-	PP	SH	PLAYOFFS Gms.	G	A	Pts.	PIM
91-92—HIFK Helsinki	Finland	6	0	0	0	0	...	...	...	—	—	—	—	—
92-93—HIFK Helsinki	Finland	46	13	24	37	16	...	...	...	4	0	2	2	2
93-94—HIFK Helsinki	Finland	43	16	22	38	14	...	...	...	3	0	0	0	2
—Fin. Olympic Team	Int'l	8	4	3	7	0	...	...	...	—	—	—	—	—
94-95—HIFK Helsinki	Finland	45	20	16	36	16	...	...	...	3	0	0	0	0
95-96—Kansas City	IHL	29	5	13	18	8	...	...	...	—	—	—	—	—
—San Jose	NHL	31	2	11	13	14	-7	0	0	—	—	—	—	—
96-97—San Jose	NHL	28	2	3	5	0	-8	1	0	—	—	—	—	—
—Kentucky	AHL	40	22	30	52	21	...	...	...	—	—	—	—	—
97-98—Vastra Frolunda	Sweden	44	22	29	51	44	...	...	...	7	4	2	6	0
—Fin. Olympic Team	Int'l	6	2	1	3	6	...	...	...	—	—	—	—	—
NHL Totals (2 years)		59	4	14	18	14	-15	1	0					

PELUSO, MIKE   LW

PERSONAL: Born November 8, 1965, in Hibbing, Minn. ... 6-4/225. ... Shoots left. ... Full name: Michael David Peluso. ... Cousin of Mike Peluso, center in Calgary Flames system. ... Name pronounced puh-LOO-soh.
HIGH SCHOOL: Greenway (Coleraine, Minn.).
COLLEGE: Alaska-Anchorage.
TRANSACTIONS/CAREER NOTES: Selected by New Jersey Devils in 10th round (10th Devils pick, 190th overall) of NHL entry draft (June 15, 1985). ... Signed as free agent by Chicago Blackhawks (September 7, 1989). ... Bruised jaw and cheek (November 8, 1990); missed five games. ... Suspended 10 games by NHL for fighting (March 17, 1991). ... Selected by Ottawa Senators in NHL expansion draft (June 18, 1992). ... Suspended one game by NHL for accumulating three game misconduct penalties (February 1, 1993). ... Pinched nerve in neck (March 27, 1993); missed two games. ... Traded by Senators to Devils (June 26, 1993) to complete deal in which Devils sent G Craig Billington, C/LW Troy Mallette and fourth-round pick (C Cosmo Dupaul) in 1993 draft to Senators for G Peter Sidorkiewicz and future considerations (June 20, 1993). ... Suffered concussion (December 18, 1993); missed two games. ... Suspended one game by NHL for non-stick related game misconduct (January 7, 1994). ... Suspended two games by NHL for non-stick related game misconduct (February 4, 1994). ... Suspended three games by NHL for non-stick related game misconduct (March 7, 1994). ... Suffered sore neck (March 8, 1995); missed one game. ... Suffered from the flu (April 5, 1995); missed one game. ... Fined $1,000 by NHL for throwing an elbow (May 12, 1995). ... Bruised shoulder (October 12, 1995); missed three games. ... Injured neck (February 1, 1996); missed one game. ... Injured leg (February 21, 1996); missed two games. ... Injured knee (February 22, 1996); missed 16 games. ... Traded by Devils with D Ricard Persson to St. Louis Blues for D Ken Sutton and second-round pick in 1999 draft (November 26, 1996). ... Injured shoulder (December 22, 1996); missed nine games. ... Traded by Blues to New York Rangers as compensation for Blues hiring Larry Pleau as general manager (June 21, 1997). ... Claimed by Calgary Flames in NHL waiver draft (September 28, 1997). ... Suffered hip pointer (October 14, 1997); missed two games. ... Strained neck (November 23, 1997); missed 16 games. ... Announced retirement (December 30, 1997).
MISCELLANEOUS: Member of Stanley Cup championship team (1995).

Season Team	League	REGULAR SEASON Gms.	G	A	Pts.	PIM	+/-	PP	SH	PLAYOFFS Gms.	G	A	Pts.	PIM
83-84—Greenway H.S.	Minn. H.S.	12	5	15	20	30	...	...	...	—	—	—	—	—
84-85—Stratford	OPJHL	52	11	45	56	114	...	...	...	—	—	—	—	—
85-86—Alaska-Anchorage	Indep.	32	2	11	13	59	...	...	...	—	—	—	—	—
86-87—Alaska-Anchorage	Indep.	30	5	21	26	68	...	...	...	—	—	—	—	—
87-88—Alaska-Anchorage	Indep.	35	4	33	37	76	...	...	...	—	—	—	—	—
88-89—Alaska-Anchorage	Indep.	33	10	27	37	75	...	...	...	—	—	—	—	—
89-90—Indianapolis	IHL	75	7	10	17	279	...	...	...	14	0	1	1	58
—Chicago	NHL	2	0	0	0	15	0	0	0	—	—	—	—	—

P

Season Team	League	REGULAR SEASON								PLAYOFFS				
		Gms.	G	A	Pts.	PIM	+/-	PP	SH	Gms.	G	A	Pts.	PIM
90-91—Indianapolis	IHL	6	2	1	3	21	...	...	...	5	0	2	2	40
—Chicago	NHL	53	6	1	7	320	-3	2	0	3	0	0	0	2
91-92—Chicago	NHL	63	6	3	9	*408	1	2	0	17	1	2	3	8
—Indianapolis	IHL	4	0	1	1	15	...			—	—	—	—	—
92-93—Ottawa	NHL	81	15	10	25	318	-35	2	0	—	—	—	—	—
93-94—New Jersey	NHL	69	4	16	20	238	19	0	0	17	1	0	1	*64
94-95—New Jersey	NHL	46	2	9	11	167	5	0	0	20	1	2	3	8
95-96—New Jersey	NHL	57	3	8	11	146	4	0	0	—	—	—	—	—
96-97—New Jersey	NHL	20	0	2	2	68	0	0	0	—	—	—	—	—
—St. Louis	NHL	44	2	3	5	158	0	0	0	5	0	0	0	25
97-98—Calgary	NHL	23	0	0	0	113	-6	0	0	—	—	—	—	—
NHL Totals (9 years)		458	38	52	90	1951	-15	6	0	62	3	4	7	107

PELUSO, MIKE C FLAMES

PERSONAL: Born September 2, 1974, in Denver, Colo. ... 6-0/200. ... Shoots right. ... Full name: Michael James Peluso. ... Cousin of Mike Peluso, left winger for six NHL teams (1989-90 through 1997-98).
HIGH SCHOOL: Bismarck (N.D.).
COLLEGE: Minnesota-Duluth.
TRANSACTIONS/CAREER NOTES: Selected by Calgary Flames in 10th round (11th Flames pick, 253rd overall) of NHL entry draft (June 29, 1994).
HONORS: Named to WCHA All-Rookie team (1994-95). ... Named to WCHA All-Star second team (1996-97).

Season Team	League	REGULAR SEASON								PLAYOFFS				
		Gms.	G	A	Pts.	PIM	+/-	PP	SH	Gms.	G	A	Pts.	PIM
91-92—Bismarck H.S.	N.D. H.S.	23	50	49	99	...	...	...	...	—	—	—	—	—
92-93—Omaha	USHL													
93-94—Omaha	USHL	48	36	29	65	77	...	...	...	—	—	—	—	—
94-95—Minnesota-Duluth	WCHA	38	11	23	34	38	...	...	...	—	—	—	—	—
96-97—Minnesota-Duluth	WCHA	37	20	20	40	53	...	...	...	—	—	—	—	—
97-98—Minnesota-Duluth	WCHA	40	24	21	45	100	...	...	...	—	—	—	—	—

(92-93—Omaha: Statistics unavailable.)

PEPPERALL, COLIN LW BLACKHAWKS

PERSONAL: Born April 28, 1978, in Niagara Falls, Ont. ... 5-10/180. ... Shoots left.
TRANSACTIONS/CAREER NOTES: Selected by New York Rangers in fifth round (fourth Rangers pick, 131st overall) of NHL entry draft (June 22, 1996). ... Traded by Rangers to Chicago Blackhawks for future considerations (June 1, 1998).
HONORS: Named to OHL All-Star second team (1997-98).

Season Team	League	REGULAR SEASON								PLAYOFFS				
		Gms.	G	A	Pts.	PIM	+/-	PP	SH	Gms.	G	A	Pts.	PIM
95-96—Niagara Falls	OHL	66	26	26	52	47	...	...	...	10	3	4	7	8
96-97—Erie	OHL	66	36	36	72	39	...	...	...	5	3	2	5	2
97-98—Erie	OHL	60	31	60	91	151	...	...	...	7	4	4	8	16
—Hartford	AHL	3	1	0	1	2	...	...	...	—	—	—	—	—

PEPPERALL, RYAN RW MAPLE LEAFS

PERSONAL: Born January 26, 1977, in Niagara Falls, Ont. ... 6-1/185. ... Shoots right.
HIGH SCHOOL: Eastwood Secondaire (Kitchener, Ont.).
TRANSACTIONS/CAREER NOTES: Selected by Toronto Maple Leafs in third round (second Maple Leafs pick, 54th overall) of NHL entry draft (July 8, 1995).

Season Team	League	REGULAR SEASON								PLAYOFFS				
		Gms.	G	A	Pts.	PIM	+/-	PP	SH	Gms.	G	A	Pts.	PIM
93-94—Chippewa	Jr. C	8	4	8	12	39	...	...	...	—	—	—	—	—
—Niagara Falls Jr. B	OHA	37	14	20	34	156	...	...	...	—	—	—	—	—
94-95—Kitchener	OHL	62	17	16	33	86	...	...	...	5	2	2	4	8
95-96—Kitchener	OHL	66	31	26	57	173	...	...	...	12	3	4	7	34
96-97—Kitchener	OHL	65	35	36	71	201	...	...	...	13	9	6	15	17
97-98—St. John's	AHL	63	3	4	7	50	...	...	...	1	0	0	0	0

PERREAULT, YANIC C KINGS

PERSONAL: Born April 4, 1971, in Sherbrooke, Que. ... 5-11/189. ... Shoots left. ... Name pronounced YAH-nihk puh-ROH.
TRANSACTIONS/CAREER NOTES: Selected by Toronto Maple Leafs in third round (first Maple Leafs pick, 47th overall) of NHL entry draft (June 22, 1991). ... Signed as free agent by Los Angeles Kings (July 14, 1994). ... Strained abdominal muscle (December 13, 1996); missed 11 games. ... Underwent kidney surgery (February 3, 1997); missed remainder of season.
HONORS: Won Can.HL Rookie of the Year Award (1988-89). ... Won Michel Bergeron Trophy (1988-89). ... Won Marcel Robert Trophy (1989-90). ... Won Michel Briere Trophy (1990-91). ... Won Jean Beliveau Trophy (1990-91). ... Won Frank J. Selke Trophy (1990-91). ... Won Shell Cup (1990-91). ... Named to QMJHL All-Star first team (1990-91).
STATISTICAL PLATEAUS: Three-goal games: 1997-98 (2).

Season Team	League	REGULAR SEASON								PLAYOFFS				
		Gms.	G	A	Pts.	PIM	+/-	PP	SH	Gms.	G	A	Pts.	PIM
88-89—Trois-Rivieres	QMJHL	70	53	55	108	48	...	...	...	—	—	—	—	—
89-90—Trois-Rivieres	QMJHL	63	51	63	114	75	...	...	...	7	6	5	11	19

P

Season Team	League	REGULAR SEASON								PLAYOFFS				
		Gms.	G	A	Pts.	PIM	+/-	PP	SH	Gms.	G	A	Pts.	PIM
90-91—Trois-Rivieres.............	QMJHL	67	*87	98	*185	103	...	...	...	6	4	7	11	6
91-92—St. John's..................	AHL	62	38	38	76	19	...	...	...	16	7	8	15	4
92-93—St. John's..................	AHL	79	49	46	95	56	...	...	...	9	4	5	9	2
93-94—St. John's..................	AHL	62	45	60	105	38	...	...	...	11	*12	6	18	14
—Toronto......................	NHL	13	3	3	6	0	1	2	0	—	—	—	—	—
94-95—Phoenix.....................	IHL	68	51	48	99	52	...	...	...	—	—	—	—	—
—Los Angeles...............	NHL	26	2	5	7	20	3	0	0	—	—	—	—	—
95-96—Los Angeles..............	NHL	78	25	24	49	16	-11	8	3	—	—	—	—	—
96-97—Los Angeles..............	NHL	41	11	14	25	20	0	1	1	—	—	—	—	—
97-98—Los Angeles..............	NHL	79	28	20	48	32	6	3	2	4	1	2	3	6
NHL Totals (5 years)...........		237	69	66	135	88	-1	14	6	4	1	2	3	6

PERSSON, RICARD — D — BLUES

PERSONAL: Born August 24, 1969, in Ostersund, Sweden. ... 6-1/203. ... Shoots left. ... Name pronounced RIH-kahrd PEER-suhn.
TRANSACTIONS/CAREER NOTES: Selected by New Jersey Devils in second round (second Devils pick, 23rd overall) of NHL entry draft (June 13, 1987). ... Traded by Devils with LW Mike Peluso to St. Louis Blues for D Ken Sutton and second-round pick in 1999 draft (November 26, 1996).

Season Team	League	REGULAR SEASON								PLAYOFFS				
		Gms.	G	A	Pts.	PIM	+/-	PP	SH	Gms.	G	A	Pts.	PIM
85-86—Ostersund..................	Swed. Dv.II	24	2	2	4	16	...	...	...	—	—	—	—	—
86-87—Ostersund..................	Swed. Dv.II	31	10	11	21	28	...	...	...	—	—	—	—	—
87-88—Leksand	Sweden	31	2	0	2	8	...	...	...	2	0	1	1	2
88-89—Leksand	Sweden	33	2	4	6	28	...	...	...	9	0	1	1	6
89-90—Leksand	Sweden	43	9	10	19	62	...	...	...	3	0	0	0	6
90-91—Leksand	Sweden	37	6	9	15	42	...	...	...	—	—	—	—	—
91-92—Leksand	Sweden	21	0	7	7	28	...	...	...	—	—	—	—	—
92-93—Leksand	Sweden	36	7	15	22	63	...	...	...	2	0	2	2	0
93-94—Malmo	Sweden	40	11	9	20	38	...	...	...	11	2	0	2	12
94-95—Malmo	Sweden	31	3	13	16	38	...	...	...	9	0	2	2	8
—Albany......................	AHL	—	—	—	—	—				9	3	5	8	7
95-96—New Jersey..............	NHL	12	2	1	3	8	5	1	0	—	—	—	—	—
—Albany......................	AHL	67	15	31	46	59	...	...	...	4	0	0	0	7
96-97—New Jersey..............	NHL	1	0	0	0	0	0	0	0	—	—	—	—	—
—Albany......................	AHL	13	1	4	5	8	...	...	...	—	—	—	—	—
—St. Louis....................	NHL	54	4	8	12	45	-2	1	0	6	0	0	0	27
97-98—Worcester	AHL	32	2	16	18	58	...	...	...	10	3	7	10	24
—St. Louis....................	NHL	1	0	0	0	0	0	0	0	—	—	—	—	—
NHL Totals (3 years)...........		68	6	9	15	53	3	2	0	6	0	0	0	27

PETERS, GEOFF — C — BLACKHAWKS

PERSONAL: Born April 30, 1978, in Hamilton, Ont. ... 6-0/174. ... Shoots left.
TRANSACTIONS/CAREER NOTES: Selected by Chicago Blackhawks in second round (third Blackhawks pick, 46th overall) of NHL entry draft (June 22, 1996).

Season Team	League	REGULAR SEASON								PLAYOFFS				
		Gms.	G	A	Pts.	PIM	+/-	PP	SH	Gms.	G	A	Pts.	PIM
94-95—Niagara Falls..............	OHL	57	11	9	20	37	...	...	...	6	2	0	2	4
95-96—Niagara Falls..............	OHL	64	25	34	59	51	...	...	...	10	4	4	8	8
96-97—Erie	OHL	28	12	10	22	39	...	...	...	5	1	3	4	7
97-98—Erie	OHL	31	15	11	26	36	...	...	...	—	—	—	—	—
—North Battleford..........	SJHL	20	11	14	25	22	...	...	...	—	—	—	—	—
—Indianapolis................	IHL	2	0	0	0	10	...	...	...	—	—	—	—	—

PETERSON, BRENT — LW — LIGHTNING

PERSONAL: Born July 20, 1972, in Calgary. ... 6-3/206. ... Shoots left. ... Name pronounced PEE-tuhr-suhn.
COLLEGE: Michigan Tech.
TRANSACTIONS/CAREER NOTES: Selected by Tampa Bay Lightning in NHL supplemental draft (June 25, 1993). ... Sprained wrist (December 4, 1996); missed four games.

Season Team	League	REGULAR SEASON								PLAYOFFS				
		Gms.	G	A	Pts.	PIM	+/-	PP	SH	Gms.	G	A	Pts.	PIM
91-92—Michigan Tech	WCHA	39	11	9	20	18	...	...	...	—	—	—	—	—
92-93—Michigan Tech	WCHA	37	24	18	42	32	...	...	...	—	—	—	—	—
93-94—Michigan Tech	WCHA	43	25	21	46	30	...	...	...	—	—	—	—	—
94-95—Michigan Tech	WCHA	39	20	16	36	27	...	...	...	—	—	—	—	—
95-96—Atlanta	IHL	69	9	19	28	33	...	...	...	3	0	0	0	0
96-97—Adirondack	AHL	52	22	23	45	56	...	...	...	4	3	1	4	2
—Tampa Bay	NHL	17	2	0	2	4	-4	0	0	—	—	—	—	—
97-98—Milwaukee..................	IHL	63	20	39	59	48	...	...	...	8	5	3	8	22
—Tampa Bay	NHL	19	5	0	5	2	-2	0	0	—	—	—	—	—
NHL Totals (2 years)...........		36	7	0	7	6	-6	0	0					

P

PETIT, MICHEL D

PERSONAL: Born February 12, 1964, in St. Malo, Que. ... 6-1/205. ... Shoots right. ... Name pronounced puh-TEE.

TRANSACTIONS/CAREER NOTES: Selected by Vancouver Canucks as underage junior in first round (first Canucks pick, 11th overall) of NHL entry draft (June 9, 1982). ... Separated shoulder (March 1984). ... Injured knee (February 1987). ... Traded by Canucks to New York Rangers for D Willie Huber and D Larry Melnyk (November 1987). ... Pulled groin (December 1987). ... Fractured right collarbone (December 27, 1988); missed 11 games. ... Traded by Rangers to Quebec Nordiques for D Randy Moller (October 5, 1989). ... Traded by Nordiques with C/LW Aaron Broten and RW Lucien DeBlois to Toronto Maple Leafs for LW Scott Pearson and second-round picks in 1991 draft (D Eric Lavigne) and 1992 draft (D Tuomas Gronman) (November 17, 1990). ... Sprained knee (February 4, 1991); missed five games. ... Sprained thumb (November 9, 1991); missed six games. ... Traded by Maple Leafs with D Alexander Godynyuk, RW Gary Leeman, LW Craig Berube and G Jeff Reese to Calgary Flames for C Doug Gilmour, D Jamie Macoun, LW Kent Manderville, D Ric Nattress and G Rick Wamsley (January 2, 1992). ... Suffered back spasms (March 3, 1992); missed four games. ... Pulled groin prior to 1992-93 season; missed first four games of season. ... Dislocated right shoulder (October 22, 1992); missed 29 games. ... Injured hip pointer (October 21, 1993); missed one game. ... Suffered concussion (January 15, 1994); missed two games. ... Pulled groin (February 2, 1994); missed four games. ... Signed as free agent by Los Angeles Kings (June 16, 1994). ... Strained groin (February 2, 1995); missed three games. ... Strained groin (February 15, 1995); missed four games. ... Sprained knee (April 17, 1995); missed one game. ... Suspended 10 games by NHL for abusing official (September 28, 1995). ... Traded by Kings to Tampa Bay Lightning for D Steven Finn (November 13, 1995). ... Bruised ribs (November 27, 1995); missed one game. ... Bruised ribs (December 19, 1995); missed two games. ... Injured right hip flexor and strained lower back (February 15, 1996); missed two games. ... Sprained back (February 21, 1996); missed 15 games. ... Signed as free agent by Edmonton Oilers (October 24, 1996). ... Bruised hand (November 9, 1996); missed two games. ... Claimed on waivers by Philadelphia Flyers (January 17, 1997). ... Suspended two games by NHL for kneeing penalty (February 25, 1997). ... Signed as free agent by Phoenix Coyotes (November 26, 1997). ... Bruised thigh (January 28, 1998); missed five games. ... Tore medial collateral knee ligament (February 28, 1998); missed 14 games.

HONORS: Won Raymond Lagace Trophy (1981-82). ... Won Association of Journalists of Hockey Trophy (1981-82). ... Named to QMJHL All-Star first team (1981-82 and 1982-83).

		REGULAR SEASON								PLAYOFFS				
Season Team	League	Gms.	G	A	Pts.	PIM	+/-	PP	SH	Gms.	G	A	Pts.	PIM
81-82—Sherbrooke	QMJHL	63	10	39	49	106	...	...	...	22	5	20	25	24
82-83—St. Jean	QMJHL	62	19	67	86	196	...	...	...	3	0	0	0	35
—Vancouver	NHL	2	0	0	0	0	-4	0	0	—	—	—	—	—
83-84—Can. Olympic Team	Int'l	19	3	10	13	58	...	...	...	—	—	—	—	—
—Vancouver	NHL	44	6	9	15	53	-6	5	0	1	0	0	0	0
84-85—Vancouver	NHL	69	5	26	31	127	-26	1	1	—	—	—	—	—
85-86—Fredericton	AHL	25	0	13	13	79	...	...	...	—	—	—	—	—
—Vancouver	NHL	32	1	6	7	27	-6	1	0	—	—	—	—	—
86-87—Vancouver	NHL	69	12	13	25	131	-5	4	0	—	—	—	—	—
87-88—Vancouver	NHL	10	0	3	3	35	-4	0	0	—	—	—	—	—
—New York Rangers	NHL	64	9	24	33	223	3	2	0	—	—	—	—	—
88-89—New York Rangers	NHL	69	8	25	33	154	-15	5	0	4	0	2	2	27
89-90—Quebec	NHL	63	12	24	36	215	-38	5	0	—	—	—	—	—
90-91—Quebec	NHL	19	4	7	11	47	-15	3	0	—	—	—	—	—
—Toronto	NHL	54	9	19	28	132	-19	3	1	—	—	—	—	—
91-92—Toronto	NHL	34	1	13	14	85	-17	1	0	—	—	—	—	—
—Calgary	NHL	36	3	10	13	79	2	3	0	—	—	—	—	—
92-93—Calgary	NHL	35	3	9	12	54	-5	2	0	—	—	—	—	—
93-94—Calgary	NHL	63	2	21	23	110	5	0	0	—	—	—	—	—
94-95—Los Angeles	NHL	40	5	12	17	84	4	2	0	—	—	—	—	—
95-96—Los Angeles	NHL	9	0	1	1	27	-1	0	0	—	—	—	—	—
—Tampa Bay	NHL	45	4	7	11	108	-10	0	0	6	0	0	0	20
96-97—Edmonton	NHL	18	2	4	6	20	-13	0	0	—	—	—	—	—
—Philadelphia	NHL	20	0	3	3	51	2	0	0	3	0	0	0	6
97-98—Detroit	IHL	9	2	3	5	24	...	...	...	—	—	—	—	—
—Phoenix	NHL	32	4	2	6	77	-4	1	0	5	0	0	0	8
NHL Totals (16 years)		827	90	238	328	1839	-172	38	2	19	0	2	2	61

PETRAKOV, ANDREI RW BLUES

PERSONAL: Born April 26, 1976, in Sverdlovsk, U.S.S.R. ... 6-0/198. ... Shoots left. ... Name pronounced PEHT-ruh-kahv.

TRANSACTIONS/CAREER NOTES: Selected by St. Louis Blues in fourth round (fourth Blues pick, 97th overall) of NHL entry draft (June 22, 1996).

		REGULAR SEASON								PLAYOFFS				
Season Team	League	Gms.	G	A	Pts.	PIM	+/-	PP	SH	Gms.	G	A	Pts.	PIM
92-93—Avtomobilist Yek.	CIS	5	0	0	0	0	...	...	...	1	0	0	0	0
93-94—Avtomobilist Yek.	CIS	35	4	2	6	10	...	...	...	—	—	—	—	—
94-95—Avtomobilist Yek.	CIS	11	1	1	2	6	...	...	...	1	0	0	0	0
95-96—Avtomobilist Yek.	CIS	52	17	6	23	14	...	...	...	—	—	—	—	—
96-97—CSKA	Rus. Div. II	55	36	32	68	73	...	...	...	—	—	—	—	—
—Metal. Magnitogorsk	Russian	18	4	0	4	8	...	...	...	9	0	0	0	0
97-98—CSK VVS Samara	Russian	9	0	0	0	4	...	...	...	—	—	—	—	—
—Metal. Magnitogorsk	Russian	29	9	11	20	0	...	...	...	—	—	—	—	—

PETRE, HENRIK D CAPITALS

PERSONAL: Born April 9, 1979, in Stockholm, Sweden. ... 6-1/187. ... Shoots left.

TRANSACTIONS/CAREER NOTES: Selected by Washington Capitals in sixth round (fifth Capitals pick, 143rd overall) of NHL entry draft (June 21, 1997).

		REGULAR SEASON								PLAYOFFS				
Season Team	League	Gms.	G	A	Pts.	PIM	+/-	PP	SH	Gms.	G	A	Pts.	PIM
95-96—Djur. Stockholm Jrs.	Sweden	32	8	6	14	16	...			—	—	—	—	—
96-97—Djur. Stockholm Jrs.	Sweden					Statistics unavailable.								
97-98—Djur. Stockholm Jrs.	Sweden					Statistics unavailable.								

P

PETROCHININ, YEVGENY   D   STARS

PERSONAL: Born February 7, 1976, in Murmansk, U.S.S.R. ... 5-9/165. ... Shoots left. ... Name pronounced ehv-GEH-nee PEHT-roh-CHEE-nihn.
TRANSACTIONS/CAREER NOTES: Selected by Dallas Stars in sixth round (fifth Stars pick, 150th overall) of NHL entry draft (June 29, 1994).

		REGULAR SEASON								PLAYOFFS				
Season Team	League	Gms.	G	A	Pts.	PIM	+/-	PP	SH	Gms.	G	A	Pts.	PIM
93-94—Spartak Moscow........	CIS	2	0	0	0	0	...	...	...	—	—	—	—	—
94-95—Spartak Moscow........	CIS	45	0	2	2	14	...	...	...	—	—	—	—	—
95-96—Spartak Moscow........	CIS	50	5	17	22	18	...	...	...	5	3	0	3	0
96-97—Spartak Moscow........	Russian	32	5	6	11	52	...	...	...	—	—	—	—	—
97-98—Spartak Moscow........	Russian	46	12	6	18	100	...	...	...	—	—	—	—	—

PETROVICKY, ROBERT   C

PERSONAL: Born October 26, 1973, in Kosice, Czechoslovakia. ... 5-11/172. ... Shoots left. ... Name pronounced peht-roh-VIH-kee.
TRANSACTIONS/CAREER NOTES: Selected by Hartford Whalers in first round (first Whalers pick, ninth overall) of NHL entry draft (June 20, 1992). ... Sprained left ankle (February 28, 1993); missed five games. ... Loaned to Slovakian Olympic team (February 11, 1994). ... Returned to Whalers (February 28, 1994). ... Traded by Whalers to Dallas Stars for Dan Kesa (November 29, 1995). ... Signed as free agent by St. Louis Blues (September 6, 1996).
HONORS: Named to Czechoslovakian League All-Star team (1991-92).

		REGULAR SEASON								PLAYOFFS				
Season Team	League	Gms.	G	A	Pts.	PIM	+/-	PP	SH	Gms.	G	A	Pts.	PIM
90-91—Dukla Trencin.............	Czech.	33	9	14	23	12	...	...	...	—	—	—	—	—
91-92—Dukla Trencin.............	Czech.	46	25	36	61		...	...	...	—	—	—	—	—
92-93—Hartford	NHL	42	3	6	9	45	-10	0	0	—	—	—	—	—
—Springfield	AHL	16	5	3	8	39	...	...	...	15	5	6	11	14
93-94—Hartford	NHL	33	6	5	11	39	-1	1	0	—	—	—	—	—
—Springfield	AHL	30	16	8	24	39	...	...	...	4	0	2	2	4
—Slov. Olympic team.....	Int'l	8	1	6	7	18	...	...	...	—	—	—	—	—
94-95—Springfield	AHL	74	30	52	82	121	...	...	...	—	—	—	—	—
—Hartford	NHL	2	0	0	0	0	0	0	0	—	—	—	—	—
95-96—Springfield	AHL	9	4	8	12	18	...	...	...	—	—	—	—	—
—Detroit......................	IHL	12	5	3	8	16	...	...	...	—	—	—	—	—
—Michigan...................	IHL	50	23	23	46	63	...	...	...	7	3	1	4	16
—Dallas.......................	NHL	5	1	1	2	0	1	1	0	—	—	—	—	—
96-97—Worcester	AHL	12	5	4	9	19	...	...	...	—	—	—	—	—
—St. Louis....................	NHL	44	7	12	19	10	2	0	0	2	0	0	0	0
97-98—Worcester	AHL	65	27	34	61	97	...	...	...	10	3	4	7	12
—Slov. Olympic team.....	Int'l	4	2	1	3	0	...	...	...	—	—	—	—	—
NHL Totals (5 years)...........		126	17	24	41	94	-8	2	0	2	0	0	0	0

PETROVICKY, RONALD   RW   FLAMES

PERSONAL: Born February 15, 1977, in Zilina, Czechoslavakia. ... 5-11/180. ... Shoots right.
TRANSACTIONS/CAREER NOTES: Signed as free agent by Calgary Flames (June 1, 1998).
HONORS: Names to WHL (East) All-Star second team (1997-98).

		REGULAR SEASON								PLAYOFFS				
Season Team	League	Gms.	G	A	Pts.	PIM	+/-	PP	SH	Gms.	G	A	Pts.	PIM
93-94—Dukla Trencin.............	Slovakia	36	28	27	55	42	...	...	...	—	—	—	—	—
94-95—Tri-City	WHL	39	4	11	15	86	...	...	...	—	—	—	—	—
—Prince George............	WHL	21	4	6	10	37	...	...	...	—	—	—	—	—
95-96—Prince George............	WHL	39	19	21	40	61	...	...	...	—	—	—	—	—
96-97—Prince George............	WHL	72	32	37	69	119	...	...	...	15	4	9	13	31
97-98—Regina	WHL	71	64	49	113	45	...	...	...	9	2	4	6	11

PETRUK, RANDY   G   HURRICANES

PERSONAL: Born April 23, 1978, in Cranbrook, B.C. ... 5-9/178. ... Catches right.
TRANSACTIONS/CAREER NOTES: Selected by Colorado Avalanche in fourth round (fifth Avalanche pick, 107th overall) of NHL entry draft (June 22, 1996). ... Rights traded by Avalanche to Carolina Hurricanes for fifth-round pick in 1999 draft (June 1, 1998).
HONORS: Named to WHL (West) All-Star second team (1997-98).

		REGULAR SEASON							PLAYOFFS					
Season Team	League	Gms.	Min	W	L	T	GA	SO	Avg.	Gms.	Min.	W	L	GA	SO	Avg.
94-95—Kamloops..................	WHL	27	1462	16	3	4	71	1	2.91	7	423	5	2	19	0	2.70
95-96—Kamloops..................	WHL	52	3071	34	15	1	181	1	3.54	16	990	9	‡6	58	0	3.52
96-97—Kamloops..................	WHL	*60	*3475	25	28	5	210	0	3.63	—						
97-98—Kamloops..................	WHL	57	3097	31	21	1	157	3	3.04	7	425	3	4	21	0	2.96

PHILLIPS, CHRIS   D   SENATORS

PERSONAL: Born March 9, 1978, in Calgary. ... 6-2/213. ... Shoots left. ... Nephew of Rod Phillips, Edmonton Oilers play-by-play announcer.
TRANSACTIONS/CAREER NOTES: Selected by Ottawa Senators in first round (first Senators pick, first overall) of NHL entry draft (June 22, 1996). ... Bruised knee (November 13, 1997); missed two games. ... Injured eye (February 25, 1998); missed five games.
HONORS: Won Can.HL Top Draft Prospect Award (1995-96). ... Won Jim Piggott Memorial Trophy (1995-96). ... Named to Can.HL All-Rookie team (1995-96). ... Named to Memorial Cup All-Star Team (1996-97). ... Named to Can.HL All-Star first team (1996-97). ... Named to WHL (East) All-Star first team (1996-97). ... Won Bill Hunter Trophy (1996-97).

P

Season Team	League	REGULAR SEASON								PLAYOFFS				
		Gms.	G	A	Pts.	PIM	+/-	PP	SH	Gms.	G	A	Pts.	PIM
93-94—Fort McMurray	AJHL	56	6	16	22	72	...	...	...	—	—	—	—	—
94-95—Fort McMurray	AJHL	48	16	32	48	127	...	...	...	—	—	—	—	—
95-96—Prince Albert	WHL	61	10	30	40	97	...	...	...	18	2	12	14	30
96-97—Prince Albert	WHL	32	3	23	26	58	...	...	...	—	—	—	—	—
—Lethbridge	WHL	26	4	18	22	28	...	...	...	19	4	*21	25	20
97-98—Ottawa	NHL	72	5	11	16	38	2	2	0	11	0	2	2	2
NHL Totals (1 year)		72	5	11	16	38	2	2	0	11	0	2	2	2

PHILLIPS, GREG   D   KINGS

PERSONAL: Born March 27, 1978, in Winnipeg. ... 6-2/190. ... Shoots right.
TRANSACTIONS/CAREER NOTES: Selected by Los Angeles Kings in third round (third Kings pick, 57th overall) of NHL entry draft (June 22, 1996).

Season Team	League	REGULAR SEASON								PLAYOFFS				
		Gms.	G	A	Pts.	PIM	+/-	PP	SH	Gms.	G	A	Pts.	PIM
94-95—Saskatoon	WHL	64	3	5	8	94	...	...	...	10	0	0	0	4
95-96—Saskatoon	WHL	67	21	24	45	132	...	...	...	4	1	2	3	2
96-97—Saskatoon	WHL	34	17	19	36	64	...	...	...	—	—	—	—	—
97-98—Brandon	WHL	69	34	49	83	165	...	...	...	18	11	11	22	58

PICARD, MICHEL   LW   BLUES

PERSONAL: Born November 7, 1969, in Beauport, Que. ... 5-11/190. ... Shoots left. ... Name pronounced pih-KAHRD.
TRANSACTIONS/CAREER NOTES: Selected by Hartford Whalers in ninth round (eighth Whalers pick, 178th overall) of NHL entry draft (June 17, 1989). ... Separated shoulder (November 14, 1991); missed seven games. ... Traded by Whalers to San Jose Sharks for future considerations (October 9, 1992); Sharks sent LW Yvon Corriveau to Whalers to complete deal (January 21, 1993). ... Signed as free agent by Portland of AHL (1993). ... Signed as free agent by Ottawa Senators (June 23, 1994). ... Suspended two games and fined $1,000 by NHL for cross-checking (March 16, 1996). ... Traded by Senators to Washington Capitals for cash (May 21, 1996). ... Signed as free agent by St. Louis Blues (January 30, 1998).
HONORS: Named to QMJHL All-Star second team (1988-89). ... Named to AHL All-Star first team (1990-91 and 1994-95). ... Named to AHL All-Star second team (1993-94). ... Named to IHL All-Star first team (1996-97).

Season Team	League	REGULAR SEASON								PLAYOFFS				
		Gms.	G	A	Pts.	PIM	+/-	PP	SH	Gms.	G	A	Pts.	PIM
86-87—Trois-Rivieres	QMJHL	66	33	35	68	53	...	...	...	—	—	—	—	—
87-88—Trois-Rivieres	QMJHL	69	40	55	95	71	...	...	...	—	—	—	—	—
88-89—Trois-Rivieres	QMJHL	66	59	81	140	107	...	...	...	4	1	3	4	2
89-90—Binghamton	AHL	67	16	24	40	98	...	...	...	—	—	—	—	—
90-91—Hartford	NHL	5	1	0	1	2	-2	0	0	—	—	—	—	—
—Springfield	AHL	77	*56	40	96	61	...	...	...	18	8	13	21	18
91-92—Hartford	NHL	25	3	5	8	6	-2	1	0	—	—	—	—	—
—Springfield	AHL	40	21	17	38	44	...	...	...	11	2	0	2	34
92-93—Kansas City	IHL	33	7	10	17	51	...	...	...	12	3	2	5	20
—San Jose	NHL	25	4	0	4	24	-17	2	0	—	—	—	—	—
93-94—Portland	AHL	61	41	44	85	99	...	...	...	17	11	10	21	22
94-95—Prin. Edward Island	AHL	57	32	57	89	58	...	...	...	8	4	4	8	6
—Ottawa	NHL	24	5	8	13	14	-1	1	0	—	—	—	—	—
95-96—Prin. Edward Island	AHL	55	37	45	82	79	...	...	...	5	5	1	6	2
—Ottawa	NHL	17	2	6	8	10	-1	0	0	—	—	—	—	—
96-97—Grand Rapids	IHL	82	46	55	101	58	...	...	...	5	2	0	2	10
97-98—Grand Rapids	IHL	58	28	41	69	42	...	...	...	—	—	—	—	—
—St. Louis	NHL	16	1	8	9	29	3	0	0	—	—	—	—	—
NHL Totals (6 years)		112	16	27	43	85	-20	4	0					

PILON, RICH   D   ISLANDERS

PERSONAL: Born April 30, 1968, in Saskatoon, Sask. ... 6-0/205. ... Shoots left. ... Full name: Richard Pilon. ... Name pronounced PEE-lahn.
TRANSACTIONS/CAREER NOTES: Selected by New York Islanders as underage junior in seventh round (ninth Islanders pick, 143rd overall) of NHL entry draft (June 21, 1986). ... Injured right leg (December 1988). ... Injured right eye (November 4, 1989); missed remainder of season. ... Injured left knee ligament (February 23, 1991). ... Suffered sore left shoulder (January 9, 1992). ... Lacerated finger (January 30, 1992); missed four games. ... Bruised hand (October 31, 1992); missed two games. ... Bruised hand (November 22, 1992); missed four games. ... Sprained left knee (December 10, 1992); missed eight games. ... Injured lower back (January 10, 1993); missed 11 games. ... Injured left shoulder (November 13, 1993); missed seven games. ... Reinjured left shoulder (December 3, 1993); missed 32 games. ... Reinjured left shoulder (March 17, 1994); missed 14 games. ... Suffered sore groin (February 22, 1995); missed four games. ... Sprained ankle (March 5, 1995); missed 17 games. ... Broke wrist (April 18, 1995); missed last seven games of season. ... Injured wrist prior to 1995-96 season; missed first 26 games of season. ... Injured groin (December 12, 1995); missed four games. ... Injured wrist (January 9, 1996); missed one game. ... Strained hip flexor (February 4, 1996); missed four games. ... Strained hip flexor (March 3, 1996); missed last 18 games of regular season. ... Aggravated groin (October 9, 1996); missed 20 games. ... Suspended two games and fined $1,000 by NHL for slashing incident (January 11, 1997). ... Sprained knee ligament (February 11, 1997); missed three games. ... Injured foot (March 26, 1997); missed four games. ... Bruised knee (April 2, 1997); missed one game. ... Injured groin (October 19, 1997); missed one game. ... Injured foot (November 14, 1997); missed four games. ... Strained triceps (March 6, 1998); missed one game.
HONORS: Named to WHL All-Star second team (1987-88).

Season Team	League	REGULAR SEASON								PLAYOFFS				
		Gms.	G	A	Pts.	PIM	+/-	PP	SH	Gms.	G	A	Pts.	PIM
85-86—Prince Albert	WHL	6	0	0	0	0	...	...	...	—	—	—	—	—
86-87—Prince Albert	WHL	68	4	21	25	192	...	...	...	7	1	6	7	17
87-88—Prince Albert	WHL	65	13	34	47	177	...	...	...	9	0	6	6	38
88-89—New York Islanders	NHL	62	0	14	14	242	-9	0	0	—	—	—	—	—
89-90—New York Islanders	NHL	14	0	2	2	31	2	0	0	—	—	—	—	—
90-91—New York Islanders	NHL	60	1	4	5	126	-12	0	0	—	—	—	—	—

P

Season Team	League	REGULAR SEASON								PLAYOFFS				
		Gms.	G	A	Pts.	PIM	+/-	PP	SH	Gms.	G	A	Pts.	PIM
91-92—New York Islanders.....	NHL	65	1	6	7	183	-1	0	0	—	—	—	—	—
92-93—New York Islanders.....	NHL	44	1	3	4	164	-4	0	0	15	0	0	0	50
—Capital District...........	AHL	6	0	1	1	8	...	...	...	—	—	—	—	—
93-94—New York Islanders.....	NHL	28	1	4	5	75	-4	0	0	—	—	—	—	—
—Salt Lake City.............	IHL	2	0	0	0	8	...	...	...	—	—	—	—	—
94-95—New York Islanders.....	NHL	20	1	1	2	40	-3	0	0	—	—	—	—	—
—Chicago....................	IHL	2	0	0	0	0	...	...	...	—	—	—	—	—
95-96—New York Islanders.....	NHL	27	0	3	3	72	-9	0	0	—	—	—	—	—
96-97—New York Islanders.....	NHL	52	1	4	5	179	4	0	0	—	—	—	—	—
97-98—New York Islanders.....	NHL	76	0	7	7	291	1	0	0	—	—	—	—	—
NHL Totals (10 years).........		448	6	48	54	1403	-35	0	0	15	0	0	0	50

PITLICK, LANCE   D   SENATORS

PERSONAL: Born November 5, 1967, in Fridley, Minn. ... 6-0/203. ... Shoots right.
HIGH SCHOOL: Cooper (New Hope, Minn.).
COLLEGE: Minnesota.
TRANSACTIONS/CAREER NOTES: Selected by Minnesota North Stars in ninth round (10th North Stars pick, 180th overall) of NHL entry draft (June 21, 1986). ... Severely pulled lower abdominal muscles (December 1, 1989). ... Underwent surgery to have tendons sewn onto his abdominal muscle for reinforcement (January 18, 1990). ... Signed as free agent by Philadelphia Flyers (September 5, 1990). ... Signed as free agent by Ottawa Senators (June 22, 1994). ... Bruised ribs (March 27, 1995); missed two games. ... Injured groin (January 5, 1996); missed one game. ... Injured groin during 1995-96 season; missed four games. ... Strained abdominal muscle (April 1, 1996); missed four games. ... Injured left knee (January 9, 1997); missed nine games. ... Strained groin (February 16, 1997); missed one game. ... Strained groin (December 2, 1997); missed one game.

Season Team	League	REGULAR SEASON								PLAYOFFS				
		Gms.	G	A	Pts.	PIM	+/-	PP	SH	Gms.	G	A	Pts.	PIM
84-85—Cooper H.S.	Minn. H.S.	23	8	4	12	...	...	...	...	—	—	—	—	—
85-86—Cooper H.S.	Minn. H.S.	21	17	8	25	...	...	...	...	—	—	—	—	—
86-87—Univ. of Minnesota......	WCHA	45	0	9	9	88	...	...	...	10	0	2	2	4
87-88—Univ. of Minnesota......	WCHA	38	3	9	12	76	...	...	...	8	1	1	2	14
88-89—Univ. of Minnesota......	WCHA	47	4	9	13	95	...	...	...	8	2	1	3	95
89-90—Univ. of Minnesota......	WCHA	14	3	2	5	26	...	...	...	—	—	—	—	—
90-91—Hershey...................	AHL	64	6	15	21	75	...	...	...	3	0	0	0	9
91-92—U.S. national team	Int'l	19	0	1	1	38	...	...	...	—	—	—	—	—
—Hershey	AHL	4	0	0	0	6	...	...	...	3	0	0	0	4
92-93—Hershey...................	AHL	53	5	10	15	77	...	...	...	—	—	—	—	—
93-94—Hershey...................	AHL	58	4	13	17	93	...	...	...	11	1	0	1	11
94-95—Prin. Edward Island	AHL	61	8	19	27	55	...	...	...	11	1	4	5	10
—Ottawa	NHL	15	0	1	1	6	-5	0	0	—	—	—	—	—
95-96—Prin. Edward Island	AHL	29	4	10	14	39	...	...	...	5	0	0	0	0
—Ottawa	NHL	28	1	6	7	20	-8	0	0	—	—	—	—	—
96-97—Ottawa	NHL	66	5	5	10	91	2	0	0	7	0	0	0	4
97-98—Ottawa	NHL	69	2	7	9	50	8	0	0	11	0	1	1	17
NHL Totals (4 years)...........		178	8	19	27	167	-3	0	0	18	0	1	1	21

PITTIS, DOMENIC   C   SABRES

PERSONAL: Born October 1, 1974, in Calgary. ... 5-11/180. ... Shoots left. ... Name pronounced PIHT-ihz.
HIGH SCHOOL: Catholic Central (Lethbridge, Alta).
TRANSACTIONS/CAREER NOTES: Selected by Pittsburgh Penguins in second round (second Penguins pick, 52nd overall) of NHL entry draft (June 26, 1993). ... Signed as free agent by Buffalo Sabres (July 30, 1998).
HONORS: Named to WHL (East) All-Star second team (1993-94).

Season Team	League	REGULAR SEASON								PLAYOFFS				
		Gms.	G	A	Pts.	PIM	+/-	PP	SH	Gms.	G	A	Pts.	PIM
91-92—Lethbridge	WHL	65	6	17	23	48	...	...	...	5	0	2	2	4
92-93—Lethbridge	WHL	66	46	73	119	69	...	...	...	4	3	3	6	8
93-94—Lethbridge	WHL	72	58	69	127	93	...	...	...	8	4	11	15	16
94-95—Cleveland	IHL	62	18	32	50	66	...	...	...	3	0	2	2	2
95-96—Cleveland	IHL	74	10	28	38	100	...	...	...	3	0	0	0	2
96-97—Pittsburgh.................	NHL	1	0	0	0	0	-1	0	0	—	—	—	—	—
—Long Beach.................	IHL	65	23	43	66	91	...	...	...	18	5	9	14	26
97-98—Syracuse...................	AHL	75	23	41	64	90	...	...	...	5	1	3	4	4
NHL Totals (1 year)............		1	0	0	0	0	-1	0	0					

PIVONKA, MICHAL   C   CAPITALS

PERSONAL: Born January 28, 1966, in Kladno, Czechoslovakia. ... 6-2/200. ... Shoots left. ... Name pronounced pih-VAHN-kuh.
TRANSACTIONS/CAREER NOTES: Selected by Washington Capitals in third round (third Capitals pick, 59th overall) of NHL entry draft (June 9, 1984). ... Strained ankle ligaments (March 1987). ... Sprained right wrist (October 1987). ... Sprained left ankle (March 1988). ... Sprained left knee (March 9, 1990). ... Pulled groin (October 10, 1992); missed three games. ... Pulled groin (October 21, 1992); missed 12 games. ... Suffered concussion (March 25, 1994); missed one game. ... Played in Europe during 1994-95 NHL lockout. ... Injured leg (April 30, 1995); missed one game. ... Missed first nine games of 1995-96 season due to contract dispute. ... Tore knee cartilage (October 26, 1996); missed 20 games. ... Suffered from the flu (March 2, 1997); missed one game. ... Suffered concussion (March 26, 1997); missed seven games. ... Injured wrist (October 23, 1997); missed four games. ... Reinjured wrist (November 11, 1997); missed 13 games. ... Injured groin (February 7, 1998); missed 24 games.
MISCELLANEOUS: Holds Washington Capitals all-time record for most assists (412).
STATISTICAL PLATEAUS: Three-goal games: 1991-92 (1).

P

Season Team	League	REGULAR SEASON								PLAYOFFS				
		Gms.	G	A	Pts.	PIM	+/-	PP	SH	Gms.	G	A	Pts.	PIM
84-85—Dukla Jihlava	Czech.	33	8	11	19	18	...	...	...	—	—	—	—	—
85-86—Dukla Jihlava	Czech.	42	5	13	18	...	...	...	...	—	—	—	—	—
86-87—Washington	NHL	73	18	25	43	41	-19	4	0	7	1	1	2	2
87-88—Washington	NHL	71	11	23	34	28	1	3	0	14	4	9	13	4
88-89—Baltimore	AHL	31	12	24	36	19	...	...	...	—	—	—	—	—
—Washington	NHL	52	8	19	27	30	9	1	0	6	3	1	4	10
89-90—Washington	NHL	77	25	39	64	54	-7	10	3	11	0	2	2	6
90-91—Washington	NHL	79	20	50	70	34	3	6	0	11	2	3	5	8
91-92—Washington	NHL	80	23	57	80	47	10	7	4	7	1	5	6	13
92-93—Washington	NHL	69	21	53	74	66	14	6	1	6	0	2	2	0
93-94—Washington	NHL	82	14	36	50	38	2	5	0	7	4	4	8	4
94-95—Klagenfurt	Austria	7	2	4	6	4	...	...	...	—	—	—	—	—
—Washington	NHL	46	10	23	33	50	3	4	2	7	1	4	5	21
95-96—Detroit	IHL	7	1	9	10	19	...	...	...	—	—	—	—	—
—Washington	NHL	73	16	65	81	36	18	6	2	6	3	2	5	18
96-97—Washington	NHL	54	7	16	23	22	-15	2	0	—	—	—	—	—
97-98—Washington	NHL	33	3	6	9	20	5	0	0	13	0	3	3	0
NHL Totals (12 years)		789	176	412	588	466	24	54	12	95	19	36	55	86

PLANTE, DAN — RW

PERSONAL: Born October 5, 1971, in Hayward, Wis. ... 5-11/202. ... Shoots right. ... Full name: Daniel Leon Plante. ... Name pronounced PLAHNT.
HIGH SCHOOL: Edina (Minn.).
COLLEGE: Wisconsin.
TRANSACTIONS/CAREER NOTES: Selected by New York Islanders in third round (third Islanders pick, 48th overall) of NHL entry draft (June 16, 1990). ... Injured knee (September 1994). ... Injured shoulder (February 10, 1996); missed one game. ... Bruised right knee (February 23, 1996); missed five games.

Season Team	League	REGULAR SEASON								PLAYOFFS				
		Gms.	G	A	Pts.	PIM	+/-	PP	SH	Gms.	G	A	Pts.	PIM
88-89—Edina High School	Minn. H.S.	27	10	26	36	12	...	...	...	—	—	—	—	—
89-90—Edina High School	Minn. H.S.	24	8	18	26	...	...	...	...	—	—	—	—	—
90-91—Univ. of Wisconsin	WCHA	33	1	2	3	54	...	...	...	—	—	—	—	—
91-92—Univ. of Wisconsin	WCHA	40	15	16	31	113	...	...	...	—	—	—	—	—
92-93—Univ. of Wisconsin	WCHA	42	26	31	57	142	...	...	...	—	—	—	—	—
93-94—Salt Lake City	IHL	66	7	17	24	148	...	...	...	—	—	—	—	—
—New York Islanders	NHL	12	0	1	1	4	-2	0	0	1	1	0	1	2
94-95—Denver	IHL	2	0	0	0	4	...	...	...	—	—	—	—	—
95-96—New York Islanders	NHL	73	5	3	8	50	-22	0	2	—	—	—	—	—
96-97—New York Islanders	NHL	67	4	9	13	75	-6	0	2	—	—	—	—	—
97-98—Utah	IHL	73	22	27	49	125	...	...	...	4	0	2	2	14
—New York Islanders	NHL	7	0	1	1	6	-1	0	0	—	—	—	—	—
NHL Totals (4 years)		159	9	14	23	135	-31	0	4	1	1	0	1	2

PLANTE, DEREK — C — SABRES

PERSONAL: Born January 17, 1971, in Cloquet, Minn. ... 5-11/181. ... Shoots left. ... Full name: Derek John Plante. ... Name pronounced PLANT.
HIGH SCHOOL: Cloquet (Minn.).
COLLEGE: Minnesota-Duluth.
TRANSACTIONS/CAREER NOTES: Broke arm (March 1988). ... Selected by Buffalo Sabres in eighth round (seventh Sabres pick, 161st overall) of NHL entry draft (June 17, 1989). ... Injured collarbone (December 15, 1989). ... Reinjured collarbone (January 20, 1990). ... Bruised left shoulder (March 8, 1994); missed two games. ... Strained back (December 15, 1995); missed three games. ... Suffered back spasms (October 7, 1997); missed three games. ... Suffered back spasms (March 1, 1998); missed four games.
HONORS: Named to NCAA All-America West first team (1992-93). ... Named WCHA Player of the Year (1992-93). ... Named to WCHA All-Star first team (1992-93).
STATISTICAL PLATEAUS: Three-goal games: 1993-94 (1).

Season Team	League	REGULAR SEASON								PLAYOFFS				
		Gms.	G	A	Pts.	PIM	+/-	PP	SH	Gms.	G	A	Pts.	PIM
87-88—Cloquet H.S.	Minn. H.S.	23	16	25	41	...	...	...	...	—	—	—	—	—
88-89—Cloquet H.S.	Minn. H.S.	24	30	33	63	...	...	...	...	—	—	—	—	—
89-90—Minnesota-Duluth	WCHA	28	10	11	21	12	...	...	...	—	—	—	—	—
90-91—Minnesota-Duluth	WCHA	36	23	20	43	6	...	...	...	—	—	—	—	—
91-92—Minnesota-Duluth	WCHA	37	27	36	63	28	...	...	...	—	—	—	—	—
92-93—Minnesota-Duluth	WCHA	37	*36	*56	*92	30	...	...	...	—	—	—	—	—
93-94—U.S. national team	Int'l	2	0	1	1	0	...	...	...	—	—	—	—	—
—Buffalo	NHL	77	21	35	56	24	4	8	1	7	1	0	1	0
94-95—Buffalo	NHL	47	3	19	22	12	-4	2	0	—	—	—	—	—
95-96—Buffalo	NHL	76	23	33	56	28	-4	4	0	—	—	—	—	—
96-97—Buffalo	NHL	82	27	26	53	24	14	5	0	12	4	6	10	4
97-98—Buffalo	NHL	72	13	21	34	26	8	5	0	11	0	3	3	10
NHL Totals (5 years)		354	87	134	221	114	18	24	1	30	5	9	14	14

PODEIN, SHJON — LW — FLYERS

PERSONAL: Born March 5, 1968, in Rochester, Minn. ... 6-2/200. ... Shoots left. ... Name pronounced SHAWN poh-DEEN.
COLLEGE: Minnesota-Duluth.

P

TRANSACTIONS/CAREER NOTES: Selected by Edmonton Oilers in eighth round (ninth Oilers pick, 166th overall) of NHL entry draft (June 11, 1988). ... Injured knee (March 9, 1994); missed five games. ... Signed as free agent by Philadelphia Flyers (July 27, 1994). ... Bruised right foot (February 22, 1996); missed three games.

		REGULAR SEASON								PLAYOFFS				
Season Team	League	Gms.	G	A	Pts.	PIM	+/-	PP	SH	Gms.	G	A	Pts.	PIM
87-88—Minnesota-Duluth	WCHA	30	4	4	8	48	...	...	...	—	—	—	—	—
88-89—Minnesota-Duluth	WCHA	36	7	5	12	46	...	...	...	—	—	—	—	—
89-90—Minnesota-Duluth	WCHA	35	21	18	39	36	...	...	...	—	—	—	—	—
90-91—Cape Breton	AHL	63	14	15	29	65	...	...	...	4	0	0	0	5
91-92—Cape Breton	AHL	80	30	24	54	46	...	...	...	5	3	1	4	2
92-93—Cape Breton	AHL	38	18	21	39	32	...	...	...	9	2	2	4	29
—Edmonton	NHL	40	13	6	19	25	-2	2	1	—	—	—	—	—
93-94—Edmonton	NHL	28	3	5	8	8	3	0	0	—	—	—	—	—
—Cape Breton	AHL	5	4	4	8	4	...	...	...	—	—	—	—	—
94-95—Philadelphia	NHL	44	3	7	10	33	-2	0	0	15	1	3	4	10
95-96—Philadelphia	NHL	79	15	10	25	89	25	0	4	12	1	2	3	50
96-97—Philadelphia	NHL	82	14	18	32	41	7	0	0	19	4	3	7	16
97-98—Philadelphia	NHL	82	11	13	24	53	8	1	1	5	0	0	0	10
NHL Totals (6 years)		355	59	59	118	249	39	3	6	51	6	8	14	86

PODKONICKY, ANDREI   C   BLUES

PERSONAL: Born May 9, 1978, in Zvolen, Czechoslovakia. ... 6-2/195. ... Shoots left. ... Name pronounced pahd-kah-NIH-kee.
TRANSACTIONS/CAREER NOTES: Selected by St. Louis Blues in eighth round (eighth Blues pick, 196th overall) of NHL entry draft (June 22, 1996).

		REGULAR SEASON								PLAYOFFS				
Season Team	League	Gms.	G	A	Pts.	PIM	+/-	PP	SH	Gms.	G	A	Pts.	PIM
95-96—ZTK Zvolen	Slov. Div. II	38	18	12	30	18	...	...	...	—	—	—	—	—
96-97—Portland	WHL	71	25	46	71	127	...	...	...	6	1	1	2	8
97-98—Portland	WHL	64	30	44	74	81	...	...	...	16	4	12	16	20

PODOLLAN, JASON   RW/C   MAPLE LEAFS

PERSONAL: Born February 18, 1976, in Vernon, B.C. ... 6-1/192. ... Shoots right. ... Name pronounced puh-DOH-lihn.
HIGH SCHOOL: University (Spokane, Wash.).
TRANSACTIONS/CAREER NOTES: Selected by Florida Panthers in second round (third Panthers pick, 31st overall) of NHL entry draft (June 28, 1994). ... Traded by Panthers to Toronto Maple Leafs for C Kirk Muller (March 18, 1997). ... Strained shoulder (March 19, 1997); missed two games.
HONORS: Named to WHL (West) All-Star second team (1995-96).

		REGULAR SEASON								PLAYOFFS				
Season Team	League	Gms.	G	A	Pts.	PIM	+/-	PP	SH	Gms.	G	A	Pts.	PIM
91-92—Penticton	Jr. A	59	20	26	46	66	...	...	...	—	—	—	—	—
—Spokane	WHL	2	0	0	0	2	...	...	...	10	3	1	4	16
92-93—Spokane	WHL	72	36	33	69	108	...	...	...	10	4	4	8	14
93-94—Spokane	WHL	69	29	37	66	108	...	...	...	3	3	0	3	2
94-95—Spokane	WHL	72	43	41	84	102	...	...	...	11	5	7	12	18
—Cincinnati	IHL	—	—	—	—	—				3	0	0	0	2
95-96—Spokane	WHL	56	37	25	62	103	...	...	...	18	*21	12	33	28
96-97—Carolina	AHL	39	21	25	46	36	...	...	...	—	—	—	—	—
—Florida	NHL	19	1	1	2	4	-3	1	0	—	—	—	—	—
—St. John's	AHL	—	—	—	—	—				11	2	3	5	6
—Toronto	NHL	10	0	3	3	6	-2	0	0	—	—	—	—	—
97-98—St. John's	AHL	70	30	31	61	116	...	...	...	4	1	0	1	10
NHL Totals (1 year)		29	1	4	5	10	-5	1	0					

POESCHEK, RUDY   D   BLUES

PERSONAL: Born September 29, 1966, in Terrace, B.C. ... 6-2/220. ... Shoots right. ... Full name: Rudolph Leopold Poeschek. ... Name pronounced POH-shehk.
TRANSACTIONS/CAREER NOTES: Injured knee (December 1984). ... Selected by New York Rangers as underage junior in 12th round (12th Rangers pick, 238th overall) of NHL entry draft (June 15, 1985). ... Injured shoulder (November 1986). ... Bruised right hand (February 1989). ... Suspended six games by AHL for pre-game fight (November 25, 1990). ... Traded by Rangers to Winnipeg Jets for C Guy Larose (January 22, 1991). ... Signed as free agent by Tampa Bay Lightning (August 13, 1993). ... Sprained ankle (February 7, 1995); missed two games. ... Reinjured ankle (February 14, 1995); missed nine games. ... Broke thumb (April 16, 1995); missed last eight games of season. ... Injured knee (October 20, 1995); missed one game. ... Sprained left knee (October 22, 1996); missed 12 games. ... Signed as free agent by St. Louis Blues (July 7, 1997). ... Suffered back spasms (January 3, 1998); missed five games. ... Injured back (January 22, 1998); missed 27 games.

		REGULAR SEASON								PLAYOFFS				
Season Team	League	Gms.	G	A	Pts.	PIM	+/-	PP	SH	Gms.	G	A	Pts.	PIM
83-84—Kamloops	WHL	47	3	9	12	93	...	...	...	8	0	2	2	7
84-85—Kamloops	WHL	34	6	7	13	100	...	...	...	15	0	3	3	56
85-86—Kamloops	WHL	32	3	13	16	92	...	...	...	16	3	7	10	40
86-87—Kamloops	WHL	54	13	18	31	153	...	...	...	15	2	4	6	37
87-88—New York Rangers	NHL	1	0	0	0	2	0	0	0	—	—	—	—	—
—Colorado	IHL	82	7	31	38	210	...	...	...	12	2	2	4	31
88-89—Denver	IHL	2	0	0	0	6	...	...	...	—	—	—	—	—
—New York Rangers	NHL	52	0	2	2	199	-8	0	0	—	—	—	—	—
89-90—Flint	IHL	38	8	13	21	109	...	...	...	4	0	0	0	16
—New York Rangers	NHL	15	0	0	0	55	-1	0	0	—	—	—	—	—
90-91—Binghamton	AHL	38	1	3	4	162	...	...	...	9	1	1	2	41
—Moncton	AHL	23	2	4	6	67	...	...	...	—	—	—	—	—
—Winnipeg	NHL	1	0	0	0	5	0	0	0	—	—	—	—	—

P

Season Team	League	REGULAR SEASON								PLAYOFFS				
		Gms.	G	A	Pts.	PIM	+/-	PP	SH	Gms.	G	A	Pts.	PIM
91-92—Moncton	AHL	63	4	18	22	170	...	...	...	11	0	2	2	46
—Winnipeg	NHL	4	0	0	0	17	-5	0	0	—	—	—	—	—
92-93—St. John's	AHL	78	7	24	31	189	...	...	...	9	0	4	4	13
93-94—Tampa Bay	NHL	71	3	6	9	118	3	0	0	—	—	—	—	—
94-95—Tampa Bay	NHL	25	1	1	2	92	0	0	0	—	—	—	—	—
95-96—Tampa Bay	NHL	57	1	3	4	88	-2	0	0	3	0	0	0	12
96-97—Tampa Bay	NHL	60	0	6	6	120	-3	0	0	—	—	—	—	—
97-98—St. Louis	NHL	50	1	7	8	64	-5	0	0	2	0	0	0	6
NHL Totals (10 years)		336	6	25	31	760	-21	0	0	5	0	0	0	18

POIRIER, GAETAN — LW — PANTHERS

PERSONAL: Born December 28, 1976, in Moncton, N.B. ... 6-2/200. ... Shoots left.
COLLEGE: Merrimack (Mass.).
TRANSACTIONS/CAREER NOTES: Selected by Florida Panthers in sixth round (sixth Panthers pick, 156th overall) of NHL entry draft (June 22, 1996).

Season Team	League	REGULAR SEASON								PLAYOFFS				
		Gms.	G	A	Pts.	PIM	+/-	PP	SH	Gms.	G	A	Pts.	PIM
94-95—Merrimack College	Hockey East	32	8	6	14	38	...	...	...	—	—	—	—	—
95-96—Merrimack College	Hockey East	33	10	14	24	52	...	...	...	—	—	—	—	—
96-97—Carolina	AHL	66	5	13	18	66	...	...	...	—	—	—	—	—
97-98—Fort Wayne	IHL	2	0	0	0	0	...	...	...	—	—	—	—	—
—Port Huron	UHL	23	5	13	18	18	...	...	...	—	—	—	—	—

POLLOCK, JAME — D — BLUES

PERSONAL: Born June 16, 1979, in Quebec City. ... 6-1/190. ... Shoots right.
TRANSACTIONS/CAREER NOTES: Selected by St. Louis Blues in fourth round (fourth Blues pick, 106th overall) of NHL entry draft (June 21, 1997).

Season Team	League	REGULAR SEASON								PLAYOFFS				
		Gms.	G	A	Pts.	PIM	+/-	PP	SH	Gms.	G	A	Pts.	PIM
95-96—Seattle	WHL	32	0	1	1	15	...	...	...	—	—	—	—	—
96-97—Seattle	WHL	66	15	19	34	94	...	...	...	15	3	5	8	16
97-98—Seattle	WHL	66	11	36	47	78	...	...	...	5	0	1	1	17

POPOVIC, PETER — D — RANGERS

PERSONAL: Born February 10, 1968, in Koping, Sweden. ... 6-6/239. ... Shoots right. ... Name pronounced PAH-poh-vihk.
TRANSACTIONS/CAREER NOTES: Selected by Montreal Canadiens in fifth round (fifth Canadiens pick, 93rd overall) of NHL entry draft (June 11, 1988). ... Injured knee (November 20, 1993); missed six games. ... Bruised shoulder (December 22, 1993); missed seven games. ... Played in Europe during 1994-95 NHL lockout. ... Cut face (March 11, 1995); missed six games. ... Broke finger on right hand (December 23, 1995); missed six games. ... Bruised foot (February 17, 1997); missed one game. ... Injured rib (April 7, 1997); missed remainder of regular season and two playoff games. ... Suffered ankle infection (October 1, 1997); missed eight games. ... Traded by Canadiens to New York Rangers for LW Sylvain Blouin and sixth-round pick in 1999 draft (June 30, 1998).

Season Team	League	REGULAR SEASON								PLAYOFFS				
		Gms.	G	A	Pts.	PIM	+/-	PP	SH	Gms.	G	A	Pts.	PIM
86-87—Vasteras	Sweden	24	1	2	3	10	...	...	...	—	—	—	—	—
87-88—Vasteras	Sweden	28	3	17	20	16	...	...	...	—	—	—	—	—
88-89—Vasteras	Sweden	22	1	4	5	32	...	...	...	—	—	—	—	—
89-90—Vasteras	Sweden	30	2	10	12	24	...	...	...	2	0	1	1	2
90-91—Vasteras	Sweden	40	3	2	5	62	...	...	...	4	0	0	0	4
91-92—Vasteras	Sweden	34	7	10	17	30	...	...	...	—	—	—	—	—
92-93—Vasteras	Sweden	39	6	12	18	46	...	...	...	3	0	1	1	2
93-94—Montreal	NHL	47	2	12	14	26	10	1	0	6	0	1	1	0
94-95—Vasteras	Sweden	11	0	3	3	10	...	...	...	—	—	—	—	—
—Montreal	NHL	33	0	5	5	8	-10	0	0	—	—	—	—	—
95-96—Montreal	NHL	76	2	12	14	69	21	0	0	6	0	2	2	4
96-97—Montreal	NHL	78	1	13	14	32	9	0	0	3	0	0	0	2
97-98—Montreal	NHL	69	2	6	8	38	-6	0	0	10	1	1	2	2
NHL Totals (5 years)		303	7	48	55	173	24	1	0	25	1	4	5	8

POSMYK, MAREK — D — MAPLE LEAFS

PERSONAL: Born September 15, 1978, in Jihlava, Czechoslovakia. ... 6-5/226. ... Shoots right.
TRANSACTIONS/CAREER NOTES: Selected by Toronto Maple Leafs in second round (first Maple Leafs pick, 36th overall) of NHL entry draft (June 22, 1996).

Season Team	League	REGULAR SEASON								PLAYOFFS				
		Gms.	G	A	Pts.	PIM	+/-	PP	SH	Gms.	G	A	Pts.	PIM
94-95—Czech Rep.	Czech Rep.	16	1	3	4		...	...	...	—	—	—	—	—
95-96—Czech Rep.	Czech Rep.	16	6	5	11		...	...	...	—	—	—	—	—
—Dukla Jihlava	Czech Rep.	18	1	2	3		...	...	...	1	0	0	0	...
—Jihlava Jrs.	Czech Rep.	16	6	5	11		...	...	...	—	—	—	—	—
96-97—Dukla Jihlava	Czech Rep.	24	1	7	8	44	...	...	...	—	—	—	—	—
—St. John's	AHL	2	0	0	0	2	...	...	...	—	—	—	—	—
97-98—St. John's	AHL	3	0	0	0	4	...	...	...	—	—	—	—	—
—Sarnia	OHL	48	8	16	24	94	...	...	...	5	0	2	2	6

P

POTI, TOM   D   OILERS

PERSONAL: Born March 22, 1977, in Worcester, Mass. ... 6-3/180. ... Shoots left.
HIGH SCHOOL: Cushing Academy (Ashburnham, Mass.).
COLLEGE: Boston University.
TRANSACTIONS/CAREER NOTES: Selected by Edmonton Oilers in third round (fourth Oilers pick, 59th overall) of NHL entry draft (June 22, 1996).
HONORS: Named to NCAA All-Tournament team (1996-97). ... Named to Hockey East All-Rookie team (1996-97). ... Named to NCAA All-America East first team (1997-98). ... Named to Hockey East All-Star first team (1997-98).

		REGULAR SEASON								PLAYOFFS				
Season Team	League	Gms.	G	A	Pts.	PIM	+/-	PP	SH	Gms.	G	A	Pts.	PIM
94-95—Cushing Academy	Mass. H.S.	36	16	47	63	35	...	...	...	—	—	—	—	—
95-96—Cushing Academy	Mass. H.S.	29	14	59	73	18	...	...	...	—	—	—	—	—
96-97—Boston University	Hockey East	38	4	17	21	54	...	...	...	—	—	—	—	—
97-98—Boston University	Hockey East	38	13	29	42	60	...	...	...	—	—	—	—	—

POTOMSKI, BARRY   LW   RED WINGS

PERSONAL: Born November 24, 1972, in Windsor, Ont. ... 6-2/215. ... Shoots left.
TRANSACTIONS/CAREER NOTES: Signed as free agent by Los Angeles Kings (July 7, 1994). ... Sprained left shoulder (March 25, 1996); missed seven games. ... Suffered herniated disc (October 17, 1996); missed 24 games. ... Signed as free agent by San Jose Sharks (August 15, 1997). ... Signed as free agent by Detroit Red Wings (July 21, 1998).

		REGULAR SEASON								PLAYOFFS				
Season Team	League	Gms.	G	A	Pts.	PIM	+/-	PP	SH	Gms.	G	A	Pts.	PIM
90-91—London	OHL	65	14	17	31	202	...	...	...	7	0	2	2	10
91-92—London	OHL	61	19	32	51	224	...	...	...	10	5	1	6	22
92-93—Toledo	ECHL	43	5	18	23	184	...	...	...	14	5	2	7	73
—Erie	ECHL	5	1	1	2	31	...	...	...	—	—	—	—	—
93-94—Adirondack	AHL	50	9	5	14	224	...	...	...	11	1	1	2	44
—Toledo	ECHL	13	9	4	13	81	...	...	...	—	—	—	—	—
94-95—Phoenix	IHL	42	5	6	11	171	...	...	...	—	—	—	—	—
95-96—Phoenix	IHL	24	5	2	7	74	...	...	...	3	1	0	1	8
—Los Angeles	NHL	33	3	2	5	104	-7	1	0	—	—	—	—	—
96-97—Los Angeles	NHL	26	3	2	5	93	-8	0	0	—	—	—	—	—
—Phoenix	IHL	28	2	11	13	58	...	...	...	—	—	—	—	—
97-98—Las Vegas	IHL	31	3	2	5	143	...	...	...	4	1	0	1	13
—San Jose	NHL	9	0	1	1	30	1	0	0	—	—	—	—	—
NHL Totals (3 years)		68	6	5	11	227	-14	1	0					

POTVIN, FELIX   G   MAPLE LEAFS

PERSONAL: Born June 23, 1971, in Anjou, Que. ... 6-1/190. ... Catches left. ... Name pronounced PAHT-vihn. ... Nickname: The Cat.
TRANSACTIONS/CAREER NOTES: Selected by Toronto Maple Leafs in second round (second Maple Leafs pick, 31st overall) of NHL entry draft (June 16, 1990).
HONORS: Named to QMJHL All-Star second team (1989-90). ... Won Can.HL Goaltender of the Year Award (1990-91). ... Won Hap Emms Memorial Trophy (1990-91). ... Won Jacques Plante Trophy (1990-91). ... Won Shell Cup (1990-91). ... Won Guy Lafleur Trophy (1990-91). ... Named to Memorial Cup All-Star team (1990-91). ... Named to QMJHL All-Star first team (1990-91). ... Won Aldege (Baz) Bastien Trophy (1991-92). ... Won Dudley (Red) Garrett Memorial Trophy (1991-92). ... Named to AHL All-Star first team (1991-92). ... Named to NHL All-Rookie team (1992-93). ... Played in NHL All-Star Game (1994 and 1996).
MISCELLANEOUS: Stopped penalty shot attempt (vs. Brian Bradley, October 22, 1992; vs. Donald Audette, November 21, 1996).

		REGULAR SEASON								PLAYOFFS					
Season Team	League	Gms.	Min.	W	L	T	GA	SO	Avg.	Gms.	Min.	W	L	GA	SO	Avg.
88-89—Chicoutimi	QMJHL	*65	*3489	25	31	1	*271	†2	4.66	—	—	—	—	—	—	—
89-90—Chicoutimi	QMJHL	*62	*3478	31	26	2	231	†2	3.99	—	—	—	—	—	—	—
90-91—Chicoutimi	QMJHL	54	3216	33	15	4	145	*6	†2.71	*16	*992	*11	5	46	0	*2.78
91-92—St. John's	AHL	35	2070	18	10	6	101	2	2.93	11	642	7	4	41	0	3.83
—Toronto	NHL	4	210	0	2	1	8	0	2.29	—	—	—	—	—	—	—
92-93—Toronto	NHL	48	2781	25	15	7	116	2	*2.50	21	1308	11	10	62	1	2.84
—St. John's	AHL	5	309	3	0	2	18	0	3.50	—	—	—	—	—	—	—
93-94—Toronto	NHL	66	3883	34	22	9	187	3	2.89	18	1124	9	†9	46	3	2.46
94-95—Toronto	NHL	36	2144	15	13	7	104	0	2.91	7	424	3	4	20	1	2.83
95-96—Toronto	NHL	69	4009	30	26	11	192	2	2.87	6	350	2	4	19	0	3.26
96-97—Toronto	NHL	*74	*4271	27	*36	7	*224	0	3.15	—	—	—	—	—	—	—
97-98—Toronto	NHL	67	3864	26	*33	7	176	5	2.73	—	—	—	—	—	—	—
NHL Totals (7 years)		364	21162	157	147	49	1007	12	2.86	52	3206	25	27	147	5	2.75

POULIN, PATRICK   C   CANADIENS

PERSONAL: Born April 23, 1973, in Vanier, Que. ... 6-1/208. ... Shoots left. ... Name pronounced POO-lai.
TRANSACTIONS/CAREER NOTES: Broke wrist (January 15, 1991). ... Selected by Hartford Whalers in first round (first Whalers pick, ninth overall) of NHL entry draft (June 22, 1991). ... Traded by Whalers with D Eric Weinrich to Chicago Blackhawks for RW Steve Larmer and D Bryan Marchment (November 2, 1993). ... Sprained ankle (December 28, 1995); missed 19 games. ... Suffered back spasms (March 5, 1996); missed two games. ... Traded by Blackhawks with D Igor Ulanov and second-round pick (traded to New Jersey) to Tampa Bay Lightning for D Enrico Ciccone (March 20, 1996). ... Injured knee (January 13, 1997); missed one game. ... Injured knee (March 6, 1997); missed six games. ... Traded by Lightning with F Mick Vukota and D Igor Ulanov to Montreal Canadiens for F Stephane Richer, F Darcy Tucker and D David Wilkie (January 15, 1998).
HONORS: Won Jean Beliveau Trophy (1991-92). ... Named to Can.HL All-Star first team (1991-92). ... Named to QMJHL All-Star first team (1991-92).

P

Season Team	League	REGULAR SEASON								PLAYOFFS				
		Gms.	G	A	Pts.	PIM	+/-	PP	SH	Gms.	G	A	Pts.	PIM
89-90—St. Hyacinthe	QMJHL	60	25	26	51	55	...	...	...	12	1	9	10	5
90-91—St. Hyacinthe	QMJHL	56	32	38	70	82	...	...	...	4	0	2	2	23
91-92—St. Hyacinthe	QMJHL	56	52	86	*138	58	...	...	...	5	2	2	4	4
—Springfield	AHL	—	—	—	—	—	...			1	0	0	0	0
—Hartford	NHL	1	0	0	0	2	-1	0	0	7	2	1	3	0
92-93—Hartford	NHL	81	20	31	51	37	-19	4	0	—				
93-94—Hartford	NHL	9	2	1	3	11	-8	1	0	—				
—Chicago	NHL	58	12	13	25	40	0	1	0	4	0	0	0	0
94-95—Chicago	NHL	45	15	15	30	53	13	4	0	16	4	1	5	8
95-96—Chicago	NHL	38	7	8	15	16	7	1	0	—				
—Indianapolis	IHL	1	0	1	1	0	...			—				
—Tampa Bay	NHL	8	0	1	1	0	0	0	0	2	0	0	0	0
96-97—Tampa Bay	NHL	73	12	14	26	56	-16	2	3	—				
97-98—Tampa Bay	NHL	44	2	7	9	19	-3	0	0	—				
—Montreal	NHL	34	4	6	10	8	-1	0	1	3	0	0	0	0
NHL Totals (7 years)		391	74	96	170	242	-28	13	4	32	6	2	8	8

PRATT, HARLAN D PENGUINS

PERSONAL: Born December 10, 1978, in Fort McMurray, Alta. ... 6-1/202. ... Shoots right. ... Brother of Nolan Pratt, defenseman, Carolina Hurricanes.

TRANSACTIONS/CAREER NOTES: Selected by Pittsburgh Penguins in fifth round (fifth Penguins pick, 124th overall) of NHL entry draft (June 21, 1997).

Season Team	League	REGULAR SEASON								PLAYOFFS				
		Gms.	G	A	Pts.	PIM	+/-	PP	SH	Gms.	G	A	Pts.	PIM
95-96—Red Deer	WHL	60	2	3	5	22	...			10	0	0	0	4
96-97—Red Deer	WHL	2	0	0	0	2	...			—				
—Prince Albert	WHL	65	7	26	33	49	...			1	1	1	2	4
97-98—Prince Albert	WHL	37	6	14	20	12	...			—				
—Regina	WHL	24	2	6	8	23	...			9	2	2	4	2

PRATT, NOLAN D HURRICANES

PERSONAL: Born August 14, 1975, in Fort McMurray, Alta. ... 6-2/208. ... Shoots left. ... Brother of Harlan Pratt, defenseman in PIttsburgh Penguins system.

HIGH SCHOOL: Sunset (Beaverton, Ore.).

TRANSACTIONS/CAREER NOTES: Selected by Hartford Whalers in fifth round (fourth Whalers pick, 115th overall) of NHL entry draft (June 26, 1993). ... Whalers franchise moved to North Carolina and renamed Carolina Hurricanes for 1997-98 season; NHL approved move on June 25, 1997.

Season Team	League	REGULAR SEASON								PLAYOFFS				
		Gms.	G	A	Pts.	PIM	+/-	PP	SH	Gms.	G	A	Pts.	PIM
91-92—Portland	WHL	22	2	9	11	13	...			6	1	3	4	12
92-93—Portland	WHL	70	4	19	23	97	...			16	2	7	9	31
93-94—Portland	WHL	72	4	32	36	105	...			10	1	2	3	14
94-95—Portland	WHL	72	6	37	43	196	...			9	1	6	7	10
95-96—Richmond	ECHL	4	1	0	1	2	...			—				
—Springfield	AHL	62	2	6	8	72	...			2	0	0	0	0
96-97—Hartford	NHL	9	0	2	2	6	0	0	0	—				
—Springfield	AHL	66	1	18	19	127	...			17	0	3	3	18
97-98—New Haven	AHL	54	3	15	18	135	...			—				
—Carolina	NHL	23	0	2	2	44	-2	0	0	—				
NHL Totals (2 years)		32	0	4	4	50	-2	0	0					

PRIMEAU, KEITH C HURRICANES

PERSONAL: Born November 24, 1971, in Toronto. ... 6-5/220. ... Shoots left. ... Brother of Wayne Primeau, center, Buffalo Sabres. ... Name pronounced PREE-moh.

TRANSACTIONS/CAREER NOTES: Selected by Detroit Red Wings in first round (first Red Wings pick, third overall) of NHL entry draft (June 16, 1990). ... Suffered from the flu (January 13, 1993); missed two games. ... Sprained right shoulder (February 9, 1993); missed one game. ... Sprained right knee (March 2, 1993); missed two games. ... Sprained right knee (April 1, 1993); missed four games. ... Injured right thumb (February 10, 1995); missed one game. ... Suffered from the flu (February 25, 1995); missed one game. ... Reinjured thumb (March 2, 1995); missed one game. ... Injured ribs (November 1, 1995); missed eight games. ... Injured left knee (January 13, 1996); missed one game. ... Traded by Red Wings with D Paul Coffey and first-round pick (traded to San Jose) in 1997 draft to Hartford Whalers for LW Brendan Shanahan and D Brian Glynn (October 9, 1996). ... Suffered from the flu (December 3, 1996); missed one game. ... Suffered concussion (December 21, 1996); missed one game. ... Suspended two games by NHL for slashing incident (January 3, 1997). ... Suffered from asthma (February 12, 1997); missed one game. ... Whalers franchise moved to North Carolina and renamed Carolina Hurricanes for 1997-98 season; NHL approved move on June 25, 1997. ... Strained hip flexor (November 13, 1997); missed one game.

HONORS: Won Eddie Powers Memorial Trophy (1989-90). ... Named to OHL All-Star second team (1989-90).

Season Team	League	REGULAR SEASON								PLAYOFFS				
		Gms.	G	A	Pts.	PIM	+/-	PP	SH	Gms.	G	A	Pts.	PIM
87-88—Hamilton	OHL	47	6	6	12	69	...			11	0	2	2	2
88-89—Niagara Falls	OHL	48	20	35	55	56	...			17	9	6	15	12
89-90—Niagara Falls	OHL	65	*57	70	*127	97	...			16	*16	17	*33	49
90-91—Detroit	NHL	58	3	12	15	106	-12	0	0	5	1	1	2	25
—Adirondack	AHL	6	3	5	8	8	...							

P

Season Team	League	REGULAR SEASON								PLAYOFFS				
		Gms.	G	A	Pts.	PIM	+/-	PP	SH	Gms.	G	A	Pts.	PIM
91-92—Detroit	NHL	35	6	10	16	83	9	0	0	11	0	0	0	14
—Adirondack	AHL	42	21	24	45	89	...	...	...	9	1	7	8	27
92-93—Detroit	NHL	73	15	17	32	152	-6	4	1	7	0	2	2	26
93-94—Detroit	NHL	78	31	42	73	173	34	7	3	7	0	2	2	6
94-95—Detroit	NHL	45	15	27	42	99	17	1	0	17	4	5	9	45
95-96—Detroit	NHL	74	27	25	52	168	19	6	2	17	1	4	5	28
96-97—Hartford	NHL	75	26	25	51	161	-3	6	3	—	—	—	—	—
97-98—Carolina	NHL	81	26	37	63	110	19	7	3	—	—	—	—	—
—Can. Olympic Team	Int'l	6	2	1	3	4	...	...	...	—	—	—	—	—
NHL Totals (8 years)		519	149	195	344	1052	77	31	12	64	6	14	20	144

PRIMEAU, WAYNE   C   SABRES

PERSONAL: Born June 4, 1976, in Scarborough, Ont. ... 6-3/220. ... Shoots left. ... Brother of Keith Primeau, center, Carolina Hurricanes. ... Name pronounced PREE-moh.

HIGH SCHOOL: St. Mary's (Owen Sound, Ont.).

TRANSACTIONS/CAREER NOTES: Selected by Buffalo Sabres in first round (first Sabres pick, 17th overall) of NHL entry draft (June 28, 1994).

Season Team	League	REGULAR SEASON								PLAYOFFS				
		Gms.	G	A	Pts.	PIM	+/-	PP	SH	Gms.	G	A	Pts.	PIM
92-93—Owen Sound	OHL	66	10	27	37	110	...	...	...	8	1	4	5	0
93-94—Owen Sound	OHL	65	25	50	75	75	...	...	...	9	1	6	7	8
94-95—Owen Sound	OHL	66	34	62	96	84	...	...	...	10	4	9	13	15
—Buffalo	NHL	1	1	0	1	0	-2	0	0	—	—	—	—	—
95-96—Buffalo	NHL	2	0	0	0	0	0	0	0	—	—	—	—	—
—Owen Sound	OHL	28	15	29	44	52	...	...	...	—	—	—	—	—
—Oshawa	OHL	24	12	13	25	33	...	...	...	3	2	3	5	2
—Rochester	AHL	8	2	3	5	6	...	...	...	17	3	1	4	11
96-97—Rochester	AHL	24	9	5	14	27	...	...	...	1	0	0	0	0
—Buffalo	NHL	45	2	4	6	64	-2	1	0	9	0	0	0	6
97-98—Buffalo	NHL	69	6	6	12	87	9	2	0	14	1	3	4	6
NHL Totals (4 years)		117	9	10	19	151	5	3	0	23	1	3	4	12

PROBERT, BOB   LW   BLACKHAWKS

PERSONAL: Born June 5, 1965, in Windsor, Ont. ... 6-3/225. ... Shoots left. ... Full name: Robert Probert. ... Name pronounced PROH-buhrt.

TRANSACTIONS/CAREER NOTES: Selected by Detroit Red Wings as underage junior in third round (third Red Wings pick, 46th overall) of NHL entry draft (June 8, 1983). ... Entered in-patient alcohol abuse treatment center (July 22, 1986). ... Suspended six games by NHL during the 1987-88 season for game misconduct penalties. ... Suspended without pay by Red Wings for skipping practice and missing team buses, flights and curfews (September 23, 1988). ... Reactivated by Red Wings (November 23, 1988). ... Suspended three games by NHL for hitting another player (December 10, 1988). ... Removed from team after showing up late for a game (January 26, 1989). ... Reactivated by Red Wings (February 15, 1989). ... Charged with smuggling cocaine into the United States (March 2, 1989). ... Expelled from the NHL (March 4, 1989). ... Reinstated by NHL (March 14, 1990). ... Unable to play any games in Canada while appealing deportation order by U.S. Immigration Department during 1990-91 and 1991-92 seasons. ... Fractured left wrist (December 1, 1990); missed 12 games. ... Suspended one game by NHL for game misconduct penalties (February 9, 1993). ... Bruised tailbone (November 20, 1993); missed eight games. ... Suspended four games by NHL for stick-swinging incident (October 16, 1993). ... Suspended two games and fined $500 by NHL for head-butting (April 7, 1994). ... Signed as free agent by Chicago Blackhawks (July 23, 1994). ... Placed on inactive status by NHL for violating substance abuse policies (September 2, 1994). ... Reinstated by NHL and declared eligible for 1995-96 season (April 28, 1995). ... Sprained knee (December 26, 1995); missed three games. ... Suspended one game by NHL for elbowing (February 10, 1996). ... Tore cartilage/sprained medial collateral ligament in right knee and underwent surgery (October 9, 1997); missed 14 games. ... Tore rotator cuff (November 19, 1997); missed 54 games.

HONORS: Played in NHL All-Star Game (1988).

MISCELLANEOUS: Holds Detroit Red Wings all-time record for most penalty minutes (2,090). ... Scored on a penalty shot (vs. Kari Takko, March 5, 1987).

STATISTICAL PLATEAUS: Three-goal games: 1987-88 (1).

Season Team	League	REGULAR SEASON								PLAYOFFS				
		Gms.	G	A	Pts.	PIM	+/-	PP	SH	Gms.	G	A	Pts.	PIM
82-83—Brantford	OHL	51	12	16	28	133	...	...	...	8	2	2	4	23
83-84—Brantford	OHL	65	35	38	73	189	...	...	...	6	0	3	3	16
84-85—Hamilton	OHL	4	0	1	1	21	...	...	...	—	—	—	—	—
—Sault Ste. Marie	OHL	44	20	52	72	172	...	...	...	15	6	11	17	*60
85-86—Adirondack	AHL	32	12	15	27	152	...	...	...	10	2	3	5	68
—Detroit	NHL	44	8	13	21	186	-14	3	0	—	—	—	—	—
86-87—Detroit	NHL	63	13	11	24	221	-6	2	0	16	3	4	7	63
—Adirondack	AHL	7	1	4	5	15	...	...	...	—	—	—	—	—
87-88—Detroit	NHL	74	29	33	62	*398	16	15	0	16	8	13	21	51
88-89—Detroit	NHL	25	4	2	6	106	-11	1	0	—	—	—	—	—
89-90—Detroit	NHL	4	3	0	3	21	0	0	0	—	—	—	—	—
90-91—Detroit	NHL	55	16	23	39	315	-3	4	0	6	1	2	3	50
91-92—Detroit	NHL	63	20	24	44	276	16	8	0	11	1	6	7	28
92-93—Detroit	NHL	80	14	29	43	292	-9	6	0	7	0	3	3	10
93-94—Detroit	NHL	66	7	10	17	275	-1	1	0	7	1	1	2	8
94-95—Chicago	NHL	Did not play.												
95-96—Chicago	NHL	78	19	21	40	237	15	1	0	10	0	2	2	23
96-97—Chicago	NHL	82	9	14	23	326	-3	1	0	6	2	1	3	41
97-98—Chicago	NHL	14	2	1	3	48	-7	2	0	—	—	—	—	—
NHL Totals (13 years)		648	144	181	325	2701	-7	44	0	79	16	32	48	274

P

PROCHAZKA, MARTIN   LW   MAPLE LEAFS

PERSONAL: Born March 3, 1972, in Slany, Czechoslovakia. ... 5-11/180. ... Shoots left. ... Name pronounced pro-HAZ-kuh.
TRANSACTIONS/CAREER NOTES: Selected by Toronto Maple Leafs in seventh round (eighth Maple Leafs pick, 135th overall) of NHL entry draft (June 22, 1991).
MISCELLANEOUS: Mermber of gold-medal-winning Czech Republic Olympic team (1998).

		REGULAR SEASON								PLAYOFFS				
Season Team	League	Gms.	G	A	Pts.	PIM	+/-	PP	SH	Gms.	G	A	Pts.	PIM
89-90—Kladno	Czech.	49	18	12	30	...	...	...	...	—	—	—	—	—
90-91—Kladno	Czech.	50	19	10	29	21	...	...	...	—	—	—	—	—
91-92—Dukla Jihlava	Czech.	44	18	11	29	2	...	...	...	—	—	—	—	—
92-93—Kladno	Czech.	46	26	12	38	38	...	...	...	—	—	—	—	—
93-94—HC Kladno	Czech Rep.	43	24	16	40	...	...	...	...	2	2	0	2	...
94-95—HC Kladno	Czech Rep.	41	25	33	58	...	...	...	...	11	8	4	12	...
95-96—HC Kladno	Czech Rep.	37	15	27	42	...	...	...	...	8	2	4	6	...
96-97—AIK	Sweden	49	16	23	39	38	...	...	...	7	2	3	5	8
97-98—Toronto	NHL	29	2	4	6	8	-1	0	0	—	—	—	—	—
—Czech Rep. Olympic....	Int'l	6	1	1	2	0	...	...	...	—	—	—	—	—
NHL Totals (1 year)		29	2	4	6	8	-1	0	0					

PROKOPEC, MIKE   RW   SENATORS

PERSONAL: Born May 17, 1974, in Toronto. ... 6-2/190. ... Shoots right. ... Name pronounced PROH-koh-pehk.
TRANSACTIONS/CAREER NOTES: Selected by Chicago Blackhawks in seventh round (seventh Blackhawks pick, 161st overall) of NHL entry draft (June 20, 1992). ... Traded by Blackhawks to Ottawa Senators for RW Denis Chaase, D Kevin Bolibruck and sixth-round pick (traded back to Ottawa) in 1998 draft (March 18, 1997).

		REGULAR SEASON								PLAYOFFS				
Season Team	League	Gms.	G	A	Pts.	PIM	+/-	PP	SH	Gms.	G	A	Pts.	PIM
91-92—Cornwall	OHL	59	12	15	27	75	...	...	...	6	0	0	0	0
92-93—Newmarket	OHL	40	6	14	20	70	...	...	...	—	—	—	—	—
—Guelph	OHL	28	10	14	24	27	...	...	...	5	1	0	1	14
93-94—Guelph	OHL	66	52	58	110	93	...	...	...	9	12	4	16	17
94-95—Indianapolis	IHL	70	21	12	33	80	...	...	...	—	—	—	—	—
95-96—Indianapolis	IHL	67	18	22	40	131	...	...	...	5	2	0	2	4
—Chicago	NHL	9	0	0	0	5	-4	0	0	—	—	—	—	—
96-97—Indianapolis	IHL	57	13	18	31	143	...	...	...	—	—	—	—	—
—Chicago	NHL	6	0	0	0	6	-1	0	0	—	—	—	—	—
—Detroit	IHL	3	2	0	2	4	...	...	...	8	2	1	3	14
97-98—Worcester	AHL	62	21	25	46	112	...	...	...	11	1	2	3	10
NHL Totals (2 years)		15	0	0	0	11	-5	0	0					

PRONGER, CHRIS   D   BLUES

PERSONAL: Born October 10, 1974, in Dryden, Ont. ... 6-6/207. ... Shoots left. ... Brother of Sean Pronger, center, Pittsburgh Penguins.
COLLEGE: Trent (Ont.).
TRANSACTIONS/CAREER NOTES: Selected by Hartford Whalers in first round (first Whalers pick, second overall) of NHL entry draft (June 26, 1993). ... Bruised left wrist (March 29, 1994); missed three games. ... Fined $500 by Whalers for involvement in bar brawl (April 1, 1994). ... Injured left shoulder (January 21, 1995); missed five games. ... Traded by Whalers to St. Louis Blues for LW Brendan Shanahan (July 27, 1995). ... Suspended four games by NHL for slashing (November 1, 1995). ... Injured hand (February 15, 1997); missed one game.
HONORS: Named to Can.HL All-Rookie team (1991-92). ... Named to OHL Rookie All-Star team (1991-92). ... Won Can.HL Plus/Minus Award (1992-93). ... Won Can.HL Top Defenseman Award (1992-93). ... Won Max Kaminsky Award (1992-93). ... Named to Can.HL All-Star first team (1992-93). ... Named to OHL All-Star first team (1992-93). ... Named to NHL All-Rookie team (1993-94). ... Named to NHL All-Star second team (1997-98).
MISCELLANEOUS: Captain of St. Louis Blues (1997-98).

		REGULAR SEASON								PLAYOFFS				
Season Team	League	Gms.	G	A	Pts.	PIM	+/-	PP	SH	Gms.	G	A	Pts.	PIM
90-91—Stratford	OPJHL	48	15	37	52	132	...	...	...	—	—	—	—	—
91-92—Peterborough	OHL	63	17	45	62	90	...	...	...	10	1	8	9	28
92-93—Peterborough	OHL	61	15	62	77	108	...	...	...	21	15	25	40	51
93-94—Hartford	NHL	81	5	25	30	113	-3	2	0	—	—	—	—	—
94-95—Hartford	NHL	43	5	9	14	54	-12	3	0	—	—	—	—	—
95-96—St. Louis	NHL	78	7	18	25	110	-18	3	1	13	1	5	6	16
96-97—St. Louis	NHL	79	11	24	35	143	15	4	0	6	1	1	2	22
97-98—St. Louis	NHL	81	9	27	36	180	*47	1	0	10	1	9	10	26
—Can. Olympic Team.....	Int'l	6	0	0	0	4	...	...	...	—	—	—	—	—
NHL Totals (5 years)		362	37	103	140	600	29	13	1	29	3	15	18	64

PRONGER, SEAN   C   PENGUINS

PERSONAL: Born November 30, 1972, in Dryden, Ont. ... 6-2/205. ... Shoots left. ... Full name: Sean James Pronger. ... Brother of Chris Pronger, defenseman, St. Louis Blues.
COLLEGE: Bowling Green State.
TRANSACTIONS/CAREER NOTES: Selected by Vancouver Canucks in third round (third Canucks pick, 51st overall) of NHL entry draft (June 22, 1991). ... Signed as free agent by Mighty Ducks of Anaheim (February 14, 1995). ... Strained abdominal muscle (February 17, 1997); missed two games. ... Traded by Mighty Ducks to Pittsburgh Penguins for rights to G Patrick Lalime (March 24, 1998). ... Fractured foot (April 4, 1998); missed seven games.

P

Season Team	League	REGULAR SEASON								PLAYOFFS				
		Gms.	G	A	Pts.	PIM	+/-	PP	SH	Gms.	G	A	Pts.	PIM
89-90—Thunder Bay Flyers.....	USHL	48	18	34	52	61	...	...	...	—	—	—	—	—
90-91—Bowling Green	CCHA	40	3	7	10	30	...	...	...	—	—	—	—	—
91-92—Bowling Green	CCHA	34	9	7	16	28	...	...	...	—	—	—	—	—
92-93—Bowling Green	CCHA	39	23	23	46	35	...	...	...	—	—	—	—	—
93-94—Bowling Green	CCHA	38	17	17	34	38	...	...	...	—	—	—	—	—
94-95—Knoxville....................	ECHL	34	18	23	41	55	...	...	...	—	—	—	—	—
—Greensboro................	ECHL	2	0	2	2	0	...	...	...	—	—	—	—	—
—San Diego	IHL	8	0	0	0	2	...	...	...	—	—	—	—	—
95-96—Baltimore	AHL	72	16	17	33	61	...	...	...	12	3	7	10	16
—Anaheim...................	NHL	7	0	1	1	6	0	0	0	—	—	—	—	—
96-97—Baltimore	AHL	41	26	17	43	17	...	...	...	—	—	—	—	—
—Anaheim...................	NHL	39	7	7	14	20	6	1	0	9	0	2	2	4
97-98—Anaheim	NHL	62	5	15	20	30	-9	1	0	—	—	—	—	—
—Pittsburgh.................	NHL	5	1	0	1	2	-1	0	0	5	0	0	0	4
NHL Totals (3 years)...........		113	13	23	36	58	-4	2	0	14	0	2	2	8

PROSPAL, VACLAV   C   SENATORS

PERSONAL: Born February 17, 1975, in Ceske Budejovice, Czechoslovakia. ... 6-2/190. ... Shoots left. ... Name pronounced VA-sla PRAHS-puhl.
TRANSACTIONS/CAREER NOTES: Selected by Philadelphia Flyers in third round (second Flyers pick, 71st overall) of NHL entry draft (June 26, 1993). ... Fractured left fibula (January 3, 1998); missed 18 games. ... Traded by Flyers with RW Pat Falloon and second round draft pick (LW Chris Bala) in 1998 draft to Ottawa Senators for RW Alexandre Daigle (January 17, 1998). ... Bruised thumb (April 2, 1998); missed two games. ... Bruised mouth (April 7, 1998); missed four games.
HONORS: Named to AHL All-Star first team (1996-97).

Season Team	League	REGULAR SEASON								PLAYOFFS				
		Gms.	G	A	Pts.	PIM	+/-	PP	SH	Gms.	G	A	Pts.	PIM
91-92—Motor Ceske-Budejo ...	Czech. Jrs.	36	16	16	32	12	...	...	...	—	—	—	—	—
92-93—Motor Ceske-Budejo ...	Czech. Jrs.	36	26	31	57	24	...	...	...	—	—	—	—	—
93-94—Hershey	AHL	55	14	21	35	38	...	...	...	2	0	0	0	2
94-95—Hershey	AHL	69	13	32	45	36	...	...	...	2	1	0	1	4
95-96—Hershey	AHL	68	15	36	51	59	...	...	...	5	2	4	6	2
96-97—Philadelphia	AHL	63	32	63	95	70	...	...	...	—	—	—	—	—
—Philadelphia	NHL	18	5	10	15	4	3	0	0	5	1	3	4	4
97-98—Philadelphia	NHL	41	5	13	18	17	-10	4	0	—	—	—	—	—
—Ottawa	NHL	15	1	6	7	4	-1	0	0	6	0	0	0	0
NHL Totals (2 years)...........		74	11	29	40	25	-8	4	0	11	1	3	4	4

PROTSENKO, BORIS   RW   PENGUINS

PERSONAL: Born August 21, 1978, in Kherson, U.S.S.R. ... 5-11/194. ... Shoots right. ... Name pronounced praht-SEHN-koh.
TRANSACTIONS/CAREER NOTES: Selected by Pittsburgh Penguins in third round (fourth Penguins pick, 77th overall) of NHL entry draft (June 22, 1996).

Season Team	League	REGULAR SEASON								PLAYOFFS				
		Gms.	G	A	Pts.	PIM	+/-	PP	SH	Gms.	G	A	Pts.	PIM
94-95—Fernie........................	Tier II Jr. A	47	27	25	52	199	...	...	...	—	—	—	—	—
95-96—Calgary	WHL	71	46	29	75	68	...	...	...	—	—	—	—	—
96-97—Calgary	WHL	67	35	32	67	136	...	...	...	—	—	—	—	—
97-98—Calgary	WHL	70	40	47	87	124	...	...	...	18	6	8	14	30

PRPIC, JOEL   C   BRUINS

PERSONAL: Born September 25, 1974, in Sudbury, Ont. ... 6-7/225. ... Shoots left. ... Name pronounced PUHR-pihk.
COLLEGE: St. Lawrence (N.Y.).
TRANSACTIONS/CAREER NOTES: Selected by Boston Bruins in ninth round (ninth Bruins pick, 233rd overall) of NHL entry draft (June 26, 1993).

Season Team	League	REGULAR SEASON								PLAYOFFS				
		Gms.	G	A	Pts.	PIM	+/-	PP	SH	Gms.	G	A	Pts.	PIM
92-93—Waterloo Jr. B.............	OHA	45	17	43	60	160	...	...	...	—	—	—	—	—
93-94—St. Lawrence Univ.......	ECAC	31	2	4	6	90	...	...	...	—	—	—	—	—
94-95—St. Lawrence Univ.......	ECAC	32	7	10	17	62	...	...	...	—	—	—	—	—
95-96—St. Lawrence Univ.......	ECAC	32	3	10	13	77	...	...	...	—	—	—	—	—
96-97—St. Lawrence Univ.......	ECAC	34	10	8	18	57	...	...	...	—	—	—	—	—
97-98—Providence.................	AHL	73	17	18	35	53	...	...	...	—	—	—	—	—
—Boston	NHL	1	0	0	0	2	0	0	0	—	—	—	—	—
NHL Totals (1 year).............		1	0	0	0	2	0	0	0					

PUPPA, DAREN   G   LIGHTNING

PERSONAL: Born March 23, 1965, in Kirkland Lake, Ont. ... 6-4/205. ... Catches right. ... Full name: Daren James Puppa. ... Name pronounced POO-puh.
COLLEGE: Rensselaer Polytechnic Institute (N.Y.).
TRANSACTIONS/CAREER NOTES: Selected by Buffalo Sabres in fourth round (sixth Sabres pick, 74th overall) of NHL entry draft (June 8, 1983). ... Injured knee (February 1986). ... Fractured left index finger (October 1987). ... Sprained right wrist (January 14, 1989). ... Broke right arm (January 27, 1989). ... Injured back (November 21, 1990); missed nine games. ... Pulled groin and stomach muscles (February 19,

P

1991). ... Fractured arm (November 12, 1991); missed 16 games. ... Suffered sore knee (January 21, 1993); missed seven games. ... Traded by Sabres with LW Dave Andreychuk and first-round pick (D Kenny Jonsson) in 1993 draft to Toronto Maple Leafs for G Grant Fuhr and fifth-round pick (D Kevin Popp) in 1995 draft (February 2, 1993). ... Selected by Florida Panthers in NHL expansion draft (June 24, 1993). ... Selected by Tampa Bay Lightning in Phase II of NHL expansion draft (June 25, 1993). ... Suffered from tonsillitis (December 11, 1993); missed two games. ... Sprained lower back (February 5, 1994); missed two games. ... Injured hand (April 2, 1995); missed two games. ... Injured right forearm (November 5, 1995); missed one game. ... Injured right knee (November 29, 1995) and underwent surgery (December 8, 1995); missed 12 games. ... Strained groin (January 6, 1996); missed one game. ... Suffered back spasms (February 10, 1996); missed two games. ... Suffered back spasms (February 13, 1996); missed two games. ... Suffered back spasms (February 23, 1996); missed one game. ... Injured back (April 12, 1996); missed one game. ... Injured groin (October 5, 1996); missed nine games. ... Underwent back surgery (November 6, 1996); missed 41 games. ... Suffered sore back (April 5, 1997); missed one game. ... Suffered back spasms (December 27, 1997); missed remainder of season.

HONORS: Named to AHL All-Star first team (1986-87). ... Named to THE SPORTING NEWS All-Star second team (1989-90). ... Named to NHL All-Star second team (1989-90). ... Played in NHL All-Star Game (1990).

MISCELLANEOUS: Holds Tampa Bay Lightning all-time records for most games played by goaltender (188), most wins (71), most shutouts (10) and goals-against average (2.63). ... Stopped penalty shot attempt (vs. Ulf Dahlen, March 17, 1992; vs. Doug Weight, January 3, 1996; vs. Radek Bonk, January 13, 1996). ... Allowed penalty shot goal (vs. Steve Yzerman, January 29, 1992).

Season Team	League	REGULAR SEASON								PLAYOFFS						
		Gms.	Min	W	L	T	GA	SO	Avg.	Gms.	Min.	W	L	GA	SO	Avg.
83-84—R.P.I.	ECAC	32	1816	24	6	0	89	0	2.94	—	—	—	—	—	—	—
84-85—R.P.I.	ECAC	32	1830	31	1	0	78	0	2.56	—	—	—	—	—	—	—
85-86—Buffalo	NHL	7	401	3	4	0	21	1	3.14	—	—	—	—	—	—	—
—Rochester	AHL	20	1092	8	11	0	79	0	4.34	—	—	—	—	—	—	—
86-87—Buffalo	NHL	3	185	0	2	1	13	0	4.22	—	—	—	—	—	—	—
—Rochester	AHL	57	3129	33	14	0	146	1	*2.80	*16	*944	10	6	*48	*1	3.05
87-88—Rochester	AHL	26	1415	14	8	2	65	2	2.76	2	108	0	1	5	0	2.78
—Buffalo	NHL	17	874	8	6	1	61	0	4.19	3	142	1	1	11	0	4.65
88-89—Buffalo	NHL	37	1908	17	10	6	107	1	3.36	—	—	—	—	—	—	—
89-90—Buffalo	NHL	56	3241	31	16	6	156	1	2.89	6	370	2	4	15	0	2.43
90-91—Buffalo	NHL	38	2092	15	11	6	118	2	3.38	2	81	0	1	10	0	7.41
91-92—Buffalo	NHL	33	1757	11	14	4	114	0	3.89	—	—	—	—	—	—	—
—Rochester	AHL	2	119	0	2	0	9	0	4.54	—	—	—	—	—	—	—
92-93—Buffalo	NHL	24	1306	11	5	4	78	0	3.58	—	—	—	—	—	—	—
—Toronto	NHL	8	479	6	2	0	18	2	2.25	1	20	0	0	1	0	3.00
93-94—Tampa Bay	NHL	63	3653	22	33	6	165	4	2.71	—	—	—	—	—	—	—
94-95—Tampa Bay	NHL	36	2013	14	19	2	90	1	2.68	—	—	—	—	—	—	—
95-96—Tampa Bay	NHL	57	3189	29	16	9	131	5	2.46	4	173	1	3	14	0	4.86
96-97—Tampa Bay	NHL	6	325	1	1	2	14	0	2.58	—	—	—	—	—	—	—
—Adirondack	AHL	1	62	1	0	0	3	0	2.90	—	—	—	—	—	—	—
97-98—Tampa Bay	NHL	26	1456	5	14	6	66	0	2.72	—	—	—	—	—	—	—
NHL Totals (13 years)		411	22879	173	153	53	1152	17	3.02	16	786	4	9	51	0	3.89

PUSHOR, JAMIE — D — MIGHTY DUCKS

PERSONAL: Born February 11, 1973, in Lethbridge, Alta. ... 6-3/225. ... Shoots right. ... Full name: James Pushor. ... Name pronounced PUSH-uhr.

TRANSACTIONS/CAREER NOTES: Selected by Detroit Red Wings in second round (second Red Wings pick, 32nd overall) of NHL entry draft (June 22, 1991). ... Strained groin (November 21, 1997); missed three games. ... Traded by Red Wings with fourth-round pick (C Viktor Wallin) in 1998 draft to Mighty Ducks of Anaheim for D Dmitri Mironov (March 24, 1998). ... Fractured right finger (April 15, 1998); missed final two games of season.

MISCELLANEOUS: Member of Stanley Cup championship team (1997).

Season Team	League	REGULAR SEASON							PLAYOFFS				
		Gms.	G	A	Pts.	PIM	+/-	PP	SH	Gms.	G	A	Pts.	PIM
89-90—Lethbridge	WHL	10	0	2	2	2	...	...	...	—	—	—	—	—
90-91—Lethbridge	WHL	71	1	13	14	193	...	...	...	—	—	—	—	—
91-92—Lethbridge	WHL	49	2	15	17	232	...	...	...	5	0	0	0	33
92-93—Lethbridge	WHL	72	6	22	28	200	...	...	...	4	0	1	1	9
93-94—Adirondack	AHL	73	1	17	18	124	...	...	...	12	0	0	0	22
94-95—Adirondack	AHL	58	2	11	13	129	...	...	...	4	0	1	1	0
95-96—Detroit	NHL	5	0	1	1	17	2	0	0	—	—	—	—	—
—Adirondack	AHL	65	2	16	18	126	...	...	...	3	0	0	0	5
96-97—Detroit	NHL	75	4	7	11	129	1	0	0	5	0	1	1	5
97-98—Detroit	NHL	54	2	5	7	71	2	0	0	—	—	—	—	—
—Anaheim	NHL	10	0	2	2	10	1	0	0	—	—	—	—	—
NHL Totals (3 years)		144	6	15	21	227	6	0	0	5	0	1	1	5

QUINT, DERON — D — COYOTES

PERSONAL: Born March 12, 1976, in Dover, N.H. ... 6-1/182. ... Shoots left.
HIGH SCHOOL: Meadowdale (Lynnwood, Wash.).
TRANSACTIONS/CAREER NOTES: Selected by Winnipeg Jets in second round (first Jets pick, 30th overall) of NHL entry draft (June 28, 1994). ... Suffered from the flu (January 29, 1996); missed two games. ... Jets franchise moved to Phoenix and renamed Coyotes for 1996-97 season; NHL approved move on January 18, 1996. ... Separated shoulder (November 27, 1997); missed six games. ... Suffered concussion (January 30, 1998); missed one game. ... Underwent hernia surgery (March 8, 1998); missed 11 games.
HONORS: Won WHL Top Draft Choice Award (1993-94). ... Named to Can.HL All-Rookie team (1993-94). ... Named to WHL (West) All-Star first team (1994-95).

Season Team	League	REGULAR SEASON								PLAYOFFS				
		Gms.	G	A	Pts.	PIM	+/-	PP	SH	Gms.	G	A	Pts.	PIM
90-91—Cardigan Prep School.	USHS (East)	31	67	54	121	...	...	...	...	—	—	—	—	—
91-92—Cardigan Prep School.	USHS (East)	32	111	68	179	...	...	...	...	—	—	—	—	—
92-93—Tabor Academy	Mass. H.S.	28	15	26	41	30	...	...	...	1	0	2	2	0
93-94—Seattle	WHL	63	15	29	44	47	...	...	...	9	4	12	16	8
94-95—Seattle	WHL	65	29	60	89	82	...	...	...	3	1	2	3	6
95-96—Winnipeg	NHL	51	5	13	18	22	-2	2	0	—	—	—	—	—
—Springfield	AHL	11	2	3	5	4	...	...	...	10	2	3	5	6
—Seattle	WHL	—	—	—	—	—	...	...	...	5	4	1	5	6
96-97—Springfield	AHL	43	6	18	24	20	...	...	...	12	2	7	9	4
—Phoenix	NHL	27	3	11	14	4	-4	1	0	7	0	2	2	0
97-98—Phoenix	NHL	32	4	7	11	16	-6	1	0	—	—	—	—	—
—Springfield	AHL	8	1	7	8	10	...	...	...	1	0	0	0	0
NHL Totals (3 years)		110	12	31	43	42	-12	4	0	7	0	2	2	0

QUINTAL, STEPHANE   D   CANADIENS

Q R

PERSONAL: Born October 22, 1968, in Boucherville, Que. ... 6-3/230. ... Shoots right. ... Name pronounced steh-FAN kay-TAHL.

HIGH SCHOOL: Polyvalente de Mortagne (Boucherville, Que.).

TRANSACTIONS/CAREER NOTES: Broke wrist (December 1985). ... Selected by Boston Bruins as underage junior in first round (second Bruins pick, 14th overall) of NHL entry draft (June 13, 1987). ... Broke bone near eye (October 1988). ... Injured knee (January 1989). ... Sprained right knee (October 17, 1989); missed eight games. ... Fractured left ankle (April 9, 1991); missed remainder of playoffs. ... Traded by Bruins with C Craig Janney to St. Louis Blues for C Adam Oates (February 7, 1992). ... Traded by Blues with RW Nelson Emerson to Winnipeg Jets for D Phil Housley (September 24, 1993). ... Sprained wrist (January 16, 1994); missed two games. ... Sprained neck (April 6, 1994); missed one game. ... Sprained ankle (February 6, 1995); missed five games. ... Traded by Jets to Montreal Canadiens for second-round pick (D Jason Doig) in 1995 draft (July 8, 1995). ... Suffered concussion (November 11, 1995); missed one game. ... Sprained right Knee (February 7, 1996); missed seven games. ... Underwent knee surgery (March 19, 1996); missed five games. ... Bruised foot (December 21, 1996); missed two games. ... Injured collarbone (January 1, 1997); missed two games. ... Sprained left knee (February 6, 1997); missed seven games. ... Suffered concussion (November 8, 1997); missed one game. ... Strained hip flexor (February 7, 1998); missed one game. ... Sprained ankle (April 1, 1998); missed nine games.

HONORS: Named to QMJHL All-Star first team (1986-87).

Season Team	League	REGULAR SEASON								PLAYOFFS				
		Gms.	G	A	Pts.	PIM	+/-	PP	SH	Gms.	G	A	Pts.	PIM
85-86—Granby	QMJHL	67	2	17	19	144	...	...	...	—	—	—	—	—
86-87—Granby	QMJHL	67	13	41	54	178	...	...	...	8	0	9	9	10
87-88—Hull	QMJHL	38	13	23	36	138	...	...	...	19	7	12	19	30
88-89—Maine	AHL	16	4	10	14	28	...	...	...	—	—	—	—	—
—Boston	NHL	26	0	1	1	29	-5	0	0	—	—	—	—	—
89-90—Boston	NHL	38	2	2	4	22	-11	0	0	—	—	—	—	—
—Maine	AHL	37	4	16	20	27	...	...	...	—	—	—	—	—
90-91—Maine	AHL	23	1	5	6	30	...	...	...	—	—	—	—	—
—Boston	NHL	45	2	6	8	89	2	1	0	3	0	1	1	7
91-92—Boston	NHL	49	4	10	14	77	-8	0	0	—	—	—	—	—
—St. Louis	NHL	26	0	6	6	32	-3	0	0	4	1	2	3	6
92-93—St. Louis	NHL	75	1	10	11	100	-6	0	1	9	0	0	0	8
93-94—Winnipeg	NHL	81	8	18	26	119	-25	1	1	—	—	—	—	—
94-95—Winnipeg	NHL	43	6	17	23	78	0	3	0	—	—	—	—	—
95-96—Montreal	NHL	68	2	14	16	117	-4	0	1	6	0	1	1	6
96-97—Montreal	NHL	71	7	15	22	100	1	1	0	5	0	1	1	6
97-98—Montreal	NHL	71	6	10	16	97	13	0	0	9	0	2	2	4
NHL Totals (10 years)		593	38	109	147	860	-46	6	3	36	1	7	8	37

RACHUNEK, KAREL   D   SENATORS

PERSONAL: Born August 27, 1979, in Zlin, Czechoslovakia. ... 6-0/183. ... Shoots right.

TRANSACTIONS/CAREER NOTES: Selected by Ottawa Senators in ninth round (eighth Senators pick, 229th overall) of 1997 NHL entry draft.

Season Team	League	REGULAR SEASON								PLAYOFFS				
		Gms.	G	A	Pts.	PIM	+/-	PP	SH	Gms.	G	A	Pts.	PIM
96-97—ZPS Zlin Jrs.	Czech. Jrs.				Statistics unavailable.									
97-98—ZPS Zlin	Czech Rep.	27	1	2	3	16	...	...	...	—	—	—	—	—

RACINE, YVES   D

PERSONAL: Born February 7, 1969, in Matane, Que. ... 6-0/200. ... Shoots left. ... Name pronounced EEV ruh-SEEN.

TRANSACTIONS/CAREER NOTES: Selected by Detroit Red Wings as underage junior in first round (first Red Wings pick, 11th overall) of NHL entry draft (June 13, 1987). ... Injured shoulder (March 22, 1991); missed four games. ... Sprained left shoulder (November 11, 1992); missed four games. ... Traded by Red Wings with fourth-round pick (LW Sebastien Vallee) in 1994 draft to Philadelphia Flyers for D Terry Carkner (October 5, 1993). ... Tore knee ligament (October 16, 1993); missed 15 games. ... Traded by Flyers to Montreal Canadiens for D Kevin Haller (June 29, 1994). ... Suffered from the flu (March 8, 1995); missed one game. ... Separated shoulder (December 2, 1995); missed 11 games. ... Claimed on waivers by San Jose Sharks (January 23, 1996). ... Injured knee (April 4, 1996); missed four games. ... Traded by San Jose Sharks to Calgary Flames for cash (December 17, 1996). ... Signed as free agent by Tampa Bay Lightning (July 16, 1997). ... Injured ankle (January 7, 1998); missed 12 games.

HONORS: Named to QMJHL All-Star first team (1987-88 and 1988-89). ... Won Emile (Butch) Bouchard Trophy (1988-89).

Season Team	League	REGULAR SEASON								PLAYOFFS				
		Gms.	G	A	Pts.	PIM	+/-	PP	SH	Gms.	G	A	Pts.	PIM
86-87—Longueuil	QMJHL	70	7	43	50	50	...	...	...	20	3	11	14	14
87-88—Victoriaville	QMJHL	69	10	84	94	150	...	...	...	5	0	0	0	13
—Adirondack	AHL	—	—	—	—	—	...	...	...	9	4	2	6	2
88-89—Victoriaville	QMJHL	63	23	85	108	95	...	...	...	18	3	*30	*33	41
—Adirondack	AHL	—	—	—	—	—	...	...	...	2	1	1	2	0
89-90—Detroit	NHL	28	4	9	13	23	-3	1	0	—	—	—	—	—
—Adirondack	AHL	46	8	27	35	31	...	...	...	—	—	—	—	—
90-91—Adirondack	AHL	16	3	9	12	10	...	...	...	—	—	—	—	—
—Detroit	NHL	62	7	40	47	33	1	2	0	7	2	0	2	0
91-92—Detroit	NHL	61	2	22	24	94	-6	1	0	11	2	1	3	10
92-93—Detroit	NHL	80	9	31	40	80	10	5	0	7	1	3	4	27
93-94—Philadelphia	NHL	67	9	43	52	48	-11	5	1	—	—	—	—	—
94-95—Montreal	NHL	47	4	7	11	42	-1	2	0	—	—	—	—	—
95-96—Montreal	NHL	25	0	3	3	26	-7	0	0	—	—	—	—	—
—San Jose	NHL	32	1	16	17	28	-3	0	0	—	—	—	—	—
96-97—Kentucky	AHL	4	0	1	1	2	...	...	...	—	—	—	—	—
—Quebec	IHL	6	0	4	4	4	...	...	...	—	—	—	—	—
—Calgary	NHL	46	1	15	16	24	4	1	0	—	—	—	—	—
97-98—Tampa Bay	NHL	60	0	8	8	41	-23	0	0	—	—	—	—	—
NHL Totals (9 years)		508	37	194	231	439	-39	17	1	25	5	4	9	37

RAGNARSSON, MARCUS   D   SHARKS

PERSONAL: Born August 13, 1971, in Ostervala, Sweden. ... 6-1/220. ... Shoots left. ... Name pronounced RAG-nuhr-suhn.
TRANSACTIONS/CAREER NOTES: Selected by San Jose Sharks in fifth round (fifth Sharks pick, 99th overall) of NHL entry draft (June 20, 1992). ... Injured foot (November 8, 1995); missed two games. ... Injured head (December 5, 1995); missed two games. ... Injured knee (January 10, 1996); missed one game. ... Suffered from the flu (January 16, 1996); missed one game. ... Injured hamstring (February 10, 1996); missed four games. ... Injured back (March 22, 1996); missed one game. ... Injured leg (November 1, 1996); missed two games. ... Broke toe (December 9, 1996); missed two games. ... Suspended one game by NHL for high-sticking incident (November 3, 1997).

Season Team	League	REGULAR SEASON								PLAYOFFS				
		Gms.	G	A	Pts.	PIM	+/-	PP	SH	Gms.	G	A	Pts.	PIM
89-90—Djur. Stockholm	Sweden	13	0	2	2	0	...	...	...	1	0	0	0	0
90-91—Djur. Stockholm	Sweden	35	4	1	5	12	...	...	...	7	0	0	0	6
91-92—Djur. Stockholm	Sweden	40	8	5	13	14	...	...	...	—	—	—	—	—
92-93—Djur. Stockholm	Sweden	35	3	3	6	53	...	...	...	6	0	2	2	...
93-94—Djur. Stockholm	Sweden	19	0	4	4	24	...	...	...	—	—	—	—	—
94-95—Djur. Stockholm	Sweden	38	7	9	16	20	...	...	...	3	0	0	0	4
95-96—San Jose	NHL	71	8	31	39	42	-24	4	0	—	—	—	—	—
96-97—San Jose	NHL	69	3	14	17	63	-18	2	0	—	—	—	—	—
97-98—San Jose	NHL	79	5	20	25	65	-11	3	0	6	0	0	0	4
—Swedish Oly. team	Int'l	3	0	1	1	0	...	...	...	—	—	—	—	—
NHL Totals (3 years)		219	16	65	81	170	-53	9	0	6	0	0	0	4

RAJAMAKI, TOMMI   D   MAPLE LEAFS

PERSONAL: Born February 29, 1976, in Pori, Finland. ... 6-2/180. ... Shoots left.
TRANSACTIONS/CAREER NOTES: Selected by Toronto Maple Leafs in seventh round (sixth Leafs pick, 178th overall) of NHL entry draft (June 29, 1994).

Season Team	League	REGULAR SEASON								PLAYOFFS				
		Gms.	G	A	Pts.	PIM	+/-	PP	SH	Gms.	G	A	Pts.	PIM
93-94—Assat Pori	Finland					Statistics unavailable.								
94-95—Assat Jrs.	Finland	29	11	17	28	30	...	...	...	—	—	—	—	—
—Assat Pori	Finland	12	4	1	5	8	...	...	...	7	0	1	1	2
95-96—Assat Pori	Finland	45	5	2	7	26	...	...	...	3	0	0	0	6
96-97—Assat Pori	Finland	46	0	1	1	16	...	...	...	4	0	0	0	2
97-98—TPS Turku	Finland	46	1	1	2	24	...	...	...	4	0	0	0	0

RAMSAY, BRUCE   LW   BLUES

PERSONAL: Born May 13, 1969, in Dryden, Ont. ... 6-1/189. ... Shoots left.
TRANSACTIONS/CAREER NOTES: Signed as free agent by St. Louis Blues (August 12, 1997).

Season Team	League	REGULAR SEASON								PLAYOFFS				
		Gms.	G	A	Pts.	PIM	+/-	PP	SH	Gms.	G	A	Pts.	PIM
92-93—Thunder Bay	Col.HL	52	3	16	19	234	...	...	...	12	1	2	3	55
93-94—Thunder Bay	Col.HL	63	9	22	31	313	...	...	...	—	—	—	—	—
94-95—Prin. Edward Island	AHL	2	0	1	1	10	...	...	...	8	1	2	3	45
—Thunder Bay	Col.HL	62	14	29	43	462	...	...	...	11	0	3	3	83
95-96—Thunder Bay	Col.HL	56	6	15	21	400	...	...	...	1	0	0	0	2
—Milwaukee	IHL	3	0	0	0	5	...	...	...	18	2	3	5	142
96-97—Thunder Bay	Col.HL	9	6	4	10	71	...	...	...	—	—	—	—	—
—Grand Rapids	IHL	66	3	5	8	306	...	...	...	—	—	—	—	—
97-98—Grand Rapids	IHL	62	5	6	11	310	...	...	...	4	0	0	0	2

PERSONAL: Born December 14, 1966, in Brandon, Man. ... 5-11/185. ... Catches left.
HIGH SCHOOL: New Westminster (B.C.).
TRANSACTIONS/CAREER NOTES: Selected by Boston Bruins as underage junior in third round (second Bruins pick, 52nd overall) of NHL entry draft (June 15, 1985). ... Traded by Bruins with LW Geoff Courtnall and second-round pick (C Petro Koivunen) in 1988 draft to Edmonton Oilers for G Andy Moog (March 1988). ... Sprained ankle (February 14, 1990); missed six games. ... Strained groin (January 4, 1992); missed two games. ... Strained hamstring (January 29, 1992); missed five games. ... Strained right quadriceps (November 12, 1992); missed two games. ... Strained left hamstring (April 7, 1993); missed two games. ... Bruised hand (March 23, 1993); missed one game. ... Strained hamstring (April 5, 1994); missed three games. ... Suffered back spasms (April 29, 1995); missed three games. ... Sprained ankle (January 3, 1996); missed two games. ... Traded by Oilers to Boston Bruins for D Sean Brown, RW Mariusz Czerkawski and first-round pick (D Matthieu Descoteaux) in 1996 draft (January 11, 1996). ... Suffered tendinitis in shoulder (December 29, 1996); missed 20 games. ... Traded by Bruins with C Adam Oates and RW Rick Tocchet to Washington Capitals for G Jim Carey, C Jason Allison, C Anson Carter and third-round pick (RW Lee Goren) in 1997 draft (March 1, 1997). ... Injured groin (October 1, 1997); missed three games. ... Injured back (October 9, 1997); missed six games. ... Injured hamstring (December 27, 1997); missed 10 games. ... Traded by Capitals to Tampa Bay Lightning for third-round pick (C Todd Hornung) in 1998 draft and second-round pick in 1999 draft (June 18, 1998).
HONORS: Named to WHL All-Star second team (1985-86). ... Won Conn Smythe Trophy (1989-90). ... Played in NHL All-Star Game (1991).
RECORDS: Shares NHL single-season playoff record for most wins by a goaltender—13 (1990).
MISCELLANEOUS: Member of Stanley Cup championship team (1988 and 1990). ... Holds Edmonton Oilers all-time record for most games played by a goaltender (433). ... Stopped penalty shot attempt (vs. Claude Loiselle, October 28, 1989; vs. Tom Kurvers, March 10, 1990; vs. Greg Adams, December 1, 1991; vs. Alexander Mogilny, January 10, 1992; vs. Mario Lemieux, March 17, 1992; vs. Dave Gagner, October 28, 1992; vs. C.J. Young, December 27, 1992; vs. Brett Hull, March 26, 1995; vs. Randy Burridge, February 3, 1996). ... Allowed penalty shot goal (vs. Robert Reichel, February 7, 1994).
STATISTICAL NOTES: Tied for NHL lead with 30 regular-season losses (1995-96).

			REGULAR SEASON							PLAYOFFS					
Season Team	League	Gms.	Min	W	L	T	GA	SO	Avg.	Gms.	Min.	W	L	GA	SO	Avg.
83-84—New Westminster.........	WHL	27	1450	10	14	0	130	0	5.38	1	27	0	0	2	0	4.44
84-85—New Westminster.........	WHL	38	2034	19	17	0	142	0	4.19	7	309	2	3	26	0	5.05
85-86—New Westminster.........	WHL	53	2791	17	29	1	225	1	4.84	—	—	—	—	—	—	—
—Boston	NHL	4	240	3	1	0	10	0	2.50	2	120	0	2	7	0	3.50
86-87—Moncton.....................	AHL	3	180	3	0	0	6	0	2.00	—	—	—	—	—	—	—
—Boston	NHL	41	2234	16	20	2	124	3	3.33	2	123	0	2	8	0	3.90
87-88—Maine	AHL	51	2856	27	16	6	165	1	3.47	—	—	—	—	—	—	—
—Edmonton	NHL	6	325	3	0	2	16	0	2.95	—	—	—	—	—	—	—
88-89—Edmonton	NHL	29	1509	15	8	2	88	1	3.50	—	—	—	—	—	—	—
89-90—Edmonton	NHL	56	3107	24	16	9	165	1	3.19	*22	*1401	*16	6	*59	1	2.53
90-91—Edmonton	NHL	60	3415	27	27	3	182	0	3.20	3	135	1	2	8	0	3.56
91-92—Edmonton	NHL	67	3822	27	26	10	228	1	3.58	16	909	8	*8	51	†2	3.37
92-93—Edmonton	NHL	67	3753	17	38	6	240	1	3.84	—	—	—	—	—	—	—
93-94—Edmonton	NHL	71	4070	22	34	11	236	1	3.48	—	—	—	—	—	—	—
94-95—Edmonton	NHL	40	2203	15	20	3	133	2	3.62	—	—	—	—	—	—	—
95-96—Edmonton	NHL	37	2015	13	†18	5	128	1	3.81	—	—	—	—	—	—	—
—Boston	NHL	40	2307	21	†12	4	109	1	2.83	4	239	1	3	16	0	4.02
96-97—Boston	NHL	37	2147	12	16	8	125	2	3.49	—	—	—	—	—	—	—
—Washington	NHL	18	1010	8	7	2	46	0	2.73	—	—	—	—	—	—	—
97-98—Washington	NHL	22	1183	7	12	2	55	0	2.79	—	—	—	—	—	—	—
NHL Totals (13 years)...........		595	33340	230	255	69	1885	14	3.39	49	2927	26	23	149	3	3.05

PERSONAL: Born January 25, 1966, in St. Louis. ... 6-1/210. ... Shoots right. ... Full name: Paul Stephen Ranheim. ... Name pronounced RAN-highm.
HIGH SCHOOL: Edina (Minn.).
COLLEGE: Wisconsin.
TRANSACTIONS/CAREER NOTES: Selected by Calgary Flames in second round (third Flames pick, 38th overall) of NHL entry draft (June 8, 1983). ... Broke right ankle (December 11, 1990); missed 41 games. ... Traded by Flames with D Gary Suter and C Ted Drury to Hartford Whalers for C Michael Nylander, D Zarley Zalapski and D James Patrick (March 10, 1994). ... Suffered finger infection on left hand (November 28, 1995); missed six games. ... Suffered abdominal strain (October 27, 1996); missed five games. ... Suffered sore groin (November 11, 1996); missed one game. ... Whalers franchise moved to North Carolina and renamed Carolina Hurricanes for 1997-98 season; NHL approved move on June 25, 1997.
HONORS: Named to WCHA All-Star second team (1986-87). ... Named to NCAA All-America West first team (1987-88). ... Named to WCHA All-Star first team (1987-88). ... Won Garry F. Longman Memorial Trophy (1988-89). ... Won Ken McKenzie Trophy (1988-89). ... Named to IHL All-Star second team (1988-89).
MISCELLANEOUS: Scored on a penalty shot (vs. Bob Essensa, October 31, 1993).
STATISTICAL PLATEAUS: Three-goal games: 1991-92 (1).

			REGULAR SEASON							PLAYOFFS				
Season Team	League	Gms.	G	A	Pts.	PIM	+/-	PP	SH	Gms.	G	A	Pts.	PIM
82-83—Edina High School	Minn. H.S.	26	12	25	37	4	...	...	...	—	—	—	—	—
83-84—Edina High School	Minn. H.S.	26	16	24	40	6	...	...	...	—	—	—	—	—
84-85—Univ. of Wisconsin......	WCHA	42	11	11	22	40	...	...	...	—	—	—	—	—
85-86—Univ. of Wisconsin......	WCHA	33	17	17	34	34	...	...	...	—	—	—	—	—
86-87—Univ. of Wisconsin......	WCHA	42	24	35	59	54	...	...	...	—	—	—	—	—
87-88—Univ. of Wisconsin......	WCHA	44	36	26	62	63	...	...	...	—	—	—	—	—
88-89—Calgary	NHL	5	0	0	0	0	-3	0	0	—	—	—	—	—
—Salt Lake City.............	IHL	75	*68	29	97	16	...	...	...	14	5	5	10	8
89-90—Calgary	NHL	80	26	28	54	23	27	1	3	6	1	3	4	2
90-91—Calgary	NHL	39	14	16	30	4	20	2	0	7	2	2	4	0
91-92—Calgary	NHL	80	23	20	43	32	16	1	3	—	—	—	—	—

		REGULAR SEASON								PLAYOFFS				
Season Team	League	Gms.	G	A	Pts.	PIM	+/-	PP	SH	Gms.	G	A	Pts.	PIM
92-93—Calgary	NHL	83	21	22	43	26	-4	3	4	6	0	1	1	0
93-94—Calgary	NHL	67	10	14	24	20	-7	0	2	—	—	—	—	—
—Hartford	NHL	15	0	3	3	2	-11	0	0	—	—	—	—	—
94-95—Hartford	NHL	47	6	14	20	10	-3	0	0	—	—	—	—	—
95-96—Hartford	NHL	73	10	20	30	14	-2	0	1	—	—	—	—	—
96-97—Hartford	NHL	67	10	11	21	18	-13	0	3	—	—	—	—	—
97-98—Carolina	NHL	73	5	9	14	28	-11	0	1	—	—	—	—	—
NHL Totals (10 years)		629	125	157	282	177	9	7	17	19	3	6	9	2

RASMUSSEN, ERIK — C — SABRES

PERSONAL: Born February 28, 1977, in Minneapolis. ... 6-2/205. ... Shoots left. ... Name pronounced RAS-muh-suhn.
HIGH SCHOOL: Saint Louis (Minn.) Park.
COLLEGE: Minnesota.
TRANSACTIONS/CAREER NOTES: Selected by Buffalo Sabres in first round (first Sabres pick, seventh overall) of NHL entry draft (June 22, 1996). ... Injured shoulder (October 26, 1997); missed one game.
HONORS: Named to WCHA All-Rookie team (1995-96).

		REGULAR SEASON								PLAYOFFS				
Season Team	League	Gms.	G	A	Pts.	PIM	+/-	PP	SH	Gms.	G	A	Pts.	PIM
92-93—Saint Louis Park	Minn. H.S.	23	16	24	40	50	...	...	...	—	—	—	—	—
93-94—Saint Louis Park	Minn. H.S.	18	25	18	43	60	...	...	...	—	—	—	—	—
94-95—Saint Louis Park	Minn. H.S.	23	19	33	52	80	...	...	...	—	—	—	—	—
95-96—Univ. of Minnesota	WCHA	40	16	32	48	55	...	...	...	—	—	—	—	—
96-97—Univ. of Minnesota	WCHA	34	15	12	27	123	...	...	...	—	—	—	—	—
97-98—Buffalo	NHL	21	2	3	5	14	2	0	0	—	—	—	—	—
—Rochester	AHL	53	9	14	23	83				1	0	0	0	5
NHL Totals (1 year)		21	2	3	5	14	2	0	0					

RATHJE, MIKE — D — SHARKS

PERSONAL: Born May 11, 1974, in Manville, Alta. ... 6-5/230. ... Shoots left. ... Full name: Michael Rathje. ... Name pronounced RATH-jee.
HIGH SCHOOL: Medicine Hat (Alta.).
TRANSACTIONS/CAREER NOTES: Selected by San Jose Sharks in first round (first Sharks pick, third overall) of NHL entry draft (June 20, 1992). ... Strained abdomen (February 19, 1994); missed three games. ... Sprained knee (February 26, 1994); missed four games. ... Sprained knee (February 2, 1995); missed three games. ... Injured foot (February 15, 1995); missed one game. ... Injured hip flexor (April 25, 1995); missed two games. ... Strained abdomen (October 6, 1995); missed first two games of season. ... Injured shoulder (November 14, 1995); missed 12 games. ... Strained groin (November 8, 1996); missed 50 games.
HONORS: Named to Can.HL All-Star second team (1992-93). ... Named to WHL (East) All-Star second team (1991-92 and 1992-93).

		REGULAR SEASON								PLAYOFFS				
Season Team	League	Gms.	G	A	Pts.	PIM	+/-	PP	SH	Gms.	G	A	Pts.	PIM
90-91—Medicine Hat	WHL	64	1	16	17	28	...	...	...	12	0	4	4	2
91-92—Medicine Hat	WHL	67	11	23	34	109	...	...	...	4	0	1	1	2
92-93—Medicine Hat	WHL	57	12	37	49	103	...	...	...	10	3	3	6	12
—Kansas City	IHL	—	—	—	—	—	...	...	...	5	0	0	0	12
93-94—San Jose	NHL	47	1	9	10	59	-9	1	0	1	0	0	0	0
—Kansas City	IHL	6	0	2	2	0	...	...	...	—	—	—	—	—
94-95—Kansas City	IHL	6	0	1	1	7	...	...	...	—	—	—	—	—
—San Jose	NHL	42	2	7	9	29	-1	0	0	11	5	2	7	4
95-96—Kansas City	IHL	36	6	11	17	34	...	...	...	—	—	—	—	—
—San Jose	NHL	27	0	7	7	14	-16	0	0	—	—	—	—	—
96-97—San Jose	NHL	31	0	8	8	21	-1	0	0	—	—	—	—	—
97-98—San Jose	NHL	81	3	12	15	59	-4	1	0	6	1	0	1	6
NHL Totals (5 years)		228	6	43	49	182	-31	2	0	18	6	2	8	10

RAY, ROB — RW — SABRES

PERSONAL: Born June 8, 1968, in Belleville, Ont. ... 6-0/203. ... Shoots left.
TRANSACTIONS/CAREER NOTES: Broke jaw (January 1987). ... Selected by Buffalo Sabres in fifth round (fifth Sabres pick, 97th overall) of NHL entry draft (June 11, 1988). ... Tore right knee ligament (April 11, 1993); missed remainder of season. ... Suffered from the flu (March 11, 1995); missed one game. ... Broke right cheekbone (November 27, 1995); missed eight games. ... Fractured thumb (November 22, 1997); missed nineteen games. ... Suspended one playoff game by NHL for verbally abusing officials (April 26, 1998).
MISCELLANEOUS: Holds Buffalo Sabres all-time record for most penalty minutes (2,268).

		REGULAR SEASON								PLAYOFFS				
Season Team	League	Gms.	G	A	Pts.	PIM	+/-	PP	SH	Gms.	G	A	Pts.	PIM
84-85—Whitby Lawmen	OPJHL	35	5	10	15	318	...	...	...	—	—	—	—	—
85-86—Cornwall	OHL	53	6	13	19	253	...	...	...	6	0	0	0	26
86-87—Cornwall	OHL	46	17	20	37	158	...	...	...	5	1	1	2	16
87-88—Cornwall	OHL	61	11	41	52	179	...	...	...	11	2	3	5	33
88-89—Rochester	AHL	74	11	18	29	*446	...	...	...	—	—	—	—	—
89-90—Buffalo	NHL	27	2	1	3	99	-2	0	0	—	—	—	—	—
—Rochester	AHL	43	2	13	15	335	...	...	...	17	1	3	4	*115
90-91—Rochester	AHL	8	1	1	2	15	...	...	...	—	—	—	—	—
—Buffalo	NHL	66	8	8	16	*350	-11	0	0	6	1	1	2	56
91-92—Buffalo	NHL	63	5	3	8	354	-9	0	0	7	0	0	0	2

Season Team	League	Gms.	G	A	Pts.	PIM	+/-	PP	SH	Gms.	G	A	Pts.	PIM
				REGULAR SEASON								PLAYOFFS		
92-93—Buffalo	NHL	68	3	2	5	211	-3	1	0	—	—	—	—	—
93-94—Buffalo	NHL	82	3	4	7	274	2	0	0	7	1	0	1	43
94-95—Buffalo	NHL	47	0	3	3	173	-4	0	0	5	0	0	0	14
95-96—Buffalo	NHL	71	3	6	9	287	-8	0	0	—	—	—	—	—
96-97—Buffalo	NHL	82	7	3	10	286	3	0	0	12	0	1	1	28
97-98—Buffalo	NHL	63	2	4	6	234	2	1	0	10	0	0	0	24
NHL Totals (9 years)		569	33	34	67	2268	-30	2	0	47	2	2	4	167

RAZIN, GENNADY — D — CANADIENS

PERSONAL: Born February 3, 1978, in Kharkov, U.S.S.R. ... 6-3/175. ... Shoots left.
TRANSACTIONS/CAREER NOTES: Selected by Montreal Canadiens in fifth round (sixth Canadiens pick, 122nd overall) of NHL entry draft (June 21, 1997).

Season Team	League	Gms.	G	A	Pts.	PIM	+/-	PP	SH	Gms.	G	A	Pts.	PIM
				REGULAR SEASON								PLAYOFFS		
95-96—St. Albert	AJHL	52	3	16	19	113	...	...	...	18	1	10	11	8
96-97—Kamloops	WHL	63	7	19	26	56	...	...	...	3	0	0	0	4
97-98—Kamloops	WHL	70	2	11	13	64	...	...	...	7	0	0	0	4

READY, RYAN — LW — FLAMES

PERSONAL: Born November 7, 1978, in Peterborough, Ont. ... 6-1/185. ... Shoots left.
TRANSACTIONS/CAREER NOTES: Selected by Calgary Flames in fourth round (eighth Flames pick, 100th overall) of NHL entry draft (June 21, 1997).

Season Team	League	Gms.	G	A	Pts.	PIM	+/-	PP	SH	Gms.	G	A	Pts.	PIM
				REGULAR SEASON								PLAYOFFS		
94-95—Trentway	Jr. A	48	20	33	53	56	...	...	...	—	—	—	—	—
95-96—Belleville	OHL	63	5	13	18	54	...	...	...	10	0	2	2	2
96-97—Belleville	OHL	66	23	24	47	102	...	...	...	6	1	3	4	4
97-98—Belleville	OHL	66	33	39	72	80	...	...	...	10	5	2	7	12

REASONER, MARTY — C — BLUES

PERSONAL: Born February 26, 1977, in Rochester, N.Y. ... 6-1/185. ... Shoots left.
HIGH SCHOOL: Deerfield Academy (Mass.).
COLLEGE: Boston College.
TRANSACTIONS/CAREER NOTES: Selected by St. Louis Blues in first round (first Blues pick, 14th overall) of NHL entry draft (June 22, 1996).
HONORS: Named to Hockey East All-Rookie team (1995-96). ... Named Hockey East Rookie of the Year (1995-96). ... Named to Hockey East All-Star team (1996-97). ... Named to NCAA All-America East first team (1997-98). ... Named to NCAA All-Tournament team (1997-98). ... Named Hockey East Tournament Most Valuable Player (1997-98). ... Named to Hockey East All-Star first team (1997-98).

Season Team	League	Gms.	G	A	Pts.	PIM	+/-	PP	SH	Gms.	G	A	Pts.	PIM
				REGULAR SEASON								PLAYOFFS		
93-94—Deerfield Academy	Mass. H.S.	22	27	24	51	...	...	...	...	—	—	—	—	—
94-95—Deerfield Academy	Mass. H.S.	26	25	32	57	14	...	...	...	—	—	—	—	—
95-96—Boston College	Hockey East	34	16	29	45	32	...	...	...	—	—	—	—	—
96-97—Boston College	Hockey East	35	20	24	44	31	...	...	...	—	—	—	—	—
97-98—Boston College	Hockey East	42	33	40	73	56	...	...	...	—	—	—	—	—

RECCHI, MARK — RW — CANADIENS

PERSONAL: Born February 1, 1968, in Kamloops, B.C. ... 5-10/185. ... Shoots left. ... Name pronounced REH-kee.
TRANSACTIONS/CAREER NOTES: Broke ankle (January 1987). ... Selected by Pittsburgh Penguins in fourth round (fourth Penguins pick, 67th overall) of NHL entry draft (June 11, 1988). ... Injured left shoulder (December 23, 1990). ... Sprained right knee (March 30, 1991). ... Traded by Penguins with D Brian Benning and first-round pick (LW Jason Bowen) in 1992 draft to Philadelphia Flyers for RW Rick Tocchet, D Kjell Samuelsson, G Ken Wregget and third-round pick in 1992 draft (February 19, 1992). ... Traded by Flyers with third-round pick (C Martin Hohenberger) in 1995 draft to Montreal Canadiens for D Eric Desjardins, LW Gilbert Dionne and LW John LeClair (February 9, 1995).
HONORS: Named to WHL (West) All-Star team (1987-88). ... Named to IHL All-Star second team (1988-89). ... Named to NHL All-Star second team (1991-92). ... Played in NHL All-Star Game (1991, 1993, 1994, 1997 and 1998). ... Named All-Star Game Most Valuable Player (1997).
MISCELLANEOUS: Member of Stanley Cup championship team (1991). ... Failed to score on a penalty shot (vs. Don Beaupre, February 6, 1995; vs. Dominik Hasek, March 8, 1995).
STATISTICAL PLATEAUS: Three-goal games: 1991-92 (1), 1996-97 (1), 1997-98 (1). Total: 3.

Season Team	League	Gms.	G	A	Pts.	PIM	+/-	PP	SH	Gms.	G	A	Pts.	PIM
				REGULAR SEASON								PLAYOFFS		
84-85—Langley Eagles	BCJHL	51	26	39	65	39	...	...	...	—	—	—	—	—
85-86—New Westminster	WHL	72	21	40	61	55	...	...	...	—	—	—	—	—
86-87—Kamloops	WHL	40	26	50	76	63	...	...	...	13	3	16	19	17
87-88—Kamloops	WHL	62	61	*93	154	75	...	...	...	17	10	*21	†31	18
88-89—Pittsburgh	NHL	15	1	1	2	0	-2	0	0	—	—	—	—	—
—Muskegon	IHL	63	50	49	99	86	...	...	...	14	7	*14	†21	28
89-90—Muskegon	IHL	4	7	4	11	2	...	...	...	—	—	—	—	—
—Pittsburgh	NHL	74	30	37	67	44	6	6	2	—	—	—	—	—
90-91—Pittsburgh	NHL	78	40	73	113	48	0	12	0	24	10	24	34	33

Season Team	League	REGULAR SEASON								PLAYOFFS				
		Gms.	G	A	Pts.	PIM	+/-	PP	SH	Gms.	G	A	Pts.	PIM
91-92—Pittsburgh	NHL	58	33	37	70	78	-16	16	1	—	—	—	—	—
—Philadelphia	NHL	22	10	17	27	18	-5	4	0	—	—	—	—	—
92-93—Philadelphia	NHL	84	53	70	123	95	1	15	4	—	—	—	—	—
93-94—Philadelphia	NHL	84	40	67	107	46	-2	11	0	—	—	—	—	—
94-95—Philadelphia	NHL	10	2	3	5	12	-6	1	0	—	—	—	—	—
—Montreal	NHL	39	14	29	43	16	-3	8	0	—	—	—	—	—
95-96—Montreal	NHL	82	28	50	78	69	20	11	2	6	3	3	6	0
96-97—Montreal	NHL	82	34	46	80	58	-1	7	2	5	4	2	6	2
97-98—Montreal	NHL	82	32	42	74	51	11	9	1	10	4	8	12	6
—Can. Olympic Team	Int'l	5	0	2	2	0	...	...	...					
NHL Totals (10 years)		710	317	472	789	535	3	100	12	45	21	37	58	41

R

REDDEN, WADE — D — SENATORS

PERSONAL: Born June 12, 1977, in Lloydminster, Sask. ... 6-2/205. ... Shoots left.

HIGH SCHOOL: Crocus Plaines (Brandon, Man.).

TRANSACTIONS/CAREER NOTES: Selected by New York Islanders in first round (first Islanders pick, second overall) of NHL entry draft (July 8, 1995). ... Traded by Islanders with G Damian Rhodes to Ottawa Senators for G Don Beaupre, D Bryan Berard and C Martin Straka (January 23, 1996). ... Bruised left foot (January 29, 1998); missed one game.

HONORS: Won Jim Piggott Memorial Trophy (1993-94). ... Won WHL Top Draft Prospect Award (1994-95). ... Named to Can.HL All-Star second team (1994-95 and 1995-96). ... Named to WHL (East) All-Star second team (1994-95). ... Named to WHL (Central/East) All-Star first team (1995-96). ... Named to Memorial Cup All-Star team (1995-96).

Season Team	League	REGULAR SEASON								PLAYOFFS				
		Gms.	G	A	Pts.	PIM	+/-	PP	SH	Gms.	G	A	Pts.	PIM
92-93—Lloydminster	SJHL	34	4	11	15	64	...	...	...	—	—	—	—	—
93-94—Brandon	WHL	64	4	35	39	98	...	...	...	14	2	4	6	10
94-95—Brandon	WHL	64	14	46	60	83	...	...	...	18	5	10	15	8
95-96—Brandon	WHL	51	9	45	54	55	...	...	...	19	5	10	15	19
96-97—Ottawa	NHL	82	6	24	30	41	1	2	0	7	1	3	4	2
97-98—Ottawa	NHL	80	8	14	22	27	17	3	0	9	0	2	2	2
NHL Totals (2 years)		162	14	38	52	68	18	5	0	16	1	5	6	4

REEKIE, JOE — D — CAPITALS

PERSONAL: Born February 22, 1965, in Victoria, B.C. ... 6-3/220. ... Shoots left. ... Full name: Joseph James Reekie.

TRANSACTIONS/CAREER NOTES: Selected by Hartford Whalers as underage junior in seventh round (eighth Whalers pick, 124th overall) of NHL entry draft (June 8, 1983). ... Selected by Buffalo Sabres in sixth round (sixth Sabres pick, 119th overall) of NHL entry draft (June 15, 1985). ... Injured ankle (March 14, 1987). ... Injured shoulder (October 1987). ... Broke kneecap (November 15, 1987). ... Underwent surgery to left knee (September 1988). ... Traded by Sabres to New York Islanders for sixth-round pick (G Bill Pye) in 1989 draft (June 17, 1989). ... Sprained right knee (November 1989). ... Broke two bones in left hand and suffered facial cuts in automobile accident and underwent surgery (December 7, 1989). ... Broke left middle finger (March 21, 1990). ... Injured eye (January 12, 1991); missed six games. ... Fractured knuckle on left hand (January 3, 1992); missed 22 games. ... Selected by Tampa Bay Lightning in NHL expansion draft (June 18, 1992). ... Broke left leg (January 16, 1993); missed remainder of season. ... Traded by Lightning to Washington Capitals for D Enrico Ciccone, third-round pick (RW Craig Reichert) in 1994 draft and conditional draft pick (March 21, 1994). ... Bruised foot (April 4, 1996); missed four games. ... Fractured heel (February 14, 1997); missed 17 games. ... Injured back (October 9, 1997); missed four games. ... Strained hip flexor (April 4, 1998); missed five games.

Season Team	League	REGULAR SEASON								PLAYOFFS				
		Gms.	G	A	Pts.	PIM	+/-	PP	SH	Gms.	G	A	Pts.	PIM
81-82—Nepean	COJHL	16	2	5	7	4	...	...	...	—	—	—	—	—
82-83—North Bay	OHL	59	2	9	11	49	...	...	...	8	0	1	1	11
83-84—North Bay	OHL	9	1	0	1	18	...	...	...					
—Cornwall	OHL	53	6	27	33	166	...	...	...	3	0	0	0	4
84-85—Cornwall	OHL	65	19	63	82	134	...	...	...	9	4	13	17	18
85-86—Rochester	AHL	77	3	25	28	178	...	...	...	—	—	—	—	—
—Buffalo	NHL	3	0	0	0	14	-2	0	0	—	—	—	—	—
86-87—Buffalo	NHL	56	1	8	9	82	6	0	0	—	—	—	—	—
—Rochester	AHL	22	0	6	6	52	...	...	...	—	—	—	—	—
87-88—Buffalo	NHL	30	1	4	5	68	-3	0	0	2	0	0	0	4
88-89—Rochester	AHL	21	1	2	3	56	...	...	...	—	—	—	—	—
—Buffalo	NHL	15	1	3	4	26	6	1	0	—	—	—	—	—
89-90—New York Islanders	NHL	31	1	8	9	43	13	0	0	—	—	—	—	—
—Springfield	AHL	15	1	4	5	24	...	...	...	—	—	—	—	—
90-91—Capital District	AHL	2	1	0	1	0	...	...	...	—	—	—	—	—
—New York Islanders	NHL	66	3	16	19	96	17	0	0	—	—	—	—	—
91-92—New York Islanders	NHL	54	4	12	16	85	15	0	0	—	—	—	—	—
—Capital District	AHL	3	2	2	4	2	...	...	...	—	—	—	—	—
92-93—Tampa Bay	NHL	42	2	11	13	69	2	0	0	—	—	—	—	—
93-94—Tampa Bay	NHL	73	1	11	12	127	8	0	0	—	—	—	—	—
—Washington	NHL	12	0	5	5	29	7	0	0	11	2	1	3	29
94-95—Washington	NHL	48	1	6	7	97	10	0	0	7	0	0	0	4
95-96—Washington	NHL	78	3	7	10	149	7	0	0	—	—	—	—	—
96-97—Washington	NHL	65	1	8	9	107	8	0	0	—	—	—	—	—
97-98—Washington	NHL	68	2	8	10	70	15	0	0	21	1	2	3	20
NHL Totals (13 years)		641	21	107	128	1062	109	1	0	41	3	3	6	55

REHNBERG, HENRIK D DEVILS

PERSONAL: Born July 20, 1977, in Grava, Sweden. ... 6-2/194. ... Shoots left.
TRANSACTIONS/CAREER NOTES: Selected by New Jersey Devils in fourth round (sixth Devils pick, 96th overall) of NHL entry draft (July 8, 1995).

		REGULAR SEASON								PLAYOFFS				
Season Team	League	Gms.	G	A	Pts.	PIM	+/-	PP	SH	Gms.	G	A	Pts.	PIM
94-95—Farjestad Jrs.	Sweden	24	1	2	3	...	...	...	...	—	—	—	—	—
95-96—Farjestad Karlstad	Sweden	4	0	0	0	0	...	...	...	—	—	—	—	—
96-97—Farjestad Karlstad	Sweden	42	2	3	5	38	...	...	...	14	1	1	2	16
97-98—Farjestad Karlstad	Sweden	32	0	1	1	24	...	...	...	10	0	0	0	12

REICH, JEREMY C BLACKHAWKS

R

PERSONAL: Born February 11, 1979, in Craik, Sask. ... 6-1/188. ... Shoots left. ... Nephew of Jim Archibald, right winger with Minnesota North Stars (1984-85 through 1986-87). ... Name pronounced REECH.
TRANSACTIONS/CAREER NOTES: Selected by Chicago Blackhawks in second round (third Blackhawks pick, 39th overall) of NHL entry draft (June 21, 1997).

		REGULAR SEASON								PLAYOFFS				
Season Team	League	Gms.	G	A	Pts.	PIM	+/-	PP	SH	Gms.	G	A	Pts.	PIM
94-95—Saskatoon	SJHL	35	13	20	33	81	...	...	...	—	—	—	—	—
95-96—Seattle	WHL	65	11	11	22	88	...	...	...	5	0	1	1	10
96-97—Seattle	WHL	62	19	31	50	134	...	...	...	15	2	5	7	36
97-98—Swift Current	WHL	35	32	31	63	168	...	...	...	12	5	6	11	37

REICHEL, ROBERT C ISLANDERS

PERSONAL: Born June 25, 1971, in Litvinov, Czechoslovakia. ... 5-10/185. ... Shoots right. ... Brother of Martin Reichel, right winger in Edmonton Oilers system. ... Name pronounced RIGH-kuhl.
TRANSACTIONS/CAREER NOTES: Selected by Calgary Flames in fourth round (fifth Flames pick, 70th overall) of NHL entry draft (June 17, 1989). ... Strained right knee (March 16, 1993); missed three games. ... Played in Europe during 1994-95 NHL lockout. ... Traded by Flames to New York Islanders for LW Marty McInnis, G Tyrone Garner and sixth-round pick (D Ilja Demidov) in 1997 draft (March 18, 1997).
HONORS: Named to Czechoslovakian League All-Star team (1989-90).
MISCELLANEOUS: Scored on a penalty shot (vs. Bill Ranford, February 7, 1994; vs. Tom Barrasso, October 24, 1996; vs. Zac Bierk, January 14, 1998). ... Mermber of gold-medal-winning Czech Republic Olympic team (1998).
STATISTICAL PLATEAUS: Three-goal games: 1992-93 (2), 1993-94 (2), 1997-98 (1). Total: 5.

		REGULAR SEASON								PLAYOFFS				
Season Team	League	Gms.	G	A	Pts.	PIM	+/-	PP	SH	Gms.	G	A	Pts.	PIM
88-89—Litvinov	Czech.	...	20	31	51	...	...	...	...	—	—	—	—	—
89-90—Litvinov	Czech.	52	49	34	*83	...	...	...	...	—	—	—	—	—
90-91—Calgary	NHL	66	19	22	41	22	17	3	0	6	1	1	2	0
91-92—Calgary	NHL	77	20	34	54	32	1	8	0	—	—	—	—	—
92-93—Calgary	NHL	80	40	48	88	54	25	12	0	6	2	4	6	2
93-94—Calgary	NHL	84	40	53	93	58	20	14	0	7	0	5	5	0
94-95—Frankfurt	Germany	21	19	24	43	41	...	...	...	—	—	—	—	—
—Calgary	NHL	48	18	17	35	28	-2	5	0	7	2	4	6	4
95-96—Frankfurt	Germany	46	47	54	101	84	...	...	...	3	1	3	4	0
96-97—Calgary	NHL	70	16	27	43	22	-2	6	0	—	—	—	—	—
—New York Islanders	NHL	12	5	14	19	4	7	0	1	—	—	—	—	—
97-98—New York Islanders	NHL	82	25	40	65	32	-11	8	0	—	—	—	—	—
—Czech Rep. Olympic	Int'l	6	3	0	3	0	...	...	...	—	—	—	—	—
NHL Totals (7 years)		519	183	255	438	252	55	56	1	26	5	14	19	6

REID, DAVE LW STARS

PERSONAL: Born May 15, 1964, in Toronto. ... 6-1/217. ... Shoots left. ... Full name: David Reid.
TRANSACTIONS/CAREER NOTES: Selected by Boston Bruins as underage junior in third round (fourth Bruins pick, 60th overall) of NHL entry draft (June 9, 1982). ... Underwent knee surgery (December 1986). ... Separated shoulder (November 1987); missed 10 games. ... Signed as free agent by Toronto Maple Leafs (August 1988). ... Suffered from pneumonia (March 1992); missed 10 games. ... Injured knee (March 25, 1993); missed remainder of season. ... Signed as free agent by Bruins (November 22, 1991). ... Injured hip (April 1995); missed two games. ... Fractured finger (February 1, 1996); missed 16 games. ... Signed as free agent by Dallas Stars (July 3, 1996). ... Strained lower back (January 29, 1998); missed three games. ... Strained lower back (February 7, 1998); missed 13 games.
STATISTICAL PLATEAUS: Three-goal games: 1995-96 (1), 1996-97 (1). Total: 2.

		REGULAR SEASON								PLAYOFFS				
Season Team	League	Gms.	G	A	Pts.	PIM	+/-	PP	SH	Gms.	G	A	Pts.	PIM
81-82—Peterborough	OHL	68	10	32	42	41	...	...	...	9	2	3	5	11
82-83—Peterborough	OHL	70	23	34	57	33	...	...	...	4	3	1	4	0
83-84—Peterborough	OHL	60	33	64	97	12	...	...	...	—	—	—	—	—
—Boston	NHL	8	1	0	1	2	1	0	0	—	—	—	—	—
84-85—Hershey	AHL	43	10	14	24	6	...	...	...	—	—	—	—	—
—Boston	NHL	35	14	13	27	27	-1	2	0	5	1	0	1	0
85-86—Moncton	AHL	26	14	18	32	4	...	...	...	—	—	—	—	—
—Boston	NHL	37	10	10	20	10	2	4	0	—	—	—	—	—
86-87—Boston	NHL	12	3	3	6	0	-1	0	0	2	0	0	0	0
—Moncton	AHL	40	12	22	34	23	...	...	...	5	0	1	1	0
87-88—Maine	AHL	63	21	37	58	40	...	...	...	10	6	7	13	0
—Boston	NHL	3	0	0	0	0	0	0	0	—	—	—	—	—

Season Team	League	REGULAR SEASON								PLAYOFFS				
		Gms.	G	A	Pts.	PIM	+/-	PP	SH	Gms.	G	A	Pts.	PIM
88-89—Toronto	NHL	77	9	21	30	22	12	1	1	—	—	—	—	—
89-90—Toronto	NHL	70	9	19	28	9	-8	0	4	3	0	0	0	0
90-91—Toronto	NHL	69	15	13	28	18	-10	1	*8	—	—	—	—	—
91-92—Maine	AHL	12	1	5	6	4	...	...	...	—	—	—	—	—
—Boston	NHL	43	7	7	14	27	5	2	1	15	2	5	7	4
92-93—Boston	NHL	65	20	16	36	10	12	1	5	—	—	—	—	—
93-94—Boston	NHL	83	6	17	23	25	10	0	2	13	2	1	3	2
94-95—Boston	NHL	38	5	5	10	8	0	0	0	5	0	0	0	0
95-96—Boston	NHL	63	23	21	44	4	14	1	6	5	0	2	2	2
96-97—Dallas	NHL	82	19	20	39	10	12	1	1	7	1	0	1	4
97-98—Dallas	NHL	65	6	12	18	14	-15	3	0	5	0	3	3	2
NHL Totals (15 years)		750	147	177	324	188	41	16	28	60	6	11	17	14

R

RENBERG, MIKAEL   RW   LIGHTNING

PERSONAL: Born May 5, 1972, in Pitea, Sweden. ... 6-2/218. ... Shoots left.
TRANSACTIONS/CAREER NOTES: Selected by Philadelphia Flyers in second round (third Flyers pick, 40th overall) of NHL entry draft (June 16, 1990). ... Played in Europe during 1994-95 NHL lockout. ... Suffered sore shoulder (March 25, 1995); missed one game. ... Strained abdominal muscles (December 30, 1995); missed one game. ... Strained lower abdominal muscles (January 22, 1996); missed 17 games. ... Strained lower abdominal muscles (March 12, 1996); missed one game. ... Strained lower abdominal muscles (March 16, 1996); missed one game. ... Reinjured lower abdominal muscle (March 19, 1996); missed 11 games. ... Underwent abdominal surgery (May 1996). ... Strained groin (March 8, 1997); missed one game. ... Cut face (April 6, 1997); missed remainder of regular season. ... Traded by Flyers with D Karl Dykhuis to Tampa Bay Lightning for C Chris Gratton (August 20, 1997). ... Suffered from the flu (October 15, 1997); missed one game. ... Fractured wrist (December 13, 1997); missed 13 games.
HONORS: Named to NHL All-Rookie team (1993-94).
MISCELLANEOUS: Captain of Tampa Bay Lightning (1997-98).
STATISTICAL PLATEAUS: Three-goal games: 1993-94 (1), 1997-98 (1). Total: 2.

Season Team	League	REGULAR SEASON								PLAYOFFS				
		Gms.	G	A	Pts.	PIM	+/-	PP	SH	Gms.	G	A	Pts.	PIM
88-89—Pitea	Sweden	12	6	3	9	...	...	...	...	—	—	—	—	—
89-90—Pitea	Sweden	29	15	19	34	...	...	...	...	—	—	—	—	—
90-91—Lulea	Sweden	29	11	6	17	12	...	...	...	5	1	1	2	4
91-92—Lulea	Sweden	38	8	15	23	20	...	...	...	2	0	0	0	0
92-93—Lulea	Sweden	39	19	13	32	61	...	...	...	11	4	4	8	...
93-94—Philadelphia	NHL	83	38	44	82	36	8	9	0	—	—	—	—	—
94-95—Lulea	Sweden	10	9	4	13	16	...	...	...	—	—	—	—	—
—Philadelphia	NHL	47	26	31	57	20	20	8	0	15	6	7	13	6
95-96—Philadelphia	NHL	51	23	20	43	45	8	9	0	11	3	6	9	14
96-97—Philadelphia	NHL	77	22	37	59	65	36	1	0	18	5	6	11	4
97-98—Tampa Bay	NHL	68	16	22	38	34	-37	6	3	—	—	—	—	—
—Swedish Oly. team	Int'l	4	1	2	3	4	...	...	...	—	—	—	—	—
NHL Totals (5 years)		326	125	154	279	200	35	33	3	44	14	19	33	24

RENNETTE, TYLER   C   BLUES

PERSONAL: Born April 16, 1979, in North Bay, Ont. ... 6-2/180. ... Shoots right.
TRANSACTIONS/CAREER NOTES: Selected by St. Louis Blues in second round (first Blues pick, 40th overall) of NHL entry draft (June 21, 1997).

Season Team	League	REGULAR SEASON								PLAYOFFS				
		Gms.	G	A	Pts.	PIM	+/-	PP	SH	Gms.	G	A	Pts.	PIM
95-96—Waterloo Jr. B	OHA	45	27	47	74	64	...	...	...	—	—	—	—	—
96-97—North Bay	OHL	63	24	34	58	42	...	...	...	—	—	—	—	—
97-98—North Bay	OHL	31	17	14	31	37	...	...	...	—	—	—	—	—
—Erie	OHL	24	16	17	33	20	...	...	...	6	3	3	6	2

RHEAUME, PASCAL   LW   BLUES

PERSONAL: Born June 21, 1973, in Quebec City. ... 6-1/200. ... Shoots left. ... Name pronounced ray-OHM.
TRANSACTIONS/CAREER NOTES: Signed as free agent by New Jersey Devils (October 1, 1992). ... Claimed by St. Louis Blues from Devils in NHL waiver draft (September 28, 1997).

Season Team	League	REGULAR SEASON								PLAYOFFS				
		Gms.	G	A	Pts.	PIM	+/-	PP	SH	Gms.	G	A	Pts.	PIM
91-92—Trois-Rivieres	QMJHL	65	17	20	37	84	...	...	...	14	5	4	9	23
92-93—Sherbrooke	QMJHL	65	28	34	62	88	...	...	...	14	6	5	11	31
93-94—Albany	AHL	55	17	18	35	43	...	...	...	5	0	1	1	0
94-95—Albany	AHL	78	19	25	44	46	...	...	...	14	3	6	9	19
95-96—Albany	AHL	68	26	42	68	50	...	...	...	4	1	2	3	2
96-97—Albany	AHL	51	22	23	45	40	...	...	...	16	2	8	10	16
—New Jersey	NHL	2	1	0	1	0	1	0	0	—	—	—	—	—
97-98—St. Louis	NHL	48	6	9	15	35	4	1	0	10	1	3	4	8
NHL Totals (2 years)		50	7	9	16	35	5	1	0	10	1	3	4	8

RHODES, DAMIAN   G   SENATORS

PERSONAL: Born May 28, 1969, in St. Paul, Minn. ... 6-0/180. ... Catches left. ... Full name: Damian G. Rhodes.
HIGH SCHOOL: Richfield (Minn.).
COLLEGE: Michigan Tech.
TRANSACTIONS/CAREER NOTES: Selected by Toronto Maple Leafs in sixth round (sixth Maple Leafs pick, 112th overall) of NHL entry draft (June 13, 1987). ... Traded by Maple Leafs with LW Ken Belanger to New York Islanders for LW Kirk Muller (January 23, 1996). ... Traded by Islanders with D Wade Redden to Ottawa Senators for D Bryan Berard and C Martin Straka (January 23, 1996). ... Bruised calf (February 23, 1997); missed 10 games.
MISCELLANEOUS: Stopped a penalty shot attempt (vs. Scott Pearson, November 20, 1993; vs. Geoff Courtnall, March 21, 1995; vs. Martin Straka, April 3, 1996; vs. Todd Marchant, November 13, 1996). ... Holds Ottawa Senators all-time records for most games played by goaltender (136), most wins (33), lowest goals-against average (2.60) and most shutouts (8). ... Allowed a penalty shot goal (vs. Pavel Bure, February 28, 1998; vs. Dixon Ward, April 11, 1998).

				REGULAR SEASON								PLAYOFFS					
Season Team	League	Gms.	Min	W	L	T	GA	SO	Avg.	Gms.	Min.	W	L	GA	SO	Avg.
85-86—Richfield H.S.	Minn. H.S.	16	720	...	...	...	56	0	4.67	—	—	—	—	—	—	—
86-87—Richfield H.S.	Minn. H.S.	19	673	...	...	...	51	1	4.55	—	—	—	—	—	—	—
87-88—Michigan Tech	WCHA	29	1623	16	10	1	114	0	4.21	—	—	—	—	—	—	—
88-89—Michigan Tech	WCHA	37	2216	15	22	0	163	0	4.41	—	—	—	—	—	—	—
89-90—Michigan Tech	WCHA	25	1358	6	17	0	119	0	5.26	—	—	—	—	—	—	—
90-91—Toronto	NHL	1	60	1	0	0	1	0	1.00	—	—	—	—	—	—	—
—Newmarket	AHL	38	2154	8	24	3	144	1	4.01	—	—	—	—	—	—	—
91-92—St. John's	AHL	43	2454	20	16	5	148	1	3.62	6	331	4	1	16	0	2.90
92-93—St. John's	AHL	52	*3074	27	16	8	184	1	3.59	9	538	4	5	37	0	4.13
93-94—Toronto	NHL	22	1213	9	7	3	53	0	2.62	1	0	0	0	0	0	0.00
94-95—Toronto	NHL	13	760	6	6	1	34	0	2.68	—	—	—	—	—	—	—
95-96—Toronto	NHL	11	624	4	5	1	29	0	2.79	—	—	—	—	—	—	—
—Ottawa	NHL	36	2123	10	22	4	98	2	2.77	—	—	—	—	—	—	—
96-97—Ottawa	NHL	50	2934	14	20	*14	133	1	2.72	—	—	—	—	—	—	—
97-98—Ottawa	NHL	50	2743	19	19	7	107	5	2.34	10	590	5	5	21	0	2.14
NHL Totals (6 years)		183	10457	63	79	30	455	8	2.61	11	590	5	5	21	0	2.14

RICCI, MIKE   C   SHARKS

PERSONAL: Born October 27, 1971, in Scarborough, Ont. ... 6-0/190. ... Shoots left. ... Name pronounced REE-chee.
TRANSACTIONS/CAREER NOTES: Separated right shoulder (December 1989). ... Selected by Philadelphia Flyers in first round (first Flyers pick, fourth overall) of NHL entry draft (June 16, 1990). ... Broke right index finger and thumb (October 4, 1990); missed nine games. ... Traded by Flyers with G Ron Hextall, C Peter Forsberg, D Steve Duchesne, D Kerry Huffman, first-round pick (G Jocelyn Thibault) in 1993 draft, cash and future considerations to Quebec Nordiques for C Eric Lindros (June 20, 1992); Flyers sent LW Chris Simon and first-round pick (traded to Toronto) in 1994 draft to Nordiques to complete deal (July 21, 1992). ... Sprained left wrist (November 3, 1992); missed four games. ... Suffered from the flu (January 5, 1993); missed two games. ... Nordiques franchise moved to Colorado and renamed Avalanche for 1995-96 season (July 21, 1995). ... Underwent sinus surgery (October 15, 1995); missed one game. ... Injured ankle (November 5, 1995); missed one game. ... Sprained left ankle (December 11, 1995); missed two games. ... Suffered back spasms (January 4, 1996); missed 16 games. ... Strained shoulder (October 30, 1996); missed 11 games. ... Broke thumb (January 6, 1997); missed four games. ... Underwent shoulder surgery prior to 1997-98 season; missed first 16 games of season. ... Traded by Avalanche with second-round pick (RW Jonathan Cheechoo) in 1998 draft to San Jose Sharks for RW Shean Donovan and first-round pick (C Alex Tanguay) in 1998 draft (November 20, 1997).
HONORS: Named to OHL All-Star second team (1988-89). ... Won Can.HL Player of the Year Award (1989-90). ... Won Red Tilson Trophy (1989-90). ... Won William Hanley Trophy (1989-90). ... Named to OHL All-Star first team (1989-90).
MISCELLANEOUS: Member of Stanley Cup championship team (1996). ... Failed to score on a penalty shot (vs. Chris Terreri, November 17, 1990).
STATISTICAL PLATEAUS: Five-goal games: 1993-94 (1).

				REGULAR SEASON							PLAYOFFS			
Season Team	League	Gms.	G	A	Pts.	PIM	+/-	PP	SH	Gms.	G	A	Pts.	PIM
87-88—Peterborough	OHL	41	24	37	61	20	...	...	...	8	5	5	10	4
88-89—Peterborough	OHL	60	54	52	106	43	...	...	...	17	19	16	35	18
89-90—Peterborough	OHL	60	52	64	116	39	...	...	...	12	5	7	12	26
90-91—Philadelphia	NHL	68	21	20	41	64	-8	9	0	—	—	—	—	—
91-92—Philadelphia	NHL	78	20	36	56	93	-10	11	2	—	—	—	—	—
92-93—Quebec	NHL	77	27	51	78	123	8	12	1	6	0	6	6	8
93-94—Quebec	NHL	83	30	21	51	113	-9	13	3	—	—	—	—	—
94-95—Quebec	NHL	48	15	21	36	40	5	9	0	6	1	3	4	8
95-96—Colorado	NHL	62	6	21	27	52	1	3	0	22	6	11	17	18
96-97—Colorado	NHL	63	13	19	32	59	-3	5	0	17	2	4	6	17
97-98—Colorado	NHL	6	0	4	4	2	0	0	0	—	—	—	—	—
—San Jose	NHL	59	9	14	23	30	-4	5	0	6	1	3	4	6
NHL Totals (8 years)		544	141	207	348	576	-20	67	6	57	10	27	37	57

RICE, STEVE   RW   HURRICANES

PERSONAL: Born May 26, 1971, in Waterloo, Ont. ... 6-0/223. ... Shoots right. ... Full name: Steven Rice.
TRANSACTIONS/CAREER NOTES: Underwent knee surgery (October 1986). ... Selected by New York Rangers in first round (first Rangers pick, 20th overall) of NHL entry draft (June 17, 1989). ... Suffered back spasms (September 14, 1989). ... Injured left shoulder (October 1990). ... Traded by Rangers with C Bernie Nicholls, LW Louie DeBrusk and future considerations to Edmonton Oilers for C Mark Messier and future considerations (October 4, 1991); Rangers later traded D David Shaw to Oilers for D Jeff Beukeboom to complete deal (November 12, 1991). ... Bruised right hip (March 1993); missed two games. ... Fractured hand (February 12, 1994); missed 16 games. ... Signed as free agent by Hartford Whalers (August 18, 1994); D Bryan Marchment awarded to Oilers as compensation (August 30, 1994). ... Injured shoulder (April 4, 1995); missed three games. ... Suffered concussion (April 26, 1995); missed three games. ... Bruised shoulder (December 10, 1995); missed four games. ... Injured shoulder (December 29, 1995); missed 11 games. ... Suffered back spasms (February 8, 1997); missed

two games. ... Whalers franchise moved to North Carolina and renamed Carolina Hurricanes for 1997-98 season; NHL approved move on June 25, 1997. ... Strained neck (November 23, 1997); missed one game. ... Suffered sore back (December 12, 1997); missed one game. ... Suffered sore neck (March 12, 1998); missed four games.

HONORS: Named to Memorial Cup All-Star team (1989-90). ... Named to OHL All-Star second team (1990-91). ... Named to AHL All-Star second team (1992-93).

STATISTICAL PLATEAUS: Three-goal games: 1994-95 (1).

Season Team	League	REGULAR SEASON								PLAYOFFS				
		Gms.	G	A	Pts.	PIM	+/-	PP	SH	Gms.	G	A	Pts.	PIM
87-88—Kitchener	OHL	59	11	14	25	43	...	...	...	4	0	1	1	0
88-89—Kitchener	OHL	64	36	31	67	42	...	...	...	5	2	1	3	8
89-90—Kitchener	OHL	58	39	37	76	102	...	...	...	16	4	8	12	24
90-91—Kitchener	OHL	29	30	30	60	43	...	...	...	6	5	6	11	2
—Binghamton	AHL	8	4	1	5	12	...	...	...	5	2	0	2	2
—New York Rangers	NHL	11	1	1	2	4	2	0	0	2	2	1	3	6
91-92—Edmonton	NHL	3	0	0	0	2	-2	0	0	—	—	—	—	—
—Cape Breton	AHL	45	32	20	52	38	...	...	...	5	4	4	8	10
92-93—Cape Breton	AHL	51	34	28	62	63	...	...	...	14	4	6	10	22
—Edmonton	NHL	28	2	5	7	28	-4	0	0	—	—	—	—	—
93-94—Edmonton	NHL	63	17	15	32	36	-10	6	0	—	—	—	—	—
94-95—Hartford	NHL	40	11	10	21	61	2	4	0	—	—	—	—	—
95-96—Hartford	NHL	59	10	12	22	47	-4	1	0	—	—	—	—	—
96-97—Hartford	NHL	78	21	14	35	59	-11	5	0	—	—	—	—	—
97-98—Carolina	NHL	47	2	4	6	38	-16	0	0	—	—	—	—	—
NHL Totals (8 years)		329	64	61	125	275	-43	16	0	2	2	1	3	6

RICHARDSON, LUKE — D — FLYERS

PERSONAL: Born March 26, 1969, in Ottawa. ... 6-4/210. ... Shoots left. ... Full name: Luke Glen Richardson.

TRANSACTIONS/CAREER NOTES: Selected by Toronto Maple Leafs as underage junior in first round (first Maple Leafs pick, seventh overall) of NHL entry draft (June 13, 1987). ... Traded by Maple Leafs with LW Vincent Damphousse, G Peter Ing, C Scott Thornton and future considerations to Edmonton Oilers for G Grant Fuhr, LW Glenn Anderson and LW Craig Berube (September 19, 1991). ... Strained clavicular joint (February 11, 1992); missed three games. ... Suffered from the flu (March 1993); missed one game. ... Fractured cheekbone (January 7, 1994); missed 15 games. ... Suffered from the flu (February 28, 1995); missed two games. ... Signed as free agent by Philadelphia Flyers (July 14, 1997).

Season Team	League	REGULAR SEASON								PLAYOFFS				
		Gms.	G	A	Pts.	PIM	+/-	PP	SH	Gms.	G	A	Pts.	PIM
84-85—Ottawa Jr. B	ODHA	35	5	26	31	72	...	...	...	—	—	—	—	—
85-86—Peterborough	OHL	63	6	18	24	57	...	...	...	16	2	1	3	50
86-87—Peterborough	OHL	59	13	32	45	70	...	...	...	12	0	5	5	24
87-88—Toronto	NHL	78	4	6	10	90	-25	0	0	2	0	0	0	0
88-89—Toronto	NHL	55	2	7	9	106	-15	0	0	—	—	—	—	—
89-90—Toronto	NHL	67	4	14	18	122	-1	0	0	5	0	0	0	22
90-91—Toronto	NHL	78	1	9	10	238	-28	0	0	—	—	—	—	—
91-92—Edmonton	NHL	75	2	19	21	118	-9	0	0	16	0	5	5	45
92-93—Edmonton	NHL	82	3	10	13	142	-18	0	2	—	—	—	—	—
93-94—Edmonton	NHL	69	2	6	8	131	-13	0	0	—	—	—	—	—
94-95—Edmonton	NHL	46	3	10	13	40	-6	1	1	—	—	—	—	—
95-96—Edmonton	NHL	82	2	9	11	108	-27	0	0	—	—	—	—	—
96-97—Edmonton	NHL	82	1	11	12	91	9	0	0	12	0	2	2	14
97-98—Philadelphia	NHL	81	2	3	5	139	7	2	0	5	0	0	0	0
NHL Totals (11 years)		795	26	104	130	1325	-126	3	3	40	0	7	7	81

RICHER, STEPHANE — RW — LIGHTNING

PERSONAL: Born June 7, 1966, in Buckingham, Que. ... 6-3/226. ... Shoots right. ... Full name: Stephane Joseph Jean Richer. ... Name pronounced REE-shay.

TRANSACTIONS/CAREER NOTES: Selected by Montreal Canadiens as underage junior in second round (third Canadiens pick, 29th overall) of NHL entry draft (June 9, 1984). ... Traded by Granby Bisons with LW Greg Choules to Chicoutimi Sagueneens for C Stephane Roy, RW Marc Bureau, Lee Duhemee, Sylvain Demers and D Rene L'Ecuyer (January 1985). ... Sprained ankle (November 18, 1985); missed 13 games. ... Bruised right hand (March 12, 1988). ... Broke right thumb (April 1988). ... Sprained right thumb (September 1988). ... Suspended 10 games by NHL for slashing (November 16, 1988). ... Suffered from the flu (March 15, 1989). ... Bruised right shoulder (September 1989). ... Bruised left foot (February 1990). ... Injured left ankle (April 21, 1990). ... Injured knee (December 12, 1990). ... Traded by Canadiens with RW Tom Chorske to New Jersey Devils for LW Kirk Muller and G Roland Melanson (September 20, 1991). ... Injured groin (October 22, 1991); missed two games. ... Injured left knee (March 24, 1992); missed three games. ... Injured back (December 6, 1992); missed two games. ... Pulled groin (March 14, 1995); missed two games. ... Reinjured groin (March 22, 1995); missed one game. ... Injured groin (October 17, 1995); missed one game. ... Bruised wrist (December 6, 1995); missed seven games. ... Suffered from the flu (February 11, 1996); missed one game. ... Traded by Devils to Canadiens for D Lyle Odelein (August 22, 1996). ... Suffered back spasms (November 25, 1996); missed six games. ... Bruised foot (January 20, 1997); missed five games. ... Suffered hairline fracture in foot (February 17, 1997); missed four games. ... Suffered back spasms (April 5, 1997); missed four games. ... Suffered lacerated calf (October 15, 1997); missed four games. ... Sprained ankle (November 8, 1997); missed one game. ... Sprained ankle (December 6, 1997); missed 17 games. ... Traded by Canadiens with F Darcy Tucker and D David Wilkie to Tampa Bay Lightning for F Patrick Poulin, F Mick Vukota and D Igor Ulanov (January 15, 1998). ... Reinjured left ankle (April 2, 1998); missed final 10 games of season.

HONORS: Won Michel Bergeron Trophy (1983-84). ... Named to QMJHL All-Star second team (1984-85). ... Played in NHL All-Star Game (1990).

MISCELLANEOUS: Member of Stanley Cup championship team (1986 and 1993).

STATISTICAL NOTES: Led NHL with 11 game-winning goals (1987-88).

STATISTICAL PLATEAUS: Three-goal games: 1987-88 (1), 1989-90 (2), 1990-91 (1), 1991-92 (1), 1992-93 (1), 1995-96 (1). Total: 7. ... Four-goal games: 1985-86 (1), 1987-88 (1). Total: 2. ... Total hat tricks: 9.

Season Team	League	REGULAR SEASON								PLAYOFFS				
		Gms.	G	A	Pts.	PIM	+/-	PP	SH	Gms.	G	A	Pts.	PIM
83-84—Granby	QMJHL	67	39	37	76	58	...	...	...	3	1	1	2	4
84-85—Granby/Chicoutimi	QMJHL	57	61	59	120	71	...	...	...	12	13	13	26	25
—Montreal	NHL	1	0	0	0	0	0	0	0	—	—	—	—	—
—Sherbrooke	AHL	—	—	—	—	—	...	...	...	9	6	3	9	10
85-86—Montreal	NHL	65	21	16	37	50	1	5	0	16	4	1	5	23
86-87—Sherbrooke	AHL	12	10	4	14	11	...	...	...	—	—	—	—	—
—Montreal	NHL	57	20	19	39	80	11	4	0	5	3	2	5	0
87-88—Montreal	NHL	72	50	28	78	72	12	16	0	8	7	5	12	6
88-89—Montreal	NHL	68	25	35	60	61	4	11	0	21	6	5	11	14
89-90—Montreal	NHL	75	51	40	91	46	35	9	0	9	7	3	10	2
90-91—Montreal	NHL	75	31	30	61	53	0	9	0	13	9	5	14	6
91-92—New Jersey	NHL	74	29	35	64	25	-1	5	1	7	1	2	3	0
92-93—New Jersey	NHL	78	38	35	73	44	-1	7	1	5	2	2	4	2
93-94—New Jersey	NHL	80	36	36	72	16	31	7	3	20	7	5	12	6
94-95—New Jersey	NHL	45	23	16	39	10	8	1	2	19	6	15	21	2
95-96—New Jersey	NHL	73	20	12	32	30	-8	3	4	—	—	—	—	—
96-97—Montreal	NHL	63	22	24	46	32	0	2	0	5	0	0	0	0
97-98—Montreal	NHL	14	5	4	9	5	1	2	0	—	—	—	—	—
—Tampa Bay	NHL	26	9	11	20	36	-7	3	0	—	—	—	—	—
NHL Totals (14 years)		866	380	341	721	560	86	84	11	128	52	45	97	61

R

RICHTER, BARRY — D — BRUINS

PERSONAL: Born September 11, 1970, in Madison, Wis. ... 6-2/200. ... Shoots left. ... Full name: Barron Patrick Richter. ... Son of Pat Richter, tight end with Washington Redskins (1963-1970). ... Name pronounced RIHK-tuhr.

HIGH SCHOOL: Culver (Ind.) Military Academy.

COLLEGE: Wisconsin.

TRANSACTIONS/CAREER NOTES: Selected by Hartford Whalers in second round (second Whalers pick, 32nd overall) of NHL entry draft (June 11, 1988). ... Traded by Whalers with RW Steve Larmer, LW Nick Kypreos and sixth-round pick (C Yuri Litvinov) in 1994 draft to New York Rangers for D James Patrick and C Darren Turcotte (November 2, 1993). ... Signed as free agent by Boston Bruins (July 17, 1996). ... Strained groin (November 4, 1996); missed four games.

HONORS: Named to NCAA All-Tournament team (1991-92). ... Named to NCAA All-America West first team (1992-93). ... Named to WCHA All-Star first team (1992-93). ... Named to AHL All-Star first team (1995-96). ... Won Eddie Shore Plaque (1995-96).

Season Team	League	REGULAR SEASON								PLAYOFFS				
		Gms.	G	A	Pts.	PIM	+/-	PP	SH	Gms.	G	A	Pts.	PIM
86-87—Culver Military	Indiana H.S.	35	19	26	45		...	...	...	—	—	—	—	—
87-88—Culver Military	Indiana H.S.	35	24	29	53	18	...	...	...	—	—	—	—	—
88-89—Culver Military	Indiana H.S.	19	21	29	50	16	...	...	...	—	—	—	—	—
89-90—Univ. of Wisconsin	WCHA	42	13	23	36	26	...	...	...	—	—	—	—	—
90-91—Univ. of Wisconsin	WCHA	43	15	20	35	42	...	...	...	—	—	—	—	—
91-92—Univ. of Wisconsin	WCHA	39	10	25	35	62	...	...	...	—	—	—	—	—
92-93—Univ. of Wisconsin	WCHA	42	14	32	46	74	...	...	...	—	—	—	—	—
93-94—U.S. national team	Int'l	56	7	16	23	50	...	...	...	—	—	—	—	—
—U.S. Olympic Team	Int'l	8	0	3	3	4	...	...	...	—	—	—	—	—
—Binghamton	AHL	21	0	9	9	12	...	...	...	—	—	—	—	—
94-95—Binghamton	AHL	73	15	41	56	54	...	...	...	11	4	5	9	12
95-96—Binghamton	AHL	69	20	61	81	64	...	...	...	3	0	3	3	0
—New York Rangers	NHL	4	0	1	1	0	2	0	0	—	—	—	—	—
96-97—Boston	NHL	50	5	13	18	32	-7	1	0	—	—	—	—	—
—Providence	AHL	19	2	6	8	4	...	...	...	10	4	4	8	4
97-98—Providence	AHL	75	16	29	45	47	...	...	...	—	—	—	—	—
NHL Totals (2 years)		54	5	14	19	32	-5	1	0					

RICHTER, MIKE — G — RANGERS

PERSONAL: Born September 22, 1966, in Philadelphia. ... 5-11/185. ... Catches left. ... Full name: Michael Thomas Richter. ... Name pronounced RIHK-tuhr.

HIGH SCHOOL: Northwood School (Lake Placid, N.Y.).

COLLEGE: Wisconsin.

TRANSACTIONS/CAREER NOTES: Selected by New York Rangers in second round (second Rangers pick, 28th overall) of NHL entry draft (June 15, 1985). ... Bruised thigh (January 30, 1992); missed 12 games. ... Injured groin (December 30, 1995); missed 15 games. ... Reinjured groin (February 18, 1996); missed eight games. ... Separated left shoulder (January 19, 1997); missed two games. ... Selected by Nashville Predators in NHL expansion draft (June 26, 1998). ... Signed as free agent by Rangers (July 14, 1998).

HONORS: Won WCHA Rookie of the Year Award (1985-86). ... Named to WCHA All-Star second team (1985-86 and 1986-87). ... Played in NHL All-Star Game (1992 and 1994). ... Named All-Star Game Most Valuable Player (1994).

RECORDS: Shares NHL single-season playoff record for most wins by goaltender—16 (1994).

MISCELLANEOUS: Member of Stanley Cup championship team (1994). ... Stopped a penalty shot attempt (vs. Kevin Dineen, October 19, 1989; vs. Pelle Eklund, January 14, 1990; vs. Troy Murray, November 27, 1991; vs. Steve Konowalchuk, March 5, 1995; vs. Ken Klee, March 12, 1997; vs. Marc Bureau, January 10, 1998). ... Allowed a penalty shot goal (vs. Doug Weight, October 8, 1997).

Season Team	League	REGULAR SEASON								PLAYOFFS						
		Gms.	Min	W	L	T	GA	SO	Avg.	Gms.	Min.	W	L	GA	SO	Avg.
84-85—Northwood School	N.Y. H.S.	24	1374	...	...	...	52	2	2.27	—	—	—	—	—	—	—
85-86—Univ. of Wisconsin	WCHA	24	1394	14	9	0	92	1	3.96	—	—	—	—	—	—	—
86-87—Univ. of Wisconsin	WCHA	36	2136	19	16	1	126	0	3.54	—	—	—	—	—	—	—
87-88—U.S. national team	Int'l	29	1559	17	7	2	86	0	3.31	—	—	—	—	—	—	—
—U.S. Olympic Team	Int'l	4	230	2	2	0	15	0	3.91	—	—	—	—	—	—	—
—Colorado	IHL	22	1298	16	5	‡0	68	1	3.14	10	536	5	3	35	0	3.92

Season Team	League	REGULAR SEASON								PLAYOFFS						
		Gms.	Min	W	L	T	GA	SO	Avg.	Gms.	Min.	W	L	GA	SO	Avg.
88-89—Denver	IHL	*57	3031	23	26	‡0	*217	1	4.30	4	210	0	4	21	0	6.00
—New York Rangers	NHL	—	—	—	—	—	—	—	—	1	58	0	1	4	0	4.14
89-90—New York Rangers	NHL	23	1320	12	5	5	66	0	3.00	6	330	3	2	19	0	3.45
—Flint	IHL	13	782	7	4	‡2	49	0	3.76	—	—	—	—	—	—	—
90-91—New York Rangers	NHL	45	2596	21	13	7	135	0	3.12	6	313	2	4	14	†1	2.68
91-92—New York Rangers	NHL	41	2298	23	12	2	119	3	3.11	7	412	4	2	24	1	3.50
92-93—New York Rangers	NHL	38	2105	13	19	3	134	1	3.82	—	—	—	—	—	—	—
—Binghamton	AHL	5	305	4	0	1	6	0	1.18	—	—	—	—	—	—	—
93-94—New York Rangers	NHL	68	3710	*42	12	6	159	5	2.57	23	1417	*16	7	49	†4	2.07
94-95—New York Rangers	NHL	35	1993	14	17	2	97	2	2.92	7	384	2	5	23	0	3.59
95-96—New York Rangers	NHL	41	2396	24	13	3	107	3	2.68	11	661	5	6	36	0	3.27
96-97—New York Rangers	NHL	61	3598	33	22	6	161	4	2.68	15	939	9	6	33	†3	2.11
97-98—New York Rangers	NHL	72	4143	21	31	*15	†184	0	2.66	—	—	—	—	—	—	—
—U.S. Olympic Team	Int'l	4	237	1	3	0	14	0	3.54	—	—	—	—	—	—	—
NHL Totals (10 years)		424	24159	203	144	49	1162	18	2.89	76	4514	41	33	202	9	2.68

RIESEN, MICHEL — LW — OILERS

PERSONAL: Born April 11, 1979, in Oberbalm, Switzerland. ... 6-2/183. ... Shoots right. ... Name pronounced REE-sihn.
TRANSACTIONS/CAREER NOTES: Selected by Edmonton Oilers in first round (first Oilers pick, 14th overall) of NHL entry draft (June 21, 1997).

Season Team	League	REGULAR SEASON								PLAYOFFS				
		Gms.	G	A	Pts.	PIM	+/-	PP	SH	Gms.	G	A	Pts.	PIM
94-95—Biel-Bienne	Switzerland	12	0	2	2	0	...	...	...	6	2	0	2	0
95-96—Biel-Bienne	Switz. Div. II	34	9	6	15	2	...	...	...	3	1	0	1	0
96-97—Biel-Bienne	Switz. Div. II	38	16	16	32	49	...	...	...	—	—	—	—	—
97-98—Davos HC	Switzerland	32	16	9	25	8	...	...	...	18	5	5	10	4

RITCHIE, BYRON — C — HURRICANES

PERSONAL: Born April 24, 1977, in North Delta, B.C. ... 5-10/188. ... Shoots left.
TRANSACTIONS/CAREER NOTES: Selected by Hartford Whalers in seventh round (sixth Whalers pick, 165th overall) of NHL entry draft (July 8, 1995).
HONORS: Named to WHL (East) All-Star second team (1995-96 and 1996-97). ... Named to Memorial Cup All-Star Team (1996-97).

Season Team	League	REGULAR SEASON								PLAYOFFS				
		Gms.	G	A	Pts.	PIM	+/-	PP	SH	Gms.	G	A	Pts.	PIM
93-94—Lethbridge	WHL	44	4	11	15	44	...	...	...	6	0	0	0	14
94-95—Lethbridge	WHL	58	22	28	50	132	...	...	...	—	—	—	—	—
95-96—Lethbridge	WHL	66	55	51	106	163	...	...	...	4	0	2	2	4
—Springfield	AHL	6	2	1	3	4	...	...	...	8	0	3	3	0
96-97—Lethbridge	WHL	63	50	76	126	115	...	...	...	18	16	12	*28	28
97-98—New Haven	AHL	65	13	18	31	97	...	...	...	—	—	—	—	—

RIVERS, JAMIE — D — BLUES

PERSONAL: Born March 16, 1975, in Ottawa. ... 6-0/200. ... Shoots left. ... Brother of Shawn Rivers, defenseman with Tampa Bay Lightning (1992-93).
HIGH SCHOOL: Lasalle Secondary (Sudbury, Ont.).
TRANSACTIONS/CAREER NOTES: Selected by St. Louis Blues in third round (second Blues pick, 63rd overall) of NHL entry draft (June 26, 1993).
HONORS: Won Max Kaminsky Award (1993-94). ... Named to OHL All-Star first team (1993-94). ... Named to Can.HL All-Star second team (1993-94). ... Named to OHL All-Star second team (1994-95). ... Named to AHL All-Star second team (1996-97).

Season Team	League	REGULAR SEASON								PLAYOFFS				
		Gms.	G	A	Pts.	PIM	+/-	PP	SH	Gms.	G	A	Pts.	PIM
90-91—Ottawa	OHA Jr. A	55	4	30	34	74	...	...	...	—	—	—	—	—
91-92—Sudbury	OHL	55	3	13	16	20	...	...	...	8	0	0	0	0
92-93—Sudbury	OHL	62	12	43	55	20	...	...	...	14	7	19	26	4
93-94—Sudbury	OHL	65	32	*89	121	58	...	...	...	10	1	9	10	14
94-95—Sudbury	OHL	46	9	56	65	30	...	...	...	18	7	26	33	22
95-96—St. Louis	NHL	3	0	0	0	2	-1	0	0	—	—	—	—	—
—Worcester	AHL	75	7	45	52	130	...	...	...	4	0	1	1	4
96-97—Worcester	AHL	63	8	35	43	83	...	...	...	5	1	2	3	14
—St. Louis	NHL	15	2	5	7	6	-4	1	0	—	—	—	—	—
97-98—St. Louis	NHL	59	2	4	6	36	5	1	0	—	—	—	—	—
NHL Totals (3 years)		77	4	9	13	44	0	2	0					

RIVET, CRAIG — D — CANADIENS

PERSONAL: Born September 13, 1974, in North Bay, Ont. ... 6-2/195. ... Shoots right. ... Name pronounced REE-vay.
TRANSACTIONS/CAREER NOTES: Selected by Montreal Canadiens in third round (fourth Canadiens pick, 68th overall) of NHL entry draft (June 20, 1992). ... Separated shoulder (January 20, 1997); missed six games. ... Bruised back (November 1, 1997); missed one game. ... Suffered concussion (December 19, 1997); missed seven games.

Season Team	League	REGULAR SEASON								PLAYOFFS				
		Gms.	G	A	Pts.	PIM	+/-	PP	SH	Gms.	G	A	Pts.	PIM
90-91—Barrie Jr. B	OHA	42	9	17	26	55	...	...	...	—	—	—	—	—
91-92—Kingston	OHL	66	5	21	26	97	...	...	...	—	—	—	—	—

Season Team	League	REGULAR SEASON								PLAYOFFS				
		Gms.	G	A	Pts.	PIM	+/-	PP	SH	Gms.	G	A	Pts.	PIM
92-93—Kingston	OHL	64	19	55	74	117	...	...	...	16	5	7	12	39
93-94—Fredericton	AHL	4	0	2	2	2	...	...	...	—	—	—	—	—
—Kingston	OHL	61	12	52	64	100	...	...	...	6	0	3	3	6
94-95—Fredericton	AHL	78	5	27	32	126	...	...	...	12	0	4	4	17
—Montreal	NHL	5	0	1	1	5	2	0	0	—	—	—	—	—
95-96—Fredericton	AHL	49	5	18	23	189	...	...	...	6	0	0	0	12
—Montreal	NHL	19	1	4	5	54	4	0	0	—	—	—	—	—
96-97—Montreal	NHL	35	0	4	4	54	7	0	0	5	0	1	1	14
—Fredericton	AHL	23	3	12	15	99	...	...	...	—	—	—	—	—
97-98—Montreal	NHL	61	0	2	2	93	-3	0	0	5	0	0	0	2
NHL Totals (4 years)		120	1	11	12	206	10	0	0	10	0	1	1	16

ROBERTS, DAVE　　　　LW　　　　STARS

PERSONAL: Born May 28, 1970, in Alameda, Calif. ... 6-0/185. ... Shoots left. ... Full name: David Lance Roberts. ... Son of Doug Roberts, defenseman for four NHL teams (1965-66 through 1974-75) and New England Whalers of WHA (1975-76 and 1976-77); and nephew of Gord Roberts, defenseman for New England Whalers of WHA (1975-76 through 1978-79) and seven NHL teams (1979-80 through 1994-95).
HIGH SCHOOL: Avon (Conn.) Old Farms School for Boys.
COLLEGE: Michigan.
TRANSACTIONS/CAREER NOTES: Selected by St. Louis Blues in sixth round (fifth Blues pick, 114th overall) of NHL entry draft (June 17, 1989). ... Injured elbow (March 7, 1995); missed one game. ... Suffered illness (April 9, 1995); missed one game. ... Traded by Blues to Edmonton Oilers for future considerations (March 12, 1996). ... Fractured cheekbone (March 19, 1996); missed 10 games. ... Signed as free agent by Vancouver Canucks (July 10, 1996). ... Suffered from the flu (December 11, 1996); missed one game. ... Strained hip flexor and groin (February 8, 1997); missed 12 games. ... Strained hip flexor (March 11, 1997); missed seven games. ... Strained abdomen (October 23, 1997); missed 15 games. ... Signed as free agent by Dallas Stars (July 30, 1998).
HONORS: Named CCHA Rookie of the Year (1989-90). ... Named to CCHA All-Rookie team (1989-90). ... Named to NCAA All-America West second team (1990-91). ... Named to CCHA All-Star second team (1990-91 and 1992-93).

Season Team	League	REGULAR SEASON								PLAYOFFS				
		Gms.	G	A	Pts.	PIM	+/-	PP	SH	Gms.	G	A	Pts.	PIM
87-88—Avon Old Farms H.S.	Conn. H.S.	...	18	39	57	...	...	...	...	—	—	—	—	—
88-89—Avon Old Farms H.S.	Conn. H.S.	...	28	48	76	...	...	...	...	—	—	—	—	—
89-90—Univ. of Michigan	CCHA	42	21	32	53	46	...	...	...	—	—	—	—	—
90-91—Univ. of Michigan	CCHA	43	40	35	75	58	...	...	...	—	—	—	—	—
91-92—Univ. of Michigan	CCHA	44	16	42	58	68	...	...	...	—	—	—	—	—
92-93—Univ. of Michigan	CCHA	40	27	38	65	40	...	...	...	—	—	—	—	—
93-94—U.S. national team	Int'l	49	17	28	45	68	...	...	...	—	—	—	—	—
—U.S. Olympic Team	Int'l	8	1	5	6	4	...	...	...	—	—	—	—	—
—Peoria	IHL	10	4	6	10	4	...	...	...	—	—	—	—	—
—St. Louis	NHL	1	0	0	0	2	0	0	0	3	0	0	0	12
94-95—Peoria	IHL	65	30	38	68	65	...	...	...	—	—	—	—	—
—St. Louis	NHL	19	6	5	11	10	2	3	0	6	0	0	0	4
95-96—Worcester	AHL	22	8	17	25	46	...	...	...	—	—	—	—	—
—St. Louis	NHL	28	1	6	7	12	-7	1	0	—	—	—	—	—
—Edmonton	NHL	6	2	4	6	6	0	0	0	—	—	—	—	—
96-97—Vancouver	NHL	58	10	17	27	51	11	1	1	—	—	—	—	—
97-98—Vancouver	NHL	13	1	1	2	4	-1	0	0	—	—	—	—	—
—Syracuse	AHL	37	17	22	39	44	...	...	...	5	2	1	3	2
NHL Totals (5 years)		125	20	33	53	85	5	5	1	9	0	0	0	16

ROBERTS, GARY　　　　LW　　　　HURRICANES

PERSONAL: Born May 23, 1966, in North York, Ont. ... 6-1/190. ... Shoots left.
TRANSACTIONS/CAREER NOTES: Selected by Calgary Flames as underage junior in first round (first Flames pick, 12th overall) of NHL entry draft (June 9, 1984). ... Injured back (January 1989). ... Suffered whiplash (November 9, 1991); missed one game. ... Suffered from the flu (January 19, 1993); missed one game. ... Suffered left quadricep hematoma (February 16, 1993); missed 25 games. ... Suspended one game by NHL for high-sticking (November 19, 1993). ... Suspended four games and fined $500 by NHL for two slashing incidents and fined $500 for high-sticking (January 7, 1994). ... Fractured thumb (March 20, 1994); missed one game. ... Fractured thumb (April 3, 1994); missed last five games of season. ... Suffered neck and spinal injury (February 4, 1995); underwent surgery and missed last 40 games of 1994-95 season and first 42 games of 1995-96 season. ... Injured neck (April 3, 1996); missed five games. ... Announced retirement (June 17, 1996); did not play during 1996-97 season. ... Traded by Flames with G Trevor Kidd to Carolina Hurricanes for G Jean-Sebastion Giguere and C Andrew Cassels (August 25, 1997). ... Strained abdomen (November 12, 1997); missed six games. ... Strained rib muscle (January 11, 1998); missed 10 games. ... Suffered from the flu (March 31, 1998); missed one game. ... Injured groin (April 13, 1998); missed final three games of season.
HONORS: Named to OHL All-Star second team (1984-85 and 1985-86). ... Played in NHL All-Star Game (1992 and 1993). ... Won Bill Masterton Memorial Trophy (1995-96).
MISCELLANEOUS: Member of Stanley Cup championship team (1989).
STATISTICAL PLATEAUS: Three-goal games: 1989-90 (1), 1991-92 (2), 1992-93 (2), 1993-94 (1), 1995-96 (3), 1997-98 (1). Total: 10. ... Four-goal games: 1993-94 (1). ... Total hat tricks: 11.

Season Team	League	REGULAR SEASON								PLAYOFFS				
		Gms.	G	A	Pts.	PIM	+/-	PP	SH	Gms.	G	A	Pts.	PIM
82-83—Ottawa	OHL	53	12	8	20	83	...	...	...	5	1	0	1	19
83-84—Ottawa	OHL	48	27	30	57	144	...	...	...	13	10	7	17	*62
84-85—Ottawa	OHL	59	44	62	106	186	...	...	...	5	2	8	10	10
—Moncton	AHL	7	4	2	6	7	...	...	...	—	—	—	—	—
85-86—Ottawa	OHL	24	26	25	51	83	...	...	...	—	—	—	—	—
—Guelph	OHL	23	18	15	33	65	...	...	...	20	18	13	31	43
86-87—Moncton	AHL	38	20	18	38	72	...	...	...	—	—	—	—	—
—Calgary	NHL	32	5	10	15	85	6	0	0	2	0	0	0	4

Season Team	League	REGULAR SEASON								PLAYOFFS				
		Gms.	G	A	Pts.	PIM	+/-	PP	SH	Gms.	G	A	Pts.	PIM
87-88—Calgary	NHL	74	13	15	28	282	24	0	0	9	2	3	5	29
88-89—Calgary	NHL	71	22	16	38	250	32	0	1	22	5	7	12	57
89-90—Calgary	NHL	78	39	33	72	222	31	5	0	6	2	5	7	41
90-91—Calgary	NHL	80	22	31	53	252	15	0	0	7	1	3	4	18
91-92—Calgary	NHL	76	53	37	90	207	32	15	0	—	—	—	—	—
92-93—Calgary	NHL	58	38	41	79	172	32	8	3	5	1	6	7	43
93-94—Calgary	NHL	73	41	43	84	145	37	12	3	7	2	6	8	24
94-95—Calgary	NHL	8	2	2	4	43	1	2	0	—	—	—	—	—
95-96—Calgary	NHL	35	22	20	42	78	15	9	0	—	—	—	—	—
96-97—					Did not play.									
97-98—Carolina	NHL	61	20	29	49	103	3	4	0	—	—	—	—	—
NHL Totals (11 years)		646	277	277	554	1839	218	55	7	58	13	30	43	216

R

ROBERTSSON, BERT   D   CANUCKS

PERSONAL: Born June 30, 1974, in Sodertalje, Sweden. ... 6-3/205. ... Shoots left. ... Name pronounced ROH-behrt-suhn.
TRANSACTIONS/CAREER NOTES: Selected by Vancouver Canucks in 10th round (eighth Canucks pick, 254th overall) of NHL entry draft (June 29, 1993).

Season Team	League	REGULAR SEASON								PLAYOFFS				
		Gms.	G	A	Pts.	PIM	+/-	PP	SH	Gms.	G	A	Pts.	PIM
92-93—Sodertalje	Swed. Dv.II	23	1	2	3	24	...	...	...	—	—	—	—	—
93-94—Sodertalje	Swed. Dv.II	28	0	1	1	12	...	...	...	—	—	—	—	—
94-95—Sodertalje	Swed. Dv.II	23	1	2	3	24	...	...	...	—	—	—	—	—
95-96—Syracuse	AHL	65	1	7	8	109	...	...	...	16	0	1	1	26
96-97—Syracuse	AHL	†80	4	9	13	132	...	...	...	3	1	0	1	4
97-98—Syracuse	AHL	42	5	9	14	87	...	...	...	3	0	0	0	6
—Vancouver	NHL	30	2	4	6	24	2	0	0	—	—	—	—	—
NHL Totals (1 year)		30	2	4	6	24	2	0	0					

ROBIDAS, STEPHANE   D   CANADIENS

PERSONAL: Born March 3, 1973, in Sherbrooke, Que. ... 5-11/195. ... Shoots right.
TRANSACTIONS/CAREER NOTES: Selected by Montreal Canadiens in seventh round (seventh Canadiens pick, 164th overall) of NHL entry draft (June 26, 1993).
HONORS: Won Emile Bouchard Trophy (1996-97). ... Named to Can.HL All-Star second team (1996-97). ... Named to QMJHL All-Star first team (1996-97).

Season Team	League	REGULAR SEASON								PLAYOFFS				
		Gms.	G	A	Pts.	PIM	+/-	PP	SH	Gms.	G	A	Pts.	PIM
93-94—Shawinigan	QMJHL	67	3	18	21	33	...	...	...	1	0	0	0	0
94-95—Shawinigan	QMJHL	71	13	56	69	44	...	...	...	15	7	12	19	4
95-96—Shawinigan	QMJHL	67	23	56	79	53	...	...	...	6	1	5	6	10
96-97—Shawinigan	QMJHL	67	24	51	75	59	...	...	...	7	4	6	10	14
97-98—Fredericton	AHL	79	10	21	31	50	...	...	...	4	0	2	2	0

ROBITAILLE, LUC   LW   KINGS

PERSONAL: Born February 17, 1966, in Montreal. ... 6-1/204. ... Shoots left. ... Name pronounced LOOK ROH-bih-tigh.
TRANSACTIONS/CAREER NOTES: Selected by Los Angeles Kings as underage junior in ninth round (ninth Kings pick, 171st overall) of NHL entry draft (June 9, 1984). ... Suspended four games by NHL for crosschecking from behind (November 10, 1990). ... Underwent surgery to repair slight fracture of right ankle (June 15, 1994). ... Traded by Kings to Pittsburgh Penguins for RW Rick Tocchet and second-round pick (RW Pavel Rosa) in 1995 draft (July 29, 1994). ... Suspended by NHL for two games for high-sticking (February 7, 1995). ... Traded by Penguins with D Ulf Samuelsson to New York Rangers for D Sergei Zubov and C Petr Nedved (August 31, 1995). ... Suffered stress fracture in ankle (December 15, 1995); missed five games. ... Fractured foot (March 12, 1997); missed final 13 games of regular season. ... Traded by Rangers to Kings for LW Kevin Stevens (August 28, 1997). ... Injured right groin and abdomen (February 25, 1998) and underwent surgery (March 2, 1998); missed 25 games.
HONORS: Named to QMJHL All-Star second team (1984-85). ... Won Can.HL Player of the Year Award (1985-86). ... Shared Guy Lafleur Trophy with Sylvain Cote (1985-86). ... Named to QMJHL All-Star first team (1985-86). ... Named to Memorial Cup All-Star team (1985-86). ... Won Calder Memorial Trophy (1986-87). ... Named to THE SPORTING NEWS All-Star second team (1986-87 and 1991-92). ... Named to NHL All-Rookie team (1986-87). ... Named to THE SPORTING NEWS All-Star first team (1987-88 through 1990-91 and 1992-93). ... Played in NHL All-Star Game (1988-1993). ... Named to NHL All-Star first team (1987-88 through 1990-91 and 1992-93).
RECORDS: Holds NHL single-season records for most points by a left-winger—125 (1992-93); and most goals by a left-winger—63 (1992-93).
STATISTICAL PLATEAUS: Three-goal games: 1986-87 (1), 1987-88 (3), 1988-89 (1), 1989-90 (2), 1992-93 (2). Total: 9. ... Four-goal games: 1991-92 (1), 1993-94 (1), 1994-95 (1). Total: 3. ... Total hat tricks: 12.
MISCELLANEOUS: Scored on a penalty shot (vs. Eldon Reddick, October 25, 1987; vs. Kay Whitmore, February 6, 1992). ... Failed to score on a penalty shot (vs. Sean Burke, February 2, 1989; vs. Jon Casey, April 3, 1993).

Season Team	League	REGULAR SEASON								PLAYOFFS				
		Gms.	G	A	Pts.	PIM	+/-	PP	SH	Gms.	G	A	Pts.	PIM
83-84—Hull	QMJHL	70	32	53	85	48	...	...	...	—	—	—	—	—
84-85—Hull	QMJHL	64	55	94	149	115	...	...	...	5	4	2	6	27
85-86—Hull	QMJHL	63	68	*123	†191	93	...	...	...	15	17	27	*44	28
86-87—Los Angeles	NHL	79	45	39	84	28	-18	18	0	5	1	4	5	2
87-88—Los Angeles	NHL	80	53	58	111	82	-9	17	0	5	2	5	7	18
88-89—Los Angeles	NHL	78	46	52	98	65	5	10	0	11	2	6	8	10

Season Team	League	REGULAR SEASON Gms.	G	A	Pts.	PIM	+/-	PP	SH	PLAYOFFS Gms.	G	A	Pts.	PIM
89-90—Los Angeles	NHL	80	52	49	101	38	8	20	0	10	5	5	10	10
90-91—Los Angeles	NHL	76	45	46	91	68	28	11	0	12	12	4	16	22
91-92—Los Angeles	NHL	80	44	63	107	95	-4	26	0	6	3	4	7	12
92-93—Los Angeles	NHL	84	63	62	125	100	18	24	2	24	9	13	22	28
93-94—Los Angeles	NHL	83	44	42	86	86	-20	24	0	—	—	—	—	—
94-95—Pittsburgh	NHL	46	23	19	42	37	10	5	0	12	7	4	11	26
95-96—New York Rangers	NHL	77	23	46	69	80	13	11	0	11	1	5	6	8
96-97—New York Rangers	NHL	69	24	24	48	48	16	5	0	15	4	7	11	4
97-98—Los Angeles	NHL	57	16	24	40	66	5	5	0	4	1	2	3	6
NHL Totals (12 years)		889	478	524	1002	793	52	176	2	115	47	59	106	146

ROBITAILLE, MARC   G   MAPLE LEAFS   R

PERSONAL: Born June 7, 1976, in Gloucester, Ont. ... 5-10/185. ... Catches left.
COLLEGE: Northeastern.
TRANSACTIONS/CAREER NOTES: Signed as free agent by Toronto Maple Leafs (June 4, 1998).
HONORS: Named to NCAA All-America East first team (1997-98). ... Named to Hockey East All-Star first team (1997-98).

Season Team	League	REGULAR SEASON Gms.	Min.	W	L	T	GA	SO	Avg.	PLAYOFFS Gms.	Min.	W	L	GA	SO	Avg.
96-97—Northeastern Univ.	Hockey East	34	1928	7	24	3	135	3	4.20	—	—	—	—	—	—	—
97-98—Northeastern Univ.	Hockey East	39	2313	21	15	3	123	1	3.19	—	—	—	—	—	—	—

ROBITAILLE, RANDY   C   BRUINS

PERSONAL: Born October 12, 1975, in Ottawa. ... 5-11/190. ... Shoots left. ... Name pronounced ROH-bih-tigh.
COLLEGE: Miami of Ohio.
TRANSACTIONS/CAREER NOTES: Signed as free agent by Boston Bruins (March 27, 1997). ... Injured shoulder (March 27, 1997); missed final seven games of regular season.
HONORS: Named to CCHA All-Rookie team (1995-96). ... Named to CCHA All-Star first team (1996-97). ... Named to NCAA All-America West first team (1996-97).

Season Team	League	REGULAR SEASON Gms.	G	A	Pts.	PIM	+/-	PP	SH	PLAYOFFS Gms.	G	A	Pts.	PIM
94-95—Ottawa	CJHL	54	48	77	125	111	...	...	...	—	—	—	—	—
95-96—Miami of Ohio	CCHA	36	14	31	45	26	...	...	...	—	—	—	—	—
96-97—Miami of Ohio	CCHA	39	27	34	61	44	...	...	...	—	—	—	—	—
—Boston	NHL	1	0	0	0	0	0	0	0	—	—	—	—	—
97-98—Providence	AHL	48	15	29	44	16	...	...	...	—	—	—	—	—
—Boston	NHL	4	0	0	0	0	-2	0	0	—	—	—	—	—
NHL Totals (2 years)		5	0	0	0	0	-2	0	0					

ROCHE, DAVE   LW   FLAMES

PERSONAL: Born June 13, 1975, in Lindsay, Ont. ... 6-4/224. ... Shoots left. ... Brother of Scott Roche, goaltender in St. Louis Blues system. ... Name pronounced ROHCH.
TRANSACTIONS/CAREER NOTES: Selected by Pittsburgh Penguins in third round (third Penguins pick, 62nd overall) of NHL entry draft (June 26, 1993). ... Sprained ankle (November 21, 1995); missed three games. ... Injured shoulder (April 10, 1996); missed eight games. ... Suspended one playoff game and fined $1,000 by NHL for butt-ending opponent (May 26, 1996). ... Traded by Penguins with G Ken Wregget to Calgary Flames for C German Titov and C Todd Hlushko (June 17, 1998).

Season Team	League	REGULAR SEASON Gms.	G	A	Pts.	PIM	+/-	PP	SH	PLAYOFFS Gms.	G	A	Pts.	PIM
90-91—Peterborough Jr. B	OHA	40	22	17	39	85	...	...	...	—	—	—	—	—
91-92—Peterborough	OHL	62	10	17	27	105	...	...	...	10	0	0	0	34
92-93—Peterborough	OHL	56	40	60	100	105	...	...	...	21	14	15	29	42
93-94—Peterborough	OHL	34	15	22	37	127	...	...	...	—	—	—	—	—
—Windsor	OHL	29	14	20	34	73	...	...	...	4	1	1	2	15
94-95—Windsor	OHL	66	55	59	114	180	...	...	...	10	9	6	15	16
95-96—Pittsburgh	NHL	71	7	7	14	130	-5	0	0	16	2	7	9	26
96-97—Pittsburgh	NHL	61	5	5	10	155	-13	2	0	—	—	—	—	—
—Cleveland	IHL	18	5	5	10	25	...	...	...	13	6	3	9	*87
97-98—Syracuse	AHL	73	12	20	32	307	...	...	...	5	2	0	2	10
NHL Totals (2 years)		132	12	12	24	285	-18	2	0	16	2	7	9	26

ROCHE, SCOTT   G   BLUES

PERSONAL: Born March 19, 1977, in Peterborough, Ont. ... 6-6/234. ... Catches left. ... Brother of Dave Roche, left winger in Calgary Flames system. ... Name pronounced ROHCH.
HIGH SCHOOL: Chippewa (North Bay, Ont.).
TRANSACTIONS/CAREER NOTES: Selected by St. Louis Blues in third round (second Blues pick, 75th overall) of NHL entry draft (July 8, 1995).
HONORS: Shared Dave Pinkney Trophy with Sandy Allan (1993-94). ... Won F.W. (Dinty) Moore Trophy (1993-94). ... Named to OHL All-Star first team (1994-95).

Season Team	League	REGULAR SEASON								PLAYOFFS						
		Gms.	Min	W	L	T	GA	SO	Avg.	Gms.	Min.	W	L	GA	SO	Avg.
93-94 —North Bay	OHL	32	1587	15	5	4	93	0	3.52	5	191	2	1	9	0	2.83
94-95 —North Bay	OHL	47	2599	24	17	2	167	2	3.86	6	348	2	4	30	0	5.17
95-96 —North Bay	OHL	53	2859	12	29	5	232	1	4.87	—	—	—	—	—	—	—
96-97 —Windsor	OHL	47	2496	20	16	4	152	1	3.65	5	267	1	4	26	0	5.84
97-98 —Detroit	IHL	4	147	0	1	‡0	8	0	3.27	—	—	—	—	—	—	—
—Peoria	ECHL	38	2228	23	11	‡3	109	1	2.94	2	121	0	2	6	0	2.98

ROENICK, JEREMY — C — COYOTES

PERSONAL: Born January 17, 1970, in Boston. ... 6-0/192. ... Shoots right. ... Brother of Trevor Roenick, center in Carolina Hurricanes system. ... Name pronounced ROH-nihk.

HIGH SCHOOL: Thayer Academy (Braintree, Mass.).

TRANSACTIONS/CAREER NOTES: Selected by Chicago Blackhawks in first round (first Blackhawks pick, eighth overall) of NHL entry draft (June 11, 1988). ... Sprained knee ligaments (January 9, 1989); missed one month. ... Played in Europe during 1994-95 NHL lockout. ... Sprained knee ligament (April 2, 1995); missed remainder of season and first eight games of playoffs. ... Pulled thigh muscle (March 4, 1996); missed three games. ... Sprained ankle (March 17, 1996); missed 12 games. ... Traded by Blackhawks to Phoenix Coyotes for C Alexei Zhamnov, RW Craig Mills and first-round pick (RW Ty Jones) in 1997 draft (August 16, 1996). ... Missed first four games of 1996-97 season due to contract dispute. ... Sprained knee (November 23, 1996); missed six games. ... Suffered mild concussion (December 5, 1997); missed one game.

HONORS: Named to QMJHL All-Star second team (1988-89). ... Named NHL Rookie of the Year by THE SPORTING NEWS (1989-90). ... Played in NHL All-Star Game (1991-1994).

MISCELLANEOUS: Failed to score on a penalty shot (vs. Andrei Trefilov, March 7, 1995).

STATISTICAL NOTES: Led NHL with 13 game-winning goals (1991-92).

STATISTICAL PLATEAUS: Three-goal games: 1989-90 (1), 1990-91 (2), 1992-93 (1). Total: 4. ... Four-goal games: 1991-92 (1), 1993-94 (1). Total: 2. ... Total hat tricks: 6.

Season Team	League	REGULAR SEASON								PLAYOFFS				
		Gms.	G	A	Pts.	PIM	+/-	PP	SH	Gms.	G	A	Pts.	PIM
87-88 —Thayer Academy	Mass. H.S.	24	34	50	84	...				—	—	—	—	—
88-89 —U.S. national team	Int'l	11	8	8	16	0		...	...	—	—	—	—	—
—Chicago	NHL	20	9	9	18	4	4	2	0	10	1	3	4	7
—Hull	QMJHL	28	34	36	70	14	...	...	...	—	—	—	—	—
89-90 —Chicago	NHL	78	26	40	66	54	2	6	0	20	11	7	18	8
90-91 —Chicago	NHL	79	41	53	94	80	38	15	4	6	3	5	8	4
91-92 —Chicago	NHL	80	53	50	103	98	23	22	3	18	12	10	22	12
92-93 —Chicago	NHL	84	50	57	107	86	15	22	3	4	1	2	3	2
93-94 —Chicago	NHL	84	46	61	107	125	21	24	5	6	1	6	7	2
94-95 —Koln	Germany	3	3	1	4	2	...	...	...	—	—	—	—	—
—Chicago	NHL	33	10	24	34	14	5	5	0	8	1	2	3	16
95-96 —Chicago	NHL	66	32	35	67	109	9	12	4	10	5	7	12	2
96-97 —Phoenix	NHL	72	29	40	69	115	-7	10	3	6	2	4	6	4
97-98 —Phoenix	NHL	79	24	32	56	103	5	6	1	6	5	3	8	4
—U.S. Olympic Team	Int'l	4	0	1	1	6	...	...	...					
NHL Totals (10 years)		675	320	401	721	788	115	124	23	94	42	49	91	61

ROEST, STACY — C — RED WINGS

PERSONAL: Born March 15, 1974, in Lethbridge, Alta. ... 5-9/192. ... Shoots right.

TRANSACTIONS/CAREER NOTES: Signed as free agent by Detroit Red Wings (June 9, 1997).

HONORS: Named to WHL All-Star East first team (1993-94). ... Named to WHL All-Star East second team (1994-95).

Season Team	League	REGULAR SEASON								PLAYOFFS				
		Gms.	G	A	Pts.	PIM	+/-	PP	SH	Gms.	G	A	Pts.	PIM
92-93 —Medicine Hat	WHL	72	33	73	106	30	...	...	...	10	3	10	13	6
93-94 —Medicine Hat	WHL	72	48	72	120	48	...	...	...	3	1	0	1	4
94-95 —Medicine Hat	WHL	69	37	78	115	32	...	...	...	5	2	7	9	2
—Adirondack	AHL	3	0	0	0	0	...	...	...	—	—	—	—	—
95-96 —Adirondack	AHL	76	16	39	55	40	...	...	...	3	0	0	0	0
96-97 —Adirondack	AHL	78	25	41	66	30	...	...	...	4	1	1	2	0
97-98 —Adirondack	AHL	80	34	58	92	30	...	...	...	3	2	1	3	6

ROHLOFF, JON — D — SHARKS

PERSONAL: Born October 3, 1969, in Mankato, Minn. ... 5-11/220. ... Shoots right. ... Full name: Jon Richard Rohloff. ... Name pronounced ROH-lahf.

HIGH SCHOOL: Grand Rapids (Minn.).

COLLEGE: Minnesota-Duluth.

TRANSACTIONS/CAREER NOTES: Selected by Boston Bruins in ninth round (seventh Bruins pick, 186th overall) of NHL entry draft (June 11, 1988). ... Sprained ankle prior to 1996-97 season; missed 17 games. ... Strained groin (January 9, 1997); missed 23 games. ... Signed as free agent by San Jose Sharks (July 23, 1998).

HONORS: Named to WCHA All-Star second team (1992-93).

Season Team	League	REGULAR SEASON								PLAYOFFS				
		Gms.	G	A	Pts.	PIM	+/-	PP	SH	Gms.	G	A	Pts.	PIM
87-88 —Grand Rapids H.S.	Minn. H.S.	23	10	13	23	...	...	...	...	—	—	—	—	—
88-89 —Minnesota-Duluth	WCHA	39	1	2	3	44	...	...	...	—	—	—	—	—
89-90 —Minnesota-Duluth	WCHA	5	0	1	1	6	...	...	...	—	—	—	—	—
90-91 —Minnesota-Duluth	WCHA	32	6	11	17	38	...	...	...	—	—	—	—	—

Season Team	League	REGULAR SEASON								PLAYOFFS				
		Gms.	G	A	Pts.	PIM	+/-	PP	SH	Gms.	G	A	Pts.	PIM
91-92—Minnesota-Duluth	WCHA	27	9	9	18	48	...	...	...	—	—	—	—	—
92-93—Minnesota-Duluth	WCHA	36	15	19	34	87	...	...	...	—	—	—	—	—
93-94—Providence	AHL	55	12	23	35	59	...	...	...	—	—	—	—	—
94-95—Boston	NHL	34	3	8	11	39	1	0	0	5	0	0	0	6
—Providence	AHL	4	2	1	3	6	...	...	...	—	—	—	—	—
95-96—Boston	NHL	79	1	12	13	59	-8	1	0	5	1	2	3	2
96-97—Providence	AHL	3	1	1	2	0	...	...	...	—	—	—	—	—
—Boston	NHL	37	3	5	8	31	-14	1	0	—	—	—	—	—
97-98—Providence	AHL	58	6	17	23	46	...	...	...	—	—	—	—	—
NHL Totals (3 years)..........		150	7	25	32	129	-21	2	0	10	1	2	3	8

ROLOSON, DWAYNE   G   SABRES

PERSONAL: Born October 12, 1969, in Simcoe, Ont. ... 6-1/190. ... Catches left. ... Name pronounced ROH-luh-suhn.
COLLEGE: Massachusetts-Lowell.
TRANSACTIONS/CAREER NOTES: Signed as free agent by Calgary Flames (July 4, 1994). ... Signed as free agent by Buffalo Sabres (July 9, 1998).
HONORS: Named Hockey East Tournament Most Valuable Player (1993-94).
MISCELLANEOUS: Stopped a penalty shot attempt (vs. Rob Blake, April 13, 1998).

Season Team	League	REGULAR SEASON								PLAYOFFS						
		Gms.	Min	W	L	T	GA	SO	Avg.	Gms.	Min.	W	L	GA	SO	Avg.
90-91—Mass.-Lowell................	Hockey East	15	823	5	9	0	63	0	4.59	—	—	—	—	—	—	—
91-92—Mass.-Lowell................	Hockey East	12	660	3	8	0	52	0	4.73	—	—	—	—	—	—	—
92-93—Mass.-Lowell................	Hockey East	39	2342	20	17	2	150	0	3.84	—	—	—	—	—	—	—
93-94—Mass.-Lowell................	Hockey East	40	2305	23	10	7	106	0	2.76	—	—	—	—	—	—	—
94-95—Saint John....................	AHL	46	2734	16	21	8	156	1	3.42	5	299	1	4	13	0	2.61
95-96—Saint John....................	AHL	67	4026	33	22	11	190	1	2.83	16	1027	10	6	49	1	2.86
96-97—Calgary........................	NHL	31	1618	9	14	3	78	1	2.89	—	—	—	—	—	—	—
—Saint John........................	AHL	8	481	6	2	0	22	1	2.74	—	—	—	—	—	—	—
97-98—Saint John....................	AHL	4	245	3	0	1	8	0	1.96	—	—	—	—	—	—	—
—Calgary............................	NHL	39	2205	11	16	8	110	0	2.99	—	—	—	—	—	—	—
NHL Totals (2 years).............		70	3823	20	30	11	188	1	2.95							

ROLSTON, BRIAN   LW   DEVILS

PERSONAL: Born February 21, 1973, in Flint, Mich. ... 6-2/200. ... Shoots left.
COLLEGE: Lake Superior State (Mich.).
TRANSACTIONS/CAREER NOTES: Selected by New Jersey Devils in first round (second Devils pick, 11th overall) of NHL entry draft (June 22, 1991). ... Loaned by Devils to U.S. Olympic Team (November 2, 1993). ... Broke foot (October 17, 1995); missed 11 games. ... Injured hamstring (January 12, 1998); missed one game. ... Suffered from the flu (January 28, 1998); missed one game.
HONORS: Named to NCAA All-Tournament team (1991-92 and 1992-93). ... Named to NCAA All-America West second team (1992-93). ... Named to CCHA All-Star first team (1992-93).
MISCELLANEOUS: Member of Stanley Cup championship team (1995).
STATISTICAL PLATEAUS: Three-goal games: 1996-97 (1).

Season Team	League	REGULAR SEASON								PLAYOFFS				
		Gms.	G	A	Pts.	PIM	+/-	PP	SH	Gms.	G	A	Pts.	PIM
89-90—Detroit Compuware.....	NAJHL	40	36	37	73	57	...	...	...	—	—	—	—	—
90-91—Detroit Compuware.....	NAJHL	36	49	46	95	14	...	...	...	—	—	—	—	—
91-92—Lake Superior	CCHA	41	18	28	46	16	...	...	...	—	—	—	—	—
92-93—Lake Superior	CCHA	39	33	31	64	20	...	...	...	—	—	—	—	—
—U.S. Jr. national	Int'l	7	6	2	8	2	...	...	...	—	—	—	—	—
93-94—U.S. national team	Int'l	41	20	28	48	36	...	...	...	—	—	—	—	—
—U.S. Olympic Team	Int'l	8	7	0	7	8	...	...	...	—	—	—	—	—
—Albany........................	AHL	17	5	5	10	8	...	...	...	5	1	2	3	0
94-95—Albany........................	AHL	18	9	11	20	10	...	...	...	—	—	—	—	—
—New Jersey	NHL	40	7	11	18	17	5	2	0	6	2	1	3	4
95-96—New Jersey	NHL	58	13	11	24	8	9	3	1	—	—	—	—	—
96-97—New Jersey	NHL	81	18	27	45	20	6	2	2	10	4	1	5	6
97-98—New Jersey	NHL	76	16	14	30	16	7	0	2	6	1	0	1	2
NHL Totals (4 years)..........		255	54	63	117	61	27	7	5	22	7	2	9	12

RONNING, CLIFF   C   COYOTES

PERSONAL: Born October 1, 1965, in Vancouver. ... 5-8/167. ... Shoots left.
HIGH SCHOOL: Burnaby North (B.C.).
TRANSACTIONS/CAREER NOTES: Selected by St. Louis Blues as underage junior in seventh round (ninth Blues pick, 134th overall) of NHL entry draft (June 9, 1984). ... Injured groin (November 1988). ... Agreed to play in Italy for 1989-90 season (August 1989). ... Fractured right index finger (November 12, 1990); missed 12 games. ... Traded by Blues with LW Geoff Courtnall, D Robert Dirk, LW Sergio Momesso and fifth-round pick (RW Brian Loney) in 1992 draft to Vancouver Canucks for C Dan Quinn and D Garth Butcher (March 5, 1991). ... Sprained hand (January 4, 1993); missed five games. ... Separated shoulder (January 8, 1994); missed eight games. ... Strained groin (February 9, 1995); missed four games. ... Injured groin (October 8, 1995); missed two games. ... Signed as free agent by Phoenix Coyotes (July 2, 1996). ... Fractured hand (October 10, 1996); missed 12 games. ... Suffered from the flu (December 17, 1996); missed one game.
HONORS: Won Stewart (Butch) Paul Memorial Trophy (1983-84). ... Named to WHL All-Star second team (1983-84). ... Won WHL Most Valuable Player Trophy (1984-85). ... Won Bob Brownridge Memorial Trophy (1984-85). ... Won Frank Boucher Memorial Trophy (1984-85). ... Named to WHL (West) All-Star first team (1984-85).
STATISTICAL PLATEAUS: Three-goal games: 1986-87 (1), 1992-93 (1), 1995-96 (1). Total: 3.

Season Team	League	Gms.	G	A	Pts.	PIM	+/-	PP	SH	Gms.	G	A	Pts.	PIM
				REGULAR SEASON								**PLAYOFFS**		
82-83—New Westminster	BCJHL	52	82	68	150	42	...	...	...	—	—	—	—	—
83-84—New Westminster	WHL	71	69	67	136	10	...	...	...	9	8	13	21	10
84-85—New Westminster	WHL	70	*89	108	*197	20	...	...	...	11	10	14	24	4
85-86—Canadian nat'l team ...	Int'l	71	55	63	118	53	...	...	...	—	—	—	—	—
—St. Louis	NHL	—	—	—	—	—	...	...	...	5	1	1	2	2
86-87—Canadian nat'l team ...	Int'l	26	16	16	32	12	...	...	...	—	—	—	—	—
—St. Louis	NHL	42	11	14	25	6	-1	2	0	4	0	1	1	0
87-88—St. Louis	NHL	26	5	8	13	12	6	1	0	—	—	—	—	—
88-89—St. Louis	NHL	64	24	31	55	18	3	16	0	7	1	3	4	0
—Peoria	IHL	12	11	20	31	8	...	...	...	—	—	—	—	—
89-90—Asiago	Italy	42	76	60	136	30	...	...	...	6	7	12	19	4
90-91—St. Louis	NHL	48	14	18	32	10	2	5	0	—	—	—	—	—
—Vancouver..................	NHL	11	6	6	12	0	-2	2	0	6	6	3	9	12
91-92—Vancouver..............	NHL	80	24	47	71	42	18	6	0	13	8	5	13	6
92-93—Vancouver..............	NHL	79	29	56	85	30	19	10	0	12	2	9	11	6
93-94—Vancouver..............	NHL	76	25	43	68	42	7	10	0	24	5	10	15	16
94-95—Vancouver..............	NHL	41	6	19	25	27	-4	3	0	11	3	5	8	2
95-96—Vancouver..............	NHL	79	22	45	67	42	16	5	0	6	0	2	2	6
96-97—Phoenix................	NHL	69	19	32	51	26	-9	8	0	7	0	7	7	12
97-98—Phoenix................	NHL	80	11	44	55	36	5	3	0	6	1	3	4	4
NHL Totals (12 years).........		695	196	363	559	291	60	71	0	101	27	49	76	66

ROSA, PAVEL   RW   KINGS

PERSONAL: Born June 7, 1977, in Most, Czechoslovakia. ... 5-11/178. ... Shoots right.
TRANSACTIONS/CAREER NOTES: Selected by Los Angeles Kings in second round (third Kings pick, 50th overall) of NHL entry draft (July 8, 1995).
HONORS: Won Michel Bergeron Trophy (1995-96). ... Named to QMJHL All-Rookie team (1995-96). ... Won Can.HL Top Scorer Award (1996-97). ... Won Jean Beliveau Trophy (1996-97). ... Named to Can.HL All-Star first team (1996-97). ... Named to QMJHL All-Star first team (1996-97).

Season Team	League	Gms.	G	A	Pts.	PIM	+/-	PP	SH	Gms.	G	A	Pts.	PIM
				REGULAR SEASON								**PLAYOFFS**		
94-95—Chemo. Litvinov Jrs....	Czech Rep.	40	56	42	98	...	...	...	...	—	—	—	—	—
—Chem. Litvinov...........	Czech Rep.	—	—	—	—	...	...	...	...	1	0	0	0	0
95-96—Hull.....................	QMJHL	61	46	70	116	39	...	...	...	18	14	22	36	25
96-97—Hull.....................	QMJHL	68	*63	*89	*152	56	...	...	...	14	18	13	31	16
97-98—Fredericton	AHL	1	0	0	0	0	...	...	...	—	—	—	—	—
—Long Beach...............	IHL	2	0	1	1	0	...	...	...	1	1	1	2	0

ROUSE, BOB   D   SHARKS

PERSONAL: Born June 18, 1964, in Surrey, B.C. ... 6-2/220. ... Shoots right. ... Name pronounced ROWZ.
TRANSACTIONS/CAREER NOTES: Selected by Minnesota North Stars as underage junior in fourth round (third North Stars pick, 80th overall) of NHL entry draft (June 9, 1982). ... Suffered hip contusions (January 1988). ... Traded by North Stars with RW Dino Ciccarelli to Washington Capitals for RW Mike Gartner and D Larry Murphy (March 7, 1989). ... Sprained right knee (December 12, 1989); missed eight games. ... Traded by Capitals with C Peter Zezel to Toronto Maple Leafs for D Al Iafrate (January 16, 1991). ... Broke collarbone (February 16, 1991). ... Suspended four games by NHL for stick-swinging incident (October 14, 1993). ... Strained knee (December 29, 1993); missed three games. ... Tore knee cartilage (January 29, 1994); missed 14 games. ... Signed as free agent by Detroit Red Wings (August 5, 1994). ... Underwent hernia surgery (September 9, 1995); missed five games. ... Fractured orbital bone (May 14, 1996); missed remainder of playoffs. ... Strained groin (December 27, 1996); missed four games. ... Suffered from the flu (March 26, 1997); missed two games. ... Signed as free agent by San Jose Sharks (July 13, 1998).
HONORS: Won Top Defenseman Trophy (1983-84). ... Named to WHL (East) All-Star first team (1983-84).
MISCELLANEOUS: Member of Stanley Cup championship team (1997 and 1998). ... Captain of Minnesota North Stars (1988-89).

Season Team	League	Gms.	G	A	Pts.	PIM	+/-	PP	SH	Gms.	G	A	Pts.	PIM
				REGULAR SEASON								**PLAYOFFS**		
80-81—Billings...................	WHL	70	0	13	13	116	...	...	...	5	0	0	0	2
81-82—Billings...................	WHL	71	7	22	29	209	...	...	...	5	0	2	2	10
82-83—Nanaimo	WHL	29	7	20	27	86	...	...	...	—	—	—	—	—
—Lethbridge	WHL	42	8	30	38	82	...	...	...	20	2	13	15	55
83-84—Lethbridge	WHL	71	18	42	60	101	...	...	...	5	0	1	1	28
—Minnesota................	NHL	1	0	0	0	0	0	0	0	—	—	—	—	—
84-85—Springfield	AHL	8	0	3	3	6	...	...	...	—	—	—	—	—
—Minnesota................	NHL	63	2	9	11	113	-14	0	0	—	—	—	—	—
85-86—Minnesota..............	NHL	75	1	14	15	151	15	0	0	3	0	0	0	2
86-87—Minnesota..............	NHL	72	2	10	12	179	6	0	0	—	—	—	—	—
87-88—Minnesota..............	NHL	74	0	12	12	168	-30	0	0	—	—	—	—	—
88-89—Minnesota..............	NHL	66	4	13	17	124	-5	0	1	—	—	—	—	—
—Washington..............	NHL	13	0	2	2	36	2	0	0	6	2	0	2	4
89-90—Washington............	NHL	70	4	16	20	123	-2	0	0	15	2	3	5	47
90-91—Washington............	NHL	47	5	15	20	65	-7	1	0	—	—	—	—	—
—Toronto	NHL	13	2	4	6	10	-11	1	0	—	—	—	—	—
91-92—Toronto	NHL	79	3	19	22	97	-20	1	0	—	—	—	—	—
92-93—Toronto	NHL	82	3	11	14	130	7	0	1	21	3	8	11	29
93-94—Toronto	NHL	63	5	11	16	101	8	1	1	18	0	3	3	29
94-95—Detroit..................	NHL	48	1	7	8	36	14	0	0	18	0	3	3	8
95-96—Detroit..................	NHL	58	0	6	6	48	5	0	0	7	0	1	1	4
96-97—Detroit..................	NHL	70	4	9	13	58	8	0	2	20	0	0	0	55
97-98—Detroit..................	NHL	71	1	11	12	57	-9	0	0	22	0	3	3	16
NHL Totals (15 years).........		965	37	169	206	1496	-33	4	5	130	7	21	28	194

ROY, ANDRE — LW

PERSONAL: Born February 8, 1975, in Port Chester, N.Y. ... 6-3/202. ... Shoots left. ... Full name: Andre Christopher Roy. ... Name pronounced WAH.

TRANSACTIONS/CAREER NOTES: Selected by Boston Bruins in sixth round (fifth Bruins pick, 151st overall) of NHL entry draft (June 29, 1994).

		REGULAR SEASON								PLAYOFFS				
Season Team	League	Gms.	G	A	Pts.	PIM	+/-	PP	SH	Gms.	G	A	Pts.	PIM
93-94—Beauport	QMJHL	33	6	7	13	125	...	...	...	—	—	—	—	—
—Chicoutimi	QMJHL	32	4	14	18	152	...	...	...	25	3	6	9	94
94-95—Chicoutimi	QMJHL	20	15	8	23	90	...	...	...	—	—	—	—	—
—Drummondville	QMJHL	34	18	13	31	233	...	...	...	4	2	0	2	34
95-96—Providence	AHL	58	7	8	15	167	...	...	...	1	0	0	0	10
—Boston	NHL	3	0	0	0	0	0	0	0	—	—	—	—	—
96-97—Providence	AHL	50	17	11	28	234	...	...	...	—	—	—	—	—
—Boston	NHL	10	0	2	2	12	-5	0	0	—	—	—	—	—
97-98—Providence	AHL	36	3	11	14	154	...	...	...	—	—	—	—	—
—Charlotte	ECHL	27	10	8	18	132	...	...	...	7	2	3	5	34
NHL Totals (2 years)		13	0	2	2	12	-5	0	0					

ROY, JEAN-YVES — RW — BRUINS

PERSONAL: Born February 17, 1969, in Rosemere, Que. ... 5-10/180. ... Shoots left. ... Name pronounced ZHAHN-eev WAH.

COLLEGE: Maine.

TRANSACTIONS/CAREER NOTES: Signed as free agent by New York Rangers (July 20, 1997). ... Traded by Rangers to Ottawa Senators for C Steve Larouche (October 6, 1995). ... Signed as free agent by Boston Bruins (July 9, 1996). ... Injured nose (October 7, 1997); missed three games.

HONORS: Named to NCAA All-America East second team (1989-90). ... Named to Hockey East All-Rookie team (1989-90). ... Named to NCAA All-America East first team (1990-91 and 1991-92). ... Named to NCAA All-Tournament team (1990-91). ... Named to Hockey East All-Star first team (1990-91). ... Named to Hockey East All-Star second team (1991-92).

MISCELLANEOUS: Member of silver-medal-winning Canadian Olympic team (1994).

		REGULAR SEASON								PLAYOFFS				
Season Team	League	Gms.	G	A	Pts.	PIM	+/-	PP	SH	Gms.	G	A	Pts.	PIM
89-90—Univ. of Maine	Hockey East	46	39	26	65	52	...	...	...	—	—	—	—	—
90-91—Univ. of Maine	Hockey East	43	37	45	82	26	...	...	...	—	—	—	—	—
91-92—Univ. of Maine	Hockey East	35	32	24	56	62	...	...	...	—	—	—	—	—
92-93—Canadian nat'l team	Int'l	23	9	6	15	35	...	...	...	—	—	—	—	—
—Binghamton	AHL	49	13	15	28	21	...	...	...	14	5	2	7	4
93-94—Binghamton	AHL	65	41	24	65	33	...	...	...	—	—	—	—	—
—Canadian nat'l team	Int'l	6	3	2	5	2	...	...	...	—	—	—	—	—
—Can. Olympic Team	Int'l	8	1	0	1	19	...	...	...	—	—	—	—	—
94-95—Binghamton	AHL	67	41	36	77	28	...	...	...	11	4	6	10	12
—New York Rangers	NHL	3	1	0	1	2	-1	0	0	—	—	—	—	—
95-96—Prin. Edward Island	AHL	67	40	55	95	64	...	...	...	5	4	9	13	6
—Ottawa	NHL	4	1	1	2	2	3	0	0	—	—	—	—	—
96-97—Providence	AHL	27	9	16	25	30	...	...	...	10	2	7	9	2
—Boston	NHL	52	10	15	25	22	-8	2	0	—	—	—	—	—
97-98—Providence	AHL	65	28	34	62	60	...	...	...	—	—	—	—	—
—Boston	NHL	2	0	0	0	0	0	0	0	—	—	—	—	—
NHL Totals (4 years)		61	12	16	28	26	-6	2	0					

ROY, PATRICK — G — AVALANCHE

PERSONAL: Born October 5, 1965, in Quebec City. ... 6-0/192. ... Catches left. ... Name pronounced WAH.

TRANSACTIONS/CAREER NOTES: Selected by Montreal Canadiens as underage junior in third round (fourth Canadiens pick, 51st overall) of NHL entry draft (June 9, 1984). ... Suspended eight games by NHL for slashing (October 19, 1987). ... Sprained left knee ligaments (December 12, 1990); missed nine games. ... Tore left ankle ligaments (January 27, 1991); missed 14 games. ... Reinjured left ankle (March 16, 1991). ... Strained hip flexor (March 6, 1993); missed two games. ... Suffered stiff neck (December 11, 1993); missed two games. ... Strained neck (December 22, 1993); missed four games. ... Traded by Canadiens with RW Mike Keane to Colorado Avalanche for G Jocelyn Thibault, LW Martin Rucinsky and RW Andrei Kovalenko (December 6, 1995). ... Sprained thumb (January 23, 1997); missed two games. ... Injured shoulder (March 26, 1997); missed two games. ... Partially dislocated shoulder (November 17, 1997); missed two games.

HONORS: Won Conn Smythe Trophy (1985-86 and 1992-93). ... Named to NHL All-Rookie team (1985-86). ... Shared William M. Jennings Trophy with Brian Hayward (1986-87 through 1988-89). ... Named to NHL All-Star second team (1987-88 and 1990-91). ... Named to THE SPORTING NEWS All-Star first team (1988-89, 1989-90 and 1991-92). ... Won Trico Goaltender Award (1988-89 and 1989-90). ... Named to NHL All-Star first team (1988-89, 1989-90 and 1991-92). ... Won Vezina Trophy (1988-89, 1989-90 and 1991-92). ... Played in NHL All-Star Game (1988, 1990-1994, 1997 and 1998). ... Named to THE SPORTING NEWS All-Star second team (1990-91). ... Won William M. Jennings Trophy (1991-92).

RECORDS: Holds NHL career playoff record for most games played by goaltender—160. ... Shares NHL single-season playoff records for most wins by goaltender—16 (1993 and 1996); and most consecutive wins by goaltender—11 (1993).

MISCELLANEOUS: Member of Stanley Cup championship team (1986, 1993 and 1996). ... Holds Colorado Avalanche franchise all-time records for most shutouts (12) and goals-against average (2.43). ... Stopped a penalty shot attempt (vs. Dan Daoust, January 1, 1986; vs. Ville Peltonen, March 5, 1996; vs. Jamie Baker, March 28, 1996). ... Allowed a penalty shot goal (vs. Michel Goulet, January 10, 1987; vs. Jock Callender, March 18, 1989; vs. Pierre Turgeon, October 17, 1990; vs. Kevin Miller, October 10, 1991; vs. Theoren Fleury, October 22, 1996; vs. Tom Chorske, March 7, 1998).

STATISTICAL NOTES: Led NHL in save percentage with .900 in 1987-88, .908 in 1988-89, .912 in 1989-90 and .914 in 1991-92.

Season Team	League	REGULAR SEASON							PLAYOFFS						
		Gms.	Min	W	L	T	GA	SO	Avg.	Gms.	Min.	W	L	GA	SO	Avg.
82-83—Granby	QMJHL	54	2808	...	...	...	293	0	6.26	—	—	—	—	—	—	—
83-84—Granby	QMJHL	61	3585	29	29	1	265	0	4.44	4	244	0	4	22	0	5.41
84-85—Granby	QMJHL	44	2463	16	25	1	228	0	5.55	—	—	—	—	—	—	—
—Montreal	NHL	1	20	1	0	0	0	0		—	—	—	—	—	—	—
—Sherbrooke	AHL	1	60	1	0	0	4	0	4.00	*13	*769	10	3	37	0	*2.89
85-86—Montreal	NHL	47	2651	23	18	3	148	1	3.35	20	1218	*15	5	39	†1	1.92
86-87—Montreal	NHL	46	2686	22	16	6	131	1	2.93	6	330	4	2	22	0	4.00
87-88—Montreal	NHL	45	2586	23	12	9	125	3	2.90	8	430	3	4	24	0	3.35
88-89—Montreal	NHL	48	2744	33	5	6	113	4	*2.47	19	1206	13	6	42	2	*2.09
89-90—Montreal	NHL	54	3173	31	16	5	134	3	2.53	11	641	5	6	26	1	2.43
90-91—Montreal	NHL	48	2835	25	15	6	128	1	2.71	13	785	7	5	40	0	3.06
91-92—Montreal	NHL	67	3935	36	22	8	155	†5	*2.36	11	686	4	7	30	1	2.62
92-93—Montreal	NHL	62	3595	31	25	5	192	2	3.20	20	1293	*16	4	46	0	*2.13
93-94—Montreal	NHL	68	3867	35	17	11	161	†7	2.50	6	375	3	3	16	0	2.56
94-95—Montreal	NHL	†43	2566	17	20	6	127	1	2.97	—	—	—	—	—	—	—
95-96—Montreal	NHL	22	1260	12	9	1	62	1	2.95	—	—	—	—	—	—	—
—Colorado	NHL	39	2305	22	15	1	103	1	2.68	22	*1454	*16	6	*51	*3	2.10
96-97—Colorado	NHL	62	3698	*38	15	7	143	7	2.32	17	1034	10	†7	*38	†3	2.21
97-98—Colorado	NHL	65	3835	31	19	13	153	4	2.39	7	430	3	4	18	0	2.51
—Can. Olympic Team	Int'l	6	369	4	2	0	9	1	1.46	—	—	—	—	—	—	—
NHL Totals (14 years)		717	41756	380	224	87	1875	41	2.69	160	9882	99	59	392	11	2.38

ROY, STEPHANE   C   BLUES

PERSONAL: Born January 26, 1976, in Ste.-Martine, Que. ... 5-11/183. ... Shoots left. ... Name pronounced WAH.
TRANSACTIONS/CAREER NOTES: Selected by St. Louis Blues in third round (first Blues pick, 68th overall) of NHL entry draft (June 29, 1994).

Season Team	League	REGULAR SEASON								PLAYOFFS				
		Gms.	G	A	Pts.	PIM	+/-	PP	SH	Gms.	G	A	Pts.	PIM
93-94—Val-d'Or	QMJHL	72	25	28	53	116	...	...	...	—	—	—	—	—
94-95—St. Jean	QMJHL	68	19	52	71	113	...	...	...	—	—	—	—	—
95-96—Val-d'Or	QMJHL	62	43	72	115	89	...	...	...	13	9	15	24	10
—Worcester	AHL	1	0	0	0	2	...	...	...	—	—	—	—	—
96-97—Worcester	AHL	66	24	23	47	57	...	...	...	5	2	0	2	4
97-98—Worcester	AHL	77	21	27	48	95	...	...	...	10	4	4	8	10
—Macon	CHL	4	1	6	7	8	...	...	...	3	1	0	1	10

ROYER, REMI   D   BLACKHAWKS

PERSONAL: Born February 12, 1978, in Donnacona, Que. ... 6-1/183. ... Shoots right. ... Brother of Gaetan Royer, right winger in Chicago Blackhawks system.
TRANSACTIONS/CAREER NOTES: Selected by Chicago Blackhawks in second round (first Blackhawks pick, 31st overall) of NHL entry draft (June 22, 1996).
HONORS: Named to Can.HL All-Star second team (1997-98). ... Named to QMJHL Al-Star first team (1997-98).

Season Team	League	REGULAR SEASON								PLAYOFFS				
		Gms.	G	A	Pts.	PIM	+/-	PP	SH	Gms.	G	A	Pts.	PIM
94-95—Victoriaville	QMJHL	57	3	17	20	144	...	...	...	4	0	1	1	7
95-96—Victoriaville	QMJHL	43	12	14	26	209	...	...	...	—	—	—	—	—
—St. Hyacinthe	QMJHL	19	10	9	19	80	...	...	...	12	1	4	5	29
96-97—Rouyn-Noranda	QMJHL	29	3	12	15	87	...	...	...	—	—	—	—	—
—Indianapolis	IHL	10	0	1	1	17	...	...	...	—	—	—	—	—
97-98—Rouyn-Noranda	QMJHL	66	20	48	68	205	...	...	...	6	1	3	4	8
—Indianapolis	IHL	5	0	2	2	4	...	...	...	5	1	2	3	12

ROZSIVAL, MICHAL   D   PENGUINS

PERSONAL: Born September 3, 1978, in Vlasim, Czechoslovakia. ... 6-1/194. ... Shoots right. ... Name pronounced RAH-sih-vahl.
TRANSACTIONS/CAREER NOTES: Selected by Pittsburgh Penguins in fourth round (fifth Penguins pick, 105th overall) of NHL entry draft (June 22, 1996).
HONORS: Named to Can.HL All-Star second team (1997-98). ... Won Bill Hunter Trophy (1997-98). ... Named to WHL (East) All-Star first team (1997-98).

Season Team	League	REGULAR SEASON								PLAYOFFS				
		Gms.	G	A	Pts.	PIM	+/-	PP	SH	Gms.	G	A	Pts.	PIM
94-95—Jihlava Jr.	Czech Rep.	31	8	13	21	...	...	...	...	—	—	—	—	—
95-96—Jihlava Jr.	Czech Rep.	36	3	4	7	...	...	...	...	—	—	—	—	—
96-97—Swift Current	WHL	63	8	31	39	80	...	...	...	10	0	6	6	15
97-98—Swift Current	WHL	71	14	55	69	122	...	...	...	12	0	5	5	33

RUCCHIN, STEVE   C   MIGHTY DUCKS

PERSONAL: Born July 4, 1971, in Thunder Bay, Ont. ... 6-3/215. ... Shoots left. ... Full name: Steven Andrew Rucchin. ... Name pronounced ROO-chihn.
COLLEGE: Western Ontario.
TRANSACTIONS/CAREER NOTES: Selected by Mighty Ducks of Anaheim in first round (first Mighty Ducks pick, second overall) of NHL supplemental draft (June 28, 1994). ... Suffered from the flu (March 7, 1995); missed two games. ... Sprained left knee (November 27, 1995); missed 18 games. ... Strained groin (October 3, 1997); missed eight games. ... Strained left knee (April 9, 1998); missed two games.
HONORS: Named OUAA Player of the Year (1993-94). ... Named to CIAU All-Star first team (1993-94).

Season Team	League	REGULAR SEASON								PLAYOFFS				
		Gms.	G	A	Pts.	PIM	+/-	PP	SH	Gms.	G	A	Pts.	PIM
90-91—Univ. of W. Ontario	OUAA	34	13	16	29	14	...	...	...	—	—	—	—	—
91-92—Univ. of W. Ontario	OUAA	37	28	34	62	36	...	...	...	—	—	—	—	—
92-93—Univ. of W. Ontario	OUAA	34	22	26	48	16	...	...	...	—	—	—	—	—
93-94—Univ. of W. Ontario	OUAA	35	30	23	53	30	...	...	...	—	—	—	—	—
94-95—San Diego	IHL	41	11	15	26	14	...	...	...	—	—	—	—	—
—Anaheim	NHL	43	6	11	17	23	7	0	0	—	—	—	—	—
95-96—Anaheim	NHL	64	19	25	44	12	3	8	1	—	—	—	—	—
96-97—Anaheim	NHL	79	19	48	67	24	26	6	1	8	1	2	3	10
97-98—Anaheim	NHL	72	17	36	53	13	8	8	1	—	—	—	—	—
NHL Totals (4 years)...........		258	61	120	181	72	44	22	3	8	1	2	3	10

RUCINSKI, MIKE   D   HURRICANES

PERSONAL: Born March 30, 1975, in Trenton, Mich. ... 5-11/188. ... Shoots left.
TRANSACTIONS/CAREER NOTES: Selected by Hartford Whalers in ninth round (eighth Whalers pick, 217th overall) of NHL entry draft (July 8, 1995). ... Whalers franchise moved to North Carolina and renamed Carolina Hurricanes for 1997-98 season; NHL approved move on June 25, 1997.

Season Team	League	REGULAR SEASON								PLAYOFFS				
		Gms.	G	A	Pts.	PIM	+/-	PP	SH	Gms.	G	A	Pts.	PIM
92-93—Detroit........................	OHL	66	6	13	19	59	...	...	...	15	0	4	4	12
93-94—Detroit........................	OHL	66	2	26	28	58	...	...	...	17	0	7	7	15
94-95—Detroit........................	OHL	64	9	18	27	61	...	...	...	21	3	3	6	8
95-96—Detroit........................	OHL	51	10	26	36	65	...	...	...	11	2	4	6	14
96-97—Springfield	AHL	6	0	1	1	0	...			—	—	—	—	—
—Richmond	ECHL	61	20	23	43	85	...	...	...	8	2	6	8	18
97-98—New Haven	AHL	65	5	17	22	50	...	...	...	1	0	0	0	0
—Carolina	NHL	9	0	1	1	2	0	0	0	—	—	—	—	—
—Cleveland	IHL	2	0	0	0	4	...			—	—	—	—	—
NHL Totals (1 year)............		9	0	1	1	2	0	0	0					

RUCINSKY, MARTIN   LW   CANADIENS

PERSONAL: Born March 11, 1971, in Most, Czechoslovakia. ... 6-1/205. ... Shoots left. ... Name pronounced roo-SHIHN-skee.
TRANSACTIONS/CAREER NOTES: Selected by Edmonton Oilers in first round (second Oilers pick, 20th overall) of NHL entry draft (June 22, 1991). ... Traded by Oilers to Quebec Nordiques for G Ron Tugnutt and LW Brad Zavisha (March 10, 1992). ... Suffered from the flu (February 28, 1993); missed one game. ... Bruised buttocks (December 3, 1994); missed one game. ... Sprained right wrist (January 11, 1994); missed one game. ... Broke left cheek (January 30, 1994); missed four games. ... Suffered hairline fracture of right wrist (March 7, 1994); missed one game. ... Suffered hairline fracture of right wrist (March 21, 1994); missed six games. ... Suffered hairline fracture of right wrist (April 5, 1994); missed one game. ... Played in Europe during 1994-95 NHL lockout. ... Separated shoulder (February 25, 1995); missed 17 games. ... Reinjured shoulder (April 6, 1995); missed last 11 games of season and playoffs. ... Nordiques franchise moved to Colorado and renamed Avalanche for 1995-96 season (June 21, 1995). ... Injured groin (November 28, 1995); missed one game. ... Traded by Avalanche with G Jocelyn Thibault and RW Andrei Kovalenko to Montreal Canadiens for G Patrick Roy and RW Mike Keane (December 6, 1995). ... Sprained right knee (April 6, 1996); missed two games. ... Injured hand (October 19, 1996); missed one game. ... Strained knee (November 25, 1996); missed one game. ... Separated shoulder (December 28, 1996); missed 10 games. ... Bruised foot (October 17, 1997); missed one game. ... Sprained ankle (April 4, 1998); missed three games.
MISCELLANEOUS: Member of gold-medal-winning Czech Republic Olympic team (1998).
STATISTICAL PLATEAUS: Three-goal games: 1995-96 (1), 1996-97 (1). Total: 2.

Season Team	League	REGULAR SEASON								PLAYOFFS				
		Gms.	G	A	Pts.	PIM	+/-	PP	SH	Gms.	G	A	Pts.	PIM
88-89—CHZ Litvinov	Czech.	3	1	0	1	2	...	...	...	—	—	—	—	—
89-90—CHZ Litvinov	Czech.	47	12	6	18	...	...	...	...	—	—	—	—	—
90-91—CHZ Litvinov	Czech.	49	23	18	41	79	...	...	...	—	—	—	—	—
—Czechoslovakia Jr. ..	Czech.	7	9	5	14	2	...	...	...	—	—	—	—	—
91-92—Cape Breton	AHL	35	11	12	23	34	...	...	...	—	—	—	—	—
—Edmonton	NHL	2	0	0	0	0	-3	0	0	—	—	—	—	—
—Halifax	AHL	7	1	1	2	6	...	...	...	—	—	—	—	—
—Quebec	NHL	4	1	1	2	2	1	0	0	—	—	—	—	—
92-93—Quebec	NHL	77	18	30	48	51	16	4	0	6	1	1	2	4
93-94—Quebec	NHL	60	9	23	32	58	4	4	0	—	—	—	—	—
94-95—Chemo. Litvinov........	Czech Rep.	13	12	10	22	34	...	...	...	—	—	—	—	—
—Quebec	NHL	20	3	6	9	14	5	0	0	—	—	—	—	—
95-96—Colorado	NHL	22	4	11	15	14	10	0	0	—	—	—	—	—
—Montreal	NHL	56	25	35	60	54	8	9	2	—	—	—	—	—
96-97—Montreal	NHL	70	28	27	55	62	1	6	3	5	0	0	0	4
97-98—Montreal	NHL	78	21	32	53	84	13	5	3	10	3	0	3	4
—Czech Rep. Olympic....	Int'l	6	3	1	4	4	...	...	...	—	—	—	—	—
NHL Totals (7 years)...........		389	109	165	274	339	55	28	8	21	4	1	5	12

RUSSELL, CAM   D   BLACKHAWKS

PERSONAL: Born January 12, 1969, in Halifax, Nova Scotia ... 6-4/200. ... Shoots left.
TRANSACTIONS/CAREER NOTES: Selected by Chicago Blackhawks as underage junior in third round (third Blackhawks pick, 50th overall) of NHL entry draft (June 13, 1987). ... Suffered from the flu (December 26, 1992); missed one game. ... Suspended one game by NHL for accumulating three game misconduct penalties (February 11, 1993). ... Underwent surgery for herniated disc in neck (March 18, 1994); missed remainder of season. ... Broke bone in hand (April 2, 1995); missed remainder of season. ... Bruised shoulder (November 2, 1995); missed five games. ... Broke left orbital bone (December 23, 1995); missed five games. ... Suffered concussion (January 10, 1997); missed two games. ... Bruised knee (September 29, 1997); missed first game of season. ... Strained shoulder (December 7, 1997); missed 15 games. ... Suffered concussion (April 15, 1998); missed two games.

Season Team	League	REGULAR SEASON								PLAYOFFS				
		Gms.	G	A	Pts.	PIM	+/-	PP	SH	Gms.	G	A	Pts.	PIM
85-86—Hull	QMJHL	56	3	4	7	24	...	...	...	15	0	2	2	4
86-87—Hull	QMJHL	66	3	16	19	119	...	...	...	8	0	1	1	16
87-88—Hull	QMJHL	53	9	18	27	141	...	...	...	19	2	5	7	39
88-89—Hull	QMJHL	66	8	32	40	109	...	...	...	9	2	6	8	6
89-90—Indianapolis	IHL	46	3	15	18	114	...	...	...	9	0	1	1	24
—Chicago	NHL	19	0	1	1	27	-3	0	0	1	0	0	0	0
90-91—Indianapolis	IHL	53	5	9	14	125	...	...	...	6	0	2	2	30
—Chicago	NHL	3	0	0	0	5	1	0	0	1	0	0	0	0
91-92—Indianapolis	IHL	41	4	9	13	78	...	...	...	—	—	—	—	—
—Chicago	NHL	19	0	0	0	34	-8	0	0	12	0	2	2	2
92-93—Chicago	NHL	67	2	4	6	151	5	0	0	4	0	0	0	0
93-94—Chicago	NHL	67	1	7	8	200	10	0	0	—	—	—	—	—
94-95—Chicago	NHL	33	1	3	4	88	4	0	0	16	0	3	3	8
95-96—Chicago	NHL	61	2	2	4	129	8	0	0	6	0	0	0	2
96-97—Chicago	NHL	44	1	1	2	65	-8	0	0	4	0	0	0	4
97-98—Chicago	NHL	41	1	1	2	79	3	0	0	—	—	—	—	—
NHL Totals (9 years)		354	8	19	27	778	12	0	0	44	0	5	5	16

RYAN, TERRY — LW — CANADIENS

PERSONAL: Born January 14, 1977, in St. John's, Nfld. ... 6-1/201. ... Shoots left.
TRANSACTIONS/CAREER NOTES: Selected by Montreal Canadiens in first round (first Canadiens pick, eighth overall) of NHL entry draft (July 8, 1995). ... Suffered post-concussion headaches (November 6, 1996); missed 37 games.
HONORS: Named to WHL (West) All-Star second team (1994-95).

Season Team	League	REGULAR SEASON								PLAYOFFS				
		Gms.	G	A	Pts.	PIM	+/-	PP	SH	Gms.	G	A	Pts.	PIM
91-92—Quesnel	PCJHL	65	35	40	75	260	...	...	...	—	—	—	—	—
92-93—Quesnel	PCJHL	46	45	40	85	222	...	...	...	—	—	—	—	—
—Tri-City	WHL	1	0	0	0	0	...	...	...	1	0	1	1	5
93-94—Tri-City	WHL	61	16	17	33	176	...	...	...	4	0	1	1	25
94-95—Tri-City	WHL	70	50	60	110	207	...	...	...	17	12	15	27	36
95-96—Fredericton	AHL	—	—	—	—	—				3	0	0	0	2
—Tri-City	WHL	59	32	37	69	133	...	...	...	5	0	0	0	4
96-97—Montreal	NHL	3	0	0	0	0	0	0	0	—	—	—	—	—
—Red Deer	WHL	16	13	22	35	10	...	...	...	16	*18	6	24	32
97-98—Montreal	NHL	4	0	0	0	31	0	0	0	—	—	—	—	—
—Fredericton	AHL	71	21	18	39	256	...	...	...	3	1	1	2	0
NHL Totals (2 years)		7	0	0	0	31	0	0	0					

RYCHEL, WARREN — LW — AVALANCHE

PERSONAL: Born May 12, 1967, in Tecumseh, Ont. ... 6-0/205. ... Shoots left. ... Full name: Warren Stanley Rychel. ... Name pronounced RIGH-kuhl.
TRANSACTIONS/CAREER NOTES: Signed as free agent by Chicago Blackhawks (September 19, 1986). ... Hyperextended left knee (February 1989). ... Traded by Blackhawks with C Troy Murray to Winnipeg Jets for D Bryan Marchment and D Chris Norton (July 22, 1991). ... Traded by Jets to Minnesota North Stars for RW Tony Joseph and future considerations (December 30, 1991). ... Signed as free agent by San Diego Gulls (August 11, 1992). ... Signed as free agent by Los Angeles Kings (October 3, 1992). ... Bruised ankle (December 1, 1992); missed 14 games. ... Traded by Kings to Washington Capitals for LW Randy Burridge (February 10, 1995). ... Traded by Capitals to Toronto Maple Leafs for fourth-round pick (G Sebastien Charpentier) in 1995 draft (February 10, 1995). ... Suspended two games and fined $500 by NHL for spearing (March 2, 1995). ... Strained groin (April 17, 1995); missed three games. ... Traded by Maple Leafs to Colorado Avalanche for cash (October 2, 1995). ... Suffered back spasms (January 14, 1996); missed two games. ... Signed as free agent by Mighty Ducks of Anaheim (July 23, 1996). ... Suffered back spasms (January 27, 1997); missed four games. ... Suffered back spasms (February 8, 1997); missed four games. ... Traded by Mighty Ducks with conditional pick in 1999 draft to Colorado Avalanche for C Josef Marha (March 24, 1998).
MISCELLANEOUS: Member of Stanley Cup championship team (1996).

Season Team	League	REGULAR SEASON								PLAYOFFS				
		Gms.	G	A	Pts.	PIM	+/-	PP	SH	Gms.	G	A	Pts.	PIM
83-84—Essex Jr. C	OHA	24	11	16	27	86	...	...	...	—	—	—	—	—
84-85—Sudbury	OHL	35	5	8	13	74	...	...	...	—	—	—	—	—
—Guelph	OHL	29	1	3	4	48	...	...	...	—	—	—	—	—
85-86—Guelph	OHL	38	14	5	19	119	...	...	...	—	—	—	—	—
—Ottawa	OHL	29	11	18	29	54	...	...	...	—	—	—	—	—
86-87—Ottawa	OHL	28	11	7	18	57	...	...	...	—	—	—	—	—
—Kitchener	OHL	21	5	5	10	39	...	...	...	4	0	0	0	9
87-88—Saginaw	IHL	51	2	7	9	113	...	...	...	1	0	0	0	0
—Peoria	IHL	7	2	1	3	7	...	...	...	—	—	—	—	—
88-89—Saginaw	IHL	50	15	14	29	226	...	...	...	6	0	0	0	51
—Chicago	NHL	2	0	0	0	17	-1	0	0	—	—	—	—	—
89-90—Indianapolis	IHL	77	23	16	39	374	...	...	...	14	1	3	4	64
90-91—Indianapolis	IHL	68	33	30	63	338	...	...	...	5	2	1	3	30
—Chicago	NHL	—	—	—	—	—				3	1	3	4	2
91-92—Moncton	AHL	36	14	15	29	211	...	...	...	—	—	—	—	—
—Kalamazoo	IHL	45	15	20	35	165	...	...	...	8	0	3	3	51
92-93—Los Angeles	NHL	70	6	7	13	314	-15	0	0	23	6	7	13	39
93-94—Los Angeles	NHL	80	10	9	19	322	-19	0	0	—	—	—	—	—
94-95—Los Angeles	NHL	7	0	0	0	19	-5	0	0	—	—	—	—	—
—Toronto	NHL	26	1	6	7	101	1	0	0	3	0	0	0	0
95-96—Colorado	NHL	52	6	2	8	147	6	0	0	12	1	0	1	23
96-97—Anaheim	NHL	70	10	7	17	218	6	1	1	11	0	2	2	19
97-98—Anaheim	NHL	63	5	6	11	198	-10	1	0	—	—	—	—	—
—Colorado	NHL	8	0	0	0	23	-1	0	0	6	0	0	0	24
NHL Totals (8 years)		378	38	37	75	1359	-38	2	1	58	8	12	20	107

PERSONAL: Born February 4, 1969, in Medford, Mass. ... 6-1/195. ... Shoots left. ... Full name: Joseph William Sacco. ... Brother of David Sacco, left winger in Mighty Ducks of Anaheim system. ... Name pronounced SA-koh.

HIGH SCHOOL: Medford (Mass.).

COLLEGE: Boston University.

TRANSACTIONS/CAREER NOTES: Selected by Toronto Maple Leafs in fourth round (fourth Maple Leafs pick, 71st overall) of NHL entry draft (June 13, 1987). ... Selected by Mighty Ducks of Anaheim in NHL expansion draft (June 24, 1993). ... Bruised left thumb (February 5, 1995); missed seven games. ... Strained chest muscle (January 22, 1997); missed five games. ... Traded by Mighty Ducks with D J.J. Daigneault and C Mark Janssens to New York Islanders for C Travis Green, D Doug Houda and RW Tony Tuzzolino (February 6, 1998). ... Strained hip flexor (March 14, 1998); missed one game.

MISCELLANEOUS: Scored on a penalty shot (vs. Jocelyn Thibault, November 12, 1997). ... Holds Mighty Ducks of Anaheim all-time record for most games played (333).

		REGULAR SEASON							PLAYOFFS				
Season Team	League	Gms.	G	A	Pts.	PIM	+/-	PP	SH	Gms.	G	A	Pts.	PIM
85-86—Medford H.S.	Mass. H.S.	20	30	30	60	...	...	...	...	—	—	—	—	—
86-87—Medford H.S.	Mass. H.S.	21	22	32	54	...	...	...	...	—	—	—	—	—
87-88—Boston University	Hockey East	34	14	22	36	38	...	...	...	—	—	—	—	—
88-89—Boston University	Hockey East	33	21	19	40	66	...	...	...	—	—	—	—	—
89-90—Boston University	Hockey East	44	28	24	52	70	...	...	...	—	—	—	—	—
90-91—Newmarket	AHL	49	18	17	35	24	...	...	...	—	—	—	—	—
—Toronto	NHL	20	0	5	5	2	-5	0	0	—	—	—	—	—
91-92—U.S. national team	Int'l	50	11	26	37	51	...	...	...	—	—	—	—	—
—U.S. Olympic Team	Int'l	8	0	2	2	0	...	...	...	—	—	—	—	—
—Toronto	NHL	17	7	4	11	4	8	0	0	—	—	—	—	—
—St. John's	AHL	—	—	—	—	...	...	...	...	1	1	1	2	0
92-93—Toronto	NHL	23	4	4	8	8	-4	0	0	—	—	—	—	—
—St. John's	AHL	37	14	16	30	45	...	...	...	7	6	4	10	2
93-94—Anaheim	NHL	84	19	18	37	61	-11	3	1	—	—	—	—	—
94-95—Anaheim	NHL	41	10	8	18	23	-8	2	0	—	—	—	—	—
95-96—Anaheim	NHL	76	13	14	27	40	1	1	2	—	—	—	—	—
96-97—Anaheim	NHL	77	12	17	29	35	1	1	1	11	2	0	2	2
97-98—Anaheim	NHL	55	8	11	19	24	-1	0	2	—	—	—	—	—
—New York Islanders	NHL	25	3	3	6	10	1	0	0	—	—	—	—	—
NHL Totals (8 years)		418	76	84	160	207	-18	7	6	11	2	0	2	2

PERSONAL: Born December 2, 1977, in Jindrichuv Hradec, Czechoslovakia. ... 6-1/194. ... Shoots left.

TRANSACTIONS/CAREER NOTES: Selected by New York Islanders in fifth round (sixth Islanders pick, 128th overall) of NHL entry draft (June 22, 1996).

		REGULAR SEASON							PLAYOFFS				
Season Team	League	Gms.	G	A	Pts.	PIM	+/-	PP	SH	Gms.	G	A	Pts.	PIM
94-95—Czech Rep.	Czech Rep.	40	6	8	14	...	...	...	...	—	—	—	—	—
95-96—Czech Rep.	Czech Rep.	39	19	17	36	...	...	...	...	—	—	—	—	—
—HC Ceske Budejovice	Czech Rep.	—	—	—	—	...	...	...	...	2	0	0	0	...
96-97—Tri-City	WHL	63	13	24	37	32	...	...	...	—	—	—	—	—
—HC Ceske Budejovice	Czech Rep.	2	0	0	0	0	...	...	...	—	—	—	—	—
97-98—Motor-Ceske Bude.	Czech Rep.	20	1	3	4	4	...	...	...	—	—	—	—	—

PERSONAL: Born July 7, 1969, in Burnaby, B.C. ... 5-11/185. ... Shoots left. ... Full name: Joseph Steve Sakic. ... Brother of Brian Sakic, left winger in New York Rangers system. ... Name pronounced SAK-ihk.

TRANSACTIONS/CAREER NOTES: Selected by Quebec Nordiques as underage junior in first round (second Nordiques pick, 15th overall) of NHL entry draft (June 13, 1987). ... Sprained right ankle (November 28, 1988). ... Developed bursitis in left ankle (January 21, 1992); missed three games. ... Suffered recurrence of bursitis in left ankle (January 30, 1992); missed eight games. ... Injured eye (January 2, 1993); missed six games. ... Nordiques franchise moved to Colorado and renamed Avalanche for 1995-96 season (June 21, 1995). ... Cut calf (January 4, 1997); missed 17 games. ... Injured knee (February 18, 1998); missed 18 games. ... Suspended one game and fined $1,000 by NHL for kneeing incident (April 21, 1998).

HONORS: Won WHL (East) Most Valuable Player Trophy (1986-87). ... Won WHL (East) Stewart (Butch) Paul Memorial Trophy (1986-87). ... Won Can.HL Player of the Year Award (1987-88). ... Won Four Broncos Memorial Trophy (1987-88). ... Shared Bob Clarke Trophy with Theoren Fleury (1987-88). ... Won WHL Player of the Year Award (1987-88). ... Named to WHL (East) All-Star first team (1987-88). ... Played in NHL All-Star Game (1990-1994, 1996 and 1998). ... Won Conn Smythe Trophy (1995-96). ... Named to play in NHL All-Star Game (1997); replaced by RW Teemu Selanne due to injury.

MISCELLANEOUS: Member of Stanley Cup championship team (1996). ... Captain of Quebec Nordiques (1990-91 through 1994-95). ... Scored on a penalty shot (vs. Ken Wregget, December 9, 1989; vs. Trevor Kidd, January 14, 1996; vs. Tyler Moss, November 1, 1997). ... Captain of Colorado Avalanche (1995-96 through 1997-98).

STATISTICAL PLATEAUS: Three-goal games: 1988-89 (2), 1989-90 (1), 1990-91 (1), 1996-97 (1). Total: 5. ... Four-goal games: 1991-92 (1). ... Total hat tricks: 6.

		REGULAR SEASON							PLAYOFFS				
Season Team	League	Gms.	G	A	Pts.	PIM	+/-	PP	SH	Gms.	G	A	Pts.	PIM
86-87—Swift Current	WHL	72	60	73	133	31	...	...	...	4	0	1	1	0
87-88—Swift Current	WHL	64	†78	82	†160	64	...	...	...	10	11	13	24	12
88-89—Quebec	NHL	70	23	39	62	24	-36	10	0	—	—	—	—	—
89-90—Quebec	NHL	80	39	63	102	27	-40	8	1	—	—	—	—	—
90-91—Quebec	NHL	80	48	61	109	24	-26	12	3	—	—	—	—	—

Season Team	League	REGULAR SEASON								PLAYOFFS				
		Gms.	G	A	Pts.	PIM	+/-	PP	SH	Gms.	G	A	Pts.	PIM
91-92—Quebec	NHL	69	29	65	94	20	5	6	3	—	—	—	—	—
92-93—Quebec	NHL	78	48	57	105	40	-3	20	2	6	3	3	6	2
93-94—Quebec	NHL	84	28	64	92	18	-8	10	1	—	—	—	—	—
94-95—Quebec	NHL	47	19	43	62	30	7	3	2	6	4	1	5	0
95-96—Colorado	NHL	82	51	69	120	44	14	17	6	22	*18	16	*34	14
96-97—Colorado	NHL	65	22	52	74	34	-10	10	2	17	8	*17	25	14
97-98—Colorado	NHL	64	27	36	63	50	0	12	1	6	2	3	5	6
—Can. Olympic Team	Int'l	4	1	2	3	4	...	...	...	—	—	—	—	—
NHL Totals (10 years)		719	334	549	883	311	-97	108	21	57	35	40	75	36

SALEI, RUSLAN   D   MIGHTY DUCKS

PERSONAL: Born November 2, 1974, in Minsk, U.S.S.R. ... 6-2/205. ... Shoots left. ... Name pronounced ROO-slahn suh-LAY.

TRANSACTIONS/CAREER NOTES: Selected by Mighty Ducks of Anaheim in first round (first Mighty Ducks pick, ninth overall) of NHL entry draft (June 22, 1996). ... Suffered charley horse (November 22, 1997); missed one game. ... Suspended two games and fined $1,000 by NHL for head-butting incident (February 4, 1998).

Season Team	League	REGULAR SEASON								PLAYOFFS				
		Gms.	G	A	Pts.	PIM	+/-	PP	SH	Gms.	G	A	Pts.	PIM
92-93—Dynamo Minsk	CIS	9	1	0	1	10	...	...	...	—	—	—	—	—
93-94—Tivali Minsk	CIS	39	2	3	5	50	...	...	...	—	—	—	—	—
94-95—Tivali Minsk	CIS	51	4	2	6	44	...	...	...	—	—	—	—	—
95-96—Las Vegas	IHL	76	7	23	30	123	...	...	...	15	3	7	10	18
96-97—Anaheim	NHL	30	0	1	1	37	-8	0	0	—	—	—	—	—
—Baltimore	AHL	12	1	4	5	12	...	...	...	—	—	—	—	—
—Las Vegas	IHL	8	0	2	2	24	...	...	...	3	2	1	3	6
97-98—Anaheim	NHL	66	5	10	15	70	7	1	0	—	—	—	—	—
—Cincinnati	AHL	6	3	6	9	14	...	...	...	—	—	—	—	—
—Belarus Oly. team	Int'l	7	1	0	1	4	...	...	...	—	—	—	—	—
NHL Totals (2 years)		96	5	11	16	107	-1	1	0					

SALO, SAMI   RW   SENATORS

PERSONAL: Born September 2, 1974, in Turku, Finland. ... 6-3/189. ... Shoots right.

TRANSACTIONS/CAREER NOTES: Selected by Ottawa Senators in ninth round (seventh Senators pick, 239th overall) of NHL entry draft (June 22, 1996).

Season Team	League	REGULAR SEASON								PLAYOFFS				
		Gms.	G	A	Pts.	PIM	+/-	PP	SH	Gms.	G	A	Pts.	PIM
94-95—TPS Turku	Finland	7	1	2	3	6	...	...	...	—	—	—	—	—
—Kiekko-67	Finland Dv.II	19	4	2	6	4	...	...	...	—	—	—	—	—
95-96—TPS Turku	Finland	47	7	14	21	32	...	...	...	11	1	3	4	8
96-97—TPS Turku	Finland	48	9	6	15	10	...	...	...	10	2	3	5	4
97-98—Jokerit Helsinki	Finland	35	3	5	8	10	...	...	...	8	0	1	1	2

SALO, TOMMY   G   ISLANDERS

PERSONAL: Born February 1, 1971, in Surahammar, Sweden. ... 5-11/173. ... Catches left. ... Name pronounced SAH-loh.

TRANSACTIONS/CAREER NOTES: Selected by New York Islanders in third round (fifth Islanders pick, 118th overall) of NHL entry draft (June 26, 1993). ... Suffered from tonsillitis (February 8, 1997); missed one game.

HONORS: Won James Gatchene Memorial Trophy (1994-95). ... Won James Norris Memorial Trophy (1994-95). ... Won Garry F. Longman Memorial Trophy (1994-95). ... Named to IHL All-Star first team (1994-95). ... Won N.R. (Bud) Poile Trophy (1995-96).

MISCELLANEOUS: Member of gold-medal-winning Swedish Olympic team (1994). ... Allowed penalty shot goal (vs. Rob Zamuner, January 11, 1997).

Season Team	League	REGULAR SEASON							PLAYOFFS					
		Gms.	Min	W	L	T	GA	SO	Avg.	Gms.	Min.	W	L	GA	SO	Avg.
90-91—Vasteras	Sweden	2	100	...	...	...	11	0	6.60	—	—	—	—	—	—	—
91-92—Vasteras	Sweden								Did not play.							
92-93—Vasteras	Sweden	24	1431	...	...	...	59	2	2.47	—	—	—	—	—	—	—
93-94—Vasteras	Sweden	32	1896	...	...	...	106	1	3.35	—	—	—	—	—	—	—
—Swedish Oly. team	Int'l	6	370	...	...	...	13	1	2.11	—	—	—	—	—	—	—
94-95—Denver	IHL	65	*3810	*45	14	‡4	165	†3	*2.60	8	390	7	0	20	0	3.08
—New York Islanders	NHL	6	358	1	5	0	18	0	3.02	—	—	—	—	—	—	—
95-96—New York Islanders	NHL	10	523	1	7	1	35	0	4.02	—	—	—	—	—	—	—
—Utah	IHL	45	2695	28	15	‡2	119	†4	2.65	22	1341	*15	7	51	*3	2.28
96-97—New York Islanders	NHL	58	3208	20	27	8	151	5	2.82	—	—	—	—	—	—	—
97-98—New York Islanders	NHL	62	3461	23	29	5	152	4	2.64	—	—	—	—	—	—	—
—Swedish Oly. team	Int'l	4	238	2	2	0	9	0	2.27	—	—	—	—	—	—	—
NHL Totals (4 years)		136	7550	45	68	14	356	9	2.83							

SALVADOR, BRYCE   D   LIGHTNING

PERSONAL: Born February 11, 1994, in Brandon, Man. ... 6-1/194. ... Shoots left.

TRANSACTIONS/CAREER NOTES: Selected by Tampa Bay Lightning in sixth round (sixth Lightning pick, 138th overall) of NHL entry draft (June 29, 1994).

S

Season Team	League	REGULAR SEASON								PLAYOFFS				
		Gms.	G	A	Pts.	PIM	+/-	PP	SH	Gms.	G	A	Pts.	PIM
92-93—Lethbridge	WHL	64	1	4	5	29	...	...	...	4	0	0	0	0
93-94—Lethbridge	WHL	61	4	14	18	36	...	...	...	9	0	1	1	2
94-95—Lethbridge	WHL	67	1	9	10	88	...	...	...	—	—	—	—	—
95-96—Lethbridge	WHL	56	4	12	16	75	...	...	...	3	0	1	1	2
96-97—Lethbridge	WHL	63	8	32	40	81	...	...	...	19	0	7	7	14
97-98—Worcester	AHL	46	2	8	10	74	...	...	...	11	0	1	1	45

SAMSONOV, SERGEI · LW · BRUINS

PERSONAL: Born October 27, 1978, in Moscow, U.S.S.R. ... 5-8/184. ... Shoots right. ... Name pronounced sam-SAH-nahf.
TRANSACTIONS/CAREER NOTES: Selected by Boston Bruins in first round (second Bruins pick, eighth overall) of NHL entry draft (June 21, 1997). ... Sufffered from the flu (December 20, 1997); missed one game.
HONORS: Won Garry F. Longman Memorial Trophy (1996-97). ... Named to IHL All-Rookie first team (1996-97). ... Named NHL Rookie of the Year by The Sporting News (1997-98). ... Won Calder Memorial Trophy (1997-98). ... Named to NHL All-Rookie team (1997-98).
STATISTICAL PLATEAUS: Three-goal games: 1997-98 (1).

Season Team	League	REGULAR SEASON								PLAYOFFS				
		Gms.	G	A	Pts.	PIM	+/-	PP	SH	Gms.	G	A	Pts.	PIM
94-95—CSKA Moscow Jrs.	CIS	50	110	72	182		...	...	...	—	—	—	—	—
95-96—CSKA Moscow	CIS	51	21	17	38	12	...	...	...	3	1	1	2	4
96-97—Detroit	IHL	73	29	35	64	18	...	...	...	19	8	4	12	12
97-98—Boston	NHL	81	22	25	47	8	9	7	0	6	2	5	7	0
NHL Totals (1 year)		81	22	25	47	8	9	7	0	6	2	5	7	0

SAMUELSSON, KJELL · D

PERSONAL: Born October 18, 1958, in Tyngsryd, Sweden. ... 6-6/235. ... Shoots right. ... Name pronounced SHEHL SAM-yuhl-suhn.
TRANSACTIONS/CAREER NOTES: Selected by New York Rangers in sixth round (fifth Rangers pick, 119th overall) of NHL entry draft (June 9, 1984). ... Traded by Rangers with second-round pick (LW Patrik Juhlin) in 1989 draft to Philadelphia Flyers for G Bob Froese (December 18, 1986). ... Pulled groin (February 1988). ... Suffered herniated disc (October 1988). ... Bruised hand (March 1989). ... Bruised right shoulder (November 22, 1989); missed 13 games. ... Underwent shoulder surgery (March 1990). ... Traded by Flyers with RW Rick Tocchet, G Ken Wregget and third-round pick in 1992 draft to Pittsburgh Penguins for RW Mark Recchi, D Brian Benning and first-round pick (LW Jason Bowen) in 1992 draft (February 19, 1992). ... Bruised knee (November 27, 1992); missed one game. ... Broke bone in foot (December 1, 1992); missed nine games. ... Fractured cheekbone (December 27, 1992); missed nine games. ... Suffered from the flu (March 18, 1993); missed one game. ... Injured groin (October 19, 1993); missed nine games. ... Injured groin (December 28, 1993); missed 13 games. ... Suffered from the flu (February 27, 1995); missed four games. ... Injured groin (April 8, 1995); missed one game. ... Suffered from the flu (April 28, 1995); missed two games. ... Signed as free agent by Flyers (July 7, 1995). ... Suffered from the flu (November 10, 1995); missed one game. ... Sprained right thumb (December 22, 1995); missed one game. ... Strained neck (February 22, 1996); missed one game. ... Suffered from the flu (March 26, 1996); missed two games. ... Suffered from the flu (April 3, 1996); missed two games. ... Suffered from a virus (October 26, 1996); missed one game. ... Suffered sore back (November 7, 1996); missed four games. ... Suffered sore ribs (November 16, 1996); missed three games. ... Strained neck (January 9, 1997); missed final 39 games of regular season.
HONORS: Played in NHL All-Star Game (1988).
MISCELLANEOUS: Member of Stanley Cup championship team (1992).

Season Team	League	REGULAR SEASON								PLAYOFFS				
		Gms.	G	A	Pts.	PIM	+/-	PP	SH	Gms.	G	A	Pts.	PIM
82-83—Tyngsryd	Sweden	32	11	6	17	57	...	...	...	—	—	—	—	—
83-84—Leksand	Sweden	36	6	7	13	59	...	...	...	—	—	—	—	—
84-85—Leksand	Sweden	35	9	5	14	34	...	...	...	—	—	—	—	—
85-86—New York Rangers	NHL	9	0	0	0	10	-1	0	0	9	0	1	1	8
—New Haven	AHL	56	6	21	27	87	...	...	...	3	0	0	0	10
86-87—New York Rangers	NHL	30	2	6	8	50	-2	0	0	—	—	—	—	—
—Philadelphia	NHL	46	1	6	7	86	-9	0	0	26	0	4	4	25
87-88—Philadelphia	NHL	74	6	24	30	184	28	3	0	7	2	5	7	23
88-89—Philadelphia	NHL	69	3	14	17	140	13	0	1	19	1	3	4	24
89-90—Philadelphia	NHL	66	5	17	22	91	20	0	0	—	—	—	—	—
90-91—Philadelphia	NHL	78	9	19	28	82	4	1	0	—	—	—	—	—
91-92—Philadelphia	NHL	54	4	9	13	76	1	0	0	—	—	—	—	—
—Pittsburgh	NHL	20	1	2	3	34	0	0	0	15	0	3	3	12
92-93—Pittsburgh	NHL	63	3	6	9	106	25	0	0	12	0	3	3	2
93-94—Pittsburgh	NHL	59	5	8	13	118	18	1	0	6	0	0	0	26
94-95—Pittsburgh	NHL	41	1	6	7	54	8	0	0	11	0	1	1	32
95-96—Philadelphia	NHL	75	3	11	14	81	20	0	0	12	1	0	0	24
96-97—Philadelphia	NHL	34	4	3	7	47	17	0	0	5	0	0	0	2
97-98—Philadelphia	NHL	49	0	3	3	28	9	0	0	1	0	0	0	0
NHL Totals (13 years)		767	47	134	181	1187	151	5	1	123	4	20	24	178

SAMUELSSON, ULF · D · RANGERS

PERSONAL: Born March 26, 1964, in Fagersta, Sweden. ... 6-1/200. ... Shoots left. ... Name pronounced UHLF SAM-yuhl-suhn.
TRANSACTIONS/CAREER NOTES: Selected by Hartford Whalers in fourth round (fourth Whalers pick, 67th overall) of NHL entry draft (June 9, 1982). ... Suffered from the flu (December 1988); missed nine games. ... Tore ligaments in right knee and underwent surgery (August 1989); missed part of 1989-90 season. ... Traded by Whalers with C Ron Francis and D Grant Jennings to Pittsburgh Penguins for C John Cullen, D Zarley Zalapski and RW Jeff Parker (March 4, 1991). ... Injured hip flexor (October 29, 1991); missed six games. ... Underwent surgery to right elbow (December 1991); missed four games. ... Bruised left hand (February 8, 1992); missed one game. ... Suffered from the flu (February 1992); missed one game. ... Strained shoulder (November 10, 1992); missed two games. ... Broke cheekbone (November 27, 1992); missed two games. ... Bruised knee (January 1993); missed one game. ... Suspended one game by NHL (February 1993). ... Suspended three off-days

S

by NHL for stick-swinging incident (March 18, 1993). ... Suffered back spasms (April 4, 1993); missed one game. ... Injured knee (November 2, 1993); missed one game. ... Bruised foot (December 14, 1993); missed two games. ... Played in Europe during 1994-95 NHL lockout. ... Strained right elbow (March 21, 1995) and underwent elbow surgery (March 23, 1995); missed three games. ... Bruised knee (April 28, 1995); missed one game. ... Traded by Penguins with LW Luc Robitaille to New York Rangers for D Sergei Zubov and C Petr Nedved (August 31, 1995). ... Suffered mild concussion (October 14, 1995); missed two games. ... Separated shoulder (October 22, 1995); missed two games. ... Underwent elbow surgery (December 28, 1995); missed four games. ... Sprained knee (October 25, 1996); missed nine games. ... Suffered from the flu (October 3, 1997); missed one game. ... Strained rib muscle (November 28, 1997); missed one game. ... Sprained right knee (January 3, 1998); missed four games. ... Suffered laceration above left eye (March 28, 1998); missed two games.

MISCELLANEOUS: Member of Stanley Cup championship team (1991 and 1992).

Season Team	League	REGULAR SEASON								PLAYOFFS				
		Gms.	G	A	Pts.	PIM	+/-	PP	SH	Gms.	G	A	Pts.	PIM
81-82—Leksand	Sweden	31	3	1	4	40	...	...	...	—	—	—	—	—
82-83—Leksand	Sweden	33	9	6	15	72	...	...	...	—	—	—	—	—
83-84—Leksand	Sweden	36	5	10	15	53	...	...	...	—	—	—	—	—
84-85—Binghamton	AHL	36	5	11	16	92	...	...	...	—	—	—	—	—
—Hartford	NHL	41	2	6	8	83	-6	0	0	—	—	—	—	—
85-86—Hartford	NHL	80	5	19	24	174	8	0	1	10	1	2	3	38
86-87—Hartford	NHL	78	2	31	33	162	29	0	0	5	0	1	1	41
87-88—Hartford	NHL	76	8	33	41	159	-10	3	0	5	0	0	0	8
88-89—Hartford	NHL	71	9	26	35	181	23	3	0	4	0	2	2	4
89-90—Hartford	NHL	55	2	11	13	177	15	0	0	7	1	0	1	2
90-91—Hartford	NHL	62	3	18	21	174	13	0	0	—	—	—	—	—
—Pittsburgh	NHL	14	1	4	5	37	4	0	0	20	3	2	5	34
91-92—Pittsburgh	NHL	62	1	14	15	206	2	1	0	21	0	2	2	39
92-93—Pittsburgh	NHL	77	3	26	29	199	36	0	0	12	1	5	6	24
93-94—Pittsburgh	NHL	80	5	24	29	199	23	1	0	6	0	1	1	18
94-95—Leksand	Sweden	2	0	0	0	8	...	...	...	—	—	—	—	—
—Pittsburgh	NHL	44	1	15	16	113	11	0	0	7	0	2	2	8
95-96—New York Rangers	NHL	74	1	18	19	122	9	0	0	11	1	5	6	16
96-97—New York Rangers	NHL	73	6	11	17	138	3	1	0	15	0	2	2	30
97-98—New York Rangers	NHL	73	3	9	12	122	1	0	0	—	—	—	—	—
—Swedish Oly. team	Int'l	3	0	1	1	4	...	...	...	—	—	—	—	—
NHL Totals (14 years)		960	52	265	317	2296	161	9	1	123	7	24	31	262

SANDERSON, GEOFF   LW   SABRES

PERSONAL: Born February 1, 1972, in Hay River, Northwest Territories. ... 6-0/190. ... Shoots left.

TRANSACTIONS/CAREER NOTES: Selected by Hartford Whalers in second round (second Whalers pick, 36th overall) of NHL entry draft (June 16, 1990). ... Bruised shoulder (October 14, 1991); missed one game. ... Injured groin (November 13, 1991); missed three games. ... Bruised knee (December 7, 1991); missed five games. ... Suffered from the flu (February 1, 1994). ... Fined $500 by Whalers for involvement in bar brawl (April 1, 1994). ... Played in Europe during 1994-95 NHL lockout. ... Whalers franchise moved to North Carolina and renamed Carolina Hurricanes for 1997-98 season; NHL approved move on June 25, 1997. ... Traded by Hurricanes to Vancouver Canucks with D Enrico Ciccone and G Sean Burke for LW Martin Gelinas and G Kirk McLean (January 3, 1998). ... Injured shoulder (January 21, 1998); missed eight games. ... Traded by Canucks to Buffalo Sabres for LW Brad May and a third-round pick in the 1999 draft (February 4, 1998). ... Bruised hip (April 13, 1998); missed one game.

HONORS: Played in NHL All-Star Game (1994 and 1997).

STATISTICAL PLATEAUS: Three-goal games: 1992-93 (2), 1994-95 (1), 1995-96 (2). Total: 5.

Season Team	League	REGULAR SEASON								PLAYOFFS				
		Gms.	G	A	Pts.	PIM	+/-	PP	SH	Gms.	G	A	Pts.	PIM
88-89—Swift Current	WHL	58	17	11	28	16	...	...	...	12	3	5	8	6
89-90—Swift Current	WHL	70	32	62	94	56	...	...	...	4	1	4	5	8
90-91—Swift Current	WHL	70	62	50	112	57	...	...	...	3	1	2	3	4
—Hartford	NHL	2	1	0	1	0	-2	0	0	3	0	0	0	0
—Springfield	AHL	—	—	—	—	—	...	...	...	1	0	0	0	2
91-92—Hartford	NHL	64	13	18	31	18	5	2	0	7	1	0	1	2
92-93—Hartford	NHL	82	46	43	89	28	-21	21	2	—	—	—	—	—
93-94—Hartford	NHL	82	41	26	67	42	-13	15	1	—	—	—	—	—
94-95—HPK Hameenlinna	Finland	12	6	4	10	24	...	...	...	—	—	—	—	—
—Hartford	NHL	46	18	14	32	24	-10	4	0	—	—	—	—	—
95-96—Hartford	NHL	81	34	31	65	40	0	6	0	—	—	—	—	—
96-97—Hartford	NHL	82	36	31	67	29	-9	12	1	—	—	—	—	—
97-98—Carolina	NHL	40	7	10	17	14	-4	2	0	—	—	—	—	—
—Vancouver	NHL	9	0	3	3	4	-1	0	0	—	—	—	—	—
—Buffalo	NHL	26	4	5	9	20	6	0	0	14	3	1	4	4
NHL Totals (8 years)		514	200	181	381	219	-49	62	4	24	4	1	5	6

SANDSTROM, TOMAS   RW   MIGHTY DUCKS

PERSONAL: Born September 4, 1964, in Jakobstad, Finland. ... 6-2/205. ... Shoots left.

TRANSACTIONS/CAREER NOTES: Selected by New York Rangers in second round (second Rangers pick, 36th overall) of NHL entry draft (June 9, 1982). ... Suffered concussion (February 24, 1986). ... Fractured right ankle (February 11, 1987). ... Fractured right index finger (November 1987). ... Traded by Rangers with LW Tony Granato to Los Angeles Kings for C Bernie Nicholls (January 20, 1990). ... Fractured vertebrae (November 29, 1990); missed 10 games. ... Partially dislocated shoulder (December 28, 1991); missed 26 games. ... Fractured left forearm (November 21, 1992); missed 24 games. ... Fractured jaw (February 28, 1993); missed 21 games. ... Pulled hamstring (October 26, 1993); missed four games. ... Traded by Kings to Pittsburgh Penguins for D Marty McSorley and D Jim Peak (February 15, 1994). ... Played in Europe during 1994-95 NHL lockout. ... Sprained foot (January 22, 1995); missed one game. ... Underwent ankle surgery (February 20, 1996); missed nine games. ... Injured shoulder (March 13, 1996); missed 15 games. ... Pulled groin (October 11, 1996); missed seven games. ... Traded by Penguins to Detroit Red Wings for C Greg Johnson (January 27, 1997). ... Signed as free agent by Mighty Ducks of Anaheim (August 1, 1997). ... Separated right shoulder (April 18, 1998); missed final game of season.

HONORS: Named to NHL All-Rookie team (1984-85). ... Played in NHL All-Star Game (1988 and 1991).
MISCELLANEOUS: Member of Stanley Cup championship team (1997). ... Scored on a penalty shot (vs. Wendell Young, February 10, 1990).
STATISTICAL PLATEAUS: Three-goal games: 1986-87 (3), 1990-91 (3), 1992-93 (1). Total: 7. ... Four-goal games: 1986-87 (1). ... Total hat tricks: 8.

		REGULAR SEASON							PLAYOFFS				
Season Team	League	Gms.	G	A	Pts.	PIM	+/-	PP	SH	Gms.	G	A	Pts.	PIM
81-82—Fagersta	Sweden 2	32	28	11	39	74	...	...	...	—	—	—	—	—
82-83—Brynas Gavle	Sweden	36	22	14	36	36	...	...	...	—	—	—	—	—
83-84—Brynas Gavle	Sweden	34	20	10	30	...	...	...	...	—	—	—	—	—
—Swedish Oly. team	Int'l	7	2	1	3	6	...	...	...	—	—	—	—	—
84-85—New York Rangers	NHL	74	29	29	58	51	3	5	0	3	0	2	2	0
85-86—New York Rangers	NHL	73	25	29	54	109	-4	8	2	16	4	6	10	20
86-87—New York Rangers	NHL	64	40	34	74	60	8	13	0	6	1	2	3	20
87-88—New York Rangers	NHL	69	28	40	68	95	-6	11	0	—	—	—	—	—
88-89—New York Rangers	NHL	79	32	56	88	148	5	11	2	4	3	2	5	12
89-90—New York Rangers	NHL	48	19	19	38	100	-10	6	0	—	—	—	—	—
—Los Angeles	NHL	28	13	20	33	28	-1	1	1	10	5	4	9	19
90-91—Los Angeles	NHL	68	45	44	89	106	27	16	0	10	4	4	8	14
91-92—Los Angeles	NHL	49	17	22	39	70	-2	5	0	6	0	3	3	8
92-93—Los Angeles	NHL	39	25	27	52	57	12	8	0	24	8	17	25	12
93-94—Los Angeles	NHL	51	17	24	41	59	-12	4	0	—	—	—	—	—
—Pittsburgh	NHL	27	6	11	17	24	5	0	0	6	0	0	0	4
94-95—Malmo	Sweden	12	10	5	15	14	...	...	...	—	—	—	—	—
—Pittsburgh	NHL	47	21	23	44	42	1	4	1	12	3	3	6	16
95-96—Pittsburgh	NHL	58	35	35	70	69	4	17	1	18	4	2	6	30
96-97—Pittsburgh	NHL	40	9	15	24	33	4	1	1	20	0	4	4	24
—Detroit	NHL	34	9	9	18	36	2	0	1	—	—	—	—	—
97-98—Anaheim	NHL	77	9	8	17	64	-25	2	1	—	—	—	—	—
—Swedish Oly. team	Int'l	4	0	1	1	0	...	...	...	—	—	—	—	—
NHL Totals (14 years)		925	379	445	824	1151	11	112	10	135	32	49	81	179

SANDWITH, TERRAN — D — MIGHTY DUCKS

PERSONAL: Born April 17, 1972, in Edmonton. ... 6-4/220. ... Shoots left.
TRANSACTIONS/CAREER NOTES: Selected by Philadelphia Flyers in second round (fourth Flyers pick, 42nd overall) of NHL entry draft (June 16, 1990). ... Suffered blood disorder (September 1990). ... Loaned to Canadian national team prior to 1995-96 season. ... Signed as free agent by Mighty Ducks of Anaheim (July 14, 1998).

		REGULAR SEASON							PLAYOFFS				
Season Team	League	Gms.	G	A	Pts.	PIM	+/-	PP	SH	Gms.	G	A	Pts.	PIM
87-88—Hobbema	AJHL	58	5	8	13	106	...	...	...	—	—	—	—	—
88-89—Tri-City	WHL	31	0	0	0	29	...	...	...	6	0	0	0	4
89-90—Tri-City	WHL	70	4	14	18	92	...	...	...	7	0	2	2	14
90-91—Tri-City	WHL	46	5	17	22	132	...	...	...	7	1	0	1	14
91-92—Brandon	WHL	41	6	14	20	145	...	...	...	—	—	—	—	—
—Saskatoon	WHL	18	2	5	7	53	...	...	...	18	2	1	3	28
92-93—Hershey	AHL	61	1	12	13	140	...	...	...	—	—	—	—	—
93-94—Hershey	AHL	62	3	5	8	169	...	...	...	2	0	1	1	4
94-95—Hershey	AHL	11	1	1	2	32	...	...	...	—	—	—	—	—
—Kansas City	IHL	25	0	3	3	73	...	...	...	—	—	—	—	—
95-96—Canadian nat'l team	Int'l	47	3	12	15	63	...	...	...	—	—	—	—	—
—Cape Breton	AHL	5	0	2	2	4	...	...	...	—	—	—	—	—
96-97—Hamilton	AHL	78	3	6	9	213	...	...	...	22	0	2	2	27
97-98—Hamilton	AHL	54	4	8	12	131	...	...	...	9	0	0	0	10
—Edmonton	NHL	8	0	0	0	6	-4	0	0	—	—	—	—	—
NHL Totals (1 year)		8	0	0	0	6	-4	0	0					

SARAULT, YVES — LW — FLAMES

PERSONAL: Born December 23, 1972, in Valleyfield, Que. ... 6-1/200. ... Shoots left. ... Name pronounced EEV suh-ROH.
TRANSACTIONS/CAREER NOTES: Traded by Victoriaville Tigers with D Jason Downey to St. Jean Lynx for D Sylvain Bourgeois (May 26, 1990). ... Selected by Montreal Canadiens in third round (third Canadiens pick, 61st overall) of NHL entry draft (June 22, 1991). ... Traded by Canadiens with RW Craig Ferguson to Calgary Flames for eighth-round pick (D Petr Kubos) in 1997 draft (November 25, 1995). ... Signed as free agent by Colorado Avalanche (September 7, 1996). ... Signed as free agent by Ottawa Senators (July 28, 1998).
HONORS: Named to QMJHL All-Star second team (1991-92).

		REGULAR SEASON							PLAYOFFS				
Season Team	League	Gms.	G	A	Pts.	PIM	+/-	PP	SH	Gms.	G	A	Pts.	PIM
89-90—Victoriaville	QMJHL	70	12	28	40	140	...	...	...	16	0	3	3	26
90-91—St. Jean	QMJHL	56	22	24	46	113	...	...	...	—	—	—	—	—
91-92—St. Jean	QMJHL	50	28	38	66	96	...	...	...	—	—	—	—	—
—Trois-Rivieres	QMJHL	18	16	14	30	10	...	...	...	15	10	10	20	18
92-93—Fredericton	AHL	59	14	17	31	41	...	...	...	3	0	1	1	2
—Wheeling	ECHL	2	1	3	4	0	...	...	...	—	—	—	—	—
93-94—Fredericton	AHL	60	13	14	27	72	...	...	...	—	—	—	—	—
94-95—Fredericton	AHL	69	24	21	45	96	...	...	...	13	2	1	3	33
—Montreal	NHL	8	0	1	1	0	-1	0	0	—	—	—	—	—
95-96—Montreal	NHL	14	0	0	0	4	-7	0	0	—	—	—	—	—
—Calgary	NHL	11	2	1	3	4	-2	0	0	—	—	—	—	—
—Saint John	AHL	26	10	12	22	34	...	...	...	16	6	2	8	33

Season Team	League	REGULAR SEASON								PLAYOFFS				
		Gms.	G	A	Pts.	PIM	+/-	PP	SH	Gms.	G	A	Pts.	PIM
96-97—Colorado	NHL	28	2	1	3	6	0	0	0	5	0	0	0	2
—Hershey	AHL	6	2	3	5	8	...	...	...	—	—	—	—	—
97-98—Hershey	AHL	63	23	36	59	43	...	...	...	7	1	2	3	14
—Colorado	NHL	2	1	0	1	0	1	0	0	—	—	—	—	—
NHL Totals (4 years)		63	5	3	8	14	-9	0	0	5	0	0	0	2

SARICH, COREY — D — SABRES

PERSONAL: Born August 16, 1978, in Saskatoon, Sask. ... 6-3/175. ... Shoots right. ... Name pronounced SAIRCH.
TRANSACTIONS/CAREER NOTES: Selected by Buffalo Sabres in second round (second Sabres pick, 27th overall) of NHL entry draft (June 22, 1996).
HONORS: Named to WHL (West) All-Star second team (1997-98).

Season Team	League	REGULAR SEASON								PLAYOFFS				
		Gms.	G	A	Pts.	PIM	+/-	PP	SH	Gms.	G	A	Pts.	PIM
94-95—Saskatoon	WHL	6	0	0	0	4	...	...	...	3	0	1	1	0
95-96—Saskatoon	WHL	59	5	18	23	54	...	...	...	3	0	0	0	4
96-97—Saskatoon	WHL	58	6	27	33	158	...	...	...	—	—	—	—	—
97-98—Seattle	WHL	46	8	40	48	137	...	...	...	—	—	—	—	—

SARNO, PETER — C — OILERS

PERSONAL: Born July 26, 1979, in Toronto ... 5-11/180. ... Shoots left.
TRANSACTIONS/CAREER NOTES: Selected by Edmonton Oilers in sixth round (sixth Oilers pick, 141st overall) of NHL entry draft (June 21, 1997).
HONORS: Won Emms Family Award (1996-97). ... Named to OHL All-Rookie first team (1996-97). ... Won Eddie Powers Memorial Trophy (1997-98).

Season Team	League	REGULAR SEASON								PLAYOFFS				
		Gms.	G	A	Pts.	PIM	+/-	PP	SH	Gms.	G	A	Pts.	PIM
95-96—North York Flames	OPJHL	52	39	57	96	27	...	...	...	—	—	—	—	—
96-97—Windsor	OHL	66	20	63	83	59	...	...	...	5	0	3	3	6
97-98—Windsor	OHL	64	33	*88	*121	18	...	...	...	—	—	—	—	—
—Hamilton	AHL	8	1	1	2	2	...	...	...	—	—	—	—	—

SATAN, MIROSLAV — LW/RW — SABRES

PERSONAL: Born October 22, 1974, in Topolcany, Czechoslovakia. ... 6-1/185. ... Shoots left. ... Name pronounced shuh-TAN.
TRANSACTIONS/CAREER NOTES: Selected by Edmonton Oilers in fifth round (sixth Oilers pick, 111th overall) of NHL entry draft (June 26, 1993). ... Suffered collapsed lung (October 1, 1995); missed two games. ... Separated right shoulder (January 13, 1996); missed four games. ... Suffered from the flu (March 9, 1997); missed one game. ... Traded by Oilers to Buffalo Sabres for D Craig Millar and LW Barrie Moore (March 18, 1997). ... Fined $1,000 by NHL for high-sticking incident (May 28, 1998).
STATISTICAL NOTES: Led NHL with 21.0 shooting percentage (1996-97).
STATISTICAL PLATEAUS: Three-goal games: 1996-97 (1), 1997-98 (1). Total: 2.

Season Team	League	REGULAR SEASON								PLAYOFFS				
		Gms.	G	A	Pts.	PIM	+/-	PP	SH	Gms.	G	A	Pts.	PIM
91-92—VTJ Topolcany	Czech Dv.II	9	2	1	3	6	...	...	...	—	—	—	—	—
—VTJ Topolcany Jrs	Czech. Jrs.	31	30	22	52		...	...	...	—	—	—	—	—
92-93—Dukla Trencin	Czech.	38	11	6	17	...	...	...	...	—	—	—	—	—
93-94—Dukla Trencin	Slovakia	30	32	16	48	16	...	...	...	—	—	—	—	—
—Slovakian Oly. team	Int'l	8	9	0	9	0	...	...	...	—	—	—	—	—
94-95—Detroit	IHL	8	1	3	4	4	...	...	...	—	—	—	—	—
—San Diego	IHL	6	0	2	2	6	...	...	...	—	—	—	—	—
—Cape Breton	AHL	25	24	16	40	15	...	...	...	—	—	—	—	—
95-96—Edmonton	NHL	62	18	17	35	22	0	6	0	—	—	—	—	—
96-97—Edmonton	NHL	64	17	11	28	22	-4	5	0	—	—	—	—	—
—Buffalo	NHL	12	8	2	10	4	1	2	0	7	0	0	0	0
97-98—Buffalo	NHL	79	22	24	46	34	2	9	0	14	5	4	9	4
NHL Totals (3 years)		217	65	54	119	82	-1	22	0	21	5	4	9	4

SAVAGE, ANDRE — C — BRUINS

PERSONAL: Born May 27, 1975, in Ottawa. ... 6-0/195. ... Shoots right.
COLLEGE: Michigan Tech.
TRANSACTIONS/CAREER NOTES: Signed as free agent by Boston Bruins (June 12, 1998).
HONORS: Named to WCHA All-Star first team (1997-98).

Season Team	League	REGULAR SEASON								PLAYOFFS				
		Gms.	G	A	Pts.	PIM	+/-	PP	SH	Gms.	G	A	Pts.	PIM
94-95—Michigan Tech	WCHA	39	7	17	24	56	...	...	...	—	—	—	—	—
95-96—Michigan Tech	WCHA	40	13	27	40	42	...	...	...	—	—	—	—	—
96-97—Michigan Tech	WCHA	37	18	20	38	34	...	...	...	—	—	—	—	—
97-98—Michigan Tech	WCHA	33	14	27	41	34	...	...	...	—	—	—	—	—

SAVAGE, BRIAN   LW   CANADIENS

PERSONAL: Born February 24, 1971, in Sudbury, Ont. ... 6-2/192. ... Shoots left.
HIGH SCHOOL: Lo-Ellen Park Secondary (Sudbury, Ont.).
COLLEGE: Miami of Ohio.
TRANSACTIONS/CAREER NOTES: Selected by Montreal Canadiens in eighth round (11th Canadiens pick, 171st overall) of NHL entry draft (June 22, 1991). ... Bruised knee (February 4, 1995); missed 10 games. ... Bruised knee (April 5, 1995); missed one game. ... Suffered hip pointer (February 17, 1996); missed six games. ... Suffered from the flu (April 1, 1996); missed one game. ... Injured groin (October 26, 1996); missed one game. ... Fractured hand (October 1, 1997); missed seven games. ... Bruised thigh (November 26, 1997); missed one game. ... Fractured thumb (March 21, 1998); missed 10 games.
HONORS: Named to NCAA All-America West second team (1992-93). ... Named CCHA Player of the Year (1992-93). ... Named to CCHA All-Star first team (1992-93).
MISCELLANEOUS: Member of silver-medal-winning Canadian Olympic team (1994).
STATISTICAL PLATEAUS: Three-goal games: 1995-96 (1), 1996-97 (1). Total: 2. ... Four-goal games: 1997-98 (1). ... Total hat tricks: 3.

		REGULAR SEASON								PLAYOFFS				
Season Team	League	Gms.	G	A	Pts.	PIM	+/-	PP	SH	Gms.	G	A	Pts.	PIM
90-91—Miami of Ohio	CCHA	28	5	6	11	26	...	...	...	—	—	—	—	—
91-92—Miami of Ohio	CCHA	40	24	16	40	43	...	...	...	—	—	—	—	—
92-93—Miami of Ohio	CCHA	38	37	21	58	44	...	...	...	—	—	—	—	—
—Canadian nat'l team	Int'l	9	3	0	3	12	...	...	...	—	—	—	—	—
93-94—Canadian nat'l team	Int'l	51	20	26	46	38	...	...	...	—	—	—	—	—
—Can. Olympic Team	Int'l	8	2	2	4	6	...	...	...	—	—	—	—	—
—Fredericton	AHL	17	12	15	27	4	...	...	...	—	—	—	—	—
—Montreal	NHL	3	1	0	1	0	0	0	0	3	0	2	2	0
94-95—Montreal	NHL	37	12	7	19	27	5	0	0	—	—	—	—	—
95-96—Montreal	NHL	75	25	8	33	28	-8	4	0	6	0	2	2	2
96-97—Montreal	NHL	81	23	37	60	39	-14	5	0	5	1	1	2	0
97-98—Montreal	NHL	64	26	17	43	36	11	8	0	9	0	2	2	6
NHL Totals (5 years)		260	87	69	156	130	-6	17	0	23	1	7	8	8

SAVARD, MARC   C   RANGERS

PERSONAL: Born July 17, 1977, in Ottawa. ... 5-11/185. ... Shoots left. ... Name pronounced suh-VAHRD.
HIGH SCHOOL: Henry Street (Whitby, Ont.).
TRANSACTIONS/CAREER NOTES: Selected by New York Rangers in fourth round (third Rangers pick, 91st overall) of NHL entry draft (July 8, 1995).
HONORS: Won Can.HL Top Scorer Award (1994-95). ... Won Eddie Powers Memorial Trophy (1994-95). ... Named to OHL All-Star second team (1994-95).

		REGULAR SEASON								PLAYOFFS				
Season Team	League	Gms.	G	A	Pts.	PIM	+/-	PP	SH	Gms.	G	A	Pts.	PIM
92-93—Metcalfe	Jr. B	31	46	53	99	26	...	...	...	—	—	—	—	—
93-94—Oshawa	OHL	61	18	39	57	24	...	...	...	5	4	3	7	8
94-95—Oshawa	OHL	66	43	96	*139	78	...	...	...	7	5	6	11	8
95-96—Oshawa	OHL	48	28	59	87	77	...	...	...	5	4	5	9	6
96-97—Oshawa	OHL	64	43	*87	*130	94	...	...	...	18	13	†24	*37	20
97-98—New York Rangers	NHL	28	1	5	6	4	-4	0	0	—	—	—	—	—
—Hartford	AHL	58	21	53	74	66	...	...	...	15	8	19	27	24
NHL Totals (1 year)		28	1	5	6	4	-4	0	0					

SCATCHARD, DAVE   C   CANUCKS

PERSONAL: Born February 20, 1976, in Hinton, Alta. ... 6-2/217. ... Shoots right. ... Name pronounced SKATCH-uhrd.
TRANSACTIONS/CAREER NOTES: Selected by Vancouver Canucks in second round (third Canucks pick, 42nd overall) of NHL entry draft (June 28, 1994). ... Suffered hip pointer (December 15, 1997); missed two games.

		REGULAR SEASON								PLAYOFFS				
Season Team	League	Gms.	G	A	Pts.	PIM	+/-	PP	SH	Gms.	G	A	Pts.	PIM
92-93—Kimberley	RMJHL	51	20	23	43	61	...	...	...	—	—	—	—	—
93-94—Portland	WHL	47	9	11	20	46	...	...	...	10	2	1	3	4
94-95—Portland	WHL	71	20	30	50	148	...	...	...	8	0	3	3	21
95-96—Portland	WHL	59	19	28	47	146	...	...	...	7	1	8	9	14
—Syracuse	AHL	1	0	0	0	0	...	...	...	15	2	5	7	29
96-97—Syracuse	AHL	26	8	7	15	65	...	...	...	—	—	—	—	—
97-98—Vancouver	NHL	76	13	11	24	165	-4	0	0	—	—	—	—	—
NHL Totals (1 year)		76	13	11	24	165	-4	0	0					

SCHAEFER, PETER   LW   CANUCKS

PERSONAL: Born July 12, 1977, in Yellow Grass, Sask. ... 5-11/190. ... Shoots left.
HIGH SCHOOL: Crocus Plains (Brandon, Man.).
TRANSACTIONS/CAREER NOTES: Selected by Vancouver Canucks in third round (third Canucks pick, 66th overall) of NHL entry draft (July 8, 1995).
HONORS: Named to WHL (East) All-Star first team (1995-96 and 1996-97). ... Won Four Broncos Memorial Trophy (1996-97). ... Named to Can.HL All-Star first team (1996-97).

S

Season Team	League	REGULAR SEASON								PLAYOFFS				
		Gms.	G	A	Pts.	PIM	+/-	PP	SH	Gms.	G	A	Pts.	PIM
93-94—Brandon	WHL	2	1	0	1	0	...	...	...	—	—	—	—	—
94-95—Brandon	WHL	68	27	32	59	34	...	...	...	18	5	3	8	18
95-96—Brandon	WHL	69	47	61	108	53	...	...	...	19	10	13	23	5
96-97—Brandon	WHL	61	49	74	123	85	...	...	...	6	1	4	5	4
—Syracuse	AHL	5	0	3	3	0	...	...	...	3	1	3	4	14
97-98—Syracuse	AHL	73	19	44	63	41	...	...	...	5	2	1	3	2

SCHAFER, PAXTON　　　G　　　BRUINS

PERSONAL: Born February 26, 1976, in Medicine Hat, Alta. ... 5-9/164. ... Catches left.
COLLEGE: Medicine Hat (Alta.).
TRANSACTIONS/CAREER NOTES: Selected by Boston Bruins in second round (third Bruins pick, 47th overall) of NHL entry draft (July 8, 1995).
HONORS: Won Del Wilson Trophy (1994-95). ... Named to Can.HL All-Star first team (1994-95). ... Named to WHL (East) All-Star first team (1994-95).

Season Team	League	REGULAR SEASON							PLAYOFFS					
		Gms.	Min	W	L	T	GA	SO	Avg.	Gms.	Min.	W	L	GA	SO	Avg.
93-94—Medicine Hat	WHL	19	909	6	9	1	67	0	4.42	—	—	—	—	—	—	—
94-95—Medicine Hat	WHL	61	3519	32	26	2	185	0	3.15	5	339	1	4	18	0	3.19
95-96—Medicine Hat	WHL	60	3256	24	30	3	200	1	3.69	5	251	1	4	25	0	5.98
96-97—Providence	AHL	22	1206	9	10	0	75	1	3.73	—	—	—	—	—	—	—
—Charlotte	ECHL	4	239	3	1	‡0	7	0	1.76	—	—	—	—	—	—	—
97-98—Charlotte	ECHL	44	2538	21	17	‡5	131	1	3.10	7	428	3	4	21	0	2.94
—Providence	AHL	3	159	1	1	0	11	0	4.15	—	—	—	—	—	—	—

SCHMIDT, CHRIS　　　LW　　　KINGS

PERSONAL: Born March 1, 1976, in Beaverlodge, Alta. ... 6-3/193. ... Shoots left.
HIGH SCHOOL: Meadowdale (Lynwood, Wash.).
TRANSACTIONS/CAREER NOTES: Selected by Los Angeles Kings in fifth round (fourth Kings pick, 111th overall) of NHL entry draft (June 29, 1994).

Season Team	League	REGULAR SEASON								PLAYOFFS				
		Gms.	G	A	Pts.	PIM	+/-	PP	SH	Gms.	G	A	Pts.	PIM
92-93—Seattle	WHL	61	6	7	13	17	...	...	...	5	0	1	1	0
93-94—Seattle	WHL	68	7	17	24	26	...	...	...	9	3	1	4	2
94-95—Seattle	WHL	61	21	11	32	31	...	...	...	3	0	0	0	0
95-96—Seattle	WHL	61	39	23	62	135	...	...	...	5	1	5	6	9
96-97—Mississippi	ECHL	18	7	7	14	35	...	...	...	—	—	—	—	—
—Phoenix	IHL	37	3	6	9	60	...	...	...	—	—	—	—	—
97-98—Fredericton	AHL	69	8	5	13	67	...	...	...	4	0	0	0	2

SCHNEIDER, MATHIEU　　　D　　　MAPLE LEAFS

PERSONAL: Born June 12, 1969, in New York. ... 5-10/192. ... Shoots left.
HIGH SCHOOL: Mount St. Charles Academy (Woonsocket, R.I.).
TRANSACTIONS/CAREER NOTES: Selected by Montreal Canadiens in third round (fourth Canadiens pick, 44th overall) of NHL entry draft (June 13, 1987). ... Bruised left shoulder (February 1990). ... Sprained left ankle (January 26, 1991); missed nine games. ... Sprained ankle (January 27, 1993); missed 24 games. ... Separated shoulder (April 18, 1993); missed seven playoff games. ... Injured ankle (December 6, 1993); missed two games. ... Underwent arthroscopic elbow surgery (March 29, 1994); missed five games. ... Suffered from cold (February 27, 1995); missed one game. ... Traded by Canadiens with LW Kirk Muller and C Craig Darby to New York Islanders for D Vladimir Malakhov and C Pierre Turgeon (April 5, 1995). ... Bruised ribs (October 28, 1995); missed one game. ... Traded by Islanders with LW Wendel Clark and D D.J. Smith to Toronto Maple Leafs for LW Sean Haggerty, C Darby Hendrickson, D Kenny Jonsson and first-round pick (G Roberto Luongo) in 1997 draft (March 13, 1996). ... Suspended three games by NHL for elbowing incident (November 14, 1996). ... Strained groin (December 12, 1996); missed 27 games. ... Reinjured groin (February 12, 1997); underwent groin surgery (March 7, 1997) and missed final 26 games of season. ... Suffered concussion and cut face (December 2, 1997); missed two games. ... Bruised shoulder (January 6, 1998); missed two games. ... Strained upper abdomen (February 2, 1998); missed one game. ... Strained groin (April 6, 1998); missed one game.
HONORS: Named to OHL All-Star first team (1987-88 and 1988-89). ... Played in NHL All-Star Game (1996).
MISCELLANEOUS: Member of Stanley Cup championship team (1993). ... Captain of New York Islanders (1995-96).

Season Team	League	REGULAR SEASON								PLAYOFFS				
		Gms.	G	A	Pts.	PIM	+/-	PP	SH	Gms.	G	A	Pts.	PIM
85-86—Mt. St. Charles H.S.	R.I.H.S.	19	3	27	30	...	...	...	...	—	—	—	—	—
86-87—Cornwall	OHL	63	7	29	36	75	...	...	...	5	0	0	0	22
87-88—Montreal	NHL	4	0	0	0	2	-2	0	0	—	—	—	—	—
—Cornwall	OHL	48	21	40	61	85	...	...	...	11	2	6	8	14
—Sherbrooke	AHL	—	—	—	—	—	...	...	...	3	0	3	3	12
88-89—Cornwall	OHL	59	16	57	73	96	...	...	...	18	7	20	27	30
89-90—Sherbrooke	AHL	28	6	13	19	20	...	...	...	—	—	—	—	—
—Montreal	NHL	44	7	14	21	25	2	5	0	9	1	3	4	31
90-91—Montreal	NHL	69	10	20	30	63	7	5	0	13	2	7	9	18
91-92—Montreal	NHL	78	8	24	32	72	10	2	0	10	1	4	5	6
92-93—Montreal	NHL	60	13	31	44	91	8	3	0	11	1	2	3	16
93-94—Montreal	NHL	75	20	32	52	62	15	11	0	1	0	0	0	0
94-95—Montreal	NHL	30	5	15	20	49	-3	2	0	—	—	—	—	—
—New York Islanders	NHL	13	3	6	9	30	-5	1	0	—	—	—	—	—
95-96—New York Islanders	NHL	65	11	36	47	93	-18	7	0	—	—	—	—	—
—Toronto	NHL	13	2	5	7	10	-2	0	0	6	0	4	4	8
96-97—Toronto	NHL	26	5	7	12	20	3	1	0	—	—	—	—	—
97-98—Toronto	NHL	76	11	26	37	44	-12	4	1	—	—	—	—	—
—U.S. Olympic Team	Int'l	4	0	0	0	6	...	...	...	—	—	—	—	—
NHL Totals (10 years)		553	95	216	311	561	3	41	1	50	5	20	25	79

S

SCHULTZ, RAY — D — ISLANDERS

PERSONAL: Born November 14, 1976, in Red Deer, Alta. ... 6-2/200. ... Shoots left. ... Cousin of Rene Chapdelaine, defenseman with Los Angeles Kings (1989-90 through 1991-92).
TRANSACTIONS/CAREER NOTES: Selected by Ottawa Senators in eighth round (eighth Senators pick, 184th overall) of NHL entry draft (July 8, 1995). ... Signed as free agent by New York Islanders (June 17, 1997).

		REGULAR SEASON								PLAYOFFS				
Season Team	League	Gms.	G	A	Pts.	PIM	+/-	PP	SH	Gms.	G	A	Pts.	PIM
93-94—Tri-City	WHL	3	0	0	0	11	...	...	...	—	—	—	—	—
94-95—Tri-City	WHL	63	1	8	9	209	...	...	...	11	0	0	0	16
95-96—Calgary	WHL	66	3	17	20	282	...	...	...	—	—	—	—	—
96-97—Calgary	WHL	32	3	17	20	141	...	...	...	—	—	—	—	—
—Kelowna	WHL	23	3	11	14	63	...	...	...	6	0	2	2	12
97-98—Kentucky	AHL	51	2	4	6	179	...	...	...	1	0	0	0	25
—New York Islanders	NHL	13	0	1	1	45	3	0	0	—	—	—	—	—
NHL Totals (1 year)		13	0	1	1	45	3	0	0					

SCHUTZ, DEREK — C — FLAMES

PERSONAL: Born March 5, 1979, in Yorkton, Sask. ... 6-2/185. ... Shoots right.
TRANSACTIONS/CAREER NOTES: Selected by Calgary Flames in third round (fifth Flames pick, 60th overall) of NHL entry draft (June 21, 1997).

		REGULAR SEASON								PLAYOFFS				
Season Team	League	Gms.	G	A	Pts.	PIM	+/-	PP	SH	Gms.	G	A	Pts.	PIM
94-95—Spokane	WHL	2	0	0	0	2	...	...	...	—	—	—	—	—
95-96—Spokane	WHL	70	10	7	17	121	...	...	...	18	1	4	5	37
96-97—Spokane	WHL	61	20	21	41	126	...	...	...	9	1	3	4	9
97-98—Spokane	WHL	67	22	34	56	113	...	...	...	18	1	5	6	21

SCHWAB, COREY — G — LIGHTNING

PERSONAL: Born November 4, 1970, in Battleford, Sask. ... 6-0/180. ... Catches left. ... Name pronounced SHWAHB.
TRANSACTIONS/CAREER NOTES: Selected by New Jersey Devils in 10th round (12th Devils pick, 200th overall) of NHL entry draft (June 16, 1990). ... Injured groin (October 12, 1995); missed six games. ... Traded by Devils to Tampa Bay Lightning for G Jeff Reese and second-(LW Pierre Dagenais) and eighth-(RW Jason Bertsch) round picks in 1996 draft (June 22, 1996). ... Injured groin (January 9, 1997); missed one game. ... Injured groin (December 23, 1997); missed one game. ... Injured ankle (December 31, 1997); missed remainder of season.
HONORS: Shared Harry (Hap) Holmes Memorial Trophy with Mike Dunham (1994-95). ... Shared Jack Butterfield Trophy with Mike Dunham (1994-95). ... Named to AHL All-Star second team (1994-95).
MISCELLANEOUS: Allowed a penalty shot goal (vs. Mike Keane, October 24, 1997). ... Stopped a penalty shot attempt (vs. Steve Heinze, December 17, 1997).

		REGULAR SEASON								PLAYOFFS						
Season Team	League	Gms.	Min	W	L	T	GA	SO	Avg.	Gms.	Min.	W	L	GA	SO	Avg.
88-89—Seattle	WHL	10	386	2	2	0	31	0	4.82	—	—	—	—	—	—	—
89-90—Seattle	WHL	27	1150	15	2	1	69	0	3.60	3	49	0	0	2	0	2.45
90-91—Seattle	WHL	58	3289	32	18	3	224	1	4.09	6	382	1	5	25	0	3.93
91-92—Utica	AHL	24	1322	9	12	1	95	1	4.31	—	—	—	—	—	—	—
—Cincinnati	AHL	8	450	6	0	1	31	0	4.13	9	540	6	3	29	0	3.22
92-93—Cincinnati	IHL	3	185	1	2	‡0	17	0	5.51	—	—	—	—	—	—	—
—Utica	AHL	40	2387	18	16	5	169	2	4.25	1	59	0	1	6	0	6.10
93-94—Albany	AHL	51	3059	27	21	3	184	0	3.61	5	298	1	4	20	0	4.03
94-95—Albany	AHL	45	2711	25	10	9	117	3	*2.59	7	425	6	1	19	0	2.68
95-96—Albany	AHL	5	298	3	2	0	13	0	2.62	—	—	—	—	—	—	—
—New Jersey	NHL	10	331	0	3	0	12	0	2.18	—	—	—	—	—	—	—
96-97—Tampa Bay	NHL	31	1462	11	12	1	74	2	3.04	—	—	—	—	—	—	—
97-98—Tampa Bay	NHL	16	821	2	9	1	40	1	2.92	—	—	—	—	—	—	—
NHL Totals (3 years)		57	2614	13	24	2	126	3	2.89							

SCISSONS, JEFF — C — CANUCKS

PERSONAL: Born November 24, 1976, in Saskatoon, Sask. ... 6-1/190. ... Shoots left.
COLLEGE: Minnesota-Duluth.
TRANSACTIONS/CAREER NOTES: Selected by Vancouver Canucks in eighth round (seventh Canucks pick, 201st overall) of NHL entry draft (June 22, 1996).

		REGULAR SEASON								PLAYOFFS				
Season Team	League	Gms.	G	A	Pts.	PIM	+/-	PP	SH	Gms.	G	A	Pts.	PIM
95-96—Vernon	Tier II Jr. A	60	26	48	74	28	...	...	...	—	—	—	—	—
96-97—Minnesota-Duluth	WCHA	38	3	14	17	30	...	...	...	—	—	—	—	—
97-98—Minnesota-Duluth	WCHA	40	17	24	41	50	...	...	...	—	—	—	—	—

SEELEY, RICHARD — D — KINGS

PERSONAL: Born April 30, 1979, in Powell River, B.C. ... 6-2/217. ... Shoots left.
TRANSACTIONS/CAREER NOTES: Selected by Los Angeles Kings in sixth round (sixth Kings pick, 137th overall) of NHL entry draft (June 21, 1997).

Season Team	League	REGULAR SEASON								PLAYOFFS				
		Gms.	G	A	Pts.	PIM	+/-	PP	SH	Gms.	G	A	Pts.	PIM
95-96—Powell River	BCJHL	44	1	8	9	42	...	...	...	—	—	—	—	—
96-97—Lethbridge	WHL	3	0	0	0	11	...	...	...	—	—	—	—	—
—Prince Albert	WHL	18	0	1	1	9	...	...	...	4	0	0	0	2
97-98—Prince Albert	WHL	65	8	21	29	114	...	...	...	—	—	—	—	—

SELANNE, TEEMU   RW   MIGHTY DUCKS

PERSONAL: Born July 3, 1970, in Helsinki, Finland. ... 6-0/200. ... Shoots right. ... Name pronounced TAY-moo suh-LAH-nay. ... Nickname: The Finnish Flash.

TRANSACTIONS/CAREER NOTES: Selected by Winnipeg Jets in first round (first Jets pick, 10th overall) of NHL entry draft (June 11, 1988). ... Broke left leg (October 19, 1989). ... Severed Achilles' tendon (January 26, 1994); missed 33 games. ... Played in Europe during 1994-95 NHL lockout. ... Suffered from patella tendonitis (February 28, 1995); missed one game. ... Suspended two games and fined $500 by NHL (March 28, 1995). ... Traded by Jets with C Marc Chouinard and fourth-round pick (traded to Toronto) in 1996 draft to Mighty Ducks of Anaheim for C Chad Kilger, D Oleg Tverdovsky and third-round pick (D Per-Anton Lundstrom) in 1996 draft (Febraury 7, 1996). ... Strained abdominal muscle (March 23, 1997); missed four games. ... Strained abdomen (February 7, 1998); missed five games. ... Strained groin (April 9, 1998); missed final four games of season.

HONORS: Named to Finnish League All-Star team (1990-91 and 1991-92). ... Named NHL Rookie of the Year by THE SPORTING NEWS (1992-93). ... Won Calder Memorial Trophy (1992-93). ... Named to THE SPORTING NEWS All-Star first team (1992-93). ... Named to NHL All-Star first team (1992-93 and 1996-97). ... Named to NHL All-Rookie team (1992-93). ... Played in NHL All-Star Game (1993, 1994 and 1996-1998). ... Named to THE SPORTING NEWS All-Star team (1996-97 and 1997-98). ... Named All-Star Game Most Valuable Player (1998). ... Named to NHL All-Star second team (1997-98).

RECORDS: Holds NHL rookie-season records for most points—132; and goals—76 (1993).

STATISTICAL NOTES: Tied for league lead with three game-tying goals (1997-98).

STATISTICAL PLATEAUS: Three-goal games: 1992-93 (4), 1993-94 (2), 1995-96 (2), 1996-97 (1), 1997-98 (3). Total: 12. ... Four-goal games: 1992-93 (1), 1995-96 (1). Total: 2. ... Total hat tricks: 14.

MISCELLANEOUS: Scored on a penalty shot (vs. Wendell Young, March 9, 1993). ... Failed to score on a penalty shot (vs. Trevor Kidd, February 6, 1995). ... Member of bronze-medal-winning Finnish Olympic team (1998). ... Captain of Mighty Ducks of Anaheim (October 1-December 10, 1997 and February 4, 1998 through remainder of season).

Season Team	League	REGULAR SEASON								PLAYOFFS				
		Gms.	G	A	Pts.	PIM	+/-	PP	SH	Gms.	G	A	Pts.	PIM
87-88—Jokerit Helsinki	Finland	33	42	23	65	18	...	...	...	5	4	3	7	2
88-89—Jokerit Helsinki	Finland	34	35	33	68	12	...	...	...	5	7	3	10	4
89-90—Jokerit Helsinki	Finland	11	4	8	12	0	...	...	...	—	—	—	—	—
90-91—Jokerit Helsinki	Finland	42	*33	25	58	12	...	...	...	—	—	—	—	—
91-92—Fin. Olympic Team	Int'l	8	7	4	11	...	...	...	...	—	—	—	—	—
—Jokerit Helsinki	Finland	44	39	23	62	20	...	...	...	—	—	—	—	—
92-93—Winnipeg	NHL	84	†76	56	132	45	8	24	0	6	4	2	6	2
93-94—Winnipeg	NHL	51	25	29	54	22	-23	11	0	—	—	—	—	—
94-95—Jokerit Helsinki	Finland	20	7	12	19	6	...	...	...	—	—	—	—	—
—Winnipeg	NHL	45	22	26	48	2	1	8	2	—	—	—	—	—
95-96—Winnipeg	NHL	51	24	48	72	18	3	6	1	—	—	—	—	—
—Anaheim	NHL	28	16	20	36	4	2	3	0	—	—	—	—	—
96-97—Anaheim	NHL	78	51	58	109	34	28	11	1	11	7	3	10	4
97-98—Anaheim	NHL	73	†52	34	86	30	12	10	1	—	—	—	—	—
—Fin. Olympic Team	Int'l	5	4	6	10	8	...	...	...	—	—	—	—	—
NHL Totals (6 years)		410	266	271	537	155	31	73	5	17	11	5	16	6

SELIVANOV, ALEXANDER   RW   LIGHTNING

PERSONAL: Born March 23, 1971, in Moscow, U.S.S.R. ... 6-0/208. ... Shoots left. ... Name pronounced sehl-ih-VAH-nahf.

TRANSACTIONS/CAREER NOTES: Selected by Philadelphia Flyers in sixth round (sixth Flyers pick, 140th overall) of NHL entry draft (June 29, 1994). ... Rights traded by Flyers to Tampa Bay Lightning for fourth-round pick in 1995 draft (September 6, 1994). ... Loaned by Lightning to Chicago Wolves (December 14, 1994). ... Sprained ankle (February 10, 1996); missed two games. ... Injured back (November 25, 1996); missed one game. ... Injured wrist (December 14, 1996); missed one game. ... Sprained knee (February 4, 1997); missed one game. ... Underwent knee surgery (February 25, 1997); missed eight games. ... Suffered a partial facial fracture (April 2, 1998); missed remainder of season.

Season Team	League	REGULAR SEASON								PLAYOFFS				
		Gms.	G	A	Pts.	PIM	+/-	PP	SH	Gms.	G	A	Pts.	PIM
88-89—Spartak Moscow	USSR	1	0	0	0	0	...	...	...	—	—	—	—	—
89-90—Spartak Moscow	USSR	4	0	0	0	0	...	...	...	—	—	—	—	—
90-91—Spartak Moscow	USSR	21	3	1	4	6	...	...	...	—	—	—	—	—
91-92—Spartak Moscow	CIS	31	6	7	13	16	...	...	...	—	—	—	—	—
92-93—Spartak Moscow	CIS	42	12	19	31	16	...	...	...	3	2	0	2	2
93-94—Spartak Moscow	CIS	45	30	11	41	50	...	...	...	6	5	1	6	2
94-95—Atlanta	IHL	4	0	3	3	2	...	...	...	—	—	—	—	—
—Chicago	IHL	14	4	1	5	8	...	...	...	—	—	—	—	—
—Tampa Bay	NHL	43	10	6	16	14	-2	4	0	—	—	—	—	—
95-96—Tampa Bay	NHL	79	31	21	52	93	3	13	0	6	2	2	4	6
96-97—Tampa Bay	NHL	69	15	18	33	61	-3	3	0	—	—	—	—	—
97-98—Tampa Bay	NHL	70	16	19	35	85	-38	4	0	—	—	—	—	—
NHL Totals (4 years)		261	72	64	136	253	-40	24	0	6	2	2	4	6

SESSA, JASON   RW   MAPLE LEAFS

PERSONAL: Born July 17, 1977, in Long Island, N.Y. ... 6-1/190. ... Shoots right.
COLLEGE: Lake Superior State (Mich.).

		REGULAR SEASON								PLAYOFFS				
Season Team	League	Gms.	G	A	Pts.	PIM	+/-	PP	SH	Gms.	G	A	Pts.	PIM
94-95—Rochester	USHL	47	45	22	67	81	...	...	...	—	—	—	—	—
95-96—Lake Superior	CCHA	28	8	5	13	12	...	...	...	—	—	—	—	—
96-97—Lake Superior	CCHA	34	22	22	44	91	...	...	...	—	—	—	—	—
97-98—Lake Superior	CCHA	32	16	13	29	55	...	...	...	—	—	—	—	—
—St. John's..................	AHL	5	0	0	0	6	...	...	...	—	—	—	—	—

SEVERYN, BRENT   RW   S

PERSONAL: Born February 22, 1966, in Vegreville, Alta. ... 6-2/212. ... Shoots left. ... Full name: Brent Leonard Severyn. ... Name pronounced SEHV-rihn.
COLLEGE: Alberta.
TRANSACTIONS/CAREER NOTES: Selected by Winnipeg Jets in fifth round (fifth Jets pick, 99th overall) of NHL entry draft (June 9, 1984). ... Injured knee (October 1985). ... Signed as free agent by Quebec Nordiques (July 15, 1988). ... Traded by Nordiques to New Jersey Devils for D Dave Marcinyshyn (June 3, 1991). ... Traded by Devils to Jets for sixth-round pick (C Ryan Smart) in 1994 draft (September 30, 1993). ... Traded by Jets to Florida Panthers for D Milan Tichy (October 3, 1993). ... Suffered left eye abrasion (November 23, 1993); missed one game. ... Traded by Panthers to New York Islanders for fourth-round pick (LW Dave Duerden) in 1995 draft (March 3, 1995). ... Suspended three games by NHL for shoving a linesman (October 26, 1995). ... Injured back (February 15, 1996); missed six games. ... Injured neck (March 16, 1996); missed two games. ... Traded by Islanders to Colorado Avalanche for third-round pick (traded to Calgary) in 1997 draft (September 4, 1996). ... Suspended two games by NHL for initiating an altercation (February 18, 1997). ... Selected by Mighty Ducks of Anaheim from Avalanche in NHL waiver draft (September 28, 1997). ... Suffered herniated disk in back (October 22, 1997); missed 32 games.
HONORS: Named to CWUAA All-Star team (1987-88). ... Named to AHL All-Star first team (1992-93).

		REGULAR SEASON								PLAYOFFS				
Season Team	League	Gms.	G	A	Pts.	PIM	+/-	PP	SH	Gms.	G	A	Pts.	PIM
82-83—Vegreville....................	CAJHL	21	20	22	42	10	...	...	...	—	—	—	—	—
83-84—Seattle........................	WHL	72	14	22	36	49	...	...	...	5	2	1	3	2
84-85—Seattle........................	WHL	38	8	32	40	54	...	...	...	—	—	—	—	—
—Brandon......................	WHL	26	7	16	23	57	...	...	...	—	—	—	—	—
85-86—Seattle........................	WHL	33	11	20	31	164	...	...	...	5	0	4	4	4
—Saskatoon..................	WHL	9	1	4	5	38	...	...	...	—	—	—	—	—
86-87—Univ. of Alberta..........	CWUAA	43	7	19	26	171	...	...	...	—	—	—	—	—
87-88—Univ. of Alberta..........	CWUAA	46	21	29	50	178	...	...	...	—	—	—	—	—
88-89—Halifax........................	AHL	47	2	12	14	141	...	...	...	—	—	—	—	—
89-90—Quebec......................	NHL	35	0	2	2	42	-19	0	0	—	—	—	—	—
—Halifax......................	AHL	43	6	9	15	105	...	...	...	6	1	2	3	49
90-91—Halifax......................	AHL	50	7	26	33	202	...	...	...	—	—	—	—	—
91-92—Utica.........................	AHL	80	11	33	44	211	...	...	...	4	0	1	1	4
92-93—Utica.........................	AHL	77	20	32	52	240	...	...	...	5	0	0	0	35
93-94—Florida.......................	NHL	67	4	7	11	156	-1	1	0	—	—	—	—	—
94-95—Florida.......................	NHL	9	1	1	2	37	-3	1	0	—	—	—	—	—
—New York Islanders........	NHL	19	1	3	4	34	1	0	0	—	—	—	—	—
95-96—New York Islanders.....	NHL	65	1	8	9	180	3	0	0	—	—	—	—	—
96-97—Colorado	NHL	66	1	4	5	193	-6	0	0	8	0	0	0	12
97-98—Anaheim	NHL	37	1	3	4	133	-3	0	0	—	—	—	—	—
NHL Totals (6 years)...........		298	9	28	37	775	-28	2	0	8	0	0	0	12

SEVIGNY, PIERRE   LW   RANGERS

PERSONAL: Born September 8, 1971, in Trois-Rivieres, Que. ... 6-1/210. ... Shoots left. ... Name pronounced SEH-vihn-yee.
TRANSACTIONS/CAREER NOTES: Selected by Montreal Canadiens in third round (fourth Canadiens pick, 51st overall) of NHL entry draft (June 17, 1989). ... Severed knee ligament in off-ice accident (March 25, 1991). ... Tore knee ligaments (December 6, 1993); missed 23 games. ... Cut elbow (January 9, 1997); missed nine games. ... Signed as free agent by New York Rangers (August 27, 1997).
HONORS: Named to QMJHL All-Star second team (1989-90 and 1990-91).

		REGULAR SEASON								PLAYOFFS				
Season Team	League	Gms.	G	A	Pts.	PIM	+/-	PP	SH	Gms.	G	A	Pts.	PIM
88-89—Verdun	QMJHL	67	27	43	70	88	...	...	...	—	—	—	—	—
89-90—St. Hyacinthe	QMJHL	67	47	72	119	205	...	...	...	12	8	8	16	42
90-91—St. Hyacinthe	QMJHL	60	36	46	82	203	...	...	...	—	—	—	—	—
91-92—Fredericton	AHL	74	22	37	59	145	...	...	...	7	1	1	2	26
92-93—Fredericton	AHL	80	36	40	76	113	...	...	...	5	1	1	2	2
93-94—Montreal	NHL	43	4	5	9	42	6	1	0	3	0	1	1	0
94-95—Montreal	NHL	19	0	0	0	15	-5	0	0	—	—	—	—	—
95-96—Fredericton	AHL	76	39	42	81	188	...	...	...	10	5	9	14	20
96-97—Fredericton	AHL	32	9	17	26	58	...	...	...	—	—	—	—	—
—Montreal	NHL	13	0	0	0	5	0	0	0	—	—	—	—	—
97-98—Hartford	AHL	40	18	13	31	94	...	...	...	12	3	5	8	14
—New York Rangers......	NHL	3	0	0	0	2	0	0	0	—	—	—	—	—
NHL Totals (4 years)...........		78	4	5	9	64	1	1	0	3	0	1	1	0

SHAFIKOV, RUSLAN   C   FLYERS

PERSONAL: Born May 11, 1976, in Ufa, U.S.S.R. ... 6-1/176. ... Shoots right.
TRANSACTIONS/CAREER NOTES: Selected by Philadelphia Flyers in eighth round (eighth Flyers pick, 204th overall) of 1995 NHL entry draft (July 8, 1995).

Season Team	League	REGULAR SEASON								PLAYOFFS				
		Gms.	G	A	Pts.	PIM	+/-	PP	SH	Gms.	G	A	Pts.	PIM
94-95—Salavat Yulayev Ufa	CIS	30	2	0	2	10	...	...	...	7	1	1	2	4
95-96—Salavat Yulayev Ufa	CIS	51	9	2	11	18	...	...	...	3	0	0	0	4
96-97—Salavat Yulayev Ufa	Russian	31	11	7	18	22	...	...	...	10	3	2	5	12
97-98—Salavat Yulayev Ufa	Russian	40	12	4	16	16	...	...	...	—	—	—	—	—

SHAFRANOV, KONSTANTIN   RW

PERSONAL: Born September 11, 1968, in Magnitogorsk, U.S.S.R. ... 6-0/196. ... Shoots left. ... Name pronounced shuh-FRAH-nahv.
TRANSACTIONS/CAREER NOTES: Selected by St. Louis Blues in ninth round (10th Blues pick, 229th overall) of NHL entry draft (June 22, 1996).

Season Team	League	REGULAR SEASON								PLAYOFFS				
		Gms.	G	A	Pts.	PIM	+/-	PP	SH	Gms.	G	A	Pts.	PIM
89-90—Torpedo Ust.	USSR	28	6	8	14	16	...	...	...	—	—	—	—	—
90-91—Torpedo Ust.	USSR	40	16	6	22	32	...	...	...	—	—	—	—	—
91-92—Torpedo Ust.	CIS	36	10	6	16	40	...	...	...	—	—	—	—	—
92-93—Torpedo Ust.	CIS	42	19	19	38	26	...	...	...	1	0	1	1	0
93-94—Detroit	CHL	4	3	2	5	0	...	...	...	—	—	—	—	—
—Torpedo Ust.	CIS	27	18	21	39	6	...	...	...	—	—	—	—	—
94-95—Magnitogorsk	CIS	47	21	30	51	24	...	...	...	5	1	2	3	4
95-96—Magnitogorsk	CIS	6	3	3	6	0	...	...	...	—	—	—	—	—
95-96—Fort Wayne	IHL	74	46	28	74	26	...	...	...	5	1	2	3	4
96-97—Worcester	AHL	62	23	25	48	16	...	...	...	5	0	2	2	0
—St. Louis	NHL	5	2	1	3	0	1	0	0	—	—	—	—	—
97-98—Fort Wayne	IHL	67	28	52	80	50	...	...	...	4	2	4	6	2
—Kazakhstan Oly. team..	Int'l	7	4	3	7	6	...	...	...	—	—	—	—	—
NHL Totals (1 year)		5	2	1	3	0	1	0	0					

SHALDYBIN, YEVGENY   D   BRUINS

PERSONAL: Born July 29, 1975, in Novosibirsk, U.S.S.R. ... 6-2/198. ... Shoots left. ... Name pronounced ev-GEH-nee SHALD-yuh-bihn.
TRANSACTIONS/CAREER NOTES: Selected by Boston Bruins in sixth round (fifth Bruin pick, 151st overall) of NHL entry draft (July 8, 1995).

Season Team	League	REGULAR SEASON								PLAYOFFS				
		Gms.	G	A	Pts.	PIM	+/-	PP	SH	Gms.	G	A	Pts.	PIM
93-94—Torpedo Yaroslavl	CIS	14	0	0	0	0	...	...	...	—	—	—	—	—
94-95—Torpedo Yaroslavl	CIS	42	2	5	7	10	...	...	...	4	0	1	1	0
95-96—Torpedo Yaroslavl	CIS	41	0	2	2	10	...	...	...	—	—	—	—	—
96-97—Providence	AHL	65	4	13	17	28	...	...	...	3	0	0	0	0
—Boston	NHL	3	1	0	1	0	-2	0	0	—	—	—	—	—
97-98—Providence	AHL	63	5	7	12	54	...	...	...	—	—	—	—	—
NHL Totals (1 year)		3	1	0	1	0	-2	0	0					

SHANAHAN, BRENDAN   LW   RED WINGS

PERSONAL: Born January 23, 1969, in Mimico, Ont. ... 6-3/220. ... Shoots right. ... Full name: Brendan Frederick Shanahan.
HIGH SCHOOL: Michael Power/St. Joseph's (Islington, Ont.).
TRANSACTIONS/CAREER NOTES: Bruised tendons in shoulder (January 1987). ... Selected by New Jersey Devils as underage junior in first round (first Devils pick, second overall) of NHL entry draft (June 13, 1987). ... Broke nose (December 1987). ... Suffered back spasms (March 1989). ... Suspended five games by NHL for stick-fighting (January 13, 1990). ... Suffered lower abdominal strain (February 1990). ... Suffered lacerations to lower right side of face and underwent surgery (January 8, 1991); missed five games. ... Signed as free agent by St. Louis Blues (July 25, 1991); D Scott Stevens awarded to Devils as compensation (September 3, 1991). ... Pulled groin (October 24, 1992); missed 12 games. ... Suspended six off-days and fined $500 by NHL for hitting another player in face with his stick (January 7, 1993). ... Suspended one game by NHL for high-sticking incident (February 23, 1993). ... Suffered viral infection (November 18, 1993); missed one game. ... Injured hamstring (March 22, 1994); missed two games. ... Played in Europe during 1994-95 NHL lockout. ... Suffered viral infection (January 20, 1995); missed three games. ... Broke ankle (May 15, 1995); missed last two games of playoffs. ... Traded by Blues to Hartford Whalers for D Chris Pronger (July 27, 1995). ... Sprained wrist (November 11, 1995); missed eight games. ... Traded by Whalers with D Brian Glynn to Detroit Red Wings for C Keith Primeau, D Paul Coffey and first-round pick (traded to San Jose) in 1997 draft (October 9, 1996). ... Suspended one game and fined $1,000 by NHL for crosschecking (October 11, 1996). ... Pulled groin (October 30, 1996); missed one game. ... Suffered stiff neck (October 12, 1997); missed four games. ... Suffered back spasms (April 15, 1998); missed final game of regular season and two playoff games.
HONORS: Played in NHL All-Star Game (1994 and 1996-1998). ... Named to NHL All-Star first team (1993-94).
MISCELLANEOUS: Member of Stanley Cup championship team (1997 and 1998). ... Captain of Hartford Whalers (1995-96). ... Failed to score on a penalty shot (vs. Grant Fuhr, December 27, 1992; vs. Trevor Kidd, November 5, 1997).
STATISTICAL PLATEAUS: Three-goal games: 1992-93 (1), 1993-94 (4), 1995-96 (1), 1996-97 (3). Total: 9.

Season Team	League	REGULAR SEASON								PLAYOFFS				
		Gms.	G	A	Pts.	PIM	+/-	PP	SH	Gms.	G	A	Pts.	PIM
84-85—Mississauga	MTHL	36	20	21	41	26	...	...	...	—	—	—	—	—
85-86—London	OHL	59	28	34	62	70	...	...	...	5	5	5	10	5
86-87—London	OHL	56	39	53	92	128	...	...	...	—	—	—	—	—
87-88—New Jersey	NHL	65	7	19	26	131	-20	2	0	12	2	1	3	44
88-89—New Jersey	NHL	68	22	28	50	115	2	9	0	—	—	—	—	—
89-90—New Jersey	NHL	73	30	42	72	137	15	8	0	6	3	3	6	20
90-91—New Jersey	NHL	75	29	37	66	141	4	7	0	7	3	5	8	12
91-92—St. Louis	NHL	80	33	36	69	171	-3	13	0	6	2	3	5	14
92-93—St. Louis	NHL	71	51	43	94	174	10	18	0	11	4	3	7	18
93-94—St. Louis	NHL	81	52	50	102	211	-9	15	*7	4	2	5	7	4
94-95—Dusseldorf	Germany	3	5	3	8	4	...	...	...	—	—	—	—	—
—St. Louis	NHL	45	20	21	41	136	7	6	2	5	4	5	9	14

- 330 -

Season Team	League	REGULAR SEASON								PLAYOFFS				
		Gms.	G	A	Pts.	PIM	+/-	PP	SH	Gms.	G	A	Pts.	PIM
95-96—Hartford	NHL	74	44	34	78	125	2	17	2	—	—	—	—	—
96-97—Hartford	NHL	2	1	0	1	0	1	0	1	—	—	—	—	—
—Detroit	NHL	79	46	41	87	131	31	†20	2	20	9	8	17	43
97-98—Detroit	NHL	75	28	29	57	154	6	15	1	20	5	4	9	22
—Can. Olympic Team	Int'l	6	2	0	2	0	...	...	...	—	—	—	—	—
NHL Totals (11 years)		788	363	380	743	1626	46	130	15	91	34	37	71	191

SHANNON, DARRIN   LW

PERSONAL: Born December 8, 1969, in Barrie, Ont. ... 6-2/207. ... Shoots left. ... Full name: Darrin A. Shannon. ... Brother of Darryl Shannon, defenseman, Buffalo Sabres.
TRANSACTIONS/CAREER NOTES: Separated right shoulder (November 1986). ... Dislocated left elbow (November 1987). ... Separated left shoulder (January 1988). ... Selected by Pittsburgh Penguins in first round (first Penguins pick, fourth overall) of NHL entry draft (June 11, 1988). ... Traded by Penguins with D Doug Bodger to Buffalo Sabres for G Tom Barrasso and third-round pick (LW Joe Dziedzic) in 1990 draft (November 12, 1988). ... Strained knee ligaments (May 1990). ... Injured jaw (January 8, 1991); missed five games. ... Traded by Sabres with LW Mike Hartman and D Dean Kennedy to Winnipeg Jets for RW Dave McLlwain, D Gordon Donnelly, fifth-round pick (LW Yuri Khmylev) in 1992 draft and future considerations (October 11, 1991). ... Injured knee (November 20, 1991). ... Injured eye (November 25, 1991); missed one game. ... Sprained leg (December 31, 1991); missed seven games. ... Strained calf (October 12, 1993); missed five games. ... Fractured rib (February 4, 1995); missed seven games. ... Strained abdomen (March 11, 1995); missed one game. ... Strained left groin (March 20, 1995); missed remainder of season. ... Sprained knee (December 6, 1995); missed four games. ... Strained groin (January 8, 1996); missed five games. ... Injured ribs (March 7, 1996); missed two games. ... Jets franchise moved to Phoenix and renamed Coyotes for 1996-97 season; NHL approved move on January 18, 1996. ... Fractured hand (October 23, 1997); missed 13 games. ... Injured ankle (December 3, 1997); missed nine games.
HONORS: Named to OHL All-Scholastic team (1986-87). ... Won Bobby Smith Trophy (1987-88). ... Named to Memorial Cup All-Star team (1987-88).

Season Team	League	REGULAR SEASON								PLAYOFFS				
		Gms.	G	A	Pts.	PIM	+/-	PP	SH	Gms.	G	A	Pts.	PIM
85-86—Barrie Jr. B	OHA	40	13	22	35	21	...	...	...					
86-87—Windsor	OHL	60	16	67	83	116	...	...	...	14	4	6	10	8
87-88—Windsor	OHL	43	33	41	74	49	...	...	...	12	6	12	18	9
88-89—Windsor	OHL	54	33	48	81	47	...	...	...	4	1	6	7	2
—Buffalo	NHL	3	0	0	0	0	-2	0	0	2	0	0	0	0
89-90—Buffalo	NHL	17	2	7	9	4	6	0	0	6	0	1	1	4
—Rochester	AHL	50	20	23	43	25	...	...	...	9	4	1	5	2
90-91—Rochester	AHL	49	26	34	60	56	...	...	...	10	3	5	8	22
—Buffalo	NHL	34	8	6	14	12	-11	1	0	6	1	2	3	4
91-92—Buffalo	NHL	1	0	1	1	0	1	0	0					
—Winnipeg	NHL	68	13	26	39	41	5	3	0	7	0	1	1	10
92-93—Winnipeg	NHL	84	20	40	60	91	-4	12	0	6	2	4	6	6
93-94—Winnipeg	NHL	77	21	37	58	87	-18	9	0					
94-95—Winnipeg	NHL	19	5	3	8	14	-6	3	0	—	—	—	—	—
95-96—Winnipeg	NHL	63	5	18	23	28	-5	0	0	6	1	0	1	6
96-97—Phoenix	NHL	82	11	13	24	41	4	1	0	7	3	1	4	4
97-98—Phoenix	NHL	58	2	12	14	26	4	0	0	5	0	1	1	4
NHL Totals (10 years)		506	87	163	250	344	-26	29	0	45	7	10	17	38

SHANNON, DARRYL   D   SABRES

PERSONAL: Born June 21, 1968, in Barrie, Ont. ... 6-2/208. ... Shoots left. ... Brother of Darrin Shannon, left winger with Buffalo Sabres (1988-89 through 1991-92), Winnipeg Jets (1991-92 through 1995-96) and Phoenix Coyotes (1996-97 and 1997-98).
TRANSACTIONS/CAREER NOTES: Selected by Toronto Maple Leafs in second round (second Maple Leafs pick, 36th overall) of NHL entry draft (June 21, 1986). ... Broke right leg and right thumb, bruised chest and suffered slipped disk in automobile accident (June 20, 1990). ... Signed as free agent with Winnipeg Jets (July 8, 1993). ... Traded by Jets with LW Michael Grosek to Buffalo Sabres for D Craig Muni (February 15, 1996). ... Injured right knee (April 10, 1996); missed one game. ... Bruised knee (December 29, 1997); missed four games.
HONORS: Named to OHL All-Star second team (1986-87). ... Won Max Kaminsky Trophy (1987-88). ... Named to OHL All-Star first team (1987-88). ... Named to Memorial Cup All-Star team (1987-88).

Season Team	League	REGULAR SEASON								PLAYOFFS				
		Gms.	G	A	Pts.	PIM	+/-	PP	SH	Gms.	G	A	Pts.	PIM
84-85—Barrie Jr. B	OHA	39	5	23	28	50	...	...	...	—	—	—	—	—
85-86—Windsor	OHL	57	6	21	27	52	...	...	...	16	5	6	11	22
86-87—Windsor	OHL	64	23	27	50	83	...	...	...	14	4	8	12	18
87-88—Windsor	OHL	60	16	70	86	116	...	...	...	12	3	8	11	17
88-89—Toronto	NHL	14	1	3	4	6	5	0	0	—	—	—	—	—
—Newmarket	AHL	61	5	24	29	37	...	...	...	5	0	3	3	10
89-90—Newmarket	AHL	47	4	15	19	58	...	...	...	—	—	—	—	—
—Toronto	NHL	10	0	1	1	12	-10	0	0	—	—	—	—	—
90-91—Toronto	NHL	10	0	1	1	0	1	0	0	—	—	—	—	—
—Newmarket	AHL	47	2	14	16	51	...	...	...	—	—	—	—	—
91-92—Toronto	NHL	48	2	8	10	23	-17	1	0	—	—	—	—	—
92-93—Toronto	NHL	16	0	0	0	11	-5	0	0	—	—	—	—	—
—St. John's	AHL	7	1	1	2	4	...	...	...	—	—	—	—	—
93-94—Moncton	AHL	37	1	10	11	62	...	...	...	20	1	7	8	32
—Winnipeg	NHL	20	0	4	4	18	-6	0	0	—	—	—	—	—
94-95—Winnipeg	NHL	40	5	9	14	48	1	0	1	—	—	—	—	—
95-96—Winnipeg	NHL	48	2	7	9	72	5	0	0	—	—	—	—	—
—Buffalo	NHL	26	2	6	8	20	10	0	0	—	—	—	—	—
96-97—Buffalo	NHL	82	4	19	23	112	23	1	0	12	2	3	5	8
97-98—Buffalo	NHL	76	3	19	22	56	26	1	0	15	2	4	6	8
NHL Totals (10 years)		390	19	77	96	378	33	3	1	27	4	7	11	16

SHANTZ, JEFF   C   BLACKHAWKS

PERSONAL: Born October 10, 1973, in Edmonton. ... 6-0/185. ... Shoots right.
HIGH SCHOOL: Robert Usher (Regina, Sask.).
TRANSACTIONS/CAREER NOTES: Selected by Chicago Blackhawks in second round (second Blackhawks pick, 36th overall) of NHL entry draft (June 20, 1992). ... Bruised right shoulder (1993-94 season); missed six games. ... Suffered swollen eye (November 30, 1996); missed one game. ... Sprained knee (February 25, 1997); missed 10 games. ... Separated shoulder (January 4, 1998); missed six games. ... Tore anterior cruciate ligament in left knee (March 19, 1998); missed remainder of season.
HONORS: Named to WHL (East) All-Star first team (1992-93).

		REGULAR SEASON								PLAYOFFS				
Season Team	League	Gms.	G	A	Pts.	PIM	+/-	PP	SH	Gms.	G	A	Pts.	PIM
89-90—Regina	WHL	1	0	0	0	0	...	...	...	—	—	—	—	—
90-91—Regina	WHL	69	16	21	37	22	...	...	...	8	2	2	4	2
91-92—Regina	WHL	72	39	50	89	75	...	...	...	—	—	—	—	—
92-93—Regina	WHL	64	29	54	83	75	...	...	...	13	2	12	14	14
93-94—Chicago	NHL	52	3	13	16	30	-14	0	0	6	0	0	0	6
—Indianapolis	IHL	19	5	9	14	20	...	...	...	—	—	—	—	—
94-95—Indianapolis	IHL	32	9	15	24	20	...	...	...	—	—	—	—	—
—Chicago	NHL	45	6	12	18	33	11	0	2	16	3	1	4	2
95-96—Chicago	NHL	78	6	14	20	24	12	1	2	10	2	3	5	6
96-97—Chicago	NHL	69	9	21	30	28	11	0	1	6	0	4	4	6
97-98—Chicago	NHL	61	11	20	31	36	0	1	2	—	—	—	—	—
NHL Totals (5 years)		305	35	80	115	151	20	2	7	38	5	8	13	20

S

SHAPLEY, LARRY   D   CANUCKS

PERSONAL: Born February 6, 1978, in Dunnville, Ont. ... 6-6/215. ... Shoots right. ... Name pronounced SHAP-lee.
TRANSACTIONS/CAREER NOTES: Selected by Vancouver Canucks in sixth round (ninth Canucks pick, 148th overall) of NHL entry draft (June 21, 1997).

		REGULAR SEASON								PLAYOFFS				
Season Team	League	Gms.	G	A	Pts.	PIM	+/-	PP	SH	Gms.	G	A	Pts.	PIM
96-97—Welland	Jr. B	35	3	10	13	27	...	...	...	—	—	—	—	—
—Peterborough	OHL	8	0	0	0	30	...	...	...	—	—	—	—	—
97-98—Peterborough	OHL	63	1	1	2	211	...	...	...	4	0	0	0	0

SHARIFIJANOV, VADIM   RW   DEVILS

PERSONAL: Born December 23, 1975, in Ufa, U.S.S.R. ... 5-11/210. ... Shoots left. ... Name pronounced vah-DEEM shuh-RIH-fee-AH-nahf.
TRANSACTIONS/CAREER NOTES: Selected by New Jersey Devils in first round (first Devils pick, 25th overall) of NHL entry draft (June 28, 1994).

		REGULAR SEASON								PLAYOFFS				
Season Team	League	Gms.	G	A	Pts.	PIM	+/-	PP	SH	Gms.	G	A	Pts.	PIM
92-93—Salavat Yulayev Ufa	CIS	37	6	4	10	16	...	...	...	2	1	0	1	0
93-94—Salavat Yulayev Ufa	CIS	46	10	6	16	36	...	...	...	5	3	0	3	4
94-95—CSKA Moscow	CIS	34	7	3	10	26	...	...	...	2	0	0	0	0
—Albany	AHL	1	1	1	2	0	...	...	...	9	3	3	6	10
95-96—Albany	AHL	69	14	28	42	28	...	...	...	—	—	—	—	—
96-97—Albany	AHL	70	14	27	41	89	...	...	...	10	3	3	6	6
—New Jersey	NHL	2	0	0	0	0	0	0	0	—	—	—	—	—
97-98—Albany	AHL	72	23	27	50	69	...	...	...	12	4	9	13	6
NHL Totals (1 year)		2	0	0	0	0	0	0	0					

SHAW, DAVID   D   SHARKS

PERSONAL: Born May 25, 1964, in St. Thomas, Ont. ... 6-2/204. ... Shoots right.
TRANSACTIONS/CAREER NOTES: Selected by Quebec Nordiques as underage junior in first round (first Nordiques pick, 13th overall) of NHL entry draft (June 9, 1982). ... Sprained wrist (December 18, 1985). ... Traded by Nordiques with LW John Ogrodnick to New York Rangers for LW Jeff Jackson and D Terry Carkner (September 30, 1987). ... Separated shoulder (October 1987). ... Suspended 12 games by NHL for slashing (October 27, 1988). ... Bruised shoulder (March 15, 1989). ... Dislocated right shoulder (November 2, 1989). ... Reinjured right shoulder (November 22, 1989); missed 10 games. ... Underwent surgery to right shoulder (February 7, 1990). ... Bruised finger (September 1990). ... Bruised left big toe (October 31, 1990). ... Sprained knee (October 20, 1991). ... Traded by Rangers to Edmonton Oilers for D Jeff Beukeboom (November 12, 1991) to complete deal in which Rangers traded C Bernie Nicholls, LW Louie DeBrusk, RW Steven Rice and future considerations to Oilers for C Mark Messier and future considerations (October 4, 1991). ... Traded by Oilers to Minnesota North Stars for D Brian Glynn (January 21, 1992). ... Traded by North Stars to Boston Bruins for future considerations (September 2, 1992). ... Injured thigh (October 1992); missed one game. ... Injured foot (December 1992); missed one game. ... Injured ribs (March 1993); missed five games. ... Suffered pinched nerve (December 26, 1993); missed three games. ... Suffered charley horse (January 6, 1994); missed seven games. ... Injured knee (January 28, 1994); missed 17 games. ... Injured shoulder (April 1995); missed three games. ... Traded by Bruins to Tampa Bay Lightning for third-round pick (RW Jason Doyle) in 1996 draft (August 17, 1995). ... Injured left shoulder prior to 1995-96 season; missed one game. ... Injured shoulder (October 21, 1995); missed five games. ... Suffered bruised left shoulder (January 2, 1996); missed one game. ... Sprained left knee (February 19, 1996); missed seven games. ... Injured back (October 12, 1996); missed one game. ... Injured left knee (November 27, 1996); missed three games. ... Traded by Lightning with D Bryan Marchment and first-round pick (traded to Nashville) in 1998 draft to San Jose Sharks for LW Andrei Nazarov, first-round pick (C Vincent Lecavalier) in 1998 draft and future considerations (March 24, 1998).
HONORS: Named to OHL All-Star first team (1983-84). ... Named to Memorial Cup All-Star team (1983-84).

		REGULAR SEASON								PLAYOFFS				
Season Team	League	Gms.	G	A	Pts.	PIM	+/-	PP	SH	Gms.	G	A	Pts.	PIM
80-81—Stratford Jr. B	OHA	41	12	19	31	30	...	...	...	—	—	—	—	—
81-82—Kitchener	OHL	68	6	25	31	99	...	...	...	15	2	2	4	51
82-83—Kitchener	OHL	57	18	56	74	78	...	...	...	12	2	10	12	18
—Quebec	NHL	2	0	0	0	0	-1	0	0	—	—	—	—	—

Season Team	League	REGULAR SEASON								PLAYOFFS				
		Gms.	G	A	Pts.	PIM	+/-	PP	SH	Gms.	G	A	Pts.	PIM
83-84—Kitchener	OHL	58	14	34	48	73	...	...	...	16	4	9	13	12
—Quebec	NHL	3	0	0	0	0	2	0	0	—	—	—	—	—
84-85—Guelph	OHL	2	0	0	0	0	...	...	...	—	—	—	—	—
—Fredericton	AHL	48	7	6	13	73	...	...	...	2	0	0	0	7
—Quebec	NHL	14	0	0	0	11	-5	0	0	—	—	—	—	—
85-86—Quebec	NHL	73	7	19	26	78	14	2	0	—	—	—	—	—
86-87—Quebec	NHL	75	0	19	19	69	-35	0	0	—	—	—	—	—
87-88—New York Rangers	NHL	68	7	25	32	100	-8	5	0	—	—	—	—	—
88-89—New York Rangers	NHL	63	6	11	17	88	14	3	1	4	0	2	2	30
89-90—New York Rangers	NHL	22	2	10	12	22	-3	1	1	—	—	—	—	—
90-91—New York Rangers	NHL	77	2	10	12	89	8	0	0	6	0	0	0	11
91-92—New York Rangers	NHL	10	0	1	1	15	1	0	0	—	—	—	—	—
—Edmonton	NHL	12	1	1	2	8	-8	0	0	—	—	—	—	—
—Minnesota	NHL	37	0	7	7	49	-5	0	0	7	2	2	4	10
92-93—Boston	NHL	77	10	14	24	108	10	1	1	4	0	1	1	6
93-94—Boston	NHL	55	1	9	10	85	-11	0	0	13	1	2	3	16
94-95—Boston	NHL	44	3	4	7	36	-9	1	0	5	0	1	1	4
95-96—Tampa Bay	NHL	66	1	11	12	64	5	0	0	6	0	1	1	4
96-97—Tampa Bay	NHL	57	1	10	11	72	1	0	0	—	—	—	—	—
97-98—Tampa Bay	NHL	14	0	2	2	12	-2	0	0	—	—	—	—	—
—Las Vegas	IHL	26	6	13	19	28	...	...	...	—	—	—	—	—
NHL Totals (16 years)		769	41	153	194	906	-32	13	3	45	3	9	12	81

SHEPPARD, RAY   RW   HURRICANES   S

PERSONAL: Born May 27, 1966, in Pembroke, Ont. ... 6-1/195. ... Shoots right.

TRANSACTIONS/CAREER NOTES: Selected by Buffalo Sabres as underage junior in third round (third Sabres pick, 60th overall) of NHL entry draft (June 9, 1984). ... Injured left knee (September 1986); missed Sabres training camp. ... Bruised back during training camp (September 1988). ... Suffered facial lacerations (November 25, 1988). ... Suffered facial lacerations (November 27, 1988). ... Suffered from the flu (December 1988). ... Sprained ankle (January 30, 1989). ... Injured left knee (March 16, 1990). ... Traded by Sabres to New York Rangers for future considerations and cash (July 10, 1990). ... Sprained medial collateral ligaments of right knee (February 18, 1991); missed 13 games. ... Dislocated left shoulder (March 24, 1991). ... Signed as free agent by Detroit Red Wings (August 5, 1991). ... Strained lower abdomen (March 20, 1992); missed five games. ... Injured knee (October 8, 1992); missed five games. ... Reinjured knee (October 28, 1992); missed two games. ... Suffered back spasms (February 13, 1993); missed three games. ... Strained back (March 2, 1993); missed two games. ... Injured left knee (October 6, 1995); missed two games. ... Injured back (February 22, 1995); missed two games. ... Traded by Red Wings to San Jose Sharks for C Igor Larionov and second-round pick (traded to St. Louis) in 1998 draft (October 25, 1995). ... Injured groin (November 2, 1995); missed one game. ... Injured knee (December 16, 1995); missed two games. ... Injured shoulder (February 5, 1996); missed nine games. ... Traded by Sharks with fourth-round pick (D Joey Tetarenko) in 1996 draft to Florida Panthers for second-(traded to Chicago) and fourth-(RW Matt Bradley) round picks in 1996 draft (March 16, 1996). ... Sprained right shoulder (September 27, 1996); missed two games. ... Sprained knee ligament (February 1, 1997); missed 11 games. ... Sprained knee (January 7, 1998); missed one game. ... Traded by Panthers to Carolina Hurricanes for G Kirk McLean (March 24, 1998). ... Pulled groin (April 13, 1998); missed three games.

HONORS: Won Red Tilson Trophy (1985-86). ... Won Eddie Powers Memorial Trophy (1985-86). ... Won Jim Mahon Memorial Trophy (1985-86). ... Named to OHL All-Star first team (1985-86). ... Named to NHL All-Rookie team (1987-88).

STATISTICAL PLATEAUS: Three-goal games: 1987-88 (2), 1991-92 (1), 1993-94 (2), 1994-95 (1), 1995-96 (1), 1995-96 (1), 1996-97 (3), 1997-98 (1). Total: 12.

Season Team	League	REGULAR SEASON								PLAYOFFS				
		Gms.	G	A	Pts.	PIM	+/-	PP	SH	Gms.	G	A	Pts.	PIM
82-83—Brockville	COJHL	48	27	36	63	81	...	...	...	—	—	—	—	—
83-84—Cornwall	OHL	68	44	36	80	69	...	...	...	—	—	—	—	—
84-85—Cornwall	OHL	49	25	33	58	51	...	...	...	9	2	12	14	4
85-86—Cornwall	OHL	63	*81	61	*142	25	...	...	...	6	7	4	11	0
86-87—Rochester	AHL	55	18	13	31	11	...	...	...	15	12	3	15	2
87-88—Buffalo	NHL	74	38	27	65	14	-6	15	0	6	1	1	2	2
88-89—Buffalo	NHL	67	22	21	43	15	-7	7	0	1	0	1	1	0
89-90—Buffalo	NHL	18	4	2	6	0	3	1	0	—	—	—	—	—
—Rochester	AHL	5	3	5	8	2	...	...	...	17	8	7	15	9
90-91—New York Rangers	NHL	59	24	23	47	21	8	7	0	—	—	—	—	—
91-92—Detroit	NHL	74	36	26	62	27	7	11	1	11	6	2	8	4
92-93—Detroit	NHL	70	32	34	66	29	7	10	0	7	2	3	5	0
93-94—Detroit	NHL	82	52	41	93	26	13	19	0	7	2	1	3	4
94-95—Detroit	NHL	43	30	10	40	17	11	11	0	17	4	3	7	5
95-96—Detroit	NHL	5	2	2	4	2	0	0	0	—	—	—	—	—
—San Jose	NHL	51	27	19	46	10	-19	12	0	—	—	—	—	—
—Florida	NHL	14	8	2	10	4	0	2	0	21	8	8	16	0
96-97—Florida	NHL	68	29	31	60	4	4	13	0	5	2	0	2	0
97-98—Florida	NHL	61	14	17	31	21	-13	5	0	—	—	—	—	—
—Carolina	NHL	10	4	2	6	2	2	2	0	—	—	—	—	—
NHL Totals (11 years)		696	322	257	579	192	10	115	1	75	25	19	44	15

SHIELDS, STEVE   G   SHARKS

PERSONAL: Born July 19, 1972, in Toronto. ... 6-3/210. ... Catches left.

COLLEGE: Michigan.

TRANSACTIONS/CAREER NOTES: Selected by Buffalo Sabres in fifth round (fifth Sabres pick, 101st overall) of NHL entry draft (June 22, 1991). ... Traded by Sabres with fourth-round pick (RW Miroslav Zalesak) in 1998 draft to San Jose Sharks for G Kay Whitmore, second-round pick (RW Jaroslav Kristek) in 1998 draft and fifth-round pick in 2000 draft (June 18, 1998).

HONORS: Named to NCCA All-America West second team (1992-93 and 1993-94). ... Named to CCHA All-Star first team (1992-93 and 1993-94).

MISCELLANEOUS: Allowed penalty shot goal (vs. Eric Lindros, May 11, 1997 (playoffs)).

Season Team	League	REGULAR SEASON								PLAYOFFS						
		Gms.	Min	W	L	T	GA	SO	Avg.	Gms.	Min.	W	L	GA	SO	Avg.
90-91 —Univ. of Michigan	CCHA	37	1963	26	6	3	106	0	3.24	—	—	—	—	—	—	—
91-92 —Univ. of Michigan	CCHA	37	2091	27	7	2	98	1	2.81	—	—	—	—	—	—	—
92-93 —Univ. of Michigan	CCHA	39	2027	30	6	2	75	...	2.22	—	—	—	—	—	—	—
93-94 —Univ. of Michigan	CCHA	36	1961	28	6	1	87	2	2.66	—	—	—	—	—	—	—
94-95 —South Carolina	ECHL	21	1158	11	5	‡2	52	2	2.69	3	144	0	2	11	0	4.58
—Rochester	AHL	13	673	3	8	0	53	0	4.73	1	20	0	0	3	0	9.00
95-96 —Rochester	AHL	43	2356	20	17	2	140	1	3.57	*19	*1126	*15	3	47	1	2.50
—Buffalo	NHL	2	75	1	0	0	4	0	3.20	—	—	—	—	—	—	—
96-97 —Rochester	AHL	23	1331	14	6	2	60	1	2.70	—	—	—	—	—	—	—
—Buffalo	NHL	13	789	3	8	2	39	0	2.97	10	570	4	6	26	1	2.74
97-98 —Buffalo	NHL	16	785	3	6	4	37	0	2.83	—	—	—	—	—	—	—
—Rochester	AHL	1	59	0	1	0	3	0	3.05	—	—	—	—	—	—	—
NHL Totals (3 years)		31	1649	7	14	6	80	0	2.91	10	570	4	6	26	1	2.74

SHTALENKOV, MIKHAIL   G   PREDATORS

PERSONAL: Born October 20, 1965, in Moscow, U.S.S.R. ... 6-2/185. ... Catches left. ... Name pronounced mih-KIGHL shtuh-LEHN-kahf.
TRANSACTIONS/CAREER NOTES: Selected by Mighty Ducks of Anaheim in fifth round (fifth Mighty Ducks pick, 108th overall) of NHL entry draft (June 26, 1993). ... Selected by Nashville Predators in NHL expansion draft (June 26, 1998).
HONORS: Named Soviet League Rookie of the Year (1986-87). ... Won Garry F. Longman Memorial Trophy (1992-93).
MISCELLANEOUS: Stopped penalty shot attempt (vs. Peter Bondra, December 13, 1996). ... Allowed penalty shot goal (vs. Dan Quinn, March 21, 1995). ... Member of silver-medal-winning Russian Olympic team (1998).

Season Team	League	REGULAR SEASON								PLAYOFFS						
		Gms.	Min	W	L	T	GA	SO	Avg.	Gms.	Min.	W	L	GA	SO	Avg.
86-87 —Dynamo Moscow	USSR	17	893	...	...	...	36	1	2.42	—	—	—	—	—	—	—
87-88 —Dynamo Moscow	USSR	25	1302	...	...	...	72	1	3.32	—	—	—	—	—	—	—
88-89 —Dynamo Moscow	USSR	4	80	...	...	...	3	0	2.25	—	—	—	—	—	—	—
89-90 —Dynamo Moscow	USSR	6	20	...	...	...	1	0	3.00	—	—	—	—	—	—	—
90-91 —Dynamo Moscow	USSR	31	1568	...	...	...	56	2	2.14	—	—	—	—	—	—	—
91-92 —Dynamo Moscow	CIS	27	1268	...	...	...	45	1	2.13	—	—	—	—	—	—	—
—Unif. Olympic Team	Int'l	8	440	...	...	...	12	3	1.64	—	—	—	—	—	—	—
92-93 —Milwaukee	IHL	47	2669	26	14	‡5	135	2	3.03	3	209	1	1	11	0	3.16
93-94 —San Diego	IHL	28	1616	15	11	‡2	93	0	3.45	—	—	—	—	—	—	—
—Anaheim	NHL	10	543	3	4	1	24	0	2.65	—	—	—	—	—	—	—
94-95 —Anaheim	NHL	18	810	4	7	1	49	0	3.63	—	—	—	—	—	—	—
95-96 —Anaheim	NHL	30	1637	7	16	3	85	0	3.12	—	—	—	—	—	—	—
96-97 —Anaheim	NHL	24	1079	7	8	1	52	2	2.89	4	211	0	3	10	0	2.84
97-98 —Anaheim	NHL	40	2049	13	18	5	110	1	3.22	—	—	—	—	—	—	—
—Russian Olympic team	Int'l	5	290	4	1	0	8	0	1.66	—	—	—	—	—	—	—
NHL Totals (5 years)		122	6118	34	53	11	320	3	3.14	4	211	0	3	10	0	2.84

SHULMISTRA, RICH   G   AVALANCHE

PERSONAL: Born April 1, 1971, in Sudbury, Ont. ... 6-2/186. ... Catches right. ... Full name: Richard Shulmistra. ... Name pronounced SHOOL-mih-struh.
HIGH SCHOOL: LaSalle Secondary (Kingston, Ont.).
COLLEGE: Miami of Ohio.
TRANSACTIONS/CAREER NOTES: Selected by Quebec Nordiques in NHL supplemental draft (June 19, 1992). ... Nordiques franchise moved to Colorado and renamed Avalanche for 1995-96 season (June 21, 1995).
HONORS: Named to CCHA All-Star second team (1992-93). ... Named to AHL All-Star second team (1997-98).

Season Team	League	REGULAR SEASON								PLAYOFFS						
		Gms.	Min	W	L	T	GA	SO	Avg.	Gms.	Min.	W	L	GA	SO	Avg.
90-91 —Miami of Ohio	CCHA	20	920	2	12	2	80	0	5.22	—	—	—	—	—	—	—
91-92 —Miami of Ohio	CCHA	19	850	3	5	2	67	0	4.73	—	—	—	—	—	—	—
92-93 —Miami of Ohio	CCHA	33	1949	22	6	4	88	...	2.71	—	—	—	—	—	—	—
93-94 —Miami of Ohio	CCHA	27	1521	13	12	1	74	0	2.92	—	—	—	—	—	—	—
94-95 —Cornwall	AHL	20	937	4	9	2	58	0	3.71	8	447	4	3	22	0	2.95
95-96 —Cornwall	AHL	36	1844	9	18	2	100	0	3.25	1	8	0	0	1	0	7.50
96-97 —Albany	AHL	23	1063	5	9	2	43	2	2.43	2	77	1	0	2	0	1.56
97-98 —Fort Wayne	IHL	11	657	3	8	‡0	34	1	3.11	—	—	—	—	—	—	—
—Albany	AHL	35	2022	20	8	4	78	2	*2.31	13	696	8	3	32	1	2.76
—New Jersey	NHL	1	62	0	1	0	2	0	1.94	—	—	—	—	—	—	—
NHL Totals (1 year)		1	62	0	1	0	2	0	1.94							

SIDORKIEWICZ, PETER   G

PERSONAL: Born June 29, 1963, in Dabrown Bialostocka, Poland. ... 5-9/185. ... Catches left. ... Full name: Peter Paul Sidorkiewicz. ... Name pronounced sih-DOHR-kuh-VIHCH.
HIGH SCHOOL: O'Neill (Oshawa, Ont.).
TRANSACTIONS/CAREER NOTES: Selected by Washington Capitals as underage junior in fifth round (fifth Capitals pick, 91st overall) of NHL entry draft (June 10, 1981). ... Sprained right ankle (March 3, 1991). ... Traded by Capitals with C Dean Evason to Hartford Whalers for LW David Jensen (March 1985). ... Selected by Ottawa Senators in NHL expansion draft (June 18, 1992). ... Traded by Senators with future considerations to New Jersey Devils for G Craig Billington and C/LW Troy Mallette and fourth-round pick (C Cosmo Dupaul) in 1993 draft (June 20, 1993); Senators sent LW Mike Peluso to Devils to complete deal (June 26, 1993). ... Loaned to Fort Wayne Komets of IHL (February 2, 1995).

HONORS: Shared Dave Pinkney Trophy with Jeff Hogg (1982-83). ... Named to Memorial Cup All-Star team (1982-83). ... Named to AHL All-Star second team (1986-87). ... Named to NHL All-Rookie team (1988-89). ... Played in NHL All-Star Game (1993).
MISCELLANEOUS: Allowed penalty shot goal (vs. Bob Sweeney, December 12, 1990; vs. Pat LaFontaine, November 29, 1992). ... Stopped penalty shot attempt (vs. Stu Barnes, February 23, 1993).

		REGULAR SEASON								PLAYOFFS						
Season Team	League	Gms.	Min	W	L	T	GA	SO	Avg.	Gms.	Min.	W	L	GA	SO	Avg.
80-81—Oshawa	OMJHL	7	308	3	3	0	24	0	4.68	5	266	2	2	20	0	4.51
81-82—Oshawa	OHL	29	1553	14	11	1	123	*2	4.75	1	13	0	0	1	0	4.62
82-83—Oshawa	OHL	60	3536	36	20	3	213	0	3.61	*17	*1020	15	1	*60	0	3.53
83-84—Oshawa	OHL	52	2966	28	21	1	205	1	4.15	7	420	3	4	27	†1	3.86
84-85—Fort Wayne	IHL	10	590	4	4	‡2	43	0	4.37	—						
—Binghamton	AHL	45	2691	31	9	5	137	3	3.05	8	481	4	4	31	0	3.87
85-86—Binghamton	AHL	49	2819	21	22	3	150	2	*3.19	4	235	1	3	12	0	3.06
86-87—Binghamton	AHL	57	3304	23	16	0	161	4	2.92	13	794	6	7	36	0	*2.72
87-88—Hartford	NHL	1	60	0	1	0	6	0	6.00	—						
—Binghamton	AHL	42	2346	19	17	3	144	0	3.68	3	147	0	2	8	0	3.27
88-89—Hartford	NHL	44	2635	22	18	4	133	4	3.03	2	124	0	2	8	0	3.87
89-90—Hartford	NHL	46	2703	19	19	7	161	1	3.57	7	429	3	4	23	0	3.22
90-91—Hartford	NHL	52	2953	21	22	7	164	1	3.33	6	359	2	4	24	0	4.01
91-92—Hartford	NHL	35	1995	9	19	6	111	2	3.34	—						
92-93—Ottawa	NHL	64	3388	8	*46	3	*250	0	4.43	—						
93-94—Fort Wayne	IHL	11	591	6	3	‡0	27	†2	2.74	18	*1054	10	*6	59	†1	3.36
—Albany	AHL	15	908	6	7	2	60	0	3.96	—						
—New Jersey	NHL	3	130	0	3	0	6	0	2.77	—						
94-95—Fort Wayne	IHL	16	942	8	6	‡1	58	1	3.69	3	144	1	2	12	0	5.00
95-96—Albany	AHL	32	1809	19	7	5	89	3	2.95	1	58	0	1	3	0	3.10
96-97—Albany	AHL	62	3539	31	23	6	171	2	2.90	16	921	7	8	48	0	3.13
97-98—Albany	AHL	43	2423	21	15	5	115	3	2.85	2	90	1	1	6	0	4.00
—New Jersey	NHL	1	20	0	0	0	1	0	3.00	—						
NHL Totals (8 years)		246	13884	79	128	27	832	8	3.60	15	912	5	10	55	0	3.62

SIDULOV, KONSTANTIN   D   CANADIENS

PERSONAL: Born January 1, 1977, in Chelyabinsk, U.S.S.R. ... 6-1/176. ... Shoots left.
TRANSACTIONS/CAREER NOTES: Selected by Montreal Canadiens in fifth round (fifth Canadiens pick, 118th overall) of NHL entry draft (June 21, 1997).

		REGULAR SEASON								PLAYOFFS				
Season Team	League	Gms.	G	A	Pts.	PIM	+/-	PP	SH	Gms.	G	A	Pts.	PIM
94-95—Traktor Chelyabinsk	CIS	2	0	0	0	0	...	...	...	—				
95-96—Traktor Chelyabinsk	CIS	52	1	0	1	58	...	...	...	—				
96-97—Traktor Chelyabinsk	Russian	42	0	0	0	28	...	...	...	—				
97-98—Traktor Chelyabinsk	Russian	43	1	3	4	36	...	...	...	—				

SILLINGER, MIKE   C/RW   FLYERS

PERSONAL: Born June 29, 1971, in Regina, Sask. ... 5-10/190. ... Shoots right. ... Name pronounced SIHL-in-juhr.
TRANSACTIONS/CAREER NOTES: Selected by Detroit Red Wings in first round (first Red Wings pick, 11th overall) of NHL entry draft (June 17, 1989). ... Fractured rib in training camp (September 1990). ... Suffered from the flu (March 5, 1993); missed three games. ... Strained rotator cuff (October 9, 1993); missed four games. ... Played in Europe during 1994-95 NHL lockout. ... Injured eye (January 17, 1995); missed four games. ... Traded by Red Wings with D Jason York to Mighty Ducks of Anaheim for LW Stu Grimson, D Mark Ferner and sixth-round pick (LW Magnus Nilsson) in 1996 draft (April 4, 1995). ... Traded by Mighty Ducks to Vancouver Canucks for RW Roman Oksuita (March 15, 1996). ... Suffered concussion (March 26, 1997); missed two games. ... Traded by Canucks to Flyers for sixth-round pick (traded back to Philadelphia) in 1998 draft (February 5, 1998).
HONORS: Named to WHL All-Star second team (1989-90). ... Named to WHL (East) All-Star first team (1990-91).
MISCELLANEOUS: Scored on a penalty shot (vs. Mark Fitzpatrick, January 14, 1997).

		REGULAR SEASON								PLAYOFFS				
Season Team	League	Gms.	G	A	Pts.	PIM	+/-	PP	SH	Gms.	G	A	Pts.	PIM
87-88—Regina	WHL	67	18	25	43	17	...	...	...	4	2	2	4	0
88-89—Regina	WHL	72	53	78	131	52	...	...	...	—				
89-90—Regina	WHL	70	57	72	129	41	...	...	...	11	12	10	22	2
—Adirondack	AHL	—					...	...	...	1	0	0	0	0
90-91—Regina	WHL	57	50	66	116	42	...	...	...	8	6	9	15	4
—Detroit	NHL	3	0	1	1	0	-2	0	0	3	0	1	1	0
91-92—Adirondack	AHL	64	25	41	66	26	...	...	...	15	9	*19	*28	12
—Detroit	NHL	—								8	2	2	4	2
92-93—Detroit	NHL	51	4	17	21	16	0	0	0	—				
—Adirondack	AHL	15	10	20	30	31	...	...	...	11	5	13	18	10
93-94—Detroit	NHL	62	8	21	29	10	2	0	1	—				
94-95—Wien	Austria	13	13	14	27	10	...	...	...	—				
—Detroit	NHL	13	2	6	8	2	3	0	0	—				
—Anaheim	NHL	15	2	5	7	6	1	2	0	—				
95-96—Anaheim	NHL	62	13	21	34	32	-20	7	0	—				
—Vancouver	NHL	12	1	3	4	6	2	0	1	6	0	0	0	2
96-97—Vancouver	NHL	78	17	20	37	25	-3	3	3	—				
97-98—Vancouver	NHL	48	10	9	19	34	-14	1	2	—				
—Philadelphia	NHL	27	11	11	22	16	3	1	2	3	1	0	1	0
NHL Totals (8 years)		371	68	114	182	147	-28	14	9	20	3	3	6	4

SIM, JON   C   STARS

PERSONAL: Born September 29, 1977, in New Glasgow, Nova Scotia. ... 5-9/175. ... Shoots left. ... Full name: Jonathan Sim.
TRANSACTIONS/CAREER NOTES: Selected by Dallas Stars in third round (fifth Capitals pick, 70th overall) of NHL entry draft (June 22, 1996).
HONORS: Named to OHL All-Star second team (1997-98).

		REGULAR SEASON								PLAYOFFS				
Season Team	League	Gms.	G	A	Pts.	PIM	+/-	PP	SH	Gms.	G	A	Pts.	PIM
94-95—Sarnia	OHL	25	9	12	21	19	...	...	...	4	3	2	5	2
95-96—Sarnia	OHL	63	56	46	102	130	...	...	...	10	8	7	15	26
96-97—Sarnia	OHL	64	†56	39	95	109	...	...	...	12	9	5	14	32
97-98—Sarnia	OHL	59	44	50	94	95	...	...	...	5	1	4	5	14

SIMON, BEN   C   BLACKHAWKS

PERSONAL: Born June 14, 1978, in Cleveland. ... 5-11/178. ... Shoots left. ... Full name: Benjamin Clarke Simon.
HIGH SCHOOL: Shaker Heights (Cleveland).
COLLEGE: Notre Dame.
TRANSACTIONS/CAREER NOTES: Selected by Chicago Blackhawks in fifth round (fifth Blackhawks pick, 110th overall) of NHL entry draft (June 21, 1997).

		REGULAR SEASON								PLAYOFFS				
Season Team	League	Gms.	G	A	Pts.	PIM	+/-	PP	SH	Gms.	G	A	Pts.	PIM
92-93—Shaker Heights	Ohio H.S.	...	15	21	36	...	...	...	...	—	—	—	—	—
93-94—Shaker Heights	Ohio H.S.	...	45	41	86	...	...	...	...	—	—	—	—	—
94-95—Shaker Heights	Ohio H.S.	...	61	68	129	...	...	...	...	—	—	—	—	—
95-96—Cleveland	NAHL	50	45	46	91	...	...	...	...	—	—	—	—	—
96-97—Univ. of Notre Dame	CCHA	30	4	15	19	79	...	...	...	—	—	—	—	—
97-98—Univ. of Notre Dame	CCHA	37	9	28	37	91	...	...	...	—	—	—	—	—

S

SIMON, CHRIS   LW   CAPITALS

PERSONAL: Born January 30, 1972, in Wawa, Ont. ... 6-3/235. ... Shoots left. ... Name pronounced SIGH-muhn.
TRANSACTIONS/CAREER NOTES: Suspended six games by OHL for shooting the puck in frustration and striking another player (January 20, 1990). ... Selected by Philadelphia Flyers in second round (second Flyers pick, 25th overall) of NHL entry draft (June 16, 1990). ... Underwent surgery to repair left rotator cuff and torn muscle (September 1990). ... Traded by Flyers with first-round pick (traded to Toronto) in 1994 draft to Quebec Nordiques (July 21, 1992) to complete deal in which Flyers sent G Ron Hextall, C Mike Ricci, C Peter Forsberg, D Steve Duchesne, first-round pick (G Jocelyn Thibault) in 1993 draft and cash to Nordiques for C Eric Lindros (June 20, 1992). ... Suffered from the flu (March 13, 1993); missed one game. ... Injured back (December 1, 1993); missed 31 games. ... Injured back (February 16, 1994); missed one game. ... Injured back (March 6, 1994); missed one game. ... Injured back (March 18, 1994); missed remainder of season. ... Injured back (January 31, 1995); missed six games. ... Injured shoulder (March 22, 1995); missed 13 games. ... Nordiques franchise moved to Colorado and renamed Avalanche for 1995-96 season (June 21, 1995). ... Suffered back spasms (January 6, 1996); missed two games. ... Injured shoulder (February 5, 1996); missed four games. ... Traded by Avalanche with D Curtis Leschyshyn to Washington Capitals for RW Keith Jones and first- (D Scott Parker) and fourth-round (traded back to Washington) picks in 1998 draft (November 2, 1996). ... Injured arm (December 20, 1996); missed two games. ... Suffered back spasms (January 24, 1997); missed 17 games. ... Suffered back spasms (March 22, 1997); missed one game. ... Strained shoulder (March 29, 1997); missed six games. ... Injured shoulder (October 25, 1997); missed five games. ... Suspended three games by NHL for alleged racial remarks (November 9, 1997). ... Reinjured shoulder (December 20, 1997) and underwent shoulder surgery (January 12, 1998); missed remainder of regular season.
MISCELLANEOUS: Member of Stanley Cup championship team (1996).

		REGULAR SEASON								PLAYOFFS				
Season Team	League	Gms.	G	A	Pts.	PIM	+/-	PP	SH	Gms.	G	A	Pts.	PIM
87-88—Sault Ste. Marie	OHA	55	42	36	78	172	...	...	...	—	—	—	—	—
88-89—Ottawa	OHL	36	4	2	6	31	...	...	...	—	—	—	—	—
89-90—Ottawa	OHL	57	36	38	74	146	...	...	...	3	2	1	3	4
90-91—Ottawa	OHL	20	16	6	22	69	...	...	...	17	5	9	14	59
91-92—Ottawa	OHL	2	1	1	2	24	...	...	...	—	—	—	—	—
—Sault Ste. Marie	OHL	31	19	25	44	143	...	...	...	11	5	8	13	49
92-93—Halifax	AHL	36	12	6	18	131	...	...	...	—	—	—	—	—
—Quebec	NHL	16	1	1	2	67	-2	0	0	5	0	0	0	26
93-94—Quebec	NHL	37	4	4	8	132	-2	0	0	—	—	—	—	—
94-95—Quebec	NHL	29	3	9	12	106	14	0	0	6	1	1	2	19
95-96—Colorado	NHL	64	16	18	34	250	10	4	0	12	1	2	3	11
96-97—Washington	NHL	42	9	13	22	165	-1	3	0	—	—	—	—	—
97-98—Washington	NHL	28	7	10	17	38	-1	4	0	18	1	0	1	26
NHL Totals (6 years)		216	40	55	95	758	18	11	0	41	3	3	6	82

SIMONS, MIKAEL   C   KINGS

PERSONAL: Born January 15, 1978, in Falun, Sweden. ... 6-2/187. ... Shoots left. ... Name pronounced see-MOHNS.
TRANSACTIONS/CAREER NOTES: Selected by Los Angeles Kings in fourth round (fourth Kings pick, 84th overall) of NHL entry draft (June 22, 1996).

		REGULAR SEASON								PLAYOFFS				
Season Team	League	Gms.	G	A	Pts.	PIM	+/-	PP	SH	Gms.	G	A	Pts.	PIM
94-95—Mora Jrs.	Sweden Jr.	26	5	3	8	57	...	...	...	—	—	—	—	—
95-96—Mora Jrs.	Sweden Jr.	10	4	4	8	12	...	...	...	—	—	—	—	—
—Mora	Swed. Dv.II	33	6	3	9	22	...	...	...	6	0	2	2	2
96-97—Mora	Swed. Dv.II	29	11	8	19	38	...	...	...	—	—	—	—	—
97-98—Mora	Swed. Dv.II	42	13	11	29	7	...	...	...	—	—	—	—	—

SIMPSON, REID   LW   BLACKHAWKS

PERSONAL: Born May 21, 1969, in Flin Flon, Man. ... 6-2/220. ... Shoots left.
TRANSACTIONS/CAREER NOTES: Selected by Philadelphia Flyers in fourth round (third Flyers pick, 72nd overall) of NHL entry draft (June 17, 1989). ... Signed as free agent by Minnesota North Stars (December 13, 1992). ... North Stars franchise moved from Minnesota to Dallas and renamed Stars for 1993-94 season. ... Traded by Stars with D Roy Mitchell to New Jersey Devils for future considerations (March 21, 1994). ... Bruised right shoulder (November 27, 1995); missed six games. ... Strained groin (September 9, 1996); missed first two games of season. ... Reinjured groin (October 16, 1996); underwent groin surgery (November 22, 1996) and missed 38 games. ... Injured hamstring (November 8, 1997); missed 13 games. ... Traded by Devils to Chicago Blackhawks for fourth-round pick (D Mikko Jokela) in 1998 draft and future considerations (January 8, 1998). ... Strained hip flexor (March 12, 1998); missed two games.

		REGULAR SEASON								PLAYOFFS				
Season Team	League	Gms.	G	A	Pts.	PIM	+/-	PP	SH	Gms.	G	A	Pts.	PIM
85-86—Flin Flon	MJHL	40	20	21	41	200	...	...	...	—	—	—	—	—
—New Westminster	WHL	2	0	0	0	0	...	...	...	—	—	—	—	—
86-87—Prince Albert	WHL	47	3	8	11	105	...	...	...	—	—	—	—	—
87-88—Prince Albert	WHL	72	13	14	27	164	...	...	...	10	1	0	1	43
88-89—Prince Albert	WHL	59	26	29	55	264	...	...	...	4	2	1	3	30
89-90—Prince Albert	WHL	29	15	17	32	121	...	...	...	14	4	7	11	34
—Hershey	AHL	28	2	2	4	175	...	...	...	—	—	—	—	—
90-91—Hershey	AHL	54	9	15	24	183	...	...	...	1	0	0	0	0
91-92—Hershey	AHL	60	11	7	18	145	...	...	...	—	—	—	—	—
—Philadelphia	NHL	1	0	0	0	0	0	0	0	—	—	—	—	—
92-93—Kalamazoo	IHL	45	5	5	10	193	...	...	...	—	—	—	—	—
—Minnesota	NHL	1	0	0	0	5	0	0	0	—	—	—	—	—
93-94—Kalamazoo	IHL	5	0	0	0	16	...	...	...	—	—	—	—	—
—Albany	AHL	37	9	5	14	135	...	...	...	5	1	1	2	18
94-95—Albany	AHL	70	18	25	43	268	...	...	...	14	1	8	9	13
—New Jersey	NHL	9	0	0	0	27	-1	0	0	—	—	—	—	—
95-96—New Jersey	NHL	23	1	5	6	79	2	0	0	—	—	—	—	—
—Albany	AHL	6	1	3	4	17	...	...	...	—	—	—	—	—
96-97—Albany	AHL	3	0	0	0	10	...	...	...	—	—	—	—	—
—New Jersey	NHL	27	0	4	4	60	0	0	0	5	0	0	0	29
97-98—New Jersey	NHL	6	0	0	0	16	-2	0	0	—	—	—	—	—
—Chicago	NHL	38	3	2	5	102	-1	1	0	—	—	—	—	—
NHL Totals (6 years)		105	4	11	15	289	-2	1	0	5	0	0	0	29

SIMPSON, TODD   D   FLAMES

PERSONAL: Born May 28, 1973, in Edmonton. ... 6-3/215. ... Shoots left.
TRANSACTIONS/CAREER NOTES: Signed as free agent by Calgary Flames (July 6, 1994). ... Injured knee (October 1, 1997) and underwent arthroscopic knee surgery (October 8, 1997); missed 10 games. ... Injured shoulder (November 15, 1997); missed four games. ... Suffered concussion (March 19, 1998); missed remainder of season.
MISCELLANEOUS: Captain of Calgary Flames (1997-98).

		REGULAR SEASON								PLAYOFFS				
Season Team	League	Gms.	G	A	Pts.	PIM	+/-	PP	SH	Gms.	G	A	Pts.	PIM
92-93—Tri-City	WHL	69	5	18	23	196	...	...	...	4	0	0	0	13
93-94—Tri-City	WHL	12	2	3	5	32	...	...	...	—	—	—	—	—
—Saskatoon	WHL	51	7	19	26	175	...	...	...	16	1	5	6	42
94-95—Saint John	AHL	80	3	10	13	321	...	...	...	5	0	0	0	4
95-96—Calgary	NHL	6	0	0	0	32	0	0	0	—	—	—	—	—
—Saint John	AHL	66	4	13	17	277	...	...	...	16	2	3	5	32
96-97—Calgary	NHL	82	1	13	14	208	-14	0	0	—	—	—	—	—
97-98—Calgary	NHL	53	1	5	6	109	-10	0	0	—	—	—	—	—
NHL Totals (3 years)		141	2	18	20	349	-24	0	0	—	—	—	—	—

SKALDE, JARROD   C   SHARKS

PERSONAL: Born February 26, 1971, in Niagara Falls, Ont. ... 6-0/190. ... Shoots left. ... Name pronounced SKAHL-dee.
TRANSACTIONS/CAREER NOTES: Selected by New Jersey Devils in second round (third Devils pick, 26th overall) of NHL entry draft (June 17, 1989). ... Traded by Oshawa Generals to Belleville Bulls for RW Rob Pearson (November 18, 1990). ... Selected by Mighty Ducks of Anaheim in NHL expansion draft (June 24, 1993). ... Signed as free agent by Las Vegas Thunder (August 18, 1994). ... Signed as free agent by Mighty Ducks (May 31, 1995). ... Traded by Mighty Ducks to Calgary Flames for D Bobby Marshall (October 30, 1995). ... Signed as free agent by San Jose Sharks (August 13, 1997). ... Claimed on waivers by Dallas Stars (January 27, 1998). ... Claimed on waivers by Chicago Blackhawks (February 12, 1998). ... Claimed on waivers by Sharks (March 6, 1998).
HONORS: Named to OHL All-Star second team (1990-91).

		REGULAR SEASON								PLAYOFFS				
Season Team	League	Gms.	G	A	Pts.	PIM	+/-	PP	SH	Gms.	G	A	Pts.	PIM
86-87—Fort Erie Jr. B	OHA	41	27	34	61	36	...	...	...	—	—	—	—	—
87-88—Oshawa	OHL	60	12	16	28	24	...	...	...	7	2	1	3	2
88-89—Oshawa	OHL	65	38	38	76	36	...	...	...	6	1	5	6	2
89-90—Oshawa	OHL	62	40	52	92	66	...	...	...	17	10	7	17	6
90-91—New Jersey	NHL	1	0	1	1	0	0	0	0	—	—	—	—	—
—Utica	AHL	3	3	2	5	0	...	...	...	—	—	—	—	—
—Oshawa	OHL	15	8	14	22	14	...	...	...	—	—	—	—	—
—Belleville	OHL	40	30	52	82	21	...	...	...	6	9	6	15	10
91-92—Utica	AHL	62	20	20	40	56	...	...	...	4	3	1	4	8
—New Jersey	NHL	15	2	4	6	4	-1	0	0	—	—	—	—	—

S

Season Team	League	REGULAR SEASON Gms.	G	A	Pts.	PIM	+/-	PP	SH	PLAYOFFS Gms.	G	A	Pts.	PIM
92-93—Cincinnati	IHL	4	1	2	3	4	...	...	...	—	—	—	—	—
—Utica	AHL	59	21	39	60	76	...	...	...	5	0	2	2	19
—New Jersey	NHL	11	0	2	2	4	-3	0	0	—	—	—	—	—
93-94—San Diego	IHL	57	25	38	63	79	...	...	...	9	3	12	15	10
—Anaheim	NHL	20	5	4	9	10	-3	2	0	—	—	—	—	—
94-95—Las Vegas	IHL	74	34	41	75	103	...	...	...	9	2	4	6	8
95-96—Baltimore	AHL	11	2	6	8	55	...	...	...	—	—	—	—	—
—Saint John	AHL	68	27	40	67	98	...	...	...	16	4	9	13	6
—Calgary	NHL	1	0	0	0	0	0	0	0	—	—	—	—	—
96-97—Saint John	AHL	65	32	36	68	94	...	...	...	3	0	0	0	14
97-98—Kentucky	AHL	23	5	15	20	48	...	...	...	3	3	0	3	6
—San Jose	NHL	22	4	6	10	14	-2	0	0	—	—	—	—	—
—Chicago	NHL	7	0	1	1	4	0	0	0	—	—	—	—	—
—Indianapolis	IHL	2	0	2	2	0	...	...	...	—	—	—	—	—
—Dallas	NHL	1	0	0	0	0	0	0	0	—	—	—	—	—
NHL Totals (6 years)		78	11	18	29	36	-9	2	0					

SKOPINTSEV, ANDREI   D   LIGHTNING

PERSONAL: Born September 28, 1971, in Elektrostal, U.S.S.R. ... 6-0/185. ... Shoots right.
TRANSACTIONS/CAREER NOTES: Selected by Tampa Bay Lightning in sixth round (seventh Lightning pick, 153rd overall) of NHL entry draft (June 21, 1997).

Season Team	League	REGULAR SEASON Gms.	G	A	Pts.	PIM	+/-	PP	SH	PLAYOFFS Gms.	G	A	Pts.	PIM
89-90—Krylja Sov. Moscow	USSR	20	0	0	0	10	...	...	...	—	—	—	—	—
90-91—Krylja Sov. Moscow	USSR	16	0	1	1	2	...	...	...	—	—	—	—	—
91-92—Krylja Sov. Moscow	CIS	36	1	1	2	14	...	...	...	—	—	—	—	—
92-93—Krylja Sov. Moscow	CIS	12	1	0	1	4	...	...	...	7	1	0	1	2
93-94—Krylja Sov. Moscow	CIS	43	4	8	12	14	...	...	...	3	1	0	1	0
94-95—Krylja Sov. Moscow	CIS	52	8	12	20	55	...	...	...	4	1	1	2	0
95-96—Augsburg	Germany	46	10	20	30	32	...	...	...	7	3	2	5	22
96-97—TPS Turku	Finland	46	3	6	9	80	...	...	...	10	1	1	2	4
97-98—TPS Turku	Finland	48	2	9	11	8	...	...	...	4	0	1	1	4

SKOREPA, ZDENEK   RW   DEVILS

PERSONAL: Born August 10, 1976, in Duchcov, Czechoslovakia. ... 6-0/185. ... Shoots left. ... Name pronounced skorh-AY-puh.
TRANSACTIONS/CAREER NOTES: Selected by New Jersey Devils in fourth round (fourth Devils pick, 103rd overall) of NHL entry draft (June 29, 1994).

Season Team	League	REGULAR SEASON Gms.	G	A	Pts.	PIM	+/-	PP	SH	PLAYOFFS Gms.	G	A	Pts.	PIM
93-94—Chemo. Litvinov	Czech Rep.	20	4	7	11	...	...	...	...	4	0	0	0	...
94-95—Chemo. Litvinov	Czech Rep.	28	3	3	6	20	...	...	...	3	0	0	0	2
95-96—Kingston	OHL	37	21	18	39	13	...	...	...	6	5	2	7	5
96-97—Albany	AHL	60	12	12	24	38	...	...	...	13	3	2	5	14
97-98—Albany	AHL	28	2	2	4	4	...	...	...	1	0	0	0	0
—Detroit	IHL	8	0	0	0	2	...	...	...	—	—	—	—	—

SKRBEK, PAVEL   D   PENGUINS

PERSONAL: Born August 9, 1978, in Kladno, Czechoslovakia. ... 6-3/200. ... Shoots left.
TRANSACTIONS/CAREER NOTES: Selected by Pittsburgh Penguins in second round (second Penguins pick, 28th overall) of NHL entry draft (June 22, 1996).

Season Team	League	REGULAR SEASON Gms.	G	A	Pts.	PIM	+/-	PP	SH	PLAYOFFS Gms.	G	A	Pts.	PIM
94-95—HC Kladno Jrs.	Czech Rep.	29	7	6	13	...	...	...	...	—	—	—	—	—
95-96—HC Kladno Jrs.	Czech Rep.	29	10	12	22	...	...	...	...	—	—	—	—	—
—HC Kladno	Czech Rep.	13	0	1	1	...	...	...	...	5	0	0	0	...
96-97—HC Kladno	Czech Rep.	35	1	5	6	26	...	...	...	3	0	0	0	4
97-98—HC Kladno	Czech Rep.	47	4	10	14	126	...	...	...	—	—	—	—	—

SKRUDLAND, BRIAN   C   STARS

PERSONAL: Born July 31, 1963, in Peace River, Alta. ... 6-0/200. ... Shoots left. ... Cousin of Barry Pederson, center for four NHL teams (1980-81 through 1991-92). ... Name pronounced SKROOD-luhnd.
TRANSACTIONS/CAREER NOTES: Signed as free agent by Montreal Canadiens (August 1983). ... Injured groin (February 1988). ... Strained left knee ligaments (December 27, 1988). ... Bruised right foot (January 1989). ... Sprained right ankle (October 7, 1989); missed 21 games. ... Pulled hip muscle (November 4, 1990); missed six games. ... Broke foot (January 17, 1991); missed 14 games including All-Star Game. ... Broke left thumb (October 5, 1991); missed five games. ... Sprained knee (October 26, 1991); missed 25 games. ... Broke nose (January 25, 1992); missed eight games. ... Tore right knee ligaments (October 6, 1992); missed 27 games. ... Injured shoulder (January 14, 1993); missed one game. ... Traded by Canadiens to Calgary Flames for RW Gary Leeman (January 28, 1993). ... Sprained ankle (February 16, 1993); missed four games. ... Broke thumb (March 2, 1993); missed 12 games. ... Lacerated right ear (April 11, 1993); missed one game. ... Selected by Florida Panthers in NHL expansion draft (June 24, 1993). ... Sprained right ankle (April 4, 1994); missed five games. ... Injured left hip flexor (March 22, 1995); missed one game. ... Suspended one game for high-sticking (February 13, 1996). ... Injured left hip flexor (April 12,

1996); missed one game. ... Cracked rib (October 30, 1996); missed three games. ... Suffered from the flu (December 10, 1996); missed one game. ... Bruised right shoulder (January 23, 1997); missed five games. ... Fractured ribs (February 7, 1997); missed six games. ... Sprained knee ligament (March 7, 1997); missed remainder of season. ... Signed as free agent by New York Rangers (July 7, 1997). ... Traded by Rangers with RW Mike Keane and sixth-round pick (RW Pavel Patera) in 1998 draft to Dallas Stars for LW Bob Errey, RW Todd Harvey and fourth-round pick (LW Boyd Kane) in 1998 draft (March 24, 1998).

HONORS: Won Jack Butterfield Trophy (1984-85).

MISCELLANEOUS: Member of Stanley Cup championship team (1986). ... Captain of Florida Panthers (1994-95 and 1996-97).

		REGULAR SEASON								PLAYOFFS				
Season Team	League	Gms.	G	A	Pts.	PIM	+/-	PP	SH	Gms.	G	A	Pts.	PIM
80-81—Saskatoon..................	WHL	66	15	27	42	97	...	...	...	—	—	—	—	—
81-82—Saskatoon..................	WHL	71	27	29	56	135	...	...	...	5	0	1	1	2
82-83—Saskatoon..................	WHL	71	35	59	94	42	...	...	...	6	1	3	4	19
83-84—Nova Scotia	AHL	56	13	12	25	55	...	...	...	12	2	8	10	14
84-85—Sherbrooke	AHL	70	22	28	50	109	...	...	...	17	9	8	17	23
85-86—Montreal	NHL	65	9	13	22	57	3	2	0	20	2	4	6	76
86-87—Montreal	NHL	79	11	17	28	107	18	0	1	14	1	5	6	29
87-88—Montreal	NHL	79	12	24	36	112	44	0	1	11	1	5	6	24
88-89—Montreal	NHL	71	12	29	41	84	22	1	1	21	3	7	10	40
89-90—Montreal	NHL	59	11	31	42	56	21	4	0	11	3	5	8	30
90-91—Montreal	NHL	57	15	19	34	85	12	1	1	13	3	10	13	42
91-92—Montreal	NHL	42	3	3	6	36	-4	0	0	11	1	1	2	20
92-93—Montreal	NHL	23	5	3	8	55	1	0	2	—	—	—	—	—
—Calgary	NHL	16	2	4	6	10	3	0	0	6	0	3	3	12
93-94—Florida	NHL	79	15	25	40	136	13	0	2	—	—	—	—	—
94-95—Florida	NHL	47	5	9	14	88	0	1	0	—	—	—	—	—
95-96—Florida	NHL	79	7	20	27	129	6	0	1	21	1	3	4	18
96-97—Florida	NHL	51	5	13	18	48	4	0	0	—	—	—	—	—
97-98—New York Rangers	NHL	59	5	6	11	39	-4	0	0	—	—	—	—	—
—Dallas....................	NHL	13	2	0	2	10	-2	0	0	17	0	1	1	16
NHL Totals (13 years).........		**819**	**119**	**216**	**335**	**1052**	**137**	**9**	**9**	**145**	**15**	**44**	**59**	**307**

SKUDRA, PETER · G · PENGUINS

PERSONAL: Born April 24, 1973, in Riga, U.S.S.R. ... 6-1/182. ... Catches left. ... Name pronounced SKOO-druh.

TRANSACTIONS/CAREER NOTES: Signed as free agent by Pittsburgh Penguins (September 25, 1997).

		REGULAR SEASON								PLAYOFFS						
Season Team	League	Gms.	Min	W	L	T	GA	SO	Avg.	Gms.	Min.	W	L	GA	SO	Avg.
94-95—Greensboro	ECHL	33	1812	13	9	‡5	113	0	4.20	6	341	2	2	28	0	4.92
95-96—Erie..........................	ECHL	30	681	3	8	‡1	47	0	4.14	—	—	—	—	—	—	—
—Johnstown	ECHL	30	1557	12	11	‡4	98	0	3.55	—	—	—	—	—	—	—
96-97—Johnstown	ECHL	4	200	2	1	‡1	11	0	3.30	—	—	—	—	—	—	—
—Hamilton	AHL	32	1615	8	16	2	101	0	3.75	—	—	—	—	—	—	—
97-98—Houston	IHL	9	499	5	3	‡1	23	0	2.77	—	—	—	—	—	—	—
—Pittsburgh	NHL	17	851	6	4	3	26	0	1.83	—	—	—	—	—	—	—
—Kansas City	IHL	13	776	10	3	‡0	37	0	2.86	8	513	4	4	20	1	*2.34
NHL Totals (1 year)..............		**17**	**851**	**6**	**4**	**3**	**26**	**0**	**1.83**							

SLANEY, JOHN · D · PREDATORS

PERSONAL: Born February 7, 1972, in St. John's, Nfld. ... 6-0/185. ... Shoots left. ... Full name: John G. Slaney.

TRANSACTIONS/CAREER NOTES: Selected by Washington Capitals in first round (first Capitals pick, ninth overall) of NHL entry draft (June 16, 1990). ... Sprained right ankle (March 9, 1994); missed six games. ... Traded by Capitals to Colorado Avalanche for third-round pick (C Shawn McNeil) in 1996 draft (July 12, 1995). ... Traded by Avalanche to Los Angeles Kings for sixth-round pick (RW Brian Willsie) in 1996 draft (December 28, 1995). ... Broke right hand (March 6, 1996); missed 12 games. ... Suffered concussion (November 17, 1996); missed one game. ... Signed as free agent by Phoenix Coyotes (August 18, 1997). ... Bruised thigh (October 30, 1997); missed one game. ... Suffered from the flu (December 10, 1997); missed one game. ... Fractured thumb (January 24, 1998); missed seven games. ... Injured hamstring (April 18, 1998); missed one game. ... Selected by Nashville Predators in NHL expansion draft (June 26, 1998).

HONORS: Won Max Kaminsky Trophy (1989-90). ... Named to OHL All-Star first team (1989-90). ... Named to OHL All-Star second team (1990-91).

		REGULAR SEASON								PLAYOFFS				
Season Team	League	Gms.	G	A	Pts.	PIM	+/-	PP	SH	Gms.	G	A	Pts.	PIM
88-89—Cornwall	OHL	66	16	43	59	23	...	...	...	18	8	16	24	10
89-90—Cornwall	OHL	64	38	59	97	60	...	...	...	6	0	8	8	11
90-91—Cornwall	OHL	34	21	25	46	28	...	...	...	—	—	—	—	—
91-92—Cornwall	OHL	34	19	41	60	43	...	...	...	6	3	8	11	0
—Baltimore	AHL	6	2	4	6	0	...	...	...	—	—	—	—	—
92-93—Baltimore	AHL	79	20	46	66	60	...	...	...	7	0	7	7	8
93-94—Portland	AHL	29	14	13	27	17	...	...	...	—	—	—	—	—
—Washington	NHL	47	7	9	16	27	3	3	0	11	1	1	2	2
94-95—Washington	NHL	16	0	3	3	6	-3	0	0	—	—	—	—	—
—Portland	AHL	8	3	10	13	4	...	...	...	7	1	3	4	4
95-96—Colorado	NHL	7	0	3	3	4	2	0	0	—	—	—	—	—
—Cornwall	AHL	5	0	4	4	2	...	...	...	—	—	—	—	—
—Los Angeles	NHL	31	6	11	17	10	5	3	1	—	—	—	—	—
96-97—Los Angeles	NHL	32	3	11	14	4	-10	4	0	—	—	—	—	—
—Phoenix	IHL	35	9	25	34	8	...	...	...	—	—	—	—	—
97-98—Las Vegas	IHL	5	2	2	4	10	...	...	...	—	—	—	—	—
—Phoenix	NHL	55	3	14	17	24	-3	1	0	—	—	—	—	—
NHL Totals (5 years)...........		**188**	**19**	**51**	**70**	**75**	**-6**	**8**	**1**	**11**	**1**	**1**	**2**	**2**

SLEGR, JIRI — D — PENGUINS

PERSONAL: Born May 30, 1971, in Litvinov, Czechoslovakia. ... 6-0/217. ... Shoots left. ... Son of Jiri Bubla, defenseman with Vancouver Canucks (1981-82 through 1985-86). ... Name pronounced YIH-ree SLAY-guhr.
TRANSACTIONS/CAREER NOTES: Selected by Vancouver Canucks in second round (third Canucks pick, 23rd overall) of NHL entry draft (June 16, 1990). ... Played in Europe during 1994-95 NHL lockout. ... Traded by Canucks to Edmonton Oilers for RW Roman Oksiuta (April 7, 1995). ... Sprained ligaments in left knee (December 27, 1995); missed 19 games. ... Traded by Oilers to Pittsburgh Penguins for third-round pick (traded to New Jersey) in 1998 draft (August 12, 1997). ... Suffered hip pointer (November 14, 1997); missed four games. ... Suffered from the flu (December 16, 1997); missed one game. ... Injured shoulder (March 2, 1998); missed one game.
HONORS: Named to Czechoslovakian League All-Star team (1990-91).
MISCELLANEOUS: Member of gold-medal-winning Czech Republic Olympic team (1998).

Season Team	League	REGULAR SEASON								PLAYOFFS				
		Gms.	G	A	Pts.	PIM	+/-	PP	SH	Gms.	G	A	Pts.	PIM
88-89—Litvinov	Czech.	8	0	0	0	...	...	...	...	—	—	—	—	—
89-90—Litvinov	Czech.	51	4	15	19	...	...	...	...	—	—	—	—	—
90-91—Litvinov	Czech.	39	10	33	43	26	...	...	...	—	—	—	—	—
91-92—Litvinov	Czech.	38	7	22	29	30	...	...	...	—	—	—	—	—
—Czech. Oly. Team	Czech.	8	1	1	2	...	...	...	...	—	—	—	—	—
92-93—Vancouver	NHL	41	4	22	26	109	16	2	0	5	0	3	3	4
—Hamilton	AHL	21	4	14	18	42	...	...	...	—	—	—	—	—
93-94—Vancouver	NHL	78	5	33	38	86	0	1	0	—	—	—	—	—
94-95—Chemo. Litvinov	Czech Rep.	11	3	10	13	43	...	...	...	—	—	—	—	—
—Vancouver	NHL	19	1	5	6	32	0	0	0	—	—	—	—	—
—Edmonton	NHL	12	1	5	6	14	-5	1	0	—	—	—	—	—
95-96—Edmonton	NHL	57	4	13	17	74	-1	0	1	—	—	—	—	—
—Cape Breton	AHL	4	1	2	3	4	...	...	...	—	—	—	—	—
96-97—Chemo. Litvinov	Czech Rep.	1	0	0	0	0	...	...	...	—	—	—	—	—
—Sodertalje SK	Sweden	30	4	14	18	62	...	...	...	—	—	—	—	—
97-98—Pittsburgh	NHL	73	5	12	17	109	10	1	1	6	0	4	4	2
—Czech Rep. Olympic	Int'l	6	1	0	1	8	...	...	...	—	—	—	—	—
NHL Totals (5 years)		280	20	90	110	424	20	5	2	11	0	7	7	6

SMEHLIK, RICHARD — D — SABRES

PERSONAL: Born January 23, 1970, in Ostrava, Czechoslovakia. ... 6-3/222. ... Shoots left. ... Name pronounced SHMEHL-ihk.
TRANSACTIONS/CAREER NOTES: Selected by Buffalo Sabres in fifth round (third Sabres pick, 97th overall) of NHL entry draft (June 16, 1990). ... Injured hip (October 30, 1992); missed two games. ... Played in Europe during 1994-95 NHL lockout. ... Bruised shoulder (January 27, 1995); missed six games. ... Tore knee ligaments (August 10, 1995); missed entire 1995-96 season. ... Suffered tendonitis in knee (January 12, 1996); missed five games. ... Sore knee (November 19, 1996); missed six games. ... Suffered sore knee (February 23, 1997); missed one game. ... Strained groin (March 30, 1997); missed three games. ... Injured wrist (February 4, 1998); missed two games. ... Bruised eye (February 25, 1998); missed seven games.
MISCELLANEOUS: Member of gold-medal-winning Czech Republic Olympic team (1998).

Season Team	League	REGULAR SEASON								PLAYOFFS				
		Gms.	G	A	Pts.	PIM	+/-	PP	SH	Gms.	G	A	Pts.	PIM
88-89—Vitkovice	Czech.	38	2	5	7	12	...	...	...	—	—	—	—	—
89-90—Vitkovice	Czech.	43	4	3	7	...	...	...	...	—	—	—	—	—
90-91—Dukla Jihlava	Czech.	51	4	2	6	22	...	...	...	—	—	—	—	—
91-92—Vitkovice	Czech.	47	9	10	19	...	...	...	...	—	—	—	—	—
—Czech. Oly. Team	Int'l.	8	0	1	1	2	...	...	...	—	—	—	—	—
92-93—Buffalo	NHL	80	4	27	31	59	9	0	0	8	0	4	4	2
93-94—Buffalo	NHL	84	14	27	41	69	22	3	3	7	0	2	2	10
94-95—HC Vitkovice	Czech Rep.	13	5	2	7	12	...	...	...	—	—	—	—	—
—Buffalo	NHL	39	4	7	11	46	5	0	1	5	0	0	0	2
95-96—Buffalo	NHL							Did not play.						
96-97—Buffalo	NHL	62	11	19	30	43	19	2	0	12	0	2	2	4
97-98—Buffalo	NHL	72	3	17	20	62	11	0	1	15	0	2	2	6
—Czech Rep. Olympic	Int'l	6	0	1	1	4	...	...	...	—	—	—	—	—
NHL Totals (6 years)		337	36	97	133	279	66	5	5	47	0	10	10	24

SMITH, D.J. — D — MAPLE LEAFS

PERSONAL: Born May 13, 1977, in Windsor, Ont. ... 6-1/200. ... Shoots left. ... Full name: Denis Smith.
HIGH SCHOOL: Holy Names (Windsor, Ont.).
TRANSACTIONS/CAREER NOTES: Selected by New York Islanders in second round (third Islanders pick, 41st overall) of NHL entry draft (July 8, 1995). ... Rights traded by Islanders with LW Wendel Clark and D Mathieu Schneider to Toronto Maple Leafs for LW Sean Haggerty, C Darby Hendrickson, D Kenny Jonsson and first-round pick (G Roberto Luongo) in 1997 draft (March 13, 1996).
HONORS: Named to OHL All-Star second team (1996-97).

Season Team	League	REGULAR SEASON								PLAYOFFS				
		Gms.	G	A	Pts.	PIM	+/-	PP	SH	Gms.	G	A	Pts.	PIM
92-93—Belle River	Jr. C	50	11	29	40	101	...	...	...	—	—	—	—	—
93-94—Windsor	Jr. B	51	8	34	42	267	...	...	...	—	—	—	—	—
94-95—Windsor	OHL	61	4	13	17	201	...	...	...	10	1	3	4	41
95-96—Windsor	OHL	64	14	45	59	260	...	...	...	7	1	7	8	23
96-97—Windsor	OHL	63	15	52	67	190	...	...	...	5	1	7	8	11
—Toronto	NHL	8	0	1	1	7	-5	0	0	—	—	—	—	—
—St. John's	AHL	—	—	—	—	—	...	...	...	1	0	0	0	0
97-98—St. John's	AHL	65	4	11	15	237	...	...	...	4	0	0	0	4
NHL Totals (1 year)		8	0	1	1	7	-5	0	0					

SMITH, DAN — D — AVALANCHE

PERSONAL: Born October 19, 1976, in Fernie, B.C. ... 6-2/195. ... Shoots left.
COLLEGE: British Columbia.
TRANSACTIONS/CAREER NOTES: Selected by Colorado Avalanche in seventh round (seventh Avalanche pick, 181st overall) of NHL entry draft (July 8, 1995).

Season Team	League	REGULAR SEASON								PLAYOFFS				
		Gms.	G	A	Pts.	PIM	+/-	PP	SH	Gms.	G	A	Pts.	PIM
94-95—British Columbia	CWUAA	28	1	2	3	26	...	...	...	—	—	—	—	—
95-96—Tri-City	WHL	58	1	21	22	70	...	...	...	11	1	3	4	14
96-97—Tri-City	WHL	72	5	19	24	174	...	...	...	—	—	—	—	—
97-98—Hershey	AHL	50	1	2	3	71	...	...	...	6	0	0	0	4

SMITH, GEOFF — D — RANGERS

PERSONAL: Born March 7, 1969, in Edmonton. ... 6-2/200. ... Shoots left. ... Full name: Geoff Arthur Smith.
HIGH SCHOOL: Harry Ainlay (Edmonton).
COLLEGE: North Dakota.
TRANSACTIONS/CAREER NOTES: Selected by Edmonton Oilers in third round (third Oilers pick, 63rd overall) of NHL entry draft (June 13, 1987). ... Fractured ankle (October 1988); missed first 10 games of season. ... Left University of North Dakota and signed to play with Kamloops Blazers (January 1989). ... Broke jaw (March 1989); missed eight games. ... Bruised shoulder (April 26, 1992). ... Traded by Oilers to Florida Panthers for third- (D Corey Neilson) and sixth-round picks in 1994 draft (December 6, 1993). ... Lacerated left leg (December 10, 1993); missed two games. ... Separated left shoulder (February 15, 1997); missed 23 games. ... Signed as free agent by New York Rangers (September 29, 1997).
HONORS: Named to WHL All-Star first team (1988-89). ... Named to NHL All-Rookie team (1989-90).
MISCELLANEOUS: Member of Stanley Cup championship team (1990).

Season Team	League	REGULAR SEASON								PLAYOFFS				
		Gms.	G	A	Pts.	PIM	+/-	PP	SH	Gms.	G	A	Pts.	PIM
86-87—St. Albert	AJHL	57	7	28	35	101	...	...	...	—	—	—	—	—
87-88—North Dakota	WCHA	42	4	12	16	34	...	...	...	—	—	—	—	—
88-89—North Dakota	WCHA	9	0	1	1	8	...	...	...	—	—	—	—	—
—Kamloops	WHL	32	4	31	35	29	...	...	...	6	1	3	4	12
89-90—Edmonton	NHL	74	4	11	15	52	13	1	0	3	0	0	0	0
90-91—Edmonton	NHL	59	1	12	13	55	13	0	0	4	0	0	0	0
91-92—Edmonton	NHL	74	2	16	18	43	-5	0	0	5	0	1	1	6
92-93—Edmonton	NHL	78	4	14	18	30	-11	0	1	—	—	—	—	—
93-94—Edmonton	NHL	21	0	3	3	12	-10	0	0	—	—	—	—	—
—Florida	NHL	56	1	5	6	38	-3	0	0	—	—	—	—	—
94-95—Florida	NHL	47	2	4	6	22	-5	0	0	—	—	—	—	—
95-96—Florida	NHL	31	3	7	10	20	-4	2	0	1	0	0	0	2
96-97—Carolina	AHL	27	3	4	7	20	...	...	...	—	—	—	—	—
—Florida	NHL	3	0	0	0	2	1	0	0	—	—	—	—	—
97-98—Hartford	AHL	59	1	12	13	34	...	...	...	—	—	—	—	—
—New York Rangers	NHL	15	1	1	2	6	-4	1	0	—	—	—	—	—
NHL Totals (9 years)		458	18	73	91	280	-15	4	1	13	0	1	1	8

SMITH, JARRETT — C — ISLANDERS

PERSONAL: Born June 15, 1979, in Edmonton. ... 6-1/190. ... Shoots left.
TRANSACTIONS/CAREER NOTES: Selected by New York Islanders in third round (fourth Islanders pick, 59th overall) of NHL entry draft (June 21, 1997).

Season Team	League	REGULAR SEASON								PLAYOFFS				
		Gms.	G	A	Pts.	PIM	+/-	PP	SH	Gms.	G	A	Pts.	PIM
94-95—Prince George	WHL	1	0	0	0	0	...	...	...	—	—	—	—	—
95-96—Prince George	WHL	18	2	0	2	6	...	...	...	—	—	—	—	—
96-97—Prince George	WHL	67	20	22	42	58	...	...	...	15	2	2	4	5
97-98—Prince George	WHL	42	12	22	34	21	...	...	...	11	3	1	4	8

SMITH, JASON — D — MAPLE LEAFS

PERSONAL: Born November 2, 1973, in Calgary. ... 6-3/205. ... Shoots right.
TRANSACTIONS/CAREER NOTES: Selected by New Jersey Devils in first round (first Devils pick, 18th overall) of NHL entry draft (June 20, 1992). ... Injured right knee (November 5, 1994); missed 37 games. ... Bruised hand (November 5, 1995); missed 15 games. ... Traded by Devils with C Steve Sullivan and C Alyn McCauley to Toronto Maple Leafs for C Doug Gilmour, D Dave Ellett and third-round pick in 1999 draft (February 25, 1997). ... Fractured toe (March 30, 1998); missed one game.
HONORS: Named to Can.HL All-Rookie team (1991-92). ... Won Bill Hunter Trophy (1992-93). ... Named to Can.HL All-Star first team (1992-93). ... Named to WHL (East) All-Star first team (1992-93).

Season Team	League	REGULAR SEASON								PLAYOFFS				
		Gms.	G	A	Pts.	PIM	+/-	PP	SH	Gms.	G	A	Pts.	PIM
90-91—Calgary Canucks	AJHL	45	3	15	18	69	...	...	...	—	—	—	—	—
—Regina	WHL	2	0	0	0	7	...	...	...	—	—	—	—	—
91-92—Regina	WHL	62	9	29	38	168	...	...	...	—	—	—	—	—
92-93—Utica	AHL	—	—	—	—	—	...	...	...	1	0	0	0	2
—Regina	WHL	64	14	52	66	175	...	...	...	13	4	8	12	39
93-94—New Jersey	NHL	41	0	5	5	43	7	0	0	6	0	0	0	7
—Albany	AHL	20	6	3	9	31	...	...	...	—	—	—	—	—

Season Team	League	REGULAR SEASON Gms.	G	A	Pts.	PIM	+/-	PP	SH	PLAYOFFS Gms.	G	A	Pts.	PIM
94-95—Albany	AHL	7	0	2	2	15	...	...	...	11	2	2	4	19
—New Jersey	NHL	2	0	0	0	0	-3	0	0	—	—	—	—	—
95-96—New Jersey	NHL	64	2	1	3	86	5	0	0	—	—	—	—	—
96-97—New Jersey	NHL	57	1	2	3	38	-8	0	0	—	—	—	—	—
—Toronto	NHL	21	0	5	5	16	-4	0	0	—	—	—	—	—
97-98—Toronto	NHL	81	3	13	16	100	-5	0	0	—	—	—	—	—
NHL Totals (5 years)		266	6	26	32	283	-8	0	0	6	0	0	0	7

SMITH, MARK   C   SHARKS

PERSONAL: Born October 24, 1977, in Edmonton. ... 5-10/190. ... Shoots left.
TRANSACTIONS/CAREER NOTES: Selected by San Jose Sharks in ninth round (seventh Sharks pick, 219th overall) in NHL entry draft (June 21, 1997).
HONORS: Named to WHL (East) All-Star second team (1997-98).

Season Team	League	REGULAR SEASON Gms.	G	A	Pts.	PIM	+/-	PP	SH	PLAYOFFS Gms.	G	A	Pts.	PIM
94-95—Lethbridge	WHL	49	3	4	7	25	...	...	...	—	—	—	—	—
95-96—Lethbridge	WHL	71	11	24	35	59	...	...	...	19	7	13	20	51
96-97—Lethbridge	WHL	62	19	38	57	125	...	...	...	19	7	13	20	51
97-98—Lethbridge	WHL	70	42	67	109	206	...	...	...	3	0	2	2	18

SMITH, NICK   C   PANTHERS

PERSONAL: Born March 23, 1979, in Hamilton, Ont. ... 6-1/165. ... Shoots left.
TRANSACTIONS/CAREER NOTES: Selected by Florida Panthers in third round (fourth Panthers pick, 74th overall) of NHL entry draft (June 21, 1997).

Season Team	League	REGULAR SEASON Gms.	G	A	Pts.	PIM	+/-	PP	SH	PLAYOFFS Gms.	G	A	Pts.	PIM
95-96—Shelburne	Jr. A	42	13	18	31	12	...	...	...	—	—	—	—	—
96-97—Barrie	OHL	63	10	18	28	15	...	...	...	9	3	8	11	13
97-98—Barrie	OHL	63	13	21	34	21	...	...	...	6	1	2	3	4

SMOLINSKI, BRYAN   C   ISLANDERS

PERSONAL: Born December 27, 1971, in Toledo, Ohio. ... 6-1/202. ... Shoots right. ... Full name: Bryan Anthony Smolinski.
COLLEGE: Michigan State.
TRANSACTIONS/CAREER NOTES: Selected by Boston Bruins in first round (first Bruins pick, 21st overall) of NHL entry draft (June 16, 1990). ... Injured knee (April 14, 1994); missed one game. ... Suffered charley horse (April 1995); missed four games. ... Traded by Bruins with RW Glen Murray to Pittsburgh Penguins for LW Kevin Stevens and C Shawn McEachern (August 2, 1995). ... Bruised knee (January 16, 1996); missed one game. ... Traded by Penguins to New York Islanders for D Darius Kasparaitis and C Andreas Johansson (November 17, 1996).
HONORS: Named to CCHA All-Rookie team (1989-90). ... Named to NCAA All-America West first team (1992-93). ... Named to CCHA All-Star first team (1992-93).
STATISTICAL PLATEAUS: Three-goal games: 1994-95 (1).

Season Team	League	REGULAR SEASON Gms.	G	A	Pts.	PIM	+/-	PP	SH	PLAYOFFS Gms.	G	A	Pts.	PIM
87-88—Detroit Little Caesars	MNHL	80	43	77	120	...	...	...	...	—	—	—	—	—
88-89—Stratford Jr. B	OHA	46	32	62	94	132	...	...	...	—	—	—	—	—
89-90—Michigan State	CCHA	39	10	17	27	45	...	...	...	—	—	—	—	—
90-91—Michigan State	CCHA	35	9	12	21	24	...	...	...	—	—	—	—	—
91-92—Michigan State	CCHA	44	30	35	65	59	...	...	...	—	—	—	—	—
92-93—Michigan State	CCHA	40	31	37	68	93	...	...	...	—	—	—	—	—
—Boston	NHL	9	1	3	4	0	3	0	0	4	1	0	1	2
93-94—Boston	NHL	83	31	20	51	82	4	4	3	13	5	4	9	4
94-95—Boston	NHL	44	18	13	31	31	-3	6	0	5	0	1	1	4
95-96—Pittsburgh	NHL	81	24	40	64	69	6	8	2	18	5	4	9	10
96-97—Detroit	IHL	6	5	7	12	10	...	...	...	—	—	—	—	—
—New York Islanders	NHL	64	28	28	56	25	9	9	0	—	—	—	—	—
97-98—New York Islanders	NHL	81	13	30	43	34	-16	3	0	—	—	—	—	—
NHL Totals (6 years)		362	115	134	249	241	3	30	5	40	11	9	20	20

SMYTH, BRAD   RW   PREDATORS

PERSONAL: Born March 13, 1973, in Ottawa. ... 6-0/200. ... Shoots right. ... Name pronounced SMIHTH.
TRANSACTIONS/CAREER NOTES: Signed as free agent by Florida Panthers (October 4, 1993). ... Traded by Panthers to Los Angeles Kings for third-round pick (D Vratislav Cech) in 1997 draft (November 28, 1996). ... Traded by Kings to New York Rangers for conditional draft pick (November 14, 1997). ... Signed as free agent by Nashville Predators (July 16, 1998).
HONORS: Named to AHL All-Star first team (1995-96). ... Won John B. Sollenberger Trophy (1995-96). ... Won Les Cunningham Plaque (1995-96).

Season Team	League	REGULAR SEASON Gms.	G	A	Pts.	PIM	+/-	PP	SH	PLAYOFFS Gms.	G	A	Pts.	PIM
90-91—London	OHL	29	2	6	8	22	...	...	...	—	—	—	—	—
91-92—London	OHL	58	17	18	35	93	...	...	...	10	2	0	2	8

Season Team	League	Gms.	G	A	Pts.	PIM	+/-	PP	SH	Gms.	G	A	Pts.	PIM
					REGULAR SEASON							PLAYOFFS		
92-93—London	OHL	66	54	55	109	118	...	...	...	12	7	8	15	25
93-94—Cincinnati	IHL	30	7	3	10	54	...	...	...	—	—	—	—	—
—Birmingham	ECHL	29	26	30	56	38	...	...	...	10	8	8	16	19
94-95—Cincinnati	IHL	26	2	11	13	34	...	...	...	1	0	0	0	2
—Birmingham	ECHL	36	33	35	68	52	...	...	...	3	5	2	7	0
—Springfield	AHL	3	0	0	0	7	...	...	...	—	—	—	—	—
95-96—Carolina	AHL	68	*68	58	*126	80	...	...	...	—	—	—	—	—
—Florida	NHL	7	1	1	2	4	-3	1	0	—	—	—	—	—
96-97—Florida	NHL	8	1	0	1	2	-3	0	0	—	—	—	—	—
—Los Angeles	NHL	44	8	8	16	74	-7	0	0	—	—	—	—	—
—Phoenix	IHL	3	5	2	7	0	...	...	...	—	—	—	—	—
97-98—Los Angeles	NHL	9	1	3	4	4	-1	0	0	—	—	—	—	—
—Hartford	AHL	57	29	33	62	79	...	...	...	15	12	8	20	11
—New York Rangers	NHL	1	0	0	0	0	0	0	0	—	—	—	—	—
NHL Totals (3 years)		69	11	12	23	84	-14	1	0					

SMYTH, RYAN — LW — OILERS

PERSONAL: Born February 21, 1976, in Banff, Alta. ... 6-1/195. ... Shoots left. ... Brother of Kevin Smyth, left winger with Hartford Whalers (1993-94 through 1995-96). ... Name pronounced SMIHTH.
HIGH SCHOOL: Vanier Comm. Catholic (Edson, Alta.).
TRANSACTIONS/CAREER NOTES: Selected by Edmonton Oilers in first round (second Oilers pick, sixth overall) of NHL entry draft (June 28, 1994). ... Tore medial collateral knee ligament (January 20, 1998); missed 15 games.
HONORS: Named to Can.HL All-Star first team (1994-95). ... Named to WHL (East) All-Star second team (1994-95).
STATISTICAL PLATEAUS: Three-goal games: 1996-97 (1).

Season Team	League	Gms.	G	A	Pts.	PIM	+/-	PP	SH	Gms.	G	A	Pts.	PIM
					REGULAR SEASON							PLAYOFFS		
91-92—Moose Jaw	WHL	2	0	0	0	0	...	...	...	—	—	—	—	—
92-93—Moose Jaw	WHL	64	19	14	33	59	...	...	...	—	—	—	—	—
93-94—Moose Jaw	WHL	72	50	55	105	88	...	...	...	—	—	—	—	—
94-95—Moose Jaw	WHL	50	41	45	86	66	...	...	...	10	6	9	15	22
—Edmonton	NHL	3	0	0	0	0	-1	0	0	—	—	—	—	—
95-96—Edmonton	NHL	48	2	9	11	28	-10	1	0	—	—	—	—	—
—Cape Breton	AHL	9	6	5	11	4	...	...	...	—	—	—	—	—
96-97—Edmonton	NHL	82	39	22	61	76	-7	†20	0	12	5	5	10	12
97-98—Edmonton	NHL	65	20	13	33	44	-24	10	0	12	1	3	4	16
NHL Totals (4 years)		198	61	44	105	148	-42	31	0	24	6	8	14	28

SNOW, GARTH — G — CANUCKS

PERSONAL: Born July 28, 1969, in Wrentham, Mass. ... 6-3/200. ... Catches left.
HIGH SCHOOL: Mount St. Charles Academy (Woonsocket, R.I.).
COLLEGE: Maine.
TRANSACTIONS/CAREER NOTES: Selected by Quebec Nordiques in sixth round (sixth Nordiques pick, 114th overall) of NHL entry draft (June 13, 1987). ... Nordiques franchise moved to Colorado and renamed Avalanche for 1995-96 season (June 21, 1995). ... Rights traded by Avalanche to Philadelphia Flyers for third-(traded to Washington) and sixth-(G Kai Fischer) round picks in 1996 draft (July 12, 1995). ... Pulled groin (March 27, 1997); missed three games. ... Traded by Flyers to Vancouver Canucks for G Sean Burke (March 4, 1998). ... Strained hip flexor (March 18, 1998); missed three games.
HONORS: Named to NCAA All-Tournament team (1992-93). ... Named to Hockey East All-Star second team (1992-93).

Season Team	League	Gms.	Min.	W	L	T	GA	SO	Avg.	Gms.	Min.	W	L	GA	SO	Avg.
					REGULAR SEASON								PLAYOFFS			
88-89—Univ. of Maine	Hockey East	5	241	2	2	0	14	1	3.49	—	—	—	—	—	—	—
89-90—Univ. of Maine	Hockey East							Did not play.								
90-91—Univ. of Maine	Hockey East	25	1290	18	4	0	64	0	2.98	—	—	—	—	—	—	—
91-92—Univ. of Maine	Hockey East	31	1792	25	4	2	73	2	2.44	—	—	—	—	—	—	—
92-93—Univ. of Maine	Hockey East	23	1210	21	0	1	42	1	2.08	—	—	—	—	—	—	—
93-94—U.S. national team	Int'l	23	1324	13	5	3	71	1	3.22	—	—	—	—	—	—	—
—Quebec	NHL	5	279	3	2	0	16	0	3.44	—	—	—	—	—	—	—
—U.S. Olympic Team	Int'l	5	299	1	2	2	17	0	3.41	—	—	—	—	—	—	—
—Cornwall	AHL	16	927	6	5	3	51	0	3.30	13	790	8	5	42	0	3.19
94-95—Cornwall	AHL	62	3558	*32	20	7	162	3	2.73	8	402	4	3	14	†2	*2.09
—Quebec	NHL	2	119	1	1	0	11	0	5.55	1	9	0	1	0	0	6.67
95-96—Philadelphia	NHL	26	1437	12	8	4	69	0	2.88	1	1	0	0	0	0	0.00
96-97—Philadelphia	NHL	35	1884	14	8	8	79	2	2.52	12	699	8	4	33	0	2.83
97-98—Philadelphia	NHL	29	1651	14	9	4	67	1	2.43	—	—	—	—	—	—	—
—Vancouver	NHL	12	504	3	6	0	26	0	3.10	—	—	—	—	—	—	—
NHL Totals (5 years)		109	5874	47	34	16	268	3	2.74	14	709	8	4	34	0	2.88

SOLING, JONAS — RW — CANUCKS

PERSONAL: Born September 7, 1978, in Stockholm, Sweden. ... 6-4/192. ... Shoots left. ... Name pronounced YOH-nuhz SOH-lihng.
TRANSACTIONS/CAREER NOTES: Selected by Vancouver Canucks in fourth round (third Canucks pick, 93rd overall) of NHL entry draft (June 22, 1996).

Season Team	League	REGULAR SEASON								PLAYOFFS				
		Gms.	G	A	Pts.	PIM	+/-	PP	SH	Gms.	G	A	Pts.	PIM
94-95—Huddinge Jrs.	Sweden	1	3	1	4	6	...	...	...	—	—	—	—	—
95-96—Huddinge Jrs.	Sweden	24	8	4	12	18	...	...	...	—	—	—	—	—
—Huddinge	Swed. Dv.II	5	0	0	0	0	...	...	...	—	—	—	—	—
96-97—Sudbury	OHL	66	18	22	40	60	...	...	...	—	—	—	—	—
97-98—Sudbury	OHL	56	9	25	34	67	...	...	...	10	0	7	7	10

SOMIK, RADOVAN   LW   FLYERS

PERSONAL: Born May 5, 1977, in Martin, Czechoslovakia. ... 6-2/194. ... Shoots right.
TRANSACTIONS/CAREER NOTES: Selected by Philadelphia Flyers in fourth round (third Flyers pick, 100th overall) of NHL entry draft (July 8, 1995).

Season Team	League	REGULAR SEASON								PLAYOFFS				
		Gms.	G	A	Pts.	PIM	+/-	PP	SH	Gms.	G	A	Pts.	PIM
93-94—Martimex ZTS Martin..	Slovakia	1	0	0	0	0	...	...	...	—	—	—	—	—
94-95—Martimex ZTS Martin..	Slovakia	28	4	0	4	31	...	...	...	3	1	0	1	2
95-96—Martimex ZTS Martin..	Slovakia	25	3	6	9	8	...	...	...	9	1	0	1	...
96-97—Martimex ZTS Martin..	Slovakia	35	3	5	8	...	...	...	...	3	0	0	0	...
97-98—Martimex ZTS Martin..	Slovakia	26	6	9	15	10	...	...	...	3	0	0	0	0

SOPEL, BRENT   D   CANUCKS

PERSONAL: Born January 7, 1977, in Calgary. ... 6-1/190. ... Shoots right. ... Name pronounced SOH-puhl.
TRANSACTIONS/CAREER NOTES: Selected by Vancouver Canucks in sixth round (sixth Canucks pick, 144th overall) of NHL entry draft (July 8, 1995).

Season Team	League	REGULAR SEASON								PLAYOFFS				
		Gms.	G	A	Pts.	PIM	+/-	PP	SH	Gms.	G	A	Pts.	PIM
93-94—Saskatoon	WHL	11	2	2	4	2	...	...	...	—	—	—	—	—
94-95—Saskatoon	WHL	22	1	10	11	31	...	...	...	—	—	—	—	—
—Swift Current	WHL	41	4	19	23	50	...	...	...	3	0	3	3	0
95-96—Swift Current	WHL	71	13	48	61	87	...	...	...	6	1	2	3	4
—Syracuse	AHL	1	0	0	0	0	...	...	...	—	—	—	—	—
96-97—Swift Current	WHL	62	15	41	56	109	...	...	...	10	5	11	16	32
—Syracuse	AHL	2	0	0	0	0	...	...	...	3	0	0	0	0
97-98—Syracuse	AHL	76	10	33	43	70	...	...	...	5	0	7	7	12

SOURAY, SHELDON   D   DEVILS

PERSONAL: Born July 13, 1976, in Elk Point, Alta. ... 6-4/235. ... Shoots left. ... Name pronounced SOOR-ay.
TRANSACTIONS/CAREER NOTES: Selected by New Jersey Devils in third round (third Devils pick, 71st overall) of NHL entry draft (June 29, 1994). ... Suffered head injury (September 27, 1997); missed five games. ... Bruised right wrist (October 17, 1997); missed four games. ... Suffered from the flu (December 18, 1997); missed one game. ... Suffered from the flu (January 30, 1998); missed one game.
HONORS: Named to WHL (West) All-Star second team (1995-96).

Season Team	League	REGULAR SEASON								PLAYOFFS				
		Gms.	G	A	Pts.	PIM	+/-	PP	SH	Gms.	G	A	Pts.	PIM
92-93—Fort Saskatchewan	AJHL	35	0	12	12	125	...	...	...	—	—	—	—	—
—Tri-City	WHL	2	0	0	0	0	...	...	...	—	—	—	—	—
93-94—Tri-City	WHL	42	3	6	9	122	...	...	...	—	—	—	—	—
94-95—Tri-City	WHL	40	2	24	26	140	...	...	...	—	—	—	—	—
—Prince George	WHL	11	2	3	5	23	...	...	...	—	—	—	—	—
—Albany	AHL	7	0	2	2	8	...	...	...	—	—	—	—	—
95-96—Prince George	WHL	32	9	18	27	91	...	...	...	—	—	—	—	—
—Kelowna	WHL	27	7	20	27	94	...	...	...	6	0	5	5	2
—Albany	AHL	6	0	2	2	12	...	...	...	4	0	1	1	4
96-97—Albany	AHL	70	2	11	13	160	...	...	...	16	2	3	5	47
97-98—New Jersey	NHL	60	3	7	10	85	18	0	0	3	0	1	1	2
—Albany	AHL	6	0	0	0	8	...	...	...	—	—	—	—	—
NHL Totals (1 year)		60	3	7	10	85	18	0	0	3	0	1	1	2

SOUZA, MIKE   LW/C   BLACKHAWKS

PERSONAL: Born January 28, 1978, in Melrose, Mass. ... 6-1/190. ... Shoots left.
HIGH SCHOOL: Wakefield (Mass.).
COLLEGE: New Hampshire.
TRANSACTIONS/CAREER NOTES: Selected by Chicago Blackhawks in third round (fourth Blackhawks pick, 67th overall) of NHL entry draft (June 21, 1997).
HONORS: Named to the Hockey East All-Rookie team (1996-97).

Season Team	League	REGULAR SEASON								PLAYOFFS				
		Gms.	G	A	Pts.	PIM	+/-	PP	SH	Gms.	G	A	Pts.	PIM
95-96—Wakefield HS	Mass. H.S.	21	25	31	56	22	...	...	...	—	—	—	—	—
96-97—New Hampshire	Hockey East	33	14	10	24	14	...	...	...	—	—	—	—	—
97-98—New Hampshire	Hockey East	38	13	12	25	36	...	...	...	—	—	—	—	—

SPRING, COREY   RW   LIGHTNING

PERSONAL: Born May 31, 1971, in Cranbrook, B.C. ... 6-4/214. ... Shoots right.
COLLEGE: Alaska-Fairbanks.
TRANSACTIONS/CAREER NOTES: Signed as free agent by Tampa Bay Lightning (July 25, 1995).

		REGULAR SEASON							PLAYOFFS				
Season Team	League	Gms.	G	A	Pts.	PIM	+/-	PP	SH	Gms.	G	A	Pts.	PIM
91-92—Alaska-Fairbanks........	CCHA	35	3	8	11	30	...	...	...	—	—	—	—	—
92-93—Alaska-Fairbanks........	CCHA	28	5	5	10	20	...	...	...	—	—	—	—	—
93-94—Alaska-Fairbanks........	CCHA	38	19	18	37	34	...	...	...	—	—	—	—	—
94-95—Alaska-Fairbanks........	CCHA	33	18	14	32	56	...	...	...	—	—	—	—	—
95-96—Atlanta	IHL	73	14	14	28	104	...	...	...	—	—	—	—	—
96-97—Adirondack	AHL	69	20	26	46	118	...	...	...	4	0	0	0	14
97-98—Adirondack	AHL	57	19	25	44	120	...	...	...	3	0	0	0	6
—Tampa Bay	NHL	8	1	0	1	10	-1	0	0	—	—	—	—	—
NHL Totals (1 year)............		8	1	0	1	10	-1	0	0					

SRDINKO, JAN   D   DEVILS

PERSONAL: Born February 22, 1974, in Vsetin, Czechoslovakia. ... 5-11/195. ... Shoots left.
TRANSACTIONS/CAREER NOTES: Selected by New Jersey Devils in ninth round (eighth Devils pick, 241st overall) of NHL entry draft (June 21, 1997).

		REGULAR SEASON							PLAYOFFS				
Season Team	League	Gms.	G	A	Pts.	PIM	+/-	PP	SH	Gms.	G	A	Pts.	PIM
94-95—Vsetin	Czech Rep.	1	0	0	0	...	...	...	...	—	—	—	—	—
95-96—Vsetin	Czech Rep.	31	0	3	3	...	...	...	...	9	0	0	0	0
96-97—Vsetin	Czech Rep.	49	2	8	10	71	...	...	...	10	0	3	3	29
97-98—Petra Vsetin	Czech Rep.	47	1	4	5	95	...	...	...	10	0	3	3	4

ST. CROIX, CHRIS   D   FLAMES

PERSONAL: Born May 2, 1979, in Voorhees, N.J. ... 6-1/186. ... Shoots right.
TRANSACTIONS/CAREER NOTES: Selected by Calgary Flames in fourth round (seventh Flames pick, 92nd overall) of NHL entry draft (June 21, 1997).

		REGULAR SEASON							PLAYOFFS				
Season Team	League	Gms.	G	A	Pts.	PIM	+/-	PP	SH	Gms.	G	A	Pts.	PIM
95-96—Kamloops	WHL	61	4	6	10	27	...	...	...	13	0	2	2	4
96-97—Kamloops	WHL	67	11	39	50	67	...	...	...	5	0	1	1	2
97-98—Kamloops	WHL	46	3	13	16	51	...	...	...	7	1	1	2	6

STAIOS, STEVE   D   CANUCKS

PERSONAL: Born July 28, 1973, in Hamilton, Ont. ... 6-0/185. ... Shoots right. ... Name pronounced STAY-ohz.
TRANSACTIONS/CAREER NOTES: Selected by St. Louis Blues in second round (first Blues pick, 27th overall) of NHL entry draft (June 22, 1991). ... Traded by Blues with LW Kevin Sawyer to Boston Bruins for RW Steve Leach (March 8, 1996). ... Strained groin (November 6, 1996); missed 13 games. ... Claimed on waivers by Vancouver Canucks (March 18, 1997).

		REGULAR SEASON							PLAYOFFS				
Season Team	League	Gms.	G	A	Pts.	PIM	+/-	PP	SH	Gms.	G	A	Pts.	PIM
89-90—Hamilton Jr. B...........	OHA	40	9	27	36	66	...	...	...	—	—	—	—	—
90-91—Niagara Falls	OHL	66	17	29	46	115	...	...	...	12	2	3	5	10
91-92—Niagara Falls	OHL	65	11	42	53	122	...	...	...	17	7	8	15	27
92-93—Niagara Falls	OHL	12	4	14	18	30	...	...	...	—	—	—	—	—
—Sudbury......................	OHL	53	13	44	57	67	...	...	...	11	5	6	11	22
93-94—Peoria	IHL	38	3	9	12	42	...	...	...	—	—	—	—	—
94-95—Peoria	IHL	60	3	13	16	64	...	...	...	6	0	0	0	10
95-96—Peoria	IHL	6	0	1	1	14	...	...	...	—	—	—	—	—
—Worcester..................	AHL	57	1	11	12	114	...	...	...	—	—	—	—	—
—Providence................	AHL	7	1	4	5	8	...	...	...	—	—	—	—	—
—Boston.......................	NHL	12	0	0	0	4	-5	0	0	3	0	0	0	0
96-97—Boston......................	NHL	54	3	8	11	71	-26	0	0	—	—	—	—	—
—Vancouver..................	NHL	9	0	6	6	20	2	0	0	—	—	—	—	—
97-98—Vancouver.................	NHL	77	3	4	7	134	-3	0	0	—	—	—	—	—
NHL Totals (3 years)...........		152	6	18	24	229	-32	0	0	3	0	0	0	0

STANLEY, CHRIS   C   CANUCKS

PERSONAL: Born June 18, 1979, in Parry Sound, Ont. ... 6-1/200. ... Shoots left.
TRANSACTIONS/CAREER NOTES: Selected by Vancouver Canucks in fourth round (fifth Canucks pick, 90th overall) of NHL entry draft (June 21, 1997).

		REGULAR SEASON							PLAYOFFS				
Season Team	League	Gms.	G	A	Pts.	PIM	+/-	PP	SH	Gms.	G	A	Pts.	PIM
95-96—Wellington	OJHL	52	27	29	56	30	...	...	...	—	—	—	—	—
96-97—Belleville	OHL	66	19	24	43	16	...	...	...	6	1	0	1	0
97-98—Belleville	OHL	66	21	23	44	31	...	...	...	10	3	2	5	4

PERSONAL: Born May 5, 1966, in Sarnia, Ont. ... 5-10/182. ... Shoots right. ... Son of Pat Stapleton, defenseman with Boston Bruins and Chicago Blackhawks (1961-62 through 1972-73) and Chicago Cougars, Indianapolis Racers and Cincinnati Stingers of WHA (1973-74 through 1977-78).

TRANSACTIONS/CAREER NOTES: Selected by Chicago Blackhawks in seventh round (seventh Blackhawks pick, 132nd overall) of NHL entry draft (June 9, 1984). ... Signed as free agent by Pittsburgh Penguins (September 4, 1992). ... Claimed on waivers by Edmonton Oilers (February 19, 1994). ... Signed as free agent by Winnipeg Jets (August 9, 1995). ... Suffered charley horse (October 12, 1995); missed one game. ... Broke jaw (November 1, 1995); missed 16 games. ... Strained groin (March 27, 1996); missed five games. ... Jets franchise moved to Phoenix and renamed Coyotes for 1996-97 season; NHL approved move on January 18, 1996. ... Suffered eye abrasion (January 30, 1998); missed four games. ... Fractured foot (March 28, 1998); missed five games.

		REGULAR SEASON								PLAYOFFS				
Season Team	League	Gms.	G	A	Pts.	PIM	+/-	PP	SH	Gms.	G	A	Pts.	PIM
82-83—Strathroy Jr. B	OHA	40	39	38	77	99	...	...	...	—	—	—	—	—
83-84—Cornwall	OHL	70	24	45	69	94	...	...	...	3	1	2	3	4
84-85—Cornwall	OHL	56	41	44	85	68	...	...	...	9	2	4	6	23
85-86—Cornwall	OHL	56	39	65	104	74	...	...	...	6	2	3	5	2
86-87—Canadian nat'l team	Int'l	21	2	4	6	4	...	...	...	—	—	—	—	—
—Chicago	NHL	39	3	6	9	6	-9	0	0	4	0	0	0	2
87-88—Saginaw	IHL	31	11	19	30	52	...	...	...	10	5	6	11	10
—Chicago	NHL	53	2	9	11	59	-10	0	0	—	—	—	—	—
88-89—Chicago	NHL	7	0	1	1	7	-1	0	0	—	—	—	—	—
—Saginaw	IHL	69	21	47	68	162	...	...	...	6	1	3	4	4
89-90—Arvika	Sweden	30	15	18	33	...	...	...	...	—	—	—	—	—
—Indianapolis	IHL	16	5	10	15	6	...	...	...	13	9	10	19	38
90-91—Chicago	NHL	7	0	1	1	2	0	0	0	—	—	—	—	—
—Indianapolis	IHL	75	29	52	81	76	...	...	...	7	1	4	5	0
91-92—Indianapolis	IHL	59	18	40	58	65	...	...	...	—	—	—	—	—
—Chicago	NHL	19	4	4	8	8	0	1	0	—	—	—	—	—
92-93—Pittsburgh	NHL	78	4	9	13	10	-8	0	1	4	0	0	0	0
93-94—Pittsburgh	NHL	58	7	4	11	18	-4	3	0	—	—	—	—	—
—Edmonton	NHL	23	5	9	14	28	-1	1	0	—	—	—	—	—
94-95—Edmonton	NHL	46	6	11	17	21	-12	3	0	—	—	—	—	—
95-96—Winnipeg	NHL	58	10	14	24	37	-4	3	1	6	0	0	0	21
96-97—Phoenix	NHL	55	4	11	15	36	-4	2	0	7	0	0	0	14
97-98—Phoenix	NHL	64	5	5	10	36	-4	1	1	6	0	0	0	2
NHL Totals (11 years)		507	50	84	134	268	-57	14	3	27	0	0	0	39

PERSONAL: Born November 25, 1967, in Duluth, Minn. ... 5-11/175. ... Catches left. ... Brother of Pete Stauber, left winger with Detroit Red Wings and Florida Panthers organizations (1990-91 through 1992-93). ... Name pronounced STAH-buhr.

HIGH SCHOOL: Denfeld (Duluth, Minn.).

COLLEGE: Minnesota.

TRANSACTIONS/CAREER NOTES: Selected by Los Angeles Kings in sixth round (fifth Kings pick, 107th overall) of NHL entry draft (June 21, 1986). ... Twisted left knee and ankle (December 3, 1988); missed 14 games. ... Injured groin and back (October 1989). ... Underwent knee surgery (March 1991). ... Strained shoulder (November 6, 1993); missed four games. ... Broke tip of right ring-finger (January 22, 1995); missed nine games. ... Traded by Kings with D Alexei Zhitnik, D Charlie Huddy and fifth-round pick (D Marian Menhart) in 1995 draft to Buffalo Sabres for G Grant Fuhr, D Philippe Boucher and D Denis Tsygurov (February 14, 1995). ... Sprained knee (April 24, 1995); missed two games. ... Signed as free agent by Washington Capitals (August 20, 1996). ... Signed as free agent by New York Rangers (September 3, 1997).

HONORS: Won Hobey Baker Memorial Award (1987-88). ... Won WCHA Most Valuable Player Award (1987-88). ... Won WCHA Goaltender of the Year Award (1987-88 and 1988-89). ... Named to NCAA All-America West first team (1987-88). ... Named to WCHA All-Star first team (1987-88). ... Named to WCHA All-Star second team (1988-89).

MISCELLANEOUS: Stopped penalty shot attempt (vs. Craig Janney, March 20, 1993; vs. Alexander Mogilny, December 17, 1993). ... Allowed penalty shot goal (vs. Paul Ysebaert, November 27, 1992; vs. Mikael Andersson, December 15, 1992).

		REGULAR SEASON							PLAYOFFS						
Season Team	League	Gms.	Min	W	L	T	GA	SO	Avg.	Gms.	Min.	W	L	GA	SO	Avg.
84-85—Duluth Denfeld H.S.	Minn. H.S.	22	990	...	...	...	37	0	2.24	—	—	—	—	—	—	—
85-86—Duluth Denfeld H.S.	Minn. H.S.	27	1215	...	...	...	66	0	3.26	—	—	—	—	—	—	—
86-87—Univ. of Minnesota	WCHA	20	1072	13	5	0	63	0	3.53	—	—	—	—	—	—	—
87-88—Univ. of Minnesota	WCHA	44	2621	34	10	0	119	5	2.72	—	—	—	—	—	—	—
88-89—Univ. of Minnesota	WCHA	34	2024	26	8	0	82	0	2.43	—	—	—	—	—	—	—
89-90—New Haven	AHL	14	851	6	6	2	43	0	3.03	5	302	2	3	24	0	4.77
—Los Angeles	NHL	2	83	0	1	0	11	0	7.95	—	—	—	—	—	—	—
90-91—Phoenix	IHL	4	160	1	2	‡0	11	0	4.13	—	—	—	—	—	—	—
—New Haven	AHL	33	1882	13	16	4	115	1	3.67	—	—	—	—	—	—	—
91-92—Phoenix	IHL	22	1242	8	12	‡1	80	0	3.86	—	—	—	—	—	—	—
92-93—Los Angeles	NHL	31	1735	15	8	4	111	0	3.84	4	240	3	1	16	0	4.00
93-94—Phoenix	IHL	3	121	1	1	‡0	13	0	6.45	—	—	—	—	—	—	—
—Los Angeles	NHL	22	1144	4	11	5	65	1	3.41	—	—	—	—	—	—	—
94-95—Los Angeles	NHL	1	16	0	0	0	2	0	7.50	—	—	—	—	—	—	—
—Buffalo	NHL	6	317	2	3	0	20	0	3.79	—	—	—	—	—	—	—
95-96—Rochester	AHL	16	832	6	7	1	49	0	3.53	—	—	—	—	—	—	—
96-97—Portland	AHL	30	1606	13	13	2	82	0	3.06	—	—	—	—	—	—	—
97-98—Hartford	AHL	39	2221	20	10	6	89	2	2.40	7	420	3	4	30	0	4.29
NHL Totals (4 years)		62	3295	21	23	9	209	1	3.81	4	240	3	1	16	0	4.00

PERSONAL: Born January 11, 1967, in Ste. Agatha Des Mont, Que. ... 6-0/201. ... Shoots right. ... Full name: Ronald Stern.

TRANSACTIONS/CAREER NOTES: Selected by Vancouver Canucks as underage junior in fourth round (third Canucks pick, 70th overall) of NHL entry draft (June 21, 1986). ... Bruised shoulder (April 1989). ... Suffered laceration near eye and dislocated shoulder (March 19, 1990). ... Fractured wrist (October 30, 1990); missed 10 weeks. ... Traded by Canucks with D Kevan Guy and option to switch fourth-round picks in 1992 draft to Calgary Flames for D Dana Murzyn; Flames did not exercise option (March 5, 1991). ... Suffered back spasms (October 15, 1992); missed 11 games. ... Broke bone in right foot (October 11, 1993); missed three games. ... Bruised shoulder (December 7, 1993); missed one game. ... Bruised shoulder (December 28, 1993); missed six games. ... Sprained left ankle (February 6, 1995); missed four games. ... Strained thigh (April 25, 1995); missed three games. ... Suspended two games by NHL for accumulating four game misconduct penalties (March 22, 1995). ... Suspended four games by NHL for slashing (December 19, 1995). ... Suffered back spasms (December 27, 1995); missed five games. ... Suspended four games and fined $1,000 by NHL for slashing (December 19, 1995). ... Injured neck and shoulder (January 14, 1996); missed 21 games. ... Sore lower back (October 19, 1996); missed three games. ... Injured knee (September 14, 1997) and underwent surgery (October 7, 1997); missed entire 1997-98 season.

STATISTICAL PLATEAUS: Three-goal games: 1991-92 (1), 1992-93 (1), 1994-95 (1). Total: 3.

		REGULAR SEASON								PLAYOFFS				
Season Team	League	Gms.	G	A	Pts.	PIM	+/-	PP	SH	Gms.	G	A	Pts.	PIM
84-85—Longueuil	QMJHL	67	6	14	20	176	...	...	...	—	—	—	—	—
85-86—Longueuil	QMJHL	70	39	33	72	317	...	...	...	—	—	—	—	—
86-87—Longueuil	QMJHL	56	32	39	71	266	...	...	...	19	11	9	20	55
87-88—Fredericton	AHL	2	1	0	1	4	...	...	...	—	—	—	—	—
—Flint	IHL	55	14	19	33	294	...	...	...	16	8	8	16	94
—Vancouver	NHL	15	0	0	0	52	-7	0	0	—	—	—	—	—
88-89—Milwaukee	IHL	45	19	23	42	280	...	...	...	5	1	0	1	11
—Vancouver	NHL	17	1	0	1	49	-6	0	0	3	0	1	1	17
89-90—Milwaukee	IHL	26	8	9	17	165	...	...	...	—	—	—	—	—
—Vancouver	NHL	34	2	3	5	208	-17	0	0	—	—	—	—	—
90-91—Milwaukee	IHL	7	2	2	4	81	...	...	...	—	—	—	—	—
—Vancouver	NHL	31	2	3	5	171	-14	0	0	—	—	—	—	—
—Calgary	NHL	13	1	3	4	69	0	0	0	7	1	3	4	14
91-92—Calgary	NHL	72	13	9	22	338	0	0	1	—	—	—	—	—
92-93—Calgary	NHL	70	10	15	25	207	4	0	0	6	0	0	0	43
93-94—Calgary	NHL	71	9	20	29	243	6	0	1	7	2	0	2	12
94-95—Calgary	NHL	39	9	4	13	163	4	1	0	7	3	1	4	8
95-96—Calgary	NHL	52	10	5	15	111	2	0	0	4	0	2	2	8
96-97—Calgary	NHL	79	7	10	17	157	-4	0	1	—	—	—	—	—
97-98—Calgary	NHL	Did not play.												
NHL Totals (10 years)		493	64	72	136	1768	-32	1	3	34	6	7	13	102

PERSONAL: Born April 15, 1965, in Brockton, Mass. ... 6-3/230. ... Shoots left. ... Full name: Kevin Michael Stevens.

HIGH SCHOOL: Silver Lake (Mass.).

COLLEGE: Boston College.

TRANSACTIONS/CAREER NOTES: Selected by Los Angeles Kings in sixth round (sixth Kings pick, 108th overall) of NHL entry draft (June 8, 1983). ... Traded by Kings to Pittsburgh Penguins for LW Anders Hakansson (September 9, 1983). ... Damaged cartilage in left knee (November 5, 1992) and underwent arthroscopic surgery (November 6, 1992); missed nine games. ... Suspended one game by NHL (March 1993). ... Suffered from bronchitis (April 3, 1993); missed two games. ... Fractured left ankle (February 4, 1995); missed 21 games. ... Traded by Penguins with C Shawn McEachern to Boston Bruins for C Bryan Smolinski and RW Glen Murray (August 2, 1995). ... Traded by Bruins to Los Angeles Kings for RW Rick Tocchet (January 25, 1996). ... Fractured left fibula (February 29, 1996); missed 10 games. ... Suffered concussion (October 15, 1996); missed one game. ... Suffered back spasms (November 27, 1996); missed one game. ... Bruised ankle (February 20, 1997); missed seven games. ... Injured knee (April 9, 1997); missed two games. ... Traded by Kings to New York Rangers for LW Luc Robitaille (August 28, 1997). ... Strained groin (October 8, 1997); missed one game. ... Suffered from the flu (March 21, 1998); missed one game.

HONORS: Named to NCAA All-America East second team (1986-87). ... Named to Hockey East All-Star first team (1986-87). ... Named to THE SPORTING NEWS All-Star second team (1990-91 and 1992-93). ... Named to NHL All-Star second team (1990-91 and 1992-93). ... Named to THE SPORTING NEWS All-Star first team (1991-92). ... Named to NHL All-Star first team (1991-92). ... Played in NHL All-Star Game (1991-1993).

MISCELLANEOUS: Member of Stanley Cup championship team (1991 and 1992). ... Failed to score on a penalty shot (vs. Nikolai Khabibulin, February 26, 1996; vs. Sean Burke, March 22, 1998).

STATISTICAL PLATEAUS: Three-goal games: 1989-90 (1), 1990-91 (1), 1991-92 (3), 1992-93 (2), 1993-94 (1). Total: 8. ... Four-goal games: 1991-92 (1), 1992-93 (1). Total: 2. ... Total hat tricks: 10.

		REGULAR SEASON								PLAYOFFS				
Season Team	League	Gms.	G	A	Pts.	PIM	+/-	PP	SH	Gms.	G	A	Pts.	PIM
82-83—Silver Lake H.S.	Minn. H.S.	18	24	27	51	...	...	...	...	—	—	—	—	—
83-84—Boston College	ECAC	37	6	14	20	36	...	...	...	—	—	—	—	—
84-85—Boston College	Hockey East	40	13	23	36	36	...	...	...	—	—	—	—	—
85-86—Boston College	Hockey East	42	17	27	44	56	...	...	...	—	—	—	—	—
86-87—Boston College	Hockey East	39	*35	35	70	54	...	...	...	—	—	—	—	—
87-88—U.S. national team	Int'l	44	22	23	45	52	...	...	...	—	—	—	—	—
—U.S. Olympic Team	Int'l	5	1	3	4	2	...	...	...	—	—	—	—	—
—Pittsburgh	NHL	16	5	2	7	8	-6	2	0	—	—	—	—	—
88-89—Pittsburgh	NHL	24	12	3	15	19	-8	4	0	11	3	7	10	16
—Muskegon	IHL	45	24	41	65	113	...	...	...	—	—	—	—	—
89-90—Pittsburgh	NHL	76	29	41	70	171	-13	12	0	—	—	—	—	—
90-91—Pittsburgh	NHL	80	40	46	86	133	-1	18	0	24	*17	16	33	53
91-92—Pittsburgh	NHL	80	54	69	123	254	8	19	0	21	13	15	28	28
92-93—Pittsburgh	NHL	72	55	56	111	177	17	26	0	12	5	11	16	22
93-94—Pittsburgh	NHL	83	41	47	88	155	-24	21	0	6	1	1	2	10
94-95—Pittsburgh	NHL	27	15	12	27	51	0	6	0	12	4	7	11	21

S

Season Team	League	REGULAR SEASON								PLAYOFFS				
		Gms.	G	A	Pts.	PIM	+/-	PP	SH	Gms.	G	A	Pts.	PIM
95-96—Boston	NHL	41	10	13	23	49	1	3	0	—	—	—	—	—
—Los Angeles	NHL	20	3	10	13	22	-11	3	0	—	—	—	—	—
96-97—Los Angeles	NHL	69	14	20	34	96	-27	4	0	—	—	—	—	—
97-98—New York Rangers	NHL	80	14	27	41	130	-7	5	0	—	—	—	—	—
NHL Totals (11 years)		668	292	346	638	1265	-71	123	0	86	43	57	100	150

STEVENS, SCOTT — D — DEVILS

PERSONAL: Born April 1, 1964, in Kitchener, Ont. ... 6-1/215. ... Shoots left. ... Brother of Mike Stevens, center/left winger for four NHL teams (1984-85 and 1987-88 through 1989-90).

TRANSACTIONS/CAREER NOTES: Selected by Washington Capitals as underage junior in first round (first Capitals pick, fifth overall) of NHL entry draft (June 9, 1982). ... Bruised right knee (November 6, 1985); missed seven games. ... Broke right index finger (December 14, 1986). ... Bruised shoulder (April 1988). ... Suffered from poison oak (November 1988). ... Lacerated face during World Cup (April 21, 1989). ... Broke left foot (December 29, 1989); missed 17 games. ... Suspended three games by NHL for scratching (February 27, 1990). ... Bruised left shoulder (March 27, 1990). ... Dislocated left shoulder (May 3, 1990). ... Signed as free agent by St. Louis Blues (July 9, 1990); Blues owed Capitals two first-round draft picks among the top seven over next two years and $100,000 cash; upon failing to get a pick in the top seven in 1991, Blues forfeited their first-round pick in 1991 (LW Trevor Halverson), 1992 (D Sergei Gonchar), 1993 (D Brendan Witt), 1994 (traded to Toronto Maple Leafs) and 1995 (LW Miikka Elomo) drafts to Capitals (July 9, 1990). ... Awarded to New Jersey Devils as compensation for Blues signing free agent RW/LW Brendan Shanahan (September 3, 1991). ... Strained right knee (February 20, 1992); missed 12 games. ... Suffered concussion (December 27, 1992); missed three games. ... Strained knee (November 19, 1993); missed one game. ... Suspended one game by NHL for highsticking incident (October 7, 1996). ... Suffered from the flu (December 23, 1996); missed one game. ... Suffered hip pointer (February 28, 1998); missed one game.

HONORS: Named to NHL All-Rookie team (1982-83). ... Named to THE SPORTING NEWS All-Star second team (1987-88). ... Named to NHL All-Star first team (1987-88 and 1993-94). ... Named to NHL All-Star second team (1991-92 and 1996-97). ... Played in NHL All-Star Game (1985, 1989, 1991-1994 and 1996-1998). ... Named to THE SPORTING NEWS All-Star first team (1993-94).

MISCELLANEOUS: Member of Stanley Cup championship team (1995). ... Captain of St. Louis Blues (1990-91). ... Captain of New Jersey Devils (1992-93, 1995-96 through 1997-98). ... Holds Washington Capitals all-time record for most penalty minutes (1,630).

Season Team	League	REGULAR SEASON								PLAYOFFS				
		Gms.	G	A	Pts.	PIM	+/-	PP	SH	Gms.	G	A	Pts.	PIM
80-81—Kitchener Jr. B	OHA	39	7	33	40	82	...	...	...	—	—	—	—	—
—Kitchener	OHL	1	0	0	0	0	...	...	...	—	—	—	—	—
81-82—Kitchener	OHL	68	6	36	42	158	...	...	...	15	1	10	11	71
82-83—Washington	NHL	77	9	16	25	195	15	0	0	4	1	0	1	26
83-84—Washington	NHL	78	13	32	45	201	26	7	0	8	1	8	9	21
84-85—Washington	NHL	80	21	44	65	221	19	16	0	5	0	1	1	20
85-86—Washington	NHL	73	15	38	53	165	0	3	0	9	3	8	11	12
86-87—Washington	NHL	77	10	51	61	283	13	2	0	7	0	5	5	19
87-88—Washington	NHL	80	12	60	72	184	14	5	1	13	1	11	12	46
88-89—Washington	NHL	80	7	61	68	225	1	6	0	6	1	4	5	11
89-90—Washington	NHL	56	11	29	40	154	1	7	0	15	2	7	9	25
90-91—St. Louis	NHL	78	5	44	49	150	23	1	0	13	0	3	3	36
91-92—New Jersey	NHL	68	17	42	59	124	24	7	1	7	2	1	3	29
92-93—New Jersey	NHL	81	12	45	57	120	14	8	0	5	2	2	4	10
93-94—New Jersey	NHL	83	18	60	78	112	*53	5	1	20	2	9	11	42
94-95—New Jersey	NHL	48	2	20	22	56	4	1	0	20	1	7	8	24
95-96—New Jersey	NHL	82	5	23	28	100	7	2	1	—	—	—	—	—
96-97—New Jersey	NHL	79	5	19	24	70	26	0	0	10	0	4	4	2
97-98—New Jersey	NHL	80	4	22	26	80	19	1	0	6	1	0	1	8
—Can. Olympic Team	Int'l	6	0	0	0	2	...	...	...	—	—	—	—	—
NHL Totals (16 years)		1200	166	606	772	2440	259	71	4	148	17	70	87	331

STEVENSON, JEREMY — LW — MIGHTY DUCKS

PERSONAL: Born July 28, 1974, in San Bernardino, Calif. ... 6-2/220. ... Shoots left. ... Full name: Jeremy Joseph Stevenson.
HIGH SCHOOL: St. Lawrence (Cornwall, Ont.).
TRANSACTIONS/CAREER NOTES: Selected by Winnipeg Jets in third round (third Jets pick, 60th overall) of NHL entry draft (June 20, 1992). ... Returned to draft pool by Jets and selected by Mighty Ducks of Anaheim in 11th round (10th Mighty Ducks pick, 262nd overall) of NHL entry draft (June 28, 1994). ... Fractured ankle (October 24, 1996); missed 33 games. ... Suffered concussion prior to 1997-98 season; missed first four games of season.

Season Team	League	REGULAR SEASON								PLAYOFFS				
		Gms.	G	A	Pts.	PIM	+/-	PP	SH	Gms.	G	A	Pts.	PIM
90-91—Cornwall	OHL	58	13	20	33	124	...	...	...	—	—	—	—	—
91-92—Cornwall	OHL	63	15	23	38	176	...	...	...	6	3	1	4	4
92-93—Newmarket	OHL	54	28	28	56	144	...	...	...	5	5	1	6	28
93-94—Newmarket	OHL	9	2	4	6	27	...	...	...	—	—	—	—	—
—Sault Ste. Marie	OHL	48	18	19	37	183	...	...	...	14	1	1	2	23
94-95—Greensboro	ECHL	43	14	13	27	231	...	...	...	17	6	11	17	64
95-96—Baltimore	AHL	60	11	10	21	295	...	...	...	12	4	2	6	23
—Anaheim	NHL	3	0	1	1	12	1	0	0	—	—	—	—	—
96-97—Baltimore	AHL	25	8	8	16	125	...	...	...	3	0	0	0	8
—Anaheim	NHL	5	0	0	0	14	-1	0	0	—	—	—	—	—
97-98—Anaheim	NHL	45	3	5	8	101	-4	0	0	—	—	—	—	—
—Cincinnati	AHL	10	5	0	5	34	...	...	...	—	—	—	—	—
NHL Totals (3 years)		53	3	6	9	127	-4	0	0					

STEVENSON, TURNER RW CANADIENS

PERSONAL: Born May 18, 1972, in Port Alberni, B.C. ... 6-3/220. ... Shoots right.
TRANSACTIONS/CAREER NOTES: Underwent surgery to remove growth in chest (August 1987). ... Injured shoulder (December 1987). ... Selected by Montreal Canadiens in first round (first Canadiens pick, 12th overall) of NHL entry draft (June 16, 1990). ... Suffered from the flu (October 21, 1995); missed two games. ... Sprained knee (October 7, 1996); missed five games. ... Sprained knee (October 26, 1996); missed four games. ... Sprained knee (November 11, 1996); missed seven games. ... Sprained shoulder (November 12, 1997); missed eight games. ... Tore cartilage in ribs (December 19, 1997); missed five games. ... Strained hamstring (April 15, 1998); missed three games.
HONORS: Named to Can.HL All-Star second team (1991-92). ... Named to Memorial Cup All-Star team (1991-92). ... Named to WHL (West) All-Star first team (1991-92).

		REGULAR SEASON							PLAYOFFS				
Season Team	League	Gms.	G	A	Pts.	PIM	+/-	PP	SH	Gms.	G	A	Pts.	PIM
88-89—Seattle	WHL	69	15	12	27	84	...	...	...	—	—	—	—	—
89-90—Seattle	WHL	62	29	32	61	276	...	...	...	13	3	2	5	35
90-91—Seattle	WHL	57	36	27	63	222	...	...	...	6	1	5	6	15
—Fredericton	AHL	—	—	—	—	—	...	...	...	4	0	0	0	5
91-92—Seattle	WHL	58	20	32	52	264	...	...	...	15	9	3	12	55
92-93—Fredericton	AHL	79	25	34	59	102	...	...	...	5	2	3	5	11
—Montreal	NHL	1	0	0	0	0	-1	0	0	—	—	—	—	—
93-94—Fredericton	AHL	66	19	28	47	155	...	...	...	—	—	—	—	—
—Montreal	NHL	2	0	0	0	2	-2	0	0	3	0	2	2	0
94-95—Fredericton	AHL	37	12	12	24	109	...	...	...	—	—	—	—	—
—Montreal	NHL	41	6	1	7	86	0	0	0	—	—	—	—	—
95-96—Montreal	NHL	80	9	16	25	167	-2	0	0	6	0	1	1	2
96-97—Montreal	NHL	65	8	13	21	97	-14	1	0	5	1	1	2	2
97-98—Montreal	NHL	63	4	6	10	110	-8	1	0	10	3	4	7	12
NHL Totals (6 years)		252	27	36	63	462	-27	2	0	24	4	8	12	16

STILLMAN, CORY C FLAMES

PERSONAL: Born December 20, 1973, in Peterborough, Ont. ... 6-0/190. ... Shoots left.
HIGH SCHOOL: Herman E. Fawcett (Brantford, Ont.).
TRANSACTIONS/CAREER NOTES: Selected by Calgary Flames in first round (first Flames pick, sixth overall) of NHL entry draft (June 20, 1992). ... Suspended four games by AHL for incident involving on-ice official (March 29, 1995). ... Suffered from the flu (October 8, 1995); missed one game. ... Bruised knee (January 14, 1996); missed two games. ... Injured shoulder (December 16, 1996); missed five games. ... Bruised ribs (October 11, 1997); missed six games.
HONORS: Won Emms Family Award (1990-91).
STATISTICAL PLATEAUS: Three-goal games: 1997-98 (1).

		REGULAR SEASON							PLAYOFFS				
Season Team	League	Gms.	G	A	Pts.	PIM	+/-	PP	SH	Gms.	G	A	Pts.	PIM
89-90—Peterborough Jr. B	OHA	41	30	54	84	76	...	...	...	—	—	—	—	—
90-91—Windsor	OHL	64	31	70	101	31	...	...	...	11	3	6	9	8
91-92—Windsor	OHL	53	29	61	90	59	...	...	...	7	2	4	6	8
92-93—Peterborough	OHL	61	25	55	80	55	...	...	...	18	3	8	11	18
—Canadian nat'l team	Int'l	1	0	0	0	0	...	...	...	—	—	—	—	—
93-94—Saint John	AHL	79	35	48	83	52	...	...	...	7	2	4	6	16
94-95—Saint John	AHL	63	28	53	81	70	...	...	...	5	0	2	2	2
—Calgary	NHL	10	0	2	2	2	1	0	0	—	—	—	—	—
95-96—Calgary	NHL	74	16	19	35	41	-5	4	1	2	1	1	2	0
96-97—Calgary	NHL	58	6	20	26	14	-6	2	0	—	—	—	—	—
97-98—Calgary	NHL	72	27	22	49	40	-9	9	4	—	—	—	—	—
NHL Totals (4 years)		214	49	63	112	97	-19	15	5	2	1	1	2	0

STOCK, P.J. C RANGERS

PERSONAL: Born May 26, 1975, in Victoriaville, Quebec. ... 5-10/190. ... Shoots left.
TRANSACTIONS/CAREER NOTES: Signed as free agent by New York Rangers (September 2, 1997).

		REGULAR SEASON							PLAYOFFS				
Season Team	League	Gms.	G	A	Pts.	PIM	+/-	PP	SH	Gms.	G	A	Pts.	PIM
94-95—Victoriaville	QMJHL	70	9	46	55	386	...	...	...	4	0	0	0	60
95-96—Victoriaville	QMJHL	67	19	43	62	432	...	...	...	12	5	4	9	79
96-97—St. Francis Xavier	CIAU	27	11	20	31	110	...	...	...	3	0	4	4	14
97-98—Hartford	AHL	41	8	8	16	202	...	...	...	11	1	3	4	79
—New York Rangers	NHL	38	2	3	5	114	4	0	0	—	—	—	—	—
NHL Totals (1 year)		38	2	3	5	114	4	0	0					

STOJANOV, ALEK LW

PERSONAL: Born April 25, 1973, in Windsor, Ont. ... 6-4/225. ... Shoots left. ... Full name: Aleksander Stojanov. ... Name pronounced STOY-ih-nahf.
TRANSACTIONS/CAREER NOTES: Dislocated shoulder (July 1989). ... Selected by Vancouver Canucks in first round (first Canucks pick, seventh overall) of NHL entry draft (June 22, 1991). ... Strained neck (December 8, 1995); missed two games. ... Traded by Canucks to Pittsburgh Penguins for RW Markus Naslund (March 20, 1996). ... Suffered concussion (April 11, 1996); missed one game. ... Cracked rib prior to 1996-97 season; missed first two games of season. ... Suffered from the flu (November 12, 1996); missed three games. ... Suffered head and shoulder injuries in an auto accident (December 28, 1996); missed 21 games. ... Strained groin (March 5, 1997); missed 18 games. ... Injured pelvis (October 1, 1997); missed 10 games.

Season Team	League	REGULAR SEASON								PLAYOFFS				
		Gms.	G	A	Pts.	PIM	+/-	PP	SH	Gms.	G	A	Pts.	PIM
89-90—Dukes of Hamilton	OHL	37	4	4	8	91	...	...	...	—	—	—	—	—
90-91—Dukes of Hamilton	OHL	62	25	20	45	179	...	...	...	4	1	1	2	14
91-92—Guelph	OHL	33	12	15	27	91	...	...	...	—	—	—	—	—
92-93—Guelph	OHL	35	27	28	55	11	...	...	...	—	—	—	—	—
—Newmarket	OHL	14	9	7	16	21	...	...	...	7	1	3	4	26
—Hamilton	AHL	4	4	0	4	0	...	...	...	—	—	—	—	—
93-94—Hamilton	AHL	4	0	1	1	5	...	...	...	—	—	—	—	—
94-95—Syracuse	AHL	73	18	12	30	270	...	...	...	—	—	—	—	—
—Vancouver	NHL	4	0	0	0	13	-2	0	0	5	0	0	0	2
95-96—Vancouver	NHL	58	0	1	1	123	-12	0	0	—	—	—	—	—
—Pittsburgh	NHL	10	1	0	1	7	-1	0	0	9	0	0	0	19
96-97—Pittsburgh	NHL	35	1	4	5	79	3	0	0	—	—	—	—	—
97-98—Syracuse	AHL	41	5	4	9	215	...	...	...	3	1	0	1	4
NHL Totals (3 years)		165	2	6	8	345	-12	0	0	14	0	0	0	21

STORR, JAMIE   G   KINGS

PERSONAL: Born December 28, 1975, in Brampton, Ont. ... 6-1/197. ... Catches left. ... Name pronounced STOHR.
HIGH SCHOOL: West Hill (Owen Sound, Ont.).
TRANSACTIONS/CAREER NOTES: Selected by Los Angeles Kings in first round (first Kings pick, seventh overall) of NHL entry draft (June 28, 1994). ... Strained right groin (October 1, 1997); missed 12 games.
HONORS: Named to OHL All-Star first team (1993-94). ... Named to NHL All-Rookie team (1997-98).

Season Team	League	REGULAR SEASON							PLAYOFFS					
		Gms.	Min	W	L	T	GA	SO	Avg.	Gms.	Min.	W	L	GA	SO	Avg.
90-91—Brampton	Jr. B	24	1145	...	...	...	91	0	4.77	—						—
91-92—Owen Sound	OHL	34	1733	11	16	1	128	0	4.43	5	299	1	4	28	0	5.62
92-93—Owen Sound	OHL	41	2362	20	17	3	180	0	4.57	8	454	4	4	35	0	4.63
93-94—Owen Sound	OHL	35	2004	21	11	1	120	1	3.59	9	547	4	5	44	0	4.83
94-95—Owen Sound	OHL	17	977	5	9	2	64	0	3.93	—						—
—Los Angeles	NHL	5	263	1	3	1	17	0	3.88	—						—
—Windsor	OHL	4	241	3	1	0	8	1	1.99	10	520	6	3	34	1	3.92
95-96—Los Angeles	NHL	5	262	3	1	0	12	0	2.75	—						—
—Phoenix	IHL	48	2711	22	20	‡4	139	2	3.08	2	118	1	1	4	1	2.03
96-97—Phoenix	IHL	44	2441	16	22	‡4	147	0	3.61	—						—
—Los Angeles	NHL	5	265	2	1	1	11	0	2.49	—						—
97-98—Los Angeles	NHL	17	920	9	5	1	34	2	2.22	3	145	0	2	9	0	3.72
—Long Beach	IHL	11	629	7	2	‡1	31	0	2.96	—						—
NHL Totals (4 years)		32	1710	15	10	3	74	2	2.60	3	145	0	2	9	0	3.72

STRAKA, MARTIN   C   PENGUINS

PERSONAL: Born September 3, 1972, in Plzen, Czechoslovakia. ... 5-10/175. ... Shoots left. ... Name pronounced STRAH-kuh.
TRANSACTIONS/CAREER NOTES: Selected by Pittsburgh Penguins in first round (first Penguins pick, 19th overall) of NHL entry draft (June 20, 1992). ... Played in Europe during 1994-95 NHL lockout. ... Suffered from the flu (February 14, 1995); missed four games. ... Traded by Penguins to Ottawa Senators for D Norm Maciver and C Troy Murray (April 7, 1995). ... Strained knee (April 19, 1995); missed remainder of season. ... Injured hamstring (November 11, 1995); missed one game. ... Traded by Senators with D Bryan Berard to New York Islanders for D Wade Redden and G Damian Rhodes (January 23, 1996). ... Claimed on waivers by Florida Panthers (March 15, 1996). ... Bruised buttocks (April 10, 1996); missed last two games of season. ... Strained groin (January 1, 1997); missed one game. ... Strained groin (January 8, 1997); missed two games. ... Strained groin (January 22, 1997); missed four games. ... Strained groin (March 5, 1997); missed nine games. ... Signed as free agent by Penguins (August 7, 1997). ... Fractured foot (December 29, 1997); missed seven games.
HONORS: Named to Czechoslovakian League All-Star team (1991-92).
MISCELLANEOUS: Failed to score on a penalty shot (vs. Jocelyn Thibault, March 16, 1995; vs. Damian Rhodes, April 3, 1996). ... Mermber of gold-medal-winning Czech Republic Olympic team (1998).
STATISTICAL PLATEAUS: Three-goal games: 1993-94 (1), 1997-98 (1). Total: 2.

Season Team	League	REGULAR SEASON								PLAYOFFS				
		Gms.	G	A	Pts.	PIM	+/-	PP	SH	Gms.	G	A	Pts.	PIM
89-90—Skoda Plzen	Czech.	1	0	3	3		...	...	...	—	—	—	—	—
90-91—Skoda Plzen	Czech.	47	7	24	31	6	...	...	...	—	—	—	—	—
91-92—Skoda Plzen	Czech.	50	27	28	55	20	...	...	...	—	—	—	—	—
92-93—Pittsburgh	NHL	42	3	13	16	29	2	0	0	11	2	1	3	2
—Cleveland	IHL	4	4	3	7	0	...	...	...	—	—	—	—	—
93-94—Pittsburgh	NHL	84	30	34	64	24	24	2	0	6	1	0	1	2
94-95—Interconex Plzen	Czech Rep.	19	10	11	21	18	...	...	...	—	—	—	—	—
—Pittsburgh	NHL	31	4	12	16	16	0	0	0	—	—	—	—	—
—Ottawa	NHL	6	1	1	2	0	-1	0	0	—	—	—	—	—
95-96—Ottawa	NHL	43	9	16	25	29	-14	5	0	—	—	—	—	—
—New York Islanders	NHL	22	2	10	12	6	-6	0	0	—	—	—	—	—
—Florida	NHL	12	2	4	6	6	1	1	0	13	2	2	4	2
96-97—Florida	NHL	55	7	22	29	12	9	2	0	4	0	0	0	0
97-98—Pittsburgh	NHL	75	19	23	42	28	-1	4	3	6	2	0	2	2
—Czech Rep. Olympic	Int'l	6	1	2	3	0	...	...	...	—	—	—	—	—
NHL Totals (6 years)		370	77	135	212	150	14	14	3	40	7	3	10	8

STRUDWICK, JASON   D   CANUCKS

PERSONAL: Born July 17, 1975, in Edmonton. ... 6-3/207. ... Shoots left. ... Name pronounced STRUHD-wihk.
COLLEGE: Cariboo University-College (Kamloops, B.C.).
TRANSACTIONS/CAREER NOTES: Selected by New York Islanders in third round (third Islanders pick, 63rd overall) of NHL entry draft (June 29, 1994). ... Traded by Islanders to Vancouver Canucks for LW Gino Odjick (March 23, 1998).

		REGULAR SEASON								PLAYOFFS				
Season Team	League	Gms.	G	A	Pts.	PIM	+/-	PP	SH	Gms.	G	A	Pts.	PIM
93-94—Kamloops	WHL	61	6	8	14	118	...	...	...	19	0	4	4	24
94-95—Kamloops	WHL	72	3	11	14	183	...	...	...	21	1	1	2	39
95-96—Worcester	AHL	60	2	7	9	119	...	...	...	4	0	1	1	0
—New York Islanders.....	NHL	1	0	0	0	7	0	0	0	—	—	—	—	—
96-97—Kentucky....................	AHL	80	1	9	10	198	...	...	...	4	0	0	0	0
97-98—Kentucky....................	AHL	39	3	1	4	87	...	...	...	—	—	—	—	—
—New York Islanders.....	NHL	17	0	1	1	36	1	0	0	—	—	—	—	—
—Vancouver..................	NHL	11	0	1	1	29	-3	0	0	—	—	—	—	—
NHL Totals (2 years)...........		29	0	2	2	72	-2	0	0					

STUMPEL, JOZEF   C   KINGS

PERSONAL: Born June 20, 1972, in Nitra, Czechoslovakia. ... 6-3/216. ... Shoots right. ... Name pronounced JOH-sehf STUHM-puhl.
TRANSACTIONS/CAREER NOTES: Selected by Boston Bruins in second round (second Bruins pick, 40th overall) of NHL entry draft (June 22, 1991). ... Injured shoulder (December 1992); missed nine games. ... Injured knee (March 17, 1994); missed nine games. ... Played in Europe during 1994-95 NHL lockout. ... Injured knee (April 1995). ... Fractured cheek bone (February 27, 1996); missed three games. ... Suffered back spasms (January 4, 1997); missed one game. ... Suffered back spasms (February 1, 1997); missed three games. ... Traded by Bruins with RW Sandy Moger and fourth-round pick (traded to New Jersey) in 1998 draft to Los Angeles Kings for LW Dimitri Khristich and G Byron Dafoe (August 29, 1997). ... Suffered from the flu (February 7, 1998); missed one game. ... Bruised kidney (March 5, 1998); missed four games.
STATISTICAL PLATEAUS: Three-goal games: 1995-96 (1), 1997-98 (1). Total: 2.

		REGULAR SEASON								PLAYOFFS				
Season Team	League	Gms.	G	A	Pts.	PIM	+/-	PP	SH	Gms.	G	A	Pts.	PIM
89-90—Nitra..........................	Czech.	38	12	11	23	0	...	...	...	—	—	—	—	—
90-91—Nitra..........................	Czech.	49	23	22	45	14	...	...	...	—	—	—	—	—
91-92—Boston	NHL	4	1	0	1	0	1	0	0	—	—	—	—	—
—Koln	Germany	33	19	18	37	35	...	...	...	—	—	—	—	—
92-93—Providence.................	AHL	56	31	61	92	26	...	...	...	6	4	4	8	0
—Boston	NHL	13	1	3	4	4	-3	0	0	—	—	—	—	—
93-94—Boston	NHL	59	8	15	23	14	4	0	0	13	1	7	8	4
—Providence....................	AHL	17	5	12	17	4	...	...	...	—	—	—	—	—
94-95—Koln	Germany	25	16	23	39	18	...	...	...	—	—	—	—	—
—Boston	NHL	44	5	13	18	8	4	1	0	5	0	0	0	0
95-96—Boston	NHL	76	18	36	54	14	-8	5	0	5	1	2	3	0
96-97—Boston	NHL	78	21	55	76	14	-22	6	0	—	—	—	—	—
97-98—Los Angeles...............	NHL	77	21	58	79	53	17	4	0	4	1	2	3	2
NHL Totals (7 years)...........		351	75	180	255	107	-7	16	0	27	3	11	14	6

STURM, MARCO   C   SHARKS

PERSONAL: Born September 8, 1978, in Dingolfing, West Germany. ... 6-0/190. ... Shoots left.
TRANSACTIONS/CAREER NOTES: Selected by San Jose Sharks in first round (second Sharks pick, 21st overall) of NHL entry draft (June 22, 1996). ... Sprained wrist (April 1, 1998); missed six games.

		REGULAR SEASON								PLAYOFFS				
Season Team	League	Gms.	G	A	Pts.	PIM	+/-	PP	SH	Gms.	G	A	Pts.	PIM
95-96—Landshut...................	Germany	47	12	20	32	50	...	...	...	—	—	—	—	—
96-97—Landshut...................	Germany	46	16	27	43	40	...	...	...	7	1	4	5	6
97-98—San Jose....................	NHL	74	10	20	30	40	-2	2	0	2	0	0	0	0
—German Oly. team..........	Int'l	2	0	0	0	0	...	...	...	—	—	—	—	—
NHL Totals (1 year).............		74	10	20	30	40	-2	2	0	2	0	0	0	0

SULC, JAN   C   LIGHTNING

PERSONAL: Born February 17, 1979, in Litvinov, Czechoslovakia. ... 6-2/183. ... Shoots right. ... Name pronounced SOOLTZ.
TRANSACTIONS/CAREER NOTES: Selected by Tampa Bay Lightning in fifth round (fifth Lightning pick, 109th overall) of NHL entry draft (June 21, 1997).

		REGULAR SEASON								PLAYOFFS				
Season Team	League	Gms.	G	A	Pts.	PIM	+/-	PP	SH	Gms.	G	A	Pts.	PIM
95-96—Chemo. Litvinov Jrs....	Czech Rep.	40	13	23	36	...	...	...	...	—	—	—	—	—
96-97—Chemo. Litvinov Jrs....	Czech Rep.	37	14	17	31	...	...	...	...	—	—	—	—	—
97-98—Toronto St. Michael's..	OHL	34	3	10	13	11	...	...	...	—	—	—	—	—
—Kingston	OHL	29	6	8	14	7	...	...	...	12	0	0	0	0

SULLIVAN, JEFFREY   D   SENATORS

PERSONAL: Born September 18, 1978, in St. John's, Nfld. ... 6-1/185. ... Shoots left.
TRANSACTIONS/CAREER NOTES: Selected by Ottawa Senators in sixth round (fifth Senators pick, 146th overall) of NHL entry draft (June 21, 1997).
HONORS: Named to QMJHL All-Rookie team (1996-97).

S

Season Team	League	REGULAR SEASON								PLAYOFFS				
		Gms.	G	A	Pts.	PIM	+/-	PP	SH	Gms.	G	A	Pts.	PIM
96-97—Granby	QMJHL	25	4	8	12	47	...	...	...					
—Halifax	QMJHL	45	4	23	27	220	...	...	...	18	0	5	5	86
97-98—Halifax	QMJHL	69	9	27	36	*377	...	...	...	5	0	1	1	21

SULLIVAN, MIKE   C   COYOTES

PERSONAL: Born February 28, 1968, in Marshfield, Mass. ... 6-2/190. ... Shoots left. ... Full name: Michael Barry Sullivan.
HIGH SCHOOL: Boston College.
COLLEGE: Boston University.
TRANSACTIONS/CAREER NOTES: Selected by New York Rangers in fourth round (fourth Rangers pick, 69th overall) of NHL entry draft (June 13, 1987). ... Traded by Rangers with D Mark Tinordi, D Paul Jerrard, RW Brett Barnett and third-round pick (C Murray Garbutt) in 1989 draft to Minnesota North Stars for LW Igor Liba, C Brian Lawton and rights to LW Eric Bennett (October 11, 1988). ... Signed as free agent by San Jose Sharks (August 9, 1991). ... Sprained left knee (April 6, 1993); missed remainder of season. ... Claimed on waivers by Calgary Flames (January 6, 1994). ... Pulled groin (January 29, 1994); missed 13 games. ... Bruised knee (April 6, 1994); missed one game. ... Bruised left foot (March 17, 1995); missed two games. ... Sprained right ankle (April 13, 1995); missed last eight games of season. ... Suffered concussion (February 15, 1997); missed two games. ... Suffered back spasms (March 16, 1997); missed two games. ... Traded by Flames to Boston Bruins for seventh-round pick (RW Radek Duda) in 1998 draft (June 21, 1997). ... Injured wrist (February 4, 1998); missed two games. ... Selected by Nashville Predators in NHL expansion draft (June 26, 1998). ... Traded by Predators to Phoenix Coyotes for seventh-round pick in 1999 draft (June 30, 1998).

Season Team	League	REGULAR SEASON								PLAYOFFS				
		Gms.	G	A	Pts.	PIM	+/-	PP	SH	Gms.	G	A	Pts.	PIM
85-86—Boston College H.S.	Mass. H.S.	22	26	33	59	...	...	...	...	—	—	—	—	—
86-87—Boston University	Hockey East	37	13	18	31	18	...	...	...	—	—	—	—	—
87-88—Boston University	Hockey East	30	18	22	40	30	...	...	...	—	—	—	—	—
88-89—Boston University	Hockey East	36	19	17	36	30	...	...	...	—	—	—	—	—
—Virginia	ECHL	2	0	0	0	0	...	...	...	—	—	—	—	—
90-91—San Diego	IHL	74	12	23	35	27	...	...	...	—	—	—	—	—
91-92—Kansas City	IHL	10	2	8	10	8	...	...	...	—	—	—	—	—
—San Jose	NHL	64	8	11	19	15	-18	1	0	—	—	—	—	—
92-93—San Jose	NHL	81	6	8	14	30	-42	0	2	—	—	—	—	—
93-94—San Jose	NHL	26	2	2	4	4	-3	0	2	—	—	—	—	—
—Kansas City	IHL	6	3	3	6	0	...	...	...	—	—	—	—	—
—Saint John	AHL	5	2	0	2	4	...	...	...	—	—	—	—	—
—Calgary	NHL	19	2	3	5	6	2	0	0	7	1	1	2	8
94-95—Calgary	NHL	38	4	7	11	14	-2	0	0	7	3	5	8	2
95-96—Calgary	NHL	81	9	12	21	24	-6	0	1	4	0	0	0	0
96-97—Calgary	NHL	67	5	6	11	10	-11	0	3	—	—	—	—	—
97-98—Boston	NHL	77	5	13	18	34	-1	0	0	6	0	1	1	2
NHL Totals (7 years)		453	41	62	103	137	-81	1	8	24	4	7	11	12

SULLIVAN, STEVE   C   MAPLE LEAFS

PERSONAL: Born July 6, 1974, in Timmins, Ont. ... 5-9/155. ... Shoots right.
TRANSACTIONS/CAREER NOTES: Selected by New Jersey Devils in ninth round (10th Devils pick, 233rd overall) of NHL entry draft (June 29, 1994). ... Traded by Devils with D Jason Smith and C Alyn McCauley to Toronto Maple Leafs for C Doug Gilmour, D Dave Ellett and third-round pick in 1999 draft (February 25, 1997). ... Suffered from the flu (March 7, 1997); missed three games.
HONORS: Named to AHL All-Star first team (1995-96).

Season Team	League	REGULAR SEASON								PLAYOFFS				
		Gms.	G	A	Pts.	PIM	+/-	PP	SH	Gms.	G	A	Pts.	PIM
92-93—Sault Ste. Marie	OHL	62	36	27	63	44	...	...	...	16	3	8	11	18
93-94—Sault Ste. Marie	OHL	63	51	62	113	82	...	...	...	14	9	16	25	22
94-95—Albany	AHL	75	31	50	81	124	...	...	...	14	4	7	11	10
95-96—Albany	AHL	53	33	42	75	127	...	...	...	4	3	0	3	6
—New Jersey	NHL	16	5	4	9	8	3	2	0	—	—	—	—	—
96-97—Albany	AHL	15	8	7	15	16	...	...	...	—	—	—	—	—
—New Jersey	NHL	33	8	14	22	14	9	2	0	—	—	—	—	—
—Toronto	NHL	21	5	11	16	23	5	1	0	—	—	—	—	—
97-98—Toronto	NHL	63	10	18	28	40	-8	1	0	—	—	—	—	—
NHL Totals (3 years)		133	28	47	75	85	9	6	0					

SUNDIN, MATS   C   MAPLE LEAFS

PERSONAL: Born February 13, 1971, in Sollentuna, Sweden. ... 6-4/228. ... Shoots right. ... Full name: Mats Johan Sundin. ... Name pronounced suhn-DEEN.
TRANSACTIONS/CAREER NOTES: Selected by Quebec Nordiques in first round (first Nordiques pick, first overall) of NHL entry draft (June 17, 1989). ... Separated right shoulder (January 2, 1993); missed three games. ... Suspended one game by NHL for second stick-related infraction (March 2, 1993). ... Traded by Nordiques with D Garth Butcher, LW Todd Warriner and first-round pick (traded to Washington Capitals who selected D Nolan Baumgartner) in 1994 draft to Toronto Maple Leafs for LW Wendel Clark, D Sylvain Lefebvre, RW Landon Wilson and first-round pick (D Jeffrey Kealty) in 1994 draft (June 28, 1994). ... Played in Europe during 1994-95 NHL lockout. ... Sprained shoulder (March 25, 1995); missed one game. ... Suffered slight tear of knee cartilage (October 24, 1995); missed four games.
HONORS: Named to Swedish League All-Star team (1990-91 and 1991-92). ... Played in NHL All-Star Game (1996-1998).
MISCELLANEOUS: Scored on a penalty shot (vs. Tom Draper, March 3, 1992; vs. Arturs Irbe, March 15, 1995). ... Failed to score on a penalty shot (vs. Kelly Hrudey, February 2, 1993; vs. Andrei Trefilov, January 10, 1998). ... Captain of Toronto Maple Leafs (1997-98).
STATISTICAL PLATEAUS: Three-goal games: 1990-91 (2), 1992-93 (1), 1996-97 (1). Total: 4. ... Five-goal games: 1991-92 (1). ... Total hat tricks: 5.

Season Team	League	REGULAR SEASON								PLAYOFFS				
		Gms.	G	A	Pts.	PIM	+/-	PP	SH	Gms.	G	A	Pts.	PIM
88-89—Nacka	Sweden	25	10	8	18	18	...	...	...	—	—	—	—	—
89-90—Djur. Stockholm	Sweden	34	10	8	18	16	...	...	...	8	7	0	7	4
90-91—Quebec	NHL	80	23	36	59	58	-24	4	0	—	—	—	—	—
91-92—Quebec	NHL	80	33	43	76	103	-19	8	2	—	—	—	—	—
92-93—Quebec	NHL	80	47	67	114	96	21	13	4	6	3	1	4	6
93-94—Quebec	NHL	84	32	53	85	60	1	6	2	—	—	—	—	—
94-95—Djur. Stockholm	Sweden	12	7	2	9	14	...	...	...	—	—	—	—	—
—Toronto	NHL	47	23	24	47	14	-5	9	0	7	5	4	9	4
95-96—Toronto	NHL	76	33	50	83	46	8	7	6	6	3	1	4	4
96-97—Toronto	NHL	82	41	53	94	59	6	7	4	—	—	—	—	—
97-98—Toronto	NHL	82	33	41	74	49	-3	9	1	—	—	—	—	—
—Swedish Oly. team	Int'l	4	3	0	3	4	...	...	...	—	—	—	—	—
NHL Totals (8 years)		611	265	367	632	485	-15	63	19	19	11	6	17	14

SUNDIN, RONNIE D RANGERS

PERSONAL: Born March 10, 1970, in Frolunda, Sweden. ... 6-2/210. ... Shoots left. ... Name pronounced suhn-DEEN.
TRANSACTIONS/CAREER NOTES: Selected by New York Rangers in ninth round (eighth Rangers pick, 237th overall) of NHL entry draft (June 22, 1996).

Season Team	League	REGULAR SEASON								PLAYOFFS				
		Gms.	G	A	Pts.	PIM	+/-	PP	SH	Gms.	G	A	Pts.	PIM
91-92—Mora	Swed. Dv.II	35	2	5	7	18	...	...	...	2	0	0	0	0
92-93—Vastra Frolunda	Sweden	17	2	3	5	12	...	...	...	—	—	—	—	—
93-94—Vastra Frolunda	Sweden	38	0	9	9	42	...	...	...	4	0	0	0	0
94-95—Vastra Frolunda	Sweden	11	3	4	7	6	...	...	...	—	—	—	—	—
95-96—Vastra Frolunda	Sweden	40	3	6	9	18	...	...	...	13	1	4	5	10
96-97—Vastra Frolunda	Sweden	47	3	14	17	24	...	...	...	3	1	0	1	2
97-98—Hartford	AHL	67	3	19	22	59	...	...	...	14	2	5	7	15
—New York Rangers	NHL	1	0	0	0	0	0	0	0	—	—	—	—	—
NHL Totals (1 year)		1	0	0	0	0	0	0	0					

SUNDSTROM, NIKLAS LW RANGERS

PERSONAL: Born June 6, 1975, in Ornskoldsvik, Sweden. ... 6-0/195. ... Shoots left.
TRANSACTIONS/CAREER NOTES: Selected by New York Rangers in first round (first Rangers pick, eighth overall) of NHL entry draft (June 26, 1993). ... Fractured finger and sprained knee (December 5, 1997); missed 10 games.

Season Team	League	REGULAR SEASON								PLAYOFFS				
		Gms.	G	A	Pts.	PIM	+/-	PP	SH	Gms.	G	A	Pts.	PIM
91-92—MoDo Ornskoldvik	Sweden	9	1	3	4	0	...	...	...	—	—	—	—	—
92-93—MoDo Ornskoldvik	Sweden	40	7	11	18	18	...	...	...	—	—	—	—	—
93-94—MoDo Ornskoldvik	Sweden	37	7	12	19	28	...	...	...	11	4	3	7	2
94-95—MoDo Ornskoldvik	Sweden	33	8	13	21	30	...	...	...	—	—	—	—	—
95-96—New York Rangers	NHL	82	9	12	21	14	2	1	1	11	4	3	7	4
96-97—New York Rangers	NHL	82	24	28	52	20	23	5	1	9	0	5	5	2
97-98—New York Rangers	NHL	70	19	28	47	24	0	4	0	—	—	—	—	—
—Swedish Oly. team	Int'l	4	1	1	2	2	...	...	...	—	—	—	—	—
NHL Totals (3 years)		234	52	68	120	58	25	10	2	20	4	8	12	6

SUTER, CURTIS D COYOTES

PERSONAL: Born August 5, 1979, in Kerroberi, Sask. ... 6-4/220. ... Shoots left.
TRANSACTIONS/CAREER NOTES: Selected by Phoenix Coyotes in fifth round (third Coyotes pick, 123rd overall) of NHL entry draft (June 21, 1997).

Season Team	League	REGULAR SEASON								PLAYOFFS				
		Gms.	G	A	Pts.	PIM	+/-	PP	SH	Gms.	G	A	Pts.	PIM
96-97—Spokane	WHL	56	2	2	4	133	...	...	...	2	0	0	0	0
97-98—Spokane	WHL	62	9	8	17	216	...	...	...	18	0	1	1	9

SUTER, GARY D SHARKS

PERSONAL: Born June 24, 1964, in Madison, Wis. ... 6-0/190. ... Shoots left. ... Full name: Gary Lee Suter. ... Name pronounced SOO-tuhr.
COLLEGE: Wisconsin.
TRANSACTIONS/CAREER NOTES: Selected by Calgary Flames in ninth round (ninth Flames pick, 180th overall) of NHL entry draft (June 9, 1984). ... Stretched knee ligament (December 1986). ... Suspended first four games of regular season and next six international games in which NHL participates for high-sticking during Canada Cup (September 4, 1987). ... Injured left knee (February 1988). ... Pulled hamstring (February 1989). ... Ruptured appendix (February 22, 1989); missed 16 games. ... Broke jaw (April 11, 1989). ... Bruised knee (December 12, 1991); missed 10 games. ... Injured ribs (March 16, 1993); missed one game. ... Suffered from the flu (March 30, 1993); missed one game. ... Tore left knee ligaments (November 4, 1993); missed 33 games. ... Strained left leg muscle (January 24, 1994); missed 10 games. ... Traded by Flames with LW Paul Ranheim and C Ted Drury to Hartford Whalers for C Michael Nylander, D Zarley Zalapski and D James Patrick (March 10, 1994). ... Traded by Hartford with LW Randy Cunneyworth and third-round pick (traded to Vancouver) in 1995 draft to Chicago Blackhawks for D Frantisek Kucera and LW Jocelyn Lemieux (March 11, 1994). ... Cracked bone in hand (May 25, 1995); missed four play-off games. ... Strained groin (December 14, 1997); missed five games. ... Suspended four games and fined $1,000 by NHL for cross-checking incident (February 3, 1998). ... Signed as free agent by San Jose Sharks (July 1, 1998).

HONORS: Named USHL Top Defenseman (1982-83). ... Named to USHL All-Star first team (1982-83). ... Won Calder Memorial Trophy (1985-86). ... Named to NHL All-Rookie team (1985-86). ... Played in NHL All-Star Game (1986, 1988, 1989 and 1991). ... Named to THE SPORTING NEWS All-Star first team (1987-88). ... Named to NHL All-Star second team (1987-88). ... Named to THE SPORTING NEWS All-Star second team (1988-89). ... Named to play in NHL All-Star Game (1996); replaced by D Larry Murphy due to injury.
RECORDS: Shares NHL single-game record for most assists by a defenseman—6 (April 4, 1986).
MISCELLANEOUS: Member of Stanley Cup championship team (1989).

		REGULAR SEASON								PLAYOFFS				
Season Team	League	Gms.	G	A	Pts.	PIM	+/-	PP	SH	Gms.	G	A	Pts.	PIM
81-82—Dubuque	USHL	18	3	4	7	32	...	...	...	—	—	—	—	—
82-83—Dubuque	USHL	41	9	10	19	112	...	...	...	—	—	—	—	—
83-84—Univ. of Wisconsin	WCHA	35	4	18	22	68	...	...	...	—	—	—	—	—
84-85—Univ. of Wisconsin	WCHA	39	12	39	51	110	...	...	...	—	—	—	—	—
85-86—Calgary	NHL	80	18	50	68	141	11	9	0	10	2	8	10	8
86-87—Calgary	NHL	68	9	40	49	79	-10	4	0	6	0	3	3	10
87-88—Calgary	NHL	75	21	70	91	124	39	6	1	9	1	9	10	6
88-89—Calgary	NHL	63	13	49	62	78	26	8	0	5	0	3	3	10
89-90—Calgary	NHL	76	16	60	76	97	4	5	0	6	0	1	1	14
90-91—Calgary	NHL	79	12	58	70	102	26	6	0	7	1	6	7	12
91-92—Calgary	NHL	70	12	43	55	128	1	4	0	—	—	—	—	—
92-93—Calgary	NHL	81	23	58	81	112	-1	10	1	6	2	3	5	8
93-94—Calgary	NHL	25	4	9	13	20	-3	2	1	—	—	—	—	—
—Chicago	NHL	16	2	3	5	18	-9	2	0	6	3	2	5	6
94-95—Chicago	NHL	48	10	27	37	42	14	5	0	12	2	5	7	10
95-96—Chicago	NHL	82	20	47	67	80	3	12	2	10	3	3	6	8
96-97—Chicago	NHL	82	7	21	28	70	-4	3	0	6	1	4	5	8
97-98—Chicago	NHL	73	14	28	42	74	1	5	2	—	—	—	—	—
—U.S. Olympic Team	Int'l	4	0	0	0	2	...	...	...	—	—	—	—	—
NHL Totals (13 years)		918	181	563	744	1156	98	81	7	83	15	47	62	100

SUTTER, BRENT   C   BLACKHAWKS

PERSONAL: Born June 10, 1962, in Viking, Alta. ... 5-11/190. ... Shoots right. ... Full name: Brent Colin Sutter. ... Brother of Brian Sutter, left winger with St. Louis Blues (1976-77 through 1987-88) and head coach, Calgary Flames; brother of Darryl Sutter, left winger with Chicago Blackhawks (1979-80 through 1986-87) and head coach, San Jose Sharks; brother of Duane Sutter, right winger with New York Islanders and Blackhawks (1979-80 through 1989-90); brother of Rich Sutter, right winger with seven NHL teams (1982-83 through 1994-95) and brother of Ron Sutter, center, San Jose Sharks. ... Name pronounced SUH-tuhr.
TRANSACTIONS/CAREER NOTES: Selected by New York Islanders as underage junior in first round (first Islanders pick, 17th overall) of NHL entry draft (June 11, 1980). ... Damaged tendon and developed infection in right hand (January 1984); missed 11 games. ... Separated shoulder (March 1985). ... Bruised left shoulder (October 19, 1985); missed 12 games. ... Bruised shoulder (December 21, 1985); missed seven games. ... Strained abductor muscle in right leg (March 1987). ... Suffered non-displaced fracture of right thumb (December 1987). ... Lacerated right leg (January 19, 1990). ... Hospitalized with an infection in right leg after stitches were removed (January 28, 1990); missed seven games. ... Traded by Islanders with RW Brad Lauer to Chicago Blackhawks for C Adam Creighton and LW Steve Thomas (October 25, 1991). ... Injured abdomen (March 11, 1992). ... Broke foot (September 25, 1992); missed 14 games. ... Bruised index finger (January 19, 1993); missed three games. ... Injured eye (March 9, 1993); missed two games. ... Strained back (February 1994); missed five games. ... Pulled groin (October 30, 1996); missed 36 games. ... Sprained knee (March 26, 1997); missed six games. ... Tore anterior cruciate knee ligament prior to 1997-98 season; missed first four games of season. ... Suffered sore shoulder (November 11, 1997); missed nine games. ... Strained groin (January 9, 1998); missed 17 games.
HONORS: Played in NHL All-Star Game (1985).
MISCELLANEOUS: Member of Stanley Cup championship team (1982 and 1983). ... Captain of New York Islanders (1987-88 through 1991-92). ... Failed to score on a penalty shot (vs. Al Jensen, December 26, 1986).
STATISTICAL PLATEAUS: Three-goal games: 1981-82 (1), 1983-84 (1), 1984-85 (2), 1986-87 (1), 1989-90 (1). Total: 6.

		REGULAR SEASON								PLAYOFFS				
Season Team	League	Gms.	G	A	Pts.	PIM	+/-	PP	SH	Gms.	G	A	Pts.	PIM
77-78—Red Deer	AJHL	60	12	18	30	33	...	...	...	—	—	—	—	—
78-79—Red Deer	AJHL	60	42	42	84	79	...	...	...	—	—	—	—	—
79-80—Red Deer	AJHL	59	70	101	171	131	...	...	...	—	—	—	—	—
—Lethbridge	WHL	5	1	0	1	2	...	...	...	—	—	—	—	—
80-81—New York Islanders	NHL	3	2	2	4	0	2	1	0	—	—	—	—	—
—Lethbridge	WHL	68	54	54	108	116	...	...	...	9	6	4	10	51
81-82—Lethbridge	WHL	34	46	34	80	162	...	...	...	—	—	—	—	—
—New York Islanders	NHL	43	21	22	43	114	28	3	0	19	2	6	8	36
82-83—New York Islanders	NHL	80	21	19	40	128	14	1	0	20	10	11	21	26
83-84—New York Islanders	NHL	69	34	15	49	69	4	7	0	20	4	10	14	18
84-85—New York Islanders	NHL	72	42	60	102	51	42	12	0	10	3	3	6	14
85-86—New York Islanders	NHL	61	24	31	55	74	11	10	0	3	0	1	1	2
86-87—New York Islanders	NHL	69	27	36	63	73	23	6	3	5	1	0	1	4
87-88—New York Islanders	NHL	70	29	31	60	55	13	11	2	6	2	1	3	18
88-89—New York Islanders	NHL	77	29	34	63	77	-12	17	2	—	—	—	—	—
89-90—New York Islanders	NHL	67	33	35	68	65	9	17	3	5	2	3	5	2
90-91—New York Islanders	NHL	75	21	32	53	49	-8	6	2	—	—	—	—	—
91-92—New York Islanders	NHL	8	4	6	10	6	-5	1	0	—	—	—	—	—
—Chicago	NHL	61	18	32	50	30	-5	7	1	18	3	5	8	22
92-93—Chicago	NHL	65	20	34	54	67	10	8	2	4	1	1	2	4
93-94—Chicago	NHL	73	9	29	38	43	17	3	2	6	0	0	0	2
94-95—Chicago	NHL	47	7	8	15	51	6	1	0	16	1	2	3	4
95-96—Chicago	NHL	80	13	27	40	56	14	0	0	10	1	1	2	6
96-97—Chicago	NHL	39	7	7	14	18	10	0	0	2	0	0	0	6
97-98—Chicago	NHL	52	2	6	8	28	-6	0	1	—	—	—	—	—
NHL Totals (18 years)		1111	363	466	829	1054	167	111	18	144	30	44	74	164

SUTTER, RON   C   SHARKS

PERSONAL: Born December 2, 1963, in Viking, Alta. ... 6-0/180. ... Shoots right. ... Full name: Ronald Sutter. ... Brother of Brian Sutter, left winger with St. Louis Blues (1976-77 through 1987-88) and head coach, Calgary Flames; brother of Brent Sutter, center, Chicago Blackhawks; brother of Darryl Sutter, left winger with Blackhawks (1979-80 through 1986-87) and head coach, San Jose Sharks; brother of Duane Sutter, right winger with New York Islanders and Blackhawks (1979-80 through 1989-90); and twin brother of Rich Sutter, right winger with seven NHL teams (1982-83 through 1994-95). ... Name pronounced SUH-tuhr.
HIGH SCHOOL: Winston Churchill (Lethbridge, Ont.).
TRANSACTIONS/CAREER NOTES: Selected by Philadelphia Flyers as underage junior in first round (first Flyers pick, fourth overall) of NHL entry draft (June 9, 1982). ... Broke ankle (November 27, 1981). ... Bruised ribs (March 1985). ... Suffered stress fracture in lower back (January 1987). ... Tore rib cartilage (March 1988). ... Fractured jaw (October 29, 1988). ... Pulled groin (March 1989). ... Traded by Flyers with D Murray Baron to St. Louis Blues for C Rod Brind'Amour and C Dan Quinn (September 22, 1991). ... Strained ligament in right knee (February 1, 1992); missed 10 games. ... Suffered abdominal pull (September 1992); missed first 18 games of season. ... Separated shoulder (March 30, 1993); missed remainder of season. ... Underwent abdominal surgery during off-season; missed nine games. ... Traded by Blues with C Bob Bassen and D Garth Butcher to Quebec Nordiques for D Steve Duchesne and RW Denis Chasse (January 23, 1994). ... Suffered sore neck (November 16, 1993); missed two games. ... Traded by Nordiques with first-round pick (RW Brett Lindros) in 1994 draft to New York Islanders for D Uwe Krupp and first-round pick (D Wade Belak) in 1994 draft (June 28, 1994). ... Sprained right ankle (February 7, 1995); missed 18 games. ... Signed as free agent by Boston Bruins (March 8, 1996). ... Signed as free agent by San Jose Sharks (October 12, 1996). ... Strained groin (November 10, 1997); missed eight games. ... Injured groin (December 2, 1997); missed eight games.
MISCELLANEOUS: Captain of Philadelphia Flyers (1989-90 and 1990-91). ... Failed to score on a penalty shot (vs. Kelly Hrudey, November 18, 1984; vs. Grant Fuhr, May 28, 1985 (playoffs)).

		REGULAR SEASON								PLAYOFFS				
Season Team	League	Gms.	G	A	Pts.	PIM	+/-	PP	SH	Gms.	G	A	Pts.	PIM
79-80—Red Deer	AJHL	60	12	33	45	44	...	...	...	—	—	—	—	—
80-81—Lethbridge	WHL	72	13	32	45	152	...	...	...	9	2	5	7	29
81-82—Lethbridge	WHL	59	38	54	92	207	...	...	...	12	6	5	11	28
82-83—Lethbridge	WHL	58	35	48	83	98	...	...	...	20	*22	†19	*41	45
—Philadelphia	NHL	10	1	1	2	9	0	0	0	—	—	—	—	—
83-84—Philadelphia	NHL	79	19	32	51	101	4	5	3	3	0	0	0	22
84-85—Philadelphia	NHL	73	16	29	45	94	13	2	0	19	4	8	12	28
85-86—Philadelphia	NHL	75	18	42	60	159	26	0	0	5	0	2	2	10
86-87—Philadelphia	NHL	39	10	17	27	69	10	0	0	16	1	7	8	12
87-88—Philadelphia	NHL	69	8	25	33	146	-9	1	0	7	0	1	1	26
88-89—Philadelphia	NHL	55	26	22	48	80	25	4	1	19	1	9	10	51
89-90—Philadelphia	NHL	75	22	26	48	104	2	0	2	—	—	—	—	—
90-91—Philadelphia	NHL	80	17	28	45	92	2	2	0	—	—	—	—	—
91-92—St. Louis	NHL	68	19	27	46	91	9	5	4	6	1	3	4	8
92-93—St. Louis	NHL	59	12	15	27	99	-11	4	0	—	—	—	—	—
93-94—St. Louis	NHL	36	6	12	18	46	-1	1	0	—	—	—	—	—
—Quebec	NHL	37	9	13	22	44	3	4	0	—	—	—	—	—
94-95—New York Islanders	NHL	27	1	4	5	21	-8	0	0	—	—	—	—	—
95-96—Phoenix	IHL	25	6	13	19	28	...	...	...	—	—	—	—	—
—Boston	NHL	18	5	7	12	24	10	0	1	5	0	0	0	8
96-97—San Jose	NHL	78	5	7	12	65	-8	1	2	—	—	—	—	—
97-98—San Jose	NHL	57	2	7	9	22	-2	0	0	6	1	0	1	14
NHL Totals (16 years)		935	196	314	510	1266	65	29	13	86	8	30	38	179

SUTTON, ANDY   LW   SHARKS

PERSONAL: Born March 10, 1975, in London, Ont. ... 6-6/234. ... Shoots left. ... Full name: Andy Cameron Sutton.
HIGH SCHOOL: St. Michael's (Toronto).
COLLEGE: Michigan Tech.
TRANSACTIONS/CAREER NOTES: Signed as free agent by San Jose Sharks (March 20, 1998).
HONORS: Named to WCHA All-Star second team (1997-98).

		REGULAR SEASON								PLAYOFFS				
Season Team	League	Gms.	G	A	Pts.	PIM	+/-	PP	SH	Gms.	G	A	Pts.	PIM
94-95—Michigan Tech	WCHA	19	2	1	3	42	...	...	...	—	—	—	—	—
95-96—Michigan Tech	WCHA	32	2	2	4	38	...	...	...	—	—	—	—	—
96-97—Michigan Tech	WCHA	32	2	7	9	73	...	...	...	—	—	—	—	—
97-98—Michigan Tech	WCHA	38	16	24	40	97	...	...	...	—	—	—	—	—
—Kentucky	AHL	7	0	0	0	33	...	...	...	—	—	—	—	—

SUTTON, KEN   D   SHARKS

PERSONAL: Born November 5, 1969, in Edmonton. ... 6-2/205. ... Shoots left. ... Full name: Kenneth Sutton.
TRANSACTIONS/CAREER NOTES: Selected by Buffalo Sabres in fifth round (fourth Sabres pick, 98th overall) of NHL entry draft (June 17, 1989). ... Separated shoulder (March 3, 1992); missed six games. ... Broke ankle (September 15, 1992); missed first 19 games of season. ... Broke finger (February 15, 1995); missed 10 games. ... Traded by Sabres to Edmonton Oilers for LW Scott Pearson (April 7, 1995). ... Traded by Oilers with D Igor Kravchuk to St. Louis Blues for D Donald Dufresne and D Jeff Norton (January 4, 1996). ... Loaned by Blues to Manitoba Moose of IHL (September 11-November 26, 1996). ... Traded by Blues with second-round pick in 1999 draft to New Jersey Devils for LW Mike Peluso and D Ricard Persson (November 26, 1996). ... Traded by Devils with RW John MacLean to San Jose Sharks for D Doug Bodger and LW Dody Wood (December 7, 1997).
HONORS: Named to Memorial Cup All-Star team (1988-89).

		REGULAR SEASON								PLAYOFFS				
Season Team	League	Gms.	G	A	Pts.	PIM	+/-	PP	SH	Gms.	G	A	Pts.	PIM
87-88—Calgary Canucks	AJHL	53	13	43	56	228	...	...	...	—	—	—	—	—
88-89—Saskatoon	WHL	71	22	31	53	104	...	...	...	8	2	5	7	12

S

| Season Team | League | REGULAR SEASON | | | | | | | | PLAYOFFS | | | | |
		Gms.	G	A	Pts.	PIM	+/-	PP	SH	Gms.	G	A	Pts.	PIM
89-90—Rochester	AHL	57	5	14	19	83	...	...	...	11	1	6	7	15
90-91—Buffalo	NHL	15	3	6	9	13	2	2	0	6	0	1	1	2
—Rochester	AHL	62	7	24	31	65	...	...	...	3	1	1	2	14
91-92—Buffalo	NHL	64	2	18	20	71	5	0	0	7	0	2	2	4
92-93—Buffalo	NHL	63	8	14	22	30	-3	1	0	8	3	1	4	8
93-94—Buffalo	NHL	78	4	20	24	71	-6	1	0	4	0	0	0	2
94-95—Buffalo	NHL	12	1	2	3	30	-2	0	0	—	—	—	—	—
—Edmonton	NHL	12	3	1	4	12	-1	0	0	—	—	—	—	—
95-96—Edmonton	NHL	32	0	8	8	39	-12	0	0	—	—	—	—	—
—St. Louis	NHL	6	0	0	0	4	-1	0	0	1	0	0	0	0
—Worcester	AHL	32	4	16	20	60	...	...	...	4	0	2	2	21
96-97—Manitoba	IHL	20	3	10	13	48	...	...	...	—	—	—	—	—
—Albany	AHL	61	6	13	19	79	...	...	...	16	4	8	12	55
97-98—Albany	AHL	10	0	7	7	15	...	...	...	—	—	—	—	—
—New Jersey	NHL	13	0	0	0	6	1	0	0	—	—	—	—	—
—San Jose	NHL	8	0	0	0	15	-4	0	0	—	—	—	—	—
NHL Totals (7 years)		303	21	69	90	291	-21	4	0	26	3	4	7	16

SVEHLA, ROBERT   D   PANTHERS

PERSONAL: Born January 2, 1969, in Martin, Czechoslovakia. ... 6-1/190. ... Shoots right. ... Name pronounced SVAY-luh.

TRANSACTIONS/CAREER NOTES: Selected by Calgary Flames in fourth round (fourth Flames pick, 78th overall) of NHL entry draft (June 20, 1992). ... Traded by Flames with D Magnus Svensson to Florida Panthers for third-round pick (LW Dmitri Vlasenkov) in 1996 draft and future considerations (September 29, 1994). ... Sprained left rotator cuff (April 22, 1995); missed two games. ... Reinjured left rotator cuff (April 28, 1995); missed one game. ... Suffered back spasms (March 4, 1998); missed three games.

HONORS: Named Czechoslovakian League Player of the Year (1991-92). ... Named to Czechoslovakian League All-Star team (1991-92). ... Played in NHL All-Star Game (1997).

MISCELLANEOUS: Member of bronze-medal-winning Czechoslovakian Olympic team (1992).

| Season Team | League | REGULAR SEASON | | | | | | | | PLAYOFFS | | | | |
		Gms.	G	A	Pts.	PIM	+/-	PP	SH	Gms.	G	A	Pts.	PIM
89-90—Dukla Trencin	Czech.	29	4	3	7		...	...	...	—	—	—	—	—
90-91—Dukla Trencin	Czech.	58	16	9	25		...	...	...	—	—	—	—	—
91-92—Dukla Trencin	Czech.	51	23	28	51	0	...	...	...	—	—	—	—	—
—Czech. Olympic team	Int'l	8	2	1	3		...	...	...	—	—	—	—	—
92-93—Malmo	Sweden	40	19	10	29	86	...	...	...	6	0	1	1	14
93-94—Malmo	Sweden	37	14	25	39	*127	...	...	...	10	5	1	6	23
—Slovakian Oly. team	Int'l	8	2	4	6	26	...	...	...	—	—	—	—	—
94-95—Malmo	Sweden	32	11	13	24	83	...	...	...	9	2	3	5	6
—Florida	NHL	5	1	1	2	0	3	1	0	—	—	—	—	—
95-96—Florida	NHL	81	8	49	57	94	-3	7	0	22	0	6	6	32
96-97—Florida	NHL	82	13	32	45	86	2	5	0	5	1	4	5	4
97-98—Florida	NHL	79	9	34	43	113	-3	3	0	—	—	—	—	—
—Slovakian Oly. team	Int'l	2	0	1	1	0	...	...	...	—	—	—	—	—
NHL Totals (4 years)		247	31	116	147	293	-1	16	0	27	1	10	11	36

SVEJKOVSKY, JAROSLAV   LW   CAPITALS

PERSONAL: Born October 1, 1976, in Plzen, Czechoslovakia. ... 6-0/195. ... Shoots right. ... Name pronounced svay-KAHF-skee.

TRANSACTIONS/CAREER NOTES: Selected by Washington Capitals in first round (second Capitals pick, 17th overall) of NHL entry draft (June 22, 1996). ... Injured ankle (October 23, 1997); missed 14 games. ... Reinjured ankle (November 26, 1997); missed 29 games.

HONORS: Named to WHL (West) All-Star second team (1995-96). ... Won Dudley (Red) Garrett Memorial Trophy (1996-97). ... Named to AHL All-Rookie team (1996-97).

STATISTICAL PLATEAUS: Four-goal games: 1996-97 (1).

| Season Team | League | REGULAR SEASON | | | | | | | | PLAYOFFS | | | | |
		Gms.	G	A	Pts.	PIM	+/-	PP	SH	Gms.	G	A	Pts.	PIM
93-94—Czech Rep.	Czech Rep.	8	0	0	0	8		...	...	—	—	—	—	—
94-95—Czech Rep.	Czech Rep.	25	18	19	37	30		...	...	—	—	—	—	—
—Ta'Bor	Czech Rep.	11	6	7	13			...	...	—	—	—	—	—
95-96—Tri-City	WHL	70	58	43	101	118		...	...	11	10	9	19	8
96-97—Portland	AHL	54	38	28	66	56		...	...	5	2	0	2	6
—Washington	NHL	19	7	3	10	4	-1	2	0	—	—	—	—	—
97-98—Washington	NHL	17	4	1	5	10	-5	2	0	1	0	0	0	4
—Portland	AHL	16	12	7	19	16		...	...	7	1	2	3	2
NHL Totals (2 years)		36	11	4	15	14	-6	4	0	1	0	0	0	4

SVOBODA, PETR   D   FLYERS

PERSONAL: Born February 14, 1966, in Most, Czechoslovakia. ... 6-1/195. ... Shoots left. ... Name pronounced svuh-BOH-duh.

TRANSACTIONS/CAREER NOTES: Selected by Montreal Canadiens in first round (first Canadiens pick, fifth overall) of NHL entry draft (June 9, 1984). ... Suffered back spasms (January 1988). ... Suffered hip pointer (March 1988). ... Sprained right wrist (November 21, 1988); missed five games. ... Injured back (March 1989). ... Separated shoulder (November 1989). ... Pulled groin (November 22, 1989). ... Aggravated groin injury (December 11, 1989); missed 15 games. ... Bruised left foot (March 11, 1990). ... Suffered stomach disorder (November 28, 1990); missed five games. ... Broke left foot (January 15, 1991); missed 15 games. ... Injured mouth (December 14, 1991). ... Sprained ankle (February 17, 1992); missed seven games. ... Traded by Canadiens to Buffalo Sabres for D Kevin Haller (March 10, 1992). ... Bruised knee (October 28, 1992); missed four games. ... Tore ligament in right knee (January 17, 1993); missed remainder of season. ...

Injured knee (October 12, 1993); missed three games. ... Suffered knee inflammation (October 16, 1993); missed seven games. ... Sprained left knee (March 17, 1994); missed 12 games. ... Played in Europe during 1994-95 NHL lockout. ... Separated shoulder (March 2, 1995); missed two games. ... Fractured jaw (March 16, 1995); missed one game. ... Traded by Sabres to Philadelphia Flyers for D Garry Galley (April 7, 1995). ... Strained neck (April 26, 1995); missed one game. ... Injured groin (October 31, 1995); missed one game. ... Suffered pinched nerve in neck (November 16, 1995); missed three games. ... Pulled hamstring (January 11, 1996); missed two games. ... Suffered concussion (February 2, 1996); missed one game. ... Strained shoulder (April 4, 1996); missed two games. ... Separated left shoulder (October 15, 1996); missed six games. ... Strained groin (December 31, 1996); missed four games. ... Suffered pinched nerve in neck (January 28, 1997); missed three games. ... Strained groin (March 13, 1997); missed two games. ... Fractured finger (October 1, 1997); missed 11 games. ... Strained neck (January 3, 1998); missed four games. ... Strained right elbow (March 5, 1998); missed four games. ... Bruised left thumb (March 24, 1998); missed seven games.

MISCELLANEOUS: Member of Stanley Cup championship team (1986). ... Member of gold-medal-winning Czech Republic Olympic team (1998).

		REGULAR SEASON								PLAYOFFS				
Season Team	League	Gms.	G	A	Pts.	PIM	+/-	PP	SH	Gms.	G	A	Pts.	PIM
83-84—Czechoslovakia Jr.	Czech.	40	15	21	36	14	—	—	—	—	—	—	—	—
84-85—Montreal	NHL	73	4	27	31	65	16	0	0	7	1	1	2	12
85-86—Montreal	NHL	73	1	18	19	93	24	0	0	8	0	0	0	21
86-87—Montreal	NHL	70	5	17	22	63	14	1	0	14	0	5	5	10
87-88—Montreal	NHL	69	7	22	29	149	46	2	0	10	0	5	5	12
88-89—Montreal	NHL	71	8	37	45	147	28	4	0	21	1	11	12	16
89-90—Montreal	NHL	60	5	31	36	98	20	2	0	10	0	5	5	2
90-91—Montreal	NHL	60	4	22	26	52	5	3	0	2	0	1	1	2
91-92—Montreal	NHL	58	5	16	21	94	9	1	0	—	—	—	—	—
—Buffalo	NHL	13	1	6	7	52	-8	0	0	7	1	4	5	6
92-93—Buffalo	NHL	40	2	24	26	59	3	1	0	—	—	—	—	—
93-94—Buffalo	NHL	60	2	14	16	89	11	1	0	3	0	0	0	4
94-95—Chemo. Litvinov..........	Czech Rep.	8	2	0	2	40	...	...	...	—	—	—	—	—
—Buffalo	NHL	26	0	5	5	60	-5	0	0	—	—	—	—	—
—Philadelphia	NHL	11	0	3	3	10	0	0	0	14	0	4	4	8
95-96—Philadelphia	NHL	73	1	28	29	105	28	0	0	12	0	6	6	22
96-97—Philadelphia	NHL	67	2	12	14	94	10	1	0	16	1	2	3	16
97-98—Philadelphia	NHL	56	3	15	18	83	19	2	0	3	0	1	1	4
—Czech Rep. Olympic....	Int'l	6	1	1	2	39	...	...	...	—	—	—	—	—
NHL Totals (14 years)..........		880	50	297	347	1313	220	18	0	127	4	45	49	135

SWANSON, BRIAN   C   RANGERS

PERSONAL: Born March 24, 1976, in Eagle River, Alaska. ... 5-10/180. ... Shoots left.
COLLEGE: Colorado College.
TRANSACTIONS/CAREER NOTES: Selected by San Jose Sharks in fifth round (fifth Sharks pick, 115th overall) of NHL entry draft (June 29, 1994). ... Traded by Sharks with D Jayson More and fourth-round pick (D Tomi Kallarsson) in 1997 draft to New York Rangers for D Marty McSorley (August 20, 1996).
HONORS: Named to WCHA All-Star second team (1995-96). ... Named WCHA Rookie of the Year (1995-96). ... Named to WCHA All-Rookie team (1995-96). ... Named to WCHA All-Star first team (1996-97 and 1997-98). ... Named to NCAA All-America West second team (1997-98).

		REGULAR SEASON								PLAYOFFS				
Season Team	League	Gms.	G	A	Pts.	PIM	+/-	PP	SH	Gms.	G	A	Pts.	PIM
93-94—Omaha	USHL	47	38	42	80	40	...	...	...	—	—	—	—	—
94-95—Portland	WHL	65	3	18	21	91	...	...	...	9	2	1	3	18
95-96—Colorado College	WCHA	40	26	33	59	24	...	...	...	—	—	—	—	—
96-97—Colorado College	WCHA	43	19	32	51	47	...	...	...	—	—	—	—	—
97-98—Colorado College	WCHA	42	18	38	56	26	...	...	...	—	—	—	—	—

SWANSON, SCOTT   D   CAPITALS

PERSONAL: Born February 15, 1975, in St. Paul, Minn. ... 6-2/190. ... Shoots left.
COLLEGE: Colorado College.
TRANSACTIONS/CAREER NOTES: Selected by Washington Capitals in ninth round (10th Capitals pick, 225th overall) of NHL entry draft (July 8, 1995).

		REGULAR SEASON								PLAYOFFS				
Season Team	League	Gms.	G	A	Pts.	PIM	+/-	PP	SH	Gms.	G	A	Pts.	PIM
94-95—Omaha	Jr. A	48	14	46	60	22	...	...	...	—	—	—	—	—
95-96—Colorado College	WCHA	42	13	35	48	16	...	...	...	—	—	—	—	—
96-97—Colorado College	WCHA	44	4	16	20	22	...	...	...	—	—	—	—	—
97-98—Colorado College	WCHA	42	7	32	39	24	...	...	...	—	—	—	—	—

SWEENEY, DON   D   BRUINS

PERSONAL: Born August 17, 1966, in St. Stephen, N.B. ... 5-10/184. ... Shoots left. ... Full name: Donald Clark Sweeney.
HIGH SCHOOL: St. Paul (N.B.).
COLLEGE: Harvard.
TRANSACTIONS/CAREER NOTES: Selected by Boston Bruins in eighth round (eighth Bruins pick, 166th overall) of NHL entry draft (June 9, 1984). ... Bruised left heel (February 22, 1990). ... Injured knee (October 12, 1991); missed four games. ... Sprained knee (October 5, 1993); missed six games. ... Injured ribs (December 15, 1993); missed three games. ... Injured shoulder (October 17, 1995); missed three games. ... Injured shoulder (October 31, 1995); missed two games. ... Fractured shoulder (March 1, 1998); missed remainder of season.
HONORS: Named to NCAA All-America East second team (1987-88). ... Named to ECAC All-Star first team (1987-88).

Season Team	League	REGULAR SEASON								PLAYOFFS				
		Gms.	G	A	Pts.	PIM	+/-	PP	SH	Gms.	G	A	Pts.	PIM
83-84—St. Paul N.B. H.S.	N.B. H.S.	22	33	26	59	...	...	...	...	—	—	—	—	—
84-85—Harvard University	ECAC	29	3	7	10	30	...	...	...	—	—	—	—	—
85-86—Harvard University	ECAC	31	4	5	9	29	...	...	...	—	—	—	—	—
86-87—Harvard University	ECAC	34	7	14	21	22	...	...	...	—	—	—	—	—
87-88—Harvard University	ECAC	30	6	23	29	37	...	...	...	—	—	—	—	—
—Maine.........................	AHL	—	—	—	—	—	...	...	...	6	1	3	4	0
88-89—Maine.........................	AHL	42	8	17	25	24	...	...	...	—	—	—	—	—
—Boston........................	NHL	36	3	5	8	20	-6	0	0	—	—	—	—	—
89-90—Boston........................	NHL	58	3	5	8	58	11	0	0	21	1	5	6	18
—Maine.........................	AHL	11	0	8	8	8	...	...	...	—	—	—	—	—
90-91—Boston........................	NHL	77	8	13	21	67	2	0	1	19	3	0	3	25
91-92—Boston........................	NHL	75	3	11	14	74	-9	0	0	15	0	0	0	10
92-93—Boston........................	NHL	84	7	27	34	68	34	0	1	4	0	0	0	4
93-94—Boston........................	NHL	75	6	15	21	50	29	1	2	12	2	1	3	4
94-95—Boston........................	NHL	47	3	19	22	24	6	1	0	5	0	0	0	4
95-96—Boston........................	NHL	77	4	24	28	42	-4	2	0	5	0	2	2	6
96-97—Boston........................	NHL	82	3	23	26	39	-5	0	0	—	—	—	—	—
97-98—Boston........................	NHL	59	1	15	16	24	12	0	0	—	—	—	—	—
NHL Totals (10 years).........		670	41	157	198	466	70	4	4	81	6	8	14	71

SWEENEY, TIM — RW

S

PERSONAL: Born April 12, 1967, in Boston. ... 5-11/185. ... Shoots left. ... Full name: Timothy Paul Sweeney. ... Brother of Bob Sweeney, center for four NHL teams (1986-87 through 1995-96).
HIGH SCHOOL: Weymouth (Mass.).
COLLEGE: Boston College.
TRANSACTIONS/CAREER NOTES: Selected by Calgary Flames in sixth round (seventh Flames pick, 122nd overall) of NHL entry draft (June 15, 1985). ... Fractured index finger (January 26, 1988). ... Bruised ankle (May 1990). ... Signed as free agent by Boston College (September 1992). ... Selected by Mighty Ducks of Anaheim in NHL expansion draft (June 24, 1993). ... Suffered injury (November 26, 1993); missed four games. ... Signed as free agent by Providence Bruins of AHL, Boston Bruins organization (April 9, 1995). ... Fractured foot (December 27, 1996); missed 15 games. ... Strained abdominal muscle (February 23, 1997); missed one game. ... Signed as free agent by New York Rangers (September 11, 1997). ... Suffered from the flu (January 9, 1998); missed two games. ... Partially dislocated right shoulder (March 30, 1998); missed eight games.
HONORS: Named to NCAA All-America East second team (1988-89). ... Named to Hockey East All-Star first team (1988-89). ... Won Ken McKenzie Trophy (1989-90). ... Named to IHL All-Star second team (1989-90). ... Named to AHL All-Star second team (1992-93).

Season Team	League	REGULAR SEASON								PLAYOFFS				
		Gms.	G	A	Pts.	PIM	+/-	PP	SH	Gms.	G	A	Pts.	PIM
83-84—Weymouth North H.S. ...	Mass. H.S.	23	33	26	59	...	...	...	...	—	—	—	—	—
84-85—Weymouth North H.S. ...	Mass. H.S.	22	32	56	88	...	...	...	...	—	—	—	—	—
85-86—Boston College	Hockey East	32	8	4	12	8	...	...	...	—	—	—	—	—
86-87—Boston College	Hockey East	38	31	16	47	28	...	...	...	—	—	—	—	—
87-88—Boston College	Hockey East	18	9	11	20	18	...	...	...	—	—	—	—	—
88-89—Boston College	Hockey East	39	29	44	73	26	...	...	...	—	—	—	—	—
89-90—Salt Lake City.............	IHL	81	46	51	97	32	...	...	...	11	5	4	9	4
90-91—Calgary	NHL	42	7	9	16	8	1	0	0	—	—	—	—	—
—Salt Lake City.............	IHL	31	19	16	35	8	...	...	...	4	3	3	6	0
91-92—Calgary	NHL	11	1	2	3	4	0	0	0	—	—	—	—	—
—U.S. national team......	Int'l	21	9	11	20	10	...	...	...	—	—	—	—	—
—U.S. Olympic Team	Int'l	8	3	4	7	6	...	...	...	—	—	—	—	—
92-93—Providence.................	AHL	60	41	55	96	32	...	...	...	3	2	2	4	0
—Boston........................	NHL	14	1	7	8	6	1	0	0	3	0	0	0	0
93-94—Anaheim	NHL	78	16	27	43	49	3	6	1	—	—	—	—	—
94-95—Anaheim	NHL	13	1	1	2	2	-3	0	0	—	—	—	—	—
—Providence.................	AHL	2	2	2	4	0	...	...	...	13	8	*17	*25	6
95-96—Boston........................	NHL	41	8	8	16	14	4	1	0	1	0	0	0	2
—Providence.................	AHL	34	17	22	39	12	...	...	...	—	—	—	—	—
96-97—Providence.................	AHL	23	11	22	33	6	...	...	...	—	—	—	—	—
—Boston........................	NHL	36	10	11	21	14	0	2	0	—	—	—	—	—
97-98—Hartford	AHL	7	2	6	8	8	...	...	...	—	—	—	—	—
—New York Rangers......	NHL	56	11	18	29	26	7	2	0	—	—	—	—	—
NHL Totals (8 years)...........		291	55	83	138	123	13	11	1	4	0	0	0	2

SYDOR, DARRYL — D — STARS

PERSONAL: Born May 13, 1972, in Edmonton. ... 6-0/200. ... Shoots left. ... Full name: Darryl Marion Sydor. ... Name pronounced sih-DOHR.
TRANSACTIONS/CAREER NOTES: Selected by Los Angeles Kings in first round (first Kings pick, seventh overall) of NHL entry draft (June 16, 1990). ... Bruised hip (November 27, 1992); missed two games. ... Sprained right shoulder (March 15, 1993); missed two games. ... Traded by Kings with seventh-round pick (G Eoin McInerney) in 1996 draft to Dallas Stars for RW Shane Churla and D Doug Zmolek (February 17, 1996).
HONORS: Named to WHL (West) All-Star first team (1989-90 through 1991-92). ... Won Bill Hunter Trophy (1990-91). ... Named to Can.HL All-Star second team (1991-92) ... Played in NHL All-Star game (1998).
STATISTICAL PLATEAUS: Three-goal games: 1997-98 (1).

Season Team	League	REGULAR SEASON								PLAYOFFS				
		Gms.	G	A	Pts.	PIM	+/-	PP	SH	Gms.	G	A	Pts.	PIM
88-89—Kamloops	WHL	65	.12	14	26	86	...	...	...	15	1	4	5	19
89-90—Kamloops	WHL	67	29	66	95	129	...	...	...	17	2	9	11	28
90-91—Kamloops	WHL	66	27	78	105	88	...	...	...	12	3	*22	25	10

Season Team	League	REGULAR SEASON								PLAYOFFS				
		Gms.	G	A	Pts.	PIM	+/-	PP	SH	Gms.	G	A	Pts.	PIM
91-92—Kamloops	WHL	29	9	39	48	43	...	...	...	17	3	15	18	18
—Los Angeles	NHL	18	1	5	6	22	-3	0	0	—	—	—	—	—
92-93—Los Angeles	NHL	80	6	23	29	63	-2	0	0	24	3	8	11	16
93-94—Los Angeles	NHL	84	8	27	35	94	-9	1	0	—	—	—	—	—
94-95—Los Angeles	NHL	48	4	19	23	36	-2	3	0	—	—	—	—	—
95-96—Los Angeles	NHL	58	1	11	12	34	-11	1	0	—	—	—	—	—
—Dallas	NHL	26	2	6	8	41	-1	1	0	—	—	—	—	—
96-97—Dallas	NHL	82	8	40	48	51	37	2	0	7	0	2	2	0
97-98—Dallas	NHL	79	11	35	46	51	17	4	1	17	0	5	5	14
NHL Totals (7 years)		475	41	166	207	392	26	12	1	48	3	15	18	30

SYKORA, MICHAL · D · LIGHTNING

PERSONAL: Born July 5, 1973, in Pardubice, Czechoslovakia. ... 6-5/225. ... Shoots left. ... Name pronounced sih-KOHR-uh.
TRANSACTIONS/CAREER NOTES: Selected by San Jose Sharks in sixth round (sixth Sharks pick, 123rd overall) of NHL entry draft (June 20, 1992). ... Strained knee (November 11, 1993); missed four games. ... Injured shoulder (February 24, 1995); missed remainder of season. ... Injured foot (February 17, 1996); missed one game. ... Traded by Sharks with G Chris Terreri and F Ulf Dahlen to Chicago Blackhawks for G Ed Belfour (January 25, 1997). ... Bruised left shoulder (March 10, 1997); missed three games. ... Suffered collapsed lung (March 15, 1998); missed remainder of season. ... Traded by Blackhawks to Lightning for G Mark Fitzpatrick and fourth-round pick in 1999 draft (July 17, 1998).
HONORS: Named to Can.HL All-Star second team (1992-93). ... Named to WHL (West) All-Star first team (1992-93).

Season Team	League	REGULAR SEASON								PLAYOFFS				
		Gms.	G	A	Pts.	PIM	+/-	PP	SH	Gms.	G	A	Pts.	PIM
90-91—Pardubice	Czech.	2	0	0	0	...	...	...	...	—	—	—	—	—
91-92—Tacoma	WHL	61	13	23	36	66	...	...	...	4	0	2	2	2
92-93—Tacoma	WHL	70	23	50	73	73	...	...	...	7	4	8	12	2
93-94—San Jose	NHL	22	1	4	5	14	-4	0	0	—	—	—	—	—
—Kansas City	IHL	47	5	11	16	30	...	...	...	—	—	—	—	—
94-95—Kansas City	IHL	36	1	10	11	30	...	...	...	—	—	—	—	—
—San Jose	NHL	16	0	4	4	10	6	0	0	—	—	—	—	—
95-96—San Jose	NHL	79	4	16	20	54	-14	1	0	—	—	—	—	—
96-97—San Jose	NHL	35	2	5	7	59	0	1	0	—	—	—	—	—
—Chicago	NHL	28	1	9	10	10	4	0	0	1	0	0	0	0
97-98—Chicago	NHL	28	1	3	4	12	-10	0	0	—	—	—	—	—
—Indianapolis	IHL	6	0	0	0	4	...	...	...	—	—	—	—	—
NHL Totals (5 years)		208	9	41	50	159	-18	2	0	1	0	0	0	0

SYKORA, PETR · C · DEVILS

PERSONAL: Born November 19, 1976, in Plzen, Czechoslovakia. ... 5-11/185. ... Shoots left. ... Name pronounced sih-KOHR-uh.
TRANSACTIONS/CAREER NOTES: Signed as free agent by Cleveland Lumberjacks (January 31, 1994). ... Rights traded by Lumberjacks to Detroit Vipers for cash and future considerations (July 27, 1994). ... Injured shoulder (1995); missed remainder of season. ... Selected by New Jersey Devils in first round (first Devils pick, 18th overall) of NHL entry draft (July 8, 1995). ... Injured back (February 21, 1996); missed two games. ... Sore groin (October 5, 1996); missed two games. ... Reinjured groin (November 9, 1996); missed four games. ... Reinjured groin (November 30, 1996); missed three games. ... Bruised shoulder (November 5, 1997); missed two games. ... Sprained ankle (November 29, 1997); missed 20 games.
HONORS: Named to NHL All-Rookie team (1995-96).

Season Team	League	REGULAR SEASON								PLAYOFFS				
		Gms.	G	A	Pts.	PIM	+/-	PP	SH	Gms.	G	A	Pts.	PIM
91-92—Skoda Plzen	Czech.	30	50	50	100	...	...	...	...	—	—	—	—	—
92-93—Skoda Plzen	Czech.	19	12	5	17	...	...	...	...	—	—	—	—	—
93-94—Skoda Plzen	Czech Rep.	37	10	16	26	...	...	...	...	4	0	1	1	...
—Cleveland	AHL	13	4	5	9	8	...	...	...	—	—	—	—	—
—Cleveland	IHL	13	4	5	9	8	...	...	...	—	—	—	—	—
94-95—Detroit	IHL	29	12	17	29	16	...	...	...	—	—	—	—	—
95-96—Albany	AHL	5	4	1	5	0	...	...	...	—	—	—	—	—
—New Jersey	NHL	63	18	24	42	32	7	8	0	2	0	0	0	2
96-97—New Jersey	NHL	19	1	2	3	4	-8	0	0	—	—	—	—	—
—Albany	AHL	43	20	25	45	48	...	...	...	4	1	4	5	2
97-98—New Jersey	NHL	58	16	20	36	22	0	3	1	2	0	0	0	0
—Albany	AHL	2	4	1	5	0	...	...	...	—	—	—	—	—
NHL Totals (3 years)		140	35	46	81	58	-1	11	1	4	0	0	0	2

SYKORA, PETR · C · PREDATORS

PERSONAL: Born December 21, 1978, in Pardubice, Czechoslovakia. ... 6-2/180. ... Shoots right.
TRANSACTIONS/CAREER NOTES: Selected by Detroit Red Wings in third round (second Red Wings pick, 76th overall) of NHL entry draft (June 21, 1997). ... Traded by Red Wings with third-round pick in 1999 draft and future considerations to Nashville Predators for RW Doug Brown (July 14, 1998).

Season Team	League	REGULAR SEASON								PLAYOFFS				
		Gms.	G	A	Pts.	PIM	+/-	PP	SH	Gms.	G	A	Pts.	PIM
94-95—HC Pardubice Jrs.	Czech Rep.	38	35	33	68	...	...	...	...	—	—	—	—	—
95-96—HC Pardubice Jrs.	Czech Rep.	26	13	9	22	...	...	...	...	—	—	—	—	—
96-97—Pojistovna Pardubice	Czech Rep.	29	1	3	4	4	...	...	...	—	—	—	—	—
—Poji. Pardubice Jrs.	Czech Rep.	12	14	4	18	...	...	...	...	—	—	—	—	—
97-98—Pojistovna Pardubice	Czech Rep.	39	4	5	9	8	...	...	...	3	0	0	0	0

TABARACCI, RICK   G   CAPITALS

PERSONAL: Born January 2, 1969, in Toronto. ... 5-11/190. ... Catches left. ... Full name: Richard Stephen Tabaracci. ... Name pronounced TA-buh-RA-chee.

TRANSACTIONS/CAREER NOTES: Selected by Pittsburgh Penguins as underage junior in second round (second Penguins pick, 26th overall) of NHL entry draft (June 13, 1987). ... Traded by Penguins with C/LW Randy Cunneyworth and RW Dave McLlwain to Winnipeg Jets for RW Andrew McBain, D Jim Kyte and LW Randy Gilhen (June 17, 1989). ... Pulled right hamstring (December 11, 1990); missed seven games. ... Strained back (October 10, 1992); missed one game. ... Suffered back spasms (December 1, 1992); missed one game. ... Suffered back spasms (January 19, 1993); missed seven games. ... Traded by Jets to Washington Capitals for G Jim Hrivnak and future considerations (March 22, 1993). ... Tore knee ligaments (September 16, 1993); missed seven games. ... Sprained knee (February 20, 1994); missed 21 games. ... Strained hamstring (February 13, 1995). ... Loaned by Capitals to Chicago Wolves (March 27, 1995). ... Traded by Capitals to Calgary Flames for fifth-round pick (D Joel Cort) in 1995 draft (April 7, 1995). ... Traded by Flames to Tampa Bay Lightning for C Aaron Gavey (November 19, 1996). ... Bruised sternum (January 8, 1997); missed one game. ... Traded by Lightning to Flames for fourth-round pick (LW Eric Beaudoin) in 1998 draft (June 21, 1997). ... Separated shoulder (January 9, 1998); missed six games. ... Injured knee (January 31, 1998); missed three games. ... Pulled groin (April 9, 1998); missed remainder of season. ... Traded by Flames to Washington Capitals for conditional draft pick and future considerations (August 7, 1998).

HONORS: Named to OHL All-Star first team (1987-88). ... Named to OHL All-Star second team (1988-89).

MISCELLANEOUS: Stopped a penalty shot attempt (vs. Jeff Beukeboom, October 6, 1990; vs. Darren Turcotte, March 22, 1998). ... Allowed a penalty shot goal (vs. Pavel Bure, February 28, 1992). ... Holds Calgary Flames all-time record for lowest goals-against average (2.80).

			REGULAR SEASON							PLAYOFFS						
Season Team	League	Gms.	Min	W	L	T	GA	SO	Avg.	Gms.	Min.	W	L	GA	SO	Avg.
85-86 —Markham Jr. B	OHA	40	2176	...	...	...	188	1	5.18	—	—	—	—	—	—	—
86-87 —Cornwall	OHL	*59	*3347	23	32	3	*290	1	5.20	5	303	1	4	26	0	5.15
87-88 —Cornwall	OHL	58	3448	33	18	6	200	†3	3.48	11	642	5	6	37	0	3.46
—Muskegon	IHL	—	—	—	—	—	—	—	—	1	13	0	0	1	0	4.62
88-89 —Cornwall	OHL	50	2974	24	20	5	*210	1	4.24	18	1080	10	8	65	†1	3.61
—Pittsburgh	NHL	1	33	0	0	0	4	0	7.27	—	—	—	—	—	—	—
89-90 —Moncton	AHL	27	1580	10	15	2	107	2	4.06	—	—	—	—	—	—	—
—Fort Wayne	IHL	22	1064	8	9	‡1	73	0	4.12	3	159	1	2	19	0	7.17
90-91 —Moncton	AHL	11	645	4	5	2	41	0	3.81	—	—	—	—	—	—	—
—Winnipeg	NHL	24	1093	4	9	4	71	1	3.90	—	—	—	—	—	—	—
91-92 —Moncton	AHL	23	1313	10	11	1	80	0	3.66	—	—	—	—	—	—	—
—Winnipeg	NHL	18	966	6	7	3	52	0	3.23	7	387	3	4	26	0	4.03
92-93 —Winnipeg	NHL	19	959	5	10	0	70	0	4.38	—	—	—	—	—	—	—
—Moncton	AHL	5	290	2	1	2	18	0	3.72	—	—	—	—	—	—	—
—Washington	NHL	6	343	3	2	0	10	2	1.75	4	304	1	3	14	0	2.76
93-94 —Washington	NHL	32	1770	13	14	2	91	2	3.08	2	111	0	2	6	0	3.24
—Portland	AHL	3	177	3	0	0	8	0	2.71	—	—	—	—	—	—	—
94-95 —Washington	NHL	8	394	1	3	2	16	0	2.44	—	—	—	—	—	—	—
—Chicago	IHL	2	120	1	1	‡0	9	0	4.50	—	—	—	—	—	—	—
—Calgary	NHL	5	202	2	0	1	5	0	1.49	1	19	0	0	0	0	...
95-96 —Calgary	NHL	43	2391	19	16	3	117	3	2.94	3	204	0	3	7	0	2.06
96-97 —Calgary	NHL	7	361	2	4	0	14	1	2.33	—	—	—	—	—	—	—
—Tampa Bay	NHL	55	3012	20	25	6	138	4	2.75	—	—	—	—	—	—	—
97-98 —Calgary	NHL	42	2419	13	22	6	116	0	2.88	—	—	—	—	—	—	—
NHL Totals (9 years)		**260**	**13943**	**88**	**112**	**27**	**704**	**13**	**3.03**	**17**	**1025**	**4**	**12**	**53**	**0**	**3.10**

TALLAS, ROB   G   BRUINS

PERSONAL: Born March 20, 1973, in Edmonton. ... 6-0/170. ... Catches left. ... Name pronounced TAL-ihz.

TRANSACTIONS/CAREER NOTES: Signed as free agent by Boston Bruins (September 13, 1995). ... Injured ankle (March 24, 1997); missed eight games. ... Injured hamstring (January 24, 1998); missed eight games.

			REGULAR SEASON							PLAYOFFS						
Season Team	League	Gms.	Min	W	L	T	GA	SO	Avg.	Gms.	Min.	W	L	GA	SO	Avg.
92-93 —Seattle	WHL	52	3151	24	23	3	194	2	3.69	5	333	1	4	18	0	3.24
93-94 —Seattle	WHL	51	2849	23	21	3	188	0	3.96	9	567	5	4	40	0	4.23
94-95 —Charlotte	ECHL	36	2011	21	9	‡3	114	0	3.40	—	—	—	—	—	—	—
—Providence	AHL	2	82	1	0	0	4	1	2.93	—	—	—	—	—	—	—
95-96 —Boston	NHL	1	60	1	0	0	3	0	3.00	—	—	—	—	—	—	—
—Providence	AHL	37	2136	12	16	7	117	1	3.29	2	135	0	2	9	0	4.00
96-97 —Providence	AHL	24	1423	9	14	1	83	0	3.50	—	—	—	—	—	—	—
—Boston	NHL	28	1244	8	12	1	69	1	3.33	—	—	—	—	—	—	—
97-98 —Providence	AHL	10	575	1	8	1	39	0	4.07	—	—	—	—	—	—	—
—Boston	NHL	14	788	6	3	3	24	1	1.83	—	—	—	—	—	—	—
NHL Totals (3 years)		**43**	**2092**	**15**	**15**	**4**	**96**	**2**	**2.75**							

TALLINDER, HENRIK   D   SABRES

PERSONAL: Born January 10, 1979, in Stockholm, Sweden. ... 6-3/194. ... Shoots left.

TRANSACTIONS/CAREER NOTES: Selected by Buffalo Sabres in second round (second Sabres pick, 48th overall) of NHL entry draft (June 21, 1997).

			REGULAR SEASON							PLAYOFFS				
Season Team	League	Gms.	G	A	Pts.	PIM	+/-	PP	SH	Gms.	G	A	Pts.	PIM
95-96 —AIK Solna Jrs.	Sweden	40	4	13	17	55	...	...	...	—	—	—	—	—
96-97 —AIK Jrs.	Sweden					Statistics unavailable.				—	—	—	—	—
—AIK	Sweden	1	0	0	0	0	...	...	...	—	—	—	—	—
97-98 —AIK Solna	Sweden	34	0	0	0	26	...	...	...	—	—	—	—	—

TAMER, CHRIS — D — PENGUINS

PERSONAL: Born November 17, 1970, in Dearborn, Mich. ... 6-2/212. ... Shoots left. ... Full name: Chris Thomas Tamer. ... Name pronounced TAY-muhr.
COLLEGE: Michigan.
TRANSACTIONS/CAREER NOTES: Selected by Pittsburgh Penguins in fourth round (third Penguins pick, 68th overall) of NHL entry draft (June 16, 1990). ... Injured shoulder (March 27, 1994); missed four games. ... Fractured ankle (May 6, 1995); missed eight playoff games. ... Pulled abdominal muscle (December 17, 1995); missed five games. ... Sprained wrist (December 30, 1995); missed five games. ... Fractured jaw (January 17, 1996); missed two games. ... Pulled abdominal muscle (November 22, 1996); missed 20 games. ... Strained hip flexor (January 4, 1997); missed 13 games. ... Strained hip flexor (March 4, 1997); missed four games.

		REGULAR SEASON								PLAYOFFS				
Season Team	League	Gms.	G	A	Pts.	PIM	+/-	PP	SH	Gms.	G	A	Pts.	PIM
87-88—Redford	NAJHL	40	10	20	30	217	...	...	...	—	—	—	—	—
88-89—Redford	NAJHL	31	6	13	19	79	...	...	...	—	—	—	—	—
89-90—Univ. of Michigan	CCHA	42	2	7	9	147	...	...	...	—	—	—	—	—
90-91—Univ. of Michigan	CCHA	45	8	19	27	130	...	...	...	—	—	—	—	—
91-92—Univ. of Michigan	CCHA	43	4	15	19	125	...	...	...	—	—	—	—	—
92-93—Univ. of Michigan	CCHA	39	5	18	23	113	...	...	...	—	—	—	—	—
93-94—Cleveland	IHL	53	1	2	3	160	...	...	...	—	—	—	—	—
—Pittsburgh	NHL	12	0	0	0	9	3	0	0	5	0	0	0	2
94-95—Cleveland	IHL	48	4	10	14	204	...	...	...	—	—	—	—	—
—Pittsburgh	NHL	36	2	0	2	82	0	0	0	4	0	0	0	18
95-96—Pittsburgh	NHL	70	4	10	14	153	20	0	0	18	0	7	7	24
96-97—Pittsburgh	NHL	45	2	4	6	131	-25	0	1	4	0	0	0	4
97-98—Pittsburgh	NHL	79	0	7	7	181	4	0	0	6	0	1	1	4
NHL Totals (5 years)		242	8	21	29	556	2	0	1	37	0	8	8	52

TANCILL, CHRIS — RW

PERSONAL: Born February 7, 1968, in Livonia, Mich. ... 5-10/185. ... Shoots left. ... Full name: Christopher William Tancill.
COLLEGE: Wisconsin.
TRANSACTIONS/CAREER NOTES: Selected by Hartford Whalers in NHL supplemental draft (June 16, 1989). ... Traded by Whalers to Detroit Red Wings for RW Daniel Shank (December 18, 1991). ... Signed as free agent by Dallas Stars (August 27, 1993). ... Signed as free agent by San Jose Sharks (August 31, 1994). ... Injured toe (January 9, 1996); missed one game. ... Injured foot (February 17, 1996); missed four games. ... Signed as free agent by Stars (July 25, 1997). ... Suffered concussion (March 20, 1998); missed two games.
HONORS: Named NCAA Tournament Most Valuable Player (1989-90). ... Named to NCAA All-Tournament team (1989-90). ... Named to AHL All-Star first team (1991-92 and 1992-93).

		REGULAR SEASON								PLAYOFFS				
Season Team	League	Gms.	G	A	Pts.	PIM	+/-	PP	SH	Gms.	G	A	Pts.	PIM
86-87—Univ. of Wisconsin	WCHA	40	9	23	32	26	...	...	...	—	—	—	—	—
87-88—Univ. of Wisconsin	WCHA	44	13	14	27	48	...	...	...	—	—	—	—	—
88-89—Univ. of Wisconsin	WCHA	44	20	23	43	50	...	...	...	—	—	—	—	—
89-90—Univ. of Wisconsin	WCHA	45	39	32	71	44	...	...	...	—	—	—	—	—
90-91—Hartford	NHL	9	1	1	2	4	2	0	1	—	—	—	—	—
—Springfield	AHL	72	37	35	72	46	...	...	...	17	8	4	12	32
91-92—Springfield	AHL	17	12	7	19	20	...	...	...	—	—	—	—	—
—Hartford	NHL	10	0	0	0	2	-6	0	0	—	—	—	—	—
—Adirondack	AHL	50	36	34	70	42	...	...	...	19	7	9	16	31
—Detroit	NHL	1	0	0	0	0	0	0	0	—	—	—	—	—
92-93—Adirondack	AHL	68	*59	43	102	62	...	...	...	10	7	7	14	10
—Detroit	NHL	4	1	0	1	2	-2	0	0	—	—	—	—	—
93-94—Dallas	NHL	12	1	3	4	8	-7	0	0	—	—	—	—	—
—Kalamazoo	IHL	60	41	54	95	55	...	...	...	5	0	2	2	8
94-95—San Jose	NHL	26	3	11	14	10	1	0	1	11	1	1	2	8
—Kansas City	IHL	64	31	28	59	40	...	...	...	—	—	—	—	—
95-96—Kansas City	IHL	27	12	16	28	18	...	...	...	—	—	—	—	—
—San Jose	NHL	45	7	16	23	20	-12	0	1	—	—	—	—	—
96-97—San Jose	NHL	25	4	0	4	8	-5	1	0	—	—	—	—	—
—Kentucky	AHL	42	19	26	45	31	...	...	...	4	2	0	2	2
97-98—Michigan	IHL	70	30	39	69	86	...	...	...	4	3	0	3	14
—Dallas	NHL	2	0	1	1	0	-1	0	0	—	—	—	—	—
NHL Totals (8 years)		134	17	32	49	54	-30	1	3	11	1	1	2	8

TARDIF, STEVE — C — BLACKHAWKS

PERSONAL: Born March 29, 1977, in St. Anges, Que. ... 5-11/178. ... Shoots left.
TRANSACTIONS/CAREER NOTES: Selected by Chicago Blackhawks in seventh round (eighth Blackhawks pick, 175th overall) of NHL entry draft (July 8, 1995).

		REGULAR SEASON								PLAYOFFS				
Season Team	League	Gms.	G	A	Pts.	PIM	+/-	PP	SH	Gms.	G	A	Pts.	PIM
93-94—Drummondville	QMJHL	71	5	16	21	117	...	...	...	10	0	1	1	19
94-95—Drummondville	QMJHL	64	10	33	43	313	...	...	...	4	1	2	3	9
95-96—Drummondville	QMJHL	54	17	33	50	291	...	...	...	6	2	3	5	58
96-97—Drummondville	QMJHL	65	24	40	64	357	...	...	...	6	1	5	6	52
97-98—Indianapolis	IHL	42	3	4	7	113	...	...	...	—	—	—	—	—
—Jacksonville	ECHL	15	4	3	7	48	...	...	...	—	—	—	—	—

PERSONAL: Born February 6, 1969, in Stratford, Ont. ... 6-1/185. ... Shoots left. ... Full name: Tim Robertson Taylor. ... Brother of Chris Taylor, center in New York Islanders system.

TRANSACTIONS/CAREER NOTES: Suffered from mononucleosis (October 1986). ... Selected by Washington Capitals in second round (second Capitals pick, 36th overall) of NHL entry draft (June 11, 1988). ... Traded by Capitals to Vancouver Canucks for C Eric Murano (January 29, 1993). ... Signed as free agent by Detroit Red Wings (July 28, 1993). ... Injured right shoulder (April 5, 1996); missed three games. ... Sprained shoulder (October 15, 1996); missed 16 games. ... Suffered from an illness (April 9, 1997); missed two games. ... Selected by Boston Bruins from Red Wings in NHL waiver draft (September 28, 1997). ... Injured ribs (March 21, 1998); missed one game. ... Injured hip (March 22, 1998); missed two games.

HONORS: Won John B. Sollenberger Trophy (1993-94). ... Named to AHL All-Star first team (1993-94).

MISCELLANEOUS: Member of Stanley Cup championship team (1997). ... Scored on a penalty shot (vs. Jocelyn Thibault, April 15, 1998).

		REGULAR SEASON								PLAYOFFS				
Season Team	League	Gms.	G	A	Pts.	PIM	+/-	PP	SH	Gms.	G	A	Pts.	PIM
86-87—London	OHL	34	7	9	16	11	...	...	...	—	—	—	—	—
87-88—London	OHL	64	46	50	96	66	...	...	...	12	9	9	18	26
88-89—London	OHL	61	34	80	114	93	...	...	...	21	*21	25	*46	58
89-90—Baltimore	AHL	74	22	21	43	63	...	...	...	9	2	2	4	13
90-91—Baltimore	AHL	79	25	42	67	75	...	...	...	5	0	1	1	4
91-92—Baltimore	AHL	65	9	18	27	131	...	...	...	—	—	—	—	—
92-93—Baltimore	AHL	41	15	16	31	49	...	...	...	—	—	—	—	—
—Hamilton	AHL	36	15	22	37	37	...	...	...	—	—	—	—	—
93-94—Adirondack	AHL	79	36	*81	117	86	...	...	...	12	2	10	12	12
—Detroit	NHL	1	1	0	1	0	-1	0	0	—	—	—	—	—
94-95—Detroit	NHL	22	0	4	4	16	3	0	0	6	0	1	1	12
95-96—Detroit	NHL	72	11	14	25	39	11	1	1	18	0	4	4	4
96-97—Detroit	NHL	44	3	4	7	52	-6	0	1	2	0	0	0	0
97-98—Boston	NHL	79	20	11	31	57	-16	1	3	6	0	0	0	10
NHL Totals (5 years)		218	35	33	68	164	-9	2	5	32	0	5	5	26

PERSONAL: Born November 15, 1964, in Warwick, R.I. ... 5-8/160. ... Catches left. ... Full name: Christopher Arnold Terreri. ... Name pronounced tuh-RAIR-ee.

COLLEGE: Providence.

TRANSACTIONS/CAREER NOTES: Selected by New Jersey Devils in fifth round (third Devils pick, 87th overall) of NHL entry draft (June 8, 1983). ... Strained knee (October 1986). ... Strained lower back (March 21, 1992); missed five games. ... Traded by Devils to San Jose Sharks for second-round pick (traded to Pittsburgh) in 1996 draft (November 14, 1995). ... Injured wrist (October 20, 1996); missed 12 games. ... Traded by Sharks with D Michal Sykora and RW Ulf Dahlen to Chicago Blackhawks for G Ed Belfour (January 25, 1997). ... Fractured finger (November 11, 1997); missed 20 games. ... Strained groin (January 1, 1998); missed 23 games.

HONORS: Named NCAA Tournament Most Valuable Player (1984-85). ... Named Hockey East Player of the Year (1984-85). ... Named Hockey East Tournament Most Valuable Player (1984-85). ... Named to NCAA All-Tournament team (1984-85). ... Named to NCAA All-America East first team (1984-85). ... Named to Hockey East All-Star first team (1984-85). ... Named to NCAA All-America East second team (1985-86). ... Named to Hockey East All-Decade team (1994).

MISCELLANEOUS: Member of Stanley Cup championship team (1995). ... Holds New Jersey Devils franchise all-time records for most games played by goaltender (268). ... Stopped a penalty shot attempt (vs. Mike Ricci, November 17, 1990; vs. Murray Craven, October 13, 1991; vs. Rob Zamuner, October 9, 1997). ... Allowed a penalty shot goal (vs. Mario Lemieux, December 31, 1988; vs. Bob Errey, January 5, 1991; vs. Ray Bourque, March 19, 1994).

		REGULAR SEASON							PLAYOFFS						
Season Team	League	Gms.	Min	W	L	T	GA	SO	Avg.	Gms.	Min.	W	L	GA	SO	Avg.
82-83—Providence College	ECAC	11	529	7	1	0	17	2	1.93	—						
83-84—Providence College	ECAC	10	391	4	2	0	20	0	3.07	—						
84-85—Providence College	Hockey East	41	2515	15	13	5	131	1	3.13	—						
85-86—Providence College	Hockey East	27	1540	6	16	0	96	0	3.74	—						
86-87—Maine	AHL	14	765	4	9	1	57	0	4.47	—						
—New Jersey	NHL	7	286	0	3	1	21	0	4.41	—						
87-88—U.S. national team	Int'l	26	1430	17	7	2	81	0	3.40	—						
—U.S. Olympic Team	Int'l	3	128	1	1	0	14	0	6.56	—						
—Utica	AHL	7	399	5	1	0	18	0	2.71	—						
88-89—New Jersey	NHL	8	402	0	4	2	18	0	2.69	—						
—Utica	AHL	39	2314	20	15	3	132	0	3.42	2	80	0	1	6	0	4.50
89-90—New Jersey	NHL	35	1931	15	12	3	110	0	3.42	4	238	2	2	13	0	3.28
90-91—New Jersey	NHL	53	2970	24	21	7	144	1	2.91	7	428	3	4	21	0	2.94
91-92—New Jersey	NHL	54	3186	22	22	10	169	1	3.18	7	386	3	3	23	0	3.58
92-93—New Jersey	NHL	48	2672	19	21	3	151	2	3.39	4	219	1	3	17	0	4.66
93-94—New Jersey	NHL	44	2340	20	11	4	106	2	2.72	4	200	3	0	9	0	2.70
94-95—New Jersey	NHL	15	734	3	7	2	31	0	2.53	1	8	0	0	0	0	0.00
95-96—New Jersey	NHL	4	210	3	0	0	9	0	2.57	—						
—San Jose	NHL	46	2516	13	29	1	155	0	3.70	—						
96-97—San Jose	NHL	22	1200	6	10	3	55	0	2.75	—						
—Chicago	NHL	7	429	4	1	2	19	0	2.66	2	44	0	0	3	0	4.09
97-98—Chicago	NHL	21	1222	8	10	2	49	2	2.41	—						
—Indianapolis	IHL	3	180	2	0	‡1	3	1	1.00	—						
NHL Totals (11 years)		364	20098	137	151	40	1037	8	3.10	29	1523	12	12	86	0	3.39

TERTYSHNY, DMITRI   D   FLYERS

PERSONAL: Born July 25, 1976, in Chelyabinsk, U.S.S.R. ... 5-10/174. ... Shoots left. ... Name pronounced tair-TIHSH-nee.
TRANSACTIONS/CAREER NOTES: Selected by Philadelphia Flyers in sixth round (fourth Flyers pick, 132nd overall) of NHL entry draft (July 8, 1995).

		REGULAR SEASON								PLAYOFFS				
Season Team	League	Gms.	G	A	Pts.	PIM	+/-	PP	SH	Gms.	G	A	Pts.	PIM
94-95—Traktor Chelyabinsk	CIS	38	0	3	3	14	...	...	...	—	—	—	—	—
95-96—Traktor Chelyabinsk	CIS	44	1	5	6	50	...	...	...	—	—	—	—	—
96-97—Traktor Chelyabinsk	Russian	40	2	5	7	32	...	...	...	2	0	0	0	2
97-98—Traktor Chelyabinsk	Russian	46	3	7	10	18	...	...	...	—	—	—	—	—

TETARENKO, JOEY   D   PANTHERS

PERSONAL: Born March 3, 1978, in Prince Albert, Sask. ... 6-1/202. ... Shoots right.
TRANSACTIONS/CAREER NOTES: Selected by Florida Panthers in fourth round (fourth Panthers pick, 82nd overall) of NHL entry draft (June 22, 1996).

		REGULAR SEASON								PLAYOFFS				
Season Team	League	Gms.	G	A	Pts.	PIM	+/-	PP	SH	Gms.	G	A	Pts.	PIM
94-95—Portland	WHL	59	0	1	1	134	...	...	...	9	0	0	0	8
95-96—Portland	WHL	71	4	11	15	190	...	...	...	7	0	1	1	17
96-97—Portland	WHL	68	8	18	26	182	...	...	...	2	0	0	0	2
97-98—Portland	WHL	49	2	12	14	148	...	...	...	16	0	2	2	30

TETRAULT, DANIEL   D   CANADIENS

PERSONAL: Born September 4, 1979, in St. Boniface, Manitoba. ... 6-0/198. ... Shoots right.
TRANSACTIONS/CAREER NOTES: Selected by Montreal Canadiens in fourth round (fourth Canadiens pick, 91st overall) of NHL entry draft (June 21, 1997).

		REGULAR SEASON								PLAYOFFS				
Season Team	League	Gms.	G	A	Pts.	PIM	+/-	PP	SH	Gms.	G	A	Pts.	PIM
95-96—Brandon	WHL	72	6	13	19	91	...	...	...	19	1	1	2	25
96-97—Brandon	WHL	64	5	24	29	136	...	...	...	6	0	0	0	14
97-98—Brandon	WHL	16	2	3	5	32	...	...	...	18	0	5	5	25

TEZIKOV, ALEXEI   D   SABRES

PERSONAL: Born June 22, 1978, in Togliatti, U.S.S.R. ... 6-1/198. ... Shoots left. ... Name pronounced TEHS-ih-kahf.
TRANSACTIONS/CAREER NOTES: Selected by Buffalo Sabres in fifth round (seventh Sabres pick, 115th overall) of NHL entry draft (June 22, 1996).
HONORS: Named to QMJHL All-Star second team (1997-98). ... Named to QMJHL All-Rookie Team (1997-98). ... Won Raymond Lagace Trophy (1997-98).

		REGULAR SEASON								PLAYOFFS				
Season Team	League	Gms.	G	A	Pts.	PIM	+/-	PP	SH	Gms.	G	A	Pts.	PIM
95-96—Lada Togliatti	CIS	14	0	0	0	8	...	...	...	—	—	—	—	—
96-97—Lada Togliatti	Russian	7	0	0	0	4	...	...	...	—	—	—	—	—
—Torpedo Nichny Nov. ..	Russian	5	0	2	2	2	...	...	...	—	—	—	—	—
97-98—Moncton	QMJHL	60	15	33	48	144	...	...	...	10	3	8	11	20

THEODORE, JOSE   G   CANADIENS

PERSONAL: Born September 13, 1976, in Laval, Que. ... 5-11/179. ... Catches right. ... Name pronounced ZOH-zhay TAY-uh-dohr.
TRANSACTIONS/CAREER NOTES: Selected by Montreal Canadiens in second round (second Canadiens pick, 44th overall) of NHL entry draft (June 28, 1994).
HONORS: Named to QMJHL All-Star second team (1994-95 and 1995-96).

		REGULAR SEASON							PLAYOFFS					
Season Team	League	Gms.	Min	W	L	T	GA	SO	Avg.	Gms.	Min.	W	L	GA	SO	Avg.
92-93—St. Jean	QMJHL	34	1776	12	16	2	112	0	3.78	3	175	0	2	11	0	3.77
93-94—St. Jean	QMJHL	57	3225	20	29	6	194	0	3.61	5	296	1	4	18	1	3.65
94-95—Hull	QMJHL	58	3348	32	22	2	193	5	3.46	21	1263	15	6	59	1	2.80
—Fredericton	AHL	—	—	—	—	—	—	—	—	1	60	0	1	3	0	3.00
95-96—Hull	QMJHL	48	2803	33	11	2	158	0	3.38	5	300	2	3	20	0	4.00
—Montreal	NHL	1	9	0	0	0	1	0	6.67	—	—	—	—	—	—	—
96-97—Fredericton	AHL	26	1469	12	12	0	87	0	3.55	—	—	—	—	—	—	—
—Montreal	NHL	16	821	5	6	2	53	0	3.87	2	168	1	1	7	0	2.50
97-98—Fredericton	AHL	53	3053	20	23	8	145	2	2.85	4	237	1	3	13	0	3.29
—Montreal	NHL	—	—	—	—	—	—	—	—	3	120	0	1	1	0	0.50
NHL Totals (3 years).............		17	830	5	6	2	54	0	3.90	5	288	1	2	8	0	1.67

THEORET, LUC   D   SABRES

PERSONAL: Born July 30, 1979, in Winnipeg. ... 6-2/197. ... Shoots left.
TRANSACTIONS/CAREER NOTES: Selected by Buffalo Sabres in fourth round (fifth Sabres pick, 101st overall) of NHL entry draft (June 21, 1997).

Season Team	League	REGULAR SEASON								PLAYOFFS				
		Gms.	G	A	Pts.	PIM	+/-	PP	SH	Gms.	G	A	Pts.	PIM
95-96—Lethbridge	WHL	47	4	13	17	41	...	...	...	4	0	0	0	6
96-97—Lethbridge	WHL	43	3	7	10	51	...	...	...	19	1	5	6	8
97-98—Lethbridge	WHL	65	12	37	49	98	...	...	...	4	0	1	1	8

THERIEN, CHRIS D FLYERS

PERSONAL: Born December 14, 1971, in Ottawa. ... 6-5/235. ... Shoots left. ... Name pronounced TAIR-ee-uhn.
HIGH SCHOOL: Northwood School (Lake Placid, N.Y.).
COLLEGE: Providence.
TRANSACTIONS/CAREER NOTES: Selected by Philadelphia Flyers in third round (seventh Flyers pick, 47th overall) of NHL entry draft (June 16, 1990). ... Suffered from the flu (November 3, 1997); missed one game. ... Sprained left knee (April 8, 1998); missed three games.
HONORS: Named to Hockey East All-Rookie Team (1990-91). ... Named to Hockey East All-Star second team (1992-93). ... Named to NHL All-Rookie team (1994-95).

Season Team	League	REGULAR SEASON								PLAYOFFS				
		Gms.	G	A	Pts.	PIM	+/-	PP	SH	Gms.	G	A	Pts.	PIM
89-90—Northwood School	N.Y. H.S.	31	35	37	72	54	...	...	...	—	—	—	—	—
90-91—Providence College	Hockey East	36	4	18	22	36	...	...	...	—	—	—	—	—
91-92—Providence College	Hockey East	36	16	25	41	38	...	...	...	—	—	—	—	—
92-93—Providence College	Hockey East	33	8	11	19	52	...	...	...	—	—	—	—	—
—Canadian nat'l team	Int'l	8	1	4	5	8	...	...	...	—	—	—	—	—
93-94—Canadian nat'l team	Int'l	59	7	15	22	46	...	...	...	—	—	—	—	—
—Can. Olympic Team	Int'l	4	0	0	0	4	...	...	...	—	—	—	—	—
—Hershey	AHL	6	0	0	0	2	...	...	...	—	—	—	—	—
94-95—Hershey	AHL	34	3	13	16	27	...	...	...	—	—	—	—	—
—Philadelphia	NHL	48	3	10	13	38	8	1	0	15	0	0	0	10
95-96—Philadelphia	NHL	82	6	17	23	89	16	3	0	12	0	0	0	18
96-97—Philadelphia	NHL	71	2	22	24	64	27	0	0	19	1	6	7	6
97-98—Philadelphia	NHL	78	3	16	19	80	5	1	0	5	0	1	1	4
NHL Totals (4 years)		279	14	65	79	271	56	5	0	51	1	7	8	38

THERRIEN, PIERRE-LUC G CAPITALS

PERSONAL: Born September 3, 1979, in Terrebonne, Que. ... 6-0/170. ... Catches left.
TRANSACTIONS/CAREER NOTES: Selected by Washington Capitals in eighth round (sixth Capitals pick, 200th overall) of NHL entry draft (June 21, 1997).

Season Team	League	REGULAR SEASON							PLAYOFFS					
		Gms.	Min	W	L	T	GA	SO	Avg.	Gms.	Min.	W	L	GA	SO	Avg.
95-96—Drummondville	QMJHL	37	2066	15	17	1	117	1	3.40	6	368	1	5	39	0	6.36
96-97—Drummondville	QMJHL	37	2235	16	17	1	147	2	3.95	5	154	1	0	16	0	6.22
97-98—Drummondville	QMJHL	16	856	5	8	0	68	0	4.77	—	—	—	—	—	—	—
—Victoriaville	QMJHL	10	571	6	1	2	26	0	2.73	1	16	0	0	5	0	18.75

THIBAULT, JOCELYN G CANADIENS

PERSONAL: Born January 12, 1975, in Montreal. ... 5-11/170. ... Catches left. ... Name pronounced TEE-boh.
TRANSACTIONS/CAREER NOTES: Selected by Quebec Nordiques in first round (first Nordiques pick, 10th overall) of NHL entry draft (June 26, 1993). ... Sprained shoulder (March 28, 1995); missed 10 games. ... Nordiques franchise moved to Colorado and renamed Avalanche for 1995-96 season (June 21, 1995). ... Traded by Avalanche with LW Martin Rucinsky and RW Andrei Kovalenko to Montreal Canadiens for G Patrick Roy and RW Mike Keane (December 6, 1995). ... Bruised right hand (February 21, 1996); missed two games. ... Fractured finger (October 24, 1996); missed nine games. ... Suffered from the flu (February 3, 1997); missed two games. ... Bruised collarbone (January 8, 1998); missed one game.
HONORS: Named to QMJHL All-Rookie team (1991-92). ... Won Can.HL Goaltender-of-the-Year Award (1992-93). ... Won Jacques Plante Trophy (1992-93). ... Won Michel Briere Trophy (1992-93). ... Won Marcel Robert Trophy (1992-93). ... Named to Can.HL All-Star first team (1992-93). ... Named to QMJHL All-Star first team (1992-93).
MISCELLANEOUS: Stopped a penalty shot attempt (vs. Tony Granato, November 25, 1993; vs. Martin Straka, March 16, 1995). ... Allowed a penalty shot goal (vs. Joe Sacco, November 12, 1997; vs. Tim Taylor, April 15, 1998).

Season Team	League	REGULAR SEASON							PLAYOFFS					
		Gms.	Min	W	L	T	GA	SO	Avg.	Gms.	Min.	W	L	GA	SO	Avg.
91-92—Trois-Rivieres	QMJHL	30	1497	14	7	1	77	0	3.09	3	300	...	...	20	0	4.00
92-93—Sherbrooke	QMJHL	56	3190	34	14	5	159	*3	*2.99	15	883	9	6	57	0	3.87
93-94—Quebec	NHL	29	1504	8	13	3	83	0	3.31	—	—	—	—	—	—	—
—Cornwall	AHL	4	240	4	0	0	9	1	2.25	—	—	—	—	—	—	—
94-95—Sherbrooke	QMJHL	13	776	6	6	1	38	1	2.94	—	—	—	—	—	—	—
—Quebec	NHL	18	898	12	2	2	35	1	2.34	3	148	1	2	8	0	3.24
95-96—Colorado	NHL	10	558	3	4	2	28	0	3.01	—	—	—	—	—	—	—
—Montreal	NHL	40	2334	23	13	3	110	3	2.83	6	311	2	4	18	0	3.47
96-97—Montreal	NHL	61	3397	22	24	11	164	1	2.90	3	179	0	3	13	0	4.36
97-98—Montreal	NHL	47	2652	19	15	8	109	2	2.47	2	43	0	0	4	0	5.58
NHL Totals (5 years)		205	11343	87	71	29	529	7	2.80	14	681	3	9	43	0	3.79

THOMAS, STEVE LW MAPLE LEAFS

PERSONAL: Born July 15, 1963, in Stockport, England. ... 5-11/185. ... Shoots left.
TRANSACTIONS/CAREER NOTES: Signed as free agent by Toronto Maple Leafs (June 1984). ... Broke wrist during training camp (September 1984). ... Traded by Maple Leafs with RW Rick Vaive and D Bob McGill to Chicago Blackhawks for LW Al Secord and RW Ed Olczyk

(September 3, 1987). ... Pulled stomach muscle (October 1987). ... Separated left shoulder (February 20, 1988); underwent surgery (May 1988). ... Pulled back muscle (October 18, 1988). ... Separated right shoulder (December 21, 1988). ... Underwent surgery to repair chronic shoulder separation problem (January 25, 1989). ... Strained knee ligaments during training camp (September 1990); missed first 11 games of season. ... Traded by Blackhawks with C Adam Creighton to New York Islanders for C Brent Sutter and RW Brad Lauer (October 25, 1991). ... Bruised ribs (March 10, 1992); missed one game. ... Bruised ribs (November 21, 1992); missed three games. ... Suffered neck muscle spasms (January 4, 1994); missed five games. ... Injured back and thumb (January 24, 1995); missed one game. ... Traded by Islanders to New Jersey Devils for RW Claude Lemieux (October 3, 1995). ... Injured head (February 1, 1996); missed one game. ... Suffered from the flu (October 24, 1996); missed two games. ... Strained ankle (November 30, 1996); missed 10 games. ... Strained knee (December 31, 1996); missed 12 games. ... Strained groin (October 23, 1997); missed 20 games. ... Bruised ribs (January 5, 1998); missed four games. ... Suffered back spasms (April 5, 1998); missed three games. ... Signed as free agent by Toronto Maple Leafs (July 12, 1998).

HONORS: Won Dudley (Red) Garrett Memorial Trophy (1984-85). ... Named to AHL All-Star first team (1984-85).
STATISTICAL PLATEAUS: Three-goal games: 1987-88 (1), 1989-90 (1), 1990-91 (1), 1993-94 (1). Total: 4. ... Four-goal games: 1989-90 (1), 1991-92 (1). Total: 2. ... Total hat tricks: 6.

			REGULAR SEASON								PLAYOFFS				
Season Team	League	Gms.	G	A	Pts.	PIM	+/-	PP	SH		Gms.	G	A	Pts.	PIM
81-82—Markham Tier II Jr. A..	OHA	48	68	57	125	113	...	...	...		—	—	—	—	—
82-83—Toronto	OHL	61	18	20	38	42	...	...	...		—	—	—	—	—
83-84—Toronto	OHL	70	51	54	105	77	...	...	...		—	—	—	—	—
84-85—Toronto	NHL	18	1	1	2	2	-13	0	0		—	—	—	—	—
—St. Catharines	AHL	64	42	48	90	56	...	...	...		—	—	—	—	—
85-86—St. Catharines	AHL	19	18	14	32	35	...	...	...		—	—	—	—	—
—Toronto	NHL	65	20	37	57	36	-15	5	0		10	6	8	14	9
86-87—Toronto	NHL	78	35	27	62	114	-3	3	0		13	2	3	5	13
87-88—Chicago	NHL	30	13	13	26	40	1	5	0		3	1	2	3	6
88-89—Chicago	NHL	45	21	19	40	69	-2	8	0		12	3	5	8	10
89-90—Chicago	NHL	76	40	30	70	91	-3	13	0		20	7	6	13	33
90-91—Chicago	NHL	69	19	35	54	129	8	2	0		6	1	2	3	15
91-92—Chicago	NHL	11	2	6	8	26	-3	0	0		—	—	—	—	—
—New York Islanders	NHL	71	28	42	70	71	11	3	0		—	—	—	—	—
92-93—New York Islanders	NHL	79	37	50	87	111	3	12	0		18	9	8	17	37
93-94—New York Islanders	NHL	78	42	33	75	139	-9	17	0		4	1	0	1	8
94-95—New York Islanders	NHL	47	11	15	26	60	-14	3	0		—	—	—	—	—
95-96—New Jersey	NHL	81	26	35	61	98	-2	6	0		—	—	—	—	—
96-97—New Jersey	NHL	57	15	19	34	46	9	1	0		10	1	1	2	18
97-98—New Jersey	NHL	55	14	10	24	32	4	3	0		6	0	3	3	2
NHL Totals (14 years)		860	324	372	696	1064	-28	81	0		102	31	38	69	151

THOMAS, TIM   G   AVALANCHE

PERSONAL: Born April 15, 1974, in Flint, Mich. ... 5-11/182. ... Catches left.
COLLEGE: Vermont.
TRANSACTIONS/CAREER NOTES: Selected by Quebec Nordiques in ninth round (11th Nordiques pick, 217th overall) of NHL entry draft (June 29, 1994). ... Nordiques franchise moved to Colorado and renamed Avalanche for 1995-96 season (June 21, 1995). ... Signed as free agent by Edmonton Oilers (June 4, 1998).
HONORS: Named to NCAA All-America East second team (1994-95 and 1995-96). ... Named to ECAC All-Star first team (1994-95). ... Named to ECAC All-Star first team (1995-96).

			REGULAR SEASON								PLAYOFFS					
Season Team	League	Gms.	Min	W	L	T	GA	SO	Avg.		Gms.	Min.	W	L	GA	SO	Avg.
92-93—Lakeland	Tier II	27	1580	...	...	...	87	...	3.30		—	—	—	—	—	—	—
93-94—Univ. of Vermont	ECAC	33	1863	15	11	6	95	1	3.06		—	—	—	—	—	—	—
94-95—Univ. of Vermont	ECAC	34	2011	18	14	2	90	3	2.69		—	—	—	—	—	—	—
95-96—Univ. of Vermont	ECAC	37	2254	26	7	4	88	3	2.34		—	—	—	—	—	—	—
96-97—Univ. of Vermont	ECAC	36	2158	22	11	3	101	2	2.81		—	—	—	—	—	—	—
97-98—Birmingham	ECHL	6	360	4	1	1	13	1	2.17		—	—	—	—	—	—	—
—Houston	IHL	1	60	0	1	‡0	4	0	4.00		—	—	—	—	—	—	—
—HIFK Helsinki	Finland	22	1035	22	4	1	28	2	1.62		9	551	9	0	14	3	1.52

THOMPSON, MARK   D   LIGHTNING

PERSONAL: Born April 26, 1979, in St. Albert, Alta. ... 6-6/205. ... Shoots right.
TRANSACTIONS/CAREER NOTES: Selected by Tampa Bay Lightning in fifth round (fourth Lightning pick, 108th overall) of NHL entry draft (June 21, 1997).

			REGULAR SEASON								PLAYOFFS				
Season Team	League	Gms.	G	A	Pts.	PIM	+/-	PP	SH		Gms.	G	A	Pts.	PIM
96-97—Regina	WHL	32	1	5	6	20	...	...	...		3	0	1	1	2
97-98—Regina	WHL	46	0	2	2	44	...	...	...		2	0	0	0	0

THOMPSON, ROCKY   D   FLAMES

PERSONAL: Born August 8, 1977, in Calgary. ... 6-2/205. ... Shoots right.
HIGH SCHOOL: Medicine Hat (Alta.).
TRANSACTIONS/CAREER NOTES: Selected by Calgary Flames in third round (third Flames pick, 72nd overall) of NHL entry draft (July 8, 1995). ... Injured neck (February 3, 1998); missed two games.

			REGULAR SEASON								PLAYOFFS				
Season Team	League	Gms.	G	A	Pts.	PIM	+/-	PP	SH		Gms.	G	A	Pts.	PIM
93-94—Medicine Hat	WHL	68	1	4	5	166	...	...	...		3	0	0	0	2
94-95—Medicine Hat	WHL	63	1	6	7	220	...	...	...		5	0	0	0	17

Season Team	League	REGULAR SEASON								PLAYOFFS				
		Gms.	G	A	Pts.	PIM	+/-	PP	SH	Gms.	G	A	Pts.	PIM
95-96—Medicine Hat	WHL	71	9	20	29	260	...	...	...	5	2	3	5	26
—Saint John	AHL	4	0	0	0	33	...	...	...	—	—	—	—	—
96-97—Medicine Hat	WHL	47	6	9	15	170	...	...	...	—	—	—	—	—
—Swift Current	WHL	22	3	5	8	90	...	...	...	10	1	2	3	22
97-98—Saint John	AHL	51	3	0	3	187	...	...	...	18	1	1	2	47
—Calgary	NHL	12	0	0	0	61	0	0	0	—	—	—	—	—
NHL Totals (1 year)		12	0	0	0	61	0	0	0					

THORNTON, JOE   C   BRUINS

PERSONAL: Born July 2, 1979, in London, Ont. ... 6-4/210. ... Shoots left. ... Cousin of Scott Thornton, left winger, Montreal Canadiens.
TRANSACTIONS/CAREER NOTES: Selected by Boston Bruins in first round (first Bruins pick, first overall) of NHL entry draft (June 21, 1997). ... Suffered broken forearm prior to 1997-98 season; missed first three games. ... Injured ankle (December 13, 1997); missed 10 games. ... Suffered from viral infection (March 28, 1998); missed six games.
HONORS: Won Can.HL Rookie of the Year Award (1995-96). ... Won Emms Family Trophy (1995-96). ... Won Can.HL Top Prospect Award (1996-97). ... Named to Can.HL All-Star second team (1996-97). ... Named to OHL All-Star second team (1996-97).

Season Team	League	REGULAR SEASON								PLAYOFFS				
		Gms.	G	A	Pts.	PIM	+/-	PP	SH	Gms.	G	A	Pts.	PIM
94-95—St. Thomas	Jr. B	50	40	64	104	53	...	...	...	—	—	—	—	—
95-96—Sault Ste. Marie	OHL	66	30	46	76	51	...	...	...	4	1	1	2	11
96-97—Sault Ste. Marie	OHL	59	41	81	122	123	...	...	...	11	11	8	19	24
97-98—Boston	NHL	55	3	4	7	19	-6	0	0	6	0	0	0	9
NHL Totals (1 year)		55	3	4	7	19	-6	0	0	6	0	0	0	9

THORNTON, SCOTT   LW   CANADIENS

PERSONAL: Born January 9, 1971, in London, Ont. ... 6-3/219. ... Shoots left. ... Full name: Scott C. Thornton. ... Cousin of Joe Thornton, center, Boston Bruins.
TRANSACTIONS/CAREER NOTES: Selected by Toronto Maple Leafs in first round (first Maple Leafs pick, third overall) of NHL entry draft (June 17, 1989). ... Suspended 12 games by OHL for refusing to leave ice following penalty (February 7, 1990). ... Separated shoulder (January 24, 1991); missed eight games. ... Traded by Maple Leafs with LW Vincent Damphousse, D Luke Richardson, G Peter Ing and future considerations to Edmonton Oilers for G Grant Fuhr, RW/LW Glenn Anderson and LW Craig Berube (September 19, 1991). ... Suffered concussion (November 23, 1991); missed one game. ... Sprained ankle (October 6, 1993); missed 13 games. ... Suffered back spasms (November 21, 1993); missed one game. ... Suffered wrist contusion (April 14, 1994); missed one game. ... Suffered from Cytomegalo virus (January 9, 1996); missed three games. ... Traded by Oilers to Montreal Canadiens for RW Andrei Kovalenko (September 6, 1996). ... Bruised hand (December 28, 1996); missed three games. ... Suffered from the flu (February 10, 1997); missed one game. ... Underwent arthroscopic knee surgery (March 6, 1997); missed five games. ... Separated shoulder (January 3, 1998); missed two games. ... Injured neck (February 7, 1998); missed one game. ... Fractured rib (March 18, 1998); missed eight games. ... Injured shoulder (April 15, 1998); missed three games.

Season Team	League	REGULAR SEASON								PLAYOFFS				
		Gms.	G	A	Pts.	PIM	+/-	PP	SH	Gms.	G	A	Pts.	PIM
86-87—London Diamonds	OPJHL	31	10	7	17	10	...	...	...	—	—	—	—	—
87-88—Belleville	OHL	62	11	19	30	54	...	...	...	6	0	1	1	2
88-89—Belleville	OHL	59	28	34	62	103	...	...	...	5	1	1	2	6
89-90—Belleville	OHL	47	21	28	49	91	...	...	...	11	2	10	12	15
90-91—Belleville	OHL	3	2	1	3	2	...	...	...	6	0	7	7	14
—Newmarket	AHL	5	1	0	1	4	...	...	...	—	—	—	—	—
—Toronto	NHL	33	1	3	4	30	-15	0	0	—	—	—	—	—
91-92—Edmonton	NHL	15	0	1	1	43	-6	0	0	1	0	0	0	0
—Cape Breton	AHL	49	9	14	23	40	...	...	...	5	1	0	1	8
92-93—Cape Breton	AHL	58	23	27	50	102	...	...	...	16	1	2	3	35
—Edmonton	NHL	9	0	1	1	0	-4	0	0	—	—	—	—	—
93-94—Edmonton	NHL	61	4	7	11	104	-15	0	0	—	—	—	—	—
—Cape Breton	AHL	2	1	1	2	31	...	...	...	—	—	—	—	—
94-95—Edmonton	NHL	47	10	12	22	89	-4	0	1	—	—	—	—	—
95-96—Edmonton	NHL	77	9	9	18	149	-25	0	2	—	—	—	—	—
96-97—Montreal	NHL	73	10	10	20	128	-19	1	1	5	1	0	1	2
97-98—Montreal	NHL	67	6	9	15	158	0	1	0	9	0	2	2	10
NHL Totals (8 years)		382	40	52	92	701	-88	2	4	15	1	2	3	12

TIKKANEN, ESA   LW

PERSONAL: Born January 25, 1968, in Helsinki, Finland. ... 6-1/200. ... Shoots left. ... Full name: Esa Kalervo Tikkanen. ... Name pronounced EH-suh TEE-kuh-nehn.
TRANSACTIONS/CAREER NOTES: Selected by Edmonton Oilers in fourth round (fourth Oilers pick, 82nd overall) of NHL entry draft (August 8, 1983). ... Broke foot (December 10, 1985). ... Lacerated elbow, developed bursitis and underwent surgery (December 9, 1986). ... Fractured left wrist (January 1989). ... Injured right knee (October 28, 1989). ... Underwent left knee surgery (August 1990); missed first 10 days of training camp. ... Sprained wrist (December 1, 1991); missed one game. ... Sprained wrist (December 20, 1991); missed one game. ... Fractured shoulder (January 4, 1992); missed 37 games. ... Suffered from the flu (December 1992); missed one game. ... Suffered elbow infection (February 1993); missed two games. ... Traded by Oilers to New York Rangers for C Doug Weight (March 17, 1993). ... Bruised knee (January 14, 1994); missed one game. ... Traded by Rangers with D Doug Lidster to St. Louis Blues for C Petr Nedved (July 24, 1994); trade arranged as compensation for Blues signing Coach Mike Keenan. ... Played in Europe during 1994-95 NHL lockout. ... Injured shoulder (April 3, 1995); missed one game. ... Suffered illness (April 28, 1995); missed two games. ... Injured leg (May 1, 1995); missed two games. ... Traded by Blues to New Jersey Devils for third-round pick (traded to Colorado) in 1997 draft (November 1, 1995). ... Injured knee (November 23, 1995); missed 15 games. ... Traded by Devils to Vancouver Canucks for second-round pick (LW Wesley Mason) in 1996 draft (November 23, 1995). ... Traded by Canucks with RW Russ Courtnall to Rangers for C Sergei Nemchinov and RW Brian Noonan (March 8, 1997). ... Signed as free agent by Florida Panthers (September 5, 1997). ... Fractured left leg (November 5, 1997); missed 26 games. ... Traded by Panthers to Washington Capitals for LW Dwayne Hay and conditional pick in 1999 draft (March 9, 1998).

MISCELLANEOUS: Member of Stanley Cup championship team (1985, 1987, 1988, 1990 and 1994). ... Member of bronze-medal-winning Finnish Olympic team (1998).
STATISTICAL PLATEAUS: Three-goal games: 1986-87 (2), 1987-88 (1), 1988-89 (1), 1990-91 (1). Total: 5.

Season Team	League	REGULAR SEASON								PLAYOFFS				
		Gms.	G	A	Pts.	PIM	+/-	PP	SH	Gms.	G	A	Pts.	PIM
81-82—Regina	WHL	2	0	0	0	0	...	...	...	—	—	—	—	—
82-83—Helsinki Junior IFK	Finland	30	34	31	65	104	...	...	...	4	4	3	7	10
—Helsinki IFK	Finland	—	—	—	—	—	...	...	...	1	0	0	0	2
83-84—Helsinki IFK	Finland	36	19	11	30	30	...	...	...	2	0	0	0	0
—Helsinki Junior IFK	Finland	6	5	9	14	13	...	...	...	4	4	3	7	8
84-85—Helsinki IFK	Finland	36	21	33	54	42	...	...	...	—	—	—	—	—
—Edmonton	NHL	—	—	—	—	—	—	—	—	3	0	0	0	2
85-86—Nova Scotia	AHL	15	4	8	12	17	...	...	...	—	—	—	—	—
—Edmonton	NHL	35	7	6	13	28	5	0	0	8	3	2	5	7
86-87—Edmonton	NHL	76	34	44	78	120	44	6	0	21	7	2	9	22
87-88—Edmonton	NHL	80	23	51	74	153	21	6	1	19	10	17	27	72
88-89—Edmonton	NHL	67	31	47	78	92	10	6	8	7	1	3	4	12
89-90—Edmonton	NHL	79	30	33	63	161	17	6	4	22	13	11	24	26
90-91—Edmonton	NHL	79	27	42	69	85	22	3	2	18	12	8	20	24
91-92—Edmonton	NHL	40	12	16	28	44	-8	6	2	16	5	3	8	8
92-93—Edmonton	NHL	66	14	19	33	76	-11	2	4	—	—	—	—	—
—New York Rangers	NHL	15	2	5	7	18	-13	0	0	—	—	—	—	—
93-94—New York Rangers	NHL	83	22	32	54	114	5	5	3	23	4	4	8	34
94-95—HIFK Helsinki	Finland	19	2	11	13	16	...	...	...	—	—	—	—	—
—St. Louis	NHL	43	12	23	35	22	13	5	2	7	2	2	4	20
95-96—St. Louis	NHL	11	1	4	5	18	1	0	1	—	—	—	—	—
—New Jersey	NHL	9	0	2	2	4	-6	0	0	—	—	—	—	—
—Vancouver	NHL	38	13	24	37	14	6	8	0	6	3	2	5	2
96-97—Vancouver	NHL	62	12	15	27	66	-9	4	1	—	—	—	—	—
—New York Rangers	NHL	14	1	2	3	6	0	0	1	15	9	3	12	26
97-98—Florida	NHL	28	1	8	9	16	-7	0	0	—	—	—	—	—
—Fin. Olympic Team	Int'l	6	1	1	2	0	...	...	...	—	—	—	—	—
—Washington	NHL	20	2	10	12	2	-4	1	0	21	3	3	6	20
NHL Totals (14 years)		845	244	383	627	1039	86	58	29	186	72	60	132	275

TILEY, BRAD   D   COYOTES

PERSONAL: Born July 5, 1971, in Markdale, Ont. ... 6-1/185. ... Shoots left. ... Name pronounced TIGH-lee.
TRANSACTIONS/CAREER NOTES: Selected by Boston Bruins in fourth round (fourth Bruins pick, 84th overall) of NHL entry draft (June 22, 1991). ... Signed as free agent by New York Rangers (September 4, 1992). ... Traded by Rangers to Los Angeles Kings for 11th-round pick (Jamie Butt) in 1994 draft (January 28, 1994). ... Selected by Orlando Solar Bears in IHL Expansion Draft (July 13, 1995). ... Rights traded by Solar Bears to Phoenix Roadrunners of IHL (October 6, 1996). ... Signed as free agent by Phoenix Coyotes (September 5, 1997).
HONORS: Named to Memorial Cup All-Star team (1990-91).

Season Team	League	REGULAR SEASON								PLAYOFFS				
		Gms.	G	A	Pts.	PIM	+/-	PP	SH	Gms.	G	A	Pts.	PIM
87-88—Owen Sound Jr. B	OHA	40	19	25	44	68	...	...	...	—	—	—	—	—
88-89—Sault Ste. Marie	OHL	50	4	11	15	31	...	...	...	—	—	—	—	—
89-90—Sault Ste. Marie	OHL	66	9	32	41	47	...	...	...	—	—	—	—	—
90-91—Sault Ste. Marie	OHL	66	11	55	66	29	...	...	...	—	—	—	—	—
91-92—Maine	AHL	62	7	22	29	36	...	...	...	—	—	—	—	—
92-93—Binghamton	AHL	26	6	10	16	19	...	...	...	8	0	1	1	2
—Phoenix	IHL	46	11	27	38	35	...	...	...	—	—	—	—	—
93-94—Binghamton	AHL	29	6	10	16	6	...	...	...	—	—	—	—	—
—Phoenix	IHL	35	8	15	23	21	...	...	...	—	—	—	—	—
94-95—Detroit	IHL	56	7	19	26	32	...	...	...	—	—	—	—	—
—Fort Wayne	IHL	14	1	6	7	2	...	...	...	3	1	2	3	0
95-96—Orlando	IHL	69	11	23	34	82	...	...	...	23	2	4	6	16
96-97—Phoenix	IHL	66	8	28	36	34	...	...	...	—	—	—	—	—
—Long Beach	IHL	3	1	0	1	2	...	...	...	—	—	—	—	—
97-98—Springfield	AHL	60	10	31	41	36	...	...	...	4	0	4	4	2
—Phoenix	NHL	1	0	0	0	0	1	0	0	—	—	—	—	—
NHL Totals (1 year)		1	0	0	0	0	1	0	0					

TIMANDER, MATTIAS   D   BRUINS

PERSONAL: Born April 16, 1974, in Solleftea, Sweden. ... 6-3/210. ... Shoots left. ... Name pronounced tih-MAN-duhr.
TRANSACTIONS/CAREER NOTES: Selected by Boston Bruins in seventh round (seventh Bruins pick, 208th overall) of NHL entry draft (June 21, 1992). ... Injured shoulder (November 26, 1996); missed four games. ... Injured finger (November 17, 1997); missed two games.

Season Team	League	REGULAR SEASON								PLAYOFFS				
		Gms.	G	A	Pts.	PIM	+/-	PP	SH	Gms.	G	A	Pts.	PIM
92-93—MoDo Ornskoldvik	Sweden	1	0	0	0	0	...	...	...	—	—	—	—	—
93-94—MoDo Ornskoldvik	Sweden	23	2	2	4	6	...	...	...	11	2	0	2	10
94-95—MoDo Ornskoldvik	Sweden	39	8	9	17	24	...	...	...	—	—	—	—	—
95-96—MoDo Ornskoldvik	Sweden	37	4	10	14	34	...	...	...	7	1	1	2	8
96-97—Boston	NHL	41	1	8	9	14	-9	0	0	—	—	—	—	—
—Providence	AHL	32	3	11	14	20	...	...	...	10	1	1	2	12
97-98—Boston	NHL	23	1	1	2	6	-9	0	0	—	—	—	—	—
—Providence	AHL	31	3	7	10	25	...	...	...	—	—	—	—	—
NHL Totals (2 years)		64	2	9	11	20	-18	0	0					

TIMKIN, ALEXEI — RW — STARS

PERSONAL: Born April 21, 1979, in Kirov, U.S.S.R. ... 6-2/194. ... Shoots left.
TRANSACTIONS/CAREER NOTES: Selected by Dallas Stars in sixth round (sixth Stars pick, 160th overall) of NHL entry draft (June 21, 1997).

Season Team	League	REGULAR SEASON								PLAYOFFS				
		Gms.	G	A	Pts.	PIM	+/-	PP	SH	Gms.	G	A	Pts.	PIM
95-96—Torpedo-2 Yaroslavl....	CIS Div. II	20	2	2	4	10	...	...	...	—	—	—	—	—
96-97—Torpedo-2 Yaroslav.....	Rus. Div. III	47	16	6	22	54	...	...	...	—	—	—	—	—
—Torpedo Yaroslavl	Russian	3	0	1	1	0	...	...	...	—	—	—	—	—
97-98—Torpedo Yaroslavl	Russian	16	4	5	9	14	...	...	...	—	—	—	—	—

TIMOFEYEV, DENIS — D — BRUINS

PERSONAL: Born January 14, 1979, in Moscow, U.S.S.R. ... 6-5/198. ... Shoots left.
TRANSACTIONS/CAREER NOTES: Selected by Boston Bruins in sixth round (seventh Bruins pick, 135th overall) of NHL entry draft (June 21, 1997).

Season Team	League	REGULAR SEASON								PLAYOFFS				
		Gms.	G	A	Pts.	PIM	+/-	PP	SH	Gms.	G	A	Pts.	PIM
96-97—CSKA Jrs.	Russia	41	6	8	14		...	...	...	—	—	—	—	—
—CSKA-2 Moscow.........	Rus. Div. III	11	0	0	0	2	...	...	...	—	—	—	—	—
97-98—						Statistics unavailable.								

TINORDI, MARK — D — CAPITALS

PERSONAL: Born May 9, 1966, in Red Deer, Alta. ... 6-4/218. ... Shoots left. ... Name pronounced tuh-NOHR-dee.
TRANSACTIONS/CAREER NOTES: Signed as free agent by New York Rangers (January 4, 1987). ... Suffered abdominal pains (January 1988). ... Underwent left knee surgery (October 6, 1988). ... Traded by Rangers with D Paul Jerrard, C Mike Sullivan, RW Brett Barnett and third-round pick (C Murray Garbutt) in 1989 draft to Minnesota North Stars for LW Igor Liba, C Brian Lawton and rights to LW Eric Bennett (October 11, 1988). ... Bruised ribs (December 1988). ... Underwent knee surgery (April 1989). ... Suspended four games by NHL for cross-checking in a preseason game (September 27, 1989). ... Bruised shoulder (December 1989). ... Fined $500 by NHL for fighting (December 28, 1989). ... Suffered concussion (January 17, 1990); missed six games. ... Suspended 10 games by NHL for leaving penalty box to fight during a pre-season game (September 26, 1990). ... Suffered from foot palsy (October 15, 1991); missed 17 games. ... Sprained knee (January 19, 1993); missed four games. ... Broke collarbone (March 16, 1993); missed remainder of season. ... North Stars franchise moved from Minnesota to Dallas and renamed Stars for 1993-94 season. ... Suffered from the flu (December 27, 1993); missed one game. ... Fractured femur (February 23, 1994); missed 22 games. ... Traded by Stars with rights to D Rick Mrozik to Washington Capitals for D Kevin Hatcher (January 18, 1995). ... Bruised ribs (February 24, 1995); missed two games. ... Sprained knee (April 24, 1995); missed last four games of season. ... Suffered concussion (February 8, 1996); missed three games. ... Suffered concussion (February 15, 1996); missed eight games. ... Suffered from the flu (November 27, 1996); missed one game. ... Fractured ankle (January 9, 1997); missed 20 games. ... Strained hip (March 18, 1997); missed five games. ... Injured knee (October 31, 1997); missed three games. ... Strained abdomen (January 15, 1998); missed 32 games.
HONORS: Named to WHL (East) All-Star first team (1986-87). ... Played in NHL All-Star Game (1992).
MISCELLANEOUS: Captain of Minnesota North Stars (1991-92 and 1992-93). ... Captain of Dallas Stars (1993-94).

Season Team	League	REGULAR SEASON								PLAYOFFS				
		Gms.	G	A	Pts.	PIM	+/-	PP	SH	Gms.	G	A	Pts.	PIM
82-83—Lethbridge	WHL	64	0	4	4	50	...	...	...	20	1	1	2	6
83-84—Lethbridge	WHL	72	5	14	19	53	...	...	...	5	0	1	1	7
84-85—Lethbridge	WHL	58	10	15	25	134	...	...	...	4	0	2	2	12
85-86—Lethbridge	WHL	58	8	30	38	139	...	...	...	8	1	3	4	15
86-87—Calgary	WHL	61	29	37	66	148	...	...	...	—	—	—	—	—
—New Haven	AHL	2	0	0	0	2	...	...	...	2	0	0	0	0
87-88—New York Rangers	NHL	24	1	2	3	50	-5	0	0	—	—	—	—	—
—Colorado	IHL	41	8	19	27	150	...	...	...	11	1	5	6	31
88-89—Minnesota....................	NHL	47	2	3	5	107	-9	0	0	5	0	0	0	0
—Kalamazoo	IHL	10	0	0	0	35	...	...	...	—	—	—	—	—
89-90—Minnesota....................	NHL	66	3	7	10	240	0	1	0	7	0	1	1	16
90-91—Minnesota....................	NHL	69	5	27	32	189	1	1	0	23	5	6	11	78
91-92—Minnesota....................	NHL	63	4	24	28	179	-13	4	0	7	1	2	3	11
92-93—Minnesota....................	NHL	69	15	27	42	157	-1	7	0	—	—	—	—	—
93-94—Dallas...........................	NHL	61	6	18	24	143	6	1	0	—	—	—	—	—
94-95—Washington	NHL	42	3	9	12	71	-5	2	0	1	0	0	0	2
95-96—Washington	NHL	71	3	10	13	113	26	2	0	6	0	0	0	16
96-97—Washington	NHL	56	2	6	8	118	3	0	0	—	—	—	—	—
97-98—Washington	NHL	47	8	9	17	39	9	0	1	21	1	2	3	42
NHL Totals (11 years).........		615	52	142	194	1406	12	18	1	70	7	11	18	165

TITOV, GERMAN — C — PENGUINS

PERSONAL: Born October 16, 1965, in Borovsk, U.S.S.R. ... 6-1/190. ... Shoots left. ... Name pronounced GAIR-muhn TEE-tahf.
TRANSACTIONS/CAREER NOTES: Selected by Calgary Flames in 10th round (10th Flames pick, 252nd overall) of NHL entry draft (June 26, 1993). ... Fractured nose (December 31, 1993); missed four games. ... Bruised hand (February 18, 1994); missed two games. ... Bruised hand (April 2, 1994); missed one game. ... Played in Europe during 1994-95 NHL lockout. ... Pulled groin (March 28, 1995); missed eight games. ... Sore lower back (October 13, 1996); missed one game. ... Injured ankle (January 22, 1997); missed one game. ... Reinjured ankle (March 7, 1997); missed one game. ... Bruised hand (March 11, 1998); missed two games. ... Injured knee (April 7, 1998); missed remainder of season. ... Traded by Flames with C Todd Hlushko to Pittsburgh Penguins for G Ken Wregget and LW Dave Roche (June 17, 1998).
MISCELLANEOUS: Member of silver-medal-winning Russian Olympic team (1998).
STATISTICAL PLATEAUS: Three-goal games: 1994-95 (1), 1996-97 (1). Total: 2.

Season Team	League	REGULAR SEASON								PLAYOFFS				
		Gms.	G	A	Pts.	PIM	+/-	PP	SH	Gms.	G	A	Pts.	PIM
82-83—Khimik	USSR	16	0	2	2	4	...			—	—	—	—	—
83-84—Khimik	USSR							Did not play.						
84-85—Khimik	USSR							Did not play.						
85-86—Khimik	USSR							Did not play.						
86-87—Khimik	USSR	23	1	0	1	10	...	...	...	—	—	—	—	—
87-88—Khimik	USSR	39	6	5	11	10	...	...	...	—	—	—	—	—
88-89—Khimik	USSR	44	10	3	13	24	...	...	...	—	—	—	—	—
89-90—Khimik	USSR	44	6	14	20	19	...	...	...	—	—	—	—	—
90-91—Khimik	USSR	45	13	11	24	28	...	...	...	—	—	—	—	—
91-92—Khimik	CIS	42	18	13	31	35	...	...	...	—	—	—	—	—
92-93—TPS Turku	Finland	47	25	19	44	49	...	...	...	—	—	—	—	—
93-94—Calgary	NHL	76	27	18	45	28	20	8	3	7	2	1	3	4
94-95—TPS Turku	Finland	14	6	6	12	20	...	...	...	—	—	—	—	—
—Calgary	NHL	40	12	12	24	16	6	3	2	7	5	3	8	10
95-96—Calgary	NHL	82	28	39	67	24	9	13	2	4	0	2	2	0
96-97—Calgary	NHL	79	22	30	52	36	-12	12	0	—	—	—	—	—
97-98—Calgary	NHL	68	18	22	40	38	-1	6	1	—	—	—	—	—
—Russian Oly. team	Int'l	6	1	0	1	6	...	...	...	—	—	—	—	—
NHL Totals (5 years)		345	107	121	228	142	22	42	8	18	7	6	13	14

TJARNQVIST, DANIEL D PANTHERS

PERSONAL: Born October 14, 1976, in Umea, Sweden. ... 6-2/176. ... Shoots left. ... Name pronounced TAHRN-kuh-vihst.
TRANSACTIONS/CAREER NOTES: Selected by Florida Panthers in fourth round (fifth Panthers pick, 88th overall) of NHL draft (July 8, 1995).

Season Team	League	REGULAR SEASON								PLAYOFFS				
		Gms.	G	A	Pts.	PIM	+/-	PP	SH	Gms.	G	A	Pts.	PIM
94-95—Rogle Angelholm	Sweden	33	2	4	6	2	...	...	...	—	—	—	—	—
95-96—Rogle Angelholm	Sweden	22	1	7	8	6	...	...	...	—	—	—	—	—
96-97—Jokerit Helsinki	Finland	44	3	8	11	4	...	...	...	9	0	3	3	4
97-98—Djur. Stockholm	Sweden	40	5	9	14	12	...	...	...	15	1	1	2	2

TKACHUK, KEITH LW COYOTES

PERSONAL: Born March 28, 1972, in Melrose, Mass. ... 6-2/220. ... Shoots left. ... Full name: Keith Matthew Tkachuk. ... Name pronounced kuh-CHUHK.
HIGH SCHOOL: Malden (Mass.) Catholic.
COLLEGE: Boston University.
TRANSACTIONS/CAREER NOTES: Selected by Winnipeg Jets in first round (first Jets pick, 19th overall) of NHL entry draft (June 16, 1990). ... Lacerated forearm (November 12, 1993); missed one game. ... Strained groin (October 9, 1995); missed three games. ... Suffered concussion (November 26, 1995); missed one game. ... Suspended two games and fined $1,000 by NHL for stick-swinging incident (March 16, 1996). ... Jets franchise moved to Phoenix and renamed Coyotes for 1996-97 season; NHL approved move on January 18, 1996. ... Suffered from the flu (March 5, 1997); missed one game. ... Injured groin (March 2, 1998); missed two games. ... Suffered hairline fracture of rib (March 12, 1998); missed seven games.
HONORS: Named to Hockey East All-Rookie team (1990-91). ... Named to NHL All-Star second team (1994-95 and 1997-98). ... Named to THE SPORTING NEWS All-Star first team (1995-96). ... Played in NHL All-Star Game (1997 and 1998).
MISCELLANEOUS: Captain of Winnipeg Jets (1993-94 and 1994-95). ... Captain of Phoenix Coyotes (1996-97 and 1997-98). ... Failed to score on a penalty shot (vs. Bob Essensa, January 24, 1998).
STATISTICAL PLATEAUS: Three-goal games: 1993-94 (1), 1996-97 (1), 1997-98 (3). Total: 5. ... Four-goal games: 1995-96 (1), 1996-97 (1). Total: 2. ... Total hat tricks: 7.

Season Team	League	REGULAR SEASON								PLAYOFFS				
		Gms.	G	A	Pts.	PIM	+/-	PP	SH	Gms.	G	A	Pts.	PIM
88-89—Malden Catholic H.S.	Mass. H.S.	21	30	16	46	...	...	...	...	—	—	—	—	—
89-90—Malden Catholic H.S.	Mass. H.S.	6	12	14	26	...	...	...	...	—	—	—	—	—
90-91—Boston University	Hockey East	36	17	23	40	70	...	...	...	—	—	—	—	—
91-92—U.S. national team	Int'l	45	10	10	20	141	...	...	...	—	—	—	—	—
—U.S. Olympic Team	Int'l	8	1	1	2	12	...	...	...	—	—	—	—	—
—Winnipeg	NHL	17	3	5	8	28	0	2	0	7	3	0	3	30
92-93—Winnipeg	NHL	83	28	23	51	201	-13	12	0	6	4	0	4	14
93-94—Winnipeg	NHL	84	41	40	81	255	-12	22	3	—	—	—	—	—
94-95—Winnipeg	NHL	48	22	29	51	152	-4	7	2	—	—	—	—	—
95-96—Winnipeg	NHL	76	50	48	98	156	11	20	2	6	1	2	3	22
96-97—Phoenix	NHL	81	*52	34	86	228	-1	9	2	7	6	0	6	7
97-98—Phoenix	NHL	69	40	26	66	147	9	11	0	6	3	3	6	10
—U.S. Olympic Team	Int'l	4	0	2	2	6	...	...	...	—	—	—	—	—
NHL Totals (7 years)		458	236	205	441	1167	-10	83	9	32	17	5	22	83

TKACZUK, DANIEL C FLAMES

PERSONAL: Born June 10, 1979, in Toronto. ... 6-0/190. ... Shoots left. ... Name pronounced kuh-CHOOK.
TRANSACTIONS/CAREER NOTES: Selected by Calgary Flames in first round (first Flames pick, sixth overall) of NHL entry draft (June 21, 1997).

Season Team	League	REGULAR SEASON								PLAYOFFS				
		Gms.	G	A	Pts.	PIM	+/-	PP	SH	Gms.	G	A	Pts.	PIM
95-96—Barrie	OHL	61	22	39	61	38	...	...	...	7	1	2	3	8
96-97—Barrie	OHL	62	45	48	93	49	...	...	...	9	7	2	9	2
97-98—Barrie	OHL	57	35	40	75	38	...	...	...	6	2	3	5	8

PERSONAL: Born April 9, 1964, in Scarborough, Ont. ... 6-0/214. ... Shoots right. ... Name pronounced TAH-kiht.

TRANSACTIONS/CAREER NOTES: Selected by Philadelphia Flyers as underage junior in sixth round (fifth Flyers pick, 121st overall) of NHL entry draft (June 8, 1983). ... Bruised right knee (November 23, 1985); missed seven games. ... Separated left shoulder (February 1988). ... Suspended 10 games by NHL for injuring an opposing player during a fight (October 27, 1988). ... Hyperextended right knee (April 21, 1989). ... Suffered viral infection (November 1989). ... Tore tendon in left groin area (January 26, 1991); missed five games. ... Reinjured groin (March 1991); missed five games. ... Sprained knee (November 29, 1991); missed five games. ... Bruised heel (January 18, 1991); missed 10 games. ... Traded by Flyers with G Ken Wregget, D Kjell Samuelsson and third-round pick in 1992 draft to Pittsburgh Penguins for RW Mark Recchi, D Brian Benning and first-round pick (LW Jason Bowen) in 1992 draft (February 19, 1992). ... Fractured jaw (March 15, 1992); missed three games. ... Bruised left foot (October 10, 1992); missed two games. ... Bruised foot (February 8, 1993); missed one game. ... Bruised ribs (November 13, 1993); missed two games. ... Suffered back spasms (December 2, 1993); missed two games. ... Suffered back spasms (December 31, 1993); missed 12 games. ... Injured back (February 21, 1994); missed one game. ... Injured back (February 28, 1994); missed 10 games. ... Underwent back surgery (June 8, 1994). ... Traded by Penguins with second-round pick (RW Pavel Rosa) in 1995 draft to Los Angeles Kings for LW Luc Robitaille (July 29, 1994). ... Strained lower back (April 1, 1995); missed four games. ... Suffered back spasms (April 17, 1995); missed six games. ... Suffered back spasms (May 3, 1995); missed one game. ... Traded by Kings to Boston Bruins for LW Kevin Stevens (July 29, 1994). ... Bruised shoulder (November 7, 1996); missed two games. ... Strained knee (November 29, 1996); missed 17 games. ... Traded by Bruins with C Adam Oates and G Bill Ranford to Washington Capitals for G Jim Carey, C Jason Allison, C Anson Carter and third-round pick (RW Lee Goren) in 1997 draft (March 1, 1997). ... Bruised foot (March 1, 1997); missed three games. ... Strained back (April 6, 1997); missed four games. ... Signed as free agent by Phoenix Coyotes (July 8, 1997). ... Jammed thumb (October 13, 1997); missed four games. ... Suspended two games and fined $1,000 by NHL for injuring another player (January 23, 1998). ... Suspended five games by NHL for illegal check (January 30, 1998). ... Suspended two games and fined $1,000 by NHL for high-sticking incident (April 14, 1998).

HONORS: Played in NHL All-Star Game (1989-1991 and 1993).

RECORDS: Shares NHL All-Star Game record for fastest goal from start of period—19 seconds (1993, second period).

STATISTICAL PLATEAUS: Three-goal games: 1987-88 (2), 1988-89 (2), 1989-90 (1), 1990-91 (1), 1991-92 (1), 1992-93 (2), 1994-95 (1), 1995-96 (2). Total: 12. ... Four-goal games: 1987-88 (1), 1989-90 (1). Total: 2. ... Total hat tricks: 14.

MISCELLANEOUS: Member of Stanley Cup championship team (1992). ... Captain of Philadelphia Flyers (1991-92). ... Holds Philadelphia Flyers all-time record for most penalty minutes (1,683). ... Failed to score on a penalty shot (vs. Craig Billington, January 6, 1987; vs. Geoff Sarjeant, March 18, 1996).

Season Team	League	Gms.	G	A	Pts.	PIM	+/-	PP	SH	Gms.	G	A	Pts.	PIM
81-82—Sault Ste. Marie	OHL	59	7	15	22	184	...	...	...	11	1	1	2	28
82-83—Sault Ste. Marie	OHL	66	32	34	66	146	...	...	...	16	4	13	17	*67
83-84—Sault Ste. Marie	OHL	64	44	64	108	209	...	...	...	16	*22	14	†36	41
84-85—Philadelphia	NHL	75	14	25	39	181	6	0	0	19	3	4	7	72
85-86—Philadelphia	NHL	69	14	21	35	284	12	3	0	5	1	2	3	26
86-87—Philadelphia	NHL	69	21	26	47	286	16	1	1	26	11	10	21	72
87-88—Philadelphia	NHL	65	31	33	64	301	3	10	2	5	1	4	5	55
88-89—Philadelphia	NHL	66	45	36	81	183	-1	16	1	16	6	6	12	69
89-90—Philadelphia	NHL	75	37	59	96	196	4	15	1	—	—	—	—	—
90-91—Philadelphia	NHL	70	40	31	71	150	2	8	0	—	—	—	—	—
91-92—Philadelphia	NHL	42	13	16	29	102	3	4	0	—	—	—	—	—
—Pittsburgh	NHL	19	14	16	30	49	12	4	1	14	6	13	19	24
92-93—Pittsburgh	NHL	80	48	61	109	252	28	20	4	12	7	6	13	24
93-94—Pittsburgh	NHL	51	14	26	40	134	-15	5	1	6	2	3	5	20
94-95—Los Angeles	NHL	36	18	17	35	70	-8	7	1	—	—	—	—	—
95-96—Los Angeles	NHL	44	13	23	36	117	3	4	0	—	—	—	—	—
—Boston	NHL	27	16	8	24	64	7	6	0	5	4	0	4	21
96-97—Boston	NHL	40	16	14	30	67	-3	3	0	—	—	—	—	—
—Washington	NHL	13	5	5	10	31	0	1	0	—	—	—	—	—
97-98—Phoenix	NHL	68	26	19	45	157	1	8	0	6	6	2	8	25
NHL Totals (14 years)		909	385	436	821	2624	70	115	12	114	47	50	97	408

PERSONAL: Born May 4, 1968, in Winnipeg. ... 5-10/180. ... Shoots left. ... Full name: Kevin Lee Todd.

HIGH SCHOOL: Tec Voc (Winnipeg).

TRANSACTIONS/CAREER NOTES: Selected by New Jersey Devils as underage junior in seventh round (seventh Devils pick, 129th overall) of NHL entry draft (June 21, 1986). ... Injured thigh (October 31, 1992); missed one game. ... Reinjured thigh (November 13, 1992); missed three games. ... Bruised shoulder (December 15, 1992); missed five games. ... Traded by Devils with LW Zdeno Ciger to Edmonton Oilers for C Bernie Nicholls (January 13, 1993). ... Separated left shoulder (March 14, 1993); missed remainder of season. ... Traded by Oilers to Chicago Blackhawks for D Adam Bennett (October 7, 1993). ... Injured knee (November 18, 1993); missed 12 games. ... Traded by Blackhawks to Los Angeles Kings for fourth-round pick (D Steve McLaren) in 1994 draft (March 21, 1994). ... Tore cartilage in knee (March 9, 1995); missed 15 games. ... Sprained left ankle (January 22, 1996); missed two games. ... Injured back (April 3, 1996); missed two games. ... Signed as free agent by Pittsburgh Penguins (July 10, 1996). ... Claimed on waivers by Mighty Ducks of Anaheim (October 4, 1996). ... Suffered tendinitis in elbow (January 31, 1997); missed seven games.

HONORS: Won Les Cunningham Plaque (1990-91). ... Won John B. Sollenberger Trophy (1990-91). ... Named to AHL All-Star first team (1990-91). ... Named to NHL All-Rookie team (1991-92).

Season Team	League	Gms.	G	A	Pts.	PIM	+/-	PP	SH	Gms.	G	A	Pts.	PIM
85-86—Prince Albert	WHL	55	14	25	39	19	...	...	...	20	7	6	13	29
86-87—Prince Albert	WHL	71	39	46	85	92	...	...	...	8	2	5	7	17
87-88—Prince Albert	WHL	72	49	72	121	83	...	...	...	10	8	11	19	27
88-89—New Jersey	NHL	1	0	0	0	0	-1	0	0	—	—	—	—	—
—Utica	AHL	78	26	45	71	62	...	...	...	4	2	0	2	6
89-90—Utica	AHL	71	18	36	54	72	...	...	...	5	2	4	6	2
90-91—Utica	AHL	75	37	*81	*118	75	...	...	...	—	—	—	—	—
—New Jersey	NHL	1	0	0	0	0	-1	0	0	1	0	0	0	6

Season Team	League	REGULAR SEASON Gms.	G	A	Pts.	PIM	+/-	PP	SH	PLAYOFFS Gms.	G	A	Pts.	PIM
91-92—New Jersey	NHL	80	21	42	63	69	8	2	0	7	3	2	5	8
92-93—New Jersey	NHL	30	5	5	10	16	-4	0	0	—	—	—	—	—
—Utica	AHL	2	2	1	3	0	...	...	...	—	—	—	—	—
—Edmonton	NHL	25	4	9	13	10	-5	0	0	—	—	—	—	—
93-94—Chicago	NHL	35	5	6	11	16	-2	1	0	—	—	—	—	—
—Los Angeles	NHL	12	3	8	11	8	-1	3	0	—	—	—	—	—
94-95—Los Angeles	NHL	33	3	8	11	12	-5	0	0	—	—	—	—	—
95-96—Los Angeles	NHL	74	16	27	43	38	6	0	2	—	—	—	—	—
96-97—Anaheim	NHL	65	9	21	30	44	-7	0	0	4	0	0	0	2
97-98—Anaheim	NHL	27	4	7	11	12	-5	3	0	—	—	—	—	—
—Long Beach	IHL	30	18	28	46	54	...	...	...	13	1	10	11	38
NHL Totals (9 years)		383	70	133	203	225	-17	9	2	12	3	2	5	16

TOMS, JEFF LW CAPITALS

PERSONAL: Born June 4, 1974, in Swift Current, Sask. ... 6-5/200. ... Shoots left.
TRANSACTIONS/CAREER NOTES: Selected by New Jersey Devils in ninth round (10th Devils pick, 210th overall) of NHL entry draft (June 26, 1993). ... Traded by Devils to Tampa Bay Lightning for fourth-round pick (traded to Calgary) in 1994 draft (May 31, 1994). ... Claimed on waivers by Washington Capitals (November 19, 1997). ... Injured knee (December 12, 1997); missed 11 games.

Season Team	League	REGULAR SEASON Gms.	G	A	Pts.	PIM	+/-	PP	SH	PLAYOFFS Gms.	G	A	Pts.	PIM
91-92—Sault Ste. Marie	OHL	36	9	5	14	0	...	...	...	16	0	1	1	2
92-93—Sault Ste. Marie	OHL	59	16	23	39	20	...	...	...	16	4	4	8	7
93-94—Sault Ste. Marie	OHL	64	52	45	97	19	...	...	...	14	11	4	15	2
94-95—Atlanta	IHL	40	7	8	15	10	...	...	...	4	0	0	0	4
95-96—Atlanta	IHL	68	16	18	34	18	...	...	...	1	0	0	0	0
—Tampa Bay	NHL	1	0	0	0	0	0	0	0	—	—	—	—	—
96-97—Adirondack	AHL	37	11	16	27	8	...	...	...	4	1	2	3	0
—Tampa Bay	NHL	34	2	8	10	10	2	0	0	—	—	—	—	—
97-98—Tampa Bay	NHL	13	1	2	3	7	-6	0	0	—	—	—	—	—
—Washington	NHL	33	3	4	7	8	-11	0	0	1	0	0	0	0
NHL Totals (3 years)		81	6	14	20	25	-15	0	0	1	0	0	0	0

TOPOROWSKI, SHAYNE RW BLUES

PERSONAL: Born August 6, 1975, in Prince Albert, Sask. ... 6-2/216. ... Shoots right. ... Name pronounced toh-poh-ROW-skee.
HIGH SCHOOL: Carlton Comprehensive (Paddockwood, Sask.).
TRANSACTIONS/CAREER NOTES: Selected by Los Angeles Kings in second round (first Kings pick, 42nd overall) of NHL entry draft (June 26, 1993). ... Traded by Kings with RW Dixon Ward, C Guy Leveque and C Kelly Fairchild to Toronto Maple Leafs for LW Eric Lacroix, D Chris Snell and fourth-round pick (C Eric Belanger) in 1996 draft (October 3, 1994). ... Signed as free agent by St. Louis Blues (August 29, 1997).

Season Team	League	REGULAR SEASON Gms.	G	A	Pts.	PIM	+/-	PP	SH	PLAYOFFS Gms.	G	A	Pts.	PIM
91-92—Prince Albert	WHL	6	2	0	2	2	...	...	...	7	2	1	3	6
92-93—Prince Albert	WHL	72	25	32	57	235	...	...	...	—	—	—	—	—
93-94—Prince Albert	WHL	68	37	45	82	183	...	...	...	—	—	—	—	—
94-95—Prince Albert	WHL	72	36	38	74	151	...	...	...	15	10	8	18	25
95-96—St. John's	AHL	72	11	26	37	216	...	...	...	4	1	1	2	4
96-97—St. John's	AHL	72	20	17	37	210	...	...	...	11	3	2	5	16
—Toronto	NHL	3	0	0	0	7	0	0	0	—	—	—	—	—
97-98—Worcester	AHL	73	9	21	30	128	...	...	...	11	5	3	8	44
NHL Totals (1 year)		3	0	0	0	7	0	0	0	—	—	—	—	—

TOSKALA, VESA G SHARKS

PERSONAL: Born May 20, 1977, in Tampere, Finland. ... 5-9/172. ... Catches left.
TRANSACTIONS/CAREER NOTES: Selected by San Jose Sharks in fourth round (fourth Sharks pick, 90th overall) of NHL entry draft (July 8, 1995).

Season Team	League	REGULAR SEASON Gms.	Min	W	L	T	GA	SO	Avg.	PLAYOFFS Gms.	Min.	W	L	GA	SO	Avg.
93-94—Ilves Jrs.	Finland	2	...	...	...	...	...	...	...	—	—	—	—	—	—	—
94-95—Ilves Jrs.	Finland	17	956	...	...	...	36	...	2.26	—	—	—	—	—	—	—
95-96—Ilves Tampere	Finland	37	2073	...	...	...	109	1	3.15	2	78	...	...	11	0	8.46
—Koo Vee	Finland	2	119	...	...	...	5	...	2.52	—	—	—	—	—	—	—
—Ilves Jrs.	Finland	3	180	...	...	...	3	...	1.00	—	—	—	—	—	—	—
96-97—Ilves Tampere	Finland	40	22	12	5	2270	108	0	2.85	8	3	5	479	29	0	3.63
97-98—Ilves Tampere	Finland	48	26	13	3	2555	118	1	2.77	9	6	3	519	18	1	2.08

TREBIL, DAN D MIGHTY DUCKS

PERSONAL: Born April 10, 1974, in Bloomington, Minn. ... 6-3/210. ... Shoots right. ... Full name: Daniel Trebil. ... Name pronounced TREH-buhl.
HIGH SCHOOL: Thomas Jefferson (Bloomington, Minn.).
COLLEGE: Minnesota.
TRANSACTIONS/CAREER NOTES: Selected by New Jersey Devils in sixth round (seventh Devils pick, 138th overall) of NHL entry draft (June 20, 1992). ... Signed as free agent by Mighty Ducks of Anaheim (May 30, 1996).
HONORS: Named to NCAA All-America West second team (1995-96). ... Named to WCHA All-Star second team (1995-96).

Season Team	League	REGULAR SEASON Gms.	G	A	Pts.	PIM	+/-	PP	SH	PLAYOFFS Gms.	G	A	Pts.	PIM
89-90—Thomas Jefferson......	Minn. H.S.	22	3	6	9	10	...	...	...	—	—	—	—	—
90-91—Thomas Jefferson......	Minn. H.S.	23	4	12	16	8	...	...	...	—	—	—	—	—
91-92—Thomas Jefferson......	Minn. H.S.	28	7	26	33	6	...	...	...	—	—	—	—	—
92-93—Univ. of Minnesota.....	WCHA	36	2	11	13	16	...	...	...	—	—	—	—	—
93-94—Univ. of Minnesota.....	WCHA	42	1	21	22	24	...	...	...	—	—	—	—	—
94-95—Univ. of Minnesota.....	WCHA	44	10	33	43	10	...	...	...	—	—	—	—	—
95-96—Univ. of Minnesota.....	WCHA	42	11	35	46	36	...	...	...	—	—	—	—	—
96-97—Baltimore	AHL	49	4	20	24	38	...	...	...	—	—	—	—	—
—Anaheim	NHL	29	3	3	6	23	5	0	0	9	0	1	1	6
97-98—Anaheim	NHL	21	0	1	1	2	-8	0	0	—	—	—	—	—
—Cincinnati..................	AHL	32	5	15	20	21	...	...	...	—	—	—	—	—
NHL Totals (2 years)...........		**50**	**3**	**4**	**7**	**25**	**-3**	**0**	**0**	**9**	**0**	**1**	**1**	**6**

TREFILOV, ANDREI   G   BLACKHAWKS

PERSONAL: Born August 31, 1969, in Moscow, U.S.S.R. ... 6-0/190. ... Catches left. ... Name pronounced AHN-dray TREH-fih-lahf.
TRANSACTIONS/CAREER NOTES: Selected by Calgary Flames in 12th round (14th Flames pick, 261st overall) of NHL entry draft (June 22, 1991). ... Twisted right knee ligament (February 2, 1994); missed 23 games. ... Signed as free agent by Buffalo Sabres (July 13, 1995). ... Sprained right knee (December 23, 1995); missed 18 games. ... Suffered labrum tear in right shoulder (December 18, 1996); underwent arthroscopic surgery (December 21, 1996); missed remainder of regular season. ... Traded by Sabres to Chicago Blackhawks for conditional draft pick (November 12, 1997).
MISCELLANEOUS: Member of gold-medal-winning Unified Olympic team (1992). ... Stopped a penalty shot attempt (vs. Jeremy Roenick, March 7, 1995; vs. Mats Sundin, January 10, 1998). ... Member of silver-medal-winning Russian Olympic team (1998).

Season Team	League	REGULAR SEASON Gms.	Min	W	L	T	GA	SO	Avg.	PLAYOFFS Gms.	Min.	W	L	GA	SO	Avg.
90-91—Dynamo Moscow..........	USSR	20	1070	...	...	...	36	0	2.02	—	—	—	—	—	—	—
91-92—Dynamo Moscow..........	CIS	28	1326	...	...	...	35	0	1.58	—	—	—	—	—	—	—
—Unif. Olympic Team.......	Int'l	4	38	...	...	...	2	2	3.16	—	—	—	—	—	—	—
92-93—Salt Lake City	IHL	44	2536	23	17	‡0	135	0	3.19	—	—	—	—	—	—	—
—Calgary	NHL	1	65	0	0	1	5	0	4.62	—	—	—	—	—	—	—
93-94—Calgary	NHL	11	623	3	4	2	26	2	2.50	—	—	—	—	—	—	—
—Saint John	AHL	28	1629	10	10	7	93	0	3.43	—	—	—	—	—	—	—
94-95—Saint John	AHL	7	383	1	5	1	20	0	3.13	—	—	—	—	—	—	—
—Calgary	NHL	6	236	0	3	0	16	0	4.07	—	—	—	—	—	—	—
95-96—Buffalo	NHL	22	1094	8	8	1	64	0	3.51	—	—	—	—	—	—	—
—Rochester.................	AHL	5	299	4	1	0	13	0	2.61	—	—	—	—	—	—	—
96-97—Buffalo	NHL	3	159	0	2	0	10	0	3.77	1	5	0	0	0	0	...
97-98—Rochester.................	AHL	3	139	1	0	1	6	0	2.59	—	—	—	—	—	—	—
—Chicago	NHL	6	299	1	4	0	17	0	3.41	—	—	—	—	—	—	—
—Russian Olympic team..	Int'l	2	69	1	0	0	4	0	3.48	—	—	—	—	—	—	—
—Indianapolis	IHL	1	59	0	1	‡0	3	0	3.05	—	—	—	—	—	—	—
NHL Totals (6 years).............		**49**	**2476**	**12**	**21**	**4**	**138**	**2**	**3.34**	**1**	**5**	**0**	**0**	**0**	**0**	...

TREMBLAY, DIDIER   D   BLUES

PERSONAL: Born May 4, 1979, in Laval, Que. ... 6-1/198. ... Shoots left.
TRANSACTIONS/CAREER NOTES: Selected by St. Louis Blues in fourth round (second Blues pick, 86th overall) of NHL entry draft (June 21, 1997).

Season Team	League	REGULAR SEASON Gms.	G	A	Pts.	PIM	+/-	PP	SH	PLAYOFFS Gms.	G	A	Pts.	PIM
95-96—Halifax........................	QMJHL	56	4	10	14	80	...	...	...	6	0	3	3	4
96-97—Halifax........................	QMJHL	68	11	26	37	79	...	...	...	12	1	2	3	6
97-98—Halifax........................	QMJHL	39	6	19	25	26	...	...	...	—	—	—	—	—
—Val-d'Or	QMJHL	31	6	24	30	43	...	...	...	19	5	13	18	8

TREMBLAY, YANNICK   D   MAPLE LEAFS

PERSONAL: Born November 15, 1975, in Pointe-aux-Trembles, Que. ... 6-2/185. ... Shoots right.
COLLEGE: St. Thomas (N.B.).
TRANSACTIONS/CAREER NOTES: Selected by Toronto Maple Leafs in sixth round (fourth Maple Leafs pick, 145th overall) of NHL entry draft (July 8, 1995).

Season Team	League	REGULAR SEASON Gms.	G	A	Pts.	PIM	+/-	PP	SH	PLAYOFFS Gms.	G	A	Pts.	PIM
93-94—St. Thomas Univ.	AUAA	25	2	3	5	10	...	...	...	—	—	—	—	—
94-95—Beauport	QMJHL	70	10	32	42	22	...	...	...	17	6	8	14	6
95-96—Beauport	QMJHL	61	12	33	45	42	...	...	...	20	3	16	19	18
—St. John's.................	AHL	3	0	1	1	0	...	...	...	—	—	—	—	—
96-97—Sherbrooke	QMJHL	42	21	25	46	212	...	...	...	—	—	—	—	—
—St. John's.................	AHL	67	7	25	32	34	...	...	...	11	2	9	11	0
—Toronto	NHL	5	0	0	0	0	-4	0	0	—	—	—	—	—
97-98—St. John's.................	AHL	17	3	6	9	4	...	...	...	4	0	1	1	5
—Toronto	NHL	38	2	4	6	6	-6	1	0	—	—	—	—	—
NHL Totals (2 years)...........		**43**	**2**	**4**	**6**	**6**	**-10**	**1**	**0**					

TREPANIER, PASCAL — D — AVALANCHE

PERSONAL: Born April 9, 1973, in Gaspe, Que. ... 6-0/205. ... Shoots right. ... Name pronounced TREH-puhn-yeh.
TRANSACTIONS/CAREER NOTES: Signed as free agent by Colorado Avalanche (August 30, 1996).
HONORS: Named to AHL All-Star second team (1996-97).

		REGULAR SEASON							PLAYOFFS				
Season Team	League	Gms.	G	A	Pts.	PIM	+/-	PP	SH	Gms.	G	A	Pts.	PIM
90-91—Hull	QMJHL	46	3	3	6	56	...	...	...	4	0	2	2	7
91-92—Trois-Rivieres	QMJHL	53	4	18	22	125	...	...	...	15	3	5	8	21
92-93—Sherbrooke	QMJHL	59	15	33	48	130	...	...	...	15	5	7	12	36
93-94—Sherbrooke	QMJHL	48	16	41	57	67	...	...	...	12	1	8	9	14
94-95—Cornwall	AHL	4	0	0	0	9	...	...	...	—	—	—	—	—
—Dayton	ECHL	36	16	28	44	113	...	...	...	—	—	—	—	—
—Kalamazoo	IHL	14	1	2	3	47	...	...	...	—	—	—	—	—
95-96—Cornwall	AHL	70	13	20	33	142	...	...	...	8	1	2	3	24
96-97—Hershey	AHL	73	14	39	53	151	...	...	...	23	6	13	19	59
97-98—Colorado	NHL	15	0	1	1	18	-2	0	0	—	—	—	—	—
—Hershey	AHL	43	13	18	31	105	...	...	...	7	4	2	6	8
NHL Totals (1 year)		15	0	1	1	18	-2	0	0					

TRIPP, JOHN — RW — FLAMES

PERSONAL: Born May 4, 1977, in Kingston, Ont. ... 6-2/208. ... Shoots right.
HIGH SCHOOL: Henry Street (Whitby, Ont.).
TRANSACTIONS/CAREER NOTES: Selected by Colorado Avalanche in third round (third Avalanche pick, 77th overall) of NHL entry draft (July 8, 1995). ... Returned to draft pool by Avalanche and selected by Calgary Flames in second round (third Flames pick, 42nd overall) of NHL entry draft (June 21, 1997).

		REGULAR SEASON							PLAYOFFS				
Season Team	League	Gms.	G	A	Pts.	PIM	+/-	PP	SH	Gms.	G	A	Pts.	PIM
93-94—St. Mary's Jr. B	OHA	42	15	29	44	116	...	...	...	—	—	—	—	—
94-95—Oshawa	OHL	58	6	11	17	53	...	...	...	7	0	1	1	4
95-96—Oshawa	OHL	56	13	14	27	95	...	...	...	5	1	1	2	13
96-97—Oshawa	OHL	59	28	20	48	126	...	...	...	18	16	10	26	42
97-98—Roanoke	ECHL	9	0	2	2	22	...	...	...	—	—	—	—	—
—Saint John	AHL	61	1	11	12	66	...	...	...	2	0	1	1	0

TRNKA, PAVEL — D — MIGHTY DUCKS

PERSONAL: Born July 27, 1976, in Plzen, Czechoslovakia. ... 6-3/200. ... Shoots left. ... Name pronounced TRIHN-kuh.
TRANSACTIONS/CAREER NOTES: Selected by Mighty Ducks of Anaheim in fifth round (fifth Mighty Ducks pick, 106th overall) of NHL entry draft (June 29, 1994). ... Suffered concussion (January 12, 1998); missed one game.

		REGULAR SEASON							PLAYOFFS				
Season Team	League	Gms.	G	A	Pts.	PIM	+/-	PP	SH	Gms.	G	A	Pts.	PIM
92-93—Skoda Plzen Jr.	Czech.								Statistics unavailable.					
93-94—Skoda Plzen	Czech Rep.	12	0	1	1	...	...	...	...	—	—	—	—	—
94-95—HC Kladno	Czech Rep.	28	0	5	5	...	...	...	...	—	—	—	—	—
—Skoda Plzen	Czech Rep.	6	0	0	0	...	...	...	...	6	0	0	0	...
95-96—Baltimore	AHL	69	2	6	8	44	...	...	...	6	0	0	0	2
96-97—Baltimore	AHL	69	6	14	20	86	...	...	...	3	0	0	0	2
97-98—Cincinnati	AHL	23	3	5	8	28	...	...	...	—	—	—	—	—
—Anaheim	NHL	48	3	4	7	40	-4	1	0	—	—	—	—	—
NHL Totals (1 year)		48	3	4	7	40	-4	1	0					

TSELIOS, NIKOS — D — HURRICANES

PERSONAL: Born January 20, 1979, in Oak Park, Ill. ... 6-4/187. ... Shoots left. ... Cousin of Chris Chelios, defenseman, Chicago Blackhawks. ... Name pronounced NEE-kohz CHEL-yoz.
TRANSACTIONS/CAREER NOTES: Selected by Carolina Hurricanes in first round (first Hurricanes pick, 22nd overall) of NHL entry draft (June 21, 1997).
HONORS: Named to Can.HL All-Rookie team (1996-97). ... Named to OHL All-Rookie first team (1996-97).

		REGULAR SEASON							PLAYOFFS				
Season Team	League	Gms.	G	A	Pts.	PIM	+/-	PP	SH	Gms.	G	A	Pts.	PIM
95-96—Chicago	MNHL	27	5	8	13	40	...	...	...	—	—	—	—	—
96-97—Belleville	OHL	64	9	37	46	61	...	...	...	—	—	—	—	—
97-98—Belleville	OHL	20	2	10	12	16	...	...	...	—	—	—	—	—
—Plymouth	OHL	41	8	20	28	27	...	...	...	15	1	8	9	27

TSYBUK, EVGUENI — D — STARS

PERSONAL: Born February 2, 1978, in Chebarkul, U.S.S.R. ... 6-0/185. ... Shoots left. ... Name pronounced ehv-GEH-nee SIGH-buk.
TRANSACTIONS/CAREER NOTES: Selected by Dallas Stars in fifth round (fourth Stars pick, 113th overall) of NHL entry draft (June 22, 1996).

Season Team	League	Gms.	G	A	Pts.	PIM	+/-	PP	SH	Gms.	G	A	Pts.	PIM
		REGULAR SEASON								PLAYOFFS				
95-96—Torpedo-2 Yaroslavl....	CIS Div. II					Statistics unavailable.								
96-97—Lethbridge	WHL	10	0	1	1	13	...	...	...	—	—	—	—	—
97-98—Lethbridge	WHL	41	5	13	18	129	...	...	...	4	1	1	2	12

TSYPLAKOV, VLADIMIR   LW   KINGS

PERSONAL: Born April 18, 1969, in Inta, U.S.S.R. ... 6-1/200. ... Shoots left. ... Name pronounced SIHP-luh-kahf.

TRANSACTIONS/CAREER NOTES: Selected by Los Angeles Kings in third round (fourth Kings pick, 59th overall) of NHL entry draft (July 8, 1995). ... Underwent reconstructive surgery on right shoulder (December 14, 1995); missed 45 games. ... Strained abdominal muscle prior to 1995-96 season; missed first nine games of season. ... Strained groin (February 13, 1997); missed three games. ... Fractured right hand (November 11, 1997); missed two games.

Season Team	League	Gms.	G	A	Pts.	PIM	+/-	PP	SH	Gms.	G	A	Pts.	PIM
		REGULAR SEASON								PLAYOFFS				
88-89—Dynamo Minsk	USSR	19	6	1	7	4	...	...	...	—	—	—	—	—
89-90—Dynamo Minsk	USSR	47	11	6	17	20	...	...	...	—	—	—	—	—
90-91—Dynamo Minsk	USSR	28	6	5	11	14	...	...	...	—	—	—	—	—
91-92—Dynamo Minsk	CIS	29	10	9	19	16	...	...	...	—	—	—	—	—
92-93—Detroit	Col.HL	44	33	43	76	20	...	...	...	6	5	4	9	6
—Indianapolis	IHL	11	6	7	13	4	...	...	...	5	1	1	2	2
93-94—Fort Wayne	IHL	63	31	32	63	51	...	...	...	14	6	8	14	16
94-95—Fort Wayne	IHL	79	38	40	78	39	...	...	...	4	2	4	6	2
95-96—Las Vegas	IHL	9	5	6	11	4	...	...	...	—	—	—	—	—
—Los Angeles	NHL	23	5	5	10	4	1	0	0	—	—	—	—	—
96-97—Los Angeles	NHL	67	16	23	39	12	8	1	0	—	—	—	—	—
97-98—Los Angeles	NHL	73	18	34	52	18	15	2	0	4	0	1	1	8
—Belarus Oly. team	Int'l	5	1	1	2	2	...	...	...	—	—	—	—	—
NHL Totals (3 years)		163	39	62	101	34	24	3	0	4	0	1	1	8

TUCKER, DARCY   C   LIGHTNING

PERSONAL: Born March 15, 1975, in Castor, Alta. ... 5-11/182. ... Shoots left.

TRANSACTIONS/CAREER NOTES: Selected by Montreal Canadiens in sixth round (eighth Canadiens pick, 151st overall) of NHL entry draft (June 26, 1993). ... Bruised knee (December 16, 1996); missed one game. ... Traded by Canadiens with F Stephane Richer and D David Wilkie to Tampa Bay Lightning for F Patrick Poulin, F Mick Vukota and D Igor Ulanov (January 15, 1998).

HONORS: Won Stafford Smythe Memorial Trophy (1993-94). ... Named to Can.HL All-Star first team (1993-94). ... Named to WHL (West) All-Star first team (1993-94 and 1994-95). ... Named to Memorial Cup All-Star team (1993-94 and 1994-95). ... Won Dudley (Red) Garrett Memorial Trophy (1995-96).

Season Team	League	Gms.	G	A	Pts.	PIM	+/-	PP	SH	Gms.	G	A	Pts.	PIM
		REGULAR SEASON								PLAYOFFS				
91-92—Kamloops	WHL	26	3	10	13	42	...	...	...	9	0	1	1	16
92-93—Kamloops	WHL	67	31	58	89	155	...	...	...	13	7	6	13	34
93-94—Kamloops	WHL	66	52	88	140	143	...	...	...	19	9	*18	*27	43
94-95—Kamloops	WHL	64	64	73	137	94	...	...	...	21	16	15	31	19
95-96—Fredericton	AHL	74	29	64	93	174	...	...	...	7	7	3	10	14
—Montreal	NHL	3	0	0	0	0	-1	0	0	—	—	—	—	—
96-97—Montreal	NHL	73	7	13	20	110	-5	1	0	4	0	0	0	0
97-98—Montreal	NHL	39	1	5	6	57	-6	0	0	—	—	—	—	—
—Tampa Bay	NHL	35	6	8	14	89	-8	1	1	—	—	—	—	—
NHL Totals (3 years)		150	14	26	40	256	-20	2	1	4	0	0	0	0

TUGNUTT, RON   G   SENATORS

PERSONAL: Born October 22, 1967, in Scarborough, Ont. ... 5-11/165. ... Catches left. ... Full name: Ronald Frederick Bradley Tugnutt.

TRANSACTIONS/CAREER NOTES: Selected by Quebec Nordiques as underage junior in fourth round (fourth Nordiques pick, 81st overall) of NHL entry draft (June 21, 1986). ... Sprained ankle (March 1989). ... Sprained knee (January 13, 1990). ... Injured hamstring (January 29, 1991); missed 11 games. ... Traded by Nordiques with LW Brad Zavisha to Edmonton Oilers for LW Martin Rucinsky (March 10, 1992). ... Selected by Mighty Ducks of Anaheim in NHL expansion draft (June 24, 1993). ... Traded by Mighty Ducks to Montreal Canadiens for C Stephan Lebeau (February 20, 1994). ... Strained knee (January 28, 1995); missed five games. ... Signed as free agent Washington Capitals prior to 1995-96 season. ... Signed as free agent by Ottawa Senators (July 17, 1996). ... Strained hip flexor (January 31, 1998); missed two games.

HONORS: Won F.W. (Dinty) Moore Trophy (1984-85). ... Shared Dave Pinkney Trophy with Kay Whitmore (1985-86). ... Named to OHL All-Star first team (1986-87).

MISCELLANEOUS: Stopped penalty shot attempt (vs. Dave McIlwain, October 12, 1991; vs. Cam Neely, October 15, 1993; vs. Brett Harkins, March 22, 1997). ... Allowed penalty shot goal (vs. Benoit Hogue, February 16, 1993). ... Holds Ottawa Senators all-time record for goals-against average (2.51).

Season Team	League	Gms.	Min	W	L	T	GA	SO	Avg.	Gms.	Min.	W	L	GA	SO	Avg.
		REGULAR SEASON								PLAYOFFS						
84-85—Peterborough	OHL	18	938	7	4	2	59	0	3.77	—	—	—	—	—	—	—
85-86—Peterborough	OHL	26	1543	18	7	0	74	1	2.88	3	133	2	0	6	0	2.71
86-87—Peterborough	OHL	31	1891	21	7	2	88	2	*2.79	6	374	3	3	21	1	3.37
87-88—Quebec	NHL	6	284	2	3	0	16	0	3.38	—	—	—	—	—	—	—
—Fredericton	AHL	34	1962	20	9	4	118	1	3.61	4	204	1	2	11	0	3.24
88-89—Quebec	NHL	26	1367	10	10	3	82	0	3.60	—	—	—	—	—	—	—
—Halifax	AHL	24	1368	14	7	2	79	1	3.46	—	—	—	—	—	—	—
89-90—Quebec	NHL	35	1978	5	24	3	152	0	4.61	—	—	—	—	—	—	—
—Halifax	AHL	6	366	1	5	0	23	0	3.77	—	—	—	—	—	—	—
90-91—Halifax	AHL	2	100	0	1	0	8	0	4.80	—	—	—	—	—	—	—
—Quebec	NHL	56	3144	12	†29	10	212	0	4.05	—	—	—	—	—	—	—

Season Team	League	REGULAR SEASON							PLAYOFFS						
		Gms.	Min	W	L	T	GA	SO	Avg.	Gms.	Min.	W	L	GA	SO	Avg.
91-92—Quebec	NHL	30	1583	6	17	3	106	1	4.02	—	—	—	—	—	—	—
—Halifax	AHL	8	447	3	3	1	30	0	4.03	—	—	—	—	—	—	—
—Edmonton	NHL	3	124	1	1	0	10	0	4.84	2	60	0	0	3	0	3.00
92-93—Edmonton	NHL	26	1338	9	12	2	93	0	4.17	—	—	—	—	—	—	—
93-94—Anaheim	NHL	28	1520	10	15	1	76	1	3.00	—	—	—	—	—	—	—
—Montreal	NHL	8	378	2	3	1	24	0	3.81	1	59	0	1	5	0	5.08
94-95—Montreal	NHL	7	346	1	3	1	18	0	3.12	—	—	—	—	—	—	—
95-96—Portland	AHL	58	3067	21	23	6	171	2	3.35	13	781	7	6	36	1	2.77
96-97—Ottawa	NHL	37	1991	17	15	1	93	3	2.80	7	425	3	4	14	1	1.98
97-98—Ottawa	NHL	42	2236	15	14	8	84	3	2.25	2	74	0	1	6	0	4.86
NHL Totals (10 years)		304	16289	90	146	33	966	8	3.56	12	618	3	6	28	1	2.72

TURCO, MARTY — G — STARS

PERSONAL: Born August 13, 1975, in Sault Ste. Marie, Ont. ... 6-0/171. ... Catches left.
HIGH SCHOOL: St. Mary's College (Sault Ste. Marie, Ont.).
COLLEGE: Michigan.
TRANSACTIONS/CAREER NOTES: Selected by Dallas Stars in fifth round (fourth Stars pick, 124th overall) of NHL entry draft (June 29, 1994).
HONORS: Named CCHA Rookie of the Year (1994-95). ... Named to NCAA All-Tournament team (1995-96). ... Named to CCHA All-Star first team (1996-1997). ... Named to NCAA All-America West first team (1996-97). ... Named NCAA Tournament Most Valuable Player (1997-98). ... Named to NCAA All-Tournament team (1997-98). ... Named to CCHA All-Star second team (1997-98).

Season Team	League	REGULAR SEASON							PLAYOFFS						
		Gms.	Min	W	L	T	GA	SO	Avg.	Gms.	Min.	W	L	GA	SO	Avg.
93-94—Cambridge Jr. B	OHA	34	1937	...	...	...	114	0	3.53	—	—	—	—	—	—	—
94-95—Univ. of Michigan	CCHA	37	2064	27	7	1	95	1	2.76	—	—	—	—	—	—	—
95-96—Univ. of Michigan	CCHA	42	2334	34	7	1	84	5	2.16	—	—	—	—	—	—	—
96-97—Univ. of Michigan	CCHA	41	2296	33	4	4	87	4	2.27	—	—	—	—	—	—	—
97-98—Univ. of Michigan	CCHA	45	2640	33	10	1	95	3	2.16	—	—	—	—	—	—	—

TURCOTTE, DARREN — C — PREDATORS

PERSONAL: Born March 2, 1968, in Boston. ... 6-0/182. ... Shoots left. ... Name pronounced TUHR-kaht.
TRANSACTIONS/CAREER NOTES: Selected by New York Rangers as underage junior in sixth round (sixth Rangers pick, 114th overall) of NHL entry draft (June 21, 1986). ... Separated shoulder (October 1987); missed 34 games. ... Suffered concussion (March 1989). ... Sprained left ankle (October 1989). ... Injured knee (April 11, 1990). ... Broke left foot (April 27, 1990). ... Suffered contusion above left ankle (November 13, 1991); missed two games. ... Bruised right foot (March 4, 1992); missed one game. ... Reinjured right foot (March 9, 1992); missed two games. ... Sprained ankle (January 2, 1993); missed one game. ... Suffered hairline fracture in foot (February 10, 1993); missed 11 games. ... Traded by Rangers with D James Patrick to Hartford Whalers for RW Steve Larmer, LW Nick Kypreos and sixth-round pick (C Yuri Litvinov) in 1994 draft (November 2, 1993). ... Underwent medial collateral ligament surgery (December 9, 1993); missed 50 games. ... Traded by Whalers to Winnipeg Jets for RW Nelson Emerson (October 6, 1995). ... Injured hand (December 19, 1995); missed one game. ... Strained right thumb (February 13, 1996); missed six games. ... Traded by Jets with second-round pick (traded to Chicago) in 1996 draft to San Jose Sharks for C Craig Janney (March 18, 1996). ... Injured back (April 6, 1996); missed one game. ... Strained knee (October 5, 1996); missed three games. ... Injured ear (January 24, 1997); missed 13 games. ... Suffered from an illness (March 11, 1997); missed one game. ... Traded by Sharks to St. Louis Blues for LW Stephane Matteau (July 25, 1997). ... Bruised shoulder (October 11, 1997); missed 11 games. ... Suffered from the flu (December 18, 1997); missed one game. ... Suffered from the flu (January 10, 1998); missed two games. ... Bruised hand (March 1, 1998); missed two games. ... Traded by Blues to Nashville Predators for future considerations (June 27, 1998).
HONORS: Played in NHL All-Star Game (1991).
MISCELLANEOUS: Failed to score on a penalty shot (vs. Wendell Young, December 29, 1991; vs. Rick Tabaracci, March 22, 1998).
STATISTICAL PLATEAUS: Three-goal games: 1988-89 (1), 1989-90 (1), 1990-91 (1), 1991-92 (1). Total: 4.

Season Team	League	REGULAR SEASON							PLAYOFFS				
		Gms.	G	A	Pts.	PIM	+/-	PP	SH	Gms.	G	A	Pts.	PIM
84-85—North Bay	OHL	62	33	32	65	28	...	...	...	8	0	2	2	0
85-86—North Bay	OHL	62	35	37	72	35	...	...	...	10	3	4	7	8
86-87—North Bay	OHL	55	30	48	78	20	...	...	...	18	12	8	20	6
87-88—Colorado	IHL	8	4	3	7	9	...	...	...	6	2	6	8	8
—North Bay	OHL	32	30	33	63	16	...	...	...	4	3	0	3	4
88-89—Denver	IHL	40	21	28	49	32	...	...	...	—	—	—	—	—
—New York Rangers	NHL	20	7	3	10	4	0	2	0	1	0	0	0	0
89-90—New York Rangers	NHL	76	32	34	66	32	3	10	1	10	1	6	7	4
90-91—New York Rangers	NHL	74	26	41	67	37	-5	15	2	6	1	2	3	0
91-92—New York Rangers	NHL	71	30	23	53	57	11	13	1	8	4	0	4	6
92-93—New York Rangers	NHL	71	25	28	53	40	-3	7	3	—	—	—	—	—
93-94—New York Rangers	NHL	13	2	4	6	13	-2	0	0	—	—	—	—	—
—Hartford	NHL	19	2	11	13	4	-11	0	0	—	—	—	—	—
94-95—Hartford	NHL	47	17	18	35	22	1	3	1	—	—	—	—	—
95-96—Winnipeg	NHL	59	16	16	32	26	-3	2	0	—	—	—	—	—
—San Jose	NHL	9	6	5	11	4	8	0	1	—	—	—	—	—
96-97—San Jose	NHL	65	16	21	37	16	-8	3	1	—	—	—	—	—
97-98—St. Louis	NHL	62	12	6	18	26	6	3	0	10	0	0	0	2
NHL Totals (10 years)		586	191	210	401	281	-3	58	10	35	6	8	14	12

TUREK, ROMAN — G — STARS

PERSONAL: Born May 21, 1970, in Strakonice, Czechoslovakia. ... 6-3/190. ... Catches right. ... Name pronounced ROH-mahn TOOR-ihk.
TRANSACTIONS/CAREER NOTES: Selected by Minnesota North Stars in sixth round (sixth North Stars pick, 113th overall) of NHL entry draft (June 16, 1990). ... Strained groin (January 8, 1997); missed three games. ... Injured knee (March 31, 1997); missed seven games. ... Strained groin (November 15, 1997); missed 12 games.

Season Team	League	REGULAR SEASON								PLAYOFFS						
		Gms.	Min	W	L	T	GA	SO	Avg.	Gms.	Min.	W	L	GA	SO	Avg.
90-91—Budejovice	Czech.	26	1244	...	...	...	98	0	4.73	—	—	—	—	—	—	—
91-92—Budejovice	Czech Dv.II							Did not play.								
92-93—Budejovice	Czech.	43	2555	...	...	...	121	...	2.84	—	—	—	—	—	—	—
93-94—Budejovice	Czech Rep.	44	2584	...	...	...	111	...	2.58	3	180	...	...	12	...	4.00
—Czech Rep. Olympic	Int'l	2	120	2	0	0	4	2	2.00	—	—	—	—	—	—	—
94-95—Budejovice	Czech Rep.	44	2587	...	...	...	119	...	2.76	9	498	...	...	25	...	3.01
95-96—Nurnberg	Germany	48	2787	...	...	...	154	...	3.32	5	338	...	...	14	...	2.49
96-97—Michigan	IHL	29	1555	8	13	‡4	77	0	2.97	—	—	—	—	—	—	—
—Dallas	NHL	6	263	3	1	0	9	0	2.05	—	—	—	—	—	—	—
97-98—Dallas	NHL	23	1324	11	10	1	49	1	2.22	—	—	—	—	—	—	—
—Michigan	IHL	2	119	1	1	‡0	5	0	2.52	—	—	—	—	—	—	—
NHL Totals (2 years)		29	1587	14	11	1	58	1	2.19							

TURGEON, PIERRE   C   BLUES

PERSONAL: Born August 29, 1969, in Rouyn, Que. ... 6-1/195. ... Shoots left. ... Brother of Sylvain Turgeon, left winger with four NHL teams (1983-84 through 1994-95). ... Name pronounced TUHR-zhaw.

TRANSACTIONS/CAREER NOTES: Underwent knee surgery (June 1985). ... Selected by Buffalo Sabres as underage junior in first round (first Sabres pick, first overall) of NHL entry draft (June 13, 1987). ... Traded by Sabres with RW Benoit Hogue, D Uwe Krupp and C Dave McLlwain to New York Islanders for C Pat LaFontaine, LW Randy Wood, D Randy Hillier and future considerations; Sabres later received fourth-round pick (D Dean Melanson) in 1992 draft to complete deal (October 25, 1991). ... Injured right knee (January 3, 1992); missed three games. ... Separated shoulder (April 28, 1993); missed six playoff games. ... Suffered from tendinitis in right wrist (October 5, 1993); missed one game. ... Suffered from the flu (December 29, 1993); missed one game. ... Fractured cheekbone (January 26, 1994); missed 12 games. ... Traded by Islanders with D Vladimir Malakhov to Montreal Canadiens for LW Kirk Muller, D Mathieu Schneider and C Craig Darby (April 5, 1995). ... Strained shoulder (November 8, 1995); missed two games. ... Bruised thigh (October 24, 1996); missed one game. ... Traded by Canadiens with C Craig Conroy and D Rory Fitzpatrick to St. Louis Blues for LW Shayne Corson, D Murray Baron and fifth-round pick (D Gennady Razin) in 1997 draft (October 29, 1996). ... Fractured right forearm (October 4, 1997); missed 22 games.

HONORS: Won Michel Bergeron Trophy (1985-86). ... Won Michael Bossy Trophy (1986-87). ... Played in NHL All-Star Game (1990, 1993, 1994 and 1996). ... Won Lady Byng Memorial Trophy (1992-93).

MISCELLANEOUS: Captain of Montreal Canadiens (1995-96 through October 29, 1996). ... Scored on a penalty shot (vs. Patrick Roy, October 17, 1990; vs. Pat Jablonski, November 7, 1992).

STATISTICAL PLATEAUS: Three-goal games: 1989-90 (1), 1990-91 (1), 1991-92 (2), 1992-93 (4), 1993-94 (2), 1994-95 (1), 1995-96 (1). Total: 12.

Season Team	League	REGULAR SEASON								PLAYOFFS				
		Gms.	G	A	Pts.	PIM	+/-	PP	SH	Gms.	G	A	Pts.	PIM
85-86—Granby	QMJHL	69	47	67	114	31	...	...	...	—	—	—	—	—
86-87—Granby	QMJHL	58	69	85	154	8	...	...	...	7	9	6	15	15
87-88—Buffalo	NHL	76	14	28	42	34	...	...	...	6	4	3	7	4
88-89—Buffalo	NHL	80	34	54	88	26	-2	19	0	5	3	5	8	2
89-90—Buffalo	NHL	80	40	66	106	29	10	17	1	6	2	4	6	2
90-91—Buffalo	NHL	78	32	47	79	26	14	13	2	6	3	1	4	6
91-92—Buffalo	NHL	8	2	6	8	4	-1	0	0	—	—	—	—	—
—New York Islanders	NHL	69	38	49	87	16	8	13	0	—	—	—	—	—
92-93—New York Islanders	NHL	83	58	74	132	26	-1	24	0	11	6	7	13	0
93-94—New York Islanders	NHL	69	38	56	94	18	14	10	4	4	0	1	1	0
94-95—New York Islanders	NHL	34	13	14	27	10	-12	3	2	—	—	—	—	—
—Montreal	NHL	15	11	9	20	4	12	2	0	—	—	—	—	—
95-96—Montreal	NHL	80	38	58	96	44	19	17	1	6	2	4	6	2
96-97—Montreal	NHL	9	1	10	11	2	4	0	0	—	—	—	—	—
—St. Louis	NHL	69	25	49	74	12	4	5	0	5	1	1	2	0
97-98—St. Louis	NHL	60	22	46	68	24	13	6	0	10	4	4	8	2
NHL Totals (11 years)		810	366	566	932	275	82	129	10	59	25	30	55	20

TUZZOLINO, TONY   RW   MIGHTY DUCKS

PERSONAL: Born October 9, 1975, in Buffalo, N.Y. ... 6-2/200. ... Shoots right. ... Name pronounced TUZZ-oh-LEEN-oh.

COLLEGE: Michigan State.

TRANSACTIONS/CAREER NOTES: Selected by Quebec Nordiques in fifth round (seventh Nordiques pick, 113th overall) of NHL entry draft (June 29, 1994). ... Nordiques franchise moved to Colorado and renamed Avalanche for 1995-96 season (June 21, 1995). ... Signed as free agent by New York Islanders (April 23, 1997). ... Traded by Islanders with C Travis Green and D Doug Houda to Mighty Ducks of Anaheim for D J.J. Daigneault, C Mark Janssens and RW Joe Sacco (February 6, 1998).

Season Team	League	REGULAR SEASON								PLAYOFFS				
		Gms.	G	A	Pts.	PIM	+/-	PP	SH	Gms.	G	A	Pts.	PIM
91-92—Niagara	NAJHL	45	19	27	46	82	...	...	...	—	—	—	—	—
92-93—Niagara	NAJHL	50	36	41	77	134	...	...	...	—	—	—	—	—
93-94—Michigan State	CCHA	38	4	3	7	50	...			—	—	—	—	—
94-95—Michigan State	CCHA	39	9	19	28	81	...			—	—	—	—	—
95-96—Michigan State	CCHA	41	12	17	29	120	...			—	—	—	—	—
96-97—Michigan State	CCHA	39	14	18	32	45	...			—	—	—	—	—
97-98—Kentucky	AHL	35	9	14	23	83	...			—	—	—	—	—
—Cincinnati	AHL	13	3	3	6	6	...			—	—	—	—	—
—Anaheim	NHL	1	0	0	0	2	-2	0	0	—	—	—	—	—
NHL Totals (1 year)		1	0	0	0	2	-2	0	0					

T

TVERDOVSKY, OLEG   D   COYOTES

PERSONAL: Born May 18, 1976, in Donetsk, U.S.S.R. ... 6-0/195. ... Shoots left. ... Name pronounced OH-lehg teh-vuhr-DAHV-skee.
TRANSACTIONS/CAREER NOTES: Selected by Mighty Ducks of Anaheim in first round (first Mighty Ducks pick, second overall) of NHL entry draft (June 28, 1994). ... Suffered from pink eye (March 15, 1995); missed two games. ... Traded by Mighty Ducks with C Chad Kilger and third-round pick (D Per-Anton Lundstrom) in 1996 draft to Winnipeg Jets for C Marc Chouinard, RW Teemu Selanne and fourth-round pick (traded to Toronto) in 1996 draft (February 7, 1996). ... Jets franchise moved to Phoenix and renamed Coyotes for 1996-97 season; NHL approved move on January 18, 1996. ... Injured rib (December 23, 1997); missed one game.
HONORS: Played in NHL All-Star Game (1997).

Season Team	League	REGULAR SEASON								PLAYOFFS				
		Gms.	G	A	Pts.	PIM	+/-	PP	SH	Gms.	G	A	Pts.	PIM
92-93—Soviet Wings	CIS	21	0	1	1	6	...	...	...	6	0	0	0	...
93-94—Soviet Wings	CIS	46	4	10	14	22	...	...	...	3	1	0	1	2
94-95—Brandon	WHL	7	1	4	5	4	...	...	...	—	—	—	—	—
—Anaheim	NHL	36	3	9	12	14	-6	1	1	—	—	—	—	—
95-96—Anaheim	NHL	51	7	15	22	35	0	2	0	—	—	—	—	—
—Winnipeg	NHL	31	0	8	8	6	-7	0	0	6	0	1	1	0
96-97—Phoenix	NHL	82	10	45	55	30	-5	3	1	7	0	1	1	0
97-98—Hamilton	AHL	9	8	6	14	2	...	...	...	—	—	—	—	—
—Phoenix	NHL	46	7	12	19	12	1	4	0	6	0	7	7	0
NHL Totals (4 years)		246	27	89	116	97	-17	10	2	19	0	9	9	0

TWIST, TONY   LW   BLUES

PERSONAL: Born May 9, 1968, in Sherwood Park, Alta. ... 6-1/242. ... Shoots left. ... Full name: Anthony Rory Twist.
TRANSACTIONS/CAREER NOTES: Suspended three games and fined $250 by WHL for leaving the penalty box to fight (January 28, 1988). ... Selected by St. Louis Blues in ninth round (ninth Blues pick, 177th overall) of NHL entry draft (June 11, 1988). ... Suspended 13 games by IHL for checking goaltender after play stopped (December 15, 1990). ... Traded by Blues with RW Herb Raglan and LW Andy Rymsha to Quebec Nordiques for RW Darin Kimble (February 4, 1991). ... Injured shoulder (December 18, 1993); missed six games. ... Hyperextended right elbow (March 30, 1994); missed five games. ... Signed as free agent by Blues (August 3, 1994). ... Injured shoulder (March 26, 1995); missed last 20 games of season. ... Underwent bicep surgery (September 22, 1995); missed 21 games. ... Bruised knee (January 16, 1996); missed one game. ... Sprained ankle (March 26, 1996); missed seven games. ... Suffered back spasms (December 18, 1996); missed nine games. ... Suffered from a virus (February 20, 1997); missed four games. ... Suffered back spasms (October 20, 1997); missed one game. ... Suffered from the flu (November 29, 1997); missed one game. ... Sprained left knee (December 22, 1997); missed 11 games. ... Strained upper abdomen (March 26, 1998); missed eight games.

Season Team	League	REGULAR SEASON								PLAYOFFS				
		Gms.	G	A	Pts.	PIM	+/-	PP	SH	Gms.	G	A	Pts.	PIM
86-87—Saskatoon	WHL	64	0	8	8	181	...	...	...	—	—	—	—	—
87-88—Saskatoon	WHL	55	1	8	9	226	...	...	...	10	1	1	2	6
88-89—Peoria	IHL	67	3	8	11	312	...	...	...	—	—	—	—	—
89-90—St. Louis	NHL	28	0	0	0	124	-2	0	0	—	—	—	—	—
—Peoria	IHL	36	1	5	6	200	...	...	...	5	0	1	1	8
90-91—Peoria	IHL	38	2	10	12	244	...	...	...	—	—	—	—	—
—Quebec	NHL	24	0	0	0	104	-4	0	0	—	—	—	—	—
91-92—Quebec	NHL	44	0	1	1	164	-3	0	0	—	—	—	—	—
92-93—Quebec	NHL	34	0	2	2	64	0	0	0	—	—	—	—	—
93-94—Quebec	NHL	49	0	4	4	101	-1	0	0	—	—	—	—	—
94-95—St. Louis	NHL	28	3	0	3	89	0	0	0	1	0	0	0	6
95-96—St. Louis	NHL	51	3	2	5	100	-1	0	0	10	1	1	2	16
96-97—St. Louis	NHL	64	1	2	3	121	-8	0	0	6	0	0	0	0
97-98—St. Louis	NHL	60	1	1	2	105	-4	0	0	—	—	—	—	—
NHL Totals (9 years)		382	8	12	20	972	-23	0	0	17	1	1	2	22

ULANOV, IGOR   D   CANADIENS

PERSONAL: Born October 1, 1969, in Kraskokamsk, U.S.S.R. ... 6-2/205. ... Shoots right. ... Name pronounced EE-gohr yoo-LAH-nahf.
TRANSACTIONS/CAREER NOTES: Selected by Winnipeg Jets in 10th round (eighth Jets pick, 203rd overall) of NHL entry draft (June 22, 1991). ... Suffered back spasms (March 7, 1992); missed five games. ... Fractured foot (March 16, 1995); missed 19 games. ... Traded by Jets with C Mike Eagles to Washington Capitals for third-round (traded to Dallas Stars) and fifth-round (G Brian Elder) picks in 1995 draft (April 7, 1995). ... Traded by Capitals to Chicago Blackhawks for third-round pick (G Dave Weninger) in 1996 draft (October 17, 1995). ... Traded by Blackhawks with LW Patrick Poulin and second-round pick (D Jeff Paul) in 1996 draft to Tampa Bay Lightning for D Enrico Ciccone (March 20, 1996). ... Injured ribs (October 5, 1996); missed three games. ... Strained groin (February 14, 1997); missed six games. ... Traded by Lightning with F Patrick Poulin and F Mick Vukota to Montreal Canadiens for F Stephane Richer, F Darcy Tucker and D David Wilkie (January 15, 1998). ... Tore ligaments in left knee (January 21, 1998); missed final 30 games of regular season.

Season Team	League	REGULAR SEASON								PLAYOFFS				
		Gms.	G	A	Pts.	PIM	+/-	PP	SH	Gms.	G	A	Pts.	PIM
90-91—Khimik	USSR	41	2	2	4	52	...	...	...	—	—	—	—	—
91-92—Khimik	CIS	27	1	4	5	24	...	...	...	—	—	—	—	—
—Winnipeg	NHL	27	2	9	11	67	5	0	0	7	0	0	0	39
—Moncton	AHL	3	0	1	1	16	...	...	...	—	—	—	—	—
92-93—Moncton	AHL	9	1	3	4	26	...	...	...	—	—	—	—	—
—Fort Wayne	IHL	3	0	1	1	29	...	...	...	—	—	—	—	—
—Winnipeg	NHL	56	2	14	16	124	6	0	0	4	0	0	0	4
93-94—Winnipeg	NHL	74	0	17	17	165	-11	0	0	—	—	—	—	—
94-95—Winnipeg	NHL	19	1	3	4	27	-2	0	0	—	—	—	—	—
—Washington	NHL	3	0	1	1	2	3	0	0	2	0	0	0	4

T
U

Season Team	League	REGULAR SEASON								PLAYOFFS				
		Gms.	G	A	Pts.	PIM	+/-	PP	SH	Gms.	G	A	Pts.	PIM
95-96—Indianapolis	IHL	1	0	0	0	0	...	...	...	—	—	—	—	—
—Chicago	NHL	53	1	8	9	92	12	0	0	—	—	—	—	—
—Tampa Bay	NHL	11	2	1	3	24	-1	0	0	5	0	0	0	15
96-97—Tampa Bay	NHL	59	1	7	8	108	2	0	0	—	—	—	—	—
97-98—Tampa Bay	NHL	45	2	7	9	85	-5	1	0	—	—	—	—	—
—Montreal	NHL	4	0	1	1	12	-2	0	0	10	1	4	5	12
NHL Totals (7 years)		351	11	68	79	706	7	1	0	28	1	4	5	74

VAIC, LUBOMIR   C   CANUCKS

PERSONAL: Born March 6, 1977, in Spisska Nova Ves, Slovakia. ... 5-9/178. ... Shoots right. ... Name pronounced VAZ.
TRANSACTIONS/CAREER NOTES: Selected by Vancouver Canucks in ninth round (eighth Canucks pick, 227th overall) of the NHL entry draft (June 22, 1996).

Season Team	League	REGULAR SEASON								PLAYOFFS				
		Gms.	G	A	Pts.	PIM	+/-	PP	SH	Gms.	G	A	Pts.	PIM
93-94—Poprad	Slovakia	28	10	6	16	10	...	...	...	—	—	—	—	—
94-95—Spisska N.V.	Slovakia	19	5	4	9	2	...	...	...	—	—	—	—	—
95-96—HC Kosice	Slovakia	36	7	19	26	10	...	...	...	—	—	—	—	—
96-97—HC Kosice	Slovakia	36	13	12	25	...	...	...	...	7	2	0	2	...
97-98—Syracuse	AHL	50	12	15	27	22	...	...	...	3	0	0	0	4
—Vancouver	NHL	5	1	1	2	2	-2	0	0	—	—	—	—	—
NHL Totals (1 year)		5	1	1	2	2	-2	0	0					

VAILLANCOURT, LUC   G   MIGHTY DUCKS

PERSONAL: Born June 13, 1978, in Ferme-Nueve, Que. ... 6-1/190. ... Catches left.
TRANSACTIONS/CAREER NOTES: Selected by Mighty Ducks of Anaheim in fifth round (fourth Mighty Ducks pick, 125th overall) of NHL entry draft (June 21, 1997).
HONORS: Won Marcel Robert Trophy (1996-97).

Season Team	League	REGULAR SEASON								PLAYOFFS						
		Gms.	Min	W	L	T	GA	SO	Avg.	Gms.	Min.	W	L	GA	SO	Avg.
95-96—Beauport	QMJHL	22	882	7	8	0	71	0	4.83	2	80	1	0	3	0	2.25
96-97—Beauport	QMJHL	51	2668	18	26	1	161	0	3.62	4	239	1	3	20	0	5.02
97-98—Quebec	QMJHL	22	1196	11	8	1	73	0	3.66	—	—	—	—	—	—	—
—Rouyn-Noranda	QMJHL	30	1762	19	10	1	93	0	3.17	6	362	2	4	26	0	4.31

VALK, GARRY   LW   PENGUINS

PERSONAL: Born November 27, 1967, in Edmonton. ... 6-1/221. ... Shoots left. ... Full name: Garry P. Valk. ... Name pronounced VAHLK.
COLLEGE: North Dakota.
TRANSACTIONS/CAREER NOTES: Selected by Vancouver Canucks in sixth round (fifth Canucks pick, 108th overall) of NHL entry draft (June 13, 1987). ... Sprained thumb (November 24, 1991); missed one game. ... Sprained shoulder (January 21, 1992); missed eight games. ... Sprained knee (February 26, 1993); missed 12 games. ... Selected by Mighty Ducks of Anaheim in NHL waiver draft (October 3, 1993). ... Suffered concussion (December 5, 1993); missed one game. ... Suffered post-concussion syndrome (December 5, 1993); missed four games. ... Sprained left knee (January 16, 1995); missed 10 games. ... Injured right eye (December 7, 1995); missed one game. ... Injured ear (December 22, 1995); missed one game. ... Traded by Mighty Ducks to Pittsburgh Penguins for D J.J. Daigneault (February 21, 1997). ... Bruised ribs (March 16, 1997); missed five games. ... Injured knee (April 11, 1997); missed one game. ... Suffered charley horse (October 1, 1997); missed two games. ... Injured groin (October 24, 1997); missed three games. ... Strained abdomen (March 5, 1998); missed 13 games.
STATISTICAL PLATEAUS: Three-goal games: 1995-96 (1).

Season Team	League	REGULAR SEASON								PLAYOFFS				
		Gms.	G	A	Pts.	PIM	+/-	PP	SH	Gms.	G	A	Pts.	PIM
85-86—Sherwood Park	AJHL	40	20	26	46	116	...	...	...	—	—	—	—	—
86-87—Sherwood Park	AJHL	59	42	44	86	204	...	...	...	—	—	—	—	—
87-88—U. of North Dakota	WCHA	38	23	12	35	64	...	...	...	—	—	—	—	—
88-89—U. of North Dakota	WCHA	40	14	17	31	71	...	...	...	—	—	—	—	—
89-90—U. of North Dakota	WCHA	43	22	17	39	92	...	...	...	—	—	—	—	—
90-91—Vancouver	NHL	59	10	11	21	67	-23	1	0	5	0	0	0	20
—Milwaukee	IHL	10	12	4	16	13	...	...	...	3	0	0	0	2
91-92—Vancouver	NHL	65	8	17	25	56	3	2	1	4	0	0	0	5
92-93—Vancouver	NHL	48	6	7	13	77	6	0	0	7	0	1	1	12
—Hamilton	AHL	7	3	6	9	6	...	...	...	—	—	—	—	—
93-94—Anaheim	NHL	78	18	27	45	100	8	4	1	—	—	—	—	—
94-95—Anaheim	NHL	36	3	6	9	34	-4	0	0	—	—	—	—	—
95-96—Anaheim	NHL	79	12	12	24	125	8	1	1	—	—	—	—	—
96-97—Anaheim	NHL	53	7	7	14	53	-2	0	0	—	—	—	—	—
—Pittsburgh	NHL	17	3	4	7	25	-6	0	0	—	—	—	—	—
97-98—Pittsburgh	NHL	39	2	1	3	33	-3	0	0	—	—	—	—	—
NHL Totals (8 years)		474	69	92	161	570	-13	8	3	16	0	1	1	37

U
V

VAN ALLEN, SHAUN   C   SENATORS

PERSONAL: Born August 29, 1967, in Shaunavon, Sask. ... 6-1/200. ... Shoots left. ... Full name: Shaun Kelly Van Allen.
HIGH SCHOOL: Walter Murray (Saskatoon, Sask.).
TRANSACTIONS/CAREER NOTES: Selected by Edmonton Oilers in fifth round (fifth Oilers pick, 105th overall) of NHL entry draft (June 13, 1987). ... Suffered concussion (January 9, 1993); missed 11 games. ... Signed as free agent by Mighty Ducks of Anaheim (July 22, 1993). ... Suffered back spasms (February 7, 1995); missed two games. ... Suffered from the flu (May 1, 1995); missed one game. ... Dislocated right thumb (November 15, 1995); missed 21 games. ... Suffered back spasms (February 7, 1996); missed four games. ... Traded by Mighty Ducks with D Jason York to Ottawa Senators for C Ted Drury and rights to D Marc Moro (October 1, 1996). ... Suffered back spasms (February 2, 1998); missed one game.
HONORS: Named to AHL All-Star second team (1990-91). ... Won John B. Sollenberger Trophy (1991-92). ... Named to AHL All-Star first team (1991-92).

		REGULAR SEASON								PLAYOFFS				
Season Team	League	Gms.	G	A	Pts.	PIM	+/-	PP	SH	Gms.	G	A	Pts.	PIM
84-85—Swift Current	SAJHL	61	12	20	32	136	...	...	...	—	—	—	—	—
85-86—Saskatoon	WHL	55	12	11	23	43	...	...	...	13	4	8	12	28
86-87—Saskatoon	WHL	72	38	59	97	116	...	...	...	11	4	6	10	24
87-88—Nova Scotia	AHL	19	4	10	14	17	...	...	...	4	1	1	2	4
—Milwaukee	IHL	40	14	28	42	34	...	...	...	—	—	—	—	—
88-89—Cape Breton	AHL	76	32	42	74	81	...	...	...	—	—	—	—	—
89-90—Cape Breton	AHL	61	25	44	69	83	...	...	...	4	0	2	2	8
90-91—Edmonton	NHL	2	0	0	0	0	0	0	0	—	—	—	—	—
—Cape Breton	AHL	76	25	75	100	182	...	...	...	4	0	1	1	8
91-92—Cape Breton	AHL	77	29	*84	*113	80	...	...	...	5	3	7	10	14
92-93—Cape Breton	AHL	43	14	62	76	68	...	...	...	15	8	9	17	18
—Edmonton	NHL	21	1	4	5	6	-2	0	0	—	—	—	—	—
93-94—Anaheim	NHL	80	8	25	33	64	0	2	2	—	—	—	—	—
94-95—Anaheim	NHL	45	8	21	29	32	-4	1	1	—	—	—	—	—
95-96—Anaheim	NHL	49	8	17	25	41	13	0	0	—	—	—	—	—
96-97—Ottawa	NHL	80	11	14	25	35	-8	1	1	7	0	1	1	4
97-98—Ottawa	NHL	80	4	15	19	48	4	0	0	11	0	1	1	10
NHL Totals (7 years)		357	40	96	136	226	3	4	4	18	0	2	2	14

VANBIESBROUCK, JOHN   G   FLYERS

PERSONAL: Born September 4, 1963, in Detroit. ... 5-8/176. ... Catches left. ... Name pronounced van-BEES-bruk.
TRANSACTIONS/CAREER NOTES: Selected by New York Rangers in fourth round (fifth Rangers pick, 72nd overall) of NHL entry draft (June 10, 1981). ... Fractured jaw (October 1987). ... Severely lacerated wrist (June 1988). ... Underwent knee surgery (May 11, 1990). ... Suffered lower back spasms (February 25, 1992); missed 11 games. ... Pulled groin (November 2, 1992); missed four games. ... Traded by Rangers to Vancouver Canucks for future considerations (June 20, 1993); Canucks sent D Doug Lidster to Rangers to complete deal (June 25, 1993). ... Selected by Florida Panthers in NHL expansion draft (June 24, 1993). ... Lacerated hand (February 1, 1994); missed seven games. ... Signed as free agent by Philadelphia Flyers (July 7, 1998).
HONORS: Won F.W. (Dinty) Moore Trophy (1980-81). ... Shared Dave Pinkney Trophy with Marc D'Amour (1981-82). ... Named to OHL All-Star second team (1982-83). ... Shared Tommy Ivan Trophy with D Bruce Affleck (1983-84). ... Shared Terry Sawchuk Trophy with Ron Scott (1983-84). ... Named to CHL All-Star first team (1983-84). ... Won Vezina Trophy (1985-86). ... Named to THE SPORTING NEWS All-Star first team (1985-86 and 1993-94). ... Named to NHL All-Star first team (1985-86). ... Played in NHL All-Star Game (1994, 1996 and 1997). ... Named to NHL All-Star second team (1993-94).
MISCELLANEOUS: Holds Florida Panthers all-time records for most games played by goalie (268), most wins (106), most shutouts (13) and goals-against average (2.58). ... Stopped a penalty shot attempt (vs. Petr Klima, February 17, 1987; vs. Ray Bourque, November 11, 1988; vs. Pavel Bure, February 17, 1992; vs. Trent Klatt, October 1, 1997). ... Allowed a penalty shot goal (vs. Pat Verbeek, March 27, 1988; vs. Keith Acton, March 25, 1990; vs. Mario Lemieux, April 11, 1997; vs. Derek King, February 7, 1998).

		REGULAR SEASON							PLAYOFFS						
Season Team	League	Gms.	Min	W	L	T	GA	SO	Avg.	Gms.	Min.	W	L	GA	SO	Avg.
80-81—Sault Ste. Marie	OMJHL	56	2941	31	16	1	203	0	4.14	11	457	3	3	24	1	3.15
81-82—Sault Ste. Marie	OHL	31	1686	12	12	2	102	0	3.63	7	276	1	4	20	0	4.35
—New York Rangers	NHL	1	60	1	0	0	1	0	1.00	—	—	—	—	—	—	—
82-83—Sault Ste. Marie	OHL	*62	3471	39	21	1	209	0	3.61	16	944	7	6	56	*1	3.56
83-84—New York Rangers	NHL	3	180	2	1	0	10	0	3.33	1	1	0	0	0	0	...
—Tulsa	CHL	37	2153	20	13	2	124	*3	3.46	4	240	4	0	10	0	*2.50
84-85—New York Rangers	NHL	42	2358	12	24	3	166	1	4.22	1	20	0	0	0	0	...
85-86—New York Rangers	NHL	61	3326	31	21	5	184	3	3.32	16	899	8	8	49	*1	3.27
86-87—New York Rangers	NHL	50	2656	18	20	5	161	0	3.64	4	195	1	3	11	1	3.38
87-88—New York Rangers	NHL	56	3319	27	22	7	187	2	3.38	—	—	—	—	—	—	—
88-89—New York Rangers	NHL	56	3207	28	21	4	197	0	3.69	2	107	0	1	6	0	3.36
89-90—New York Rangers	NHL	47	2734	19	19	7	154	1	3.38	6	298	2	3	15	0	3.02
90-91—New York Rangers	NHL	40	2257	15	18	6	126	3	3.35	1	52	0	1	1	0	1.15
91-92—New York Rangers	NHL	45	2526	27	13	3	120	2	2.85	7	368	2	5	23	0	3.75
92-93—New York Rangers	NHL	48	2757	20	18	7	152	4	3.31	—	—	—	—	—	—	—
93-94—Florida	NHL	57	3440	21	25	11	145	1	2.53	—	—	—	—	—	—	—
94-95—Florida	NHL	37	2087	14	15	4	86	4	2.47	—	—	—	—	—	—	—
95-96—Florida	NHL	57	3178	26	20	7	142	2	2.68	22	1332	12	*10	50	1	2.25
96-97—Florida	NHL	57	3347	27	19	10	128	2	2.29	5	328	1	4	13	1	2.38
97-98—Florida	NHL	60	3451	18	29	11	165	4	2.87	—	—	—	—	—	—	—
—U.S. Olympic Team	Int'l	1	1	0	0	0	0	0	0.00	—	—	—	—	—	—	—
NHL Totals (16 years)		717	40883	306	285	90	2124	29	3.12	65	3600	26	34	168	4	2.80

V

VANDENBUSSCHE, RYAN — RW — BLACKHAWKS

PERSONAL: Born February 28, 1973, in Simcoe, Ontario. ... 5-11/187. ... Shoots right. ... Name pronounced VAN-dihn-bush.
TRANSACTIONS/CAREER NOTES: Selected by Toronto Maple Leafs in eighth round (173rd overall) of NHL entry draft (June 20, 1992). ... Signed as free agent by New York Rangers (August 22, 1995). ... Traded by Rangers to Chicago Blackhawks for D Ryan Risidore (March 24, 1998).

		REGULAR SEASON								PLAYOFFS				
Season Team	League	Gms.	G	A	Pts.	PIM	+/-	PP	SH	Gms.	G	A	Pts.	PIM
90-91—Cornwall	OHL	49	3	8	11	139	...		...	—	—	—	—	—
91-92—Cornwall	OHL	61	13	15	28	232	...		...	6	0	2	2	9
92-93—Newmarket	OHL	30	15	12	27	161	...		...	—	—	—	—	—
—Guelph	OHL	29	3	14	17	99	...		...	5	1	3	4	13
—St. John's	AHL	1	0	0	0	0	...		...	—	—	—	—	—
93-94—St. John's	AHL	44	4	10	14	124	...		...	—	—	—	—	—
—Springfield	AHL	9	1	2	3	29	...		...	5	0	0	0	16
94-95—St. John's	AHL	53	2	13	15	239	...		...	—	—	—	—	—
95-96—Binghamton	AHL	68	3	17	20	240	...		...	4	0	0	0	9
96-97—Binghamton	AHL	38	8	11	19	133	...		...	—	—	—	—	—
—New York Rangers	NHL	11	1	0	1	30	-2	0	0	—	—	—	—	—
97-98—New York Rangers	NHL	16	1	0	1	38	-2	0	0	—	—	—	—	—
—Hartford	AHL	15	2	0	2	45	...		...	—	—	—	—	—
—Chicago	NHL	4	0	1	1	5	0	0	0	—	—	—	—	—
—Indianapolis	IHL	3	1	1	2	4	...		...	—	—	—	—	—
NHL Totals (2 years)		31	2	1	3	73	-4	0	0					

VAN DRUNEN, DAVID — D — SENATORS

PERSONAL: Born January 31, 1976 ... 6-0/200. ... Shoots right. ... Name pronounced van DROO-nehn.
TRANSACTIONS/CAREER NOTES: Signed as free agent by Ottawa Senators (May 2, 1997).
HONORS: Named to WHL (East) All-Star second team (1996-97).

		REGULAR SEASON								PLAYOFFS				
Season Team	League	Gms.	G	A	Pts.	PIM	+/-	PP	SH	Gms.	G	A	Pts.	PIM
92-93—Sherwood Park	AJHL	32	3	16	19	114	...		...	—	—	—	—	—
93-94—Prince Albert	WHL	63	3	10	13	95	...		...	—	—	—	—	—
94-95—Prince Albert	WHL	71	2	14	16	132	...		...	15	3	4	7	36
95-96—Prince Albert	WHL	70	10	23	33	172	...		...	18	1	5	6	37
96-97—Prince Albert	WHL	72	18	47	65	216	...		...	0	0	4	4	24
97-98—Prince Albert	WHL	59	8	22	30	107	...		...	—	—	—	—	—
—Detroit	IHL	1	0	0	0	2	...		...	—	—	—	—	—
—Hershey	AHL	5	0	0	0	2	...		...	—	—	—	—	—
—Portland	AHL	4	0	0	0	2	...		...	—	—	—	—	—

VAN IMPE, DARREN — D — BRUINS

PERSONAL: Born May 18, 1973, in Saskatoon, Sask. ... 6-1/205. ... Shoots left. ... Name pronounced VAN-IHMP.
TRANSACTIONS/CAREER NOTES: Selected by New York Islanders in seventh round (seventh Islanders pick, 170th overall) of NHL entry draft (June 26, 1993). ... Traded by Islanders to Mighty Ducks of Anaheim for ninth-round pick (LW Mike Broda) in 1995 draft (September 2, 1994). ... Claimed on waivers by Boston Bruins (November 26, 1997). ... Strained shoulder (January 7, 1998); missed one game.
HONORS: Named to WHL (East) All-Star first team (1992-93 and 1993-94).

		REGULAR SEASON								PLAYOFFS				
Season Team	League	Gms.	G	A	Pts.	PIM	+/-	PP	SH	Gms.	G	A	Pts.	PIM
92-93—Red Deer	WHL	54	23	47	70	118	...		...	4	2	5	7	16
93-94—Red Deer	WHL	58	20	64	84	125	...		...	4	2	4	6	6
94-95—San Diego	IHL	76	6	17	23	74	...		...	5	0	0	0	0
—Anaheim	NHL	1	0	1	1	4	0	0	0	—	—	—	—	—
95-96—Baltimore	AHL	63	11	47	58	79	...		...	—	—	—	—	—
—Anaheim	NHL	16	1	2	3	14	8	0	0	—	—	—	—	—
96-97—Anaheim	NHL	74	4	19	23	90	3	2	0	9	0	2	2	16
97-98—Anaheim	NHL	19	1	3	4	4	-10	0	0	—	—	—	—	—
—Boston	NHL	50	2	8	10	36	4	2	0	6	2	1	3	0
NHL Totals (4 years)		160	8	33	41	148	5	4	0	15	2	3	5	16

VAN OENE, DARREN — LW — SABRES

PERSONAL: Born January 18, 1978, in Edmonton. ... 6-3/207. ... Shoots left. ... Name pronounced van OH-ihn.
TRANSACTIONS/CAREER NOTES: Selected by Buffalo Sabres in second round (third Sabres pick, 33rd overall) of NHL entry draft (June 22, 1996).

		REGULAR SEASON								PLAYOFFS				
Season Team	League	Gms.	G	A	Pts.	PIM	+/-	PP	SH	Gms.	G	A	Pts.	PIM
94-95—Brandon	WHL	59	5	13	18	108	...		...	18	1	1	2	34
95-96—Brandon	WHL	47	10	18	28	126	...		...	18	1	6	7	*78
96-97—Brandon	WHL	56	21	27	48	139	...		...	6	2	3	5	19
97-98—Brandon	WHL	51	23	24	47	161	...		...	17	6	7	13	51

V

VARADA, VACLAV   RW   SABRES

PERSONAL: Born April 26, 1976, in Valasske Mezirici, Czechoslovakia. ... 6-0/209. ... Shoots left. ... Name pronounced vuh-RAH-duh.
TRANSACTIONS/CAREER NOTES: Selected by San Jose Sharks in fourth round (fourth Sharks pick, 89th overall) of NHL entry draft (June 29, 1994). ... Fractured left hand (February 2, 1997); missed 15 games. ... Traded by Sharks with LW Martin Spahnel and fourth-round pick (D Mike Martone) in 1996 draft to Buffalo Sabres for D Doug Bodger (November 16, 1995).

Season Team	League		REGULAR SEASON								PLAYOFFS			
		Gms.	G	A	Pts.	PIM	+/-	PP	SH		Gms.	G	A	Pts.	PIM
92-93—TJ Vitkovice	Czech.	1	0	0	0	...	...	...	...		—	—	—	—	—
93-94—HC Vitkovice	Czech Rep.	24	6	7	13	...	...	...	...		5	1	1	2	...
94-95—Tacoma	WHL	68	50	38	88	108	...	...	...		4	4	3	7	11
95-96—Kelowna	WHL	59	39	46	85	100	...	...	...		6	3	3	6	16
—Rochester	AHL	5	3	0	3	4	...	...	...		—	—	—	—	—
—Buffalo	NHL	1	0	0	0	0	0	0	0		—	—	—	—	—
96-97—Rochester	AHL	53	23	25	48	81	...	...	...		10	1	6	7	27
—Buffalo	NHL	5	0	0	0	2	0	0	0		—	—	—	—	—
97-98—Rochester	AHL	45	30	26	56	74	...	...	...		15	3	4	7	18
—Buffalo	NHL	27	5	6	11	15	0	0	0		15	3	4	7	18
NHL Totals (3 years)		33	5	6	11	17	0	0	0		15	3	4	7	18

VARIS, PETRI   LW   BLACKHAWKS

PERSONAL: Born May 13, 1969, in Varkaus, Finland. ... 6-1/200. ... Shoots left. ... Name pronounced PEHT-ree VAIR-ihz.
TRANSACTIONS/CAREER NOTES: Selected by San Jose Sharks in sixth round (seventh Sharks pick, 132nd overall) of NHL entry draft (June 26, 1993). ... Signed as free agent by Chicago Blackhawks (August 6, 1997).
HONORS: Named Finnish League Rookie of the Year (1991-92).
MISCELLANEOUS: Member of bronze-medal-winning Finnish Olympic team (1994).

Season Team	League		REGULAR SEASON								PLAYOFFS			
		Gms.	G	A	Pts.	PIM	+/-	PP	SH		Gms.	G	A	Pts.	PIM
90-91—KooKoo Kouvola	Finland Dv.II	44	20	31	51	42	...	...	...		—	—	—	—	—
91-92—Assat Pori	Finland	36	13	23	36	24	...	...	...		—	—	—	—	—
92-93—Assat Pori	Finland	46	14	35	49	42	...	...	...		8	2	2	4	12
93-94—Jokerit Helsinki	Finland	31	14	15	29	16	...	...	...		11	3	4	7	6
—Fin. Olympic Team	Int'l	5	1	1	2	2	...	...	...		—	—	—	—	—
94-95—Jokerit Helsinki	Finland	47	21	20	41	53	...	...	...		11	7	2	9	10
95-96—Jokerit Helsinki	Finland	50	28	28	56	22	...	...	...		11	12	7	19	6
96-97—Jokerit Helsinki	Finland	50	36	23	59	38	...	...	...		9	7	4	11	14
97-98—Indianapolis	IHL	77	18	54	72	32	...	...	...		5	3	4	7	4
—Chicago	NHL	1	0	0	0	0	0	0	0		—	—	—	—	—
NHL Totals (1 year)		1	0	0	0	0	0	0	0						

VARLAMOV, SERGEI   RW   FLAMES

PERSONAL: Born July 21, 1978, in Kiev, U.S.S.R. ... 5-11/190. ... Shoots left. ... Name pronounced VAHR-luh-mahf.
TRANSACTIONS/CAREER NOTES: Signed as free agent by Calgary Flames (September 18, 1996).
HONORS: Named to Can.HL All-Star first team (1997-98). ... Won Bob Clarke Trophy (1997-98). ... Won Four Broncos Memorial Trophy (1997-98). ... Won Can.HL Player of the Year Award (1997-98). ... Named to WHL (East) All-Star first team (1997-98).

Season Team	League		REGULAR SEASON								PLAYOFFS			
		Gms.	G	A	Pts.	PIM	+/-	PP	SH		Gms.	G	A	Pts.	PIM
95-96—Swift Current	WHL	55	23	21	44	65	...	...	...		—	—	—	—	—
96-97—Swift Current	WHL	72	46	39	85	94	...	...	...		—	—	—	—	—
—Saint John	AHL	1	0	0	0	2	...	...	...		—	—	—	—	—
97-98—Swift Current	WHL	72	*66	53	*119	132	...	...	...		12	10	5	15	28
—Calgary	NHL	1	0	0	0	0	0	0	0		—	—	—	—	—
NHL Totals (1 year)		1	0	0	0	0	0	0	0						

VASILIEV, ALEXEI   D   ISLANDERS

PERSONAL: Born September 1, 1977, in Yaroslavl, U.S.S.R. ... 6-1/190. ... Shoots left.
TRANSACTIONS/CAREER NOTES: Selected by New York Rangers in fifth round (fourth Rangers pick, 110th overall) of NHL entry draft (July 8, 1995).

Season Team	League		REGULAR SEASON								PLAYOFFS			
		Gms.	G	A	Pts.	PIM	+/-	PP	SH		Gms.	G	A	Pts.	PIM
93-94—Yaroslavl	CIS	2	0	1	1	4	...	...	...		—	—	—	—	—
94-95—Yaroslavl 2	CIS.2					Statistics unavailable.									
95-96—Yaroslavl	CIS	40	4	7	11	4	...	...	...		—	—	—	—	—
96-97—Yaroslavl	Russian	44	2	8	10	10	...	...	...		9	1	1	2	8
97-98—						Statistics unavailable.									

VASILJEVS, HERBERT   C   PANTHERS

PERSONAL: Born May 27, 1976, in Rigo, U.S.S.R. ... 5-11/170. ... Shoots right.
TRANSACTIONS/CAREER NOTES: Signed as free agent by Florida Panthers (October 3, 1997).

V

Season Team	League	REGULAR SEASON								PLAYOFFS				
		Gms.	G	A	Pts.	PIM	+/-	PP	SH	Gms.	G	A	Pts.	PIM
95-96—Guelph	OHL	65	34	33	67	63	...	...	...	16	6	13	19	6
96-97—Carolina	AHL	54	13	18	31	30	...	...	...	—	—	—	—	—
—Port Huron	Col.HL	3	3	2	5	4	...	...	...	—	—	—	—	—
97-98—New Haven	AHL	76	36	30	66	60	...	...	...	3	1	0	1	2

VASKE, DENNIS D

PERSONAL: Born October 11, 1967, in Rockford, Ill. ... 6-2/215. ... Shoots left. ... Full name: Dennis James Vaske. ... Name pronounced VAS-kee.
HIGH SCHOOL: Armstrong (Plymouth, Minn.).
COLLEGE: Minnesota-Duluth.
TRANSACTIONS/CAREER NOTES: Selected by New York Islanders in second round (second Islanders pick, 38th overall) of NHL entry draft (June 21, 1986). ... Lacerated forehead (April 8, 1993); missed three games. ... Broke foot (December 19, 1993); missed 13 games. ... Broke ankle (April 18, 1995); missed last seven games of season. ... Suffered concussion and lacerated face (November 22, 1995); missed remainder of season. ... Separated shoulder (September 17, 1996); missed 18 games. ... Suffered concussion (November 29, 1996); missed 48 games. ... Suffered concussion (November 14, 1997); missed remainder of season.

Season Team	League	REGULAR SEASON								PLAYOFFS				
		Gms.	G	A	Pts.	PIM	+/-	PP	SH	Gms.	G	A	Pts.	PIM
84-85—Armstrong H.S.	Minn. H.S.	22	5	18	23		...	...	...	—	—	—	—	—
85-86—Armstrong H.S.	Minn. H.S.	20	9	13	22		...	...	...	—	—	—	—	—
86-87—Minnesota-Duluth	WCHA	33	0	2	2	40	...	...	...	—	—	—	—	—
87-88—Minnesota-Duluth	WCHA	39	1	6	7	90	...	...	...	—	—	—	—	—
88-89—Minnesota-Duluth	WCHA	37	9	19	28	86	...	...	...	—	—	—	—	—
89-90—Minnesota-Duluth	WCHA	37	5	24	29	72	...	...	...	—	—	—	—	—
90-91—New York Islanders	NHL	5	0	0	0	2	4	0	0	—	—	—	—	—
—Capital District	AHL	67	10	10	20	65	...	...	...	—	—	—	—	—
91-92—Capital District	AHL	31	1	11	12	59	...	...	...	—	—	—	—	—
—New York Islanders	NHL	39	0	1	1	39	5	0	0	—	—	—	—	—
92-93—Capital District	AHL	42	4	15	19	70	...	...	...	—	—	—	—	—
—New York Islanders	NHL	27	1	5	6	32	9	0	0	18	0	6	6	14
93-94—New York Islanders	NHL	65	2	11	13	76	21	0	0	4	0	1	1	2
94-95—New York Islanders	NHL	41	1	11	12	53	3	0	0	—	—	—	—	—
95-96—New York Islanders	NHL	19	1	6	7	21	-13	1	0	—	—	—	—	—
96-97—New York Islanders	NHL	17	0	4	4	12	3	0	0	—	—	—	—	—
97-98—New York Islanders	NHL	19	0	3	3	12	2	0	0	—	—	—	—	—
NHL Totals (8 years)		232	5	41	46	247	34	1	0	22	0	7	7	16

VERBEEK, PAT RW STARS

PERSONAL: Born May 24, 1964, in Sarnia, Ont. ... 5-9/190. ... Shoots right.
TRANSACTIONS/CAREER NOTES: Selected by New Jersey Devils as underage junior in third round (third Devils pick, 43rd overall) of NHL entry draft (June 9, 1982). ... Suffered severed left thumb between knuckles in a corn-planting machine on his farm and underwent surgery to have thumb reconnected (May 15, 1985). ... Pulled side muscle (March 1987). ... Bruised chest (October 28, 1988). ... Traded by Devils to Hartford Whalers for LW Sylvain Turgeon (June 17, 1989). ... Missed first three games of 1991-92 season due to contract dispute. ... Fined $500 by Whalers for involvement in bar brawl (April 1, 1994). ... Traded by Whalers to New York Rangers for D Glen Featherstone, D Michael Stewart, first-round pick (G Jean-Sebastien Giguere) in 1995 draft and fourth-round pick (C Steve Wasylko) in 1996 draft (March 23, 1995). ... Injured knee (February 17, 1996); missed two games. ... Separated shoulder (March 1, 1996); missed nine games. ... Suffered back spasms (April 7, 1996); missed two games. ... Signed as free agent by Dallas Stars (July 3, 1996). ... Sprained knee (January 4, 1997); missed one game.
HONORS: Won Emms Family Award (1981-82). ... Played in NHL All-Star Game (1991 and 1996).
MISCELLANEOUS: Scored on a penalty shot (vs. John Vanbiesbrouck, March 27, 1988).
STATISTICAL NOTES: Only player in NHL history to lead team in goals scored and penalty minutes (1989-90 and 1990-91). ... Captain of Hartford Whalers (1992-93 through 1993-94).
STATISTICAL PLATEAUS: Three-goal games: 1985-86 (1), 1986-87 (1), 1987-88 (1), 1988-89 (1), 1992-93 (2), 1993-94 (2), 1995-96 (2), 1997-98 (1). Total: 11. ... Four-goal games: 1987-88 (1). ... Total hat tricks: 12.

Season Team	League	REGULAR SEASON								PLAYOFFS				
		Gms.	G	A	Pts.	PIM	+/-	PP	SH	Gms.	G	A	Pts.	PIM
80-81—Petrolia Jr. B.	OPJHL	42	44	44	88	155	...	...	...	—	—	—	—	—
81-82—Sudbury	OHL	66	37	51	88	180	...	...	...	—	—	—	—	—
82-83—Sudbury	OHL	61	40	67	107	184	...	...	...	—	—	—	—	—
—New Jersey	NHL	6	3	2	5	8	-2	0	0	—	—	—	—	—
83-84—New Jersey	NHL	79	20	27	47	158	-19	5	1	—	—	—	—	—
84-85—New Jersey	NHL	78	15	18	33	162	-24	5	1	—	—	—	—	—
85-86—New Jersey	NHL	76	25	28	53	79	-25	4	1	—	—	—	—	—
86-87—New Jersey	NHL	74	35	24	59	120	-23	17	0	—	—	—	—	—
87-88—New Jersey	NHL	73	46	31	77	227	29	13	0	20	4	8	12	51
88-89—New Jersey	NHL	77	26	21	47	189	-18	9	0	—	—	—	—	—
89-90—Hartford	NHL	80	44	45	89	228	1	14	0	7	2	2	4	26
90-91—Hartford	NHL	80	43	39	82	246	0	15	0	6	3	2	5	40
91-92—Hartford	NHL	76	22	35	57	243	-16	10	0	7	0	2	2	12
92-93—Hartford	NHL	84	39	43	82	197	-7	16	0	—	—	—	—	—
93-94—Hartford	NHL	84	37	38	75	177	-15	15	1	—	—	—	—	—
94-95—Hartford	NHL	29	7	11	18	53	0	3	0	—	—	—	—	—
—New York Rangers	NHL	19	10	5	15	18	-2	4	0	10	4	6	10	20
95-96—New York Rangers	NHL	69	41	41	82	129	29	17	0	11	3	6	9	12
96-97—Dallas	NHL	81	17	36	53	128	3	5	0	7	1	3	4	16
97-98—Dallas	NHL	82	31	26	57	170	15	9	0	17	3	2	5	26
NHL Totals (16 years)		1147	461	470	931	2532	-74	161	4	85	20	31	51	203

PERSONAL: Born February 24, 1963, in Calgary. ... 5-9/170. ... Catches left.

TRANSACTIONS/CAREER NOTES: Selected by Calgary Flames in third round (second Flames pick, 56th overall) of NHL entry draft (June 10, 1981). ... Injured hip (March 2, 1988). ... Suffered back spasms (February 1989). ... Suffered back spasms (March 1990); missed 10 games. ... Suffered lacerated forehead (October 25, 1992); missed five games. ... Suffered from the flu (November 15, 1993); missed two games. ... Twisted knee (December 30, 1993); missed 14 games. ... Traded by Flames to Detroit Red Wings for D Steve Chiasson (June 29, 1994). ... Pulled groin (December 29, 1995); missed 12 games. ... Suffered from the flu (October 23, 1996); missed three games. ... Injured knee (March 12, 1997); missed three games. ... Traded by Red Wings to San Jose Sharks for second-round pick (D Maxim Linnik) in 1998 draft and third-round pick in 1999 draft (August 18, 1997).

HONORS: Won WHL Most Valuable Player Trophy (1981-82 and 1982-83). ... Won WHL Top Goaltender Trophy (1981-82 and 1982-83). ... Won WHL Player of the Year Award (1981-82). ... Named to WHL All-Star first team (1981-82 and 1982-83). ... Named to CHL All-Star second team (1983-84). ... Named to THE SPORTING NEWS All-Star second team (1988-89). ... Named to NHL All-Star second team (1988-89). ... Played in NHL All-Star Game (1988-1991 and 1993). ... Shared William M. Jennings Trophy with Chris Osgood (1995-96). ... Won Conn Smythe Trophy (1996-97).

RECORDS: Shares NHL single-season playoff record for most wins by a goaltender—16 (1989 and 1997).

MISCELLANEOUS: Member of Stanley Cup championship team (1989 and 1997). ... Stopped a penalty shot attempt (vs. Kirk Muller, March 14, 1989; vs. Jim Cummins, April 7, 1996). ... Allowed a penalty shot goal (vs. Stan Smyl, January 16, 1987; vs. Craig MacTavish, December 23, 1988; vs. Gino Odjick, October 19, 1991; vs. Paul Broten, January 16, 1992; vs. Pavel Bure, November 12, 1997). ... Holds Calgary Flames all-time records for games played by a goaltender (467) and most wins (225).. ... Holds San Jose Sharks all-time records for goals-against average (2.46).

Season Team	League	REGULAR SEASON							PLAYOFFS						
		Gms.	Min	W	L	T	GA	SO	Avg.	Gms.	Min.	W	L	GA	SO	Avg.
80-81—Calgary	WHL	59	3154	33	17	1	198	1	3.77	22	1271	...	...	82	1	3.87
81-82—Calgary	WHL	42	2329	22	14	2	143	*3	*3.68	9	527	...	...	30	0	*3.42
—Oklahoma City	CHL	—	—	—	—	—	—	—	—	1	70	0	1	4	0	3.43
82-83—Calgary	WHL	50	2856	19	18	2	155	*3	*3.26	16	925	9	7	60	0	3.89
—Calgary	NHL	2	100	0	2	0	11	0	6.60	—	—	—	—	—	—	—
83-84—Calgary	NHL	1	11	0	1	0	4	0	21.82	—	—	—	—	—	—	—
—Colorado	CHL	*46	*2648	30	13	2	148	1	*3.35	6	347	2	4	21	0	3.63
84-85—Moncton	AHL	41	2050	10	20	4	134	0	3.92	—	—	—	—	—	—	—
85-86—Salt Lake City	IHL	10	601	...	...	...	34	1	3.39	—	—	—	—	—	—	—
—Moncton	AHL	6	374	3	1	2	21	0	3.37	—	—	—	—	—	—	—
—Calgary	NHL	18	921	9	3	3	52	1	3.39	*21	*1229	12	*9	*60	0	2.93
86-87—Calgary	NHL	54	2957	30	21	1	178	1	3.61	5	263	2	3	16	0	3.65
87-88—Calgary	NHL	64	3565	39	16	7	210	1	3.53	9	515	4	4	34	0	3.96
88-89—Calgary	NHL	52	2938	*37	6	5	130	0	2.65	*22	*1381	*16	5	*52	*3	2.26
89-90—Calgary	NHL	47	2795	23	14	9	146	0	3.13	6	342	2	3	19	0	3.33
90-91—Calgary	NHL	54	3121	31	19	3	172	1	3.31	7	427	3	4	21	0	2.95
91-92—Calgary	NHL	63	3640	24	30	9	217	0	3.58	—	—	—	—	—	—	—
92-93—Calgary	NHL	64	3732	29	26	9	203	2	3.26	4	150	1	1	15	0	6.00
93-94—Calgary	NHL	48	2798	26	17	5	131	3	2.81	7	466	3	4	23	0	2.96
94-95—Detroit	NHL	30	1807	19	6	4	76	1	2.52	18	1063	12	6	41	1	2.31
95-96—Detroit	NHL	32	1855	21	7	2	70	3	2.26	4	243	2	2	11	0	2.72
96-97—Detroit	NHL	33	1952	13	11	8	79	0	2.43	20	*1229	*16	4	36	1	1.76
97-98—San Jose	NHL	62	3564	30	22	8	146	5	2.46	6	348	2	4	14	1	2.41
NHL Totals (15 years)		624	35756	331	201	73	1825	18	3.06	129	7656	75	49	342	6	2.68

PERSONAL: Born April 10, 1969, in Sault Ste. Marie, Ont. ... 6-1/220. ... Shoots left. ... Name pronounced vee-AL.

TRANSACTIONS/CAREER NOTES: Suspended three games by OHL for spearing (October 1986). ... Selected by New York Rangers in sixth round (fifth Rangers pick, 110th overall) of NHL entry draft (June 11, 1988). ... Suspended indefinitely by OHL for leaving the bench to fight (March 23, 1989). ... Traded by Rangers with C Kevin Miller and RW Jim Cummins to Detroit Red Wings for RW Joe Kocur and D Per Djoos (March 5, 1991). ... Injured right knee and ankle (December 7, 1991); missed two games. ... Traded by Red Wings with D Doug Crossman to Quebec Nordiques for cash (June 15, 1992). ... Traded by Nordiques to Red Wings for cash (September 9, 1992). ... Separated right shoulder (January 19, 1993); missed 15 games. ... Traded by Red Wings to Tampa Bay Lightning for LW Steve Maltais (June 8, 1993). ... Selected by Mighty Ducks of Anaheim in NHL expansion draft (June 24, 1993). ... Selected by Ottawa Senators in Phase II of NHL expansion draft (June 25, 1993). ... Injured left foot (November 10, 1993); missed 12 games. ... Fractured left hand (December 21, 1993); missed 13 games. ... Suspended one game and fined $500 by NHL for shooting a puck into opposing team's bench (March 23, 1994). ... Suffered ankle contusion (March 27, 1995); missed one game. ... Broke thumb (September 18, 1995); missed 11 games. ... Suffered from the flu during 1995-96 season; missed two games. ... Bruised right ankle (March 6, 1996); missed one game. ... Sprained right ankle (September 15, 1996); missed one game. ... Suffered bone chip in right hand (October 19, 1996); missed 15 games. ... Broke finger (November 30, 1996); missed 12 games. ... Underwent finger surgery (January 20, 1997); missed remainder of the season. ... Dislocated left knee cap (October 17, 1997); missed 22 games.

MISCELLANEOUS: Holds Ottawa Senators all-time record for most penalty minutes (625).

Season Team	League	REGULAR SEASON								PLAYOFFS				
		Gms.	G	A	Pts.	PIM	+/-	PP	SH	Gms.	G	A	Pts.	PIM
85-86—Hamilton	OHL	31	1	1	2	66	...	...	...	—	—	—	—	—
86-87—Hamilton	OHL	53	1	8	9	194	...	...	...	8	0	0	0	8
87-88—Hamilton	OHL	52	3	17	20	229	...	...	...	13	2	2	4	49
88-89—Niagara Falls	OHL	50	10	27	37	227	...	...	...	15	1	7	8	44
89-90—Flint	IHL	79	6	29	35	351	...	...	...	4	0	0	0	10
90-91—Binghamton	AHL	40	2	7	9	250	...	...	...	—	—	—	—	—
—New York Rangers	NHL	21	0	0	0	61	-4	0	0	—	—	—	—	—
—Detroit	NHL	9	0	0	0	16	-3	0	0	—	—	—	—	—
91-92—Detroit	NHL	27	1	0	1	72	1	0	0	—	—	—	—	—
—Adirondack	AHL	20	2	4	6	107	...	...	...	17	1	3	4	43
92-93—Detroit	NHL	9	0	1	1	20	1	0	0	—	—	—	—	—
—Adirondack	AHL	30	2	11	13	177	...	...	...	11	1	1	2	14

Season Team	League	Gms.	G	A	Pts.	PIM	+/-	PP	SH	Gms.	G	A	Pts.	PIM
93-94—Ottawa	NHL	55	2	5	7	214	-9	0	0	—	—	—	—	—
94-95—Ottawa	NHL	27	0	4	4	65	0	0	0	—	—	—	—	—
95-96—Ottawa	NHL	64	1	4	5	276	-13	0	0	—	—	—	—	—
96-97—Ottawa	NHL	11	0	1	1	25	0	0	0	—	—	—	—	—
97-98—Ottawa	NHL	19	0	0	0	45	0	0	0	—	—	—	—	—
—Chicago	IHL	24	1	3	4	86	...	...	...	1	0	0	0	2
NHL Totals (8 years)		242	4	15	19	794	-27	0	0					

VIRTUE, TERRY   D   BLUES

PERSONAL: Born August 8, 1970, in Scarborough, Ont. ... 6-0/197. ... Shoots right.
TRANSACTIONS/CAREER NOTES: Signed as free agent by St. Louis Blues (January 29, 1996).

Season Team	League	Gms.	G	A	Pts.	PIM	+/-	PP	SH	Gms.	G	A	Pts.	PIM
88-89—Victoria	WHL	8	1	1	2	13	...	...	...	—	—	—	—	—
89-90—Tri-City	WHL	58	2	19	21	167	...	...	...	—	—	—	—	—
90-91—Tri-City	WHL	11	1	8	9	24	...	...	...	—	—	—	—	—
—Portland	WHL	59	9	44	53	127	...	...	...	—	—	—	—	—
91-92—Roanoke	ECHL	38	4	22	26	165	...	...	...	—	—	—	—	—
—Louisville	ECHL	23	1	15	16	58	...	...	...	13	0	8	8	49
92-93—Louisville	ECHL	28	0	17	17	84	...	...	...	—	—	—	—	—
—Wheeling	ECHL	31	3	15	18	86	...	...	...	16	3	5	8	18
93-94—Wheeling	ECHL	34	5	28	33	61	...	...	...	6	2	2	4	4
—Cape Breton	AHL	26	4	6	10	10	...	...	...	5	0	0	0	17
94-95—Worcester	AHL	73	14	25	39	183	...	...	...	—	—	—	—	—
95-96—Worcester	AHL	76	7	31	38	234	...	...	...	4	0	0	0	4
96-97—Worcester	AHL	80	16	26	42	220	...	...	...	5	0	4	4	8
97-98—Worcester	AHL	74	8	26	34	233	...	...	...	11	1	4	5	41

VOKOUN, TOMAS   G   PREDATORS

PERSONAL: Born July 2, 1976, in Karlovy Vary, Czechoslovakia. ... 6-0/202. ... Catches right. ... Name pronounced TOH-mahz voh-KOON.
TRANSACTIONS/CAREER NOTES: Selected by Montreal Canadiens in ninth round (11th Canadiens pick, 226th overall) of NHL entry draft (June 29, 1994). ... Selected by Nashville Predators in NHL expansion draft (June 26, 1998).

Season Team	League	Gms.	Min	W	L	T	GA	SO	Avg.	Gms.	Min.	W	L	GA	SO	Avg.
93-94—Poldi Kladno	Czech Rep.	1	20	...	...	...	2	0	6.00	—	—	—	—	—	—	—
94-95—Poldi Kladno	Czech Rep.	26	1368	...	...	...	70	...	3.07	5	240	...	...	19	...	4.75
95-96—Wheeling	ECHL	35	1911	20	10	‡2	117	0	3.67	7	436	4	3	19	0	2.61
—Fredericton	AHL	—	—	—	—	—	—	—	—	1	59	0	1	4	0	4.07
96-97—Fredericton	AHL	47	2645	12	26	7	154	2	3.49	—	—	—	—	—	—	—
—Montreal	NHL	1	20	0	0	0	4	0	12.00	—	—	—	—	—	—	—
97-98—Fredericton	AHL	31	1735	13	13	2	90	0	3.11	—	—	—	—	—	—	—
NHL Totals (1 year)		1	20	0	0	0	4	0	12.00							

VOLCHKOV, ALEXANDRE   LW   CAPITALS

PERSONAL: Born September 15, 1977, in Moscow, U.S.S.R. ... 6-2/214. ... Shoots left. ... Name pronounced VOHLCH-kahv.
TRANSACTIONS/CAREER NOTES: Selected by Washington Capitals in first round (first Capitals pick, fourth overall) of NHL entry draft (June 22, 1996).
HONORS: Named to Can.HL All-Rookie team (1995-96). ... Named to OHL All-Rookie first team (1995-96). ... Named to OHL All-Star second team (1996-97).

Season Team	League	Gms.	G	A	Pts.	PIM	+/-	PP	SH	Gms.	G	A	Pts.	PIM
94-95—CSKA Moscow Jrs.	CIS	50	20	30	50	20	...	...	...	—	—	—	—	—
95-96—Barrie	OHL	47	37	27	64	36	...	...	...	7	2	3	5	12
96-97—Barrie	OHL	56	29	53	82	76	...	...	...	9	6	9	15	12
—Portland	AHL	—	—	—	—	—	...	...	...	4	0	0	0	0
97-98—Portland	AHL	34	2	5	7	20	...	...	...	1	0	0	0	0

VOPAT, JAN   D   PREDATORS

PERSONAL: Born March 22, 1973, in Most, Czechoslovakia. ... 6-0/207. ... Shoots left. ... Brother of Roman Vopat, center, Los Angeles Kings. ... Name pronounced YAHN VOH-paht.
TRANSACTIONS/CAREER NOTES: Selected by Hartford Whalers in third round (third Whalers pick, 57th overall) of NHL entry draft (June 20, 1992). ... Traded by Whalers to Los Angeles Kings for fourth-round pick (C Ian MacNeil) in 1995 draft (May 31, 1995). ... Underwent back surgery (October 22, 1996); missed 30 games. ... Sprained ankle (January 24, 1997); missed six games. ... Sprained ankle (Febraury 15, 1997); missed one game. ... Bruised thigh (April 7, 1997); missed one game. ... Traded by Kings with rights to D Kimmo Timonen to Nashville Predators for future considerations (June 26, 1998).

Season Team	League	Gms.	G	A	Pts.	PIM	+/-	PP	SH	Gms.	G	A	Pts.	PIM
90-91—CHZ Litvinov	Czech.	25	1	4	5	4	...	...	...	—	—	—	—	—
91-92—Chemopetrol Litvinov	Czech.	46	4	2	6	6	...	...	...	—	—	—	—	—
92-93—Chemopetrol Litvinov	Czech.	45	12	10	22		...	...	...	—	—	—	—	—
93-94—Chemopetrol Litvinov	Czech Rep.	41	9	19	28		...	...	...	4	1	1	2	...
—Czech Rep. Olympic	Int'l	8	0	1	1	8	...	...	...	—	—	—	—	—

Season Team	League	REGULAR SEASON								PLAYOFFS				
		Gms.	G	A	Pts.	PIM	+/-	PP	SH	Gms.	G	A	Pts.	PIM
94-95—Chemopetrol Litvinov .	Czech Rep.	42	7	18	25	...	...	...	...	4	0	2	2	...
95-96—Phoenix	IHL	47	0	9	9	34	...	...	...	4	0	2	2	4
—Los Angeles	NHL	11	1	4	5	4	3	0	0	—	—	—	—	—
96-97—Los Angeles	NHL	33	4	5	9	22	3	0	0	—	—	—	—	—
—Phoenix	IHL	4	0	6	6	6	...	...	...	—	—	—	—	—
97-98—Los Angeles	NHL	21	1	5	6	10	8	0	0	2	0	1	1	2
—Utah	IHL	38	8	13	21	24	...	...	...	—	—	—	—	—
NHL Totals (3 years)		65	6	14	20	36	14	0	0	2	0	1	1	2

VOPAT, ROMAN — C — KINGS

PERSONAL: Born April 21, 1976, in Litvinov, Czechoslovakia. ... 6-3/221. ... Shoots left. ... Brother of Jan Vopat, defenseman, Nashville Predators. ... Name pronounced ROH-muhn VOH-paht.

TRANSACTIONS/CAREER NOTES: Selected by St. Louis Blues in seventh round (fourth Blues pick, 172nd overall) of NHL entry draft (June 29, 1994). ... Traded by Blues with LW Craig Johnson, RW/C Patrice Tardiff, fifth-round pick (D Peter Hogan) in 1996 draft and first-round pick (LW Matt Zultek) in 1997 draft to Los Angeles Kings for C Wayne Gretzky (February 27, 1996). ... Suffered concussion (March 22, 1997); missed one game.

Season Team	League	REGULAR SEASON								PLAYOFFS				
		Gms.	G	A	Pts.	PIM	+/-	PP	SH	Gms.	G	A	Pts.	PIM
93-94—Litvinov	Czech Rep.	7	0	0	0	...	...	...	...	—	—	—	—	—
—Chemopetrol Litvinov .	Czech Rep.	7	0	0	0	...	...	...	...	—	—	—	—	—
94-95—Moose Jaw	WHL	72	23	20	43	141	...	...	...	10	4	1	5	28
—Peoria	IHL	—	—	—	—	—	...	...	...	6	0	2	2	2
95-96—St. Louis	NHL	25	2	3	5	48	-8	1	0	—	—	—	—	—
—Worcester	AHL	5	2	0	2	14	...	...	...	—	—	—	—	—
—Moose Jaw	WHL	7	0	4	4	34	...	...	...	—	—	—	—	—
—Prince Albert	WHL	22	15	5	20	81	...	...	...	18	9	8	17	57
96-97—Phoenix	IHL	50	8	8	16	139	...	...	...	—	—	—	—	—
—Los Angeles	NHL	29	4	5	9	60	-7	1	0	—	—	—	—	—
97-98—Los Angeles	NHL	25	0	3	3	55	-7	0	0	—	—	—	—	—
—Fredericton	AHL	29	10	10	20	93	...	...	...	—	—	—	—	—
NHL Totals (3 years)		79	6	11	17	163	-22	2	0	—	—	—	—	—

VOROBIEV, VLADIMIR — LW — RANGERS

PERSONAL: Born October 2, 1972, in Cherepovets, U.S.S.R. ... 6-3/205. ... Shoots right. ... Name pronounced vuh-ROH-bee-yehf.

TRANSACTIONS/CAREER NOTES: Selected by New York Rangers in 10th round (10th Rangers pick, 240th overall) of NHL entry draft (June 20, 1992).

Season Team	League	REGULAR SEASON								PLAYOFFS				
		Gms.	G	A	Pts.	PIM	+/-	PP	SH	Gms.	G	A	Pts.	PIM
92-93—Metallurg Cherepovets	CIS	42	18	5	23	18	...	...	...	—	—	—	—	—
93-94—Dynamo Moscow	CIS	11	3	1	4	2	...	...	...	—	—	—	—	—
94-95—Dynamo Moscow	CIS	48	9	20	29	28	...	...	...	14	1	7	8	2
95-96—Dynamo Moscow	CIS	42	19	9	28	49	...	...	...	9	2	8	10	2
96-97—Binghamton	AHL	61	22	27	49	6	...	...	...	4	1	1	2	2
—New York Rangers	NHL	16	5	5	10	6	4	2	0	—	—	—	—	—
97-98—Hartford	AHL	56	20	28	48	18	...	...	...	15	11	8	19	4
—New York Rangers	NHL	15	2	2	4	6	-10	0	0	—	—	—	—	—
NHL Totals (2 years)		31	7	7	14	12	-6	2	0	—	—	—	—	—

VUJTEK, VLADIMIR — LW

PERSONAL: Born February 17, 1972, in Ostrava, Czechoslovakia. ... 6-1/190. ... Shoots left. ... Name pronounced VWEE-tehk.

TRANSACTIONS/CAREER NOTES: Selected by Montreal Canadiens in fourth round (fifth Canadiens pick, 73rd overall) of NHL entry draft (June 22, 1991). ... Traded by Canadiens with LW Shayne Corson and C Brent Gilchrist to Edmonton Oilers for LW Vincent Damphousse and fourth-round pick (D Adam Wiesel) in 1993 draft (August 27, 1992). ... Suffered charley horse (October 6, 1992); missed eight games. ... Suspended by Oilers after failing to report to assigned team (January 4, 1993). ... Strained lower back (March 17, 1993); missed five games. ... Injured shoulder (January 11, 1994); missed seven games. ... Injured shoulder and underwent surgery (February 14, 1994); missed remainder of season. ... Played in Europe during 1994-95 NHL lockout. ... Traded by Oilers to Tampa Bay Lightning for RW Brantt Myhres and conditional draft pick (July 16, 1997). ... Suffered from the flu (October 3, 1997); missed one game. ... Suffered from chest virus (November 8, 1997); missed 42 games.

HONORS: Named to WHL (West) All-Star first team (1991-92).

Season Team	League	REGULAR SEASON								PLAYOFFS				
		Gms.	G	A	Pts.	PIM	+/-	PP	SH	Gms.	G	A	Pts.	PIM
89-90—Vitkovice	Czech.	29	3	4	7	...	...	...	...	—	—	—	—	—
90-91—Tri-City	WHL	37	26	18	44	25	...	...	...	—	—	—	—	—
—Vitkovice	Czech.	26	7	4	11	...	...	...	...	—	—	—	—	—
91-92—Tri-City	WHL	53	41	61	102	114	...	...	...	—	—	—	—	—
—Montreal	NHL	2	0	0	0	0	...	...	...	—	—	—	—	—
92-93—Edmonton	NHL	30	1	10	11	8	-1	0	0	—	—	—	—	—
—Cape Breton	AHL	20	10	9	19	14	...	...	...	1	0	0	0	0
93-94—Edmonton	NHL	40	4	15	19	14	-7	1	0	—	—	—	—	—
94-95—HC Vitkovice	Czech Rep.	18	5	7	12	51	...	...	...	—	—	—	—	—
—Cape Breton	AHL	30	10	11	21	30	...	...	...	—	—	—	—	—
—Las Vegas	IHL	1	0	0	0	0	...	...	...	—	—	—	—	—
95-96—TJ Vitkovice	Czech Rep.	26	6	7	13	0	...	...	...	4	1	1	2	0
96-97—Assat Pori	Finland	50	27	31	58	48	...	...	...	4	1	2	3	2
97-98—Tampa Bay	NHL	30	2	4	6	16	-2	0	0	—	—	—	—	—
—Adirondack	AHL	2	1	2	3	0	...	...	...	—	—	—	—	—
NHL Totals (4 years)		102	7	29	36	38	...	...	...	—	—	—	—	—

V

VUKOTA, MICK   RW

PERSONAL: Born September 14, 1966, in Saskatoon, Sask. ... 6-1/225. ... Shoots right. ... Name pronounced vuh-KOH-tuh.
TRANSACTIONS/CAREER NOTES: Signed as free agent by New York Islanders (September 1987). ... Suspended six games by AHL for returning from locker room to fight (November 20, 1987). ... Suffered sore back (February 1990). ... Separated left shoulder (March 18, 1990). ... Suspended 10 games by NHL for fighting (April 5, 1990); missed final four games of 1989-90 season and first six games of 1990-91 season. ... Injured shoulder prior to 1992-93 season; missed first two games of season. ... Bruised left hand (October 26, 1993); missed two games. ... Suspended 10 games and fined $10,000 by NHL for leaving bench to fight (January 7, 1994). ... Suspended two games without pay and fined $500 by NHL for improper conduct in playoff game (May 17, 1994). ... Injured knee (November 28, 1995); missed one game. ... Fractured right thumb (December 23, 1995); missed 43 games. ... Selected by Tampa Bay Lightning from Islanders in NHL waiver draft (September 28, 1997). ... Traded by Lightning with F Patrick Poulin and D Igor Ulanov to Montreal Canadiens for F Stephane Richer, F Darcy Tucker and D David Wilkie (January 15, 1998). ... Injured hand (February 1, 1998); missed one game.
MISCELLANEOUS: Holds New York Islanders all-time record for most penalty minutes (1,879).
STATISTICAL PLATEAUS: Three-goal games: 1989-90 (1).

		REGULAR SEASON								PLAYOFFS				
Season Team	League	Gms.	G	A	Pts.	PIM	+/-	PP	SH	Gms.	G	A	Pts.	PIM
83-84—Winnipeg	WHL	3	1	1	2	10	...	...	...	—	—	—	—	—
84-85—Kelowna	WHL	66	10	6	16	247	...	...	...	—	—	—	—	—
85-86—Spokane	WHL	64	19	14	33	369	...	...	...	9	6	4	10	68
86-87—Spokane	WHL	61	25	28	53	*337	...	...	...	4	0	0	0	40
87-88—New York Islanders	NHL	17	1	0	1	82	1	0	0	2	0	0	0	23
—Springfield	AHL	52	7	9	16	372	...	...	...	—	—	—	—	—
88-89—Springfield	AHL	3	1	0	1	33	...	...	...	—	—	—	—	—
—New York Islanders	NHL	48	2	2	4	237	-17	0	0	—	—	—	—	—
89-90—New York Islanders	NHL	76	4	8	12	290	10	0	0	1	0	0	0	17
90-91—Capital District	AHL	2	0	0	0	9	...	...	...	—	—	—	—	—
—New York Islanders	NHL	60	2	4	6	238	-13	0	0	—	—	—	—	—
91-92—New York Islanders	NHL	74	0	6	6	293	-6	0	0	—	—	—	—	—
92-93—New York Islanders	NHL	74	2	5	7	216	3	0	0	15	0	0	0	16
93-94—New York Islanders	NHL	72	3	1	4	237	-5	0	0	4	0	0	0	17
94-95—New York Islanders	NHL	40	0	2	2	109	1	0	0	—	—	—	—	—
95-96—New York Islanders	NHL	32	1	1	2	106	-3	0	0	—	—	—	—	—
96-97—New York Islanders	NHL	17	1	0	1	71	-2	0	0	—	—	—	—	—
—Utah	IHL	43	11	11	22	185	...	...	...	7	1	2	3	20
97-98—Tampa Bay	NHL	42	1	0	1	116	0	0	0	—	—	—	—	—
—Montreal	NHL	22	0	0	0	76	-4	0	0	1	0	0	0	0
NHL Totals (11 years)		**574**	**17**	**29**	**46**	**2071**	**-35**	**0**	**0**	**23**	**0**	**0**	**0**	**73**

WAITE, JIM   G

PERSONAL: Born April 15, 1969, in Sherbrooke, Que. ... 6-1/180. ... Catches left. ... Name pronounced WAYT.
TRANSACTIONS/CAREER NOTES: Selected by Chicago Blackhawks as underage junior in first round (first Blackhawks pick, eighth overall) of NHL entry draft (June 13, 1987). ... Broke collarbone (December 6, 1988). ... Sprained ankle (October 12, 1991); missed one game. ... Loaned to Hershey Bears for part of 1991-92 season. ... Traded by Blackhawks to San Jose Sharks for future considerations (June 18, 1993); Sharks sent D Neil Wilkinson to Blackhawks to complete deal (July 9, 1993). ... Sprained knee (January 11, 1994); missed two games. ... Underwent arthroscopic knee surgery (March 7, 1994); missed eight games. ... Traded by Sharks to Blackhawks for fourth-round pick (traded to Rangers) in 1997 draft (February 6, 1995). ... Selected by Phoenix Coyotes from Blackhawks in NHL waiver draft (September 28, 1997). ... Sprained thumb (January 9, 1998); missed 18 games.
HONORS: Won Raymond Lagace Trophy (1986-87). ... Named to QMJHL All-Star second team (1986-87). ... Won James Norris Memorial Trophy (1989-90). ... Named to IHL All-Star first team (1989-90).

		REGULAR SEASON								PLAYOFFS						
Season Team	League	Gms.	Min	W	L	T	GA	SO	Avg.	Gms.	Min.	W	L	GA	SO	Avg.
86-87—Chicoutimi	QMJHL	50	2569	23	17	3	209	†2	4.88	11	576	4	6	54	*1	5.63
87-88—Chicoutimi	QMJHL	36	2000	17	16	1	150	0	4.50	4	222	1	2	17	0	4.59
88-89—Chicago	NHL	11	494	0	7	1	43	0	5.22	—	—	—	—	—	—	—
—Saginaw	IHL	5	304	3	1	‡0	10	0	1.97	—	—	—	—	—	—	—
89-90—Indianapolis	IHL	54	*3207	34	14	‡5	135	*5	*2.53	†10	*602	9	1	19	†1	*1.89
—Chicago	NHL	4	183	2	0	0	14	0	4.59	—	—	—	—	—	—	—
90-91—Indianapolis	IHL	49	2888	26	18	‡4	167	3	3.47	6	369	2	4	20	0	3.25
—Chicago	NHL	1	60	1	0	0	2	0	2.00	—	—	—	—	—	—	—
91-92—Chicago	NHL	17	877	4	7	4	54	0	3.69	—	—	—	—	—	—	—
—Indianapolis	IHL	13	702	4	7	‡1	53	0	4.53	—	—	—	—	—	—	—
—Hershey	AHL	11	631	6	4	1	44	0	4.18	6	360	2	4	19	0	3.17
92-93—Chicago	NHL	20	996	6	7	1	49	2	2.95	—	—	—	—	—	—	—
93-94—San Jose	NHL	15	697	3	7	0	50	0	4.30	2	40	0	0	3	0	4.50
94-95—Chicago	NHL	2	119	1	1	0	5	0	2.52	—	—	—	—	—	—	—
—Indianapolis	IHL	4	239	2	1	‡1	13	0	3.26	—	—	—	—	—	—	—
95-96—Indianapolis	IHL	56	3157	28	18	‡6	179	0	3.40	5	297	2	3	15	1	3.03
—Chicago	NHL	1	31	0	0	0	0	0	...	—	—	—	—	—	—	—
96-97—Chicago	NHL	2	105	0	1	1	7	0	4.00	—	—	—	—	—	—	—
—Indianapolis	IHL	41	2450	22	15	‡4	112	4	2.74	4	222	1	3	13	0	3.51
97-98—Phoenix	NHL	17	793	5	6	1	28	1	2.12	4	171	0	3	11	0	3.86
NHL Totals (10 years)		**90**	**4355**	**22**	**36**	**8**	**252**	**3**	**3.47**	**6**	**211**	**0**	**3**	**14**	**0**	**3.98**

V
W

WALKER, SCOTT   C   PREDATORS

PERSONAL: Born July 19, 1973, in Montreal. ... 5-10/189. ... Shoots right.
TRANSACTIONS/CAREER NOTES: Selected by Vancouver Canucks in fifth round (fourth Canucks pick, 124th overall) of NHL entry draft (June 26, 1993). ... Strained abdominal muscle (October 12, 1996); missed eight games. ... Strained groin (December 13, 1996); missed six games. ... Fractured nasal bone (November 16, 1997); missed four games. ... Selected by Nashville Predators in NHL expansion draft (June 26, 1998).
HONORS: Named to OHL All-Star second team (1992-93).

Season Team	League	Gms.	G	A	Pts.	PIM	+/-	PP	SH	Gms.	G	A	Pts.	PIM
				REGULAR SEASON								PLAYOFFS		
89-90—Kitch.-Cambridge Jr....	OHA	33	7	27	34	91	...	...	...	—	—	—	—	—
90-91—Cambridge Jr. B.........	OHA	45	10	27	37	241	...	...	...	—	—	—	—	—
91-92—Owen Sound...............	OHL	53	7	31	38	128	...	...	...	5	0	7	7	8
92-93—Owen Sound...............	OHL	57	23	68	91	110	...	...	...	8	1	5	6	16
—Canadian nat'l team	Int'l	2	3	0	3	0	...	...	...	—	—	—	—	—
93-94—Hamilton....................	AHL	77	10	29	39	272	...	...	...	4	0	1	1	25
94-95—Syracuse...................	AHL	74	14	38	52	334	...	...	...	—	—	—	—	—
—Vancouver..................	NHL	11	0	1	1	33	0	0	0	—	—	—	—	—
95-96—Vancouver..................	NHL	63	4	8	12	137	-7	0	1	—	—	—	—	—
—Syracuse...................	AHL	15	3	12	15	52	...	...	...	16	9	8	17	39
96-97—Vancouver..................	NHL	64	3	15	18	132	2	0	0	—	—	—	—	—
97-98—Vancouver..................	NHL	59	3	10	13	164	-8	0	1	—	—	—	—	—
NHL Totals (4 years)..........		197	10	34	44	466	-13	0	2					

WALLIN, JESSE   D   RED WINGS

PERSONAL: Born March 10, 1978, in Saskatoon, Sask. ... 6-2/190. ... Shoots left. ... Name pronounced WAH-lihn.
TRANSACTIONS/CAREER NOTES: Selected by Detroit Red Wings in first round (first Red Wings pick, 26th overall) of NHL entry draft (June 22, 1996).
HONORS: Won Can.HL Humanitarian of the Year Award (1996-97). ... Won WHL Humanitarian Award (1996-97).

Season Team	League	Gms.	G	A	Pts.	PIM	+/-	PP	SH	Gms.	G	A	Pts.	PIM
				REGULAR SEASON								PLAYOFFS		
94-95—Red Deer....................	WHL	72	4	16	20	72	...	...	...	—	—	—	—	—
95-96—Red Deer....................	WHL	70	5	19	24	61	...	...	...	9	0	3	3	4
96-97—Red Deer....................	WHL	59	6	33	39	70	...	...	...	16	1	4	5	10
97-98—Red Deer....................	WHL	14	1	6	7	17	...	...	...	5	0	1	1	2

WARD, AARON   D   RED WINGS

PERSONAL: Born January 17, 1973, in Windsor, Ont. ... 6-2/225. ... Shoots right. ... Full name: Aaron Christian Ward.
COLLEGE: Michigan.
TRANSACTIONS/CAREER NOTES: Selected by Winnipeg Jets in first round (first Jets pick, fifth overall) of NHL entry draft (June 22, 1991). ... Traded by Jets with fourth-round pick (D John Jakopin) in 1993 draft and future considerations to Detroit Red Wings for RW Paul Ysebaert (June 11, 1993); Jets sent RW Alan Kerr to Red Wings to complete deal (June 18, 1993). ... Suffered bronchitis (December 22, 1996); missed three games. ... Suffered from the flu (October 26, 1997); missed two games. ... Bruised knee (November 26, 1997); missed one game. ... Fractured right foot (December 3, 1997); missed 19 games. ... Sprained shoulder (February 7, 1998); missed two games.
HONORS: Named to CCHA All-Rookie Team (1990-91).
MISCELLANEOUS: Member of Stanley Cup championship team (1997).

Season Team	League	Gms.	G	A	Pts.	PIM	+/-	PP	SH	Gms.	G	A	Pts.	PIM
				REGULAR SEASON								PLAYOFFS		
88-89—Nepean	COJHL	56	2	17	19	44	...	...	...	—	—	—	—	—
89-90—Nepean	COJHL	52	6	33	39	85	...	...	...	—	—	—	—	—
90-91—Univ. of Michigan........	CCHA	46	8	11	19	126	...	...	...	—	—	—	—	—
91-92—Univ. of Michigan........	CCHA	42	7	12	19	64	...	...	...	—	—	—	—	—
92-93—Univ. of Michigan........	CCHA	30	5	8	13	73	...	...	...	—	—	—	—	—
—Canadian nat'l team	Int'l	4	0	0	0	8	...	...	...	—	—	—	—	—
93-94—Detroit.......................	NHL	5	1	0	1	4	2	0	0	—	—	—	—	—
—Adirondack	AHL	58	4	12	16	87	...	...	...	9	2	6	8	6
94-95—Adirondack	AHL	76	11	24	35	87	...	...	...	4	0	1	1	0
—Detroit....................	NHL	1	0	1	1	2	1	0	0	—	—	—	—	—
95-96—Adirondack	AHL	74	5	10	15	133	...	...	...	3	0	0	0	6
96-97—Detroit.......................	NHL	49	2	5	7	52	-9	0	0	19	0	0	0	17
97-98—Detroit.......................	NHL	52	5	5	10	47	-1	0	0	—	—	—	—	—
NHL Totals (4 years)..........		107	8	11	19	105	-7	0	0	19	0	0	0	17

W

WARD, DIXON   RW/LW   SABRES

PERSONAL: Born September 23, 1968, in Leduc, Alta. ... 6-0/200. ... Shoots right. ... Full name: Dixon M. Ward Jr.
COLLEGE: North Dakota.
TRANSACTIONS/CAREER NOTES: Selected by Vancouver Canucks in seventh round (sixth Canucks pick, 128th overall) of NHL entry draft (June 11, 1988). ... Separated left shoulder (December 1990). ... Sprained ankle (March 14, 1993); missed four games. ... Suspended three games and fined $500 by NHL for checking from behind (October 15, 1993). ... Traded by Canucks with future considerations to Los Angeles Kings for C Jimmy Carson (January 8, 1994). ... Traded by Kings with C Guy Leveque, RW Shayne Toporowski and C Kelly Fairchild to Toronto Maple Leafs for LW Eric Lacroix, D Chris Snell and fourth-round pick (C Eric Belanger) in 1996 draft (October 3, 1994). ... Loaned by Maple Leafs to Chicago Wolves of IHL (March 16, 1995). ... Signed as free agent by Buffalo Sabres (August 24, 1995).
HONORS: Named to WCHA All-Star second team (1990-91 and 1991-92). ... Won Jack Butterfield Trophy (1995-96).
MISCELLANEOUS: Scored on a penalty shot (vs. Damian Rhodes, April 11, 1998).

Season Team	League	REGULAR SEASON Gms.	G	A	Pts.	PIM	+/-	PP	SH	PLAYOFFS Gms.	G	A	Pts.	PIM
86-87—Red Deer	AJHL	59	46	40	86	153	...	...	...	—	—	—	—	—
87-88—Red Deer	AJHL	51	60	71	131	167	...	...	...	—	—	—	—	—
88-89—U. of North Dakota	WCHA	37	8	9	17	26	...	...	...	—	—	—	—	—
89-90—U. of North Dakota	WCHA	45	35	34	69	44	...	...	...	—	—	—	—	—
90-91—U. of North Dakota	WCHA	43	34	35	69	84	...	...	...	—	—	—	—	—
91-92—U. of North Dakota	WCHA	38	33	31	64	90	...	...	...	—	—	—	—	—
92-93—Vancouver	NHL	70	22	30	52	82	34	4	1	9	2	3	5	0
93-94—Vancouver	NHL	33	6	1	7	37	-14	2	0	—	—	—	—	—
—Los Angeles	NHL	34	6	2	8	45	-8	2	0	—	—	—	—	—
94-95—Toronto	NHL	22	0	3	3	31	-4	0	0	—	—	—	—	—
—St. John's	AHL	6	3	3	6	19	...	...	...	—	—	—	—	—
—Detroit	IHL	7	3	6	9	7	...	...	...	5	3	0	3	7
95-96—Rochester	AHL	71	38	56	94	74	...	...	...	19	11	*24	*35	8
—Buffalo	NHL	8	2	2	4	6	1	0	0	—	—	—	—	—
96-97—Buffalo	NHL	79	13	32	45	36	17	1	2	12	2	3	5	6
97-98—Buffalo	NHL	71	10	13	23	42	9	0	2	15	3	8	11	6
NHL Totals (6 years)		**317**	**59**	**83**	**142**	**279**	**35**	**9**	**5**	**36**	**7**	**14**	**21**	**12**

WARD, ED — RW — FLAMES

PERSONAL: Born November 10, 1969, in Edmonton. ... 6-3/215. ... Shoots right. ... Full name: Edward John Ward.
COLLEGE: Northern Michigan.
TRANSACTIONS/CAREER NOTES: Tore knee cartilage (August 1987). ... Selected by Quebec Nordiques in sixth round (seventh Nordiques pick, 108th overall) of NHL entry draft (June 11, 1988). ... Traded by Nordiques to Calgary Flames for D Francois Groleau (March 24, 1995). ... Bruised ribs (December 3, 1995); missed one game. ... Lacerated elbow (December 13, 1995); missed one game.

Season Team	League	REGULAR SEASON Gms.	G	A	Pts.	PIM	+/-	PP	SH	PLAYOFFS Gms.	G	A	Pts.	PIM
86-87—Sherwood Park	AJHL	60	18	28	46	272	...	...	...	—	—	—	—	—
87-88—N. Michigan Univ.	WCHA	25	0	2	2	40	...	...	...	—	—	—	—	—
88-89—N. Michigan Univ.	WCHA	42	5	15	20	36	...	...	...	—	—	—	—	—
89-90—N. Michigan Univ.	WCHA	39	5	11	16	77	...	...	...	—	—	—	—	—
90-91—N. Michigan Univ.	WCHA	46	13	18	31	109	...	...	...	—	—	—	—	—
91-92—Halifax	AHL	51	7	11	18	65	...	...	...	—	—	—	—	—
—Greensboro	ECHL	12	4	8	12	21	...	...	...	—	—	—	—	—
92-93—Halifax	AHL	70	13	19	32	56	...	...	...	—	—	—	—	—
93-94—Cornwall	AHL	60	12	30	42	65	...	...	...	12	1	3	4	14
—Quebec	NHL	7	1	0	1	5	0	0	0	—	—	—	—	—
94-95—Cornwall	AHL	56	10	14	24	118	...	...	...	—	—	—	—	—
—Saint John	AHL	11	4	5	9	20	...	...	...	5	1	0	1	10
—Calgary	NHL	2	1	1	2	2	-2	0	0	—	—	—	—	—
95-96—Saint John	AHL	12	1	2	3	45	...	...	...	16	4	4	8	27
—Calgary	NHL	41	3	5	8	44	-2	0	0	—	—	—	—	—
96-97—Saint John	AHL	1	0	0	0	0	...	...	...	—	—	—	—	—
—Detroit	IHL	31	7	6	13	45	...	...	...	—	—	—	—	—
—Calgary	NHL	40	5	8	13	49	-3	0	0	—	—	—	—	—
97-98—Calgary	NHL	64	4	5	9	122	-1	0	0	—	—	—	—	—
NHL Totals (5 years)		**154**	**14**	**19**	**33**	**222**	**-8**	**0**	**0**					

WARD, JASON — RW/C — CANADIENS

PERSONAL: Born January 16, 1979, in Chapleau, Ont. ... 6-2/184. ... Shoots right.
TRANSACTIONS/CAREER NOTES: Selected by Montreal Canadiens in first round (first Canadiens pick, 11th overall) of NHL entry draft (June 21, 1997).

Season Team	League	REGULAR SEASON Gms.	G	A	Pts.	PIM	+/-	PP	SH	PLAYOFFS Gms.	G	A	Pts.	PIM
94-95—Oshawa	Tier II Jr. A	47	30	31	61	75	...	...	...	—	—	—	—	—
95-96—Niagara Falls	OHL	64	15	35	50	139	...	...	...	10	6	4	10	23
96-97—Erie	OHL	58	25	39	64	137	...	...	...	5	1	2	3	2
97-98—Erie	OHL	21	7	9	16	42	...	...	...	—	—	—	—	—
—Windsor	OHL	26	19	27	46	34	...	...	...	—	—	—	—	—
—Fredericton	AHL	7	1	0	1	2	...	...	...	1	0	0	0	2

W

WARE, JEFF — D — MAPLE LEAFS

PERSONAL: Born May 19, 1977, in Toronto. ... 6-4/220. ... Shoots left.
HIGH SCHOOL: Henry Street (Whitby, Ont.).
TRANSACTIONS/CAREER NOTES: Selected by Toronto Maple Leafs in first round (first Maple Leafs pick, 15th overall) of NHL entry draft (July 8, 1995).

Season Team	League	REGULAR SEASON Gms.	G	A	Pts.	PIM	+/-	PP	SH	PLAYOFFS Gms.	G	A	Pts.	PIM
93-94—Wexford	Tier II Jr. A	45	1	9	10	75	...	...	...	—	—	—	—	—
94-95—Oshawa	OHL	55	2	11	13	86	...	...	...	7	1	1	2	6
95-96—Oshawa	OHL	62	4	19	23	128	...	...	...	5	0	1	1	8
—St. John's	AHL	4	0	0	0	4	...	...	...	4	0	0	0	2
96-97—Toronto	NHL	13	0	0	0	6	2	0	0	—	—	—	—	—
—Oshawa	OHL	24	1	10	11	38	...	...	...	13	0	3	3	34

Season Team	League	REGULAR SEASON								PLAYOFFS				
		Gms.	G	A	Pts.	PIM	+/-	PP	SH	Gms.	G	A	Pts.	PIM
97-98—St. John's..................	AHL	67	0	3	3	182	...	...	...	4	0	0	0	4
—Toronto	NHL	2	0	0	0	0	1	0	0	—	—	—	—	—
NHL Totals (2 years)...........		15	0	0	0	6	3	0	0					

WARRENER, RHETT   D   PANTHERS

PERSONAL: Born January 27, 1976, in Shaunavon, Sask. ... 6-1/209. ... Shoots right. ... Name pronounced REHT WAHR-uh-nuhr.
TRANSACTIONS/CAREER NOTES: Selected by Florida Panthers in second round (second Panthers pick, 27th overall) of NHL entry draft (June 28, 1994). ... Strained groin (October 20, 1996); missed four games. ... Strained groin (November 11, 1996); missed two games. ... Strained groin (December 22, 1996); missed 10 games.

Season Team	League	REGULAR SEASON								PLAYOFFS				
		Gms.	G	A	Pts.	PIM	+/-	PP	SH	Gms.	G	A	Pts.	PIM
91-92—Saskatoon..................	WHL	2	0	0	0	0	...	...	...	—	—	—	—	—
92-93—Saskatoon..................	WHL	68	2	17	19	100	...	...	...	9	0	0	0	14
93-94—Saskatoon..................	WHL	61	7	19	26	131	...	...	...	16	0	5	5	33
94-95—Saskatoon..................	WHL	66	13	26	39	137	...	...	...	10	0	3	3	6
95-96—Carolina	AHL	9	0	0	0	4	...	...	...	—	—	—	—	—
—Florida..........................	NHL	28	0	3	3	46	4	0	0	21	0	3	3	10
96-97—Florida..........................	NHL	62	4	9	13	88	20	1	0	5	0	0	0	0
97-98—Florida..........................	NHL	79	0	4	4	99	-16	0	0	—	—	—	—	—
NHL Totals (3 years)...........		169	4	16	20	233	8	1	0	26	0	3	3	10

WARRINER, TODD   LW   MAPLE LEAFS

PERSONAL: Born January 3, 1974, in Chatham, Ont. ... 6-1/188. ... Shoots left. ... Name pronounced WAHR-ih-nuhr.
HIGH SCHOOL: Herman E. Fawcett (Brantford, Ont.).
TRANSACTIONS/CAREER NOTES: Selected by Quebec Nordiques in first round (first Nordiques pick, fourth overall) of NHL entry draft (June 20, 1992). ... Traded by Nordiques with C Mats Sundin, D Garth Butcher and first-round pick (traded to Washington Capitals who selected D Nolan Baumgartner) in 1994 draft to Toronto Maple Leafs for LW Wendel Clark, D Sylvain Lefebvre, RW Landon Wilson and first-round pick (D Jeffrey Kealty) in 1994 draft (June 28, 1994). ... Suffered hip pointer (December 7, 1995); missed eight games. ... Injured hip flexor (October 3, 1996); missed one game. ... Injured hip flexor (November 19, 1996); missed four games. ... Suffered from the flu (April 2, 1997); missed one game. ... Sprained shoulder (October 15, 1997); missed three games. ... Bruised thigh (November 17, 1997); missed 27 games.
HONORS: Won Can.HL Top Draft Prospect Award (1991-92). ... Won OHL Top Draft Prospect Award (1991-92). ... Named to Can.HL All-Star second team (1991-92). ... Named to OHL All-Star first team (1991-92).
MISCELLANEOUS: Member of silver-medal-winning Canadian Olympic team (1994).

Season Team	League	REGULAR SEASON								PLAYOFFS				
		Gms.	G	A	Pts.	PIM	+/-	PP	SH	Gms.	G	A	Pts.	PIM
88-89—Blenheim Jr. C	OHA	10	1	4	5	0	...	...	...	—	—	—	—	—
89-90—Chatham Jr. B.............	OHA	40	24	21	45	12	...	...	...	—	—	—	—	—
90-91—Windsor......................	OHL	57	36	28	64	26	...	...	...	11	5	6	11	12
91-92—Windsor......................	OHL	50	41	42	83	66	...	...	...	7	5	4	9	6
92-93—Windsor......................	OHL	23	13	21	34	29	...	...	...	—	—	—	—	—
—Kitchener.......................	OHL	32	19	24	43	35	...	...	...	7	5	14	19	14
93-94—Canadian nat'l team	Int'l	50	11	20	31	33	...	...	...	—	—	—	—	—
—Can. Olympic Team......	Int'l	4	1	1	2	0	...	...	...	—	—	—	—	—
—Kitchener.......................	OHL	—	—	—	—	—	...	...	...	1	0	1	1	0
—Cornwall	AHL	—	—	—	—	—	...	...	...	10	1	4	5	4
94-95—St. John's..................	AHL	46	8	10	18	22	...	...	...	4	1	0	1	2
—Toronto	NHL	5	0	0	0	0	-3	0	0	—	—	—	—	—
95-96—St. John's..................	AHL	11	5	6	11	16	...	...	...	—	—	—	—	—
—Toronto	NHL	57	7	8	15	26	-11	1	0	6	1	1	2	2
96-97—Toronto	NHL	75	12	21	33	41	-3	2	2	—	—	—	—	—
97-98—Toronto	NHL	45	5	8	13	20	5	0	0	—	—	—	—	—
NHL Totals (4 years)...........		182	24	37	61	87	-12	3	2	6	1	1	2	2

WASHBURN, STEVE   C   PANTHERS

PERSONAL: Born April 10, 1975, in Ottawa. ... 6-2/191. ... Shoots left.
TRANSACTIONS/CAREER NOTES: Selected by Florida Panthers in third round (fifth Panthers pick, 78th overall) of NHL entry draft (June 26, 1993). ... Sprained knee (April 11, 1997); missed remainder of season. ... Separated right shoulder (October 28, 1997); missed nine games.

Season Team	League	REGULAR SEASON								PLAYOFFS				
		Gms.	G	A	Pts.	PIM	+/-	PP	SH	Gms.	G	A	Pts.	PIM
90-91—Gloucester	OPJHL	56	21	30	51	47	...	...	...	—	—	—	—	—
91-92—Ottawa	OHL	59	5	17	22	10	...	...	...	11	2	3	5	4
92-93—Ottawa	OHL	66	20	38	58	54	...	...	...	—	—	—	—	—
93-94—Ottawa	OHL	65	30	50	80	88	...	...	...	17	7	16	23	10
94-95—Ottawa	OHL	63	43	63	106	72	...	...	...	—	—	—	—	—
—Cincinnati.....................	IHL	6	3	1	4	0	...	...	...	9	1	3	4	4
95-96—Carolina	AHL	78	29	54	83	45	...	...	...	—	—	—	—	—
—Florida..........................	NHL	1	0	1	1	0	1	0	0	1	0	1	1	0
96-97—Carolina	AHL	60	23	40	63	66	...	...	...	—	—	—	—	—
—Florida..........................	NHL	18	3	6	9	4	2	1	0	—	—	—	—	—
97-98—Florida..........................	NHL	58	11	8	19	32	-6	4	0	—	—	—	—	—
—New Haven	AHL	6	3	5	8	4	...	...	...	3	2	0	2	15
NHL Totals (3 years)...........		77	14	15	29	36	-3	5	0	1	0	1	1	0

W

WATT, MIKE   LW/C   ISLANDERS

PERSONAL: Born March 31, 1976, in Seaforth, Ont. ... 6-2/212. ... Shoots left.
COLLEGE: Michigan State.
TRANSACTIONS/CAREER NOTES: Selected by Edmonton Oilers in second round (third Oilers pick, 32nd overall) of NHL entry draft (June 28, 1994). ... Traded by Oilers to New York Islanders for G Eric Fichaud (June 18, 1998).

		REGULAR SEASON									PLAYOFFS				
Season Team	League	Gms.	G	A	Pts.	PIM	+/-	PP	SH		Gms.	G	A	Pts.	PIM
91-92—Stratford Jr. B	OHA	46	5	26	31	...	...	...	...		—	—	—	—	—
92-93—Stratford Jr. B	OHA	45	20	35	55	100	...	...	...		—	—	—	—	—
93-94—Stratford Jr. B	OHA	48	34	34	68	165	...	...	...		—	—	—	—	—
94-95—Michigan State	CCHA	39	12	6	18	64	...	...	...		—	—	—	—	—
95-96—Michigan State	CCHA	37	17	22	39	60	...	...	...		—	—	—	—	—
96-97—Michigan State	CCHA	39	24	17	41	109	...	...	...		—	—	—	—	—
97-98—Hamilton	AHL	63	24	25	49	65	...	...	...		9	2	2	4	8
—Edmonton	NHL	14	1	2	3	4	-4	0	0		—	—	—	—	—
NHL Totals (1 year)		14	1	2	3	4	-4	0	0						

WEBB, STEVE   RW   ISLANDERS

PERSONAL: Born April 30, 1975, in Peterborough, Ont. ... 6-0/195. ... Shoots right.
TRANSACTIONS/CAREER NOTES: Selected by Buffalo Sabres in seventh round (eighth Sabres pick, 176th overall) of NHL entry draft (June 29, 1994). ... Signed as free agent by New York Islanders (October 14, 1996).

		REGULAR SEASON									PLAYOFFS				
Season Team	League	Gms.	G	A	Pts.	PIM	+/-	PP	SH		Gms.	G	A	Pts.	PIM
91-92—Peterborough	Jr. B	37	9	9	18	195	...	...	...		—	—	—	—	—
92-93—Windsor	OHL	63	14	25	39	181	...	...	...		—	—	—	—	—
93-94—Windsor	OHL	33	6	15	21	117	...	...	...		—	—	—	—	—
—Peterborough	OHL	2	0	1	1	9	...	...	...		—	—	—	—	—
94-95—Peterborough	OHL	42	8	16	24	109	...	...	...		11	3	3	6	22
95-96—Muskegon	Col.HL	58	18	24	42	263	...	...	...		5	1	2	3	22
—Detroit	IHL	4	0	0	0	24	...	...	...		—	—	—	—	—
96-97—Kentucky	AHL	25	6	6	12	103	...	...	...		2	0	0	0	19
—New York Islanders	NHL	41	1	4	5	144	-10	1	0		—	—	—	—	—
97-98—Kentucky	AHL	37	5	13	18	139	...	...	...		3	0	1	1	10
—New York Islanders	NHL	20	0	0	0	35	-2	0	0		—	—	—	—	—
NHL Totals (2 years)		61	1	4	5	179	-12	1	0						

WEEKES, KEVIN   G   PANTHERS

PERSONAL: Born April 4, 1975, in Toronto. ... 6-0/175. ... Catches left. ... Name pronounced WEEKS.
HIGH SCHOOL: West Hill (Ont.) Secondary.
TRANSACTIONS/CAREER NOTES: Selected by Florida Panthers in second round (second Panthers pick, 41st overall) of NHL entry draft (June 26, 1993). ... Sprained right knee (March 19, 1998); missed remainder of season.
MISCELLANEOUS: Allowed a penalty shot goal (vs. Paul Kariya, January 21, 1998).

		REGULAR SEASON								PLAYOFFS					
Season Team	League	Gms.	Min	W	L	T	GA	SO	Avg.		Gms.	Min.	W	L	GA	SO	Avg.
91-92—St. Michael's	Tier II Jr. A	2	127	...	...	...	11	0	5.20		—	—	—	—	—	—	—
92-93—Owen Sound	OHL	29	1645	9	12	5	143	0	5.22		1	26	0	0	5	0	11.54
93-94—Owen Sound	OHL	34	1974	13	19	1	158	0	4.80		—	—	—	—	—	—	—
94-95—Ottawa	OHL	41	2266	13	23	4	154	1	4.08		—	—	—	—	—	—	—
95-96—Carolina	AHL	60	3403	24	25	8	229	2	4.04		—	—	—	—	—	—	—
96-97—Carolina	AHL	51	2899	17	†28	4	172	1	3.56		—	—	—	—	—	—	—
97-98—Fort Wayne	IHL	12	719	9	2	‡1	34	1	2.84		—	—	—	—	—	—	—
—Florida	NHL	11	485	0	5	1	32	0	3.96		—	—	—	—	—	—	—
NHL Totals (1 year)		11	485	0	5	1	32	0	3.96								

WEIGHT, DOUG   C   OILERS

PERSONAL: Born January 21, 1971, in Warren, Mich. ... 5-11/200. ... Shoots left. ... Full name: Douglas D. Weight. ... Name pronounced WAYT.
COLLEGE: Lake Superior State (Mich.).
TRANSACTIONS/CAREER NOTES: Selected by New York Rangers in second round (second Rangers pick, 34th overall) of NHL entry draft (June 16, 1990). ... Sprained elbow (October 14, 1991); missed three games. ... Damaged ligaments (January 11, 1991). ... Suspended four off-days and fined $500 by NHL for cross-checking (November 5, 1992). ... Traded by Rangers to Edmonton Oilers for LW Esa Tikkanen (March 17, 1993). ... Played in Europe during 1994-95 NHL lockout. ... Sprained ankle (February 15, 1997); missed one game. ... Injured ankle (February 21, 1997); missed one game. ... Sprained left shoulder (March 15, 1998); missed two games.
HONORS: Named to CCHA All-Rookie team (1989-90). ... Named to NCAA All-America West second team (1990-91). ... Named to CCHA All-Star first team (1990-91). ... Played in NHL All-Star Game (1996 and 1998).
MISCELLANEOUS: Failed to score on a penalty shot (vs. Daren Puppa, January 3, 1996). ... Scored on a penalty shot (vs. Mike Richter, October 8, 1997).
STATISTICAL PLATEAUS: Three-goal games: 1995-96 (1).

		REGULAR SEASON									PLAYOFFS				
Season Team	League	Gms.	G	A	Pts.	PIM	+/-	PP	SH		Gms.	G	A	Pts.	PIM
88-89—Bloomfield	NAJHL	34	26	53	79	105	...	...	...		—	—	—	—	—
89-90—Lake Superior	CCHA	46	21	48	69	44	...	...	...		—	—	—	—	—

W

		REGULAR SEASON								PLAYOFFS				
Season Team	League	Gms.	G	A	Pts.	PIM	+/-	PP	SH	Gms.	G	A	Pts.	PIM
90-91—Lake Superior	CCHA	42	29	46	75	86	...	...	...	—	—	—	—	—
—New York Rangers	NHL	—	—	—	—	—	—	—	—	1	0	0	0	0
91-92—New York Rangers	NHL	53	8	22	30	23	-3	0	0	7	2	2	4	0
—Binghamton	AHL	9	3	14	17	2	...	...	...	4	1	4	5	6
92-93—New York Rangers	NHL	65	15	25	40	55	4	3	0	—	—	—	—	—
—Edmonton	NHL	13	2	6	8	10	-2	0	0	—	—	—	—	—
93-94—Edmonton	NHL	84	24	50	74	47	-22	4	1	—	—	—	—	—
94-95—Rosenheim	Germany	8	2	3	5	18	...	...	...	—	—	—	—	—
—Edmonton	NHL	48	7	33	40	69	-17	1	0	—	—	—	—	—
95-96—Edmonton	NHL	82	25	79	104	95	-19	9	0	—	—	—	—	—
96-97—Edmonton	NHL	80	21	61	82	80	1	4	0	12	3	8	11	8
97-98—Edmonton	NHL	79	26	44	70	69	1	9	0	12	2	7	9	14
—U.S. Olympic Team	Int'l	4	0	2	2	2	...	...	...	—	—	—	—	—
NHL Totals (8 years)		504	128	320	448	448	-57	30	1	32	7	17	24	22

WEINRICH, ERIC — D — BLACKHAWKS

PERSONAL: Born December 19, 1966, in Roanoke, Va. ... 6-1/210. ... Shoots left. ... Full name: Eric John Weinrich. ... Name pronounced WIGHN-rihch.

HIGH SCHOOL: North Yarmouth (Maine) Academy.

COLLEGE: Maine.

TRANSACTIONS/CAREER NOTES: Dislocated shoulder (December 1984). ... Selected by New Jersey Devils in second round (third Devils pick, 32nd overall) of NHL entry draft (June 15, 1985). ... Traded by Devils with G Sean Burke to Hartford Whalers for RW Bobby Holik, second-round pick (LW Jay Pandolfo) in 1993 draft and future considerations (August 28, 1992). ... Suffered concussion (November 25, 1992); missed two games. ... Sprained knee (September 22, 1993); missed five games. ... Signed as free agent by Hartford Whalers (September 25, 1993). ... Injured right knee (October 5, 1993); missed five games. ... Traded with LW Patrick Poulin by Whalers to the Chicago Blackhawks for RW Steve Larmer and D Bryan Marchment (November 2, 1993). ... Broke jaw (February 24, 1994); missed 17 games. ... Cut eye (November 1, 1995); missed three games. ... Cut thigh (December 31, 1996); missed one game.

HONORS: Named to NCAA All-America East second team (1986-87). ... Named to Hockey East All-Star first team (1986-87). ... Won Eddie Shore Plaque (1989-90). ... Named to AHL All-Star first team (1989-90). ... Named to NHL All-Rookie team (1990-91).

		REGULAR SEASON								PLAYOFFS				
Season Team	League	Gms.	G	A	Pts.	PIM	+/-	PP	SH	Gms.	G	A	Pts.	PIM
83-84—North Yarmouth Acad.	Maine H.S.	17	23	33	56	...	...	...	...	—	—	—	—	—
84-85—North Yarmouth Acad.	Maine H.S.	20	6	21	27	...	...	...	...	—	—	—	—	—
85-86—Univ. of Maine	Hockey East	34	0	15	15	26	...	...	...	—	—	—	—	—
86-87—Univ. of Maine	Hockey East	41	12	32	44	59	...	...	...	—	—	—	—	—
87-88—Univ. of Maine	Hockey East	8	4	7	11	22	...	...	...	—	—	—	—	—
—U.S. national team	Int'l	39	3	9	12	24	...	...	...	—	—	—	—	—
—U.S. Olympic Team	Int'l	3	0	0	0	24	...	...	...	—	—	—	—	—
88-89—Utica	AHL	80	17	27	44	70	...	...	...	5	0	1	1	8
—New Jersey	NHL	2	0	0	0	0	-1	0	0	—	—	—	—	—
89-90—Utica	AHL	57	12	48	60	38	...	...	...	—	—	—	—	—
—New Jersey	NHL	19	2	7	9	11	1	1	0	6	1	3	4	17
90-91—New Jersey	NHL	76	4	34	38	48	10	1	0	7	1	2	3	6
91-92—New Jersey	NHL	76	7	25	32	55	10	5	0	7	0	2	2	4
92-93—Hartford	NHL	79	7	29	36	76	-11	0	2	—	—	—	—	—
93-94—Hartford	NHL	8	1	1	2	2	-5	1	0	—	—	—	—	—
—Chicago....................	NHL	54	3	23	26	31	6	1	0	6	0	2	2	6
94-95—Chicago....................	NHL	48	3	10	13	33	1	1	0	16	1	5	6	4
95-96—Chicago....................	NHL	77	5	10	15	65	14	0	0	10	1	4	5	10
96-97—Chicago....................	NHL	81	7	25	32	62	19	1	0	6	0	1	1	4
97-98—Chicago....................	NHL	82	2	21	23	106	10	0	0	—	—	—	—	—
NHL Totals (10 years)		602	41	185	226	489	54	11	2	58	4	19	23	51

WELLS, CHRIS — C — PANTHERS

PERSONAL: Born November 12, 1975, in Calgary. ... 6-6/223. ... Shoots left.

HIGH SCHOOL: Meadowdale (Lynnwood, Wash.).

TRANSACTIONS/CAREER NOTES: Selected by Pittsburgh Penguins in first round (first Penguins pick, 24th overall) of NHL entry draft (June 28, 1994). ... Suffered tendinitis in knee (October 9, 1995); missed two games. ... Traded by Penguins to Florida Panthers for C Stu Barnes and D Jason Woolley (November 19, 1996). ... Strained groin (March 15, 1998); missed one game. ... Reinjured groin (March 26, 1998); missed remainder of season.

HONORS: Named to WHL (West) All-Star first team (1994-95).

		REGULAR SEASON								PLAYOFFS				
Season Team	League	Gms.	G	A	Pts.	PIM	+/-	PP	SH	Gms.	G	A	Pts.	PIM
90-91—Calgary Royals...........	AJHL	35	13	14	27	33	...	...	...	—	—	—	—	—
91-92—Seattle......................	WHL	64	13	8	21	70	...	...	...	11	0	0	0	15
92-93—Seattle......................	WHL	63	18	37	55	111	...	...	...	5	2	3	5	4
93-94—Seattle......................	WHL	69	30	44	74	150	...	...	...	9	6	5	11	23
94-95—Seattle......................	WHL	69	45	63	108	148	...	...	...	3	0	1	1	4
—Cleveland	IHL	3	0	1	1	2	...	...	...	—	—	—	—	—
95-96—Pittsburgh	NHL	54	2	2	4	59	-6	0	1	—	—	—	—	—
96-97—Cleveland	IHL	15	4	6	10	9	...	...	...	—	—	—	—	—
—Florida	NHL	47	2	6	8	42	5	0	0	3	0	0	0	0
97-98—Florida......................	NHL	61	5	10	15	47	4	0	1	—	—	—	—	—
NHL Totals (3 years)		162	9	18	27	148	3	0	2	3	0	0	0	0

W

WERENKA, BRAD　　　　　　　　D　　　　　　　　PENGUINS

PERSONAL: Born February 12, 1969, in Two Hills, Alta. ... 6-1/221. ... Shoots left. ... Full name: John Bradley Werenka. ... Name pronounced wuh-REHN-kuh.
HIGH SCHOOL: Fort Saskatchewan (Alta.).
COLLEGE: Northern Michigan.
TRANSACTIONS/CAREER NOTES: Selected by Edmonton Oilers as underage junior in second round (second Oilers pick, 42nd overall) of NHL entry draft (June 13, 1987). ... Tore stomach muscles (October 1988). ... Sprained right knee (November 3, 1989). ... Loaned by Oilers to Canadian Olympic team (February 10, 1994). ... Traded by Oilers to Quebec Nordiques for G Steve Passmore (March 21, 1994). ... Signed as free agent by Chicago Blackhawks (August 10, 1995). ... Signed as free agent by Pittsburgh Penguins (July 31, 1997). ... Sprained ankle (October 17, 1997); missed 10 games. ... Bruised shoulder (November 22, 1997); missed one game.
HONORS: Named to NCAA All-America West first team (1990-91). ... Named to NCAA All-Tournament team (1990-91). ... Named to WCHA All-Star first team (1990-91). ... Won Governors Trophy (1996-97). ... Named to IHL All-Star first team (1996-97).
MISCELLANEOUS: Member of silver-medal-winning Canadian Olympic team (1994).

			REGULAR SEASON							PLAYOFFS			
Season Team	League	Gms.	G	A	Pts.	PIM	+/-	PP	SH	Gms.	G	A	Pts.	PIM
85-86—Fort Saskatchewan	AJHL	29	12	23	35	24	...	...	...	—	—	—	—	—
86-87—N. Michigan Univ.	WCHA	30	4	4	8	35	...	...	...	—	—	—	—	—
87-88—N. Michigan Univ.	WCHA	34	7	23	30	26	...	...	...	—	—	—	—	—
88-89—N. Michigan Univ.	WCHA	28	7	13	20	16	...	...	...	—	—	—	—	—
89-90—N. Michigan Univ.	WCHA	8	2	5	7	8	...	...	...	—	—	—	—	—
90-91—N. Michigan Univ.	WCHA	47	20	43	63	36	...	...	...	—	—	—	—	—
91-92—Cape Breton...............	AHL	66	6	21	27	95	...	...	...	5	0	3	3	6
92-93—Canadian nat'l team	Int'l	18	3	7	10	10	...	...	...	—	—	—	—	—
—Edmonton	NHL	27	5	3	8	24	1	0	1	—	—	—	—	—
—Cape Breton..............	AHL	4	1	1	2	4	...	...	...	16	4	17	21	12
93-94—Cape Breton...............	AHL	25	6	17	23	19	...	...	...	—	—	—	—	—
—Edmonton	NHL	15	0	4	4	14	-1	0	0	—	—	—	—	—
—Can. Olympic Team.....	Int'l	8	2	2	4	8	...	...	...	—	—	—	—	—
—Quebec	NHL	11	0	7	7	8	4	0	0	—	—	—	—	—
—Cornwall	AHL	—	—	—	—	—	...	...	...	12	2	10	12	36
94-95—Milwaukee.................	IHL	80	8	45	53	161	...	...	...	15	3	10	13	36
95-96—Indianapolis	IHL	73	15	42	57	85	...	...	...	5	1	3	4	8
—Chicago.....................	NHL	9	0	0	0	8	-2	0	0	—	—	—	—	—
96-97—Indianapolis	IHL	82	20	56	76	83	...	...	...	4	1	4	5	6
97-98—Pittsburgh..................	NHL	71	3	15	18	46	15	2	0	6	1	0	1	8
NHL Totals (4 years)...........		133	8	29	37	100	17	2	1	6	1	0	1	8

WESENBERG, BRIAN　　　　　　　RW　　　　　　　　FLYERS

PERSONAL: Born May 9, 1977, in Peterborough, Ont. ... 6-3/173. ... Shoots right.
HIGH SCHOOL: Bishop MacDonnell (Guelph, Ont.).
TRANSACTIONS/CAREER NOTES: Selected by Mighty Ducks of Anaheim in second round (second Mighty Ducks pick, 29th overall) of NHL entry draft (July 8, 1995). ... Traded by Mighty Ducks to Philadelphia Flyers for C Anatoli Semenov and D Mike Crowley (March 19, 1996).

			REGULAR SEASON							PLAYOFFS			
Season Team	League	Gms.	G	A	Pts.	PIM	+/-	PP	SH	Gms.	G	A	Pts.	PIM
93-94—Cobourg....................	Tier II Jr. A	40	14	18	32	81	...	...	...	—	—	—	—	—
94-95—Guelph	OHL	66	17	27	44	81	...	...	...	14	2	3	5	18
95-96—Guelph	OHL	66	25	33	58	161	...	...	...	16	4	11	15	34
96-97—Guelph	OHL	64	37	43	80	186	...	...	...	18	4	9	13	59
—Philadelphia	AHL	—	—	—	—	—	...	...	...	3	0	0	0	7
97-98—Philadelphia	AHL	74	17	22	39	93	...	...	...	19	1	4	5	34

WESLEY, GLEN　　　　　　　　D　　　　　　　　HURRICANES

PERSONAL: Born October 2, 1968, in Red Deer, Alta. ... 6-1/201. ... Shoots left.
TRANSACTIONS/CAREER NOTES: Selected by Boston Bruins as underage junior in first round (first Bruins pick, third overall) of NHL entry draft (June 13, 1987). ... Sprained left knee (October 1988). ... Broke foot (November 24, 1992); missed 14 games. ... Injured groin (February 1993); missed one game. ... Injured groin (March 1993); missed three games. ... Injured groin (April 1993); missed two games. ... Injured kidney (March 3, 1994); missed three games. ... Traded by Bruins to Hartford Whalers for first-round picks in 1995 (D Kyle McLaren), 1996 (D Johnathan Aitken) and 1997 (C Sergei Samsonov) drafts (August 26, 1994). ... Bruised shin (November 4, 1995); missed two games. ... Injured groin (December 28, 1995); missed three games. ... Sprained knee (January 6, 1996); missed three games. ... Injured groin (January 17, 1996); missed four games. ... Injured groin (January 25, 1996); missed three games. ... Strained hip flexor (November 4, 1996); missed one game. ... Broke foot (November 16, 1996); missed ten games. ... Suffered from the flu (February 5, 1997); missed one game. ... Whalers franchise moved to North Carolina and renamed Carolina Hurricanes for 1997-98 season; NHL approved move on June 25, 1997.
HONORS: Won WHL West Top Defenseman Trophy (1985-86 and 1986-87). ... Named to WHL (West) All-Star first team (1985-86 and 1986-87). ... Named to NHL All-Rookie team (1987-88). ... Played in NHL All-Star Game (1989).
MISCELLANEOUS: Captain of Hartford Whalers (1994-95).
STATISTICAL PLATEAUS: Three-goal games: 1993-94 (1).

			REGULAR SEASON							PLAYOFFS			
Season Team	League	Gms.	G	A	Pts.	PIM	+/-	PP	SH	Gms.	G	A	Pts.	PIM
83-84—Red Deer..................	AJHL	57	9	20	29	40	...	...	...	—	—	—	—	—
—Portland....................	WHL	3	1	2	3	0	...	...	...	—	—	—	—	—
84-85—Portland....................	WHL	67	16	52	68	76	...	...	...	6	1	6	7	8
85-86—Portland....................	WHL	69	16	75	91	96	...	...	...	15	3	11	14	29
86-87—Portland....................	WHL	63	16	46	62	72	...	...	...	20	8	18	26	27
87-88—Boston.....................	NHL	79	7	30	37	69	21	1	2	23	6	8	14	22
88-89—Boston.....................	NHL	77	19	35	54	61	23	8	1	10	0	2	2	4
89-90—Boston.....................	NHL	78	9	27	36	48	6	5	0	21	2	6	8	36

W

Season Team	League	REGULAR SEASON								PLAYOFFS				
		Gms.	G	A	Pts.	PIM	+/-	PP	SH	Gms.	G	A	Pts.	PIM
90-91—Boston	NHL	80	11	32	43	78	0	5	1	19	2	9	11	19
91-92—Boston	NHL	78	9	37	46	54	-9	4	0	15	2	4	6	16
92-93—Boston	NHL	64	8	25	33	47	-2	4	1	4	0	0	0	0
93-94—Boston	NHL	81	14	44	58	64	1	6	1	13	3	3	6	12
94-95—Hartford	NHL	48	2	14	16	50	-6	1	0	—	—	—	—	—
95-96—Hartford	NHL	68	8	16	24	88	-9	6	0	—	—	—	—	—
96-97—Hartford	NHL	68	6	26	32	40	0	3	1	—	—	—	—	—
97-98—Carolina	NHL	82	6	19	25	36	7	1	0	—	—	—	—	—
NHL Totals (11 years)		803	99	305	404	635	32	44	7	105	15	32	47	109

WHITE, COLIN — D — DEVILS

PERSONAL: Born December 12, 1977, in New Glasgow, Nova Scotia. ... 6-3/215. ... Shoots left. ... Full name: John Colin White.
TRANSACTIONS/CAREER NOTES: Selected by New Jersey Devils in second round (fifth Devils pick, 49th overall) of NHL entry draft (June 22, 1996).
HONORS: Named to QMJHL All-Rookie team (1995-96).

Season Team	League	REGULAR SEASON								PLAYOFFS				
		Gms.	G	A	Pts.	PIM	+/-	PP	SH	Gms.	G	A	Pts.	PIM
94-95—Hull	QMJHL	5	0	1	1	4	...	...	...	12	0	0	0	23
95-96—Hull	QMJHL	62	2	8	10	303	...	...	...	18	0	4	4	42
96-97—Hull	QMJHL	63	3	12	15	297	...	...	...	14	3	12	15	65
97-98—Albany	AHL	76	3	13	16	235	...	...	...	13	0	0	0	55

WHITE, PETER — C — FLYERS

PERSONAL: Born March 15, 1969, in Montreal. ... 5-11/200. ... Shoots left. ... Full name: Peter Toby White.
COLLEGE: Michigan State.
TRANSACTIONS/CAREER NOTES: Selected by Edmonton Oilers in fifth round (fourth Oilers pick, 92nd overall) of NHL entry draft (June 17, 1989). ... Traded by Oilers with fourth-round pick (RW Jason Sessa) in 1996 draft to Toronto Maple Leafs for LW Kent Manderville (December 4, 1995). ... Signed as free agent by Philadelphia Flyers (July 17, 1996).
HONORS: Named to CCHA All-Rookie team (1988-89). ... Named CCHA Playoff Most Valuable Player (1989-90). ... Won John B. Sellenberger Trophy (1994-95 and 1996-97). ... Named to AHL All-Star second team (1994-95 and 1996-97). ... Won John B. Sollenberger trophy (1997-98).

Season Team	League	REGULAR SEASON								PLAYOFFS				
		Gms.	G	A	Pts.	PIM	+/-	PP	SH	Gms.	G	A	Pts.	PIM
87-88—Pembroke	COJHL	56	90	136	226	32	...	...	...	—	—	—	—	—
88-89—Michigan State	CCHA	46	20	33	53	17	...	...	...	—	—	—	—	—
89-90—Michigan State	CCHA	45	22	40	62	6	...	...	...	—	—	—	—	—
90-91—Michigan State	CCHA	37	7	31	38	28	...	...	...	—	—	—	—	—
91-92—Michigan State	CCHA	44	26	51	77	32	...	...	...	—	—	—	—	—
92-93—Cape Breton	AHL	64	12	28	40	10	...	...	...	16	3	3	6	12
93-94—Cape Breton	AHL	45	21	49	70	12	...	...	...	5	2	3	5	2
—Edmonton	NHL	26	3	5	8	2	1	0	0	—	—	—	—	—
94-95—Cape Breton	AHL	65	36	†69	*105	30	...	...	...	—	—	—	—	—
—Edmonton	NHL	9	2	4	6	0	1	2	0	—	—	—	—	—
95-96—Edmonton	NHL	26	5	3	8	0	-14	1	0	—	—	—	—	—
—Toronto	NHL	1	0	0	0	0	0	0	0	—	—	—	—	—
—St. John's	AHL	17	6	7	13	6	...	...	...	—	—	—	—	—
—Atlanta	IHL	36	21	20	41	4	...	...	...	3	0	3	3	2
96-97—Philadelphia	AHL	80	*44	61	*105	28	...	...	...	10	6	8	14	6
97-98—Philadelphia	AHL	80	27	*78	*105	28	...	...	...	20	9	9	18	6
NHL Totals (3 years)		62	10	12	22	2	-12	3	0					

WHITE, TODD — C — BLACKHAWKS

PERSONAL: Born May 21, 1975, in Kanata, Ont. ... 5-10/181. ... Shoots left.
COLLEGE: Clarkson (N.Y.).
TRANSACTIONS/CAREER NOTES: Signed as free agent by Chicago Blackhawks (August 6, 1997). ... Suffered charley horse (October 4, 1997); missed one game.
HONORS: Named to ECAC All-Star second team (1995-96). ... Named to NCAA All-America East first team (1996-97). ... Named to ECAC All-Star first team (1996-97). ... Won Garry F. Longman Trophy (1997-98).

Season Team	League	REGULAR SEASON								PLAYOFFS				
		Gms.	G	A	Pts.	PIM	+/-	PP	SH	Gms.	G	A	Pts.	PIM
93-94—Clarkson	ECAC	33	10	12	22	28	...	...	...	—	—	—	—	—
94-95—Clarkson	ECAC	34	13	16	29	44	...	...	...	—	—	—	—	—
95-96—Clarkson	ECAC	38	29	43	72	36	...	...	...	—	—	—	—	—
96-97—Clarkson	ECAC	37	38	36	74	22	...	...	...	—	—	—	—	—
97-98—Chicago	NHL	7	1	0	1	2	0	0	0	—	—	—	—	—
—Indianapolis	IHL	65	†46	36	82	28	...	...	...	5	2	3	5	4
NHL Totals (1 year)		7	1	0	1	2	0	0	0					

W

WHITMORE, KAY   G   RANGERS

PERSONAL: Born April 10, 1967, in Sudbury, Ont. ... 5-11/180. ... Catches left.
TRANSACTIONS/CAREER NOTES: Selected by Hartford Whalers as underage junior in second round (second Whalers pick, 26th overall) of NHL entry draft (June 15, 1985). ... Traded by Whalers to Vancouver Canucks for G Corrie D'Alessio and conditional pick in 1993 draft (October 1, 1992). ... Signed as free agent by San Jose Sharks (September 2, 1997). ... Traded by Sharks with second-round pick (RW Jaroslav Kristek) in 1998 draft and future considerations to Buffalo Sabres for G Steve Shields and fourth-round pick (RW Miroslav Zalesak) in 1998 draft (June 19, 1998). ... Signed as free agent by New York Rangers (August 17, 1998).
HONORS: Shared Dave Pinkney Trophy with Ron Tugnutt (1985-86). ... Named to OHL All-Star first team (1985-86). ... Won Jack Butterfield Trophy (1990-91). ... Shared James Norris Trophy with Mike Buzak (1997-98).
MISCELLANEOUS: Stopped penalty shot attempt (vs. Randy Burridge, March 31, 1991). ... Allowed penalty shot goal (vs. Luc Robitaille, February 6, 1992).

			REGULAR SEASON							PLAYOFFS						
Season Team	League	Gms.	Min	W	L	T	GA	SO	Avg.	Gms.	Min.	W	L	GA	SO	Avg.
83-84—Peterborough	OHL	29	1471	17	8	0	110	0	4.49	—	—	—	—	—	—	—
84-85—Peterborough	OHL	*53	*3077	35	16	2	172	†2	3.35	*17	*1020	10	4	58	0	3.41
85-86—Peterborough	OHL	41	2467	27	12	2	114	†3	*2.77	14	837	8	5	40	0	2.87
86-87—Peterborough	OHL	36	2159	14	17	5	118	1	3.28	7	366	3	3	17	1	2.79
87-88—Binghamton	AHL	38	2137	17	15	4	121	3	3.40	2	118	0	2	10	0	5.08
88-89—Binghamton	AHL	*56	*3200	21	29	4	*241	1	4.52	—	—	—	—	—	—	—
—Hartford	NHL	3	180	2	1	0	10	0	3.33	2	135	0	2	10	0	4.44
89-90—Binghamton	AHL	24	1386	3	19	2	109	0	4.72	—	—	—	—	—	—	—
—Hartford	NHL	9	442	4	2	1	26	0	3.53	—	—	—	—	—	—	—
90-91—Hartford	NHL	18	850	3	9	3	52	0	3.67	—	—	—	—	—	—	—
—Springfield	AHL	33	1916	22	9	1	98	1	3.07	*15	*926	11	4	*37	0	*2.40
91-92—Hartford	NHL	45	2567	14	21	6	155	3	3.62	1	19	0	0	1	0	3.16
92-93—Vancouver	NHL	31	1817	18	8	4	94	1	3.10	—	—	—	—	—	—	—
93-94—Vancouver	NHL	32	1921	18	14	0	113	0	3.53	—	—	—	—	—	—	—
94-95—Vancouver	NHL	11	558	0	6	2	37	0	3.98	1	20	0	0	2	0	6.00
95-96—Los Angeles	IHL	30	1562	10	9	‡7	99	1	3.80	—	—	—	—	—	—	—
—Detroit	IHL	10	501	3	5	0	33	0	3.95	—	—	—	—	—	—	—
—Syracuse	AHL	11	662	6	4	1	37	0	3.35	—	—	—	—	—	—	—
97-98—Long Beach	IHL	46	2516	28	12	‡3	109	3	2.60	14	839	9	5	43	0	3.08
NHL Totals (7 years)		149	8335	59	61	16	487	4	3.51	4	174	0	2	13	0	4.48

WHITNEY, RAY   LW/C   PANTHERS

PERSONAL: Born May 8, 1972, in Fort Saskatchewan, Alta. ... 5-10/175. ... Shoots right.
TRANSACTIONS/CAREER NOTES: Selected by San Jose Sharks in second round (second Sharks pick, 23rd overall) of NHL entry draft (June 22, 1991). ... Sprained knee (October 30, 1993); missed 18 games. ... Suffered from the flu (December 15, 1993); missed one game. ... Injured ankle (February 20, 1995) and suffered eye infection (February 28, 1995); missed seven games. ... Suffered eye infection (March 21, 1995); missed one game. ... Suffered from the flu (April 9, 1995); missed one game. ... Injured groin (December 15, 1995); missed three games. ... Injured wrist (February 18, 1996); missed 17 games. ... Signed as free agent by Edmonton Oilers (October 1, 1997). ... Claimed on waivers by Florida Panthers (November 6, 1997).
HONORS: Won Four Broncos Memorial Trophy (1990-91). ... Won Bob Clarke Trophy (1990-91). ... Won WHL (West) Player of the Year Award (1990-91). ... Won George Parsons Trophy (1990-91). ... Named to Memorial Cup All-Star team (1990-91). ... Named to WHL (West) All-Star first team (1990-91).

			REGULAR SEASON							PLAYOFFS				
Season Team	League	Gms.	G	A	Pts.	PIM	+/-	PP	SH	Gms.	G	A	Pts.	PIM
88-89—Spokane	WHL	71	17	33	50	16	...	...	...	—	—	—	—	—
89-90—Spokane	WHL	71	57	56	113	50	...	...	...	6	3	4	7	6
90-91—Spokane	WHL	72	67	118	*185	36	...	...	...	15	13	18	*31	12
91-92—San Diego	IHL	63	36	54	90	12	...	...	...	4	0	0	0	0
—San Jose	NHL	2	0	3	3	0	-1	0	0	—	—	—	—	—
—Koln	Germany	10	3	6	9	4	...	...	...	—	—	—	—	—
92-93—Kansas City	IHL	46	20	33	53	14	...	...	...	12	5	7	12	2
—San Jose	NHL	26	4	6	10	4	-14	1	0	—	—	—	—	—
93-94—San Jose	NHL	61	14	26	40	14	2	1	0	14	0	4	4	8
94-95—San Jose	NHL	39	13	12	25	14	-7	4	0	11	4	4	8	2
95-96—San Jose	NHL	60	17	24	41	16	-23	4	2	—	—	—	—	—
96-97—Kentucky	AHL	9	1	7	8	2	...	...	...	—	—	—	—	—
—Utah	IHL	43	13	35	48	34	...	...	...	7	3	1	4	6
—San Jose	NHL	12	0	2	2	4	-6	0	0	—	—	—	—	—
97-98—Edmonton	NHL	9	1	3	4	0	-1	0	0	—	—	—	—	—
—Florida	NHL	68	32	29	61	28	10	12	0	—	—	—	—	—
NHL Totals (7 years)		277	81	105	186	80	-40	22	2	25	4	8	12	10

WIDMER, JASON   D   BLUES

PERSONAL: Born August 1, 1973, in Calgary. ... 6-0/200. ... Shoots left. ... Name pronounced WIHD-muhr.
TRANSACTIONS/CAREER NOTES: Selected by New York Islanders in eighth round (eighth Islanders pick, 176th overall) of the NHL entry draft (June 20, 1992). ... Signed as free agent by San Jose Sharks (August 26, 1996). ... Signed as free agent by St. Louis Blues (July 24, 1998).

			REGULAR SEASON							PLAYOFFS				
Season Team	League	Gms.	G	A	Pts.	PIM	+/-	PP	SH	Gms.	G	A	Pts.	PIM
89-90—Moose Jaw	WHL	58	1	8	9	33	...	...	...	—	—	—	—	—
90-91—Lethbridge	WHL	58	2	12	14	55	...	...	...	16	0	1	1	12

W

Season Team	League	REGULAR SEASON								PLAYOFFS				
		Gms.	G	A	Pts.	PIM	+/-	PP	SH	Gms.	G	A	Pts.	PIM
91-92—Lethbridge	WHL	40	2	19	21	181	...	...	...	5	0	4	4	9
92-93—Lethbridge	WHL	55	3	15	18	140	...	...	...	4	0	3	3	2
—Capital District	AHL	4	0	0	0	2	...	...	...	—	—	—	—	—
93-94—Lethbridge	WHL	64	11	31	42	191	...	...	...	9	3	5	8	34
94-95—Canadian nat'l team	Int'l	6	1	4	5	4	...	...	...	—	—	—	—	—
—Worcester	AHL	73	8	26	34	136	...	...	...	—	—	—	—	—
—New York Islanders	NHL	1	0	0	0	0	-1	0	0	—	—	—	—	—
95-96—Worcester	AHL	76	6	21	27	129	...	...	...	4	2	0	2	9
—New York Islanders	NHL	4	0	0	0	7	0	0	0	—	—	—	—	—
96-97—Kentucky	AHL	76	4	24	28	105	...	...	...	4	0	0	0	8
—San Jose	NHL	2	0	1	1	0	1	0	0	—	—	—	—	—
97-98—Kentucky	AHL	71	5	13	18	176	...	...	...	3	0	0	0	6
NHL Totals (3 years)		7	0	1	1	7	0	0	0					

WIEMER, JASON — LW — FLAMES

PERSONAL: Born April 14, 1976, in Kimberley, B.C. ... 6-2/219. ... Shoots left. ... Name pronounced WEE-muhr.
TRANSACTIONS/CAREER NOTES: Selected by Tampa Bay Lightning in first round (first Lightning pick, eighth overall) of NHL entry draft (June 28, 1994). ... Suffered from the flu (March 2, 1995); missed one game. ... Injured jaw (November 3, 1995); missed one game. ... Injured back (April 12, 1996); missed one game. ... Broke bursa sac in elbow (November 30, 1996); missed 14 games. ... Traded by Lightning to Calgary Flames for RW Sandy McCarthy and third- (LW Brad Richards) and fifth-round (D Curtis Rich) picks in 1998 draft (March 24, 1998).
STATISTICAL PLATEAUS: Three-goal games: 1995-96 (1).

Season Team	League	REGULAR SEASON								PLAYOFFS				
		Gms.	G	A	Pts.	PIM	+/-	PP	SH	Gms.	G	A	Pts.	PIM
91-92—Kimberley	RMJHL	45	34	33	67	211	...	...	...	—	—	—	—	—
—Portland	WHL	2	0	1	1	0	...	...	...	—	—	—	—	—
92-93—Portland	WHL	68	18	34	52	159	...	...	...	16	7	3	10	27
93-94—Portland	WHL	72	45	51	96	236	...	...	...	10	4	4	8	32
94-95—Portland	WHL	16	10	14	24	63	...	...	...	—	—	—	—	—
—Tampa Bay	NHL	36	1	4	5	44	-2	0	0	—	—	—	—	—
95-96—Tampa Bay	NHL	66	9	9	18	81	-9	4	0	6	1	0	1	28
96-97—Tampa Bay	NHL	63	9	5	14	134	-13	2	0	—	—	—	—	—
—Adirondack	AHL	4	1	0	1	7	...	...	...	—	—	—	—	—
97-98—Tampa Bay	NHL	67	8	9	17	132	-9	2	0	—	—	—	—	—
—Calgary	NHL	12	4	1	5	28	-1	1	0	—	—	—	—	—
NHL Totals (4 years)		244	31	28	59	419	-34	9	0	6	1	0	1	28

WIKSTROM, JOHN — D — RED WINGS

PERSONAL: Born January 30, 1979, in Lulea, Sweden. ... 6-3/200. ... Shoots left.
TRANSACTIONS/CAREER NOTES: Selected by Detroit Red Wings in fifth round (fourth Red Wings pick, 129th overall) of NHL entry draft (June 21, 1997).

Season Team	League	REGULAR SEASON								PLAYOFFS				
		Gms.	G	A	Pts.	PIM	+/-	PP	SH	Gms.	G	A	Pts.	PIM
95-96—Lulea	Sweden	9	0	0	0	2	...	...	...	—	—	—	—	—
96-97—Lulea	Sweden	9	0	0	0	0	...	...	...	3	0	0	0	0
97-98—Lulea	Sweden	1	0	0	0	0	...	...	...	—	—	—	—	—

WILFORD, MARTY — D — BLACKHAWKS

PERSONAL: Born April 17, 1977, in Cobourg, Ont. ... 6-0/207. ... Shoots left.
HIGH SCHOOL: Henry Street (Whitby, Ont.).
TRANSACTIONS/CAREER NOTES: Selected by Chicago Blackhawks in sixth round (seventh Blackhawks pick, 149th overall) of NHL entry draft (July 8, 1995).
HONORS: Named to OHL All-Star second team (1996-97).

Season Team	League	REGULAR SEASON								PLAYOFFS				
		Gms.	G	A	Pts.	PIM	+/-	PP	SH	Gms.	G	A	Pts.	PIM
93-94—Peterborough	OHA Jr. A	40	3	19	22	107	...	...	...	—	—	—	—	—
94-95—Oshawa	OHL	63	1	6	7	95	...	...	...	7	1	1	2	4
95-96—Oshawa	OHL	65	3	24	27	107	...	...	...	5	0	1	1	4
96-97—Oshawa	OHL	62	19	43	62	126	...	...	...	16	2	18	20	28
97-98—Indianapolis	IHL	26	0	4	4	16	...	...	...	—	—	—	—	—
—Columbus	ECHL	46	8	27	35	123	...	...	...	—	—	—	—	—

W

WILKIE, DAVID — D — LIGHTNING

PERSONAL: Born May 30, 1974, in Ellensburg, Wash. ... 6-2/207. ... Shoots right.
COLLEGE: Cariboo University-College (B.C.).
TRANSACTIONS/CAREER NOTES: Selected by Montreal Canadiens in first round (first Canadiens pick, 20th overall) of NHL entry draft (June 20, 1992). ... Injured right thigh (April 14, 1995); missed remainder of season. ... Injured groin (October 16, 1996); missed one game. ... Suffered concussion (February 1, 1997); missed four games. ... Traded by Canadiens with F Stephane Richer and F Darcy Tucker to Tampa Bay Lightning for F Patrick Poulin, F Mick Vukota and D Igor Ulanov (January 15, 1998). ... Suffered from the flu (February 4, 1998); missed one game.

Season Team	League	REGULAR SEASON Gms.	G	A	Pts.	PIM	+/-	PP	SH	PLAYOFFS Gms.	G	A	Pts.	PIM
89-90—NW Americans Jr.	WCHL	41	21	27	48	59	...	...	...	—	—	—	—	—
90-91—Seattle	WHL	25	1	1	2	22	...	...	...	—	—	—	—	—
91-92—Kamloops	WHL	71	12	28	40	153	...	...	...	16	6	5	11	19
92-93—Kamloops	WHL	53	11	26	37	109	...	...	...	6	4	2	6	2
93-94—Kamloops	WHL	27	11	18	29	18	...	...	...	—	—	—	—	—
—Regina	WHL	29	27	21	48	16	...	...	...	4	1	4	5	4
94-95—Fredericton	AHL	70	10	43	53	34	...	...	...	1	0	0	0	0
—Montreal	NHL	1	0	0	0	0	0	0	0	—	—	—	—	—
95-96—Fredericton	AHL	23	5	12	17	20	...	...	...	—	—	—	—	—
—Montreal	NHL	24	1	5	6	10	-10	1	0	6	1	2	3	12
96-97—Montreal	NHL	61	6	9	15	63	-9	3	0	2	0	0	0	2
97-98—Montreal	NHL	5	1	0	1	4	-1	0	0	—	—	—	—	—
—Tampa Bay	NHL	29	1	5	6	17	-21	0	0	—	—	—	—	—
NHL Totals (4 years)		120	9	19	28	94	-41	4	0	8	1	2	3	14

WILKINSON, DEREK   G   LIGHTNING

PERSONAL: Born July 29, 1974, in Windsor, Ont. ... 6-0/174. ... Catches left.
TRANSACTIONS/CAREER NOTES: Selected by Tampa Bay Lightning in eighth round (eighth Lightning pick, 170th overall) of NHL entry draft (June 20, 1992). ... Broke right foot (November 13, 1995); missed 14 games.

Season Team	League	REGULAR SEASON Gms.	Min	W	L	T	GA	SO	Avg.	PLAYOFFS Gms.	Min.	W	L	GA	SO	Avg.
91-92—Detroit	OHL	38	1943	16	17	1	138	1	4.26	7	313	3	2	28	0	5.37
92-93—Detroit	OHL	4	245	1	2	1	18	0	4.41	—	—	—	—	—	—	—
—Belleville	OHL	59	3370	21	24	11	237	0	4.22	7	434	3	4	29	0	4.01
93-94—Belleville	OHL	56	2860	24	16	4	179	2	3.76	12	700	6	†6	39	*1	3.34
94-95—Atlanta	IHL	46	2415	22	17	‡2	121	1	3.01	4	197	2	1	8	0	2.44
95-96—Atlanta	IHL	28	1433	11	11	‡2	98	1	4.10	—	—	—	—	—	—	—
—Tampa Bay	NHL	4	200	0	3	0	15	0	4.50	—	—	—	—	—	—	—
96-97—Tampa Bay	NHL	5	169	0	2	1	12	0	4.26	—	—	—	—	—	—	—
—Cleveland	IHL	46	2595	20	17	‡6	138	1	3.19	14	893	8	*6	*44	0	2.96
97-98—Cleveland	IHL	25	1295	9	12	‡2	63	1	2.92	1	27	0	0	1	0	2.22
—Tampa Bay	NHL	8	311	2	4	1	17	0	3.28	—	—	—	—	—	—	—
NHL Totals (3 years)		17	680	2	9	2	44	0	3.88							

WILKINSON, NEIL   D   PENGUINS

PERSONAL: Born August 15, 1967, in Selkirk, Man. ... 6-3/194. ... Shoots right. ... Full name: Neil John Wilkinson.
COLLEGE: Michigan State.
TRANSACTIONS/CAREER NOTES: Suffered concussion and broken nose (January 1986). ... Selected by Minnesota North Stars in second round (second North Stars pick, 30th overall) of NHL entry draft (June 21, 1986). ... Twisted knee ligaments during training camp (September 1988). ... Bruised left instep (November 9, 1989). ... Strained back (January 1990). ... Tore left thumb ligaments (March 6, 1991); missed five games. ... Selected by San Jose Sharks in NHL dispersal draft (May 30, 1991). ... Injured groin (December 16, 1991). ... Injured eye (January 8, 1992); missed three games. ... Strained back (February 4, 1992); missed 13 games. ... Suffered facial contusions (October 28, 1992); missed two games. ... Strained back (November 10, 1992); missed 14 games. ... Injured hand (December 18, 1992); missed one game. ... Strained back (February 10, 1993); missed six games. ... Traded by Sharks to Chicago Blackhawks to complete deal in which Blackhawks sent G Jimmy Waite to Sharks for future considerations (June 18, 1993). ... Traded by Blackhawks to Winnipeg Jets for third-round pick in 1995 draft (June 3, 1994). ... Bruised back (April 7, 1995); missed six games. ... Broke foot (November 10, 1995); missed 14 games. ... Traded by Jets to Pittsburgh Penguins for D Norm Maciver (December 28, 1995). ... Bruised shoulder (January 31, 1996); missed three games. ... Bruised heel (February 14, 1996); missed two games. ... Underwent abdominal surgery (October 2, 1996); missed 38 games. ... Fractured cheekbone (January 15, 1997); missed nine games. ... Bruised shoulder (February 15, 1997); missed two games. ... Suffered abdominal pain (March 8, 1997); missed four games. ... Suffered recurring abdominal pain (April 5, 1997); missed five games. ... Reinjured abdomen prior to 1997-98 season; missed first 12 games of season. ... Reinjured abdomen (November 26, 1997); missed four games. ... Reinjured abdomen (December 19, 1997); missed one game. ... Reinjured abdomen (March 26, 1998); missed remainder of season.

Season Team	League	REGULAR SEASON Gms.	G	A	Pts.	PIM	+/-	PP	SH	PLAYOFFS Gms.	G	A	Pts.	PIM
85-86—Selkirk	MJHL	42	14	35	49	91	...	...	...	—	—	—	—	—
86-87—Michigan State	CCHA	19	3	4	7	18	...	...	...	—	—	—	—	—
87-88—Medicine Hat	WHL	55	11	21	32	157	...	...	...	5	1	0	1	2
88-89—Kalamazoo	IHL	39	5	15	20	96	...	...	...	—	—	—	—	—
89-90—Kalamazoo	IHL	20	6	7	13	62	...	...	...	—	—	—	—	—
—Minnesota	NHL	36	0	5	5	100	-1	0	0	7	0	2	2	11
90-91—Kalamazoo	IHL	10	0	3	3	38	...	...	...	—	—	—	—	—
—Minnesota	NHL	50	2	9	11	117	-5	0	0	22	3	3	6	12
91-92—San Jose	NHL	60	4	15	19	107	-11	1	0	—	—	—	—	—
92-93—San Jose	NHL	59	1	7	8	96	-50	0	1	—	—	—	—	—
93-94—Chicago	NHL	72	3	9	12	116	2	1	0	4	0	0	0	0
94-95—Winnipeg	NHL	40	1	4	5	75	-26	0	0	—	—	—	—	—
95-96—Winnipeg	NHL	21	1	4	5	33	0	0	1	—	—	—	—	—
—Pittsburgh	NHL	41	2	10	12	87	12	0	0	15	0	1	1	14
96-97—Pittsburgh	NHL	23	0	0	0	36	-12	0	0	5	0	0	0	4
—Cleveland	IHL	2	0	1	1	0	...	...	...	—	—	—	—	—
97-98—Pittsburgh	NHL	34	2	4	6	24	0	1	0	—	—	—	—	—
NHL Totals (9 years)		436	16	67	83	791	-91	3	2	53	3	6	9	41

W

WILLIS, SHANE — RW — HURRICANES

PERSONAL: Born June 13, 1977, in Edmonton. ... 6-0/176. ... Shoots right.
TRANSACTIONS/CAREER NOTES: Selected by Tampa Bay Lightning in third round (third Lightning pick, 56th overall) of NHL entry draft (July 8, 1995). ... Returned to draft pool by Lightning and selected by Carolina Hurricanes in fourth round (fourth Hurricanes pick, 88th overall) of NHL entry draft (June 21, 1997).
HONORS: Named to Can.HL All-Rookie team (1994-95). ... Named to WHL (East) All-Star first team (1996-97). ... Named to WHL (East) All-Star first team (1997-98).

			REGULAR SEASON							PLAYOFFS				
Season Team	League	Gms.	G	A	Pts.	PIM	+/-	PP	SH	Gms.	G	A	Pts.	PIM
94-95—Prince Albert	WHL	65	24	19	43	38	...	...	...	13	3	4	7	6
95-96—Prince Albert	WHL	69	41	40	81	47	...	...	...	18	11	10	21	18
96-97—Prince Albert	WHL	41	34	22	56	63	...	...	...	—	—	—	—	—
—Lethbridge	WHL	26	22	17	39	24	...	...	...	19	13	11	24	20
97-98—New Haven	AHL	1	0	1	1	2	...	...	...	—	—	—	—	—
—Lethbridge	WHL	64	58	54	112	73	...	...	...	4	2	3	5	6

WILLSIE, BRIAN — RW — AVALANCHE

PERSONAL: Born March 16, 1978, in London, Ont. ... 6-0/179. ... Shoots right.
TRANSACTIONS/CAREER NOTES: Selected by Colorado Avalanche in sixth round (seventh Avalanche pick, 146th overall) of NHL entry draft (June 22, 1996).
HONORS: Named to OHL All-Star first team (1997-98).

			REGULAR SEASON							PLAYOFFS				
Season Team	League	Gms.	G	A	Pts.	PIM	+/-	PP	SH	Gms.	G	A	Pts.	PIM
95-96—Guelph	OHL	65	13	21	34	18	...	...	...	16	4	2	6	6
96-97—Guelph	OHL	64	37	31	68	37	...	...	...	18	15	4	19	10
97-98—Guelph	OHL	57	45	31	76	41	...	...	...	12	9	5	14	18

WILM, CLARKE — C — FLAMES

PERSONAL: Born October 24, 1976, in Central Butte, Sask. ... 5-11/204. ... Shoots left. ... Name pronounced WIHLM.
TRANSACTIONS/CAREER NOTES: Selected by Calgary Flames in sixth round (fifth Flames pick, 150th overall) of NHL entry draft (July 8, 1995).

			REGULAR SEASON							PLAYOFFS				
Season Team	League	Gms.	G	A	Pts.	PIM	+/-	PP	SH	Gms.	G	A	Pts.	PIM
91-92—Saskatoon	WHL	—	—	—	—	—	...	...	...	1	0	0	0	0
92-93—Saskatoon	WHL	69	14	19	33	71	...	...	...	9	4	2	6	13
93-94—Saskatoon	WHL	70	18	32	50	181	...	...	...	16	0	9	9	19
94-95—Saskatoon	WHL	71	20	39	59	179	...	...	...	10	6	1	7	21
95-96—Saskatoon	WHL	72	49	61	110	83	...	...	...	4	1	1	2	4
96-97—Saint John	AHL	62	9	19	28	107	...	...	...	5	2	0	2	15
97-98—Saint John	AHL	68	13	26	39	112	...	...	...	21	5	9	14	8

WILSON, LANDON — RW — BRUINS

PERSONAL: Born March 15, 1975, in St. Louis. ... 6-2/216. ... Shoots right. ... Son of Rick Wilson, defenseman with Montreal Canadiens, St. Louis Blues and Detroit Red Wings (1973-74 through 1976-77).
COLLEGE: North Dakota.
TRANSACTIONS/CAREER NOTES: Selected by Toronto Maple Leafs in first round (second Maple Leafs pick, 19th overall) of NHL entry draft (June 26, 1993). ... Traded by Maple Leafs with LW Wendel Clark, D Sylvain Lefebvre and first-round pick (D Jeffrey Kealty) in 1994 draft to Quebec Nordiques for C Mats Sundin, D Garth Butcher, LW Todd Warriner and first-round pick (traded to Washington Capitals who selected D Nolan Baumgartner) in 1994 draft (June 28, 1994). ... Nordiques franchise moved to Colorado and renamed Avalanche for 1995-96 season (June 21, 1995). ... Traded by Avalanche with D Anders Myrvold to Boston Bruins for first-round pick (D Robyn Regehr) in 1998 draft (November 22, 1996). ... Sprained shoulder (December 12, 1996); missed 10 games. ... Suffered charley horse (January 7, 1997); missed 12 games. ... Strained abdomen (April 15, 1998); missed final two games of regular season and first two games of playoffs.
HONORS: Named WCHA Rookie of the Year (1993-94). ... Named to WCHA All-Rookie team (1993-94).

			REGULAR SEASON							PLAYOFFS				
Season Team	League	Gms.	G	A	Pts.	PIM	+/-	PP	SH	Gms.	G	A	Pts.	PIM
92-93—Dubuque	USHL	43	29	36	65	284	...	...	...	—	—	—	—	—
93-94—U. of North Dakota	WCHA	35	18	15	33	147	...	...	...	—	—	—	—	—
94-95—U. of North Dakota	WCHA	31	7	16	23	141	...	...	...	—	—	—	—	—
—Cornwall	AHL	8	4	4	8	25	...	...	...	13	3	4	7	68
95-96—Cornwall	AHL	53	21	13	34	154	...	...	...	8	1	3	4	22
—Colorado	NHL	7	1	0	1	6	3	0	0	—	—	—	—	—
96-97—Colorado	NHL	9	1	2	3	23	1	0	0	—	—	—	—	—
—Boston	NHL	40	7	10	17	49	-6	0	0	—	—	—	—	—
—Providence	AHL	2	2	1	3	2	...	...	...	10	3	4	7	16
97-98—Boston	NHL	28	1	5	6	7	3	0	0	1	0	0	0	0
—Providence	AHL	42	18	10	28	146	...	...	...	—	—	—	—	—
NHL Totals (3 years)		84	10	17	27	85	1	0	0	1	0	0	0	0

W

WILSON, MIKE — D — SABRES

PERSONAL: Born February 26, 1975, in Brampton, Ont. ... 6-6/212. ... Shoots left.
TRANSACTIONS/CAREER NOTES: Selected by Vancouver Canucks in first round (first Canucks pick, 20th overall) of NHL entry draft (June 26, 1993). ... Traded by Canucks with RW Mike Peca and first-round pick (D Jay McKee) in 1995 draft to Buffalo Sabres for RW Alexander Mogilny and fifth-round pick (LW Todd Norman) in 1995 draft (July 8, 1995). ... Suffered concussion (January 26, 1996); missed two games. ... Bruised chest (November 13, 1997); missed one game. ... Suffered mild concussion (January 8, 1998); missed two games.
HONORS: Named to Can.HL All-Rookie team (1992-93). ... Named to OHL All-Rookie team (1992-93).

		REGULAR SEASON								PLAYOFFS				
Season Team	League	Gms.	G	A	Pts.	PIM	+/-	PP	SH	Gms.	G	A	Pts.	PIM
91-92—Georgetown Jr. B	OHA	41	9	13	22	65	...	...	...	—	—	—	—	—
92-93—Sudbury	OHL	53	6	7	13	58	...	...	...	14	1	1	2	21
93-94—Sudbury	OHL	60	4	22	26	62	...	...	...	9	1	3	4	8
94-95—Sudbury	OHL	64	13	34	47	46	...	...	...	18	1	8	9	10
95-96—Rochester	AHL	15	0	5	5	38	...	...	...	—	—	—	—	—
—Buffalo	NHL	58	4	8	12	41	13	1	0	—	—	—	—	—
96-97—Buffalo	NHL	77	2	9	11	51	13	0	0	10	0	1	1	2
97-98—Buffalo	NHL	66	4	4	8	48	13	0	0	15	0	1	1	13
NHL Totals (3 years)		201	10	21	31	140	39	1	0	25	0	2	2	15

WITT, BRENDAN — D — CAPITALS

PERSONAL: Born February 20, 1975, in Humboldt, Sask. ... 6-1/215. ... Shoots left.
HIGH SCHOOL: Meadowdale (Lynnwood, Wash.).
TRANSACTIONS/CAREER NOTES: Selected by Washington Capitals in first round (first Capitals pick, 11th overall) of NHL entry draft (June 26, 1993). ... Missed entire 1994-95 season due to contract dispute. ... Broke wrist (January 28, 1996); missed 34 games. ... Suffered from the flu (November 15, 1996); missed five games. ... Bruised shoulder (November 27, 1997); missed seven games. ... Suffered illness (January 6, 1998); missed three games. ... Injured wrist (April 6, 1998); missed final six games of regular season and five playoff games.
HONORS: Named to WHL (West) All-Star first team (1992-93 and 1993-94). ... Won Bill Hunter Trophy (1993-94). ... Named to Can.HL All-Star first team (1993-94).

		REGULAR SEASON								PLAYOFFS				
Season Team	League	Gms.	G	A	Pts.	PIM	+/-	PP	SH	Gms.	G	A	Pts.	PIM
90-91—Seattle	WHL	—					...	...	...	1	0	0	0	...
91-92—Seattle	WHL	67	3	9	12	212	...	...	...	15	1	1	2	84
92-93—Seattle	WHL	70	2	26	28	239	...	...	...	5	1	2	3	30
93-94—Seattle	WHL	56	8	31	39	235	...	...	...	9	3	8	11	23
94-95—							Did not play.							
95-96—Washington	NHL	48	2	3	5	85	-4	0	0	—	—	—	—	—
96-97—Washington	NHL	44	3	2	5	88	-20	0	0	—	—	—	—	—
—Portland	AHL	30	2	4	6	56	...	...	...	5	1	0	1	30
97-98—Washington	NHL	64	1	7	8	112	-11	0	0	16	1	0	1	14
NHL Totals (4 years)		156	6	12	18	285	-35	0	0	16	1	0	1	14

WOLANIN, CRAIG — D — MAPLE LEAFS

PERSONAL: Born July 27, 1967, in Grosse Point, Mich. ... 6-4/215. ... Shoots left. ... Brother of Chris Wolanin, defenseman with Vancouver Canucks organizations (1988-89 through 1991-92). ... Name pronounced woh-LAN-ihn.
TRANSACTIONS/CAREER NOTES: Selected by New Jersey Devils as underage junior in first round (first Devils pick, third overall) of NHL entry draft (June 15, 1985). ... Bruised left shoulder (October 31, 1985). ... Broke ring finger on left hand (February 1, 1986). ... Underwent surgery to finger (February 19, 1986). ... Suffered sore left hip (December 1987). ... Sprained right knee (November 15, 1988). ... Underwent surgery to right knee (December 1988). ... Injured finger (November 22, 1989). ... Traded by Devils with future considerations to Quebec Nordiques for C Peter Stastny (March 6, 1990). ... Devils sent D Randy Velischek to Nordiques to complete deal (August 13, 1990). ... Injured knee (April 1, 1990). ... Injured groin (October 17, 1991); missed three games. ... Injured knee (January 8, 1992); missed four games. ... Pulled muscle in right thigh (October 13, 1992); missed 24 games. ... Bruised ribs (December 20, 1992); missed six games. ... Injured groin (January 16, 1993); missed 28 games. ... Pulled groin (April 1, 1993); missed one game. ... Strained left groin (October 18, 1993); missed 11 games. ... Bruised right knee (November 27, 1993); missed one game. ... Strained left hip flexor (January 4, 1994); missed six games. ... Injured groin (January 21, 1995); missed four games. ... Bruised knee (February 25, 1995); missed four games. ... Nordiques franchise moved to Colorado and renamed Avalanche for 1995-96 season (June 21, 1995). ... Injured shoulder (December 18, 1995); missed five games. ... Traded by Avalanche to Tampa Bay Lightning for future considerations (July 29, 1996). ... Reinjured shoulder (October 5, 1996); missed 23 games. ... Traded by Lightning to Toronto Maple Leafs for third-round pick (traded to Edmonton) in 1998 draft (January 31, 1997). ... Sprained knee (March 26, 1997); missed seven games. ... Strained groin (October 1, 1997); missed two games. ... Underwent knee surgery (November 4, 1997); missed remainder of season.
MISCELLANEOUS: Member of Stanley Cup championship team (1996).

		REGULAR SEASON								PLAYOFFS				
Season Team	League	Gms.	G	A	Pts.	PIM	+/-	PP	SH	Gms.	G	A	Pts.	PIM
84-85—Kitchener	OHL	60	5	16	21	95	...	...	...	4	1	1	2	2
85-86—New Jersey	NHL	44	2	16	18	74	-7	0	0	—	—	—	—	—
86-87—New Jersey	NHL	68	4	6	10	109	-31	0	0	—	—	—	—	—
87-88—New Jersey	NHL	78	6	25	31	170	0	1	1	18	2	5	7	51
88-89—New Jersey	NHL	56	3	8	11	69	-9	0	0	—	—	—	—	—
89-90—Utica	AHL	6	2	4	6	2	...	...	...	—	—	—	—	—
—New Jersey	NHL	37	1	7	8	47	-13	0	0	—	—	—	—	—
—Quebec	NHL	13	0	3	3	10	2	0	0	—	—	—	—	—
90-91—Quebec	NHL	80	5	13	18	89	-13	0	1	—	—	—	—	—
91-92—Quebec	NHL	69	2	11	13	80	-12	0	0	—	—	—	—	—
92-93—Quebec	NHL	24	1	4	5	49	9	0	0	4	0	0	0	4
93-94—Quebec	NHL	63	6	10	16	80	16	0	0	—	—	—	—	—

Season Team	League	REGULAR SEASON Gms.	G	A	Pts.	PIM	+/-	PP	SH	PLAYOFFS Gms.	G	A	Pts.	PIM
94-95—Quebec	NHL	40	3	6	9	40	12	0	0	6	1	1	2	4
95-96—Colorado	NHL	75	7	20	27	50	25	0	3	7	1	0	1	8
96-97—Tampa Bay	NHL	15	0	0	0	8	-9	0	0	—	—	—	—	—
—Toronto	NHL	23	0	4	4	13	3	0	0	—	—	—	—	—
97-98—Toronto	NHL	10	0	0	0	6	-9	0	0	—	—	—	—	—
NHL Totals (13 years)		695	40	133	173	894	-36	1	5	35	4	6	10	67

WOOD, DODY   C   DEVILS

PERSONAL: Born May 8, 1972, in Chetwynd, B.C. ... 6-0/200. ... Shoots left.
TRANSACTIONS/CAREER NOTES: Selected by San Jose Sharks in third round (fourth Sharks pick, 45th overall) of NHL entry draft (June 22, 1991). ... Injured hand (November 29, 1995); missed two games. ... Injured back (February 10, 1996); missed seven games ... Injured back (March 5, 1996); missed 11 games. ... Sore foot (October 30, 1996); missed five games. ... Underwent wrist surgery (April 1, 1997); missed remainder of season. ... Traded by Sharks with D Doug Bodger to New Jersey Devils for RW John MacLean and D Ken Sutton (December 7, 1997).

Season Team	League	REGULAR SEASON Gms.	G	A	Pts.	PIM	+/-	PP	SH	PLAYOFFS Gms.	G	A	Pts.	PIM
89-90—Fort St. John	PCJHL	44	51	73	124	270	...	...	...	—	—	—	—	—
—Seattle	WHL	—					...	...	...	5	0	0	0	2
90-91—Seattle	WHL	69	28	37	65	272	...	...	...	6	0	1	1	2
91-92—Seattle	WHL	37	13	19	32	232	...	...	...	—	—	—	—	—
—Swift Current	WHL	3	0	2	2	14	...	...	...	7	2	1	3	37
92-93—Kansas City	IHL	36	3	2	5	216	...	...	...	6	0	1	1	15
—San Jose	NHL	13	1	1	2	71	-5	0	0	—	—	—	—	—
93-94—Kansas City	IHL	48	5	15	20	320	...	...	...	—	—	—	—	—
94-95—Kansas City	IHL	44	5	13	18	255	...	...	...	21	7	10	17	87
—San Jose	NHL	9	1	1	2	29	0	0	0	—	—	—	—	—
95-96—San Jose	NHL	32	3	6	9	138	0	0	1	—	—	—	—	—
96-97—San Jose	NHL	44	3	2	5	193	-3	0	0	—	—	—	—	—
—Kansas City	IHL	6	3	6	9	35	...	...	...	—	—	—	—	—
97-98—San Jose	NHL	8	0	0	0	40	-3	0	0	—	—	—	—	—
—Kansas City	IHL	2	0	1	1	31	...	...	...	—	—	—	—	—
—Albany	AHL	34	4	13	17	185	...	...	...	13	2	0	2	55
NHL Totals (5 years)		106	8	10	18	471	-11	0	1					

WOOLLEY, JASON   D   SABRES

PERSONAL: Born July 27, 1969, in Toronto. ... 6-1/188. ... Shoots left. ... Full name: Jason Douglas Woolley.
COLLEGE: Michigan State.
TRANSACTIONS/CAREER NOTES: Selected by Washington Capitals in third round (fourth Capitals pick, 61st overall) of NHL entry draft (June 17, 1989). ... Broke wrist (October 12, 1992); missed 24 games. ... Signed as free agent by Detroit Vipers (October 7, 1994). ... Contract sold by Vipers to Florida Panthers (February 14, 1995). ... Separated left shoulder (October 15, 1995); missed two games. ... Broke left thumb (November 18, 1995); missed 13 games. ... Traded by Panthers with C Stu Barnes to Pittsburgh Penguins for C Chris Wells (November 19, 1996). ... Injured groin (November 22, 1996); missed one game. ... Strained groin (February 27, 1997); missed one game. ... Strained groin (March 4, 1997); missed two games. ... Bruised wrist (March 18, 1997); missed two games. ... Traded by Penguins to Buffalo Sabres for fifth-round pick (D Robert Scuderi) in 1998 draft (September 24, 1997). ... Fractured thumb (October 1, 1997); missed nine games.
HONORS: Named to CCHA All-Rookie team (1988-89). ... Named to NCAA All-America West first team (1990-91). ... Named to CCHA All-Star first team (1990-91).
MISCELLANEOUS: Member of silver-medal-winning Canadian Olympic team (1992).

Season Team	League	REGULAR SEASON Gms.	G	A	Pts.	PIM	+/-	PP	SH	PLAYOFFS Gms.	G	A	Pts.	PIM
87-88—St. Michael's Jr. B	ODHA	31	19	37	56	22	...	...	...	—	—	—	—	—
88-89—Michigan State	CCHA	47	12	25	37	26	...	...	...	—	—	—	—	—
89-90—Michigan State	CCHA	45	10	38	48	26	...	...	...	—	—	—	—	—
90-91—Michigan State	CCHA	40	15	44	59	24	...	...	...	—	—	—	—	—
91-92—Canadian nat'l team	Int'l	60	14	30	44	36	...	...	...	—	—	—	—	—
—Can. Olympic Team	Int'l	8	0	5	5	4	...	...	...	—	—	—	—	—
—Baltimore	AHL	15	1	10	11	6	...	...	...	—	—	—	—	—
—Washington	NHL	1	0	0	0	0	1	0	0	—	—	—	—	—
92-93—Baltimore	AHL	29	14	27	41	22	...	...	...	1	0	2	2	0
—Washington	NHL	26	0	2	2	10	3	0	0	—	—	—	—	—
93-94—Portland	AHL	41	12	29	41	14	...	...	...	9	2	2	4	4
—Washington	NHL	10	1	2	3	4	2	0	0	4	1	0	1	4
94-95—Detroit	IHL	48	8	28	36	38	...	...	...	—	—	—	—	—
—Florida	NHL	34	4	9	13	18	-1	1	0	—	—	—	—	—
95-96—Florida	NHL	52	6	28	34	32	-9	3	0	13	2	6	8	14
96-97—Florida	NHL	3	0	0	0	2	1	0	0	—	—	—	—	—
—Pittsburgh	NHL	57	6	30	36	28	3	2	0	5	0	3	3	0
97-98—Buffalo	NHL	71	9	26	35	35	8	3	0	15	2	9	11	12
NHL Totals (7 years)		254	26	97	123	129	8	9	0	37	5	18	23	30

W

WORRELL, PETER   LW   PANTHERS

PERSONAL: Born August 18, 1977, in Pierrefonds, Quebec. ... 6-6/225. ... Shoots left. ... Name pronounced wuh-REHL.
TRANSACTIONS/CAREER NOTES: Selected by Florida Panthers in seventh round (seventh Panthers pick, 166th overall) of NHL entry draft (July 8, 1995).

Season Team	League	REGULAR SEASON								PLAYOFFS				
		Gms.	G	A	Pts.	PIM	+/-	PP	SH	Gms.	G	A	Pts.	PIM
94-95—Hull	QMJHL	56	1	8	9	243	...	...	...	21	0	1	1	91
95-96—Hull	QMJHL	63	23	36	59	464	...	...	...	18	11	8	19	81
96-97—Hull	QMJHL	62	18	45	63	*495	...	...	...	14	3	13	16	83
97-98—New Haven	AHL	50	15	12	27	309	...	...	...	1	0	1	1	6
—Florida	NHL	19	0	0	0	153	-4	0	0	—	—	—	—	—
NHL Totals (1 year)		19	0	0	0	153	-4	0	0					

WOTTON, MARK   D   CANUCKS

PERSONAL: Born November 16, 1973, in Foxwarren, Man. ... 5-11/192. ... Shoots left. ... Name pronounced WAH-tehn.
TRANSACTIONS/CAREER NOTES: Selected by Vancouver Canucks in 10th round (11th Canucks pick, 237th overall) of NHL entry draft (June 20, 1992). ... Suffered blood clot in eye (May 17, 1995); missed six playoff games.
HONORS: Named to WHL (East) All-Star second team (1993-94).

Season Team	League	REGULAR SEASON								PLAYOFFS				
		Gms.	G	A	Pts.	PIM	+/-	PP	SH	Gms.	G	A	Pts.	PIM
90-91—Saskatoon	WHL	45	4	11	15	37	...	...	...	—	—	—	—	—
91-92—Saskatoon	WHL	64	11	25	36	92	...	...	...	—	—	—	—	—
92-93—Saskatoon	WHL	71	15	51	66	90	...	...	...	9	6	5	11	18
93-94—Saskatoon	WHL	65	12	34	46	108	...	...	...	16	3	12	15	32
94-95—Syracuse	AHL	75	12	29	41	50	...	...	...	—	—	—	—	—
—Vancouver	NHL	1	0	0	0	0	1	0	0	5	0	0	0	4
95-96—Syracuse	AHL	80	10	35	45	96	...	...	...	15	1	12	13	20
96-97—Syracuse	AHL	27	2	8	10	25	...	...	...	2	0	0	0	4
—Vancouver	NHL	36	3	6	9	19	8	0	1	—	—	—	—	—
97-98—Vancouver	NHL	5	0	0	0	6	-2	0	0	—	—	—	—	—
—Syracuse	AHL	56	12	21	33	80	...	...	...	5	0	0	0	12
NHL Totals (3 years)		42	3	6	9	25	7	0	1	5	0	0	0	4

WREGGET, KEN   G   FLAMES

PERSONAL: Born March 25, 1964, in Brandon, Man. ... 6-1/205. ... Catches left.
TRANSACTIONS/CAREER NOTES: Selected by Toronto Maple Leafs as underage junior in third round (fourth Maple Leafs pick, 45th overall) of NHL entry draft (June 9, 1982). ... Injured knee (December 26, 1985). ... Traded by Maple Leafs to Philadelphia Flyers for two first-round picks (RW Rob Pearson and D Steve Bancroft) in 1989 draft (March 6, 1989). ... Tore hamstring (November 1, 1989); missed seven games. ... Pulled hamstring (March 24, 1990). ... Strained right hip flexor (November 4, 1990); missed 15 games. ... Traded by Flyers with RW Rick Tocchet, D Kjell Samuelsson and conditional pick in 1992 draft to Pittsburgh Penguins for RW Mark Recchi, D Brian Benning and first-round pick (LW Jason Bowen) in 1992 draft (February 19, 1992). ... Bruised right knee (February 27, 1993); missed one game. ... Injured foot (April 4, 1994); missed five games. ... Strained ankle (March 24, 1995); missed two games. ... Strained ankle (April 5, 1995); missed four games. ... Pulled hamstring (December 26, 1996); missed nine games. ... Reinjured hamstring (March 18, 1997); missed four games. ... Reinjured hamstring (April 5, 1997); missed three games. ... Bruised knee (October 25, 1997); missed one game. ... Herniated disk in back (November 5, 1997); missed 23 games. ... Bruised knee and back (March 14, 1998); missed five games. ... Traded by Penguins with LW Dave Roche to Calgary Flames for C German Titov and C Todd Hlushko (June 17, 1998).
HONORS: Won WHL Top Goaltender Trophy (1983-84). ... Named to WHL (East) All-Star first team (1983-84).
MISCELLANEOUS: Member of Stanley Cup championship team (1992). ... Stopped penalty shot attempt (vs. Christian Ruuttu, November 15, 1987; vs. Lane Lambert, March 15, 1988; vs. Joe Nieuwendyk, January 23, 1993; vs. Scott Niedermayer, February 7, 1996). ... Allowed penalty shot goal (vs. Rick Meagher, December 7, 1986; vs. Joe Sakic, December 9, 1989; vs. Doug Brown, November 23, 1991).

Season Team	League	REGULAR SEASON							PLAYOFFS					
		Gms.	Min	W	L	T	GA	SO	Avg.	Gms.	Min.	W	L	GA	SO	Avg.
81-82—Lethbridge	WHL	36	1713	19	12	0	118	1	4.13	3	84	...	...	3	0	2.14
82-83—Lethbridge	WHL	48	2696	26	17	1	157	1	3.49	*20	*1154	14	5	58	*1	*3.02
83-84—Lethbridge	WHL	53	*3053	32	20	0	161	0	*3.16	4	210	1	3	18	0	5.14
—Toronto	NHL	3	165	1	1	1	14	0	5.09	—	—	—	—	—	—	—
84-85—Toronto	NHL	23	1278	2	15	3	103	0	4.84	—	—	—	—	—	—	—
—St. Catharines	AHL	12	688	2	8	1	48	0	4.19	—	—	—	—	—	—	—
85-86—St. Catharines	AHL	18	1058	8	9	0	78	1	4.42	—	—	—	—	—	—	—
—Toronto	NHL	30	1566	9	13	4	113	0	4.33	10	607	6	4	32	†1	3.16
86-87—Toronto	NHL	56	3026	22	28	3	200	0	3.97	13	761	7	6	29	1	*2.29
87-88—Toronto	NHL	56	3000	12	35	4	222	2	4.44	2	108	0	1	11	0	6.11
88-89—Toronto	NHL	32	1888	9	20	2	139	0	4.42	—	—	—	—	—	—	—
—Philadelphia	NHL	3	130	1	1	0	13	0	6.00	5	268	2	2	10	0	2.24
89-90—Philadelphia	NHL	51	2961	22	24	3	169	0	3.42	—	—	—	—	—	—	—
90-91—Philadelphia	NHL	30	1484	10	14	3	88	0	3.56	—	—	—	—	—	—	—
91-92—Philadelphia	NHL	23	1259	9	8	3	75	0	3.57	—	—	—	—	—	—	—
—Pittsburgh	NHL	9	448	5	3	0	31	0	4.15	1	40	0	0	4	0	6.00
92-93—Pittsburgh	NHL	25	1368	13	7	2	78	0	3.42	—	—	—	—	—	—	—
93-94—Pittsburgh	NHL	42	2456	21	12	7	138	1	3.37	—	—	—	—	—	—	—
94-95—Pittsburgh	NHL	38	2208	*25	9	2	118	0	3.21	11	661	5	6	33	1	3.00
95-96—Pittsburgh	NHL	37	2132	20	13	2	115	3	3.24	9	599	7	2	23	0	2.30
96-97—Pittsburgh	NHL	46	2514	17	17	6	136	2	3.25	5	297	1	4	18	0	3.64
97-98—Pittsburgh	NHL	15	611	3	6	2	28	0	2.75	—	—	—	—	—	—	—
NHL Totals (15 years)		519	28494	201	226	47	1780	8	3.75	56	3341	28	25	160	3	2.87

WREN, BOB   LW   MIGHTY DUCKS

PERSONAL: Born September 16, 1974, in Preston, Ont. ... 5-10/185. ... Shoots left.
TRANSACTIONS/CAREER NOTES: Selected by Los Angeles Kings in fourth round (third Kings pick, 94th overall) of NHL entry draft (June 26, 1993). ... Signed as free agent by Hartford Whalers (September 6, 1994). ... Signed as free agent by Mighty Ducks of Anaheim (October 17, 1996).
HONORS: Named to OHL All-Star second team (1992-93 and 1993-94).

W

Season Team	League	Gms.	G	A	Pts.	PIM	+/-	PP	SH	Gms.	G	A	Pts.	PIM
			REGULAR SEASON								PLAYOFFS			
89-90—Guelph	Jr. B	48	24	36	60	12	...	...	...	—	—	—	—	—
90-91—Kingston	Jr. B	32	27	28	55	85	...	...	...	—	—	—	—	—
91-92—Detroit	OHL	62	13	36	49	58	...	...	...	7	3	4	7	19
92-93—Detroit	OHL	63	57	88	145	91	...	...	...	15	4	11	15	20
93-94—Detroit	OHL	57	45	64	109	81	...	...	...	17	12	18	30	20
94-95—Springfield	AHL	61	16	15	31	118	...	...	...	—	—	—	—	—
—Richmond	ECHL	2	0	1	1	0	...	...	...	—	—	—	—	—
95-96—Detroit	IHL	1	0	0	0	0	...	...	...	—	—	—	—	—
—Knoxville	ECHL	50	21	35	56	257	...	...	...	8	4	11	15	32
96-97—Baltimore	AHL	72	23	36	59	97	...	...	...	3	1	1	2	0
97-98—Cincinnati	AHL	77	*42	58	100	151	...	...	...	—	—	—	—	—
—Anaheim	NHL	3	0	0	0	0	0	0	0	—	—	—	—	—
NHL Totals (1 year)		3	0	0	0	0	0	0	0					

WRIGHT, JAMIE — LW — STARS

PERSONAL: Born May 13, 1976, in Kitchener, Ont. ... 6-0/172. ... Shoots left.
HIGH SCHOOL: Bishop MacDonnell (Guelph, Ont.).
TRANSACTIONS/CAREER NOTES: Selected by Dallas Stars in fourth round (third Stars pick, 98th overall) of NHL entry draft (June 29, 1994).
HONORS: Won Bobby Smith Trophy (1994-95).

Season Team	League	Gms.	G	A	Pts.	PIM	+/-	PP	SH	Gms.	G	A	Pts.	PIM
			REGULAR SEASON								PLAYOFFS			
91-92—Elmira Jr. B	OHA	44	17	11	28	46	...	...	...	—	—	—	—	—
92-93—Elmira Jr. B	OHA	47	22	32	54	52	...	...	...	—	—	—	—	—
93-94—Guelph	OHL	65	17	15	32	34	...	...	...	8	2	1	3	10
94-95—Guelph	OHL	65	43	39	82	36	...	...	...	14	6	8	14	6
95-96—Guelph	OHL	55	30	36	66	45	...	...	...	16	10	12	22	35
96-97—Michigan	IHL	60	6	8	14	34	...	...	...	1	0	0	0	0
97-98—Michigan	IHL	53	15	11	26	31	...	...	...	—	—	—	—	—
—Dallas	NHL	21	4	2	6	2	8	0	0	5	0	0	0	0
NHL Totals (1 year)		21	4	2	6	2	8	0	0	5	0	0	0	0

WRIGHT, TYLER — C — PENGUINS

PERSONAL: Born April 6, 1973, in Canora, Sask. ... 5-11/185. ... Shoots right.
TRANSACTIONS/CAREER NOTES: Selected by Edmonton Oilers in first round (first Oilers pick, 12th overall) of NHL entry draft (June 22, 1991). ... Traded by Oilers to Pittsburgh Penguins for seventh-round pick (RW Brandon LaFrance) in 1996 draft (June 22, 1996). ... Bruised ribs (December 13, 1996); missed one game.

Season Team	League	Gms.	G	A	Pts.	PIM	+/-	PP	SH	Gms.	G	A	Pts.	PIM
			REGULAR SEASON								PLAYOFFS			
89-90—Swift Current	WHL	67	14	18	32	119	...	...	...	4	0	0	0	12
90-91—Swift Current	WHL	66	41	51	92	157	...	...	...	3	0	0	0	6
91-92—Swift Current	WHL	63	36	46	82	295	...	...	...	8	2	5	7	16
92-93—Swift Current	WHL	37	24	41	65	76	...	...	...	17	9	17	26	49
—Edmonton	NHL	7	1	1	2	19	-4	0	0	—	—	—	—	—
93-94—Cape Breton	AHL	65	14	27	41	160	...	...	...	5	2	0	2	11
—Edmonton	NHL	5	0	0	0	4	-3	0	0	—	—	—	—	—
94-95—Cape Breton	AHL	70	16	15	31	184	...	...	...	—	—	—	—	—
—Edmonton	NHL	6	1	0	1	14	1	0	0	—	—	—	—	—
95-96—Edmonton	NHL	23	1	0	1	33	-7	0	0	—	—	—	—	—
—Cape Breton	AHL	31	6	12	18	158	...	...	...	—	—	—	—	—
96-97—Pittsburgh	NHL	45	2	2	4	70	-7	0	0	—	—	—	—	—
—Cleveland	IHL	10	4	3	7	34	...	...	...	14	4	2	6	44
97-98—Pittsburgh	NHL	82	3	4	7	112	-3	1	0	6	0	1	1	4
NHL Totals (6 years)		168	8	7	15	252	-23	1	0	6	0	1	1	4

YACHMENEV, VITALI — RW — PREDATORS

PERSONAL: Born January 8, 1975, in Chelyabinsk, U.S.S.R. ... 5-9/191. ... Shoots left. ... Name pronounced vee-TAL-ee YAHCH-mih-nehf.
TRANSACTIONS/CAREER NOTES: Selected by Los Angeles Kings in third round (third Kings pick, 59th overall) of NHL entry draft (June 29, 1994). ... Sprained left shoulder (October 4, 1996); missed eight games. ... Sprained ankle (December 27, 1996); missed seven games. ... Suffered from the flu (February 11, 1997); missed one game. ... Traded by Kings to Nashville Predators for future considerations (July 7, 1998).
HONORS: Named Can.HL Rookie of the Year (1993-94). ... Won Emms Family Award (1993-94). ... Named to Can.HL All-Rookie team (1993-94). ... Named to OHL All-Rookie team (1993-94). ... Won William Hanley Trophy (1994-95).
STATISTICAL PLATEAUS: Three-goal games: 1995-96 (1).

Season Team	League	Gms.	G	A	Pts.	PIM	+/-	PP	SH	Gms.	G	A	Pts.	PIM
			REGULAR SEASON								PLAYOFFS			
90-91—Traktor Chelyabinsk	USSR	80	88	60	148	72	...	...	...	—	—	—	—	—
91-92—Traktor Chelyabinsk	CIS	80	82	70	152	20	...	...	...	—	—	—	—	—
92-93—Mechel Chelyabinsk	CIS Div. II	51	23	20	43	12	...	...	...	—	—	—	—	—
93-94—North Bay	OHL	66	*61	52	113	18	...	...	...	18	13	19	32	12
94-95—North Bay	OHL	59	53	52	105	8	...	...	...	6	1	8	9	2
—Phoenix	IHL	—	—	—	—	—	...	...	...	4	1	0	1	0
95-96—Los Angeles	NHL	80	19	34	53	16	-3	6	1	—	—	—	—	—
96-97—Los Angeles	NHL	65	10	22	32	10	-9	2	0	—	—	—	—	—
97-98—Los Angeles	NHL	4	0	1	1	4	1	0	0	—	—	—	—	—
—Long Beach	IHL	59	23	28	51	14	...	...	...	17	8	9	17	4
NHL Totals (3 years)		149	29	57	86	30	-11	8	1					

W
Y

YAKE, TERRY   C   BLUES

PERSONAL: Born October 22, 1968, in New Westminster, B.C. ... 5-11/185. ... Shoots right.
TRANSACTIONS/CAREER NOTES: Selected by Hartford Whalers in fourth round (third Whalers pick, 81st overall) of NHL entry draft (June 13, 1987). ... Selected by Mighty Ducks of Anaheim in NHL expansion draft (June 24, 1993). ... Traded by Mighty Ducks to Toronto Maple Leafs for RW David Sacco (September 28, 1994). ... Loaned by Maple Leafs to Denver Grizzlies of IHL (April 5, 1995). ... Signed as free agent by Buffalo Sabres (August 5, 1996). ... Signed as free agent by St. Louis Blues (August 12, 1997).
STATISTICAL PLATEAUS: Three-goal games: 1993-94 (1).

Season Team	League	REGULAR SEASON								PLAYOFFS				
		Gms.	G	A	Pts.	PIM	+/-	PP	SH	Gms.	G	A	Pts.	PIM
84-85—Brandon	WHL	11	1	1	2	0	...	...	...	—	—	—	—	—
85-86—Brandon	WHL	72	26	26	52	49	...	...	...	—	—	—	—	—
86-87—Brandon	WHL	71	44	58	102	64	...	...	...	—	—	—	—	—
87-88—Brandon	WHL	72	55	85	140	59	...	...	...	3	4	2	6	7
88-89—Hartford	NHL	2	0	0	0	0	1	0	0	—	—	—	—	—
—Binghamton	AHL	75	39	56	95	57	...	...	...	—	—	—	—	—
89-90—Hartford	NHL	2	0	1	1	0	-1	0	0	—	—	—	—	—
—Binghamton	AHL	77	13	42	55	37	...	...	...	—	—	—	—	—
90-91—Hartford	NHL	19	1	4	5	10	-3	0	0	6	1	1	2	16
—Springfield	AHL	60	35	42	77	56	...	...	...	15	9	9	18	10
91-92—Hartford	NHL	15	1	1	2	4	-2	0	0	—	—	—	—	—
—Springfield	AHL	53	21	34	55	63	...	...	...	8	3	4	7	2
92-93—Springfield	AHL	16	8	14	22	27	...	...	...	—	—	—	—	—
—Hartford	NHL	66	22	31	53	46	3	4	1	—	—	—	—	—
93-94—Anaheim	NHL	82	21	31	52	44	2	5	0	—	—	—	—	—
94-95—Toronto	NHL	19	3	2	5	2	1	1	0	—	—	—	—	—
—Denver	IHL	2	0	3	3	2	...	...	...	17	4	11	15	16
95-96—Milwaukee	IHL	70	32	56	88	70	...	...	...	5	3	6	9	4
96-97—Rochester	AHL	78	34	*67	101	77	...	...	...	10	8	8	16	2
97-98—St. Louis	NHL	65	10	15	25	38	1	3	1	10	2	1	3	6
NHL Totals (8 years)		270	58	85	143	144	2	13	2	16	3	2	5	22

YAKUSHIN, DMITRI   D   MAPLE LEAFS

PERSONAL: Born January 21, 1978, in Kharkov, U.S.S.R. ... 6-0/200. ... Shoots left.
TRANSACTIONS/CAREER NOTES: Selected by Toronto Maple Leafs in sixth round (ninth Maple Leafs pick, 140th overall) of NHL entry draft (June 22, 1996).

Season Team	League	REGULAR SEASON								PLAYOFFS				
		Gms.	G	A	Pts.	PIM	+/-	PP	SH	Gms.	G	A	Pts.	PIM
95-96—Pembroke	CJHL	31	8	5	13	62	...	...	...	—	—	—	—	—
96-97—Edmonton	WHL	63	3	14	17	103	...	...	...	—	—	—	—	—
97-98—Regina	WHL	42	1	24	25	57	...	...	...	9	2	8	10	12

YASHIN, ALEXEI   C   SENATORS

PERSONAL: Born November 5, 1973, in Sverdlovsk, U.S.S.R. ... 6-3/225. ... Shoots right. ... Name pronounced uh-LEK-see YA-shihn.
TRANSACTIONS/CAREER NOTES: Selected by Ottawa Senators in first round (first Senators pick, second overall) of NHL entry draft (June 20, 1992). ... Suffered strep throat (December 4, 1993); missed one game.
HONORS: Named to CIS All-Star team (1992-93). ... Played in NHL All-Star Game (1994).
MISCELLANEOUS: Holds Ottawa Senators all-time records for most games played (340), most goals (134), most assists (175) and most points (309). ... Member of silver-medal-winning Russian Olympic team (1998).
STATISTICAL PLATEAUS: Three-goal games: 1993-94 (1), 1994-95 (1), 1995-96 (1), 1997-98 (1). Total: 4.

Season Team	League	REGULAR SEASON								PLAYOFFS				
		Gms.	G	A	Pts.	PIM	+/-	PP	SH	Gms.	G	A	Pts.	PIM
90-91—Avtomo. Sverdlovsk	USSR	26	2	1	3	10	...	...	...	—	—	—	—	—
91-92—Dynamo Moscow	CIS	35	7	5	12	19	...	...	...	—	—	—	—	—
92-93—Dynamo Moscow	CIS	27	10	12	22	18	...	...	...	10	7	3	10	18
93-94—Ottawa	NHL	83	30	49	79	22	-49	11	2	—	—	—	—	—
94-95—Las Vegas	IHL	24	15	20	35	32	...	...	...	—	—	—	—	—
—Ottawa	NHL	47	21	23	44	20	-20	11	0	—	—	—	—	—
95-96—Ottawa	NHL	46	15	24	39	28	-15	8	0	—	—	—	—	—
96-97—Ottawa	NHL	82	35	40	75	44	-7	10	0	7	1	5	6	2
97-98—Ottawa	NHL	82	33	39	72	24	6	5	0	11	5	3	8	8
—Russian Oly. team	Int'l	6	3	3	6	0	...	...	...	—	—	—	—	—
NHL Totals (5 years)		340	134	175	309	138	-85	45	2	18	6	8	14	10

YAWNEY, TRENT   D   BLACKHAWKS

PERSONAL: Born September 29, 1965, in Hudson Bay, Sask. ... 6-3/195. ... Shoots left.
TRANSACTIONS/CAREER NOTES: Selected by Chicago Blackhawks as underage junior in third round (second Blackhawks pick, 45th overall) of NHL entry draft (June 9, 1984). ... Bruised left shoulder (March 1989). ... Strained right knee (April 24, 1989). ... Bruised kidney (November 11, 1989). ... Bruised thigh (January 1990). ... Strained knee (October 1990). ... Traded by Blackhawks to Calgary Flames for LW Stephane Matteau (December 16, 1991). ... Fractured right clavicle (September 26, 1992); missed first 20 games of season. ... Tore muscle in shoulder (September 9, 1993); missed 25 games. ... Strained left thumb ligaments (January 28, 1995); missed five games. ... Reinjured left thumb (February 11, 1995); missed two games. ... Strained right thumb ligaments (March 22, 1995); missed one game. ... Suffered from the flu (November 8, 1995); missed two games. ... Lacerated hand (January 5, 1996); missed one game. ... Injured knee (February 3, 1996); missed one game. ... Signed as free agent by St. Louis Blues (July 6, 1996). ... Signed as free agent by Blackhawks (September 25, 1997). ... Sprained thumb (March 14, 1998); missed eight games.

Y

Season Team	League	REGULAR SEASON Gms.	G	A	Pts.	PIM	+/-	PP	SH	PLAYOFFS Gms.	G	A	Pts.	PIM
81-82—Saskatoon	WHL	6	1	0	1	0	...	...	...	—	—	—	—	—
82-83—Saskatoon	WHL	59	6	31	37	44	...	...	...	6	0	2	2	0
83-84—Saskatoon	WHL	72	13	46	59	81	...	...	...	—	—	—	—	—
84-85—Saskatoon	WHL	72	16	51	67	158	...	...	...	3	1	6	7	7
85-86—Canadian nat'l team	Int'l	73	6	15	21	60	...	...	...	—	—	—	—	—
86-87—Canadian nat'l team	Int'l	51	4	15	19	37	...	...	...	—	—	—	—	—
87-88—Canadian nat'l team	Int'l	60	4	12	16	81	...	...	...	—	—	—	—	—
—Can. Olympic Team	Int'l	8	1	1	2	6	...	...	...	—	—	—	—	—
—Chicago	NHL	15	2	8	10	15	1	2	0	5	0	4	4	8
88-89—Chicago	NHL	69	5	19	24	116	-5	3	1	15	3	6	9	20
89-90—Chicago	NHL	70	5	15	20	82	-6	1	0	20	3	5	8	27
90-91—Chicago	NHL	61	3	13	16	77	6	3	0	1	0	0	0	0
91-92—Indianapolis	IHL	9	2	3	5	12	...	...	...	—	—	—	—	—
—Calgary	NHL	47	4	9	13	45	-5	1	0	—	—	—	—	—
92-93—Calgary	NHL	63	1	16	17	67	9	0	0	6	3	2	5	6
93-94—Calgary	NHL	58	6	15	21	60	21	1	1	7	0	0	0	16
94-95—Calgary	NHL	37	0	2	2	108	-4	0	0	2	0	0	0	2
95-96—Calgary	NHL	69	0	3	3	88	-1	0	0	4	0	0	0	2
96-97—St. Louis	NHL	39	0	2	2	17	2	0	0	—	—	—	—	—
97-98—Chicago	NHL	45	1	0	1	76	-5	0	0	—	—	—	—	—
NHL Totals (11 years)		573	27	102	129	751	13	11	2	60	9	17	26	81

YEGOROV, ALEXEI   LW   SHARKS

PERSONAL: Born May 21, 1975, in Leningrad, U.S.S.R. ... 5-11/185. ... Shoots left. ... Name pronounced yuh-GOHR-ahf.
TRANSACTIONS/CAREER NOTES: Selected by San Jose Sharks in third round (third Sharks pick, 66th overall) of NHL entry draft (June 29, 1994).
STATISTICAL PLATEAUS: Three-goal games: 1995-96 (1).

Season Team	League	REGULAR SEASON Gms.	G	A	Pts.	PIM	+/-	PP	SH	PLAYOFFS Gms.	G	A	Pts.	PIM
92-93—SKA St. Petersburg	CIS	17	1	2	3	10	...	...	...	6	3	1	4	6
93-94—SKA St. Petersburg	CIS	23	5	3	8	18	...	...	...	6	0	0	0	4
94-95—SKA St. Petersburg	CIS	10	2	1	3	10	...	...	...	—	—	—	—	—
—Fort Worth	CHL	18	4	10	14	15	...	...	...	—	—	—	—	—
95-96—Kansas City	IHL	65	31	25	56	84	...	...	...	5	2	0	2	8
—San Jose	NHL	9	3	2	5	2	-5	2	0	—	—	—	—	—
96-97—Kentucky	AHL	75	26	32	58	59	...	...	...	4	0	1	1	2
—San Jose	NHL	2	0	1	1	0	1	0	0	—	—	—	—	—
97-98—Kentucky	AHL	79	32	52	84	56	...	...	...	3	2	0	2	0
NHL Totals (2 years)		11	3	3	6	2	-4	2	0					

YELLE, STEPHANE   C   AVALANCHE

PERSONAL: Born May 9, 1974, in Ottawa. ... 6-1/191. ... Shoots left. ... Name pronounced YEHL.
TRANSACTIONS/CAREER NOTES: Selected by New Jersey Devils in eighth round (ninth Devils pick, 186th overall) of NHL entry draft (June 20, 1992). ... Traded by Devils with 11th-round pick (D Stephen Low) in 1994 draft to Quebec Nordiques for 11th-round pick (C Mike Hansen) in 1994 draft (June 1, 1994). ... Nordiques franchise moved to Colorado and renamed Avalanche for 1995-96 season (June 21, 1995). ... Pulled groin (February 15, 1996); missed nine games. ... Strained hip flexor (December 14, 1996); missed three games.
MISCELLANEOUS: Member of Stanley Cup championship team (1996).

Season Team	League	REGULAR SEASON Gms.	G	A	Pts.	PIM	+/-	PP	SH	PLAYOFFS Gms.	G	A	Pts.	PIM
91-92—Oshawa	OHL	55	12	14	26	20	...	...	...	7	2	0	2	1
92-93—Oshawa	OHL	66	24	50	74	20	...	...	...	10	2	4	6	4
93-94—Oshawa	OHL	66	35	69	104	22	...	...	...	5	1	7	8	2
94-95—Cornwall	AHL	40	18	15	33	22	...	...	...	13	7	7	14	8
95-96—Colorado	NHL	71	13	14	27	30	15	0	2	22	1	4	5	8
96-97—Colorado	NHL	79	9	17	26	38	1	0	1	12	1	6	7	2
97-98—Colorado	NHL	81	7	15	22	48	-10	0	1	7	1	0	1	12
NHL Totals (3 years)		231	29	46	75	116	6	0	4	41	3	10	13	22

YERKOVICH, SERGEI   D   OILERS

PERSONAL: Born March 9, 1974, in Minsk, U.S.S.R. ... 6-3/210. ... Shoots left. ... Name pronounced YUHR-koh-vihch.
TRANSACTIONS/CAREER NOTES: Selected by Edmonton Oilers in third round (third Oilers pick, 68th overall) of NHL entry draft (June 21, 1997).

Season Team	League	REGULAR SEASON Gms.	G	A	Pts.	PIM	+/-	PP	SH	PLAYOFFS Gms.	G	A	Pts.	PIM
92-93—Dynamo Minsk	CIS	1	0	0	0	0	...	...	...	—	—	—	—	—
93-94—Tivali Minsk	CIS	39	2	1	3	34	...	...	...	—	—	—	—	—
94-95—Tivali Minsk	CIS	45	3	1	4	52	...	...	...	—	—	—	—	—
95-96—Tivali Minsk	CIS	41	5	3	8	30	...	...	...	—	—	—	—	—
96-97—Las Vegas	IHL	76	6	19	25	167	...	...	...	—	—	—	—	—
97-98—Las Vegas	IHL	69	7	15	22	130	...	...	...	4	0	0	0	6

Y

YLONEN, JUHA   C   COYOTES

PERSONAL: Born February 13, 1972, in Helsinki, Finland. ... 6-1/183. ... Shoots left. ... Name pronounced YOO-hah yee-LOH-nehn.
TRANSACTIONS/CAREER NOTES: Selected by Winnipeg Jets in fifth round (fifth Jets pick, 91st overall) of NHL entry draft (June 22, 1991). ... Jets franchise moved to Phoenix and renamed Coyotes for 1996-97 season; NHL approved move on January 18, 1996. ... Bruised foot (March 10, 1998); missed two games. ... Fractured leg (March 19, 1998); missed 14 games.
MISCELLANEOUS: Member of bronze-medal-winning Finnish Olympic team (1998).

Season Team	League	Gms.	G	A	Pts.	PIM	+/-	PP	SH	Gms.	G	A	Pts.	PIM
90-91—Kiekko-Espoo	Finland Dv.II	40	12	21	33	4	...	...	...	—	—	—	—	—
91-92—HPK Hameenlinna	Finland	43	7	11	18	8	...	...	...	—	—	—	—	—
92-93—HPK Hameenlinna	Finland	48	8	18	26	22	...	...	...	12	3	5	8	2
93-94—Jokerit Helsinki	Finland	37	5	11	16	2	...	...	...	12	1	3	4	8
94-95—Jokerit Helsinki	Finland	50	13	15	28	10	...	...	...	11	3	2	5	0
95-96—Jokerit Helsinki	Finland	24	3	13	16	20	...	...	...	11	4	5	9	4
96-97—Springfield	AHL	70	20	41	61	6	...	...	...	17	5	†16	21	4
—Phoenix	NHL	2	0	0	0	0	0	0	0	—	—	—	—	—
97-98—Phoenix	NHL	55	1	11	12	10	-3	0	1	—	—	—	—	—
—Fin. Olympic Team	Int'l	6	0	0	0	8	...	...	...	—	—	—	—	—
NHL Totals (2 years)		57	1	11	12	10	-3	0	1					

YORK, HARRY   C   RANGERS

PERSONAL: Born April 4, 1974, in Panoka, Alta. ... 6-2/220. ... Shoots left.
TRANSACTIONS/CAREER NOTES: Signed as free agent by St. Louis Blues (May 1, 1996). ... Traded by Blues to New York Rangers for C Mike Eastwood (March 24, 1998). ... Partially dislocated right shoulder (March 26, 1998); missed 10 games.

Season Team	League	Gms.	G	A	Pts.	PIM	+/-	PP	SH	Gms.	G	A	Pts.	PIM
94-95—Fort McMurray	AJHL	54	35	73	108	...	...	...	...	—	—	—	—	—
95-96—Nashville	ECHL	64	33	50	83	122	...	...	...	—	—	—	—	—
—Atlanta	IHL	2	0	0	0	15	...	...	...	—	—	—	—	—
—Worcester	AHL	13	8	5	13	2	...	...	...	4	0	4	4	4
96-97—St. Louis	NHL	74	14	18	32	24	1	3	1	5	0	0	0	2
97-98—St. Louis	NHL	58	4	6	10	31	0	0	0	—	—	—	—	—
—New York Rangers	NHL	2	0	0	0	0	-1	0	0	—	—	—	—	—
NHL Totals (2 years)		134	18	24	42	55	0	3	1	5	0	0	0	2

YORK, JASON   D   SENATORS

PERSONAL: Born May 20, 1970, in Nepean, Ont. ... 6-2/198. ... Shoots right.
TRANSACTIONS/CAREER NOTES: Selected by Detroit Red Wings in seventh round (sixth Red Wings pick, 129th overall) of NHL entry draft (June 16, 1990). ... Traded by Red Wings with C/RW Mike Sillinger to Mighty Ducks of Anaheim for LW Stu Grimson, D Mark Ferner and sixth-round pick (LW Magnus Nilsson) in 1996 draft (April 4, 1995). ... Sprained right ankle (December 1, 1995); missed two games. ... Traded by Mighty Ducks with C Shaun Van Allen to Ottawa Senators for C Ted Drury and rights to D Marc Moro (October 1, 1996). ... Strained groin (December 4, 1996); missed six games. ... Suffered concussion (January 3, 1998); missed four games. ... Injured right eye (April 13, 1998); missed three games.
HONORS: Named to AHL All-Star first team (1993-94).

Season Team	League	Gms.	G	A	Pts.	PIM	+/-	PP	SH	Gms.	G	A	Pts.	PIM
89-90—Windsor	OHL	39	9	30	39	38	...	...	...	—	—	—	—	—
—Kitchener	OHL	25	11	25	36	17	...	...	...	17	3	19	22	10
90-91—Windsor	OHL	66	13	80	93	40	...	...	...	11	3	10	13	12
91-92—Adirondack	AHL	49	4	20	24	32	...	...	...	5	0	1	1	0
92-93—Adirondack	AHL	77	15	40	55	86	...	...	...	11	0	3	3	18
—Detroit	NHL	2	0	0	0	0	0	0	0	—	—	—	—	—
93-94—Adirondack	AHL	74	10	56	66	98	...	...	...	12	3	11	14	22
—Detroit	NHL	7	1	2	3	2	0	0	0	—	—	—	—	—
94-95—Adirondack	AHL	5	1	3	4	4	...	...	...	—	—	—	—	—
—Detroit	NHL	10	1	2	3	2	0	0	0	—	—	—	—	—
—Anaheim	NHL	15	0	8	8	12	4	0	0	—	—	—	—	—
95-96—Anaheim	NHL	79	3	21	24	88	-7	0	0	—	—	—	—	—
96-97—Ottawa	NHL	75	4	17	21	67	-8	1	0	7	0	0	0	4
97-98—Ottawa	NHL	73	3	13	16	62	8	0	0	7	1	1	2	7
NHL Totals (6 years)		261	12	63	75	233	-3	1	0	14	1	1	2	11

YORK, MICHAEL   C   RANGERS

PERSONAL: Born January 3, 1978, in Pontiac, Mich. ... 5-9/179. ... Shoots right.
COLLEGE: Michigan State.
TRANSACTIONS/CAREER NOTES: Selected by New York Rangers in sixth round (seventh Rangers pick, 136th overall) of NHL entry draft (June 21, 1997).
HONORS: Named to CCHA All-Rookie team (1995-96).

Season Team	League	Gms.	G	A	Pts.	PIM	+/-	PP	SH	Gms.	G	A	Pts.	PIM
95-96—Michigan State	CCHA	39	12	27	39	20	...	...	...	—	—	—	—	—
96-97—Michigan State	CCHA	37	18	29	47	42	...	...	...	—	—	—	—	—
97-98—Michigan State	CCHA	40	27	34	61	38	...	...	...	—	—	—	—	—

Y

YOUNG, B.J.　　　　　　RW　　　　　　RED WINGS

PERSONAL: Born July 23, 1977, in Anchorage, Alaska. ... 5-11/177. ... Shoots right.
TRANSACTIONS/CAREER NOTES: Selected by Detroit Red Wings in sixth round (fifth Red Wings pick, 157th overall) of NHL entry draft (June 21, 1997).
HONORS: Named to WHL (East) All-Star first team (1996-97).

		REGULAR SEASON								PLAYOFFS				
Season Team	League	Gms.	G	A	Pts.	PIM	+/-	PP	SH	Gms.	G	A	Pts.	PIM
93-94—Tri-City	WHL	54	19	24	43	66	...	...	...	2	1	1	2	2
94-95—Tri-City	WHL	30	6	3	9	39	...	...	...	—	—	—	—	—
—Red Deer	WHL	21	5	9	14	33	...	...	...	—	—	—	—	—
95-96—Red Deer	WHL	67	49	45	94	144	...	...	...	8	4	9	13	12
96-97—Red Deer	WHL	63	58	56	114	97	...	...	...	16	8	14	22	26
97-98—Adirondack	AHL	65	15	22	37	191	...	...	...	3	0	2	2	6

YOUNG, SCOTT　　　　　　RW　　　　　　BLUES

PERSONAL: Born October 1, 1967, in Clinton, Mass. ... 6-0/190. ... Shoots right. ... Full name: Scott Allen Young.
HIGH SCHOOL: St. Mark's (Southborough, Mass.).
COLLEGE: Boston University.
TRANSACTIONS/CAREER NOTES: Selected by Hartford Whalers in first round (first Whalers pick, 11th overall) of NHL entry draft (June 21, 1986). ... Suffered lacerations above right eye (October 8, 1988). ... Lacerated face (February 18, 1990). ... Traded by Whalers to Pittsburgh Penguins for RW Rob Brown (December 21, 1990). ... Traded by Penguins to Quebec Nordiques for D Bryan Fogarty (March 10, 1992). ... Injured rib (February 14, 1993); missed one game. ... Bruised right ankle (February 23, 1993); missed one game. ... Sprained right ankle (October 5, 1993); missed eight games. ... Played in Europe during 1994-95 NHL lockout. ... Nordiques franchise moved to Colorado and renamed Avalanche for 1995-96 season (June 21, 1995). ... Bruised right shoulder (December 23, 1996); missed five games. ... Traded by Avalanche to Mighty Ducks of Anaheim for third-round pick (traded to Florida) in 1998 draft (September 17, 1997). ... Bruised right foot (November 22, 1997); missed two games. ... Bruised right foot (November 29, 1997); missed five games. ... Suffered eye abrasion (March 9, 1998); missed two games. ... Signed as free agent by St. Louis Blues (July 16, 1998).
HONORS: Named Hockey East Rookie of the Year (1985-86).
MISCELLANEOUS: Member of Stanley Cup championship team (1991 and 1996).
STATISTICAL PLATEAUS: Three-goal games: 1992-93 (1), 1993-94 (1), 1994-95 (1), 1996-97 (1). Total: 4.

		REGULAR SEASON								PLAYOFFS				
Season Team	League	Gms.	G	A	Pts.	PIM	+/-	PP	SH	Gms.	G	A	Pts.	PIM
84-85—St. Marks H.S.	Mass. H.S.	23	28	41	69	...	...	...	...	—	—	—	—	—
85-86—Boston University	Hockey East	38	16	13	29	31	...	...	...	—	—	—	—	—
86-87—Boston University	Hockey East	33	15	21	36	24	...	...	...	—	—	—	—	—
87-88—U.S. Olympic Team	Int'l	59	13	53	66	...	...	...	...	—	—	—	—	—
—Hartford	NHL	7	0	0	0	2	-6	0	0	4	1	0	1	0
88-89—Hartford	NHL	76	19	40	59	27	-21	6	0	4	2	0	2	4
89-90—Hartford	NHL	80	24	40	64	47	-24	10	2	7	2	0	2	2
90-91—Hartford	NHL	34	6	9	15	8	-9	3	1	—	—	—	—	—
—Pittsburgh	NHL	43	11	16	27	33	3	3	1	17	1	6	7	2
91-92—U.S. national team	Int'l	10	2	4	6	21	...	...	...	—	—	—	—	—
—U.S. Olympic Team	Int'l	8	2	1	3	2	...	...	...	—	—	—	—	—
—Bolzano	Italy	18	22	17	39	6	...	...	...	—	—	—	—	—
92-93—Quebec	NHL	82	30	30	60	20	5	9	6	6	4	1	5	0
93-94—Quebec	NHL	76	26	25	51	14	-4	6	1	—	—	—	—	—
94-95—Frankfurt	Germany	1	1	0	1	0	...	...	...	—	—	—	—	—
—Landshut	Germany	4	6	1	7	6	...	...	...	—	—	—	—	—
—Quebec	NHL	48	18	21	39	14	9	3	3	6	3	3	6	2
95-96—Colorado	NHL	81	21	39	60	50	2	7	0	22	3	12	15	10
96-97—Colorado	NHL	72	18	19	37	14	-5	7	0	17	4	2	6	14
97-98—Anaheim	NHL	73	13	20	33	22	-13	4	2	—	—	—	—	—
NHL Totals (10 years)		672	186	259	445	251	-63	58	16	83	20	24	44	34

YSEBAERT, PAUL　　　　　　RW　　　　　　LIGHTNING

PERSONAL: Born May 15, 1966, in Sarnia, Ont. ... 6-1/194. ... Shoots left. ... Full name: Paul Robert Ysebaert. ... Name pronounced IGH-suh-BAHRT.
COLLEGE: Bowling Green State.
TRANSACTIONS/CAREER NOTES: Selected by New Jersey Devils in fourth round (fourth Devils pick, 74th overall) of NHL entry draft (June 9, 1984). ... Pulled stomach and groin muscles (December 1988). ... Suffered contusion to left thigh (March 1989). ... Traded by New Jersey Devils to Detroit Red Wings for D Lee Norwood and future considerations; Devils later received fourth-round pick (D Scott McCabe) in 1992 draft to complete deal (November 27, 1990). ... Injured knee (December 1991); missed one game. ... Suffered from the flu (December 22, 1992); missed one game. ... Suffered from the flu (March 5, 1993); missed one game. ... Suffered from the flu (March 10, 1993); missed one game. ... Traded by Red Wings to Winnipeg Jets for D Aaron Ward, fourth-round pick (D John Jakopin) in 1993 draft and future considerations (June 11, 1993); Jets sent RW Alan Kerr to Red Wings to complete deal (June 18, 1993). ... Traded by Jets to Chicago Blackhawks for third-round pick in 1995 draft (March 21, 1994). ... Traded by Blackhawks with RW Rich Sutter to Tampa Bay Lightning for RW Jim Cummins, D Jeff Buchanan and D Tom Tilley (February 22, 1995). ... Injured groin (March 24, 1995); missed two games. ... Strained groin (December 16, 1995); missed one game. ... Injured groin (January 6, 1996); missed 24 games. ... Strained groin (September 15, 1996); missed 34 games. ... Strained groin (February 15, 1997); missed nine games.
HONORS: Named CCHA Rookie of the Year (1984-85). ... Named to CCHA All-Star second team (1985-86 and 1986-87). ... Won Les Cunningham Plaque (1989-90). ... Won John B. Sollenberger Trophy (1989-90). ... Named to AHL All-Star first team (1989-90). ... Won Alka-Seltzer Plus Award (1991-92).
MISCELLANEOUS: Scored on a penalty shot (vs. Robb Stauber, November 27, 1992).
STATISTICAL PLATEAUS: Three-goal games: 1991-92 (1).

Y

		REGULAR SEASON								PLAYOFFS				
Season Team	League	Gms.	G	A	Pts.	PIM	+/-	PP	SH	Gms.	G	A	Pts.	PIM
83-84—Petrolia Jr. B	OHA	33	35	42	77	20	...	...	...	—	—	—	—	—
84-85—Bowling Green	CCHA	42	23	32	55	54	...	...	...	—	—	—	—	—
85-86—Bowling Green	CCHA	42	23	45	68	50	...	...	...	—	—	—	—	—
86-87—Bowling Green	CCHA	45	27	58	85	44	...	...	...	—	—	—	—	—
—Canadian nat'l team	Int'l	5	1	0	1	4	...	...	...	—	—	—	—	—
87-88—Utica	AHL	78	30	49	79	60	...	...	...	—	—	—	—	—
88-89—Utica	AHL	56	36	44	80	22	...	...	...	5	0	1	1	4
—New Jersey	NHL	5	0	4	4	0	2	0	0	—	—	—	—	—
89-90—New Jersey	NHL	5	1	2	3	0	0	0	0	—	—	—	—	—
—Utica	AHL	74	53	52	*105	61	...	...	...	5	2	4	6	0
90-91—New Jersey	NHL	11	4	3	7	6	1	1	0	—	—	—	—	—
—Detroit	NHL	51	15	18	33	16	-8	5	0	2	0	2	2	0
91-92—Detroit	NHL	79	35	40	75	55	*44	3	4	10	1	0	1	10
92-93—Detroit	NHL	80	34	28	62	42	19	3	3	7	3	1	4	2
93-94—Winnipeg	NHL	60	9	18	27	18	-8	1	0	—	—	—	—	—
—Chicago	NHL	11	5	3	8	8	1	2	0	6	0	0	0	8
94-95—Chicago	NHL	15	4	5	9	6	4	0	0	—	—	—	—	—
—Tampa Bay	NHL	29	8	11	19	12	-1	0	0	—	—	—	—	—
95-96—Tampa Bay	NHL	55	16	15	31	16	-19	4	1	5	0	0	0	0
96-97—Tampa Bay	NHL	39	5	12	17	4	1	2	0	—	—	—	—	—
97-98—Tampa Bay	NHL	82	13	27	40	32	-43	2	1	—	—	—	—	—
NHL Totals (10 years)		522	149	186	335	215	-7	23	9	30	4	3	7	20

YUSHKEVICH, DIMITRI   D   MAPLE LEAFS

PERSONAL: Born November 19, 1971, in Yaroslavl, U.S.S.R. ... 5-11/208. ... Shoots right. ... Name pronounced yoosh-KAY-vihch.
TRANSACTIONS/CAREER NOTES: Selected by Philadelphia Flyers in sixth round (sixth Flyers pick, 122nd overall) of NHL entry draft (June 22, 1991). ... Sprained wrist (January 28, 1993); missed two games. ... Strained groin (February 18, 1994); missed four games. ... Played in Europe during 1994-95 NHL lockout. ... Suffered from sore back (February 23, 1995); missed three games. ... Sprained left knee (April 16, 1995); missed five games. ... Traded by Flyers with secound-round pick (G Francis Larivee) in 1996 draft to Toronto Maple Leafs for first- (RW Dainius Zubrus) and fourth-(traded to Los Angeles) round picks in 1996 draft and second-round pick (G Jean-Marc Pelletier) in 1997 draft (August 30, 1995). ... Sprained knee (October 26, 1995); missed eight games. ... Bruised knee (December 30, 1995); missed two games. ... Pulled hamstring (December 14, 1996); missed four games. ... Injured knee (March 22, 1997); missed two games. ... Fractured toe (October 15, 1997); missed six games. ... Sprained knee (December 31, 1997); missed two games.
MISCELLANEOUS: Member of silver-medal-winning Russian Olympic team (1998).

		REGULAR SEASON								PLAYOFFS				
Season Team	League	Gms.	G	A	Pts.	PIM	+/-	PP	SH	Gms.	G	A	Pts.	PIM
88-89—Torpedo Yaroslavl	USSR	23	2	1	3	8	...	...	...	—	—	—	—	—
89-90—Torpedo Yaroslavl	USSR	41	2	3	5	39	...	...	...	—	—	—	—	—
90-91—Torpedo Yaroslavl	USSR	43	10	4	14	22	...	...	...	—	—	—	—	—
91-92—Dynamo Moscow	CIS	41	6	7	13	14	...	...	...	—	—	—	—	—
—Unif. Olympic Team	Int'l	8	1	2	3	4	...	...	...	—	—	—	—	—
92-93—Philadelphia	NHL	82	5	27	32	71	12	1	0	—	—	—	—	—
93-94—Philadelphia	NHL	75	5	25	30	86	-8	1	0	—	—	—	—	—
94-95—Torpedo Yaroslavl	CIS	10	3	4	7	8	...	...	...	—	—	—	—	—
—Philadelphia	NHL	40	5	9	14	47	-4	3	1	15	1	5	6	12
95-96—Toronto	NHL	69	1	10	11	54	-14	1	0	4	0	0	0	0
96-97—Toronto	NHL	74	4	10	14	56	-24	1	1	—	—	—	—	—
97-98—Toronto	NHL	72	0	12	12	78	-13	0	0	—	—	—	—	—
—Russian Oly. team	Int'l	6	0	0	0	2	...	...	...	—	—	—	—	—
NHL Totals (6 years)		412	20	93	113	392	-51	7	2	19	1	5	6	12

YZERMAN, STEVE   C   RED WINGS

PERSONAL: Born May 9, 1965, in Cranbrook, B.C. ... 5-11/185. ... Shoots right. ... Name pronounced IGH-zuhr-muhn.
TRANSACTIONS/CAREER NOTES: Selected by Detroit Red Wings as underage junior in first round (first Red Wings pick, fourth overall) of NHL entry draft (June 8, 1983). ... Fractured collarbone (January 31, 1986). ... Injured ligaments of right knee and underwent surgery (March 1, 1988). ... Injured right knee in playoff game (April 8, 1991). ... Suffered herniated disc (October 21, 1993); missed 26 games. ... Sprained knee (May 27, 1995); missed three playoff games. ... Suffered from the flu (March 17, 1996); missed one game. ... Bruised ankle (April 9, 1997); missed one game. ... Sprained medial collateral knee ligament (January 28, 1998); missed three games. ... Injured groin (April 11, 1998); missed three games.
HONORS: Named NHL Rookie of the Year by THE SPORTING NEWS (1983-84). ... Named to NHL All-Rookie team (1983-84). ... Played in NHL All-Star Game (1984, 1988-1993 and 1997). ... Won Lester B. Pearson Award (1988-89).
MISCELLANEOUS: Member of Stanley Cup championship team (1997 and 1998). ... Captain of Detroit Red Wings (1986-87 through 1997-98). ... Scored on a penalty shot (vs. Bob Essensa, February 13, 1989; vs. Grant Fuhr, January 3, 1992; vs. Daren Puppa, January 29, 1992). ... Failed to score on a penalty shot (vs. Doug Keans, November 22, 1987; vs. Darcy Wakaluk, March 19, 1993; vs. Blaine Lacher, November 2, 1995). ... Became youngest player (18 years old) to play in NHL All-Star Game (January 31, 1984).
STATISTICAL PLATEAUS: Three-goal games: 1983-84 (1), 1984-85 (1), 1987-88 (2), 1988-89 (2), 1989-90 (2), 1990-91 (3), 1991-92 (3), 1992-93 (3). Total: 17. ... Four-goal games: 1989-90 (1). ... Total hat tricks: 18.

Y

		REGULAR SEASON								PLAYOFFS				
Season Team	League	Gms.	G	A	Pts.	PIM	+/-	PP	SH	Gms.	G	A	Pts.	PIM
81-82—Peterborough	OHL	58	21	43	64	65	...	...	...	6	0	1	1	16
82-83—Peterborough	OHL	56	42	49	91	33	...	...	...	4	1	4	5	0
83-84—Detroit	NHL	80	39	48	87	33	-17	13	0	4	3	3	6	0
84-85—Detroit	NHL	80	30	59	89	58	-17	9	0	3	2	1	3	2
85-86—Detroit	NHL	51	14	28	42	16	-24	3	0	—	—	—	—	—

Season Team	League	REGULAR SEASON								PLAYOFFS				
		Gms.	G	A	Pts.	PIM	+/-	PP	SH	Gms.	G	A	Pts.	PIM
86-87—Detroit......................	NHL	80	31	59	90	43	-1	9	1	16	5	13	18	8
87-88—Detroit......................	NHL	64	50	52	102	44	30	10	6	3	1	3	4	6
88-89—Detroit......................	NHL	80	65	90	155	61	17	17	3	6	5	5	10	2
89-90—Detroit......................	NHL	79	62	65	127	79	-6	16	†7	—	—	—	—	—
90-91—Detroit......................	NHL	80	51	57	108	34	-2	12	6	7	3	3	6	4
91-92—Detroit......................	NHL	79	45	58	103	64	26	9	*8	11	3	5	8	12
92-93—Detroit......................	NHL	84	58	79	137	44	33	13	†7	7	4	3	7	4
93-94—Detroit......................	NHL	58	24	58	82	36	11	7	3	3	1	3	4	0
94-95—Detroit......................	NHL	47	12	26	38	40	6	4	0	15	4	8	12	0
95-96—Detroit......................	NHL	80	36	59	95	64	29	16	2	18	8	12	20	4
96-97—Detroit......................	NHL	81	22	63	85	78	22	8	0	20	7	6	13	4
97-98—Detroit......................	NHL	75	24	45	69	46	3	6	2	22	6	*18	*24	22
—Can. Olympic Team.....	Int'l	6	1	1	2	10	...	...	...	—	—	—	—	—
NHL Totals (15 years).........		1098	563	846	1409	740	110	152	45	135	52	83	135	68

ZABRANSKY, LIBOR   D   BLUES

PERSONAL: Born November 25, 1973, in Budejovice, Czechoslovakia ... 6-3/189. ... Shoots left.
TRANSACTIONS/CAREER NOTES: Selected by St. Louis Blues in ninth round (eighth Blues pick, 209th overall) of NHL entry draft (July 8, 1995).

Season Team	League	REGULAR SEASON								PLAYOFFS				
		Gms.	G	A	Pts.	PIM	+/-	PP	SH	Gms.	G	A	Pts.	PIM
94-95—Budejovice	Czech Rep.	44	2	6	8	54	...	...	...	9	0	4	4	6
95-96—Budejovice	Czech Rep.	40	4	7	11	...	...	...	...	10	0	1	1	...
96-97—St. Louis	NHL	34	1	5	6	44	-1	0	0	—	—	—	—	—
—Worcester	AHL	23	3	6	9	24	...	...	...	5	2	5	7	6
97-98—Worcester	AHL	54	2	17	19	61	...	...	...	6	1	1	2	8
—St. Louis	NHL	6	0	1	1	6	-3	0	0	—	—	—	—	—
NHL Totals (2 years)...........		40	1	6	7	50	-4	0	0					

ZALAPSKI, ZARLEY   D

PERSONAL: Born April 22, 1968, in Edmonton. ... 6-1/215. ... Shoots left. ... Name pronounced zuh-LAP-skee.
TRANSACTIONS/CAREER NOTES: Selected by Pittsburgh Penguins in first round (first Penguins pick, fourth overall) of NHL entry draft (June 21, 1986). ... Suffered from Spondylosis, deterioration of the structure of the spine (October 1987). ... Tore ligaments in right knee (December 29, 1988). ... Broke right collarbone (October 25, 1989). ... Sprained right knee (February 24, 1990); missed 13 games. ... Traded by Penguins with C John Cullen and RW Jeff Parker to Hartford Whalers for C Ron Francis, D Ulf Samuelsson and D Grant Jennings (March 4, 1991). ... Suffered from the flu (March 3, 1993); missed one game. ... Sprained knee (October 14, 1993); missed 10 games. ... Traded by Hartford Whalers with C Michael Nylander and D James Patrick to Calgary Flames for D Gary Suter, LW Paul Ranheim and C Ted Drury (March 10, 1994). ... Bruised thigh (February 16, 1994); missed one game. ... Suffered from the flu (November 8, 1995); missed two games. ... Tore knee ligament (October 6, 1996); underwent surgery (December 10, 1996); missed remainder of season. ... Injured knee (November 22, 1997); missed one game. ... Traded by Flames to Canadiens with RW Jonas Hoglund for RW Valeri Bure and fourth-round draft pick (C Shaun Sutter) in 1998 draft (February 1, 1998).
HONORS: Named to NHL All-Rookie team (1988-89). ... Played in NHL All-Star Game (1993).

Season Team	League	REGULAR SEASON								PLAYOFFS				
		Gms.	G	A	Pts.	PIM	+/-	PP	SH	Gms.	G	A	Pts.	PIM
84-85—Fort Saskatchewan	AJHL	23	17	30	47	14	...	...	...	—	—	—	—	—
85-86—Fort Saskatchewan	AJHL	27	20	33	53	46	...	...	...	—	—	—	—	—
—Canadian nat'l team	Int'l	32	2	4	6	10	...	...	...	—	—	—	—	—
86-87—Canadian nat'l team	Int'l	74	11	29	40	28	...	...	...	—	—	—	—	—
87-88—Canadian nat'l team	Int'l	47	3	13	16	32	...	...	...	—	—	—	—	—
—Can. Olympic Team.....	Int'l	8	1	3	4	2	...	...	...	—	—	—	—	—
—Pittsburgh...................	NHL	15	3	8	11	7	10	0	0	11	1	8	9	13
88-89—Pittsburgh...................	NHL	58	12	33	45	57	9	5	1	—	—	—	—	—
89-90—Pittsburgh...................	NHL	51	6	25	31	37	-14	5	0	—	—	—	—	—
90-91—Pittsburgh...................	NHL	66	12	36	48	59	15	5	1	—	—	—	—	—
—Hartford	NHL	11	3	3	6	6	-7	3	0	6	1	3	4	8
91-92—Hartford	NHL	79	20	37	57	120	-7	4	0	7	2	3	5	6
92-93—Hartford	NHL	83	14	51	65	94	-34	8	1	—	—	—	—	—
93-94—Hartford	NHL	56	7	30	37	56	-6	0	0	—	—	—	—	—
—Calgary	NHL	13	3	7	10	18	0	1	0	7	0	3	3	2
94-95—Calgary	NHL	48	4	24	28	46	9	1	0	7	0	4	4	4
95-96—Calgary	NHL	80	12	17	29	115	11	5	0	4	0	1	1	10
96-97—Calgary	NHL	2	0	0	0	0	-1	0	0	—	—	—	—	—
97-98—Calgary	NHL	35	2	7	9	41	-12	2	0	—	—	—	—	—
—Montreal	NHL	28	1	5	6	22	-1	0	1	6	0	1	1	4
NHL Totals (11 years).........		625	99	283	382	678	-28	39	4	48	4	23	27	47

ZAMUNER, ROB   LW   LIGHTNING

PERSONAL: Born September 17, 1969, in Oakville, Ont. ... 6-2/207. ... Shoots left. ... Name pronounced ZAM-uh-nuhr.
TRANSACTIONS/CAREER NOTES: Selected by New York Rangers in third round (third Rangers pick, 45th overall) of NHL entry draft (June 17, 1989). ... Signed as free agent by Tampa Bay Lightning (July 14, 1992); Rangers awarded third-round pick in 1993 draft as compensation (July 23, 1992). ... Hyperextended elbow (March 19, 1995); missed five games. ... Sprained knee (October 4, 1995); missed 10 games. ... Suffered sore back (April 1, 1998); missed five games.

MISCELLANEOUS: Scored on a penalty shot (vs. Tommy Salo, January 11, 1997). ... Holds Tampa Bay Lightning all-time record for most games played (417). ... Failed to score on a penalty shot (vs. Chris Terreri, October 9, 1997).
STATISTICAL PLATEAUS: Three-goal games: 1997-98 (1).

			REGULAR SEASON								PLAYOFFS				
Season Team	League	Gms.	G	A	Pts.	PIM	+/-	PP	SH	Gms.	G	A	Pts.	PIM
86-87—Guelph	OHL	62	6	15	21	8	...	...	...	—	—	—	—	—
87-88—Guelph	OHL	58	20	41	61	18	...	...	...	—	—	—	—	—
88-89—Guelph	OHL	66	46	65	111	38	...	...	...	7	5	5	10	9
89-90—Flint	IHL	77	44	35	79	32	...	...	...	4	1	0	1	6
90-91—Binghamton	AHL	80	25	58	83	50	...	...	...	9	7	6	13	35
91-92—Binghamton	AHL	61	19	53	72	42	...	...	...	11	8	9	17	8
—New York Rangers	NHL	9	1	2	3	2	0	0	0	—	—	—	—	—
92-93—Tampa Bay	NHL	84	15	28	43	74	-25	1	0	—	—	—	—	—
93-94—Tampa Bay	NHL	59	6	6	12	42	-9	0	0	—	—	—	—	—
94-95—Tampa Bay	NHL	43	9	6	15	24	-3	0	3	—	—	—	—	—
95-96—Tampa Bay	NHL	72	15	20	35	62	11	0	3	6	2	3	5	10
96-97—Tampa Bay	NHL	82	17	33	50	56	3	0	4	—	—	—	—	—
97-98—Tampa Bay	NHL	77	14	12	26	41	-31	0	3	—	—	—	—	—
—Can. Olympic Team	Int'l	6	1	0	1	8	...	...	...	—	—	—	—	—
NHL Totals (7 years)		426	77	107	184	301	-54	1	13	6	2	3	5	10

ZANUTTO, MIKE · C · SABRES

PERSONAL: Born January 1, 1977, in Burlington, Ont. ... 6-0/190. ... Shoots left. ... Name pronounced zuh-NOO-toh.
TRANSACTIONS/CAREER NOTES: Selected by Buffalo Sabres in eighth round (10th Sabres pick, 198th overall) of NHL entry draft (July 8, 1995).

			REGULAR SEASON								PLAYOFFS				
Season Team	League	Gms.	G	A	Pts.	PIM	+/-	PP	SH	Gms.	G	A	Pts.	PIM
94-95—North Bay	OHL	13	1	1	2	2	...	...	...	—	—	—	—	—
—Oshawa	OHL	42	13	17	30	2	...	...	...	7	4	1	5	0
95-96—Oshawa	OHL	66	32	38	70	6	...	...	...	5	0	2	2	0
96-97—Oshawa	OHL	62	23	33	56	18	...	...	...	18	6	6	12	12
97-98—Rochester	AHL	9	0	0	0	0	...	...	...	—	—	—	—	—
—South Carolina	ECHL	49	18	17	35	6	...	...	...	5	0	0	0	0

ZEDNIK, RICHARD · RW · CAPITALS

PERSONAL: Born January 6, 1976, in Bystrica, Czechoslovakia. ... 5-10/193. ... Shoots left. ... Name pronounced ZEHD-nihk.
TRANSACTIONS/CAREER NOTES: Selected by Washington Capitals in 10th round (10th Capitals pick, 249th overall) of NHL entry draft (June 29, 1994). ... Suffered from the flu (November 6, 1996); missed two games. ... Suffered from the flu (December 12, 1997); missed one game. ... Suffered concussion (March 18, 1998); missed six games. ... Strained abdomen (April 2, 1998); missed final eight games of regular season and four playoff games.
HONORS: Named to WHL (West) All-Star second team (1995-96).

			REGULAR SEASON								PLAYOFFS				
Season Team	League	Gms.	G	A	Pts.	PIM	+/-	PP	SH	Gms.	G	A	Pts.	PIM
93-94—Banska Bystrica	Slovakia	25	3	6	9	...	...	...	...	—	—	—	—	—
94-95—Portland	WHL	65	35	51	86	89	...	...	...	9	5	5	10	20
95-96—Portland	WHL	61	44	37	81	154	...	...	...	7	8	4	12	23
—Portland	AHL	1	1	1	2	0	...	...	...	21	4	5	9	26
—Washington	NHL	1	0	0	0	0	0	0	0	—	—	—	—	—
96-97—Washington	NHL	11	2	1	3	4	-5	1	0	—	—	—	—	—
—Portland	AHL	56	15	20	35	70	...	...	...	5	1	0	1	6
97-98—Washington	NHL	65	17	9	26	28	-2	2	0	17	7	3	10	16
NHL Totals (3 years)		77	19	10	29	32	-7	3	0	17	7	3	10	16

ZEHR, JEFF · C/LW · ISLANDERS

PERSONAL: Born December 10, 1978, in Woodstock, Ont. ... 6-3/195. ... Shoots left. ... Name pronounced ZAIR.
TRANSACTIONS/CAREER NOTES: Selected by New York Islanders in second round (third Islanders pick, 31st overall) of NHL entry draft (June 21, 1997).

			REGULAR SEASON								PLAYOFFS				
Season Team	League	Gms.	G	A	Pts.	PIM	+/-	PP	SH	Gms.	G	A	Pts.	PIM
94-95—Stratford	OPJHL	44	26	32	58	143	...	...	...	—	—	—	—	—
95-96—Windsor	OHL	56	4	21	25	103	...	...	...	7	0	1	1	2
96-97—Windsor	OHL	57	27	32	59	196	...	...	...	5	2	1	3	4
97-98—Windsor	OHL	20	12	18	30	67	...	...	...	—	—	—	—	—
—Erie	OHL	32	15	24	39	91	...	...	...	5	0	3	3	24

ZELEPUKIN, VALERI · RW · OILERS

PERSONAL: Born September 17, 1968, in Voskresensk, U.S.S.R. ... 6-0/200. ... Shoots left. ... Name pronounced vuh-LAIR-ee zehl-ih-POO-kihn.
TRANSACTIONS/CAREER NOTES: Selected by New Jersey Devils in 11th round (13th Devils pick, 221st overall) of NHL entry draft (June 22, 1990). ... Bruised shoulder (January 22, 1993); missed five games. ... Bruised left shoulder (December 22, 1993); missed one game. ... Injured chest (April 14, 1994); missed one game. ... Injured eye (January 24, 1995); missed first 42 games of season. ... Bruised finger (April 26, 1995); missed one game. ... Injured eye (October 7, 1995); missed first two games of season. ... Injured calf (November 27, 1995); missed two games. ... Injured foot (February 18, 1996); missed one game. ... Bruised right knee (March 23, 1996); missed six games. ...

Suffered from the flu (November 14, 1996); missed three games. ... Suffered infected elbow (January 2, 1997); missed four games. ... Traded by Devils with RW Bill Guerin to Edmonton Oilers for C Jason Arnott and D Bryan Muir (January 4, 1998).

MISCELLANEOUS: Member of Stanley Cup championship team (1995). ... Member of silver-medal-winning Russian Olympic team (1998).

Z

		REGULAR SEASON								PLAYOFFS				
Season Team	League	Gms.	G	A	Pts.	PIM	+/-	PP	SH	Gms.	G	A	Pts.	PIM
84-85—Khimik	USSR	5	0	0	0	2	...	...	...	—	—	—	—	—
85-86—Khimik	USSR	33	2	2	4	10	...	...	...	—	—	—	—	—
86-87—Khimik	USSR	19	1	0	1	4	...	...	...	—	—	—	—	—
87-88—SKA Leningrad	USSR	18	18	6	24	...	...	...	...	—	—	—	—	—
—CSKA Moscow	USSR	19	3	1	4	8	...	...	...	—	—	—	—	—
88-89—CSKA Moscow	USSR	17	2	3	5	2	...	...	...	—	—	—	—	—
89-90—Khimik	USSR	46	17	14	31	26	...	...	...	—	—	—	—	—
90-91—Khimik	USSR	46	12	19	31	22	...	...	...	—	—	—	—	—
91-92—Utica	AHL	22	20	9	29	8	...	...	...	—	—	—	—	—
—New Jersey	NHL	44	13	18	31	28	11	3	0	4	1	1	2	2
92-93—New Jersey	NHL	78	23	41	64	70	19	5	1	5	0	2	2	0
93-94—New Jersey	NHL	82	26	31	57	70	36	8	0	20	5	2	7	14
94-95—New Jersey	NHL	4	1	2	3	6	3	0	0	18	1	2	3	12
95-96—New Jersey	NHL	61	6	9	15	107	-10	3	0	—	—	—	—	—
96-97—New Jersey	NHL	71	14	24	38	36	-10	3	0	8	3	2	5	2
97-98—New Jersey	NHL	35	2	8	10	32	0	0	0	—	—	—	—	—
—Edmonton	NHL	33	2	10	12	57	-2	0	0	8	1	2	3	2
—Russian Oly. team	Int'l	6	1	2	3	0	...	...	...	—	—	—	—	—
NHL Totals (7 years)		408	87	143	230	406	47	22	1	63	11	11	22	32

ZENT, JASON — LW — FLYERS

PERSONAL: Born April 15, 1971, in Buffalo. ... 5-11/216. ... Shoots left. ... Full name: Jason William Zent.
HIGH SCHOOL: Nichols School (Buffalo).
COLLEGE: Wisconsin.
TRANSACTIONS/CAREER NOTES: Selected by New York Islanders in third round (third Islanders pick, 44th overall) of NHL entry draft (June 17, 1989). ... Sprained ankle playing racquetball (January 1991). ... Traded by Islanders to Ottawa Senators for fifth-round pick (D Andy Berenzweig) in 1996 draft (October 15, 1994). ... Bruised thigh (February 16, 1997); missed seven games. ... Signed by Philadelphia Flyers (August 4, 1998).
HONORS: Named to WCHA All-Rookie team (1990-91). ... Named to NCAA All-Tournament team (1991-92).

		REGULAR SEASON								PLAYOFFS				
Season Team	League	Gms.	G	A	Pts.	PIM	+/-	PP	SH	Gms.	G	A	Pts.	PIM
87-88—Nichols School	N.Y. H.S.	21	20	16	36	28	...	...	...	—	—	—	—	—
88-89—Nichols School	N.Y. H.S.	29	49	32	81	26	...	...	...	—	—	—	—	—
89-90—Nichols School	N.Y. H.S.					Statistics unavailable.								
90-91—Univ. of Wisconsin	WCHA	39	19	18	37	51	...	...	...	—	—	—	—	—
91-92—Univ. of Wisconsin	WCHA	43	27	17	44	134	...	...	...	—	—	—	—	—
92-93—Univ. of Wisconsin	WCHA	40	26	12	38	88	...	...	...	—	—	—	—	—
93-94—Univ. of Wisconsin	WCHA	42	20	21	41	120	...	...	...	—	—	—	—	—
94-95—Prin. Edward Island	AHL	55	15	11	26	46	...	...	...	9	6	1	7	6
95-96—Prin. Edward Island	AHL	68	14	5	19	61	...	...	...	5	2	1	3	4
96-97—Worcester	AHL	45	14	10	24	45	...	...	...	5	3	3	6	4
—Ottawa	NHL	22	3	3	6	9	5	0	0	—	—	—	—	—
97-98—Detroit	IHL	4	1	0	1	0	...	...	...	—	—	—	—	—
—Worcester	AHL	66	25	17	42	67	...	...	...	11	2	0	2	6
—Ottawa	NHL	3	0	0	0	4	0	0	0	—	—	—	—	—
NHL Totals (2 years)		25	3	3	6	13	5	0	0					

ZETTLER, ROB — D — PREDATORS

PERSONAL: Born March 8, 1968, in Sept-Iles, Que. ... 6-3/200. ... Shoots left.
TRANSACTIONS/CAREER NOTES: Selected by Minnesota North Stars as underage junior in fifth round (fifth North Stars pick, 55th overall) of NHL entry draft (June 21, 1986). ... Tore hip flexor (January 21, 1991); missed 11 games. ... Selected by San Jose Sharks in NHL dispersal draft (May 30, 1991). ... Strained back (October 20, 1992); missed three games. ... Injured groin (April 8, 1993); missed one game. ... Traded by Sharks to Philadelphia Flyers for C Viacheslav Butsayev (February 1, 1994). ... Traded by Flyers to Toronto Maple Leafs for fifth-round pick (G Per-Ragna Bergqvist) in 1996 draft (July 8, 1995). ... Suspended two games by NHL for checking from behind (January 4, 1996). ... Strained groin (April 3, 1997); missed three games. ... Dislocated thumb (November 11, 1997); missed three games. ... Selected by Nashville Predators in NHL expansion draft (June 26, 1998).

		REGULAR SEASON								PLAYOFFS				
Season Team	League	Gms.	G	A	Pts.	PIM	+/-	PP	SH	Gms.	G	A	Pts.	PIM
84-85—Sault Ste. Marie	OHL	60	2	14	16	37	...	...	...	—	—	—	—	—
85-86—Sault Ste. Marie	OHL	57	5	23	28	92	...	...	...	—	—	—	—	—
86-87—Sault Ste. Marie	OHL	64	13	22	35	89	...	...	...	4	0	0	0	0
87-88—Sault Ste. Marie	OHL	64	7	41	48	77	...	...	...	6	2	2	4	9
—Kalamazoo	IHL	2	0	1	1	0	...	...	...	7	0	2	2	2
88-89—Minnesota	NHL	2	0	0	0	0	1	0	0	—	—	—	—	—
—Kalamazoo	IHL	80	5	21	26	79	...	...	...	6	0	1	1	26
89-90—Minnesota	NHL	31	0	8	8	45	-7	0	0	—	—	—	—	—
—Kalamazoo	IHL	41	6	10	16	64	...	...	...	7	0	0	0	6
90-91—Kalamazoo	IHL	1	0	0	0	2	...	...	...	—	—	—	—	—
—Minnesota	NHL	47	1	4	5	119	-10	0	0	—	—	—	—	—
91-92—San Jose	NHL	74	1	8	9	99	-23	0	0	—	—	—	—	—
92-93—San Jose	NHL	80	0	7	7	150	-50	0	0	—	—	—	—	—

Z

Season Team	League	REGULAR SEASON								PLAYOFFS				
		Gms.	G	A	Pts.	PIM	+/-	PP	SH	Gms.	G	A	Pts.	PIM
93-94—San Jose	NHL	42	0	3	3	65	-7	0	0	—				
—Philadelphia	NHL	33	0	4	4	69	-19	0	0	—				
94-95—Philadelphia	NHL	32	0	1	1	34	-3	0	0	1	0	0	0	2
95-96—Toronto	NHL	29	0	1	1	48	-1	0	0	2	0	0	0	0
96-97—Utah	IHL	30	0	10	10	60	...	...	...	—				
—Toronto	NHL	48	2	12	14	51	8	0	0	—				
97-98—Toronto	NHL	59	0	7	7	108	-8	0	0	—				
NHL Totals (10 years)		477	4	55	59	788	-119	0	0	3	0	0	0	2

ZEZEL, PETER C CANUCKS

PERSONAL: Born April 22, 1965, in Toronto. ... 5-11/200. ... Shoots left. ... Name pronounced ZEH-zihl.

TRANSACTIONS/CAREER NOTES: Selected by Philadelphia Flyers as underage junior in second round (first Flyers pick, 41st overall) of NHL entry draft (June 8, 1983). ... Broke hand (November 1984). ... Tore medial cartilage in left knee (March 1987). ... Sprained right ankle (November 1987). ... Separated left shoulder (March 1988). ... Traded by Flyers to St. Louis Blues for C Mike Bullard (November 29, 1988). ... Pulled groin (December 1988). ... Bruised sternum (January 1989). ... Sprained right knee (March 5, 1989). ... Bruised right hip (March 11, 1990). ... Traded by Blues with D Mike Lalor to Washington Capitals for LW Geoff Courtnall (July 13, 1990). ... Sprained left ankle (October 23, 1990); missed 23 games. ... Reinjured ankle (December 28, 1990); missed two games. ... Traded by Capitals with D Bob Rouse to Toronto Maple Leafs for D Al Iafrate (January 16, 1991). ... Sprained knee (November 14, 1991); missed five games. ... Strained knee (March 5, 1992). ... Bruised knee (November 5, 1992); missed five games. ... Sprained wrist (January 6, 1993); missed three games. ... Sprained neck (March 25, 1993); missed five games. ... Injured back (October 16, 1993); missed 41 games. ... Suffered back spasms (January 30, 1994); missed one game. ... Awarded to Dallas Stars with RW Grant Marshall as compensation for Maple Leafs signing free-agent RW Mike Craig (August 10, 1994). ... Signed as free agent by Blues (October 19, 1995). ... Sprained wrist (January 4, 1996); missed 13 games. ... Sprained neck (February 20, 1996); missed two games. ... Sprained ankle [need date]; missed three games. ... Suffered back spasms (December 19, 1996); missed four games. ... Injured back (January 20, 1996); missed eight games. ... Traded by Blues to New Jersey Devils for D Chris McAlpine and ninth-round pick in 1999 draft (February 11, 1997). ... Stiff neck (March 15, 1997); missed one game. ... Suffered from the flu (April 1, 1997); missed three games. ... Bruised knee (April 9, 1997); missed final two games of regular season. ... Traded by Devils to Vancouver Canucks for fifth-round pick (LW Anton But) in the 1998 draft (February 5, 1998). ... Strained abdominal muscle (April 9, 1998); missed two games.

MISCELLANEOUS: Failed to score on a penalty shot (vs. Chris Osgood, March 4, 1994). ... Played three games as a striker for Toronto Blizzard in the North American Soccer League (1982).

STATISTICAL PLATEAUS: Three-goal games: 1986-87 (1).

Season Team	League	REGULAR SEASON								PLAYOFFS				
		Gms.	G	A	Pts.	PIM	+/-	PP	SH	Gms.	G	A	Pts.	PIM
81-82—Don Mills Flyers	MTHL	40	43	51	94	36	...	...	...	—				
82-83—Toronto	OHL	66	35	39	74	28	...	...	...	4	2	4	6	0
83-84—Toronto	OHL	68	47	86	133	31	...	...	...	9	7	5	12	4
84-85—Philadelphia	NHL	65	15	46	61	26	22	8	0	19	1	8	9	28
85-86—Philadelphia	NHL	79	17	37	54	76	27	4	0	5	3	1	4	4
86-87—Philadelphia	NHL	71	33	39	72	71	21	6	2	25	3	10	13	10
87-88—Philadelphia	NHL	69	22	35	57	42	7	14	0	7	3	2	5	7
88-89—Philadelphia	NHL	26	4	13	17	15	13	0	0	—				
—St. Louis	NHL	52	17	36	53	27	-1	5	1	10	6	6	12	4
89-90—St. Louis	NHL	73	25	47	72	30	-9	7	0	12	1	7	8	4
90-91—Washington	NHL	20	7	5	12	10	-13	6	0	—				
—Toronto	NHL	32	14	14	28	4	-7	6	0	—				
91-92—Toronto	NHL	64	16	33	49	26	-22	4	0	—				
92-93—Toronto	NHL	70	12	23	35	24	0	0	0	20	2	1	3	6
93-94—Toronto	NHL	41	8	8	16	19	5	0	0	18	2	4	6	8
94-95—Dallas	NHL	30	6	5	11	19	-6	0	0	3	1	0	1	0
—Kalamazoo	IHL	2	0	0	0	0	...	...	...	—				
95-96—St. Louis	NHL	57	8	13	21	12	-2	2	0	10	3	0	3	2
96-97—St. Louis	NHL	35	4	9	13	12	6	0	0	—				
—New Jersey	NHL	18	0	3	3	4	4	0	0	2	0	0	0	10
97-98—Albany	AHL	35	13	37	50	18	...	...	...	—				
—New Jersey	NHL	5	0	3	3	0	2	0	0	—				
—Vancouver	NHL	25	5	12	17	2	13	2	0	—				
NHL Totals (14 years)		832	213	381	594	419	60	64	3	131	25	39	64	83

ZHAMNOV, ALEXEI C BLACKHAWKS

PERSONAL: Born October 1, 1970, in Moscow, U.S.S.R. ... 6-1/195. ... Shoots left. ... Name pronounced ZHAM-nahf.

TRANSACTIONS/CAREER NOTES: Selected by Winnipeg Jets in fourth round (fifth Jets pick, 77th overall) of NHL entry draft (June 16, 1990). ... Suffered hip flexor (November 2, 1992); missed two games. ... Suffered back spasms (January 27, 1993); missed one game. ... Suffered back spasms (February 3, 1993); missed one game. ... Suffered back spasms (February 12, 1993); missed 12 games. ... Suffered left quad contusion (October 26, 1993); missed three games. ... Sprained back (December 27, 1993); missed eight games. ... Suffered back spasms (March 19, 1994); missed remainder of season. ... Suffered stress fracture in leg (October 12, 1995); missed eight games. ... Suffered from the flu (January 5, 1996); missed one game. ... Bruised back (March 7, 1996); missed four games. ... Injured back (March 16, 1996); missed remainder of regular season. ... Jets franchise moved to Phoenix and renamed Coyotes for 1996-97 season; NHL approved move on January 18, 1996. ... Traded by Coyotes with RW Craig Mills and first-round pick (RW Ty Jones) in 1997 draft to Chicago Blackhawks for C Jeremy Roenick (August 16, 1996). ... Fractured toe (November 2, 1997); missed four games. ... Suffered concussion (November 29, 1997); missed one game. ... Suffered concussion (March 3, 1998); missed four games. ... Bruised back (April 4, 1998); missed one game. ... Fractured finger (April 15, 1998); missed two games.

HONORS: Named to NHL All-Star second team (1994-95).

MISCELLANEOUS: Member of gold-medal-winning Unified Olympic team (1992). ... Member of silver-medal-winning Russian Olympic team (1998).

STATISTICAL PLATEAUS: Three-goal games: 1993-94 (2), 1994-95 (1), 1995-96 (1), 1996-97 (1). Total: 5. ... Five-goal games: 1994-95 (1). ... Total hat tricks: 6.

Season Team	League	REGULAR SEASON								PLAYOFFS				
		Gms.	G	A	Pts.	PIM	+/-	PP	SH	Gms.	G	A	Pts.	PIM
88-89—Dynamo Moscow.......	USSR	4	0	0	0	0	...	...	...	—	—	—	—	—
89-90—Dynamo Moscow.......	USSR	43	11	6	17	23	...	...	...	—	—	—	—	—
90-91—Dynamo Moscow.......	USSR	46	16	12	28	24	...	...	...	—	—	—	—	—
91-92—Dynamo Moscow.......	CIS	39	15	21	36	28	...	...	...	—	—	—	—	—
—Unif. Olympic Team	Int'l	8	0	3	3	8	...	...	...	—	—	—	—	—
92-93—Winnipeg	NHL	68	25	47	72	58	7	6	1	6	0	2	2	2
93-94—Winnipeg	NHL	61	26	45	71	62	-20	7	0	—	—	—	—	—
94-95—Winnipeg	NHL	48	30	35	65	20	5	9	0	—	—	—	—	—
95-96—Winnipeg	NHL	58	22	37	59	65	-4	5	0	6	2	1	3	8
96-97—Chicago...................	NHL	74	20	42	62	56	18	6	1	—	—	—	—	—
97-98—Chicago...................	NHL	70	21	28	49	61	16	6	2	—	—	—	—	—
—Russian Oly. team.......	Int'l	6	2	1	3	2	...	...	...	—	—	—	—	—
NHL Totals (6 years)...........		379	144	234	378	322	22	39	4	12	2	3	5	10

ZHITNIK, ALEXEI — D — SABRES

PERSONAL: Born October 10, 1972, in Kiev, U.S.S.R. ... 5-11/204. ... Shoots left. ... Name pronounced ZHIHT-nihk.
TRANSACTIONS/CAREER NOTES: Selected by Los Angeles Kings in fourth round (third Kings pick, 81st overall) of NHL entry draft (June 22, 1991). ... Suffered from the flu (January 12, 1993); missed five games. ... Suspended one game by NHL for cross-checking (November 30, 1993). ... Traded by Kings with D Charlie Huddy, G Robb Stauber and fifth-round pick (D Marian Menhart) in 1995 draft to Buffalo Sabres for G Grant Fuhr, D Philippe Boucher and D Denis Tsygurov (February 14, 1995). ... Broke thumb (February 19, 1995); missed three games. ... Reinjured thumb (March 8, 1995); missed one game. ... Ruptured calf muscle (March 19, 1995); missed 11 games. ... Suspended two games and fined $1,000 by NHL for high-sticking incident (November 1, 1996). ... Missed first four games of 1997-98 season due to contract dispute.
MISCELLANEOUS: Member of gold-medal-winning Unified Olympic team (1992). ... Member of silver-medal-winning Russian Olympic team (1998).

Season Team	League	REGULAR SEASON								PLAYOFFS				
		Gms.	G	A	Pts.	PIM	+/-	PP	SH	Gms.	G	A	Pts.	PIM
89-90—Sokol Kiev..................	USSR	31	3	4	7	16	...	...	...	—	—	—	—	—
90-91—Sokol Kiev..................	USSR	40	1	4	5	46	...	...	...	—	—	—	—	—
91-92—CSKA Moscow............	CIS	36	2	7	9	48	...	...	...	—	—	—	—	—
—Unif. Olympic Team	Int'l	8	1	0	1	0	...	...	...	—	—	—	—	—
92-93—Los Angeles..............	NHL	78	12	36	48	80	-3	5	0	24	3	9	12	26
93-94—Los Angeles..............	NHL	81	12	40	52	101	-11	11	0	—	—	—	—	—
94-95—Los Angeles..............	NHL	11	2	5	7	27	-3	2	0	—	—	—	—	—
—Buffalo	NHL	21	2	5	7	34	-3	1	0	5	0	1	1	14
95-96—Buffalo	NHL	80	6	30	36	58	-25	5	0	—	—	—	—	—
96-97—Buffalo	NHL	80	7	28	35	95	10	3	1	12	1	0	1	16
97-98—Buffalo	NHL	78	15	30	45	102	19	2	3	15	0	3	3	36
—Russian Oly. team.......	Int'l	6	0	2	2	2	...	...	...	—	—	—	—	—
NHL Totals (6 years)...........		429	56	174	230	497	-16	29	4	56	4	13	17	92

ZHOLTOK, SERGEI — C

PERSONAL: Born December 2, 1972, in Riga, U.S.S.R. ... 6-2/195. ... Shoots right. ... Name pronounced SAIR-gay ZOHL-tahk.
TRANSACTIONS/CAREER NOTES: Selected by Boston Bruins in third round (second Bruins pick, 56th overall) of NHL entry draft (June 20, 1992). ... Signed as free agent by Las Vegas of IHL (August 8, 1995). ... Signed as free agent by Ottawa Senators (June 25, 1996).

Season Team	League	REGULAR SEASON								PLAYOFFS				
		Gms.	G	A	Pts.	PIM	+/-	PP	SH	Gms.	G	A	Pts.	PIM
90-91—Dynamo Riga..............	USSR	39	4	0	4	16	...	...	...	—	—	—	—	—
91-92—HC Riga.....................	CIS	27	6	3	9	6	...	...	...	—	—	—	—	—
92-93—Providence.................	AHL	64	31	35	66	57	...	...	...	6	3	5	8	4
—Boston	NHL	1	0	1	1	0	1	0	0	—	—	—	—	—
93-94—Providence.................	AHL	54	29	33	62	16	...	...	...	—	—	—	—	—
—Boston	NHL	24	2	1	3	2	-7	1	0	—	—	—	—	—
94-95—Providence.................	AHL	78	23	35	58	42	...	...	...	13	8	5	13	6
95-96—Las Vegas	IHL	82	51	50	101	30	...	...	...	15	7	13	20	6
96-97—Las Vegas	IHL	19	13	14	27	20	...	...	...	—	—	—	—	—
—Ottawa	NHL	57	12	16	28	19	2	5	0	7	1	1	2	0
97-98—Ottawa	NHL	78	10	13	23	16	-7	7	0	11	0	2	2	0
NHL Totals (4 years)...........		160	24	31	55	37	-11	13	0	18	1	3	4	0

ZIMAKOV, SERGEI — D — CAPITALS

PERSONAL: Born January 15, 1978, in Moscow, U.S.S.R. ... 6-1/194. ... Shoots left.
TRANSACTIONS/CAREER NOTES: Selected by Washington Capitals in third round (fourth Capitals pick, 58th overall) of NHL entry draft (June 22, 1996).

Season Team	League	REGULAR SEASON								PLAYOFFS				
		Gms.	G	A	Pts.	PIM	+/-	PP	SH	Gms.	G	A	Pts.	PIM
94-95—Omaha	Jr. A	48	14	46	60	22	...	...	...	—	—	—	—	—
95-96—Krylja Sov. Moscow	CIS	49	2	7	9	36	...	...	...	—	—	—	—	—
96-97—Krylja Sov. Moscow	Russian	27	2	3	5	14	...	...	...	—	—	—	—	—
97-98—Krylja Sov. Moscow	Russian	42	4	1	5	48	...	...	...	—	—	—	—	—

ZMOLEK, DOUG   D   KINGS

PERSONAL: Born November 3, 1970, in Rochester, Minn. ... 6-2/220. ... Shoots left. ... Full name: Doug Allan Zmolek. ... Name pronounced ZMOH-lehk.

HIGH SCHOOL: John Marshall (Rochester, Minn.).

COLLEGE: Minnesota.

TRANSACTIONS/CAREER NOTES: Selected by Minnesota North Stars in first round (first North Stars pick, seventh overall) of NHL entry draft (June 17, 1989). ... Selected by San Jose Sharks in NHL dispersal draft (May 30, 1991). ... Traded by Sharks with D Mike Lalor to Dallas Stars for RW Ulf Dahlen and future considerations (March 19, 1994). ... Sprained thumb (March 12, 1994); missed one game. ... Separated shoulder (March 31, 1994); missed five games. ... Lacerated hand (March 6, 1995); missed no games. ... Bruised kneecap (April 7, 1995); missed six games. ... Injured shoulder (November 9, 1995); missed five games. ... Traded by Stars with RW Shane Churla to Los Angeles Kings for Darryl Sydor and seventh-round pick (G Eoin McInerney) in 1996 draft (February 17, 1996). ... Sprained left knee (March 23, 1996); missed last eight games of season. ... Bruised thigh (October 26, 1996); missed one game. ... Strained right shoulder (November 7, 1996); missed one game. ... Sprained right shoulder (December 9, 1996); missed six games. ... Bruised hand (January 14, 1997); missed one game. ... Suffered irregular heartbeat (February 17, 1997); missed five games. ... Bruised left foot (November 11, 1997); missed one game. ... Suffered concussion (January 5, 1998); missed two games. ... Sprained right shoulder (March 7, 1998); missed eight games.

HONORS: Named to NCAA All-America West second team (1991-92). ... Named to WCHA All-Star second team (1991-92).

Season Team	League	REGULAR SEASON								PLAYOFFS				
		Gms.	G	A	Pts.	PIM	+/-	PP	SH	Gms.	G	A	Pts.	PIM
87-88—John Marshall	Minn. H.S.	27	4	32	36	...	...	...	...	—	—	—	—	—
88-89—John Marshall	Minn. H.S.	29	17	41	58	...	...	...	...	—	—	—	—	—
89-90—Univ. of Minnesota	WCHA	40	1	10	11	52	...	...	...	—	—	—	—	—
90-91—Univ. of Minnesota	WCHA	42	3	15	18	94	...	...	...	—	—	—	—	—
91-92—Univ. of Minnesota	WCHA	44	6	21	27	88	...	...	...	—	—	—	—	—
92-93—San Jose	NHL	84	5	10	15	229	-50	2	0	—	—	—	—	—
93-94—San Jose	NHL	68	0	4	4	122	-9	0	0	—	—	—	—	—
—Dallas	NHL	7	1	0	1	11	1	0	0	7	0	1	1	4
94-95—Dallas	NHL	42	0	5	5	67	-6	0	0	5	0	0	0	10
95-96—Dallas	NHL	42	1	5	6	65	1	0	0	—	—	—	—	—
—Los Angeles	NHL	16	1	0	1	22	-6	0	0	—	—	—	—	—
96-97—Los Angeles	NHL	57	1	0	1	116	-22	0	0	—	—	—	—	—
97-98—Los Angeles	NHL	46	0	8	8	111	0	0	0	2	0	0	0	2
NHL Totals (6 years)		362	9	32	41	743	-91	2	0	14	0	1	1	16

ZUBOV, SERGEI   D   STARS

PERSONAL: Born July 22, 1970, in Moscow, U.S.S.R. ... 6-1/200. ... Shoots right. ... Name pronounced SAIR-gay ZOO-bahf.

TRANSACTIONS/CAREER NOTES: Selected by New York Rangers in fifth round (sixth Rangers pick, 85th overall) of NHL entry draft (June 16, 1990). ... Suffered concussion (February 26, 1993); missed one game. ... Suffered from the flu (February 4, 1995); missed one game. ... Underwent wrist surgery (February 27, 1995); missed nine games. ... Traded by Rangers with C Petr Nedved to Pittsburgh Penguins for LW Luc Robitaille and D Ulf Samuelsson (August 31, 1995). ... Broke finger (October 9, 1995); missed nine games. ... Reinjured finger (November 11, 1995); missed seven games. ... Bruised shoulder (March 31, 1996); missed one game. ... Traded by Penguins to Dallas Stars for D Kevin Hatcher (June 22, 1996). ... Suffered from the flu (November 20, 1996); missed one game. ... Suffered back spasms (January 24, 1997); missed two games. ... Sprained neck (March 4, 1998); missed nine games.

HONORS: Played in NHL All-Star Game (1998).

MISCELLANEOUS: Member of Stanley Cup championship team (1994). ... Member of gold-medal-winning Unified Olympic team (1992).

Season Team	League	REGULAR SEASON								PLAYOFFS				
		Gms.	G	A	Pts.	PIM	+/-	PP	SH	Gms.	G	A	Pts.	PIM
88-89—CSKA Moscow	USSR	29	1	4	5	10	...	...	...	—	—	—	—	—
89-90—CSKA Moscow	USSR	48	6	2	8	16	...	...	...	—	—	—	—	—
90-91—CSKA Moscow	CIS	41	6	5	11	12	...	...	...	—	—	—	—	—
91-92—CSKA Moscow	CIS	36	4	7	11	6	...	...	...	—	—	—	—	—
—Unif. Olympic Team	Int'l	8	0	1	1	0	...	...	...	—	—	—	—	—
92-93—CSKA Moscow	CIS	1	0	1	1	0	...	...	...	—	—	—	—	—
—Binghamton	AHL	30	7	29	36	14	...	...	...	11	5	5	10	2
—New York Rangers	NHL	49	8	23	31	4	-1	3	0	—	—	—	—	—
93-94—New York Rangers	NHL	78	12	77	89	39	20	9	0	22	5	14	19	0
—Binghamton	AHL	2	1	2	3	0	...	...	...	—	—	—	—	—
94-95—New York Rangers	NHL	38	10	26	36	18	-2	6	0	10	3	8	11	2
95-96—Pittsburgh	NHL	64	11	55	66	22	28	3	2	18	1	14	15	26
96-97—Dallas	NHL	78	13	30	43	24	19	1	0	7	0	3	3	2
97-98—Dallas	NHL	73	10	47	57	16	16	5	1	17	4	5	9	2
NHL Totals (6 years)		380	64	258	322	123	80	27	3	74	13	44	57	32

ZUBRUS, DAINIUS   RW   FLYERS

PERSONAL: Born June 16, 1978, in Elektrenai, U.S.S.R. ... 6-3/215. ... Shoots left. ... Name pronounced DIGH-nuhz ZOO-bruhz.

TRANSACTIONS/CAREER NOTES: Selected by Philadelphia Flyers in first round (first Flyers pick, 15th overall) of NHL entry draft (June 22, 1996). ... Bruised right hand (October 8, 1997); missed two games. ... Bruised right hand (October 15, 1997); missed five games. ... Suspended two games and fined $1,000 by NHL for slashing incident (April 2, 1998). ... Strained left hamstring (December 15, 1997); missed one game.

Season Team	League	REGULAR SEASON								PLAYOFFS				
		Gms.	G	A	Pts.	PIM	+/-	PP	SH	Gms.	G	A	Pts.	PIM
95-96—Pembroke	CJHL	28	19	13	32	73	...	...	...	—	—	—	—	—
—Caledon	Jr. A	7	3	7	10	2	...	...	...	17	11	12	23	4
96-97—Philadelphia	NHL	68	8	13	21	22	3	1	0	19	5	4	9	12
97-98—Philadelphia	NHL	69	8	25	33	42	29	1	0	5	0	1	1	2
NHL Totals (2 years)		137	16	38	54	64	32	2	0	24	5	5	10	14

ZULTEK, MATT   LW   KINGS

PERSONAL: Born March 12, 1979, in Windsor, Ont. ... 6-4/218. ... Shoots left. ... Name pronounced ZOHL-tehk.
TRANSACTIONS/CAREER NOTES: Selected by Los Angeles Kings in first round (second Kings pick, 15th overall) of NHL entry draft (June 21, 1997).
HONORS: Named to OHL All-Rookie second team (1996-97).

		REGULAR SEASON								PLAYOFFS				
Season Team	League	Gms.	G	A	Pts.	PIM	+/-	PP	SH	Gms.	G	A	Pts.	PIM
95-96—Caledon	Jr. A	50	19	14	33	40	...	...	...	—	—	—	—	—
96-97—Ottawa	OHL	63	27	13	40	76	...	...	...	21	7	6	13	27
97-98—Ottawa	OHL	62	28	28	56	156	...	...	...	13	6	12	18	20

ZYUZIN, ANDREI   D   SHARKS

PERSONAL: Born January 21, 1978, in Ufa, U.S.S.R. ... 6-1/195. ... Shoots left. ... Name pronounced ZYOO-zihn.
TRANSACTIONS/CAREER NOTES: Selected by San Jose Sharks in first round (first Sharks pick, second overall) of NHL entry draft (June 22, 1996).

		REGULAR SEASON								PLAYOFFS				
Season Team	League	Gms.	G	A	Pts.	PIM	+/-	PP	SH	Gms.	G	A	Pts.	PIM
94-95—Salavat Yulayev Ufa	CIS	30	3	0	3	16	...	...	...	—	—	—	—	—
95-96—Salavat Yulayev Ufa	CIS	41	6	3	9	24	...	...	...	2	0	0	0	4
96-97—Salavat Yulayev Ufa	USSR	32	7	10	17	28	...	...	...	7	1	1	2	4
97-98—San Jose	NHL	56	6	7	13	66	8	2	0	6	1	0	1	14
—Kentucky	AHL	17	4	5	9	28	...	...	...	—	—	—	—	—
NHL Totals (1 year)		56	6	7	13	66	8	2	0	6	1	0	1	14

ABID, RAMZI — LW — AVALANCHE

PERSONAL: Born March 24, 1980, in Montreal. ... 6-2/195. ... Shoots left.
TRANSACTIONS/CAREER NOTES: Selected by Colorado Avalanche in second round (fifth Avalanche pick, 28th overall) of NHL entry draft (June 27, 1998).
HONORS: Named to Can.HL All-Star second team (1997-98). ... Named to QMJHL All-Star first team (1997-98). ... Won Jean Beliveau Trophy (1997-98). ... Won Michel Briere Trophy (1997-98).

		REGULAR SEASON					PLAYOFFS				
Season Team	League	Gms.	G	A	Pts.	PIM	Gms.	G	A	Pts.	PIM
96-97—Chicoutimi	QMJHL	65	13	24	37	151	—	—	—	—	—
97-98—Chicoutimi	QMJHL	68	50	†85	*135	266	6	3	4	7	10

AFANASENKOV, DMITRI — LW — LIGHTNING

PERSONAL: Born May 12, 1980, in Arkhangelsk, U.S.S.R. ... 6-1/180. ... Shoots right.
TRANSACTIONS/CAREER NOTES: Selected by Tampa Bay Lightning in third round (third Lightning pick, 72nd overall) of NHL entry draft (June 27, 1998).

		REGULAR SEASON					PLAYOFFS				
Season Team	League	Gms.	G	A	Pts.	PIM	Gms.	G	A	Pts.	PIM
95-96—Torpedo-2 Yaroslavl	CIS Div. II	25	10	5	15	10	—	—	—	—	—
—Torpedo Yaroslavl	CIS Jr.	35	28	16	44	8	—	—	—	—	—
96-97—Torpedo-2 Yaroslavl	Rus. Div. III	45	20	15	35	14	—	—	—	—	—
97-98—Yaroslavl	Russian	45	19	11	30	28	—	—	—	—	—

ALLEN, BOBBY — D — BRUINS

PERSONAL: Born November 14, 1978, in Braintree, Mass. ... 6-1/198. ... Shoots left.
HIGH SCHOOL: Cushing Academy (Ashburnham, Mass.).
COLLEGE: Boston College.
TRANSACTIONS/CAREER NOTES: Selected by Boston Bruins in second round (second Bruins pick, 52nd overall) of NHL entry draft (June 27, 1998).

		REGULAR SEASON					PLAYOFFS				
Season Team	League	Gms.	G	A	Pts.	PIM	Gms.	G	A	Pts.	PIM
96-97—Cushing	USHS	36	11	33	44	28	—	—	—	—	—
97-98—Boston College	Hockey East	37	7	19	26	34	—	—	—	—	—

ALLEN, BRYAN — D — CANUCKS

PERSONAL: Born August 21, 1980, in Kingston, Ont. ... 6-4/208. ... Shoots left.
TRANSACTIONS/CAREER NOTES: Selected by Vancouver Canucks in first round (first Canucks pick, fourth overall) of NHL entry draft (June 27, 1998).

		REGULAR SEASON					PLAYOFFS				
Season Team	League	Gms.	G	A	Pts.	PIM	Gms.	G	A	Pts.	PIM
95-96—Ernestown	Jr. C	36	1	16	17	71	—	—	—	—	—
96-97—Oshawa	OHL	60	2	4	6	76	18	1	3	4	26
97-98—Oshawa	OHL	48	6	13	19	126	5	0	5	5	18

ANTILA, KRISTIAN — G — OILERS

PERSONAL: Born January 10, 1980, in Vammala, Finland. ... 6-3/207. ... Catches left.
TRANSACTIONS/CAREER NOTES: Selected by Edmonton Oilers in fourth round (fourth Oilers pick, 113th overall) of NHL entry draft (June 27, 1998).

		REGULAR SEASON							PLAYOFFS						
Season Team	League	Gms.	Min	W	L	T	GA	SO	Avg.	Gms.	Min.	W	L	GA	SO	Avg.
96-97—Ilves Tampere	Finland Jr.	24	...	...	...	...	...	...	...	3	...	...	...	...	...	...
97-98—Ilves Tampere	Finland Jr.	11	564	...	...	...	28	0	2.98	—	—	—	—	—	—	—

ANTROPOV, NIKOLAI — C — MAPLE LEAFS

PERSONAL: Born February 18, 1980, in Ust-Kamenogorsk, U.S.S.R. ... 6-5/191. ... Shoots left.
TRANSACTIONS/CAREER NOTES: Selected by Toronto Maple Leafs in first round (first Maple Leafs pick, 10th overall) of NHL entry draft (June 27, 1998).

		REGULAR SEASON					PLAYOFFS				
Season Team	League	Gms.	G	A	Pts.	PIM	Gms.	G	A	Pts.	PIM
95-96—Torpedo Ust-Kamenogorsk	CIS Jr.	20	18	20	38	30	—	—	—	—	—
96-97—Torpedo Ust-Kamenogorsk	Rus. Div. II	8	2	1	3	6	—	—	—	—	—
97-98—Torpedo Ust-Kamenogorsk	Rus. Div. II	42	15	24	39	62	—	—	—	—	—

ARKHIPOV, DENIS   RW   PREDATORS

PERSONAL: Born May 19, 1979, in Kazan, U.S.S.R. ... 6-3/196. ... Shoots left.
TRANSACTIONS/CAREER NOTES: Selected by Nashville Predators in third round (second Predators pick, 60th overall) of NHL entry draft (June 27, 1998).

Season Team	League	REGULAR SEASON					PLAYOFFS				
		Gms.	G	A	Pts.	PIM	Gms.	G	A	Pts.	PIM
94-95—Ak Bars Kazan	CIS Jr.	40	20	12	32	10	—	—	—	—	—
95-96—Ak Bars Kazan	CIS Jr.	40	15	8	23	30	—	—	—	—	—
—Ak Bars-2 Kazan	CIS Div. II	15	10	8	18	10	—	—	—	—	—
96-97—Ak Bars-2 Kazan	Rus. Div. III	50	17	23	40	20	—	—	—	—	—
—Ak Bars Kazan	Russian	1	1	0	1	0	—	—	—	—	—
97-98—Ak Bars Kazan	Russian	29	2	2	4	2	—	—	—	—	—

BACKMAN, CHRISTIAN   D   BLUES

PERSONAL: Born April 28, 1980, in Alingsas, Sweden. ... 6-2/187. ... Shoots left.
TRANSACTIONS/CAREER NOTES: Selected by St. Louis Blues in first round (first Blues pick, 24th overall) of NHL entry draft (June 27, 1998).

Season Team	League	REGULAR SEASON					PLAYOFFS				
		Gms.	G	A	Pts.	PIM	Gms.	G	A	Pts.	PIM
96-97—V. Frolunda Goteborg	Sweden Jr.	26	2	5	7	16	—	—	—	—	—
97-98—V. Frolunda Goteborg	Sweden Jr.	28	5	14	19	12	2	0	1	1	4

BALA, CHRIS   LW   SENATORS

PERSONAL: Born September 24, 1978, in Alexandria, Va. ... 6-1/180. ... Shoots left.
HIGH SCHOOL: Phoenixville (Pa.), then The Hill School (Pottstown, Pa.).
COLLEGE: Harvard.
TRANSACTIONS/CAREER NOTES: Selected by Ottawa Senators in second round (third Senators pick, 58th overall) of NHL entry draft (June 27, 1998).

Season Team	League	REGULAR SEASON					PLAYOFFS				
		Gms.	G	A	Pts.	PIM	Gms.	G	A	Pts.	PIM
96-97—The Hill School	USHS (East)	23	28	33	61	36	—	—	—	—	—
97-98—Harvard University	ECAC	33	16	14	30	23	—	—	—	—	—

BARCH, KRYS   LW   CAPITALS

PERSONAL: Born March 26, 1980, in Guelph, Ont. ... 6-1/195. ... Shoots left. ... Full Name: Krystofer Barch.
TRANSACTIONS/CAREER NOTES: Selected by Washington Capitals in fourth round (third Capitals pick, 106th overall) of NHL entry draft (June 27, 1998).

Season Team	League	REGULAR SEASON					PLAYOFFS				
		Gms.	G	A	Pts.	PIM	Gms.	G	A	Pts.	PIM
96-97—Georgetown	Tier II Jr. A	51	18	26	44	58	—	—	—	—	—
97-98—London	OHL	65	9	27	36	62	16	4	3	7	16

BARNES, RYAN   LW   RED WINGS

PERSONAL: Born January 30, 1980, in Dunnville, Ont. ... 6-1/201. ... Shoots left.
TRANSACTIONS/CAREER NOTES: Selected by Detroit Red Wings in second round (second Red Wings pick, 55th overall) of NHL entry draft (June 27, 1998).

Season Team	League	REGULAR SEASON					PLAYOFFS				
		Gms.	G	A	Pts.	PIM	Gms.	G	A	Pts.	PIM
96-97—Quinte	Tier II Jr. A	46	15	19	34	245	—	—	—	—	—
97-98—Sudbury	OHL	46	13	18	31	111	10	0	2	2	24

BASHKIROV, ANDREI   LW   CANADIENS

PERSONAL: Born June 22, 1970, in Shelekhov, U.S.S.R. ... 6-0/198. ... Shoots left.
TRANSACTIONS/CAREER NOTES: Selected by Montreal Canadiens in fifth round (fourth Canadiens pick, 132nd overall) of NHL entry draft (June 27, 1998).

Season Team	League	REGULAR SEASON					PLAYOFFS				
		Gms.	G	A	Pts.	PIM	Gms.	G	A	Pts.	PIM
90-91—Yermak Angarsk	USSR Div. III				Statistics unavailable.		—	—	—	—	—
91-92—Khimik Voskresensk	CIS	11	2	0	2	4	—	—	—	—	—
92-93—Yermak Angarsk	CIS Div. III				Statistics unavailable.		—	—	—	—	—
93-94—Charlotte	ECHL	62	28	42	70	25	3	1	0	1	...
—Providence	AHL	1	0	0	0	2	—	—	—	—	—
94-95—Charlotte	ECHL	61	19	27	46	20	3	0	0	0	0
95-96—Huntington	ECHL	55	19	39	58	35	—	—	—	—	—
96-97—Huntington	ECHL	47	29	41	70	12	—	—	—	—	—
—Detroit	IHL	2	0	0	0	0	—	—	—	—	—
—Las Vegas	IHL	27	10	12	22	0	2	0	0	0	0
97-98—Las Vegas	IHL	15	2	3	5	5	—	—	—	—	—
—Fort Wayne	IHL	65	28	48	76	16	4	2	2	4	2

BEAUCHEMIN, FRANCOIS   D   CANADIENS

PERSONAL: Born June 4, 1980, in Sorel, Que. ... 5-11/190. ... Shoots left.
TRANSACTIONS/CAREER NOTES: Selected by Montreal Canadiens in third round (third Canadiens pick, 75th overall) of NHL entry draft (June 27, 1998).
HONORS: Named to Can.HL All-Rookie team (1996-97).

		REGULAR SEASON					PLAYOFFS				
Season Team	League	Gms.	G	A	Pts.	PIM	Gms.	G	A	Pts.	PIM
96-97—Laval	QMJHL	66	7	20	27	112	3	0	0	0	2
97-98—Laval	QMJHL	70	12	35	47	132	16	1	3	4	23

BEAUCHESNE, MARTIN   D   PREDATORS

PERSONAL: Born July 8, 1980, in Cap-de-la-Madeleine, Que. ... 6-0/200. ... Shoots left.
TRANSACTIONS/CAREER NOTES: Selected by Nashville Predators in fifth round (fifth Predators pick, 138th overall) of NHL entry draft (June 27, 1998).

		REGULAR SEASON					PLAYOFFS				
Season Team	League	Gms.	G	A	Pts.	PIM	Gms.	G	A	Pts.	PIM
96-97—Sherbrooke	QMJHL	65	1	2	3	115	3	0	0	0	4
97-98—Sherbrooke	QMJHL	37	1	3	4	105	—	—	—	—	—

BEAUDOIN, ERIC   LW   LIGHTNING

PERSONAL: Born May 3, 1980, in Ottawa. ... 6-3/180. ... Shoots left.
TRANSACTIONS/CAREER NOTES: Selected by Tampa Bay Lightning in fourth round (fourth Lightning pick, 92nd overall) of NHL entry draft (June 27, 1998).

		REGULAR SEASON					PLAYOFFS				
Season Team	League	Gms.	G	A	Pts.	PIM	Gms.	G	A	Pts.	PIM
96-97—Ottawa	Tier II Jr. A	54	12	19	31	55	—	—	—	—	—
97-98—Guelph	OHL	62	9	13	22	43	12	3	2	5	4

BECKETT, JASON   D   FLYERS

PERSONAL: Born July 23, 1980, in Lethbridge, Alta. ... 6-3/203. ... Shoots right.
TRANSACTIONS/CAREER NOTES: Selected by Philadelphia Flyers in second round (second Flyers pick, 42nd overall) of NHL entry draft (June 27, 1998).

		REGULAR SEASON					PLAYOFFS				
Season Team	League	Gms.	G	A	Pts.	PIM	Gms.	G	A	Pts.	PIM
96-97—Lethbridge	AMHL	34	7	10	17	118	—	—	—	—	—
97-98—Seattle	WHL	71	1	11	12	241	5	0	0	0	16

BELANGER, FRANCIS   LW   FLYERS

PERSONAL: Born January 15, 1978, in Bellefuille, Que. ... 6-2/216. ... Shoots left.
TRANSACTIONS/CAREER NOTES: Selected by Philadelphia Flyers in fifth round (fifth Flyers pick, 124th overall) of NHL entry draft (June 27, 1998).

		REGULAR SEASON					PLAYOFFS				
Season Team	League	Gms.	G	A	Pts.	PIM	Gms.	G	A	Pts.	PIM
96-97—Hull	QMJHL	53	13	13	26	134	8	2	2	4	29
97-98—Hull	QMJHL	33	22	23	45	133	—	—	—	—	—
—Rimouski	QMJHL	30	18	10	28	248	—	—	—	—	—

BELL, MARK   C/LW   BLACKHAWKS

PERSONAL: Born August 5, 1980, in Stratford, Ont. ... 6-3/185. ... Shoots left.
TRANSACTIONS/CAREER NOTES: Selected by Chicago Blackhawks in first round (first Blackhawks pick, eighth overall) of NHL entry draft (June 27, 1998).

		REGULAR SEASON					PLAYOFFS				
Season Team	League	Gms.	G	A	Pts.	PIM	Gms.	G	A	Pts.	PIM
95-96—Stratford Jr. B	OHA	47	8	15	23	32	—	—	—	—	—
96-97—Ottawa	OHL	65	8	12	20	40	24	4	7	11	13
97-98—Ottawa	OHL	55	34	26	60	87	13	6	5	11	14

BERGLUND, CHRISTIAN   RW   DEVILS

PERSONAL: Born March 12, 1980, in Orebro, Sweden. ... 5-11/183. ... Shoots left.
TRANSACTIONS/CAREER NOTES: Selected by New Jersey Devils in second round (third Devils pick, 37th overall) of NHL entry draft (June 27, 1998).

		REGULAR SEASON					PLAYOFFS				
Season Team	League	Gms.	G	A	Pts.	PIM	Gms.	G	A	Pts.	PIM
94-95—Karlskoga	Sweden Dv. 4	20	14	13	27	...	—	—	—	—	—
95-96—Kristinehamn	Sweden Dv. 3	23	8	8	16	12	—	—	—	—	—
96-97—Farjestad Karlstad	Sweden Jr.	21	2	3	5	24	—	—	—	—	—
97-98—Farjestad Karlstad	Sweden Jr.	29	23	19	42	88	2	0	0	0	0
—Farjestad Karlstad	Sweden	1	0	0	0	0	—	—	—	—	—

BERTRAN, RICK — D — CANUCKS

PERSONAL: Born March 12, 1980, in Niagara Falls, Ont. ... 6-3/180. ... Shoots left.
TRANSACTIONS/CAREER NOTES: Selected by Vancouver Canucks in fifth round (seventh Canucks pick, 140th overall) of NHL entry draft (June 27, 1998).

		REGULAR SEASON					PLAYOFFS				
Season Team	League	Gms.	G	A	Pts.	PIM	Gms.	G	A	Pts.	PIM
96-97—Fort Erie Jr. B	OHA	42	6	10	16	68	15	2	2	4	6
97-98—Kitchener	OHL	56	0	9	9	149	6	0	0	0	11

BETTS, BLAIR — C — FLAMES

PERSONAL: Born February 16, 1980, in Edmonton. ... 6-1/183. ... Shoots left.
TRANSACTIONS/CAREER NOTES: Selected by Calgary Flames in second round (second Flames pick, 33rd overall) of NHL entry draft (June 27, 1998).

		REGULAR SEASON					PLAYOFFS				
Season Team	League	Gms.	G	A	Pts.	PIM	Gms.	G	A	Pts.	PIM
96-97—Prince George	WHL	58	12	18	30	19	—	—	—	—	—
97-98—Prince George	WHL	71	35	41	76	38	11	4	6	10	8

BIRON, MATHIEU — D — KINGS

PERSONAL: Born April 29, 1980, in Lac St. Charles, Que. ... 6-6/212. ... Shoots right.
TRANSACTIONS/CAREER NOTES: Selected by Los Angeles Kings in first round (first Kings pick, 21st overall) of NHL entry draft (June 27, 1998).
HONORS: Named to QMJHL All-Rookie Team (1997-98).

		REGULAR SEASON					PLAYOFFS				
Season Team	League	Gms.	G	A	Pts.	PIM	Gms.	G	A	Pts.	PIM
97-98—Shawinigan	QMJHL	59	8	28	36	60	6	0	1	1	10

BLACKBURN, JOSH — G — COYOTES

PERSONAL: Born November 13, 1978, in Del Rio, Texas. ... 6-0/185. ... Catches left.
TRANSACTIONS/CAREER NOTES: Selected by Phoenix Coyotes in fifth round (sixth Coyotes pick, 116th overall) of NHL entry draft (June 27, 1998).

		REGULAR SEASON							PLAYOFFS						
Season Team	League	Gms.	Min	W	L	T	GA	SO	Avg.	Gms.	Min.	W	L	GA	SO	Avg.
96-97—Dubuque-Lincoln	USHL	52	2979	...	...	...	185	1	3.72	—	—	—	—	—	—	—
97-98—Lincoln	USHL	45	2609	...	...	...	135	1	3.10	—	—	—	—	—	—	—

BOUCK, TYLER — RW — STARS

PERSONAL: Born January 13, 1980, in Camrose, Alta. ... 6-0/185. ... Shoots left.
TRANSACTIONS/CAREER NOTES: Selected by Dallas Stars in second round (second Stars pick, 57th overall) of NHL entry draft (June 27, 1998).

		REGULAR SEASON					PLAYOFFS				
Season Team	League	Gms.	G	A	Pts.	PIM	Gms.	G	A	Pts.	PIM
96-97—Prince George	WHL	12	0	2	2	11	—	—	—	—	—
97-98—Prince George	WHL	65	11	26	37	90	11	1	0	1	21

BRENNAN, KIP — D — KINGS

PERSONAL: Born August 27, 1980, in Kingston, Ont. ... 6-4/196. ... Shoots left.
TRANSACTIONS/CAREER NOTES: Selected by Los Angeles Kings in fourth round (fourth Kings pick, 103rd overall) of NHL entry draft (June 27, 1998).

		REGULAR SEASON					PLAYOFFS				
Season Team	League	Gms.	G	A	Pts.	PIM	Gms.	G	A	Pts.	PIM
96-97—Windsor	OHL	42	0	10	10	156	5	0	1	1	16
97-98—Windsor	OHL	24	0	7	7	103	—	—	—	—	—
—Sudbury	OHL	24	0	3	3	85	—	—	—	—	—

BRUNEL, CRAIG — RW — PREDATORS

PERSONAL: Born November 12, 1979, in Winnipeg. ... 6-0/201. ... Shoots right.
TRANSACTIONS/CAREER NOTES: Selected by Nashville Predators in sixth round (sixth Predators pick, 147th overall) of NHL entry draft (June 27, 1998).

		REGULAR SEASON					PLAYOFFS				
Season Team	League	Gms.	G	A	Pts.	PIM	Gms.	G	A	Pts.	PIM
96-97—Prince Albert	WHL	57	5	2	7	208	4	0	0	0	13
97-98—Prince Albert	WHL	58	6	12	18	247	—	—	—	—	—

BURNHAM, ANDY   RW   ISLANDERS

PERSONAL: Born July 2, 1980, in New Lidkeard, Ont. ... 6-4/201. ... Shoots right.
TRANSACTIONS/CAREER NOTES: Selected by New York Islanders in fourth round (third Islanders pick, 95th overall) of NHL entry draft (June 27, 1998).

		REGULAR SEASON					PLAYOFFS				
Season Team	League	Gms.	G	A	Pts.	PIM	Gms.	G	A	Pts.	PIM
97-98—Plymouth	OHL	28	1	3	4	55	—	—	—	—	—
—Windsor	OHL	10	1	1	2	23	—	—	—	—	—

BUT, ANTON   LW   DEVILS

PERSONAL: Born July 3, 1980, in Kharkov, U.S.S.R. ... 6-1/187. ... Shoots right.
TRANSACTIONS/CAREER NOTES: Selected by New Jersey Devils in fifth round (seventh Devils pick, 119th overall) of NHL entry draft (June 27, 1998).

		REGULAR SEASON					PLAYOFFS				
Season Team	League	Gms.	G	A	Pts.	PIM	Gms.	G	A	Pts.	PIM
95-96—Torpedo-2 Yaroslavl	CIS Div. II	60	30	12	42	10	—	—	—	—	—
96-97—Torpedo-2 Yaroslavl	Rus. Div. III	70	30	20	50	20	—	—	—	—	—
97-98—Torpedo-2 Yaroslavl	Rus. Div. II	48	12	5	17	28	—	—	—	—	—

CABANA, PAUL   RW   CANUCKS

PERSONAL: Born September 28, 1978. ... 6-0/180.
TRANSACTIONS/CAREER NOTES: Selected by Vancouver Canucks in sixth round (eighth Canucks pick, 149th overall) of NHL entry draft (June 27, 1998).

		REGULAR SEASON					PLAYOFFS				
Season Team	League	Gms.	G	A	Pts.	PIM	Gms.	G	A	Pts.	PIM
97-98—Fort McMurray	AJHL	50	48	32	80	112	—	—	—	—	—

CAMERON, DAVID   C   PENGUINS

PERSONAL: Born April 27, 1980, in Winnipeg. ... 6-1/180. ... Shoots right.
TRANSACTIONS/CAREER NOTES: Selected by Pittsburgh Penguins in third round (third Penguins pick, 80th overall) of NHL entry draft (June 27, 1998).

		REGULAR SEASON					PLAYOFFS				
Season Team	League	Gms.	G	A	Pts.	PIM	Gms.	G	A	Pts.	PIM
96-97—Lethbridge	WHL	38	3	3	6	5	—	—	—	—	—
—Prince Albert	WHL	18	3	4	7	11	3	0	2	2	0
97-98—Prince Albert	WHL	69	20	36	56	42	—	—	—	—	—

CHEECHOO, JONATHAN   RW   SHARKS

PERSONAL: Born July 15, 1980, in Moose Factory, Ont. ... 6-0/205. ... Shoots right.
TRANSACTIONS/CAREER NOTES: Selected by San Jose Sharks in second round (second Sharks pick, 29th overall) of NHL entry draft (June 27, 1998).

		REGULAR SEASON					PLAYOFFS				
Season Team	League	Gms.	G	A	Pts.	PIM	Gms.	G	A	Pts.	PIM
96-97—Kitchener Jr. B	OHA	43	35	41	76	33	—	—	—	—	—
97-98—Belleville	OHL	64	31	45	76	62	10	4	2	6	10

CHOUINARD, ERIC   C   CANADIENS

PERSONAL: Born July 8, 1980, in Atlanta. ... 6-2/195. ... Shoots left. ... Son of Guy Chouinard, center with Atlanta/Calgary Flames (1974-75 through 1982-83); and cousin of Marc Chouinard, center, Mighty Ducks of Anaheim system.
TRANSACTIONS/CAREER NOTES: Selected by Montreal Canadiens in first round (first Canadiens pick, 16th overall) of NHL entry draft (June 27, 1998).

		REGULAR SEASON					PLAYOFFS				
Season Team	League	Gms.	G	A	Pts.	PIM	Gms.	G	A	Pts.	PIM
97-98—Quebec	QMJHL	68	41	42	83	18	14	7	10	17	6

CHOUINARD, MATHIEU   G   SENATORS

PERSONAL: Born April 11, 1980, in Laval, Que. ... 6-1/200. ... Catches left.
TRANSACTIONS/CAREER NOTES: Selected by Ottawa Senators in first round (first Senators pick, 15th overall) of NHL entry draft (June 27, 1998).

		REGULAR SEASON							PLAYOFFS						
Season Team	League	Gms.	Min	W	L	T	GA	SO	Avg.	Gms.	Min.	W	L	GA	SO	Avg.
96-97—Shawinigan	QMJHL	17	793	4	7	1	51	0	3.86	4	264	1	3	15	0	3.42
97-98—Shawinigan	QMJHL	55	3055	*32	18	3	142	2	2.79	6	348	2	4	24	0	4.14

CHUBAROV, ARTEM — C — CANUCKS

PERSONAL: Born December 13, 1979, in Gorky, U.S.S.R. ... 6-1/189. ... Shoots left.
TRANSACTIONS/CAREER NOTES: Selected by Vancouver Canucks in second round (second Canucks pick, 31st overall) of NHL entry draft (June 27, 1998).

		REGULAR SEASON					PLAYOFFS				
Season Team	League	Gms.	G	A	Pts.	PIM	Gms.	G	A	Pts.	PIM
94-95—Torpedo Nizhny Novgorod	CIS Jr.	60	20	30	50	20	—	—	—	—	—
95-96—Torpedo Nizhny Novgorod	CIS Jr.	60	22	25	47	20	—	—	—	—	—
96-97—Torpedo-2 Nizhny Novgorod	Rus. Div. III	40	24	5	29	16	—	—	—	—	—
—Torpedo Nizhny Novgorod	Rus. Div. II	15	1	1	2	8	—	—	—	—	—
97-98—Dynamo Moscow	Russian	30	1	4	5	4	—	—	—	—	—

CLAUSON, KEVIN — D — ISLANDERS

PERSONAL: Born November 13, 1978, in Lebanon, N.H. ... 6-5/210. ... Shoots left.
COLLEGE: Western Michigan.
TRANSACTIONS/CAREER NOTES: Selected by New York Islanders in sixth round (fifth Islanders pick, 155th overall) of NHL entry draft (June 27, 1998).

		REGULAR SEASON					PLAYOFFS				
Season Team	League	Gms.	G	A	Pts.	PIM	Gms.	G	A	Pts.	PIM
97-98—Western Michigan U.	CCHA	36	1	1	2	56	—	—	—	—	—

COALTER, BRANDON — LW — SHARKS

PERSONAL: Born June 22, 1978, in Richmond Hill, Ont. ... 6-2/201. ... Shoots left.
TRANSACTIONS/CAREER NOTES: Selected by San Jose Sharks in fifth round (sixth Sharks pick, 127th overall) of NHL entry draft (June 27, 1998).

		REGULAR SEASON					PLAYOFFS				
Season Team	League	Gms.	G	A	Pts.	PIM	Gms.	G	A	Pts.	PIM
95-96—Oshawa	OHL	37	1	5	6	40	5	0	0	0	0
96-97—Oshawa	OHL	63	4	9	13	98	18	2	1	3	12
97-98—Oshawa	OHL	64	8	13	21	143	7	3	3	6	6

COLE, ERIK — LW — HURRICANES

PERSONAL: Born November 6, 1978, in Oswego, N.Y. ... 6-0/185. ... Shoots left.
HIGH SCHOOL: Oswego (N.Y.).
COLLEGE: Clarkson (N.Y.).
TRANSACTIONS/CAREER NOTES: Selected by Carolina Hurricanes in third round (third Hurricanes pick, 71st overall) of NHL entry draft (June 27, 1998).

		REGULAR SEASON					PLAYOFFS				
Season Team	League	Gms.	G	A	Pts.	PIM	Gms.	G	A	Pts.	PIM
96-97—Des Moines	USHL	48	30	34	64	185	—	—	—	—	—
97-98—Clarkson	ECAC	34	11	20	31	55	—	—	—	—	—

COPLEY, RANDY — RW — RANGERS

PERSONAL: Born October 4, 1979, in Inverness, Nova Scotia. ... 6-1/205. ... Shoots right.
TRANSACTIONS/CAREER NOTES: Selected by New York Rangers in second round (second Rangers pick, 40th overall) of NHL entry draft (June 27, 1998).

		REGULAR SEASON					PLAYOFFS				
Season Team	League	Gms.	G	A	Pts.	PIM	Gms.	G	A	Pts.	PIM
96-97—Granby	QMJHL	70	7	14	21	114	5	0	0	0	5
97-98—Cape Breton	QMJHL	69	34	42	76	194	4	0	0	0	16

CORRINET, CHRIS — RW — CAPITALS

PERSONAL: Born October 29, 1978, in Derby, Conn. ... 6-3/220. ... Shoots right.
HIGH SCHOOL: Deerfield (Mass.) Academy.
COLLEGE: Princeton.
TRANSACTIONS/CAREER NOTES: Selected by Washington Capitals in fourth round (fourth Capitals pick, 107th overall) of NHL entry draft (June 27, 1998).

		REGULAR SEASON					PLAYOFFS				
Season Team	League	Gms.	G	A	Pts.	PIM	Gms.	G	A	Pts.	PIM
96-97—Deerfield	USHSE	16	6	15	21	10	—	—	—	—	—
97-98—Princeton University	ECAC	31	3	6	9	22	—	—	—	—	—

CRUZ, JOMAR — G — CAPITALS

PERSONAL: Born April 5, 1980, in The Pas, Man. ... 6-1/177. ... Catches left.
TRANSACTIONS/CAREER NOTES: Selected by Washington Capitals in second round (first Capitals pick, 49th overall) of NHL entry draft (June 27, 1998).

Season Team	League	REGULAR SEASON Gms.	Min	W	L	T	GA	SO	Avg.	PLAYOFFS Gms.	Min.	W	L	GA	SO	Avg.
96-97—Notre Dame	SMHL	20	1107	...	...	...	...	2	3.84	—	—	—	—	—	—	—
97-98—Brandon	WHL	20	1596	16	9	1	81	3	3.05	14	749	7	6	41	0	3.28

DAGENAIS, PIERRE — LW — DEVILS

PERSONAL: Born March 4, 1978, in Blainville, Que. ... 6-4/200. ... Shoots left. ... Name pronounced da-zhih-NAY.
TRANSACTIONS/CAREER NOTES: Selected by New Jersey Devils in second round (fourth Devils pick, 47th overall) of NHL entry draft (June 22, 1996). ... Returned to draft pool by Devils and selected by Devils in fourth round (sixth Devils pick, 105th overall) of NHL entry draft (June 27, 1998).
HONORS: Named to Can.HL All-Rookie team (1995-96). ... Named to QMJHL All-Rookie team (1995-96). ... Named to QMJHL All-Star second team (1997-98).

Season Team	League	REGULAR SEASON Gms.	G	A	Pts.	PIM	PLAYOFFS Gms.	G	A	Pts.	PIM
95-96—Moncton	QMJHL	67	43	25	68	59	—	—	—	—	—
96-97—Moncton	QMJHL	6	4	2	6	0	—	—	—	—	—
—Laval	QMJHL	37	16	14	30	22	—	—	—	—	—
—Rouyn-Noranda	QMJHL	27	21	8	29	22	—	—	—	—	—
97-98—Rouyn-Noranda	QMJHL	60	*66	67	133	50	6	6	2	8	2

DARBY, REGAN — D — CANUCKS

PERSONAL: Born July 17, 1980, in Estevan, Sask. ... 6-2/200. ... Shoots left.
TRANSACTIONS/CAREER NOTES: Selected by Vancouver Canucks in fourth round (fifth Canucks pick, 90th overall) of NHL entry draft (June 27, 1998).

Season Team	League	REGULAR SEASON Gms.	G	A	Pts.	PIM	PLAYOFFS Gms.	G	A	Pts.	PIM
97-98—Spokane	WHL	7	0	1	1	28	—	—	—	—	—
—Tri-City	WHL	32	1	2	3	125	—	—	—	—	—

DATSYUK, PAVEL — C — RED WINGS

PERSONAL: Born July 20, 1978, in Sverdlovsk, U.S.S.R. ... 5-11/180. ... Shoots left.
TRANSACTIONS/CAREER NOTES: Selected by Detroit Red Wings in sixth round (eighth Red Wings pick, 171st overall) of NHL entry draft (June 27, 1998).

Season Team	League	REGULAR SEASON Gms.	G	A	Pts.	PIM	PLAYOFFS Gms.	G	A	Pts.	PIM
96-97—Spartak Yekaterinburg	Russian	18	2	2	4	4	—	—	—	—	—
—Spartak Yekaterinburg	Rus. Div. II	36	12	10	22	12	—	—	—	—	—
97-98—Dynamo-Energiya	Russian	24	3	5	8	4	—	—	—	—	—
—Dynamo-Energiya	Rus. Div. II	22	7	8	15	4	—	—	—	—	—

DAVISON, ROB — D — SHARKS

PERSONAL: Born May 1, 1980, in St. Catharines, Ont. ... 6-2/210. ... Shoots left.
TRANSACTIONS/CAREER NOTES: Selected by San Jose Sharks in fourth round (fourth Sharks pick, 98th overall) of NHL entry draft (June 27, 1998).

Season Team	League	REGULAR SEASON Gms.	G	A	Pts.	PIM	PLAYOFFS Gms.	G	A	Pts.	PIM
96-97—St. Michael's	Tier II Jr. A	45	2	6	8	93	—	—	—	—	—
97-98—North Bay	OHL	59	0	11	11	200	—	—	—	—	—

DELEEUW, ADAM — LW — RED WINGS

PERSONAL: Born February 29, 1980, in Brampton, Ont. ... 6-0/206. ... Shoots left.
TRANSACTIONS/CAREER NOTES: Selected by Detroit Red Wings in sixth round (seventh Red Wings pick, 151st overall) of NHL entry draft (June 27, 1998).

Season Team	League	REGULAR SEASON Gms.	G	A	Pts.	PIM	PLAYOFFS Gms.	G	A	Pts.	PIM
96-97—Brampton	Tier II Jr. A	45	11	17	28	97	—	—	—	—	—
97-98—Barrie	OHL	56	10	6	16	224	—	—	—	—	—

DesROCHERS, PATRICK — G — COYOTES

PERSONAL: Born October 27, 1979, in Penetang, Ont. ... 6-3/195. ... Catches left.
TRANSACTIONS/CAREER NOTES: Selected by Phoenix Coyotes in first round (first Coyotes pick, 14th overall) of NHL entry draft (June 27, 1998).

Season Team	League	REGULAR SEASON Gms.	Min	W	L	T	GA	SO	Avg.	PLAYOFFS Gms.	Min.	W	L	GA	SO	Avg.
95-96—Sarnia	OHL	29	1265	12	6	2	96	0	4.55	3	71	0	1	5	0	4.23
96-97—Sarnia	OHL	50	2667	22	17	4	154	1	3.46	11	576	6	5	42	0	4.38
97-98—Sarnia	OHL	56	3205	26	17	11	179	1	3.35	4	160	1	2	12	0	4.50

DiPENTA, JOE   D   PANTHERS

PERSONAL: Born February 25, 1979, in Barrie, Ont. ... 6-2/205. ... Shoots right.
COLLEGE: Boston University.
TRANSACTIONS/CAREER NOTES: Selected by Florida Panthers in third round (second Panthers pick, 61st overall) of NHL entry draft (June 27, 1998).

		REGULAR SEASON					PLAYOFFS				
Season Team	League	Gms.	G	A	Pts.	PIM	Gms.	G	A	Pts.	PIM
97-98—Boston University	Hockey East	38	2	16	18	50	—	—	—	—	—

DOPITA, JIRI   C   ISLANDERS

PERSONAL: Born December 2, 1968, in Sumperk, Czechoslovakia. ... 6-3/209. ... Shoots left.
TRANSACTIONS/CAREER NOTES: Selected by Boston Bruins in sixth round (fourth Bruins pick, 133rd overall) of NHL entry draft (June 20, 1992). ... Returned to draft pool by Bruins and selected by New York Islanders in fifth round (fourth Islanders pick, 123rd overall) of NHL entry draft (June 27, 1998).

		REGULAR SEASON					PLAYOFFS				
Season Team	League	Gms.	G	A	Pts.	PIM	Gms.	G	A	Pts.	PIM
88-89—DS Olomouc	Czech Dv.II					Statistics unavailable.					
89-90—Dukla Jihlava	Czech.	5	1	2	3	...	—	—	—	—	—
90-91—DS Olomouc	Czech.	42	11	13	24	...	—	—	—	—	—
91-92—DS Olomouc	Czech.	38	23	20	43	...	—	—	—	—	—
92-93—DS Olomouc	Czech.	28	12	17	29	...	—	—	—	—	—
—Eisbaren Berlin	Germany	11	7	8	15	49	4	3	5	8	5
94-95—Eisbaren Berlin	Germany	42	28	40	68	55	—	—	—	—	—
95-96—Petra Vsetin	Czech Rep.	38	19	20	39	20	13	9	11	20	10
96-97—Petra Vsetin	Czech Rep.	52	30	31	61	55	10	7	4	11	22
97-98—Petra Vsetin	Czech Rep.	50	21	34	55	64	10	12	6	18	4
—Czech Rep. Olympic team	Int'l	6	1	2	3	0	—	—	—	—	—

DWYER, GORDIE   LW   CANADIENS

PERSONAL: Born January 25, 1978, in Dalhousie, N.B. ... 6-2/218. ... Shoots left.
TRANSACTIONS/CAREER NOTES: Selected by St. Louis Blues in third round (second Blues pick, 67th overall) of NHL entry draft (June 22, 1996). ... Returned to draft pool by Blues and selected by Montreal Canadiens in sixth round (fifth Canadiens pick, 152nd overall) of NHL entry draft (June 27, 1998).

		REGULAR SEASON					PLAYOFFS				
Season Team	League	Gms.	G	A	Pts.	PIM	Gms.	G	A	Pts.	PIM
94-95—Hull	QMJHL	57	3	7	10	204	17	1	3	4	54
95-96—Hull	QMJHL	25	5	9	14	199	—	—	—	—	—
—Laval	QMJHL	22	5	17	22	72	—	—	—	—	—
—Beauport	QMJHL	22	4	9	13	87	20	3	5	8	104
96-97—Drummondville	QMJHL	66	21	48	69	391	8	6	1	7	39
97-98—Quebec	QMJHL	59	18	27	45	365	14	4	9	13	67

ELLIOTT, PAUL   D   OILERS

PERSONAL: Born June 2, 1980, in White Rock, B.C. ... 6-0/202. ... Shoots left.
TRANSACTIONS/CAREER NOTES: Selected by Edmonton Oilers in fifth round (fifth Oilers pick, 128th overall) of NHL entry draft (June 27, 1998).

		REGULAR SEASON					PLAYOFFS				
Season Team	League	Gms.	G	A	Pts.	PIM	Gms.	G	A	Pts.	PIM
96-97—Lethbridge	WHL	46	0	8	8	17	1	0	0	0	0
97-98—Lethbridge	WHL	48	4	18	22	35	—	—	—	—	—
—Medicine Hat	WHL	24	7	9	16	12	—	—	—	—	—

ERSKINE, JOHN   D   STARS

PERSONAL: Born June 26, 1980, in Kingston, Ont. ... 6-4/197. ... Shoots left.
TRANSACTIONS/CAREER NOTES: Selected by Dallas Stars in second round (first Stars pick, 39th overall) of NHL entry draft (June 27, 1998).
HONORS: Named to OHL All-Rookie second team (1997-98).

		REGULAR SEASON					PLAYOFFS				
Season Team	League	Gms.	G	A	Pts.	PIM	Gms.	G	A	Pts.	PIM
96-97—Quinte	Tier II Jr. A	48	4	16	20	241	—	—	—	—	—
97-98—London	OHL	55	0	9	9	205	16	0	5	5	25

ETTINGER, TREVOR   D   OILERS

PERSONAL: Born July 13, 1980, in Truro, Nova Scotia. ... 6-5/240. ... Shoots left.
TRANSACTIONS/CAREER NOTES: Selected by Edmonton Oilers in sixth round (seventh Oilers pick, 159th overall) of NHL entry draft (June 27, 1998).

		REGULAR SEASON					PLAYOFFS				
Season Team	League	Gms.	G	A	Pts.	PIM	Gms.	G	A	Pts.	PIM
97-98—Cape Breton	QMJHL	50	1	2	3	181	3	0	0	0	7

FADRNY, JAN   C   PENGUINS

PERSONAL: Born June 14, 1980, in Brno, Czechoslovakia. ... 6-0/176. ... Shoots right.
TRANSACTIONS/CAREER NOTES: Selected by Pittsburgh Penguins in sixth round (sixth Penguins pick, 169th overall) of NHL entry draft (June 27, 1998).

		REGULAR SEASON					PLAYOFFS				
Season Team	League	Gms.	G	A	Pts.	PIM	Gms.	G	A	Pts.	PIM
95-96—Kometa Brno Jrs.	Czech Rep.	36	22	15	37	26	—	—	—	—	—
96-97—HC Olomouc Jrs.	Czech Rep.	38	16	24	40	32	—	—	—	—	—
97-98—Slavia Praha Jrs.....................	Czech Rep.	14	7	4	11	12	—	—	—	—	—
—Slavia Praha........................	Czech Rep.	18	1	1	2	2	3	0	0	0	4

FATA, RICO   RW   FLAMES

PERSONAL: Born February 12, 1980, in Sault Ste. Marie, Ont. ... 5-11/202. ... Shoots left.
TRANSACTIONS/CAREER NOTES: Selected by Calgary Flames in first round (first Flames pick, sixth overall) of NHL entry draft (June 27, 1998).

		REGULAR SEASON					PLAYOFFS				
Season Team	League	Gms.	G	A	Pts.	PIM	Gms.	G	A	Pts.	PIM
95-96—Sault Ste. Marie	OMJHL	62	11	15	26	52	—	—	—	—	—
96-97—London	OHL	59	19	34	53	76	—	—	—	—	—
97-98—London	OHL	64	43	33	76	110	16	9	5	14	*49

FISCHER, JIRI   D   RED WINGS

PERSONAL: Born July 31, 1980, in Horovice, Czechoslovakia. ... 6-5/210. ... Shoots left.
TRANSACTIONS/CAREER NOTES: Selected by Detroit Red Wings in first round (first Red Wings pick, 25th overall) of NHL entry draft (June 27, 1998).

		REGULAR SEASON					PLAYOFFS				
Season Team	League	Gms.	G	A	Pts.	PIM	Gms.	G	A	Pts.	PIM
95-96—Poldi Kladno	Czech Rep.	39	6	10	16	...	—	—	—	—	—
96-97—Poldi Kladno	Czech Rep.	38	11	16	27	...	—	—	—	—	—
97-98—Hull	QMJHL	70	3	19	22	112	11	1	4	5	16

FISHER, MIKE   C   SENATORS

PERSONAL: Born June 5, 1980, in Peterborough, Ont. ... 6-0/180. ... Shoots right.
TRANSACTIONS/CAREER NOTES: Selected by Ottawa Senators in second round (second Senators pick, 44th overall) of NHL entry draft (June 27, 1998).

		REGULAR SEASON					PLAYOFFS				
Season Team	League	Gms.	G	A	Pts.	PIM	Gms.	G	A	Pts.	PIM
96-97—Peterborough..........................	Tier II Jr. A	51	26	30	56	33	—	—	—	—	—
97-98—Sudbury.................................	OHL	66	24	25	49	65	9	2	2	4	13

FLINN, RYAN   LW   DEVILS

PERSONAL: Born April 20, 1980, in Halifax, Nova Scotia. ... 6-4/210. ... Shoots left.
TRANSACTIONS/CAREER NOTES: Selected by New Jersey Devils in fifth round (eighth Devils pick, 143rd overall) of NHL entry draft (June 27, 1998).

		REGULAR SEASON					PLAYOFFS				
Season Team	League	Gms.	G	A	Pts.	PIM	Gms.	G	A	Pts.	PIM
96-97—Laval	QMJHL	23	3	2	5	66	2	0	0	0	0
97-98—Laval	QMJHL	59	4	12	16	217	15	1	0	1	63

FORBES, IAN   D   FLYERS

PERSONAL: Born August 2, 1980, in Brampton, Ont. ... 6-6/180. ... Shoots left.
TRANSACTIONS/CAREER NOTES: Selected by Philadelphia Flyers in second round (third Flyers pick, 51st overall) of NHL entry draft (June 27, 1998).

		REGULAR SEASON					PLAYOFFS				
Season Team	League	Gms.	G	A	Pts.	PIM	Gms.	G	A	Pts.	PIM
97-98—Guelph	OHL	61	2	3	5	164	12	0	0	0	16

GAGNE, SIMON   C   FLYERS

PERSONAL: Born February 29, 1980, in Ste. Foy, Quebec. ... 6-0/165. ... Shoots left.
TRANSACTIONS/CAREER NOTES: Selected by Philadelphia Flyers in first round (first Flyers pick, 22nd overall) of NHL entry draft (June 27, 1998).

		REGULAR SEASON					PLAYOFFS				
Season Team	League	Gms.	G	A	Pts.	PIM	Gms.	G	A	Pts.	PIM
96-97—Beauport	QMJHL	51	9	22	31	39	—	—	—	—	—
97-98—Quebec	QMJHL	53	30	39	69	26	12	11	5	16	23

GAUVREAU, BRENT — RW — FLAMES

PERSONAL: Born June 29, 1980, in Sudbury, Ont. ... 6-3/191. ... Shoots right.
TRANSACTIONS/CAREER NOTES: Selected by Calgary Flames in fifth round (sixth Flames pick, 120th overall) of NHL entry draft (June 27, 1998).

Season Team	League	Gms.	G	A	Pts.	PIM	Gms.	G	A	Pts.	PIM
		REGULAR SEASON					PLAYOFFS				
96-97—Oshawa	OHL	59	8	13	21	13	18	1	5	6	2
97-98—Oshawa	OHL	66	25	42	67	39	7	3	1	4	2

GIONTA, BRIAN — RW — DEVILS

PERSONAL: Born January 18, 1979, in Rochester, N.Y. ... 5-7/160. ... Shoots right.
COLLEGE: Boston College.
TRANSACTIONS/CAREER NOTES: Selected by New Jersey Devils in third round (fourth Devils pick, 82nd overall) of NHL entry draft (June 27, 1998).
HONORS: Named to NCAA All-America East second team (1997-98). ... Named to Hockey East All-Star second team (1997-98). ... Named Hockey East Rookie of the Year (1997-98).

Season Team	League	Gms.	G	A	Pts.	PIM	Gms.	G	A	Pts.	PIM
		REGULAR SEASON					PLAYOFFS				
97-98—Boston College	ECAC	40	30	32	62	44	—	—	—	—	—

GIRARD, JONATHAN — D — BRUINS

PERSONAL: Born May 27, 1980, in Joliette, Que. ... 5-11/192. ... Shoots right.
TRANSACTIONS/CAREER NOTES: Selected by Boston Bruins in second round (first Bruins pick, 48th overall) of NHL entry draft (June 27, 1998).
HONORS: Named to QMJHL All-Rookie team (1996-97). ... Named to QMJHL All-Star second team (1997-98).

Season Team	League	Gms.	G	A	Pts.	PIM	Gms.	G	A	Pts.	PIM
		REGULAR SEASON					PLAYOFFS				
96-97—Laval	QMJHL	38	11	21	32	23	3	0	3	3	0
97-98—Laval	QMJHL	64	20	47	67	44	16	2	16	18	13

GOLDADE, AARON — C — SABRES

PERSONAL: Born July 30, 1980, in Prince Albert, Sask. ... 6-0/180. ... Shoots left.
TRANSACTIONS/CAREER NOTES: Selected by Buffalo Sabres in fifth round (sixth Sabres pick, 137th overall) of NHL entry draft (June 27, 1998).

Season Team	League	Gms.	G	A	Pts.	PIM	Gms.	G	A	Pts.	PIM
		REGULAR SEASON					PLAYOFFS				
96-97—Brandon	WHL	59	4	10	14	51	6	0	1	1	0
97-98—Brandon	WHL	66	19	16	35	58	16	0	2	2	22

GOMEZ, SCOTT — C — DEVILS

PERSONAL: Born December 23, 1979, in Anchorage, Alaska. ... 5-11/180. ... Shoots left.
TRANSACTIONS/CAREER NOTES: Selected by New Jersey Devils in first round (second Devils pick, 27th overall) of NHL entry draft (June 27, 1998).
HONORS: Named to WHL All-Rookie Team (1997-98).

Season Team	League	Gms.	G	A	Pts.	PIM	Gms.	G	A	Pts.	PIM
		REGULAR SEASON					PLAYOFFS				
96-97—Surrey Jr. A	BCJHL	56	48	76	124	94	—	—	—	—	—
97-98—Tri-City	WHL	45	12	37	49	57	—	—	—	—	—

HEEREMA, JEFF — RW — HURRICANES

PERSONAL: Born January 17, 1980, in Thunder Bay, Ont.. ... 6-1/171. ... Shoots right.
TRANSACTIONS/CAREER NOTES: Selected by Carolina Hurricanes in first round (first Hurricanes pick, 11th overall) of NHL entry draft (June 27, 1998).
HONORS: Named to OHL Second All-Rookie Team (1997-98).

Season Team	League	Gms.	G	A	Pts.	PIM	Gms.	G	A	Pts.	PIM
		REGULAR SEASON					PLAYOFFS				
97-98—Sarnia	OHL	63	32	40	72	88	5	4	1	5	10

HENRICH, MICHAEL — RW — OILERS

PERSONAL: Born March 3, 1980, in Thornhill, Ont. ... 6-2/206. ... Shoots right.
TRANSACTIONS/CAREER NOTES: Selected by Edmonton Oilers in first round (first Oilers pick, 13th overall) of NHL entry draft (June 27, 1998).

Season Team	League	Gms.	G	A	Pts.	PIM	Gms.	G	A	Pts.	PIM
		REGULAR SEASON					PLAYOFFS				
96-97—Barrie	OHL	52	9	15	24	19	9	0	5	5	0
97-98—Barrie	OHL	66	41	22	63	75	5	1	3	4	4

HENRY, ALEX   D   OILERS

PERSONAL: Born October 18, 1979, in Elliot Lake, Ont. ... 6-5/216. ... Shoots left.
TRANSACTIONS/CAREER NOTES: Selected by Edmonton Oilers in third round (second Oilers pick, 67th overall) of NHL entry draft (June 27, 1998).

		REGULAR SEASON					PLAYOFFS				
Season Team	League	Gms.	G	A	Pts.	PIM	Gms.	G	A	Pts.	PIM
96-97—London	OHL	61	1	10	11	65	—	—	—	—	—
97-98—London	OHL	62	5	9	14	97	16	0	3	3	14

HOBDAY, BRENT   C/LW   RED WINGS

PERSONAL: Born August 26, 1979, in Winnipeg. ... 6-1/192. ... Shoots left.
TRANSACTIONS/CAREER NOTES: Selected by Detroit Red Wings in fourth round (fifth Red Wings pick, 111th overall) of NHL entry draft (June 27, 1998).

		REGULAR SEASON					PLAYOFFS				
Season Team	League	Gms.	G	A	Pts.	PIM	Gms.	G	A	Pts.	PIM
96-97—Moose Jaw	WHL	45	5	7	12	26	2	0	0	0	0
97-98—Moose Jaw	WHL	68	21	22	43	122	4	2	0	2	4

HODSON, JAMIE   G   MAPLE LEAFS

PERSONAL: Born April 8, 1980, in Brandon, Man. ... 6-1/180. ... Catches left.
TRANSACTIONS/CAREER NOTES: Selected by Toronto Maple Leafs in third round (third Maple Leafs pick, 69th overall) of NHL entry draft (June 27, 1998).

		REGULAR SEASON							PLAYOFFS						
Season Team	League	Gms.	Min	W	L	T	GA	SO	Avg.	Gms.	Min.	W	L	GA	SO	Avg.
97-98—Brandon	WHL	20	964	12	2	2	52	2	3.24	6	337	5	0	16	0	2.85

HOLDRIDGE, KEVIN   D   HURRICANES

PERSONAL: Born September 9, 1980, in Syracuse, N.Y. ... 6-2/202. ... Shoots left.
TRANSACTIONS/CAREER NOTES: Selected by Carolina Hurricanes in third round (second Hurricanes pick, 70th overall) of NHL entry draft (June 27, 1998).

		REGULAR SEASON					PLAYOFFS				
Season Team	League	Gms.	G	A	Pts.	PIM	Gms.	G	A	Pts.	PIM
96-97—Detroit	OHL	55	0	9	9	49	5	0	0	0	2
97-98—Plymouth	OHL	61	4	15	19	106	15	0	3	3	30

HORCOFF, SHAWN   C   OILERS

PERSONAL: Born September 17, 1978, in Trail, B.C. ... 6-1/194. ... Shoots left.
HIGH SCHOOL: Stanley Humphres Secondary (Castlegar, B.C.).
COLLEGE: Michigan State.
TRANSACTIONS/CAREER NOTES: Selected by Edmonton Oilers in fourth round (third Oilers pick, 99th overall) of NHL entry draft (June 27, 1998).

		REGULAR SEASON					PLAYOFFS				
Season Team	League	Gms.	G	A	Pts.	PIM	Gms.	G	A	Pts.	PIM
96-97—Michigan State	CCHA	40	10	13	23	20	—	—	—	—	—
97-98—Michigan State	CCHA	34	14	13	27	50	—	—	—	—	—

HORNUNG, TODD   C   CAPITALS

PERSONAL: Born September 3, 1980, in Swift Current, Sask. ... 6-0/200. ... Shoots left.
TRANSACTIONS/CAREER NOTES: Selected by Washington Capitals in third round (second Capitals pick, 59th overall) of NHL entry draft (June 27, 1998).

		REGULAR SEASON					PLAYOFFS				
Season Team	League	Gms.	G	A	Pts.	PIM	Gms.	G	A	Pts.	PIM
96-97—Portland	WHL	59	3	3	6	51	6	0	0	0	0
97-98—Portland	WHL	64	19	18	37	96	16	6	6	12	26

HUNTER, TRENT   RW   MIGHTY DUCKS

PERSONAL: Born July 5, 1980, in Red Deer, Alta. ... 6-3/191. ... Shoots right.
TRANSACTIONS/CAREER NOTES: Selected by Mighty Ducks of Anaheim in sixth round (fourth Mighty Ducks pick, 150th overall) of NHL entry draft (June 27, 1998).

		REGULAR SEASON					PLAYOFFS				
Season Team	League	Gms.	G	A	Pts.	PIM	Gms.	G	A	Pts.	PIM
96-97—Red Deer	AMHL	42	30	25	55	50	—	—	—	—	—
97-98—Prince George	WHL	60	13	14	27	34	8	1	0	1	4

HUSKINS, KENT   D   BLACKHAWKS

PERSONAL: Born May 4, 1979, in Ottawa. ... 6-2/190. ... Shoots left.
COLLEGE: Clarkson (N.Y.).
TRANSACTIONS/CAREER NOTES: Selected by Chicago Blackhawks in sixth round (third Blackhawks pick, 156th overall) of NHL entry draft (June 27, 1998).

		REGULAR SEASON					PLAYOFFS				
Season Team	League	Gms.	G	A	Pts.	PIM	Gms.	G	A	Pts.	PIM
97-98—Clarkson	ECAC	35	2	8	10	46	—	—	—	—	—

JARDINE, RYAN   LW   PANTHERS

PERSONAL: Born March 15, 1980, in Ottawa. ... 6-0/178. ... Shoots left.
TRANSACTIONS/CAREER NOTES: Selected by Florida Panthers in fourth round (fourth Panthers pick, 89th overall) of NHL entry draft (June 27, 1998).
HONORS: Named to OHL All-Rookie first team (1997-98).

		REGULAR SEASON					PLAYOFFS				
Season Team	League	Gms.	G	A	Pts.	PIM	Gms.	G	A	Pts.	PIM
96-97—Kanata Valley	Tier II Jr. A	52	30	27	57	70	—	—	—	—	—
97-98—Sault Ste. Marie	OHL	65	28	32	60	16	—	—	—	—	—

JOKELA, MIKKO   D   DEVILS

PERSONAL: Born March 4, 1980, in Lappeenranta, Finland. ... 6-1/212. ... Shoots right.
TRANSACTIONS/CAREER NOTES: Selected by New Jersey Devils in fourth round (fifth Devils pick, 96th overall) of NHL entry draft (June 27, 1998).

		REGULAR SEASON					PLAYOFFS				
Season Team	League	Gms.	G	A	Pts.	PIM	Gms.	G	A	Pts.	PIM
95-96—KalPa Kuopio	Finland Jr.	11	2	1	3	20	—	—	—	—	—
96-97—KalPa Kuopio	Finland Jr.	45	5	7	12	26	5	1	1	2	4
97-98—Helsinki IFK	Finland	16	0	0	0	0	—	—	—	—	—
—Helsinki IFK	Finland Jr.	22	2	5	7	14	—	—	—	—	—

JONSSON, DAVID   D   CANUCKS

PERSONAL: Born September 29, 1979, in Ornskoldsvik, Sweden. ... 6-0/187. ... Shoots left.
TRANSACTIONS/CAREER NOTES: Selected by Vancouver Canucks in fifth round (sixth Canucks pick, 136th overall) of NHL entry draft (June 27, 1998).

		REGULAR SEASON					PLAYOFFS				
Season Team	League	Gms.	G	A	Pts.	PIM	Gms.	G	A	Pts.	PIM
96-97—Leksand Jrs.	Sweden Jr.	25	3	5	8	...	—	—	—	—	—
97-98—Leksand	Sweden	10	0	0	0	2	—	—	—	—	—
—Leksand Jrs.	Sweden Jr.	23	13	10	23	101	—	—	—	—	—

KALININ, DMITRI   D   SABRES

PERSONAL: Born July 22, 1980, in Chelyabinsk, U.S.S.R. ... 6-2/198. ... Shoots left.
TRANSACTIONS/CAREER NOTES: Selected by Buffalo Sabres in first round (first Sabres pick, 18th overall) of NHL entry draft (June 27, 1998).

		REGULAR SEASON					PLAYOFFS				
Season Team	League	Gms.	G	A	Pts.	PIM	Gms.	G	A	Pts.	PIM
95-96—Traktor Chelyabinsk	CIS Jr.	30	10	10	20	60	—	—	—	—	—
—Nadezhda Chelyabinsk	CIS Div. II	20	0	3	3	10	—	—	—	—	—
96-97—Traktor Chelyabinsk	Russian	2	0	0	0	0	2	0	0	0	0
—Traktor-2 Chelyabinsk	Rus. Div. III	20	0	0	0	10	—	—	—	—	—
97-98—Traktor Chelyabinsk	Russian	26	0	2	2	24	—	—	—	—	—

KANE, BOYD   LW   RANGERS

PERSONAL: Born April 18, 1978, in Swift Current, Sask. ... 6-2/218. ... Shoots left.
TRANSACTIONS/CAREER NOTES: Selected by Pittsburgh Penguins in third round (third Penguins pick, 72nd overall) of NHL entry draft (June 22, 1996). ... Returned to draft pool by Penguins and selected by New York Rangers in fourth round (fourth Rangers pick, 114th overall) of NHL entry draft (June 27, 1998).

		REGULAR SEASON					PLAYOFFS				
Season Team	League	Gms.	G	A	Pts.	PIM	Gms.	G	A	Pts.	PIM
94-95—Regina	WHL	25	6	5	11	6	4	0	0	0	0
95-96—Regina	WHL	72	21	42	63	155	11	5	7	12	12
96-97—Regina	WHL	66	25	50	75	154	5	1	1	2	15
97-98—Regina	WHL	68	48	45	93	133	9	5	7	12	29

KAPANEN, NIKO   C   STARS

PERSONAL: Born April 29, 1978, in Hattula, Finland. ... 5-10/185. ... Shoots left.
TRANSACTIONS/CAREER NOTES: Selected by Dallas Stars in sixth round (fifth Stars pick, 173rd overall) of NHL entry draft (June 27, 1998).

Season Team	League	REGULAR SEASON					PLAYOFFS				
		Gms.	G	A	Pts.	PIM	Gms.	G	A	Pts.	PIM
93-94—HPK Hameenlinna	Finland Jr.	31	17	33	50	34	—	—	—	—	—
94-95—HPK Hameenlinna	Finland Jr.	37	19	44	63	40	—	—	—	—	—
95-96—HPK Hameenlinna	Finland Jr.	26	15	22	37	34	—	—	—	—	—
—HPK Hameenlinna	Finland	7	1	0	1	0	—	—	—	—	—
96-97—HPK Hameenlinna	Finland	41	6	9	15	12	10	4	5	9	2
—HPK Hameenlinna	Finland Jr.	5	1	7	8	2	2	0	1	1	2
97-98—HPK Hameenlinna	Finland	48	8	18	26	44	—	—	—	—	—
—HPK Hameenlinna	Finland Jr.	2	1	1	2	0	—	—	—	—	—

KARLSSON, GABRIEL   C   STARS

PERSONAL: Born January 22, 1980, in Borlange, Sweden. ... 6-1/189. ... Shoots left.
TRANSACTIONS/CAREER NOTES: Selected by Dallas Stars in third round (third Stars pick, 86th overall) of NHL entry draft (June 27, 1998).

Season Team	League	REGULAR SEASON					PLAYOFFS				
		Gms.	G	A	Pts.	PIM	Gms.	G	A	Pts.	PIM
96-97—HV 71 Jonkoping	Sweden Jr.	25	7	9	16	...	—	—	—	—	—
97-98—HV 71 Jonkoping	Sweden Jr.	27	11	15	26	32	—	—	—	—	—
—HV 71 Jonkoping	Sweden	1	0	0	0	0	—	—	—	—	—

KLOUCEK, TOMAS   D   RANGERS

PERSONAL: Born March 7, 1980, in Prague, Czechoslovakia. ... 6-2/205. ... Shoots left.
TRANSACTIONS/CAREER NOTES: Selected by New York Rangers in fifth round (sixth Rangers pick, 131st overall) of NHL entry draft (June 27, 1998).

Season Team	League	REGULAR SEASON					PLAYOFFS				
		Gms.	G	A	Pts.	PIM	Gms.	G	A	Pts.	PIM
95-96—Slavia Praha Jrs.	Czech Rep.	40	2	8	10	...	—	—	—	—	—
96-97—Slavia Praha Jrs.	Czech Rep.	43	4	14	18	44	—	—	—	—	—
97-98—Slavia Praha Jrs.	Czech Rep.	43	1	9	10	...	—	—	—	—	—

KOCH, GEOFF   LW   PREDATORS

PERSONAL: Born June 27, 1979, in Burlington, Va. ... 6-1/190. ... Shoots left.
HIGH SCHOOL: Phillips Exeter (N.H.) Academy.
COLLEGE: Michigan.
TRANSACTIONS/CAREER NOTES: Selected by Nashville Predators in third round (third Predators pick, 85th overall) of NHL entry draft (June 27, 1998).

Season Team	League	REGULAR SEASON					PLAYOFFS				
		Gms.	G	A	Pts.	PIM	Gms.	G	A	Pts.	PIM
96-97—Phillips Exeter	USHS (East)	27	22	38	60	45	—	—	—	—	—
97-98—Univ. of Michigan	CCHA	43	5	6	11	51	—	—	—	—	—

KOTALIK, ALES   RW   SABRES

PERSONAL: Born December 23, 1978, in Jindrichuv Hradec, Czechoslovakia. ... 6-1/194. ... Shoots right.
TRANSACTIONS/CAREER NOTES: Selected by Buffalo Sabres in sixth round (seventh Sabres pick, 164th overall) of NHL entry draft (June 27, 1998).

Season Team	League	REGULAR SEASON					PLAYOFFS				
		Gms.	G	A	Pts.	PIM	Gms.	G	A	Pts.	PIM
93-94—HC Ceske Budejovice Jrs.	Czech Rep.	28	12	12	24	...	—	—	—	—	—
94-95—HC Ceske Budejovice Jrs.	Czech Rep.	36	26	17	43	...	—	—	—	—	—
95-96—HC Ceske Budejovice Jrs.	Czech Rep.	28	6	7	13	...	—	—	—	—	—
96-97—HC Ceske Budejovice Jrs.	Czech Rep.	36	15	16	31	24	—	—	—	—	—
97-98—HC Ceske Budejovice	Czech Rep.	47	9	7	16	14	—	—	—	—	—

KRAFT, MILAN   C   PENGUINS

PERSONAL: Born January 17, 1980, in Plzen, Czechoslovakia. ... 6-2/191. ... Shoots right.
TRANSACTIONS/CAREER NOTES: Selected by Pittsburgh Penguins in first round (first Penguins pick, 23rd overall) of NHL entry draft (June 27, 1998).

Season Team	League	REGULAR SEASON					PLAYOFFS				
		Gms.	G	A	Pts.	PIM	Gms.	G	A	Pts.	PIM
96-97—Plzen Jrs.	Czech Rep.	36	26	17	43	...	—	—	—	—	—
97-98—Plzen Jrs.	Czech Rep.	24	22	23	45	12	—	—	—	—	—

KRISTEK, JAROSLOV   RW   SABRES

PERSONAL: Born March 16, 1980, in Gottwaldov, Czechoslovakia. ... 6-0/183. ... Shoots left.
TRANSACTIONS/CAREER NOTES: Selected by Buffalo Sabres in second round (fourth Sabres pick, 50th overall) of NHL entry draft (June 27, 1998).

		REGULAR SEASON					PLAYOFFS				
Season Team	League	Gms.	G	A	Pts.	PIM	Gms.	G	A	Pts.	PIM
95-96—ZPS Zlin Jrs.	Czech Rep.	34	33	20	53	...	—	—	—	—	—
96-97—ZPS Zlin Jrs.	Czech Rep.	44	28	27	55	...	—	—	—	—	—
97-98—ZPS Zlin Jrs.	Czech Rep.	7	8	5	13	...	—	—	—	—	—
—ZPS Zlin	Czech Rep.	37	2	8	10	20	—	—	—	—	—
—Prostejov	Czech Rep. Dv. II	4	0	0	0	0	—	—	—	—	—

KUZNETSOV, SERGEI   C   LIGHTNING

PERSONAL: Born January 29, 1980, in Yaroslavl, U.S.S.R. ... 6-0/180. ... Shoots left.
TRANSACTIONS/CAREER NOTES: Selected by Tampa Bay Lightning in sixth round (sixth Lightning pick, 146th overall) of NHL entry draft (June 27, 1998).

		REGULAR SEASON					PLAYOFFS				
Season Team	League	Gms.	G	A	Pts.	PIM	Gms.	G	A	Pts.	PIM
95-96—Torpedo Yaroslavl	CIS Jr.	28	14	14	28	20	—	—	—	—	—
96-97—Torpedo-2 Yaroslavl	Rus. Div. III	62	16	15	31	35	—	—	—	—	—
97-98—Torpedo-2 Yaroslavl	Rus. Div. II	42	10	13	23	30	—	—	—	—	—

LABARBERA, JASON   G   RANGERS

PERSONAL: Born January 18, 1980, in Burnaby, B.C. ... 6-2/205. ... Catches left.
TRANSACTIONS/CAREER NOTES: Selected by New York Rangers in third round (third Rangers pick, 66th overall) of NHL entry draft (June 27, 1998).

		REGULAR SEASON							PLAYOFFS					
Season Team	League	Gms.	Min	W	L	T	GA	SO	Avg.	Gms.	Min.	W	L	GA	SO	Avg.
96-97—Portland	WHL	9	443	5	1	1	18	0	2.44	—	—	—	—	—	—	—
97-98—Portland	WHL			18	4	0	...	1	3.31	—	—	—	—	—	—	—

LAPLANTE, ERIC   LW   SHARKS

PERSONAL: Born December 1, 1979, in St.-Louis-France, Que. ... 6-0/185. ... Shoots left.
TRANSACTIONS/CAREER NOTES: Selected by San Jose Sharks in third round (third Sharks pick, 65th overall) of NHL entry draft (June 27, 1998).

		REGULAR SEASON					PLAYOFFS				
Season Team	League	Gms.	G	A	Pts.	PIM	Gms.	G	A	Pts.	PIM
96-97—Halifax	QMJHL	68	20	30	50	253	18	3	10	13	28
97-98—Halifax	QMJHL	40	19	22	41	193	—	—	—	—	—

LARIVIERE, JACQUES   LW   DEVILS

PERSONAL: Born December 18, 1979, in Sorel, Que. ... 6-1/210. ... Shoots left.
TRANSACTIONS/CAREER NOTES: Selected by New Jersey Devils in sixth round (ninth Devils pick, 172nd overall) of NHL entry draft (June 27, 1998).

		REGULAR SEASON					PLAYOFFS				
Season Team	League	Gms.	G	A	Pts.	PIM	Gms.	G	A	Pts.	PIM
96-97—Moncton	QMJHL	3	0	0	0	5	—	—	—	—	—
97-98—Moncton	QMJHL	68	3	1	4	249	9	0	0	0	15

LAZAREV, YEVGENY   LW   AVALANCHE

PERSONAL: Born April 25, 1980, in Kharkov, U.S.S.R. ... 6-2/215. ... Shoots left.
TRANSACTIONS/CAREER NOTES: Selected by Colorado Avalanche in third round (eighth Avalanche pick, 79th overall) of NHL entry draft (June 27, 1998).

		REGULAR SEASON					PLAYOFFS				
Season Team	League	Gms.	G	A	Pts.	PIM	Gms.	G	A	Pts.	PIM
96-97—Torpedo Yaroslavl	Russian	1	0	0	0	0	—	—	—	—	—
—Torpedo-2 Yaroslavl	Rus. Div. III	44	18	15	33	38	—	—	—	—	—
97-98—Kitchener Jr. B	OHA	11	9	13	22	22	5	5	2	7	17

LEACH, JAY   D   COYOTES

PERSONAL: Born September 2, 1979, in Syracuse, N.Y. ... 6-3/202. ... Shoots left. ... Full Name: Jay C. Leach. ... Nephew of Steve Leach, right winger, Carolina Hurricanes; nephew of Jay Leach, assistant coach, L.A. Kings; and nephew of Mark Leach, scout, Detroit Red Wings.
COLLEGE: Providence.
TRANSACTIONS/CAREER NOTES: Selected by Phoenix Coyotes in fifth round (fifth Coyotes pick, 115th overall) of NHL entry draft (June 27, 1998).

Season Team	League	REGULAR SEASON Gms.	G	A	Pts.	PIM	PLAYOFFS Gms.	G	A	Pts.	PIM
96-97—Capital District	Jr. A	57	8	50	58	140	—	—	—	—	—
97-98—Providence College	Hockey East	32	0	8	8	33	—	—	—	—	—

LEAHY, PATRICK   RW   RANGERS

PERSONAL: Born June 9, 1979, in Brighton, Mass. ... 6-3/190. ... Shoots right.
COLLEGE: Miami of Ohio.
TRANSACTIONS/CAREER NOTES: Selected by New York Rangers in fifth round (fifth Rangers pick, 122nd overall) of NHL entry draft (June 27, 1998).

Season Team	League	REGULAR SEASON Gms.	G	A	Pts.	PIM	PLAYOFFS Gms.	G	A	Pts.	PIM
97-98—Miami of Ohio	CCHA	28	0	1	1	24	—	—	—	—	—

LECAVALIER, VINCENT   C   LIGHTNING

PERSONAL: Born April 21, 1980, in Ile-Bizard, Que. ... 6-4/180. ... Shoots left.
TRANSACTIONS/CAREER NOTES: Selected by Tampa Bay Lightning in first round (first Lightning pick, first overall) of NHL entry draft (June 27, 1998).
HONORS: Won Can.HL Rookie of the Year Award (1996-97). ... Won Michel Bergeron Trophy (1996-97). ... Named to Can.HL All-Rookie team (1996-97). ... Named to QMJHL All-Rookie team (1996-97). ... Won Michael Bossy Trophy (1997-98). ... Won Can.HL Top Draft Prospect Award (1997-98). ... Named to Can.HL All-Star first team (1997-98). ... Named to QMJHL All-Star first team (1997-98).

Season Team	League	REGULAR SEASON Gms.	G	A	Pts.	PIM	PLAYOFFS Gms.	G	A	Pts.	PIM
96-97—Rimouski	QMJHL	64	42	60	102	36	4	4	3	7	2
97-98—Rimouski	QMJHL	58	44	71	115	117	18	15	†26	41	46

LEGWAND, DAVID   C   PREDATORS

PERSONAL: Born August 17, 1980, in Detroit. ... 6-1/175. ... Shoots left.
TRANSACTIONS/CAREER NOTES: Selected by Nashville Predators in first round (first Predators pick, second overall) of NHL entry draft (June 27, 1998).
HONORS: Named to Can.HL All-Star second team (1997-98). ... Won Red Tilson Trophy (1997-98). ... Named OHL Rookie of the Year (1997-98). ... Named to OHL All-Star first team (1997-98). ... Named to OHL All-Rookie first team (1997-98). ... Won Can.HL Rookie of the Year Award (1997-98).

Season Team	League	REGULAR SEASON Gms.	G	A	Pts.	PIM	PLAYOFFS Gms.	G	A	Pts.	PIM
96-97—Detroit	Jr. A	44	21	41	62	58	—	—	—	—	—
97-98—Plymouth	OHL	59	54	51	105	56	15	8	12	20	24

LINNIK, MAXIM   D   BLUES

PERSONAL: Born September 6, 1979, in Kiev, U.S.S.R. ... 6-3/190. ... Shoots left.
TRANSACTIONS/CAREER NOTES: Selected by St. Louis Blues in second round (second Blues pick, 41st overall) of NHL entry draft (June 27, 1998).

Season Team	League	REGULAR SEASON Gms.	G	A	Pts.	PIM	PLAYOFFS Gms.	G	A	Pts.	PIM
96-97—Sokol Kiev	EEHL	7	0	0	0	0	—	—	—	—	—
97-98—St. Thomas Jr. B	OHA	35	4	14	18	130	—	—	—	—	—

MADDEN, CHRIS   G   HURRICANES

PERSONAL: Born March 10, 1979, in Syracuse, N.Y. ... 6-0/177. ... Catches left.
TRANSACTIONS/CAREER NOTES: Selected by Carolina Hurricanes in fourth round (sixth Hurricanes pick, 97th overall) of NHL entry draft (June 27, 1998).

Season Team	League	REGULAR SEASON Gms.	Min	W	L	T	GA	SO	Avg.	PLAYOFFS Gms.	Min.	W	L	GA	SO	Avg.
95-96—Weatfield	Jr. B						Statistics unavailable.									
96-97—Guelph	OHL	21	1128	11	5	1	68	1	3.62	3	72	1	1	4	0	3.33
97-98—Guelph	OHL	51	2906	*33	11	3	132	4	2.73	12	688	*11	1	20	0	*1.74

MALHOTRA, MANNY   C   RANGERS

PERSONAL: Born May 18, 1980, in Mississauga, Ont. ... 6-1/210. ... Shoots left.
TRANSACTIONS/CAREER NOTES: Selected by New York Rangers in first round (first Rangers pick, seventh overall) of NHL entry draft (June 27, 1998).

Season Team	League	REGULAR SEASON Gms.	G	A	Pts.	PIM	PLAYOFFS Gms.	G	A	Pts.	PIM
96-97—Guelph	OHL	61	16	28	44	26	18	7	7	14	11
97-98—Guelph	OHL	57	16	35	51	29	12	7	6	13	8

MANNING, PAUL   D   FLAMES

PERSONAL: Born April 15, 1979, in Red Deer, Alta. ... 6-4/193. ... Shoots left.
COLLEGE: Colorado College.
TRANSACTIONS/CAREER NOTES: Selected by Calgary Flames in third round (third Flames pick, 62nd overall) of NHL entry draft (June 27, 1998).

		REGULAR SEASON					PLAYOFFS				
Season Team	League	Gms.	G	A	Pts.	PIM	Gms.	G	A	Pts.	PIM
97-98—Colorado College	WCHA	26	1	5	6	16	—	—	—	—	—

MARKOV, ANDREI   D   CANADIENS

PERSONAL: Born December 20, 1978, in Voskresensk, U.S.S.R. ... 6-0/185. ... Shoots left.
TRANSACTIONS/CAREER NOTES: Selected by Montreal Canadiens in sixth round (sixth Canadiens pick, 162nd overall) of NHL entry draft (June 27, 1998).

		REGULAR SEASON					PLAYOFFS				
Season Team	League	Gms.	G	A	Pts.	PIM	Gms.	G	A	Pts.	PIM
95-96—Khimik Voskresensk	CIS	36	0	0	0	14	—	—	—	—	—
96-97—Khimik Voskresensk	Russian	43	8	4	12	32	2	1	1	2	0
97-98—Khimik Voskresensk	Russian	43	10	5	15	83	—	—	—	—	—

McCRACKEN, JAKE   G   RED WINGS

PERSONAL: Born January 15, 1980, in London, Ont. ... 5-10/180. ... Catches left.
TRANSACTIONS/CAREER NOTES: Selected by Detroit Red Wings in third round (fourth Red Wings pick, 84th overall) of NHL entry draft (June 27, 1998).
HONORS: Named to OHL All-Rookie first team (1996-97). ... Won Bobby Smith Trophy (1996-97). ... Won F. W. (Dinty) Moore Trophy (1996-97).

		REGULAR SEASON							PLAYOFFS						
Season Team	League	Gms.	Min	W	L	T	GA	SO	Avg.	Gms.	Min.	W	L	GA	SO	Avg.
95-96—St. Thomas Jr. B	OHA	33	1754	...	...	...	126	0	4.31	—	—	—	—	—	—	—
96-97—Sault Ste. Marie	OHL	29	1389	13	3	6	80	0	3.46	1	28	0	1	4	0	8.57
97-98—Sault Ste. Marie	OHL	55	3102	16	31	5	216	0	4.18	—	—	—	—	—	—	—

McLEOD, GAVIN   D   SENATORS

PERSONAL: Born January 1, 1980, in Fort Saskatchewan, Alta. ... 6-4/187. ... Shoots left.
TRANSACTIONS/CAREER NOTES: Selected by Ottawa Senators in fifth round (sixth Senators pick, 130th overall) of NHL entry draft (June 27, 1998).

		REGULAR SEASON					PLAYOFFS				
Season Team	League	Gms.	G	A	Pts.	PIM	Gms.	G	A	Pts.	PIM
96-97—Kelowna	WHL	60	0	6	6	44	—	—	—	—	—
97-98—Kelowna	WHL	70	3	17	20	98	7	0	0	0	14

MILANOVIC, RYAN   LW   BRUINS

PERSONAL: Born September 3, 1980, in Toronto. ... 6-2/201. ... Shoots left.
TRANSACTIONS/CAREER NOTES: Selected by Boston Bruins in sixth round (fifth Bruins pick, 165th overall) of NHL entry draft (June 27, 1998).

		REGULAR SEASON					PLAYOFFS				
Season Team	League	Gms.	G	A	Pts.	PIM	Gms.	G	A	Pts.	PIM
96-97—Kitchener	OHL	59	3	10	13	59	13	1	2	3	0
97-98—Kitchener	OHL	42	1	8	9	72	6	1	3	4	19

MILLEY, NORMAN   RW   SABRES

PERSONAL: Born February 14, 1980, in Toronto. ... 5-11/185. ... Shoots right.
TRANSACTIONS/CAREER NOTES: Selected by Buffalo Sabres in second round (third Sabres pick, 47th overall) of NHL entry draft (June 27, 1998).
HONORS: Named to Can.HL All-Rookie team (1996-97). ... Named to OHL All-Rookie first team (1996-97).

		REGULAR SEASON					PLAYOFFS				
Season Team	League	Gms.	G	A	Pts.	PIM	Gms.	G	A	Pts.	PIM
95-96—Toronto Red Wings	MTHL	42	42	36	78	109	—	—	—	—	—
96-97—Sudbury	OHL	61	30	32	62	15	—	—	—	—	—
97-98—Sudbury	OHL	62	33	41	74	48	10	0	1	1	4

MOORE, STEVE   C   AVALANCHE

PERSONAL: Born September 22, 1978, in Windsor, Ont. ... 6-2/190. ... Shoots right.
COLLEGE: Harvard.
TRANSACTIONS/CAREER NOTES: Selected by Colorado Avalanche in second round (seventh Avalanche pick, 53rd overall) of NHL entry draft (June 27, 1998).
HONORS: Named Ivy League Rookie of the Year (1997-98). ... Named to ECAC All-Rookie Team (1997-98).

Season Team	League	REGULAR SEASON					PLAYOFFS				
		Gms.	G	A	Pts.	PIM	Gms.	G	A	Pts.	PIM
95-96—Thornhill	OHA Jr. A	77	30	43	73	90	—	—	—	—	—
96-97—Thornhill	OHA Jr. A	50	34	52	86	52	—	—	—	—	—
97-98—Harvard University	ECAC	33	10	23	33	46	—	—	—	—	—

MORIN, JEAN-PHILIPPE — D — FLYERS

PERSONAL: Born February 6, 1980, in Gaspe, Que. ... 6-1/188. ... Shoots left.
TRANSACTIONS/CAREER NOTES: Selected by Philadelphia Flyers in fourth round (fourth Flyers pick, 109th overall) of NHL entry draft (June 27, 1998).

Season Team	League	REGULAR SEASON					PLAYOFFS				
		Gms.	G	A	Pts.	PIM	Gms.	G	A	Pts.	PIM
96-97—Victoriaville	QMJHL	56	3	5	8	20	1	0	0	0	0
97-98—Victoriaville	QMJHL	35	3	11	14	79	—	—	—	—	—
—Drummondville	QMJHL	18	1	4	5	16					

MORRISON, JUSTIN — RW — CANUCKS

PERSONAL: Born September 10, 1979, in Los Angeles. ... 6-3/205. ... Shoots right.
COLLEGE: Colorado College.
TRANSACTIONS/CAREER NOTES: Selected by Vancouver Canucks in third round (fourth Canucks pick, 81st overall) of NHL entry draft (June 27, 1998).

Season Team	League	REGULAR SEASON					PLAYOFFS				
		Gms.	G	A	Pts.	PIM	Gms.	G	A	Pts.	PIM
96-97—Omaha	USHL	62	12	24	36	44	—	—	—	—	—
97-98—Colorado College	WCHA	42	4	9	13	8	—	—	—	—	—

MYERS, SCOTT — G — PENGUINS

PERSONAL: Born June 11, 1979, in Winnipeg. ... 5-10/172. ... Catches right.
TRANSACTIONS/CAREER NOTES: Selected by Pittsburgh Penguins in fourth round (fourth Penguins pick, 110th overall) of NHL entry draft (June 27, 1998).

Season Team	League	REGULAR SEASON							PLAYOFFS						
		Gms.	Min	W	L	T	GA	SO	Avg.	Gms.	Min.	W	L	GA	SO	Avg.
96-97—Prince George	WHL	25	1284	6	14	1	94	0	4.39	—	—	—	—	—	—	—
97-98—Prince George	WHL	48	2822	29	13	4	139	2	2.96	11	665	5	6	25	†2	2.26

NEIL, CHRISTOPHER — RW — SENATORS

PERSONAL: Born June 18, 1979, in Markdale, Ont. ... 6-0/210. ... Shoots right.
TRANSACTIONS/CAREER NOTES: Selected by Ottawa Senators in sixth round (seventh Senators pick, 161st overall) of NHL entry draft (June 27, 1998).

Season Team	League	REGULAR SEASON					PLAYOFFS				
		Gms.	G	A	Pts.	PIM	Gms.	G	A	Pts.	PIM
96-97—North Bay	OHL	65	13	16	29	150	—	—	—	—	—
97-98—North Bay	OHL	59	26	29	55	231	—	—	—	—	—

NIELSEN, CHRIS — C — ISLANDERS

PERSONAL: Born February 16, 1980, in Moshi, Tanzania. ... 6-2/185. ... Shoots right.
TRANSACTIONS/CAREER NOTES: Selected by New York Islanders in second round (second Islanders pick, 36th overall) of NHL entry draft (June 27, 1998).

Season Team	League	REGULAR SEASON					PLAYOFFS				
		Gms.	G	A	Pts.	PIM	Gms.	G	A	Pts.	PIM
96-97—Calgary	WHL	62	11	19	30	39	18	2	4	6	10
97-98—Calgary	WHL	68	22	29	51	31	—	—	—	—	—

NIITTYMAKI, ANTERO — G — FLYERS

PERSONAL: Born June 18, 1980, in Turku, Finland. ... 6-0/176. ... Catches left.
TRANSACTIONS/CAREER NOTES: Selected by Philadelphia Flyers in sixth round (seventh Flyers pick, 168th overall) of NHL entry draft (June 27, 1998).

Season Team	League	REGULAR SEASON							PLAYOFFS						
		Gms.	Min	W	L	T	GA	SO	Avg.	Gms.	Min.	W	L	GA	SO	Avg.
96-97—TPS Turku	Finland Jr.	22	...	...	...	...	...	...	...	6	—	—	—	—	—	—
97-98—TPS Turku	Finland Jr.	33	...	...	...	...	...	...	...	—	—	—	—	—	—	—

NORDSTROM, PETER RW BRUINS

PERSONAL: Born July 26, 1974, in Munkfors, Sweden. ... 6-1/200.
TRANSACTIONS/CAREER NOTES: Selected by Boston Bruins in third round (third Bruins pick, 78th overall) of NHL entry draft (June 27, 1998).

		REGULAR SEASON					PLAYOFFS				
Season Team	League	Gms.	G	A	Pts.	PIM	Gms.	G	A	Pts.	PIM
91-92—Munkfors	Sweden Dv. 3	31	12	20	32	42	—	—	—	—	—
92-93—Munkfors	Sweden Dv. 3	35	19	11	30	44	—	—	—	—	—
93-94—Munkfors	Sweden Dv. 3	31	17	26	43	87	—	—	—	—	—
94-95—Munkfors	Sweden Dv. 2	21	8	17	25	30	—	—	—	—	—
95-96—Farjestad Karlstad	Sweden	40	6	5	11	36	8	0	3	3	12
96-97—Farjestad Karlstad	Sweden	44	9	5	14	32	14	1	2	3	6
97-98—Farjestad Karlstad	Sweden	45	6	19	25	46	12	5	7	12	8

O'LEARY, PAT C COYOTES

PERSONAL: Born September 2, 1979, in Minneapolis. ... 6-2/190. ... Shoots left.
HIGH SCHOOL: Armstrong (Plymouth, Minn.).
TRANSACTIONS/CAREER NOTES: Selected by Phoenix Coyotes in third round (third Coyotes pick, 73rd overall) of NHL entry draft (June 27, 1998).

		REGULAR SEASON					PLAYOFFS				
Season Team	League	Gms.	G	A	Pts.	PIM	Gms.	G	A	Pts.	PIM
96-97—Armstrong	USHSW	22	28	27	55	42	—	—	—	—	—
97-98—Armstrong	USHSW	24	22	27	49	28	—	—	—	—	—

OVINGTON, CHRIS D PANTHERS

PERSONAL: Born August 15, 1980, in Vernon, B.C. ... 6-3/173. ... Shoots right.
TRANSACTIONS/CAREER NOTES: Selected by Florida Panthers in sixth round (sixth Panthers pick, 148th overall) of NHL entry draft (June 27, 1998).

		REGULAR SEASON					PLAYOFFS				
Season Team	League	Gms.	G	A	Pts.	PIM	Gms.	G	A	Pts.	PIM
96-97—Saskatoon	WHL	33	0	3	3	17	7	0	1	1	2
97-98—Red Deer	WHL	68	2	13	15	72	5	0	0	0	2

PANDOLFO, MIKE LW SABRES

PERSONAL: Born September 15, 1979, in Winchester, Mass. ... 6-3/226. ... Shoots left.
HIGH SCHOOL: St. Sebastian's Country Day (Needham, Mass.).
TRANSACTIONS/CAREER NOTES: Selected by Buffalo Sabres in third round (fifth Sabres pick, 77th overall) of NHL entry draft (June 27, 1998).

		REGULAR SEASON					PLAYOFFS				
Season Team	League	Gms.	G	A	Pts.	PIM	Gms.	G	A	Pts.	PIM
96-97—St. Sebastien's	USHS (East)	32	27	28	55	30	—	—	—	—	—
97-98—St. Sebastien's	USHS (East)	28	29	23	52	18	—	—	—	—	—

PAPINEAU, JUSTIN C KINGS

PERSONAL: Born January 15, 1980, in Ottawa. ... 5-10/160. ... Shoots left.
TRANSACTIONS/CAREER NOTES: Selected by Los Angeles Kings in second round (second Kings pick, 46th overall) of NHL entry draft (June 27, 1998).
HONORS: Named to OHL All-Rookie second team (1996-97).

		REGULAR SEASON					PLAYOFFS				
Season Team	League	Gms.	G	A	Pts.	PIM	Gms.	G	A	Pts.	PIM
95-96—Ottawa	OHA Jr. A	52	31	19	50	51	—	—	—	—	—
96-97—Belleville	OHL	40	10	32	42	32	—	—	—	—	—
97-98—Belleville	OHL	66	41	53	94	34	10	5	9	14	6

PARKER, SCOTT LW AVALANCHE

PERSONAL: Born January 29, 1978, in Hanford, Calif. ... 6-4/218. ... Shoots right.
TRANSACTIONS/CAREER NOTES: Selected by New Jersey Devils in third round (sixth Devils pick, 63rd overall) of NHL entry draft (June 22, 1996). ... Returned to draft pool by Devils and selected by Colorado Avalanche in first round (fourth Avalanche pick, 20th overall) of NHL entry draft (June 27, 1998).

		REGULAR SEASON					PLAYOFFS				
Season Team	League	Gms.	G	A	Pts.	PIM	Gms.	G	A	Pts.	PIM
95-96—Kelowna	WHL	64	3	4	7	159	6	0	0	0	12
96-97—Kelowna	WHL	68	18	8	26	*330	6	0	2	2	4
97-98—Kelowna	WHL	71	30	22	52	243	7	6	0	6	23

PATERA, PAVEL   C   STARS

PERSONAL: Born September 6, 1971, in Kladno, Czechoslovakia. ... 6-1/176. ... Shoots left.
TRANSACTIONS/CAREER NOTES: Selected by Dallas Stars in sixth round (fourth Stars pick, 153rd overall) of NHL entry draft (June 27, 1998).

		REGULAR SEASON					PLAYOFFS				
Season Team	League	Gms.	G	A	Pts.	PIM	Gms.	G	A	Pts.	PIM
90-91—Poldi Kladno	Czech.	3	0	0	0	...	—	—	—	—	—
91-92—Poldi Kladno	Czech.	38	12	13	25	26	8	8	4	12	0
92-93—Poldi Kladno	Czech.	42	9	23	32	...	—	—	—	—	—
93-94—HC Kladno	Czech Rep.	43	21	39	60	...	11	5	10	15	...
94-95—HC Kladno	Czech Rep.	43	26	49	75	24	11	5	7	12	6
95-96—Poldi Kladno	Czech Rep.	40	24	31	55	38	8	3	1	4	34
96-97—AIK Solna	Sweden	50	19	24	43	44	7	2	3	5	6
97-98—AIK Solna	Sweden	46	8	17	25	50	—	—	—	—	—

PEAT, STEPHEN   D   MIGHTY DUCKS

PERSONAL: Born March 10, 1980, in Princeton, B.C. ... 6-2/205. ... Shoots right.
TRANSACTIONS/CAREER NOTES: Selected by Mighty Ducks of Anaheim in second round (second Mighty Ducks pick, 32nd overall) of NHL entry draft (June 27, 1998).

		REGULAR SEASON					PLAYOFFS				
Season Team	League	Gms.	G	A	Pts.	PIM	Gms.	G	A	Pts.	PIM
96-97—Red Deer	WHL	68	3	14	17	161	16	0	2	2	22
97-98—Red Deer	WHL	63	6	12	18	189	5	0	0	0	8

PELLETIER, JONATHAN   G   BLACKHAWKS

PERSONAL: Born April 14, 1980, in Riviere-du-Loup, Que. ... 5-11/165. ... Catches left.
TRANSACTIONS/CAREER NOTES: Selected by Chicago Blackhawks in sixth round (fifth Blackhawks pick, 166th overall) of NHL entry draft (June 27, 1998).

		REGULAR SEASON							PLAYOFFS						
Season Team	League	Gms.	Min	W	L	T	GA	SO	Avg.	Gms.	Min.	W	L	GA	SO	Avg.
96-97—Victoriaville	QMJHL	25	1223	14	5	1	65	0	3.19	2	31	0	0	1	0	1.94
97-98—Victoriaville	QMJHL	16	902	7	4	3	58	0	3.86	—	—	—	—	—	—	—
—Drummondville	QMJHL	29	1571	5	17	1	116	0	4.43	—	—	—	—	—	—	—

PETERS, ANDREW   LW   SABRES

PERSONAL: Born May 5, 1980, in St. Catharines, Ont. ... 6-4/195. ... Shoots left.
TRANSACTIONS/CAREER NOTES: Selected by Buffalo Sabres in second round (second Sabres pick, 34th overall) of NHL entry draft (June 27, 1998).

		REGULAR SEASON					PLAYOFFS				
Season Team	League	Gms.	G	A	Pts.	PIM	Gms.	G	A	Pts.	PIM
96-97—Georgetown	Tier II Jr. A	46	11	16	27	105	—	—	—	—	—
97-98—Oshawa	OHL	60	11	7	18	220	7	2	0	2	19

PONIKAROVKSY, ALEXEI   RW   MAPLE LEAFS

PERSONAL: Born April 9, 1980, in Kiev, U.S.S.R. ... 6-4/196. ... Shoots left.
TRANSACTIONS/CAREER NOTES: Selected by Toronto Maple Leafs in fourth round (fourth Maple Leafs pick, 87th overall) of NHL entry draft (June 27, 1998).

		REGULAR SEASON					PLAYOFFS				
Season Team	League	Gms.	G	A	Pts.	PIM	Gms.	G	A	Pts.	PIM
95-96—Dynamo Moscow	CIS Jr.	70	14	10	24	20	—	—	—	—	—
96-97—Dynamo Moscow	Russian Jr.	60	12	15	27	30	—	—	—	—	—
—Dynamo-2 Moscow	Rus. Div. III	2	0	0	0	2	—	—	—	—	—
97-98—Dynamo-2 Moscow	Rus. Div. II	24	1	2	3	30	—	—	—	—	—

PROSOFSKY, GARRETT   C   FLYERS

PERSONAL: Born May 19, 1980, in Saskatoon, Sask. ... 5-11/180. ... Shoots left.
TRANSACTIONS/CAREER NOTES: Selected by Philadelphia Flyers in fifth round (sixth Flyers pick, 139th overall) of NHL entry draft (June 27, 1998).

		REGULAR SEASON					PLAYOFFS				
Season Team	League	Gms.	G	A	Pts.	PIM	Gms.	G	A	Pts.	PIM
96-97—Saskatoon	WHL	66	20	45	65	67	—	—	—	—	—
97-98—Saskatoon	WHL	71	28	42	70	76	6	6	3	9	4

RAYCROFT, ANDREW   G   BRUINS

PERSONAL: Born May 4, 1980, in Belleville, Ont. ... 6-0/150. ... Catches left.
TRANSACTIONS/CAREER NOTES: Selected by Boston Bruins in fifth round (fourth Bruins pick, 135th overall) of NHL entry draft (June 27, 1998).

Season Team	League	REGULAR SEASON							PLAYOFFS					
		Gms.	Min	W	L	T	GA	SO	Avg.	Gms.	Min.	W	L	GA	SO	Avg.
96-97—Wellington	Tier II Jr. A	27	1402	...	...	...	92	0	3.94						
97-98—Sudbury	OHL	33	1802	8	16	5	125	0	4.16	2	89	0	1	8	0	5.39

REGEHR, ROBYN — D — AVALANCHE

PERSONAL: Born April 19, 1980, in Recife, Brazil. ... 6-2/211. ... Shoots left.
TRANSACTIONS/CAREER NOTES: Selected by Colorado Avalanche in first round (third Avalanche pick, 19th overall) of NHL entry draft (June 27, 1998).

Season Team	League	REGULAR SEASON					PLAYOFFS				
		Gms.	G	A	Pts.	PIM	Gms.	G	A	Pts.	PIM
96-97—Kamloops	WHL	64	4	19	23	96	5	0	1	1	18
97-98—Kamloops	WHL	65	4	10	14	120	5	0	3	3	8

RIBEIRO, MIKE — C — CANADIENS

PERSONAL: Born February 10, 1980, in Montreal. ... 5-11/150. ... Shoots left.
TRANSACTIONS/CAREER NOTES: Selected by Montreal Canadiens in second round (second Canadiens pick, 45th overall) of NHL entry draft (June 27, 1998).
HONORS: Won Michel Bergeron Trophy (1997-98). ... Named to QMJHL All-Star second team (1997-98). ... Named to QMJHL All-Rookie Team (1997-98).

Season Team	League	REGULAR SEASON					PLAYOFFS				
		Gms.	G	A	Pts.	PIM	Gms.	G	A	Pts.	PIM
97-98—Rouyn-Noranda	QMJHL	67	40	†85	125	55	—	—	—	—	—

RICH, CURTIS — D — LIGHTNING

PERSONAL: Born October 6, 1979, in Edmonton. ... 6-4/200. ... Shoots left.
TRANSACTIONS/CAREER NOTES: Selected by Tampa Bay Lightning in fifth round (fifth Lightning pick, 121st overall) of NHL entry draft (June 27, 1998).

Season Team	League	REGULAR SEASON					PLAYOFFS				
		Gms.	G	A	Pts.	PIM	Gms.	G	A	Pts.	PIM
95-96—Calgary	WHL	24	0	0	0	10	—	—	—	—	—
96-97—Calgary	WHL	45	1	6	7	73	—	—	—	—	—
97-98—Calgary	WHL	70	3	12	15	204	17	0	0	0	36

RICHARDS, BRAD — LW — LIGHTNING

PERSONAL: Born May 2, 1980, in Montague, P.E.I. ... 6-0/170. ... Shoots left.
TRANSACTIONS/CAREER NOTES: Selected by Tampa Bay Lightning in third round (second Lightning pick, 64th overall) of NHL entry draft (June 27, 1998).
HONORS: Named to QMJHL All-Rookie Team (1997-98).

Season Team	League	REGULAR SEASON					PLAYOFFS				
		Gms.	G	A	Pts.	PIM	Gms.	G	A	Pts.	PIM
96-97—Notre Dame	SJHL	63	39	48	87	73	—	—	—	—	—
97-98—Rimouski	QMJHL	68	33	82	115	44	19	8	24	32	2

ROSSITER, KYLE — D — PANTHERS

PERSONAL: Born June 9, 1980, in Edmonton. ... 6-2/200. ... Shoots left.
TRANSACTIONS/CAREER NOTES: Selected by Florida Panthers in second round (first Panthers pick, 30th overall) of NHL entry draft (June 27, 1998).
HONORS: Won Can.HL Scholastic Player of the Year Award (1997-98).

Season Team	League	REGULAR SEASON					PLAYOFFS				
		Gms.	G	A	Pts.	PIM	Gms.	G	A	Pts.	PIM
96-97—Spokane	WHL	50	0	2	2	65	9	0	0	0	6
97-98—Spokane	WHL	61	6	16	22	190	15	0	3	3	28

ROURKE, ALLAN — D — MAPLE LEAFS

PERSONAL: Born March 6, 1980, in Mississauga, Ont. ... 6-1/214. ... Shoots left.
TRANSACTIONS/CAREER NOTES: Selected by Toronto Maple Leafs in sixth round (sixth Maple Leafs pick, 154th overall) of NHL entry draft (June 27, 1998).

Season Team	League	REGULAR SEASON					PLAYOFFS				
		Gms.	G	A	Pts.	PIM	Gms.	G	A	Pts.	PIM
96-97—Kitchener	OHL	25	1	1	2	12	6	0	0	0	0
97-98—Kitchener	OHL	48	5	17	22	59	6	1	1	2	6

RULLIER, JOE   D   KINGS

PERSONAL: Born January 28, 1980, in Montreal. ... 6-3/198. ... Shoots right.
TRANSACTIONS/CAREER NOTES: Selected by Los Angeles Kings in fifth round (fifth Kings pick, 133rd overall) of NHL entry draft (June 27, 1998).

		REGULAR SEASON					PLAYOFFS				
Season Team	League	Gms.	G	A	Pts.	PIM	Gms.	G	A	Pts.	PIM
96-97—Rimouski	QMJHL	23	0	3	3	77	4	0	0	0	11
97-98—Rimouski	QMJHL	55	1	10	11	176	16	1	4	5	34

RUPP, MICHAEL   LW   ISLANDERS

PERSONAL: Born January 13, 1980, in Cleveland. ... 6-5/218. ... Shoots left.
TRANSACTIONS/CAREER NOTES: Selected by New York Islanders in first round (first Islanders pick, ninth overall) of NHL entry draft (June 27, 1998).

		REGULAR SEASON					PLAYOFFS				
Season Team	League	Gms.	G	A	Pts.	PIM	Gms.	G	A	Pts.	PIM
96-97—St. Edward's	USHS (East)	20	26	24	50	...	—	—	—	—	—
97-98—Windsor	OHL	38	9	8	17	60	—	—	—	—	—
—Erie	OHL	26	7	3	10	57	7	3	1	4	6

RUUTU, JARKKO   LW   CANUCKS

PERSONAL: Born August 23, 1975, in Vantaa, Finland. ... 6-2/194. ... Shoots left.
COLLEGE: Michigan Tech.
TRANSACTIONS/CAREER NOTES: Selected by Vancouver Canucks in third round (third Canucks pick, 68th overall) of NHL entry draft (June 27, 1998).

		REGULAR SEASON					PLAYOFFS				
Season Team	League	Gms.	G	A	Pts.	PIM	Gms.	G	A	Pts.	PIM
91-92—HIFK Helsinki	Finland Jr.	1	0	0	0	0	—	—	—	—	—
92-93—HIFK Helsinki	Finland Jr.	34	26	21	47	53	—	—	—	—	—
93-94—HIFK Helsinki	Finland Jr.	19	9	12	21	44	—	—	—	—	—
94-95—HIFK Helsinki	Finland Jr.	35	26	22	48	117	—	—	—	—	—
95-96—Michigan Tech	WCHA	39	12	10	22	96	—	—	—	—	—
96-97—HIFK Helsinki	Finland	48	11	10	21	155	—	—	—	—	—
97-98—HIFK Helsinki	Finland	37	10	10	20	87	8	7	4	11	10

RYAZANTSEV, ALEXANDER   D   AVALANCHE

PERSONAL: Born March 15, 1980, in Moscow, U.S.S.R. ... 5-11/196. ... Shoots right.
TRANSACTIONS/CAREER NOTES: Selected by Colorado Avalanche in sixth round (10th Avalanche pick, 167th overall) of NHL entry draft (June 27, 1998).

		REGULAR SEASON					PLAYOFFS				
Season Team	League	Gms.	G	A	Pts.	PIM	Gms.	G	A	Pts.	PIM
96-97—Spartak Moscow	Russian	20	1	2	3	4	—	—	—	—	—
—SAK Moscow	Rus. Div. III	18	0	0	0	8	—	—	—	—	—
97-98—Spartak-2 Moscow	Rus. Div. III	31	3	8	11	26	—	—	—	—	—
—Victoriaville	QMJHL	22	6	9	15	14	4	0	0	0	0

SABOURIN, DANY   G   FLAMES

PERSONAL: Born September 2, 1980, in Val d'Or, Que. ... 6-2/165. ... Catches left.
TRANSACTIONS/CAREER NOTES: Selected by Calgary Flames in fourth round (fifth Flames pick, 108th overall) of NHL entry draft (June 27, 1998).

		REGULAR SEASON							PLAYOFFS						
Season Team	League	Gms.	Min	W	L	T	GA	SO	Avg.	Gms.	Min.	W	L	GA	SO	Avg.
97-98—Sherbrooke	QMJHL	37	1906	15	15	2	128	1	4.03	—	—	—	—	—	—	—

SAMUELSSON, MIKAEL   C   SHARKS

PERSONAL: Born December 23, 1976, in Mariefred, Sweden. ... 6-1/200.
TRANSACTIONS/CAREER NOTES: Selected by San Jose Sharks in fifth round (seventh Sharks pick, 145th overall) of NHL entry draft (June 27, 1998).

		REGULAR SEASON					PLAYOFFS				
Season Team	League	Gms.	G	A	Pts.	PIM	Gms.	G	A	Pts.	PIM
94-95—Sodertalje	Sweden Jr.	30	8	6	14	12	—	—	—	—	—
95-96—Sodertalje	Sweden Dv. 2	18	5	1	6	0	4	0	0	0	0
—Sodertalje	Sweden Jr.	22	13	12	25	20	—	—	—	—	—
96-97—Sodertalje	Sweden	29	3	2	5	10	—	—	—	—	—
—Sodertalje	Sweden Jr.	2	2	1	3	...	—	—	—	—	—
97-98—Sodertalje	Sweden	31	8	8	16	47	—	—	—	—	—

SAUER, KEN — D — PREDATORS

PERSONAL: Born May 10, 1979, in St. Cloud, Minn. ... 6-2/226. ... Shoots right.
TRANSACTIONS/CAREER NOTES: Selected by Nashville Predators in fourth round (fourth Predators pick, 88th overall) of NHL entry draft (June 27, 1998).

Season Team	League	REGULAR SEASON Gms.	G	A	Pts.	PIM	PLAYOFFS Gms.	G	A	Pts.	PIM
96-97—St. Cloud-Appolo	USHS (West)	23	14	15	29	20	—	—	—	—	—
97-98—North Iowa	USHL	54	4	19	23	99	—	—	—	—	—

SAUVE, PHILIPPE — G — AVALANCHE

PERSONAL: Born February 27, 1980, in Buffalo. ... 6-0/175. ... Catches left.
TRANSACTIONS/CAREER NOTES: Selected by Colorado Avalanche in second round (sixth Avalanche pick, 38th overall) of NHL entry draft (June 27, 1998).

Season Team	League	REGULAR SEASON Gms.	Min	W	L	T	GA	SO	Avg.	PLAYOFFS Gms.	Min.	W	L	GA	SO	Avg.
96-97—Rimouski	QMJHL	26	1332	11	9	2	84	0	3.78	1	14	0	0	3	0	12.82
97-98—Rimouski	QMJHL	40	2326	23	16	0	131	1	3.38	7	262	0	5	33	0	7.56

SCHASTLIVY, PETR — LW — SENATORS

PERSONAL: Born April 18, 1979, in Angarsk, U.S.S.R. ... 6-0/191. ... Shoots left.
TRANSACTIONS/CAREER NOTES: Selected by Ottawa Senators in fourth round (fifth Senators pick, 101st overall) of NHL entry draft (June 27, 1998).

Season Team	League	REGULAR SEASON Gms.	G	A	Pts.	PIM	PLAYOFFS Gms.	G	A	Pts.	PIM
96-97—Yermak Angarsk	Rus. Div. III			Statistics unavailable.							
97-98—Torpedo-2 Yaroslavl	Rus. Div. II	47	15	9	24	34	—	—	—	—	—
—Torpedo Yaroslavl	Russian	4	0	0	0	0	—	—	—	—	—

SCHNABEL, ROBERT — D — COYOTES

PERSONAL: Born November 10, 1978, in Prague, Czechoslovakia. ... 6-6/216. ... Shoots left. ... Name pronounced SHNAY-buhl.
TRANSACTIONS/CAREER NOTES: Selected by New York Islanders in third round (fifth Islanders pick, 79th overall) of NHL entry draft (June 21, 1997). ... Returned to draft pool by Islanders and selected by Phoenix Coyotes in sixth round (seventh Coyotes pick, 129th overall) of NHL entry draft (June 27, 1998).

Season Team	League	REGULAR SEASON Gms.	G	A	Pts.	PIM	PLAYOFFS Gms.	G	A	Pts.	PIM
94-95—Slavia Praha Jrs.	Czech Rep.	35	11	6	17	14	—	—	—	—	—
95-96—Slavia Praha Jrs.	Czech Rep.	38	3	5	8	...	—	—	—	—	—
96-97—Slavia Praha Jrs.	Czech Rep.	36	5	2	7	...	—	—	—	—	—
—Slavia Praha	Czech Rep.	4	0	0	0	4	1	0	0	0	0
97-98—Red Deer	WHL	61	1	22	23	143	5	0	0	0	16

SCUDERI, ROBERT — D — PENGUINS

PERSONAL: Born December 30, 1978, in Syosset, N.Y. ... 6-1/194. ... Shoots left.
HIGH SCHOOL: St. Anthony's (South Huntington, N.Y.).
COLLEGE: Boston College.
TRANSACTIONS/CAREER NOTES: Selected by Pittsburgh Penguins in fifth round (fifth Penguins pick, 134th overall) of NHL entry draft (June 27, 1998).

Season Team	League	REGULAR SEASON Gms.	G	A	Pts.	PIM	PLAYOFFS Gms.	G	A	Pts.	PIM
96-97—NY Apple Core	Jr. B	80	42	70	112	52	—	—	—	—	—
97-98—Boston College	Hockey East	42	0	24	24	12	—	—	—	—	—

SIKLENKA, MIKE — D — CAPITALS

PERSONAL: Born December 18, 1979, in Meadow Lake, Sask. ... 6-4/215. ... Shoots right.
TRANSACTIONS/CAREER NOTES: Selected by Washington Capitals in fifth round (fifth Capitals pick, 118th overall) of NHL entry draft (June 27, 1998).

Season Team	League	REGULAR SEASON Gms.	G	A	Pts.	PIM	PLAYOFFS Gms.	G	A	Pts.	PIM
97-98—Olds	AJHL	54	10	17	27	120	—	—	—	—	—
—Seattle	WHL	1	0	0	0	0	5	0	0	0	6

SKOULA, MARTIN — D — AVALANCHE

PERSONAL: Born October 28, 1979, in Litomerice, Czechoslovakia. ... 6-2/195. ... Shoots left.
TRANSACTIONS/CAREER NOTES: Selected by Colorado Avalanche in first round (second Avalanche pick, 17th overall) of NHL entry draft (June 27, 1998).

Season Team	League	REGULAR SEASON					PLAYOFFS				
		Gms.	G	A	Pts.	PIM	Gms.	G	A	Pts.	PIM
95-96—Litvinov Jrs............................	Czech Rep.	38	0	4	4	...	—	—	—	—	—
—Litvinov...............................	Czech Rep.	—	—	—	—	—	1	0	0	0	0
96-97—Litvinov Jrs............................	Czech Rep.	38	2	9	11	...	—	—	—	—	—
—Litvinov...............................	Czech Rep.	—	—	—	—	—	1	0	0	0	0
97-98—Barrie.................................	COJHL	66	8	36	44	36	6	1	3	4	4

SMIRNOV, OLEG　　　　　LW　　　　　OILERS

PERSONAL: Born April 8, 1980, in Elektrostal, U.S.S.R. ... 5-11/176. ... Shoots right.
TRANSACTIONS/CAREER NOTES: Selected by Edmonton Oilers in fifth round (sixth Oilers pick, 144th overall) of NHL entry draft (June 27, 1998).

Season Team	League	REGULAR SEASON					PLAYOFFS				
		Gms.	G	A	Pts.	PIM	Gms.	G	A	Pts.	PIM
96-97—Kristall-2 Elektrostal	Rus. Div. III	38	2	2	4	8	—	—	—	—	—
97-98—Kristall Elektrostal...................	Russian	6	0	2	2	0	—	—	—	—	—
—Kristall Elektrostal...............	Rus. Div. II	10	0	0	0	2	—	—	—	—	—

SPACEK, JAROSLAV　　　　　D　　　　　PANTHERS

PERSONAL: Born February 11, 1974, in Rokycany, Czechoslovakia. ... 6-0/198. ... Shoots left.
TRANSACTIONS/CAREER NOTES: Selected by Florida Panthers in fifth round (fifth Panthers pick, 117th overall) of NHL entry draft (June 27, 1998).

Season Team	League	REGULAR SEASON					PLAYOFFS				
		Gms.	G	A	Pts.	PIM	Gms.	G	A	Pts.	PIM
92-93—Skoda Plzen..........................	Czech.	16	1	3	4	...	—	—	—	—	—
93-94—Skoda Plzen..........................	Czech Rep.	34	2	10	12	...	—	—	—	—	—
94-95—Interconex Plzen	Czech Rep.	38	4	8	12	14	3	1	0	1	2
95-96—ZKZ Pleen	Czech Rep.	40	3	10	13	42	3	0	1	1	4
96-97—ZKZ Pleen	Czech Rep.	52	9	29	38	44	—	—	—	—	—
97-98—Farjestad Karlstad	Sweden	45	10	16	26	63	12	2	5	7	14

STEEN, CALLE　　　　　RW　　　　　RED WINGS

PERSONAL: Born May 16, 1980, in Stockholm, Sweden. ... 5-11/198. ... Shoots left.
TRANSACTIONS/CAREER NOTES: Selected by Detroit Red Wings in fifth round (sixth Red Wings pick, 142nd overall) of NHL entry draft (June 27, 1998).

Season Team	League	REGULAR SEASON					PLAYOFFS				
		Gms.	G	A	Pts.	PIM	Gms.	G	A	Pts.	PIM
95-96—Hammarby	Sweden Jr.	5	0	0	0	0	—	—	—	—	—
96-97—Hammarby	Sweden Jr.	24	4	9	13		—	—	—	—	—
97-98—Hammarby	Sweden Jr.					Statistics unavailable.					

STUART, BRAD　　　　　D　　　　　SHARKS

PERSONAL: Born November 6, 1979, in Rocky Mountain House, Alta. ... 6-2/215. ... Shoots left.
TRANSACTIONS/CAREER NOTES: Selected by San Jose Sharks in first round (first Sharks pick, third overall) of NHL entry draft (June 27, 1998).
HONORS: Named to WHL (East) All-Star second team (1997-98).

Season Team	League	REGULAR SEASON					PLAYOFFS				
		Gms.	G	A	Pts.	PIM	Gms.	G	A	Pts.	PIM
96-97—Regina	WHL	57	7	36	43	58	5	0	4	4	14
97-98—Regina	WHL	72	20	45	65	82	9	3	4	7	10

SUTTER, SHAUN　　　　　C　　　　　FLAMES

PERSONAL: Born June 2, 1980, in Red Deer, Alta. ... 5-11/160. ... Shoots right.
TRANSACTIONS/CAREER NOTES: Selected by Calgary Flames in fourth round (fourth Flames pick, 102nd overall) of NHL entry draft (June 27, 1998).

Season Team	League	REGULAR SEASON					PLAYOFFS				
		Gms.	G	A	Pts.	PIM	Gms.	G	A	Pts.	PIM
96-97—Red Deer	AMHL	33	15	24	39	143	—	—	—	—	—
97-98—Lethbridge	WHL	69	11	9	20	146	4	0	0	0	4

SVOBODA, PETR　　　　　D　　　　　MAPLE LEAFS

PERSONAL: Born June 20, 1980, in Jihlava, Czechoslovakia. ... 6-2/194. ... Shoots right.
TRANSACTIONS/CAREER NOTES: Selected by Toronto Maple Leafs in second round (second Maple Leafs pick, 35th overall) of NHL entry draft (June 27, 1998).

Season Team	League	REGULAR SEASON					PLAYOFFS				
		Gms.	G	A	Pts.	PIM	Gms.	G	A	Pts.	PIM
95-96—Jihlava Jrs.	Czech Rep.	38	4	12	16	50	—	—	—	—	—
96-97—Jihlava Jrs.	Czech Rep.	29	1	3	4	...	—	—	—	—	—
97-98—Dukla Jihlava	Czech Rep.	1	0	0	0	0	—	—	—	—	—
—Havlickuv Brod	Czech Rep.Dv.II	18	1	2	3	16	—	—	—	—	—
—Jihlava Jrs.	Czech Rep.	12	0	2	2	...	—	—	—	—	—

TANGUAY, ALEX — C — AVALANCHE

PERSONAL: Born November 21, 1979, in Ste.-Justine, Que. ... 6-0/180. ... Shoots left.
TRANSACTIONS/CAREER NOTES: Selected by Colorado Avalanche in first round (first Avalanche pick, 12th overall) of NHL entry draft (June 27, 1998).
HONORS: Named to Can.HL All-Rookie team (1996-97). ... Named to QMJHL All-Rookie team (1996-97).

		REGULAR SEASON					PLAYOFFS				
Season Team	League	Gms.	G	A	Pts.	PIM	Gms.	G	A	Pts.	PIM
96-97—Halifax	QMJHL	70	27	41	68	50	12	4	8	12	8
97-98—Halifax	QMJHL	51	47	38	85	32	5	7	6	13	4

TIMMONS, K.C. — LW — AVALANCHE

PERSONAL: Born April 6, 1980, in Victoria, B.C. ... 6-2/205. ... Shoots left. ... Full Name: Kristinn Timmons.
TRANSACTIONS/CAREER NOTES: Selected by Colorado Avalanche in fifth round (ninth Avalanche pick, 141st overall) of NHL entry draft (June 27, 1998).

		REGULAR SEASON					PLAYOFFS				
Season Team	League	Gms.	G	A	Pts.	PIM	Gms.	G	A	Pts.	PIM
96-97—Tri-City	WHL	52	0	5	5	27	—	—	—	—	—
97-98—Tri-City	WHL	72	11	7	18	139	—	—	—	—	—

TRATTNIG, MATTHIAS — C — BLACKHAWKS

PERSONAL: Born April 22, 1979, in Graz, Austria. ... 6-1/208. ... Shoots left.
COLLEGE: Maine.
TRANSACTIONS/CAREER NOTES: Selected by Chicago Blackhawks in fourth round (second Blackhawks pick, 94th overall) of NHL entry draft (June 27, 1998).

		REGULAR SEASON					PLAYOFFS				
Season Team	League	Gms.	G	A	Pts.	PIM	Gms.	G	A	Pts.	PIM
95-96—Graz	Austria	17	0	1	1	0	—	—	—	—	—
96-97—Capital District (N.Y.)	Jr. A	51	30	54	84	64	—	—	—	—	—
97-98—Univ. of Maine	Hockey East	34	8	9	17	30	—	—	—	—	—

TROSCHINSKY, ANDREI — C — BLUES

PERSONAL: Born February 14, 1978, in Ust-Kamenogorsk, U.S.S.R. ... 6-5/187. ... Shoots left.
TRANSACTIONS/CAREER NOTES: Selected by St. Louis Blues in sixth round (fifth Blues pick, 170th overall) of NHL entry draft (June 27, 1998).

		REGULAR SEASON					PLAYOFFS				
Season Team	League	Gms.	G	A	Pts.	PIM	Gms.	G	A	Pts.	PIM
95-96—Dynamo-2 Moscow	CIS Div. III				Statistics unavailable.						
96-97—Torpedo Ust-Kamenogorsk	Rus. Div. II	9	1	1	2	8	—	—	—	—	—
97-98—Torpedo Ust-Kamenogorsk	Rus. Div. II	47	10	16	26	34	—	—	—	—	—

VAANANEN, OSSI — D — COYOTES

PERSONAL: Born August 18, 1980, in Vantaa, Finland. ... 6-3/200. ... Shoots left.
TRANSACTIONS/CAREER NOTES: Selected by Phoenix Coyotes in second round (second Coyotes pick, 43rd overall) of NHL entry draft (June 27, 1998).

		REGULAR SEASON					PLAYOFFS				
Season Team	League	Gms.	G	A	Pts.	PIM	Gms.	G	A	Pts.	PIM
95-96—Jokerit Helsinki	Finland Jr.	2	0	0	0	0	—	—	—	—	—
96-97—Jokerit Helsinki	Finland Jr.	19	1	2	3	43	—	—	—	—	—
97-98—Jokerit Helsinki	Finland Jr.	31	0	6	6	24	—	—	—	—	—

VALTONEN, TOMEK — LW — RED WINGS

PERSONAL: Born January 8, 1980, in Piotrkow Trybunalski, Poland. ... 6-1/198. ... Shoots left.
TRANSACTIONS/CAREER NOTES: Selected by Detroit Red Wings in second round (third Red Wings pick, 56th overall) of NHL entry draft (June 27, 1998).

		REGULAR SEASON					PLAYOFFS				
Season Team	League	Gms.	G	A	Pts.	PIM	Gms.	G	A	Pts.	PIM
95-96—Ilves Tampere	Finland Jr.	12	7	7	14	28	—	—	—	—	—
96-97—Ilves Tampere	Finland Jr.	27	10	9	19	82	3	0	1	1	6
97-98—Ilves Tampere	Finland	19	1	0	1	14	3	0	0	0	0
—Kiekko-Karhut Joensuu	Finland Div. 2	6	1	2	3	39	—	—	—	—	—
—Ilves Tampere	Finland Jr.	13	3	2	5	36	—	—	—	—	—

VAN RYN, MIKE — D — DEVILS

PERSONAL: Born May 14, 1979, in London, Ont. ... 6-1/190. ... Shoots right.
COLLEGE: Michigan.

TRANSACTIONS/CAREER NOTES: Selected by New Jersey Devils in first round (first Devils pick, 26th overall) of NHL entry draft (June 27, 1998).
HONORS: Named to CCHA All-Rookie Team (1997-98).

		REGULAR SEASON					PLAYOFFS				
Season Team	League	Gms.	G	A	Pts.	PIM	Gms.	G	A	Pts.	PIM
95-96—London Jr. B	OHA	44	9	14	23	24	—	—	—	—	—
96-97—London Jr. B	OHA	46	14	31	45	32	—	—	—	—	—
97-98—University of Michigan	WCHA	25	4	14	18	36	—	—	—	—	—

VANBUSKIRK, RYAN   D   COYOTES

PERSONAL: Born January 12, 1980, in Sault Ste. Marie, Mich. ... 6-1/190. ... Shoots left.
TRANSACTIONS/CAREER NOTES: Selected by Phoenix Coyotes in fourth round (fourth Coyotes pick, 100th overall) of NHL entry draft (June 27, 1998).

		REGULAR SEASON					PLAYOFFS				
Season Team	League	Gms.	G	A	Pts.	PIM	Gms.	G	A	Pts.	PIM
96-97—Petrolia	Jr. B	43	7	28	35	133	—	—	—	—	—
97-98—Sarnia	OHL	61	8	17	25	84	5	1	2	3	4

VASICEK, JOSEF   C   HURRICANES

PERSONAL: Born September 12, 1980, in Havlickuv Brod, Czechoslovakia. ... 6-4/189. ... Shoots left.
TRANSACTIONS/CAREER NOTES: Selected by Carolina Hurricanes in fourth round (fourth Hurricanes pick, 91st overall) of NHL entry draft (June 27, 1998).

		REGULAR SEASON					PLAYOFFS				
Season Team	League	Gms.	G	A	Pts.	PIM	Gms.	G	A	Pts.	PIM
95-96—Havlickuv Brod Jrs.	Czech Rep.	36	25	25	50	...	—	—	—	—	—
96-97—Slavia Praha Jrs.	Czech Rep.	37	20	40	60	...	—	—	—	—	—
97-98—Slavia Praha Jrs.	Czech Rep.	34	13	20	33	...	—	—	—	—	—

VAUCLAIR, JULIEN   D   SENATORS

PERSONAL: Born October 2, 1979, in Delemont, Switzerland. ... 6-1/198. ... Shoots left.
TRANSACTIONS/CAREER NOTES: Selected by Ottawa Senators in third round (fourth Senators pick, 74th overall) of NHL entry draft (June 27, 1998).

		REGULAR SEASON					PLAYOFFS				
Season Team	League	Gms.	G	A	Pts.	PIM	Gms.	G	A	Pts.	PIM
95-96—Ajoie	Switz. Div. 3	20	4	10	14	...	—	—	—	—	—
96-97—Ajoie	Switz. Div. 3	40	0	6	6	24	9	0	2	2	8
97-98—Lugano	Switzerland	36	1	2	3	12	7	0	0	0	25

VISHNEVSKY, VITALI   D   MIGHTY DUCKS

PERSONAL: Born March 18, 1980, in Kharkov, U.S.S.R. ... 6-1/187. ... Shoots left.
TRANSACTIONS/CAREER NOTES: Selected by Mighty Ducks of Anaheim in first round (first Mighty Ducks pick, fifth overall) of NHL entry draft (June 27, 1998).

		REGULAR SEASON					PLAYOFFS				
Season Team	League	Gms.	G	A	Pts.	PIM	Gms.	G	A	Pts.	PIM
95-96—Torpedo-2 Yaroslavl	CIS Div. II	40	4	4	8	20	—	—	—	—	—
96-97—Torpedo-2 Yaroslavl	Rus. Div. III	45	0	2	2	30	—	—	—	—	—
97-98—Torpedo-2 Yaroslavl	Rus. Div. II	47	8	9	17	164	—	—	—	—	—

VIUHKOLA, JARI   C   BLACKHAWKS

PERSONAL: Born February 27, 1980, in Oulu, Finland. ... 6-0/165. ... Shoots left.
TRANSACTIONS/CAREER NOTES: Selected by Chicago Blackhawks in sixth round (fourth Blackhawks pick, 158th overall) of NHL entry draft (June 27, 1998).

		REGULAR SEASON					PLAYOFFS				
Season Team	League	Gms.	G	A	Pts.	PIM	Gms.	G	A	Pts.	PIM
96-97—Karpat Oulu	Finland Jr.	32	8	11	19	74	—	—	—	—	—
97-98—Karpat Oulu	Finland Jr.	28	8	18	26	57	—	—	—	—	—

VOLKOV, ALEXEI   G   KINGS

PERSONAL: Born March 15, 1980, in Sverdlovsk, U.S.S.R. ... 6-0/174. ... Catches left.
TRANSACTIONS/CAREER NOTES: Selected by Los Angeles Kings in third round (third Kings pick, 76th overall) of NHL entry draft (June 27, 1998).

		REGULAR SEASON							PLAYOFFS						
Season Team	League	Gms.	Min.	W	L	T	GA	SO	Avg.	Gms.	Min.	W	L	GA	SO	Avg.
95-96—SKA-Avto-2 Yekat.	CIS Div. II	42	...	...	...	...	78	...	...	—	—	—	—	—	—	—
96-97—SKA Yekaterinburg	Rus. Div. III	34	...	...	...	...	66	...	...	—	—	—	—	—	—	—
—Krylja Sov. Moscow	Russian Jr.	8	...	...	...	...	9	...	...	—	—	—	—	—	—	—
97-98—Krylja Sov.-2 Moscow	Rus. Div. III	27	...	...	...	...	72	...	...	—	—	—	—	—	—	—

VOTH, BRAD — D — BLUES

PERSONAL: Born February 25, 1980, in Saskatoon, Sask. ... 6-4/223. ... Shoots right.
TRANSACTIONS/CAREER NOTES: Selected by St. Louis Blues in sixth round (fourth Blues pick, 157th overall) of NHL entry draft (June 27, 1998).

Season Team	League	REGULAR SEASON Gms.	G	A	Pts.	PIM	PLAYOFFS Gms.	G	A	Pts.	PIM
96-97—Calgary	AMHL	30	3	10	13	190	—	—	—	—	—
—Medicine Hat	WHL	2	0	0	0	2	—	—	—	—	—
97-98—Medicine Hat	WHL	70	8	5	13	244	—	—	—	—	—

WALKER, MATT — D — BLUES

PERSONAL: Born April 7, 1980, in Beaverlodge, Alta. ... 6-2/212. ... Shoots right.
TRANSACTIONS/CAREER NOTES: Selected by St. Louis Blues in third round (third Blues pick, 83rd overall) of NHL entry draft (June 27, 1998).

Season Team	League	REGULAR SEASON Gms.	G	A	Pts.	PIM	PLAYOFFS Gms.	G	A	Pts.	PIM
97-98—Portland	WHL	64	2	13	15	124	16	0	0	0	21

WALLIN, RICKARD — C — COYOTES

PERSONAL: Born April 9, 1980, in Stockholm, Sweden. ... 6-2/183. ... Shoots left.
TRANSACTIONS/CAREER NOTES: Selected by Phoenix Coyotes in sixth round (eighth Coyotes pick, 160th overall) of NHL entry draft (June 27, 1998).

Season Team	League	REGULAR SEASON Gms.	G	A	Pts.	PIM	PLAYOFFS Gms.	G	A	Pts.	PIM
96-97—Vasteras	Sweden Jr.	26	3	3	6	...	—	—	—	—	—
97-98—Farjestad Karlstad	Sweden Jr.	29	20	20	40	32	2	1	1	2	2

WALLIN, VIKTOR — C — MIGHTY DUCKS

PERSONAL: Born January 17, 1980, in Jonkoping, Sweden. ... 6-3/198. ... Shoots left.
TRANSACTIONS/CAREER NOTES: Selected by Mighty Ducks of Anaheim in fourth round (third Mighty Ducks pick, 112th overall) of NHL entry draft (June 27, 1998).

Season Team	League	REGULAR SEASON Gms.	G	A	Pts.	PIM	PLAYOFFS Gms.	G	A	Pts.	PIM
96-97—HV 71 Jonkoping	Sweden Jr.	16	1	2	3	...	—	—	—	—	—
97-98—HV 71 Jonkoping	Sweden Jr.	28	9	15	24	42	—	—	—	—	—

WARD, LANCE — D — PANTHERS

PERSONAL: Born June 2, 1978, in Lloydminster, Alta. ... 6-2/195. ... Shoots left.
TRANSACTIONS/CAREER NOTES: Selected by New Jersey Devils in first round (first Devils pick, 10th overall) of NHL entry draft (June 22, 1996). ... Returned to draft pool by Devils and selected by Florida Panthers in third round (third Panthers pick, 63rd overall) of NHL entry draft (June 27, 1998).

Season Team	League	REGULAR SEASON Gms.	G	A	Pts.	PIM	PLAYOFFS Gms.	G	A	Pts.	PIM
94-95—Red Deer	WHL	28	0	0	0	57	—	—	—	—	—
95-96—Red Deer	WHL	72	4	13	17	127	10	0	4	4	10
96-97—Red Deer	WHL	70	5	34	39	229	16	0	3	3	36
97-98—Red Deer	WHL	71	8	25	33	233	5	0	0	0	16

WARREN, MORGAN — RW — MAPLE LEAFS

PERSONAL: Born March 6, 1980, in Summerside, P.E.I. ... 6-1/190. ... Shoots right.
TRANSACTIONS/CAREER NOTES: Selected by Toronto Maple Leafs in fifth round (fifth Maple Leafs pick, 126th overall) of NHL entry draft (June 27, 1998).

Season Team	League	REGULAR SEASON Gms.	G	A	Pts.	PIM	PLAYOFFS Gms.	G	A	Pts.	PIM
97-98—Moncton	QMJHL	58	11	10	21	80	10	2	2	4	2

WENDELL, ERIK — C/LW — CAPITALS

PERSONAL: Born August 23, 1979, in Minneapolis. ... 6-1/197. ... Shoots left.
HIGH SCHOOL: Maple Grove (Minn.).
TRANSACTIONS/CAREER NOTES: Selected by Washington Capitals in fifth round (sixth Capitals pick, 125th overall) of NHL entry draft (June 27, 1998).

Season Team	League	REGULAR SEASON Gms.	G	A	Pts.	PIM	PLAYOFFS Gms.	G	A	Pts.	PIM
97-98—Maple Grove H.S.	USHS (West)	24	24	23	47	28	—	—	—	—	—

WESTLUND, TOMMY — RW — HURRICANES

PERSONAL: Born December 29, 1974, in Fors, Sweden. ... 6-1/207. ... Shoots right.
TRANSACTIONS/CAREER NOTES: Selected by Carolina Hurricanes in fourth round (fifth Hurricanes pick, 93rd overall) of NHL entry draft (June 27, 1998).

| Season Team | League | REGULAR SEASON | | | | | PLAYOFFS | | | | |
		Gms.	G	A	Pts.	PIM	Gms.	G	A	Pts.	PIM
91-92—Avesta	Sweden Dv. 3	27	11	9	20	8	—	—	—	—	—
92-93—Avesta	Sweden Dv. 2	32	9	5	14	32	—	—	—	—	—
93-94—Avesta	Sweden Dv. 2	31	20	11	31	34	—	—	—	—	—
94-95—Avesta	Sweden Dv. 2	32	17	13	30	22	—	—	—	—	—
95-96—Brynas Gavle	Sweden	18	2	1	3	2	—	—	—	—	—
—Brynas Gavle	Sweden Dv. 2	18	10	10	20	4	8	1	0	1	4
96-97—Brynas Gavle	Sweden	50	21	13	34	16	—	—	—	—	—
97-98—Brynas Gavle	Sweden	46	29	9	38	45	3	0	1	1	0

ZALESAK, MIROSLAV — RW — SHARKS

PERSONAL: Born January 2, 1980, in Skalica, Czechoslovakia. ... 6-1/183. ... Shoots left.
TRANSACTIONS/CAREER NOTES: Selected by San Jose Sharks in fourth round (fifth Sharks pick, 104th overall) of NHL entry draft (June 27, 1998).

| Season Team | League | REGULAR SEASON | | | | | PLAYOFFS | | | | |
		Gms.	G	A	Pts.	PIM	Gms.	G	A	Pts.	PIM
95-96—HC Nitra	Slovakia Jrs.	49	53	29	82	...	—	—	—	—	—
96-97—HC Nitra	Slovakia Jrs.	58	51	31	82	...	—	—	—	—	—
97-98—HC Nitra	Slovakia Jrs.	23	33	23	56	16	—	—	—	—	—
—Plastika Nitra	Slovakia	30	8	6	14	0	—	—	—	—	—

ZEVAKHIN, ALEXANDER — C — PENGUINS

PERSONAL: Born June 4, 1980, in Perm, U.S.S.R. ... 6-0/187. ... Shoots left.
TRANSACTIONS/CAREER NOTES: Selected by Pittsburgh Penguins in second round (second Penguins pick, 54th overall) of NHL entry draft (June 27, 1998).

| Season Team | League | REGULAR SEASON | | | | | PLAYOFFS | | | | |
		Gms.	G	A	Pts.	PIM	Gms.	G	A	Pts.	PIM
95-96—CSKA	CIS Jr.	65	52	30	82	30	—	—	—	—	—
96-97—CSKA Moscow	Rus. Div. II	29	7	3	10	10	—	—	—	—	—
—CSKA-2 Moscow	Rus. Div. III	30	15	18	33	10	—	—	—	—	—
97-98—CSKA-2 Moscow	Rus. Div. III	32	13	14	27	20	—	—	—	—	—
—CSKA Moscow	Russian	10	1	0	1	0	—	—	—	—	—

ZIZKA, TOMAS — D — KINGS

PERSONAL: Born October 10, 1979, in Sternberk, Czechoslovakia. ... 6-1/198. ... Shoots left.
TRANSACTIONS/CAREER NOTES: Selected by Los Angeles Kings in sixth round (sixth Kings pick, 163rd overall) of NHL entry draft (June 27, 1998).

| Season Team | League | REGULAR SEASON | | | | | PLAYOFFS | | | | |
		Gms.	G	A	Pts.	PIM	Gms.	G	A	Pts.	PIM
94-95—ZPS Zlin Jrs.	Czech Rep.	39	1	10	11	...	—	—	—	—	—
95-96—ZPS Zlin Jrs.	Czech Rep.	47	2	8	10	...	—	—	—	—	—
96-97—ZPS Zlin Jrs.	Czech Rep.	14	1	0	1	...	—	—	—	—	—
97-98—ZPS Zlin	Czech Rep.	33	0	3	3	2	—	—	—	—	—
—ZPS Zlin Jrs.	Czech Rep.	11	3	4	7	...	—	—	—	—	—

BOWMAN, SCOTTY   RED WINGS

PERSONAL: Born September 18, 1933, in Montreal. ... Full name: William Scott Bowman.
HONORS: Inducted into Hall of Fame (1991).

HEAD COACHING RECORD
BACKGROUND: Minor league hockey supervisor, Montreal Canadiens organization (1954-55 through 1956-57). ... Coach, Team Canada (1976 and 1981). ... Director of hockey operations/general manager, Buffalo Sabres (1979-80 through 1986-87). ... Director of player development, Pittsburgh Penguins (1990-91). ... Director of player personnel, Detroit Red Wings (1994-95 through present).
HONORS: Won Jack Adams Award (1976-77 and 1995-96). ... Named NHL Executive of the Year by THE SPORTING NEWS (1979-80). ... Named NHL Coach of the Year by THE SPORTING NEWS (1995-96).
RECORDS: Holds NHL career regular-season records for wins—1,057; and winning percentage—.658. ... Holds NHL career playoff records for wins—194; and games—305.

		REGULAR SEASON						PLAYOFFS		
Season Team	League	W	L	T	Pct.	Finish		W	L	Pct.
67-68—St. Louis	NHL	23	21	14	.517	3rd/Western Division		8	10	.444
68-69—St. Louis	NHL	37	25	14	.579	1st/Western Division		8	4	.667
69-70—St. Louis	NHL	37	27	12	.566	1st/Western Division		8	8	.500
70-71—St. Louis	NHL	13	10	5	.554	2nd/West Division		2	4	.333
71-72—Montreal	NHL	46	16	16	.692	3rd/Eastern Division		2	4	.333
72-73—Montreal	NHL	52	10	16	.769	1st/East Division		12	5	.706
73-74—Montreal	NHL	45	24	9	.635	2nd/East Division		2	4	.333
74-75—Montreal	NHL	47	14	19	.706	1st/Adams Division		6	5	.545
75-76—Montreal	NHL	58	11	11	.794	1st/Adams Division		12	1	.923
76-77—Montreal	NHL	60	8	12	.825	1st/Adams Division		12	2	.857
77-78—Montreal	NHL	59	10	11	.806	1st/Adams Division		12	3	.800
78-79—Montreal	NHL	52	17	11	.719	1st/Adams Division		12	4	.750
79-80—Buffalo	NHL	47	17	16	.688	1st/Adams Division		9	5	.643
81-82—Buffalo	NHL	18	10	7	.614	3rd/Adams Division		1	3	.250
82-83—Buffalo	NHL	38	29	13	.556	3rd/Adams Division		6	4	.600
83-84—Buffalo	NHL	48	25	7	.644	2nd/Adams Division		0	3	.000
84-85—Buffalo	NHL	38	28	14	.563	3rd/Adams Division		2	3	.400
85-86—Buffalo	NHL	18	18	1	.500	5th/Adams Division		—	—	—
86-87—Buffalo	NHL	3	7	2	.333	5th/Adams Division		—	—	—
91-92—Pittsburgh	NHL	39	32	9	.544	3rd/Patrick Division		16	5	.762
92-93—Pittsburgh	NHL	56	21	7	.708	1st/Patrick Division		7	5	.583
93-94—Detroit	NHL	46	30	8	.595	1st/Central Division		3	4	.429
94-95—Detroit	NHL	33	11	4	.729	1st/Central Division		12	6	.667
95-96—Detroit	NHL	62	13	7	.799	1st/Central Division		10	9	.526
96-97—Detroit	NHL	38	26	18	.573	2nd/Central Division		16	4	.800
97-98—Detroit	NHL	44	23	15	.628	2nd/Central Division		16	6	.727
NHL Totals (26 years)		**1057**	**483**	**278**	**.658**	**NHL Totals (24 years)**		**194**	**111**	**.636**

NOTES:
67-68—Defeated Philadelphia in Western Division finals; defeated Minnesota in Stanley Cup semifinals; lost to Montreal in Stanley Cup finals.
68-69—Defeated Philadelphia in Stanley Cup quarterfinals; defeated Los Angeles in Stanley Cup semifinals; lost to Montreal in Stanley Cup finals.
69-70—Defeated Minnesota in Stanley Cup quarterfinals; defeated Pittsburgh in Stanley Cup semifinals; lost to Montreal in Stanley Cup finals.
70-71—Lost to Minnesota in Stanley Cup quarterfinals.
71-72—Lost to New York Rangers in Stanley Cup quarterfinals.
72-73—Defeated Buffalo in Stanley Cup quarterfinals; defeated Philadelphia in Stanley Cup semifinals; defeated Chicago in Stanley Cup finals.
73-74—Lost to New York Rangers in Stanley Cup quarterfinals.
74-75—Defeated Vancouver in Stanley Cup quarterfinals; lost to Buffalo in Stanley Cup semifinals.
75-76—Defeated Chicago in Stanley Cup quarterfinals; defeated New York Islanders in Stanley Cup semifinals; defeated Philadelphia in Stanley Cup finals.
76-77—Defeated St. Louis in Stanley Cup quarterfinals; defeated New York Islanders in Stanley Cup semifinals; defeated Boston in Stanley Cup finals.
77-78—Defeated Detroit in Stanley Cup quarterfinals; defeated Toronto in Stanley Cup semifinals; defeated Boston in Stanley Cup finals.
78-79—Defeated Toronto in Stanley Cup quarterfinals; defeated Boston in Stanley Cup semifinals; defeated New York Rangers in Stanley Cup finals.
79-80—Defeated Vancouver in Stanley Cup preliminary round; defeated Chicago in Stanley Cup quarterfinals; lost to New York Islanders in Stanley Cup semi-finals.
81-82—Lost to Boston in Stanley Cup preliminary round.
82-83—Defeated Montreal in Adams Division semifinals; lost to Boston in Adams Division finals.
83-84—Lost to Quebec in Adams Division semifinals.
84-85—Lost to Quebec in Adams Division semifinals.
91-92—Defeated Washington in Patrick Division semifinals; defeated New York Rangers in Patrick Division finals; defeated Boston in Wales Conference finals; defeated Chicago in Stanley Cup finals.
92-93—Defeated New Jersey in Patrick Division semifinals; lost to New York Islanders in Patrick Division finals.
93-94—Lost to San Jose in Western Conference quarterfinals.
94-95—Defeated Dallas in Western Conference quarterfinals; defeated San Jose in Western Conference semifinals; defeated Chicago in Western Conference finals; lost to New Jersey in Stanley Cup finals.
95-96—Defeated Winnipeg in Western Conference quarterfinals; defeated St. Louis in Western Conference semifinals; lost to Colorado in Western Conference finals.
96-97—Defeated St. Louis in Western Conference quarterfinals; defeated Anaheim in Western Conference semifinals; defeated Colorado in Western Conference finals; defeated Philadelphia in Stanley Cup finals.
97-98—Defeated Phoenix in Western Conference quarterfinals; defeated St. Louis in Western Conference semifinals; defeated Dallas in Western Conference finals; defeated Washington in Stanley Cup finals.

BURNS, PAT   BRUINS

PERSONAL: Born April 4, 1952, in St.-Henri, Que.
MISCELLANEOUS: Served 17 years with the Gastineau (Quebec) and Ottawa Police Departments before assuming a professional hockey coaching career.

HEAD COACHING RECORD

BACKGROUND: Assistant coach, Canadian national team (1986). ... Assistant coach, Canadian Jr. national team (1987).
HONORS: Named NHL Coach of the Year by THE SPORTING NEWS (1988-89, 1992-93 and 1997-98). ... Won Jack Adams Award (1988-89, 1992-93 and 1997-98). ... Only coach in NHL history to win Coach of the Year award for three different NHL teams.

Season Team	League	REGULAR SEASON						PLAYOFFS		
		W	L	T	Pct.	Finish		W	L	Pct.
83-84—Hull	QMJHL	25	45	0	.357	6th/LeBel Division		—	—	—
84-85—Hull	QMJHL	33	34	1	.493	2nd/LeBel Division		1	4	.200
85-86—Hull	QMJHL	54	18	0	.750	1st/LeBel Division		15	0	1.000
86-87—Hull	QMJHL	26	39	5	.407	4th/LeBel Division		4	4	.500
87-88—Sherbrooke	AHL	42	34	4	.550	3rd/North Division		2	4	.333
88-89—Montreal	NHL	53	18	9	.719	1st/Adams Division		14	7	.667
89-90—Montreal	NHL	41	28	11	.581	3rd/Adams Division		5	6	.455
90-91—Montreal	NHL	39	30	11	.556	2nd/Adams Division		7	6	.538
91-92—Montreal	NHL	41	28	11	.581	1st/Adams Division		4	7	.364
92-93—Toronto	NHL	44	29	11	.589	3rd/Norris Division		11	10	.524
93-94—Toronto	NHL	43	29	12	.583	2nd/Central Division		9	9	.500
94-95—Toronto	NHL	21	19	8	.521	4th/Central Division		3	4	.429
95-96—Toronto	NHL	25	30	10	.462			—	—	—
97-98—Boston	NHL	39	30	13	.555	2nd/Northeast Division		2	4	.333
NHL Totals (9 years)		**346**	**241**	**96**	**.577**	**NHL Totals (8 years)**		**55**	**53**	**.509**

NOTES:
84-85—Lost to Verdun in quarterfinals of President Cup playoffs.
85-86—Defeated Shawinigan in quarterfinals of Presiden Cup playoffs; defeated St. Jean in semifinals of President Cup playoffs; defeated Drummondville in President Cup finals.
86-87—Eliminated in President Cup quarterfinal round-robin series.
87-88—Lost to Fredericton in quarterfinals of Calder Cup playoffs.
88-89—Defeated Hartford in Adams Division semifinals; defeated Boston in Adams Division finals; defeated Philadelphia in Wales Conference finals; lost to Calgary in Stanley Cup finals.
89-90—Defeated Buffalo in Adams Division semifinals; lost to Boston in Adams Division finals.
90-91—Defeated Buffalo in Adams Division semifinals; lost to Boston in Adams Division finals.
91-92—Defeated Hartford in Adams Division semifinals; lost to Boston in Adams Division finals.
92-93—Defeated Detroit in Norris Division semifinals; defeated St. Louis in Norris Division finals; lost to Los Angeles in Campbell Conference finals.
93-94—Defeated Chicago in Western Conference quarterfinals; defeated San Jose in Western Conference semifinals; lost to Vancouver in Western Conference finals.
94-95—Lost to Chicago in Western Conference quarterfinals.
95-96—Replaced as head coach by Nick Beverley (March 4) with club in fifth place.
97-98—Lost to Washington in Eastern Conference quarterfinals.

CONSTANTINE, KEVIN   PENGUINS

PERSONAL: Born December 27, 1958, in International Falls, Minn. ... Full Name: Kevin Lars Constantine.
HIGH SCHOOL: International Falls (Minn.).
COLLEGE: Rensselaer Polytechnic Institute (N.Y.), then Nevada-Reno.
TRANSACTIONS/CAREER NOTES: Selected by Montreal Canadiens in ninth round (11th Canadiens pick, 154th overall) in NHL entry draft (June 15, 1978). ... Invited to Canadiens tryout camp (1980).
MISCELLANEOUS: Played goaltender.

Season Team	League	REGULAR SEASON								PLAYOFFS						
		Gms.	Min	W	L	T	GA	SO	Avg.	Gms.	Min.	W	L	GA	SO	Avg.
77-78—R.P.I.	ECAC	6	229	2	2	0	13	0	3.41	—	—	—	—	—	—	—
78-79—R.P.I.	ECAC	5	233	3	2	0	15	0	3.86	—	—	—	—	—	—	—
79-80—R.P.I.	ECAC	24	1342	11	9	0	89	1	3.98	—	—	—	—	—	—	—

HEAD COACHING RECORD

BACKGROUND: Junior varsity coach, Northwood Prep School, Lake Placid, N.Y. (1986-87). ... Assistant coach, Kalamazoo of IHL, Minnesota North Stars organization (1988-89 through 1990-91). ... Assistant coach, Calgary Flames (1996-97).
HONORS: IHL Coach of the Year (1991-92). ... Won Commissioner's Trophy (1991-92).

Season Team	League	REGULAR SEASON						PLAYOFFS		
		W	L	T	Pct.	Finish		W	L	Pct.
85-86—North Iowa	USHL	17	31	0	.354	6th/USHL		2	3	.400
87-88—Rochester	USHL	39	7	2	.833	T1st/USHL		7	4	.636
91-92—Kansas City	IHL	56	22	4	.707	1st/West Division		12	3	.800
92-93—Kansas City	IHL	46	26	10	.622	2nd/Midwest Division		6	6	.500
93-94—San Jose	NHL	33	35	16	.488	3rd/Pacific Division		7	7	.500
94-95—San Jose	NHL	19	25	4	.438	3rd/Pacific Division		4	7	.364
95-96—San Jose	NHL	3	18	4	.200			—	—	—
97-98—Pittsburgh	NHL	40	24	18	.598	1st/Northeast Division		2	4	.333
NHL Totals (4 years)		**95**	**102**	**42**	**.485**	**NHL Totals (3 years)**		**13**	**18**	**.419**

NOTES:
85-86—Lost to Sioux City in USHL quarterfinals.
87-88—Defeated Sioux City in USHL quarterfinals; defeated St. Paul in USHL semifinals; lost to Thunder Bay in USHL finals. Finished first in USA Jr. A Championships.
91-92—Defeated Salt Lake City in quarterfinals of Turner Cup playoffs; defeated Peoria in semifinals of Turner Cup playoffs; defeated Muskegon in Turner Cup finals.
92-93—Defeated Milwaukee in quarterfinals of Turner Cup playoffs; lost to San Diego in semifinals of Turner Cup playoffs.
93-94—Defeated Detroit in Western Conference quarterfinals; lost to Toronto in Western Conference semifinals.
94-95—Defeated Calgary in Western Conference quarterfinals; lost to Detroit in Western Conference semifinals. Replaced as head coach by Jim Wiley (December 2) with club in seventh place.
95-96—Replaced as head coach by Jim Wiley (December 2) with club in seventh place.
97-98—Lost to Montreal in Eastern Conference quarterfinals.

DEMERS, JACQUES   LIGHTNING

PERSONAL: Born August 25, 1944, in Montreal.

HEAD COACHING RECORD
BACKGROUND: Director of player personnel, Chicago Cougars of WHA (1972-73). ... Scout, Montreal Canadiens (October 21, 1995 through November 12, 1997).

HONORS: Won Louis A.R. Pieri Memorial Award (1982-83). ... Named NHL Coach of the Year by THE SPORTING NEWS (1985-86 and 1986-87). ... Won Jack Adams Award (1986-87 and 1987-88).

Season Team	League	W	L	T	Pct.	Finish	W	L	Pct.
75-76—Indianapolis	WHA	35	39	6	.475	1st/Eastern Division	3	4	.429
76-77—Indianapolis	WHA	36	37	8	.494	3rd/Eastern Division	5	4	.556
77-78—Cincinnati	WHA	35	42	3	.456	7th/WHA	—	—	—
78-79—Quebec	WHA	41	34	5	.544	2nd/WHA	0	4	.000
79-80—Quebec	NHL	25	44	11	.381	5th/Adams Division	—	—	—
81-82—Fredericton	AHL	20	55	5	.281	5th/Northern Division	—	—	—
82-83—Fredericton	AHL	45	27	8	.613	1st/Northern Division	6	6	.500
83-84—St. Louis	NHL	32	41	7	.444	2nd/Norris Division	6	5	.545
84-85—St. Louis	NHL	37	31	12	.538	1st/Norris Division	0	3	.000
85-86—St. Louis	NHL	37	34	9	.519	3rd/Norris Division	10	9	.526
86-87—Detroit	NHL	34	36	10	.488	2nd/Norris Division	9	7	.563
87-88—Detroit	NHL	41	28	11	.581	1st/Norris Division	9	7	.563
88-89—Detroit	NHL	34	34	12	.500	1st/Norris Division	2	4	.333
89-90—Detroit	NHL	28	38	14	.438	5th/Norris Division	—	—	—
92-93—Montreal	NHL	48	30	6	.607	3rd/Adams Division	16	4	.800
93-94—Montreal	NHL	41	29	14	.571	3rd/Northeast Division	3	4	.429
94-95—Montreal	NHL	18	23	7	.448	6th/Northeast Division	—	—	—
95-96—Montreal	NHL	0	5	0	.000		—	—	—
97-98—Tampa Bay	NHL	15	43	8	.288	7th/Atlantic Division	—	—	—
WHA Totals (4 years)		**147**	**152**	**22**	**.492**				
NHL Totals (13 years)		**390**	**416**	**121**	**.486**	**NHL Totals (8 years)**	**55**	**43**	**.561**

NOTES:
75-76—Lost to New England in Avco World Cup quarterfinals.
76-77—Defeated Cincinnati in Avco World Cup quarterfinals; lost to Quebec in Avco World Cup semifinals.
78-79—Lost to Winnipeg in Avco World Cup semifinals.
82-83—Defeated Adirondack in Calder Cup quarterfinals; lost to Maine in Calder Cup semifinals.
83-84—Defeated Detroit in Norris Division semifinals; lost to Minnesota in Norris Division finals.
84-85—Lost to Minnesota in Norris Division finals.
85-86—Defeated Minnesota in Norris Division semifinals; defeated Toronto in Norris Division finals; lost to Calgary in Campbell Conference finals.
86-87—Defeated Chicago in Norris Division semifinals; defeated Toronto in Norris Division finals; lost to Edmonton in Campbell Conference finals.
87-88—Defeated Toronto in Norris Division semifinals; defeated St. Louis in Norris Division finals; lost to Edmonton in Campbell Conference finals.
88-89—Lost to Chicago in Norris Division semifinals.
92-93—Defeated Quebec in Adams Division semifinals; defeated Buffalo in Adams Division finals; defeated New York Islanders in Wales Conference finals; defeated Los Angeles in Stanley Cup finals.
93-94—Lost to Boston in Eastern Conference quarterfinals.
95-96—Replaced as head coach by Mario Tremblay (October 21) with club in sixth place.
97-98—Replaced interim head coach Rick Paterson (November 12) with club in seventh place.

FTOREK, ROBBIE   DEVILS

PERSONAL: Born January 2, 1952, in Needham, Mass. ... Full Name: Robert Brian Ftorek.

TRANSACTIONS/CAREER NOTES: Signed as a free agent by the Detroit Red Wings (1972). ... Signed as a free agent by the Phoenix Roadrunners of the World Hockey Association (1974). ... Sold to Cincinatti Stingers by Phoenix Roadrunners (April 1977). ... Claimed by Quebec Nordiques in the World Hockey Association dispersal draft (June 1979). ... Traded by Nordiques with eighth round pick (D Bryan Glynn) in 1982 draft to New York Rangers for Jere Gillis and Dean Talafous (December 1981). ... Named player/assistant coach of the New Haven Nighthawks of the AHL (October 1984). ... Announced retirement to become head coach of New Haven Nighthawks (July 1985).

HONORS: Named Most Valuable Player in WHA (1976-77). ... Named THE SPORTING NEWS WHA Player of the Year (1978-79).

Season Team	League	Gms.	G	A	Pts.	PIM	+/-	PP	SH	Gms.	G	A	Pts.	PIM
72-73—Virginia	AHL	55	17	42	59	36	...	...	...	5	2	2	4	4
—Detroit	NHL	3	0	0	0	0	—	—	—	—	—	—	—	—
73-74—Virginia	AHL	65	24	42	66	37	...	...	...	—	—	—	—	—
—Detroit	NHL	12	2	5	7	4	...	...	...	—	—	—	—	—
74-75—Tulsa	CHL	11	6	10	16	14	...	...	...	—	—	—	—	—
—Phoenix	WHA	53	31	37	68	29	...	...	...	5	2	5	7	2
75-76—Phoenix	WHA	80	41	72	113	109	...	...	...	5	1	3	4	2
76-77—Phoenix	WHA	80	46	71	117	86	...	...	...	—	—	—	—	—
77-78—Cincinnati	WHA	80	59	50	109	54	...	...	...	—	—	—	—	—
78-79—Cincinnati	WHA	80	39	77	116	87	...	...	...	3	3	2	5	6
79-80—Quebec	NHL	52	18	33	51	28	...	...	...	—	—	—	—	—
80-81—Quebec	NHL	78	24	49	73	104	...	...	...	5	1	2	3	17
81-82—Quebec	NHL	19	1	8	9	4	...	...	...	—	—	—	—	—
—New York Rangers	NHL	30	8	24	32	24	...	...	...	10	7	4	11	11
82-83—New York Rangers	NHL	61	12	19	31	41	...	...	...	4	1	0	1	0
83-84—New York Rangers	NHL	31	3	2	5	22	...	...	...	—	—	—	—	—
—Tulsa	CHL	25	11	11	22	10	...	...	...	9	4	5	9	2
84-85—New Haven	AHL	17	9	10	19	35	...	...	...	—	—	—	—	—
—New York Rangers	NHL	48	9	10	19	35	...	...	...	—	—	—	—	—
WHA Totals (4 years)		**293**	**170**	**236**	**406**	**279**	...	...	...	**13**	**6**	**10**	**16**	**10**
NHL Totals (8 years)		**331**	**77**	**153**	**230**	**262**	...	...	...	**19**	**9**	**6**	**15**	**28**

HEAD COACHING RECORD

BACKGROUND: Assistant coach, Quebec Nordiques (1989-90 and 1990-91). ... Assistant coach, New Jersey Devils (1991-92, 1996-97 and 1997-98).

HONORS: Won Louis A. R. Pieri Memorial Award (1994-95 and 1995-96).

Season Team	League	REGULAR SEASON					PLAYOFFS		
		W	L	T	Pct.	Finish	W	L	Pct.
85-86—New Haven	AHL	36	37	7	.494	4th/South Division	1	4	.200
86-87—New Haven	AHL	44	25	11	.619	3rd/South Division	3	4	.429
87-88—New Haven	AHL	16	8	3	.648	—	—	—	—
—Los Angeles	NHL	23	25	4	.481	4th/Smythe Division	1	4	.200
88-89—Los Angeles	NHL	42	31	7	.569	2nd/Smythe Division	4	7	.364
89-90—Halifax	AHL	25	19	4	.563	—	—	—	—
92-93—Utica	AHL	33	36	11	.481	3rd/Southern Division	1	4	.200
93-94—Albany	AHL	38	34	8	.525	3rd/Northern Division	1	4	.200
94-95—Albany	AHL	46	17	17	.681	1st/Northern Division	12	2	.857
95-96—Albany	AHL	54	19	17	.694	1st/Central Division	1	3	.250
NHL Totals (2 years)		65	56	11	.534	**NHL Totals (2 years)**	17	13	.567

NOTES:
85-86—Lost to Hershey in quarterfinals of Calder Cup playoffs.
87-88—Replaced Mike Murphy as head coach (December 9, 1987) with club in fifth place; lost to Calgary in Smythe Division semifinals in Stanley Cup playoffs.
88-89—Defeated Edmonton in Smythe Division semifinals of Stanley Cup playoffs; lost to Calgary in Smythe Division finals of Stanley Cup playoffs.
89-90—Hired as an assistant coach by Quebec Nordiques (January, 1990).
92-93—Lost to Rochester in quarterfinals of Calder Cup playoffs.
93-94—Lost to Portland in quarterfinals of Calder Cup playoffs.
94-95—Defeated Adirondack in division semifinals of Calder Cup playoffs; defeated Providence in division finals of Calder Cup playoffs; defeated Fredericton in Calder Cup finals.
95-96—Lost to Cornwall in conference quarterfinals of Calder Cup playoffs.

GRAHAM, DIRK   BLACKHAWKS

PERSONAL: Born July 29, 1959, in Regina, Sask. ... Played left wing. ... Shot right. ... Full name: Dirk Milton Graham.

TRANSACTIONS/CAREER NOTES: Selected by Vancouver Canucks in fifth round (fifth Canucks pick, 89th overall) of NHL entry draft (August 9, 1979). ... Signed as free agent by Minnesota North Stars (August 17, 1983). ... Sprained wrist (November 1987); missed seven games. ... Traded by North Stars to Chicago Blackhawks for LW Curt Fraser (January 4, 1988). ... Fined $500 by NHL for fighting (December 28, 1989). ... Fractured left kneecap (March 17, 1990); missed six weeks. ... Underwent surgery to left knee (May 1990). ... Separated shoulder (February 18, 1994); missed 17 games. ... Sprained knee (February 19, 1995); missed eight games. ... Announced retirement and named assistant coach of Blackhawks (August 7, 1995).

HONORS: Named to WHL All-Star second team (1978-79). ... Named to IHL All-Star second team (1980-81). ... Named to IHL All-Star first team (1982-83). ... Named to CHL All-Star first team (1983-84). ... Won Frank J. Selke Trophy (1990-91).

MISCELLANEOUS: Captain of Chicago Blackhawks (1988-1989 through 1994-95). ... Failed to score on a penalty shot (vs. Kelly Hrudey, March 9, 1995).

STATISTICAL PLATEAUS: Three-goal games: 1989-90 (1).

Season Team	League	REGULAR SEASON								PLAYOFFS				
		Gms.	G	A	Pts.	PIM	+/-	PP	SH	Gms.	G	A	Pts.	PIM
75-76—Regina Blues	SJHL	54	36	32	68	82	...	...	...	—	—	—	—	—
—Regina	WCHL	2	0	0	0	0	...	...	...	6	1	1	2	5
76-77—Regina	WCHL	65	37	28	65	66	...	...	...	—	—	—	—	—
77-78—Regina	WCHL	72	49	61	110	87	...	...	...	13	15	19	34	37
78-79—Regina	WHL	71	48	60	108	252	...	...	...	—	—	—	—	—
79-80—Dallas	CHL	62	17	15	32	96	...	...	...	—	—	—	—	—
80-81—Fort Wayne	IHL	6	1	2	3	12	...	...	...	—	—	—	—	—
—Toledo	IHL	61	40	45	85	88	...	...	...	—	—	—	—	—
81-82—Toledo	IHL	72	49	56	105	68	...	...	...	13	10	11	21	8
82-83—Toledo	IHL	78	70	55	125	86	...	...	...	11	13	7	†20	30
83-84—Minnesota	NHL	6	1	1	2	0	...	...	...	1	0	0	0	2
—Salt Lake City	CHL	57	37	57	94	72	...	...	...	5	3	8	11	2
84-85—Springfield	AHL	37	20	28	48	41	...	...	...	—	—	—	—	—
—Minnesota	NHL	36	12	11	23	23	...	...	...	9	0	4	4	7
85-86—Minnesota	NHL	80	22	33	55	87	...	...	...	5	3	1	4	2
86-87—Minnesota	NHL	76	25	29	54	142	...	...	...	—	—	—	—	—
87-88—Minnesota	NHL	28	7	5	12	39	...	...	...	—	—	—	—	—
—Chicago	NHL	42	17	19	36	32	...	...	...	4	1	2	3	4
88-89—Chicago	NHL	80	33	45	78	89	...	...	...	16	2	4	6	38
89-90—Chicago	NHL	73	22	32	54	102	1	2	3	5	1	5	6	2
90-91—Chicago	NHL	80	24	21	45	88	...	...	...	6	1	2	3	17
91-92—Chicago	NHL	80	17	30	47	89	...	...	...	18	7	5	12	8
92-93—Chicago	NHL	84	20	17	37	139	0	1	2	4	0	0	0	0
93-94—Chicago	NHL	67	15	18	33	45	13	0	2	6	0	1	1	4
94-95—Chicago	NHL	40	4	9	13	42	2	1	1	16	2	3	5	8
NHL Totals (12 years)		772	219	270	489	917	...	...	...	90	17	27	44	92

HEAD COACHING RECORD

BACKGROUND: Assistant coach, Chicago Blackhawks (1995-96). ... Scout, Blackhawks (1997-98).

HARTLEY, BOB — AVALANCHE

PERSONAL: Born September 7, 1960, in Hawksbury, Ont. ... Full name: Robert Hartley.

HEAD COACHING RECORD

		REGULAR SEASON						PLAYOFFS		
Season Team	League	W	L	T	Pct.	Finish		W	L	Pct.
92-93—Laval	QMJHL	43	25	2	.629	1st/Robert Le Bel Division		12	1	.923
94-95—Cornwall	AHL	38	33	9	.531	2nd/Southern Division		8	6	.571
95-96—Cornwall	AHL	34	39	7	.469	4th/Central Division		3	5	.375
96-97—Hershey	AHL	43	22	10	.640	2nd/Mid-Atlantic Division		15	8	.652
97-98—Hershey	AHL	36	31	7	.534	2nd/Mid-Atlantic Division		3	4	.429

NOTES:

92-93—Defeated Verdun in quarterfinals of President Cup playoffs; defeated Drummondville in semifinals of President Cup playoffs; defeated Sherbrooke in finals of President Cup playoffs.

94-95—Defeated Hershey in division semifinals in Calder Cup playoffs; defeated Binghamton in division finals in Calder Cup playoffs; lost to Fredericton in league semifinals in Calder Cup playoffs.

95-96—Defeated Albany in conference quarterfinals in Calder Cup playoffs; lost to Rochester in conference finals in Calder Cup playoffs.

96-97—Defeated Kentucky in conference quarterfinals in Calder Cup playoffs; defeated Philadelphia in conference semifinals in Calder Cup playoffs; defeated Springfield in conference finals in Calder Cup playoffs; defeated Hamilton in Calder Cup finals.

97-98—Defeated Kentucky in conference quarterfinals in Calder Cup playoffs; lost to Philadelphia in conference semifinals in Calder Cup playoffs.

HARTSBURG, CRAIG — MIGHTY DUCKS

PERSONAL: Born June 29, 1959, in Stratford, Ont. ... Played defense. ... Shot left.

TRANSACTIONS/CAREER NOTES: Selected by Minnesota North Stars in first round (first North Stars pick, sixth overall) of NHL entry draft (August 9, 1979). ... Tore ligaments in left knee (September 1977). ... Separated shoulder (September 1980). ... Underwent surgery to remove bone spur on knee (October 10, 1983). ... Injured ligaments in left knee (January 10, 1984). ... Suffered hip pointer (October 1984). ... Suffered fractured femur (December 1984). ... Injured groin (January 16, 1986); missed four games. ... Suffered herniated disc (February 1987). ... Strained knee ligaments (March 1987). ... Suffered concussion (November 7, 1987). ... Injured left hip and separated shoulder (March 1988). ... Underwent shoulder surgery (March 1988). ... Suffered staph infection on right ankle and required hospitalization (October 11, 1988). ... Reinjured right ankle (January 2, 1989).

HONORS: Won Max Kaminsky Memorial Trophy (1976-77). ... Named to OHA All-Star second team (1976-77). ... Played in NHL All-Star game (1980, 1982 and 1983).

MISCELLANEOUS: Played defense. ... Captain of Minnesota North Stars (1982-83 through 1987-88).

STATISTICAL PLATEAUS: Three-goal games: 1986-87 (1).

		REGULAR SEASON								PLAYOFFS				
Season Team	League	Gms.	G	A	Pts.	PIM	+/-	PP	SH	Gms.	G	A	Pts.	PIM
75-76—Sault Ste. Marie	OHA	64	9	19	28	65	...	...	...	—	—	—	—	—
76-77—Sault Ste. Marie	OHA	61	29	64	93	142	...	...	...	9	0	11	11	27
77-78—Sault Ste. Marie	OHA	36	15	42	57	101	...	...	...	13	4	8	12	24
78-79—Birmingham	WHA	77	9	40	49	73	...	...	...	—	—	—	—	—
79-80—Minnesota	NHL	79	14	30	44	81	...	7	0	15	3	1	4	17
80-81—Minnesota	NHL	74	13	30	43	124	-9	8	0	19	3	12	15	16
81-82—Minnesota	NHL	76	17	60	77	117	11	5	0	4	1	2	3	14
82-83—Minnesota	NHL	78	12	50	62	109	7	3	1	9	3	8	11	7
83-84—Minnesota	NHL	26	7	7	14	37	-2	5	0	—	—	—	—	—
84-85—Minnesota	NHL	32	7	11	18	54	-5	1	1	9	5	3	8	14
85-86—Minnesota	NHL	75	10	47	57	127	7	4	0	5	0	1	1	2
86-87—Minnesota	NHL	73	11	50	61	93	-2	4	0	—	—	—	—	—
87-88—Minnesota	NHL	27	3	16	19	29	-2	2	0	—	—	—	—	—
88-89—Minnesota	NHL	30	4	14	18	47	-8	1	0	—	—	—	—	—
WHA Totals (1 year)		77	9	40	49	73	...	...	...					
NHL Totals (10 years)		570	98	315	413	818	...	40	2	61	15	27	42	70

HEAD COACHING RECORD

BACKGROUND: Assistant coach, Minnesota North Stars (1989-90). ... Assistant coach, Philadelphia Flyers (1990-91 through 1993-94).

		REGULAR SEASON						PLAYOFFS		
Season Team	League	W	L	T	Pct.	Finish		W	L	Pct.
94-95—Guelph	OHL	47	14	5	.750	1st/Central Division		10	4	.714
95-96—Chicago	NHL	40	28	14	.573	2nd/Central Division		6	4	.600
96-97—Chicago	NHL	34	35	13	.494	5th/Central Division		2	4	.333
97-98—Chicago	NHL	30	39	13	.445	5th/Central Division		—	—	—
NHL Totals (3 years)		104	102	40	.504	NHL Totals (2 years)		8	8	.500

NOTES:

94-95—Defeated Owen Sound in second round of OHL playoffs; defeated Belleville in third round of OHL playoffs; lost to Detroit in J. Ross Robertson Cup finals.

95-96—Defeated Calgary in Western Conference quarterfinals; lost to Colorado in Western Conference semifinals.

96-97—Lost to Colorado in Western Conference quarterfinals.

HITCHCOCK, KEN — STARS

PERSONAL: Born December 17, 1951, in Edmonton.

COLLEGE: University of Alberta.

HEAD COACHING RECORD

BACKGROUND: Assistant coach, Philadelphia Flyers (1990-91 through 1992-93).
HONORS: Named NHL Coach of the Year by THE SPORTING NEWS (1996-97).

Season Team	League	REGULAR SEASON					PLAYOFFS		
		W	L	T	Pct.	Finish	W	L	Pct.
84-85—Kamloops	WHL	52	17	2	.746	1st/West Division	10	5	.667
85-86—Kamloops	WHL	49	19	4	.708	1st/West Division	14	2	.875
86-87—Kamloops	WHL	55	14	3	.785	1st/West Division	8	5	.615
87-88—Kamloops	WHL	45	26	1	.632	1st/West Division	12	6	.667
88-89—Kamloops	WHL	34	33	5	.507	3rd/West Division	8	8	.500
89-90—Kamloops	WHL	56	16	0	.778	1st/West Division	14	3	.824
93-94—Kalamazoo	IHL	48	26	7	.636	1st/Atlantic Division	1	4	.200
94-95—Kalamazoo	IHL	43	24	14	.617	2nd/Northern Division	10	6	.625
95-96—Dallas	NHL	15	23	5	.407	6th/Central Division	—	—	—
—Michigan	IHL	19	10	11	.613	2nd/Northern Division	—	—	—
96-97—Dallas	NHL	48	26	8	.634	1st/Central Division	2	4	.333
97-98—Dallas	NHL	49	22	11	.665	1st/Central Division	10	7	.588
NHL Totals (3 years)		112	71	24	.599	**NHL Totals (2 years)**	12	11	.522

NOTES:
84-85—Defeated Portland in West Division semifinals; defeated New Westminster in West Division finals; lost to Prince Albert in WHL finals.
85-86—Defeated Seattle in West Division semifinals; defeated Portland in West Division finals; defeated Medicine Hat in WHL finals.
86-87—Defeated Victoria in West Division semifinals; lost to Portland in West Division finals.
87-88—Defeated New Westminster in West Division semifinals; defeated Spokane in West Division finals; lost to Medicine Hat in WHL finals.
88-89—Defeated Victoria in West Division semifinals; lost to Portland in West Division finals.
89-90—Defeated Spokane in West Division semifinals; defeated Seattle in West Division finals; defeated Lethbridge in WHL finals.
93-94—Lost to Cincinnati in Eastern Conference quarterfinals.
94-95—Defeated Chicago in Eastern Conference quarterfinals; defeated Cincinnati in Eastern Conference semifinals; lost to Kansas City in Eastern Conference finals.
95-96—Replaced Bob Gainey as head coach (January 8) with club in sixth place.
96-97—Lost to Edmonton in Western Conference quarterfinals.
97-98—Defeated San Jose in Western Conference quarterfinals; defeated Edmonton in Western Conference semifinals; lost to Detroit in Western Conference finals.

KEENAN, MIKE   CANUCKS

PERSONAL: Born October 21, 1949, in Whitby, Ont. ... Played left wing. ... Shot right. ... Full name: Michael Edward Keenan.
HIGH SCHOOL: Denis O'Connor (Ajax, Ont.).
COLLEGE: St. Lawrence (N.Y.).

Season Team	League	REGULAR SEASON								PLAYOFFS				
		Gms.	G	A	Pts.	PIM	+/-	PP	SH	Gms.	G	A	Pts.	PIM
69-70—St. Lawrence Univ.	ECAC	10	0	4	4	32	...	...	...	—	—	—	—	—
70-71—St. Lawrence Univ.	ECAC	22	4	12	16	35	...	...	...	—	—	—	—	—
71-72—St. Lawrence Univ.	ECAC	25	13	16	29	52	...	...	...	—	—	—	—	—

HEAD COACHING RECORD

BACKGROUND: Coach, Canadian national junior team (1980). ... Coach, NHL All-Star team (1985-86, 1987-88 and 1992-93). ... Coach, Team Canada (1987). ... General manager, Chicago Blackhawks (1989-90 through 1991-92). ... General manager/coach, Team Canada (1991). ... Coach, Canadian national team (1993). ... General manager, St. Louis Blues (1994-95 through December 18, 1996).
HONORS: Named NHL Coach of the Year by THE SPORTING NEWS (1984-85). ... Won Jack Adams Award (1984-85).

Season Team	League	REGULAR SEASON					PLAYOFFS		
		W	L	T	Pct.	Finish	W	L	Pct.
79-80—Peterborough	OHL	47	20	1	.699	1st/Leyden Division	15	3	.833
80-81—Rochester	AHL	30	42	8	.425	5th/Southern Division	—	—	—
81-82—Rochester	AHL	40	31	9	.556	2nd/Southern Division	4	5	.444
82-83—Rochester	AHL	46	25	9	.631	1st/Southern Division	12	4	.750
83-84—University of Toronto	OUAA	41	5	3	.867	1st/OUAA	9	0	1.000
84-85—Philadelphia	NHL	53	20	7	.706	1st/Patrick Division	12	7	.632
85-86—Philadelphia	NHL	53	23	4	.688	1st/Patrick Division	2	3	.400
86-87—Philadelphia	NHL	46	26	8	.625	1st/Patrick Division	15	11	.577
87-88—Philadelphia	NHL	38	33	9	.531	3rd/Patrick Division	3	4	.429
88-89—Chicago	NHL	27	41	12	.413	4th/Norris Division	9	7	.563
89-90—Chicago	NHL	41	33	6	.550	1st/Norris Division	10	10	.500
90-91—Chicago	NHL	49	23	8	.663	1st/Norris Division	2	4	.333
91-92—Chicago	NHL	36	29	15	.544	2nd/Norris Division	12	6	.667
92-93—Canadian nat'l team	Int'l	—	—	—	.000	Record unavailable.	—	—	—
93-94—New York Rangers	NHL	52	24	8	.667	1st/Atlantic Division	16	7	.696
94-95—St. Louis	NHL	28	15	5	.635	2nd/Central Division	3	4	.429
95-96—St. Louis	NHL	32	34	16	.488	4th/Central Division	7	6	.538
96-97—St. Louis	NHL	15	17	1	.470	—	—	—	—
97-98—Vancouver	NHL	21	30	12	.429	7th/Pacific Division	—	—	—
NHL Totals (13 years)		491	348	111	.575	**NHL Totals (11 years)**	91	69	.569

NOTES:
81-82—Defeated New Haven in Calder Cup quarterfinals; lost to Binghamton in Calder Cup semifinals.
82-83—Defeated Binghamton in Calder Cup quarterfinals; defeated New Haven in Calder Cup semifinals; defeated Maine in Calder Cup finals.
83-84—Defeated Guelph in OUAA semifinals; defeated Western Ontario in OUAA finals; defeated New Brunswick in East Regional Qualifying Round; defeated Trois-Rivieres in CIAU Championship Tournament semifinals; defeated Concordia in CIAU Championship Tournament finals.
84-85—Defeated New York Rangers in Patrick Division semifinals; defeated New York Islanders in Patrick Division finals; defeated Quebec in Wales Conference finals; lost to Edmonton in Stanley Cup finals.

85-86—Lost to New York Rangers in Patrick Division semifinals.
86-87—Defeated New York Rangers in Patrick Division semifinals; defeated New York Islanders in Patrick Division finals; defeated Montreal in Wales Conference finals; lost to Edmonton in Stanley Cup finals.
87-88—Lost to Washington in Patrick Division semifinals.
88-89—Defeated Detroit in Norris Division semifinals; defeated St. Louis in Norris Division finals; lost to Calgary in Campbell Conference finals.
89-90—Defeated Minnesota in Norris Division semifinals; defeated St. Louis in Norris Division finals; lost to Edmonton in Campbell Conference finals.
90-91—Lost to Minnesota in Norris Division semifinals.
91-92—Defeated St. Louis in Norris Division semifinals; defeated Detroit in Norris Division finals; defeated Edmonton in Campbell Conference finals; lost to Pittsburgh in Stanley Cup finals.
92-93—Finished fourth in World Championships.
93-94—Defeated New York Islanders in Eastern Conference quarterfinals; defeated Washington in Eastern Conference semifinals; defeated New Jersey in Eastern Conference finals; defeated Vancouver in Stanley Cup finals.
94-95—Lost to Vancouver in Western Conference quarterfinals.
95-96—Defeated Toronto in Western Conference quarterfinals; lost to Detroit in Western Conference semifinals.
96-97—Replaced by interim Jimmy Roberts as head coach (December 18).
97-98—Replaced Tom Renney as head coach (November 13) with club in seventh place.

LOW, RON   OILERS

PERSONAL: Born June 21, 1950, in Birtle, Man. Played goaltender. ... Caught right. ... Full Name: Ron Albert Low. ... Name pronounced LOH.
TRANSACTIONS/CAREER NOTES: Selected by Toronto Maple Leafs in eighth round (eighth Maple Leafs pick, 103rd overall) of NHL amateur draft (June 11, 1970). ... Claimed by Washington Capitals from Maple Leafs in expansion draft (June 12, 1974). ... Signed as free agent by Detroit Red Wings (August 17, 1977). ... Claimed by Quebec Nordiques from Red Wings in expansion draft (June 13, 1979). ... Traded by Nordiques to Edmonton Oilers for C Ron Chipperfield (March 11, 1980). ... Traded by Oilers to New Jersey Devils with D Jim McTaggart for G Lindsay Middlebrook and C Paul Miller (February 19, 1983).
HONORS: Named to CHL All-Star second team (1973-74). ... Won Tommy Ivan Trophy (1978-79). ... Named to CHL All-Star first team (1978-79).
MISCELLANEOUS: Played goaltender.

			REGULAR SEASON							PLAYOFFS						
Season Team	League	Gms.	Min	W	L	T	GA	SO	Avg.	Gms.	Min.	W	L	GA	SO	Avg.
70-71—Jacksonville	EHL	49	2940	...	...	...	293	1	5.98	—	—	—	—	—	—	—
—Tulsa	CHL	4	192	...	...	...	11	0	3.44	—	—	—	—	—	—	—
71-72—Richmond	AHL	1	60	...	...	...	2	0	2.00	—	—	—	—	—	—	—
—Tulsa	CHL	43	2428	...	...	...	135	1	3.34	8	474	...	...	15	1	1.90
72-73—Toronto	NHL	42	2343	12	24	4	152	1	3.89	—	—	—	—	—	—	—
73-74—Tulsa	CHL	56	3213	...	...	...	169	1	3.16	—	—	—	—	—	—	—
74-75—Washington	NHL	48	2588	8	36	2	235	1	5.45	—	—	—	—	—	—	—
75-76—Washington	NHL	43	2289	6	31	2	208	0	5.45	—	—	—	—	—	—	—
76-77—Washington	NHL	54	2918	16	27	5	188	0	3.87	—	—	—	—	—	—	—
77-78—Detroit	NHL	32	1816	9	12	9	102	1	3.37	4	240	1	3	17	0	4.25
78-79—Kansas City	CHL	63	3795	...	...	...	244	0	3.86	4	237	...	...	15	...	3.80
79-80—Syracuse	AHL	15	905	5	9	1	70	0	4.64	—	—	—	—	—	—	—
—Quebec	NHL	15	828	5	7	2	51	0	3.70	—	—	—	—	—	—	—
—Edmonton	NHL	11	650	8	2	1	37	0	3.42	3	212	0	3	12	...	3.40
80-81—Edmonton	NHL	24	1260	5	13	3	93	0	4.43	—	—	—	—	—	—	—
—Wichita	CHL	2	120	0	2	0	10	0	5.00	—	—	—	—	—	—	—
81-82—Edmonton	NHL	29	1554	17	7	1	100	0	3.86	—	—	—	—	—	—	—
82-83—Edmonton	NHL	3	104	0	1	0	10	0	5.77	—	—	—	—	—	—	—
—New Jersey	NHL	11	608	2	7	1	41	0	4.05	—	—	—	—	—	—	—
83-84—New Jersey	NHL	44	2218	8	25	4	161	0	4.36	—	—	—	—	—	—	—
84-85—New Jersey	NHL	26	1326	6	11	4	85	1	3.85	—	—	—	—	—	—	—
NHL Totals (11 years)		382	20,502	102	203	38	1463	4	4.28	7	452	1	6	29	0	3.85

HEAD COACHING RECORD

BACKGROUND: Player/assistant coach, Nova Scotia Oilers (1985-86). ... Assistant coach, Nova Scotia Oilers (1986-87). ... Assistant coach, Edmonton Oilers (August 3, 1989 through 1994-95).

		REGULAR SEASON					PLAYOFFS		
Season Team	League	W	L	T	Pct.	Finish	W	L	Pct.
87-88—Nova Scotia	AHL	35	36	9	.494	4th/Northern Division	—	—	—
88-89—Cape Breton	AHL	27	47	6	.375	7th/Northern Division	—	—	—
94-95—Edmonton	NHL	5	7	1	.423	5th/Pacific Division	—	—	—
95-96—Edmonton	NHL	30	44	8	.415	5th/Pacific Division	—	—	—
96-97—Edmonton	NHL	36	37	9	.494	3rd/Pacific Division	5	6	.455
97-98—Edmonton	NHL	35	37	10	.488	3rd/Pacific Division	5	7	.417
NHL Totals (4 years)		106	125	28	.463	**NHL Totals (2 years)**	10	13	.435

NOTES:
96-97—Defeated Dallas in western Conference quarterfinals; lost to Colorado in Western Conferenece semifinals.
97-98—Defeated Colorado in Western Conference quarterfinals; lost to Dallas in Western Conference semifinals.

MARTIN, JACQUES   SENATORS

PERSONAL: Born October 1, 1952, in Rockland, Ont.

HEAD COACHING RECORD

BACKGROUND: Assistant coach, Chicago Blackhawks (1988-89 through 1989-90). ... Assistant coach, Quebec Nordiques (1990-91 through 1992-93 and 1994-95). ... Assistant coach, Colorado Avalanche (1995 through January 24, 1996).

Season Team	League	REGULAR SEASON W	L	T	Pct.	Finish	PLAYOFFS W	L	Pct.
85-86—Guelph	OHL	41	23	2	.636	2nd/Emms Division	15	3	.833
86-87—St. Louis	NHL	32	33	15	.494	1st/Norris Division	2	4	.333
87-88—St. Louis	NHL	34	38	8	.475	2nd/Norris Division	5	5	.500
93-94—Cornwall	AHL	33	36	11	.481	T3rd/Southern Division	4	2	.667
95-96—Ottawa	NHL	10	24	4	.316	6th/Northeast Division	—	—	—
96-97—Ottawa	NHL	31	36	15	.470	T3rd/Northeast Division	3	4	.429
97-98—Ottawa	NHL	34	33	15	.506	5th/Northeast Division	5	6	.455
NHL Totals (5 years)		141	164	57	.468	**NHL Totals (4 years)**	15	19	.441

NOTES:

85-86—Defeated Sudbury in OHL quarterfinals; defeated Windsor in OHL semifinals; defeated Belleville in J. Ross Robertson Cup finals.

86-87—Lost to Toronto in Norris Division semifinals.

87-88—Defeated Chicago in Norris Division semifinals; lost to Detroit in Norris Division finals.

93-94—Defeated Hamilton in quarterfinals of Calder Cup playoffs; defeated Hershey in division finals of Calder Cup playoffs; lost to Moncton in semifinals of Calder Cup playoffs.

96-97—Lost to Buffalo in Eastern Conference quarterfinals.

97-98—Defeated New Jersey in Eastern Conference quarterfinals; lost to Washington in Eastern Conference semifinals.

MAURICE, PAUL — HURRICANES

PERSONAL: Born January 30, 1967, in Sault Ste. Marie, Ont.

HEAD COACHING RECORD

BACKGROUND: Assistant coach, Hartford Whalers (June 9-November 6, 1995). ... Whalers franchise moved to North Carolina and renamed Carolina Hurricanes for 1997-98 season; NHL approved move on June 25, 1997.

Season Team	League	REGULAR SEASON W	L	T	Pct.	Finish	PLAYOFFS W	L	Pct.
93-94—Detroit	OHL	42	20	4	.667	1st/West Division	11	6	.647
94-95—Detroit	OHL	44	18	4	.697	1st/West Division	16	5	.762
95-96—Hartford	NHL	29	33	8	.471	4th/Northeast Division	—	—	—
96-97—Hartford	NHL	32	39	11	.457	5th/Northeast Division	—	—	—
97-98—Carolina	NHL	33	41	8	.451	6th/Northeast Division	—	—	—
NHL Totals (3 years)		94	113	27	.459				

NOTES:

93-94—Defeated Owen Sound in quarterfinals of OHL playoffs; defeated Sault Ste. Marie in semifinals of OHL playoffs; lost to North Bay in OHL finals.

94-95—Defeated London in first round of OHL playoffs; defeated Peterborough in second round of OHL playoffs; defeated Sudbury in third round of OHL playoffs; defeated Guelph in J. Ross Robertson Cup finals.

MILBURY, MIKE — ISLANDERS

PERSONAL: Born June 17, 1952, in Brighton, Mass. ... Full name: Michael James Milbury. ... Cousin of Dave Silk, center with New York Rangers, Boston Bruins and Detroit Red Wings (1979-80 through 1984-85).

COLLEGE: Colgate.

TRANSACTIONS/CAREER NOTES: Signed as free agent by Boston Bruins (September 1974). ... Suspended six games by NHL for fighting in stands (December 26, 1979). ... Strained ligaments in right knee (March 11, 1982). ... Broke kneecap (March 29, 1983). ... Underwent surgery to repair ligament damage in right knee (October 26, 1986).

MISCELLANEOUS: Played defense.

Season Team	League	REGULAR SEASON Gms.	G	A	Pts.	PIM	+/-	PP	SH	PLAYOFFS Gms.	G	A	Pts.	PIM
72-73—Colgate University	ECAC	27	4	25	29	81	...	...	...	—	—	—	—	—
73-74—Colgate University	ECAC	23	2	19	21	68	...	...	...	—	—	—	—	—
—Boston	AHL	5	0	0	0	7	...	...	...	—	—	—	—	—
74-75—Rochester	AHL	71	2	15	17	246	...	...	...	8	0	3	3	24
75-76—Rochester	AHL	73	3	15	18	199	...	...	...	3	0	1	1	13
—Boston	NHL	3	0	0	0	9	...	...	...	11	0	0	0	29
76-77—Boston	NHL	77	6	18	24	166	...	...	...	13	2	2	4	47
77-78—Boston	NHL	80	8	30	38	151	...	...	...	15	1	8	9	27
78-79—Boston	NHL	74	1	34	35	149	...	...	...	11	1	7	8	7
79-80—Boston	NHL	72	10	13	23	59	...	...	...	10	0	2	2	50
80-81—Boston	NHL	77	0	18	18	222	...	...	...	2	0	1	1	10
81-82—Boston	NHL	51	2	10	12	71	...	...	...	11	0	4	4	6
82-83—Boston	NHL	78	9	15	24	216	...	...	...	—	—	—	—	—
83-84—Boston	NHL	74	2	17	19	159	...	...	...	3	0	0	0	12
84-85—Boston	NHL	78	3	13	16	152	...	...	...	5	0	0	0	10
85-86—Boston	NHL	22	2	5	7	102	...	...	...	1	0	0	0	17
86-87—Boston	NHL	68	6	16	22	96	...	...	...	4	0	0	0	4
NHL Totals (12 years)		754	49	189	238	1552	...	...	...	86	4	24	28	219

HEAD COACHING RECORD

BACKGROUND: Assistant coach, Boston Bruins (May 6, 1985 through February 1986). ... Co-coach, Bruins (November 8, 1986). ... Player/assistant coach, Bruins (November 8, 1986 through 1987). ... Assistant general manager, Bruins (May 16, 1989 through 1993-94). ... Head coach, Boston College (March 30-June 2, 1994; never coached a game). ... Hockey analyst, ESPN television (1994-95). ... General manager, New York Islanders (December 12, 1995 to present).

HONORS: Named AHL Coach of the Year (1987-88). ... Named NHL Coach of the Year by The Sporting News (1989-90).

Season Team	League	REGULAR SEASON							PLAYOFFS		
		W	L	T	Pct.	Finish			W	L	Pct.
87-88—Maine	AHL	44	29	7	.594	1st/North Division			5	5	.500
88-89—Maine	AHL	32	40	8	.450	5th/North Division			—	—	—
89-90—Boston	NHL	46	25	9	.631	1st/Adams Division			13	8	.619
90-91—Boston	NHL	44	24	12	.625	1st/Adams Division			10	9	.526
95-96—New York Islanders	NHL	22	50	10	.329	7th/Atlantic Division			—	—	—
96-97—New York Islanders	NHL	14	23	9	.402	—			—	—	—
97-98—New York Islanders	NHL	8	9	2	.474	4th/Atlantic Division			—	—	—
NHL Totals (5 years)		134	131	42	.505	**NHL Totals (2 years)**			23	17	.575

NOTES:
87-88—Defeated Nova Scotia in quarterfinals of Calder Cup playoffs; lost to Fredericton in semifinals of Calder Cup playoffs.
89-90—Defeated Hartford in Adams Division semifinals; defeated Montreal in Adams Division finals; defeated Washington in Wales Conference finals; lost to Edmonton in Stanley Cup finals.
90-91—Defeated Hartford in Adams Division semifinals; defeated Montreal in Adams Division finals; lost to Pittsburgh in Wales Conference finals.
96-97—Replaced as head coach by Rick Bowness (January 24) with club in seventh place.
97-98—Replaced Rick Bowness as head coach (March 11) with club in fifth place.

MUCKLER, JOHN   RANGERS

PERSONAL: Born April 13, 1934, in Midland, Ont. ... Full name: John Ernest Muckler.
HONORS: Named EHL Coach of the Year (1964-65). ... Won Louis A. R. Pieri Trophy (1974-75). ... Won Jake Milford Trophy with Jack Evans (1978-79). ... Named NHL Executive of the Year by THE SPORTING NEWS (1996-97).
MISCELLANEOUS: Played defense.

Season Team	League	REGULAR SEASON							PLAYOFFS				
		Gms.	G	A	Pts.	PIM	+/-	PP	SH	Gms.	G	A	Pts.	PIM
49-50—Detroit	IHL	32	3	4	7	24	...	...	...	—	—	—	—	—
50-51—Windsor	OJHA						Statistics unavailable.			—	—	—	—	—
51-52—Windsor	OJHA	48	2	3	5	...	...	...	...	—	—	—	—	—
52-53—Windsor	OJHA						Statistics unavailable.			—	—	—	—	—
53-54—Guelph	OJHA						Statistics unavailable.			—	—	—	—	—
54-55—Chatham	OHA	7	0	1	1	...	...	...	...	—	—	—	—	—
—Belleville	OHA						Statistics unavailable.			—	—	—	—	—
55-56—Baltimore	EHL	62	11	34	45	82	...	...	...	—	—	—	—	—

HEAD COACHING RECORD
BACKGROUND: Director of player personnel, New York Rangers (1966-67). ... Scout, Vancouver Canucks (1979-80 and 1980-81). ... Assistant coach, Edmonton Oilers (1982-83 and 1984-85). ... Co-coach, Oilers (1985-86 through 1988-89). ... Director of hockey operations, Buffalo Sabres (1991-92). ... Head coach/general manager, Buffalo Sabres (1991-92 through 1994-95). ... General manager, Buffalo Sabres (1995-96 and 1996-97).

Season Team	League	REGULAR SEASON							PLAYOFFS		
		W	L	T	Pct.	Finish			W	L	Pct.
59-60—New York	EHL	18	41	1	.308	—			—	—	—
60-61—New York	EHL	18	45	1	.289	—			—	—	—
61-62—Long Island	EHL	26	41	1	.390	—			—	—	—
62-63—Long Island	EHL					Record unavailable.					
63-64—Long Island	EHL	32	24	6	.565	—			—	—	—
64-65—Long Island	EHL	42	29	1	.590	—			—	—	—
65-66—Long Island	EHL	46	23	3	.660	—			—	—	—
68-69—Memphis	CHL	3	5	1	.389	4th/Northern Division			—	—	—
—Minnesota	NHL	6	23	6	.257	6th/West Division			—	—	—
71-72—Cleveland	AHL	32	34	10	.487	4th/ Western Division			2	4	.333
72-73—Cleveland-Jacksonville	AHL	23	44	9	.362	5th/Western Division			—	—	—
73-74—Providence	AHL	38	26	12	.579	2nd/Northern Division			9	6	.600
74-75—Providence	AHL	43	21	12	.645	1st/North Division			2	4	.333
75-76—Providence	AHL	34	34	8	.500	3rd/North Division			0	3	.000
76-77—Rhode Island	AHL	21	30	2	.415	6th/AHL			—	—	—
78-79—Dallas	CHL	45	28	3	.612	2nd/CHL			8	1	.889
81-82—Wichita	CHL	44	33	3	.569	1st/Southern Division			3	4	.429
89-90—Edmonton	NHL	38	28	14	.563	2nd/Smythe Division			16	4	.800
90-91—Edmonton	NHL	37	37	6	.500	3rd/Smythe Division			9	9	.500
91-92—Buffalo	NHL	22	22	8	.500	3rd/Adams Division			3	4	.429
92-93—Buffalo	NHL	38	36	10	.512	4th/Adams Division			4	4	.500
93-94—Buffalo	NHL	43	32	9	.565	4th/Northeast Division			3	4	.429
94-95—Buffalo	NHL	22	19	7	.531	4th/Northeast Division			1	4	.200
97-98—New York Rangers	NHL	8	15	2	.360	5th/Atlantic Division			—	—	—
NHL Totals (8 years)		214	212	62	.502	**NHL Totals (6 years)**			36	29	.554

NOTES:
71-72—Lost to Baltimore in Calder Cup semifinals.
73-74—Defeated Nova Scotia in Calder Cup quarterfinals; defeated New Haven in Calder Cup semifinals; lost to Hershey in Calder Cup finals.
74-75—Lost to Springfield in Calder Cup quarterfinals.
75-76—Lost to Rochester in Calder Cup quarterfinals.
78-79—Defeated Kansas City in Adams Cup semifinals; defeated Salt Lake City in Adams Cup finals.
81-82—Defeated Nashville in Adams Cup quarterfinals; lost to Indianapolis in Adams Cup semifinals.
89-90—Defeated Winnipeg in Smythe Division semifinals; defeated Los Angeles in Smythe Division finals; defeated Chicago in Clarence Campbell finals; defeated Boston in Stanley Cup finals.
90-91—Defeated Calgary in Smythe Division semifinals; defeated Los Angeles in Smythe Division finals; lost to Minnesota in Clarence Campbell finals.
91-92—Lost to Boston in Adams Division semifinals.
92-93—Defeated Boston in Adams Division semifinals; lost to Montreal in Adams Division finals.
93-94—Lost to New Jersey in Eastern Conference quarterfinals.
94-95—Lost to Philadelphia in Eastern Conference quarterfinals.
97-98—Replaced Colin Campbell as head coach (February 18) with club in fourth place.

PERSONAL: Born July 20, 1950, in Shawville, Que. ... Full name: Terry Rodney Murray. ... Brother of Bryan Murray, general manager, Florida Panthers.

HIGH SCHOOL: Shawville (Que.).

TRANSACTIONS/CAREER NOTES: Selected by Oakland Seals from Ottawa 67's in seventh round (seventh Seals pick, 88th overall) of NHL amateur draft (June 11, 1970). ... Loaned to Boston Braves (February 1972). ... Broke leg (1973-74). ... Traded by Philadelphia Flyers with RW Dave Kelly, RW Steve Coates and LW Bob Ritchie to Detroit Red Wings for D Mike Korney and D Rick LaPointe (February 1977). ... Contract sold by Red Wings to Flyers (November 1977). ... Selected by Washington Capitals in NHL waiver draft (October 1981).

HONORS: Won Eddie Shore Plaque (1977-78 and 1978-79). ... Named to AHL All-Star first team (1975-76, 1977-78 and 1978-79).

MISCELLANEOUS: Played defense.

		REGULAR SEASON								PLAYOFFS				
Season Team	League	Gms.	G	A	Pts.	PIM	+/-	PP	SH	Gms.	G	A	Pts.	PIM
67-68—Ottawa	OHA JR. A	52	0	4	4	59	...	...	...	—	—	—	—	—
68-69—Ottawa	OHA JR. A	50	1	16	17	39	...	...	...	—	—	—	—	—
69-70—Ottawa	OHA JR. A	50	4	24	28	43	...	...	...	—	—	—	—	—
70-71—Providence	AHL	57	1	22	23	47	...	...	...	10	0	1	1	5
71-72—Baltimore	AHL	30	0	5	5	13	...	...	...	—	—	—	—	—
—Boston	AHL	9	0	0	0	0	...	...	...	—	—	—	—	—
—Oklahoma City	CPHL	17	1	1	2	19	...	...	...	6	0	0	0	2
72-73—Salt Lake City	WHL	39	3	8	11	30	...	...	...	9	0	6	6	14
—California	NHL	23	0	3	3	4	...	...	...	—	—	—	—	—
73-74—California	NHL	58	0	12	12	48	...	...	...	—	—	—	—	—
74-75—Salt Lake City	CHL	62	5	30	35	122	...	...	...	11	2	2	4	30
—California	NHL	9	0	2	2	8	...	...	...	—	—	—	—	—
75-76—Richmond	AHL	67	8	48	56	95	...	...	...	6	1	4	5	2
—Philadelphia	NHL	3	0	0	0	2	...	...	...	6	0	1	1	0
76-77—Philadelphia	NHL	36	0	13	13	14	...	...	...	—	—	—	—	—
—Detroit	NHL	23	0	7	7	10	...	...	...	—	—	—	—	—
77-78—Philadelphia	AHL	7	2	1	3	13	...	...	...	—	—	—	—	—
—Maine	AHL	68	9	40	49	53	...	...	...	12	1	7	8	28
78-79—Philadelphia	NHL	5	0	0	0	0	...	...	...	—	—	—	—	—
—Maine	AHL	55	14	23	37	14	...	...	...	10	1	5	6	6
79-80—Maine	AHL	68	3	19	22	26	...	...	...	12	2	2	4	10
80-81—Maine	AHL	2	0	1	1	0	...	...	...	—	—	—	—	—
—Philadelphia	NHL	71	1	17	18	53	...	...	...	12	2	1	3	10
81-82—Washington	NHL	74	3	22	25	60	...	...	...	—	—	—	—	—
NHL Totals (8 years)		**302**	**4**	**76**	**80**	**199**	...	...	...	**18**	**2**	**2**	**4**	**10**

HEAD COACHING RECORD

BACKGROUND: Assistant coach, Washington Capitals (1982-83 through 1987-88). ... Scout, Philadelphia Flyers (1997-98).

		REGULAR SEASON					PLAYOFFS		
Season Team	League	W	L	T	Pct.	Finish	W	L	Pct.
88-89—Baltimore	AHL	30	46	4	.400	6th/South Division	—	—	—
89-90—Baltimore	AHL	26	17	1	.602	—	—	—	—
—Washington	NHL	18	14	2	.559	3rd/Patrick Division	8	7	.533
90-91—Washington	NHL	37	36	7	.506	3rd/Patrick Division	5	6	.455
91-92—Washington	NHL	45	27	8	.613	2nd/Patrick Division	3	4	.429
92-93—Washington	NHL	43	34	7	.554	2nd/Patrick Division	2	4	.333
93-94—Washington	NHL	20	23	4	.468	—	—	—	—
—Cincinnati	ECHL	17	7	‡4	.679	2nd/Central Division	6	5	.545
94-95—Philadelphia	NHL	28	16	4	.625	1st/Atlantic Division	10	5	.667
95-96—Philadelphia	NHL	45	24	13	.628	1st/Atlantic Division	6	6	.500
96-97—Philadelphia	NHL	45	24	13	.628	2nd/Atlantic Division	12	7	.632
NHL Totals (8 years)		**281**	**198**	**58**	**.577**	**NHL Totals (7 years)**	**46**	**39**	**.541**

NOTES:

89-90—Replaced Bryan Murray as head coach (January 15) with club in fourth place; defeated New Jersey in Patrick Division semifinals; defeated New York Rangers in Patrick Division finals; lost to Boston in Wales Conference finals.

90-91—Defeated New York Rangers in Patrick Division semifinals; lost to Pittsburgh in Patrick Division finals.

91-92—Lost to Pittsburgh in Patrick Division semifinals.

92-93—Lost to New York Islanders in Patrick Division semifinals.

93-94—Replaced as head coach by Jim Schoenfeld (January 27) with club in fifth place. Loaned to Florida Panthers (February 18) to coach Cincinnati Cyclones of IHL. Defeated Kalamazoo in Turner Cup quarterfinals; lost to Fort Wayne in Turner Cup semifinals.

94-95—Defeated Buffalo in Atlantic Division quarterfinals; defeated New York Rangers in Atlantic Division semifinals; lost to New Jersey in Atlantic Division finals.

95-96—Defeated Tampa Bay in Eastern Conference quarterfinals; lost to Florida in Eastern Conference semifinals.

96-97—Defeated Pittsburgh in Eastern Conference quarterfinals; defeated Sabres in Eastern Conference semifinals; defeated New York Rangers in Eastern Conference finals; lost to Detroit in Stanley Cup finals.

NEILSON, ROGER   FLYERS

PERSONAL: Born June 16, 1934, in Toronto. ... Name pronounced NEEL-suhn.

COLLEGE: McMaster University.

HEAD COACHING RECORD

BACKGROUND: Scout, Peterborough, Montreal Canadiens organization (1964-65 through 1966-67). ... Assistant coach, Buffalo Sabres (1979-80). ... Assistant coach, Vancouver Canucks (1981-82). ... Assistant coach, Chicago Blackhawks (1984-85 through 1986-87). ... Scout, Blackhawks (1987-88 and 1988-89). ... Assistant coach, St. Louis Blues (1995-96 through March 9, 1998).

Season Team	League	REGULAR SEASON					PLAYOFFS		
		W	L	T	Pct.	Finish	W	L	Pct.
66-67—Peterborough	OHA	7	8	3	.472	—	—	—	—
67-68—Peterborough	OHA	13	30	11	.343	8th/OHA	—	—	—
68-69—Peterborough	OHA	27	18	9	.583	3rd/OHA	4	6	.400
69-70—Peterborough	OHA	29	13	12	.648	2nd/OHA	2	4	.333
70-71—Peterborough	OHA	41	13	8	.726	1st/OHA	1	4	.200
71-72—Peterborough	OHA	34	20	9	.611	3rd/OHA	13	2	.824
72-73—Peterborough	OHA	42	13	8	.730	2nd/OHA	9	4	.639
73-74—Peterborough	OHA	35	21	14	.600	3rd/OHA	7	7	.500
74-75—Peterborough	OHA	37	20	13	.621	2nd/OHA	5	4	.545
75-76—Peterborough	OHA	18	37	11	.356	6th/Leyden Division	—	—	—
76-77—Dallas	CHL	35	25	16	.566	2nd/CHL	1	4	.200
77-78—Toronto	NHL	41	29	10	.575	3rd/Adams Division	6	7	.462
78-79—Toronto	NHL	34	33	13	.506	3rd/Adams Division	2	4	.333
79-80—Buffalo	NHL	14	6	6	.654	1st/Adams Division	—	—	—
80-81—Buffalo	NHL	39	20	21	.619	1st/Adams Division	4	4	.500
81-82—Vancouver	NHL	4	0	1	.900	2nd/Smythe Division	11	6	.647
82-83—Vancouver	NHL	30	35	15	.469	3rd/Smythe Division	1	3	.250
83-84—Vancouver	NHL	17	26	5	.406	3rd/Smythe Division	—	—	—
—Los Angeles	NHL	8	17	3	.339	5th/Smythe Division	—	—	—
89-90—New York Rangers	NHL	36	31	13	.531	1st/Patrick Division	5	5	.500
90-91—New York Rangers	NHL	36	31	13	.531	2nd/Patrick Division	2	4	.333
91-92—New York Rangers	NHL	50	25	5	.656	1st/Patrick Division	6	7	.462
92-93—New York Rangers	NHL	19	17	4	.525	—	—	—	—
93-94—Florida	NHL	33	34	17	.494	5th/Atlantic Division	—	—	—
94-95—Florida	NHL	20	22	6	.479	5th/Atlantic Division	—	—	—
97-98—Philadelphia	NHL	10	9	2	.524	2nd/Atlantic Division	1	4	.200
NHL Totals (14 years)		**391**	**335**	**134**	**.533**	**NHL Totals (9 years)**	**38**	**44**	**.468**

NOTES:

68-69—Defeated London in OHA quarterfinals; lost to Montreal in OHA semifinals.

69-70—Lost to London in OHA quarterfinals.

70-71—Lost to Toronto in OHA quarterfinals.

71-72—Defeated St. Catharines in OHA quarterfinals; defeated Toronto in OHA semifinals; defeated Ottawa in OHA finals; lost to Cornwall in Memorial Cup finals. Peterborough had two playoff ties.

72-73—Defeated Oshawa in OHA quarterfinals; defeated London in OHA semifinals; lost to Toronto in OHA finals. Peterborough had five playoff ties.

73-74—Defeated Oshawa in OHA quarterfinals; defeated Kitchener in OHA semifinals; lost to St. Catharines in OHA finals. Peterborough had four playoff ties.

74-75—Defeated Oshawa in OHA quarterfinals; lost to Hamilton in OHA finals. Peterborough had two playoff ties.

76-77—Lost to Tulsa in Adams Cup semifinals.

77-78—Defeated Los Angeles in Stanley Cup preliminary round; defeated New York Islanders in Stanley Cup quarterfinals; lost to Montreal in Stanley Cup semifinals.

78-79—Defeated Atlanta in Stanley Cup preliminary round; lost to Montreal in Stanley Cup quarterfinals.

80-81—Defeated Vancouver in Stanley Cup preliminary round; lost to Minnesota in Stanley Cup quarterfinals.

81-82—Defeated Calgary in Smythe Division semifinals; defeated Los Angeles in Smythe Division finals; defeated Chicago in Campbell Conference finals; lost to New York Islanders in Stanley Cup finals.

82-83—Lost to Calgary in Smythe Division semifinals.

89-90—Defeated New York Islanders in Patrick Division semifinals; lost to Washington in Patrick Division finals.

90-91—Lost to Washington in Patrick Division semifinals.

91-92—Defeated New Jersey in Patrick Division semifinals; lost to Pittsburgh in Patrick Division finals.

97-98—Replaced Wayne Cashman as head coach (March 9) with club in second place; lost to Buffalo in Eastern Conference quarterfinals.

QUENNEVILLE, JOEL — BLUES

PERSONAL: Born September 15, 1958, in Windsor, Ont. ... Full name: Joel Norman Quenneville.

TRANSACTIONS/CAREER NOTES: Selected by Toronto Maple Leafs from Windsor Spitfires in second round (first Maple Leafs pick, 21st overall) of NHL amateur draft (June 15, 1978). ... Traded by Maple Leafs with RW Lanny McDonald to Colorado Rockies for RW Wilf Paiement and LW Pat Hickey (December 1979). ... Injured rib cage (March 1980). ... Underwent surgery to repair torn ligaments in ring finger of left hand (March 1980). ... Sprained ankle, twisted knee and suffered facial lacerations (January 4, 1982). ... Rockies franchise moved to New Jersey and became the Devils (June 30, 1982). ... Traded by Devils with C Steve Tambellini to Calgary Flames for C Mel Bridgman and D Phil Russell (July 1983). ... Traded by Flames with D Richie Dunn to Hartford Whalers for D Mickey Volcan and third-round pick in 1984 draft (August 1983). ... Broke right shoulder (December 18, 1986); missed 42 games. ... Separated left shoulder (January 19, 1989); missed nine games. ... Traded by Whalers to Washington Capitals for future considerations (October 3, 1990). ... Signed as free agent by Maple Leafs (July 30, 1991).

HONORS: Named to OMJHL All-Star second team (1977-78). ... Named to AHL All-Star second team (1991-92).

Season Team	League	REGULAR SEASON							PLAYOFFS				
		Gms.	G	A	Pts.	PIM	+/-	PP	SH	Gms.	G	A	Pts.	PIM
75-76—Windsor	OHA Mj. Jr.	66	15	33	48	61	...	...	...	—	—	—	—	—
76-77—Windsor	OMJHL	65	19	59	78	169	...	...	...	9	6	5	11	112
77-78—Windsor	OMJHL	66	27	76	103	114	...	...	...	6	2	3	5	17
78-79—Toronto	NHL	61	2	9	11	60	...	...	...	6	0	1	1	4
—New Brunswick	AHL	16	1	10	11	10	...	...	...	—	—	—	—	—
79-80—Toronto	NHL	32	1	4	5	24	...	...	...	—	—	—	—	—
—Colorado Rockies	NHL	35	5	7	12	26	...	...	...	—	—	—	—	—
80-81—Colorado Rockies	NHL	71	10	24	34	86	-24	3	0	—	—	—	—	—
81-82—Colorado Rockies	NHL	64	5	10	15	55	...	0	0	—	—	—	—	—
82-83—New Jersey	NHL	74	5	12	17	46	-13	0	1	—	—	—	—	—
83-84—Hartford	NHL	80	5	8	13	95	-11	0	2	—	—	—	—	—
84-85—Hartford	NHL	79	6	16	22	96	-15	0	0	—	—	—	—	—
85-86—Hartford	NHL	71	5	20	25	83	20	1	0	10	0	2	2	12
86-87—Hartford	NHL	37	3	7	10	24	8	0	1	6	0	0	0	0

Season Team	League	REGULAR SEASON								PLAYOFFS				
		Gms.	G	A	Pts.	PIM	+/-	PP	SH	Gms.	G	A	Pts.	PIM
87-88—Hartford	NHL	77	1	8	9	44	-13	0	0	6	0	2	2	2
88-89—Hartford	NHL	69	4	7	11	32	3	0	0	4	0	3	3	4
89-90—Hartford	NHL	44	1	4	5	34	9	0	0	—	—	—	—	—
90-91—Washington	NHL	9	1	0	1	0	-8	0	0	—	—	—	—	—
—Baltimore	AHL	59	6	13	19	58	...	...	...	6	1	1	2	6
91-92—St. John's	AHL	73	7	23	30	58	...	...	...	16	0	1	1	10
NHL Totals (13 years).........		803	54	136	190	705	...	...	...	32	0	8	8	22

HEAD COACHING RECORD

BACKGROUND: Player/coach, St. John's of the AHL (1991-92). ... Assistant coach, St. John's (1992-93). ... Assistant coach, Quebec Nordiques (1994-95). ... Quebec franchise moved to Denver and renamed Colorado Avalanche for 1995-96 season. ... Assistant coach, Avalanche (1995-96 through January 5, 1997).

Season Team	League	REGULAR SEASON					PLAYOFFS		
		W	L	T	Pct.	Finish	W	L	Pct.
93-94—Springfield	AHL	29	38	13	.444	4th/Northern Division	2	4	.333
96-97—St. Louis	NHL	18	15	7	.538	4th/Central Division	2	4	.333
97-98—St. Louis	NHL	45	29	8	.598	3rd/Central Division	6	4	.600
NHL Totals (2 years)		63	44	15	.578	**NHL Totals (2 years)**	8	8	.500

NOTES:
93-94—Lost to Adirondack in division semifinals of Calder Cup playoffs.
96-97—Replaced Mike Keenan as coach (January 6). Lost to Detroit in Western Conference quarterfinals.
97-98—Defeated Los Angeles in Western Conference quarterfinals; lost to Detroit in Western Conference semifinals.

QUINN, PAT — MAPLE LEAFS

PERSONAL: Born January 29, 1943, in Hamilton, Ont. ... Full name: John Brian Patrick Quinn.
HIGH SCHOOL: Central (Hamilton, Ont.).
COLLEGE: UC San Diego, then Widener University (degree in law).
TRANSACTIONS/CAREER NOTES: Suspended eight games for stick-swinging (November 1960). ... Loaned by Detroit Red Wings to Tulsa Oilers for 1964-65 season. ... Broke ankle (1965). ... Selected by Montreal Canadiens from Red Wings in intraleague draft (June 1966). ... Sold by Canadiens to St. Louis Blues (June 1967). ... Loaned to Oilers for 1967-68 season. ... Sold by Blues to Toronto Maple Leafs for rights to LW Dickie Moore (March 1968). ... Selected by Vancouver Canucks in NHL expansion draft (June 1970). ... Selected by Atlanta Flames in NHL expansion draft (June 1972). ... Broke leg (1976).
MISCELLANEOUS: Played defense. ... Captain of Calgary Flames (1975-76 through 1976-77).

Season Team	League	REGULAR SEASON								PLAYOFFS				
		Gms.	G	A	Pts.	PIM	+/-	PP	SH	Gms.	G	A	Pts.	PIM
58-59—Hamilton Jr. A............	OHA	20	0	1	1	...				—	—	—	—	—
59-60—Hamilton Jr. A............	OHA	27	0	1	1	...				—	—	—	—	—
60-61—Hamilton Jr. B............	OHA					Statistics unavailable.				—	—	—	—	—
61-62—						Did not play.								
62-63—Edmonton................	CAHL					Statistics unavailable.								
63-64—Knoxville	EHL	72	6	31	37	217	...	...	...	3	0	0	0	9
64-65—Tulsa	CPHL	70	3	32	35	202	...	...	...	—	—	—	—	—
65-66—Memphis	CPHL	67	2	16	18	135	...	...	...	—	—	—	—	—
66-67—Houston	CPHL	15	0	3	3	66	...	...	...	—	—	—	—	—
—Seattle......................	WHL	35	1	3	4	49	...	...	...	5	0	0	0	2
67-68—Tulsa	CPHL	51	3	15	18	178	...	...	...	11	1	4	5	19
68-69—Tulsa	CHL	17	0	6	6	25	...	...	...	—	—	—	—	—
—Toronto....................	NHL	40	2	7	9	95	...	...	...	4	0	0	0	13
69-70—Tulsa	CHL	2	0	1	1	6	...	...	...	—	—	—	—	—
—Toronto....................	NHL	59	0	5	5	88	...	...	...	—	—	—	—	—
70-71—Vancouver.................	NHL	76	2	11	13	149	...	...	...	—	—	—	—	—
71-72—Vancouver.................	NHL	57	2	3	5	63	...	...	...	—	—	—	—	—
72-73—Atlanta	NHL	78	2	18	20	113	...	...	...	—	—	—	—	—
73-74—Atlanta	NHL	77	5	27	32	94	...	...	...	4	0	0	0	6
74-75—Atlanta	NHL	80	2	19	21	156	...	...	...	—	—	—	—	—
75-76—Atlanta	NHL	80	2	11	13	134	...	...	...	2	0	1	1	2
76-77—Atlanta	NHL	59	1	12	13	58	...	...	...	1	0	0	0	0
NHL Totals (10 years).........		606	18	113	131	950	...	...	...	11	0	1	1	21

HEAD COACHING RECORD

BACKGROUND: Assistant coach, Philadelphia Flyers (1977-78). ... Coach, Team Canada (1986). ... President/general manager, Vancouver Canucks (1987-88 through November 4, 1997). ... Assistant general manager, Team Canada (1996 and 1997).
HONORS: Named NHL Coach of the Year by THE SPORTING NEWS (1979-80 and 1991-92). ... Won Jack Adams Award (1979-80 and 1991-92).

Season Team	League	REGULAR SEASON					PLAYOFFS		
		W	L	T	Pct.	Finish	W	L	Pct.
78-79—Philadelphia	NHL	18	8	4	.667	2nd/Patrick Division	3	5	.375
79-80—Philadelphia	NHL	48	12	20	.725	1st/Patrick Division	13	6	.684
80-81—Philadelphia	NHL	41	24	15	.606	2nd/Patrick Division	6	6	.500
81-82—Philadelphia	NHL	34	29	9	.535	3rd/Patrick Division	—	—	—
84-85—Los Angeles	NHL	34	32	14	.513	4th/Smythe Division	0	3	.000
85-86—Los Angeles	NHL	23	49	8	.338	5th/Smythe Division	—	—	—
86-87—Los Angeles	NHL	18	20	4	.476	4th/Smythe Division	—	—	—
90-91—Vancouver	NHL	9	13	4	.423	4th/Smythe Division	2	4	.333
91-92—Vancouver	NHL	42	26	12	.600	1st/Smythe Division	6	7	.462
92-93—Vancouver	NHL	46	29	9	.601	1st/Smythe Division	6	6	.500
93-94—Vancouver	NHL	41	40	3	.506	2nd/Pacific Division	15	9	.625
95-96—Vancouver	NHL	3	3	0	.500	3rd/Pacific Division	2	4	.333
NHL Totals (12 years)		357	285	102	.548	**NHL Totals (9 years)**	53	50	.515

NOTES:

78-79—Defeated Vancouver in Stanley Cup preliminary round; lost to New York Rangers in Stanley Cup quarterfinals.
79-80—Defeated Edmonton in Stanley Cup preliminary round; defeated New York Rangers in Stanley Cup quarterfinals; defeated Minnesota in Stanley Cup semifinals; lost to New York Islanders in Stanley Cup finals.
80-81—Defeated Quebec in Stanley Cup preliminary round; lost to Calgary in Stanley Cup quarterfinals.
84-85—Lost to Edmonton in Smythe Division semifinals.
90-91—Replaced Bob McCammon as head coach (January) with club in fifth place; lost to Los Angeles in Smythe Division semifinals.
91-92—Defeated Winnipeg in Smythe Division semifinals; lost to Edmonton in Smythe Division finals.
92-93—Defeated Winnipeg in Smythe Division semifinals; lost to Los Angeles in Smythe Division finals.
93-94—Defeated Calgary in Western Conference quarterfinals; defeated Dallas in Western Conference semifinals; defeated Toronto in Western Conference finals; lost to New York Rangers in Stanley Cup finals.
95-96—Replaced Rick Ley as head coach (March 28) with club in third place; lost to Colorado in Western Conference quarterfinals.

ROBINSON, LARRY — KINGS

PERSONAL: Born June 2, 1951, in Winchester, Ont. ... Full name: Larry Clark Robinson. ... Brother of Moe Robinson, defenseman with Montreal Canadiens (1979-80).

TRANSACTIONS/CAREER NOTES: Selected by Montreal Canadiens from Kitchener Rangers in second round (fourth Canadiens pick, 20th overall) of NHL amateur draft (June 10, 1971). ... Injured knee; missed part of 1978-79 season. ... Separated right shoulder (March 6, 1980). ... Injured groin (October 1980). ... Separated left shoulder (November 14, 1980). ... Broke nose (January 8, 1981). ... Injured left shoulder (October 1982). ... Suffered skin infection behind right knee (October 1983). ... Hyperextended left elbow (March 1985). ... Strained ligaments in right ankle (March 9, 1987). ... Broke right leg (August 1987). ... Sprained right wrist (December 1987). ... Hyperextended knee (May 23, 1989). ... Signed as free agent by Los Angeles Kings (July 26, 1989). ... Suffered food poisoning (March 1990). ... Injured eye (November 26, 1991); missed two games.

HONORS: Named to COJHL All-Star first team (1969-70). ... Played in NHL All-Star Game (1974, 1976-1978, 1980, 1982, 1986, 1988, 1989 and 1992). ... Won James Norris Memorial Trophy (1976-77 and 1979-80). ... Named to THE SPORTING NEWS All-Star first team (1976-77 through 1979-80). ... Named to NHL All-Star first team (1976-77, 1978-79 and 1979-80). ... Won Conn Smythe Trophy (1977-78). ... Named to NHL All-Star second team (1977-78, 1980-81 and 1985-86). ... Named to THE SPORTING NEWS All-Star second team (1980-81, 1981-82 and 1985-86).

RECORDS: Holds NHL career playoff records for most games—227; and most consecutive years in playoffs—20 (1972-73 through 1991-92). ... Shares NHL career playoff record for most years in playoffs—20 (1972-73 through 1991-92).

STATISTICAL PLATEAUS: Three-goal games: 1985-86 (1).

MISCELLANEOUS: Member of Stanley Cup championship team (1973, 1976-1979 and 1986).

Season Team	League	REGULAR SEASON								PLAYOFFS				
		Gms.	G	A	Pts.	PIM	+/-	PP	SH	Gms.	G	A	Pts.	PIM
68-69—Brockville	COJHL						Statistics unavailable.							
69-70—Brockville	COJHL	40	22	29	51	74	...	...	...	—	—	—	—	—
70-71—Kitchener	OHA Jr. A	61	12	39	51	65	...	...	...	—	—	—	—	—
71-72—Nova Scotia	AHL	74	10	14	24	54	...	...	...	15	2	10	12	31
72-73—Nova Scotia	AHL	38	6	33	39	33	...	...	...	—	—	—	—	—
—Montreal	NHL	36	2	4	6	20	...	...	...	11	1	4	5	9
73-74—Montreal	NHL	78	6	20	26	66	...	...	...	6	0	1	1	26
74-75—Montreal	NHL	80	14	47	61	76	...	...	...	11	0	4	4	27
75-76—Montreal	NHL	80	10	30	40	59	...	...	...	13	3	3	6	10
76-77—Montreal	NHL	77	19	66	85	45	...	...	...	14	2	10	12	12
77-78—Montreal	NHL	80	13	52	65	39	...	...	...	15	4	17	21	6
78-79—Montreal	NHL	67	16	45	61	33	...	...	...	16	6	9	15	8
79-80—Montreal	NHL	72	14	61	75	39	...	...	...	10	0	4	4	2
80-81—Montreal	NHL	65	12	38	50	37	46	7	0	3	0	1	1	2
81-82—Montreal	NHL	71	12	47	59	41	57	5	1	5	0	1	1	8
82-83—Montreal	NHL	71	14	49	63	33	33	6	0	3	0	0	0	2
83-84—Montreal	NHL	74	9	34	43	39	4	4	0	15	0	5	5	22
84-85—Montreal	NHL	76	14	33	47	44	32	6	0	12	3	8	11	8
85-86—Montreal	NHL	78	19	63	82	39	29	10	0	20	0	13	13	22
86-87—Montreal	NHL	70	13	37	50	44	24	6	0	17	3	17	20	6
87-88—Montreal	NHL	53	6	34	40	30	26	2	0	11	1	4	5	4
88-89—Montreal	NHL	74	4	26	30	22	23	0	0	21	2	8	10	12
89-90—Los Angeles	NHL	64	7	32	39	34	7	1	0	10	2	3	5	10
90-91—Los Angeles	NHL	62	1	22	23	16	22	0	0	12	1	4	5	15
91-92—Los Angeles	NHL	56	3	10	13	37	1	0	0	2	0	0	0	0
NHL Totals (20 years)		1384	208	750	958	793	...	...	...	227	28	116	144	211

HEAD COACHING RECORD

BACKGROUND: Assistant coach, New Jersey Devils (1993-94 and 1994-95).

Season Team	League	REGULAR SEASON					PLAYOFFS		
		W	L	T	Pct.	Finish	W	L	Pct.
95-96—Los Angeles	NHL	24	40	18	.402	6th/Pacific Division	—	—	—
96-97—Los Angeles	NHL	28	43	11	.409	6th/Pacific Division	—	—	—
97-98—Los Angeles	NHL	38	33	11	.530	2nd/Pacific Division	0	4	.000
NHL Totals (3 years)		90	116	40	.447	**NHL Totals (1 year)**	0	4	.000

NOTES:

97-98—Lost to St. Louis Blues in Western Conference quarterfinals.

RUFF, LINDY — SABRES

PERSONAL: Born February 17, 1960, in Warburg, Alta. ... Played defense. ... Shot left. ... Full name: Lindy Cameron Ruff.

TRANSACTIONS/CAREER NOTES: Selected by Buffalo Sabres as underage junior in second round (second Sabres pick, 32nd overall) of NHL entry draft (August 9, 1979). ... Fractured ankle (December 1980). ... Broke hand (March 1983). ... Injured shoulder (January 14, 1984). ...

Separated shoulder (October 26, 1984). ... Broke left clavicle (March 5, 1986). ... Sprained shoulder (November 1988). ... Traded by Sabres to New York Rangers for fifth-round pick (D Richard Smehlik) in 1990 draft (March 7, 1989). ... Fractured rib (January 23, 1990); missed seven games. ... Broke nose (March 21, 1990). ... Bruised left thigh (April 1990). ... Signed as free agent by Sabres (September 1991). ... Signed as free agent by San Diego Gulls (August 24, 1992).

HONORS: Named to IHL All-Star team (1992-93).

MISCELLANEOUS: Captain of Buffalo Sabres (1986-87 through 1988-89). ... Scored on a penalty shot (vs. Mario Brunetta, November 26, 1989).

		REGULAR SEASON								PLAYOFFS				
Season Team	League	Gms.	G	A	Pts.	PIM	+/-	PP	SH	Gms.	G	A	Pts.	PIM
76-77—Taber	AJHL	60	13	33	46	112	...	...	...	—	—	—	—	—
—Lethbridge	WCHL	2	0	2	2	0	...	...	...	—	—	—	—	—
77-78—Lethbridge	WCHL	66	9	24	33	219	...	...	...	8	2	8	10	4
78-79—Lethbridge	WHL	24	9	18	27	108	...	...	...	6	0	1	1	0
79-80—Buffalo	NHL	63	5	14	19	38	-2	1	0	8	1	1	2	19
80-81—Buffalo	NHL	65	8	18	26	121	3	1	0	6	3	1	4	23
81-82—Buffalo	NHL	79	16	32	48	194	1	3	0	4	0	0	0	28
82-83—Buffalo	NHL	60	12	17	29	130	14	2	0	10	4	2	6	47
83-84—Buffalo	NHL	58	14	31	45	101	15	3	0	3	1	0	1	9
84-85—Buffalo	NHL	39	13	11	24	45	-1	2	0	5	2	4	6	15
85-86—Buffalo	NHL	54	20	12	32	158	8	5	1	—	—	—	—	—
86-87—Buffalo	NHL	50	6	14	20	74	-12	0	0	—	—	—	—	—
87-88—Buffalo	NHL	77	2	23	25	179	-9	0	0	6	0	2	2	23
88-89—Buffalo	NHL	63	6	11	17	86	-17	0	0	—	—	—	—	—
—New York Rangers	NHL	13	0	5	5	31	-6	0	0	2	0	0	0	17
89-90—New York Rangers	NHL	56	3	6	9	80	-10	0	0	8	0	3	3	12
90-91—New York Rangers	NHL	14	0	1	1	27	-2	0	0	—	—	—	—	—
91-92—Rochester	AHL	62	10	24	34	110	...	...	...	13	0	4	4	16
92-93—San Diego	IHL	81	10	32	42	100	43	0	1	14	1	6	7	26
NHL Totals (12 years)		691	105	195	300	1264	-18	17	1	52	11	13	24	193

HEAD COACHING RECORD

BACKGROUND: Assistant coach, Florida Panthers (1993-94 through 1996-97).

		REGULAR SEASON					PLAYOFFS		
Season Team	League	W	L	T	Pct.	Finish	W	L	Pct.
97-98—Buffalo	NHL	36	29	17	.543	3rd/Northeast Division	10	5	.667
NHL Totals (1 year)		36	29	17	.543	**NHL Totals (1 year)**	10	5	.667

NOTES:

97-98—Defeated Philadelphia in Eastern Conference quarterfinals; defeated Montreal in Eastern Conference semifinals; lost to Washington in Eastern Conference finals.

SCHOENFELD, JIM — COYOTES

PERSONAL: Born September 4, 1952, in Galt, Ont. ... Full name: James Grant Schoenfeld. ... Name pronounced SHAHN-fehld.

TRANSACTIONS/CAREER NOTES: Traded by London Knights with D Ken Southwick and RW Rick Kehoe to Hamilton Red Wings for D Gary Geldhart, RW Gordon Brooks, LW Dave Gilmour and Mike Craig (December 1969). ... Traded by Red Wings to Niagara Falls Flyers for C Russ Friesen and D Mike Healey (January 1971). ... Selected by New York Raiders in WHA player selection draft (February 1972). ... Selected by Buffalo Sabres in first round (first Sabres pick, fifth overall) of NHL amateur draft (June 8, 1972). ... Damaged nerve in leg (1972); underwent corrective surgery following season. ... Ruptured spinal disc (1973); missed most of season. ... Underwent back surgery (1973). ... Broke left foot (1974). ... Suffered from mononucleosis (1975). ... Suffered from viral pneumonia (1976). ... Broke right foot (1978). ... Separated shoulder (1978). ... Strained knee (1978). ... Injured hand and suffered from the flu (December 1980); missed nine games. ... Broke left little finger (September 1981). ... Broke metatarsal bone in right foot (October 18, 1981). ... Traded by Sabres with RW Danny Gare, G Bob Sauve and C Derek Smith to Detroit Red Wings for C Dale McCourt, RW Mike Foligno, C Brent Peterson and future considerations (December 1981). ... Separated ribs (October 1982). ... Released by Red Wings (June 1983). ... Signed as free agent by Boston Bruins (August 1983). ... Fractured and separated left shoulder (November 11, 1983); underwent surgery. ... Injured shoulder (February 27, 1984). ... Announced retirement (September 1984). ... Recalled to active player status by Sabres (December 19, 1984). ... Suffered stress fracture in right foot (January, 1985); missed 13 games. ... Announced retirement (June 1985).

HONORS: Named to NHL All-Star second team (1979-80). ... Played in NHL All-Star Game (1976-77 and 1979-80).

MISCELLANEOUS: Played defense. ... Captain of Buffalo Sabres (1974-75 through 1976-77).

		REGULAR SEASON								PLAYOFFS				
Season Team	League	Gms.	G	A	Pts.	PIM	+/-	PP	SH	Gms.	G	A	Pts.	PIM
69-70—London	OHA Mjr.Jr.A	16	1	4	5	81	...	...	...	—	—	—	—	—
—Hamilton Jr. A.	OHA	32	2	12	14	54	...	...	...	—	—	—	—	—
70-71—Hamilton Jr. A.	OHA	25	3	19	22	120	...	...	...	—	—	—	—	—
—Niagara Falls	OHA	30	3	9	12	85	...	...	...	—	—	—	—	—
71-72—Niagara Falls	OHA	40	6	46	52	225	...	...	...	—	—	—	—	—
72-73—Buffalo	NHL	66	4	15	19	178	...	...	...	6	2	1	3	4
73-74—Cincinnati	AHL	2	0	2	2	4	...	...	...	—	—	—	—	—
—Buffalo	NHL	28	1	8	9	56	...	...	...	—	—	—	—	—
74-75—Buffalo	NHL	68	1	19	20	184	...	...	...	17	1	4	5	38
75-76—Buffalo	NHL	56	2	22	24	114	...	...	...	8	0	3	3	33
76-77—Buffalo	NHL	65	7	25	32	97	...	...	...	6	0	0	0	12
77-78—Buffalo	NHL	60	2	20	22	89	...	...	...	8	0	1	1	28
78-79—Buffalo	NHL	46	8	17	25	67	...	...	...	3	0	1	1	0
79-80—Buffalo	NHL	77	9	27	36	72	...	...	...	14	0	3	3	18
80-81—Buffalo	NHL	71	8	25	33	110	28	3	0	8	0	0	0	14
81-82—Buffalo	NHL	13	3	2	5	30	5	0	0	—	—	—	—	—
—Detroit	NHL	39	5	9	14	69	2	0	0	—	—	—	—	—
82-83—Detroit	NHL	57	1	10	11	18	-14	0	0	—	—	—	—	—
83-84—Boston	NHL	39	0	2	2	20	18	0	0	—	—	—	—	—
84-85—Buffalo	NHL	34	0	3	3	28	0	0	0	5	0	0	0	4
NHL Totals (13 years)		719	51	204	255	1132	...			75	3	13	16	151

BACKGROUND: ESPN analyst (1992-93 through January 27, 1994).

		REGULAR SEASON					PLAYOFFS		
Season Team	League	W	L	T	Pct.	Finish	W	L	Pct.
84-85—Rochester	AHL	17	6	2	.720	3rd/South Division	—	—	—
85-86—Buffalo	NHL	19	19	5	.500	5th/Adams Division	—	—	—
87-88—New Jersey	NHL	17	12	1	.583	6th/Patrick Division	11	9	.550
88-89—New Jersey	NHL	27	41	12	.413	5th/Patrick Division	—	—	—
89-90—New Jersey	NHL	6	6	2	.500	—	—	—	—
93-94—Washington	NHL	19	12	6	.595	3rd/Atlantic Division	5	6	.455
94-95—Washington	NHL	22	18	8	.542	3rd/Atlantic Division	3	4	.429
95-96—Washington	NHL	39	32	11	.543	4th/Atlantic Division	2	4	.333
96-97—Washington	NHL	33	40	9	.457	5th/Atlantic Division	—	—	—
97-98—Phoenix	NHL	35	35	12	.500	4th/Central Division	2	4	.333
NHL Totals (9 years)		**217**	**215**	**66**	**.502**	**NHL Totals (5 years)**	**23**	**27**	**.460**

NOTES:
87-88—Defeated New York Islanders in Patrick Division semifinals; defeated Washington in Patrick Division finals; lost to Boston in Campbell Conference finals.
93-94—Replaced Terry Murray as head coach (January 27) with club in fifth place; defeated Pittsburgh Penguins in Eastern Conference quarterfinals; lost to New York Rangers in Eastern Conference semifinals.
94-95—Lost to Pittsburgh in Eastern Conference quarterfinals.
95-96—Lost to Pittsburgh in Eastern Conference quarterfinals.
97-98—Lost to Detroit in Western Conference quarterfinals.

SUTTER, BRIAN   FLAMES

PERSONAL: Born October 7, 1956, in Viking, Alta. ... Full name: Brian Louis Allen Sutter. ... Brother of Darryl Sutter, head coach, San Jose Sharks and left winger, Chicago Blackhawks (1979-80 through 1986-87); brother of Brent Sutter, center, Blackhawks; brother of Ron Sutter, center, San Jose Sharks; brother of Rich Sutter, right winger, with seven teams (1982-83 through 1994-95); and brother of Duane Sutter, right winger, New York Islanders and Blackhawks (1979-80 through 1989-90). ... Name pronounced SUH-tuhr.
TRANSACTIONS/CAREER NOTES: Selected by St. Louis Blues from Lethbridge Broncos in second round (second Blues pick, 20th overall) of NHL amateur draft (June 1, 1976). ... Suffered hairline fracture of pelvis (November 3, 1983). ... Broke left shoulder (January 16, 1986). ... Reinjured left shoulder (March 8, 1986). ... Damaged left shoulder muscle (November 1986). ... Sprained ankle (November 1987). ... Retired as player and signed as head coach of Blues (June 1988).
HONORS: Played in NHL All-Star Game (1982, 1983 and 1985).
MISCELLANEOUS: Played left wing. ... Captain of St. Louis Blues (1979-80).

		REGULAR SEASON							PLAYOFFS				
Season Team	League	Gms.	G	A	Pts.	PIM	+/-	PP	SH	Gms.	G	A	Pts.	PIM
72-73—Red Deer	AJHL	51	27	40	67	54	...	...	...	—	—	—	—	—
73-74—Red Deer	AJHL	59	42	54	96	139	...	...	...	—	—	—	—	—
74-75—Lethbridge	WCHL	53	34	47	81	134	...	...	...	6	0	1	1	39
75-76—Lethbridge	WCHL	72	36	56	92	233	...	...	...	7	3	4	7	45
76-77—Kansas City	CHL	38	15	23	38	47	...	...	...	—	—	—	—	—
—St. Louis	NHL	35	4	10	14	82	...	...	...	4	1	0	1	14
77-78—St. Louis	NHL	78	9	13	22	123	...	...	...	—	—	—	—	—
78-79—St. Louis	NHL	77	41	39	80	165	...	...	...	—	—	—	—	—
79-80—St. Louis	NHL	71	23	35	58	156	...	...	...	3	0	0	0	4
80-81—St. Louis	NHL	78	35	34	69	232	12	17	0	11	6	3	9	77
81-82—St. Louis	NHL	74	39	36	75	239	-2	14	0	10	8	6	14	49
82-83—St. Louis	NHL	79	46	30	76	254	-1	11	0	4	2	1	3	10
83-84—St. Louis	NHL	76	32	51	83	162	-6	14	2	11	1	5	6	22
84-85—St. Louis	NHL	77	37	37	74	121	11	14	0	3	2	1	3	2
85-86—St. Louis	NHL	44	19	23	42	87	-12	8	0	9	1	2	3	22
86-87—St. Louis	NHL	14	3	3	6	18	-5	3	0	—	—	—	—	—
87-88—St. Louis	NHL	76	15	22	37	147	-16	4	1	10	0	3	3	49
NHL Totals (12 years)		**779**	**303**	**333**	**636**	**1786**	...	...	...	**65**	**21**	**21**	**42**	**249**

HEAD COACHING RECORD

BACKGROUND: Assistant coach, Team Canada (1991).
HONORS: Won Jack Adams Trophy (1990-91).

		REGULAR SEASON					PLAYOFFS		
Season Team	League	W	L	T	Pct.	Finish	W	L	Pct.
88-89—St. Louis	NHL	33	35	12	.488	2nd/Norris Division	5	5	.500
89-90—St. Louis	NHL	37	34	9	.519	2nd/Norris Division	7	5	.583
90-91—St. Louis	NHL	47	22	11	.656	2nd/Norris Division	6	7	.462
91-92—St. Louis	NHL	36	33	11	.519	3rd/Norris Division	2	4	.333
92-93—Boston	NHL	51	26	7	.649	1st/Adams Division	0	4	.000
93-94—Boston	NHL	42	29	13	.577	2nd/Northeast Division	6	7	.462
94-95—Boston	NHL	27	18	3	.594	3rd/Northeast Division	1	4	.200
97-98—Calgary	NHL	26	41	15	.409	5th/Pacific Division	—	—	—
NHL Totals (8 years)		**299**	**238**	**81**	**.549**	**NHL Totals (7 years)**	**27**	**36**	**.429**

NOTES:
88-89—Defeated Minnesota in Norris Division semifinals; lost to Chicago in Norris Division finals.
89-90—Defeated Toronto in Norris Division semifinals; lost to Chicago in Norris Division finals.
90-91—Defeated Detroit in Norris Division semifinals; lost to Minnesota in Norris Division finals.
91-92—Lost to Chicago in Norris Division semifinals.
92-93—Lost to Buffalo in Adams Division semifinals.
93-94—Defeated Montreal in Eastern Conference quarterfinals; lost to New Jersey in Eastern Conference semifinals.
94-95—Lost to New Jersey in Eastern Conference quarterfinals.

NHL HEAD COACHES

SUTTER, DARRYL — SHARKS

PERSONAL: Born August 19, 1958, in Viking, Alta. ... Brother of Brian Sutter, head coach, Calgary Flames and left winger, St. Louis Blues (1976-77 through 1987-88); brother of Duane Sutter, right winger, New York Islanders and Chicago Blackhawks (1979-80 through 1989-90); brother of Rich Sutter, right winger, with seven teams (1982-83 through 1994-95); brother of Ron Sutter, center, San Jose Sharks; and brother of Brent Sutter, center, Blackhawks. ... Name pronounced SUH-tuhr.

TRANSACTIONS/CAREER NOTES: Selected by Chicago Blackhawks in 11th round (11th Blackhawks pick, 179th overall) of NHL amateur draft (June 1978). ... Lacerated left elbow, developed infection and underwent surgery (November 27, 1981). ... Broke nose (November 7, 1982). ... Broke ribs (November 1983). ... Fracture left cheekbone and injured left eye (January 2, 1984). ... Underwent arthroscopic surgery to right knee (September 1984). ... Bruised ribs (October 1984). ... Broke left ankle (December 26, 1984). ... Separated right shoulder and underwent surgery (November 13, 1985); missed 30 games. ... Injured knee (February 1987). ... Retired as player and signed as assistant coach of Blackhawks (June 1987).

HONORS: Named top rookie of Japan National League (1978-79). ... Won Dudley (Red) Garrett Memorial Trophy (1979-80). ... Named to AHL All-Star second team (1979-80).

MISCELLANEOUS: Played left wing. ... Captain of Chicago Blackhawks (1982-83 through 1986-87).

		REGULAR SEASON								PLAYOFFS				
Season Team	League	Gms.	G	A	Pts.	PIM	+/-	PP	SH	Gms.	G	A	Pts.	PIM
74-75—Red Deer	AJHL	60	16	20	36	43	...	...	...	—	—	—	—	—
75-76—Red Deer	AJHL	60	43	93	136	82	...	...	...	—	—	—	—	—
76-77—Red Deer	AJHL	56	55	78	133	131	...	...	...	—	—	—	—	—
—Lethbridge	WCHL	1	1	0	1	0	...	...	...	15	3	7	10	13
77-78—Lethbridge	WCHL	68	33	48	81	119	...	...	...	8	4	9	13	2
78-79—New Brunswick	AHL	19	7	6	13	6	...	...	...	5	1	2	3	0
—Iwakura	JAPAN	20	28	13	41	0	...	...	...	—	—	—	—	—
79-80—New Brunswick	AHL	69	35	31	66	69	...	...	...	12	6	6	12	8
—Chicago	NHL	8	2	0	2	2	...	...	...	7	3	1	4	2
80-81—Chicago	NHL	76	40	22	62	86	-1	14	0	3	3	1	4	2
81-82—Chicago	NHL	40	23	12	35	31	0	4	3	3	0	1	1	2
82-83—Chicago	NHL	80	31	30	61	53	18	10	0	13	4	6	10	8
83-84—Chicago	NHL	59	20	20	40	44	-18	8	0	5	1	1	2	0
84-85—Chicago	NHL	49	20	18	38	12	8	2	0	15	12	7	19	12
85-86—Chicago	NHL	50	17	10	27	44	-15	3	0	3	1	2	3	0
86-87—Chicago	NHL	44	8	6	14	16	-3	1	0	2	0	0	0	0
NHL Totals (8 years)		**406**	**161**	**118**	**279**	**288**				**51**	**24**	**19**	**43**	**26**

HEAD COACHING RECORD

BACKGROUND: Assistant coach, Chicago Blackhawks (1987-88). ... Associate coach, Blackhwaks (1991-92). ... Special assistant to general manager, Blackhawks (1995-96 and 1996-97).

		REGULAR SEASON					PLAYOFFS		
Season Team	League	W	L	T	Pct.	Finish	W	L	Pct.
88-89—Saginaw	IHL	46	26	10	.622	2nd/East Division	2	4	.333
89-90—Indianapolis	IHL	53	21	8	.695	1st/West Division	12	2	.857
90-91—Indianapolis	IHL	48	29	5	.616	2nd/East Division	3	4	.429
92-93—Chicago	NHL	47	25	12	.631	1st/Norris Division	0	4	.000
93-94—Chicago	NHL	39	36	9	.518	5th/Central Division	2	4	.333
94-95—Chicago	NHL	24	19	5	.552	3rd/Central Division	9	7	.563
97-98—San Jose	NHL	34	38	10	.476	4th/Pacific Division	2	4	.333
NHL Totals (4 years)		**144**	**118**	**36**	**.544**	**NHL Totals (4 years)**	**13**	**19**	**.406**

NOTES:

88-89—Lost to Fort Wayne in quarterfinals of Turner Cup playoffs.

89-90—Defeated Peoria in quarterfinals of Turner Cup playoffs; defeated Salt Lake City in semifinals of Turner Cup playoffs; defeated Muskegon in Turner Cup finals.

90-91—Lost to Fort Wayne in quarterfinals of Turner Cup playoffs.

92-93—Lost to St. Louis in Norris Division semifinals.

93-94—Lost to Toronto in Western Conference quarterfinals.

94-95—Defeated Toronto in Western Conference quarterfinals; defeated Vancouver in Western Conference semifinals; lost to Detroit in Western Conference finals.

97-98—Lost to Dallas in Western Conference quarterfinals.

TROTZ, BARRY — PREDATORS

PERSONAL: Born July 15, 1962, in Winnipeg.

		REGULAR SEASON								PLAYOFFS				
Season Team	League	Gms.	G	A	Pts.	PIM	+/-	PP	SH	Gms.	G	A	Pts.	PIM
79-80—Regina	WHL	41	4	8	12	42	...	...	...	—	—	—	—	—
80-81—Regina	WHL	62	4	13	17	115	...	...	...	—	—	—	—	—
81-82—Regina	WHL	50	6	28	34	155	...	...	...	20	1	7	8	79

HEAD COACHING RECORD

BACKGROUND: Player/assistant coach, University of Manitoba (1983-84). ... Scout, Washington Capitals (1988-89 through 1990-91). ... Assistant coach, Baltimore Skipjacks of the AHL (1991-92). ... Scout, Nashville Predators (1997-98).

HONORS: Named AHL Coach of the Year (1993-94).

		REGULAR SEASON					PLAYOFFS		
Season Team	League	W	L	T	Pct.	Finish	W	L	Pct.
92-93—Baltimore	AHL	28	40	12	.425	4th/Southern Division	3	4	.429
93-94—Portland	AHL	43	27	10	.600	2nd/Northern Division	12	5	.706
94-95—Portland	AHL	46	22	12	.650	2nd/Northern Division	3	4	.429
95-96—Portland	AHL	32	38	10	.463	3rd/Northern Division	14	10	.583
96-97—Portland	AHL	37	26	10	.575	3rd/New England Division	2	3	.400

NOTES:

92-93—Lost to Binghamton in the first round of Calder Cup playoffs.

93-94—Defeated Albany in Northern Division semifinals; defeated Adirondack in Northern Division finals; defeated Moncton in Calder Cup finals.

94-95—Lost to Providence in Northern Division semifinals.

95-96—Defeated Worcester in Eastern Conference quarterfinals; defeated Springfield in Eastern Conference semifinals; defeated Saint John in Eastern Conference finals; lost to Rochester in Calder Cup finals.

96-97—Lost to Springfield in Southern Conference quarterfinals.

VIGNEAULT, ALAIN — CANADIENS

PERSONAL: Born May 14, 1961, in Quebec City. ... Played defense. ... Shot right.

TRANSACTIONS/CAREER NOTES: Selected by St. Louis Blues in eighth round (seventh Blues pick, 167th overall) of NHL entry draft (June 1981).

Season Team	League	REGULAR SEASON								PLAYOFFS				
		Gms.	G	A	Pts.	PIM	+/-	PP	SH	Gms.	G	A	Pts.	PIM
79-80—Hull	QJHL	35	5	34	39	82	...	...	...	—	—	—	—	—
—Trois Riv. Flambeaux...	QJHL	28	6	19	25	93	...	...	...	—	—	—	—	—
80-81—Trois Riv. Flambeaux...	QJHL	67	7	55	62	181	...	...	...	—	—	—	—	—
81-82—Salt Lake City	CHL	64	2	10	12	266	...	...	...	—	—	—	—	—
—St. Louis	NHL	14	1	2	3	43	-1	0	0	—	—	—	—	—
82-83—Salt Lake City	CHL	33	1	4	5	189	...	...	...	—	—	—	—	—
—St. Louis	NHL	28	1	3	4	39	-4	0	0	—	—	—	—	—
83-84—Montana	CHL	47	2	14	16	139	...	...	...	—	—	—	—	—
—Maine	AHL	11	0	1	1	46	...	...	...	—	—	—	—	—
NHL Totals (2 years)		42	2	5	7	82	-5	0	0	—	—	—	—	—

HEAD COACHING RECORD

BACKGROUND: Assistant coach, Canadian junior national team (1989 and 1991). ... Assistant coach, Ottawa Senators (1992-93 through November 20, 1995).

HONORS: Canadian Coach of the Year (1987-88).

Season Team	League	REGULAR SEASON					PLAYOFFS		
		W	L	T	Pct.	Finish	W	L	Pct.
86-87—Trois-Rivieres	QMJHL	26	37	2	.415	5th/Frank Dilio Division	—	—	—
87-88—Hull	QMJHL	43	23	4	.643	1st Robert Le Bel Division	12	7	.632
88-89—Hull	QMJHL	40	25	5	.607	3rd/Robert Le Bel Division	5	4	.556
89-90—Hull	QMJHL	36	29	5	.550	T5th/Robert Le Bel Division	4	7	.364
90-91—Hull	QMJHL	33	25	7	.562	2nd/Robert Le Bel Division	2	4	.333
91-92—Hull	QMJHL	40	23	5	.625	2nd/Robert Le Bel Division	2	4	.333
95-96—Beauport	QMJHL	19	7	5	.694	1st/Frank Dilio Division	13	7	.650
96-97—Beauport	QMJHL	24	44	2	.357	6th/Frank Dilio Division	1	3	.250
97-98—Montreal	NHL	37	32	13	.530	4th/Northeast Division	4	6	.400
NHL Totals (1 year)		37	32	13	.530	**NHL Totals (1 year)**	4	6	.400

NOTES:

87-88—Defeated Granby in quarterfinals of President Cup playoffs; defeated Laval in semifinals of President Cup playoffs; defeated Drummondville in President Cup finals.

88-89—Defeated St. Jean in quarterfinals of President Cup playoffs; lost to Victoriaville in semifinals of President Cup playoffs.

89-90—Defeated Longueuil in quarterfinals of President Cup playoffs; lost to Laval in semifinals of President Cup playoffs.

90-91—Lost to Laval in quarterfinals of President Cup playoffs.

91-92—Lost to Laval in quarterfinals of President Cup playoffs.

95-96—Defeated Rimouski in quarterfinals of President Cup playoffs; defeated Hull in semifinals of President Cup playoffs; lost to Granby in President Cup finals.

96-97—Lost to Halifax in quarterfinals of President Cup playoffs.

97-98—Defeated Pittsburgh in Eastern Conference quarterfinals; lost to Buffalo in Eastern Conference semifinals.

WILSON, RON — CAPITALS

PERSONAL: Born May 28, 1955, in Windsor, Ont. ... Full name: Ronald Lawrence Wilson. ... Son of Larry Wilson, center with Detroit Red Wings and Chicago Blackhawks (1949-50 through 1955-56) and coach, Red Wings (1976-77); and nephew of Johnny Wilson, left winger with four NHL teams (1949-50 through 1961-62) and coach with four NHL teams and two WHA teams (1969-70 through 1979-80).

COLLEGE: Providence (degree in economics).

TRANSACTIONS/CAREER NOTES: Selected by Toronto Maple Leafs in seventh round (seventh Maple Leafs pick, 132nd overall) in NHL entry draft (June 3, 1975). ... Loaned by Davos HC to Minnesota North Stars for remainder of NHL season and playoffs (March 1985). ... Loaned by Davos HC to Minnesota North Stars for remainder of NHL season and playoffs (March 1986). ... Traded by Davos HC to Minnesota North Stars for D Craig Levie (May 1986). ... Separated shoulder (March 9, 1987).

HONORS: Named to NCAA All-America East first team (1974-75 and 1975-76). ... Named to ECAC All-Star team (1973-74 through 1976-77). ... Named ECAC Player of the Year (1974-75).

MISCELLANEOUS: Played defense.

Season Team	League	REGULAR SEASON								PLAYOFFS				
		Gms.	G	A	Pts.	PIM	+/-	PP	SH	Gms.	G	A	Pts.	PIM
73-74—Providence College	ECAC	26	16	22	38	...	...	...	...	—	—	—	—	—
74-75—Providence College	ECAC	27	26	61	87	12	...	...	...	—	—	—	—	—
—U.S. national team	Int'l	27	5	32	37	42	...	...	...	—	—	—	—	—
75-76—Providence College	ECAC	28	19	47	66	44	...	...	...	—	—	—	—	—
76-77—Providence College	ECAC	30	17	42	59	62	...	...	...	—	—	—	—	—
—Dallas	CHL	4	1	0	1	2	...	...	...	—	—	—	—	—
77-78—Dallas	CHL	67	31	38	69	18	...	...	...	—	—	—	—	—
—Toronto	NHL	13	2	1	3	0	...	...	...	—	—	—	—	—

Season Team	League	REGULAR SEASON								PLAYOFFS				
		Gms.	G	A	Pts.	PIM	+/-	PP	SH	Gms.	G	A	Pts.	PIM
78-79—New Brunswick..........	AHL	31	11	20	31	13	...	...	...	—	—	—	—	—
—Toronto	NHL	46	5	12	17	4	...	...	...	3	0	1	1	0
79-80—New Brunswick..........	AHL	43	20	43	63	10	...	...	...	—	—	—	—	—
—Toronto	NHL	5	0	2	2	0	...	...	...	3	1	2	3	2
80-81—Davos HC....................	Switzerland						Statistics unavailable.							
81-82—Davos HC....................	Switzerland						Statistics unavailable.							
82-83—Davos HC....................	Switzerland						Statistics unavailable.							
83-84—Davos HC....................	Switzerland						Statistics unavailable.							
84-85—Davos HC....................	Switzerland						Statistics unavailable.							
—Minnesota..................	NHL	13	4	8	12	2	-1	0	0	9	1	6	7	2
85-86—Davos HC....................	Switzerland						Statistics unavailable.							
—Minnesota..................	NHL	11	1	3	4	8	-2	1	0	5	2	4	6	4
86-87—Minnesota..................	NHL	65	12	29	41	36	-9	6	0	—	—	—	—	—
87-88—Minnesota..................	NHL	24	2	12	14	16	-4	1	0	—	—	—	—	—
NHL Totals (7 years)..........		177	26	67	93	66	...	...	...	20	4	13	17	8

HEAD COACHING RECORD

BACKGROUND: Assistant coach, Milwaukee, Vancouver Canucks organization (1989-90). ... Served as interim coach of Milwaukee while Ron Lapointe was hospitalized for cancer treatments (February and March 1990; team went 9-10). ... Assistant coach, Canucks (1990-91 through 1992-93).

Season Team	League	REGULAR SEASON					PLAYOFFS		
		W	L	T	Pct.	Finish	W	L	Pct.
93-94—Anaheim................................	NHL	33	46	5	.423	4th/Pacific Division	—	—	—
94-95—Anaheim................................	NHL	16	27	5	.385	6th/Pacific Division	—	—	—
95-96—Anaheim................................	NHL	35	39	8	.476	4th/Pacific Division	—	—	—
96-97—Anaheim................................	NHL	36	33	13	.518	2nd/Pacific Division	4	7	.364
97-98—Washington............................	NHL	40	30	12	.561	3rd/Atlantic Division	12	9	.571
NHL Totals (5 years)		160	175	43	.480	**NHL Totals (2 years)**.................................	16	16	.500

NOTES:

96-97—Defeated Phoenix in Western Conference quarterfinals; lost to Detroit in Western Conference semifinals.

97-98—Defeated Boston in Eastern Conference quarterfinals; defeated Ottawa in Eastern Conference semifinals; defeated Buffalo in Eastern Conference finals; lost to Detroit in Stanley Cup finals.

NHL HEAD COACHES

1997-98 NATIONAL HOCKEY LEAGUE LEADERS

Games

Mike Keane, NYR-Dal. 83
Many players with 82

Points

Jaromir Jagr, Pittsburgh 102
Peter Forsberg, Colorado 91
Pavel Bure, Vancouver 90
Wayne Gretzky, N.Y. Rangers......90
John LeClair, Philadelphia...........87
Zigmund Palffy, N.Y. Islanders.....87
Ron Francis, Pittsburgh 87
Teemu Selanne, Anaheim.............86
Jason Allison, Boston 83
Jozef Stumpel, Los Angeles........79

Points by a defenseman

Nicklas Lidstrom, Detroit 59
Scott Niedermayer, New Jersey ...57
Sergei Zubov, Dallas 57
Steve Duchesne, St. Louis 56
Larry Murphy, Detroit...................52

Goals

Peter Bondra, Washington 52
Teemu Selanne, Anaheim.............52
Pavel Bure, Vancouver 51
John LeClair, Philadelphia...........51
Zigmund Palffy, N.Y. Islanders.....45
Keith Tkachuk, Phoenix...............40
Joe Nieuwendyk, Dallas 39
Rod Brind'Amour, Philadelphia 36
Jaromir Jagr, Pittsburgh 35
Jason Allison, Boston 33
Mats Sundin, Toronto 33
Ray Whitney, Edm.-Fla. 33
Alexei Yashin, Ottawa..................33

Assists

Wayne Gretzky, N.Y. Rangers......67
Jaromir Jagr, Pittsburgh 67
Peter Forsberg, Colorado 66
Ron Francis, Pittsburgh 62
Adam Oates, Washington.............58
Jozef Stumpel, Los Angeles........58
Theoren Fleury, Calgary 51
Jason Allison, Boston 50
Sergei Zubov, Dallas 47
Pierre Turgeon, St. Louis 46

Power-play goals

Zigmund Palffy, N.Y. Islanders.....17
John LeClair, Philadelphia...........16
Stu Barnes, Pittsburgh................15
Brendan Shanahan, Detroit 15
Shayne Corson, Montreal.............14
Joe Nieuwendyk, Dallas 14

Shorthanded goals

Pavel Bure, Vancouver 6
Jeff Friesen, San Jose..................6
Peter Bondra, Washington 5
Bob Corkum, Phoenix...................5
Mike Modano, Dallas 5
Michael Peca, Buffalo...................5

Game-winning goals

Peter Bondra, Washington 13
Joe Nieuwendyk, Dallas 11
Teemu Selanne, Anaheim.............10
John LeClair, Philadelphia.............9
Brendan Shanahan, Detroit 9

Game-tying goals

Adam Deadmarsh, Colorado 3
Pat LaFontaine, N.Y. Rangers........3
Teemu Selanne, Anaheim..............3
Many tied with 2

Shots

Pavel Bure, Vancouver 329
John LeClair, Philadelphia..........303
Tony Amonte, Chicago 296
Alexei Yashin, Ottawa.................291
Peter Bondra, Washington 284

Shooting percentage
(82 shots minimum)

Mike Sillinger, Van.-Phi. 21.9
Jason Allison, Boston 20.9
Dmitri Khristich, Boston............20.1
Teemu Selanne, Anaheim..........19.4
Joe Nieuwendyk, Dallas 19.2

Plus/minus

Chris Pronger, St. Louis..............47
Larry Murphy, Detroit...................35
Jason Allison, Boston 33
Randy McKay, New Jersey...........30
John LeClair, Philadelphia...........30

Penalty minutes

Donald Brashear, Vancouver 372
Tie Domi, Toronto 365
Krzysztof Oliwa, New Jersey 295
Paul Laus, Florida 293
Richard Pilon, N.Y. Islanders......291
Matthew Barnaby, Buffalo 289
Denny Lambert, Ottawa 250
Matt Johnson, Los Angeles 249
Sandy McCarthy, Tampa Bay......241
Rob Ray, Buffalo 234

Consecutive-game point streaks

Zigmund Palffy, N.Y. Islanders 13
Pierre Turgeon, St. Louis 12
Teemu Selanne, Anaheim.............11
Peter Bondra, Washington 11

Pavel Bure, Vancouver 10
Andrew Brunette, Washington 10
Mark Messier, Vancouver............10

Consecutive-game goal streaks

Teemu Selanne, Anaheim.............11
Joe Sakic, Colorado 7
John LeClair, Philadelphia (twice) ..6
Peter Forsberg, Colorado 6
Ed Olczyk, Pittsburgh....................6
Keith Primeau, Carolina 6
Andrew Brunette, Washington 6

Consecutive-game assist streaks

Adam Oates, Washington...............8
Wayne Gretzky, N.Y. Islanders.......8
Shayne Corson, Montreal...............7
Robert Reichel, N.Y. Islanders.......7
Joe Sakic, Colorado 7
Valeri Kamensky, Colorado 7
Mike Modano, Dallas 7
Keith Primeau, Carolina 7

Most games scoring three or more goals

Pavel Bure, Vancouver 3
Teemu Selanne, Anaheim...............3
Keith Tkachuk, Phoenix..................3
Many tied with 2

Points by a rookie

Mike Johnson, Toronto 47
Sergei Samsonov, Boston...........47
Patrik Elias, New Jersey..............37
Patrick Marleau, San Jose...........32
Marco Sturm, San Jose 30
Mattias Ohlund, Vancouver 30

Goals by a rookie

Sergei Samsonov, Boston 22
Patrik Elias, New Jersey..............18
Richard Zednik, Washington 17
Mike Johnson, Toronto 15
Patrick Marleau, San Jose...........13
Alexei Morozov, Pittsburgh 13
Dave Scatchard, Vancouver 13

Assists by a rookie

Mike Johnson, Toronto 32
Sergei Samsonov, Boston...........25
Mattias Ohlund, Vancouver 23
Matt Cullen, Anaheim..................21
Marco Sturm, San Jose 20
Derek Morris, Calgary 20

GOALTENDING

Games

Dominik Hasek, Buffalo................72
Mike Richter, N.Y. Rangers..........72
Curtis Joseph, Edmonton.............71
Martin Brodeur, New Jersey.........70
Nikolai Khabibulin, Phoenix.........70

Minutes

Dominik Hasek, Buffalo............4220
Mike Richter, N.Y. Rangers......4143
Curtis Joseph, Edmonton.........4132
Martin Brodeur, New Jersey.....4128
Nikolai Khabibulin, Phoenix.....4026

Goals allowed

Nikolai Khabibulin, Phoenix.......184
Mike Richter, N.Y. Rangers.......184
Curtis Joseph, Edmonton..........181
Felix Potvin, Toronto.................176
John Vanbiesbrouck, Florida......165

Shutouts

Dominik Hasek, Buffalo...............13
Martin Brodeur, New Jersey.........10
Ed Belfour, Dallas..........................9
Jeff Hackett, Chicago....................8
Curtis Joseph, Edmonton..............8

Lowest goals-against average

(25 games played minimum)
Ed Belfour, Dallas.....................1.88
Martin Brodeur, New Jersey......1.89
Tom Barrasso, Pittsburgh.........2.07
Dominik Hasek, Buffalo.............2.09
Ron Hextall, Philadelphia.......2.165
Trevor Kidd, Carolina..............2.168
Jamie McLennan, St. Louis.....2.171

Highest goals-against average

(25 games played minimum)
Kirk McLean, Van.-Car.-Fla........3.54
Mikhail Shtalenkov, Anaheim....3.22
Mark Fitzpatrick, Fla.-T.B...........3.12
Dwayne Roloson, Calgary.........2.99
Sean Burke, Car.-Van.-Phi........2.95

Games won

Martin Brodeur, New Jersey........41
Ed Belfour, Dallas.......................37
Dominik Hasek, Buffalo...............33
Olaf Kolzig, Washington...............33
Chris Osgood, Detroit..................33

Best winning percentage

(25 games played minimum)
Ed Belfour, Dallas (37-12-10)..712
Martin Brodeur, N.J. (43-17-8).691
Jamie McLennan, St.L. (16-8-2).654
Tom Barrasso, Pit. (31-14-13)..647
Olaf Kolzig, Was. (33-18-10)...623

Worst winning percentage

(25 games played minimum)
Kelly Hrudey, San Jose (4-16-2).227
Mark Fitzpatrick, Fla.-T.B. (9-31-3).244
Daren Puppa, Tampa Bay (5-14-6).320
Guy Hebert, Anaheim (13-24-6)...372
Rick Tabaracci, Calgary (13-22-6).390

Games lost

Felix Potvin, Toronto...................33
Mark Fitzpatrick, Fla.-T.B. 31
Curtis Joseph, Edmonton.............31
Mike Richter, N.Y. Rangers..........31
John Vanbiesbrouck, Florida........29
Tommy Salo, N.Y. Islanders.........29

Shots against

Dominik Hasek, Buffalo............2149
Curtis Joseph, Edmonton.........1901
Mike Richter, N.Y. Rangers......1888
Felix Potvin, Toronto...............1882
Nikolai Khabibulin, Phoenix.....1835

Saves

Dominik Hasek, Buffalo............2002
Curtis Joseph, Edmonton.........1720
Felix Potvin, Toronto...............1706
Mike Richter, N.Y. Rangers......1704
Patrick Roy, Colorado..............1672

Highest save percentage

(25 games played minimum)
Dominik Hasek, Buffalo............ .932
Tom Barrasso, Pittsburgh....92159
Trevor Kidd, Carolina..........92158
Olaf Kolzig, Washington........... .920
Martin Brodeur, New Jersey. .91714
Jeff Hackett, Chicago........... .91711

Lowest save percentage

(25 games played minimum)
Kirk McLean, Van.-Car.-Fla....... .881
Dwayne Roloson, Calgary........ .890
Mark Fitzpatrick, Fla.-T.B......... .892
Rick Tabaracci, Calgary........ .89328
Mikhail Shtalenkov, Anaheim .89331